THE SQUADRONS OF THE FLEET AIR ARM

RAY STURTIVANT, I.S.O.
AND THEO BALLANCE

AN AIR-BRITAIN PUBLICATION

Copyright 1994 by Ray Sturtivant I.S.O.
and Theo Ballance.

Published in the United Kingdom by

Air-Britain (Historians) Ltd,
1 East Street, Tonbridge, Kent.

Sales Dept: 5 Bradley Road, Upper Norwood,
London, SE19 3NT

Correspondence to:

R.C.Sturtivant, 26 Monks Horton Way,
St.Albans, Herts, AL1 4HA
and not to the Tonbridge address

All rights reserved. No part of this publication may be reproduced, stored in a retrieval system or transmitted, in any form or by any means, electronic, mechanical, photocopying, recording or otherwise, without the prior permission of Air-Britain (Historians) Ltd

ISBN 0 85130 223 8

Printed by Unwin Brothers Ltd,
The Gresham Press
Old Woking
Surrey GU22 9LH

Cover paintings by Dugald Cameron

Front cover:
Sea Harrier FRS.1 ZD582 '124' of No.800 Squadron.
Firefly AS.6 WD871 '244/AC' of the Scottish Air Division.
Swordfish II LS326 'L2' of No.836L Flight (restored).

Back cover:
Lynx HAS.2 XZ238.
Gazelle HT.2 XX441 '538' of No.705 Squadron.
Sea King HAS.6 XV653 '500/CU. of No.810 Squadron.

CONTENTS

Credits	5
Preface	6
Introduction	7
Squadron Numbering	11
Notes on Squadron Listing	12
Glossary	13
Squadrons numbered 700 to 799	15
Squadrons numbered 800 to 1853	123
Index of Aircraft Equipment	361
Index of Locations in the United Kingdom	364
Index of Overseas Locations	367
Index of Ships	371
Index of Commanding Officers Names	374
Fleet Air Arm Flag Officers	380
Battle Honours	382
Boyd Trophy Award	383
Ships Names of Fleet Air Arm Stations	384
Fleet Air Arm Bases in the United Kingdom	385
Fleet Air Arm Bases Overseas	390
Aircraft Carriers	393
MAC-ships	403
Warships with Catapults, Cranes or Flying-off Platforms 1923-1944	404
Armed Merchant Cruisers Fitted with Aircraft Catapults	404
Fighter Catapult Ships with Fleet Air Arm Aircraft	404
Catapult Armed Merchant Ship with Fleet Air Arm Aircraft	404
Major WW2 Warships Fitted with Aircraft Catapults	405
Helicopter-carrying Ships	410
Numbered Ships Helicopter Flights	428
Fleet Air Arm Flights 1923-1936	431
Miscellaneous Fleet Air Arm Units	434
Naval Aircraft Code Markings	450
Fleet Air Arm Codes 1933-1939	453
Fleet Air Arm Codes 1939-1947	454
Fin Codes since 1945 - Shore Bases	459
Deck Letters since 1945 - Fleet Carriers	459
Deck Letters - Ships other than Carriers	460
British Pacific Fleet Codes 1945-1947	461
Fleet Air Arm Carrier Codes 1946-1956	462
Fleet Air Arm Shore Codes 1946-1956	463
Fleet Air Arm Codes 1956-1965	468
Fleet Air Arm Codes 1965-date	472
Fleet Air Arm Helicopter Codes since 1971	476
Royal Australian Navy Fleet Air Arm Codes since 1948	476
Royal Canadian Navy Aircraft Codes 1948-1952	477
Naval Aircraft Museums	479

HMS Eagle in November 1956, with Suez-striped Wyverns of No.830 Squadron and Sea Hawks of No.897 Squadron parked on the angled deck. (via Brian Lowe)

CREDITS

The authors would like to acknowledge the help given by numerous people in providing information and photographs for this book. Without their help, it would not have been possible to have given such a comprehensive coverage of many of the squadrons, since official records are either incomplete or have failed to survive. The following have given help in respect of specific gaps, but the help is equally appreciated of many others who have given assistance over the years.

Vice Admiral Sir Conolly Abel Smith; H.J.Abraham; Hank Adlam; Philip Aked; Dick Allen; W.H.Anderson; Dennis Antrobus; John Arnold; Ken Atkinson; P.E.I.Bailey; Leo Baker; George Baldwin; Francis Baring; Rick Barker; David Bay; David Berrill; Bernard Bevans; John; Dick Blackburn; Eric Bond; Alan Braidwood; Stanley Brilliant; Cecil Bristow; Ed Brown; E.M.Buchan; Douglas Buchanan; David Buchanan-Dunlop; Rear Admiral Dennis Cambell; Neville Cambell; G.J. Cardew; Peter Carmichael; John Casson; Owen Cathcart-Jones; Rodney Carver; Ralph Chalker; Philip Charlton; V.B.G.Cheesman; Pat Chilton; Don Chute; E.J.Clark; Glyn Clayton; W.G.Coates; Leslie Cooper; R.K.Cooper; Cedric Coxon; P.J.Craig; W.H.Crawford; N.B.Dale; Peter Dallosso; Les Donovan; Tony Down; Colin Drew; Graham Drucker; Lt Cdr A.C.van Duin RNIN; Leo Dunne; Paddy Edwards; Glen Evans; Kenneth Evans; Donald Eve; Robert Everett; Ivor Faulconer; John Fay; Dennis Foley; George Fowler; Philip Francklin; Freddie Gann; Dennis Gardiner; John Griffith; Richard Griffiths; S.G.Grinstead; Dick Grose; G.E Hall; Nigel Hallett; Gordon Halliday; M.E.Hamilton; L.A.Harris; Bill Harrison; Roy Hawkes; Roy Hawkeswell; Bill Hawley; Hugh Hearn; Wally Hearn; Mrs J.Heath; Dick Henderson; Robert Henley; J.M.Henry; R.G.Henton; Mrs E.Hibbert; Bruce Hocking; Bill Holdridge; Michael Hordern; Maurice Humphreys; Mrs Peggy Hutton; George Huyton; Chris Isacke; J.P.Issaverdens; Paul Jackson; P.B.Jackson; Gareth Jenkins; Stuart Jewers; Len Jeyes; David Johnson; A.Jones; H.G.Jones; R.W.Kearsley; Leslie Kemp; R.E.F.Kerrison; David Kirke; J.H.Kneale; Douglas Knight; John Lang; Hugh Langrishe; Mick Lawrence; Bob Lea; Edgar Lee; John Lees-Jones; Ken Lee-White; Geoffrey Legg; Norman Lester; Peter London; Victor Lowden; Peter Lowndes; Brian MacCaw; David McCrandles; Doug MacPhail; W.R.MacWhirter; J.E.Maddocks; Sam Manchett; A.O.Masters; John Maybank; John Menhenitt; G.J.Miller; Ron Moore; Ivor Morgan; Pat Moss; Fred Motley; Barry Nation; Hamilton Neilson; Clifford Nell; Peter Nichols; Stanley Orr; Frank Ott; A.S.Owensmith; N.S.Painter; Donald Payne; Arthur Pearcy; Bill Penlington; Dennis Phillips; Dickie Phillips; Harry Phillips; Ron Porter; Jeff Powell; W.N.Preston; Rear Admiral C.E.Price; Dick Pridham-Wippell; F.J. Rankin; Ben Rice; John Riley; R.H.S.Rodger; W.F.Rogers; Peter Rougier; Neill Rush; Bill Sabey; Harold Salisbury; Michael Schoeman; W.F.H.Schwenk; John Scott; Peter Scott; Rear Admiral E.H.Shattock; Harold Shear; Maurice Shippey; Ronald Shilcock; Rear Admiral M.F.Simpson; Sir Edward Singleton; Vice Admiral Sir Richard Smeeton; H.A.W.Smith; Jack Smith; Vic Smith; Peter Snow; Gordon Steer; John Stenning; Michael Swale; Tony Sweeting; Frederick Taylor; John Taylor; Dennis Teague; Bill Thomson; Maurice Tibby; W.A.Tofts; Rear Admiral A.D.Torlesse; John Treble; Tony Tuke; Martin Turner; Sir Walter Verco; Bruce Vibert; B.W.Vigrass; Bill Voller; R.F.Walker; F.D.Walter; Edward Walthall; M.J. Weston; Paul Whitfield; Harry Wragg; Dick Yeo; Stanley Yeo.

PREFACE

It is now more than seventy years since the formation of what was then the Fleet Air Arm of the Royal Air Force, which came into existence on 1 April 1924. Over the years there have been many books dealing with various aspects of FAA history, but much remains unrecorded. The present book attempts to fill some of the gaps, and provide a framework for further research.

This work represents the culmination of nearly fifty years investigation by the primary author into the histories of British naval air squadrons and their aircraft. Half of those years have been specifically aimed at producing a book of this nature, a target which at the outset seemed likely to be unattainable in anything like the amount of detail which has now proved possible.

The main difficulty has been that until the mid-1950s the FAA had no standardised method of recording and retaining the history of each squadron. RAF squadrons have for many years been required to make a daily record of their activities in an Operations Record Book, in standard form, one copy of which is deposited with the Air Historical Branch. It is likely that in prewar days such records were kept when naval squadrons, and the flights which preceded them, were part of the RAF, and in fact a small number of extracts from these are held in the Public Record Office. The majority probably disappeared, however, when the Admiralty regained control of naval aviation just before the outbreak of war in 1939.

For the next fifteen years or so, each squadron kept records in such form as it thought fit, generally a diary and a line book. The former could be anything from a small notebook to a heavy bound volume, and often contained mainly evidence of sporting activities or drinking sessions, but in some instances it was well kept with full details of daily activities of the aircraft and crews. The majority fell somewhere between these two. The line-book was in effect a line-shooting book, or scrap-book, mostly filled with newspapers cuttings and photographs relevant to the squadron, very often accompanied by witticisms, polite or otherwise. The only official record in standard form was the fair flying log, in which a squadron recorded daily the details of the flight times of each of its aircraft, but few of these have survived.

Such records as were maintained should have been handed in on disbandment, the intention being that they would then be reissued to the squadron if it should reform. If all this had been done, it would have been possible to reassemble the majority of histories, but unfortunately it was often not the case, particularly at the end of the war. Disbandments tended to happen rather quickly, and the person holding the records often had no idea how to dispose of them properly. Those that were correctly handed in are now in either the Public Record Office or the FAA Museum at Yeovilton. A few others are known to be in private hands, but the greater proportion of the earlier ones have vanished, especially those relating to the wartime years.

In order to fill the gap left by this absence of early records, the primary author has spent many years identifying people who served with those squadrons for which no contemporary official records have survived. He is indebted to the many hundreds of such former FAA members who have been kind enough to allow him to inspect or borrow their flying log books, photographs and other records. Particular tribute should be paid to members of the Fleet Air Arm Officers Association and the Telegraphist Air Gunners Association for their kindnesses and help in this self-imposed task.

Gratitude must also be expressed to the staff of the FAA Museum for their unfailing support over many years. Especial thanks in this respect are due to the former Museum Director, Commander D.C.B.White; the present Deputy Director, Graham Mottram; the former Curator, Lt Cdr L.A.Cox; the Keeper of Records Mrs Moira Gittos; former Librarians Mrs Anne Bell and Len Lovell; former Technical Adviser, the late Vernon Hillier, and staff members Dave Richardson and Mrs Jan Keohane. Similar thanks are due to the past and present staff of the RAF Museum, and also to the staff of The Australian Naval Aviation Museum Foundation at Nowra, especially the Curator, Lt Cdr R.E.Geale, MBE, RAN (Rtd).

Credit should also be given for the considerable help received from the many other researchers who have freely made available their records, photographs and advice in respect of their own lines of research. These include Mick Burrow for his depth of knowledge on wartime second line squadrons and wartime code markings; Eric Myall for his unrivalled knowledge of helicopters; Dick Cronin for his meticulous help with the prewar period; Joe Barr for his researches into Royal Australian Navy aviation history; and to past and present members of the British Aviation Research Group for help with the postwar period, especially Douglas Rough, John Tipp, Jim Downing and Rod Burden. Also Brian Pickering for allowing us to make use of his excellent Military Aircraft Photographs collection (his address for those wanting copies is Westfield Lodge, Aveland Way, Aslackby, near Sleaford, Lincs).

Last but certainly not least, especial thanks are due to the co-author of the present edition of this book, which first appeared in 1984. Lieutenant Commander Theo Ballance, who is at present based at Yeovilton, joined the Royal Navy from New Zealand in 1968. He has been a Fleet Air Arm observer since 1969, serving on, or working closely with, many of the Squadrons recorded in this book. He very generously offered to help with a new edition, and his invaluable efforts have made it possible to produce an updated and revised version in a relatively short time.

R.C.Sturtivant
St.Albans, England
September 1994

INTRODUCTION

The Fleet Air Arm can be said to trace its origins to the formation of the Naval Wing of the Royal Flying Corps on 13 April 1912. This in turn became the Royal Naval Air Service on 1 July 1914, only a few weeks before the outbreak of the First World War. That war lasted more than four long years, and by the time it had ended the nature of military aviation had been transformed.

For the first six years of its existence, British naval aviation was firmly in the hands of the Admiralty, but on 1 April 1918 the RNAS and RFC were combined to form the Royal Air Force. The RNAS had by that stage been built up to a strength of 55,000 officers and men, had 2,900 aircraft and 103 airships, and controlled 126 air stations at home and overseas. A number of land based units were operating in France and Belgium, and others were active in the Aegean and Mediterranean. Seaplanes, flying boats and airships were stationed all around the British Isles, protecting shipping against U-boats. All this became part of the new service.

In the postwar period, the naval element of the RAF was run down, and by 1919 there remained only one spotter-reconnaissance squadron, half a torpedo squadron, a fighter flight, a seaplane flight and a flying boat flight. However, a number of aircraft carriers were coming into service and the RAF began to make some preparations for these. By the beginning of 1923, No.3 Squadron was operating Westland Walrus spotters from Gosport, alongside No.210 Squadron which was then re-equipping from Sopwith Cuckoos to Blackburn Darts. At Leuchars, No.203 Squadron had Sopwith Camel and Nieuport Nightjar fighters, whilst No.205 Squadron was a reconnaissance unit equipped mainly with Parnall Panthers. On 1 April 1923 the naval squadrons were disbanded to form 400-series flights, each of six aircraft. Exactly a year later, on 1 April 1924, this small force was styled the Fleet Air Arm of the Royal Air Force, and the Fleet Air Arm it has been ever since, whether officially or unofficially.

These new flights fell into four categories, fleet fighter, fleet spotter, fleet reconnaissance and fleet torpedo. The first aircraft carrier to embark any of them seems to have been HMS *Argus*, soon followed by HMS *Eagle*, HMS *Furious* and HMS *Hermes*. These served in Home waters, the Mediterranean and on the China Station, being later joined by the aircraft carriers HMS *Courageous* and HMS *Glorious*, and also the seaplane carrier HMS *Vindictive*. Further new flights were formed for these as the need arose.

The carriers participated in numerous exercises, though surviving records of their activities are sparse. Newer types of aircraft came into service during the early 1920's, to replace the outmoded wartime designs. The Fairey Flycatcher became the standard fleet fighter, but the fleet spotter flights used both the Avro Bison and the Blackburn Blackburn. The fleet reconnaissance flights used the Fairey IIID, whilst the fleet torpedo flights continued to use the Blackburn Dart.

Aircraft were slow in those days, and pilots relied on the speed of the air passing over the ship to pull them up once they had landed, after cutting their engines over the round-down at the after end of the flight deck. Trials were conducted with wires running fore and aft along the deck, to prevent aircraft running over the side of the ship, but this idea was dropped around 1925. A night deck landing was first carried out in 1926 in HMS *Furious*.

The fleet spotter category was dropped in 1929, to be amalgamated into a new fleet reconnaissance category with the advent of the ubiquitous Fairey IIIF, which had the distinction of serving on every carrier and at every station, as well as being well suited for catapult work when these began to be fitted to larger warships. This resulted in some reorganisation of the flight numbering system.

During 1930 the now elderly Darts began to be replaced in the fleet torpedo flights by Blackburn Ripons. Other new types to come into service in the early 1930's included the Hawker Nimrod fleet fighter, and its two-seater fighter reconnaissance counterpart, the Hawker Osprey. The advent of these faster machines led to the introduction of transverse arrester wires, HMS *Courageous* being the first ship so fitted.

A major change occurred in April 1933, when the squadron system was reintroduced, this being the real starting point for the subject matter of this book. Most of the existing 400-series flights were then amalgamated to become 800-series squadrons originally of either nine or twelve aircraft. The only flights to retain their identities, at least for the time being, were those wholly employed on catapult duties.

1933 was also the year in which the spotter reconnaissance squadrons began to discard the IIIF in favour of its radial-engined successor the Fairey Seal, and the following year the torpedo bomber squadrons similarly re-equipped. These gradually had their Ripons withdrawn to be re-engined and refurbished to become radial-engined Baffins, some new machines of this type also being built.

During the autumn of 1935 several squadrons sailed to Egypt, where they remained during the Abyssinian crisis, returning home the following spring.

1936 was an important year for the FAA. It saw the arrival on the scene of the Fairey Swordfish, which was to re-equip all the torpedo bomber and spotter reconnaissance squadrons, to undertake the combined task of torpedo spotter reconnaissance. Another new arrival was the Supermarine Walrus, which had already been tried out as a catapult aircraft with No.444 Flight in HMS *Nelson*, and would eventually become the standard aircraft in this role. The catapult flights themselves were reorganised in that year, when in July they finally discarded the 400-series of numbers to become reorganised in a new 700-series. Thus the basis of the present system of squadron numbering was complete, although the new catapult units retained their flight status for a time, being generally still rather small.

Around 1937 the 'batsman' system was introduced, or to give it the official title, Deck Landing Control Officer. His task was to stand to one side of the deck during landings, and indicate to the pilot by a series of standard signals what changes, if any, he should make to his approach, until the final crossing of bats to indicate that the engine should be cut. In that year the Fairey Seafox began to enter service, this being a light reconnaissance aircraft for catapult use from cruisers; it gave some useful service but was not a great success.

Early in 1939 the new modern carrier HMS *Ark Royal* entered service, and became the first British carrier to carry monoplanes in the shape of the Blackburn Skua fighter. By now the Admiralty had won its battle to regain control of its air arm, and on 24 May 1939 it officially took over all naval squadrons and aircraft. With them came a number of shore bases, which were promptly given ships names in true naval style, some of these being training bases. The new training and support units were all given squadron numbers, contrary to RAF practice. They were regarded as second-line squadrons and given numbers from 750 onwards, this part of the 700-series not having been reached by the catapult units, which by then had achieved squadron status.

At the outbreak of war, on 3 September 1939, the Royal Navy was promptly in action, despite the general period of inactivity ashore at that time which gave rise to the expression 'Phoney War'. HMS *Ark Royal* soon had a near miss from a torpedo fired by a U-boat, and within a fortnight HMS *Courageous* had been lost in a similar attack. On the credit side, a Skua from HMS *Ark Royal* was able to claim the first British air success of the war when it shot down a shadowing Dornier Do 18 flying boat.

A more important success was the chase after the pocket battleship *Graf Spee*, which was eventually scuttled by her crew off Montevideo, after being damaged by gunfire whose accuracy was mainly due to the spotting efforts of the crew of a Seafox from the cruiser HMS *Ajax*.

With the German invasion of Norway in April 1940 the Fleet Air Arm was soon in action. Two Skua squadrons temporarily ashore at Hatston from HMS *Ark Royal* made a successful attack on the German cruiser *Königsberg*, sinking her within ten minutes at her berth in Bergen harbour. This was the first time that a major warship had been sunk by aircraft in a bombing attack. Four days later a Swordfish from HMS *Warspite* bombed and sank the U-boat *U-64* at Bjervik. These successes were to be more than offset, however, when in early June 1940 HMS *Glorious* was sighted and sunk by the German battle-cruisers *Scharnhorst* and *Gneisenau*. The FAA continued to be active in this theatre after the British forces had been evacuated, and in September and October carried out attacks on Trondheim and Tromsø from HMS *Furious*, the latter being the first large night torpedo attack ever carried out.

During the evacuation from Dunkirk in May and June, land-based aircraft of the FAA played a part, several squadrons operating in various roles from RAF aerodromes along the English Channel. After the fall of France, attention largely turned to the Mediterranean, Italy having entered the war on 10 June 1940. Many courageous attacks were made against both Italian and German targets in that theatre, the most notable being undoubtedly the night attack on Taranto on 11 November 1940, in which half the Italian fleet was put out of action by twenty Swordfish from HMS *Illustrious*, which had only joined the Fleet a few weeks earlier.

A major blow occurred on 10 January 1941 when HMS *Illustrious* was herself badly damaged in the eastern Mediterranean by dive-bombing Junkers Ju 87s, being saved only by her sturdy construction. It was to be a year later before she was able to rejoin the Fleet following repairs in the United States. Fortunately HMS *Formidable* came into service at this time and helped to fill the gap.

A number of FAA aircraft participated in the defence of Greece and then Crete, during late 1940 and the early months of 1941, operating from shore bases. Then in June and July 1941 other squadrons were involved in the Syrian campaign, operating from Palestine. Several FAA squadrons were attached to the Desert Air Force being particularly useful in carrying out flare dropping to mark targets for RAF night bombing. Operations against enemy shipping was carried out from Malta, despite heavy attacks against that beleaguered island, which was also the recipient of five relief convoys between May and November 1941. All of these were heavily attacked, defence being provided at different times by FAA aircraft from HMS *Argus*, HMS *Ark Royal*, HMS *Furious* and the new armoured carrier HMS *Victorious*.

Meanwhile, the FAA had participated in the search for and ultimate sinking of the German battle-cruiser *Bismarck*. Her absence from Bergen Fjord was first noted by the crew of a Maryland of No.771 Squadron from Hatston, and subsequent attacks by aircraft from HMS *Victorious* and HMS *Ark Royal* led to her destruction on 27 May 1941 by surface vessels.

From May 1941, Sea Hurricanes and Fulmars were operated from catapult-armed merchantmen, or CAM-ships, this task being later handed over to the RAF. Then in September 1941 No.802 Squadron flew its Martlets aboard the auxiliary carrier HMS *Audacity*, a captured German merchant ship fitted with a flight deck, two arrester wires and a barrier, but no hangar. This was the prototype for the many escort carriers which later entered service, most being American built.

HMS *Ark Royal* now carried the Fairey Fulmar fighter, an improvement on the Skua, but she was herself nearing the end of her life. After two years of false claims by the Germans, she was finally lost when on 13 November 1941 she was hit by a torpedo from *U-81* whilst returning to Gibraltar from a Malta run. Attempts to get her to port were unsuccessful, and she sank the following morning.

At the end of 1941 Japan entered the war, and the FAA soon became involved in the defence of Ceylon. HMS *Hermes* was joined in the Eastern Fleet by HMS

Formidable and HMS *Indomitable*, but was herself sunk on 9 April 1942 in an attack by Japanese carrier-based aircraft.

On 12 February 1942, No.825 Squadron, operating from Manston in Kent, carried out a brave attack on the German battlecruisers *Scharnhorst* and *Gneisenau*, which were making a dash through the English Channel from their refuge at Brest in poor visibility. All the aircraft were lost in this unsuccessful attack, but the CO, Lt Cdr (A) Eugene Esmonde, DSO, RN was posthumously awarded the Victoria Cross.

During May 1942, aircraft from HMS *Illustrious* and HMS *Indomitable* participated in an invasion of the Vichy French island of Madagascar. In the initial attack the FAA successfully attacked an armed merchant cruiser and a submarine. It also took part in the final assault in September.

Further Malta convoys were undertaken in 1942, several British carriers being joined by the US carrier *Wasp* during a run in April. A heavy blow was suffered on 11 August when, during Operation *Pedestal*, a particularly difficult convoy, HMS *Eagle* was sunk north of Algiers by torpedoes from *U-73*. However, this convoy was successfully defended by the FAA, despite heavy damage to HMS *Indomitable*, which had to go to the United States for repair.

The FAA also played its part in numerous Arctic convoys, which sailed for north Russian ports with valuable war materials. Many of these suffered heavily from German air and submarine attacks, and British carriers and later escort carriers flew numerous sorties, often in appalling weather conditions. British carriers were also involved in attacks on the German battleship *Tirpitz* in Norway.

In November 1942 the FAA participated in Operation *Torch*, the Allied landings in North Africa. Seven British carriers were involved, including three of the new small escort carriers, or 'Woolworth carriers' as they were known unofficially, and they provided 130 fighters and more than 30 Albacore TBR aircraft for the attack. One FAA pilot landed his American-built Martlet fighter at Blida aerodrome, and accepted its surrender from the French station commander.

One of the most effective measures against the U-boat menace was the introduction of Merchant Aircraft Carriers (MAC-ships) in May 1943. These were standard grain carriers or oil tankers fitted with an elementary flight deck on which were carried three or four Swordfish. So successful was this concept that no convoy in which they participated lost a single ship.

The Germans having been driven out of North Africa by May 1943, preparations were made for an invasion of Sicily in July, but the FAA had only a minimal involvement. They were, however, fully involved during Operation *Avalanche*, the landings at Salerno, south of Naples, in September, over 100 fighters operating from the escort carriers of Force V.

By April 1944 the Eastern Fleet had built up sufficient strength for attacks on Japanese-held territory. The first of these was on the port of Sabang, on the island of Sumatra, and this was followed by numerous similar attacks on other targets during the year. The striking force included Corsairs, a tough American-built fighter which was by then largely replacing the inadequate British designs.

Several FAA Swordfish and Avenger squadrons were attached to RAF Coastal Command during mid-1944, to operate both by day and by night over the English Channel in support of the invasion forces. Some of these continued to operate until almost of the end of the war in Europe.

In August 1944 the FAA played its part in Operation *Dragoon*, the landings in the south of France, making numerous attacks against shore targets. Bombardment spotting and other activities were carried out a few weeks later during operations in the Aegean.

During 1944 and 1945 more than 30 attacks were made from both fleet carriers and escort carriers against targets in Norway. The last such attack was made shortly before VE-day, when a U-boat and a depot ship were blown up.

By November 1944 the Eastern Fleet had sufficiently expanded to be split up. The fleet carriers became part of the new British Pacific Fleet, whilst the escort carriers joined the East Indies Fleet. Both fleets took part in numerous attacks during the last few months of the war, culminating in strikes against the Japanese mainland by the British Pacific Fleet shortly before VJ-day, 15 August 1945. The FAA won its second Victoria Cross, again posthumously, when on 9 August Lt (A) Robert Hampton Gray, RCNVR, of No.1841 Squadron in HMS *Formidable* pressed home an attack on a Japanese destroyer despite heavy fire from warships and shore batteries.

In the postwar period, the FAA gradually re-equipped. The American-built aircraft gave way to new British designs, mostly designed as naval aircraft, though adaptations of RAF aircraft continued to appear. In 1947 the first RNVR squadrons were formed, a peak strength of twelve squadrons being achieved by 1954.

The Korean war started in June 1950, and several of the Royal Navy's postwar light flight carriers were involved before the end of hostilities in July 1953. During that time 23,000 sorties were flown for the loss of 22 aircrew on operations and a further 11 in accidents.

Meanwhile the first naval jet squadron had formed in August 1951, No.802 Squadron embarking its Attackers in the new carrier HMS *Eagle* the following March. This ship headed eight other carriers during the Coronation Review of the Fleet on 15 June 1953, in which 300 naval aircraft took part in a flypast before Her Majesty the Queen, including the new Sea Hawks of No.806 Squadron.

Airborne Early Warning was introduced when No.849 Squadron reformed with American Skyraiders in July 1952, its flights being embarked as needed in all the existing carriers. Helicopters, with which the Royal Navy had been carrying out trials as early as 1944, went into general squadron use by the early 1950s, and they came into operational use in 1953, by No.848 Squadron against terrorists in Malaya.

New developments appeared around that time in both carrier design and operating techniques. Angled decks gave much greater flexibility, the consequent absence of a barrier allowing aircraft to take off again in the case of a faulty approach. Steam catapults were being fitted, after successful trials in HMS *Perseus* in 1950. The batsman technique, which could not cope with the speed of jet operations, was superseded by the Mirror Landing Aid, this being supplemented by an audio airspeed indicator. Aircraft were also being equipped with ejector seats, and the combination of these factors resulted in a marked drop in deck-landing accidents and casualties.

Towards the end of 1956, the FAA was involved in Operation *Musketeer*, the joint British/French attack on the Suez Canal area. Five British carriers took part, their aircraft attacking airfields, covering landings and ferrying Commandos ashore by helicopter before the cease-fire was declared on 5 November.

In 1958 the powerful Scimitar strike fighter came into service, bringing with it the capability of carrying a nuclear weapon. The following year appeared the Sea Vixen all-weather fighter, the first to be equipped with Firestreak missiles, a pilot attack sight and GEC radar locked to the parent carrier's radar system.

During 1961 the FAA was used to afford protection for Kuwait, which was under threat from Iraq. The newly-converted Commando carrier HMS *Bulwark* brought No.848 Squadron to the scene, to put ashore No.42 Royal Marine Commando. This was to prove the forerunner to a request the following year for British help from the newly independent Federation of Malaysia following attacks across the Brunei border from Indonesia. It was not until October 1966 that FAA helicopter squadrons could be withdrawn, these having used HMS *Albion* and HMS *Bulwark* when not ashore in jungle bases.

In March 1964 No.829 Squadron reformed as the parent squadron for helicopters carried on small ships. Initially Wasps were used in most cases, but in 1978 these began to give way to the Lynx, the latter being controlled initially by No.702 Squadron and later No.815 Squadron. Helicopters were also carried on the new Amphibious Warfare Ships which appeared during 1965, and also in 1967 on Helicopter Carriers of which two were converted from *Tiger*-class cruisers.

In 1969 the American-built Phantom entered service as a new generation of all-weather strike fighter, capable of carrying an impressive range of loads, which included both conventional and nuclear bombs. This was followed in 1970 by the twin-engined Sea King helicopter, primarily intended for the anti-submarine role, but later adapted for commando and other tasks.

1978 saw the end of conventional flying, with the withdrawal of the first postwar HMS *Ark Royal*. However, its place was soon taken by the launching in 1980 of the first of the light fleet carriers or through-deck cruisers, HMS *Invincible*. These ships are fitted with another British invention, the 'ski-jump', which enables its vertical take-off Sea Harriers to carry a much greater load when taking off with forward thrust.

The Fleet Air Arm's greatest test in recent years was undoubtedly its role with the South Atlantic Task Force in 1982. Its Sea Harriers in particular were a spectacular success against their Argentinean opponents, and the part played by all the FAA units, many of which were hastily improvised on the outbreak of hostilities, undoubtedly gave it added confidence for the future.

Equipment has largely remained the same since, though mostly with more advanced versions of each major type. On the horizon is the Merlin helicopter to replace the Lynx, with conjecture as to the possibility of supersonic replacement for the Sea Harrier.

Gloster Meteor T.7 WS103 '709/VL' of Station Flight Yeovilton around 1966/7. (Brian Lowe)

Hawker Hunter T.7s and GA.11s of No.738 Squadron at Lossiemouth around 1962/3. (via Brian Lowe)

SQUADRON NUMBERING

The numbers allotted to FAA flights and squadrons fall into the following groups. To avoid confusion, blocks of squadron numbers used since 1933 are different from those used by the Royal Air Force:

Nos.401 to 419	Fleet fighter flights.
Nos.420 to 439	Fleet spotter flights.
Nos.440 to 459	Fleet reconnaissance flights, many later becoming fleet spotter reconnaissance flights.
Nos.460 onwards	Fleet torpedo flights, later becoming fleet torpedo bomber flights.
Nos.700 to 749	Catapult flights, later becoming catapult squadrons. When these ceased to exist the range became available for training and ancillary squadrons. Nos.700 to 710 were earmarked for use by amphibian and floatplane squadrons in 1943, but this later lapsed.
Nos.750 to 799	Training and ancillary squadrons.
Nos.800 to 809	Single-seat fighter squadrons in carriers.
Nos.810 to 819	Torpedo bomber squadrons in carriers, later torpedo spotter reconnaissance and torpedo bomber reconnaissance squadrons. [810 onwards now HAS helicopter squadrons]
Nos.820 to 859	Spotter reconnaissance squadrons, later torpedo spotter reconnaissance and torpedo bomber reconnaissance squadrons. [845 onwards now Commando helicopter squadrons]
Nos.860 to 869	Torpedo bomber reconnaissance squadrons. Later reserved for Dutch-manned and then Dutch Navy squadrons.
Nos.870 to 879	Single-seat fighter squadrons. Later reserved for Royal Canadian Navy use.
Nos.880 to 899	Single - seat fighter squadrons in carriers.
Nos.1700 to 1749	Torpedo bomber reconnaissance squadrons, reallocated to amphibian bomber reconnaissance squadrons.
Nos.1750 to 1769	Single-seat fighter squadrons (not taken up).
Nos.1770 to 1799	Two-seat fighter squadrons.
Nos.1800 to 1809	Torpedo bomber reconnaissance squadrons (not taken up)
Nos.1810 to 1829	Dive-bomber squadrons.
Nos.1830 to 1899	Single-seat fighter squadrons. Later used for RNVR squadrons, and latterly RNR squadrons.

NOTES ON SQUADRON LISTINGS

Squadrons

In addition to British naval air squadrons, details are given of Australian, Canadian and Dutch naval air squadron where these have been numbered in the 700 or 800 series. Bases are listed in respect of every known movement of each squadron, including detachments. These have been culled from a considerable number of sources, including surviving squadron diaries, Navy Lists, individual flying log books, newspaper reports and the magazines of various aviation historical societies. Whilst every effort has been to ensure their completeness and accuracy, there will inevitably be errors and omissions. The date quoted against each shore base or ship is generally that on which most squadron aircraft arrived; where a significant portion of the squadron was located other than on the main base, this is shown as a detachment (Dt), and if known the actual number of aircraft (or maximum number if it varied) is also shown (e.g. Dt3). Where a particular flight or other detachment operated independently from the main squadron for any length of time, its moves are listed separately, being inset to distinguish them from those of the main squadron. Periods spent on aerodrome dummy deck landings (ADDLs), deck landing training (DLT) or deck landing practice (DLP) are indicated, even where this occupied as little as one day. Also listed are bases temporarily used by a squadron whilst in transit, especially on disembarkation. Where space permits, the parent Group or Wing, or resident unit, is shown of RAF stations to which a FAA squadron was attached.

Commanding Officers

Names are listed of the commanding officers of every first and second line squadron. There are inevitably a few gaps, mainly in the dates, but most of these relate to Commonwealth squadrons. Prewar FAA officers usually held dual RAF ranks, and these are shown in parenthesis. The dates listed are generally those on which the officer concerned actually took over command; they will in many instances be later than the date of his arrival on the squadron, since there was often a handing over period.

Aircraft types

Every type and mark of aircraft known to have been flown by each squadron or unit is listed, including those used only in small numbers. The periods of service quoted are those between which the squadron is known to have been using that particular type of aircraft, but could have been longer, especially in the case of supporting types, for which information is often sparse, particularly for 1939-1945. It has been possible with first line squadrons, and with second line squadrons since about 1955, to establish the actual overall dates of use. For the remaining second line squadrons, the dates quoted are those during which the squadron concerned is known to have flown that particular type of aircraft, but could well have used it for a longer period.

Identification Markings

The application of visual identification markings to the aircraft of each squadron is briefly summarised, the various systems being described in the section 'Naval Aircraft Code Markings'. Where letter/number/letter or number/letter codes were used, these are shown as, for instance, *A6A+*, indicating that individual aircraft were marked *A6A, A6B, A6C* and so on, though not all individual letters up to *A6Z* were necessarily used. Carrier letter/individual letter codes are shown as *E:A+*, for example.

In the case of number codes, the range of numbers is given (e.g. *150-161*), though again not all numbers in that range were necessarily used; where appropriate, the range is suffixed by any fin letters carried (e.g. *230-243/V:H:LM*). Where detailed information on such codes is lacking, it may be shown as, for instance, *150+*.

Much of the information, especially for the period 1939 to 1947, has been gleaned over many years from numerous photographs and individual flying log books. Although the details given are largely complete and accurate, there are still gaps and doubts, and the authors would be pleased to hear from anyone who might be able to help with any of these.

GLOSSARY

(A)	Air Branch
AA	Anti-aircraft
AAC	Army Air Corps
AAS	Air Armament School
ABR	Amphibian Bomber Reconnaissance (role prefix)
a/c	Aircraft
ACMI	Air Combat Manoevring Instrumentation
ACV	Auxiliary Aircraft Carrier (formerly AVG, changed to CVE on 17 July 1943)
ADCF	Air Defence Command Frigate
ADDL	Aerodrome Dummy Deck Landing
Ad F	Admiralty Flight
AEF	Air Experience Flight
AEW	Airborne Early Warning (role prefix)
AFB	Air Force Base
AFC	Air Force Cross
AFT	Advanced Flying Training
AI	Air Interception (airborne radar)
ALT	Attack Light Torpedo
AMC	Armed Merchant Cruiser
APC	Armament Practice Camp
AS	Anti-submarine (role prefix)
ASH	Air-to-surface-vessel radar (US)
ASV	Air-to-surface-vessel radar (British)
ASW	Air Sea Warfare
ASWDU	Air Sea Warfare Development Unit
ASWE	Air Sea Warfare Establishment
ATC	Armament Training Camp
ATDU	Aircraft Torpedo Development Unit
ATS	Armament Training Station
AUTEC	Atlantic Underwater Test and Evaluation Center (US Navy, Andros Island, Bahamas)
AVG	Aircraft Escort Vessel (changed to ACV on 20 August 1942)
B	Bomber (role prefix)
BEM	British Empire Medal
BPF	British Pacific Fleet
BRNC	Britannia Royal Naval College
Bt	Baronet
BUTEC	British Underwater Test & Evaluation Centre (Kyle of Lochalsh, uses airstrip at Plockton)
C	Transport (role prefix)
CAG	Carrier Air Group
CAM-ship	Catapult-armed Merchantship
CAP	Combat Air Patrol
Capt	Captain
CB	Commander of the Order of the Bath
CC	Communications (role prefix)
CCA	Carrier Controlled Approach
CD	Canadian Forces Decoration
Cdo	Commando
Cdr	Commander
CFE	Central Fighter Establishment
C-in-C	Commander-in-Chief
CJATC	Canadian Joint Air Training Centre
CMG	Companion of the Order of St.Michael and St.George
CO	Commanding Officer
COD	Carrier Onboard Delivery (formerly Courier Onboard Delivery)
CPE	Central Photographic Establishment
c/s	Call sign
CTS	Central Tactical System
CVE	Carrier Vessel Escort (US-built escort carrier) (formerly ACV and AVG)
CVO	Commander of the Royal Victorian Order
D	Pilotless drone conversion (role prefix)
DDH	Helicopter fitted destroyer (RCN)
DFC	Distinguished Flying Cross
DH	De Havilland
DLCO	Deck Landing Control Officer ('batsman')
DLG	Destroyer, Light Guided (Missile)
DLP	Deck Landing Practice
DLT	Deck Landing Training
DSC	Distinguished Service Cross
DSO	Distinguished Service Order
Dt	Detachment
E-boat	Small offensive German MTB
ECM	Electronic Counter Measures (role prefix)
F	Flight; Fighter (role prefix)
FAA	Fleet Air Arm
FAW	Fighter All Weather (role prefix)
FB	Fighter-bomber (role prefix)
FFG	Guided Missile Frigate
FFH	Helicopter fitted frigate (RCN)
FG	Fighter Ground Attack (role prefix); Fighter-General (role prefix)
FGA	Fighter Ground Attack (role prefix)
FIU	Fighter Interception Unit
Flt	Flight
FOB	Forward Operating Base
FOFT	Flag Officer Flying Training
FOMFA	Flag Officer Malaya and Forward Areas
FONA	Flag Officer Naval Aviation
FONAC	Flag Officer Naval Air Command
FONFT	Flag Officer Naval Flying Training
FORACS	NATO Naval Forces Sensor and Weapons Accuracy Check Site [near Stavangar]
FOST	Flag Officer Sea Training
FR	Fighter-reconnaissance (role prefix)
FRADTU	Fleet Requirements and Air Direction Training Unit
FRADU	Fleet Requirements and Air Direction Unit
FRS	Fighter-reconnaissance V/STOL (role prefix)
FRU	Fleet Requirements Unit
GA	Ground Attack (role prefix)
GC	George Cross
Gp	Group (RAF)
HAR	Helicopter Air Rescue (role prefix)
HAS	Helicopter Anti-Submarine (role prefix)
HMAS	Her/His Majesty's Australian Ship
HMCS	Her/His Majesty's Canadian Ship
HMNZS	Her/His Majesty's New Zealand Ship
HMS	Her/His Majesty's Ship
HMT	Her/His Majesty's Troopship
HR	Helicopter Rescue (role prefix)
HrMs	Harer Majesteits (Her Majesty's [Ship]) (Dutch Navy)

HT	Helicopter Trainer (role prefix)	RNARY	Royal Naval Aircraft Repair Yard
HU	Helicopter Utility (role prefix)	RNAY	Royal Naval Aircraft Yard
		RNethN	Royal Netherlands Navy
IF	Intensive Flying	RNR	Royal Naval Reserve
IFTU	Intensive Flying Trials Unit	RNVR	Royal Naval Volunteer Reserve
IR	Instrument Rating	RNZNVR	Royal New Zealand Naval Volunteer Reserve
JASS	Joint Anti-Submarine School	RO-RO	Roll-on/Roll-off
JOAC	Junior Officers Air Course	RP	Rocket Projectile
JSTU	Joint Services Training Unit	RSRE	Royal Signals and Radar Establishment
KCB	Knight Commander of the Order of the Bath	S	Strike (role prefix)
		SAG	Support Air Group
L	Low-altitude fighter (role prefix)	SANF(V)	South African Naval Force (Volunteer)
L/C	Lieutenant Commander	SAR	Search and Rescue
LR	Long Range	ScAD	Scottish Air Division
LSL	Landing Ship, Logistic	SEATO	South East Asia Treaty Organisation
LST	Landing Ship, Tank	Senior Pilot	Second in command of FAA squadron
Lt	Lieutenant	Sh F	Ships Flight
		SK	Sea King
MAC-ship	Merchant Aircraft Carrier	SKTF	Sea King Training Flight
MAG	Miscellaneous Air Group	SKTU	Sea King Training Unit
MBE	Member of the Order of the British Empire	SMAC	Short Maintenance Air Course
		SNAW	School of Naval Air Warfare
MEAF	Middle East Air Force	SP	Seaplane; Senior Pilot
MONAB	Mobile Naval Air Base	Sqdn	Squadron
MTB	Motor Torpedo Boat	SS	Steamship
MV	Motor Vessel	St	Station
MVO	Member of the Victorian Order	St F	Station Flight
		STU	Service Trials Unit
NAFDU	Naval Air Fighting Development Unit		
NAFS	Naval Air Fighter School	T	Trainer (role prefix)
NAFU	Naval Air Firing Unit	TacR	Tactical Reconnaissance
NAS	Naval Air Station	TAG	Telegraphist Air Gunner
NASS	Naval Anti-Submarine School	TBR	Torpedo Bomber Reconnaissance (role prefix)
NASWDU	Naval Air Sea Warfare Development Unit		
NATO	North Atlantic Treaty Organisation	TF	Torpedo Fighter (role prefix); Task Force
NF	Night Fighter (role prefix)	TLC	Tank Landing Craft
NOTU	Naval Operational Training Unit	TR	Torpedo Reconnaissance (role prefix)
		TrAG	Training Air Group
OBE	Officer of the Order of the British Empire	TSR	Torpedo Spotter Reconnaissance
OEU	Operational Evaluation Unit	TT	Target Towing (role prefix)
OFS	Operational Flying School		
OFT	Operational Flying Training	U	Unmanned (role prefix)
OTU	Operational Training Unit	U-boat	German submarine
		UK	United Kingdom
PR	Photographic Reconnaissance (role prefix)	UN	United Nations
Pt	Pennant number	USN	United States Navy
		USNS	United States Naval Ship
RAAF	Royal Australian Air Force	USS	United States Ship
RAF	Royal Air Force		
RAN	Royal Australian Navy	VC	Victoria Cross
RANAS	Royal Australian Naval Air Station	VE-Day	Victory in Europe day (8 May 1945)
RANVR	Royal Australian Naval Volunteer Reserve	VIP	Very Important Person
RCAF	Royal Canadian Air Force	VJ-Day	Victory against Japan day (15 August 1945)
RCN	Royal Canadian Navy		
RCN(R)	Royal Canadian Navy (Reserve)	VRD	Volunteer Reserve Decoration
RCNVR	Royal Canadian Naval Volunteer Reserve		
RFA	Royal Fleet Auxiliary	Westlant	Western Atlantic
RM	Royal Marines	W/T	Wireless Telegraphy
RN	Royal Navy	Wx	Wessex
RNAMY	Royal Naval Aircraft Maintenance Yard		

No.700 Squadron

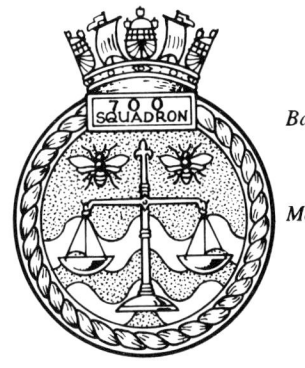

Badge: On a field per fesse blue and barry wavy white and blue, a pair of scales gold in chief two bees proper
Motto: Experienta docet (Experience teaches)

No.700 Squadron first formed at Hatston on 21 January 1940, by amalgamating the 700 series of Catapult Squadrons. Equipped initially with 42 Walruses, in addition to 11 Seafoxes and 12 Swordfish floatplanes, it acted as a pool and headquarters for all catapult aircraft embarked in battleships and cruisers. From 16 July 1940 a sub-unit of 6-8 Walruses operated from Sullom Voe as the Shetland Flight. In November 1940 a similar sub-unit was formed out of No.701 Squadron as the Stornoway Flight, moving to join the other flight at Sullom Voe in May 1941.

Several independent detachments of No.700 Squadron were set up overseas. A Mediterranean detachment was formed on 16 Oct 1941, based initially at Dekheila, with responsibility for all those Fleet Air Arm aircraft disembarked in the Middle East whose primary duty was co-operation with the Mediterranean Fleet. It came under the control of No.201 Group, RAF, becoming known as No.700 (Levant) Squadron when it reached Beirut on 11 May 1942 and absorbed part of the MEAF Air Sea Rescue Flight, only to be redesignated No.701 Squadron on 1 October 1942. From 27 November 1941, 6 Walruses which had been shipped out in HMS Argus took over from No.833 Squadron the task of carrying out daily patrols from North Front, Gibraltar, this detachment ending in April 1943. Another detachment formed on 8 November 1942 at the old Air France flying boat base at Arzeu as No.700 (Algiers) Squadron, for anti-submarine patrols with 6 Walruses, three of which embarked as required whilst the other three remained ashore, this detachment disbanding in January 1943. A detachment also operated in the Far East, with 9 Walruses and 2 Seafoxes.

The main squadron reached an establishment of 63 Walruses by June 1942, when it moved its headquarters to Twatt, to be known as 'A' Flight, No.700 Squadron. By this time the squadron was operating a ten week course for newly formed catapult flights, consisting of 3 weeks initially at Donibristle for aerodrome flying, circuits and landings, wireless telegraphy, water landings, anti-submarine practice attacks, dive bombing and photography. This was followed by 3 weeks at Dundee in which these tasks were supplemented by crew training, navigation exercises and night landings, after which a week was spent on a catapult course in HMS Pegasus in the Irish Sea area. After another week back at Donibristle, the final two weeks were spent attached to 'A' Flight at Twatt before joining the allotted ship. The various catapult flights used the nearest most convenient shore base when disembarked, including Arbroath, Donibristle, Grimsetter, Lee-on-Solent, Mount Batten, Roborough, Speke, Stornoway and Sullom Voe, as well as Hatston and later Twatt. A sub-unit known as 'W' Flight, No.700 Squadron formed at Sandbanks on 12 July 1943 with 6 Walruses and 4 Swordfish, embarking in HMS Fencer in September 1943 to participate in the occupation of the Azores, being absorbed into No.836 Squadron later in the year, after returning home. No.700 Squadron gradually ran down as the advent of MAC-ships and escort carriers made catapult aircraft superfluous, and on 24 Mar 1944 the residue of 'A' Flight, No.700 Squadron became 'B' Flight, No.771 Squadron, and No.700 Squadron disbanded.

On 11 October 1944, No.700 reformed at Donibristle as a Maintenance Test Pilot Training Squadron. Moving to Worthy Down, it operated a course, initially of 4 weeks but later extended to 10 weeks, during which each pilot was required to carry out a minimum of 5 weeks test flying on the basic types of aircraft then in service. These included the Avenger, Barracuda, Firebrand, Firefly, Hellcat, Seafire and Wildcat, and in its first eleven months the squadron trained 84 test pilots. Moving to Middle Wallop in November 1945, and then to Yeovilton in April 1946, it became part of the 50th Training Air Group when the latter formed in May 1948. The squadron disbanded on 30 September 1949.

No.700 next reformed at Ford on 18 August 1955 as the Trials and Requirements Unit, replacing Nos.703 and 771 Squadrons. Initially equipped with 9 Firefly TT.4s, 2 Sea Vampire F.20s, 2 Ansons, 2 Sea Hawks, 2 Wyverns and 2 Gannets, it also took over the task of No.787 Squadron when the latter disbanded on 16 January 1956. The Fleet Requirements element of its work was largely handed over to the Airwork FRU at Hurn in February 1957. Then shortly before Ford closed, the squadron moved to Yeovilton, in September 1958. There it disbanded on 3 July 1961, its aircraft going mainly to No.771 Squadron.

From the mid-fifties, a number of intensive flying trials units were formed, both before and after the squadron's disbandment, in preparation for new types of aircraft coming into service. These operated as independent units but under the 700 Squadron title, each being distinguished by an individual letter suffix. Brief details of these are given in the appended lists.

The most recent of these was No.700L Squadron. This originally formed on 1 September 1976 at Yeovilton as No.700L Lynx IFTU for the introduction into service of the Lynx helicopter. Its task completed, it disbanded on 16 December 1977. On 16 July 1990 No.700L Squadron reformed at Portland by redesignating the Lynx Operational Flying Trials Unit (LOFTU). Equipped with three Lynx HAS.3(CTS) helicopters, it operated for two years as an IFTU for the Racal Central Tactical System (CTS) to be fitted to the Lynx fleet. The squadron also trained three front-line CTS-fitted Lynx flights. On completion of trials the squadron was absorbed into No.815 Squadron as an Operational Evaluation Unit on 17 July 1992.

No.700M Squadron is expected to form in July 1997 as the Merlin IFTU.

Walrus W3099 from HMS Howe, flying off Inverness in July 1942. It was written off half an hour after this photograph was taken.
(L.Bailey)

Walrus L2293 of No.700 Pool Sqdn at Dekheila in March 1941.
(Dennis Phillips)

Identification Markings
Walrus & Swordfish mostly uncoded but a few had single letters and Walruses with the East Indies Fleet based at Mombasa used *9A+* for a time (code *G8A+* allocated 1.40 but not used); *Y2A+* on all types from 10.44, to *200/VL+* & *300/VL+*1946; *071-084/FD* from 8.55, to *500-524/FD:VL* 1.56.

Aircraft Equipment	Period of Service	Example	
Walrus	Jan 1940 - Mar 1944	W3072	(S)
Swordfish I/SP	Jan 1940 - Jan 1942	L9767	
Seafox I	Jan 1940 - Sep 1942	L4519	
Kingfisher I	1942 - Jan 1943	FN684	
Fulmar I	Sep 1941 - Sep 1941	N1920	
Swordfish (700W Flt)	Jul 1943 - Dec 1943		
Albacore I	Jan 1946 - Feb 1946	BF764	
Avenger I	Jun 1945 - Feb 1946	FN837	
Avenger II	Mar 1945 - May 1945	JZ321	
Barracuda II	Jan 1945 - Mar 1946	DR244	
Barracuda TR.III	May 1945 - Aug 1947	RJ763	(300/VL)
Corsair I	Mar 1945 - Nov 1945	JT106	
Corsair III	Feb 1945 - Feb 1946	JS494	
Dauntless I	Feb 1945 - Feb 1946	JT927	
Defiant TT.III	Feb 1945 - Mar 1945		
Firebrand TF.III	Jun 1945 - Mar 1946	DK412	
Firefly I	Jan 1945 - Sep 1949	MB401	(200/VL)
Fulmar II	Jan 1946 - Feb 1946	X8626	
Harvard III	Apr 1947 - Sep 1949	EZ284	(203/VL)
Hellcat I	Feb 1945 - Dec 1945	JV204	
Hellcat II	Jun 1945 - Jan 1946	JW875	
Helldiver I	Nov 1945 - Dec 1945		
Hurricane IIc	May 1945	PZ816	
Sea Hurricane IIb	Feb 1945 - Sep 1945	JS310	
Master II	Oct 1944 - Jul 1946	DL365	
Mosquito FB.VI	Feb 1946 - May 1946		
Oxford	Feb 1946 - Aug 1947	DF453	
Reliant I	Jan 1945 - Feb 1946	FL148	
Seafire Ib	Feb 1945 - Sep 1945	NX957	
Seafire IIc	Nov 1945 - Dec 1945	NM942	
Seafire III	Feb 1945 - Feb 1946	NN514	
Seafire XV	Feb 1945 - Mar 1948	SW907	('Y2C')
Seafire FR.45	1945		
Seamew	Nov 1945 - Dec 1945	JW589	
Sea Otter I	Feb 1945 - Mar 1948	JN201	
Swordfish II	Oct 1945 - Nov 1945	NE924	
Swordfish III	Jan 1945 - May 1945	NR972	
Tiger Moth II	Jan 1945 - Jun 1945	T6976	
Walrus II	Jan 1945 - Feb 1946	HD876	
Wildcat IV	Jun 1945 - Feb 1946	FN237	
Wildcat V	Feb 1945 - Mar 1945	5JV341	
Wildcat VI	Dec 1944	JV659	
Barracuda V	Feb 1948 - Jun 1948	RK557	
Firebrand TF.V	Feb 1948 -	EK787	
Sea Fury F.10	Jun 1948 - Sep 1949	TF951	
Anson 1	Aug 1955 - May 1956	NK834	(591/FD)
Attacker FB.2	Aug 1955 - Feb 1956	WZ277	(076/FD)
Avenger AS.5	1956 - Aug 1958	XB374	(507/FD)
Dragonfly HR.1	Feb 1959 - Oct 1959	VX597	
Firefly TT.4	Aug 1955 - Feb 1957	VH132	(514/FD)
Gannet AS.1	Aug 1955 - Jun 1961	WN418	(520/FD)
Gannet T.2	Mar 1959 - May 1959	XG873	
Gannet AS.4	Feb 1957 - Feb 1960	XG794	(503/FD)
Meteor TT.20	Dec 1959 - Jul 1961	WM242	(511)
Scimitar F.1	May 1958 - Feb 1959	XD221	(512/VL)
Sea Fury FB.11	Dec 1955 - Jan 1956	VW633	(523/FD)
Sea Hawk F.1	Aug 1955 - Nov 1955	WF233	(074/FD)
Sea Hawk F.2	Nov 1956 - Feb 1957	WF259	(511/FD)
Sea Hawk FB.3	Aug 1955 - Sep 1958	WM912	(512/FD)
Sea Hawk FGA.4	Aug 1955 - Sep 1959	WV904	(516/VL)
Sea Hawk FB.5	Nov 1958 - Aug 1959	WM913	(515/VL)
Sea Hawk FGA.6	Jul 1957 - 1959	XE403	(517/FD)
Seamew AS.1	Nov 1956 - Feb 1957	XE179	(507/FD)
Sea Vampire F.20	Aug 1955 - Nov 1956	VV143	(508/FD)
Sea Vampire T.22	Jul 1957 - Oct 1957	XA165	(520/FD)
Sea Venom FAW.20	Sep 1956 - 1959	WM523	(521/FD)
Sea Venom FAW.21	Jan 1956 - Mar 1961	XG607	(522/FD)
Whirlwind HAR.1	May 1960 - Nov 1960	XA869	
Whirlwind HAR.3	Sep 1958 - Jun 1961	XJ402	(501/VL)
Whirlwind HAS.7	Sep 1958 - Feb 1960	XK939	(502)
Wyvern S.4	Aug 1955 - Feb 1957	WP342	(518/FD)

Battle Honours

River Plate	1939
Norway	1940
Spartivento	1940
Atlantic	1940-41
Matapan	1941
Mediterranean	1942
North Africa	1942-43
Normandy	1944

700A

Aircraft Equipment	Period of Service	Example
Sea Harrier FRS.1	Jun 1979 - Mar 1980	XZ452 (101/VL)

700B

Aircraft Equipment	Period of Service	Example
Buccaneer S.2	Apr 1965 - Sep 1965	XN979 (727/VL)
Hunter T.8	Apr 1965 - May 1965	XE664 (739/LM)

700G

Aircraft Equipment	Period of Service	Example
Gannet AEW.3	Aug 1959 - Jan 1960	XL453

700H

Aircraft Equipment	Period of Service	Example
Whirlwind HAS.7	Mar 1957 - Sep 1957	XG596 (508 'H')
Wessex HAS.1	Apr 1960 - Jan 1962	XM839 (512)
Wessex HAS.1	1967 - 1967	XP151
Wessex HAS.3	Jan 1967 - Sep 1967	XS119 (583/CU)

700L

Aircraft Equipment	Period of Service	Example
Lynx HAS.2	Sep 1976 - Dec 1977	XZ229 (740/VL)
Lynx HAS.3(CTS)	Jul 1990 - Jul 1992	ZF557 (670/PO)

700P

Aircraft Equipment	Period of Service	Example
Phantom FG.1	Apr 1968 - Mar 1969	XT862 (722/VL)

700S

Aircraft Equipment	Period of Service	Example
Sea King HAS.1	Aug 1969 - May 1970	XV649 (587/CU)

700V

Aircraft Equipment	Period of Service	Example
Wessex HU.5	Oct 1963 - May 1964	XS480 (B)

700W

Aircraft Equipment	Period of Service	Example
Wasp HAS.1	Jun 1963 - Mar 1964	XS530 (992)

700X

Aircraft Equipment	Period of Service	Example
Scimitar F.1	Aug 1957 - Jun 1958	XD231 (806/FD)
Sea Vampire T.22	1957 - May 1958	XG769 (809)
P.531-O/N Wasp	Oct 1959 - Jun 1961	XN333

700Y

Aircraft Equipment	Period of Service	Example
Sea Vixen FAW.1	Nov 1958 - Jul 1959	XJ490
Hunter T.8	Nov 1958 - Jan 1959	XL582

700Z

Aircraft Equipment	Period of Service	Example
Buccaneer S.1	Aug 1961 - Dec 1962	XK536 (685/LM)
Hunter T.8	May 1961 - Jul 1961	WV319 (689/LM)
Hunter T.8b	Jul 1961 - Dec 1962	WW664 (686/LM)
Meteor T.7	May 1961 - Nov 1961	WS116 (935/LM)
Sea Prince T.1	Oct 1961 - Mar 1962	WP316 (936)
Dominie 1	Oct 1962	HG694

Supermarine Walrus W2714 of No.700 Squadron HMS Cornwall Flight at George airfield, South Africa in February 1942. (V.W.Clarkson)

A Curtiss Helldiver of No.700 Maintenance Test Pilot Training Squadron at Worthy Down in 1945. (via Douglas Rough)

Grumman Wildcat VI JV659 of No.700 Maintenance Test Pilot Training Squadron at Worthy Down around December 1944. (via Douglas Rough)

North American Harvard III EX447 'Y2M' of No.700 Squadron on 4 December 1946 makes a successful wheels up landing at Yeovilton with a jammed throttle. (Lt Cdr D Wilson/FAA Museum)

de Havilland Sea Venom FAW.22 XG631 '518/LM' of No.700 Squadron at Yeovilton 1961. (Arthur Pearcy)

Westland Whirlwind HAR.3 XG572 '715/R' of No.700 Squadron 'B' Flight aboard HMS Ark Royal in 1958. (MAP)

Fairey Gannet AS.4 XG797 '505/VL' of No.700 Squadron at Yeovilton in 1961. (MAP)

Hawker Sea Hawk FB.3 WM912 '512' of No.700 Squadron at Ford in 1957. (J.D.R.Rawlings)

Westland Wessex HAS.3 XS121 '(5)82/CU', the third conversion from an HAS.1, under trial by No.700H Intensive Flying Trials Flight at Culdrose in 1967. (via Brian Lowe)

Supermarine Scimitar F.1 XD230 '805/FD' of No.700X Intensive Flying Flight receiving attention in the hangar at Ford in 1958. (via Brian Lowe)

700

Squadron bases
Hatston	21 Jan	1940
Twatt (A Flt = HQ & Trg Flt)	22 Jun	1942
Squadron disbanded	24 Mar	1944
Donibristle	11 Oct	1944
Worthy Down	7 Nov	1944
Middle Wallop	23 Nov	1945
Yeovilton	1 Apr	1946
Squadron disbanded	30 Sep	1949
Ford	18 Aug	1955
Yeovilton	19 Sep	1958
Merryfield	5 Jan	1960
Yeovilton	Oct	1960
NAeL Minas Gerais (Dt)	17-26 Oct	1960
Squadron disbanded	3 Jul	1961

No.700 Sqdn Shetlands Flt
Sullom Voe	16 Jul	1940
Flt disbanded	28 May	1941

No.700 Sqdn Stornoway Flt
Stornoway	11 Nov	1940
Sullom Voe	28 May	1941

No.700 (Mediterranean) Sqdn

Squadron bases
Dekheila	16 Oct	1941
Aboukir	Jan	1942
St.Jean D'Acre	18 Apr	1942
Rayak - and became	11 May	1942
No.700(Levant) Sqdn		
Redesignated 701 Sqdn	1 Oct	1942

No.700 (Algiers) Sqdn

Squadron bases
Arzeu	8 Nov	1942
Sub-sqdn disbanded	Jan	1943

No.700 (Gibraltar) Sqdn

Squadron bases
North Front	27 Nov	1941
Sub-sqdn disbanded	27 Apr	1943

No.700 Sqdn 'W' Flt

Squadron bases
Sandbanks	12 Jul	1943
Lee-on-Solent (Dt)	23 Jul	1943
to	27 Jul	1943
Machrihanish	26 Jul	1943
Eglinton	14 Aug	1943
passage	Sep	1943
Machrihanish	15 Sep	1943
HMS Fencer	25 Sep	1943
Lagens	9 Oct	1943
HMS Fencer	24 Oct	1943
Machrihanish	19 Nov	1943
Flt disbanded into No.836 Sqdn	16 Dec	1943

No.700A Sea Harrier IFTU

Squadron bases
Yeovilton	26 Jun	1979
Redes 899 Sqdn	31 Mar	1980

No.700B Buccaneer IFTU

Squadron bases
Lossiemouth	9 Apr	1965
Flt disbanded	30 Sep	1965

No.700G Gannet AEW.3 IFTU

Squadron bases
Culdrose	17 Aug	1959
Redes 849A Flt	1 Feb	1960

No.700H Whirlwind HAS.7 IFTU

Squadron bases
Lee-on-Solent	18 Mar	1957
Flt disbanded	26 Sep	1957
Culdrose	1 Jun	1959
Flt disbanded	27 Aug	1959

No.700H Wessex IFTU

Squadron bases
Culdrose	1 Apr	1960
Flt disbanded	12 Jan	1962
Culdrose	9 Jan	1967
Flt disbanded	15 Sep	1967

No.700L Lynx IFTU

Squadron bases
Yeovilton	1 Sep	1976
Flt disbanded	16 Dec	1977

No.700L Squadron
Portland	6 Jul	1990
RFA Argus	9 Jul	1990
Portland	20 Jul	1990
Vaerlose (Dt2)	8-11 Oct	1990
HMS Boxer (Dt1)	8 Jan	1991
	to 7 Feb	1991
Aberporth (Dt2)	4-12 Mar	1991
HMS Boxer (Dt1)	9-15 Mar	1991
HMS Boxer (Dt1)	15-25 Apr	1991
passage (RORO ship)	9 Sep	1991
Cocoa Beach	6 Oct	1991
AUTEC Andros	13 Oct	1991
Cocoa Beach	28 Oct	1991
passage (RORO ship)	31 Oct	1991
Portland	18 Nov	1991
HMS London (Dt1)	7-24 Feb	1992
Squadron disbanded	17 Jul	1992

No.700M Squadron
Due to form as
Merlin IFTU   Jul 1997

No.700P Phantom IFTU

Squadron bases
Yeovilton	30 Apr	1968
Flt disbanded	31 Mar	1969

No.700S Sea King IFTU

Squadron bases
Culdrose	1 Jul	1969
Flt disbanded	29 May	1970

No.700V Wessex HU.5 IFTU

Squadron bases
Culdrose	29 Oct	1963
Redes 848 Sqdn	7 May	1964

No.700W Wasp IFTU

Squadron bases
Culdrose	4 Jun	1963
Flt disbanded	4 Mar	1964

No.700X Scimitar IFTU

Squadron bases
Ford	27 Aug	1957
Flt disbanded	29 May	1958

No.700X Wasp P.531 IFTU

Squadron bases
Yeovilton (& Merryfield)	Oct	1959
Flt disbanded	Jun	1961

No.700Y Sea Vixen IFTU

Squadron bases
Yeovilton	4 Nov	1958
Redes 892 Sqdn	1 Jul	1959

No.700Z Buccaneer IFTU

Squadron bases
Lossiemouth	7 Mar	1961
Redes 809 Sqdn	15 Jan	1963

Commanding Officers
L/C AHT Fleming RN	29 Jan	1940
L/C NS Luard DSC RN	17 May	1941
L/C GWR Nicholl RN	4 Feb	1942
L/C(A) CG Hide RNVR	16 Oct	1943
Squadron disbanded	24 Mar	1944
L/C LRE Castlemaine RNVR	11 Oct	1944
Cdr(E) PHC Illingworth RN	20 May	1946
L/C(E) GF Hawkes RN	2 Feb	1948
Lt(E) RM Orr-Ewing RN	3 May	1948
Lt(E) WJ Lovell RN	18 Feb	1949
Lt(E) GW Malpas-Finlay RN	23 Apr	1949
Squadron disbanded	30 Sep	1949
L/C RW Turral RN	18 Aug	1955
L/C DG Halliday RN	16 Jan	1956
L/C PM Lamb DSC AFC RN	23 Jan	1957
Cdr TG Innes AFC RN	27 Aug	1957
L/C RA Shilcock RN	29 Sep	1958
L/C AIR Shaw MBE RN	12 Sep	1960
Squadron disbanded	3 Jul	1961

700A

Commanding Officers
L/C ND Ward RN	26 Jun	1979
Squadron disbanded	31 Mar	1980

700B

Commanding Officers
Cdr NJP Mills RN	9 Apr	1965
Squadron disbanded	30 Sep	1965

700G

Commanding Officers
L/C W Hawley RN	17 Aug	1959
Flight disbanded	1 Feb	1960

700H

Commanding Officers
L/C JGC Williams RN	18 Mar	1957
Flight disbanded	26 Sep	1957
L/C AG Cornabe RN	1 Jun	1959
Flight disbanded	27 Aug	1959
L/C R Turpin RN	1 Apr	1960
Flight disbanded	12 Jan	1962
L/C CRV Doe RN	9 Jan	1967
Flight disbanded	15 Sep	1967

700L

Commanding Officers
L/C GA Cavalier RN	1 Sep	1976
Squadron disbanded	16 Dec	1977
L/C CE Thornton RN	16 Jul	1990
L/C M Boland RN	14 Jul	1992
Squadron disbanded	17 Jul	1992

700P

Commanding Officers
Cdr AMG Pearson RN	30 Apr	1968
Squadron disbanded	31 Mar	1969

700S

Commanding Officers
L/C VG Sirett RN	1 Jul	1969
Squadron disbanded	29 May	1970

700V

Commanding Officers
L/C CJ Isacke RN	29 Oct	1963
Flight disbanded	7 May	1964

700W

Commanding Officers
L/C K Mitchell DFC RN	4 Jun	1963
Flight disbanded	4 Mar	1964

700X

Commanding Officers
Cdr TG Innes AFC RN	27 Aug	1957
Flight disbanded	29 May	1958
Not identified	Oct	1959
Flight disbanded	Jun	1961

700Y

Commanding Officers
Cdr MHJ Petrie RN	4 Nov	1958
Flight disbanded	1 Jul	1959

700Z

Commanding Officers
L/C AJ Leahy MBE DSC RN	7 Mar	1961
Flight disbanded	15 Jan	1963

A Supermarine Walrus of No.700 Squadron of the East Indies Fleet with side marking '9A' is launched from the catapult of HMS Warspite. Also in the picture is HMS Illustrious. (FAA Museum)

No.701 Squadron

No.701 (Catapult) Flight formed on 15 July 1936, achieving squadron status some months before the outbreak of war. It inherited some of the aircraft of 447 (Catapult) Flight, and after partial re-equipment flew a miscellany of Ospreys, Fairey IIIFs, Sharks, Seals and Swordfish from ships of the 1st Battle Squadron serving with the Home and Mediterranean Fleets. Its shore base in the Mediterranean was at Kalafrana, Malta, and the aircraft embarked periodically in the battleships HMS *Barham*, HMS *Malaya*, HMS *Valiant* and later HMS *Warspite*. No.701 Squadron, as it had by then become, disbanded into No.700 Squadron on 21 January 1940, its number being then reserved for units to be temporarily formed from time to time for special duties ashore.

The first such unit formed at Donibristle on 7 May 1940 for coastal patrol duties in Norway. Embarking its 6 Walruses two days later in HMS *Glorious* it set up base at Harstad, until evacuated in HMS *Ark Royal* on 7 June, being fortunate that lack of space prevented it from being aboard HMS *Glorious* when she was sunk the following day. On return it regrouped for passage in HMS *Argus* to Iceland, where it carried out anti-submarine and reconnaissance duties until being withdrawn in October. It then performed a similar task from Stornoway and the Shetlands, the commanding officer attempting a night reconnaissance of Narvik on 26 April 1941. No.701 disbanded at Donibristle on 8 June 1941.

On 1 October 1942 No.701 was reformed by redesignating No.700 (Levant) Squadron at Beirut. Equipped with six Walruses, it carried out anti-submarine patrols under the control of No.201 Group, RAF. In October 1942 a detachment joined No.235 Wing at Latakia to carry out patrols further north after U-boats had been reported operating between Cyprus and the Turkish coast. The squadron disbanded at Beirut on 15 August 1943, its aircraft being then transferred locally to the RAF for air-sea rescue work.

No.701 next reformed at Heston on 18 April 1945 for communications duties, by expanding 'B' Flight (or Admiralty Flight) of No.781 Squadron, which had been operating from the old Fairey aerodrome at Heath Row. Coming under the administrative control of Lee-on-Solent it carried VIPs and other passengers to and from the London area. Aircraft were mainly Oxfords and Travellers, but Expediters, Dominies and other types were also flown. The squadron disbanded at Heston on 13 January 1947.

On 31 October 1957, No.701 reformed at Lee-on-Solent as a Helicopter Fleet Requirements Unit equipped with Whirlwinds and Dragonflies. Detached flights operated from fleet carriers on search and rescue duties, and later the squadron embraced the ship's flights of the ocean survey ship HMS *Vidal* and the ice patrol ship HMS *Protector*. In January 1958 No.701 took over the helicopter trials role from No.705 Squadron to become a Helicopter Trials, Communications and Fleet Requirements Unit. No.701 disbanded on 20 September 1958, its sub-units then becoming ship's flights of their respective ships.

Battle Honours
Norway   1940

Identification Markings
IIIF, Osprey, Swordfish *072-076* to 5.39, then *C8A* on Swordfish; Walrus uncoded 1940-41 & 1942-43; All types *LOA+* 1945-47; Whirlwind & Dragonfly *708-723/E:O:R:V* also *990-991*.

Aircraft Equipment	Period of Service	Example	
Osprey	Jul 1936 - Nov 1936	K3640	(073)
IIIF	Jul 1936 - Jan 1937	S1809	(072)
Shark	Feb 1937 - Aug 1937	K4362	
Seal II	Nov 1936 - Feb 1938		
Swordfish I/SP	Sep 1936 - Jan 1940	K8446	(075)
Walrus	May 1940 - Jun 1941	P5707	
Walrus	Aug 1942 - Aug 1943	W3014	
Anson C.X	Sep 1945	NK836	(LOZ)
Dominie I	Mar 1945 - Jan 1947	HG714	(LOR)
Expediter C.I	Apr 1945 - Aug 1945	FT984	(LOH)
Expediter C.II	Mar 1946	HD757	
Harvard III	Mar 1945 - Apr 1946	EZ424	(LOE)
Oxford	Apr 1945 - Jan 1947	NM641	(LOA)
Seafire XV	Mar 1946 - Jul 1946	SR485	(LOZ)
Seafire XVII	Sep 1945 - Nov 1945	SX125	
Tiger Moth II	Apr 1945 - Feb 1946	X5108	
Traveller I	Apr 1945 - Sep 1945	FT467	(LOF)
Dragonfly HR.5	Nov 1957 - Sep 1958	WG671	(720)
Whirlwind HAR.1	Jul 1958 - Sep 1958	XA868	(990)
Whirlwind HAR.3	Oct 1957 - Sep 1958	XG579	(709/V)
Whirlwind HAS.7	Nov 1957 - Sep 1958	XK939	(716)
Whirlwind HAS.22	Nov 1957 - Apr 1958	WV219	(718)

Westland Whirlwind XA869 of No.701 Squadron parked on the helicopter deck of the ice patrol ship HMS Protector on return to Portsmouth in May 1959 after a lengthy spell in the South Atlantic. (via Brian Lowe)

Squadron bases

Calafrana	15 Jul 1936
Squadron disbanded	21 Jan 1940
Donibristle	7 May 1940
HMS Glorious	9 May 1940
Harstad	18 May 1940
HMS Ark Royal	7 Jun 1940
Hatston	14 Jun 1940
Donibristle	16 Jun 1940
HMS Argus	23 Jun 1940
Reykjavik	1 Jul 1940
HMS Argus	21 Oct 1940
Donibristle	26 Oct 1940
Stornoway	6 Nov 1940
Campbeltown	12 Mar 1941
Hooton Park	13 Mar 1941
Sullom Voe (Dt3)	13 Mar 1941
	to 13 Apr 1941
Donibristle	22 Mar 1941
Squadron disbanded	8 Jun 1941
Rayak	1 Oct 1942
Latakia (Dt)	1 Oct 1942
	to Feb 1943
St.Jean D'Acre	Apr 1943
Dekheila	12 Jun 1943
Rayak	13 Jul 1943
Squadron disbanded	15 Aug 1943
Heston	18 Apr 1945
Squadron disbanded	13 Jan 1947
Lee-on-Solent	31 Oct 1957
Portland (Dt)	17-20 Sep 1958
Squadron disbanded	20 Sep 1958

'A' Flt:
HMS Eagle	31 Oct 1957
Lee-on-Solent	27 Nov 1957
HMS Eagle	27 Jan 1958
Lee-on-Solent	24 Mar 1958
HMS Eagle	20 May 1958
Redes Ships Flt	20 Sep 1958

'B' Flt:
HMS Ark Royal	27 Jan 1958
Lee-on-Solent	5 Jul 1958
Flt disbanded	5 Jul 1958

'C' Flt:
Lee-on-Solent	25 Nov 1957
HMS Victorious	3 Feb 1958
Lee-on-Solent	8 Feb 1958
HMS Victorious	15 Feb 1958
Lee-on-Solent	26 Feb 1958
HMS Victorious	28 May 1958
Lee-on-Solent	15 Jun 1958
HMS Albion	7 Jul 1958
Redes Ships Flt	20 Sep 1958

'D' Flt:
HMS Bulwark	27 Nov 1957
Lee-on-Solent	13 Dec 1957
Squadron disbanded	20 Sep 1958

'P' Flt:
| Lee-on-Solent | 21 Jul 1958 |
| HMS Protector | 20 Sep 1958 |

'V' Flt
Lee-on-Solent	
HMS Vidal	1 Apr 1958
Redes Ships Flt	20 Sep 1958

Commanding Officers

L/C ACG Ermen RN (Flt Lt RAF)	15 Jul 1936
Not identified	Apr 1937
Lt MC Hoskin RN (Flt Lt RAF)	29 Mar 1938
Lt JCM Harman RN	12 Aug 1938
L/C WLM Brown RN	24 May 1939
Squadron disbanded	21 Jan 1940
Lt HH Bracken RN	8 May 1940
Cdr RSD Armour RN	18 May 1940
L/C MA Everett RN	14 Mar 1941
Squadron disbanded	8 Jun 1941
Lt PC Chorley RN	5 Oct 1942
Squadron disbanded	15 Aug 1943
L/C(A) AB Cunningham RNVR	18 Apr 1945
Lt(A) J Lawson RNVR	10 Dec 1945
Lt(A) RH Billson RNVR	31 Jan 1946
Lt(A) HA Monk DSM RN	21 Mar 1946
Squadron disbanded	13 Jan 1947
L/C JS Sproule RN	31 Oct 1957
L/C RL Turnbull MBE RN	31 Aug 1958
Squadron disbanded	20 Sep 1958

Fairey Swordfish I L2751 of No.701 Flight being hoisted during catapult trials on HMS Barham. (Lt Col A Newson)

Supermarine Walrus L2249 of 701 Squadron at Beirut around 1942/3. (J.F.Hindley)

Westland Dragonfly HR.5 conversion WG669 '719' of No.701 Squadron was based at Lee-on-Solent in 1958. (MAP)

No.702 Squadron

Badge: (1) On a white field, a wild cat winged, issuing from flames proper (later used by No.1840 Squadron)
(2) On a field argent, in front of a roundel gyronny azure and argent a demi-lynx erased or

Motto: Cave ungues felis
(Beware the cat's paws)

No.702 (Catapult) Flight formed on 15 July 1936 to operate aircraft from ships of the 2nd Battle Squadron with the Home Fleet. Its shore base initially was at Mount Batten, and it flew Walruses and Seals, the latter being later replaced by Swordfish floatplanes. Aircraft were attached as required, mainly to HMS *Nelson*, HMS *Rodney* and later HMS *Resolution*. Squadron status was granted by early 1939, but the squadron disbanded into No.700 Squadron on 21 January 1940.

On 27 December 1940, No.702 reformed as a Long Range catapult squadron with Seafoxes for duty in Armed Merchant Cruisers. Each ship carried two aircraft, the first to be equipped being *Alcantara*, which like most of the later sub-flights formed up at Lee-on-Solent. This was followed by sub-flights in *Pretoria Castle*, *Canton*, *Queen of Bermuda* and *Asturias*. The *Canton* and *Pretoria Castle* flights were transferred to No.703 Squadron in June 1942. A flight of Sea Hurricanes was also formed on 10 May 1942 to take over from No.804 Squadron the task of operating two catapult aircraft from *Maplin*, but this disbanded two months later. By July 1943 the task was no longer required and the last sub-flight ceased to exist.

No.702 next reformed out of No.758 Squadron at Hinstock on 1 June 1945 as an Instrument Flying Training and Checking Unit, for service in support of the British Pacific Fleet. Embarking for Australia seven weeks later, it arrived at Schofields on 4 September. Owing to non-arrival of the intended beam approach equipment, its Oxfords and Harvards concentrated on the instrument flying task until the squadron was disbanded at Schofields on 10 September 1946.

On 4 April 1949, No.702 reformed at Culdrose as the Naval Jet Evaluation and Training Unit, initially equipped with four Sea Vampire F.20's. Two months later it became the first unit of either the RAF or the FAA to receive Meteor T.7s, and a few RAF-type Vampire FB.5s were also flown. Squadron aircraft were operated from HMS *Implacable* during the autumn of 1949, and also from HMS *Theseus* the following summer, gaining experience and information on the techniques of operating jet aircraft from carriers prior to their entry into service with a first line squadron. In March 1952, Attacker F.1s arrived, and with these it engaged in converting piston engined pilots to jets, but on 26 August 1952 the unit became No.738 Squadron under a reorganisation of fighter training units.

No.702 next reformed at Lee-on-Solent on 30 September 1957 from the Junior Officers Air Course Flight of No.781 Squadron. Equipped with Sea Balliols, Sea Vampire T.22s and a Sea Prince T.1, it moved two weeks later to Ford, where it disbanded on 11 August 1958 on being absorbed into No.727 Squadron.

On 3 January 1978, No.702 reformed at Yeovilton from the remnants of No.700L Squadron, the Lynx IFTU, to become the Lynx headquarters and training squadron, being commissioned on 26 January. It became responsible for Lynx pilot and observer conversion, and for advanced and operational flying training on the type. Until 1 January 1981 it also acted as the headquarters unit for ship's flights operating the Lynx, but this task was then taken over by No.815 Squadron.

The squadron moved to Portland on 19 July 1982. It continues to operate from there as a training squadron, regularly deploying detachments to sea in Royal Fleet Auxiliaries.

Westland/Aerospatiale Lynx HAS.2 XZ239 '345/NC' of No.702 Squadron bore the nickname 'WEE GEORDIE' for obvious reasons while serving aboard HMS Newcastle between 1978 and 1982. (via Brian Lowe)

Identification Markings
Believed uncoded to 5.39, then *E8A+* on Swordfish; Seafox & Sea Hurricane uncoded; Believed uncoded in Australia; Sea Vampire & Attacker *190-199/CW*; Meteor *400-404/CW*; Sea Balliol/Sea Vampire T/22/Sea Prince *750-756/FD*; Lynx small ship codes.

Aircraft Equipment	Period of Service	Example	
Walrus I	Jul 1936 - Jan 1940	K5778	
Seal	Feb 1937 - Oct 1938		
Swordfish I/SP	1939 - Jan 1940	P4199	(E8F)
Seafox I	Dec 1940 - Jul 1943	L4526	(L)
Sea Hurricane Ib	May 1942 - Jul 1942	V7050	
Harvard IIb	Sep 1945 - Feb 1946	KF519	
Oxford	Sep 1945 - Feb 1946	PH288	
Tiger Moth II	Nov 1945 - Apr 1946	A17-299	
Avenger III	Jan 1946	JZ709	
Sea Vampire F.20	Apr 1949 - Aug 1952	VV152	(195)
Meteor T.7	Jun 1949 - Aug 1952	WA652	(404/CW)
Vampire FB.5	May 1951 - May 1952	VZ142	(192/CW)
Vampire T.11/22	1952	WW458	
Attacker F.1	Mar 1952 - Aug 1952	WA473	(196/CW)
Sea Balliol T.21	Oct 1957 - Aug 1958	WL715	(752/FD)
Sea Vampire T.22	Oct 1957 - Aug 1958	XA108	(754)
Sea Prince T.1	Oct 1957 - 1958	WP318	(756)
Lynx HAS.2	Jan 1978 - Sep 1988	XZ231	(742/VL)
Lynx HAS.3/3S	Jun 1982 - to date	XZ252	(644/PO)
Lynx HAS.8	due 1995		

Squadron bases
Mount Batten	15 Jul 1936
Lee-on-Solent	1 Jan 1938
Squadron disbanded	21 Jan 1940
Lee-on-Solent	27 Dec 1940
Belfast (Sea Hurricane Flt)	10 May 1942 to 7 Jul 1942
Squadron disbanded	Jul 1943
Hinstock	1 Jun 1945
in transit	21 Jul 1945
Schofields	4 Sep 1945
Squadron disbanded	10 Sep 1946
Culdrose	4 Apr 1949
HMS Implacable	16 Sep 1949
Culdrose	11 Nov 1949
HMS Theseus	2 May 1950
Culdrose	30 Jun 1950
Perseus(Dt-trials)	29 May 1951
Redes 736 Sqdn	26 Aug 1952
Lee-on-Solent	30 Sep 1957
Ford	17 Oct 1957
Squadron disbanded	11 Aug 1958
Yeovilton	3 Jan 1978
Tirstrup (Dt1)	17-27 Apr 1978
RFA Engadine (Dt4)	22-26 May 1978
Lee-on-Solent (Dt1)	19-26 Jun 1978
Prestwick (Dt4)	15-19 Jan 1979
Aalborg (Dt3)	20 Apr 1979 to 9 May 1979
RFA Engadine (Dt4)	30 Apr 1979 to 4 May 1979
Florennes (Dt2)	21-25 Jun 1979
RFA Engadine (Dt4)	25-29 Jun 1979
RFA Engadine (Dt3)	25-29 Feb 1980
Tirstrup (Dt3)	18 Apr 1980 to 14 May 1980
Aldergrove (Dt1)	20 May 1980 to 6 Jun 1980
RFA Olna (Dt3)	21-25 Jul 1980
Aldergrove (Dt1)	20 Oct 1980 to 5 Dec 1980
RFA Fort Grange (Dt4)	27-31 Oct 1980
RFA Engadine (Dt4)	12-16 Jan 1981
RFA Engadine (Dt4)	23-27 Mar 1981
RFA Tidespring (Dt3)	12-16 Oct 1981
RFA Engadine (Dt4)	11-15 Jan 1982
RFA Engadine (Dt4)	8-12 Mar 1982
St Mawgan (Dt4)	24-28 May 1982
Portland	19 Jul 1982
Valley (Dt4)	2-6 Aug 1982
RFA Engadine (Dt4)	10-14 Jan 1983
RFA Engadine (Dt4)	6-11 Mar 1983
RFA Engadine (Dt4)	21-29 Jul 1983
RFA Engadine (Dt4)	3-14 Oct 1984

Squadron bases
Castlemartin (Dt3)	5-8 Mar 1984
Kinloss (Dt3)	19-28 Mar 1984
RFA Engadine (Dt4)	21 May 1984 to 1 Jun 1984
RFA Engadine (Dt4)	13-24 Aug 1984
RFA Engadine (Dt4)	22 Oct 1984 to 2 Nov 1984
Kinloss (Dt3)	21-31 Jan 1985
RFA Engadine (Dt4)	22 Apr 1985 to 3 May 1985
RFA Engadine (Dt4)	1-12 Jul 1985
RFA Engadine (Dt4)	7-21 Oct 1985
St Mawgan (Dt3)	11-17 Dec 1985
Castlemartin (Dt3)	20-23 Jan 1986
RFA Engadine (Dt4)	10-20 Mar 1986
RFA Engadine (Dt4)	26 May 1986 to 6 Jun 1986
RFA Engadine (Dt4)	5-16 Jul 1986
St Mandrier (Dt4)	4-8 Sep 1986
RFA Engadine (Dt5)	17-31 Oct 1986
RFA Engadine (Dt4)	9-20 Feb 1987
RFA Engadine (Dt4)	27 Apr 1987 to 8 May 1987
RFA Engadine (Dt5)	12-23 Oct 1987
RFA Engadine (Dt5)	7-17 Dec 1987
RFA Engadine (Dt5)	7-18 Mar 1988
RFA Engadine (Dt5)	25 May 1988 to 4 Jun 1988
RFA Engadine (Dt4)	18-29 Jul 1988
RFA Engadine (Dt5)	31 Oct 1988 to 11 Nov 1988
RFA Engadine (Dt4)	25 Jan 1989 to 1 Feb 1989
RFA Argus (Dt5)	10-21 Apr 1989
RFA Argus (Dt5)	17-28 Jun 1989
RFA Fort Austin (Dt4)	21 Sep 1989 to 3 Oct 1989
RFA Argus (Dt5)	4-16 Dec 1989
RFA Argus (Dt5)	12-23 Feb 1990
RFA Argus (Dt5)	27 Apr 1990 to 9 May 1990
RFA Argus (Dt5)	9-20 Jul 1990
RFA Olmeda (Dt4)	12-23 Oct 1990
St Mawgan (Dt4)	4-14 Feb 1991
RFA Olmeda (Dt4)	10-21 May 1991
RFA Olwen (Dt4)	22 Nov 1991 to 10 Dec 1991
RFA Olwen (Dt4)	22 Feb 1992 to 5 Mar 1992
RFA Argus (Dt5)	21-24 Aug 1992
RFA Argus (Dt5)	19-29 Oct 1992

Squadron bases
RFA Olmeda (Dt4)	29 Mar 1993 to 8 Apr 1993
RFA Olmeda (Dt4)	24 Nov 1993 to 8 Dec 1993
RFA Argus (Dt4)	7-18 Feb 1994
RFA Argus (Dt4)	11-25 Mar 1994
RFA Argus (Dt4)	27 May 1994 to 10 Jun 1994

Commanding Officers
Lt SWD Colls RN (Flt Lt RAF)	15 Jul 1936
None	18 Sep 1937
Lt PE O'Brien (Flt Lt RAF)	14 Nov 1938
L/C RAB Phillimore RN	24 May 1939
Squadron disbanded	21 Jan 1940
None	27 Dec 1940
Squadron disbanded	Jul 1943
L/C(A) GT Bertholdt RNVR	1 Jun 1945
Squadron disbanded	10 Sep 1946

Commanding Officers
Lt(A) ABB Clark RN	4 Apr 1949
L/C N Perrett RN	3 May 1951
Squadron disbanded	26 Aug 1952
L/C TVG Binney RN	30 Sep 1957
Squadron disbanded	11 Aug 1958
L/C BF Prendergast RN	3 Jan 1978
L/C RF Edmonds RN	29 Jan 1980
Cdr RF Edmonds RN	30 Jun 1980
L/C DHN Yates RN	29 Oct 1980
L/C HF Hatton RN	6 Jan 1981
L/C TL Bailey RN	5 May 1983
L/C CD Ferbrache RN	2 Jul 1985
Cdr CD Ferbrache RN	30 Jun 1986
L/C M Bishop-Bailey RN	30 Jul 1986
L/C RG Burrows RN	29 Sep 1988
L/C CL Palmer RN	29 Nov 1990
L/C CF Mervik RN	20 Jun 1991
L/C PJ Bryant RN	21 Feb 1992
L/C RN Wain RN	4 Feb 1994

Fairey Seafox L4526 'L' of No.702 Squadron being lowered on to the catapult of HMS Asturias. (Tony Downs)

Gloster Meteor T.7 VW436 of No.702 Squadron, then the Naval Jet Evaluation and Training Unit at Culdrose in 1951. (A.E.Hughes)

Boulton Paul Sea Balliol T.21 WL715 '752' of No.702 (Junior Officers Air Course) Squadron at Ford in 1957/8. (M.J.F.Bowyer)

No.703 Squadron

Badge: On a blue field, in chief a mailed hand white holding a balance gold over waves in base white
Motto: Experentia docet (Experience teaches)

Blackburn Firebrand TF.5 EK747 'T' of No.703 Squadron the Naval Air-Sea Warfare Development Unit at Thorney Island, around 1947.

No.703 Squadron first formed on 3 June 1942 as a long range catapult squadron with flights operating from armed merchant cruisers. These each had either one or two Kingfishers, except for *Pretoria Castle* Flight which retained its Seafoxes on being transferred from No.702 Squadron. Lee-on-Solent was used as the shore base, and a maximum strength of eleven Kingfishers was reached in April 1943, when they were operating from *Canton, Cilicia, Corfu, Fidelity* and *Ranpura* as well as the light cruisers HMS *Emerald* and HMS *Enterprise*. In addition, the squadron by then had three Walruses shore-based at Walvis Bay in South Africa. The last flight disbanded on 1 May 1944 and the squadron ceased to exist.

On 19 April 1945, No.703 reformed at Thorney Island as the Naval Flight of the RAF's Air-Sea Warfare Development Unit, being usually referred to as NASWDU. It had a variety of aircraft types, initially including Avengers, Barracudas, Fireflies, Hoverflies and Sea Mosquitoes. In May 1948 it moved to Lee-on-Solent, where it took over the Service Trials Unit task of No.778 Squadron, to become known as the NASWDU/STU. During 1948 and 1949 it was involved in trials with a flexible deck. In April 1950 it went to Ford, where it dropped the NASWDU role to become simply the STU, and on 12 July 1950 it absorbed No.739 Squadron which then became its Photographic Flight. In December 1951 its aircraft became the first to operate from the new HMS *Eagle*. By May 1953 its duties comprised the testing of catapult and arrester gear after carrier refits, and also the testing of equipment developed by the Safety Equipment School and the Medical Air School, both at Gosport.

Between February and June 1954, 'A' Flight operated as an independent unit from Arbroath, where it flew six ex-No.825 Squadron Fireflies as "clockwork mice" for Ferranti's new Carrier Controlled Approach (CCA) system, which was being developed at the Air Signals and Radar Establishment at Tantallon, 30 miles east of Edinburgh; flights took place at the seaward end of the Firth of Forth, using Bass Rock as a dummy carrier. No.703X Flight formed at Ford on 15 March 1954 for intensive flying trials of the Gannet AS1, including carrier operations and tropical trials, the aircraft being dispersed when the trials ended on 21 December 1954. No.703W Flight formed on 4 October 1954 at Ford to hold Wyvern aircraft for No.827 Squadron, which formed there on 1 November 1954. No.703 ceased to exist when on 17 August 1955 it amalgamated with No.771 Squadron to form No.700 Squadron.

No.703 reformed at Portland on 22 January 1972 from the training element of No.829 Squadron, to become the Wasp HAS.1 Training Unit. In 1973 it won the Bambara Trophy for the best safety record of any second line FAA unit, and at the beginning of 1975 it took over the Wasp element of No.706 Squadron and its advanced training role for this type, to become entirely responsible for Wasp conversion, including both Advanced Flying Training and Operational Flying Training. It operated as the Wasp Aircrew and Groundcrew Training Squadron until being disbanded into No.829 Squadron on 1 January 1981.

Identification Markings
Kingfisher uncoded; single letters on all types from 4.45, to *031-099/LP* by 11.48, to *001-099/FD* 4.50; Wasp *500-507*, also *624-637* 1975-70.

Vought Kingfisher FN734 floatplane of No.703 Squadron, nicknamed 'BRENDA', flying from the armed merchant cruiser HMS Corfu around 1943. (via Brian Lowe)

Aircraft Equipment	Period of Service	Example
Kingfisher I	May 1942 - Mar 1944	FN658
Seafox I	Jul 1942 - Nov 1942	
Swordish I/SP	Oct 1942 - Nov 1942	K5993
Barracuda II	Apr 1945 - Mar 1946	MX797 (F)
Reliant I	May 1945	FK877
Avenger II	Nov 1945 - Mar 1946	JZ518 (G)
Avenger III	Apr 1945 - Jul 1953	KE442 (064/FD)
Avenger TBM-3E	Jun 1953 - Jun 1954	XB444 (065/FD)
Avenger AS.4	Jun 1954 - Aug 1955	XB365 (065/FD)
Anson I	Dec 1945 - Apr 1952	MG741 (083/LP)
Attacker F.1	Jul 1951 - Aug 1951	WA509 (056/FD)
Attacker FB.1	Jan 1952 - Apr 1952	WA527 (054/FD)
Attacker FB.2	Apr 1955 - Aug 1955	WZ277 (076/FD)
Meteor F.8	May 1953 - Jan 1953	WK942
Sea Balliol T.21	May 1951 - Jul 1951	VR596 (031/FD)
Barracuda II	Mar 1946	MX797 (F)
Barracuda TR.III	Apr 1945 - Sep 1953	ME123 (D)
Blackburn YA.8	Feb 1951	WB788 (015)
Corsair II	Jul 1945 - Apr 1946	JT658 (K)
Dominie I	May 1947 - Oct 1948	HG709 (A)
Firebrand TF.III	Sep 1945 - Mar 1946	DK407 (L)
Firebrand TF.IV	Mar 1946 - Jun 1946	EK734 (J)
Firebrand TF.5	1946 - Mar 1952	EK636 (082/FD)
Firebrand TF.5a	Jan 1950	EK732
Firefly FR.I	Aug 1945 - May 1949	MB645 (G)
Firefly FR.4	Jul 1947 - Jul 1951	VG957 (022/FD)
Firefly 5	Nov 1948 - Jun 1954	WB259 (024/FD)
Firefly AS.6	Jul 1951 - Aug 1955	WD953 (025/FD)
Sea Fury F.10	Jun 1948 - Feb 1952	TF922 (096/FD)
Sea Fury FB.11	Jul 1948 - Mar 1955	VX608 (098/FD)
Sea Fury T.20	Jun 1951 - Oct 1951	VZ369 (097/FD)
Gannet AS.1	Oct 1953 - Aug 1955	WN453 (083/FD)
Sea Hawk F.1	Sep 1952 - Aug 1955	WF153 (033/FD)
Sea Hawk FB.3	Jul 1955	WM906 (073/FD)
Hellcat I	1945 -	JV177
Hellcat II	Oct 1945 - Nov 1945	JV278
Sea Hornet F.20	Jul 1947 - Sep 1951	TT210 (005/LP)
Sea Hornet NF.21	Oct 1948 - Dec 1951	VW958 (001/FD)
Sea Hornet PR.22	Jul 1950 - Oct 1953	WE246 (008/FD)
Hoverfly I	Jan 1946 - Sep 1947	FT837 (Z)
Meteor 3/hooked	Aug 1948 - 1952	EE337 (031/FD)
Meteor T.7	Jul 1950 - Aug 1955	WS103 (075/FD)
Mosquito FB.VI	Jun 1945 - Jul 1950	RF821 (T)
Mosquito PR.16	Sep 1947 - Jun 1948	RG171 (042)
Sea Mosquito TR.33	Jun 1946 - Oct 1950	TW233 (U)
Sea Mosquito TR.37	Dec 1948 - May 1950	VT728 (048/LP)
Sea Mosquito TT.39	Oct 1948	PF576
Oxford	Apr 1946 - Aug 1947	HN132 (Q)
Seafire F.17	1947 - Aug 1949	SX360 (011/LP)
Seafire F.45	Dec 1945 - 1946	LA496
Vampire F.1	Sep 1947 - Oct 1947	VF269
Vampire F.1/hooked	Feb 1949 - Oct 1949	TG328
Vampire FB.5	Jul 1950 - Jun 1952	VZ143
Sea Vampire F.20	Oct 1948 - Aug 1955	VV148 (071/FD)
Sea Vampire F.21		VG701 (076/FD)
Sturgeon TT.2	Jun 1951 - Aug 1951	TS477 (004)
Wyvern S.4	Jun 1954 - Aug 1955	VZ796 (081/FD)
Wasp HAS.1	Jan 1972 - Dec 1980	XT430 (501)

703A

Aircraft Equipment	Period of Service	Example
Firefly AS.5	Feb 1954 - Jul 1954	WB359 ("286/J")
Firefly AS.6	Feb 1954 - Jul 1954	WD847 ("283/J")

703W

Aircraft Equipment	Period of Service	Example
Wyvern S.4	Oct 1954 - Nov 1954	WL879

703X

Aircraft Equipment	Period of Service	Example
Gannet AS.1	Mar 1954 - Dec 1954	WN350

Grumman Avenger AS.4 XB444 '065/FD' of No.703 Squadron in 1953. (via Brian Lowe)

Fairey Firefly FR.5 WB259 '288/J' of No.703A Flight at Arbroath over the eastern Scottish Highlands in March 1954. (P.D.Lowndes)

Fairey Gannet AS.1 WN347 of No.703X Flight in 1954. (MAP)

Commanding Officers

None	
Squadron disbanded	3 Jun 1942
L/C JH Dundas	1 May 1944
DSC RN	19 Apr 1945
L/C JCN Shrubsole	
DSC RN	25 Apr 1947
L/C WJR MacWhirter	
DSC RN	22 Apr 1948
L/C NA Bartlett RN	8 May 1950
L/C JM Glaser	
DSC RN	25 Apr 1951
L/C SMdeL Longsden	
RN	8 Jan 1953
L/C FJ Sherborne	
RN	20 Jul 1953
L/C JRN Gardner	
DSC RN	4 Sep 1953
L/C FE Cowtan RN	14 Mar 1955
Squadron disbanded	17 Aug 1955
L/C HA Pawsey RN	27 Jan 1972
L/C PG Gregson RN	19 Jul 1973
L/C GA Cavalier RN	20 Dec 1974
L/C DA Blythe RN	27 May 1976
L/C PJG Clark RN	20 Feb 1978
L/C CJ Clay RN	27 Nov 1979
Squadron disbanded	1 Jan 1981

703A

Commanding Officers

Lt PD Lowndes RN	16 Feb 1954
Flight disbanded	4 Jul 1954

703W

Commanding Officers

L/C SJA Richardson RN	4 Oct 1954
Flight disbanded	1 Nov 1954

703X

Commanding Officers

L/C FE Cowtan RN	15 Mar 1954
Flight disbanded	21 Dec 1954

Grumman Avenger AS.4 XB444 '064/FD' over the south coast in 1953. (via Brian Lowe)

Squadron bases

Lee-on-Solent	3 Jun 1942
(Detts Dundee and Palisadoes)	
Walvis Bay (Dt3)	16 Feb 1943
	to 1 Mar 1943
Squadron disbanded	1 May 1944
Thorney Island	19 Apr 1945
Lee-on-Solent	25 May 1948
Ford	19 Apr 1950
Carrier trials:	
HMS Vengeance	15 Jan 1953
HMS Eagle	20 & 22 Jan 1953
HMS Theseus	22 May 1953
HMS Indomitable	19 Jun 1953
USS Antietan	30 Jun 1953
	to 1 Jul 1953
HMS Illustrious	22 Jul 1953
HMCS Warrior	2-12 Dec 1953
HMS Eagle	27 Jan 1954
HMS Illustrious	30 Jan 1954
HMS Centaur	24-28 May 1954
HMS Centaur	23 Aug 1954
HMS Bulwark	7-11 Feb 1955
HMS Eagle	18-21 Apr 1955
HMS Ark Royal	27 Jun 1955
	to 2 Jul 1955
HMS Ark Royal	18-20 Jul 1955
Wyvern Dett:	
Thurleigh	16 Jun 1954
	to 31 Oct 1954
Squadron disbanded	17 Aug 1955
Portland	22 Jan 1972
Squadron disbanded	1 Jan 1981

No.703A Flight

Squadron bases

Ford	17 Feb 1954
Arbroath	22 Feb 1954
Ford	30 Jun 1954
Flight disbanded	4 Jul 1954

No.703W Wyvern IFTU

Squadron bases

Ford	4 Oct 1954
Redes 827 Sqdn	1 Nov 1954

No.703X Gannet AS.1 IFTU

Squadron bases

Ford	15 Mar 1954
Flt disbanded	21 Dec 1954

No.704 Squadron

No.704 Squadron formed at Zeals on 11 April 1945 as a Naval Operational Training Unit for the conversion of Mosquito crews. It was mainly equipped with Mosquito FB.VIs, a few T.IIIs being also flown. Four aircraft were detached to Thorney Island in June, where they were temporarily amalgamated with No.703 Squadron for development work in conjunction with the Air-Sea Warfare Development Unit. The detachment was reabsorbed when the remainder of the squadron moved there on 4 September. No.704 disbanded at Thorney Island on 2 December 1945, being absorbed into No.762 Squadron at Halesworth.

Identification Markings
Mosquito *FD3A+*.

Aircraft Equipment	Period of Service	Example
Mosquito T.III	Oct 1945 - Dec 1945	TV963
Mosquito FB.VI	Apr 1945 - Jul 1945	RF825 (FD3B)
Mosquito B.25	1945 - Sep 1945	KB699
Oxford	Sep 1945 - 1945	PH364

Squadron bases		Commanding Officers	
Zeals	11 Apr 1945	L/C(A) SMP Walsh DSC & Bar RNVR	11 Apr 1945
Thorney Island(Dt4)	20 Jun 1945	L/C PAM Hudson DSC RN	25 Aug 1945
Thorney Island	4 Sep 1945		
Squadron disbanded	2 Dec 1945	Squadron disbanded	2 Dec 1945

de Havilland Mosquito FB.VIs of No.704 Squadron taking off at Ford in 1945. (Bill Sabey)

No.705 Squadron

Badge: *On a field barry wavy of ten white and blue, four wings conjoined in saltire gold*
Motto: *None*

No.705 (Catapult) Flight formed on 15 July 1936 from part of No.444 (Catapult) Flight for use on ships of the Battle Cruiser Squadron. Attached to the Mediterranean Fleet, Kalafrana was used as a shore base, aircraft being mainly Swordfish floatplanes, though two Sharks were also used for a time. By the beginning of 1939 it had achieved squadron status, operating only from HMS *Repulse* until she was joined by HMS *Renown* shortly before the outbreak of war. On 21 January 1940 the squadron was absorbed into No.700 Squadron.

On 7 March 1945, No.705 reformed at Ronaldsway as a Replacement Crew Training unit. Equipped with Swordfish IIIs, it operated an anti-submarine course, but this task was no longer needed after VE-Day and consequently disbanded on 24 June 1945.

No.705 reformed at Gosport on 7 May 1947 as a Helicopter Fleet Requirements Unit. It was initially equipped with Hoverflies, taking over seven of these from the Helicopter Flight of No.771 Squadron and others from Gosport Station Flight. It became the sole operating authority for all FAA helicopter operations, training pilots, crewmen and maintenance personnel, evaluating helicopter equipment, developing techniques, carrying out special trials as well as undertaking some communications work. Dragonflies were received in January 1950, and two Saro Skeeters were tested during 1952. Early in 1953, squadron aircraft played a major part in flood relief work in both Holland and eastern England after extensive gales and high tides during the night of 31 January/1 February, the CO being later awarded the MBE and a crewman the BEM.

Hiller HT.1s were received in May 1953, and around this time a Sikorsky S.55 was evaluated, later being developed by Westlands to become the Whirlwind, the first British-built example arriving the following year. Another notable event at that time was the Coronation Review flypast on 15 June 1953, which No.705 had the honour of leading. With the formation of No.706 Squadron in September 1953, No.705 lost part of its role, and it was restyled a Helicopter Training Squadron. It moved on 1 November 1955 to Lee-on-Solent, where in October 1957 it handed over the trials role to No.701 Squadron, to concentrate entirely on training. A further move was made on 7 January 1958, to Culdrose, where Hiller HT.2s arrived in September 1962. In March 1974 the first Gazelles were received, and by March 1975 the squadron was equipped entirely with these, becoming the Basic Helicopter Training unit, a role in which it continues. Its achievements were given recognition in 1983 when it was awarded the annual Boyd Trophy.

Identification Markings
Shark & Swordfish *089-093* to 5.39, then *Swordfish B8A+*; Swordfish *AR1A+* from 3.45; All types *501-515 & 700-711/GJ* from 5.47, to *520-549/CU* 7.56, to *(5)40-(5)67* 7.65.

Six Westland/Aerospatiale Gazelles of "The Sharks" display team piloted by instructors of No.705 Squadron at Culdrose in August 1975. (via Brian Lowe)

Aircraft Equipment	Period of Service	Example	
Shark II/SP	Jul 1936 - Jun 1937	K5624	(091)
Swordfish I/SP	Jul 1936 - Jan 1940	K5954	(093)
Swordfish III	Mar 1945 - Jun 1945	NS134	
Hoverfly I	May 1947 - Nov 1950	KK999	(512/GJ)
Hoverfly II	May 1947 - Jan 1950	KN879	(501/GJ)
Skeeter 3	Jul 1952	WF112	
Dragonfly HR.1	Jan 1950 - Mar 1953	VZ963	(705/GJ)
Dragonfly HR.3	Jul 1952 - Oct 1960	WG723	(706/GJ)
Dragonfly HR.5	Oct 1957 - Mar 1962	WG669	(530/CU)
Hiller HT.1	May 1953 - Jan 1963	XB513	(534)
Hiller HT.2	Sep 1962 - Mar 1975	XS700	(543)
Sikorsky S.55	Jun 1953	WW339	
Whirlwind HAS.22	Oct 1953 - Nov 1956	WV221	(701/GJ)
Whirlwind HAR.1	Oct 1954 - May 1960	XA866	(524)
Whirlwind HAR.3	Nov 1955 - Feb 1966	XJ397	(529)
Whirlwind HAS.7	Jun 1960 - Dec 1974	XN304	(522)
Wasp HAS.1	Jul 1965 - 1967	XT426	(64)
Gazelle HT.2	Mar 1974 - to date	XZ938	(45/CU)

Squadron bases
Calafrana	15 Jul	1936
Squadron disbanded	21 Jan	1940
Ronaldsway	7 Mar	1945
Squadron disbanded	24 Jun	1945
Gosport	7 May	1947
Haslemere (Dt - Hoverflies)	7 May 1947 to 3 Dec	1947
Portland (Dt)	8 Feb to 12 Jul	1950 1950
Chickerall (Dt)	15 Jan to 27 Mar	1953 1953
Lee-on-Solent	1 Nov	1955
Culdrose (satt Predannack)	7 Jan	1958
Kiel	10 Jul	1971
Culdrose	20 Jul	1971

Commanding Officers
L/C DW MacKendrick RN (Sq Ldr RAF)	15 Jul	1936
Lt PE O'Brien RN (Flt Lt RAF)	14 Nov	1938
Squadron disbanded	21 Jan	1940
L/C(A) G Bennett DSC RNVR	7 Mar	1945
Squadron disbanded	24 Jun	1945
Lt(A) KM Reed RN	7 May	1947
Lt GNC Fuller RN	20 Aug	1949
L/C SH Suthers DSC RN	29 Nov	1949
L/C HR Spedding MBE RN	28 Oct	1952

Commanding Officers
L/C JC Jacob RN	25 May	1954
L/C GCJ Knight DFC RN	1 Nov	1955
L/C GW Bricker RN	29 Nov	1957
L/C RGD Williams RN	6 Jan	1960
L/C PJ Craig RN	29 Jun	1961
L/C GA Bagnall RN	22 Oct	1962
L/C A Casdagli RN	4 Apr	1964
L/C BC Sarginson RN	10 Nov	1965
L/C GW Barras RN	14 Sep	1967
L/C DK Hale RN	2 Apr	1969
L/C EC Ashton-Johnson RN	15 Jul	1970
L/C PB Rover RN	29 Sep	1971
L/C CJS Craig RN	14 May	1973
L/C PTS Taylor RN	28 Jan	1975
L/C FA Rock RN	18 Nov	1976
L/C RJB Riley RN	17 Aug	1978
L/C WB Kirby RN	21 May	1980
L/C JT Lockwood RN	23 Apr	1982
L/C SD Pendrich RN	19 Mar	1984
L/C MR Swales RN	25 Mar	1986
L/C MC Nixon RN	19 Feb	1988
L/C DG Hale RN	28 Feb	1990
L/C AJ Eagles AFC RN	18 Dec	1990
L/C NK Bennett RN	26 Feb	1993
L/C MR Osman RAN	7 Nov	1994

Fairey Swordfish floatplane K5931 '092' of No.705 (Catapult) Flight in HMS Repulse taking off from Kalafrana seaplane base, Malta in 1937

Vought Sikorsky Hoverfly I KL100 of No.705 Squadron at Bramcote in 1948. (Tony Hughes)

Hiller HT.2 XS162 '(5)47' of No.705 Helicopter Training Squadron, Gosport around 1967/8. (MAP)

No.706 Squadron

Badge: On a field azure, over water barry wavy argent and azure a winged horse in flight supporting between the forelegs a dagger point downwards and piercing the water all gold

Motto: None

No.706 Squadron personnel took passage from the United Kingdom on 2 February 1945, assembling early in March at Jervis Bay as a Pool Squadron, and moving to Schofields on 6 March, to be officially commissioned there on 10 April 1945. Operating as a Crew Pool and Refresher Flying School, equipment comprised 36 aircraft, being six each of the operational types then in use with the British Pacific Fleet, namely the Avenger, Barracuda, Corsair, Firefly, Hellcat and Seafire. The squadron acted as a pool for aircrew destined for the British Pacific Fleet, provided refresher training for aircrew arriving from the United Kingdom and Ceylon, and undertook conversion training for pilots changing to aircraft they had not previously flown. Strength was still at 36 aircraft on VJ-Day, but after moving to Maryborough on 28 August, the squadron gradually flew its surplus aircraft to Archerfield, and by mid-October had only two left of each type. With these it moved to Nowra on 24 October, returning on 18 January 1946 to Schofields, where it disbanded on 31 May 1946.

On 7 September 1953, No.706 reformed at Gosport as an Anti-Submarine Helicopter squadron equipped with 8 American-built Whirlwind HAS.22s and two Hiller HT.1s. Trials were carried out with sonar equipment both at Portland and Belfast, during which the squadron embarked in HMS *Perseus*. Returning to Gosport, No.706 disbanded on 15 March 1954 to become No.845 Squadron.

No.706 reformed at Culdrose on 4 January 1962 from a nucleus of 700H Flight, as a Helicopter Advanced Flying Training squadron. Equipped with 8 Wessex HAS.1s, it converted helicopter pilots to this new type, gave advanced flying training to helicopter specialist pilots and providing operational flying training in the Commando role, as well as carrying out service and miscellaneous trials. Aircraft were also provided for the Aircraft Torpedo Development Unit at Culdrose.

In January 1964, 6 Wessex HAS.1s and 2 Hiller HT.2s were received for operation by 'B' Flight in HMS *Bulwark*, the former being incorporated in No.845 Squadron when the ship reached the Far East. Two Wasps were received in November 1964, and the following month the squadron took over from No.829 Squadron the task of Wasp conversion. Wessex HAS.3s arrived in 1967 and Sea Kings in 1978, the training of aircrew for these types being added to the squadron task as they came into service. Training in the Commando role ceased when this task was transferred to No.707 Squadron on its formation in December 1964. The Wasp element was transferred to No.703 Squadron in February 1975. An RFA trials flight operated with RFA *Fort Grange* from February to December 1978, transferring to No.824 Squadron on completion of the trials. The RAF Sea King Training Flight (q.v.) was parented between October 1979 and January 1982.

On 21 October 1985, observers and aircrewmen advanced flying training (AFT) was taken over from No.810 Squadron. The squadron currently operates as a conversion and advanced training squadron for Sea King pilots and maintainers, and is due to re-equip with the Merlin from 1998.

Identification Markings
Australia unknown; Whirlwind *780-787/GJ*; Wessex/Wasp *501-512/CU* to 7.65, then Wessex/Wasp/Sea King *566-599/CU*.

Aircraft Equipment	Period of Service	Example	
Avenger I	Mar 1945 - Oct 1945	FN870	
Avenger II	Mar 1945 - Sep 1945	JZ552	
Avenger III	Feb 1946 - Mar 1946	JZ704	
Barracuda II	Aug 1945 - Mar 1946	PM759	
Corsair II	Mar 1945 - Dec 1945	JT315	
Corsair IV	Dec 1945 - Jul 1946	KD810	
Firefly I	Nov 1945 - Jan 1946	MB629	
Hellcat I	Mar 1945 - Sep 1945	FN373	
Hellcat II	Dec 1945 - 1946		
Seafire III	Mar 1945 - Nov 1945	LR789	
Seafire XV	1946 - 1946		
Hiller HT.1	Sep 1953 - Oct 1953	XB479	
Whirlwind HAS.22	Sep 1953 - Mar 1954	WV218	(c/s 781)
Wessex HAS.1	Jan 1962 - Jan 1971	XM868	(574/CU)
Wessex HAS.3	Jul 1967 - Nov 1970	XP110	(567/CU)
Wasp HAS.1	Nov 1964 - Feb 1975	XT426	(80/CU)
Sea King HAS.1	Jan 1970 - Nov 1978	XV657	(596/CU)
Sea King HAS.2/2a	Jun 1978 - Mar 1990	XZ581	(593/CU)
Sea King HAR.3 (RAF SKTF)	Oct 1979 - Jan 1982	XZ585	(576)
Sea King HAS.5	Jan 1981 - to date	XV652	(581/CU)
Sea King HAS.6	1992-to date	XV673	(588)

706B

Aircraft Equipment	Period of Service	Example	
Wessex HAS.1	Jan 1964 - Feb 1964	XS150	(P)
Hiller HT.2	Jan 1964 - Apr 1964	XZ170	(Z)

Westland Sea King HAS.2A XV650 '(5)88/CU' of No.706 Squadron, Culdrose in 1979. (Westland Helicopters Ltd)

Commanding Officers
L/C(A) RE Bradshaw
  DSC & 2 Bars RN 6 Mar 1945
L/C(A) DMR
  Wynne-Roberts RN 31 Aug 1945
L/C(A) CA Fraser
          RN   22 Oct 1945
Squadron disbanded 31 May 1946
L/C H Phillips RN   7 Sep 1953
Squadron disbanded 15 Mar 1954
L/C RA Duxbury RN 4 Jan 1962
L/C CRV Doe RN   30 Jul 1963
L/C JE Kelly RN   7 Oct 1963
L/C CRV Doe RN   19 Mar 1965
L/C MJ Harvey RN 14 Sep 1966
L/C DJA Bridger RN 18 Sep 1968
L/C VG Sirett RN   24 Jun 1970
L/C GW Barras RN 15 Oct 1971
L/C HC Foster RN   6 Jun 1973
L/C MP Clark RN   29 Jan 1975
L/C NB Shaw RN   15 Mar 1976
L/C TW Loughran RN 8 Oct 1976
L/C RC Swales RN 23 Sep 1977
L/C RE Wilkinson
          RN   23 Oct 1978
L/C DR Warren RN 17 Apr 1980
L/C HS Clark RN   12 Aug 1981
L/C IC Domoney RN 4 May 1982
L/C HS Clark DSC
          RN   27 Sep 1982
L/C I Stanley DSO
          RN   20 Oct 1983
L/C RG Harrison RN 7 Jun 1985
L/C T Jane RN   1 Apr 1987
L/C NJ Hennell
        AFC RN   20 Sep 1989
L/C OMC Dismore
          RN   17 Feb 1993

Squadron bases
Jervis Bay   Mar 1945
Schofields   6 Mar 1945
Maryborough   28 Aug 1945
Nowra   24 Oct 1945
Schofields   18 Jan 1946
Squadron disbanded 31 May 1946
Gosport   7 Sep 1953
Belfast   30 Oct 1953
HMS Perseus   20 Jan 1954
HMS Relentless   9 Feb 1954
Eglinton   10 Feb 1954
Gosport   1 Mar 1954
Redes 845 Sqdn   15 Mar 1954
Culdrose   4 Jan 1962

No.706B Flight

Squadron bases
Culdrose   7 Jan 1964
Portland   5 Feb 1964
HMS Bulwark(Dt)   8 Mar 1964
- absorbed into 845 Sqdn

Westland Wessex HAS.1 XM838 '508/CU' of No.706 Squadron in 1963. (MAP)

Westland Wasp HAS.1 XS530 '(5)81' of No.706 Squadron, 1972. (MAP)

No.707 Squadron

Badge: 1. On a white field, a base barry wavy white and blue overall a dagger point downwards proper winged gold
2. On a white field, a base barry wavy blue and white overall a dagger point upwards red winged gold (from 1979)
Motto: Ne gladius dormiat
(Let the sword not sleep)

No.707 Squadron

No.707 Squadron formed at Burscough on 20 February 1945 from 'B' Flight of No.735 Squadron as a Radar Trials Unit. Otherwise known as the Naval School of Airborne Radar, it acted as the control authority in airborne radar matters, including both ASV and AI, and also the airborne radar training of flying personnel. Equipped initially with Swordfish, Barracudas and Avengers, these were supplemented later by radar-equipped Ansons. The squadron moved on 14 August to Gosport, where it disbanded on 1 October 1945 on being merged into No.778 Squadron.

On 9 December 1964, No.707 reformed at Culdrose out of the disbanded No.847 Squadron. It operated as an advanced and operational flying training (AFT/OFT) Commando helicopter squadron with Wessex HU.5s. In addition to giving instruction to RN and RM Commando pilots, No.707 undertook communications work, development flying, weapons trials, and exercises with Army units, as well as training Wessex crews for operation in Royal Fleet Auxiliary vessels. In May 1972 the squadron moved to Yeovilton, and during the summer of 1974 a search and rescue commitment was added to the squadron's duties for a time. On 29 July 1974 the Red Dragon Flight was formed with two aircraft to provide a three-months conversion course for HRH Prince Charles, The Prince of Wales, being disbanded on 12 December 1974 on completion of this task. In April 1982 much of the squadron formed the nucleus of a reformed No.848 Squadron for service in the South Atlantic. Re-equipment with Sea King HC.4s began in October 1983, and the Wessex Commando training task was transferred to No.771 Squadron in 1985.

Regular training detachments deploy to St.Raphael and Sailagouse in southern France, and Landsberg in Germany for mountain flying, to Castlemartin and Dartmoor for military and weapon training, and to RFAs for DLP training. The squadron retains a wartime role in support of Commando forces and provided aircraft and men again for No.848 Squadron which reformed and deployed to the Gulf in 1991. The squadron deployed three aircraft to Aldergrove in support of internal security operations from October 1993, reinstating a FAA presence formerly undertaken by No.845 Squadron between 1977 and 1982. In April 1994 No.707 Squadron were relieved at Aldergrove by No.846 Squadron. The squadron is to be renumbered No.848 on 9 February 1995.

Identification Markings
Swordfish *O7A+*; Barracuda *O8A+*; Avenger *AH8A+*; Wessex single letters *M-Z/CU* to 7.71, then *WA-WB,WM-WZ/CU:VL* to 4.84; Wessex/Sea King *ZA+/VL* from 4.82.

Aircraft Equipment	Period of Service	Example
Swordfish II	Feb 1945 - Sep 1945	LS445
Swordfish III	Feb 1945 - Sep 1945	NF313 (B)
Barracuda II	Feb 1945 - Sep 1945	MD703 (c/s BC)
Barracuda III	Feb 1945 - Sep 1945	ME166 (O8U)
Anson I	Feb 1945 - Sep 1945	NK210 (c/s BD)
Avenger III	Apr 1945 - Sep 1945	JZ670 (c/s BE)
Wessex HU.5	Dec 1964 - Apr 1982	XS491 (WL/VL)
	May 1982 - Sep 1985	XT479 (ZA/VL)
Sea King HC.4	Oct 1983 - Feb 1995	ZD476 (ZX/VL)

Commanding Officers
L/C(A) SS Laurie RNVR	20 Feb 1945
Squadron disbanded	1 Oct 1945
L/C DJ Lickfold MBE RN	9 Dec 1964
L/C PJ Craig RN	14 Jun 1965
L/C PD Deller RN	21 Feb 1966
L/C RE Smith MBE RN	27 Oct 1967
L/C BB Hartwell RN	4 Sep 1967
L/C NS Foster RN	12 Mar 1969
L/C RE Smith MBE RN	28 May 1970
L/C GS Clarke RN	25 Feb 1972
L/C PA Voute RN	21 Aug 1973
L/C RF Shercliff RN	19 Dec 1974
L/C PJW Stevens RN	24 Jun 1976
L/C M Kenworthy RN	6 Mar 1978
L/C SC Thornewill RN	15 Apr 1980
L/C DEP Baston RN	18 Nov 1981
L/C NPR Maddox RN	12 May 1982

Commanding Officers
L/C DEP Baston AFC RN	1 Jul 1982
L/C S Radley RN	1 Jun 1984
L/C J Beattie RN	17 Jun 1986
L/C GRN Foster RN	8 Nov 1988
L/C RI Horton AFC RN	9 Oct 1990
L/C DA Lord MBE RN	29 Sep 1993
Redes 848 Sqdn	9 Feb 1995

Squadron bases
Burscough	20 Feb 1945
Gosport	14 Aug 1945
Squadron disbanded	1 Oct 1945
Culdrose	9 Dec 1964
Yeovilton	15 May 1972
Redes 848 Sqdn	19 Apr 1982
Yeovilton	12 May 1982
Aldergrove (Z Flt)	1 Oct 1993
(Dt3)	to 31 Mar 1994
Redes 848 Sqdn	9 Feb 1995

Grumman Avenger II JZ670 'AH8X' of No.707 Squadron, Burscough being inspected by members of the public at a rather wet open day shortly after VJ-Day. (FAA Museum)

No.708 Squadron

No.708 Squadron formed at Lee-on-Solent on 1 October 1944 from 'B' Flight of No.764 Squadron as the Firebrand Tactical Trials Unit. Equipped with Firebrand TF.IIs, some of its aircraft were fitted with 8 rocket projectiles and flew combat practice sorties against Seafires which were also attached to the squadron. Moving to Gosport in January 1945, the squadron engaged in investigations to overcome problems peculiar to the Firebrand. Progress was slow due to lack of availability of aircraft, poor serviceability, work on numerous modifications, and unsuitability of the airfield for this type of aircraft. Deck landing trials were carried out in HMS *Glory* in the Clyde during May 1945, being later continued in HMS *Pretoria Castle*. In August the first Firebrand TF.IIIs arrived, these being flown to Lee-on-Solent on a daily basis to pick up torpedoes for exercises in Stokes Bay. The squadron moved to Ford at the beginning of September 1945, where the CO and several pilots provided a nucleus for the formation of No.813, the first operational Firebrand squadron. No.708 moved to Fearn towards the end of the year, then early in 1946 to Rattray, where it disbanded on 26 February 1946.

Blackburn Firebrand II DK383 'OC' and others of No.708 Squadron, the Firebrand Tactical Trials Unit, lined up around 1945. (MAP)

Identification Markings
Firebrand *OA+*.

Aircraft Equipment	Period of Service	Example
Firebrand TF.II	Oct 1944 - Aug 1945	DK375 (OK)
Firebrand TF.III	Aug 1945 - Feb 1946	DK406
Seafire Ib	May 1945 - Jun 1945	MB357
Seafire IIc	May 1945 1945	MB264
Seafire III	May 1945 - Aug 1945	NN575

Squadron bases	
Lee-on-Solent	1 Oct 1944
Gosport	15 Jan 1945
Ford	6 Sep 1945
Fearn	5 Dec 1945
Rattray	8 Jan 1946
Squadron disbanded	26 Feb 1946

Commanding Officers	
Cdr(A) WC Simpson DSC RNVR	15 Sep 1944
L/C DB Law DSC RN	5 Jan 1946
Squadron disbanded	26 Feb 1946

No.709 Squadron

No.709 Squadron formed at St Merryn on 15 September 1944 within the School of Naval Air Warfare as a Ground Attack School. Initial equipment included Seafire L.IIIs taken over from Nos.808 and 885 Squadrons of No.3 Naval Fighter Wing, which was in the process of converting to Hellcats, the CO of No.709 having been formerly in command of another squadron in that wing. The School also operated Hellcats and Harvards, on which it carried out training in the lessons learned by No.3 Wing during recent operations in support of the Normandy invasion. No.709 disbanded at St Merryn on 6 January 1946.

Early in 1965, plans were made to form a Buccaneer S.1 Operational Flying School as No.709 Squadron by renumbering No.809 Squadron at Lossiemouth, but it became No.736 Squadron instead.

Identification Markings
Seafire *S5A+*; Harvard *S3A+*; Hellcat *S5A+* & believed *S6A+*.

Aircraft Equipment	Period of Service	Example	
Seafire III	Sep 1944 - Aug 1945	NF493	(S5N)
Hellcat I	Sep 1944 - Jan 1946	JV157	(S5C)
Hellcat II	Sep 1944 - Sep 1945	JV247	(S5H)
Harvard IIb	1945 - Jan 1946	KF559	(S3V)
Harvard III	Feb 1945 - Jun 1945	EZ274	(S3N)
Seafire XV	Nov 1945 - Jan 1946	SR604	
Seafire XVII	Dec 1945 - Jan 1946	SX273	(S5O)
Seafire 45	Dec 1945 - Jan 1946	LA449	(S5A)

Commanding Officers	
Lt K White MBE RN	1 Oct 1944
Lt(A) DLR Hutchinson RNVR	20 Aug 1945
Lt(A) W Orr RNVR	2 Nov 1945
Squadron disbanded	26 Feb 1946

Squadron bases	
St.Merryn	15 Sep 1944
Squadron disbanded	6 Jan 1946

Supermarine Seafire F.XVII SX273 'S5O' of No.709 Squadron, St.Merryn in 1945. (FAA Museum)

No.710 Squadron

No.710 Squadron formed at Lee-on-Solent on 23 August 1939 as a seaplane squadron for service in the seaplane carrier HMS *Albatross*. Equipped with six Walruses plus three reserve aircraft, these were embarked on 1 September and the ship sailed for West Africa. Arriving at Freetown, Sierra Leone on 8 September, the ship was soon back at sea after a report was received of U-boats and a mother ship being sighted in mid-Atlantic. This proved fruitless, and the ship returned to Freetown, where No.710 operated as a Fleet Requirements Unit, providing drogue towing for the local anti-aircraft defences and taking aerial photographs to enable the Army to update maps and charts. The ship also operated as a repair unit for visiting catapult flights of No.700 Squadron, whilst No.710 sent detached flights to Dakar and Bathurst for anti-submarine patrols over an extended area. By the end of July 1940 a rough landing ground had been cleared at Hastings, and another at nearby Wellington, and an increasing number of Walruses were able to operate ashore. On 15 January 1941 an unsuccessful attack was made on an Italian submarine which had just sunk a freighter. From 14 May 1941 the whole squadron began to operate from Hastings, which had become a RN Air Station.

Re-embarking with six aircraft on 14 September 1941, No.710 had only short periods ashore before sailing in HMS *Albatross* during April 1942 by way of the Cape to participate in the Madagascar campaign, during which they dropped supplies to forward troops and undertook other tasks. Two aircraft went ashore to Nairobi in June to be fitted with radar, and in July five aircraft went to Mayotte to patrol the Mozambique Channel. Following the final landings in Madagascar in September, the ship remained in the area until November when she sailed to Durban, where No.710 was put ashore to Stamford Hill. In March 1943 the ship sailed for Bombay with No.710, to become a Combined Operations Training Ship. The squadron trained at Santa Cruz, carrying out exercises with the Army, until re-embarking in July to sail back to Africa. The Walruses were put ashore at Kilindini, and ferried to Nairobi before the ship sailed without aircraft, the squadron disbanding at Lee-on-Solent on 14 October 1943, soon after arrival.

No.710 reformed at Ronaldsway on 7 October 1944 as a Torpedo Training squadron. Operating as part of No.1 Naval Operational Training Unit, with No.713 Squadron it provided Part III of the Torpedo Bomber Reconnaissance Course with Barracudas and a few Swordfish. No.710 disbanded at Ronaldsway on 20 December 1945.

Identification Markings
Walrus *A9A+* later *9A+*; Barracuda *AR2A+ to AR7A+*.

Aircraft Equipment	Period of Service	Example
Walrus	Oct 1939 - Oct 1943	L2334 (A9K)
Swordfish I	- Jun 1945	L7657
Swordfish II	Apr 1945 - Dec 1945	LS459
Barracuda II	Oct 1944 - Dec 1945	LS958 (AR3K)
Barracuda III	Oct 1944 - Dec 1945	MD895
Anson I	Apr 1945 - Jul 1945	NK164

Squadron bases
Lee-on-Solent	23 Aug 1939
Mount Batten	26 Aug 1939
HMS Albatross (operated from ship at Freetown from 8 Sep 1939)	1 Sep 1939
Hastings (Flts detd Dakar and Bathurst)	12 Jan 1940
HMS Albatross	26 Jan 1940
HMS Hermes (Dt4)	1-17 May 1940
Hastings and Wellington (Dts)	31 Jul 1940 to 14 May 1941
Hastings	14 May 1941
HMS Albatross	25 Sep 1941
Hastings	17 Nov 1941
HMS Albatross	27 Nov 1941
Hastings (Dt2)	22 Dec 1941 to 23 Feb 1942
Port Stanley (Y Flt - Dt1)	Feb 1942 to 1 Mar 1942
HMS Albatross	22 Apr 1942
Kilindini	31 May 1942
Port Reitz (Dt4)	20 Jun 1942
Mayotte (Dt5)	21 Jul 1942
HMS Albatross (Dt2)	21 Jul 1942
Kilindini	5 Aug 1942
HMS Albatross (Dt2)	5 Sep 1942
Majunga	9 Sep 1942
HMS Albatross	19 Nov 1942
Stamford Hill (Dt)	29 Nov 1942
Maputo (Dt4)	5-22 Feb 1943
HMS Albatross	4 Mar 1943
Santa Cruz	31 Mar 1943
HMS Albatross	15 Jul 1943
Lee-on-Solent	12 Oct 1943
Squadron disbanded	14 Oct 1943
Ronaldsway	7 Oct 1944
Squadron disbanded	20 Dec 1945

Commanding Officers
L/C HL Hayes RN	23 Aug 1939
Capt WHC Manson RM	8 Aug 1940
L/C CE Fenwick RN	14 Jul 1941
L/C JE Smallwood RN	10 Mar 1942
Lt EF Pritchard RN	1 Sep 1942
Lt(A) MJJ Harris RNVR	13 May 1943
Squadron disbanded	14 Oct 1943
L/C(A) DR Connor RNVR	7 Oct 1944
L/C JF Arnold RN	1 Aug 1945
Squadron disbanded	20 Dec 1945

Supermarine Walrus W2738 '9A' of No.710 Squadron Falklands detachment being examined by the local canine population while beached. (FAA Museum)

Pictured on 25 August 1945, Fairey Barracuda II DR116 'R3S' of RNAS Ronaldsway was used by trainees with No.710 Squadron. (RAF Museum 6060-1)

No.711 Squadron

No.711 (Catapult) Flight formed on 15 July 1936 from part of No.447 (Catapult) Flight for use on ships of the 1st Cruiser Squadron. This formed part of the Mediterranean Fleet, and Kalafrana was used by the squadron as a shore base. Aircraft were initially Ospreys, which were embarked in HMS *London*, HMS *Devonshire*, HMS *Shropshire* and HMS *Sussex*. Walruses soon arrived as replacements, and on the outbreak of war their shore base was changed to Aboukir. By this time the parent unit had become No.711 (Catapult) Squadron, but it lost its identity when it was absorbed into No.700 Squadron on 21 January 1940.

On 9 September 1944, No.711 reformed at Crail as a Torpedo Training squadron. Equipped with Barracudas, these were partially replaced in August 1945 by Avengers, and this element of the unit operated as an Avenger Operational Training Unit. With the ending of hostilities, there was a reduced requirement for its task, and No.711 disbanded at Crail on 21 December 1945, its remnants being absorbed by No.785 Squadron.

Supermarine Walrus L2221 '069' of No.711 (Catapult) Squadron from HMS Shropshire on the flight deck of HMS Glorious in 1938 (Cross/FAA Museum)

Aircraft Equipment	Period of Service	Example	
Osprey III/SP	Jul 1936 - Dec 1936	K3641	(071)
Walrus I	Oct 1936 - Jan 1940	L2169	(UV)
Barracuda II	Sep 1944 - Dec 1945	MX561	(C6C)
Reliant I	Sep 1944 - Oct 1944	?	(C6B)
Anson I/ASV	Jan 1945 - 1945	MG860	
Avenger I	Sep 1945 - Dec 1945	JZ163	(C1J)
Avenger II	Aug 1945 - Dec 1945	JZ377	

Identification Markings
Osprey *067-071*; Walrus *067-071*, to *UM-UX* 1936, reverted to *067-071*, to *F9A+* 5.39; Barracuda *C5A+* & *C6A+*; Reliant *C6A+A+*; Avenger *C1A+, C3A+, C4A+, C5A+* & *C6A+*.

Commanding Officers
L/C AA Murray RN
 (Sq Ldr RAF)   15 Jul 1936
Lt ACR Duvall RN 28 Sep 1936
Lt RJH Stephens RN
 (Flt Lt RAF)   28 Jun 1937
Lt PA Booth RN   25 Oct 1937
L/C OS Stevinson RN
 (Sq Ldr RAF)   17 Jan 1938
L/C AHT Fleming
 RN   24 May 1939
Squadron disbanded 21 Jan 1940

Commanding Officers
L/C(A) JB Curgenven
 -Robinson DSC RNVR
       9 Sep 1944
L/C(A) DM Judd
 DSC RNVR   30 Jul 1945
Squadron disbanded 21 Dec 1945

Squadron bases
Calafrana   15 Jul 1936
Aboukir   19 Aug 1939
Squadron disbanded 21 Jan 1940
Crail   9 Sep 1944
Squadron disbanded 21 Dec 1945

Fairey Barracuda 'C6S' of No.711 Squadron flying from Crail. (via Cdr F.W.Baring)

Hawker Osprey III K3649 of No.711 (Catapult) Flight fitted with wheeled undercarriage whilst receiving attention ashore in the Mediterranean. (RAF Museum P.10882)

No.712 Squadron

No.712 (Catapult) Flight formed on 15 July 1936 by renumbering No.407 (Catapult) Flight, for service in ships of the 2nd Cruiser Squadron in the Home Fleet. Equipment was initially Ospreys, these being embarked in HMS *Leander*, HMS *Neptune* and HMS *Orion*, with a shore base at Mount Batten. With the arrival of Walruses in April 1937, aircraft in these ships became the responsibility of No.718 Squadron, and No.712 took over instead the requirement for HMS *Glasgow*, HMS *Newcastle*, HMS *Sheffield* and HMS *Southampton*, which all commissioned during 1937. The shore base was changed to Lee-on-Solent on 1 January 1938, by which time No.712 had achieved squadron status. At this time HMS *Cornwall* was added to its charges, but this ship was relinquished when it sailed to join the China Station in March 1939, to be replaced by HMS *Cumberland*. On the outbreak of war the squadron's responsibility was changed to the 18th Cruiser Squadron and the Humber Force, and it then also had control of aircraft in HMS *Belfast*, HMS *Edinburgh*, HMS *Norfolk* and HMS *Suffolk*, at which time it had 18 Walruses operating from 9 cruisers. The squadron reverted to the 2nd Cruiser Squadron by the end of the year, but lost its identity when on 21 January 1940 all the catapult squadrons were combined to form No.700 Squadron.

On 2 August 1944, No.712 reformed at Hatston as a Communications squadron out of 'B' Flight No.771 Squadron. It operated a miscellany of communications aircraft including Expeditors, Dominies, Sea Otters and Travellers until disbanding at Hatston on 23 August 1945.

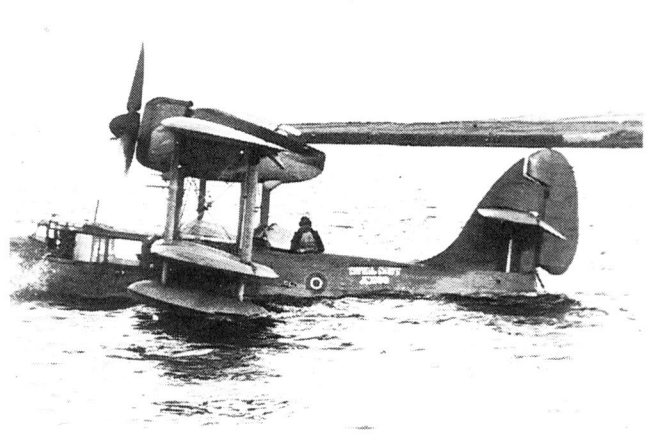

Supermarine Sea Otter 1 JM806 of No.712 Squadron, Hatston around 1944/45. (FAA Museum)

Aircraft Equipment	Period of Service	Example
Osprey SP	Jul 1936 - Jun 1937	K3918 (034)
Walrus I	Apr 1937 - Jan 1940	L2180 (G9U)
Traveller I	Aug 1944 - Apr 1945	FT502
Sea Otter	Aug 1944 - Aug 1945	JM806
Reliant I	Aug 1944 - Aug 1945	FK913 (H9.)

Identification Markings
Osprey *034*; Walrus *34-42, 147*, to *G9A+* 5.39; All types *H9A+* or uncoded 1944/5.

Squadron bases
Mount Batten	15 Jul	1936
Lee-on-Solent	1 Jan	1938
Squadron disbanded	21 Jan	1940
Hatston	2 Aug	1944
Squadron disbanded	23 Aug	1945

Commanding Officers
L/C HA Traill RN 15 Jul 1936
  (Flt Lt RAF)
Lt JC Richards RN 5 Aug 1936
  (Flt Lt RAF)

Commanding Officers
L/C OS Stevinson RN
  (Flt Lt RAF) 8 Feb 1937
L/C EH Shattock RN 3 Apr 1937
  (Sq Ldr RAF)
L/C RE Gunston RN 20 Apr 1939
  (Sq Ldr RAF)
L/C GA Tilney RN 24 May 1939
Squadron disbanded 21 Jan 1940
Lt(A) JU Reid RNVR 2 Aug 1944
Lt(A) RWM Williams
  RNZNVR 27 Mar 1945
Squadron disbanded 23 Aug 1945

Supermarine Walrus Is K8556 '34', L2195 '40' and K8546 '35' of No.712 (Catapult) Squadron in 1938. (via Rear Admiral E.H. Shattock)

No.713 Squadron

No.713 (Catapult) Flight formed on 15 July 1936 by renumbering No.445 (Catapult) Flight with the 3rd Cruiser Squadron. With a shore base at Kalafrana, it was responsible for Ospreys embarked in HMS *Arethusa*, HMS *Galatea*, and later HMS *Penelope*. These began to give way to Seafoxes in November 1937, and by early 1939 the unit had achieved squadron status, only to lose its identity when it was absorbed into No.700 Squadron on 21 January 1940.

On 12 August 1944, No.713 reformed at Ronaldsway as a Torpedo Bomber Reconnaissance Training squadron. Its Barracudas operated an anti-submarine course, and 'B' Flight acted as the Squadron Commander's Attack School, with a short course on dive bombing. No.713 provided Part III of the TBR Course in conjunction with No.710 Squadron until disbanding on 20 December 1945.

Commanding Officers
Lt JPG Bryant RN   15 Jul 1936
  (Flt Lt RAF)
Lt M Johnstone RN
  (Flt Lt RAF)   8 Nov 1937
Lt J Hamilton RN   26 Jun 1939
Squadron disbanded 21 Jan 1940
L/C(A) AG
  McWilliam RNVR 12 Aug 1944
Squadron disbanded 20 Dec 1945

Squadron bases
Kalafrana   15 Jul 1936
Squadron disbanded 21 Jan 1940
Ronaldsway   12 Aug 1944
Squadron disbanded 20 Dec 1945

Fairey Barracuda II 'AR2L' was flown by No.710 Squadron at Ronaldsway around 1945

Aircraft Equipment	Period of Service	Example
Osprey SP	Jul 1936 - Apr 1938	K5758
Seafox I	Nov 1937 - Jan 1940	K8588 (H9B)
Barracuda II	Aug 1944 - Dec 1945	MX542
Barracuda III	Nov 1944 - Dec 1945	MD892 (R3M)

Identification Markings
Osprey *078-079*; Seafox *078-079*, to *H9A+* 5.39; Barracuda *R2A+*, *R3A+*, *R5A+*, *R6A+* & *R7A+*, later *AR2A* to *AR6A+*.

Fairey Barracuda II LS683 'F2G' of No.714 Squadron from Fearn on the flight deck of HMS Ravager on 9 September 1944.
(HMS Ravager)

No.714 Squadron

No.714 (Catapult) Flight formed on 15 July 1936 by renumbering No.406 (Catapult) Flight with the 4th Cruiser Squadron in the East Indies Station. Initial equipment was Fairey IIIFs embarked in HMS *Emerald*, HMS *Enterprise* and HMS *Norfolk*, these soon being phased out in favour of Ospreys and Walruses. During manouvres at Singapore in January 1937, the flight operated from its shore base at Seletar. Seafoxes arrived in June 1937 for use in HMS *Emerald*, but by the beginning of 1939 the unit had achieved squadron status and was by then operating from HMS *Liverpool* and HMS *Manchester*, later supplemented by HMS *Gloucester*. On the outbreak of war the squadron had 6 Walruses and was using both Seletar and Trincomalee as shore bases. It was absorbed into No.700 Squadron on 21 January 1940.

On 1 August 1944, No.714 reformed at Fearn as a Torpedo Bomber Reconnaissance Training squadron. With No.717 Squadron it received aircrew from their specialist training and assembled them into crews. Equipped with Barracudas, it moved to Rattray on 30-31 October 1944, disbanding there on 29 October 1945 when its task was taken over by No.717 Squadron.

Squadron bases
Seletar	15 Jul	1936
Squadron disbanded	21 Jan	1940
Fearn	1 Aug	1944
Rattray	30 Oct	1944
Squadron disbanded	29 Oct	1945

Commanding Officers
L/C HH Caddy RN	15 Jul	1936
L/C PW Humphreys RN	26 Oct	1937
Lt HJF Lane RN	27 Jan	1939
L/C AS Webb RN	24 May	1939
Squadron disbanded	21 Jan	1940
L/C(A) VR Crane RNVR	1 Aug	1944
Lt(A) PD Buckland RNVR (temp)	15 May	1945
L/C(A) RJ Godley DSC RNVR	19 May	1945
Squadron disbanded	29 Oct	1945

Aircraft Equipment	Period of Service	Example	
Fairey IIIF	Jul 1936 - Oct 1936	S1548	
Osprey SP	Jul 1936 - Mar 1938	K4330	
Seafox I	Jun 1937 - Jul 1938	K8572	
Walrus I	Oct 1936 - Jan 1940	L2253	(J9G)
Barracuda II	Aug 1944 - Dec 1945	P9744	(I2C)
Barracuda III	Oct 1945 - Dec 1945	MD967	

Identification Markings
Osprey believed uncoded; Walrus *307*, to *J9A+* 5.39; Barracuda *F1A+* & *F2A+*, to *AT1A+* & *AT2A+* 10.44, to *I1+ I2A+*.

Supermarine Walrus L2253 '307' of No.714 Flight aboard Manchester on 19 December 1938 whilst en route from Goa to Cochin.
(FAA Museum)

No.715 Squadron

No.715 (Catapult) Flight formed on 15 July 1936 by renumbering No.403 (Catapult) Flight in ships of the 5th Cruiser Squadron in the China Station. The shore base was at Kai Tak, with Wei-Hai-Wei in northern China also being used. Initial equipment was Ospreys in HMS *Berwick*, HMS *Dorsetshire* and HMS *Kent*, but in September 1936 these began to give way to Walruses. HMS *Berwick* was withdrawn, but the squadron took over responsibility for aircraft in HMS *Birmingham*, HMS *Cornwall*, HMS *Cumberland* and HMS *Suffolk*. It achieved squadron status by early 1938, and at the outbreak of war had 7 Walruses in 5 cruisers, using both Kai Tak and Seletar as shore bases. No.714 disbanded into No.700 Squadron on 21 January 1940.

On 17 August 1944, part of No.736 Squadron at St Merryn broke away to reform No.715 Squadron within the School of Air Combat. Equipped mainly with Seafires and Corsairs it operated a Fighter Air Combat Course and also a Fighter Leaders Course until being reabsorbed by No.736 Squadron on 31 March 1946.

Aircraft Equipment	Period of Service	Example	
Osprey III/SP	Jul 1936 - Jul 1937	K3645	
Walrus I	Sep 1936 - Jan 1940	K8552	(WP)
Corsair III	Aug 1944 - Aug 1945	JS508	
Corsair IV	Aug 1944 - Jun 1946	KD801	
Harvard IIb	Jun 1945 - Nov 1945	KF557	
Harvard III	Sep 1945 - Dec 1945	EZ375	
Master II	Aug 1944 - Jun 1945	DL799	
Seafire Va	Aug 1944 - Oct 1944	R6722	
Seafire Ib	Aug 1944 - 1945	PA115	
Seafire III	Aug 1944 - Dec 1945	NF551	(S4B)
Seafire XVII	Aug 1944 - Dec 1945	SX125	(S4H)

Identification Markings
Walrus *43-45*, to *WM-WW* 1936, reverted to *43-45* 1937, to *K9A+* 5.39; Seafire *S4A+*; Corsair *S4A+*.

Commanding Officers
L/C EOF Price RN 15 Jul 1936
 (Flt Lt RAF)
Lt IR Sarel RN 11 Oct 1937
 (Sq Ldr RAF)
Lt PJ Milner-Barry
  RN 24 May 1939
Squadron disbanded 21 Jan 1940
L/C(A) RE Gardner
  DSC RNVR 17 Aug 1944
L/C DG Carlisle
  DSC SANF(V) 12 Dec 1944
L/C FRA Turnbull
  DSC & Bar RN 28 Jun 1945
Squadron disbanded 31 Mar 1946

Squadron bases
Kai Tak 15 Jul 1936
Squadron disbanded 21 Jan 1940
St Merryn 17 Aug 1944
Squadron disbanded 31 Mar 1946

Supermarine Walrus K5780 'WM' of No.715 Sqdn from HMS Cumberland in the China Station, seen on the flight deck of HMS Eagle around 1937/8. (FAA Museum)

No.716 Squadron

No.716 (Catapult) Flight formed on 15 July 1936 from part of No.443 (Catapult) Flight for ships of the 6th Cruiser Squadron in the South Africa Station. Initially equipped with Ospreys for use in HMS *Amphion*, these began to be replaced by Seafoxes in October 1937 when HMS *Neptune* arrived. Mount Batten was used as a shore base when in Home waters, until being replaced by Lee-on-Solent on 1 January 1938. By the outbreak of war the unit had achieved squadron status and was using Simonstown as a shore base, but on 21 January 1940 it was absorbed into No.700 Squadron.

On 28 June 1944, No.716 reformed at Eastleigh as the School of Safety Equipment. Equipped with a few Sea Otters and at least one Wellington, it gave instruction in Air Sea Rescue techniques, and carried out development work on equipment. A detachment of the squadron joined HMS *Ruler* at Greenock in January 1945 for a few days. No.716 disbanded on 1 September 1945.

Aircraft Equipment	Period of Service	Example	
Osprey IV/SP	Jul 1936 - Feb 1938	K5748	
Seafox I	Oct 1937 - Jan 1940	K8590	
Walrus I	Sep 1939 - Sep 1939		
Sea Otter I	Jul 1944 - Aug 1945	JM801	(10A)
Wellington XI	Jul 1944 - Aug 1945	MP524	

Identification Markings
Seafox uncoded, to *L9A+* 5.39 (no evidence of use); Sea Otter *10A+*.

Squadron bases
Mount Batten 15 Jul 1936
Lee-on-Solent 1 Jan 1938
 (South African base
  at Simonstown)
Squadron disbanded 21 Jan 1940
Eastleigh 28 Jun 1944
ASR Training Flight
 detd Lee-on-Solent 10 Mar 1945
Squadron disbanded 1 Sep 1945

Commanding Officers
Lt FEC Judd RN
 (Flt Lt RAF) 15 Jul 1936
Lt AJT Roe RN 25 Apr 1938
Squadron disbanded 21 Jan 1940
L/C JF Nicholas RN 28 Jun 1944
L/C(A) DV Robinson
  RNVR 11 May 1945
Squadron disbanded 1 Sep 1945

BEFORE - Fairey Seafox K8577 of No.716 Flight leaves the catapult of HMS Neptune. (FAA Museum)

AFTER - Fairey Seafox K8577 being ignominiously hoisted aboard HMS Neptune after a ditching in 1938. (FAA Museum)

No.717 Squadron

No.717 Squadron formed at Fearn on 1 July 1944 as a Torpedo Bomber Reconnaissance Training Squadron. With No.714 Squadron it received aircrew from their specialist training and assembled them into complete crews. Equipped with Barracuda IIs, it moved to Rattray on 30-31 October 1944 where it operated Part I of the TBR Course. It took over the task of the disbanding Nos.769 and 714 Squadrons on 22 and 29 October 1945 respectively. Then Firebrands were received in February 1946, and one flight was to have been the Firebrand Conversion Unit, but instead these aircraft went to Lee-on-Solent. No.717 Squadron was itself disbanded at Rattray on 22 March 1946.

Identification Markings
Barracuda *F1A+* & *F2A+*, to *AT3A+* & *AT4A+* 10.44, to *I1A+* & *I2A+* 1945.

Commanding Officers
L/C D Norcock RN   1 Jul 1944
L/C(A) A Brunt
　DSC RNZNVR 18 Sep 1944
L/C(A) JL Fisher
　RNVR   26 Jan 1945
Lt(A) TE Rogers
　RNVR   17 Aug 1945
Lt(A) HTT Harding
　RNVR   21 Dec 1945
Squadron disbanded 22 Mar 1946

Squadron bases
Fearn   1 Jul 1944
Rattray   30 Oct 1944
Squadron disbanded 22 Mar 1946

Aircraft Equipment	Period of Service	Example
Barracuda II	Jul 1944 - Mar 1946	DR204 (AT4Y)
Firebrand II/III/IV	Feb 1946 - Mar 1946	DK397

No.718 Squadron

No.718 (Catapult) Flight formed on 15 July 1936 from part of No.443 (Catapult) Flight for use on ships of the 8th Cruiser Squadron in the America and West Indies Station. Initial equipment was Fairey IIIFs and Ospreys, the former soon giving way to Walruses. Seafoxes arrived in August 1937, and the Ospreys were withdrawn the following year, the aircraft operating from HMS *Apollo*, HMS *Ajax*, HMS *Exeter*, and HMS *York*. By this time squadron status had been granted, and whilst in the West Indies aircraft were based at Bermuda. By the outbreak of war the squadron was operating 5 Walruses and 5 Seafoxes in 6 cruisers, the departure of HMS *Apollo* from the station having been compensated by the addition of HMS *Berwick*, HMS *Orion* and HMAS *Perth*. The squadron lost its identity when it was absorbed into No.700 Squadron on 21 January 1940.

On 5 June 1944, No.718 reformed at Henstridge as an Army Co-operation Training Unit, being referred to by October 1944 as the Army Co-operation Naval Operational Training Unit. Its initial main equipment was 9 Seafire IIIs, but it also had 6 Spitfire PR.XIIIs for training photographic reconnaissance pilots. It operated an Army Co-operation course in which suitable new pilots were trained in the various aspects of tactical reconnaissance techniques in order to supplement and replace experienced pilots in squadrons engaged in this activity. An Air Combat course was also operated. By April 1945 it had been restyled the School of Naval Air Reconnaissance, but on 17 August 1945 it moved to Ballyhalbert as No.4 Naval Air Fighting School. Here Corsairs replaced the Spitfire PR.XIIIs, some Harvards also being flown. The squadron disbanded into No.794 Squadron on 1 November 1945.

No.718 reformed at Eglinton on 23 August 1946 as a Seafire Conversion squadron. It was initially part of the 51st Training Air Group, but transferred to the 52nd Training Air Group when the former disbanded in November 1946. Type conversion was given on Seafire IIIs, a few Harvards and Masters also being flown. The squadron disbanded at Eglinton on 17 March 1947.

On 25 April 1955, No.718 reformed at Stretton in order to convert RNVR piston-engined pilots to jet aircraft. Equipped with Attackers and Sea Vampire T.22s, it was responsible for the conversion of No.1831 Squadron pilots at Stretton, after which it moved to Honiley in July 1955 in order to carry out the same task for No.1833 Squadron. This work completed, it disbanded at Honiley on 31 December 1955.

Supermarine Walrus L2278 of No.718 (Catapult) Squadron aboard HMS Berwick in 1939. (MAP)

Aircraft Equipment	Period of Service	Example
Fairey IIIF	Jul 1936 - Dec 1936	S1859 (780)
Osprey SP	Jul 1936 - Jun 1938	K5746 (791)
Walrus I	Oct 1936 - Jan 1940	K8557 (780)
Seafox I	Aug 1937 - Jan 1940	K8591 (C9M)
Martinet I	Aug 1945 - Oct 1945	PX141 (S)
Corsair III	Aug 1945 - Oct 1945	JS479 (BH2Q)
Corsair IV	Jun 1945 - Oct 1945	KD822
Harvard III	Sep 1945 - Oct 1945	EZ278
Seafire IIc	Jul 1945 - Oct 1945	NM924 (G3C)
Seafire III	Jun 1944 - Oct 1945	NF634 (G3R)
Spitfire PR.XIII	Jun 1944 - Oct 1945	R7335 (G3K)
Wildcat V	Sep 1945	JV355
Master II	Aug 1946 - Oct 1947	AZ666
Seafire L.III	Aug 1946 - Mar 1947	RX300
Attacker FB.2	Apr 1955 - Dec 1955	WP286 (165/ST)
Sea Vampire T.22	Apr 1955 - Dec 1955	XG770 (262/ST)

Identification Markings
IIIF *769, 780-781*; Osprey *790-791*; Walrus *769, 780*; Seafox *C9A+*; Seafire/Spitfire *G3A+*, to *BH1A+* 8.45; Corsair *BH2A+*; Attacker *160-173/ST*; Sea Vampire *260-264/ST*.

Hawker Osprey IV K5760 '790' of No.718 Flight from HMS Apollo during a visit to Hamilton, Ontario on 20 June 1937.

Commanding Officers
Lt TWT Blackwell RN
 (Flt Lt RAF) 15 Jul 1936
L/C AA Murray RN
 (Sq Ldr RAF) 21 Oct 1936
L/C JC Cockburn RN
 (Flt Lt RAF) 29 Mar 1939
Squadron disbanded 21 Jan 1940
L/C(A) WH Stevens
 RN 5 Jun 1944
L/C SJ Hall DSC RN 26 Nov 1944
Squadron disbanded 1 Nov 1945
Lt(A) RM Crosley
 DSC & Bar RN 23 Aug 1946
Lt AC Lindsay
 DSC RN 13 Nov 1946
Squadron disbanded 17 Mar 1947
L/C WG Cook RN 25 Apr 1955
Squadron disbanded 31 Dec 1955

Squadron bases
Bermuda 15 Jul 1936
Squadron disbanded 21 Jan 1940
Henstridge 5 Jun 1944
Ballyhalbert 17 Aug 1945
Squadron disbanded 1 Nov 1945
Eglinton 23 Aug 1946
Squadron disbanded 17 Mar 1947
Stretton 25 Apr 1955
Honiley 4 Jul 1955
Squadron disbanded 31 Dec 1955

Supermarine Spitfire PR.XIII AA739 'G3O' of No.718 Squadron Henstridge in September 1944. (Malcolm Brown)

North American Harvard III EX277 of No.718 Squadron at Ballyhalbert in October 1945. (via M.J.Brown)

No.719 Squadron

Badge: On a white field, an archer with jerkin and hat red, hose and shoes green, bow and quiver proper

Motto: None

No.719 Squadron formed at St Merryn on 15 June 1944 as an Air Firing Training squadron within the School of Air Combat. Equipped with 7 Wildcats, 12 hooked Spitfires and 6 Masters it ran a Naval Air Firing course in which pupils were given air firing exercises and weapon training. By the end of 1944 the squadron had received some Seafires and Corsairs, but on 2 January 1945 it disbanded into No.794 Squadron.

On 1 March 1946, No.719 reformed at Fearn as a Strike Training squadron equipped initially with Barracudas. On 14 May 1946 it moved to Eglinton to become part of the newly formed 51st Training Air Group, Fireflies being then added to the equipment. In October the squadron spent a week in HMS *Implacable*, after which the CO and his staff were exchanged with their counterparts in No.795 Squadron. No.719 then became an Anti-Submarine Training squadron, its task being to bring together pilots, observers and TAGs and train themas A/S crews for No.744 Squadron, which continued their tuition. When No.744 became No.815 Squadron on 1 December 1947, No.719 continued to supply it with embryo crews, until being disbanded on 27 December 1949.

No.719 next reformed on 14 June 1950, again at Eglinton, as part of the new 53rd Training Air Group. Equipped with Firefly AS.5s it operated as the Naval Air Anti-Submarine School in conjunction with No.737 Squadron. Some Firefly AS.6s were received in 1951, but both of the earlier marks were withdrawn on the arrival of Firefly T.7s in March 1953. These in turn were phased out in favour of Gannets from November 1955. On 22 November 1957 the squadron absorbed the disbanding No.737 Squadron, and adopted the alternative title of Naval Anti-Submarine Operational Flying School, but was itself disbanded on 17 March 1959.

Final production Westland Whirlwind HAS.7 XN387 '626' with No.719 Squadron, Eglinton in 1961. (MAP)

On 17 May 1960, No.719 reformed at Eglinton, as the Joint Anti-Submarine School Flight. Equipped with 3 Whirlwind HAS.7s, it spent 10 days in HMS *Hermes* in October 1960. It was accorded first line status on 5 October 1961, on re-equipping with 4 Wessexes, becoming No.819 Squadron.

Identification Markings
All types *S1A+* 1944-45; Firefly 1 *A4A+*, later *200/A+*; Barracuda *300/JR+*; Firefly 5/6 *224-279/GN* from 5.49; Firefly 7 *320-341/GN*, to *550-559* 1.56; Gannet *456-459/GN*, to *541-557/GN* 1.56; Whirlwind *625-627*.

Aircraft Equipment	Period of Service	Example	
Corsair III	1944 - Dec 1944	JS519	
Master II	Jun 1944 - Dec 1944	DM267	
Seafire Ib	1944 - Dec 1944	NX891	
Seafire IIc	1944 - Dec 1944	NM918	
Spitfire Vb	Jun 1944 - Aug 1944	BM371	
Spitfire Vb/hooked	Jun 1944 - Dec 1944	BL628	
Wildcat IV	Jun 1944 - Dec 1944	FN181	
Barracuda III	Mar 1946 - May 1949	RJ942	(318/JR)
Harvard IIb	Apr 1947 - Nov 1948	KF511	
Anson I	Dec 1947 - Nov 1949	NK834	
Firefly FR.1	Jun 1946 - Jan 1947	MB662	(A4M)
Firefly AS.5	May 1949 - Dec 1949	WB336	(227/GN)
	Jun 1950 - Mar 1953	WB361	(265/GN)
Firefly AS.6	Aug 1951 - Jun 1953	WD842	(267/GN)
Firefly T.7	Mar 1953 - Jun 1956	WM770	(330/GN)
Gannet AS.1	Nov 1955 - Mar 1959	XA363	(550/GN)
Gannet T.2	Nov 1955 - Mar 1959	XA511	(545/GN)
Whirlwind HAS.7	May 1960 - Oct 1961	XN387	(626)

Commanding Officers
L/C(A) JL Appleby RN	15 Jun 1944
Squadron disbanded	2 Jan 1945
L/C JF Arnold RN	1 Mar 1946
L/C(A) CRJ Coxon RN	23 Aug 1946
Lt(A) JM Brown RN	13 Nov 1946
L/C FGB Sheffield DSC RN	8 Jan 1947
L/C(A) RHW Blake RN	8 Dec 1947
Squadron disbanded	27 Dec 1949
L/C SS Laurie RN	14 Jun 1950
L/C DA Berrill RN	15 Sep 1950
L/C RHW Blake RN	17 Apr 1952
L/C JD Nunn RN	15 Dec 1953
L/C ERA Johnson RN	11 Jan 1956
L/C AW Sabey DSM RN	6 Aug 1957
L/C DLG James RN	13 Dec 1957
L/C AA Reid RN	21 Jan 1959
L/C JRT Bluett RN	17 May 1960
Squadron disbanded	5 Oct 1961

Squadron bases
St.Merryn	15 Jun 1944
Squadron disbanded	2 Jan 1945
Fearn	1 Mar 1946
Eglinton	14 May 1946
HMS Implacable	24 Oct 1946
Eglinton	31 Oct 1946
Squadron disbanded	27 Dec 1949
Eglinton	14 Jun 1950
Squadron disbanded	17 Mar 1959
Eglinton	17 May 1960
HMS Hermes	4 Oct 1960
Eglinton	14 Oct 1960
Redes 819 Sqdn	5 Oct 1961

No.720 Squadron

No.720 (Catapult) Flight formed at Mount Batten on 15 July 1936 to operate Walruses from ships of the New Zealand Division. Initially only HMS *Achilles* was used for this purpose, but she was joined by HMS *Leander* the following year. The squadron came under the operational control of RAF Coastal Command until being passed to HQ, RAF Far East on 1 June 1937. By the outbreak of war it had attained squadron status, and its shore base was by then at Auckland. On 21 January 1940 the squadron was absorbed into the newly formed No.700 Squadron.

In December 1940, an unnumbered photographic flight was formed at Ford with Seals and Sharks, the flight being attached to the RN Storage Section at that station. The unit carried out work with the RN School of Photography, and had received some Ansons by July 1943. Due to the airfield being needed by units involved in the Normandy invasion, the flight moved out to the satellite airfield at Cowdray Park in April 1944, but returned to Ford in October, being then incorporated in the Station Flight. The unit was elevated to squadron status when on 1 August 1945 the RN Photo Flight, as it was by then, became No.720 Squadron. Equipped with 4 Ansons, the squadron undertook many photographic commissions and requirements for the Fleet, as well as its flying task for photographic trainees at the School. The Ansons were supplemented in October 1947 by an Oxford, and on 27 May 1948 the squadron moved to Gosport, to liaise with the RAF at Tangmere. It disbanded on 5 January 1950, its aircraft and task being absorbed by No.771 Squadron.

Identification Markings
Walrus *Z1-Z4*, to *P9A+* 5.39;
Oxford *FD8A+*; Anson *FD8A+*,
to *600-603/FD/GJ* 1947.

Aircraft Equipment	Period of Service	Example
Walrus I	Jul 1936 - Jan 1940	L2222 (Z4)
Anson I	Aug 1945 - Jan 1950	MG673 (FD8P)
Oxford I	Oct 1947 - Jan 1949	V4201 (FD8F)

Commanding Officers
Lt TP Coode RN
 (Flt Lt RAF) 15 Jul 1936
Lt GWR Nicholl RN
 (Flt Lt RAF) 30 Apr 1937
L/C BEW Logan RN 24 May 1939
Squadron disbanded 21 Jan 1940
L/C(A) GN Gladish
 RNVR 1 Aug 1945
Lt(A) DG Dick
 RNVR 28 Sep 1945
Lt(A) GH Davies
 RNVR 10 Dec 1945
Lt(A) WA Murray
 RN 14 Feb 1946

Commanding Officers
Lt(A) ERG Green RN 5 Nov 1947
Lt(A) H Phillips
 RN 25 Oct 1948
Lt DJ Whitehead RN 12 Dec 1949
Squadron disbanded 5 Jan 1950

Squadron bases
Mount Batten 15 Jul 1936
Auckland 1 Jun 1937
Squadron disbanded 21 Jan 1940
Ford 1 Aug 1945
Tangmere 18 Jul 1947
Ford 25 Aug 1947
Gosport 27 May 1948
Squadron disbanded 5 Jan 1950

Supermarine Walrus K5774 'Z1' of No.720 (New Zealand) Flight. (MAP)

Avro Anson I MG721 '603/GJ' of No.720 Squadron, Gosport around 1948/9. (via Harry Phillips)

No.721 Squadron

No.721 Squadron formed up at Belfast on 1 March 1945 as a Fleet Requirements Unit for passage to the Pacific theatre. Initial equipment was 12 Vengeance target tugs, of which six were used at Belfast for pilot familiarisation, whilst the remainder were prepared for shipment in a ferry carrier. On 17 April the squadron embarked in HMS *Begum*, commencing FRU activities upon arrival at Ponam on 28 May 1945. In adddition its aircraft assisted the locally based MONAB No.4 by acting as a target for interception, and also towed drogues for air-to-air firing by pilots awaiting first line appointments. In July, six Corsairs and six Beaufighter IIs were allocated to the unit, but it is doubtful whether they ever arrived at Ponam. The Vengeances were later grounded, and the squadron closed down at Ponam.

No.721 reopened at Archerfield on 15 October 1945. Equipment was to be 12 Vengeances, 9 Corsairs, 6 Beaufighters, 2 Avengers, 6 Mosquitoes, 6 Defiants, and a Harvard, but again it is doubtful whether most of these materialised. In the New Year the squadron embarked in HMS *Speaker* for passage to Hong Kong, and on 11 January 1946 it set up residence at Kai Tak. Here it is known to have operated Seafires, Vengeances and a Tiger Moth. On 27 August 1946 it took over the remaining Sea Otters of No.1701 Squadron to form an Air Sea Rescue Flight. In December 1946, 'B' Flight embarked its Corsairs in HMS *Glory* for a time. The squadron disbanded at Kai Tak on 21 November 1947.

Identification Markings
Unknown.

Squadron bases
Belfast	1 Mar 1945
HMS Begum(transit)	17 Apr 1945
Ponam	28 May 1945
HMS Unicorn (transit)	9 Oct 1945
Archerfield	15 Oct 1945
HMS Speaker	28 Dec 1945
Kai Tak	11 Jan 1946
Squadron disbanded	21 Nov 1947

Commanding Officers
L/C(A) FA Simpson RNVR	1 Mar 1945
Lt JL Moore RN	7 Mar 1946
Lt RD Head DSC & Bar RN	19 Nov 1946
Squadron disbanded	21 Nov 1947

Aircraft Equipment	Period of Service	Example
Avenger TBF-1	Nov 1945 - Dec 1945	
Beaufighter II	Jul 1945 - Nov 1945	
Corsair III	Aug 1945 - Sep 1945	JS610
Corsair IV	Jul 1945 - Sep 1947	KD749
Defiant TT.I	Nov 1945 - 1946	
Harvard	Nov 1945 - Dec 1945	
Hellcat I	Sep 1945	FN396
Hellcat II	Aug 1945 - Sep 1945	JZ979
Mosquito	Nov 1945 - Dec 1945	
Seafire III	1946 - 1947	
Seafire XV	Nov 1946 - Nov 1947	SW854
Sea Otter I	Aug 1946 - Nov 1947	
Tiger Moth II	May 1946 - Aug 1946	A17-526
Vengeance TT.IV	Mar 1945 - May 1947	A27-545

de Havilland Tiger Moth A17-84 of No.721 Squadron at Kai Tak in 1946. (P.R.W.Cort)

No.722 Squadron

No.722 Squadron formed at Tambaram on 1 September 1944 as a Fleet Requirements Unit equipped initially with 12 Martinets, a Reliant and a Walrus. Its main task was to provide drogue and winged target towing for ships and naval fighter aircraft in coastal areas of southern India. Units on the west coast, especially those in the Bombay area were catered for by 'X' Flight, based at Juhu from September 1944, until moving to Cochin a year later. On the east coast, 'Y' Flight operated two Martinets from Vizagapatam from 24 December 1944, one pilot of this flight flying his aircraft half way to Rangoon on a reconnaissance flight during the attack on that city. Aircraft flown later at Tambaram included Swordfish and Wildcats. No.722 disbanded at Tambaram on 24 October 1945.

Identification Markings
All types probably *T9A+*.

Aircraft Equipment	Period of Service	Example
Martinet TT.I	Sep 1944 - Oct 1945	PX134 (T9Z)
Reliant I	Sep 1944 - Oct 1945	FL125
Walrus I	Sep 1944 - Oct 1944	X9509
Swordfish	May 1945 - Oct 1945	
Wildcat	Jul 1945 - Oct 1945	

Squadron bases
Tambaram	1 Sep 1944
Juhu (X Flt)	7 Sep 1944 to 18 Sep 1945
Vizagapatam (Y Flt)	24 Dec 1944 to 14 Nov 1945
Cochin (X Flt)	18 Sep 1945 to 14 Oct 1945
Sqdn HQ disbanded	24 Oct 1945

Commanding Officers
L/C(A) AFE Payen RNVR	1 Sep 1944
L/C(A) KC Johnson SANF(V)	23 Oct 1944
L/C(A) LG Morris RN	8 Mar 1945
Squadron disbanded	24 Oct 1945

Miles Martinet PX134 'T9Z' of No.722 Squadron, Tambaram in 1945. (W.H.Poole)

No.723 Squadron

Badge: On an azure field, in bend three albatrosses volant, proper within the Southern Cross argent, in base three waves argent

Motto: Wings of the albatross

No.723 Squadron personnel assembled at Townhill Camp, Fifeshire on 21 November 1944, and embarked for passage to Australia on 22 December. They arrived at Nowra on 27 January 1945, and on 28 February the squadron officially formed at Bankstown as a Fleet Requirements Unit to operate with Fleet units working up in Jervis Bay. Bankstown was only a grass airfield, and the squadron mainly used Nowra. Official establishment comprised initially eight Martinets and eight Corsairs, though an Expeditor or two was also used at first. Hellcats were added later, and with these and the Corsairs the squadron engaged in "throw off" shoots, in which the aircraft dived at warships which fired back with live ammunition, but with gunsights offset 15 degrees to port, which could be rather hair-raising at times for the pilots. It was also planned to use Beaufighter IIs for this work, and 12 were allocated in July but these never arrived. Conversion of two ex-RAAF Ansons for anti-jamming training and radar training took too long and they also failed to materialise. Some of the Martinets began to operate from Schofields in September 1945, and in January 1946 the whole squadron moved there, only to disband on 31 May 1946.

On 7 April 1952, No.723 reformed as a Royal Australian Navy unit for Fleet requirements, communications, air-sea rescue and refresher flying duties. It also co-operated with the Australian Joint Anti-Submarine School. Initial equipment comprised a Dakota, a Wirraway, two Sea Furies, a Sea Otter and three Fireflies. The first Sycamore helicopter arrived on 16 January 1953, and the following year some Vampire T.34s were received. No.723 disbanded at Nowra on 25 October 1956.

The squadron reformed at Nowra on 18 February 1957 as a helicopter training squadron with five Sycamore HR.50s and HR.51s. From time to time two of these embarked in HMAS *Melbourne*. In 1961 a fixed wing element was added to the squadron, comprising two Auster Autocars, a C-47 and some Firefly TT.6s, but these were transferred to No.724 Squadron in November 1962. In April 1963, two Westland Scouts arrived for use in the supply ship HMAS *Moresby*, and a year later six Bell UH-1B Iroquois' were received as replacement for the Sycamores, which were withdrawn in June 1965. The squadron then continued with the role of converting fixed-wing pilots to helicopters, in addition to search and rescue work. In October 1967 the RAN Helicopter Flight Vietnam formed as a subsidiary of No.723 Squadron, which provided operational training for it, the Flight being withdrawn in June 1971. In 1969 the squadron title was altered to HT-723, to conform with U.S. Navy practice. In 1974, two Bell 206B-1 Kiowas were received to replace the Scouts in HMAS *Moresby*. The squadron strength in November 1983 was four Iroquois', five Kiowas and 13 Wessex HAS.31B's, but in early 1984 the Wessex element broke away to reform No.816 Squadron. HT-723 retained its SAR and Fleet Support roles and conducted training for the frigate flights in anticipation of the arrival of Squirrels.

HT-723 Squadron is now the parent squadron for all RAN ship's flights. There are personnel designated for the four helicopter capable frigates and for HMAS *Stalwart*, HMAS *Success* and HMAS *Moresby*. HMAS *Moresby* carries a Kiowa, HMAS *Stalwart* and HMAS *Success* carry a Wessex while each frigate takes a Squirrel from the pool when it embarks.

Identification Markings
All types *N8A+* 1945/6, *901-916* from 1952, to *920-922/NW* 1955, to *841-857* 1958, to *853-858, 891-897* 1963, to *823, 891-899* 1968.

Battle Honours
Vietnam 1967-71
Kuwait 1991

Bell 206B-1 Kiowa N17-025 '891' of HT-723, Nowra. (Royal Australian Navy)

Aircraft Equipment	Period of Service	Example
Expediter II	Feb 1945 - Apr 1945	
Corsair II	Feb 1945 - Dec 1945	? (N8AL)
Hellcat	1945 - 1945	
Martinet TT.I	Feb 1945 - May 1946	RG958 (277/N)
Vengeance TT.IV	1945 - 1945	
Anson I	May 1945 - Jan 1946	NK950
Tiger Moth II	Aug 1945	A17-748
Wirraway	Sep 1945	A20-8
Autocar	Dec 1954 - Oct 1956	N11-301
C-47B	Apr 1952 - Oct 1956	? (901)
Sea Otter 2	Apr 1952 - Oct 1956	JN200
Wirraway	Apr 1952 - Oct 1956	A20-145
Sea Fury FB.11	Apr 1952 - Oct 1956	WH581 (922/NW)
Firefly Mk.5 T.2	Jan 1954 - Feb 1955	VX373 (916/NW)
Firefly TT.5	Nov 1954 - Oct 1956	WB271
Firefly 6	May 1952 - Oct 1956	WD882 (910/NW)
Sycamore HR.50	May 1953 - Oct 1956	XA219 (906)
Sycamore HR.51	Jan 1955 - Oct 1956	XD656 (905)
Vampire T.34	Sep 1954 - Oct 1956	A79-837
Autocar	Feb 1957 - Nov 1962	N11-301(857/NW)
Sycamore HR.50	Feb 1957 - Nov 1963	XA220 (849/NW)
Sycamore HR.51	Feb 1957 - Jun 1965	XN449 (853/NW)
Firefly TT.6	Dec 1961 - Nov 1962	WD826 (845/NW)
C-47B	Oct 1961 - Nov 1962	A65-43(VJ-ORA/NW)
Scout	Apr 1963 - 1973	N8-101 (891)
UH-1B Iroquois	May 1964 - Jun 1987	N9-3102(894)
Bell 206B-1 Kiowa	1973 - to date	N17-025(891)
Wessex HAS.31b	Dec 1975 - Feb 1984	N7-213 (823)
Squirrel	1984 - to date	N22-013(23)
Wessex HAS.31B	Jul 1987 - to date	N7-202 (812)
HS.748	1994	

de Havilland Tiger Moth II A17-749 of No.723 Squadron at Nowra in 1945. (FAA Museum)

Commanding Officers
L/C(A) HAP
  Bullivant RNVR 28 Feb 1945
Lt(A) GH Horne
  RNVR 11 Feb 1946
Squadron disbanded 31 May 1946
L/C JA Gledhill RAN 7 Apr 1952
L/C A Ignatieff RAN 6 Jul 1952
L/C GA Beange
  DSC RAN 27 Apr 1953
L/C JGB Campbell
  DFC RAN 7 Sep 1953
L/C KA Douglas
  RAN 23 Sep 1953
L/C JA O'Farrell
  RAN 13 Dec 1953
L/C CMA Wheatley
  RAN 23 May 1955
Squadron disbanded 25 Oct 1956
L/C JRN Salthouse
  RAN 18 Feb 1957
L/C G McPhee
  OBE RAN 1 Jul 1959
L/C JRN Salthouse
  RAN 24 Jul 1959
L/C JA O'Farrell
  RAN 27 Nov 1960
L/C A Ignatieff RAN 6 Jul 1962
L/C KA Douglas
  RAN 23 Sep 1963
L/C JA O'Farrell
  RAN 13 Dec 1963
L/C DJ Orr RAN 17 Sep 1964
Lt PJ Vickers RAN 6 Oct 1965
L/C G McPhee
  OBE RAN 25 Oct 1965

Commanding Officers
L/C N Ralph RAN 27 Mar 1967
L/C SBE Courtier
  RAN 5 Jun 1967
L/C G McPhee
  OBE RAN 3 Jul 1967
L/C GR Rohrsheim
  DSC RAN 16 Dec 1969
L/C DD Farthing
  DSC RAN 3 Nov 1970
L/C WS Lowe
  MBE RAN 10 Jul 1972
L/C IM Speedy
  DSC RAN 3 Nov 1972
L/C BC Crawford
  DSC RAN 21 Dec 1973
L/C JC Buchanan
  DFC RAN 1 Dec 1974
L/C BJ Boettcher
  DFC RAN 26 Jan 1976
L/C JM Leak RAN 12 Apr 1977
L/C CF Daley RAN 20 Oct 1978
L/C VT Battesse
  RAN 23 Jun 1980
L/C MA Perrott
  RAN 19 Oct 1981
L/C M Lehan RAN 11 Oct 1982
L/C C George RAN 17 Feb 1984
L/C R Luxton RAN 10 Jan 1986
L/C PJ Cannell RAN 4 Dec 1987
L/C PJ Machin RAN 8 Dec 1989
L/C VEB Di Pietro RAN
  10 Jan 1992
L/C AFE Di Pietro RAN
  Dec 1993

Squadron bases
Bankstown 28 Feb 1945
Jervis Bay 1 May 1945
Nowra 4 Jun 1945
Schofields 21 Jan 1946
Squadron disbanded 31 May 1946
Nowra 7 Apr 1952
Squadron disbanded 29 Oct 1956
Nowra 18 Feb 1957
HMAS Melbourne 14 Mar 1957
(723H Flt) to 11 Jul 1957

RAN Helicopter Flight, Vietnam
(sub-unit of No.723 Squadron)

Squadron bases
Nowra Aug 1967
Vung Tau 16 Oct 1967
Camp Blackhorse late Dec 1967
(Xuan Loc, Long
  Khanh Province)
Camp Bearcat 23 Nov 1968
25m NE Saigon in
Bien Hoa Province)
Dong Tam 6 Sep 1970
Flight withdrawn 8 Jun 1971
Flight disbanded 16 Jun 1971

Commanding Officers
L/C N Ralph RN 18 Sep 1967
L/C GR Rohrsheim
  DSC RAN 12 Oct 1968
L/C DD Farthing
  DSC RAN 9 Oct 1969
L/C WP James
  DSC RAN 10 Sep 1970
Flight disbanded 16 Jun 1971

Auster Autocar A11-301 '857/NW' of No.723 Squadron, Nowra. (via Joe Barr)

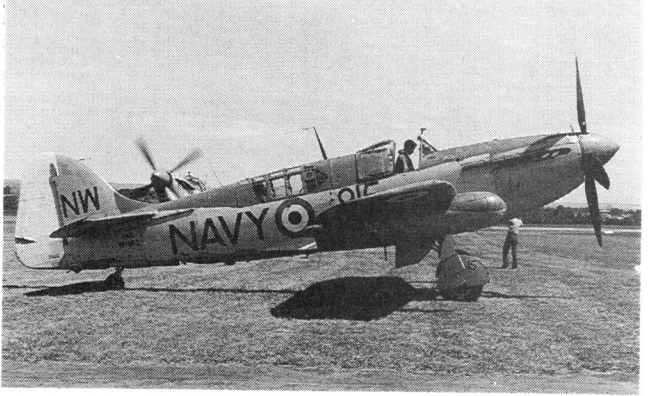

Fairey Firefly AS.6 WD892 '915/NW' of 723 Sqdn, Nowra around 1954/5. (MAP)

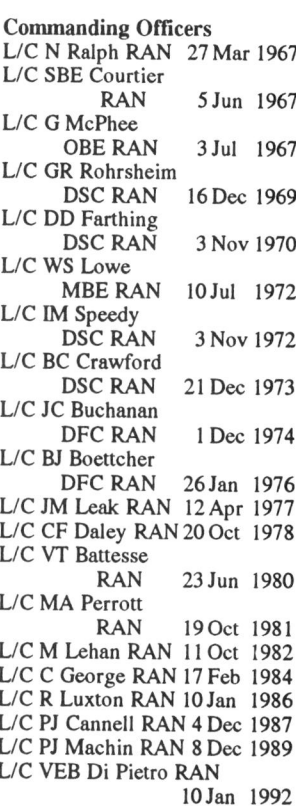

No.724 Squadron

Badge: On an azure field, a fledgling albatross close, wearing a mortar-board, proper, perched upon two closed books, arraswise, the upper leathered or and the lower argent, both garnished argent

Motto: Learn and live

No.724 Squadron formed on 10 April 1945 as a Naval Air Communications squadron at Bankstown. The grass surface of this airfield was unsuitable for this work, and at first the aircraft were flown from Mascot Airport. Aircraft were Expeditors and two Ansons, and from the beginning of May the squadron flew a service to Melbourne on five days each week, and three to Archerfield. From 1 January the Archerfield service was extended, with an overnight stop there before continuing to Maryborough, and 8 days later the Melbourne service became a daily one. A twice daily service to Jervis Bay and Nowra was inaugurated on 18 June, operating six days a week. When Bankstown was paid off on 31 March 1946 the squadron moved to Schofields, where it disbanded on 31 May 1946.

On 1 June 1955, No.724 reformed at Nowra as a Miscellaneous Air Squadron of the Royal Australian Navy. It functioned as an Operational Training School and an aircrew conversion unit, equipped initially with Fireflies, Sea Vampires, Sea Furies, Wirraways and later Gannets. When No.723 Squadron disbanded on 29 October 1956, No.724 took over its six Sycamores as No.724H Flight, which shortly afterwards transported HRH The Duke of Edinburgh during a royal tour. At this time the piston engined aircraft were transferred to Nos.805 and 851 Squadrons. In February 1957 the Sycamores returned to a reformed No.723 Squadron, and in January 1958 the Gannets were transferred to No.725 Squadron, leaving No.724 as an entirely jet squadron. When No.725 Squadron disbanded on 31 May 1961 its aircraft and task were transferred to No.724, which then operated Gannets, Sea Venoms, Vampire T.34As, Sea Furies and C-47Bs. No.724 then carried out anti-submarine and all-weather fighter training, operational flying training, fleet requirements, trials, communications and type conversion.

The Sea Furies were withdrawn in October 1962, and in June 1963, No.805 Squadron was absorbed, followed in November 1963 by the fixed-wing element of No.723, which added Autocars, Fireflies and C-47Bs to the strength. With the completion of the last all-weather fighter course in September 1965, the squadron continued with pilot conversion training. By December 1968 No.724 had again become an all-jet unit, engaged in operational flying training, fleet requirements and trials, with four Vampires, five Sea Venoms and six Douglas Skyhawks. In 1969 the squadron style was amended to VC-724 to confirm with U.S.Navy practice, and by 1972 Macchi MB.326H jet trainers had replaced the Sea Vampires and Sea Venoms, the squadron role being then weapon training using air-to-air and air-to-ground missiles, Delmar target towing and photo reconnaissance training. VF-805 was absorbed by VC-724 on 2 July 1982. On 30 June 1983, VC-724 handed over eight Macchi MB.326s to the RAAF, and the Skyhawks were reduced to four for fleet support and target towing duties. By June 1984 the Skyhawks had also been withdrawn. The squadron disbanded on 30 June 1984.

de Havilland Sea Vampire T.22 XA167 '807/NW' of No.724 Squadron at Nowra, 4 November 1968. (Joe Barr)

Douglas C-47B N2-23 '801/NW' of No.724 Squadron at Llanherne in July 1966. (via Chris Ashworth)

Identification Markings
Expediter *civil-type call signs VJ-AAA+*; All types *911, 950-972, 980-996* from *1955*, to *863-878* 1958, to *800-809, 841-860, 860-889* 1963, to *800-809, 860-889* 1968.

Aircraft Equipment	Period of Service	Example
Expediter C.II	Apr 1945 - May 1946	KP111 (VJ-AAN)
Anson I	May 1945 - Jan 1946	
Wirraway	Jun 1955 - Oct 1956	A20-752 (971/NW)
Sea Fury FB.11	Jun 1955 - Oct 1956	WH586
Firefly T.5	Jun 1955 - Oct 1956	VX373 (962/NW)
Firefly 6	Jun 1955 - Oct 1956	WB504 (965/NW)
Firefly TT.6	Nov 1962 - Mar 1966	WD901 (878/NW)
Sea Vampire T.22	Jun 1955 - 1970	XG766 (874/NW)
Sea Venom FAW.53	Jun 1955 - 1973	WZ905 (863/NW)
Gannet AS.1	Jun 1955 - Jan 1958	XA329
	May 1961 - Jul 1964	XA327 (880/NW)
Gannet T.2	Jun 1955 - Jan 1958	XG888
	May 1961 - Nov 1966	XA514 (878/NW)
Sycamore HR.50	Oct 1956 - Feb 1957	XA219
Sycamore HR.51	Oct 1956 - Feb 1957	XL507
Vampire T.34A	Jun 1957 - Jan 1966	A79-840 (804/NW)
Autocar	May 1961	A11-300
C-47B	May 1961 - 1974	N23-23 (861/NW)
Sea Fury FB.11	May 1961 - Oct 1962	WH589 (115/NW)
A-4G Skyhawk	Dec 1968 - Jun 1984	N13-154904 (883)
TA-4G Skyhawk	Dec 1968 - Jun 1984	N13-154647 (878)
Macchi MB.326H	Oct 1972 - Jun 1983	N14-076 (867)

Squadron bases
Bankstown (aircraft based Mascot) 10 Apr 1945
Schofields 31 Mar 1946
Squadron disbanded 31 May 1946
Nowra 1 Jun 1955
Squadron disbanded 30 Jun 1984

Commanding Officers
Lt(A) JHL Evans RNVR 10 Apr 1945
Squadron disbanded 31 May 1946
L/C LA Robinson RAN 1 Jun 1955
L/C PR Dallosso RN 25 Feb 1957
Lt KM Barnett RAN 1 Jul 1957
L/C AG Cordell RAN 6 Aug 1957
Lt CE Champ RAN 1 Sep 1958
L/C GHG Hanchard-Goodwin RN 24 Nov 1958
L/C MWMcD Barron RN 15 Feb 1959
L/C GHG Hanchard-Goodwin RN 20 Jul 1959
L/C IK Josselyn RAN 9 Dec 1959
L/C MWMcD Barron RN 4 Jan 1961
Lt NE Lee RAN 3 Feb 1961
L/C RA Waddell-Wood RAN 4 Apr 1961
L/C AE Payne RAN 1 Jun 1961

Commanding Officers
L/C JP Van Gelder RAN 22 Jun 1962
L/C A Ignatieff RAN 15 Jul 1963
L/C MJ Astbury RAN 1 Aug 1965
L/C KA Douglas MBE RAN 23 Aug 1965
L/C CMA Wheatley RAN 2 Jan 1968
L/C JR Da Costa RAN 2 Dec 1968
L/C WE Callan RAN 28 Jul 1969
L/C GS King RAN 21 Jul 1970
L/C BA Dutch RAN 10 Jan 1972
L/C AM Hickling RAN 22 Oct 1973
L/C G Heron RAN 17 Jan 1974
L/C PC Marshall AFC RAN 7 Jul 1975
L/C D Collingridge RAN 4 Mar 1977
L/C EM Kavanagh RAN 16 Jan 1978
L/C CC Blennerhassett RAN 11 Dec 1978
L/C BJ Daly RAN 11 Jan 1980
L/C K Johnson RAN 19 Dec 1980
L/C PL Clark RAN 23 Aug 1982
L/C JM Hamilton AFC RAN 2 Dec 1983
Squadron disbanded 30 Jun 1984

Fairey Firefly FR.5 VT504 '965/NW' of No.724 Squadron, Nowra around 1955/6

de Havilland Sea Venom FAW.53 WZ937 '862/M' of No.724 Squadron, Nowra in 1966. (MAP)

No.725 Squadron

Badge: On an azure field, a dexter mailed gauntlet clenched, or, winged argent
Motto: Be aggressive

Identification Markings
Unknown 1943-45; All types *903-907, 930-931, 973-975* from 1958, to *854, 880-894* 1958; to *810-836* 1963.

Aircraft Equipment	Period of Service	Example
Anson I	May 1945 - Aug 1945	LT944
Hellcat I	Dec 1944	JV139
Martinet TT.I	Dec 1943 - Dec 1945	EM582
Reliant I	Jul 1944 - Jul 1945	FK885
Roc I	Aug 1943 - Dec 1943	L3097
Traveller I	Dec 1944 - Aug 1945	FT515
C-47B	Jan 1958 - May 1961	A65-43
Autocar	Jan 1958 - May 1961	11-301 (931/NW)
Gannet AS.1	Jan 1958 - May 1961	XA327
Gannet T.2	Jan 1958 - May 1961	
Sea Fury FB.11	Jan 1958 - May 1959	WH590
Firefly TT.5	Jan 1958 - May 1959	
Firefly TT.6	Jan 1958 - May 1959	WB518 (903/NW)
Wessex HAS.31a/b	Nov 1962 - Dec 1975	WA203 (883)

Squadron bases
Eglinton	27 Aug 1943
Ballyhalbert (Dt2)	21 Aug 1944
Ronaldsway (Dt4) to	9 Nov 1944
Ballyhalbert (Dt4)	9 Nov 1944 to 21 Feb 1945
St.Merryn	4 Aug 1945
Squadron disbanded	27 Dec 1945
Nowra	13 Jan 1958
Squadron disbanded	31 May 1961
Nowra	1 Nov 1962
Squadron disbanded	27 Dec 1975

Commanding Officers
L/C(A) SJ McDowell RNVR		27 Aug 1943
L/C(A) R MacDermott RNVR		10 Aug 1945
Lt(A) PV Robinson RN		1 Oct 1945
Lt(A) FAH Harley RN		29 Oct 1945
Lt JL Moore RN		21 Dec 1945
Squadron disbanded		27 Dec 1945
L/C JM Wade-Brown RAN		13 Jan 1958
L/C KM Barnett RAN		5 Jan 1959
L/C P Goldrick RAN		20 Jul 1959
L/C AE Payne RAN		27 Jul 1960
Squadron disbanded		31 May 1961
L/C DG Hilliard RAN		1 Nov 1962
L/C BF Matthews RAN		8 Nov 1962
L/C NE Lee RAN		5 Oct 1965
L/C N Ralph RAN		6 Oct 1965
L/C PD Campbell RAN		19 Jun 1967
L/C SBE Courtier RAN		23 Oct 1967
L/C AG Whitton RAN		22 Jan 1968
L/C DN Rodgers RAN		5 Jan 1970
L/C ES Bell RAN		1 Jun 1970
Cdr DN Rodgers RAN		8 Mar 1971
L/C ES Bell RAN		18 Oct 1971
L/C GR Rhorsheim DSC RAN		14 Oct 1972
L/C BJ Boettcher RAN		23 Jan 1974
L/C WP James DSC RAN		17 Jan 1975
Squadron disbanded		27 Dec 1975

No.725 Squadron formed at Eglinton on 27 August 1943 as a Fleet Requirements Unit equipped initially with three Rocs. Three more arrived in October, followed in December by the first of eight Martinets. Two of the latter were detached to Ballyhalbert in August 1944 to provide target towing facilities for pilots of No.3 Naval Fighter Wing, which had recently moved there. A further four Martinets were detached to Ronaldsway, these going to Ballyhalbert in November 1944, until being withdrawn to Eglinton in February 1945. Small number of other types of aircraft were flown from time to time, these including Hellcats, Travellers, Ansons and Reliants. The squadron moved to St Merryn on 4 August 1945, and became an Air Target Towing Unit. It disbanded on 27 December 1945, its task being absorbed by No.736 Squadron.

On 13 January 1958, the squadron reformed at Nowra as HT-725, a Fleet Requirements and Communications Unit of the Royal Australian Navy. Initial equipment comprised a C-47B, an Autocar, two Fireflies, three Gannets and a Sea Fury, supplemented shortly afterwards by two more Sea Furies and some Sea Venoms. In May 1959 the role was changed to anti-submarine warfare training, but on 31 May 1961 it was disbanded into No.724 Squadron.

No.725 reformed at Nowra on 1 November 1962 as a helicopter anti-submarine operational flying squadron. Equipped with ten Wessex HAS.31s, it provided support for No.817 Squadron until being disbanded on 27 December 1975.

Fairey Firefly TT.5 WB271 '889' of No.725 Squadron, Nowra in 1959. (MAP)

No.726 Squadron

Badge: On a field per fesse blue and barry wavy of six white and blue, in front of two assegais in saltire points downwards a Zulu shield all proper

Motto: None

A Vought-Sikorsky Kingfisher of No.726 Squadron, Stamford Hill, Durban around 1943/4. (via Mike Schoeman)

No.726 Squadron formed at Durban racecourse on 7 July 1943, probably out of No.789 Squadron. Operating as a Fleet Requirements Unit, its initial equipment was officially just 2 Kingfisher landplanes for radar calibration, target towing, communications and other tasks. However, it also managed to acquire small numbers of other aircraft including Swordfish, Fulmars and a Walrus. In December 1943, 4 Defiants were allocated, to be followed in June 1944 by 8 Martinets and a Beaufighter II. The first of three Harvards arrived in May 1945, but on 3 November 1945 the squadron disbanded.

Aircraft Equipment	Period of Service	Example
Beaufighter II	Jun 1944 - Sep 1944	T3099
Defiant TT.I	Dec 1943 - May 1944	AA479
Fulmar II	Aug 1943 - Oct 1943	DR640
Harvard	May 1945 - Nov 1945	
Kingfisher I	Jul 1943 - Sep 1944	FN733
Martinet TT.I	Jun 1944 - Nov 1945	NR497
Swordfish I	Aug 1943 - Dec 1943	V4704
Swordfish II	Sep 1944 - Nov 1945	HS256

Identification Markings
Believed uncoded 1943-45.

Squadron bases
Stamford Hill 7 Jul 1943
Squadron disbanded 3 Nov 1945

Commanding Officers
L/C(A) FG Hood
  SANF(V) 7 Jul 1943
Lt(A) WA McElroy
  RNVR 4 Jan 1945
Not identified 23 Feb 1945

Commanding Officers
Lt(A) DC Langley
  SANF(V) 4 Jun 1945
Squadron disbanded 3 Nov 1945

No.727 Squadron

Badge: On a field perfesse white and barry wavy of six blue and white, the head of Britannia proper helmed gold

Motto: Regere mare regite caewm (To rule the sea one must rule the sky)

No.727 Squadron formed at North Front, Gibraltar on 26 May 1943 as a Fleet Requirements Unit, a detachment being set up at Tafaroui. Initial equipment comprised 6 Defiant target tugs, these being increased to 12 in August 1944. A detachment was also sent to Blida to carry out sleeve target, air training and dummy fighter attack exercises for the Allied Armies, Navies and Air Forces using the Defiants and also a small number of Swordfish which had been added to the strength. Some RAF Hurricanes were also loaned to the squadron. On 1 November 1944 the squadron moved to Ta Kali, where it disbanded on 7 December 1944.

On 23 Apr 1946, No.727 reformed at Gosport out of 'B' Flight of No.799 Squadron, which had functioned as a training flight to RN Air Courses. The new squadron provided the same service to Air Courses for non-flying Sub-Lieutenants and Royal Marine Officers. Equipment mainly consisted of 18 Tiger Moths, and a Seafire was also on strength at first, this being soon replaced by one, then two Harvards, a Firefly FR.4 being also added in November 1948. Glider experience was also undertaken. The squadron disbanded on 17 January 1950.

No.727 reformed at Brawdy on 4 January 1956 as the Dartmouth Cadet Air Training squadron, with 3 Sea Balliols, 3 Sea Vampire T.22s and a Sea Prince T.1. Its task was essentially the same as its predecessor, providing non-flying junior officers with air experience. From September 1958, two Dragonflies were also used by the squadron to demonstrate the use of helicopters in naval flying, but these were lost in June 1960 to the Britannia Helicopter Flight. No.727 disbanded on 16 December 1960.

Identification Markings
All types single letters, then *GP2A+* from 1.46, to *210-239/GJ* 9.47; Harvard *GP2+*, to *201-202/GJ* 9.47; Sea Prince/Sea Vampire/Sea Balliol/Dragonfly *555-568/BY*.

de Havilland Tiger Moth II NL879 '221/GJ' of No.727 Squadron, Gosport in 1948. (FAA Museum)

Percival Sea Prince T.1 WF118 '567/BY' of No.727 Squadron, Brawdy around 1956/7. (MAP)

Aircraft Equipment	Period of Service	Example	Commanding Officers		Squadron bases	
Defiant TT.I	May 1943 - Dec 1944	AA576	Lt(A) EL Meiklejohn		North Front	26 May 1943
Hurricane IIc	Aug 1943 - Aug 1944	KW731 (8V)	RNVR	26 May 1943	Tafaroui (Dt)	26 May 1943
Swordfish II	May 1943 - Sep 1944	HS424	L/C(A) MV Dyas		Blida (Dt)	26 May 1943
Tiger Moth T.2	May 1946 - Jan 1950	DE195 (GP2K)	RNVR	1 Oct 1943	Ta Kali	1 Nov 1944
Seafire XVII	Dec 1946 - Feb 1947	SX365	Squadron disbanded	1 Dec 1944	Squadron disbanded	7 Dec 1944
Harvard IIa	Jun 1947 - Jul 1947	EX687	Lt AM Dennis RN	23 Apr 1946	Gosport	23 Apr 1946
Harvard IIb	Jul 1947 - Jan 1950	KF521 (201/GJ)	Lt(A) RB Lunberg		Squadron disbanded	17 Jan 1950
Harvard III	Jul 1947 - Jan 1950	EZ442 (GP2Z)	RN	10 Jan 1947	Brawdy	4 Jan 1956
Oxford I	Jul 1947 - Aug 1947	DF460	Lt WE Cotton RN	15 Nov 1948	Squadron disbanded	16 Dec 1960
Firefly FR.4	Nov 1948 - Jan 1950	TW688	Squadron disbanded	17 Jan 1950		
Sea Balliol T.21	Jan 1956 - Jul 1959	WP330 (566/BY)	L/C HER Bain RN	4 Jan 1956		
Sea Prince T.1	Jan 1956 - Dec 1960	WM740 (567/BY)	L/C MA Tibby RN	17 Jun 1957		
Sea Vampire T.22	Jan 1956 - Dec 1960	XG748 (560/BY)	L/C PL Keighly			
Dragonfly HR.5	Sep 1958 - Jun 1960	WG752 (561/BY)	-Peach RN	6 Sep 1958		
Sea Devon C.20	Nov 1959 - Jan 1960	XJ350	L/C DG Halliday RN	11 Jun 1959		
			Squadron disbanded	16 Dec 1960		

de Havilland Sea Vampire T.22 XA126 '557/BY' of No.727 Squadron, Brawdy in 1963. (Arthur Pearcy)

No.728 Squadron

Badge: On a field blue on a base wavy white two bars, wavy blue, in chief a Maltese cross per pale red and white thereon a hurt surmounted by a plate surmounted by a roundel red pierced by an arrow point downwards in bend sinister feathered black

Motto: Descendo discimus
(We learn by teaching)

No.728 Squadron formed at North Front, Gibraltar on 1 May 1943 as a Fleet Requirements Unit, initially with 6 Defiant target tugs. A detachment was soon operating from Tafaroui using a Swordfish at first, and in June a few Defiants were sent to Oujda in French Morocco to tow for the US 80th AA Battery firing range at Nouvion. The whole squadron moved to Dekheila on 15 June, only to be absorbed there into No.775 Squadron on 4 July 1943.

On 14 August 1943, No.728 reformed out of No.775 Squadron, the pilots flying out via Tripoli to Ta Kali, to become a Fleet Requirements Unit once more. Initial equipment was again Defiants, and the squadron engaged in towing exercises, verification runs and other activities for Fleet and Shore establishments, and also the Army batteries at Bahar-ic-Chiak. In January 1944 four aircraft were detached to Capodichino to tow targets for the US Fleet at Naples, and in March 1944 Malta-based aircraft carried out exercises from Catania in Italy. New equipment was by then arriving in the shape of Martinet target tugs, and also a few Beaufighters and two RAF Hurricanes. The units became responsible for vessels of the British Pacific Fleet working up in the Mediterranean, and in the 18 months period to 1 November 1945 carried out exercises for a total of 176 ships, a peak of 715 flying hours being undertaken in May 1945.

The last of the Defiants went at the end of 1944, but new equipment during 1944 and 1945 included Beauforts, Baltimores, Seafires and Mosquitoes. The Mosquitoes were used for pilot conversion and also took over radar calibration and all other FRU commitments from No.255 Squadron RAF, which had been temporarily performing these tasks. After a spell at Luqa No.728 moved to Hal Far on 5 May 1946. Here the postwar contraction of the Mediterranean Fleet led to a reduced squadron strength, but the obsolete Martinets were replaced by Mosquito TT.39s in 1949. Later marks of Seafires continued to carry out fighter exercises, and two Expediters were used for carrying passengers and cargo of various kinds. Sea Vampires were the first jet aircraft to arrive, replacing the Seafires from 1951, and five Sea Hornets were allocated the following year. Sturgeon target tugs replaced the Mosquito TT.39s in 1952.

During the 1950's, the Mediterranean Fleet was the main user, but the Army increasingly took advantage of the target towing facilities for their AA Batteries, and the RAF Regiment also became a regular customer. A helicopter element was added with the arrival of Dragonflies in December 1952, and in 1955 Meteor T.7s were taken on charge, being followed in 1958 by Meteor TT.20s in place of the Sturgeons. Other types to be used included the Sea Devon, Heron and Whirlwind, the latter for search and rescue duties. No.728 disbanded at Hal Far on 31 May 1967.

Identification Markings
All types single letters, to *M8A+* 1944, to *500-599, 801-812, 901-903/HF* from 1946, to *570-599, 621-624, 655-659, 956-961* 1.56, to *860-866/HF 7.65*.

Beech Expediter C.2 FT994 of No.728 Squadron flying from Hal Far on 8 February 1950. (via Norman Lauchlan)

Aircraft Equipment	Period of Service	Example	
Anson I	Jul 1945 - Nov 1945	LT115	
Baltimore IV	Sep 1944 - Apr 1946	FA435	(801/HF)
Baltimore V	Nov 1944 - Oct 1946	FW352	
Beaufighter II	Feb 1944 - Nov 1945	T3157	
Beaufighter X	Oct 1945 - Jun 1946	RD166	
Beaufort I	Sep 1944 - Dec 1945	LR954	
Defiant TT.I	May 1943 - Dec 1944	DS145	
Hurricane IIc	May 1944 - Jan 1945	LB561	
Martinet TT.1	Mar 1944 - Dec 1949	RH114	(513/HF)
Mosquito B.25	Sep 1945 - Nov 1949	KB647	(M8B)
Oxford I	Jan 1946 - 1948	NM333	
Seafire L.IIc	Jan 1945 - Jan 1946	MB281	(M8A)
Seafire III	Jul 1945 - Jul 1946	NF521	(M8L)
Seafire XV	Sep 1946 - Sep 1948	PR495	
Seafire F.17	May 1948 - Mar 1952	SP327	(504/HF)
Sea Otter 2	Aug 1947 - Dec 1952	RD898	
Swordfish I	May 1943 - 1943	L2831	
	Jan 1946 - Feb 1946	V4637	
Swordfish II	Feb 1944 - Jan 1945	HS516	
Walrus	Nov 1945 - Feb 1946	L2253	
Wellington XIV	1946	NB863	
Beaufighter TT.10	Jun 1949 - Oct 1949	SR917	
Dragonfly HR.3	Dec 1952 - Oct 1959	WP501	(959/HF)
Expediter C.2	Mar 1948 - Jun 1959	KP115	(811/HF)
Gannet T.2	Jul 1957 - Nov 1957	XA526	
Harvard T.3	Aug 1948	EX913	
Heron C.2	Mar 1963 - Oct 1965	XR444	(794/HF)
Meteor T.7	Feb 1955 - May 1967	WL353	(574/HF)
Meteor TT.20	Mar 1958 - May 1967	WM147	(580/HF)
Mosquito T.3	Oct 1945 - Jun 1946	RR295	
Mosquito PR.16	May 1948 - Sep 1952	NS742	(526/HF)
Mosquito TT.39	Mar 1949 - May 1952	RV295	(511/HF)
Sea Devon C.20	Aug 1956 - Apr 1963	XJ348	(795/HF)
Sea Hornet FR.20	Feb 1952 - Feb 1957	VR854	(533/HF)
Sea Vampire F.20	Jul 1951 - Mar 1955	VV153	(582/HF)
Sturgeon TT.2	Aug 1951 - Jan 1956	TS497	(597/HF)
Sturgeon TT.3	Jul 1954 - Oct 1958	TS477	(584/HF)
Whirlwind HAR.3	Jun 1957 - Nov 1958	XG573	(958/HF)
Whirlwind HAS.22	Mar 1963 - Aug 1965	WV224	(961/HF)

de Havilland Sea Venom FAW.22 XG664 '679/HF' of No.728 Squadron, Hal Far in 1961. (Tom MacFadyen)

Squadron bases

North Front	1 May 1943
Tafaroui (Dt)	11 May 1943
Oujda (Dt)	5 Jun 1943
Dekheila	15 Jun 1943
Squadron disbanded	4 Jul 1943
Dekheila	14 Aug 1943
Ta Kali	17 Aug 1943
Capodichino (Dt4)	11 Jan 1944
Catania (Dt4)	Mar 1944
Capodichino (Dt2)	14 Mar 1944
North Front (Dt)	1 Apr 1944
to	May 1944
Pomigliano (Dt)	Aug 1945
to	Apr 1946
Ciampino (Dt)	Aug 1945
to	Apr 1946
Luqa	1 Jan 1946
Hal Far	5 May 1946
Squadron disbanded	31 May 1967

Commanding Officers

L/C(A) EH Horn RNVR	8 May 1943
Lt P Snow RN	12 Aug 1943
L/C(A) PB Pratt RNVR	8 Jan 1944
L/C EM Britton RN	5 Jan 1946
Lt(A) PJWW Cruttenden RNVR	3 Jun 1946
Lt(A) JRW Groves RN	21 Oct 1946
L/C DH Lough RN	14 Oct 1948
L/C RP Keogh RN	6 Aug 1949
L/C HA Monk DSM RN	23 Oct 1950
L/C PCS Bagley RN	6 Feb 1952
L/C AD Corkhill RN	1 Jan 1954
L/C B Bevans DSC RN	26 Jan 1955
L/C RCB Trelawney RN	27 May 1957
L/C RH Hallam RN	19 Oct 1959
L/C CR Mellor RN	17 Mar 1962
L/C AA Knight RN	16 Mar 1964
L/C PJ Wreford RN	7 Apr 1966
Squadron disbanded	31 May 1967

de Havilland Sea Hornet F.20 TT197 '531/HF' of No.728 Squadron, Hal Far in 1953. (MAP)

No.728B Squadron

No.728B Squadron formed at Ta Kali during January 1945 as a Fleet Requirements Unit equipped with five Martinets and three Seafires, increasing these in May to eight and six respectively. The relationship of this sub-unit to No.728 Squadron has not been properly established. It disbanded during July 1945.

On 13 January 1958, No.728B Squadron reformed at Stretton as a pilotless drone target unit. Equipped initially with 6 Firefly U.9s, these were flown out to Malta betweeen 17 and 26 February, and the squadron officially set up residence at Hal Far on 1 March 1958. The task of the unit was primarily to provide radio-controlled pilotless target aircraft for Seaslug missiles fired from the trials ship HMS *Girdle Ness*. The Firefly strength was increased to nine in October 1958, and the following year Meteor U.15s and U.16s began to arrive. In May 1961 a few Canberra U.14s were received, these being later known as D.14s. No.728B disbanded at Hal Far on 2 December 1961, and HMS *Girdle Ness* returned home to act as a model for future missile ships.

The title No.728B (SAR) Flight was applied to the Hal Far Search and Rescue Flight when it was absorbed into No.728 Squadron in March 1963.

Identification Markings
Firefly/Canberra *590-599*, Meteor *655-659*.

Aircraft Equipment	Period of Service	Example
Martinet I	Jan 1945 - Jul 1945	
Seafire III	Jan 1945 - Jul 1945	
Firefly U.8	Oct 1960	WJ188
Firefly U.9	Jan 1958 - Nov 1961	VX416 (599)
Meteor U.15	Jul 1959 - Oct 1961	VT310 (657)
Meteor U.16	Oct 1960 - Nov 1961	WK870 (655)
Canberra D.14	May 1961 - Dec 1961	WH704 (594)

Squadron bases		Commanding Officers	
Stretton	13 Jan 1958	L/C JG Corbett RN	13 Jan 1958
transit	26 Feb 1958	Squadron disbanded	2 Dec 1961
Hal Far	1 Mar 1958		
in transit	26 Feb 1958		
Hal Far	1 Mar 1958		
Unit disbanded	2 Dec 1961		

Fairey Firefly U.9 WB257 '591' of No.728B Squadron, Hal Far in 1959. (Grant Macdonald)

No.728C Squadron

No.728C Squadron formed at Lee-on-Solent on 7 January 1958 as the Amphibious Warfare Trials Unit. The squadron's task was to develop the capability of transporting RM commandos from ship to shore for large scale assaults on beachheads. Equipped with 4 Whirlwind HAS.22s, these were taken to Plymouth to be embarked in HMS *Eagle* and HMS *Ark Royal* for ferrying to Malta. The crews left London Airport on 2 February in a Transair Viscount, and with the arrival of their aircraft set up headquarters at Hal Far. In April they embarked in the landing ship HMS *Striker* for Tripoli, but an exercise with the Royal Marines was cut short. Joining HMS *Ark Royal* the squadron was to have returned to Malta, but instead the ship diverted to Sardinia. Planned exercises were again cut short, and the aircraft rejoined HMS *Striker* to sail back to Malta. In June the squadron was hastily sent to Cyprus, the aircraft being carried as deck cargo in HMS *Bermuda* with 45 RM Commando, returning to Malta in late July. It was redesignated No.848 Squadron on 13 October 1958 on achieving first line status.

Aircraft Equipment	Period of Service	Example
Whirlwind HAS.22	Jan 1958 - Oct 1958	WV222 (622/HF)

Identification Markings
Whirlwind *621-624/HF*.

Commanding Officers
L/C GCJ Knight DFC RN 8 Jan 1958
Squadron disbanded 13 Oct 1958

Squadron bases		Commanding Officers	
Lee-on-Solent	7 Jan 1958	Tarhuna (Tripoli)	Apr 1958
HMS Eagle/ HMS Ark Royal (transit)	24 Jan 1958	HMS Ark Royal	15 Apr 1958
		HMS Striker	21 Apr 1958
Hal Far	7 Feb 1958	Hal Far	28 Apr 1958
HMS Striker (transit)	7 Apr 1958	HMS Bermuda (transit)	16 Jun 1958
		Nicosia	19 Jun 1958
		HMS Reggio (transit)	26 Jul 1958
		Hal Far	30 Jul 1958
		Redes 848 Sqdn	13 Oct 1958

No.729 Squadron

No.729 Squadron formed at Hinstock on 1 January 1945 as an offshoot of No.758 Squadron, being an Instrument Flying Training squadron for service in the Far East. Taking passage on 16 April 1945, it arrived at Coimbatore on 15 May, and started training with Oxfords and Harvards. Three weeks later it moved to Tambaram, then in July to Puttalam, before going to Ceylon at the end of August to operate from Katukurunda. An air sea rescue flight operated briefly with the squadron in the early part of 1946, but on 24 July 1946 the squadron disbanded at Katukurunda.

Aircraft Equipment	Period of Service	Example
Harvard III	May 1945 - Jul 1946	KF494
Oxford I	May 1945 - Jul 1946	PH137 (K7B)
Sea Otter	Jan 1946 - Apr 1946	JM950

Identification Markings
All types K7A+.

Commanding Officers
L/C(A) HR Law
    RNVR 1 Jan 1945
Lt(A) AH Bender
    RNVR 23 Nov 1945
Squadron disbanded 24 Apr 1946

Squadron bases	
Hinstock	1 Jan 1945
in transit	16 Apr 1945
Coimbatore	15 May 1945
Tambaram	7 Jun 1945
Puttalam	20 Jul 1945
Katukurunda	30 Aug 1945
Squadron disbanded	24 Jul 1946

Airspeed Oxford PH137 'K7B' of No.729 Squadron, Katukurunda in 1945. (FAA Museum)

No.730 Squadron

No.730 Squadron formed at Abbotsinch on 17 April 1944 as a Communications squadron, by elevating the Flag Officer Carrier Training Flight to squadron status. The squadron moved to Ayr on 20 November 1944, and equipment then comprised Sea Otters, Reliant, Fireflies, Travellers, Walruses and a Percival Q.6 Petrel. A sub-flight operated from Donibristle, and later equipment included an Expediter which the squadron had only just polished up when to their annoyance it was taken over by No.781 Squadron. No.730 disbanded at Ayr on 1 August 1945.

Identification Markings
All types unknown, believed AR0A+ from 11.44.

Commanding Officers
Lt(A) G Windsor
    RNVR 17 Apr 1944
Lt(A) C White RNVR 1 Dec 1944
Lt JC Kennedy RN 24 May 1945
Squadron disbanded 1 Aug 1945

Squadron bases	
Abbotsinch	17 Apr 1944
Ayr	20 Nov 1944
Machrihanish (Dt)	1 Jan 1945
	to 8 Mar 1945
Squadron disbanded	1 Aug 1945

Aircraft Equipment	Period of Service	Example
Auster I	Jan 1945 - Aug 1945	LB384
Corsair II	Jul 1944 - Oct 1944	JT420
Expediter	1945 - 1945	
Firefly I	Sep 1944 - Aug 1945	Z2109
Fulmar II	Jun 1944 - Sep 1944	X8613
Oxford I	Jun 1945 - Aug 1945	..681
Q.6 Petrel	Jul 1944 - Dec 1944	P5638
Reliant	Apr 1944 - Aug 1945	FK883
Seafire IIc	Oct 1944	NM921
Sea Otter I	Sep 1944 - Aug 1945	JM878
Swordfish II	Jan 1945 - Aug 1945	NE988
Traveller I	Dec 1944 - Aug 1945	FT532
Walrus II	May 1944 - Nov 1944	HD868
Wildcat V, VI	Jun 1944 - Aug 1944	JV640

Fairey Firefly I Z2035 was flown by No.730 Squadron at Ayr in 1945. (MAP)

No.731 Squadron

Badge: On a field blue, a seagull white alighting on an anchor fesswise gold
Motto: Circum undique (From everywhere around)

Identification Markings
All types E3A+.

Aircraft Equipment	Period of Service	Example	
Barracuda II	Jul 1945 - Nov 1945	MD722	
Corsair II	1945 - Nov 1945	JT629	
Corsair III	Jun 1944 - Nov 1945	JS486	
Firefly I	Dec 1944 - Nov 1945	Z2116	(E3J)
Fulmar II	Mar 1944 - Jun 1944	BP789	
Seafire Ib	May 1944 - Feb 1945	MB335	(E3Y)
Seafire IIc	1945 - Nov 1945	MB312	
Sea Hurricane Ib	Dec 1943 - Jun 1944	R4078	
Swordfish I	Dec 1943 - Jun 1944	V4568	
Swordfish II	Dec 1943 - Nov 1945	NF247	
Swordfish III	Nov 1944 - Nov 1945	NF320	

No.731 Squadron formed at East Haven on 5 December 1943 for Deck Landing Control Officer training. The main equipment was Swordfish, but Fulmars, Sea Hurricanes and Seafires were also used. Batsmen, to give them their colloquial name, were given initial experience by squadron aircraft continuously being in circuit, executing dummy deck landings and then taking off again. This specialised function gave rise to the term "Clockwork Mice", though the pilots sometimes indulged in rather more eccentric flying in order to make things difficult for the pupil batsmen. The squadron was attached to the locally based Deck Landing Training School. It was absorbed into Nos.767 and 768 Squadrons at East Haven on 1 November 1945.

Squadron bases		Commanding Officers	
East Haven	5 Dec 1943	L/C(A) K Stilliard	
DLT:		RNVR	5 Dec 1943
HMS Smiter	2 May 1945	L/C R Pridham	
HMS Battler	6 Aug 1945	-Wippell RN	1 Jan 1945
HMS Battler	11-15 Sep 1945	Squadron disbanded	1 Nov 1945
Squadron disbanded	1 Nov 1945		

Chance Vought Corsair III JS853 'E3S' of No.731 Squadron, East Haven in 1945

No.732 Squadron

No.732 Squadron formed at Brunswick on 23 November 1943 as an Operational Training Unit. Its primary task was to provide pre-squadron training for the many Fleet Air Arm fighter pilots who had received their initial and advanced training at US Navy bases in Florida. Equipped with Corsairs, the squadron gave ADDL training, Bar Harbour being also used on occasion. The squadron disbanded on 1 July 1944.
On 15 May 1945, No.732 reformed at Drem as a Night Fighter Training School. Equipment comprised 9 Hellcats, 6 Anson Classrooms, 6 Harvards and some Firefly NF.Is. No.732 disbanded on 7 November 1945, becoming 'B' Flight of No.784 Squadron.

Identification Markings
Corsair unknown; Hellcat D2A+ (possibly also Harvard/Anson).

Squadron bases		Commanding Officers	
Brunswick	23 Nov 1943	L/C(A) MS Godson RN	23 Nov 1943
Bar Harbour(Dt)	18-30 Apr 1944	L/C WN Waller RN	31 Jan 1944
Bar Harbour(Dt)	23-31 May 1944	Squadron disbanded	1 Jul 1944
Squadron disbanded	1 Jul 1944	Lt(A) MBW Howell RNVR	15 May 1945
Drem	15 May 1945	L/C(A) AM Tritton DSC RNVR	1 Aug 1945
Squadron disbanded	7 Nov 1945	L/C(A) MBW Howell RNVR	5 Sep 1945
		Squadron disbanded	7 Nov 1945

Aircraft Equipment	Period of Service	Example	
Corsair I	Nov 1943 - Jun 1944	JT127	(5T)
Corsair II	Nov 1943 - Jun 1944	JT288	(5R)
Anson I	May 1945 - Nov 1945	LT304	(B)
Firefly NF.I	May 1945 - Nov 1945		
Harvard III	May 1945 - Nov 1945	EZ260	(S)
Hellcat IINF	May 1945 - Nov 1945	JZ907	(D2W)

No.733 Squadron

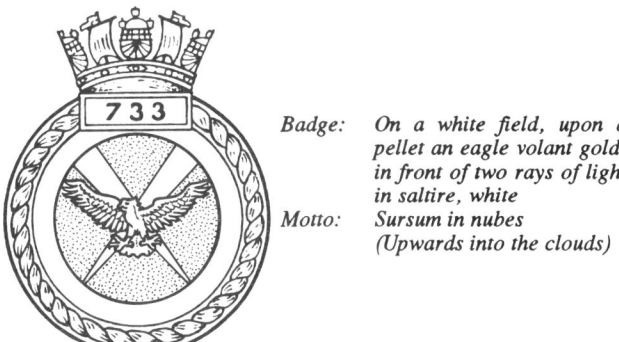

Badge: On a white field, upon a pellet an eagle volant gold, in front of two rays of light in saltire, white
Motto: Sursum in nubes (Upwards into the clouds)

Aircraft Equipment	Period of Service	Example
Albacore I	1944 - 1945	BF714
Avenger I	Jan 1944 - Apr 1944	JZ144 (C8B)
Avenger II	Mar 1944 - Nov 1945	JV357 (C8G)
Barracuda II	Sep 1944 - Apr 1945	LS672 (C8K)
Beaufighter II	Jan 1944 - Jul 1945	T3029 (C)
Beaufort I	1944 - Mar 1945	LR936
Corsair IV	Oct 1945 - Oct 1946	KD659
Defiant TT.I	Jan 1944 - Oct 1946	DR961
Expediter C.II	Aug 1946 - Dec 1947	HD775
Fulmar II	Jan 1944 - 1944	DR710
Harvard IIb	Dec 1944 - Dec 1945	FT190
Martinet TT.I	Mar 1944 - Nov 1945	PX169
Mosquito B.25	Nov 1945 - Dec 1945	KB663
Reliant I	Apr 1944 - Nov 1945	FL118
Seafire III	Oct 1946 - Dec 1946	
Seafire XV	Jan 1947 - Dec 1947	SW878
Sea Otter I	Aug 1946 - Dec 1947	JM756
Swordfish I	Jan 1944 - Dec 1944	P4143
Swordfish II	Sep 1944 - Nov 1945	HS386
Tiger Moth II	Jan 1947 - Apr 1947	NL750
Vengeance TT.II	Jul 1945 - Sep 1945	HB335
Walrus I	Mar 1946 - Nov 1946	W2775
Wildcat V	Jun 1944 - Nov 1945	JV430 (C9O)

No.733 Squadron formed at Minneriya on 1 January 1944 as a Fleet Requirements Unit, moving to China Bay in March 1944. Services were provided for the Eastern Fleet, initial equipment being mainly Martinets, Wildcats and Avengers, with a few Beaufighters, Barracudas and Swordfish. Later types included Defiants, Reliants, Mosquitoes, Corsairs, Vengeances and Seafires. One of the many tasks of the squadron was radar calibration, one pilot making a trip for this purpose halfway to Singapore and back at 30,000 ft maintaining a specific height and speed. In August the squadron was expanded by taking over some Expeditors of the disbanding No.742 Squadron, and an air sea rescue flight was added early in 1946 using Walruses and later Sea Otters. The squadron disbanded at Trincomalee, as China Bay had by then been renamed, on 31 December 1947.

Identification Markings
All types C8A+ & C9A+ 1944, uncoded from 1946.

Commanding Officers
L/C(A) RA Beard RNVR 1 Jan 1944
L/C(A) L Gilbert RNVR (temp) 1 Apr 1944
L/C(A) JA Ansell RNVR 6 Oct 1944
L/C(A) IO Robertson RNVR 9 Aug 1945
L/C(A) HJ Mortimore RNVR 15 Dec 1945
Squadron disbanded 31 Dec 1947

Squadron bases
Minneriya 1 Jan 1944
 (advance party from 15 Dec 1943)
China Bay 25 Mar 1944
Minneriya (Dt) to 12 Aug 1944
Squadron disbanded 31 Dec 1947

Grumman Wildcat V JV439 'C9N' of No.733 Squadron, piloted by Sub-Lt Griffiths, flying over the bombardment spotting range at Trincomalee in 1945. (Richard Griffiths)

No.734 Squadron

No.734 Squadron formed at Worthy Down on 14 February 1944 as an Engine Handling Unit. The unit was equipped with Whitley GR.VIIs which had been specially fitted with fuel flowmeters and other instruments. They were used as flying classrooms in which pilots could be instructed in Merlin engine handling techniques. No.734 moved to Hinstock in August 1945, and was later to have moved to its satellite at Peplow, where it would have been able to re-equip with Fortresses and Lancasters, but instead it disbanded on 21 February 1946.

Identification Markings
Whitley *W0A+*.

Aircraft Equipment	Period of Service	Example
Whitley VII	Feb 1944 - Feb 1946	LA794 (WOY)

Squadron bases	
Worthy Down	14 Feb 1944
Hinstock	21 Aug 1945
(satt Peplow)	
Squadron disbanded	21 Feb 1946

Commanding Officers
L/C(A) RC Cockburn DSO RNVR 14 Feb 1944
Lt(A) RG Parkes RNVR 5 Dec 1945
Squadron disbanded 21 Feb 1946

An Armstrong Whitworth Whitley of No.734 Squadron, Hinstock. (Molly Brown)

No.735 Squadron

No.735 Squadron formed at Inskip on 1 August 1943 as an ASV Training unit. It initially had ASV-equipped Swordfish, but later replaced these with similarly-equipped Barracudas. A number of Ansons were used, for both ASH and ASV radar training. No.735 originally comprised two flights, 'A' Flight being concerned with radar training and 'B' Flight engaged in radar trials. The squadron moved to Burscough in March 1944, and later a 'C' Flight was added for administrative convenience, though it actually operated as a mobile unit giving Rebecca training to fighter pilots, being equipped with 3 Hellcats and an Anson. In February 1945, 'B' Flight broke away to become No.707 Squadron, then on 1 March 1945, 'C' Flight became 787X Flight at Odiham. In November 1945, No.737 Squadron was absorbed, but No.735 itself disbanded at Burscough on 30 April 1946.

Aircraft Equipment	Period of Service	Example	
Swordfish I	Aug 1943 - Mar 1944	P4222	
Swordfish II	Aug 1943 - Jun 1944	HS333	
Anson I	Aug 1943 - Apr 1946	NK762	(AH7S)
Barracuda II	Dec 1944 - Apr 1946	MD767	
Barracuda III	Nov 1945 - Apr 1946	MD849	(O1X)
Hellcat I	1945 - May 1945	JV128	(AH4R)

Squadron bases	
Inskip	1 Aug 1943
Burscough	18 Mar 1944
Arbroath (Dt)	28 Aug 1944
	to 15 Apr 1945
Squadron disbanded	30 Apr 1946

Identification Markings
Swordfish unknown; Barracuda *AH4A+*, to *O4A+* by 6.45. Anson *AH7A+*, Hellcat *AH4A+*.

Commanding Officers
L/C ES Carver DSC RN 1 Aug 1943
L/C(A) RT Hayes RNVR 15 Mar 1944
L/C(A) JH Mayne RNVR 18 Aug 1944
L/C(A) SL Revett DSC RNVR 31 Mar 1945
L/C F Stovin-Bradford DSC RN 28 Dec 1945
Squadron disbanded 30 Apr 1946

A Fairey Barracuda of No.735 Squadron, Burscouch climbing into a still sky. (V.M.G.Bennett)

No.736 Squadron

Badge: On a black field, an eagle volant gold surmounting a ray of lightning white
Motto: None

No.736 Squadron formed at Yeovilton on 24 May 1943 as the School of Air Combat. Equipped with Seafires it took over from the RAF Fighter Leaders School the task of teaching the latest techniques of air combat to experienced naval fighter leaders. In September 1943 it moved to St Merryn, where it became the Fighter Combat School element of the School of Naval Air Warfare. Masters and Barracudas were added, the latter operating as its TBR Wing. By the beginning of 1945 the squadron was operating an Air Instructors Course and a TBR Air Strike Course, then in March 1945 'B' Flight was formed by absorbing 'Y' Flight of No.787 Squadron for fighter affiliation work. The latter continued to operate independently, its Seafires sailing in HMS *Colossus* to Malta to train units of the 11th Aircraft Carrier Squadron in Gyro Gunsight tactics prior to their sailing to Ceylon to join the British Pacific. Returning in June, this sub-unit operated Seafires, Beaufighters and a Dominie from Woodvale and later Fearn before disbanding at Woodvale in September 1945.

Continuing postwar, No.736 moved to Culdrose on 1 February 1950 as the Naval Air Fighter School, in the 52nd Training Air Group, equipped mainly with 50 Sea Furies. Three months later this large unit was split, half becoming No.738 Squadron, but on 13 August 1952 No.738 took over all the Sea Furies and No.736 disbanded as a piston-engined squadron.

The following day, No.736 reformed at Culdrose out of No.702 Squadron as an Advanced Jet Flying School, otherwise Operational Flying School Part II (Jet), still as part of the Naval Air Fighter School. Initial equipment was Attackers and Meteor T.7s, and with these it moved with the NAFS in November 1953 to Lossiemouth, where the airfield and weather conditions proved more suitable to flying training needs. Sea Vampires and Sea Hawks replaced the earlier aircraft at Lossiemouth, and the squadron task was increased to give experience in jet aircraft to piston engined pilots, but in March 1955 the Sea Hawks were transferred to No.738 Squadron. No.736 then became responsible for converting to British standards and aircraft types pilots trained in America, training small numbers of experienced pilots to be Air Warfare Instructors, and keeping all Lossiemouth pilots in constant instrument flying practice. Late in 1958 a reorganisation resulted in the parent formation being changed to become the Naval Air Fighter and Strike School, with No.736 becoming Sea Hawk OFS Parts I and II, and the Sea Vampires then departed. The reorganised squadron's task was to train pilots up to first-line standard, the course including experience in photographic reconnaissance, ground attack using bombs, rockets guns and Bullpup missiles, Sidewinder interceptions, low level navigation and army co-operation. Re-equipment with Scimitars began in June 1959, the last of the Sea Hawks going to No.738 Squadron in July 1960. No.736 disbanded at Lossiemouth on 26 March 1965, its remnants becoming No.764B Squadron.

No.736 reformed the same day at Lossiemouth from No.809 Squadron, as a Jet Strike Training Squadron equipped with Buccaneer S.1s, these being partially replaced by Buccaneer S.2s from May 1966. The squadron disbanded on 25 February 1972.

Identification Markings
All types *ACA+* to 1946, then *S3A+* to *S6A+* to 1947. Seafire/Sea Fury *100-109/JB*, Harvard/Firefly *201-287/JB*, Martinet *551-553* from 1947. 2.50 to 8.52 - Seafire *100-189/CW*, Firefly *270-271/CW*, Sea Fury *291-296/CW*. 8.52 to 1.56 - Attacker *100-119/CW:LM* & *150-158, 176/LM*, Seafire *180-189/CW*, Meteor *405-408/CW:LM*, Sea Hawk *150-156/LM*, Sea Vampire *211-242/LM*. 1.56 to 3.65 Sea Hawk/Hunter/Scimitar *600-625/LM*. 3.65 to 2.72 Buccaneer *630-657*.

Supermarine Seafire F.17 SX365 '173/JB' of No.736 Squadron, St.Merryn about to be launched from the catapult of HMAS Sydney in 1949. (RAF Museum 6311-4)

Aircraft Equipment	Period of Service	Example
Barracuda II	Sep 1943 - Jul 1945	LS707 (AC-G)
Master II	Sep 1943 - Jul 1945	DK950 (AC-S)
Seafire Ib	May 1943 - Aug 1944	NX942 (AC-E)
Seafire III	Apr 1944 - Aug 1944	NN511
Spitfire Va	Mar 1944 - Aug 1944	R7207
Corsair III	Jun 1944 - Aug 1944	JS535
Wellington XI	Mar 1945	? (AC-X)
Avenger II	Feb 1945 - Jul 1945	JZ312
Harvard III	Jun 1945 - Nov 1949	EZ327 (202/JB)
Firefly FR.IV	Mar 1948	
Firebrand TF.IV	Mar 1948	
Martinet TT.1	Feb 1946 - Feb 1950	RG898 (552)
Seafire III	Feb 1946 - Jul 1946	SP166
Seafire F.15	Apr 1946 - Jun 1948	SW852 (162/JB)
Seafire F.17	Jan 1946 - Apr 1951	SX237 (197/JB)
Seafire F.46	Jan 1946 - Dec 1946	LA449 (S5A)
Sea Fury F.10	Aug 1950 - Sep 1951	TF911 (118/CW)
Sea Fury FB.11	May 1949 - Aug 1952	WJ280 (111/CW)
Sea Fury T.20	Mar 1950 - Aug 1952	VZ350 (295/CW)
Firefly FR.1	Jan 1946 - Feb 1950	MB755 (S5M)
Firefly T.1	Jul 1948 - Feb 1950	DK449 (271/JB)
Sea Hornet F.20	Feb 1950 - Jun 1951	TT191
Attacker F.1	Aug 1952 - Aug 1954	WA473 (116/LM)
Attacker FB.2	1953 - Aug 1954	WZ274 (108/LM)
Meteor T.7	Aug 1952 - May 1954	WS112 (406/LM)
Sea Vampire T.22	Nov 1953 - Jul 1954	XA159 (215/LM)
	Oct 1954 - Nov 1958	XA131 (610/LM)
Sea Hawk F.1	Jul 1954 - Mar 1955	WF164 (104/LM)
Sea Hawk F.2	Jul 1954 - Mar 1955	WF273 (119/LM)
	Mar 1957 - Jul 1958	WF253 (606/LM)
Sea Hawk FB.3	Jul 1954 - Mar 1955	WF300 (156/LM)
	May 1958 - Sep 1959	WM986 (610/LM)
Sea Hawk FGA.4	May 1957 - Jun 1957	WV833 (618/LM)
	Dec 1958 - Jul 1959	WV826 (608/LM)
Sea Hawk FB.5	Mar 1959 - Sep 1959	WM913 (616/LM)
Sea Hawk FGA.6	Oct 1958 - Jul 1960	WV794 (602/LM)
Sea Venom FAW.21	Oct 1957 - Dec 1957	WW274 (653/LM)
Hunter T.8	Jul 1958 - Nov 1958	XL581 (619/LM)
Scimitar F.1	Jun 1959 - Mar 1965	XD316 (612/LM)
Buccaneer S.1	Mar 1965 - Dec 1970	XN965 (636/LM)
Buccaneer S.2	May 1966 - Feb 1972	XV865 (652/LM)
Buccaneer S.2b	Jan 1971 - Mar 1971	XV349 (B)

Hawker Sea Fury F.10 TF898 '100/CW' of No.736 Squadron at Culdrose in 1951. (Tony Hughes)

Commanding Officers	
L/C(A) RE Gardner DSC RNVR	24 May 1943
L/C DR Curry DSC RN	17 Aug 1944
L/C PD Gick RN	8 Feb 1945
L/C(A) SP Luke RN	3 Aug 1945
L/C DB Law DSC RN	6 Jan 1946
L/C W Stuart DSC RNVR	16 Apr 1946
L/C JG Baldwin DSC RN	24 Apr 1947
L/C MF Fell DSO DSC RN	21 Oct 1947
L/C PJP Leckie RN	5 Sep 1949
Lt PB Stuart RN	1 Feb 1950
L/C PM Austin RN	17 Oct 1950
L/C PH London DSC RN	24 Mar 1952
L/C N Perrett RN	26 Aug 1952
L/C PH London DSC RN	1 Dec 1952
L/C AR Rawbone AFC RN	20 Apr 1953
L/C WDD MacDonald RN	20 Oct 1954
L/C R Bellamy RN	16 Jul 1956
L/C LEA Chester -Lawrence RN	12 Dec 1957

Commanding Officers	
L/C JD Baker RN	2 Sep 1958
L/C A Mancais RN	2 May 1960
L/C PG Newman RN	9 Oct 1961
L/C JAD Ford RN	10 Jan 1963
L/C J Worth RN	9 Dec 1963
Squadron disbanded	26 Mar 1965
L/C J Worth RN	26 Mar 1965
L/C JF Kennett RN	28 Jul 1965
L/C JDHB Howard RN	15 Feb 1967
L/C DP Mears RN	23 Oct 1968
L/C R Wren RN	16 Feb 1970
L/C LA Wilkinson RN	16 Dec 1970
Squadron disbanded	25 Feb 1972

Squadron bases

Yeovilton	24 May 1943
St Merryn	2 Sep 1943
Culdrose	1 Feb 1950
Squadron disbanded	25 Aug 1952
Culdrose	26 Aug 1952
Lossiemouth	4 Nov 1953
Brawdy (Dd)	25 Jun 1960
Lossiemouth	2 Jul 1960
Squadron disbanded	26 Mar 1965
Lossiemouth	26 Mar 1965
Squadron disbanded	25 Feb 1972

No.736B Flight

Aircraft Equipment	Period of Service	Example
Seafire III	Mar 1945 - May 1945	NF586 (YΘH)
Seafire XV	Jul 1945 - Sep 1945	
Beaufighter X	Jul 1945 - Sep 1945	
Dominie I	Jul 1945 - Aug 1945	X7341

Squadron bases	
Speke	1 Mar 1945
HMS Colossus	11 Mar 1945
Hal Far	20 Mar 1945
Woodvale	28 Jun 1945
Fearn	20 Jul 1945
Woodvale	17 Aug 1945
Unit disbanded	26 Sep 1945

Commanding Officers	
L/C(A) RE Bibby DSO RNVR	1 Mar 1945
L/C(A) LGC Reece DSC RNZNVR	26 Jul 1945
Flight disbanded	26 Sep 1945

No.737 Squadron

Badge: On a field barry wavy of eight white and blue, a foil the point in base proper, the blade winged gold
Motto: Purposeful

No.737 Squadron formed at Dunino on 22 February 1943 as an Amphibious Bomber Reconnaissance Training squadron. Equipped with Walruses, the squadron provided training for crews joining catapult ships, but the need for these was diminishing and No.737 disbanded on 28 September 1943.

On 15 March 1944, the squadron reformed at Inskip as an ASV radar training unit. Equipped with Swordfish and Ansons, No.737 trained aircrew in the use of ASV Mks.X and XI radar for anti-shipping operations. It moved to Arbroath in August 1944, and then to Burscough in April 1945, where Barracudas were received in August. The squadron disbanded into No.735 Squadron on 12 November 1945.

No.737 next reformed at Eglinton on 30 March 1949 as part of the 52nd Training Air Group. It acted as Part II of the Operational Flying School Course, equipped with Seafires and Fireflies. Pupils were trained in the use of air weapons, being given basic training in anti-submarine warfare and also some deck landing training experience. In April 1950 the Seafires were transferred to No.738 Squadron, and No.737 became the basis for the Naval Anti-Submarine School. On 19 April 1950, 'X' Flight was formed at Lee-on-Solent for special trials with search receivers to detect submarine radar, operating as a separate unit equipped with a Firefly and an Anson, and spending two months in Gibraltar before moving to Eglinton where it became No.744 Squadron. On 14 June 1950 No.719 Squadron also became part of NASS, and with No.737 formed the 53rd Training Air Group. In 1955 the Fireflies gave way to Gannets, but the squadron disbanded into No.719 Squadron at Eglinton on 22 November 1957.

On 28 August 1959, No.737 became a helicopter squadron when it reformed at Portland from No.815 Squadron to take over the role of Anti-Submarine Operational Flying School. Equipment comprised Whirlwind HAR.3s and HAS.7s, two HAS.22s being added in February 1960 for search and rescue duties, these later being handed over to No.771 Squadron when it reformed in July 1961. In July 1962 No.737 converted to Wessex HAS.1s, and the remainder of the Whirlwinds went to No.771 Squadron the following month. Wessex HAS.3s arrived in 1967, and in 1970 No.737 took over from No.829 Squadron the parentage of the Wessex flights in County-class cruisers. In July 1970 the squadron partially re-equipped with Sea Kings HAS.1s, but these were withdrawn in December 1975 for first line use. The squadron then concentrated on operational training for anti-submarine warfare pilots, observers and aircrewmen, as well as conversion and refresher training for Wessex HAS.3 aircraft. No.737 was to have disbanded in the summer of 1982, but this was postponed when the Wessexes were required for use in County-class cruisers serving with the Falklands Task Force, the Flight Commander of *Antrim* Flight, Lt-Cdr Ian Stanley, being awarded the DSO for gallantry during the operation to recover the island of South Georgia. The Wessex responsibility reverted to No.829 Squadron on 1 August 1982, and No.737 disbanded at Portland on 7 February 1983.

Battle Honours
Falkland Islands   1982

Identification Markings
Walrus *D1A+*, Swordfish/Anson *K4A+* from 3.44, to *A2+* 8.44. From 3.49 to 1.56 Seafire *100-119/GN*, Firefly *200-231/GN*, Gannet *421-434/GN*. 1.56 to 11.57 Gannet *617-627/GN*. Whirlwind *760-789*. Wessex *770-776/PO*, to *520-529/PO* 7.65, to *434-437, 520-528/PO* 8.68. Sea King *524-529/PO*, to *660-666/PO* 4.73.

Westland Sea King HAS.1 XV668 '(5)26/PO' of No.737 Squadron, Portland around 1971/2. (Brian Lowe)

Aircraft Equipment	Period of Service	Example
Walrus	Feb 1943 - Sep 1943	X9571 (D1X)
Swordfish II	Mar 1944 - Jul 1945	LS446 (A2C)
Anson I	Jun 1944 - Sep 1945	NK834 (A2T)
Barracuda III	Aug 1945 - Dec 1945	ME111
Seafire F.15	Apr 1949 - Jan 1950	SR603
Seafire F.17	Apr 1949 - May 1950	SX163 (112/GN)
Firefly FR.1	Apr 1949 - Mar 1950	DV121 (225/GN)
Firefly T.1	Apr 1949 - Nov 1952	Z1943 (235/GN)
Firefly T.2	Apr 1949 - Jun 1955	MB717 (219/GN)
Firefly FR.4	Apr 1949 - Aug 1953	VH127 (216/GN)
Firefly AS.5	Apr 1949 - May 1955	VX429 (212/GN)
Firefly AS.6	May 1954 - Jun 1955	WB298 (200/GN)
Gannet AS.1	Mar 1955 - Nov 1957	XA335 (620/GN)
Gannet T.2	Mar 1955 - Nov 1957	XG878 (622/GN)
Whirlwind HAR.3	Aug 1959 - Dec 1960	XG577 (762)
Whirlwind HAS.7	Sep 1959 - Aug 1962	XK939 (789)
Whirlwind HAS.22	Feb 1960 - Jul 1961	WV223 (781)
Wessex HAS.1	Jul 1962 - May 1978	XS128 (522/PO)
Wessex HAS.3	Mar 1967 - Dec 1982	XS119 (527/PO)
Sea King HAS.1	Jul 1970 - Dec 1975	XV670 (664/PO)

737X Flight

Aircraft Equipment	Period of Service	Example
Anson 1	Apr 1950 - Jul 1951	MG731 (081/LP)
Barracuda TR.3	Jun 1951 - Jul 1951	ME292
Firefly 5	Apr 1950 - Jan 1951	WB251
Firefly AS.6	Jan 1951 - Jul 1951	WD871 (022)

Fairey Firefly AS.5 VT486 '206/GN' of No.737 Squadron, Eglinton in 1953. (J.D.R.Rawlings)

Commanding Officers
Lt(A) JR Dimsdale
    RNVR   22 Feb 1943
Squadron disbanded 28 Sep 1943
L/C(A) LP Dunne
    RNVR   15 Mar 1944
L/C(A) GJ Staveley
    RNVR   9 Nov 1944
L/C FV Jones RNVR 5 Mar 1945
Squadron disbanded 12 Nov 1945
Lt(A) JL Appleby
    RN (temp)   30 Mar 1949
L/C WC Simpson
    DSC RN   10 May 1949
L/C A Turnbull RN 15 Dec 1949
L/C LG Morris RN 14 Jun 1950
L/C JLW Thompson
    RN   31 Jan 1952
L/C JD Honywill RN 29 Jul 1953
L/C DW Pennick RN 6 Jan 1955
L/C RDR Hawkesworth
    DSC RN   3 May 1956
Squadron disbanded 22 Nov 1957
L/C HMA Hayes RN 28 Aug 1959
L/C GF Stride RN 15 Feb 1960
L/C PE Bailey RN 8 Aug 1961
L/C R Leonard
  OBE DFC AFC RN 11 Apr 1963
L/C TMB Seymour
    RN   30 Nov 1964
L/C MGW White RN 1 Oct 1965
L/C AG Claridge RN 28 Jul 1967
L/C MJ Holmes RN 11 Dec 1968
L/C KF Harding RN 16 Dec 1970
L/C JM Neville
  -Rolfe RN   7 Aug 1972
L/C GP Stock RN 28 Mar 1975
L/C M Fitzgerald
    RN   19 Dec 1975
L/C AN Law RN 5 Dec 1977
L/C CR Green RN 4 Jun 1979
L/C AB Gough RN 11 Sep 1980
L/C MS Tennant RN 18 Dec 1981
Squadron disbanded 4 Feb 1983

Squadron bases
Dunino	22 Feb 1943
Squadron disbanded	28 Sep 1943
Inskip	15 Mar 1944
Arbroath	28 Aug 1944
Burscough	15 Apr 1945
Squadron disbanded	12 Nov 1945
Eglinton	30 Mar 1949
ADDLs at Limavady early 1950s	
Squadron disbanded	22 Nov 1957
Portland	28 Aug 1959
Squadron disbanded	7 Feb 1983

No.737X Flt

Squadron bases
Lee-on-Solent	19 Apr 1950
HMS Indefatigable	27 Jan 1951
North Front	7 Feb 1951
Lee-on-Solent	25 Apr 1951
Eglinton	11 Jun 1951
Redes No.744 Sqdn	20 Jul 1951

No.737 Squadron 'O' Flight (Arctic Flight)

Squadron bases
Portland	14 Nov 1973
RFA Olna	4 Jan 1974
Portland	5 Mar 1974
Flight disbanded	10 Apr 1974

No.737 Oscar Flight

Squadron bases
Portland	19 Feb 1976
RFA Tidepool	19 Apr 1976
Portland	27 May 1976
Flight disbanded	11 Sep 1976

Fairey Gannet AS.1 WN415 '618' of No.737 Squadron, Eglinton in 1957. (Don Hannah)

Westland Wessex HAS.3 XM327 '401/KE' of HMS Kent Flight, No.737 Squadron in 1976. (MAP)

No.738 Squadron

Badge: On a blue field, a foul anchor, erect gold, in front of a ray of lightning in bend white, the whole surmounted by a Pegasus courant also white

Motto: Parare bellum (Prepare for war)

No.738 Squadron formed at Quonset Point on 1 February 1943 with Corsairs, Martlets and Harvards as a Pilot Training squadron. It moved to Lewiston on 31 July 1943 where Avengers were also used. Here No.738 provided advanced carrier training for pilots who had received their preliminary training at various US Naval Air Stations. They were taught British flying methods, and instruction included map reading, flight information, patrol formation, simulated forced landings and dummy deck landings, navigation exercises over the sea, anti-submarine bombing and night flying. TBR aircrew were also trained towards providing complete crews for Avenger squadrons. On completion of their training, pilots and crews were assigned to new first line squadrons forming up in the USA. The squadron moved on 14 February 1945 to Brunswick where it disbanded on 31 July 1945.

On 1 May 1950, No.738 reformed at Culdrose out of No.736 Squadron as part of the Naval Air Fighter School, controlled by the 52nd Training Air Group. Equipped mainly with Seafire F.17s and Sea Furies, newly qualified pilots were taught the operational techniques of air-to-air and air-to-ground firing, prior to joining first line squadrons. Part of the squadron broke away in August 1951 to become No.759 Squadron, and No.738 then standardised on Sea Furies, those of the disbanding No.736 Squadron being added as 'A' Flight in August 1952. 'A' Flight was then responsible for fighter combat training and 'B' Flight for ground attack training.

On 9 November 1953 No.738 moved to Lossiemouth, and here Sea Hawks and Sea Vampire T.22s arrived in May 1954, the Sea Furies departing in March 1955. The squadron's task was to familiarise American trained pilots with British methods and be responsible for all conversions of British-trained piston-engined pilots to jet aircraft, the Command Instrument Flight being also attached to the squadron.

The Sea Vampires left in March 1955, to be replaced by the Sea Hawks of No.736 Squadron. The Sea Hawks in turn departed in December 1958, to be replaced by Sea Venoms for all weather fighter training in the day fighter and strike role. In late 1958 the parent formation was renamed the Naval Air Fighter and Strike School, with No.738 becoming the Sea Venom OFS Parts I and II, providing refresher conversion and instrument-flying training. Sea Hawks returned from No.736 Squadron in June 1960, but were phased out when Hunter GA.11s and T.8s arrived in June 1962, and it then became an Advanced Training Squadron. Tasks included low-level navigation, ground attack and air-to-air weapons training. Owing to congestion at Lossiemouth No.738 moved on 1 January 1964 to Brawdy, where it operated purely as Phase II of the Advanced Flying Training Course, giving training in fighter tactics and weapon release to pupils from No.759 Squadron. It disbanded on 8 May 1970.

Identification Markings

Avenger *1BA+* later *1V17 to 19V17*, Harvard *1BS+*, Martlet *2BA+*, Corsair *3BA+*. From 5.50 Seafire *161-189/CW*, Firebrand *180-183/CW*, Sea Hornet *450-457/CW*, Sea Fury FB.11 *100-149/CW:CU*, T.20 *200-207/CW:CU*. From 11.53 Sea Fury FB.1/Sea Hawk *100-149/LM*, Sea Fury T.20/Sea Vampire T.22 *201-212/LM*, from 1.56 all types *629-656/LM:BY*, from 7.65 Hunter *785-795/BY*.

Hawker Sea Fury FB.11 WG603 '138/CW' of No.738 Squadron, Culdrose in 1953. (via Brian Lowe)

Hawker Sea Hawker FGA.6 WV908 '641/LM' of No.738 Squadron, Lossiemouth around 1961/2. (via Brian Lowe)

Aircraft Equipment	Period of Service	Example	
Harvard III	Feb 1943 - Jul 1945	KE307	
Corsair I	Feb 1943 - Jul 1945	JT125	
Corsair II	Jul 1944 - Jul 1945	JT187	(3BD)
Martlet I	Apr 1943 -	BJ557	
Wildcat IV	Sep 1943 - Feb 1944	FN315	
Wildcat V	Jun 1943 - Jan 1944	JV359	
Avenger I	Jun 1943 - May 1945	JZ187	(8V7)
Avenger II	Dec 1943 - May 1945	JZ395	(14V7)
Avenger III	Apr 1945 - May 1945	JZ697	(18V7)
Widgeon I	Jul 1944 - Mar 1945	FP466	
Seafire F.17	May 1950 - Sep 1951	SP341	(164/CW)
Seafire F.46	May 1950 - Aug 1950	LA564	
Sea Hornet F.20	May 1950 - Aug 1951	VR837	(454/CW)
Sea Hornet PR.22	May 1950 - Aug 1951	VZ664	(451/CW)
Firebrand TF.4	May 1950 - Aug 1951	EK745	(183/CW)
Sea Fury F.10	May 1950 - Aug 1951	TF916	(109/CW)
Sea Fury FB.11	May 1950 - Mar 1955	WG603	(138/CW)
Sea Fury T.20	May 1950 - Mar 1955	WE202	(202/LM)
Sea Hawk F.1	May 1954 - Apr 1957	WF220	(120/LM)
Sea Hawk F.2	Mar 1955 - Mar 1957	WF270	(642/LM)
Sea Hawk FB.3	Mar 1955 - Jun 1958	WM999	(630/LM)
Sea Hawk FGA.4	Oct 1955 - Dec 1958	WV845	(656/LM)
Sea Hawk FGA.6	Jun 1960 - Jul 1962	XE401	(645/LM)
Sea Venom FAW.21	Oct 1957 - Sep 1960	WW203	(650/LM)
Sea Vampire T.22	May 1954 - Mar 1955	XA107	(210/LM)
	Dec 1958 - Sep 1962	XG777	(630/LM)
Hunter T.8	Jun 1962 - May 1970	XL585	(630/BY)
Hunter GA.11	Jun 1962 - May 1970	XF291	(653/BY)

Squadron bases		Squadron bases	
Quonset Point	1 Feb 1943	HMS Triumph	19-27 Oct 1952
Lewiston	31 Jul 1943	HMS Triumph	2-11 Feb 1953
Norfolk (Dt)	2-14 Jan 1945	HMS Illustrious	
Brunswick	14 Feb 1945		13-20 Mar 1953
Bar Harbour (Dt)	14-25 Apr 1945	HMS Illustrious	
Bar Harbour (Dt)	25 May 1945		10-19 May 1953
	to 2 Jun 1945	HMS Illustrious	
Norfolk (Dt)	6-8 Jun 1945		12-21 Jul 1953
Squadron disbanded	31 Jul 1945	HMS Illustrious	29 Oct 1953
Culdrose	1 May 1950		to 3 Nov 1953
DLT:		ADDLs:	
HMS Vengeance	28 Jan 1951	Predannack	to 12 Jan 1953
	to 9 Feb 1951	St.Merryn	from 12 Jan 1953
HMS Triumph	18-27 Jul 1951	Lossiemouth	9 Nov 1953
HMS Triumph	22-30 Oct 1951	Brawdy	25 Jun 1960
HMS Triumph	10-13 Dec 1951	Lossiemouth	2 Jul 1960
HMS Illustrious	1-12 Feb 1952	Brawdy	1 Jan 1964
HMS Triumph	10-22 May 1952	Squadron disbanded	8 May 1970
HMS Illustrious	21 Jul 1952		

Commanding Officers
L/C JC Reed DSC RN 1 Feb 1943
L/C(A) JP Flood
    RNVR 24 Oct 1944
L/C(A) JL Cullen RN
    16 Mar 1945
Squadron disbanded 31 Jul 1945
L/C SFF Shotton RN 1 May 1950
L/C SA Mearns
    DSC RN 19 Jan 1951
L/C HJ Abraham RN 12 Jul 1951
L/C J Robertson 3 Apr 1954
L/C H Kenworthy RN 5 Apr 1954
L/C P Carmichael
    RN 28 Sep 1954
L/C DB Morrison RN 5 Jan 1955

Commanding Officers
L/C AJ Leahy
    DSC RN 21 May 1956
L/C RJ McCandless
    DSC RN 5 Feb 1958
L/C D Monsell RN 5 Oct 1959
L/C F Hefford
    DSC RN 7 Jul 1961
L/C JW Beard RN 17 Dec 1962
L/C JW Moore RN 22 Jun 1964
L/C CAM Comins
    RN 28 Mar 1966
L/C JF Hall RN 27 Jul 1967
L/C NG Grier
    -Rees RN 2 Dec 1968
Squadron disbanded 8 May 1970

Blackburn Firebrand TF.5 EK773 '183/CW' of No.738 Squadron, Culdrose at Gibraltar around 1951. (via M.Burrrow)

No.739 Squadron

No.739 Squadron formed at Lee-on-Solent on 15 December 1942 as the Blind Approach Development Unit. Equipped with a Swordfish and a Fulmar, it undertook trials of ground and airborne equipment used in blind landing. Oxfords and Ansons were added to the strength, and in September 1943 the squadron moved to Worthy Down. From there it went in October 1944 to Donibristle, where it disbanded on 7 March 1945 to become 'C' Flight of No.778 Squadron.

On 1 May 1947, No.739 reformed at Culham as the Photographic Development Unit. Equipped mainly with Sea Mosquito TR.33s, it was to have been attached to the Central Photographic Establishment at RAF Benson, but due to hangar shortage had to use nearby Culham instead. Its terms of reference were to maintain a close liaison with the CPE, and to keep the Royal Navy appraised of the latest techniques and developments in photographic reconnaissance. An Anson and a Dominie were also used, and a Sea Fury and a Sea Hornet were later attached for camera installation and evaluation. By 1950 it had become the Strategic Reconnaissance Photographic Development Unit, but on 12 July 1950 it disbanded to become the Photographic Flight of No.703 Squadron.

Identification Markings
1942/5 unknown, 1947/50 uncoded.

Aircraft Equipment	Period of Service	Example
Swordfish I	Dec 1942 - Nov 1943	V4711
Fulmar II	Dec 1942 - Aug 1943	DR666
Oxford I	Feb 1943 - Mar 1945	
Anson I	Feb 1943 - Mar 1945	
Sea Mosquito TR.33	May 1947 - Jul 1950	TW294
Sea Hornet F.20	Aug 1949 - Jul 1950	VR858
Sea Hornet PR.22	May 1947 - Jul 1950	VW938
Anson 1	May 1949 - Dec 1949	NK641
Dominie C.1	Feb 1948 - Jul 1950	NR782
Sea Fury FB.11	Sep 1948 - Sep 1948	VW235

Squadron bases	
Lee-on-Solent	15 Dec 1942
Hinstock (Dt) by	Jun 1943
Worthy Down	14 Sep 1943
Donibristle	5 Oct 1944
Squadron disbanded	7 Mar 1945
Culham	1 May 1947
Squadron disbanded	12 Jul 1950

Commanding Officers	
Lt(A) G Smith RN	15 Dec 1942
L/C(A) G Bennett DSC RN	17 Jan 1945
Squadron disbanded	7 Mar 1945
Lt(A) BA MacCaw DSC RN	1 May 1947
Lt PS Cole DSC RN	23 Nov 1949
Squadron disbanded	12 Jul 1950

de Havilland Sea Mosquito TR.33 TW294 of No.739 Squadron at Culham Air Day in July 1947. (via Brian Lowe)

No.740 Squadron

No.740 Squadron formed at Arbroath on 4 May 1943 for Observer Training as part of No.2 Observer School. Aircraft were mainly Walruses, but one or two Swordfish and Kingfishers were also used. Flying largely took place from the River Tay at Dundee. The squadron disbanded on 5 August 1943.

On 30 December 1943, No.740 reformed at Machrihanish from the communications element of No.772 Squadron as a Communications squadron, using a variety of types including Reliants, Travellers, Dominies, Ansons and Oxfords. Its Torpedo Training Flight, equipped with Swordfish, was detached to Ayr in January 1944. No.740 Squadron disbanded at Machrihanish on 1 September 1945.

Identification Markings
1943 Walrus unknown, 1944/5 all types *M9A+*.

Aircraft Equipment	Period of Service	Example	
Kingfisher I	May 1943 - Aug 1943	FN699	
Swordfish I	May 1943 - Aug 1943	W5971	
Walrus	May 1943 - Aug 1943	X9466	
Anson I	Jan 1945 - Aug 1945	EF825	
Dominie I	Jan 1944 - Sep 1944		
Fulmar I	Jan 1944 -	N1948	
Martinet I	Nov 1944	MS808	
Master II	Nov 1944	DL903	
Oxford I	Jan 1944 - Mar 1945	T1345	
Reliant I	Dec 1943 - Aug 1945	FL157	(M9L)
Seafire L.III	Jul 1945 - Aug 1945	..319	
Sea Otter I	Oct 1944 - Aug 1945	JM873	
Swordfish II	Sep 1944 - Aug 1945	HS621	
Swordfish III	Oct 1944 - Aug 1945	NF312	
Traveller I	Jul 1944 - Nov 1944	FT527	
Walrus	Jan 1944 - Oct 1944	W2726	(M9T)

Commanding Officers	
L/C DH Angel RN	4 May 1943
Squadron disbanded	5 Aug 1943
L/C(A) LF Diggens RNVR	30 Dec 1943
L/C(A) LT Summerfield RNVR	23 Apr 1945
Squadron disbanded	1 Sep 1945

Squadron bases	
Arbroath	4 May 1943
Squadron disbanded	5 Aug 1943
Machrihanish	30 Dec 1943
Ayr (Dt)	26 Jan 1944
Squadron disbanded	1 Sep 1945

No.741 Squadron

No.741 Squadron formed at Arbroath on 1 March 1943 as an Observer Training squadron within No.2 Observer School. Equipped with Swordfish, it trained pupils up to wings standard, then passed them to No.753 to complete their training. The squadron disbanded on 19 March 1945.

On 12 August 1946, No.741 reformed at St Merryn as an Operational Flying Training Unit. Equipped with Fireflies and a few Seafires, it took over the task of Operational Flying School Part II from 7 January 1947. By the time it disbanded on 25 November 1947 its role was officially that of a modified Part II (Strike) Operational Flying Course.

Identification Markings
Swordfish *A3A+*, Firefly/Seafire *S2A+*, *S3A+* & *S5A+*.

Fairey Fireflies of No.741 Squadron St.Merryn flying in formation around 1946/47. (via Chris Ashworth)

Aircraft Equipment	Period of Service	Example
Swordfish I	Mar 1943 - Mar 1945	W5917 (A3Z)
Swordfish II	Mar 1943 - Mar 1945	HS223 (A3C)
Firefly FR.I	Aug 1946 - Nov 1947	MB725 (S2A)
Seafire L.III	Feb 1947 - Nov 1947	NN241
Harvard III	Sep 1947 - Nov 1947	EZ413

Commanding Officers		Squadron bases	
L/C(A) OH Cantrill RNVR	1 Mar 1943	Arbroath	1 Mar 1943
L/C(A) RMcA Stratton RNVR	17 Mar 1944	Squadron disbanded	19 Mar 1945
Squadron disbanded	19 Mar 1945	St.Merryn	12 Aug 1946
L/C(A) SG Cooper RN	12 Aug 1946	Squadron disbanded	25 Nov 1947
L/C(A) TW Harrington DSC & Bar RN	25 Aug 1947		
Squadron disbanded	25 Nov 1947		

No.742 Squadron

No.742 Squadron formed at Colombo on 6 December 1943 as a Communications squadron. Equipped mainly with Expediters, its task was to link up scattered RN Air Stations in the Far East. It operated regular air services between the various air stations, including four return trips each day to nearby Trincomalee. Other daily services were operated between Colombo and Madras, Colombo and Sulur (for RNAY Coimbatore), Sulur and Cochin, and Sulur and Madras (via Bangalore).

The squadron moved its headquarters to Coimbatore on 15 September 1944, where it became the RN Air Transport Squadron on 1 November 1944, with a detachment operating from Tambaram. A further move was made on 1 February 1945, to Sulur, with detachments operating from Colombo, Ratmalana and Katukurunda. When Singapore fell, three aircraft were flown there via Burma, Siam and Malaya, where the pilots flew personal flights for Rear Admiral Morse, the Flag Officer Malaya and Forward Areas (FOMFA). On 15 January 1946, 9 of the Expediters began a 6,500 miles flight in formation from Sulur to Lee-on-Solent to be returned to the United States, whilst a further 9 were shipped by sea. A few remained for duty in India and Ceylon, the headquarters moving to Katukurunda on 26 February 1946. No.742 disbanded on 31 August 1946, having flown millions of miles with only one fatal accident.

Beech Expediter FR883 of No.742 Squadron, Sulur was mispainted as FE883. Seen here after being flown to the U.K., it was an AT-7-BH Navigator in American parlance. (RAF Museum 6116-13)

Identification Markings
Uncoded in Far East, some possibly *RAA+*.

Aircraft Equipment	Period of Service	Example
Beech AT-7	Dec 1943 - Aug 1946	FR883
Expediter C.II	Jun 1944 - Aug 1946	FT985
Anson I	1944 - 1945	NK817
Walrus I	1944 - 1945	W2674
Sea Otter I	1944 - 1945	JM756
Swordfish	Dec 1943 - Oct 1945	HS548
Reliant I	Dec 1943 - Oct 1945	FL129

Squadron bases		Commanding Officers	
Colombo Racecourse	6 Dec 1943	Lt(A) TN Stack RNR	6 Dec 1943
Coimbatore	15 Sep 1944	L/C(A) R MacDermott RNVR	8 Jan 1944
Tambaram (Dt)	21 Sep 1944	L/C TN Stack RNR	29 Sep 1944
Sulur	1 Feb 1945	L/C(A) PH Parsons RN	15 Jan 1946
Katukurunda (Dt)	14 Jan 1946 to 26 Feb 1946	Squadron disbanded	31 Aug 1946
Singapore (D Flt)	Aug 1945		
Colombo Racecourse (Dt)	2-31 Oct 1945		
Ratmalana (Dt)	1 Nov 1945 to 1 Dec 1945		
Katukurunda	26 Feb 1946		
Squadron disbanded	31 Aug 1946		

No.743 Squadron

No.743 Squadron assembled at Lee-on-Solent on 10 February 1943 for passage to Canada, where it officially formed at Yarmouth, Nova Scotia on 1 March 1943 as part of No.2 Telegraphist Air Gunners School. Known by the Canadians as No.1 Naval Air Gunners School, this supplemented the UK training of TAGs, the administration being undertaken by the RCAF, whilst the Royal Navy was responsible for the training instructors, who were a mixture of RCAF and FAA pilots. Aircraft were mainly Swordfish, and by the end of June 1943 the School was operating 40 of these plus a Walrus. No.743 disbanded at Dartmouth on 30 March 1945, all training having ceased 11 days earlier.

On 18 September 1946, No.743 reformed at Dartmouth as a Fleet Requirements Unit of the Royal Canadian Navy, becoming part of No.1 Training Air Group when it formed soon afterwards. Equipped with Swordfish and Walruses, it later also acquired Harvards and Anson 5s. On 1 May 1954 it was redesignated VU32 (Utility) Squadron.

Identification Markings
Walrus *Z1+*, Swordfish *single letters & letter/number combinations*, Harvard/Avenger/Swordfish *VG-TFA to VG-TFZ*.

Aircraft Equipment	Period of Service	Example
Swordfish II	Mar 1943 - Mar 1945	HS488(K3)
Walrus II	Mar 1943 - Oct 1944	Z1768(Z3)
Swordfish II	Sep 1946 - Nov 1948	NE926
Walrus II	Sep 1946 - Dec 1947	Z1781
Harvard II	1947 - May 1954	RCAF 2898
Anson V	Apr 1949 - Sep 1949	RCAF12435

Commanding Officers
L/C(A) R Gillett RNVR 1 Mar 1943
Squadron disbanded 30 Mar 1945
Lt JN Donaldson RCN 18 Sep 1946
L/C WE Widdows RCN 30 Aug 1947
L/C CG Smith RCN 1 Dec 1948
L/C RJ Watson RCN 12May 1952
Squadron disbanded 1 May 1954

Squadron bases
Yarmouth 1 Mar 1943
Squadron disbanded 30 Mar 1945
Dartmouth 18 Sep 1946
Sqdn redes VU32 1 May 1954

No.744 Squadron

Badge: On a field barry wavy of ten white and blue, a sun in splendor charged with an eagle's head affronte proper
Motto: *Nemo solus satis sapit* (No one (or "man") knows enough)

No.744 Squadron assembled on 10 February 1943 at Lee-on-Solent for passage to Canada, where it joined No.743 Squadron in No.2 TAG School when the squadron officially formed at Yarmouth, Nova Scotia on 1 March 1943. It operated Seamews, but these caused difficulties due to lack of strength in the tailwheels, which tended to collapse on landing. The squadron was redesignated No.754 Squadron in June 1944 because another No.744 Squadron now existed in the United Kingdom, presumably due to an administrative error.

This second No.744 had formed at Maydown on 6 March 1944, for Merchant Aircraft Carrier training. Equipped with 12 Swordfish plus 6 reserves, it provided trained crews for the locally based No.836 Squadron, live armament and anti-submarine training being given by a detachment at Machrihanish. The course included experience in deck landing aboard escort carriers in the Firth of Clyde. One flight was equipped with Barracudas by late 1944, and in May 1945 the Swordfish were withdrawn. Fireflies were briefly used from July 1945, but on 22 September the squadron reduced from 12 Barracudas and 6 Fireflies to 6 Barracuda IIIs, the Fireflies going to No.767 Squadron at East Haven.

The squadron moved in October 1945 to Eglinton, having by then become fully engaged on Anti-Submarine training. A flight of six aircraft was detached to Ballykelly from 27-28 November, returning to Eglinton in March 1946. Ansons were also flown from August 1946. The squadron operated at this stage in tandem with No.719, from which it took trainee crews. Co-operating with the Derry Squadron, which comprised *Loch*-Class frigates, and with submarines, it came under the aegis of the Joint Anti-Submarine School in the former Army barracks at Londonderry. Also involved was a sonobuoy tracking school at Maydown, which by then had ceased to be an airfield, having been turned over to married quarters, sheep and cattle. When No.744 was considered up to strength with trained crews it was elevated to first line status, and accordingly became No.815 Squadron on 1 December 1947.

Fairey Swordfish 'N7B' of No.744 Squadron, Maydown around 1944/5. (via Brian Lowe)

No.744 next reformed on 20 July 1951, by redesignating 'X' Flight of No.737 Squadron, as a Trials and Development squadron within the Naval Air Anti-Submarine School at Eglinton. Equipped with a few Fireflies, Barracudas and Ansons, it engaged in trials and development of search receivers to detect submarine radar. 'Investigation Pointer' was a trial conversion of the Barracuda ASV Mk.XI for this purpose, and another such project was code-named 'Orange Harvest', which eventually saw service in RAF Shackletons. After trials at Farnborough, two of the squadron's Fireflies were fitted with a new homing device for finding sonobuoys in the water without need of smoke markers, and these went to Malta in October 1951 for trials with submarines and ships. The squadron also acted as Station Flight by 1953, with an assortment of Firefly trainers, Sea Princes and SAR Dragonfly HR.3s, until disbanding at Eglinton on 1 March 1954.

On the same day, No.744 reformed at Culdrose as the Naval Air-Sea Warfare Development Unit, to work in conjunction with the RAFs ASWDU at St Mawgan, to where the squadron itself moved on 23 October 1954. Equipment was initially Firefly AS.6s, on which various trials were carried out under such code names as 'Talbe', 'Homer' and 'Random'. Gannets arrived in May 1955, followed two months later by Avengers, the Fireflies being withdrawn at the end of that year. An 'X' Flight was formed on 11 June 1955 for evaluation of radar jamming trials, this becoming No.745 Squadron on 23 April 1956. In October 1955, No.744 was restyled the Naval Anti-Submarine Development Squadron. The Avengers were withdrawn in February 1956, and on 20 April 1956 dummy rocket projectile dives were commenced at Lilstock Range. Due to the Suez situation, the squadron disbanded on 31 October 1956, its trials task then being carried out elsewhere within ASWDU.

Identification Markings
Seamew *letter/number combinations*, Swordfish *K7A+ & N7A+*, Avenger *N6A+*, Barracuda *N4A+ & N6A+*, later *300-311/JR*, Sea Prince/Anson *400-410/GN*, Firefly *236-239/CU*, Avenger *394-399/CU*, Gannet *401-403/CU*.

Aircraft Equipment	Period of Service	Example	
Seamew I	Mar 1943 - Feb 1944	JW614	
Swordfish II	Mar 1943 - Jun 1944	HS507	(O2)
Swordfish I	Mar 1944 - Apr 1945	W5973	
Swordfish II	Mar 1944 - Apr 1945	HS330	(N7F)
Swordfish III	Feb 1945 - May 1945	NS120	(N7X)
Reliant I	Jul 1944 - Aug 1945	FK889	
Avenger II	Oct 1944 - Sep 1945	JZ303	
Barracuda II	Nov 1944 - Aug 1945	MX681	
Barracuda TR.III	Mar 1945 - Dec 1947	RJ945	(309/JR)
Firefly I	Jul 1945 - Sep 1945	Z1955	
Anson I	Aug 1946 - Dec 1947	MH228	
Seafire III	May 1946	RX335	
Oxford I	Sep 1947	PH364	
Barracuda III	Jul 1951 - Jul 1953	RJ933	
Anson I	Jul 1951 - Nov 1953	NK833	(400/GN)
Sea Otter I	Jul 1951 - Jan 1952	RD895	(903/GN)
Dominie I	Jul 1951 - Sep 1953	NF861	(900/GN)
Firefly AS.6	Jul 1951 - Mar 1954	WD871	(022)
Firefly T.2	Oct 1953 - Feb 1954	DK478	(247/GN)
Dragonfly HR.3	Dec 1952 - Feb 1954	WG724	(901/GN)
Sea Prince T.1	Aug 1952 - Feb 1954	WP321	(406/GN)
Firefly T.1	Aug 1952 - Feb 1954	Z1943	(245/GN)
Firefly AS.6	Mar 1954 - Nov 1955	WD894	(239/CU)
Gannet AS.1	May 1955 - Oct 1956	WN393	(661/CU)
Sea Fury FB.11	May 1954 - Oct 1956	WE790	
Avenger AS.5	Jul 1955 - Feb 1956	XB395	(395/CU)

Squadron bases
Yarmouth	1 Mar 1943
Redes 754 Squadron	Jun 1944
Maydown	6 Mar 1944
(Dt Machrihanish)	
Eglinton	29 Sep 1945
Ballykelly (Dt6)	27 Nov 1945
to	1 May 1946
Maydown (Dt)	1 May 1946
to	27 Jan 1947

Squadron bases
HMS Theseus (Dt)	7-17 Nov 1946
Squadron disbanded	1 Dec 1947
Eglinton	20 Jul 1951
Hal Far (Dt)	3 Oct 1951
to	22 Nov 1951
Squadron disbanded	1 Mar 1954
Culdrose	1 Mar 1954
St.Mawgan	23 Oct 1954
Squadron disbanded	31 Oct 1956

Commanding Officers
Lt(A) EJ Trerise RN	1 Mar 1943
Squadron disbanded	Feb 1944
L/C(A) CMT Hallewell RN	6 Mar 1944
L/C(A) DW Phillips DSC RN	27 Feb 1945
Lt(A) JHB Bedells RN	27 Feb 1946

Commanding Officers
Lt(A) RHW Blake RN	20 May 1946
Squadron disbanded	1 Dec 1947
L/C FE Cowtan RN	20 Jul 1951
Squadron disbanded	1 Mar 1954
L/C FGJ Arnold RN	1 Mar 1954
L/C R Fulton RN	4 Jan 1956
Squadron disbanded	31 Oct 1956

Fairey Firefly T.1 DK478 '247/GN' of No.744 Squadron, Eglinton at White Waltham in 1953 (Don Hannah)

No.745 Squadron

No.745 Squadron assembled at Lee-on-Solent on 10 February 1943 for passage to Canada, where it officially formed at Yarmouth, Nova Scotia on 1 March 1943 as part of No.2 Telegraphist Air Gunners School, which was known somewhat confusingly by the Canadians as No.1 Naval Air Gunners School. Equipment was Swordfish and Anson IIs, plus a few Seamews. The squadron disbanded on 30 March 1945.

On 23 April 1956, No.745 reformed at Eglinton from 'X' Flight of No.744 Squadron as a Radar Jamming Trials unit. It was equipped with four Avengers modified for tactical evaluation of the 'Orange Harvest' equipment, and known as TS.5s. From time to time during 1956 aircraft were sent to St Mawgan for calibration trials with the Air Sea Warfare Development Unit. Squadron headquarters moved to Ballykelly in May 1957, whilst the Eglinton runways were being resurfaced. At the same time, the aircraft went to Culdrose for a few days, returning later to Ballykelly and then Eglinton. In the autumn of 1957 trials were carried out in HMS *Bulwark* and HMS *Albion*, but on 1 November 1957 the squadron disbanded at Eglinton.

Fairey Swordfish IV conversion HS325 'Q' of No.745 Squadron, Yarmouth, Nova Scotia around 1944/5. (Bert Joss)

Identification Markings
Swordfish/Anson *letter/number combinations*, Avenger *795-798/GN*.

Aircraft Equipment	Period of Service	Example
Seamew I	Mar 1943 - 1944	FN495
Anson I	Dec 1943 - 1944	AX288
Anson II	Mar 1943 - Mar 1945	JS162(G2)
Swordfish II	Mar 1943 - Mar 1945	HS491(P3)
Swordfish IV	1944 - Mar 1945	HS325(Q)
Avenger TS.5	Apr 1956 - Oct 1957	XB355(795/GN)

Squadron bases
Yarmouth 1 Mar 1943
Squadron disbanded 30 Mar 1945
Eglinton 23 Apr 1956
Ballykelly 2 May 1957
Culdrose 6 May 1957
Ballykelly 16 May 1957
Ford 20 Aug 1957
HMS Albion (Dt2) 3-29 Sep 1957
Eglinton 22 Sep 1957
HMS Bulwark (Dt2) 11-17 Oct 1957
Squadron disbanded 1 Nov 1957

Commanding Officers
L/C(A) RH Ovey RNVR 1 Mar 1943
L/C(A) FAH Harley RN 6 Nov 1944
L/C(A) EJ Trerise RN Dec 1944
Squadron disbanded 30 Mar 1945
L/C MF Bowen RN 16 Apr 1956
Squadron disbanded 1 Nov 1957

Grumman Avenger XB395 "795/GN" of No.745 Squadron, Maydown in 1957. (via Brian Lowe)

No.746 Squadron

No.746 Squadron formed at Lee-on-Solent on 23 November 1942 as the Naval Night Fighter Interception Unit, moving to Ford in December. The unit was formed to work with the RAF Fighter Interception Unit at Ford, initial equipment being 3 Fulmar night fighters and 3 Fulmar target aircraft. In May 1943, Fireflies were received, including some fitted out as night fighters, and the unit's tasks were redefined. It was to continue to work in close liaison with the FIU and also the Naval Fighter Direction Centre at Yeovilton, its primary task being to develop and adapt night fighter tactics for naval aircraft, and also the operational use of night fighter and interceptor equipment. It was to carry out service, operational and tactical trials of night fighter and interception equipment, and to pay visits to naval night fighter units to obtain first hand information on their experiences, so as to keep up to date the latest tactical information about equipment. In October 1943 some of the squadron pilots undertook intruder operations with the FIU under the control of RAF No.11 Group.

No.746 vacated Ford for Wittering on 6 May 1944, the aerodrome being then required for invasion work. From about that time squadron members were detached to Defford, for radar development work with the Telecommunications Flying Unit. The Firefly night fighters were used for a time against He 111/V-1 bomb carriers off the East coast. In October 1944 the squadron returned to Ford, and in January 1945 'A' Flight moved to Hatston for ADDLs and pre-embarkation exercises, prior to embarking pairs of aircraft in various escort carriers, this flight becoming an operational sub-unit shortly before VE-Day. In March 1945 No.746 was restyled the Naval Night Fighter Development Squadron, and its task redefined as testing the suitability of naval fighters and their equipment for night operations, and also testing experimental equipment. Hellcat night fighters were added to the equipment, and it continued to work in liaison with what had by then become the Fighter Interception Development Squadron of the Central Fighter Establishment, and also with the Bomber Support Development Unit at Swanton Morley. No.746 moved to West Raynham on 23 August 1945, this being the new home of the CFE, but on 30 January 1946 it disbanded into No.787 Squadron.

Identification Markings
Fulmar *LOA+*, Firefly/Hellcat unknown.

Aircraft Equipment	Period of Service	Example
Fulmar IINF	Nov 1942 - 1943	DR714 (LOF)
Fulmar IITT	Nov 1942 - 1943	X8708
Firefly INF	May 1943 - Jan 1946	X1845
Firefly NF.II	Feb 1944 - Jan 1946	Z1870
Hellcat IINF	Feb 1945 - Jan 1946	JZ895
Seafire F.17	Dec 1945	SX164
Proctor Ia	Nov 1942 - Apr 1944	BV551
Reliant	Apr 1944 - Nov 1945	FK882

Squadron bases
Lee-on-Solent 23 Nov 1942
Ford 1 Dec 1942
Wittering 3 Apr 1944
Lee-on-Solent (Dt) 24 Aug 1944 to 14 Sep 1945
Ford 1 Oct 1944
'A' Flight:
Hatston 5 Jan 1945
HMS Smiter (Dt) 5-12 Jan 1945
HMS Ravager (Dt) 25-26 Jan 1945
HMS Premier (Dt2) 17 Jan 1945 to 13 Feb 1945
HMS Searcher (Dt2) 9 Feb 1945
HMS Premier (Dt2) 17-23 Feb 1945
HMS Searcher (Dt) 14 Mar 1945 to 30 Mar 1945
HMS Premier (Dt2) 12-13 Apr 1945
HMS Searcher (Dt2) 5-13 Apr 1945
HMS Searcher (Dt2) 17-25 Apr 1945
Ford 10 May 1945
West Raynham 23 Aug 1945
Hatston (Dt) 14 Sep 1945
Squadron disbanded 30 Jan 1946

Commanding Officers
Mjr LA Harris DSC RM 23 Nov 1942
L/C(A) GLC Davies DSC RN 30 Jul 1945
Squadron disbanded 30 Jan 1946

No.747 Squadron

No.747 Squadron formed at Fearn on 22 March 1943 as a Torpedo Bomber Reconnaissance Pool squadron. Initial equipment was 3 Swordfish, 3 Barracudas and a few Ansons. The squadron soon became an Operational Training Unit, the Ansons being used for radar training. On 9 June 1943 it moved to Inskip as part of No.1 Naval OTU, and Albacores were added for an intensive crew training course. No.747 moved with No.1N.OTU back to Fearn on 26 January 1944, and then to Ronaldsway 14-17 July 1944. The squadron headquarters moved with the OTU to Crail on 15 November 1945, but 'B' Flight, equipped with Ansons, remained at Ronaldsway. The squadron disbanded on 20 December 1945, several of the aircrew being posted to No.717 Squadron.

Aircraft Equipment	Period of Service	Example
Albacore I	Mar 1943 - Sep 1943	X9215
Anson I	Mar 1943 - Dec 1945	EG309
Barracuda I	Mar 1943 - Jul 1943	DN628
Barracuda II	Mar 1943 - Dec 1945	P9828 (K2L)
Barracuda III	Jan 1945 - Dec 1945	MD901 (R3B)
Reliant	Sep 1945 - Dec 1945	FK966
Swordfish I	Mar 1943 - Feb 1944	V4644
Swordfish II	Jun 1943 - Jul 1943	HS166
Walrus II	Jul 1943 - Apr 1944	W3073

Identification Markings
Barracuda *K2A+* by 12.43, to *F2A+* 1.44, to *R2A+* to *R7A+* 7.44. Other types unknown.

Squadron bases
Fearn 22 Mar 1943
Inskip 9 Jun 1943
Fearn 26 Jan 1944
Ronaldsway 14 Jul 1944
Crail 15 Nov 1945
'B' Flt remained at Ronaldsway
Squadron disbanded 20 Dec 1945

Commanding Officers
L/C JA Ievers RN 22 Mar 1943
L/C(A) FA Swanton DSC RN 13 Sep 1943
L/C(A) TM Bassett RNZNVR 1 Mar 1944
L/C(A) RD Kingdon DSC RNVR 6 Nov 1944
Squadron disbanded 20 Dec 1945

Fairey Barracuda 'R3B' of No.747 Squadron, Ronaldsway. (RAF Museum 6061-3)

No.748 Squadron

Badge: Winged crown and wreaths, to the left a sun and four rays (unofficial design?)
Motto: We labour that others may learn

Aircraft Equipment	Period of Service	Example	
Fulmar I	Oct 1942 - Apr 1943	N2007	
Fulmar II	Oct 1942 - Mar 1943	X8775	
Hurricane I	Oct 1942 - Dec 1943	V6850	
Proctor Ia	Jan 1943 - Mar 1943	P6068	
Sea Hurricane Ib	Feb 1943 - Jul 1943	P3530	
Sea Hurricane IIc	Jun 1943 - Feb 1944	NF716	
Martlet I	Oct 1942 - Jan 1944	AX829	(S7O)
Martlet IV	Sep 1943 - Sep 1944	FN278	
Reliant I	Nov 1943 - Jul 1944	FK931	
Blenheim IV	Nov 1943 - Mar 1944	V6073	
Master I	Oct 1942 - Jan 1944	T8284	
Master GT.II	May 1944	DM443	
Spitfire I	Oct 1942 - Apr 1943	X4270	
Spitfire Va	Feb 1943 - Jul 1944	R6722	(S7H)
Spitfire Vb	Dec 1942	BL243	
Spitfire Vb/hooked	Mar 1945 - Feb 1946	P8708	
Seafire Ib	Jun 1943 - Feb 1946	PA110	(S7B)
Seafire IIc	Mar 1943 - Feb 1946	MA984	
Seafire III	Nov 1945 - Feb 1946	RX217	(S7A)
Harvard III	Jun 1945 - Feb 1946	EZ268	(W)
Corsair II	Mar 1944 - 1945	JT407	
Corsair III	May 1944 - Nov 1945	JS511	(P7AE)
Corsair IV	Mar 1944 - Jan 1945	JT401	
Wildcat V	May 1945 - Mar 1946	JV636	
Wildcat VI	Sep 1945 - Mar 1946	JV881	
Firefly I	Jun 1944 - Jun 1945	Z2023	
Hellcat I	May 1944 - May 1945	FN332	(P7AP)

No.748 Squadron formed at St Merryn on 12 October 1942 as a Fighter Pool squadron. Initial equipment was 4 Fulmars, 4 Martlets, 4 Spitfires and 4 Hurricanes, with which it undertook refresher flying. In March 1943 it become No.10 Naval Operational Training Unit, and Seafires were added to the complement soon afterwards. The squadron moved to Henstridge on 4 February 1944, and then to Yeovilton 9-10 March 1944, where Corsairs, Hellcats, and during June a few Fireflies, arrived. Moving to Dale on 1 October 1944, the squadron provided refresher courses on Corsairs, Hellcats, Wildcats and Seafires as well as a Firefly conversion course. A final move occurred on 14 August 1945, back to St Merryn, still as No.10N.OTU, and it disbanded there on 11 February 1946.

Identification Markings
All types S7A+ 1943/4, P7A+ from 10.44, to S7A+ 8.45.

Commanding Officers
L/C(A) RG French
  RNVR   12 Oct 1942
L/C(A) BHC Nation
  RN   5 Nov 1943
L/C(A) JG Smith
  RNVR   20 Jul 1944
L/C(A) PJE Nichols
  RNVR   5 Aug 1945
L/C(A) PCS Chilton
  RN   17 Dec 1945
Squadron disbanded 11 Feb 1946

Squadron bases
St.Merryn   12 Oct 1942
Chivenor (Dt)   2 Sep 1943
                       to 3 Feb 1944
Yeovilton (B Flt)   11 Oct 1943
Henstridge   4 Feb 1944
Yeovilton   9 Mar 1944
Dale   1 Oct 1944
St.Merryn   14 Aug 1945
(ADDLs Davidstowe Moor)
Squadron disbanded 11 Feb 1946

Grumman Martlet I of No.748 Squadron at St.Merryn. (Dick Yeo)

No.749 Squadron

No.749 Squadron formed at Piarco, Trinidad on 1 January 1941 as an Observer Training squadron within No.1 Observer School. The squadron flew amphibious aircraft, initial equipment being four Walruses, but the Grumman Goose was also in use by 1942. Between January and April 1942 the squadron undertook local anti-submarine patrols. By 1944 it had reached a peak strength of 27 Walruses and over 30 Gooses. Some of the Palisadoes-based Kingfishers of No.703 Squadron were also used on occasion for observer training. No.749 Squadron disbanded at Piarco on 9 October 1945.

Identification Markings
Walrus W2QA+ & W2QAA+, Goose W2A+ & W2AA+, Anson A1-A4.

Aircraft Equipment	Period of Service	Example	
Walrus	Jan 1941 - Oct 1945	W2674	
Goose I	Mar 1942 - Oct 1945	FP503	(W2W)
Anson I	Jun 1945 - Oct 1945	NL123	(A4)

Squadron bases
Piarco   1 Jan 1941
Squadron disbanded 9 Oct 1945

Commanding Officers
Lt(A) JC Moore
  RNVR   1 Jan 1941
L/C(A) GH Winn
  RNVR   1 Dec 1941
L/C(A) AE Worby
  RNVR   7 Apr 1943
L/C(A) PG Lee
  RNVR   1 Aug 1945
Squadron disbanded 9 Oct 1945

Supermarine Walrus L2739 'W2QO' of No.749 Squadron, Piarco. (FAA Museum).

No.750 Squadron

Badge: On a blue field, a Greek runner white, in his dexter hand a torch fired proper, in his sinister hand a sword white, over water barry wavy white and blue
Motto: Teach and strike

No.750 Squadron formed at Ford on 24 May 1939 out of the RN Observers School, which then became No.1 Observers School. Initial equipment was Sharks and a few Ospreys, and from about May 1940 these used Yeovilton for dispersal, prior to its completion as a naval air station. The majority of the squadron moved there when Ford was blitzed in August 1940, but this was unsatisfactory, and it was decided to send the school overseas. Accordingly training ceased after 28 September and 14 days later the personnel took passage to Trinidad, the school reopening at Piarco Savannah, to give it its full title, on 5 November. The Ospreys were left behind, but the Sharks had been shipped to Trinidad and it was intended that these should be supplemented by Swordfish, but the latter could not be spared and Albacores were issued instead. The last Shark left in 1942, around 40 being in use at the peak. These were replaced by further Albacores, of which eventually over 70 were in use. A few Barracudas were also received in late 1944, and the Albacores were retired around VE-Day. No.750 disbanded at Piarco on 10 October 1945.

On 17 April 1952 No.750 reformed at St Merryn from the Barracuda element of No.796 Squadron, the two units operating as Observer School Part II. Equipment was initially 12 Barracudas and 4 Ansons, but these were pensioned off early in 1953 with the advent of Firefly T.7s and Sea Prince T.1s. The school moved to Culdrose on 30 November 1953, where it became the Observer and Air Signal School during 1955, and under a reorganisation of duties on 13 March the Fireflies went to No.796 Squadron. No.750 then concentrated on Part I training of Observers, who had basic navigation instruction in the Sea Princes before transferring to No.796, and also undertook the training of Air Telegraphists in W/T morse and operation of the Sono-Buoy system. No.796 disbanded in October 1958, and in May 1959 No.750 reverted to the title of Observer School.

Between 12 and 14 October 1959 the squadron's 9 Sea Princes were flown out to Malta, where it began observer training from Hal Far in much kinder weather conditions. Sea Venoms arrived in July 1960 for high level navigation and some FRU work, and navigation exercises frequently took the aircraft to such places as Idris, Naples, Palma, Rome and Sigonella. In 1965 the squadron returned home, the Sea Venoms flying to Lossiemouth on 23 June, to be joined there on 5 July by the Sea Princes. Overseas navigation flights continued, though on a reduced scale, and visits were made to Amsterdam, Brussels, Copenhagen, Oslo, Vallenburg and Vaerloese. In 1969 the squadron won the Bambara Trophy for the best all round flying performance by a headquarters flight. On 26 September 1972 No.750 found itself back at Culdrose, still flying the now elderly Sea Princes until these were replaced from October 1978 by Jetstream T.2s, with which it continues in the observer training task. A number of Jetstream T.3s served with the squadron from April 1986, mainly for communications purposes, these being all transferred to Heron Flight at Yeovilton by April 1993.

Individual Markings
Swordfish *W1A+, W1AA+ & W0-A+*, Albacore *Nos.1-78*, Barracuda *B1, B2, B3+*. From 4.52 Barracuda/Firefly *300-316/MF:SR*, Anson/Sea Prince *600-612/MF:SR:CU*. From 1.56 all types *664-679/HF*, also *590-599/HF*, to *618-680/LM 7.65*, to *560-579/CU 9.72*.

Fairey Albacore N4228 '79' of No.750 Squadron, Piarco, Trinidad. (via FAA Museum)

Aircraft Equipment	Period of Service	Example
Shark II	May 1939 - Jun 1942	L2361 (W1W)
Albacore I	Dec 1940 - Apr 1945	BF615
Barracuda II	Nov 1944 - Oct 1945	LS797 (B9)
Harvard	Feb 1945 - Aug 1945	? (4)
Anson I	Apr 1952 - May 1953	NK941 (604)
Barracuda TR.3	Apr 1952 - Jul 1953	ME281 (311/MF)
Sea Prince T.1	Feb 1953 - May 1979	WM739 (574/CU)
Firefly T.7	Apr 1953 - Mar 1955	WK371 (308/SR)
Oxford I	Mar 1957 - Apr 1957	NM355 ("730/CU")
Sea Vampire T.22	Jan 1962 - May 1965	XA110 (599/HF)
Sea Venom FAW.21	Jul 1960 - Oct 1961	XG618 (678/HF)
Sea Venom FAW.22	Aug 1961 - Mar 1970	XG692 (668/LM)
Sea Devon C.20	Mar 1957 - Aug 1961	XJ349 (665/CU)
Jetstream T.1	Jan 1976 - 1976	XX475 (572)
Jetstream T.2	Oct 1978 - to date	ZA111 (574/CU)
Jetstream T.3	Apr 1986 - Apr 1993	ZK441 (579)

Commanding Officers
Cdr(A) JHF Burroughs RN 24 May 1939
L/C CA Kingsley-Rowe RN 1 Feb 1940
L/C(A) TG Stubley RN 30 Sep 1940
L/C(A) EK Lee RNVR 1 Dec 1941
L/C(A) FE Darlow RNVR 1 Oct 1943
L/C(A) JH Crook RNVR 6 Dec 1943
L/C(A) H Whitaker RNVR 15 Mar 1945
L/C(A) FB Gardner RNVR 1 Aug 1945
Squadron disbanded 10 Oct 1945
L/C PH Frudd RN 17 Apr 1952
L/C EF Pritchard RN 19 Jan 1953
L/C P A Jordan RN 10 Feb 1954 (temp)
L/C JCN Shrubsole RN 15 Mar 1954
L/C HP Allingham RN 25 Jun 1956
L/C MF Bowen RN 14 Jan 1958
L/C ATJ Dibell RN 10 Sep 1958
L/C ET Genge RN 7 Oct 1958
L/C P Cane RN 22 Sep 1960
L/C AC Whitton RN 19 Oct 1962
L/C K Sinclair MBE RN 11 Nov 1964
L/C CR Mellor RN 16 Jul 1966
L/C JS Humphreys MBE RN 16 Aug 1968
L/C NC Atkinson RN 16 Jun 1970
L/C CK Manning RN 1 Sep 1972
L/C JH Eagle RN 29 Mar 1974
L/C LA Wilkinson RN 20 Dec 1974
L/C NLC Featherstone RN 8 Nov 1976
L/C PM Burgess RN 20 Jul 1979
L/C RE Just RN 10 Apr 1981
L/C CRW Griffin RN 23 Jun 1982
L/C JDO McDonald RN 20 Aug 1984
L/C A Rees RN 6 Mar 1986
L/C DLW Sim RN 7 Oct 1988
L/C IV Munday RN 10 Mar 1991
L/C JE Ward RN 23 Mar 1993

Squadron bases
Ford	24 May 1939
(dispersal at Yeovilton from May 1940)	
in transit	12 Oct 1940
Piarco	5 Nov 1940
Squadron disbanded	10 Oct 1945
St.Merryn	17 Apr 1952
Culdrose	30 Nov 1953
Hal Far	13 Oct 1959
Lossiemouth	23 Jun 1965
Culdrose	26 Sep 1972

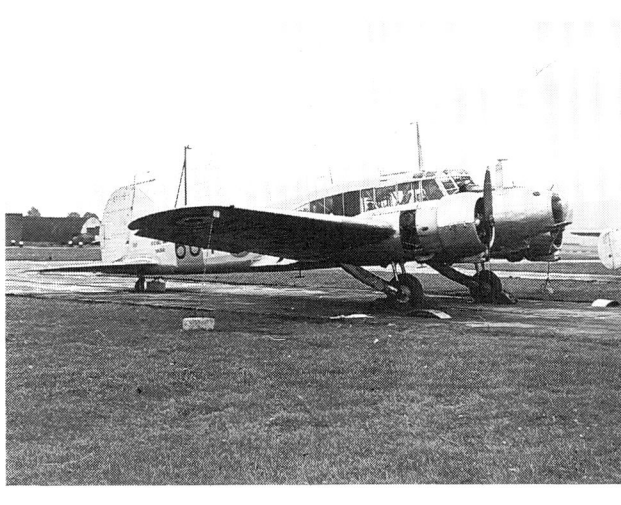
Avro Anson NK941 '604' of No.750 Squadron, St.Merryn around 1952/3. (Stan Peachey via Dave Welch)

Sea Venom XG721 '592/HF' of No.750 Squadron, Hal Far around 1964/5. (via Brian Lowe)

Percival Sea Prince WP321 '575/CU' of No 750 Squadron, Culdrose around 1972/3. (Brian Lowe)

No.751 Squadron

Badge: On a field white a base barry wavy of four blue and white, overall a lightning flash erect gold in front of two arrows in saltire points downwards black
Motto: None

No.751 Squadron formed at Ford on 24 May 1939 out of the RN Observers School, which then became No.1 Observers School, including also Nos.750 and 752 Squadrons. Equipment was Walruses, and Yeovilton was used for dispersal from May 1940, but the squadron moved north to Arbroath on 19 August 1940, following a German attack on Ford. Operating there as part of No.2 Observers School, it transferred to the satellite at Dundee on 13 August 1941, this move being considered an unqualified success. Aircraft could be kept under cover during severe weather conditions, and there were additional storage and ancillary facilities at Stannergate. Catapult crews were attached to the station for three weeks at a time during their 10 weeks training course. The squadron disbanded at Dundee on 2 May 1944.

No.751 reformed from No.846 Squadron on 22 September 1945 at Machrihanish as a trials unit, but disbanded on 31 October 1945. It next came into existence when it reformed at RAF Watton on 1 March 1947 as a Radar Trials Unit. A small number of Ansons and Oxfords were operated until disbanding on 30 September 1947.

No.751 next reformed on 3 December 1951, again at Watton, as a Radio Warfare Unit. It was formed around a small RN nucleus at the Central Signals Establishment, and undertook trials in electronic countermeasures equipment, as well as assisting in Fleet training. Aircraft comprised a miscellany of Avengers, Fireflies, Sea Furies and assorted marks of Mosquito, and these were frequently detached to participate in exercises, including occasional embarkation in carriers in later years. In February 1957 various types of radar jamming were carried out during exercises in the Gibraltar area, then in June 1957 'A' Flight re-equipped with Sea Venoms, 'B' Flight retaining its Avengers. Between 27 September and 2 October 1957 the squadron moved to Culdrose, to be restyled the Electronic Warfare Unit in March 1958. On 1 May 1958 it achieved first line status and was renumbered No.831 Squadron.

Individual Markings
Walrus W9A+, to A4A+, AA4A+ & AA5A+ 1943. 1947 unknown. From 12.51 all types uncoded, to *385-388 & 810-815* 1.56, to *680-688* 3.58.

Aircraft Equipment	Period of Service	Example	
Walrus	May 1939 - May 1944	L2231	(W9A)
Anson I	Mar 1947 - Sep 1947	NK172	
Oxford	Mar 1947 - Sep 1947	LX116	
Seafire XV	Jul 1947 - Sep 1947	PR401	
Avenger II	Sep 1945 - Oct 1945		
Mosquito FB.6	Apr 1952 - Feb 1953	RF788	
Mosquito PR.34	May 1952 - Nov 1954	PF664	
Sea Mosquito TR.33	Mar 1952 - Jun 1953	TW250	
Sea Fury FB.11	Aug 1952 - Mar 1956	TF969	
Firefly AS.6	Sep 1952 - Mar 1956	WD923	(680)
Anson I	Feb 1953 - Aug 1955	EG323	
Avenger AS.4	Dec 1952 - Jul 1957	XB388	(686)
Sea Venom 21(ECM)	Jun 1957 - Apr 1958	XG608	(813)

Squadron bases
Ford	24 May 1939
(dispersal at Yeovilton from May 1940)	
Arbroath	19 Aug 1940
Dundee	13 Aug 1941
Squadron disbanded	2 May 1944
Machrihanish	22 Sep 1945
Squadron disbanded	31 Oct 1945
Watton	1 Mar 1947
Squadron disbanded	30 Sep 1947
Watton	3 Dec 1951
HMS Illustrious (Dt)	31 Aug 1953 to 2 Oct 1953
HMS Centaur Dt)	19 Feb 1955 to 15 Mar 1955
HMS Bulwark(Dt)	7-12 Jun 1955
Hal Far (Dt)	30 Jan 1956 to 20 Feb 1956
Valkenburg (Dt2)	1-15 Oct 1956
North Front	31 Jan 1957
Watton	28 Feb 1957
Brawdy (Dt2)	13-14 May 1957
Lossiemouth (Dt2)	30 May 1957 to 6 Jun 1957
Lossiemouth(Dt4)	2-11 Sep 1957
Brawdy (Dt2)	11-19 Sep 1957
Culdrose	27 Sep 1957
Lossiemouth(Dt2)	5-13 Nov 1957
HMS Eagle (Dt3)	13-28 Nov 1957
Hal Far (B Flt)	19 Feb 1958 to 20 Mar 1958
Squadron disbanded	1 May 1958

Commanding Officers
L/C(A) JH Sender RN	24 May 1939
L/C(A) F Leach RNVR	1 Feb 1941
L/C(A) H Jones RNVR	1 Dec 1941
L/C DH Angel RN	7 Aug 1943
L/C TE Sargent RD RNVR	2 Feb 1944
Squadron disbanded	2 May 1944
Lt RFJ Forty RN	1 Mar 1947
Squadron disbanded	30 Sep 1947
L/C P Winter DSC	3 Dec 1951
L/C GR Woolston RN	25 Mar 1952
L/C WJ Cooper RN	2 Jun 1954
L/C JT Williams RN	16 Jul 1956
L/C WJ Hanks RN	24 Mar 1958
Squadron disbanded	1 May 1958

Grumman Avenger AS.5 XB357 '687' of No.751 Squadron, Watton in 1957. (MAP)

No.752 Squadron

No.752 Squadron formed at Ford on 24 May 1939 out of the RN Observers School, which then became No.1 Observers School. Equipment was mainly Proctors, but a few Albacores were also used. The squadron used Yeovilton for dispersal from May 1940, but after Ford was bombed the squadron was earmarked for overseas, moving to Lee-on-Solent on 30 September, then taking passage on 12 October to regroup at Piarco, Trinidad on 5 November 1940. Equipment continued as before, but on a larger scale, Reliants and Tiger Moths also being used later. No.752 disbanded at Piarco on 9 October 1945.

Aircraft Equipment	Period of Service	Example	
Vega Gull	Feb 1940 - Jun 1940	P5987	
Proctor Ia	Mar 1940 - Jul 1940	P6037	
Proctor II	Aug 1942 - Jul 1943	Z7239	(W3AS)
Proctor IIa	Feb 1941 - Jun 1944	BV607	
Reliant I	Dec 1942 - Oct 1945	FK978	(W5V)
Tiger Moth II	Jul 1943 - Sep 1944	T6681	

A Percival Proctor of No.753 Squadron at Piarco around 1941. (FAA Museum)

Individual Markings
Proctor W0-A+, W3A+, also W3AA, W3AB etc, Reliant W5A+, also W5AA, W5BA etc.

Squadron bases
Ford   24 May 1939
(dispersal at Yeovilton
 from May 1940)
Lee-on-Solent   30 Sep 1940
 in transit   12 Oct 1940
 sailed   17 Oct 1940
Piarco   5 Nov 1940
Squadron disbanded   9 Oct 1945

Commanding Officers
L/C GRFT Cooper
    RN   24 May 1939
L/C JHMcI Malcolm
    RNVR   21 Feb 1940
L/C(A) BAG Meads
    RNVR   31 Mar 1941

Commanding Officers
L/C(A) GM Tonge
    RNVR   1 May 1943
L/C(A) PG Lee
    RNVR   1 May 1945
Squadron disbanded 9 Oct 1945

No.753 Squadron

No.753 Squadron formed out of the School of Naval Co-operation at Lee-on-Solent on 24 May 1939, as part of No.2 Observers School. Initial equipment was Sharks, plus a few Seals. On 23 August 1940, just seven days after a German attack on the aerodrome, the school moved out to Arbroath. Equipment there became mostly Swordfish, but the Sharks continued for a time until being replaced by Albacores from August 1941, these being in turn replaced in December 1944 by ASV-equipped Barracudas. No.753 moved in November 1945 to Rattray, where it disbanded on 10 August 1946.

Individual Markings
All types W4A+, to A4A+ to A7A+ 2.43.

Aircraft Equipment	Period of Service	Example	
Shark II	May 1939 - Jan 1942	L2360	(W4A)
Seal	May 1939 - 1939	K4225	
Nimrod	Sep 1939 - May 1940	S1582	
Swordfish I	Aug 1941 - Jun 1945	V4641	(W4R)
Seal	Jan 1941 - Mar 1941	K4784	
Albacore I	Aug 1941 - Dec 1944	X9022	(A5N)
Tiger Moth II	Dec 1941	T6977	
Reliant I	Nov 1943 - Sep 1944	?	(A5H)
Barracuda II	Dec 1944 - Aug 1946	MX655	(A5B)

Blackburn Shark L2365 'W4V' of No.753 Squadron. (FAA Museum)

Commanding Officers
L/C(A) GNP Stringer
    RN   24 May 1939
Capt AC Newson
    RM   22 Oct 1940
L/C(A) LA Cubitt
    RN   6 May 1941
L/C(A) AC Mills
    RNVR   30 Sep 1941
L/C(A) FR Steggall
    RNVR   15 Jul 1942
L/C(A) RE Stewart
    RNVR   31 Mar 1944
L/C(A) AJ Phillips
    RN   12 Aug 1945
Squadron disbanded 10 Aug 1946

Squadron bases
Lee-on-Solent   24 May 1939
Arbroath   23 Aug 1940
Rattray   1 Nov 1945
Squadron disbanded   10 Aug 1946

Fairey Barracuda 'A7B' of No.753 Squadron. (FAA Museum)

No.754 Squadron

No.754 Squadron formed out of the School of Naval Co-operation at Lee-on-Solent on 24 May 1939, as part of No.2 Observers School. Equipment was mainly Walruses, plus a few Seafoxes and Vega Gulls, and Yeovilton was used as a dispersal from May 1940. Following the bombing of Lee-on-Solent the squadron moved with the school to Arbroath on 7 September 1940. Here No.754 re-equipped with Proctors, and it then trained observers and air gunners in the use of early air-to-surface vessel equipment. In June 1941 it received 18 Lysander target tugs, and these soon replaced the Proctors. A few Albacores were also received early in 1943. No.754 disbanded at Arbroath on 27 March 1944.

The squadron reformed in June 1944 at Yarmouth in No.1 Naval Air Gunners School by renumbering No.744 Squadron. It disbanded on 12 March 1945.

Individual Markings
All types *W5A*, to *A5A+* 2.43. From 6.44 Swordfish single letters and *letter/number combinations*.

Westland Lysander IIIa V9618 'E' of No.754 Squadron, Arbroath in September 1941. (via Tom Sargent)

Aircraft Equipment	Period of Service	Example	
Seafox I	May 1939 - Sep 1940	K8597	(W5J)
Walrus I	May 1939 - Sep 1940	L2210	
Vega Gull	May 1939 - Mar 1940	P5987	
Proctor Ia	Feb 1940 - Nov 1941	P6031	
Proctor II	Jul 1941 - Nov 1941	Z7246	(U)
Proctor IIa	Dec 1940 - Oct 1941	X8909	
Lysander IIIa	Jun 1941 - Mar 1944	V9618	(E)
Albacore I	Feb 1943 - Mar 1944	N4324	
Reliant I	Jan 1944 - Mar 1944	FK873	
Swordfish II	Jun 1944 - Mar 1945	HS466	(W2)
Harvard IIb	Mar 1945 - Nov 1945	FE697	

Commanding Officers
L/C(A) E Esmonde RN 24 May 1939
L/C EJE Burt RN 31 May 1940
L/C(A) HES Pritchett RNVR 10 Jan 1941
L/C(A) AFE Payen RNVR 22 Apr 1942
L/C(A) DA Horton RNVR 2 May 1942
L/C(A) WE Dunn RNVR 15 Oct 1943

Commanding Officers
Squadron disbanded 27 Mar 1944
Lt(A) EJ Trerise RNVR Jun 1944
Squadron disbanded 12 Mar 1945

Squadron bases
Lee-on-Solent 24 May 1939
Arbroath 7 Sep 1940
Squadron disbanded 27 Mar 1944
Yarmouth Jun 1944
Squadron disbanded 12 Mar 1945

No.755 Squadron

No.755 Squadron formed at Worthy Down on 24 May 1939 as a Telegraphist Air Gunner Training squadron within No.1 Air Gunners School. It undertook the initial part of the wireless course for TAGs, using Sharks and at first a few Ospreys. On 11 March 1940 the squadron moved to Jersey, but returned hurriedly when France was overrun. By July 1941 spares for the by then elderly Sharks were becoming a problem, and a number of Lysanders were taken over at short notice from the RAF. On 1 December 1942 the school was concentrated on one squadron, and No.755 then took over the Proctors of No.756 Squadron and the Lysanders of No.757 Squadron. In October 1943 the remaining Sharks were replaced by Seamews, though an attempt to standardise on these was unsuccessful. A few Tiger Moths were used to give the pilots periodic instrument checks. No.755 disbanded at Worthy Down on 31 October 1944.

On 24 March 1945 No.755 reformed at Colombo as a Communications squadron. Equipped with a small number of Expediters, it was no longer required after VJ-Day and disbanded on 31 October 1945.

Individual Markings
All types *X2A+*, to *W6A+* 1943.

Curtiss Seamew 'C' (possibly JW658 'W9C') of No.755 Squadron, Worthy Down in November 1944 (Mrs Mollie Brown)

Aircraft Equipment	Period of Service	Example	
Osprey	May 1939 - Jan 1941	K5766	
Shark II	May 1939 - Oct 1943	L2359	(F)
Proctor Ia	Nov 1939 - Oct 1944	P6105	
Skua II	Jan 1940	L2947	
Proctor II	Apr 1942 - Jan 1944	Z7247	
Proctor IIa	Oct 1941 - Oct 1944	BV629	(W6H)
Proctor III	Nov 1943 - Mar 1944	LZ761	
Proctor IV	Feb 1944 - Jun 1944	LA585?	
Lysander TT.III	Jul 1941 - Oct 1944	T1445	(W6K)
Lysander TT.IIIa	Jul 1941 - Oct 1944	V9574	(W6U)
Tiger Moth II	Sep 1943 - Dec 1943	BB805	
Seamew I	Oct 1943 - Oct 1944	FN628	(W6D)
Expediter C.2	Mar 1945 - Oct 1945	FT994	

Squadron bases
Worthy Down 24 May 1939
Jersey Airport(Dt) 11 Mar 1940 to 31 May 1940
Squadron disbanded 31 Oct 1944
Colombo 24 Mar 1945
Squadron disbanded 31 Oct 1945

Commanding Officers
L/C RA Peyton RN 24 May 1939
L/C OS Stevinson RN 17 Jul 1939
L/C(E) HP Sears RN 11 Mar 1940
L/C(A) T Coates RNVR 6 Mar 1941

Commanding Officers
L/C(A) RH Ovey RNVR 1 Dec 1942
L/C(A) JJ Dykes RNVR 15 Jan 1943
L/C(A) WHC Blake RNVR 10 Jun 1944
Squadron disbanded 31 Oct 1944
L/C(A) JGO'Sullivan RNZNVR 24 Mar 1945
L/C(A) RJ Griffith RNZNVR 4 Sep 1945
Squadron disbanded 31 Oct 1945

No.756 Squadron

No.756 Squadron was originally earmarked to form in May 1939 as a Telegraphist Air Gunner Training squadron at Worthy Down, but in the event it did not materialise there until 6 March 1941. The squadron, which formed part of No.1 Air Gunners School, was equipped entirely with Proctors on which it provided the advanced half of the TAG course, including cross-country flights, beacon flying and other instruction. No.756 disbanded on 1 December 1942 on being merged with No.755 Squadron.

On 1 October 1943 No.756 reformed at Katukurunda as a Training Squadron giving various forms of tuition, including deck landing training and refresher flying. Fulmars were used for monoplane conversion of Albacore pilots to Barracudas, both the latter types also being on strength. Colombo was used as a satellite from March 1944, and Avengers were also flown from about that time. No.756 disbanded at Katukurunda on 24 November 1945.

Swordfish LS348/KL of No.756 Sqdn Katukurunda. (via M.Bowyer)

Individual Markings
Proctor X3A + allocated. Albacore single letters. Barracuda/Swordfish KA +; Avenger K1A +.

Aircraft Equipment	Period of Service	Example	
Proctor Ia	Mar 1941 - Dec 1942	P6007	
Proctor IIa	Oct 1941 - Dec 1942	BV630	
Tiger Moth II	Dec 1941 - Jun 1942	DE200	
Albacore I	Oct 1943 - Feb 1944	X9156	(Q)
Fulmar II	Oct 1943 - May 1944	DR709	
Barracuda II	Dec 1943 - Oct 1944	P9971	
Barracuda III	Oct 1945 - Nov 1945	ME136	
Swordfish II	Mar 1944 - Feb 1945	LS348	(KL)
Hellcat I	Mar 1944	FN449	
Avenger I	Feb 1945 - Nov 1945	FN926	
Avenger II	May 1944 - May 1945	JZ393	

Commanding Officers
L/C(A) RH Ovey RNVR	6 Mar 1941	
L/C(A) WHC Blake RNVR	18 Jun 1942	
Squadron disbanded	1 Dec 1942	
L/C AD Bourke RNZNVR	1 Oct 1943	
Lt(A) WE Widdows RNVR (temp)	1 Feb 1944	
L/C(A) SMdeL Longsden RN	27 Feb 1944	
L/C(A) TT Miller RN	28 Oct 1944	
L/C(A) REF Kerrison RNVR	7 Jul 1945	
L/C(A) FW Baring RNVR	12 Aug 1945	
Squadron disbanded 24 Nov 1945		

Squadron bases
Worthy Down	6 Mar 1941
Squadron disbanded	1 Dec 1942
Katukurunda	1 Oct 1943
Colombo (Dt)	Mar 1944 to Jun 1945
HMS Unicorn (DLT)	21 Apr 1944 to 4 May 1944
HMS Victorious (DLT)	29 Oct 1944 to 12 Nov 1944
HMS Attacker (DLT)	1-31 May 1945
HMS Atheling (DLT)	15-21 Aug 1945
Squadron disbanded 24 Nov 1945	

No.757 Squadron

No.757 Squadron formed at Worthy Down on 24 May 1939 as a Telegraphist Air Gunner Training squadron within No.1 Air Gunners School, equipped with Sharks and Ospreys. The squadron went into abeyance on 15 August 1939, but reformed on 6 March 1941 with Skuas and two Nimrods. Pupils were given the initial part of the air gunnery course before going on to No.774 Squadron at St Merryn for live firing training. Lysanders replaced the Skuas in April 1942, but No.757 disbanded into No.755 Squadron on 1 December 1942.

On 2 October 1943 No.757 reformed at Puttalam as a Fighter Pool squadron. Also known as No.757 Naval Operational Training Unit, it was equipped with Corsairs, Wildcats, Hellcats and Seafires which undertook deck landing training in escort carriers. No.757 moved to Tambaram on 15 July 1945, then to Katukurunda on 12 November 1945, where it disbanded on 29 January 1946.

Aircraft Equipment	Period of Service	Example	
Osprey	May 1939 - Aug 1939	K5750	(X6D)
Shark II	May 1939 - Aug 1939		
Nimrod II	Mar 1941 - May 1941	K5058	
Skua II	Mar 1941 - Apr 1942	L2973	
Lysander III	Apr 1942 - Dec 1942	V9478	(N)
Walrus	Oct 1943 - Sep 1945	Z1821	
Barracuda II	Dec 1945 - Jan 1946	MX806	
Corsair II	Dec 1943 - Jan 1945	JT260	(P54)
Corsair III	Jan 1945 - Jan 1946	JS784	(P83)
Corsair IV	Mar 1945 - Jan 1946	KD361	(T79)
Fulmar II	Jul 1944	BP778	
Harvard IIa	Oct 1943 - Nov 1945	EX702	
Harvard IIb	Jul 1945 - Jan 1946	KF552	(P93)
Harvard III	Oct 1944 - Aug 1945	EZ139	
Hellcat I	Jul 1944 - Jul 1945	JV220	
Hellcat II	Mar 1945 - Jan 1946	JV316	
Martinet I	Apr 1945 -	?	(P47)
Wildcat V	Apr 1944 - Feb 1945	JV433	(T)
Wildcat VI	May 1945	JV772	
Seafire L.IIc	Jun 1944	LR750	
Seafire III	May 1945 - Jan 1946	NN200	(P40)

Individual Markings
All types X6A + 1939/42. All types P1-P87 + at Puttalam, T1-T93 + at Tambaram.

Commanding Officers
L/C VJ Somerset-Thomas RN	24 May 1939
Sqdn in abeyance	15 Aug 1939
L/C(A) CR Hodgson RNVR	6 Mar 1941
L/C(A) JJ Dykes RNVR	1 Jul 1942
Squadron disbanded	1 Dec 1942
L/C(A) GW Parrish DSC RNVR	2 Oct 1943
L/C(A) RW Durrant DSC RNZNVR	5 May 1945
L/C(A) FW Baring RNVR	24 Nov 1945
Squadron disbanded 29 Jan 1946	

Squadron bases
Worthy Down	24 May 1939
Squadron disbanded	15 Aug 1939
Worthy Down	6 Mar 1941
Squadron disbanded	1 Dec 1942
Puttalam	2 Oct 1943
HMS Battler (DLT)	5-6 Nov 1944
HMS Stalker (DLT)	14-20 Apr 1945
HMS Hunter (DLT)	29-30 Jun 1945
HMS Begum (DLT)	9-14 Jul 1945
Tambaram	15 Jul 1945
HMS Atheling (DLT)	15-21 Aug 1945
HMS Begum (DLT)	19-25 Aug 1945
Katukurunda	12 Nov 1945
Squadron disbanded 29 Jan 1946	

Corsair II JT260 'P54' of No.757 Sqdn on HMS Unicorn, June 1944 (CAA Rayner)

No.758 Squadron

No.758 Squadron formed by renumbering No.759 Squadron at Eastleigh on 1 July 1939 as a Telegraphist Air Gunner Training squadron, within No.2 Air Gunners School. Equipped initially with 13 Sharks and 6 Ospreys, Skuas and Proctors were also added shortly after the outbreak of war. On 14 October 1940 the squadron moved with the school to Arbroath, leaving behind the Ospreys and Sharks. The squadron disbanded on 1 February 1941.

On 25 May 1942 No.758 reformed at Donibristle as the Beam Approach School with a small number of Oxfords. Moving to Hinstock on 15 August 1942 it changed its title first to the Blind Approach School, and then by April 1943 to the Naval Advanced Instrument Flying School. Detachments were sent to the main specialist flying schools at Crail, East Haven, Fearn, Hinstock and Yeovilton to provide a short instrument flying course for pupils. By 1944 it had over 100 Oxfords, and other types were also in use. There were three Rover units, being 'X' Flight with 6 Oxfords and 2 Tiger Moths, 'Y' Flight with 2 Oxfords and a Harvard, and 'Z' Flight with 5 Ansons. 'Z' Flight was a Calibration Flight, being also responsible for the development of landing and homing aids. Peplow was used as a satellite from 28 February 1945, and on 18 March 1946 the squadron absorbed part of No.799 Squadron, but on 14 May 1946 was itself disbanded, to become 'B' Flight of No.780 Squadron.

Individual Markings

All types X5A+ 1939/41. From 5.42 all types U1A+ to U3A+, also U1AA, U1BB+ to U3AA, U3BB+.

Aircraft Equipment	Period of Service	Example	
Osprey III	Jul 1939 - Jun 1940	K3618	(X5B)
Shark II	Jul 1939 - Sep 1940	L2337	
Skua II	Oct 1939 - Feb 1941	L2909	
Roc I	Nov 1939 - 1940	L3091	
Proctor Ia	Dec 1939 - Feb 1941	P6064	
Proctor IIa	Aug 1940	X8833	
Oxford	May 1942 - May 1946	PG982	(U3EE)
Tiger Moth II	Feb 1943 - Sep 1943	BB723	(U3K)
Wellington XI	Sep 1943 - Dec 1943		
Reliant I	Nov 1943 - Jun 1945	FK923	
Anson I	Nov 1943 - Nov 1945	K6288	(U3F)
Harvard IIb	Mar 1945 - May 1946	KF528	(U3XX)
Harvard III	Nov 1944 - May 1946	FT974	(U2R)

Squadron bases

Eastleigh	1 Jul	1939
Arbroath	14 Oct	1940
Squadron disbanded	1 Feb	1941
Donibristle	25 May	1942
Hinstock	15 Aug	1942
satt Peplow from	28 Feb	1945
Burscough (F Flt)	21 Jan	1944
Crail (E Flt)	20 Jan	1944
to	26 Apr	1944
Maydown (X Flt)	22 Jul	1944
to	8 Aug	1944
Burscough (D Flt)	23 Jan	1944
to	27 Mar	1944
Burscough (C Flt)	3 Mar	1944
Eglinton (X Flt)	8 Aug	1944
to	11 Nov	1944
Eglinton (X Flt)	15-27 Jan	1945
Squadron disbanded	14 May	1946

Commanding Officers

L/C WHG Saunt RN	10 Jul	1939
L/C JM Wintour RN	22 May	1940
L/C(A) F Leach RNVR	26 Oct	1940
Squadron disbanded	1 Feb	1941
L/C(A) JBW Pugh AFC RNVR	25 May	1942
L/C(A) JCVK Watson RNVR	15 Aug	1942
Operated as separate flights	Jan	1944
Squadron disbanded	14 May	1946

758A

L/C(A) JMacD Scott OBE RN	13 Dec	1943
L/C(A) ES Barsham RNVR	1 Feb	1945
L/C DCEF Gibson DSC RN	4 Apr	1946
Flight disbanded	14 May	1946

758B

L/C(A) HR Law RNVR	13 Dec	1943
L/C(A) GT Bertholdt RNVR	1 Jan	1945
L/C(A) FG Averill RNVR	1 Jun	1945
L/C(A) RT Hargreaves RNVR	8 Feb	1946
Flight disbanded	14 May	1946

758C

L/C(A) GK Pridham RNVR	13 Dec	1943
L/C(A) T McVey RN	28 Jul	1944
L/C(A) ES Barsham RNVR	8 Nov	1944
Flight disbanded	17 Feb	1946

758D

L/C(A) ES Barsham RNVR	18 Nov	1944
L/C(A) OP Bradley RNVR	27 Feb	1945
Flight disbanded	7 Feb	1946

758E

Lt(A) AJ Phillips RN	Jan	1944

758Y

L/C(A) FG Averill RNVR		1945
L/C(A) GB O'Flynn RNVR	27 Jul	1945
Flight disbanded	28 Feb	1946

758 Rover Flt

L/C(A) RT Hargreaves RNVR	17 Jul	1944
L/C(A) HR Law RNVR by	Oct	1944
Flight disbanded	6 May	1946

No.759 Squadron

Badge: On a blue field, in front of a torch inflamed two swords in saltire winged at the hilts gold
Motto: None

No.759 Squadron commenced to form at Eastleigh on 26 May 1939 as a Telegraphist Air Gunner Training squadron, but was renumbered as No.758 Squadron on 1 July 1939.

On 1 November 1939 No.759 Squadron reformed at Eastleigh as a Fighter School and Pool squadron. Equipped initially with 9 Skuas, 5 Rocs and 4 Sea Gladiators, it absorbed No.769 Squadron on 1 December 1939 to become the Fleet Fighter School. On 16 September 1940 it moved to Yeovilton, where in 1940 it added Martlets, Fulmars and Masters, followed in June 1941 by Sea Hurricanes. In April 1943 it became the Advanced Flying School component of No.1 Naval Air Fighter School, and by May had a complement of 66 Sea Hurricanes, 8 Spitfires, 24 Fulmars and 15 Masters. A detachment was sent to Angle on 1 July 1943 to work with No.794 Squadron, being known whilst there as the Naval Air Firing Unit. Seafires arrived in August 1943, and by early 1944 'E' Flight was operating Oxfords for instrument flying, this being effectively a sub-unit of No.758 Squadron. From November 1944 the squadron largely re-equipped with Corsairs, on which 'A' Flight provided basic type conversion, 'C' Flight camera air-to-air firing and combat instruction and 'D' Flight dummy deck landings. The Corsair familiarisation element broke away in April 1945 to form No.760 Squadron. In September 1945 the squadron moved to Zeals whilst repairs were carried out to the Yeovilton runways, and on returning in January 1946 it absorbed No.761 Squadron from Henstridge, but on 5 February 1946 was itself disbanded into No.794 Squadron.

On 16 August 1951 No.759 reformed out of No.738 Squadron as No.1 Operational Flying School, an element of the Naval Air Fighter School at Culdrose. Equipped initially with Seafires and Firebrands, it added a Jet Conversion course when Meteor T.7s and Sea Vampires arrived in 1952. On 28 November it moved with the NAFS to Lossiemouth, where it disbanded into No.736 Squadron on 12 October 1954.

No.759 next reformed at Brawdy on 1 August 1963 as the Naval Advanced Flying Training School. Equipped with Hunter T.8s, it undertook Part I of the Advanced Flying Training course, pupils being then passed on to either No.738 Squadron for weapon training or to No.849 Squadron for AEW operational flying training. In 1965 the squadron received the annual Boyd Trophy award for its work in converting young Jet Provost-trained pilots to the Hunter. No.759 disbanded at Brawdy on 24 December 1969.

Aircraft Equipment	Period of Service	Example	
Skua II	Nov 1939 - Jun 1941	L2934	(N)
Roc I	Nov 1939 - Jun 1941	L3113	
Sea Gladiator	Nov 1939 - May 1943	N5546	
Swordfish I	Nov 1939 - Jun 1941	L9737	
Swordfish II	May 1943	HS544	
Nimrod I	Apr 1940	S1579	
Osprey I	Mar 1940 - Aug 1940	S1692	
Gipsy Moth	Jan 1940 - Mar 1943	K1898	
Hornet Moth	May 1940 - Jun 1940	G-ADKV	
Leopard Moth	May 1940 - Jun 1940	G-ADHB	
Buffalo I	Sep 1940 -	AS421	
Proctor Ia	Mar 1940 - Feb 1943	P6077	
Proctor II	Feb 1943	Z7243	
Proctor IIa	Aug 1943 - Dec 1943	BV657	
Fulmar I	May 1940 - Jul 1943	N2013	
Fulmar II	Feb 1941 - May 1943	X8682	
Master I	Feb 1940 - May 1944	N8055	(Y3A)
Master II	Sep 1943 - Nov 1945	DM159	
Miles M.18	Jan 1941	UO224	
Sea Hurricane Ib	May 1941 - Mar 1944	Z4847	(Y1Z)
Sea Hurricane II	Feb 1943 - Aug 1943	BX126	
Blenheim I	Oct 1943	K7113	
Blenheim IV	Jul 1943 - Sep 1944	V6073	
Tiger Moth II	Jul 1943 - Feb 1944	BB731	(Y3T)
Spitfire I	Jun 1940 - Aug 1944	X4337	(J)
Spitfire II	Aug 1943 - Oct 1943	P7786	
Spitfire Va	May 1943 - Oct 1944	X4997	
Spitfire Vb	May 1943 - Oct 1944	AD536	
Reliant I	May 1944 - Aug 1945	FK968	
Martlet I	Oct 1940 - May 1944	BJ520	
Wildcat IV	Nov 1943 - Jul 1945	FN170	(Y3S)
Wildcat V	Oct 1944 - May 1945	JV442	(Y4F)
Oxford	Jan 1944 - Feb 1946	LB416	(Y2A)
Avenger II	Jan 1945	JZ302	
Harvard III	Mar 1945 - Feb 1946	EZ433	(Y3U)
Firefly I	Jun 1944		
Corsair II	Mar 1944 - Apr 1944	JT401	
Corsair III	Sep 1944 - Feb 1946	JS823	(Y7L)
Corsair IV	Oct 1945 - Nov 1945	KE112	
Hellcat II	Jan 1946	JZ798?	
Seafire Ib	Aug 1943 - Jan 1945	MB328	
Seafire IIc	Feb 1944 - Feb 1945	MB303	
Seafire III	Dec 1945 - Feb 1946	PP999	(Y6F)
Seafire XV	Jan 1946 - Feb 1946	SW899	
Seafire F.17	Aug 1951 - Jul 1954	SX250	(179/CW)
Seafire F.47	Sep 1952 - Nov 1953	VP493	(162/CU)
Firebrand TF.5	Aug 1951 - Feb 1953	EK844	(182/CW)
Sea Hornet F.20	Aug 1951 - Feb 1953	TT191	(456/CW)
Sea Hornet NF.21	Nov 1952 - Jun 1953	VV434	
Sea Hornet PR.22	Aug 1951 - Sep 1952	VZ664	(451/CW)
Sea Fury FB.11	May 1952 - Jun 1952	WF625	
Sea Fury T.20	Feb 1952 - Jan 1954	WG625	(211/CW)
Meteor T.7	Sep 1952 - Apr 1954	VZ648	(411/CW)
Vampire T.11	Jul 1952 - Nov 1953	WW458	(221)
Sea Vampire F.20	Oct 1952 - Mar 1954	VV141	(181/CW)
Sea Vampire T.22	Nov 1953 - Oct 1954	XA108	(226/LM)
Hunter T.8/T.8c	Jul 1963 - Dec 1969	XL580	(810/BY)

Individual Markings
All types, single letters at first, to Y1A+ to Y7A+ by 1943. From 1951 Seafire *161-179/CW:CU*, Firebrand *180-183/CW*, Sea Fury T.20 *210-215/CW*, Meteor *410-417/CW:CU:LM*, Sea Hornet *451-456/CW*, Sea Vampire *180-182/CW:CU, 220-221 & 221-242/LM*, Hunter *655-664/BY* to 7.65 then *800-811/LM*.

Commanding Officers
L/C BHM Kendall RN 1 Nov 1939
L/C HP Bramwell
   DSO DSC RN 18 Nov 1940
Capt FDG Bird RM 1 Aug 1941
L/C JN Garnett RN 13 Oct 1941
L/C EWT Taylour
   DSC RN 8 Dec 1941
Not identified 7 Apr 1942
Lt EDG Lewin
   DSO DSC RN 12 Nov 1942
L/C JM Bruen
   DSO DSC RN 7 Dec 1942
L/C NG Hallett
   DSC RN 17 May 1943
Mjr FDG Bird RM 20 Dec 1943
L/C ON Bailey RN 10 Jul 1944
L/C JW Sleigh
   DSO DSC RN 14 Dec 1944
Squadron disbanded 5 Feb 1946
L/C RD Lygo RN 16 Aug 1951

Commanding Officers
L/C DRO Price RN 30 May 1953
L/C WDD MacDonald
   RN 20 Jul 1954
Squadron disbanded 12 Oct 1954
L/C CDW Pugh MBE
   RN 1 Aug 1963
L/C AH Milnes
   RN 6 Aug 1963
L/C CS Casperd RN 4 Mar 1965
L/C MI Darlington
   RN 26 Oct 1966
Cdr CCN Davis RN 10 May 1967
Squadron disbanded 24 Dec 1969

759E

Commanding Officers
Cdr(A) EAR Forwood
   RNVR 13 Dec 1943
Flight disbanded 28 Mar 1946

Fulmar II N4040 'G' of No.759 Sqdn. (R.Pridham-Wippell)

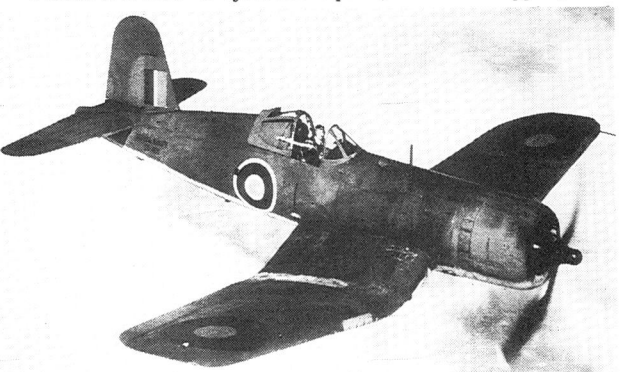
Corsair III JS499 of No.759 Sqdn, Yeovilton 1944. (Mrs P.J.Hutton)

Squadron bases
Eastleigh	26 May 1939
Redes 758 Sqdn	1 Jul 1939
Eastleigh	1 Nov 1939
Yeovilton	16 Sep 1940
(satt Haldon 1942)	
Angle (Dt)	1 Jul 1943
	to 22 Nov 1943
Zeals	19 Sep 1945
Yeovilton	7 Jan 1946
Squadron disbanded	5 Feb 1946
Culdrose	16 Aug 1951
Lossiemouth	28 Nov 1953
(satt Milltown)	
Squadron disbanded	12 Oct 1954
Brawdy	1 Aug 1963
Squadron disbanded	24 Dec 1969

Hawker Hunter T.8 XF358 '804/BY' of No.759 Squadron, Brawdy in 1968. (MAP)

No.760 Squadron

No.760 Squadron formed at Eastleigh on 1 April 1940 as Fleet Fighter Pool No.1. Initial equipment was 4 Skuas, 2 Rocs and a Sea Gladiator, with which the squadron moved to Yeovilton on 16 September 1940 as the Fighter Pool squadron. Masters and Sea Hurricanes were received, then on 1 August 1941 the Fleet Fighter pool task was dropped and the Fulmar element broke away to become No.761 Squadron. Now standardising on Sea Hurricanes as as part of the Fleet Fighter School, No.760 Squadron disbanded at Yeovilton on 31 December 1942.

On 1 May 1944 No.760 reformed at Inskip as an Anti-Submarine Operational Training squadron. Equipped with Sea Hurricane IICs, the pupils practised rocket projectile attacks and anti-flak cannon fire. The squadron disbanded into No.766 Squadron on 1 November 1944.

No.760 reformed on 10 April 1945 at Zeals out of No.759 Squadron as the Corsair Familiarization Unit, within No.1 Naval Air Fighter School. Its task was to convert fighter pilots to the Corsair, prior to joining No.759 Squadron. This was to relieve pressure on the Yeovilton circuit, which at that time was suffering an excessive number of fatal accidents due to crowded conditions and the inexperience of the pilots. On 12 September 1945 the squadron moved to Lee-on-Solent, where it joined No.2 Naval Air Fighter School, re-equipping with Seafires in October. A further move to Henstridge on 27 December was followed by disbandment on 23 January 1946.

Squadron bases

Eastleigh	1 Apr 1940
Yeovilton	16 Sep 1940
Squadron disbanded	31 Dec 1942
Inskip	1 May 1944
Squadron disbanded	1 Nov 1944
Zeals	10 Apr 1945
Lee-on-Solent	12 Sep 1945
Henstridge	27 Dec 1945
Squadron disbanded	23 Jan 1946

Identification Markings

Sea Hurricane 1941/2 *W7A+* to *W9A+*, *K1A+* 1944. Corsair *Y1A+* to *Y7A+* (used 759 Sqdn aircraft). Other types unknown.

Aircraft Equipment

Aircraft	Period of Service	Example	
Skua II	Apr 1940 - Apr 1941	L2968	
Roc I	Apr 1940 - Mar 1941	L3099	
Sea Gladiator	Apr 1940 - Sep 1940		
Fulmar I	Mar 1941 - Jun 1941	N1925	
Fulmar II	Sep 1942	X8691	
Buffalo I	Dec 1941 - Apr 1942	AS412	
Master I	Jun 1940 - Dec 1942	N7572	
Martlet I	Oct 1941	BJ556	
Hurricane I	Sep 1942 - Dec 1942	L1568	
Sea Hurricane Ib	Oct 1941 - Dec 1942	V6700	(W7E)
Sea Hurricane IIc	May 1944 - Oct 1944	NF738	
Harvard IIa	Apr 1945 - Jan 1946	EZ425	(Y6Q)
Corsair III	Apr 1945 - Oct 1945	JS852	(Y7C)
Hellcat I	Aug 1945 -	JV112	
Seafire III	Oct 1945 - Jan 1946	PP929	(S)

Commanding Officers

Lt J Casson RN (temp)	1 Apr 1940
L/C PH Havers RN	23 May 1940
L/C GN Torry RN	18 Jan 1941
Lt KVV Spurway RN	1 Aug 1941
Lt EWT Taylour RN	22 Oct 1941
Lt OJR Nicolls RN	8 Dec 1941 -@Mar 1942
Lt HP Allingham RN	bySep 1942
Squadron disbanded	31 Dec 1942
Lt(A) JD Kelsall RNVR	1 May 1944
Squadron disbanded	1 Nov 1944
L/C(A) PG Burke RNZNVR	21 Apr 1945
L/C(A) R Tebble RNVR	15 Sep 1945
Squadron disbanded	23 Jan 1946

Hawker Sea Hurricane Ib P3090 'W8E' of No.760 Squadron, Yeovilton around 1941/2. (RAF Museum 5946-1)

No.761 Squadron

No.761 Squadron was originally to have formed at Gosport in 1939 as a Torpedo School and Pool squadron. In the event it formed out of No.760 Squadron at Yeovilton on 1 August 1941 as the Advanced Training Squadron of the Fleet Fighter School. Equipped with Fulmars and a few Sea Hurricanes, these used Haldon for air firing practice. On 10 April 1943 No.761 moved to Henstridge as No.2 Naval Air Fighter School. Equipped there initially with a mixture of 18 Spitfires and Seafires, plus 6 Masters, pupils undertook deck landing training with 'D' Flight in HMS *Argus* and later HMS *Ravager*. The Seafire remained the basic equipment, through successive marks, and strength had increased to 68 by June 1944. No.761 disbanded at Henstridge on 16 January 1946, when its remnants were absorbed into No.759 Squadron at Yeovilton.

Fairey Fulmar of No.761 Sqdn, Henstridge 1943.
(via B.A.G. Woodwards)

Aircraft Equipment	Period of Service	Example	
Fulmar I	Aug 1941 - Apr 1943	N4012	
Fulmar II	Aug 1941 - Apr 1943	DR725	
Sea Hurricane Ib	Aug 1941 - Aug 1942	V7824	
Proctor Ia	May 1942 - Jul 1942	P6167	
	Apr 1943 - Nov 1943	P6167	
Master I	Apr 1943 - Nov 1943	N8077	
Master II	Apr 1943 - Jan 1946	DM159	(G1A)
Spitfire I	Sep 1942 - Jul 1944	AR238	(F)
Spitfire Va	Apr 1943 - Jan 1945	N3281	
Spitfire Vb	Apr 1943 - Jan 1945	AB201	(G1U)
Spitfire Vb/hooked	Nov 1943 - Feb 1945	AA904	
Spitfire PR.XIII	Oct 1943 - Jun 1944	AA739	(G3O)
Sea Hurricane IIc	Sep 1943 - May 1944	NF733	
Seafire Ib	Apr 1943 - Mar 1945	NX957	(G1A)
Seafire IIc	Jul 1944 - Aug 1945	LR647	
Seafire III	Apr 1944 - Jan 1946	RX288	(G3C)
Seafire XV	Jul 1945 - Jan 1946	PR339	
Seafire XVII	Nov 1945 - Jan 1946	SX125	
Harvard III	Nov 1944 - Jan 1946	EZ403	(Z)
Oxford	May 1944 - Jun 1944	V4268	
Spitfire LF.XVI	Jul 1945	RW375	

Identification Markings
All types unknown 1941/2 (*Y1A+* allocated), to *G1A+* to *G6A+*.

Squadron bases
Yeovilton 1 Aug 1941
(satt Haldon - air firing)
Henstridge 10 Apr 1943
'D' Flt (DLT):
HMS Ravager 1-5 May 1944
HMS Ravager 18-20 May 1944
HMS Argus 26-27 Aug 1944
HMS Ravager 27 Jan 1945
to 2 Feb 1945
HMS Ravager 21-22 Jun 1945
HMS Ravager 18-23 Aug 1945
Squadron disbanded 16 Jan 1946

Commanding Officers
Lt CP Campbell
 -Horsfall RN 1 Aug 1941
Capt RC Hay DSC
 RN 1 Jan 1942
Lt(A) RB Pearson 21 Jul 1942
Lt(A) WC Simpson
 RNVR 12 Sep 1942
Lt AC Wallace RN Oct 1942
Unidentified Nov 1942
L/C(A) RJ Cork
 DSO DSC RN 10 Apr 1943
L/C(A) RHP Carver
 DSC RN 15 Nov 1943
L/C(A) SG Orr
 DSC RNVR 20 Sep 1944
L/C(A) PN Charlton
 DFC RN 27 Apr 1945
Squadron disbanded 16 Jan 1946

No.762 Squadron

No.762 Squadron formed at Yeovilton on 23 March 1942 as an Advanced Flying Training School squadron. Equipped with Fulmars, it moved on 15 April 1942 to St Merryn, where Martlets and Masters were received. A further move was made to Yeovilton on 8 September 1942, where Sea Hurricanes arrived, and No.762 then undertook continuation training and conversion. The squadron disbanded into No.761 Squadron on 9 June 1943.

On 14 March 1944 No.762 reformed at Lee-on-Solent from part of No.798 Squadron as the Two Engine Conversion Unit, moving at the end of the month to Dale. Equipment consisted mainly of Beauforts and Oxfords until moving to Halesworth on 3 December 1945, where it was expanded to include a Mosquito conversion element, bringing the total strength up to 30 aircraft. A further move to Ford on 15 January 1946 saw the title changed to Heavy Twin Conversion Unit, and later in the year the Beauforts left. A final move was made on 1 May 1948 to Culdrose, where No.762 disbanded on 8 December 1949.

Identification Markings
Unknown 1942/3. All types 3.44 *P1A+* & *P2A+*, to *HA3A+* 12.45, to *FD5A+* & *FD6A+* 1.46, to *400-476/FD* 2.47. From 5.48 Oxford *650-662/CW*, Mosquito *450-466/CW*.

Squadron bases
Yeovilton 23 Mar 1942
St.Merryn 15 Apr 1942
Yeovilton 8 Sep 1942
Squadron disbanded 9 Jun 1943
Lee-on-Solent 14 Mar 1944
Dale 31 Mar 1944
Inskip (Dt) 20 Jun 1945
Halesworth 3 Dec 1945
Ford 15 Jan 1946
Culdrose 1 May 1948
Squadron disbanded 8 Dec 1949

Commanding Officers
Lt(A) R McD Hall
 RN 23 Mar 1942
Lt DBM Fiddes RN 9 Sep 1942
L/C(A) MJS Newman
 RN 29 Mar 1943
Squadron disbanded 9 Jun 1943
L/C(A) SJ Hawley
 RNVR 14 Mar 1944
L/C(A) TR Koeller
 RNVR 7 Mar 1945
L/C(A) J Mills
 RNVR 20 Jul 1945
L/C M Johnstone
 DSC RN 11 Jun 1948
Lt(A) AL Brown RN 3 Feb 1949
Squadron disbanded 8 Dec 1949

Aircraft Equipment	Period of Service	Example	
Fulmar I	Mar 1942 - Jan 1943	N1878	
Fulmar II	Mar 1942 - Jun 1943	BP814	
Martlet I	Jun 1942 - Jan 1943	BJ511	
Master I	Jun 1942 - Jun 1943	N8079	
Tiger Moth II	Oct 1942	T7610	
Spitfire I	Feb 1943 - Jun 1943	X4657	
Sea Hurricane Ia	Sep 1942 - Jun 1943	W9219	
Sea Hurricane Ib	Sep 1942 - Jun 1943	V7501	
Blenheim IV	Mar 1944 - 1945		
Beaufort I	Mar 1944 - May 1944	LR902	
Beaufort T.II	Mar 1944 - Aug 1946	ML716	(P1U)
Beaufighter II	Mar 1944 - 1945	T3050	
Wellington XI	Aug 1944 - Apr 1945	MP547	(P1Y)
Oxford	Mar 1944 - Dec 1949	ED291	(408/FD)
Mosquito T.3	Dec 1945 - Dec 1949	VA880	(458/CW)
Mosquito FB.6	Aug 1945 - Nov 1949	RF788	(FD6Q)
Sea Mosquito TR.33	Nov 1947 - Nov 1949	TW283	(466/CW)
Mosquito B.25	1946	KA962	(HA3L)
Anson 1	1948	MG725	(401/FD)

Beaufort T.II ML569 'P1K', No.762 Squadron.
(via Roger Hayward)

No.763 Squadron

No.763 Squadron formed at Worthy Down on 15 December 1939 as Torpedo Spotter Reconnaissance Pool No.1. Equipped with six Swordfish, its initial task was to fit out and give a limited amount of training to the new aircraft and crews required for HMS *Ark Royal* and HMS *Hermes*. It effectively acted as a reservoir for newly qualified pilots, who would be allocated crews so that small numbers of manned and equipped aircraft could be absorbed as required into first line squadrons. On 11 March 1940 the squadron flew to Jersey Airport, and six Albacores were added at this time. Due to the situation in France the squadron flew to Lee-on-Solent on 31 May 1940. On 4 July it returned to Worthy Down, where it disbanded four days later. Plans to reform it at Arbroath as a TSR Pool at Arbroath on 15 October 1940 were postponed, and then finally cancelled in February 1941.

On 20 April 1942 No.763 reformed aboard HMS *Pegasus* as a Seaplane Training squadron. Equipped with Walruses it provided a one-week advanced course in catapult training, including catapult launching, for crews joining the various flights of No.700 Squadron. With the declining need for this form of convoy protection, the squadron disbanded on 13 February 1944.

No.763 next reformed at Inskip on 14 April 1944 out of No.766 Squadron, as an Anti-Submarine Operational Training squadron. It was equipped with Avengers, having originally been intended as the Avenger Flight of No.766 until plans were changed. In March 1945 a small Photographic Flight was added, equipped with Swordfish, but on 31 July 1945 No.763 disbanded, its remnants being absorbed into No.785 Squadron at Crail.

Identification Markings
Swordfish *P5A+*, Avenger *K5A+*

Squadron bases
Worthy Down	15 Dec 1939
Jersey Airport	11 Mar 1940
Lee-on-Solent	31 May 1940
Worthy Down	4 Jul 1940
Squadron disbanded	8 Jul 1940
HMS Pegasus	20 Apr 1942
Squadron disbanded	13 Feb 1944
Inskip	14 Apr 1944
Squadron disbanded	31 Jul 1945

Commanding Officers
L/C PL Mortimer RN		18 Dec 1939
Squadron disbanded		8 Jul 1940
Lt(A) JRW Groves RN		9 Oct 1941
Lt SM Howard RN		20 May 1943
Squadron disbanded		13 Feb 1944
Not identified		14 Apr 1944
L/C(A) RJG Brown RNVR		13 Jul 1944
L/C(A) NG Haigh RNVR		20 Dec 1944
Squadron disbanded		31 Jul 1945

Aircraft Equipment

Aircraft	Period of Service	Example	
Swordfish I	Dec 1939 - Jul 1940	P4144	
Albacore I	Mar 1940 - Jul 1940	L7089	
Walrus	Apr 1942 - Feb 1944	W2729	
Avenger I	Apr 1944 - Aug 1945	FN836	(K5AA)
Avenger II	Apr 1944 - Jul 1945	JZ514	(K5M)
Anson I	May 1944 - Aug 1945	NK840	
Swordfish II	Mar 1945 - Jul 1945	NF151	

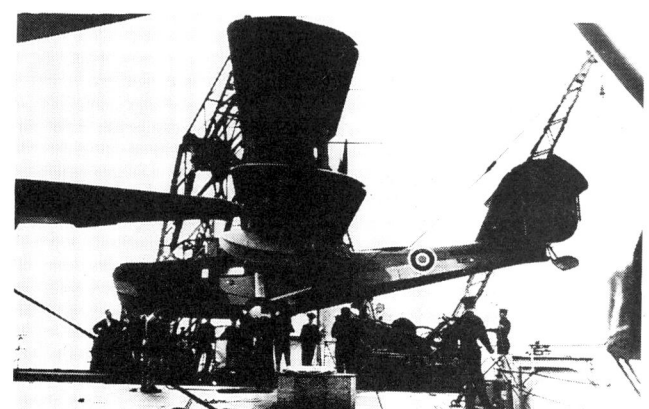

Supermarine Walrus W2743 of No.763 Squadron aboard HMS Pegasus in 1942. (FAA Museum)

No.764 Squadron

Badge: *On a field barry wavy of six white and blue, a balance gold*
Motto: *Experientia expertus (Tested by trial)*

No.764 Squadron was to have formed in 1939 at Gosport as a Torpedo School and Pool squadron. In the event it formed at Lee-on-Solent on 8 April 1940 as a Seaplane Training squadron. Equipped with Walruses and a few Swordfish and Seafoxes, it provided an advanced floatplane conversion course for both landplanes and seaplane pilots, each course culminating in catapult exercises with HMS *Pegasus*. The squadron moved to Pembroke Dock on 3 July 1940, leaving behind the Seafoxes for No.765 Squadron. In October 1941, after an air attack on Pembroke Dock, No.764 moved to nearby Lawrenny Ferry, the Swordfish being discarded about this time. In July 1942 Kingfishers arrived, and the task was then officially described as Seaplane Training Part II. No.764 disbanded at Lawrenny Ferry on 7 November 1943.

On 19 February 1944 No.764 reformed at Gosport as the User Trials Unit, equipped initially with Barracudas and Avengers. The Barracudas undertook trials of radio and other equipment, and both types were used for torpedo trials. On 1 September 1944, 'B' Flight formed at Lee-on-Solent with Firebrands for tactical trials, but this was redesignated No.708 Squadron on 1 October. Commencing on 27 September 1944, a Torpedo Trials Flight carried out net defence trials in the Clyde, being absorbed into No.778 Squadron on completion of the trials. Some Fireflies were received in June 1945, to provide flying practice on this type, but the squadron disbanded on 1 September 1945.

No.764 next reformed as an Advanced Training squadron at Lossiemouth on 18 May 1953 by redesignating No.766A Squadron. It was equipped with Seafires and Fireflies on which it provided Part I (Fighter) of the Operational Flying School course. Moving to Yeovilton on 23 September 1953, three Sea Hawks arrived in May 1954, but it continued to operate 13 Seafires and six Fireflies. The squadron disbanded at Yeovilton on 23 November 1954.

Fairey Swordfish floatplane 'Y9F' of No.764 Squadron at Lee-on-Solent in 1940. (via Chaz Bowyer)

No.764 next reformed on 1 February 1955 at Ford as a Fighter Pilot Holding Unit or Jet Fighter Pilot Pool. Equipped with 10 Sea Hawks and 10 Sea Vampires, it gave continuous flying to pilots awaiting appointment to first line squadrons, and also converted USA-trained pilots to British procedures. The Sea Vampires had dual controls and were equipped to train pilots in all forms of fighter combat and ground attack. In May 1955 two Wyverns were added to give type conversion to pilots who had completed their operational training, before joining a first line squadron. On 1 March 1956, part of the squadron became No.767 Squadron, and in February 1957 the Wyvern element also became independent, as the Wyvern Conversion Flight.

On 21 June 1957 the squadron left behind its Sea Vampires and moved to Lossiemouth. Here its role changed, and it comprised an Air Weapons Training Flight, a Commanding Officers and Senior Pilots Designate Course, and a Jet Fighter Pilot Pool and Target Towing Unit. Hunter T.8s began to arrive in December 1958, and the last Sea Hawk departed in July 1959. A few Scimitars were used briefly in 1959, but soon departed and by August the squadron equipment comprised 12 Hunter T.8s. From March 1959 the main task became Air Warfare Instructor training; the CO and SP Designates Course was retained, but the third task was now Swept Wing Conversion to Hunter T.8s. In July 1962 some of the latter were replaced by Hunter GA.11s, a few of which were later fitted out as PR.11s. Three Hunter T.8Bs arrived in 1968, and later a few T.8Cs were also used. On 26 March 1965 No.764B Squadron was formed from the remnants of No.736 Squadron, to train Airwork pilots to fly Scimitars, disbanding in November on completion of this task. No.764 itself disbanded at Lossiemouth on 27 July 1972 with a final complement of 10 Hunter GA.11s and 4 Hunter T.8Cs.

Identification Markings
Swordfish *Y9A+*, Walrus/Kingfisher unmarked. Unknown 1944/5. From 5.53 Seafire *100-116/LM:VL*, Firefly *243-250/LM:VL*. From 2.55 *251-256/FD*, Sea Hawk/Wyvern *161-175/FD*. From 1.56 all types *689-714/FD*

de Havilland Sea Vampire T.22 XG742 '254/FD' of No.764 Squadron Ford in 1955. (John Rawlings)

Squadron bases
Lee-on-Solent	8 Apr 1940
(and HMS Pegasus)	
Pembroke Dock	3 Jul 1940
(and HMS Pegasus)	
Lawrenny Ferry	4 Oct 1941
(and HMS Pegasus)	
Squadron disbanded	7 Nov 1943
Gosport	19 Feb 1944
Crail (Dt)	22 Apr 1944
to	@ May 1945
Lee-on-Solent	1 Jul 1944
(B Flt) - redes	
No.708 Sqdn	1 Oct 1944
Squadron disbanded	1 Sep 1945
Lossiemouth	18 May 1953
Yeovilton	23 Sep 1953
Squadron disbanded	23 Nov 1954
Ford	1 Feb 1955
Lossiemouth	21 Jun 1957
(satt Milltown)	
Squadron disbanded	27 Jul 1972

Commanding Officers
L/C FEC Judd RN	8 Apr 1940
L/C(A) HL McCulloch RN	16 Jul 1940
L/C H Wright RN	17 Oct 1941
Lt MBP Francklin DSC RN	1 Aug 1942
L/C(A) WJR MacWhirter RN	17 Jan 1943
Lt DH Angel RN	8 Feb 1943
L/C(A) JE Mansfield RNVR	10 Apr 1943
L/C(A) JOB Young RN	16 Jun 1943
Squadron disbanded	7 Nov 1943
Lt(A) EDJR Whatley RN (temp)	19 Feb 1944
Lt(A) DLR Hutchinson RNVR	19 Apr 1944
Lt(A) GA Donaghue RNVR	15 Nov 1944
Capt DBL Smith RM	3 Jun 1945

Commanding Officers
Squadron disbanded	1 Sep 1945
L/C PS Brewer RN	18 May 1953
L/C B Bevans DSC RN	28 Sep 1953
Squadron disbanded	23 Nov 1954
L/C DF Battison RN	1 Feb 1955
L/C JW Ayres RN	15 Apr 1957
L/C DT McKeown RN	17 Jun 1957

Commanding Officers
Lt RMP Carne RN	20 Apr 1959
L/C JC Mather RN	2 Dec 1960
L/C JNS Anderson RN	7 Jan 1963
L/C GWG Hunt RN	31 Aug 1964
L/C MF Kennett RN	22 Nov 1965
L/C E Cope RN	1 May 1967
L/C RJ Northard RN	6 Sep 1968
L/C RW Edwards RN	6 May 1970
Squadron disbanded	27 Jul 1972

Aircraft Equipment
Aircraft Equipment	Period of Service	Example	
Swordfish I/SP	Apr 1940 - Sep 1941	P4084	
Seafox I	Apr 1940 - Jul 1940	K8608	
Walrus	Apr 1940 - Nov 1943	HD832	
Kingfisher I	Jul 1942 - Nov 1943	FN688	
Barracuda II	Feb 1944 - Aug 1945	DR203	
Avenger II	Feb 1944 - Apr 1944	JZ475	
Firefly I	Jun 1945 - 1945		
Seafire XVII	1945 - Aug 1945		
Firefly T.1	May 1953 - Nov 1954	SX254	(112/VL)
Firefly T.2	Nov 1953 - Nov 1954	Z2119	(243/VL)
Sea Hawk F.1	May 1953 - Nov 1954	MB673	(244/VL)
	May 1954 - Nov 1954	WM905	(122)
	Feb 1955 - Jun 1957	WF201	(162/FD)
Sea Hawk F.2	Feb 1955 - Jun 1957	WF255	(164/FD)
Sea Hawk FB.3	Mar 1956 - Jan 1959	WM981	(702/FD)
Sea Hawk FGA.4	Jul 1957 - Jul 1959	XE327	(695/LM)
Sea Hawk FGA.6	Oct 1958 - Jul 1959	XE399	(690/LM)
Sea Vampire F.20	Jun 1955 - Feb 1956	VV151	(712/FD)
Sea Vampire F.21	Jul 1955 - Mar 1956	VG701	(179/FD)
Sea Vampire T.22	Jan 1955 - Jun 1957	XG742	(254/FD)
Wyvern S.4	May 1955 - Feb 1957	VZ788	(689/FD)
Meteor T.7	Dec 1957 - Mar 1958	VZ647	
Scimitar F.1	Feb 1959 - May 1959	XD241	
Hunter T.8/T.8b/T.8c	Dec 1958 - Jul 1972	XE664	(708/LM)
Hunter GA.11/PR.11	Jul 1962 - Jul 1972	XE673	(680/LM)

Hawker Hunter PR.11 WT723 '692/LM' of No.764 Squadron Lossiemouth in 1970. (via Brian Lowe)

764B Squadron

Aircraft Equipment	Period of Service	Example	
Firebrand F.I	Sep 1944 - Oct 1944	DK370	
Scimitar F.1	Mar 1965 - Nov 1965	XD227	(615/LM)

Squadron bases
Lossiemouth	26 Mar 1965
Unit disbanded	23 Nov 1965

Commanding Officers
L/C J Worth RN	29 Mar 1965
Squadron disbanded	23 Nov 1965

No.765 Squadron

Badge: On a blue field, a dragon volant gold in his forepaw a spear point downwards also gold
Motto: *Praesidium navibus*
(A safeguard for ships)

No.765 Squadron formed on 24 May 1939 at Lee-on-Solent as a Seaplane School and Pool squadron, to train pilots in seaplane techniques and to provide a reserve for catapult squadrons. Equipment consisted mainly of Walruses, plus a few Swordfish and Seafoxes. Some Roc seaplanes were issued early in 1940 when, following the German invasion of Norway it was proposed to form first line squadrons equipped with these, but the idea was dropped. By September 1940 the squadron had moved to Sandbanks, in Poole Harbour, where it became the Basic Seaplane Training School, providing Part I of the Seaplane Training course. As the need for this training declined the squadron was run down, to disband on 25 October 1943.

On 10 February 1944 No.765 reformed at Charlton Horethorne as a Travelling Recording Unit. It moved on 18 March to Lee-on-Solent, but the runways there were inadequate for the small number of Wellingtons with which the squadron was equipped, and they were therefore mainly based at Manston during crew training. The unit's main purpose was to record the efficiency of radar units, but the aircraft were also intended for long range reconnaissance, a number of experienced photographers being posted to the squadron. A detachment went to RAF Hornchurch in November 1944 to provide naval co-operation in liaison with No.567 Anti-Aircraft Co-operation Squadron, moving to Manston in June 1945. No.765 flew out to Hal Far in October 1945, and its aircraft were then fitted with bench-type seats for transporting troops from various parts of the the Mediterranean back to Malta for embarkation home. The squadron disbanded at Hal Far on 30 April 1946.

No.765 reformed at Culdrose on 7 February 1955 as a Piston Engine Pilot Pool squadron. Equipment comprised Firefly T.2s and T.7s, supplemented in May 1955 by Oxfords. Sea Balliols arrived during February 1957, but on 25 March 1957 the squadron disbanded, its task being shared between Nos.750 and 796 Squadrons.

Aircraft Equipment	Period of Service	Example	
Swordfish I/SP	May 1939 - Jun 1941	P4084	(Y8L)
Walrus	May 1939 - Oct 1942	X9521	(BL3S)
Seafox I	May 1939 - Jun 1942	K8613	(Y8Q)
Roc I/SP	Feb 1940 - Jun 1941	L3058	
Kingfisher I	Jun 1942 - Oct 1943	FN678	(BL3P)
Wellington X	Jul 1945 - Apr 1946	HZ470	(B)
Wellington XI	Aug 1944 - Apr 1946	HZ361	(L8B)
Firefly T.2	Feb 1955 - Mar 1957	MB745	(277/CU)
Firefly T.7	Feb 1955 - Mar 1957	WJ174	(331/CU)
Oxford T.2	May 1955 - Mar 1957	NM355	(730/CU)
Sea Balliol T.21	Feb 1957 - Mar 1957	WP325	(791/CU)
Sea Devon C.20	Feb 1957 - Mar 1957	XJ349	

Identification Markings
Swordfish/Seafox *Y8A+*, Walrus *L3A+* & *BL3A*, Kingfisher *BL3A+*, Wellington *L8A+*, Firefly *272-280, 329-336/CU*, to *717-724/CU* 1.56, Oxford *623-624/CU*, to *729-730/CU* 1.56, Sea Balliol *791-794/CU*.

Squadron bases
Lee-on-Solent	24 May 1939
Sandbanks	26 Aug 1940
Squadron disbanded	25 Oct 1943
Charlton Horethorne	10 Feb 1944
Lee-on-Solent	18 Mar 1944
Hornchurch (Dt)	14 Nov 1944 to 14 Jun 1945
Manston (Dt)	14 Jun 1945 to 6 Sep 1945
Hal Far	6 Oct 1945
Squadron disbanded	30 Apr 1946
Culdrose	7 Feb 1955
Squadron disbanded	25 Mar 1957

Commanding Officers
L/C HC Ranald RN	24 May 1939
L/C(A) HL McCulloch RN	8 Apr 1940
L/C(A) LB Wilson RN	12 Jul 1940
L/C GR Brown DSC RN	21 Apr 1941
Lt JLWM Allison RN	27 Aug 1942
L/C(A) LD Goldsmith RNVR	11 Jan 1943
Squadron disbanded	25 Oct 1943
Lt(A) DH Coates RNVR	10 Feb 1944
Lt(A) SC Abel RNVR	14 Aug 1945
Lt(A) HE Rumble RNVR	4 Feb 1946
Squadron disbanded	30 Apr 1946
L/C JI Baker RN	7 Feb 1955
L/C DW Winterton RN	12 Dec 1955
L/C WH Gunner RN	8 Mar 1957
Squadron disbanded	25 Mar 1957

Vought Sikorsky Kingfisher FN678 'BL3P' of No.765 Squadron, Sandbanks in 1943. (RAF Museum 5979-11)

No.766 Squadron

Badge: On a field blue in base two bars wavy white, a torch gold winged white inflamed proper
Motto: Festine lente (Hasten slowly)

de Havilland Sea Vixen FAW. XS583 '727/VL' of No.766 Squadron, Yeovilton around 1966/7. (via Brian Lowe)

No.766 Squadron was originally to have formed at Lee-on-Solent in 1939 as a Seaplane School and Pool, but after several postponements this plan was abandoned. Instead it formed at Machrihanish on 15 April 1942 as a Night ALT Course equipped with Swordfish. On 7 July 1943 it moved to Inskip to become part of No.1 Naval Operational Training Unit, and by May 1944 was operating 31 Swordfish, including three used by a Photographic Flight. In October 1944 Fireflies arrived, initial equipment being 14 aircraft given up by No.1772 Squadron, and on 1 November 1944 it absorbed the Sea Hurricanes of No.760 Squadron. No.766 moved to Rattray on 20 January 1946, and then to Lossiemouth on 4 August 1946 where it also received Seafires, becoming Part I of the Operational Flying School course. A few Sea Fury T.20s arrived on September 1951, these being given up ten months later. On 3 October 1953 the squadron moved to Culdrose, where it disbanded on 25 November 1954.

On 18 October 1955 No.766 reformed at Yeovilton from No.890 Squadron as an All Weather Fighter Pool, equipped with 8 Sea Venoms. Owing to reconstruction of the Yeovilton runways, it moved out to Merryfield on 24 November 1956. From October 1957 it operated as a Naval All Weather Fighter School, taking over the task of training naval pilots and observers in this work previously performed by No.238 Operational Conversion Unit at RAF North Luffenham. Moving back to Yeovilton on 20 January 1958, it became the All Weather Fighter Training squadron in May 1959. Sea Vixens FAW.1s arrived in October 1959, and these were designated No.766B Squadron until the remaining Sea Venom finally left on 24 October 1960. Sea Vixen FAW.2s began to arrive in July 1965, but the last of the FAW.1s did not depart until May 1968. The squadron disbanded at Yeovilton on 10 December 1970, its task and aircraft going to No.890 Squadron.

Identification Markings

Albacore numbers *1-10*, Swordfish *A-Q*, to *K1A+* to *K3A+* 7.43, Sea Hurricane *K1A+*, Harvard *231-248/LM*, Firefly *K1A+*, *K2A+* & *K5A+*, to *11A+* to *17A+* 1.46, to *200-258/LM:CU*, Seafire *100-140/LM*, Anson *400-402/LM*, Sea Fury *270-275/LM*, Sea Venom *200-207/VL*, to *717-739/VL* 1.56.

Aircraft Equipment	Period of Service	Example
Swordfish I	Apr 1942 - Nov 1944	V4446 (G)
Swordfish II	Apr 1943 - Nov 1944	HS293 (K1V)
Swordfish III	Mar 1944 - Nov 1944	NF267
Albacore I	Apr 1942 - Oct 1943	X9165 (3)
Fulmar I,II	Aug 1942 - Sep 1944	X8777
Anson I	Jan 1944 - Mar 1949	NK669 (402/LM)
Defiant	1944 - 1945	
Sea Hurricane IIc	Nov 1944 - Apr 1945	NF728 (K1F)
Harvard IIb	Jan 1947	KF493
Harvard III	Feb 1946 - Nov 1949	EZ403 (245/LM)
Firefly FR.1	Oct 1944 - Nov 1954	MB408 (211/CU)
Firefly T.1	Jan 1948 - Nov 1954	DK437 (254/LM)
Firefly T.2	Sep 1951 - Nov 1954	MB717 (251/CU)
Oxford	Dec 1945 - Jun 1947	V3816
Master GT.II	Oct 1945	DL437 (K3B)
Martinet TT.1	1945 - Jun 1946	MS807
Seafire III	Aug 1946 - Sep 1947	NN497 (16J)
Seafire F.15	Jun 1947 - Nov 1951	PR497 (109/MV)
Seafire F.17	Jul 1947 - Nov 1952	SW989 (122/LM)
Sea Fury T.20	Sep 1951 - Aug 1952	VX300 (274/LM)
Sea Vampire T.22	Jan 1956 - Jul 1956	XA130 (740/VL)
Sea Venom FAW.20	Oct 1955 - Aug 1956	WM563 (733/VL)
Sea Venom FAW.21	Aug 1956 - Oct 1960	XG610 (730/VL)
Sea Vixen FAW.1	Oct 1959 - May 1968	XN647 (718/VL)
Sea Vixen FAW.2	Jul 1965 - Dec 1970	XP919 (706/VL)

Squadron bases

Machrihanish	15 Apr 1942
(satt Campbeltown)	
Inskip	7 Jul 1943
Rattray	20 Jan 1946
(Martinet Flight remained to 2 Sep 1946)	
Lossiemouth	4 Aug 1946
(satt Milltown)	
Culdrose	3 Oct 1953
Squadron disbanded 25 Nov 1954	
Yeovilton	18 Oct 1955
Merryfield	24 Nov 1956
Yeovilton	20 Jan 1958
Squadron disbanded 10 Dec 1970	

Commanding Officers

L/C(A) RE Bibby DSO RNVR	15 Apr 1942
L/C(A) WFC Garthwaite DSC RNVR	24 Jul 1943
L/C EB Morgan RANVR	3 Aug 1944
Mjr VBG Cheesman DSO MBE DSC RM	20 Jan 1946
L/C TW Harrington DSC & Bar RN	1 Dec 1947
L/C AW Bloomer RN	30 Mar 1949
L/C JM Henry RN	21 Jan 1951
L/C DW Winterton RN	2 Dec 1952
L/C P Carmichael RN	30 Oct 1953
L/C EF Pritchard RN	10 Feb 1954
Squadron disbanded 25 Nov 1954	
L/C L Jeyes RN	18 Oct 1955
L/C PJ Young RN	4 Jan 1956
L/C I McKenzie RN	6 Feb 1956
L/C GJR Elgar RN	16 Apr 1956
L/C WAM Ferguson DSO RN	11 Mar 1957
L/C K Sinclair RN	1 May 1958
L/C JF Blunden RN	29 Sep 1959
L/C WJ Carter RN	14 Jan 1960
L/C K Sinclair RN	9 May 1960
L/C PB Reynolds RN	28 Apr 1961
L/C GP Carne RN	15 Feb 1963
Cdr KE Kemp RN	24 Aug 1964
L/C BG Young RN	10 Nov 1965
L/C GWG Hunt RN	14 Oct 1966
L/C DJ Dunbar-Dempsey RN	3 Jun 1968
L/C GL Shaw RN	23 Jul 1969
Squadron disbanded 10 Dec 1970	

766B

Commanding Officers

Lt K Sinclair RN	22 Oct 1959
Squadron disbanded 24 Oct 1960	

Fireflies of No.766 Sqdn, Lossiemouth. (via Brian Lowe)

No.767 Squadron

Badge: On a blue field, a hawk proper alighting on a lure gold

Motto: Cum diligentia salus (Safety with hard work or application)

No.767 Squadron formed at Donibristle on 24 May 1939 as a Deck Landing Training squadron, by redesignating No.811 Squadron. Initially equipped with Swordfish, Sharks and Moths, these embarked periodically in HMS *Furious*. Owing to poor weather at home, a detachment joined HMS *Argus* in November 1939 to continue training in the Mediterranean. Using Hyères la Palyvestre, near Toulon as a shore base, DLT continued until the fall of France. When Italy entered the war, No.767 found itself on operational service, and on 13 June 1940 nine aircraft carried out a bombing attack on Genoa and Italian lines of communication. The squadron's task could no longer be continued in the area, and on 18 June eighteen aircraft flew to Bône. Two days later twelve of these flew to Malta, to become No.830 Squadron on 1 July 1940. The other six went to Gibraltar via Rabat and were absorbed by squadrons in HMS *Ark Royal*.

On 8 July 1940 No.767 regrouped as a Deck Landing Training squadron at Arbroath, from a basis of No.763 Squadron, being also known later as the Deck Landing Training School, to which other squadrons were added during 1941. The main equipment was again Swordfish, but Albacores were also used. No.767 moved to East Haven on 5 May 1943, where it re-equipped with Barracudas in June 1944, a TBR Course Part II being undertaken during 1945. Fireflies and a few Corsairs arrived towards the end of the year, followed early in 1946 by Seafire IIIs and XVs, the last of the Barracudas being withdrawn on moving to Milltown on 15 July 1946. There it became Part I of the Operational Flying School course, some Seafire XVIIs arriving in 1947.

No.767 moved to Yeovilton on 8 September 1949, where it joined the 50th Training Air Group, to give Deck Landing Control Officer training, the continual circuits and landings giving rise to the term "Clockwork Mouse" squadron. Actual practice was undertaken in Fleet carriers, and this continued when the squadron moved to Henstridge on 4 January 1952, equipment there being mainly Firefly FR.4s and Sea Furies. A further move was made to Stretton on 20 September 1952, where Attackers were received in February 1953. From October 1953, following the introduction of the Mirror Landing Aid, No.767 became the Landing Signal Officers Training Squadron, a few Avengers and Sea Hawks being received early in 1954. The squadron disbanded at Stretton on 31 March 1955.

On 1 March 1956 No.767 again reformed, out of No.764 Squadron, this time as a Fighter Pilot Pool squadron at Ford, equipped with Sea Hawks. It initially undertook general training, but on moving to Brawdy in August provided an armament work-up course. Returning to Ford the following month, it was given the task of providing replacements pilots for squadrons engaged in the Suez operations. It disbanded into No.764 Squadron on 1 April 1957.

Reforming at Yeovilton on 14 January 1969 from a nucleus of No.700P Squadron, No.767's task was to convert RN and RAF pilots and observers to the Phantom FG.1. This task completed, it disbanded at Yeovilton on 1 August 1972, an advanced echelon having been sent the previous day to RAF Leuchars to provide a RN Detachment for the Phantom Post Operational Conversion Unit, which was to support No.892 Squadron.

Battle Honours
Mediterranean   1940

Identification Markings
Swordfish *T4A+* & *T0-A+* 1939/40. All types *T4A+* from 7.40, to *E1A+* & *E2A+* 5.43, *IT1A+* to *IT7A+* 7.46, to *201-244/MV* 1947, to *200-206/VL* 9.49, to *260-264/JA:ST* 9.52, Seafire *100-154/MV:VL*, Sea Fury *160-160/JA:ST*, Attacker *171-176/JA:ST*, Avenger *361-365/ST*, Sea Hawk *180-181/ST*, to *121-128*, then *704-715/FD* from 3.56.

Fairey Barracuda II MD771 'E1L' of No.767 Squadron, East Haven, with wings folded. (via Brian Lowe)

Aircraft Equipment	Period of Service	Example	
DH60M Moth	May 1939 - Jul 1940	J9107	
DH60X Moth	Dec 1939 - Jul 1940	G-ABBD	
Shark II	May 1939 - Jul 1939	L2358	
Swordfish I	May 1939 - Jul 1940	L2817	(T4F)
Albacore I	Feb 1940 - Jul 1940	L7076	
Sea Gladiator	Apr 1940		
Skua II	Apr 1940		
Proctor Ia	Apr 1940		
Swordfish I	Jul 1940 - May 1944	P4065	(T4N)
Swordfish II	Jan 1943 - May 1944	DK718	
Albacore I	Jul 1940 - Dec 1943	X9109	
Roc I	Sep 1940	L3078	
Fulmar I	Sep 1940 - Oct 1941	N1911	
Fulmar II	Nov 1943 - Feb 1944	X8698	
Proctor Ia	Jun 1941 - Aug 1941	P6063	
Martlet I	Nov 1941 - 1942	BJ559	
Barracuda I	Jun 1944 - Aug 1944	P9656	
Barracuda II	Jun 1944 - Jul 1946	P9891	(E1U2)
Corsair III	Dec 1945 - Feb 1946	JS475	
Corsair IV	Mar 1946	KD283	
Seafire L.III	Mar 1946 - Jun 1947	PR317	(IT3E)
Seafire F.15	May 1946 - Feb 1952	PR497	(109/MV)
Seafire F.46	Mar 1950 - Jul 1950	LA561	(129/VL)
Tiger Moth T.2	1948	T5900	(240/VL)
Dominie 1	Mar 1950 - Jan 1951	X7488	
Firefly FR.1	Sep 1945 - Mar 1952	PP506	(208/MV)
Firefly T.1	Apr 1948 - Jun 1953	MB379	
Firefly FR.4	Oct 1959 - May 1954	TW740	(260/ST)
Firefly AS.6	Mar 1951 - Dec 1951	WD881	(-/VL)
Harvard T.2b	Mar 1949 - Jul 1950	KF559	(265/VL)
Harvard T.3	Aug 1948 - Jul 1950	EZ284	(203/VL)
Sea Fury FB.11	Nov 1949 - Jun 1952	VX681	
Firebrand TF.5	Jul 1950	EK773	
Meteor T.7	Feb 1953 - Dec 1953	WL334	
Attacker F.1	Feb 1953 - Mar 1954	WA513	(176/ST)
Attacker FB.1	Feb 1953 - 1953	WA535	
Attacker FB.2	Jul 1953 - Mar 1954	WP296	(171/ST)
Sea Hawk F.1	Feb 1954 - Mar 1955	WF176	(180/ST)
Sea Hawk F.2	Dec 1954 - Mar 1955	WF261	(124)
	Mar 1956 - May 1957	WF250	(705/FD)
Sea Hawk FB.3	Mar 1956 - Jun 1957	WM930	(714/FD)
Avenger AS.4	Mar 1954 - Mar 1955	XB359	(361/ST)
Phantom FG.1	Jan 1969 - Jul 1972	XT875	(157/VL)

Hawker Sea Hawk F.1 WF176 '180/ST' of No.767 Squadron, Stretton in 1954. (Ray Williams)

McDonnell Douglas Phantom FG.1 XT876 '160/VL' of No.767 Squadron, Yeovilton in 1969. (MAP)

Commanding Officers
L/C EOF Price RN 24 May 1939
L/C JAL Drummond RN 24 Aug 1939
L/C PL Mortimer RN 8 Jul 1940
L/C JAL Drummond RN 25 Jul 1940
L/C DN Russell by Sep 1941
Lt AG Leatham RN 29 Nov 1941
Lt RL Williamson DSC RN 17 Jun 1942
Lt RS Baker-Falkner RN 1 Jul 1942
Lt CHC O'Rorke RN 10 Oct 1942
L/C WJ Mainprice RN 25 Mar 1943
L/C(A) TT Miller RN 3 Nov 1943
L/C(A) JL Fisher RNVR 7 Nov 1943
L/C(A) BW Vigrass RNVR 6 May 1944
L/C(A) DR Park RNZNVR 4 Feb 1945
L/C(A) SG Cooke RNVR 12 Aug 1945
Lt(A) DC Hill MBE RNZNVR 8 Dec 1945
L/C(A) FA Swanton DSC & Bar RN 22 Jan 1946
Lt JCS Wright RN 26 Aug 1946
L/C LD Empson RN 24 Nov 1946
Lt(A) JS Toner RN 14 Jan 1949
Lt PH Mogridge DSC RN 27 Apr 1949
L/C WE Simpson RN 29 Nov 1949

Commanding Officers
L/C CK Roberts RN 19 Apr 1950
Lt ME Stanley RN 18 Jan 1951
L/C DO'D Newbery RN 3 Sep 1951
L/C LJ Baker RN 9 Nov 1953
Lt BT Jones RN 10 Jan 1955
Squadron disbanded 31 Mar 1955
L/C GB Newby RN 13 Feb 1956
Squadron disbanded 1 Apr 1957
L/C PC Marshall RN 14 Jan 1969
L/C DA Borroman RN 23 Jun 1970
L/C MJ Doust RN 16 Jun 1971
Squadron disbanded 1 Aug 1972

Squadron bases
Donibristle 24 May 1939
HMS Furious 28 Jun 1939
 (DLT) to 7 Jul 1939
HMS Furious 26 Sep 1939
 (DLT) to 9 Oct 1939
Detachment (3 a/c):
HMS Argus 13 Nov 1939
Hyères la Palyvestre
 (for DLT in 21 Nov 1939
 HMS Argus)
HMS Argus(DLT) 4-21 Dec 1939
Hyères la Palyvestre Mar 1940
(rest of sqdn flew out)
HMS Argus (Flt) 4 Jun 1940
to Gibraltar arr 8 Jun 1940
Bone 18 Jun 1940
Medjaz-el-Bab 20 Jun 1940
Hal Far 22 Jun 1940
- Redes 830 Sqdn 1 Jul 1940

Squadron bases
HMS Ark Royal(Dt2) 27 Jun 1940
Arbroath (regroup) 8 Jul 1940
DLT:
HMS Furious 1- 3 Oct 1940
HMS Argus 25-28 Jul 1941
East Haven 5 May 1943
DLT:
HMS Activity 14 Aug 1943
HMS Rajah 12-14 Aug 1944
HMS Speaker 3-27 Nov 1944
HMS Smiter 1 Feb 1945
HMS Smiter 25 Apr 1945
HMS Battler 17 Jul 1945
HMS Ravager 8-10 Nov 1945
HMS Premier 4 Feb 1946
HMS Theseus 30 Apr 1946
 to 13 May 1946
HMS Theseus 12 Jun 1946
 to 12 Jul 1946
Milltown 15 Jul 1946
DLT:
HMS Theseus 24-25 Sep 1946
HMS Theseus 24-30 Oct 1946
HMS Theseus 25 Nov 1946
HMS Vengeance(B Flt)
 12-13 Feb 1947
HMS Vengeance(A Flt)
 26 Mar 1947
HMS Vengeance 15 May 1947
HMS Illustrious 3-1 2 Jun 1947
HMS Illustrious 11 Sep 1947
HMS Implacable 22-26 Sep 1947
HMS Implacable 4-15 Oct 1947
HMS Implacable 24 Nov 1947
 to 16 Dec 1947
HMS Implacable 8 Mar 1948
HMS Implacable 24 Apr 1948
HMS Implacable 24-25 May 1948
HMS Implacable 22 Jun 1948
HMS Implacable 20 Jul 1948

Squadron bases
HMS Vengeance 13 Sep 1948
HMS Implacable 23 Oct 1948
HMS Illustrious 2-8 Nov 1948
HMS Illustrious 17 Dec 1948
HMS Illustrious 28-29 Mar 1949
Yeovilton 8 Sep 1949
DLT:
HMS Theseus 9-13 Sep 1949
HMS Illustrious 8 Nov 1949
HMS Illustrious 28 Nov 1949
HMS Illustrious 22 May 1950
HMS Implacable 8 Jun 1950
HMS Vengeance 22 Nov 1950
HMS Illustrious
 12-15 Sep 1950
HMS Illustrious 1 May 1951
HMS Illustrious 12 Sep 1951
HMS Triumph 26 Nov 1951
 to 3 Dec 1951
Henstridge 4 Jan 1952
DLT:
HMS Triumph 19-27 Feb 1952
HMS Illustrious 2 Mar 1952
HMS Triumph 26 May 1952
 to 4 Jun 1952
HMS Triumph 8- 20 Sep 1952
Stretton 20 Sep 1952
DLT:
HMS Triumph 17-26 Nov 1952
HMS Triumph 16-25 Feb 1953
HMS Illustrious 5- 8 May 1954
Squadron disbanded 31 Mar 1955
Ford 1 Mar 1956
Brawdy 14 Aug 1956
Ford 20 Sep 1956
Brawdy 26 Feb 1957
Squadron disbanded 1 Apr 1957
Yeovilton 14 Jan 1969
Leeuwarden(Dt4) 14-17 Apr 1972
Squadron disbanded 1 Aug 1972

No.768 Squadron

Unofficial Badge:
Depicts an upright grey clockwork mouse with white wings and red eyes holding white bats, the winding handling blue, to represent the squadron's DLCO activities

Identification Markings
All types individual letters, to *B2A +* by early 1943, to *M2A +* 3.43, to *E2A +* 10.45. Firefly *213-214/JR* from 12.48.

No.768 Squadron was originally to have formed as a Deck Landing Training squadron in 1939 at Donibristle, but in the event it did not come into existence as such until 13 January 1941 at Arbroath, where it became part of the Deck Landing Training School. Initial equipment was Swordfish, with which its pupils embarked as part of their course for practical training, mainly in HMS *Argus*, a detachment being maintained at Machrihanish. Later equipment included Fulmars, Martlets, Sea Hurricanes and hooked Spitfires. The squadron moved to Machrihanish on 1 March 1943, where it also flew Albacores, Seafires and Barracudas. On 29 September 1943 No.768 moved to Ayr, where it received Hellcats, then on 19 January 1944 to Abbotsinch. Here Avengers and Corsairs arrived, followed in September by Fireflies, periods being spent on deck landing training in various escort carriers in the Firth of Clyde. No.768 Squadron continued to use Ayr, this being the nearest available airfield to the DLT carriers operating in the Clyde, and on 5 July 1945 the squadron returned there. On 28 August it moved to Ballyhalbert, and finally on 25-26 October 1945 to East Haven, where it absorbed part of No.731 Squadron on 1 November, only to be disbanded itself on 16 April 1946.

On 15 December 1948 No.768 reformed at Eglinton as a Deck Landing Control Officer Training squadron equipped with 8 Seafire F.15s and 2 Firefly 1s. At that time there were still a large number of pilots who had been trained on the old British style deck landing signals. The task of No.768 was to train sufficient DLCOs to the new American-style standard so that one DLCO could be provided for every station, to familiarise all pilots with these new signals and thus become re-eligible for carrier service. The course, known as SMAC I Part II, produced 15 trained DLCOs before being disbanded on 8 March 1949.

Aircraft Equipment	Period of Service	Example	
Swordfish I	Jan 1941 - Dec 1944	V4434	(B)
Swordfish II	Jul 1943 - Oct 1945	HS315	(M)
Swordfish III	Oct 1944	NR955	
Fulmar I	Sep 1941 - Jan 1944	N1888	
Fulmar II	Sep 1941 - Jan 1944	X8763	
Sea Hurricane Ib	Sep 1941 - Mar 1944	P2886	(M2H)
Sea Hurricane IIc	Dec 1943	NF728	(K1F)
Martlet I	Jul 1941 - Oct 1944	AL241	(M2K)
Martlet II	Jan 1943 - Sep 1944	AJ128	(D)
Martlet III	Oct 1943	AM956	
Wildcat IV	Feb 1943 - Jun 1945	FN283	
Wildcat V	May 1944 - Jul 1945	JV574	
Albacore I	Jan 1943 - Sep 1943	X9169	(E2A)
Barracuda I	Jul 1943 - Sep 1943	P9666	
Barracuda II	Jul 1943 - Oct 1945	P9887	(A)
Auster I	Aug 1943		
Spitfire Va	Jul 1943 - Feb 1944	X4846	
Spitfire Vb/hooked	Oct 1942 - Feb 1945	X4172	
Avenger I	Jan 1944 - May 1945	JZ311	
Avenger II	Jul 1944 - May 1945	FN801	
Tiger Moth II	Jan 1944 - Jun 1944	T6094	
Seafire Ib	Jul 1943 - Feb 1945	PA124	
Seafire IIc	Jan 1944 - Apr 1946	LR647	
Seafire III	Jun 1944 - Apr 1946	NF655	(E2A)
Firefly F.1	Sep 1944 - Jul 1945	Z2015	
Harvard III	Dec 1943 - 1944	FT966	
Corsair II	Mar 1944 - Sep 1945	JT670	
Corsair III	Aug 1944 - Apr 1946	JS480	
Corsair IV	Sep 1945 - Apr 1946	KD431	(E2M)
Hellcat I	Oct 1943 - Sep 1945	FN371	(N)
Seafire F.15	Dec 1948 - Mar 1949	SW795	
Firefly F.1	Dec 1948 - Mar 1949	Z2100	(213/JR)

Squadron bases		
Arbroath	13 Jan 1941	
(Dt Machrihanish) DLT:		
HMS Argus	15-18 Jul 1941	
HMS Argus	20-26 Sep 1941	
HMS Argus	1-24 Jul 1942	
HMS Furious	26 Sep 1942 to 7 Oct 1942	
HMS Activity	3 Nov 1942 to 18 Dec 1942	
HMS Argus	14 Jan 1943	
HMS Argus	25 Feb 1943 to 14 Apr 1943	
Machrihanish	1 Mar 1943	
DLT:		
HMS Activity	12 Mar 1943 to 23 Jun 1943	
HMS Argus	1 May 1943 to 24 Jun 1943	
HMS Argus	17-19 Aug 1943	
HMS Tracker	2 Sep 1943	
Ayr	29 Sep 1943	
DLT:		
HMS Ravager	28 Sep 1943 to 19 Jan 1944	
HMS Argus	20 Oct 1943 to 6 Nov 1943	
HMS Argus	27 Nov 1943 to 2 Dec 1943	
HMS Argus	13 Dec 1943 to 26 Sep 1944	
Abbotsinch	19 Jan 1944	
(also used Machrihanish) DLT:		
HMS Ravager (various dates) to	27 Jan 1944 5 Jul 1945	
HMS Trumpeter	15 Jun 1944 to 2 Jul 1944	
HMS Biter	3-10 Jul 1944	
HMS Rajah	30 Jul 1944 to 14 Aug 1944	
HMS Nairana	7 Aug 1944	
HMS Empress	6 Sep 1944	
HMS Speaker	16 Oct 1944 to 28 Nov 1944	
HMS Patroller	31 Oct 1944 to 1 Nov 1944	
HMS Slinger	3-28 Nov 1944	
HMS Ranee	23 Nov 1944 to 27 Dec 1944	
HMS Smiter	21 Dec 1944 to 18 May 1945	
HMS Reaper	1 Jan 1945	
HMS Trouncer	19 Jan 1945 to 2 Mar 1945	
HMS Pretoria Castle	8-12 Mar 1945	
HMS Battler	5 May 1945 to 31 Dec 1945	
Ayr	5 Jul 1945	
DLT:		
HMS Premier	3-16 Jul 1945	
HMS Ravager	17 Jul 1945 to 3 Aug 1945	
HMS Premier	21-25 Aug 1945	
HMS Ravager	21-23 Aug 1945	
Ballyhalbert	28 Aug 1945	
DLT:		
HMS Premier	11-27 Sep 1945	
HMS Nairana	20 Sep 1945 to 1 Oct 1945	
East Haven	25 Oct 1945	
DLT:		
HMS Ravager	29 Nov 1945 to 28 Dec 1945	
HMS Premier	18-19 Jan 1946	
HMS Premier	7 Feb 1946	
Squadron disbanded	16 Apr 1946	
Eglinton	15 Dec 1948	
Squadron disbanded	8 Mar 1949	

Commanding Officers
L/C VC Grenfell RN 13 Jan 1941
L/C(A) FDG Jennings RN 26 Jun 1941
Lt NG Hallett RN 28 Sep 1941
Lt JCM Harman RN 1 Nov 1941
Lt(A) PB Jackson RN 15 Mar 1942
L/C(A) DM Brown RNVR 29 Dec 1942
L/C(A) DJW Williams RN 1 Mar 1943
L/C(A) JS Bailey RN 8 Jul 1943
L/C(A) JM Brown DSC RNVR 29 Oct 1944
L/C R Pridham-Wippell RN 1 Nov 1945
Lt NA Bartlett RN 10 Jan 1946
Squadron disbanded 16 Apr 1946
Lt(A) DG MacQueen MBE RN 15 Dec 1948
Squadron disbanded 8 Mar 1949

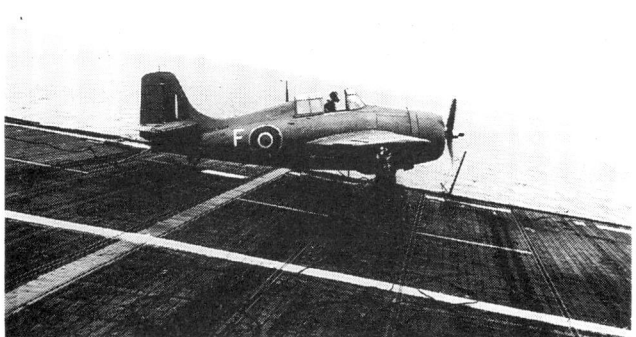

Grumman Wildcat V JV346 'F' of No.768 Sqdn into wires landing HMS Ravager on 6 June 1945.

No.769 Squadron

No.769 Squadron formed at Donibristle on 24 May 1939 as a Fighter Deck Landing Training squadron, by renumbering No.801 Squadron. Equipped with Skuas, Rocs and Sea Gladiators, deck landing training was undertaken in HMS *Furious*. Four of the Sea Gladiators broke away on 25 November to form No.804 Squadron, and No.769 disbanded on 1 December 1939.

On 29 November 1941 No.769 reformed as a Deck Landing Training squadron within the Deck Landing Training School at Arbroath. Equipped mainly with Swordfish and Albacores, it began to re-equip with Barracudas on moving to East Haven on 7 November 1943. Here it also operated a Deck Landing Training Officers course until this became No.731 Squadron on 5 December 1943. During 1944 the squadron's task changed to Torpedo Bomber Reconnaissance Training, and on 28 July 1945 it moved to Rattray. It was intended to open as a new Deck Landing Training School, but VJ-Day intervened, and it was instead absorbed into No.717 Squadron on 29 October 1945.

de Havilland DH.60M Moth J9107 of No.769 Squadron on HMS Furious in 1939. (FAA Museum)

Identification Markings
Sea Gladiator *T6+*, Swordfish individual letters, Albacore *numbers up to 78+*, Barracuda *E1A+ & E2A*, to *I4A+ to I6A+ 7.45*.

Aircraft Equipment	Period of Service	Example	
Skua II	May 1939 - Nov 1939	L2943	
Roc I	Aug 1939 - Nov 1939	L3114	(E)
Sea Gladiator	May 1939 - Nov 1939	N5500	(T6L)
DH60M Moth	Jul 1939 - Apr 1940	K1898	
Albacore I	Nov 1941 - Feb 1944	N4264	
Swordfish I	Nov 1941 - Feb 1944	L2861	(U)
Tiger Moth II	Nov 1941 - Aug 1942	T6976	
Fulmar I	Nov 1941 - Sep 1942	N1991	
Fulmar II	Dec 1942 - Dec 1943	N4127	
Sea Gladiator	Jul 1942 - Oct 1943	N2299	
Sea Hurricane Ib	Mar 1942 - Apr 1944	AF973	
Swordfish II	Oct 1943 - Feb 1944	HS592	
Barracuda II	Nov 1943 - Oct 1945	LS535	(E4K)
Barracuda III	Aug 1945 - Oct 1945	MD978	

Squadron bases
Donibristle	24 May 1939
DLT:	
HMS Furious	15-22 Jun 1939
HMS Furious	17-26 Jul 1939
HMS Furious	19-23 Sep 1939
Squadron disbanded	1 Dec 1939
Arbroath	29 Nov 1941
DLT:	
HMS Argus	19-20 Jul 1942
East Haven	7 Nov 1943
DLT:	
HMS Ravager	8-11 Oct 1943
HMS Ravager	20 Dec 1943 to 7 Jan 1944
HMS Ravager	23-30 Jan 1944
HMS Khedive	10-13 Jun 1944
HMS Rajah	11-12 Aug 1944
HMS Ranee	23-30 Nov 1944
HMS Smiter	3 Jan 1945 to 25 May 1945
Rattray	28 Jul 1945
Squadron disbanded	29 Oct 1945

Commanding Officers
L/C CA Kingsley-Rowe RN	24 May 1939
Squadron disbanded	1 Dec 1939
Lt WH Crawford RN	29 Nov 1941
L/C WH Nowell RN	1 Jan 1943
L/C(A) SP Luke RN	7 May 1943
L/C PN Medd RN	24 Jan 1943
L/C(A) D Brooks DSC RNVR	8 Jul 1944
L/C GC Edwards RCNVR	7 Apr 1945
L/C(A) G Bennett DSC RNVR	28 Jun 1945
Squadron disbanded	29 Oct 1945

Blackburn Skua L2929 'S', believed to be of No.769 Squadron, Donibristle, in 1939. (MAP)

No.770 Squadron

Badge: On a blue field, upon clouds melting white a cock proper
Motto: In alto societas
(There's company aloft)
(Badge to No.790 Squadron)

No.770 Squadron formed at Lee-on-Solent on 7 November 1939 as a Deck Landing Training squadron, equipped with two Skuas, two Sea Gladiators, a Moth, and later two Swordfish. These embarked in HMS *Argus* for the Mediterranean, where the squadron used Hyères la Palyvestre as a shore base until disbanding on 1 May 1940.

On 1 January 1941 No.770 reformed from 'X' Flight of No.771 Squadron at Donibristle as a Fleet Requirements Unit. Initial equipment was four Rocs, of which two were target tugs and the others were used for marking. The squadron moved to Crail on 1 June, where Skuas were soon added, followed in 1942 by other types including Chesapeakes and Defiants. Martinets took over the target towing task from late 1943, and on 29 January 1944 the squadron moved to Dunino. Here a few Blenheims were received, and the Chesapeakes were replaced by Hurricanes before moving to Drem on 25 July 1944. Various types of aircraft were employed during 1945, including Beaufighters, Spitfires, Mosquitoes and a Reliant. The Mosquito detachment spent a few days at Arbroath in September 1945, but on 1 October 1945 No.770 disbanded into No.772 Squadron.

Identification Markings
All types individual letters 1939/40. Individual letters from 1941, then Skua *C8A+*, Chesapeake & Martinet unknown, Blenheim *B8A+*, *D8A+* & *BR8A+*, Beaufighter *BR8A+*, Seafire *D8A+*.

*Blackburn Skuas of No.770 Squadron, Crail around 1941/42.
(via Hamilton Neilson)*

Aircraft Equipment	Period of Service	Example	
Skua II	Nov 1939 - Apr 1940	L2963	
Sea Gladiator	Nov 1939 - Apr 1940	N5508	
Moth	Nov 1939 - Apr 1940	G-ABBD	
Swordfish I	Dec 1939 - Apr 1940	L2857	
Roc I	Jan 1941 - Dec 1943	L3171	(J)
Skua II	Oct 1941 - Dec 1943	L2952	(C8S)
Proctor II	Dec 1941 - May 1942	Z7241	
Blenheim I	Mar 1942 - Jun 1942		
Botha I	Jun 1942 - Sep 1942	L6109	
Chesapeake I	Jun 1942 - Jun 1944	AL909	
Defiant TT.I	Aug 1942 - Aug 1943	DR894	
Tiger Moth II	Aug 1943 - Sep 1943	BB810	
Seafire L.IIc	Sep 1943	LR682	
Martinet TT.I	Sep 1943 - Oct 1945	MS788	
Blenheim IV	Mar 1944 - Jun 1945	Z6271	(B8X)
Hurricane IIc	Jun 1944 - Apr 1945		
Beaufighter X	May 1945 - May 1945		
Spitfire	May 1945 - Jul 1945		
Reliant	May 1945 - May 1945		
Mosquito PR.XVI	Sep 1945 - Oct 1945	MM293	
Mosquito B.25	Jul 1945 - Oct 1945	KB698	
Seafire IIc	Jul 1945 - Oct 1945	MA970	(D8R)

Squadron bases	
Lee-on-Solent	7 Nov 1939
HMS Argus (Dt)	9 Nov 1939
Hyeres La Palyvestre	21 Nov 1939
HMS Argus	13 Dec 1939
(Shore base Hyères La Palvestre)	
Squadron disbanded	1 May 1940
Donibristle	1 Jan 1941
Crail	1 Jun 1941
Evanton (Dt)	7 Dec 1943
to	1 May 1944
Dunino	29 Jan 1944
Drem	25 Jul 1944
Ouston (Dt)	19-23 Apr 1945
Ayr (Dt)	30 Jun 1945
Charter Hall (Dt)	1 Jul 1945
to	1 Oct 1945
[Mosquito B.XXV training flight]	
Arbroath (Dt)	3-14 Sep 1945
Squadron disbanded	1 Oct 1945

Commanding Officers		
None		7 Nov 1939
Lt EW Lawson RN		1 Jan 1941
Lt HER Torin RN		5 May 1941
L/C(A) WHC Blake RN (temp)		29 Oct 1941
L/C(A) HT Molyneaux RNVR		13 Nov 1941
L/C(A) AFE Payen RNVR		4 Apr 1942
L/C(A) DRM Manthorpe RNVR		5 Apr 1944
L/C(A) JML Wilson RNZNVR		13 Aug 1945
Squadron disbanded		1 Oct 1945

Fleet Requirements Unit
L/C H Wright RN		11 Aug 1938
Lt PGO Sydney-Turner RN		9 Jan 1939
Became 771 Sqdn		24 May 1939

No.771 Squadron

Badge: On a field blue in base two bars wavy white, three bees volant one and two, proper
Motto: Non nobis solum (Not unto us alone)

No.771 Squadron formed at Portland as a Fleet Requirements Unit on 24 May 1939, from a previously unnumbered FRU which had formed at Lee-on-Solent on 11 August 1938. Such units carried out various types of exercises with locally bases naval ships and provided target towing facilities for naval gunners.

Initial equipment was 14 Swordfish and a few Walruses, and the squadron had both a northern element ('X' Flight) and a southern element ('Y' Flight). This proved unsatisfactory, and 'X' Flight broke away on 28 September 1939 to become No.772 Squadron. The reshaped No.771 operated from Hatston with Swordfish, a detachment being based at Abbotsinch. It later received Henleys, Skuas and Rocs. A new 'X' Flight was based mainly at Donibristle until it became No.770 Squadron on 1 January 1941.

Blenheims and Marylands were later received, one of the latter being responsible for starting the chain of events that led to the sinking of the German battleship *Bismarck*, when, on 22 May 1941, during a reconnaissance to Bergen in weather considered by RAF Coastal Command to be unsuitable, it discovered that she had left a Norwegian fjord. On 1 July 1942 No.771 moved to Twatt, having given up the Skuas for Defiant target tugs and a few Chesapeakes. The Defiants gave way to Martinets in August 1943, and a number of Bostons and Havocs were also used. In May 1944 the Rocs and Skuas were replaced by Hurricanes, these being soon followed by Corsairs, and early in 1945 Hoverfly helicopters arrived.

After VE-Day, the Fleet moved south from Scapa Flow to Portsmouth and the anchorage at Portland. As a consequence, No.771 also moved south, but the only available airfield at that time was the rather unsuitable one at Zeals, where it arrived on 25 July 1945, Wildcats being received there. Here the squadron was mainly involved in flying for the Fighter Direction School at Yeovilton.

More convenient facilities became available at Gosport, and No.771 moved there on 12-15 September 1945, the helicopter element being based mainly at Portland. Seafires and Mosquitoes also arrived at this time, but as the grass airfield at Gosport was unsuitable the Mosquitoes were stationed at Ford. The fixed wing element of No.771 moved to Lee-on-Solent on March 1947, but the Mosquito Flight stayed at Ford with a detachment at Arbroath. The helicopter flight merged into No.705 Squadron when it formed on 7 May 1947, and the remainder of the squadron joined the 51st Miscellaneous Air Group when it formed in July 1948. In 1950 Sea Hornets, Sturgeons, Fireflies and Meteors all arrived, followed in 1951 by Sea Vampires. On 1 September 1952 the squadron moved its headquarters to Ford to become the Southern Fleet Requirements Unit, with Lee-on-Solent now becoming the detached base. On 17 August 1955 No.771 combined with No.703 Squadron to form No.700 Squadron.

On 11 July 1961 No.771 reformed at Portland from the Helicopter Flight of No.700 Squadron as a Helicopter Trials and Training squadron. Equipped with a small number of Dragonflies and Whirlwinds, it also had two Wasp prototypes. When 2 Whirlwind HAR.3s arrived it took over the SAR Portland commitment at Portland. The squadron disbanded on 1 December 1964, on being absorbed into No.829 Squadron.

No.771 reformed at Portland on 23 June 1967 from the Whirlwind Flight of No.829 Squadron. Equipped with 9 Whirlwind HAS.7s, its task was primarily that of Anti-Submarine Fleet Requirements Unit, but it also acted as the Station SAR Flight. Wessex HAS.1s began to replace the Whirlwinds in November 1969, and a year later the A/S FRU commitment was transferred to No.737 Squadron. On 4 September 1974 the squadron moved to Culdrose, leaving behind 6 aircraft to form the basis of No.772 Squadron. At Culdrose it joined the Culdrose Training School, undertaking Aircrewman Training as well as Station SAR Flight. The squadron re-equipped with Wessex HU.5s during 1979. During the Falklands conflict it provided back-up facilities, some of its aircraft being taken over by operational squadrons. On 10 January 1983 it absorbed the Station Flight, taking over two Chipmunks and two Sea Devons. In 1985 it took over the Wessex Commando training task from No.707 Squadron and replaced the Wessex helicopters with Sea King HAS.5, converted to HAR.5, in 1987. The Boyd Trophy was awarded for its activities in 1992. and the squadron continues to operate from Culdrose as Station Flight as well as providing aircrewman training and SAR duties. No.771 Squadron regularly deploys detachments throughout the UK on exercises in support of security contingency plans.

Bristol Blenheim IV R2782 'T8J' of No.771 Squadron, Twatt over the Orkney coast. (via Gregor Lamb/FAA Museum)

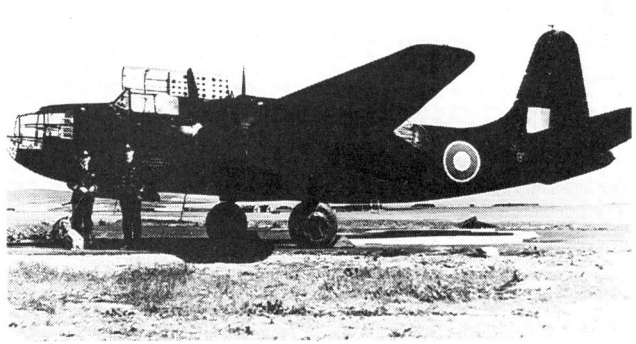

Douglas Boston I BD121 of No.771 Sqdn, Twatt. (FAA Museum)

de Havilland Sea Mosquito TR.33 TW256 '593/LP' of No.771 Squadron, Lee-on-Solent around 1957/8. (via Don Hannah)

Identification Markings
All types *R5A+*, then individual letters for a time, to *T8A+* 3.43, to *Z8A+* 7.45, to *GP8A+*, *GP9A+* & *GP0A+* 9.45, to *550-599/LP:FD* 3.47. All types *750-759/PO* from 7.61, then *420-421, 508-527/PO* from 6.67, to *516-530/CU* 9.74, to *816-826/CU* 1.84.

Aircraft Equipment	Period of Service	Example	
Swordfish	May 1939 - Apr 1945	L7679	(R5G)
Henley III	Oct 1939 - Aug 1943	L3368	(R5M)
Walrus I	Nov 1939 - Feb 1940	L2331	
Skua II	Apr 1940 - Apr 1943	L3046	(R5G)
Roc I	Apr 1940 - May 1944	L3104	(T8G)
Albacore I	Nov 1941	L7134	
Blenheim I	Apr 1941 - Jun 1943	L1146	
Blenheim IV	Apr 1944 - May 1945	V5534	(T8B)
Sea Gladiator	Dec 1941 - Jun 1944	N2277	
Maryland	Oct 1940 - Sep 1944	AR720	
Walrus	Mar 1944 - Jun 1944	X9586	
Defiant TT.I	Jun 1942 - Aug 1943	DR888	(R5R)
Chesapeake I	May 1942 - Apr 1944	AL952	(R5S)
Proctor Ia	Aug 1942 - Oct 1943	P6111	
Lysander TT.III	Jul 1943 - Dec 1943	T1443	(D)
Martinet TT.I	Aug 1943 - Oct 1951	RG882	(GP8K)
Havoc I	Dec 1942 - Sep 1944	BL227	
Boston II	Nov 1943 - Aug 1944	AH507	
Boston III	Feb 1944 - Aug 1945	W8341	(T8L)
Hurricane FB.IIc	May 1944 - Apr 1945	PG473	
Sea Otter	Apr 1944 - Aug 1949	JM761	
Corsair II	Sep 1944 - May 1945	JT487	(T8N)
Corsair III	Dec 1944 - Sep 1945	JS751	(Y6K)
Wildcat IV	Jul 1945 - Nov 1945	FN270	(Z8C)
Wildcat V	Nov 1945 - Mar 1946	JV550	
Wildcat VI	Oct 1945 - Mar 1946	JV789	
Oxford I	Mar 1946	RR361	(GP0A)
Hellcat I	Sep 1945	JV180	
Hoverfly I	Feb 1945 - May 1947	KL102	(503/GJ)
Hoverfly II	Dec 1945 - May 1947	KN879	(501/GJ)
Seafire III	Mar 1946 - Jan 1947	NN545	(GP9L)
Seafire F.15	Nov 1946 - Jan 1951	PR402	(GP9K)
Seafire F.45	Dec 1947 - Sep 1950	LA438	(560/LP)
Seafire F.46	May 1947 - Dec 1947		
Anson 1	Apr 1947 - Aug 1955	MH160	(591/FD)
Harvard T.2b	Jan 1948	KF514	
Mosquito FB.6	Jul 1950 - Apr 1952	TE705	(545/FD)
Mosquito PR.16	Dec 1948 - Aug 1952	RF986	(593/LP)
Mosquito B.25	Aug 1945 - May 1947	KA964	(GP8C)
Sea Mosquito TR.33	May 1947 - Mar 1950	TW277	(597/LP)
Mosquito PR.34	Nov 1948 - Jan 1950	RG297	(596/LP)
Sea Mosquito TR.37	Dec 1948 - Jul 1949	TW240	
Mosquito TT.39	Jan 1950 - Jan 1952	PF452	(598/FD)
Sea Hornet FR.20	May 1950 - Jun 1950	VR856	
Sea Hornet NF.21	Jan 1950 - Oct 1952	VW958	
Sea Fury T.20	Jul 1950 - Dec 1950	VX291	(590/LP)
Meteor T.7	May 1950 - Mar 1955	VZ648	(515/FD)
Sea Vampire F.20	Mar 1952 - Aug 1955	VV150	(503/FD)
Sea Vampire F.21	Jan 1951 - Sep 1951	VG701	(594/FD)
Sturgeon TT.2	Sep 1950 - Nov 1952	TS491	(586/FD)
Firefly FR.1	Jan 1950 - Jul 1955	PP594	(509/FD)
Firefly T.1	Jul 1950	Z2027	
Firefly T.2	Jul 1950 - Aug 1952	DK499	
Firefly TT.4	Nov 1951 - Aug 1955	VH127	(507/FD)
Firefly TT.5	Jun 1952	WB406	
Firefly AS.6	Oct 1950 - Dec 1953	WD850	
Dragonfly HR.5	Jul 1961 - Oct 1963	WG707	(756/PO)
Wasp P-531 O/N	Jul 1961 - Dec 1964	XN334	(758)
Wasp HAS.1	Nov 1963 - Dec 1964	XS563	(759)
Whirlwind HAR.1	Jul 1961 - Jul 1961	XA862	
Whirlwind HAR.3	Oct 1961 - Mar 1964	XG583	(751)
Whirlwind HAS.7	Aug 1962 - Jan 1965	XN358	(750)
	Jun 1967 - Jan 1970	XN259	(518/PO)
Whirlwind HAS.22	Jul 1961 - Nov 1961	WV205	(753)
Wessex HAS.1	Dec 1963 - Dec 1963	XM837	
	Nov 1969 - Jul 1979	XS886	(517/PO)
Wessex HU.5	Mar 1979 - Mar 1988	XT466	(528/CU)
Chipmunk T.10	Jan 1983 - Mar 1993	WP906	(516)
Sea Devon C.20	Jan 1983 - Dec 1989	XK895	(c/s 519)
Sea King HAR.5	Oct 1987 - to date	XV705	(821/CU)

de Havilland Sea Hornet NF.21 VW967 '553/LP' of No.771 Squadron, Lee-on-Solent around 1950/1. (N.Pritchard/MAP)

de Havilland Sea Vampire F.20 VV150 '503/FD' of No.771 Squadron, Ford in 1953. (MAP)

Supermarine Seafire LA436 '584/LP' of No.771 Squadron, Lee-on-Solent around 1949/51. (Brian Lowe)

Commanding Officers
L/C KW Beard RN 24 May 1939
L/C FEC Judd RN 13 Sep 1940
Mjr AR Burch RM 15 Jan 1941
L/C(A) NE Goddard
    DSC RNVR 15 Oct 1941
L/C(A) HT Molyneaux
    RNVR 4 May 1942
L/C(A) W Dobson
    RN 13 Feb 1944
L/C(A) CC Burke
    RNZNVR 11 Apr 1945
L/C GMT Osborn
    DSO DSC RN 24 Oct 1945
L/C CR Bateman RN 23 Feb 1948
L/C(A) RWM Walsh
    RN 7 Jan 1949
L/C JG Baldwin
    DSC RN 18 Nov 1949
L/C JA Welply RN 18 Dec 1950
L/C MW Rudorf
    DSC RN 5 May 1952
L/C R Pridham
    -Wippell RN 15 Sep 1952
L/C BE Bullivant RN 3 Jun 1953
L/C RW Turral RN 28 Mar 1955
Squadron disbanded 17 Aug 1955
L/C AIR Shaw MBE 11 Jul 1961
L/C RV Woodward
    RN 23 Mar 1962

Commanding Officers
L/C JRJ Rutherford
    RN 28 Mar 1964
Squadron disbanded 1 Dec 1964
L/C JT Rawlins
    MBE RN 23 Jun 1967
L/C R McLean
    MVO RN 14 Aug 1968
L/C I Lachlan RN 20 May 1970
L/C CL MacGregor
    RN 4 Oct 1971
L/C RN Woodard
    RN 5 Sep 1974
L/C CP West RN 16 Sep 1974
L/C KJMcK Ayres
    RN 16 Jul 1976
L/C R Mortimer RN 10 Mar 1978
L/C PA Fish RN 28 Sep 1979
L/C NB Shaw RN 19 Feb 1981
L/C GRK Gadsden
    RN 20 Sep 1982
L/C EK Bramall RN 10 Jan 1983
L/C RHS Everall RN 8 Apr 1983
L/C DR George RN 15 Oct 1985
L/C MJ Lawrence
    RN 18 Dec 1988
L/C IS Dominey RN 28 Jul 1989
L/C SD Pendrich
    AFC RN 15 Mar 1991
L/C L Matthews RN 23 Jul 1993

Squadron bases
Portland 24 May 1939
(and HMS Argus)
Mount Batten 19-23 Aug 1939
(Dt)
X Flight (ex A Flight):
Lee-on-Solent 29 Jun 1939
Evanton 29 Jul 1939
Hatston 26 Aug 1939
Became No.771 Sqn 28 Sep 1939
Y Flight (ex B Flight):
Portland
HMS Furious 1 Jul 1939
Donibristle 14 Jul 1939
Portland 31 Jul 1939
Redes No.772 Sqdn 28 Sep 1939
Hatston 28 Sep 1939
Abbotsinch (Dt) 12 Dec 1939
Abbotsinch (Dt) 23 May 1940
X Flight:
Donibristle 26 May 1940
Redes No.770 Sqdn 1 Jan 1941
Twatt 1 Jul 1942
Zeals 25 Jul 1945

Squadron bases
Gosport 12 Sep 1945
Haslemere 14 Sep 1945
(Helicopter dt)
redes No.705 Sqdn 7 May 1947
Ford (twin-engined 20 Sep 1945
detachment) to 1 Sep 1952
Evanton (Dt) 21 Sep 1946
Lee-on-Solent 9 Mar 1947
Tangmere (Dt) 12 Aug 1948
    to Dec 1949
Arbroath (Dt) 13 Oct 1948
    to 3 Sep 1951
Ford 1 Sep 1952
Lee-on-Solent (Dt) 1 Sep 1952
    to 25 Aug 1953
Lossiemouth (Dt) 13-24 Sep 1954
Squadron disbanded 17 Aug 1955
Portland 11 Jul 1961
Squadron disbanded 1 Dec 1964
Portland 23 Jun 1967
Culdrose 4 Sep 1974

Westland Wessex HAS.1 XS884 '522/CU' of No.771 Squadron, Culdrose in 1976 (MAP)

Westland Sea King HAS.5 XZ920 '822' of No.771 Squadron, Portland in 1991. (MAP)

No.772 Squadron

Badge: 1. On a white field, issuant from water barry wavy in base blue and white, an arm embowed vested white, the hand proper grasping a trident gold impaled thereon an aeroplane black
2. On an azure field, in front of a pair of wings argent a trident and shepherds crook in saltire or (From 1975)
Motto: None

No.772 Squadron formed on 28 September 1939 at Lee-on-Solent from 'Y' Flight of No.771 Squadron as a Fleet Requirements Unit. Its 4 Swordfish mainly operated as floatplanes from Portland, until moving to Campbeltown on 14 July 1940. On moving to Machrihanish on 15 June 1941 the Swordfish were replaced by Rocs. Activities included target towing, height finding exercises, photography and radar calibration. Walruses were also attached, for air sea rescue duties over a large area, one aircraft being required to stand by from dawn to dusk each day. During 1942 Fulmars, Chesapeakes and Defiants were received and the Swordfish returned. Martinets arrived in 1943, followed by Blenheims and Hurricanes in the early part of 1944.

On 27 May 1944 No.772 put up as many aircraft as possible for a dummy attack on the Fleet, as a practice for the coming invasion of Europe. On 2 July 1944 the squadron moved to Ayr, where it operated an FRU School. Towards the end of 1944, it received Corsairs, Bostons and Fireflies, and from early 1945 detachments operated from Ronaldsway. By the end of 1945 only the Martinets remained in service of the earlier aircraft, the remainder being replaced by 25 Wildcats and 12 Mosquitoes, the latter being taken over from the disbanded No.770 Squadron. On 10 January 1946 the squadron moved to Burscough, where it received Seafires, then on 3 May 1946 to Anthorn. It became the Northern FRU on moving to Arbroath on 26 June 1947, but disbanded into No.771 Squadron on 13 October 1948.

No.772 reformed at Portland on 6 September 1974 from 6 Wessex HAS.1s of No.771 Squadron as a Fleet Requirements Unit and SAR squadron. It provided search and rescue cover of the local sea areas, and helicopter support to RN and foreign warships working up in the Portland sea areas. During 1976 it re-equipped with Wessex HU.5s, and on 9 September 1977 took over responsibility for the ships flights of RFAs *Regent, Resource and Tidepool*. In 1979 this element was divided into three flights, of which 'A' Flight was for RFA *Resource*, 'B' Flight for RFA *Olmeda* and 'C' Flight for RFA *Regent*. During 1982 'A' Flight was attached to HMS *Illustrious*, and elements of the squadron were used to reform No.848 Squadron for the Falklands Task Force. From 14 February 1983 until 1988 'C' Flight was stationed at Lee-on-Solent to provide local SAR facilities. No.772 Squadron regularly deploys detachments throughout the UK on exercises in suppport of security contingency plans. The squadron is due to disband in 1995 when the FOST organisation moves to Devonport. The aircraft and personnel are to be absorbed in the Yeovilton Sea King squadrons.

Supermarine Walrus 'M8F' of No.772 Squadron, Machrihanish aboard HMS Argus around 1942/3. (FAA Museum)

Identification Markings
All types *R3A+*, to *K9A+* 1942, to *M8A+* 1943, to *AR8A+*, *AR9A+*, *BR8A+* & *BR9A+* 7.44, to *O8A+* & *O9A+* 1.46. Mosquito *501/AO+*, Wessex *510-517/PO*, Sea King *(6)21-(6)28*.

Aircraft Equipment	Period of Service	Example	
Swordfish I	Sep 1939 - Jul 1941	L9738	
Skua II	Sep 1940 - Jul 1944	L2907	(M8L)
Roc I	Jul 1941 - Apr 1944	L3156	
Chesapeake I	Jun 1942 - Aug 1943	AL951	(M8E)
Defiant TT.I	Jun 1942 - Aug 1943	DR971	
Swordfish II	Oct 1942 - Aug 1945	DK680	
Reliant I	Nov 1943 - Nov 1945	FB653	
Fulmar I	Jun 1942 - Oct 1942	N4026	
Fulmar II	Aug 1943 - Jun 1944	BP786	(M8G)
Martinet TT.I	Sep 1943 - Aug 1946	RG903	
Master II	Jul 1945	DM163	
Walrus	May 1942 - Aug 1944	W3062	
Blenheim IV	Feb 1944 - Apr 1945	V5655	(BR8J)
Hurricane IIc	Jun 1944 - Apr 1945	PG596	
Proctor II	Jun 1943	Z7251	
Corsair III	Sep 1944 - Sep 1945	JS549	(AR9R)
Boston III	Dec 1944 - Aug 1945	Z2184	(AR9J)
Havoc I	Nov 1943 - Nov 1943		
Firefly I	Sep 1944 - Feb 1946	MB564	
Firefly NF.II	Mar 1945	Z1874	(BR8W)
Beaufighter X	1945	RD308	(BR8P)
Wildcat IV	Sep 1945 -	FN188	
Wildcat V	Sep 1945 - Apr 1946	JV548	
Sea Otter	Dec 1944 - Nov 1945	JM874	
Anson I	Nov 1945 - Aug 1946	NK952	
Mosquito T.3	Sep 1945	RR318	
Mosquito PR.XVI	Oct 1945 - Nov 1946	MM364	(AR8O)
Mosquito B.25	May 1945 - Aug 1946	KA948	(AR8Q)
Mosquito PR.34	Apr 1946 - Oct 1948	RG291	(509/AO)
Seafire L.III	Mar 1946 - Aug 1946	NF450	(O9A)
Wessex HAS.1	Sep 1974 - Jul 1976	XP159	(514/PO)
Wessex HU.5	Feb 1976 - Mar 1988	XT455	(314/PO)
Sea King HC.4	Feb 1988 - Sep 1995	XF124	(624/PO)

Squadron bases
Lee-on-Solent (HQ) & Portland (aircraft)	28 Sep 1939	
Campbeltown	14 Jul 1940	
Machrihanish	15 Jun 1941	
Ballykelly (Dt)	7 Dec 1942 to 5 Feb 1943	
Ayr	2 Jul 1944	
Ronaldsway (B Flt)	5 Jan 1945 to 17 Apr 1945	
Andreas (B Flt)	17 Apr 1945 to 6 Sep 1945	
Ronaldsway (B Flt)	6 Sep 1945 to 10 Jan 1946	
Charter Hall (Dt)	1 Oct 1945 to 16 Oct 1945	
Arbroath (Dt)	16 Oct 1945 to 10 Jan 1946	
Peplow (Dt)	28 Jan 1946 to 31 Jan 1946	
Burscough (B Flt)	28 Dec 1945 to 10 Jan 1946	
Burscough	10 Jan 1946	
Arbroath (Dt)	10 Jan 1946 to Jul 1946	
Nutts Corner (Dt)	Feb 1946 to Mar 1946	
Andreas (Dt)	7 Mar 1946 to 2 May 1946	
Charter Hall (Dt)	19 Mar 1946 to Aug 1946	
Anthorn	3 May 1946	
Andreas (Dt)	3 May 1946 to 15 Aug 1946	
Jurby (Dt)	15 Aug 1946 to 21 Dec 1946	
Arbroath	26 Jun 1947	
Squadron disbanded	13 Oct 1948	
Portland	6 Sep 1974	
Lee-on-Solent (SAR dt)	14 Feb 1983 to 20 Mar 1988	
Squadron disbands	Sep 1995	

Commanding Officers
L/C MA Everett RN	28 Sep 1939
L/C REP Miers RN	16 Nov 1939
L/C KW Beard RN	6 Sep 1940
L/C CL Hill RN	25 May 1942
L/C(A) AC Mills RNVR	4 Aug 1942
L/C PJ Connolly RN	25 Aug 1943
L/C CR Holman RNR	11 Sep 1944
L/C P Snow RN	16 Jun 1945
Lt FGB Sheffield DSC RN	20 Aug 1946
L/C CH Filmer RN	15 Jan 1947
Lt(A) WC Larkins RN	6 Sep 1948
Squadron disbanded	13 Oct 1948
L/C NH Burbury AFC RN	6 Sep 1974
L/C JA Holt RN	18 Dec 1975
L/C PG Syer RN	6 Jan 1978
L/C P Barton RN	24 May 1979
L/C NT de Hartog AFC RN	13 Apr 1981
L/C BM Brock RN	17 Dec 1981
L/C RM Evans RN	20 Oct 1983
L/C AR Smith RN	3 Dec 1985
L/C ND Arnall-Culliford RN	8 Sep 1987
L/C R Lamb RN	28 Feb 1990
L/C NA King RN	12 Dec 1990
L/C EA McNair AFC RN	4 Mar 1993
Squadron disbands	Sep 1995

772B
Lt(A) AR Linstead RNVR	8 Jan 1945
Lt(A) IHM Gunn RNVR	17 Apr 1945
None	24 Sep 1945
Flight disbanded	28 Dec 1945

Chance Vought Corsair III 'BR9C̄' of No.772 Squadron, Ayr in 1945. (FAA Museum)

de Havilland Mosquito PR.34 RG294 '501/AO' of No.772 Squadron, Arbroath c.1947/8. (Tom Hollands via John Hamlin)

Westland Wessex HU.5 XS518 '516/PO' of No.772 Squadron, Portland in 1977. (MAP)

No.773 Squadron

No.773 Squadron formed at Bermuda on 3 June 1940 as a Fleet Requirements Unit to provide facilities for ships in the America and West Indies station. Equipped initially with a Swordfish floatplane and two Walruses, it later had some Seafoxes and Rocs, the latter operating as both floatplanes and landplanes. No.773 disbanded at Bermuda on 25 April 1944.

No.773 next reformed at Lee-on-Solent on 1 June 1945, probably as a Fleet Requirements Unit. It moved to Brawdy on 29 March 1946 and is known to have had at least one Queen Martinet pilotless target aircraft before being disbanded on 30 September 1946.

On 6 January 1949 No.773 reformed out of No.771 Squadron at Lee-on-Solent as a Fleet Requirements Unit, to provide for the needs of the Home Fleet during its Spring Cruise in the Western Mediterranean. Embarking in HMS *Theseus* on 27 January, it disembarked its Martinets and Sea Furies to North Front, Gibraltar until returning in HMS *Implacable* in March to be reabsorbed into No.771 Squadron on 31 March 1949.

This pattern was repeated when No.773 next reformed out of No.771 Squadron as an FRU squadron at Lee-on-Solent on 4 January 1950 for the Home Fleet's 1950 Spring Cruise. Taking passage to North Front, the squadron operated five Martinets, six Seafires and two Mosquitoes until re-embarking in HMS *Implacable* and HMS *Vengeance*, to disband into No.771 Squadron on return on 31 March 1950.

No.773 reformed for the last time for this purpose, again as an FRU squadron out of No.771 Squadron, at Lee-on-Solent on 1 September 1950. This time it had a longer existence, being based at North Front from 14 September 1950 to 27 November 1950 and again from 16 January 1951 to 1 March 1951. It finally merged back into No.771 Squadron on 31 March 1951.

Identification Markings
All types *R4A+*, later no markings. Unknown 1945/6. Sea Fury *103-106/LP* 1949. Seafire *510-515/LP* 1950.

Aircraft Equipment	Period of Service	Example
Walrus	Jun 1940 - Sep 1943	L2266 (R4C)
Swordfish I/SP	Jun 1940 - Apr 1944	P4203 (R4A)
Roc I	Sep 1941 - Apr 1944	L3109
Roc I/SP	Dec 1941 - Jul 1943	L3069
Seafox I	Aug 1940 - Sep 1941	L4530
Anson C.XII	Sep 1945 - Nov 1945	PH664
Queen Martinet TT.1	Jul 1946 - Aug 1946	RH182
Martinet TT.1	Jan 1949 - Mar 1949	PX115
Sea Fury FB.11	Jan 1949 - Mar 1949	VR949 (106)
Martinet TT.1	Jan 1950 - Mar 1950	NR573
Seafire F.15	Jan 1950 - Mar 1950	PR368 (510/LP)
Mosquito FB.VI	Jan 1950 - Mar 1950	
Martinet TT.1	Sep 1950 - Feb 1951	RG888

Squadron bases
Bermuda	3 Jun 1940
Squadron disbanded	25 Apr 1944
Lee-on-Solent	1 Jun 1945
Brawdy	29 Mar 1946
Squadron disbanded	30 Sep 1946
Lee-on-Solent	6 Jan 1949
HMS Theseus	27 Jan 1949
North Front	5 Feb 1949
HMS Implacable	18 Mar 1949
Lee-on-Solent	25 Mar 1949
Squadron disbanded	31 Mar 1949
Lee-on-Solent	4 Jan 1950
passage	3 Feb 1950
North Front	3 Feb 1950
HMS Implacable	26-31 Mar 1950
HMS Vengeance	26-30 Mar 1950
Lee-on-Solent	30 Mar 1950
Squadron disbanded	31 Mar 1950
Lee-on-Solent	1 Sep 1950
North Front	14 Sep 1950
Lee-on-Solent	27 Nov 1950
North Front	16 Jan 1951
Lee-on-Solent	1 Mar 1951
Squadron disbanded	31 Mar 1951

Commanding Officers
L/C H Wright RN	28 Jun 1940
L/C GCW Fowler RN	Sep 1941
L/C KW Beard RN	6 Aug 1943
Squadron disbanded	25 Apr 1944
L/C(E) WPT Croome RN	1 Jun 1945
L/C(E) P Richmond RN	20 Aug 1945
Squadron disbanded	30 Sep 1946
Lt(A) A Haslam RN	6 Jan 1949
Squadron disbanded	31 Mar 1949
Lt RCB Trelawney RN	4 Jan 1950
Squadron disbanded	31 Mar 1950
Lt JF Smith RN	1 Sep 1950
Squadron disbanded	31 Mar 1951

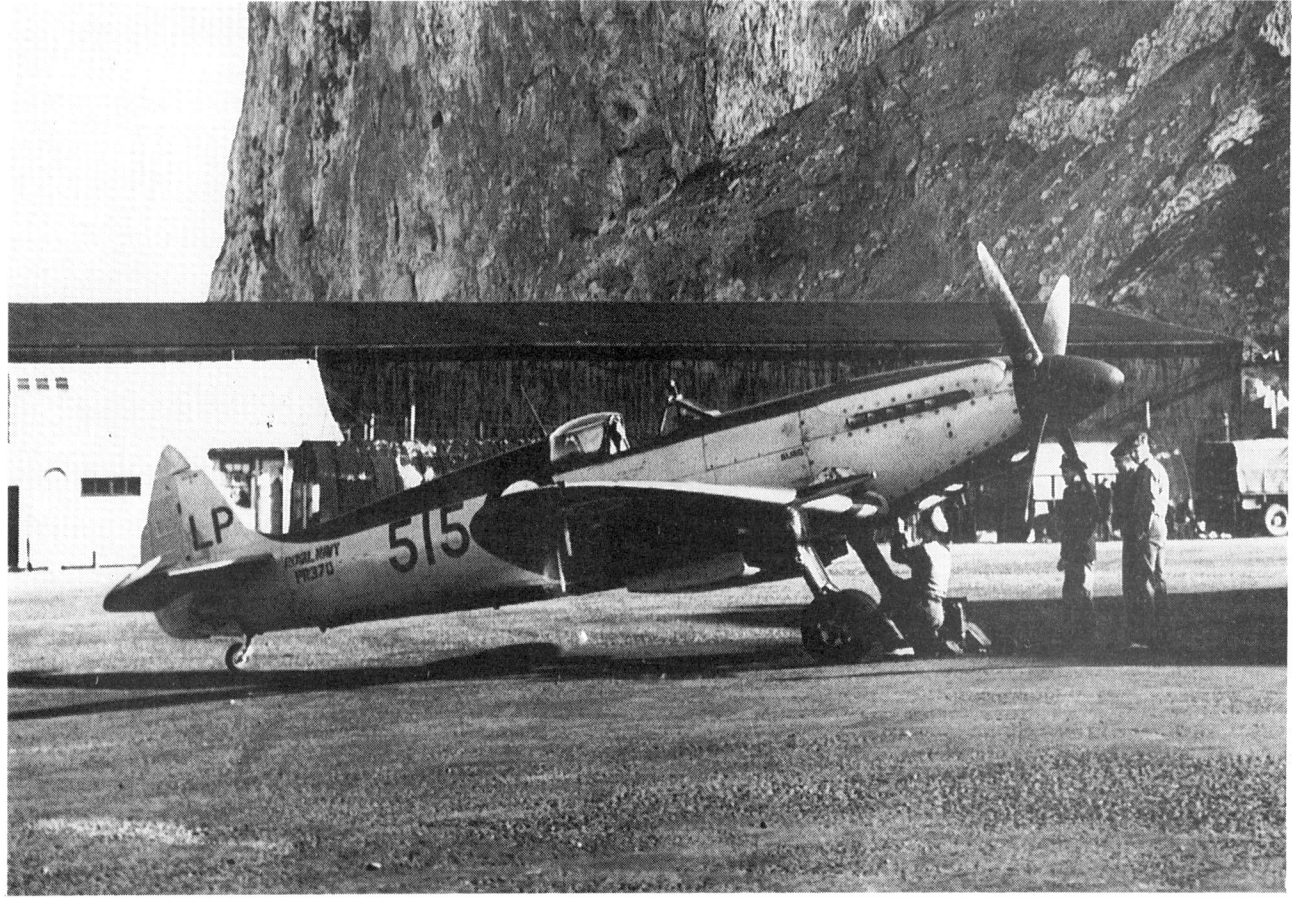

Supermarine Seafire F.15 PR370 '515/LP' of No.773 Squadron at North Front, Gibraltar in February 1950. (RAF Museum 6383-6)

No.774 Squadron

No.774 Squadron formed on 10 November 1939 as an Armament Training squadron for observers and telegraphist air gunners. Aircraft were allotted from Nos.815 and 782 Squadrons, plus others from storage to bring the initial complement up to 3 Skuas, 3 Rocs, 4 Shark target tugs and 4 Swordfish. On 25 December 1939 it moved to Aldergrove, where it was attached to No.3 Bombing and Gunnery School. On 3-4 July 1940 it moved to Evanton, and then on 17-26 September 1940 to St Merryn, where Albacores were received. The Skuas and Rocs were withdrawn early in 1941, the latter having been used for turret conversion courses. The Sharks left in 1942, and during 1944 the Albacores and Swordfish were replaced by Barracudas. Several Defiants target tugs and Sea Hurricanes were also received that year. No.774 moved to Rattray on 24 October 1944, where it disbanded on 1 August 1945.

Squadron bases
Worthy Down	10 Nov 1939
Aldergrove	16 Nov 1939
Evanton	3 Jul 1940
St.Merryn	17 Sep 1940
Rattray	24 Oct 1944
Squadron disbanded	1 Aug 1945

Commanding Officers
L/C S Borrett RN	16 Nov 1939
L/C WGC Stokes RN	24 Nov 1939
L/C PL Mortimer RN	30 Aug 1940
L/C (A) JH Gibbons RN	15 Mar 1941
L/C(A) L Gilbert RNVR	by Oct 1942
L/C PP Pardoe-Matthews RNR	16 Aug 1943
Lt (A) JO Sparke RNVR	7 Oct 1944
Squadron disbanded	1 Aug 1945

A Blackburn Skua of No.774 Squadron at Aldergrove in 1940. (A.M.McKinnon)

Identification Markings
All types O4A+, to single letters, to S6A+ 1942.

Aircraft Equipment	Period of Service	Example	
Skua II	Nov 1939 - Jan 1941	L3029	
Roc I	Nov 1939 - Jan 1941	L3138	
Shark IITT	Nov 1939 - Dec 1942	K8914	(F)
Swordfish I	Nov 1939 - Aug 1944	L2732	(S6A)
Swordfish II	Feb 1943 - May 1944	DK670	
Albacore I	Sep 1940 - Jun 1944	X9041	(S6K)
Barracuda II	Feb 1944 - Jul 1945	DR224	(G)
Defiant TT.III	Nov 1944 - Mar 1945	N1614	
Sea Hurricane Ib	Jun 1944 - Sep 1944	V7162	
Hurricane FB.IIc	Dec 1944 - Feb 1945	LF601	
Avenger	1945 - 1945		

No.775 Squadron

No.775 Squadron formed at Dekheila in November 1940 as a Fleet Requirements Unit. Equipped initially with 4 Rocs for target towing and marking, it received 7 Swordfish, 2 Fulmars, 2 Sea Gladiators and some Albacores and Queen Bees during 1941. A detachment was sent to Haifa in late 1942, and on 4 July 1943 No.728 Squadron was absorbed, only to be reformed on 14 August 1943. From October 1941 it parented the Fulmar-equipped RN Fighter Flight, until this became No 889 Squadron on 13 March 1942. No.775 received Defiants in 1943, and on 1 February 1944 moved to Gibraltar, where Martinets began to arrive, and later small numbers of Beaufighters, Hurricanes and Seafires. The squadron moved back to Dekheila on 5 August 1945, and a communications flight was formed in late 1945, this continuing to exist for a time after No.775 headquarters disbanded at Dekheila in March 1946.

Commanding Officers
Not identified	Nov 1940
Lt AH Abrams RN	27 Jul 1941
L/C(A) HL McCulloch RN	27 Oct 1941
L/C(A) JWG Wellham DSO RN	29 Nov 1942
L/C(A) JM Waddell RNVR	8 Dec 1942
L/C(A) JL Wordsworth RNVR	24 Mar 1945
Squadron disbanded	Mar 1946

Squadron bases
Dekheila	by 25 Nov 1940
Fayid (TTU a/c)	c.24-29 Mar 1942
St.Jean D'Acre (Dt)	12 Jul 1942 to Apr 1943
North Front	1 Feb 1944
Dekheila	5 Aug 1945
Maryut (Comm Flt)	Jan 1946
Aboukir (Comm Flt)	Feb 1946 to 15 May 1946
Squadron disbanded	Mar 1946

Sea Gladiator N5505 'A' of No.775 Sqdn, Dekheila. (FAA Museum)

Identification Markings
Single letters.

Aircraft Equipment	Period of Service	Example	
Roc I	Nov 1940 - Jul 1943	L3183	(X)
Swordfish I	May 1941 - Jun 1945	V4436	
Swordfish II	Nov 1943 - Feb 1944	HS180	
Albacore I	Sep 1941 - Nov 1943	T9150	
Fulmar I	Sep 1941 - Apr 1942	N4000	
Fulmar II	Apr 1943 - Feb 1944	N4119	(M)
Queen Bee	Aug 1941 - Apr 1943	P4709	(S)
Sea Gladiator	Oct 1941 - Feb 1944	N5539	
Tiger Moth II	Jun 1942 - Feb 1944	K28 (ex Kenya AF)	
Spitfire I	Jun 1943	P9311	
Spitfire Vc	Jun 1943	JK163	
Defiant TT.I	Jul 1943 - Dec 1944	AA498	
Seafire Ib	Jul 1943 - Mar 1944	MB339	
Seafire IIc	Aug 1944 - Nov 1945	LR696	
Martinet TT.I	May 1944 - Nov 1945	EM709	(O)
Beaufighter X	May 1944 - Nov 1945	NV295	
Hurricane	May 1944 - Jan 1945		
Blenheim IV	May 1945 - Aug 1945		

775 Sqdn Comm Flt

Aircraft Equipment	Period of Service	Example
Oxford	Dec 1945 - Mar 1946	NM333

Queen Bee L7727 '36' of No.775 Sqdn, Dekheila. (FAA Museum)

No.776 Squadron

Badge: On a field per fess wavy gold and black, a cormorant rising proper collared and line reflexed over the back red, the line attached to a drogue also red
Motto: None

No.776 Squadron formed at Lee-on-Solent on 1 January 1941 as a Fleet Requirements Unit. Equipped with 3 Blenheims and a number of Rocs, some of the latter were detached to Speke on 22 March 1941. Another detachment went to Woodvale on 16 May 1942, at which time Skuas were received and also 7 Chesapeakes. The squadron headquarters moved to Speke on 18 October 1942, and during 1943 detachments were sent to Waltham, Millom, Usworth and Llanbedr. In early 1944 No.776 received 14 Hurricanes, 8 Blenheims, 12 Defiant target tugs and a Swordfish. Martinets replaced the Defiants in March 1945, and on 7 April the headquarters moved to Woodvale to reabsorb the detachment which was still there. In May, 10 Seafires arrived, but on 30 October 1945 No.776 disbanded, soon after moving to Burscough.

Aircraft Equipment	Period of Service	Example	
Blenheim	Jan 1941 - Aug 1941		
Roc I	Jan 1941 - Apr 1944	L3117	(N)
Skua II	Nov 1941 - May 1944	L2892	(J)
Sea Gladiator	Jan 1942 - Jul 1942	N2276	
Chesapeake I	Jun 1942 - Apr 1944	AL930	
Dominie I	Nov 1942 - Jun 1945	X7508	
Fulmar II	Aug 1943 - Sep 1943	DR633	
Sea Hurricane Ib	Oct 1943 - Jul 1944	V6604	
Sea Hurricane IIc	Oct 1944 - Jul 1945	NF726	
Hurricane I	Nov 1943 - Apr 1944	L1998	
Hurricane FB.IIc	Apr 1944 - Jul 1945	LF656	(R7B)
Oxford	Aug 1943 - Jul 1944	HN132	(O)
Blenheim I	Apr 1944	L6764	
Blenheim IV	Jan 1944 - Apr 1945	Z6172	
Defiant TT.III	Apr 1944 - Mar 1945	V1107	
Swordfish I	Oct 1943 - Dec 1943	V4320	
Swordfish II	Jun 1944 - Dec 1944	LS234	(R8M)
Seafire IIc	May 1945 - Oct 1945	NM973	
Traveller I		FT535	(R8F)
Martinet I	Mar 1945 - Oct 1945	RG888	(V9S)

Identification Markings
All types single letters, to R7A+ & R8A+ 1942, believed also V9A+ for Woodvale detachment.

Squadron bases
Lee-on-Solent	1 Jan 1941	Usworth (Dt)	5 Mar 1943
Speke (Dt - Rocs)	22 Mar 1941		to 12 Jul 1943
	to 18 Oct 1942	Andreas (Dt)	1 Jan 1944
Woodvale (Dt)	16 May 1942		to 7 Feb 1944
	to 7 Apr 1945	Millom (Dt)	27 Oct 1944
Speke	18 Oct 1942		to 4 Jan 1945
Millom (Dt)	30 Dec 1942	Walney Island (Dt)	4 Jan 1945
	to 21 Apr 1944		to 8 Jan 1945
Waltham (Dt)	19 Jan 1943	Woodvale	7 Apr 1945
	to 7 Dec 1944	Burscough	6 Oct 1945
Llanbedr (Dt)	4 Feb 1943	Squadron disbanded	30 Oct 1945
	to 28 Jun 1943		

Commanding Officers
L/C EJE Burt RN	10 Jan 1941
L/C(A) NE Goddard DSC RNVR	7 May 1942
L/C(A) J Goodyear RNVR	19 Aug 1942
L/C(A) BAG Meads MBE RNVR	24 Jul 1943
L/C(A) RMB Ward RNVR	10 Apr 1944
L/C(A) NG Maclean RNVR	24 Jan 1945
Squadron disbanded	30 Oct 1945

Miles Martinet TT.I RG988 'R8K' of No.776 Squadron, Ronaldsway in 1945. (RAF Museum 6061-7)

No.777 Squadron

Badge: On a blue field, above a base barry wavy of four white and blue an eagle displayed gold gorged with a mural crown red grasping two tridents points downwards white

Motto: *Expertam docemus artem* (We teach the art which we have gained by experience)

No.777 Squadron was to have formed at Eastleigh on 15 December 1939 as a Reserve Fighter Pool squadron with Skuas and Rocs, but after several changes of plan this proved abortive. Instead the squadron formed at Hastings, Sierra Leone on 1 August 1941 as a Fleet Requirements Unit. Initial equipment was a few Swordfish and three Rocs, later increased to five, to which were added two Defiants and several Walruses during 1942. Between April and December 1943 the squadron was responsible for the local defence of Sierra Leone. No.777 disbanded at Hastings on 25 December 1944.

On 23 May 1945 No.777 reformed from 'B' Flight of No.778 Squadron as a Trials Unit for service aboard HMS *Pretoria Castle*. Various trials were carried out, mainly with Seafires, with Gosport, Ford and Ayr all being used whilst ashore. The squadron disbanded into No.778 Squadron on 3 January 1946.

Identification Markings
All types single letters 1941/4, also *SA+* on Defiant. Single letters 1945/6.

Aircraft Equipment	Period of Service	Example
Roc I	Aug 1941 - Aug 1943	L3067
Walrus	May 1942 - Dec 1944	W2681
Swordfish I	Aug 1941 - Mar 1944	P4220
Swordfish II	Aug 1942 - Jul 1944	HS391
Defiant TT.I	Oct 1942 - Aug 1944	DR962 (T)
Kingfisher I	Mar 1944 - Aug 1944	FN708
Firefly I	May 1945 - Jul 1945	DK427
Corsair III	Jul 1945 -	JS806
Avenger I	Jul 1945 - Dec 1945	JZ181
Barracuda II	Jul 1945 - Dec 1945	NX664
Hellcat I	Jul 1945 - Oct 1945	JV136
Auster I	Aug 1945 - Dec 1945	LB384
Seafire F.III	Oct 1945 - Dec 1945	RX344
Seafire F.XV	May 1945 - Jul 1945	PK245
Seafire F.XVII	Dec 1945 - Mar 1946	SX161
Seafire F.45	May 1945 - Dec 1945	PK245
Seafire F.46	May 1945 - Jun 1945	
Seafire F.47	May 1945 - Jun 1945	
Mosquito FB.VI	Nov 1945 - Dec 1945	LR336
Mosquito B.25	Oct 1945 - Dec 1945	KB696

Commanding Officers
L/C CE Fenwick RN 1 Aug 1941
L/C(A) HJ Gibbs RNVR 5 Aug 1941
L/C(A) FC Muir RNVR 22 Jul 1942
L/C(A) C Draper RNVR 27 Sep 1943
L/C(A) MN Stewart RN 15 Mar 1944
Squadron disbanded 25 Dec 1944
Lt(A) DR Carter RNVR 23 May 1945
L/C(A) JRN Gardner RN 4 Jun 1945
Squadron disbanded 3 Jan 1946

Squadron bases
Hastings 1 Aug 1941
(A/S detts of 2/3 Swordfish to Monrovia in 1944)
(Occasional flights to Conakry, French Guinea)
Squadron disbanded 25 Dec 1944
HMS Pretoria Castle 23 May 1945
(Used Ayr as shore base to 17.9.45, then Ford. Gosport also used)
Squadron disbanded 3 Jan 1946

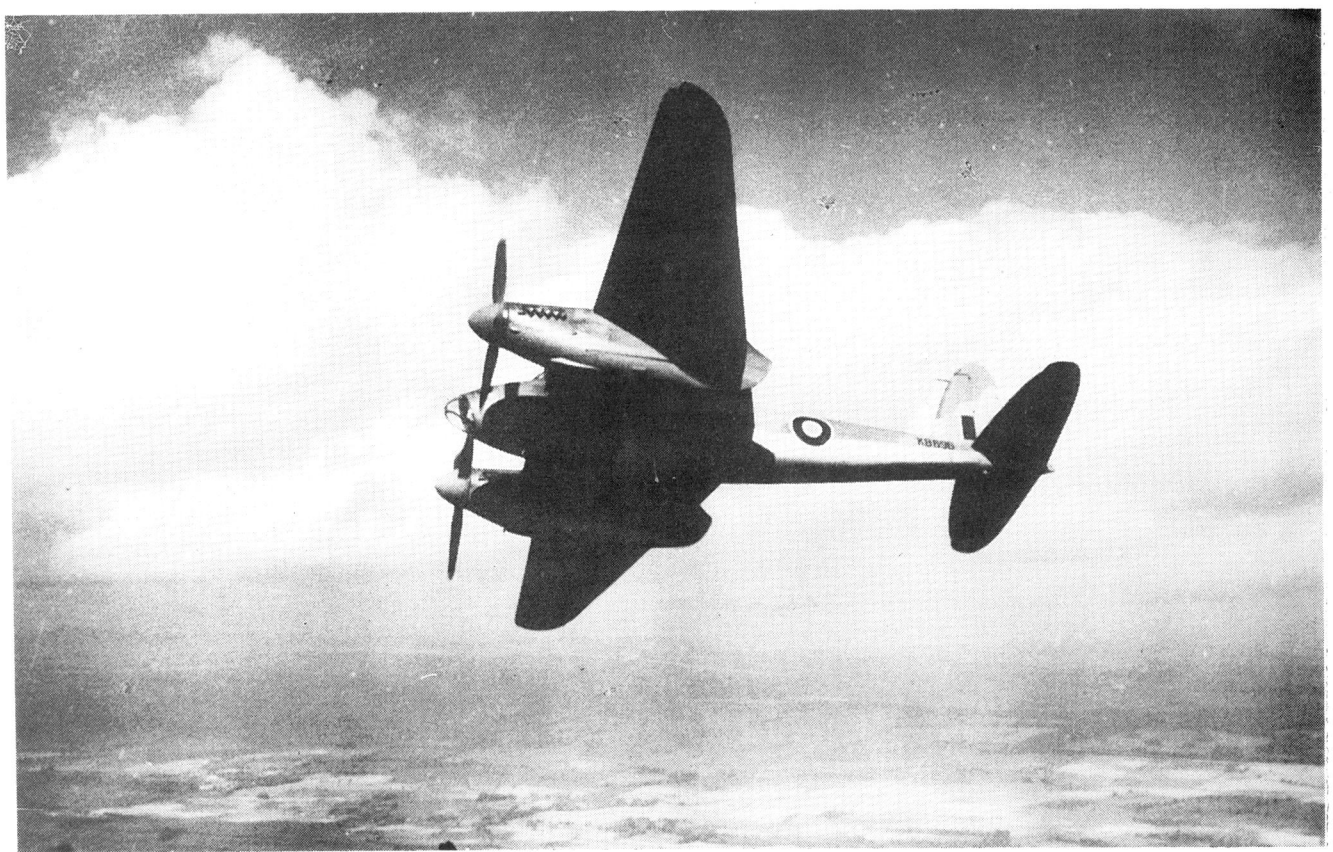

de Havilland Mosquito B.25 KB696 of No.777 Squadron, Ford in 1945 (Cliff Crellin)

No.778 Squadron

Badge: On a blue field, a pair of inside and outside callipers interlaced gold
Motto: Ex quaestione veritas (From examination truth emerges)

No.778 Squadron formed at Lee-on-Solent on 28 September 1939 as a Service Trials Unit squadron. Initial equipment was Swordfish, Walruses, Skuas and Rocs, but by the time it moved to Arbroath on 6 July 1940 it also had Albacores and Fulmars, these being soon followed by Martlets and Sea Hurricanes. Service trials were carried out on all new types of naval aircraft as well as new equipment, and aircraft types received during 1941 and 1942 included the Seafire, Chesapeake, Kingfisher and Barracuda. The squadron moved to Crail on 5 March 1943, and on 26 July 1943 'B' Flight was formed for deck trials in HMS *Pretoria Castle*. Equipment tested around that time included flame floats and aerial mines. A further move was made to Arbroath on 15 August 1944, where more new types of aircraft included Avenger, Corsair, Firebrand, and Firefly. 'C' Flight formed on 7 March 1945 from the disbanded No.739 Squadron for blind approach development work, but was soon absorbed into the main body of the squadron. 'B' Flight, which had operated largely as a separate unit aboard HMS *Pretoria Castle*, became No.777 Squadron on 23 May 1945.

Between 9 and 17 August 1945 No.778 moved south to Gosport, where on 1 October 1945 it absorbed No.707 Squadron and took over responsibility for radar trials. Moving to Ford on 3 January 1946 it reabsorbed No.777 Squadron, and adopted the dual role of Service Trials Unit and Carrier Trials Unit, Sea Mosquitoes and Sea Hornets being received about that time. Sea Furies were tested from February 1947 by the Intensive Flying Development Flight, then due to runway repairs the squadron moved out to Tangmere on 18 July 1947. Moving to Lee-on-Solent on 28 May 1948, the squadron was disbanded into No.703 Squadron on 16 August 1948.

No.778 reformed at Culdrose on 5 November 1951 as the Airborne Early Warning squadron. Equipped with 4 Skyraider AEW.1s, it disbanded on 7 July 1952 to form the basis of No.849 Squadron.

Identification Markings
All types *CO* only from 3.43 (no individual letters), to *FD9A+* 1.46, to *000-042/FD* 1946, to *001-029/LP* 1947. Skyraider *301-304/CW*.

Commanding Officers
L/C RA Kilroy RN 28 Sep 1939
L/C JPG Bryant RN 22 Apr 1940
L/C AJ Tillard RN 6 Jan 1941
L/C HP Bramwell
    DSO DSC RN 21 Jul 1941
L/C HJF Lane RN 1 Mar 1943
L/C PB Schonfield
    RN 25 Apr 1944
L/C EM Britton RN 5 Feb 1945

Commanding Officers
L/C(A) MA Lacayo
    RN 1 Oct 1945
L/C RHP Carver
    DSC RN 3 Jul 1946
L/C FRA Turnbull
    DSC & Bar RN 16 Jan 1948
Squadron disbanded 16 Aug 1948
Lt JD Treacher RN 5 Nov 1951
Squadron disbanded 7 Jul 1952

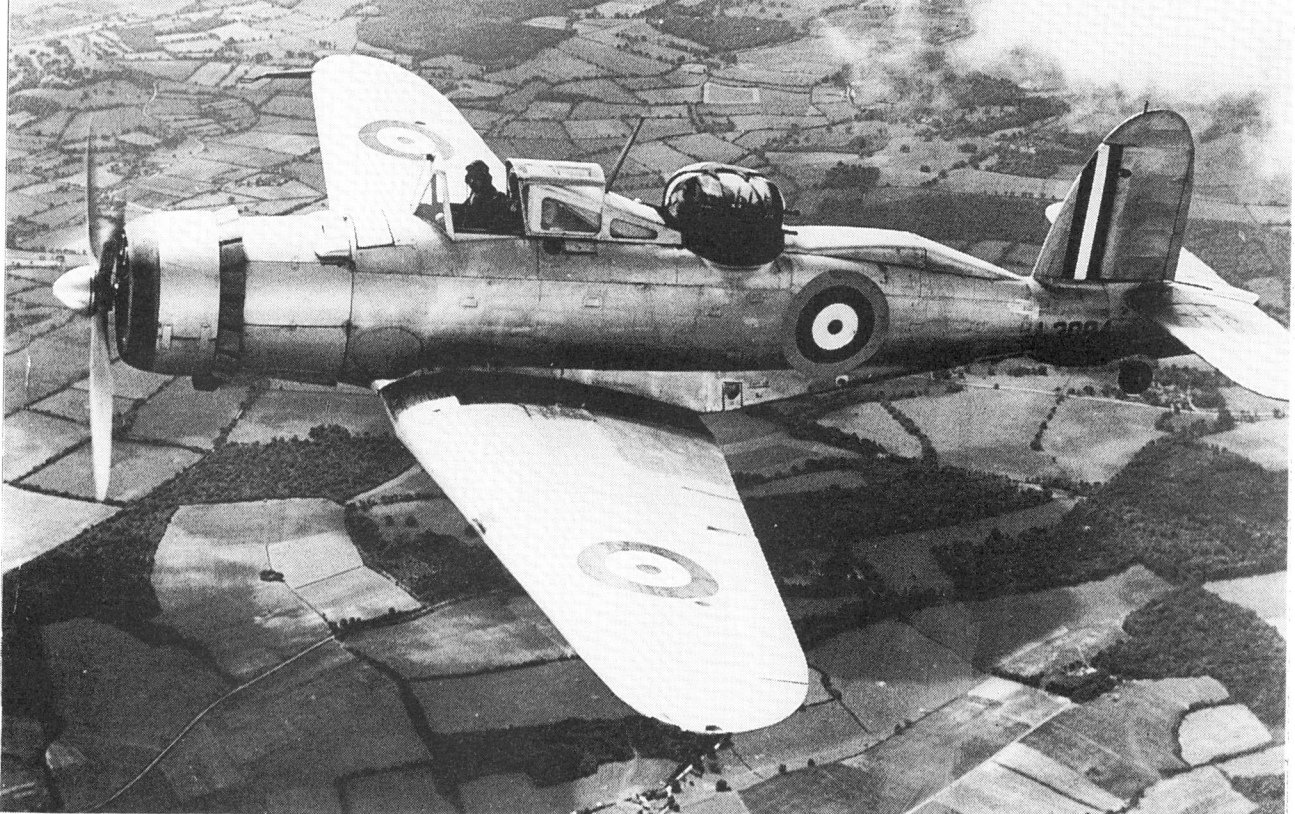

Blackburn Roc L3084 of No.778 Squadron in 1940. (Capt E.D.G.Lewin)

Aircraft Equipment	Period of Service	Example	
Swordfish I	Sep 1939 - Jan 1944	P4213	(CO)
Swordfish II	Sep 1942 - Feb 1945	DK688	
Skua II	Sep 1939 - Mar 1940	L2944	
Roc I	Dec 1939 - Feb 1942	L3141	
Walrus	Sep 1939 - Sep 1943	W2780	
Albacore I	Feb 1940 - Sep 1943	BF631	
Fulmar I	May 1940 - Sep 1944	N1861	
Fulmar II	Dec 1940 - Sep 1944	X8641	
Chesapeake I	Jun 1941 - Dec 1941	AL916	
Proctor Ia	Oct 1941	P6074	
Proctor IIa	Oct 1941 - Nov 1941	BV540	
Spitfire Vb	Nov 1941	AB986	
Spitfire IX	Apr 1944 - May 1945	NH582	
Spitfire XII	Feb 1943 - Mar 1943	EN226	
Sea Gladiator	Dec 1941 - Mar 1943	N2265	
Sea Hurricane Ib	Aug 1941 - Jun 1943	Z7082	
Sea Hurricane IIc	1943 - Oct 1943	JS233	
Kingfisher I	May 1942 - Aug 1942	FN650	
Magister (McLaren undercarriage)	Sep 1942 - Sep 1942	P6456	
Havoc I	Oct 1942 - Dec 1942	BB906	
Typhoon Ib	Feb 1943 - Feb 1943	DN419	
Sea Otter I	Nov 1943 - Jul 1946	JN185	
Helldiver I	Nov 1943 - Nov 1944	JW117	
Martlet I	Sep 1940 - Nov 1941	AX827	
Martlet II	Jan 1944	AJ114	
Martlet IV	Apr 1943 - Apr 1944	FN153	(CO)
Wildcat VI	Dec 1944 - Jun 1945	JV721	
Barracuda I	May 1942 - Nov 1943	P1770	
Barracuda II	Feb 1943 - Nov 1946	P9717	(CO)
Barracuda III	Dec 1945 - Apr 1948	RJ936	
Barracuda TR.V	Sep 1946 - Jul 1947	RK534	
Seafire Ib	Jan 1942 - Feb 1945	MB361	
Seafire IIc	Jul 1942 - Apr 1944	MA995	
Seafire III	Jun 1943 - Mar 1947	RX173	(FD9R)
Seafire XV	Mar 1944 - Aug 1946	SW862	(FD9M)
Seafire F.17	Jul 1945 - Jul 1948	SX283	(016/LP)
Seafire F.45	Jun 1945 - Oct 1947	LA450	(012/LP)
Seafire F.46	Jul 1946 - Jan 1948	LA550	
Seafire F.47	Dec 1946 - Mar 1947	PS947	
Airacobra I	Apr 1945	AH574	
Firebrand F.I	Feb 1943 -	DD815	
Firebrand TF.III	Apr 1945 - Sep 1945	DK395	
Firebrand TF.IV	Sep 1945 - May 1947	EK657	
Firebrand TF.V	Oct 1947 - Nov 1947	EK692	
Avenger I	1942 - Apr 1945	JZ181	
Avenger II	Apr 1944 - Jun 1947	JZ516	
Avenger III	Apr 1946 - Jan 1948	JZ638	
Traveller I	Jan 1945 - Aug 1945	FT491	
Hellcat I	Oct 1943 - Sep 1945	FN330	
Hellcat II	Feb 1945 - Aug 1945	JV264	
Corsair II	Apr 1944 - Nov 1945	JT612	
Corsair III	Feb 1945 - May 1945	JS580	
Corsair IV	Oct 1945 - 1945	KD180	
Auster I	Jan 1945 - Jan 1948	LB384	
Seafang F.32	May 1947	VB895	
Mosquito FB.VI	Nov 1944 - Nov 1945	LR336	
Mosquito PR.16	Dec 1946 - Sep 1947	RG171	(042/FD)
Mosquito B.25	May 1945 -	KB696	
Sea Mosquito TR.33	Apr 1946 - Jul 1948	TW285	(041/FD)
Anson I	1945 - 1946	NK201	
Sea Vampire F.10	Jul 1946	LZ551	
Vampire F.1	Sep 1947 - Apr 1948	VV269	
Harvard III	Dec 1947 - Feb 1948	FT972	
Oxford I	Apr 1946 - Aug 1947	PH185	(002/FD)
Dominie I	Oct 1947 - Mar 1948	NF871	(002/FD)
Firefly FR.1	Feb 1943 - Jul 1948	Z1955	(026/FD)
Firefly T.1	Jun 1947	MB750	
Firefly FR.4	Feb 1947 - Nov 1947	VG968	(028/LP)
Firefly 5	May 1948	VT363	
Sea Hornet F.20	Mar 1946 - Jul 1948	TT210	(005/LP)
Sea Fury F.10	Feb 1947 - Jul 1947	TF907	
Sea Fury FB.11	Feb 1948 - Sep 1949	TF969	
Skyraider AEW.1	Nov 1951 - Jul 1952	WT946	(303/CW)

Fairey Barracuda II MX727 '8M' of No.778 Squadron, Arbroath during trials with an air-sea rescue launch in 1945

Supermarine Sea Otter JN185 of No.778 Squadron. (MAP)

Gloster Meteor F.3 EE337 '051/FD' of No.778 Squadron, Ford in 1959. (John Rawlings)

Squadron bases		Squadron bases	
Lee-on-Solent	28 Sep 1939	HMS Illustrious	14 Nov 1946
Arbroath	6 Jul 1940	(Dt)	to 12 Dec 1946
Crail	5 Mar 1943	(known as Night	
HMS Pretoria Castle (B Flt)	14 Aug 1943 to 23 May 1945	Fighter Trials Unit) Tangmere	18 Jul 1947
Arbroath	15 Aug 1944	Lee-on-Solent	28 May 1948
Gosport	9 Aug 1945	Squadron disbanded	16 Aug 1948
Ford	3 Jan 1946	Culdrose	5 Nov 1951
		Squadron disbanded	7 Jul 1952

No.779 Squadron

Badge: On a field bendy of four gold and black, a roundel per fess white and green in chief the battlements of a tower issuant proper and in base a key fesswise wards downwards gold

Motto: Finis coronat opus
(The end crowns the work)

No.779 Squadron formed at North Front, Gibraltar on 1 October 1941 as a Fleet Requirements Unit. Initially it had only 2 Skuas, with which it undertook drogue towing and coastal defence during 1942. Small numbers of Swordfish, Fulmars and Sea Hurricanes were later used, the Skuas being replaced by Defiant target tugs in April 1943. Shortly afterwards a few Beaufighter IIs arrived, and in August and September 1943 a detachment was in Italy for operational work based at Taranto. On return from this the Beaufighters were detached to numerous places in North Africa. Martinets replaced the Defiants in June 1944, and by January 1945 the strength was 2 Swordfish, 3 Beaufighters, 2 Hurricanes and 9 Martinets. No.779 disbanded at North Front on 5 August 1945.

Aircraft Equipment	Period of Service	Example	
Skua II	Oct 1941 - Apr 1943	L3006	
Swordfish I	Oct 1941 - Aug 1942	V4380	(G)
Swordfish II	Oct 1941 - Jan 1945	HS410	
Fulmar II	Feb 1942 - Jan 1943	X8768	(Q)
Sea Hurricane Ib	Feb 1942	V7433	
Defiant TT.III	Apr 1943 - May 1944	DR986	
Seafire Ib	May 1943 - Oct 1944	MB348	(Z)
Beaufighter II	Jun 1943 - Aug 1945	V8169	
Hurricane IIc	Jun 1944 - Apr 1945	LB623	
Martinet TT.I	Jun 1944 - Aug 1945	NR479	
Seafire	May 1945 - Aug 1945		

Identification Markings
Some aircraft single letters.

Commanding Officers
L/C(A) BF Cox RNVR 1 Oct 1941
L/C(A) L Gilbert RNVR 17 Jan 1942
L/C(A) JM Keene-Miller RNVR 22 Jun 1942
L/C CR Holman RNR 1 May 1943
L/C(A) EL Meiklejohn RNVR 14 Sep 1943
Squadron disbanded 5 Aug 1945

Squadron bases
North Front	1 Oct 1941
Taranto (Dt)	18-22 Sep 1943
Blida (Dt)	19 Oct 1943 to 12 Oct 1944
Tafaroui (Dt)	27 Oct 1943 to 21 May 1944
Oujda (Dt)	26 Jan 1944 to 16 Feb 1944
Maison Blanche (Dt)	22 Feb 1944 to 23 May 1944
La Senia (Dt)	3 Mar 1944 to 3 Aug 1944
Squadron disbanded	5 Aug 1945

No.780 Squadron

No.780 Squadron formed at Eastleigh on 2 October 1939 as a Conversion Course Unit. Its task was to convert to naval standards civilian trained volunteer pilots, being equipped with a mixture of aircraft which included the Hart Trainer, Osprey, Nimrod, Shark, Swordfish, Proctor, Hornet Moth, Gipsy Moth, Tiger Moth and Vega Gull. It had been envisaged that this task would be completed within a few months, but a need was found for other kinds of conversion work, and it therefore continued in existence, moving to Lee-on-Solent on 7 October 1940. From August 1943 one of its main tasks was to convert biplane pilots to the Barracuda, but this task was taken over by No.798 Squadron two months later, and on 9 October 1943 No.780 moved to Charlton Horethorne as a Pilot Training squadron. A further move was made to Lee-on-Solent on 28 November 1944, where it disbanded into No.794 Squadron on 2 January 1945.

On 28 March 1946 No.780 reformed at Hinstock as an Advanced Flying Training Unit, being styled the Naval Advanced Flying School. Equipped with an assortment of Oxfords, Harvards, Fireflies and Tiger Moths, it also had a few Lancasters based at the Peplow satellite, these being used for testing and experience in dropping loads. The remnants of No.758 Squadron were absorbed on 14 May 1946 as 'B' Flight, and on 17 December 1946 this moved to Crail to operate as the Naval Instrument Flying Instructional Flight. On 27 March 1947 the squadron moved to Donibristle, then on 27 May 1947 to Culdrose, where the Crail detachment was reabsorbed. On 16 November 1949 No.780 disbanded at Culdrose, and its task of Naval Instrument Flying School, which was known as the SMAC 14 Course, was taken over by the Shorts-operated Admiralty Flight at Rochester.

Identification Markings
Individual numbers up to 1941, to L1A+ 1942, to BY1A+ 10.43, to L1A+ 11.44. U1A+ to U3A+ from 3.46 to 1947, then 201/CW+ on Harvard & 601/CW+ on Oxford.

Aircraft Equipment	Period of Service	Example	
Hart Trainer	Oct 1939 - Aug 1942	K6433	
Seal	Oct 1939 -	K4201	
Magister I	Oct 1939 - May 1941	L8204	
Nimrod II	Oct 1939 - Jun 1940	K3654	
Osprey	Oct 1939 - Feb 1942	K5744	
Shark II	Oct 1939 - Nov 1941	L2367	
Vega Gull	Jun 1940 - Jul 1940	G-AFIT	
Gipsy Moth	Jun 1940 - Aug 1940	K1898	
Hornet Moth	Mar 1941 - Apr 1941	P6788	
Tutor	May 1940 - Aug 1942	K5602	
Magister	May 1940 - Apr 1941	L8204	
Tiger Moth II	Jun 1940 - Jan 1945	DE197	(L1A)
Proctor Ia	Jun 1940 - Aug 1943	P6006	
Proctor IIa	Aug 1943 - Sep 1944	BV551	
Master I	Sep 1940 - Oct 1943	N8045	
Master II	Jul 1944 - Oct 1944	DL905	
Audax	Dec 1941 - Aug 1942	K5221	
Skua II	Apr 1943 - Sep 1943	L2949	
Harvard I	Sep 1940		
Harvard III	Dec 1943 - Jan 1945	FT965	(X)
Whitney Straight	Jan 1944 -	BS355	
Barracuda II	Aug 1943 - Oct 1943	P9721	
Blenheim I	Jun 1943 - Dec 1943	L6764	(L1N)
Swordfish I	Jun 1940 - Jul 1943	L2765	(BY1S)
Swordfish II	Jul 1943 - Sep 1944	HS329	(BY1U)
Fulmar I	Jun 1943 - Oct 1943	N1923	
Tiger Moth II	Mar 1946 - Sep 1946	X5106	
Seafire XV	Apr 1946 - Nov 1946	SW902	(U1E)
Seafire F.45	Nov 1946 - Dec 1946	LA489	
Firefly F.1	Mar 1946 - Dec 1946	MB475	(U1L)
Mosquito T.III	Oct 1946 - Dec 1946	VA879	
Mosquito FB.VI	Sep 1946 - Dec 1946	RF901	
Oxford I	Mar 1946 - Nov 1949	LB413	(604/CW)
Harvard IIb	Mar 1946 - Nov 1949	KF522	(U2R)
Harvard III	Mar 1946 - Nov 1949	EZ345	(U2B)
Lancaster I	Mar 1946 - Jan 1947	NG232	

Commanding Officers		Squadron bases	
L/C(E) HS Cooper RN	2 Oct 1939	Eastleigh	2 Oct 1939
L/C(A) J Goodyear RNVR	7 Oct 1940	Lee-on-Solent (Dts Hamble)	7 Oct 1940
L/C(A) TG Stubley RNVR	17 Aug 1942	Charlton Horethorne	9 Oct 1943
		Lee-on-Solent	28 Nov 1944
Squadron disbanded	2 Jan 1945	Squadron disbanded	2 Jan 1945
L/C DCEF Gibson DSC RN	28 Mar 1946	Hinstock (satt Peplow)	28 Mar 1946
Lt(A) WE Cotton RN	17 Dec 1946	Crail (Dt - IF Instl Flt) to	17 Dec 1946 23 May 1947
Lt SP Luke RN(temp)	2 Oct 1947	Donibristle	27 Mar 1947
L/C GR Humphries RN	5 Jan 1948	Culdrose	27 May 1947
		Squadron disbanded	16 Nov 1949
Lt(A) RB Lunberg RN	16 Nov 1948		
Lt(A) MA Birrell RN	31 Mar 1949		
Squadron disbanded 16 Nov 1949			

Fairey Swordfish II HS228 dual-control trainer of No.780 Squadron, Lee-on-Solent around 1943/4. (FAA Museum).

No.781 Squadron

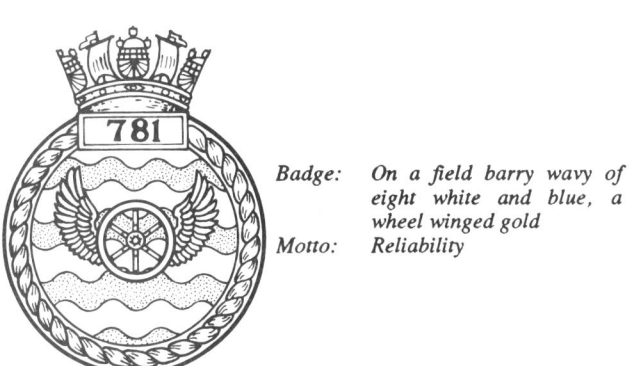

Badge: On a field barry wavy of eight white and blue, a wheel winged gold
Motto: Reliability

No.781 Squadron was originally earmarked to form at Lee-on-Solent in late 1939 as a Reserve Amphibious Bomber Reconnaissance squadron equipped with 6 Walruses. In the event it actually formed there on 20 March 1940 as a Communications Unit, equipped with various types of aircraft including the Swordfish, Fulmar, Walrus and Hornet Moth in the first instance. Later types to be introduced included the Vega Gull, Dominie, Tiger Moth, Proctor, Hudson and Oxford. A few Beaufighter IIs were received in June 1943 for a Beaufighter Conversion Course, but these broke away on 11 October to help form No.798 Squadron. The squadron's duties gradually increased to include both training and refresher flying.

From February 1944 'B' Flight, which usually consisted of 2 Swordfish and a Proctor, was based at Fairey's Heath Row aerodrome for the use of officers at the Admiralty. During the summer of 1944 an Anson was based at Rochester for use by the Commander-in-Chief The Nore during the invasion period. 'X' Flight went to the Continent on 3 May 1945, but on 31 July 1945 No.781 disbanded into Nos.782 and 799 Squadrons. Three of the Dominies remained at Lee-on-Solent as a detached flight of No.782, and the Continental detachment became 'X' Flight of No.799 Squadron.

On 27 June 1946 No.781 Squadron reformed at Lee-on-Solent from 'B' Flight of No.799 Squadron, again as a Communications squadron, being known for some time as the Southern Communications Squadron. The Continental 'X' Flight returned to the squadron, equipped with Expediters and an Anson XIX, until disbanding on 17 November 1947. The main equipment of the reformed No.781 was Dominies and Expediters, plus Sea Otters for a Search and Rescue Flight. By September 1951 the squadron's task consisted of providing communications aircraft for VIPs, and operating an Instrument Examining Flight and also a Bad Weather Flying Training Flight which undertook day and night training of all naval pilots in flying in adverse weather conditions. The refresher flying task was restored when No.799 Squadron disbanded on 12 August 1952. No.781 by then comprised a Communications Section, a Training and Miscellaneous Section, and an Instrument Flying Examining Section. Equipment consisted of the Sea Prince, Expeditor, Dominie, Firefly, Harvard, Sea Fury, Meteor T.7 and Oxford. The SAR commitment was dropped when the Sea Otters were withdrawn on 3 October 1952.

On 21 November 1952 No.781 took over the Junior Officers Air Course, forming a JOAC Flight equipped with four Firefly Trainers, two Meteor T.7s an Anson 1 and a Sea Prince, all except the latter being later replaced by Sea Vampires and Sea Balliols. An Admiralty Flight was formed on 6 September 1954, with two Firefly Trainers, and four Sea Furies, on which staff and Admiralty pilots could keep in flying practice. The first Sea Devons arrived in April 1955, and on 30 September 1957 the JOAC Flight became No.702 Squadron. At the end of 1958 the task of the Northern Communications Squadron was taken over by No.781, which then ceased to be known as the Southern Communications Squadron. The 1959 Boyd Trophy award was made to the squadron for its efficiency in carrying out communications flights, and the first Whirlwind arrived in 1959, followed in 1961 by Sea Herons. Strength in January 1967 consisted of five Sea Devons, three Sea Herons, two Whirlwinds and a Sea Hawk, the latter for use by the Flag Officer Air (Home), who had previously flown a Sea Vampire T.22. Wessex HU.5s arrived in June 1969 for use by the SAR Flight, in place of Whirlwinds. By the time the squadron disbanded on 31 March 1981 its aircraft comprised Wessex HU.5s for both VIP and SAR work, Sea Herons, Sea Devons and a Chipmunk.

Identification Markings
All types *L8A+*, *L9A+* & *L0A+* from 1942, also Beaufighter *L1A+* 1943. From 6.46 Seafire *101-167/LP*, Firefly/Seafire/Harvard/Sea Balliol *201-293*, Sea Otter *301-306/LP*, Meteor/Sea Vampire *441-453*, Oxford *606-608*, Expeditor/Dominie/Oxford/Anson/Sea Prince/Sea Devon *850-869/LP*. From 1.56 all types *740-755/LP*, to *814-829* 7.65.

Walrus L2219 'L9Z' of No.781 Sqdn, Lee-on-Solent. (FAA Museum)

Supermarine Sea Otter JN202 '314/LP' of No.781 Squadron, Lee-on-Solent in 1951. (MAP)

Aircraft Equipment	Period of Service	Example	
Walrus I	Sep 1940 - Nov 1942	L2219	
Fulmar I	Sep 1940		
Swordfish I	Sep 1940 - Dec 1941	V4378	(L9S)
Swordfish II	Mar 1942 - Feb 1943	HS314	
Hornet Moth	Jun 1940 - Jan 1943	P6785	
Q.6 Petrel	Dec 1940 - Oct 1942	AX860	
Falcon	Jun 1940	W9373	
DH.86b	Jul 1940 -	AX841	
Fox Moth	Jun 1941 -	DZ213	
Nimrod II	Apr 1941		
Vega Gull	Jul 1941 - Aug 1943	P5987	(L9H)
Hart	Jul 1941 - Aug 1941		
Albacore I	Jun 1942 - Dec 1942	X9282	
Sea Hurricane Ib	Nov 1942 - Feb 1945	Z4550	
Sea Hurricane IIc	Oct 1943	NF733	
Chesapeake I	Dec 1942	AL926	
Proctor Ia	Dec 1942 - Aug 1944	P6068	(L9F)
Proctor II	Mar 1942 - Aug 1943	Z7242	
Proctor IIa	Nov 1943 - Oct 1944	BV535	
Barracuda II	May 1943 - Sep 1943	P9807	
Beaufighter II	Jun 1943 - Oct 1943	T3223	(L1P)
Oxford I	Feb 1943 - Jul 1945	V3390	(L9B)
Martlet I	May 1943	BJ518	
Fulmar II	Oct 1943	X8746	
Tiger Moth II	Dec 1943 - Jul 1945	BB723	
Dominie I	Jan 1944 - Jul 1945	X7350	(L9C)
Seafire Ib	Jul 1943	NX963	
Seafire III	Aug 1944		
Hudson III	Mar 1945 - Jun 1945	T9410	
Hudson IV	Sep 1944 - May 1946	AE635	(LOB)
Hudson V	Jul 1944 - Jan 1945	AM550	
Anson I	1945 - Jul 1945	DJ561	(L8J)
Reliant I	1945 - Jul 1945	FL145	
Sea Otter	1945 - Jul 1945	JM813	
Expediter C.I	Jun 1945 - Jul 1945	HB162	
Expediter C.II	Jun 1945 - Jul 1945	KP110	
Traveller I	Jun 1944 - Jul 1945	FT505	(OM)
Avro 652	Mar 1942	DG655	
Anson C.XII	Jun 1946 - Nov 1946	PH655	
Hellcat II	Jul 1946	KE210	
Expediter C.2	Jun 1946 - Jan 1955	KP107	(851/LP)
Sea Otter	Jun 1946 - Oct 1952	RD878	(313/LP)
Dominie 1	Jun 1946 - Jun 1963	NF871	(859/LP)

Aircraft Equipment	Period of Service	Example	
Oxford 1	Mar 1948 - May 1954	DF518	(608/LP)
Anson 1	Dec 1951 - Sep 1953	NK837	(869/LP)
Seafire F.15	Dec 1949 - Feb 1950	SW818	
Seafire F.17	May 1949 - Oct 1949	SX161	(166/LP)
Seafire F.46	Mar 1947 - 1947	LA560	
Auster I	Dec 1949 - Feb 1950	LB440?	
Firefly FR.1	Sep 1949 - Mar 1954	MB614	(207/LP)
Firefly T.1	Nov 1949 - Jan 1954	DK453	(221/LP)
Firefly T.2	Oct 1950 - Nov 1956	DK550	(226/LP)
Firefly FR.4	1946 - Dec 1949	TW750	(238/LP)
Firefly FR.5		?	(239/LP)
Harvard T.2b	Nov 1947 - Feb 1954	KF504	(267/LP)
Harvard T.3	Apr 1953 - May 1953	EZ376	
Sea Fury F.10	Oct 1948 - Mar 1950	TF908	
Sea Fury FB.11	Dec 1953 - Feb 1955	VR928	(120/LP)
Sea Fury T.20	May 1950 - Sep 1954	VX299	(206/LP)
Meteor T.7	Apr 1951 - Jun 1954	WL352	(442)
Swordfish TS.3	Mar 1953 - Nov 1963	NF389	("5B")
Vampire T.11/22	Nov 1953 - May 1954	WW458	(-/LS)
Sea Vampire T.22	Oct 1953 - Dec 1964	XG771	(754)
Sea Balliol T.21	Apr 1954 - Dec 1958	WL723	(291)
Sea Devon C.20	Apr 1955 - Mar 1981	XK895	(c/s749)
Sea Prince C.1	Jul 1953 - Feb 1965	WF137	(c/s850)
Sea Prince C.2	Jul 1953 - Jun 1961	WJ349	(c/s852)
Sea Prince T.1	Sep 1953 - Sep 1957	WP319	(c/s857)
Tiger Moth T.2	Aug 1960 - Mar 1972	BB814	
Whirlwind HAR.1	Jul 1961 - Mar 1962	XA862	(c/s747)
Whirlwind HAR.3	Jul 1963 - Sep 1963	XG583	
Whirlwind HAS.7	Jun 1965	XL881	
Whirlwind HAS.22	Jan 1959 - Mar 1970	WV223	(c/s827)
Sea Hawk FGA.6	May 1962 - May 1967	XE390	(c/s928)
Wessex HU.5	Jun 1969 - Mar 1981	XT770	(c/s816)
Sea Heron C.2	Jul 1961 - Mar 1981	XR444	(c/s824)
Heron C.4	Sep 1969 - Jun 1970	XR391	(c/s821)
Heron CC.4	Jul 1972 - Mar 1981	XM296	(c/s824)
Chipmunk T.10	Jun 1971 - Mar 1981	WK635	(c/s814)

781X

Aircraft Equipment	Period of Service	Example
Dominie C.I	May 1945 - Jul 1945	NF847
Expediter C.II	Jun 1946 - Nov 1947	KP110
Anson C.XIX	Jun 1946 - Nov 1947	TX157

Percival Sea Prince C.2 WH348 of No.781 Squadron, Lee-on-Solent painted up as an Admiral's Barge for the use of the Flag Officer Air (Home) in 1954. (MAP)

Squadron bases
Lee-on-Solent 20 Mar 1940
B Flt:
 Heath Row 17 Feb 1944
 Redes 701 Sqdn 18 Apr 1945
X Flt:
 Toussus 3 May 1945
 Wunstorf 11 Jun 1945
 (operating Buckeburg)
 Redes 799X Flt 31 Jul 1945
Squadron disbanded 31 Jul 1945
Lee-on-Solent 27 Jun 1946
X Flt:
 Wunstorf 27 Jun 1946
 Fuhlsbuttel 17 Sep 1946
 Flt disbanded 17 Nov 1947
 Ford (Dt) 24- 31 May 1950
Squadron disbanded 31 Mar 1981

Commanding Officers
L/C EJE Burt RN 20 Mar 1940
L/C(A) ACS Irwin
  RNVR 7 Sep 1940
L/C(A) JM Keene-Miller
  RNVR 15 Feb 1941
L/C(A) Sir George
  JE Lewis Bt RNVR 7 Nov 1941
L/C(A) WB Caldwell
  RNVR 1 Dec 1944
Squadron disbanded 31 Jul 1945
None 27 Jun 1946
L/C(E) PF Clayton
  RN 19 Aug 1946
Lt(A) LWA
  Barrington RN 7 Jul 1948
L/C DL Stirling RN 19 Jul 1950
L/C DH Richards RN 9 Jul 1953
L/C MW Rudorf
  DSC RN 28 Apr 1954

Commanding Officers
L/C H Cureton RN 15 Jun 1956
L/C JS Barnes RN 13 Jul 1957
L/C RC Stock RN 22 Nov 1960
L/C SW Birse
  OBE DSC RN 30 Nov 1962
L/C FP Curry RN 2 Sep 1963
L/C PGW Morris RN 28 Sep 1964
L/C RA Shilcock RN 22 Mar 1965
L/C AMcK Sinclair
  RN 4 Oct 1967
L/C PGW Morris RN 3 Apr 1969
L/C DM Rouse RN 15 May 1970
L/C R Garvin RN 24 Mar 1975
L/C R King RN 13 Dec 1976
L/C GD Varley RN 25 May 1979
Squadron disbanded 31 Mar 1981

781X

Commanding Officers
L.V. AE Bret
 (French Navy) 3 May 1945
Flight to 799 Sqdn 31 Jul 1945
L.V. AE Bret
 (French Navy) 27 Jun 1946
L/C(A) TE Sargent
  RN 1 Aug 1946
Flight disbanded 17 Nov 1947

Sikorsky Whirlwind HAS.22 WV204 of No.781 Squadron, Lee-on-Solent in 1968. (MAP)

Handley Page 'Sparrow' Harrow K6906 named 'Merlin XV' of No.782 Squadron, Donibristle around 1942/3. (Tom Sargent)

Flag bedecked de Havilland Dominies 'Merlin I' and 'Merlin IX' of No.782 Squadron, Donibristle. (via Cecil Bristow)

No.782 Squadron

Badge: On a green field, a horse's head erased and winged white gorged with a chaplet of roses, thistles and shamrock proper
Motto: None

No.782 Squadron formed at Ford on 23 October 1939 as an Armament Training squadron. It was intended to have Swordfish, but before these could be delivered the squadron disbanded on 10 November 1939, its personnel being amalgamated with those of No.815 Squadron to form No.774 Squadron.

On 1 December 1940 No.782 reformed from a Communications Flight at Donibristle which had itself formed on 1 July 1940 with Jersey Airways crews who had accepted RN commissions. Aircraft initially comprised Flamingos, DH.86s and Proctors.

Known as the Northern Communications Squadron, it established a link between isolated air stations in mainland Scotland, Shetlands, Orkneys and Northern Ireland by operating regular services between them and also to Lee-on-Solent. Its aircraft, many of which carried as identification the station name 'Merlin' plus an individual number, later included Expediters, Oxfords, Travellers and 'Sparrow'-type Harrows. The latter as well as being used for passenger carrying were also equipped to carry engines and urgently required spares.

When No.781 Squadron disbanded on 31 July 1945, No.782 took over part of its task, detached flights of Dominies being by then stationed at Lee-on-Solent, Eglinton and Inverness. The squadron at that time operated mainly in support of the new Flag Officer Flying Training headquarters, and several Fireflies were received for a High Speed Flight. Small numbers of Seafires and Sea Furies were also flown. Following the transfer of FOFT to Yeovilton in July 1953, the need for the squadron diminished and it was consequently disbanded on 9 October 1953, its communications role being continued by a civilian-operated Northern Communications Squadron, which took over the Dominies.

Identification Markings
Names *Merlin 1+*, to *B8A+* 1946, to *201-205/DO & 801-815/DO* 1946.

de Havilland Flamingo R2766 served with No.782 Squadron at Donibristle between 1940 and 1945, being originally named 'Merlin VI' and later 'Merlin 27'.

Aircraft Equipment	Period of Service	Example	Commanding Officers		Squadron bases	
Flamingo	Dec 1940 - Aug 1945	BT312 (Merlin 27)	L/C(A) A Goodfellow		Ford	23 Oct 1939
DH.86/DH.86b	Dec 1940 - Mar 1945	X9442	RNVR	23 Sep 1940	Squadron disbanded 10 Nov 1939	
Proctor Ia	Dec 1940 - Apr 1942	P6074	L/C(A) WTD Gairdner		Donibristle	1 Dec 1940
Albacore I	Dec 1940 - 1941	N4240	RNVR	21 Mar 1941	Inverness (Dt)	22 Jan 1942
Skua II	Dec 1940 - 1941	L2887	L/C(A) GHGS Rayer			to 24 Aug 1942
Swordfish I	Dec 1940 - Mar 1941	P4219	OBE RNVR	7 Dec 1944	Inverness (Dt)	27 Jul 1944
Seal I	Dec 1940 - Jan 1941	K4795	L/C(A) JKN Evans			to 27 Jul 1945
Fulmar II	Feb 1941 - Mar 1941	N4100	RNVR	27 Jul 1945	Lee-on-Solent (Dt)	20 Jul 1945
Dominie I	Jul 1941 - Oct 1953	NF881 (B8H)	L/C(A) GP Barlass			to 27 Jun 1946
Q.6 Petrel		X9336	RN	28 Dec 1945	Eglinton (Dt)	1 Aug 1945
Moth	Oct 1941	W9368	L/C(A) H Whitaker			to 6 May 1946
'Sparrow' Harrow	Jun 1941 - Jul 1943	K6946 (Merlin XV)	RNVR	1 Oct 1946	Squadron disbanded	9 Oct 1953
Tiger Moth II	Dec 1941 - Jun 1946	T7796	L/C(A) TE Sargent			
Vega Gull	Jan 1942 - Aug 1943	W9377	RN	2 Dec 1947		
Oxford I	Jun 1942 - Apr 1953	PH187 (Merlin II)	L/C CC Thornton			
Reliant I	Nov 1943 - Apr 1944	FK906	RN	26 Oct 1949		
Expediter C.1	Oct 1944 - Oct 1945	HB162 (Merlin 23)	L/C V Barrington RN 1 Apr 1953			
Expediter C.2	May 1944 - Jul 1953	KP103 (807/DO)	Squadron disbanded 9 Oct 1953			
Traveller I	May 1944 - Sep 1945	FT500				
Dakota C.III	1944	FD904				
Hudson IV	Aug 1945 - May 1946	AE628				
Firefly FR.1	Aug 1945 - May 1953	PP584 (812/DO)				
Firefly T.1	May 1950 - Sep 1950	DK449 (203/DO)				
Firefly T.2	Sep 1950 - May 1953	DK540 (811/DO)				
Firefly FR.4	Dec 1948 - Apr 1953	VG985 (201/DO)				
Firefly 5	May 1948 - Jan 1949	VT398				
Firefly 6	Jul 1952 - Jan 1953	VX393				
Anson I	Apr 1946 - Sep 1949	NK505				
Anson C.XII	Feb 1947 - May 1947	PH656				
Harvard IIa/IIb	May 1946 - Sep 1949	EZ431				
Harvard III	Aug 1946 - Nov 1946	EZ254				
Avenger II	Nov 1946	JZ490				
Swordfish III	Nov 1946	NF399				
Seafire III	May 1947 - Jan 1948	NN189				
Seafire F.17	Dec 1947 - Oct 1948	SX238				
Sea Fury FB.11	Jun 1948 - Jun 1950	TF989				
Sea Fury T.20	May 1951 - Oct 1951	VZ352 (205/DO)				

Beech Expediter C.2 KP116 of No.782 Squadron visiting Culdrose in 1952. (Tony Hughes)

No.783 Squadron

No.783 Squadron formed at Arbroath on 9 January 1941 as an Air-to-Surface-Vessel Radar Training squadron. Equipped mainly with Swordfish, Albacores and Walruses, it also used a DH.86 fitted out as an ASV flying classroom, until this was damaged in July 1942 by 'friendly' gunfire from a minesweeper off Bell Rock, being then replaced by an ASV-equipped Wellington. The main equipment from early 1942, however, was Ansons, most of which were fitted with ASV. From March 1943 the squadron operated in conjunction with the Naval Air Signals School. Fireflies, Barracudas and Avengers arrived in 1945, but were withdrawn the following year.

The squadron moved to Lee-on-Solent on 15 May 1947, continuing to meet the diverse needs of the Naval Air Signal School at nearby Seafield Park. In December 1947 six Barracuda Vs were received as temporary equipment, pending the arrival of eight new Ansons fitted out as flying classrooms, in which guise they were known as Anson Type C in naval parlance. These were for exercise in Search, Homing Beacon and Air Interception using radar. The squadron also operated a staff Anson for use by the Flag Officer Air (Home) Communications Officer. From July 1948 No.783 formed part of the 51st Miscellaneous Air Group, sharing maintenance facilities with No.771 Squadron. The following year the squadron was engaged in providing a Radio Refresher and Aircrewman's Course, but on 18 November 1949 it disbanded, its aircraft and radar training task being transferred to Air Service Training Ltd at Hamble.

Squadron bases
Arbroath 9 Jan 1941
Lee-on-Solent 15 May 1947
Squadron disbanded 18 Nov 1949

Commanding Officers
L/C(A) JM Waddell
  RNVR 9 Jan 1941
L/C(A) JM Keene
  -Miller RNVR 7 Nov 1941
L/C(A) DM Brown
  RNVR 15 Jun 1942
L/C(A) RP Mason
  RNVR 29 Dec 1942
L/C(A) TB Horsley
  RNVR 30 Aug 1944

Identification Markings
All types numbers *1 onwards*, to A6A+ & AOA+ 1943. Post-war, Anson 601/LP+, Barracuda 323/LP+.

Commanding Officers
Lt(A) WLM Daubney
  RNVR 10 Nov 1945
Lt(A) EHG Child
  RNVR 10 Dec 1945
L/C(A) AM Tuke RN 1 Dec 1946
L/C(A) KC
  Winstanley RN 1 Dec 1947
Lt(A) GH Colles RN 27 May 1948
Lt PH Parsons
  MBE RN 24 May 1949
Squadron disbanded 18 Nov 1949

Aircraft Equipment	Period of Service	Example
Swordfish I	Jun 1942 - Oct 1943	L2797
Swordfish II	1942 - Jul 1945	LS442 (AOR)
Albacore I	Dec 1942 - Feb 1943	BF597
Walrus	Jun 1942 - Jan 1944	X9569
DH.86	Aug 1941 - Jul 1942	AX840 (6)
Wellington I	Feb 1944 - Jun 1945	L4244 (AOF)
Wellington II	Feb 1944 - Sep 1944	W5357
Anson I	Jan 1942 - Nov 1949	EF810 (AOA)
Firefly F.1/FR.1	Sep 1944 - Dec 1946	PP425
Avenger I	Dec 1944 - Jul 1945	FN897 (AOF)
Avenger II	Dec 1945 - Mar 1949	JZ582
Barracuda II	Oct 1944 - Dec 1946	MD652 (AOM)
Barracuda III	Mar 1946 - Dec 1946	RK403
Barracuda V	Dec 1947 - Oct 1948	RK558 (325/LP)

Fairey Firefly FR.1 MB758 'A' of No.783 Squadron at Arbroath in 1946. (Richard Griffiths)

No.784 Squadron

Badge: On a black field, a bat gold breathing flames proper in chief and issuant from water barry wavy in base proper a torch gold inflamed also proper

Motto: *Illumina tenebras*
(Lighten our darkness)

Aircraft Equipment	Period of Service	Example	
Chesapeake I	Jun 1942 - Aug 1943	AL943	
Fulmar I	Jun 1942 - Nov 1943	N4012	
Fulmar IINF	Jun 1942 - Nov 1944	DR746	(BOH)
Proctor Ia	Jun 1942 - Sep 1943	P6135	
Anson I	Aug 1942 - Sep 1946	EG697	(BOAD)
Reliant I	Sep 1943 - Aug 1944	FK904	
Hurricane IIc	Jul 1944	LF647	
Firefly INF	Sep 1944 - Sep 1946	MB558	(D1E)
Hellcat IINF	Nov 1945 - Sep 1946	JZ907	(D2W)
Harvard III	Nov 1945 - Jul 1946	EZ373	(T)

No.784 Squadron formed at Lee-on-Solent on 1 June 1942 as a Night Fighter Training squadron. Initial equipment was 2 Chesapeakes and 6 Fulmars, the latter being increased considerably in number after the squadron had moved to Drem on 18 October 1942. Several Ansons were also used from August 1942. Some squadron members were attached to Christchurch by January 1943, this being the home of the Naval Air Radio Installation Unit. From about October 1943 trained crews were attached to RAF night fighter squadrons, the most successful such crew being Lt(A) D.R.O.Price, RNVR and Sub Lt(A) R.E.Armitage, RNVR who were awarded DFCs for their exploits with No.29 Squadron.

From early 1944 detachments of 3 Fulmars from 'B' Flight were attached to Nos.813, 825 and 835 Squadrons for service in HMS *Campania*, HMS *Vindex* and HMS *Nairana* respectively for protection during convoy runs, being known as 'B1', 'B2 and 'B3' Flights, though not in that order. Firefly INFs arrived in September 1944, these being fitted with US AI radar. Hellcat IINFs and Harvard were added to the strength when a new 'B' Flight was formed on 7 November 1945 from the disbanded No.732 Squadron. No.784 moved to Dale on 15 January 1946, only to disband there on 10 September 1946, becoming 'B' Flight of No.790 Squadron.

Identification Markings
All types *AOA+* from 10.42, to *D1A+ to D3A+ & D5A+* 1945, also *B0A+*, to *P3A+ & P8A+* 1.46.

Squadron bases
Lee-on-Solent	1 Jun 1942
Drem	18 Oct 1942
Detd Flights (B1,B2,B3) in HMS Campania, HMS Nairana and HMS Vindex:	
HMS Campania (B3 Flight - attd 813 Sqdn):	
HMS Campania	13 Mar 1944
Ballyhalbert	3 Apr 1944
HMS Campania	26 Apr 1944
HMS Ravager (Dt2)	9-16 Apr 1944
Drem	21 Jul 1944
HMS Campania	3 Aug 1944
Drem	18 Aug 1944
HMS Campania	6 Sep 1944
Machrihanish	1 Mar 1945
- flight disbanded	
HMS Nairana (attd 835 Sqdn)	
HMS Nairana	24 Feb 1944
disembarked	15 Mar 1944
HMS Vindex (B2 Flight - attd 825 Sqdn)	
Ballyhalbert	3 Apr 1944
HMS Vindex	15 Apr 1944
disembarked	23 Apr 1944
Donibristle (Dt)	28 Apr 1944 to 20 Apr 1945
Burscough(Dt)	18 Aug 1945
Dale	15 Jan 1946
(satt Brawdy)	
Squadron disbanded 10 Sep 1946	

Commanding Officers
Capt LA Harris DSC RM	1 Jun 1942
L/C PN Humphreys GC RN	1 Dec 1942
L/C(A) JEM Hoare RCNVR	10 Sep 1943
L/C(A) RO Davies RN	18 Jan 1944
L/C(A) PRV Wheeler RNVR	3 Sep 1944
L/C(A) GE Fenner RNVR	9 Apr 1945
L/C(A) GLC Davies DSC RNVR	30 Jan 1946
Mjr JO Armour RM	1 Jun 1946
Lt(A) ES Griffiths RN (temp)	30 Aug 1946
Squadron disbanded 10 Sep 1946	

Fairey Fulmar II DR726 'B0X' of No.784 Squadron comes to grief during a night deck landing on HMS Ravager on 23 February 1944. (via Ivor Faulconer)

No.785 Squadron

Badge: On a white field, a jackdaw rising upon a torpedo all proper
Motto: None

No.785 Squadron formed at Crail on 4 November 1940 from the naval element of the Torpedo Training Unit, Abbotsinch as a Torpedo Bomber Reconnaissance Training squadron. Equipped initially with 13 Sharks and 5 Swordfish, the former had departed within a few months to be replaced from August 1941 by Albacores. Barracudas began to arrive in December 1942, and by late 1943 the squadron was operating both an anti-submarine course and a Barracuda familiarisation course. By the end of 1944 the squadron had become part of No.1 Naval Operational Training Unit, Avengers being added to the strength when it absorbed No.763 Squadron from Inskip on 31 July 1945. The squadron was further enlarged on 21 December 1945 when it also absorbed Nos.711 and 786 Squadrons, but it was itself disbanded on 1 March 1946.

Identification Markings
Swordfish *individual letters A-Q, also AA-EE, also individual numbers*, Albacore *individual letters R-Z also RR-ZZ, also individual numbers*. Later all types *C1A+ to C5A+*.

Aircraft Equipment	Period of Service	Example	
Shark II	Nov 1940 - Apr 1941	K8909	
Swordfish I	Nov 1940 - May 1944	L9739	(C4X)
Swordfish II	Apr 1942 - Feb 1944	HS427	(C1X)
Albacore	Aug 1941 - Nov 1943	L7148	(18)
Tiger Moth II	Dec 1941 - 1943		
Barracuda I	Dec 1942 - Jan 1944	P9722	(C1A)
Barracuda II	Apr 1943 - Feb 1946	BV684	(C3A)
Barracuda TR.III	Jan 1946 - Feb 1946	ME135	
Master I	Jun 1943 - Jan 1944	N7878	
Avenger I	Aug 1945 - Feb 1946	FN795	(C2Y)
Avenger II	Aug 1945 - Feb 1946	JZ537	
Anson I	Nov 1945 - Feb 1946	MH228	

Squadron bases
Crail 4 Nov 1940
 (satt Dunino)
Squadron disbanded 1 Mar 1946

Fairey Barracuda 'C3G' of No.785 Squadron, Crail receiving attention. (FAA Museum)

Commanding Officers		Commanding Officers	
L/C PGO Sydney-Turner RN	4 Nov 1940	L/C(A) RB Lunberg RN	31 Jan 1944
Capt O Patch DSO DSC RM	22 Aug 1941	L/C(A) MW Rudorf DSC RN	5 Dec 1944
Lt RW Thorne RN	1 Jan 1942	L/C LC Watson DSC RN	13 Jun 1945
Lt AH Abrams DSC RN	7 Sep 1942	L/C(A) NG Haigh RNVR	31 Jul 1945
Lt JH Stenning RN	22 Oct 1942	L/C JF Arnold RN	15 Dec 1945
L/C(A) KG Sharp RN	2 Dec 1942	Squadron disbanded	1 Mar 1946
L/C(A) M Thorpe RN	1 Jul 1943		

Fairey Albacores of No.785 Sqdn being armed with torpedoes at Crail. (Roger Kerrison)

No.786 Squadron

No.786 Squadron formed at Crail on on 4 November 1940 from the naval element of the Torpedo Training Unit, Abbotsinch as a Torpedo Bomber Reconnaissance Training squadron, to operate alongside No.785 Squadron. Initial equipment was 9 Albacores, these being supplemented early in 1941 by Swordfish and Chesapeakes. The first Barracudas arrived in December 1942, and the Swordfish and Albacores mainly departed. A few Anson were in use from 1944. No.786 disbanded into No.785 Squadron at Crail on 21 December 1945.

Identification Markings

Albacore individual numbers. Later all types *C1A+ to C5A+*.

Aircraft Equipment	Period of Service	Example	
Albacore I	Nov 1940 - Dec 1942	N4287	(14)
Swordfish I	May 1941 - Dec 1942	L9739	(C4X)
Swordfish II	Jun 1942 - 1943	DK745	
Chesapeake I	Jun 1941 - Jul 1943	AL928	
Tiger Moth II	Dec 1941	T6972	
Barracuda I	Dec 1942 - Dec 1943	BV661	
Barracuda II	Dec 1943 - Dec 1945	BV684	(C3A)
Anson I	Aug 1944 - Dec 1945	MG731	

Squadron bases
Crail 4 Nov 1940
 (satt Dunino)
Squadron disbanded 21 Dec 1945

Fairey Swordfish 'C1P' of No.786 Sqdn, Crail in formation. (Bill Penlington)

Commanding Officers		Commanding Officers	
Capt FW Brown RM	6 Dec 1940	L/C(A) RJ Fisher	
Lt(A) S Keane RN	28 Jul 1941	RNZNVR	30 Jun 1944
Lt RW Little RN	by Nov 1941	L/C(A) FH Franklin	
Lt RCB Stallard -Penoyre RN	23 Feb 1942	RNVR	30 Oct 1944
L/C BE Boulding DSC RN	15 Oct 1942	L/C LC Watson DSC RN	13 Jun 1945
L/C D Norcock RN	10 Aug 1943	Squadron disbanded 21 Dec 1945	

Fairey Albacore N4257 '4' of No.786 Sqdn Crail. (MAP)

Barracuda P9789 'C2V' of No.786 Sqdn, believed on HMS Rajah, February 1944. (FAA Museum)

No.787 Squadron

Badge: On a field per fesse wavy blue and barry wavy of four white and blue, a key the wards in chief gold and a sword white hilted gold in saltire
Motto: None

Albacore X9220 of No.787 Sqdn at Duxford in 1942 (F.E.Wheeler)

No.787 Squadron formed at Yeovilton out of No.804 Squadron as a Fleet Fighter Development Unit on 5 March 1941. Initial equipment was Sea Gladiators, Fulmars, Sea Hurricanes and Martlets, but as new types of naval fighter appeared the squadron received these for testing. An early task was comparative testing of captured aircraft, including a Fulmar II against a Fiat CR.42 and a Martlet I against a Messerschmitt Bf 109e. No.787 moved to Duxford on 18 June 1941 to become the Naval Air Fighting Development Unit, being attached there to the RAFs Air Fighting Development Unit, whose aircraft were also flown during trials. In January 1943 'Z' Flight formed with Swordfish, Fulmars and Sea Hurricanes as a development unit for the use of rocket projectiles on naval aircraft, moving to St Merryn the following month to conduct trials at the Treligga Range under the code-name 'Glowworm', and also to train first line squadrons in the use of RPs.

On 26 March 1943 No.787 moved with AFDU to Wittering, where soon afterwards it received Hellcats, Corsairs and Fireflies, plus some Barracudas and Avengers. 'Z' Flight disbanded on 1 July 1944, but 'Y' Flight had formed three weeks earlier at Arbroath as a Fighter Affiliation Flight equipped mainly with Seafires. Its task was to visit first line squadrons to keep them up to date on fighter tactics, and in the case of TBR squadrons to teach them defensive tactics against fighters. For this purpose it was successively based at Burscough, Ballyhalbert and Machrihanish, disbanding at the latter on 1 March 1945 after training Nos. 814 and 837 Squadron.

On 17 January 1945 No.787 moved to Tangmere, the new home of AFDU, the latter then becoming the Air Fighting Development Squadron of the Central Fighter Establishment. No.787 became at the same time the Air Support Development Section of the Naval Air Fighting Development Unit. 'X' Flight was formed on 1 March 1945 at Odiham from 'C' Flight of No.735 Squadron, equipped with three Hellcats and an Anson for Rebecca radar trials, disbanding on completion of this task on 4 June 1945. On 29 April 1945 five Fireflies were detached to Ford for ASH radar trials. After VE-Day it was proposed to set up a branch of the unit in the Far East as a new 'Z' Flight, and the squadron commander went out to Colombo for this purpose, but VJ-Day intervened before it could materialize. No.787 moved to Westhampnett on 12 July 1945, but some aircraft returned to Tangmere for about ten days from 27 October to allow Westhampnett to be cleared of mines. The squadron went to West Raynham on 16-27 November 1945, where No.746 Squadron was absorbed when it disbanded on 30 January 1946. No.787 continued its trials task in the postwar years, successively flying Sea Hornets, Sea Furies, Sea Vampires, Attackers, Wyverns and Sea Hawks before disbanding at West Raynham on 16 January 1956.

Identification Markings
All types YθA+ from 1943.

Bristol Blenheim I L1255 of No.787 Squadron, Wittering in 1943. (C.Hall via A.S.Thomas)

Chance Vought Corsair I JT104 of No.787 Squadron, Wittering in 1943. (via Peter Green)

Aircraft Equipment	Period of Service	Example	
Sea Gladiator	Mar 1941 - Nov 1942	N2272	
Fulmar I	Mar 1941 - Nov 1943	N1910	
Fulmar II	Nov 1941 - Apr 1944	DR714	
Skua II	Mar 1941 - Mar 1942	L2935	
Whitney Straight	Mar 1941 -	BS755	
Sea Hurricane Ia	Mar 1941 -	W9313	
Sea Hurricane Ib	Jul 1941 - Sep 1943	AF951	
Sea Hurricane IIc	Apr 1943 - Sep 1944	NF721	(YθF)
Martlet I	Mar 1941 - Mar 1943	BJ556	
Martlet II	Jan 1942 -	AM968	
Chesapeake I	Jul 1941 -	AL929	
Roc I	Oct 1941	L3079	
Spitfire Vb	Mar 1942	BL366	
Dominie I	May 1942 - Oct 1945	NF879	
Albacore I	May 1942 - Mar 1943	X9220	
Kingfisher I	Jun 1942 - Jul 1942	FN651	
Seafire Ib	Jul 1942 - Aug 1944	NX962	
Seafire L.IIc	Nov 1942 - Mar 1945	LR729	
Seafire III	Dec 1943 - Jun 1946	PR332	
Seafire XV	Sep 1944 - Jun 1946	SR447	
Seafire XVII	Apr 1945 - Jan 1948	SP348	
Seafire F.45	Mar 1946 - Feb 1948	LA442	
Seafire F.47	May 1947 - Sep 1949	VP428	
Blenheim I	Oct 1942 - Feb 1944	L6674	
Q.6 Petrel	Oct 1942 - May 1944	AX860	
Walrus I	Sep 1942 - Dec 1942	K8547	
Proctor Ia	Jan 1943 - Jul 1943	P6034	
Blenheim IV	Mar 1943 - May 1945	R3888	
Barracuda I	Apr 1943 - Jun 1943	P9644	
Barracuda II	Jun 1943 - Jun 1945	BV788	
Avenger I	May 1943 - Apr 1945	FN785	(YθP)
Avenger II	Sep 1944 - Feb 1945	JX569	
Avenger III	Jan 1945 - 1947	KE431	
Wildcat IV	Oct 1942 - Aug 1943	FN224	
Wildcat V	Jul 1943 - Mar 1945	JV334	
Wildcat VI	May 1944 - Sep 1945	JV652	
Hellcat I	Jun 1943 - Mar 1945	FN326	
Hellcat II	Sep 1944 - Nov 1945	JX899	
Hellcat IINF	Jan 1946 - May 1946	JZ898	
Firefly I	Aug 1943 - Jun 1945	DK425	
Firefly FR.4	Apr 1947 - Jan 1949	VG965	
Reliant I	Dec 1943 - Nov 1945	FK960	
Dauntless I	Jul 1944 - Oct 1944	JS999	
Corsair I	Jul 1943 - Aug 1943	JT112	
Corsair II	Apr 1944 - Nov 1945	JT563	
Corsair III	Jul 1943 - Nov 1945	JS492	
Traveller I	Nov 1944	FT528	
Swordfish I	Jan 1945	NE957	
Tigercat	Feb 1945 - Apr 1945	TT346	
Anson I	Sep 1945 - Sep 1946	MG863	

Aircraft Equipment	Period of Service	Example
Oxford I	May 1946 - Mar 1954	DF413
Mosquito FB.VI	Dec 1946 - May 1948	TE708
Sea Mosquito TR.33	Mar 1946 - Dec 1946	TW234
Sea Hornet F.20	Mar 1947 - Mar 1950	TT186
Sea Hornet PR.22	Aug 1949	VW935
Firebrand TF.5	May 1947 - Oct 1947	
Sea Fury F.10	May 1947 - Jul 1948	TF946
Sea Fury FB.11	Feb 1949 - 1954	VX608
Sea Fury T.20	1949 - 1949	VX283
Vampire F.1	Sep 1947 - Feb 1950	VF269
Vampire F.5	Sep 1949 - Aug 1953	VZ146
Sea Vampire F.20	Feb 1949 - Apr 1951	VV143
Attacker F.1	Jan 1951 - Apr 1952	WA486
Attacker FB.1	Sep 1952 - Sep 1954	WP282
Attacker FB.2	Apr 1954 - Sep 1954	WZ297
Sea Hawk F.1	May 1953 - Nov 1954	WF179
Sea Hawk FB.3	Apr 1954 - Oct 1955	WF287
Sea Hawk FGA.4	Nov 1954 - Jan 1956	WV836
Wyvern S.4	Mar 1954 - Nov 1954	VZ799
Dominie 1	Aug 1954 - Jan 1956	NF872
Sea Venom FAW.21	Jun 1955 - Jan 1956	WW148

787X

Aircraft Equipment	Period of Service	Example
Hellcat	Mar 1945 - May 1945	
Anson I	Mar 1945 - May 1945	

787Y

Aircraft Equipment	Period of Service	Example
Avenger I	Jun 1944 - Oct 1944	FN905
Seafire Ib	Jun 1944 - Oct 1944	NX885
Seafire IIc	Jun 1944 - Oct 1944	LR651
Seafire III	Jun 1944 - Feb 1945	NF601
Blenheim IV	Jun 1944 - Feb 1945	Z5991
Dominie I	Jun 1944 - Feb 1945	NF850
Swordfish	Jun 1944 - Oct 1944	HS216

787Z

Aircraft Equipment	Period of Service	Example	
Swordfish I	Mar 1943 - Jun 1944	L2805	
Swordfish II	Jan 1943 -	DK747/G	(YθG)
Fulmar I	Apr 1943 -	N1925	
Fulmar II	Jan 1944	N4023	(YθE)
Sea Hurricane Ia	May 1943 - Jun 1944	V6794	
Sea Hurricane IIc	Nov 1943 -	NF721	(YθF)
Hurricane IV	Jun 1943 - Nov 1943	KZ573	

Squadron bases
Yeovilton	5 Mar 1941
Duxford	18 Jun 1941
Machrihanish(Dt)	9-27 Mar 1943
Wittering	26 Mar 1943
Tangmere	17 Jan 1945
Ford (Dt)	29 Apr 1945

X Flt:
- Odiham — 1 Mar 1945
- Flt disbanded — 4 Jun 1945

Y Flt:
- Arbroath — 12 Jun 1944
- Burscough — 6 Aug 1944
- Speke — 12 Nov 1944
- Machrihanish — 15 Jan 1945
- Ballyhalbert — 7 Feb 1945
- Machrihanish — 20 Feb 1945
- Flt disbanded — 1 Mar 1945

Squadron bases

Z Flt:
- Lee-on-Solent — 15 Jan 1943
- St.Merryn — 24 Feb 1943
- Inskip — 16 Nov 1943
- St.Merryn (satt Treligga) — 14 Jan 1944
- Flt disbanded — 1 Jul 1944
- Westhampnett — 12 Jul 1945
- Tangmere (Dt) — 27 Oct 1945 to 5 Nov 1945
- West Raynham — 16 Nov 1945
- St Davids (Dt) — 22 Apr 1952 to 24 Jul 1952
- Squadron disbanded 16 Jan 1956

Commanding Officers

Cdr BHM Kendall OBE RN — 5 Mar 1941
Cdr RA Kilroy DSC RN — 6 May 1946
L/C PEI Bailey RN — 3 Dec 1946 (temp)
Cdr RJH Stephens RN — 11 Feb 1947
Cdr EA Shaw RN — 21 Apr 1948
L/C BHC Nation RN — 16 May 1950
L/C WI Campbell RN — 24 Sep 1951
L/C SG Orr DSC AFC RN — 4 Mar 1953
L/C RE Bourke RN — 8 Oct 1953
L/C RD Taylor RN — 1 Jan 1954
L/C RA Shilcock RN — 24 Jul 1954
Squadron disbanded 16 Jan 1956

787X

Commanding Officers
Lt(A) RJ Sturges RNVR — 1 Mar 1945
Flight disbanded — 4 Jun 1945

787Y

L/C(A) RE Bibby DSO RNVR — 28 Jul 1944
Flight disbanded — 1 Mar 1945

787Z

L/C(A) GH Bates RNVR — 15 Jan 1943
Lt(A) TG Davison RNVR — 6 Jun 1944
Flight disbanded — 1 Jul 1944

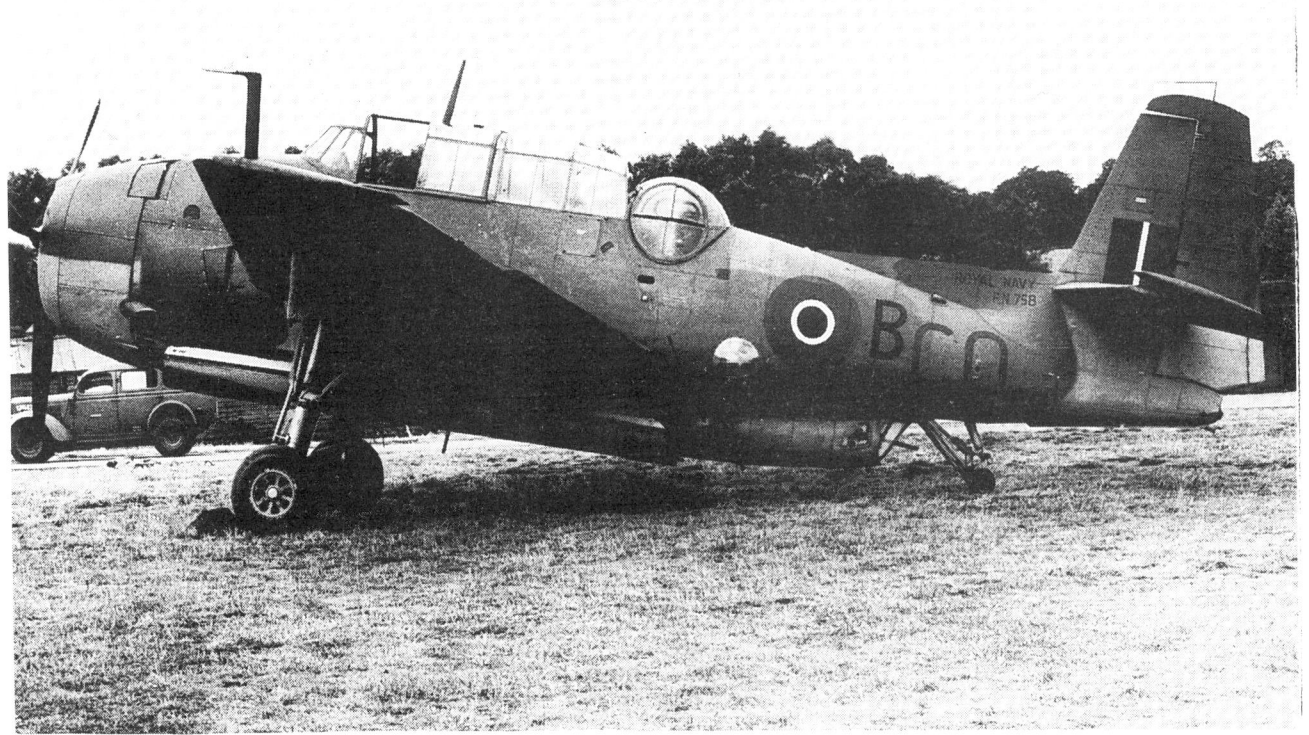

Grumman Avenger I FN758 of No.787 Squadron, still bearing No.778 Sqdn code 'C0B' at Wittering in 1943. (via J.D.Buchanan)

de Havilland Sea Hornet F.20 TT186 of No.787 Sqdn, West Raynham in 1947. (B.C.Lyons)

de Havilland Vampire FB.5 VV548 of No.787 Squadron visiting Culdrose in 1951. (Tony Hughes)

No.788 Squadron

Badge: On a field blue, over water barry wavy in base white and blue and in front of two rays of lightning also white in saltire a target proper pierced in the centre by an arrow gold flighted also white

Motto: *Tayari saa yote*
(Ready at all hours)

Aircraft Equipment	Period of Service	Example
Albacore I	Feb 1942 - Mar 1944	X9081
Swordfish I	Feb 1942 - Jun 1944	P4275
Swordfish II	Feb 1942 - Jun 1944	HS165
Fulmar II	May 1942 - Jul 1943	X8528
Walrus	May 1942 - Jul 1945	L2264
Skua II	Jun 1942 - Jan 1944	L2973
Tiger Moth II		VP-CAG
Sea Hurricane Ib	1942 - 1942	V7502
Hurricane IIb	Aug 1942 - Nov 1942	BP695
Blenheim	1942 - 1942	
SM.79	1942 - 1942	
Defiant TT.I	Feb 1944 - Jul 1945	DR872
Beaufighter II	Apr 1944 - Jan 1945	T3429
Beaufort I	1945 - Jun 1945	

A rather motley strike force assembled at China Bay on 18 January 1942, and was numbered No.788 Squadron on 16 February as the Eastern Fleet TBR Pool. Initial equipment was Swordfish, but all 6 aircraft were shot down during Japanese carrier raids on Ceylon on 5 April 1942. The remnants of the squadron then took passage to East Africa, where it regrouped at Tanga on 20 May before moving to Mombasa on 24 June to become a Fleet Requirements Unit. Equipment comprised a miscellany of Swordfish, Albacores, Fulmars, Sea Hurricanes Skuas and a captured SM 79. A detached section operated from Eastleigh, Nairobi between May and November 1942. During 1944 the squadron re-equipped, and by the end of the year had 4 Defiant target tugs, 2 Beaufighter IIs and a Walrus. A Beaufort was operated briefly during mid-1945, but No.788 disbanded on 11 June 1945.

Squadron bases
China Bay 16 Feb 1942
HMT Athene and HMS
Cornwall (transit) 8 May 1942
Tanga 20 May 1942
Mombasa 24 Jun 1942
Eastleigh (Dt) 1 May 1942
to 7 Nov 1942
Squadron disbanded 11 Jun 1945

Commanding Officers
L/C CA Kingsley-Rowe
RN 16 Feb 1942
Mjr VBG Cheesman
RM 1 May 1942
Lt EM Britton RN 7 Aug 1942
Lt WN Waller RN 25 Aug 1942
L/C(A) EH Horn
RNVR 12 Aug 1943
L/C(A) JA Ansell
RNVR 25 Oct 1943
L/C(A) FG Hood
SANF(V) 15 Aug 1944
Squadron disbanded 11 Jun 1945

Identification Markings
Believed uncoded throughout.

Fairey Fulmar II DR711 of No.788 Squadron, Tanga en route to Nairobi. (R.Pridham-Wippell)

No.789 Squadron

Badge: (Heraldic description lacking) (Probably not approved)
Motto: Ex culta robur (Strength from culture)

No.789 Squadron formed at Wingfield on 1 July 1942 as a Fleet Requirements Unit. Initial equipment was officially one Walrus, but other local aircraft were used including Albacores, Sea Hurricanes, Swordfish and Fulmars. In September 1943 two Skuas were allocated to the squadron, and around that time they held a few Kingfishers as spares for HM ships and for No.726 Squadron. Also from that time they largely shared aircraft with No.799 Squadron which had just formed as a Pool squadron. Four Defiants arrived early in 1944, and these were followed in September by Beaufighter IIs, Martinets, Harvards and Ansons. The earlier aircraft were then withdrawn. No.789 disbanded at Wingfield on 25 November 1945.

Aircraft Equipment	Period of Service	Example	
Walrus	Jul 1942 - Dec 1944	W3045	(C)
Albacore I	Jul 1942 - Sep 1944	BF642	(D)
Sea Hurricane Ib	Jul 1942 -	V6944	
Swordfish I	Jul 1942 - Jun 1943	V4430	
Swordfish II	Oct 1942 - Nov 1945	DK783	
Fulmar II	May 1943 - Jul 1943	DR640	(AC)
Roc ITT	1943 - 1943	L3127	
Skua II	Sep 1943 - Sep 1944		
Kingfisher I	Nov 1943 - Feb 1944	FN725	
Defiant TT.I	Feb 1944 - Dec 1944	DR883	
Beaufighter II	Sep 1944 - Nov 1945	T3099	(W9Q)
Martinet TT.I	Sep 1944 - Nov 1945	NR456	(W8B)
Anson I	Sep 1944 - Nov 1945	NK872	
Harvard IIa	Sep 1944 - Nov 1945	EX687	
Harvard III	Feb 1945 - Nov 1945	SAAF7568	
Oxford I	Feb 1945 - Aug 1945	SAAF3657	
Dakota	Feb 1945 - 1945		

Miles Martinet NR646 ('W8A') of No.789 Sqdn, Wingfield in 1944. (Harry Hands via Chris Thomas)

Identification Markings
All types single letters, except Fulmar *AA, AB, AC etc*, to *W8A+* & *W9A+* 1943.

Squadron bases
Wingfield 1 Jul 1942
Squadron disbanded 25 Nov 1945

Commanding Officers
L/C(A) KC Johnston RNVR 1 Jul 1942
L/C WTE White SANF(V) 11 Jun 1943
Lt(A) B Sinclair MBE RN 10 Sep 1943
L/C WTE White SANF(V) 20 Jun 1944
Squadron disbanded 25 Nov 1945

Fairey Albacore X9218 of No.789 Squadron, Wingfield releasing a practice torpedo. (via Ken Smy)

No.790 Squadron

Badge: On a blue field, upon clouds melting white a cock proper
Motto: In alto societas (There's company aloft)

Fairey Firefly 1 Z2030 'Z8M' of No.790 Sqdn, Zeals in 1945. (FAA Museum)

No.790 Squadron formed at Machrihanish as an Air Target Towing Squadron on 15 June 1941. It took over elements of the task of Nos.768 and 772 Squadrons, whose complements were then adjusted accordingly. It was short-lived, however, being disbanded into No.772 Squadron on 30 September 1941.

On 27 July 1942 No.790 Squadron reformed at Charlton Horethorne with Oxfords and Fulmars. It was attached to the Fighter Direction School and helped to train Fighter Direction Officers, the Oxfords acting as bombers for this purpose and the Fulmars as fighters. Fireflies replaced the Fulmars in June 1944, and on 10 August No.790 was detached to Culmhead, returning to Charlton Horethorne on 26 September 1944. A move was made to Zeals on 1-4 April 1945, and Seafires arrived about that time, followed by Wildcats on moving to Dale on 30 August 1945. Mosquitoes were received in July 1946, and on 10 September 1946 No.784 Squadron was absorbed to become a new 'B' Flight. On 13 December 1947 the No.790 moved to Culdrose, where it disbanded on 15 November 1949.

Commanding Officers
L/C(A) CR Hodgson RNVR 27 Jul 1942
L/C(A) RP Demuth RNVR 26 Jun 1944
L/C(A) GK Pridham RNVR 13 Nov 1944
L/C(A) R Williams RNVR 24 Apr 1945
L/C MJA O'Sullivan RN 16 Nov 1945
L/C(A) H Muir-MacKenzie RN 15 Jun 1947
L/C(A) DWH Gardner RN 25 Jun 1947
L/C(A) B Sinclair MBE RN 14 Aug 1948
Lt PA Jordan RN 27 May 1949
Squadron disbanded 15 Nov 1949

Squadron bases
Machrihanish 15 Jun 1941
Squadron disbanded 30 Sep 1941
Charlton Horethorne 27 Jul 1942 (also used Yeovilton)
Culmhead 10 Aug 1944
Charlton Horethorne 26 Sep 1944
Zeals 1 Apr 1945
Dale 30 Aug 1945
Culdrose 13 Dec 1947
Squadron disbanded 15 Nov 1949

Identification Markings
All types Y0A+ & BY0A+, to Z8A+ & Z0A+ 4.45, to P3A+ & P8A+ 8.45, to 100/DL:CW+ & 401/DL:CW+ 1946.

Aircraft Equipment	Period of Service	Example	
Oxford I	Jul 1942 - Oct 1947	MP293	(BYOX)
Fulmar I	Jul 1942 - Jun 1944	N1863	
Fulmar II	Oct 1942 - Jun 1944	X8814	
Firefly I	Jun 1944 - Apr 1947	MB577	(P8P)
Spitfire Vb	Feb 1945	AD426	
Seafire Ib	Mar 1945	NX907	
Seafire IIc	Mar 1945	NM982	
Seafire III	Nov 1946 - Feb 1947	NN123	
Seafire XV	May 1947 - Jan 1949	PR424	(152/CW)
Wildcat V	Sep 1945 - Feb 1946	JV558	
Dominie I	Dec 1945 - Jul 1946	X7499	
Anson I	Jan 1946 - Sep 1947	MG473	
Anson C.XII	Nov 1945	PH656	
Mosquito FB.6	Jul 1946 - Dec 1948	TE720	(402/DL)
Mosquito B.25	Oct 1946 - Feb 1948	KB576	
Sea Mosquito TR.33	Dec 1946 - Nov 1949	TW281	(407/CW)
Auster I	Jun 1948 - Jul 1948	LB384	
Auster V	Nov 1948	TJ651	

de Havilland Mosquito TR.33 TW270 '413/CU' of No.790 Squadron, Culdrose around 1948/9. (FAA Museum)

No.791 Squadron

No.791 Squadron formed at Arbroath on 15 October 1940 as an Air Target Towing Unit, equipped initially with two Rocs. As the unit expanded it received Skuas, Swordfish, Defiants and other types before disbanding on 10 December 1944.

On 1 November 1945 No.791 reformed at Trincomalee as a Fleet Requirements Unit. On 23 December 1945 it embarked with No.888 Squadron in HMS *Smiter* for passage to Singapore, where it disembarked four days later to Sembawang. Initial equipment comprised 6 Corsairs, six Vengeance target tugs and a Harvard. During 1946 it also received two Seafires, three Austers and two Expediters, and in addition to its requirements duties was operating an air-sea-rescue flight and a communications flight. No.791 disbanded at Sembawang on 16 June 1947.

Identification Markings
All types *A8A*+ from 1942. Single letters 1945/7.

Aircraft Equipment	Period of Service	Example	
Roc I	Oct 1940 - Mar 1944	L3092	(A8A)
Skua II	Mar 1942 - Mar 1944	L3034	(A8Q)
Albacore I	Mar 1941	N4246	
Swordfish I	Apr 1942 - Dec 1944	P4232	(A8M)
Swordfish II	Dec 1943 - Jan 1944	HS367	(A8T)
Sea Gladiator	Mar 1942	N2298	
Spitfire I	Oct 1942 - May 1943	R7155	
Sea Hurricane Ia	Dec 1943 - Jan 1944	Z6997	
Sea Hurricane Ib	Apr 1942	AE962	
Sea Hurricane IIc	Oct 1943	NF697	
Defiant TT.III	Apr 1944 - Jun 1944	N1617	(A8N)
Corsair IV	Nov 1945 - Nov 1946	KD647	(E)
Vengeance TT.IV	Dec 1945 - Dec 1946	A27-520	
Harvard IIb	Dec 1945 - May 1947	KF534	
Expediter	Apr 1946 - Apr 1947		
Auster V	Oct 1946 - Jun 1947	TJ651	(2)
Seafire XV	Dec 1946 - Jun 1947	SR633	

Commanding Officers
L/C(A) L Gilbert RNVR 19 Oct 1940
L/C(A) KB Brotchie RNVR 6 Dec 1941
Lt JCM Harman RN 10 Sep 1942
L/C(A) CA Crighton RNVR 12 May 1943
L/C(A) APT Pierssene RNVR 7 Apr 1944
Squadron disbanded 10 Dec 1944
L/C(A) CMT Hallewell RN 1 Nov 1945

Commanding Officers
Lt(A) RA Shilcock RN 1 Aug 1946
Lt(A) DM Jeram RN 26 Apr 1947
Squadron disbanded 16 Jun 1947

Squadron bases
Arbroath 15 Oct 1940
Squadron disbanded 10 Dec 1944
Trincomalee 1 Nov 1945
HMS Smiter(transit) 23 Dec 1945
Sembawang 27 Dec 1945
Squadron disbanded 16 Jun 1947

Vultee Vengeance TT.IV HB462 of No.791 Squadron, Sembawang in 1946. (R.A.Shilcok)

Chance Vought Corsair IV KD647 'E' of No.791 Squadron, Sembawang in 1946. (FAA Museum)

No.792 Squadron

Badge (1): On a white field, a lion rampant red holding between the fore-paws a target proper
Motto: Patimur ut discant alii (We suffer that others may learn)
(Badge transferred to No.794 Squadron on disbandment)

Badge (2): On gold field, a panther's head caboshed black
Motto: Sapianta vincit tenebras (Wisdom conquers darkness)

No.792 Squadron formed at St Merryn on 15 August 1940 as an Air Target Towing Unit. Equipped initially with six Rocs and Skuas, these were replaced later with Defiants and then Martinets. The squadron disbanded on 2 January 1945 on being merged with No.794 Squadron.

On 15 January 1948 No.792 Squadron reformed at Culdrose as a Night Fighter Training Unit. Equipped initially with Firefly NF.1s plus 3 Ansons fitted for AI radar training, these gave way in May 1950 to Sea Hornets NF.21s. No.792 disbanded on 16 August 1950, its aircraft and task being taken over by No.809 Squadron.

Identification Markings
All types *S8A+* by 1944. Firefly *220-227/CW*, Sea Hornet *491-49/CW* & Anson/Oxford *640-642/CW* 1948/50.

Aircraft Equipment	Period of Service	Example	
Roc ITT	Aug 1940 - May 1942	L3045	
Skua II	Aug 1940 - May 1943	L2943	
Master I	Aug 1940 - Sep 1940		
Sea Gladiator	Jun 1941 - Jun 1942	N5500	
Proctor Ia	Dec 1941 - Jul 1942	P6131	
Lysander III	Mar 1942 - May 1942	W6951	
Fulmar II	Apr 1942 - Jul 1944	BP838	
Whitney Straight	Jul 1942	BS755	
Defiant TT.III	Dec 1943 - Jan 1945	N3379	
Martinet TT.I	Jul 1943 - Jan 1945	MS660	(S8C)
Sea Hurricane Ia	May 1944	Z7162	
Firefly NF.1	Jan 1948 - Jul 1950	PP435	(221/CW)
Anson I	Jan 1948 - Aug 1950	MG673	(641/CW)
Oxford I	Jan 1948 - Mar 1948	PH140	(640/CW)
Sea Hornet NF.21	May 1950 - Aug 1950	VZ672	(491/CW)

Fairey Firefly FR.1 PP586 '227' of No.792 Squadron, Culdrose in 1949. (R.G.Dennison)

Squadron bases
St.Merryn   15 Aug 1940
Squadron disbanded 2 Jan 1945
Culdrose   15 Jan 1948
Squadron disbanded 16 Aug 1950

Commanding Officers
Lt HER Torin DSC RN   15 Aug 1940
Lt(A) HR Dimock RNVR   9 Dec 1940
Lt EW Lawson RN   5 May 1941
L/C(A) TJ Archer RNVR   30 Sep 1941
L/C(A) GV Oddy RNVR   8 Dec 1941
None   7 Feb 1944
L/C(A) NG Maclean RNVR   12 Jun 1944
Squadron disbanded   2 Jan 1945
Lt(A) BC Lyons RN   15 Jan 1948
Lt JA McColgan RN   28 Nov 1949
Squadron disbanded   16 Aug 1950

Miles Martinet MS660 'S8C' of No.792 Squadron St.Merryn in 1944. (Ken Atkinson)

No.793 Squadron

Badge: On a white field, a falcon rising holding in its talons a target pierced in the centre by two arrows all proper
Motto: Believed none

No.793 Squadron formed at Ford on 25 October 1939 as an Air Target Towing Unit. Equipped with Rocs, it towed targets for other squadrons in the English Channel, out from Littlehampton. It also provided aircraft for observers' gunnery training. During July 1940 it sent a detachment to Warmwell to tow for a FAA squadron then based at Exeter, but on returning to Ford found that an enemy raid on 18 August had destroyed its remaining aircraft. It was considered unwise to continue its activities in this area, and consequently the squadron moved to Lee-on-Solent for passage overseas. It eventually reassembled on 18 November 1940 at Piarco, Trinidad, where it was attached to No.1 Observer School. It was equipped for some time with Rocs shipped out from the UK, until these were supplemented with Fulmars and Albacores in 1943. In June 1944 No.793 took over Exchange Field at Piarco and two months later the last Rocs left, Martinets replacements having arrived a few weeks earlier. The Fulmars were scrapped early in 1945, and the squadron continued with Albacores and Martinets until being disbanded on 10 October 1945.

Fairey Fulmar 'W7C' of No.793 Squadron. Piarco, Trinidad. (via R.C.Jones)

Commanding Officers
Lt(A) JM Gladish
    RNVR   25 Oct 1939
None   28 Aug 1940
L/C(A) KDR Davis
    RNVR   8 Nov 1940
L/C(A) FC Booth
    RNVR   8 Jun 1944
L/C(A) FB Gardner
    RNVR   7 Dec 1944
Squadron disbanded 10 Oct 1945

Identification Markings
All types W6A+ to W8A+

Squadron bases
Ford   25 Oct 1939
Warmwell (Dt)   14-24 Aug 1940
Lee-on-Solent   1 Oct 1940
passage   12 Oct 1940
Piarco   18 Nov 1940
Squadron disbanded 10 Oct 1945

Aircraft Equipment	Period of Service	Example
Roc I	Oct 1939 - Aug 1940	L3181
	Nov 1940 - Aug 1944	L3163
Fulmar II	Sep 1943 - May 1945	X8778
Albacore I	Nov 1943 - Oct 1945	T9167
Martinet TT.I	Apr 1944 - Oct 1945	MS915

No.794 Squadron

Badge: On a white field, a lion rampant red holding between the fore-paws a target proper
Motto: Fungar vice cotis
(I will do duty as a whetstone)
OR Patimur ut discant alii
(We suffer that others may learn)

No.794 Squadron formed at Yeovilton on 1 August 1940 as an Air Target Towing Unit. Initially equipped with Rocs and Swordfish, it later received a few Skuas, Spitfires, Defiants, Tiger Moths and Blenheims. A detachment was sent to Warmwell on 10 April 1943 to act as an Air Firing Unit, but on 1 July 1943 the whole squadron moved to Angle to be retitled the Naval Air Firing Unit. The establishment here was 16 Sea Hurricanes, 4 Master IIs, 4 Defiants and 8 Martinets, with which it acted as a target towing and air firing training unit in conjunction with the Fighter School at Yeovilton. It moved successively to Dale on 10 September, Henstridge on 22 November and Charlton Horethorne on 1 December 1943, being by then known as No.1 NAFU. No.794 disbanded at Charlton Horethorne on 30 June 1944.

On 2 January 1945 No.794 formed at St Merryn out of Nos.719, 780 and 792 Squadrons as the School of Air Firing. Equipped with Seafires, Fireflies, Corsairs, Wildcats, Martinets and Harvards, it provided air firing training. When the Ground Attack School formed in June 1945 it commenced ground attack courses, and on moving to Eglinton on 9 August 1945 it had three flights respectively giving instruction in ground attack, air combat and photo reconnaissance. During the Spring of 1946 it also gave Seafire conversion and refresher courses. In August 1946 it became part of the newly formed 52nd Training Air Group. By October 1945 it had become No.3 Naval Air Fighter School, with an ADDLs flight operating at Maydown. On 5 February 1946 it absorbed No.1 NAFS, otherwise No.759 Squadron, and periods were later spent on deck landing training in both HMS *Implacable* and HMS *Theseus* before disbanding on 26 Febuary 1947.

Identification Markings
All types P8A+ from 8.43, to Y8A+ 12.43. S1A+ from 1.45, to J1A+ to J4A+ 8.45, to A4A+ & A5A+ 1946.

Aircraft Equipment	Period of Service	Example
Swordfish I	Aug 1940 - Jun 1944	K8438
Swordfish II	Apr 1944 - Jun 1945	NF584
Roc I	Aug 1940 - Jan 1943	
Skua II	Dec 1941 - Jul 1943	L3056
Blenheim IV	Jul 1942 - Jul 1943	Z6244
Defiant TT.I	Nov 1942 - Jan 1944	DR917
Defiant TT.III	Dec 1943 - Jun 1944	AA321
Proctor Ia	Apr 1943	P6023
Tiger Moth II	1943 - Jul 1943	
Master I	Apr 1943 - Jun 1943	T8459
Master II	Sep 1943 - Nov 1943	W9026 (P2)
Martinet TT.I	Jun 1943 - Jun 1944	MS682
Sea Hurricane Ib	Aug 1943 - Sep 1943	V7421
Hurricane IIb	Sep 1943 - Oct 1943	JS235
Spitfire I	Apr 1943 - Nov 1943	R6835
Spitfire Va	Sep 1942 - Dec 1942	R6759
Spitfire Vb/hooked	Nov 1943 - May 1945	P8708
Seafire L.IIc	Jan 1945 - Feb 1945	LR661
Reliant I	Apr 1944 - Nov 1945	FK867
Fulmar II	1944 - Jun 1944	X8550
Firefly NF.I	Dec 1945 - Jan 1947	MB662 (A4M)
Corsair III	Jan 1945 - Feb 1946	JS793 (J1R)
Corsair IV	Dec 1945 - Feb 1946	KD988
Wildcat IV	Jan 1945 - Oct 1945	FN237
Wildcat VI	Oct 1945 - Jan 1946	JV851 (J3V)
Harvard IIb	Jun 1945 - Jan 1946	KF522 (A)
Harvard III	Jan 1945 - Jun 1946	EZ167 (N)
Martinet TT.I	Jan 1945 - Apr 1946	NR654 (J4M)
Master II	Jan 1945 - 1945	DM267
Spitfire Vb/hooked	Jan 1945 - May 1945	W3846
Seafire L.III	Jun 1946 - Feb 1947	RX248 (A5G)

Squadron bases

Yeovilton	1 Aug 1940
(satt Haldon)	
Warmwell (Dt)	6 Mar 1943
	to 7 Jul 1943
Angle	1 Jul 1943
Dale	10 Sep 1943
Henstridge	22 Nov 1943
Charlton Horethorne	1 Dec 1943
Squadron disbanded	30 Jun 1944
St.Merryn	2 Jan 1945
Eglinton	9 Aug 1945
(satt Maydown)	
HMS Theseus (Dt)	21-31 May 1946
HMS Implacable(Dt)	13 Aug 1946
	to 1 Oct 1946
HMS Implacable (Dt)	22-31 Oct 1946
HMS Theseus (Dt)	7-15 Nov 1946
HMS Implacable	13 Jan 1947
Squadron disbanded	26 Feb 1947

Commanding Officers

Lt(A) RWH Everett		
	RNVR	3 Aug 1940
L/C(A) FC Muir		
	RNVR	22 Jul 1942
Lt(A) WH Stevens		
	RN	16 Nov 1942
L/C(A) AL Hill		
	RNVR	10 Apr 1943
L/C(A) TL Crookston		
	RN	6 Jan 1944
Squadron disbanded		30 Jun 1944
L/C(A) JL Appleby		
	RN	2 Jan 1945
L/C RA Bird		
	DSC RN	3 Jul 1945
L/C(A) G Dennison		
	RNVR	11 Apr 1946
Lt AC Lindsay DSC		
	RN	1 Aug 1946
Lt(A) RM Crosley		
	DSC & Bar RN	13 Nov 1946
Squadron disbanded		26 Feb 1947

Supermarine Seafire L.III 'A5G' of No.794 Sqdn in trouble on HMS Implacable in 1946. (J.A.Greenfield)

The result of a towing accident involving Seafire III SP195 'J2.' and Miles Martinet NR654 'J4M' of No.794 Squadron at Eglinton in September 1945.

No.795 Squadron

No.795 Squadron formed at Tanga on 24 June 1942 as the Eastern Fleet Fighter Pool equipped with Martlets and Fulmars. On 29 August 'A' Flight, equipped with six Fulmars, embarked in HMS *Illustrious* to participate in the Madagascar invasion. These were put ashore to Majunga on 11 September for anti-submarine patrols and tactical reconnaissance under the control of RAF No.207 Group, and carried out 45 operational sorties before returning in HMS *Albatross* in November. The squadron headquarters had in the meantime moved to Mackinnon Road, where it disbanded on 11 August 1943, its aircraft being by then obsolescent.

On 1 August 1946 No.795 reformed at Eglinton as a Refresher Training squadron in the 52nd Training Air Group. Equipped with Fireflies, its task was to provide refresher training to carrier standard. The squadron embarked in HMS *Implacable* on 14 January 1947, but on disembarking to Ford on 24 March 1947 it was disbanded, the aircraft being flown into storage at Stretton the same day.

Martlets of No.795 Squadron at Mackinnon Road around 1942/3. (R.Pridham-Wippell)

Identification Markings
Believed uncoded 1942/3. Firefly types *A4A+, later 201/A+*.

Aircraft Equipment	Period of Service	Example
Fulmar II	Jun 1942 - Jun 1943	DR644
Martlet I	1942	AX828
Martlet II	Sep 1942 - Apr 1943	AJ122
Martlet III	Nov 1942 - Aug 1943	HK841
Martlet IV	Jun 1943 - Aug 1943	FN156
Harvard IIa	- Aug 1943	EX598
Sea Hurricane Ib	Dec 1942 - Jan 1943	Z4649
Firefly FR.1	Aug 1946 - Mar 1947	DK479 (209/A)

Squadron bases
Tanga	24 Jun 1942
A Flt (6 Fulmars):	
HMS Illustrious	29 Aug 1942
Majunga	11 Sep 1942
Antisarbe (Dt3)	12 Oct 1942
HMS Albatross	13 Nov 1942
Tanga	15 Nov 1942
Mackinnon Road	19 Sep 1942
Detd Flt:	26 Apr 1943
Nakuru to	15 May 1943
(attd 70 OTU RAF)	
Squadron disbanded	11 Aug 1943
Eglinton	1 Aug 1946
'A' Flight	
HMS Illustrious	29 Aug 1946

Squadron bases
HMS Implacable	14 Jan 1947
Ford (Sqdn disbanded)	24 Mar 1947

Commanding Officers
Lt ON Bailey RN	24 Jun 1942
L/C(A) GW Parish DSC RNVR	7 Jun 1943
Squadron disbanded	11 Aug 1943
Lt(A) JM Brown DSC RN	10 Aug 1946
Lt(A) CRJ Coxon RN	13 Nov 1946
Squadron disbanded	24 Mar 1947

No.796 Squadron

Badge: On a field per fesse blue and barry wavy of four white and blue, a pair of dividers gold winged white

Motto: *Ubi imus cognoscimus* (We know where we are going)

No.796 Squadron formed at Port Reitz on 25 July 1942 from aircraft of No.818 Squadron as the Eastern Fleet Torpedo Bomber Reconnaissance Pool. Equipped with Swordfish and Albacores, a detachment embarked in HMS *Indomitable* on 29 August 1942 to take part in the Madagascar operations. Disembarking to Majunga on 10 September they contributed 89 sorties, five Albacores operating from Antisarbe from 12 October. The aircraft embarked in HMS *Albatross* on 13 November, to rejoin the main squadron, by then based at Tanga. No.796 continued as a Torpedo Spotter Reconnaissance pool, being effectively an operational training unit, until disbanding at Tanga on 28 April 1944, its task and remnants being taken over by No.756 Squadron in Ceylon.

On 13 November 1947 No.796 reformed at St Merryn as an Aircrewmans School. Equipped with Barracuda IIIs its task changed to Observers School Part II in March 1950. Firefly T.3s arrived in July 1950, though these had the disadvantage that they could only carry one trainee observer as against two in the Barracuda. The latter were detached in April 1952 to form No.750 Squadron, and three-seater Firefly T.7s began to replace the T.3s in June 1953, the squadron being temporarily divided at this time as Nos.796A and 796B Squadrons. No.796 moved to Culdrose between 9 and 18 February 1954, to operate with No.750 Squadron as the Observers School, this becoming the Observer and Air Signals School by the beginning of 1956. The school took over the task of No.765 Squadron when it disbanded in March 1957, its Sea Balliols going to No.796. The Fireflies were gradually replaced during that year by Gannets, and in March 1958 two of the Sea Balliols were used to help convert ex-Gannet pilots to Skyraiders. The squadron disbanded at Culdrose on 1 October 1958.

Fairey Albacore X9253 of No.796 Squadron, Tanga in January 1943. (M.A.Swale)

Aircraft Equipment	Period of Service	Example	
Swordfish I	Jul 1942 - Dec 1943	W5857	(P)
Swordfish II	Sep 1943 - Mar 1944	HS165	
Albacore I	Jul 1942 - Jul 1943	BF588	(M)
Walrus	Mar 1943 - Feb 1944	Z1812	
Firefly FR.1	Nov 1947 - May 1951	DK504	(254/MF)
Firefly T.3	Jul 1950 - May 1954	PP609	(267/MF)
Firefly AS.5	Jul 1950 - May 1952	VT479	(231/MF)
Firefly AS.6	Dec 1951 - Jun 1953	WD892	(217/MF)
Firefly T.7	Jun 1953 - Dec 1957	WK348	(374/CU)
Barracuda III	Nov 1949 - Feb 1952	ME179	(310/MF)
Tiger Moth T.2	Jan 1950	T6094	
Sea Balliol T.21	Mar 1957 - Jun 1958	WP325	(791/CU)
Gannet AS.1	Apr 1957 - Sep 1958	XA353	(761/CU)
Gannet T.2	Feb 1957 - Sep 1958	XG876	(770/CU)

Identification Markings
Single letter 1942/4. From 11.47 Firefly *210-290/MF & 360-378/MF*, Barracuda *300-313/MF*, to Firefly *360-380/CU* 2.54. All types *761-794/CU* from 7.1.56.

Squadron bases
Port Reitz	25 Jul 1942
A Flight:	
HMS Indomitable	29 Aug 1942
Majunga	10 Sep 1942
Antisarbe (Dt5)	12 Oct 1942
HMS Albatross	13 Nov 1942
Tanga	17 Nov 1942
B Flight:	
Mackinnon Road	29 Aug 1942
Tanga (whole sqdn)	30 Sep 1942
Eastleigh (Dt)	22 Jun 1943
	to 22 Nov 1943
Squadron disbanded	28 Apr 1944
St.Merryn	13 Nov 1947
St Eval (Dt10)	28 Aug 1948
	to 28 Sep 1948
HMS Illustrious	28 Sep 1948
(Dt - DLT)	to 2 Oct 1948
Culdrose	9 Feb 1954
Squadron disbanded	1 Oct 1958

Commanding Officers
Lt(A) HE Shilbach RNVR	25 Jul 1942
Lt NT O'Neil RN	19 Aug 1942
Lt(A) AJI Temple -West RN	12 Jan 1943
L/C(A) MW Rudorf DSC RN	14 Jul 1943
Squadron disbanded	28 Apr 1944
Lt(A) PJ Hutton DSC RN	13 Nov 1947
L/C RD Henderson RN	2 Nov 1949
L/C TJ Harris RN	18 Dec 1950
Lt(E) SE Adams RN (temp)	7 Dec 1951
L/C JS Barnes RN	16 Jan 1952
L/C LR Tivy RN	15 Aug 1953
L/C P Cane RN (temp)	17 Jan 1955
L/C AM Dennis RN	21 Feb 1955
L/C NJ Ovenden RN	3 Dec 1956
L/C WL Hughes RN	14 Mar 1957
L/C AH Smith RN	6 Jan 1958
L/C LDM Searson RN	10 Jan 1958
Squadron disbanded	1 Oct 1958

Fairey Barracuda III ME256 '314/MF' of No.796 Squadron, St.Merryn around 1952/3. (Tony Hughes)

No.797 Squadron

No.797 Squadron formed at Katukurunda in July 1942 as a Fleet Requirements Unit squadron with two Skuas. A few Swordfish and Sea Gladiators were later used, and also three Albacores during 1943, but shortly after moving to Colombo on 1 October 1943 the Skuas were replaced by Defiants. 'X' Flight was detached to Juhu on 1 July 1944, and during that year numbers of Harvards, Barracudas, Avengers, and Beaufighter IIs were received. In July 1945 six Mosquito B.25s were used for a few days before being withdrawn, then on 24 October 1945 No.797 disbanded.

Identification Markings
Defiant *R8A+*, Beaufighter *L9A+*, remainder uncertain.

Aircraft Equipment	Period of Service	Example
Skua II	Jul 1942 - Nov 1943	
Swordfish I	Nov 1942 - Aug 1945	L9723
Sea Gladiator	1943	N5500
Albacore I	Apr 1943 - Oct 1943	BF724
Defiant TT.I	Nov 1943 - Aug 1945	DR915
Harvard III	Jan 1944	EX913
Avenger I	Mar 1944 - May 1944	
Beaufighter II	Mar 1944 - Aug 1945	T3431 (L9Y)
Martinet TT.I	Sep 1944 - Oct 1944	EM506
Barracuda II	Nov 1944	DP973
Corsair III	Jan 1945	KD333
Mosquito B.25	Jul 1945 - Jul 1945	

Squadron bases
Katukurunda	by 24 Jul 1942
Juhu (X Flt)	8 Aug 1943
	to 7 Sep 1944
Colombo Racecourse	1 Oct 1943
Squadron disbanded	24 Oct 1945

Commanding Officers
Lt(A) FL Page RNVR	Jul 1942
Lt(A) KC Winstanley RNVR	9 Dec 1943
Squadron disbanded	24 Oct 1945

Miles Martinets of No.797 Squadron lined up at Colombo Racecourse in 1945. (Topham)

No.798 Squadron

No.798 Squadron formed out of the conversion elements of Nos.780 and 781 Squadrons at Lee-on-Solent on 11 October 1943. Operating as an Advanced Conversion Course, it initially flew an assortment of aircraft which included Fulmars, Barracudas, Blenheims, Beaufighters, Beauforts, Masters, Tiger Moths and Oxfords. The twin engined element broke away in March 1944 to form No.762 Squadron, taking with it the Beauforts, Beaufighters, Blenheims and Oxfords. A detachment was based at Stretton from 20 April 1944, converting crews of newly formed Barracuda squadrons, before returning to Lee-on-Solent between 30 July and 2 August. Harvards and Fireflies arrived during 1944, and in 1945 the squadron concentrated on refresher and familiarisation training. Moving to Halesworth on 6 September, FAA ex-prisoners of war were given refresher flying courses on Harvards, following their return home. A further move was made to Hinstock on 28 November 1945, but on 18 March 1946 the squadron disbanded.

Identification Markings
All types *L1A+* to *L4A+* from 10.43, to *U2A+* 11.45.

Commanding Officers
L/C(A) IJ Wallace
    OBE RNVR   11 Oct 1943
L/C(A) SW Birse
    DSC RNR   8 Aug 1945
Squadron disbanded 18 Mar 1946

Squadron bases
Lee-on-Solent   11 Oct 1943
Stretton (Dt)   20 Apr 1944
              to 30 Jul 1944
Halesworth   6 Sep 1945
Hinstock   28 Nov 1945
  (satt Peplow)
Burscough (Dt)   5 Dec 1945
              to 19 Feb 1946
Squadron disbanded 18 Mar 1946

Aircraft Equipment	Period of Service	Example	
Oxford	Oct 1943 - Mar 1944	T1098	
Beaufighter II	Oct 1943 - Mar 1944	T3223	(L1P)
Master I	Oct 1943 - Aug 1944	N9003	(N)
Master II	Jul 1944 - Oct 1945	DM130	
Tiger Moth II	Oct 1943 - Apr 1945	T7034	(L3D)
Blenheim IV	Oct 1943 - Mar 1944	N1984	
Beaufort I	Oct 1943 - Mar 1944	LR929	
Barracuda II	Oct 1943 - Oct 1945	LS849	
Barracuda III	Jun 1945	MD972	
Fulmar II	Oct 1943 - Apr 1945	X8799	
Avenger II	Apr 1944 - Jun 1945	JZ438	(L3B)
Firefly I	Nov 1944 - Nov 1945	DK420	
Anson I	Apr 1945	DJ561	
Spitfire Vb	Apr 1945 - Jun 1945	W3370	
Spitfire IX	Dec 1944 - Feb 1945	BS390	
Seafire Ib	May 1945 - Jul 1945	NX894	
Seafire IIc	Jun 1945	MB117	
Harvard IIb	Jan 1945 - Oct 1945	KF511	(L3C)
Harvard III	Jul 1944 - Oct 1945	EZ379	(U2F)
Oxford	Nov 1945 - Mar 1946	NM524	(U3OO)

No.799 Squadron

Badge: On a field barry wavy of twelve white and blue, a roundel per fesse black and blue charged with an eagle volant gold in the claws a torpedo white in chief three estoiles also gold
Motto: To 'ey nicata
(May the right prevail)

No.799 Squadron formed at Wingfield on 10 September 1943 as a Pool squadron. Equipped with Albacores, which it shared with No.789 Squadron, it provided training for spare aircrew awaiting posting to first line squadrons, until being disbanded on 20 June 1944.

On 30 July 1945 No.799 reformed out of elements of Nos.781 Squadron and 'B' Flight of No.798 Squadron as a Flying Check and Conversion Refresher squadron. On 17 December 1945 it was divided into three flights, of which 'A' Flight was based with the headquarters at Lee-on-Solent, 'B' Flight was based at Gosport and gave junior RN and RM officers flying experience in its 15 Tiger Moths, whilst 'C' Flight gave Sea Otter refresher and conversion courses at Henstridge. 'C' Flight joined the main squadron at Lee-on-Solent in the New Year, and from here its courses included an embarked period in HMS *Indefatigable*. In addition, the former 'X' Flight of No.781 was loosely attached to the squadron as No.799X Flight, or Germany Flight.

On 23 April 1946, 'B' Flight broke away to become No.727 Squadron, and the remainder of the squadron was reorganised. The Sea Otter course became 'B' Flight, and a new 'C' Flight was formed from the Refresher Flying and Instrument Flying element. When No.781 Squadron reformed on 27 June 1946, 'X' Flight was returned to it. At the end of August 1946 the system of each flight being regarded as a separate sub-unit ceased. No.799 moved to Yeovilton on 13 May 1948, where it became part of the newly-formed 50th Training Air Group. Its task was officially described as Flying Check and Conversion Refresher until early 1951 when it became the Refresher Flying Training Unit. Under the latter title it moved to Machrihanish on 3-6 December 1951, disbanding there on 12 August 1952.

Identification Markings
Believed uncoded 1943/4. All types *L8A+* & *L9A+* from 7.45, to 751-787/LP 1946 until 5.48 then Seafire/Sea Fury *100-154/VL*, Firefly/Harvard *200-206/VL* until 12.51, then Firefly/Harvard *201-235/MA*.

Aircraft Equipment	Period of Service	Example	
Albacore I	Sep 1943 - Jun 1944	X9283	
Seafire L.IIc	Aug 1945 -	MB299	
Seafire III	Aug 1945 - Jul 1947	PP928	(769/LP)
Seafire F.15	Oct 1945 - Nov 1951	PR377	(772/LP)
Seafire F.17	Dec 1947 - Jun 1952	SX134	(107/VL)
Dakota C.IV	Nov 1945 - Jun 1946	KP222	
Traveller I	Aug 1945 - Nov 1945	FT520	
Anson I	Aug 1945 - May 1946	DJ561	(L8J)
Anson C.XII	Aug 1945 - Sep 1945	PH655	
Oxford I	Aug 1945 - Jul 1946	PG980	
Dominie I	Aug 1945 - Mar 1946	X7452	(L9B)
Expediter C.II	Aug 1945 - Aug 1946	KP110	
Sea Otter II	Aug 1945 - Dec 1947	RD899	(F)
Tiger Moth II	Aug 1945 - Apr 1946	BB798	
Firefly FR.1	Aug 1945 - Aug 1952	Z2051	(L8A)
Firefly T.1	May 1949 - Aug 1952	MB412	(222/MA)
Firefly T.2	Dec 1951 - Aug 1952	DK489	
Firefly FR.4	Nov 1949 - Jan 1952	VH126	(-/VL)
Leopard Moth	Jan 1946 - Apr 1946	ES945	
Barracuda III	May 1946 - Sep 1947	RK446	(787/LP)
Harvard T.2b	May 1946 - Aug 1952	KF550	(206/MA)
Harvard T.3	Dec 1945 - Jul 1951	FT971	
Firebrand TF.5	Sep 1949 - Jul 1950	EK777	(-/VL)
Sea Fury F.10	Sep 1948 - Oct 1949	TF912	(120/VL)
Sea Fury FB.11	May 1949 - Nov 1951	VR946	
Sea Fury T.20	Apr 1951 - May 1951	VX300	

Squadron bases	Squadron bases	Commanding Officers
Wingfield 10 Sep 1943	C Flt (Sea Otter Course):	L/C WTE White
Squadron disbanded 20 Jun 1944	Henstridge 17 Dec 1945	SANF(V) 10 Sep 1943
Lee-on-Solent 30 Jul 1945	Lee-on-Solent 23 Jan 1946	Squadron disbanded 20 Jun 1944
(HQ and A Flt)	HMS Indefatigable 17 Mar 1946	L/C TE Sargent RNR 30 Jul 1945
B Flt (RN Air Course-	Lee-on-Solent 7 Apr 1946	L/C NR Quill RNR 4 Jan 1946
Tiger Moths):	Redes 799B Flt 29 Apr 1946	L/C PW Compton
Gosport 17 Dec 1945	C Flt (Refresher Flying	DSC RN 4 Nov 1946
Redes 727 Sqdn 23 Apr 1946	and IF Course):	L/C JB Harrowar
B Flt (Sea Otter Course):	Lee-on-Solent 29 Apr 1946	DFC RNVR 1 Jul 1947
Lee-on-Solent 29 Apr 1946	Merged into sqdn 27 Aug 1946	L/C JN Ball
HMS Indefatigable 27 May 1946	X Flt (Germany Flight):	DSC RN 16 Jan 1948
Lee-on-Solent 16 Jun 1946	Wunstorf 31 Jul 1945	Lt(A) TJ Harris RN 13 May 1948
HMS Indefatigable 21 Jun 1946	(operating Buckeburg)	Lt JD Nunn RN 28 Oct 1948
Lee-on-Solent 13 Jul 1946	Redes 781X Flt 27 Jun 1946	Lt KG Talbot RN 6 Jun 1949
Merged into sqdn 28 Aug 1946	HMS Indefatigable	L/C GR Callingham
	(Dt) 6-18 Sep 1946	RN 26 Apr 1950
	Yeovilton 13 May 1948	L/C BH Harriss RN 1 Mar 1951
	Machrihanish 3 Dec 1951	L/C GF Birch RN 12 Nov 1951
	Squadron disbanded 12 Aug 1952	Squadron disbanded 12 Aug 1952

Supermarine Sea Otter II RD874 was flown by No. 799 Squadron at Lee-on-Solent in 1946. (MAP)

Blackburn Firebrand TF.5 EK798 of No. 799 Squadron, Yeovilton in 1950. (D.W.Warne)

No.800 Squadron

Badge: On a blue field, in front of a trident erect, two winged swords in saltire, gold

Motto: Nunquam non paratus (Never unprepared)

No.800 Squadron formed from Nos.402 and 404 Flights on 3 April 1933 as a Fleet Fighter squadron with 9 Nimrods and 3 Ospreys. It embarked the following month in HMS *Courageous*, serving in Home Waters apart from a period in the Mediterranean during the Abyssinian crisis of 1935/36. In October 1938 the squadron began to re-equip with Skuas, and these embarked in HMS *Ark Royal* in the New Year, a few Rocs being also received in May 1939.

On the outbreak of war, fighter patrols were carried out off Norway and anti-submarine patrols in the North West Approaches, then the ship sailed for the South Atlantic to search for enemy shipping. On return, whilst ashore at Hatston, Skuas of Nos.800 and 803 Squadrons dive bombed the cruiser *Königsberg* at Bergen, during the German invasion of Norway. Later, squadron pilots shot down 6 He 111's, but in an abortive attack on the battle cruiser *Scharnhorst* four aircraft were lost and the CO was taken prisoner.

In July 1940 the squadron provided fighter patrols and escorts during an attack on the French Fleet at Oran, and then helped to shoot down two SM 79 bombers during attacks on Italian ships off Sardinia. Transferring to HMS *Furious* at Gibraltar in April 1941, the squadron regrouped with nine Fulmars, of which three embarked in HMS *Argus* as No.800Y Flight, whilst the remainder formed No.800Z Flight in HMS *Victorious* to help search for the Bismarck. A further nine Fulmars were added when the disbanding No.801 Squadron became No.800X Flight in May 1941, sailing in HMS *Furious* for a six months spell in Malta.

The squadron regrouped at St.Merryn in June 1941, and in July joined HMS *Furious* for an attack on the Arctic port of Petsamo, in which it lost two aircraft to German fighters, before transferring to HMS *Indomitable* for a spell in the West Indies. The ship then sailed for the Indian Ocean to participate in the Madagascar operations. Sea Hurricanes were received in June 1942, and with these the squadron returned to the United Kingdom before taking part in the North African landings in HMS *Biter* during November.

In July 1943 the squadron became the first to receive Hellcats, and later joining No.7 Naval Fighter Wing it embarked at the end of the year in HMS *Emperor*. On 3 April 1944, escort was provided for an attack on the battleship *Tirpitz*, and during the next two months strikes were made on shipping off Norway. On 18 June, No.804 Squadron was absorbed and its strength increased from 10 to 20 Hellcats. It later sailed to the Mediterranean to take part in the invasion of the south of France in August.

Following this, shore targets and shipping were attacked in the Aegean before returning to the United Kingdom, where the squadron re-equipped with new Hellcats prior to re-embarking for the Far East. In May 1945 came participation in the recapture of Rangoon, followed by attacks on shore targets and shipping off the Tenasserim coast, during which eight aircraft were operated from HMS *Shah*. VE-Day prevented participation in an assault on Malaya, and No.800 Squadron returned home without its aircraft, disbanding on arrival on 5 December 1945.

On 15 August 1946, a new No.800 assembled at Eglinton, then officially reformed there on 1 October 1946 as a fighter squadron with 12 Seafire XVs, these being replaced in January 1947 by Seafire XVIIs for service with the 13th CAG in HMS *Triumph* in the Mediterranean Fleet. Returning home in March 1949 to re-equip with Mk.47s, the squadron re-embarked for the Far East to take part in strikes against Malayan terrorists, and later operated in Korean waters before returning home to disband on 10 November 1950.

When No.800 next reformed on 21 August 1951 at Ford it received eight Attacker F.1 jet fighters. Strength was increased to 12 FB.2s when No.890 Squadron disbanded in December 1952, the squadron serving in HMS *Eagle* in both Home waters and the Mediterranean before disbanding at Ford on 1 June 1954.

Twelve Sea Hawk FB.3s were the equipment on reforming at Brawdy on 8 November 1954, these being replaced in June 1955

Hawker Nimrod I S1582 '102' of No.800 Squadron, HMS Courageous around 1937/8. (RAF Museum P.8300)

Grumman Hellcat I JV131 'E:L' of No.800 Squadron in 1944. (MAP)

by FGA.4s and FGA.6s for service in HMS *Ark Royal* in the Mediterranean. In November 1956, operating from HMS *Albion*, the squadron attacked Egyptian airfields and other targets during the Suez Crisis. Early in 1958 No.800 rejoined HMS *Ark Royal* for a spell in the Mediterranean before returning to Brawdy where it disbanded on 3 March 1959.

Reformed at Lossiemouth on 1 July 1959 with six Scimitar F.1s, the squadron spent four years with HMS *Ark Royal*, much of it in the Far East, until being disbanded into No.803 Squadron on 25 February 1964.

On 18 March 1964, No.800 reformed at Lossiemouth in the strike role with eight Buccaneer S.1s for service in HMS *Eagle*. The associated but separate No.800B Flight formed at Lossiemouth on 9 September 1964 for investigation into the operational techniques of air to air refuelling with four Scimitar F.1s before disbanding on 14 August 1966. No.800 continued in service, both in the Far East and in Home waters, Buccaneers S.2s being received late in 1966, the squadron eventually disbanding on 23 February 1972.

The number then remained in abeyance until 31 March 1980, when No.800 reformed at Yeovilton with 4 Sea Harrier FRS.1s for service in HMS *Invincible*. In June 1981 the squadron transferred to HMS *Hermes*, from which it played an active role the following year with the Falklands Task Force. It continued operating from that carrier after hostilities ended, until joining HMS *Illustrious* in September 1983.

The squadron operated from HMS *Illustrious* until 1989, deploying to Westlant in autumn 1985, around the world on *Global 86* between July and December 1986, a Mediterranean cruise in the spring of 1988 and again to Westlant in the late autumn of 1988. Transferring to HMS *Invincible* in June 1989, they deployed back to Westlant between October 1989 and February 1990, disembarking to Cecil Field over Christmas and New Year. Operating mainly in home waters during 1991 they deployed to the Far East on *Orient 92* from May to November 1992, and after a work-up in home waters during the first half of 1993. *Invincible* relieved *Ark Royal* on patrol in the Adriatic from August, returning to the UK in January 1994. No.800 Squadron deployed to the Adriatic again in August 1994 and is planned to return in March 1995. It is due to re-equip with Sea Harrier FA.2s in April 1995.

Identification Markings

Nimrod *501-510*, to *102-109, 120* 5.36; Osprey *208-210*, to *123-125* to 5.36, to *102-109* 12.38; Skua single letters, to *A6A+* 5.39, to *6A+* 10.40; Fulmar single letters from 5.41, to *6A+* 2.42; Sea Hurricane single letters throughout; Hellcat single letters, to *E:A+* on *Emperor* 12.43, to *C3A+* 2.45, to *K3A+* by 5.45; Seafire single letters briefly, then *171-182/P*; Attacker *101-112/J*; Sea Hawk *100-113/O:J:Z:R*; Scimitar *100-113/R*, also 800B Sqdn *114-117/E*; Buccaneer *100-115/E*; Sea Harrier *250-254*, to *123-126/N:H:L* 4.81.

Supermarine Seafire FR.47 VP453 '171/P', the aircraft of the CO of No.800 Squadron, equipped with rocket projectiles and RATOG gear, aboard HMS Triumph around 1948/9. (via Mike Schoeman)

Aircraft Equipment	Period of Service	Example	Battle Honours		Squadron bases	
Nimrod I,II	Apr 1933 - Jan 1939	K2826 (106)	Norway	1940-44	Hal Far	25 Jan 1935
Osprey	Apr 1933 - 1939	K2779 (208)	Mediterranean	1940-41	HMS Courageous	4 Feb 1935
AW.XVI	Oct 1933 - Jan 1934	S1591	Spartivento	1940	Upavon	25 Mar 1935
Skua II	Oct 1938 - Apr 1941	L2877 (C)	Malta Convoys	1941-42	Sutton Bridge(3ATC)	27 Apr 1935
Gladiator I	Oct 1938 - Feb 1939	K8039	*'Bismarck'*	1941	Upavon	15 May 1935
Roc I	May 1939 - Nov 1939	L3061	Diego Suarez	1942	HMS Courageous	22 May 1935
	May 1940 - May 1940		North Africa	1942	Upavon	10 Jun 1935
Fulmar I	May 1941 - Jun 1941	N1875 (6H)	Normandy	1944	HMS Courageous	29 Aug 1935
Fulmar II	Jun 1941 - Jul 1942	X8650	South France	1944	Hal Far	15 Dec 1935
Sea Hurricane Ib	Jun 1942 - Oct 1942	P5206 (7C)	Aegean	1944	HMS Courageous	21 Dec 1935
Sea Hurricane IIb	Sep 1942 - Oct 1942	AG334	Burma	1945	Aboukir	23 Dec 1935
Sea Hurricane IIc	Oct 1942 - Nov 1943	NF695 (H)	Korea	1950	HMS Courageous	20 Feb 1936
Hellcat I	Jul 1943 - May 1945	JV134 (EZ)	Falkland Islands	1982	Gosport	28 Feb 1936
Hellcat II	Oct 1944 - Nov 1945	JV304 (K3G)			Eastleigh	29 Feb 1936
Seafire F.XV	Aug 1946 - Feb 1947		**Squadron bases**		Leuchars (ATC)	24 May 1936
Seafire F.XVII	Jan 1947 - Apr 1949	SX112 (M)	Netheravon	3 Apr 1933	Eastleigh	6 Jun 1936
Seafire FR.47	Apr 1949 - Nov 1950	VP459 (179/P)	HMS Courageous	5 May 1933	HMS Courageous	13 Jul 1936
Attacker F.1	Aug 1951 - May 1952	WA496 (101/J)	Northolt	6 Jul 1933	Eastleigh	20 Jul 1936
Attacker FB.1	Feb 1952 - Jan 1953	WA528 (104/J)	Sutton Bridge(3ATC)	10 Jul 1933	HMS Courageous	
Attacker FB.2	Sep 1952 - Jun 1954	WP298 (102/J)	Gosport	19 Jul 1933	(Dt6)	18-24 Aug 1936
Sea Hawk FB.3	Nov 1954 - Jul 1955	WN108 (108/O)	HMS Ark Royal	26 Jul 1933	HMS Courageous	1 Sep 1936
Sea Hawk FGA.4	Jun 1955 - Aug 1956	WV849 (113/O)	Netheravon	31 Aug 1933	Eastleigh	17 Nov 1936
Sea Hawk FGA.6	Jun 1955 - Mar 1959	XE455 (100/Z)	HMS Courageous	20 Feb 1934	HMS Courageous	19 Jan 1937
Scimitar F.1	Jul 1959 - Feb 1964	XD317 (112/R)	Netheravon	12 Apr 1934	Eastleigh	22 Mar 1937
Buccaneer S.1	Mar 1964 - Nov 1966	XN959 (103/E)	HMS Courageous	14 May 1934	Leuchars (ATC)	22 May 1937
Buccaneer S.2	Jun 1966 - Feb 1972	XV336 (115/E)	Sutton Bridge(3ATC)	25 Jun 1934	Eastleigh	13 Jun 1937
Sea Harrier FRS.1	Mar 1980 - Apr 1994	ZD579 (126/L)	Upavon	13 Jul 1934	HMS Courageous	25 Jun 1937
Sea Harrier FA.2	from Apr 1995	ZD612	HMS Courageous	2 Sep 1934	Eastleigh	22 Jul 1937
			Upavon	30 Sep 1934	HMS Courageous	1 Sep 1937
			Leuchars	5 Oct 1934	Evanton (8 ATC)	16 Sep 1937
			HMS Courageous	8 Oct 1934	Leuchars	25 Sep 1937
			Upavon	6 Nov 1934	HMS Courageous	29 Sep 1937
			HMS Courageous	15 Nov 1934	Eastleigh	1 Nov 1937

800B

Aircraft Equipment	Period of Service	Example
Scimitar F.1	Sep 1964 - Aug 1966	XD274 (114/E)

Supermarine Attacker F.1s WA496 '101', WA494 '105' and WA473 '102' of No.800 Squadron in flight soon after reforming in August 1951. (RAF Museum 6456-1)

Squadron bases

HMS Courageous	10 Jan 1938
Aboukir (Dt)	15-17 Feb 1938
Eastleigh	29 Mar 1938
Leuchars (transit)	7 Jun 1938
Evanton (8 ATC)	8 Jun 1938
Abbotsinch (transit)	1 Jul 1938
HMS Courageous	3 Jul 1938
Worthy Down	7 Jul 1938
HMS Courageous	6 Sep 1938
(Dt5) to	27 Oct 1938
HMS Ark Royal	11 Jan 1939
Worthy Down	24 Mar 1939
HMS Ark Royal	3 Apr 1939
Worthy Down	24 May 1939
Lympne	9 Jul 1939
HMS Ark Royal	29 Jul 1939
Hatston	27 Aug 1939
HMS Ark Royal	31 Aug 1939
Worthy Down	27 Sep 1939
HMS Ark Royal	2 Oct 1939
Hatston	15 Feb 1940
HMS Ark Royal	22 Apr 1940
Hatston	2 May 1940
HMS Ark Royal	4 May 1940
Hatston	25 May 1940
HMS Ark Royal	31 May 1940
Hatston	14 Jun 1940
HMS Ark Royal	17 Jun 1940
Gibraltar Racecourse	25 Aug 1940
HMS Ark Royal	29 Aug 1940
Crail	8 Oct 1940
Prestwick	27 Oct 1940
HMS Ark Royal	31 Oct 1940
North Front (Dt)	17 Jan 1941
to	6 Feb 1941
North Front (Dt)	23-24 Mar 1941
HMS Furious	5 Apr 1941
Lee-on-Solent	12 Apr 1941
flights separated	2 May 1941
'X' Flight:	
Donibristle	3 May 1941
Sealand	5 May 1941
HMS Furious	10 May 1941
Hal Far	21 May 1941
Flight disbanded	13 Nov 1941
'Y' Flight:	
Arbroath	2 May 1941
Abbotsinch	12 May 1941
HMS Argus	17 May 1941
North Front	31 May 1941
HMS Furious	5 Jun 1941
HMS Ark Royal	8 Jun 1941
Lee-on-Solent	14 Jun 1941
'Z' Flight:	
Donibristle	2 May 1941
HMS Victorious	11 May 1941
Lee-on-Solent	2 Jun 1941

Squadron bases

Squadron regrouped at Lee-on-Solent	14 Jun 1941
St Merryn	16 Jun 1941
Yeovilton	30 Jun 1941
Machrihanish	12 Jul 1941
HMS Furious	21 Jul 1941
Arbroath	5 Aug 1941
Lee-on-Solent	11 Aug 1941
St Merryn	19 Sep 1941
Machrihanish	14 Oct 1941
HMS Indomitable	15 Oct 1941
Norfolk	10 Nov 1941
HMS Indomitable	22 Nov 1941
Palisadoes	28 Nov 1941
HMS Indomitable	3 Dec 1941
Palisadoes	6 Dec 1941
HMS Indomitable	12 Dec 1941
Khormaksar	11 Jan 1942
HMS Indomitable	16 Mar 1942
Ratmalana	14 Apr 1942
HMS Indomitable	24 Apr 1942
Tanga	22 May 1942
Port Reitz (transit)	8 Jul 1942
Lee-on-Solent	27 Aug 1942
Hatston	23 Sep 1942
Lee-on-Solent	1 Oct 1942
Hatston	8 Oct 1942
HMS Biter	9 Oct 1942
Machrihanish	19 Nov 1942
Grimsetter	1 Jan 1943
HMS Argus (DLP)	13 Jan 1943
Grimsetter	14 Jan 1943
Machrihanish	12 Mar 1943
HMS Unicorn	24 Mar 1943
Donibristle	16 Apr 1943
Hatston	30 Apr 1943
Donibristle	8 May 1943
Eglinton	3 Jun 1943
HMS Ravager (DLT)	28 Oct 1943
Eglinton	4 Nov 1943
HMS Emperor	5 Dec 1943
Eglinton	11 Dec 1943
HMS Emperor	11 Jan 1944
Norfolk	25 Jan 1944
HMS Emperor	5 Feb 1944
Eglinton	2 Mar 1944
HMS Emperor	6 Mar 1944
Hatston	6 Apr 1944
HMS Emperor	11 Apr 1944
Hatston	28 Apr 1944
HMS Emperor	6 May 1944
Belfast	5 Jun 1944
HMS Emperor	7 Jun 1944
Ayr	19 Jun 1944
Ballyhalbert	28 Jun 1944
HMS Emperor	9 Jul 1944
Ta Kali (Dt)	25 Jul 1944
to	6 Aug 1944

Squadron bases

Dekheila	10 Sep 1944
HMS Emperor	14 Sep 1944
Long Kesh	29 Nov 1944
Belfast	23 Feb 1945
HMS Emperor	25 Feb 1945
Colombo Racecourse	25 Mar 1945
HMS Emperor	21 Apr 1945
HMS Shah (Dt8)	11-19 May 1945
HMS Khedive (Dt3)	11-19 May 1945
Cochin	23 May 1945
HMS Emperor	9 Jun 1945
Colombo	11 Jun 1945
HMS Emperor	18 Jun 1945
HMS Shah (Dt8)	24 Jun 1945
to	1 Jul 1945
Katukurunda	19 Jul 1945
HMS Emperor	7 Aug 1945
Trincomalee	15 Aug 1945
HMS Emperor	4 Sep 1945
Coimbatore	18 Sep 1945
Trincomalee	3 Oct 1945
HMS Emperor (no a/c)	5 Nov 1945
Sqdn disbanded UK	5 Dec 1945
Lee-on-Solent	15 Aug 1946
Eglinton	1 Oct 1946
HMS Triumph	1 Feb 1947
Hal Far (Dt6)	16 Feb 1947
to	14 Apr 1947
Hal Far	15 May 1947
HMS Triumph	24 Jun 1947
Hal Far	4 Jul 1947
HMS Triumph	15 Jul 1947
Hal Far	22 Aug 1947
HMS Triumph	15 Sep 1947
Hal Far	16 Oct 1947
Castel Benito	5 Nov 1947
HMS Triumph	16 Dec 1947
Hal Far	19 Dec 1947
HMS Triumph	12 Jan 1948
Hal Far	23 Mar 1948
HMS Triumph	6 Apr 1948
Hal Far (Dt5)	11 Jun 1948
Hal Far	29 Jul 1948
HMS Triumph	18 Aug 1948
Hal Far	28 Sep 1948
HMS Triumph	18 Dec 1948
Hal Far	5 Feb 1949
HMS Triumph	24 Feb 1949
Donibristle	30 Mar 1949
HMS Triumph	25 Apr 1949
Hal Far	6 May 1949
HMS Triumph	30 Jun 1949
Sembawang	3 Oct 1949
HMS Triumph	1 Nov 1949
Kai Tak	5 Nov 1949
HMS Triumph	3 Dec 1949
Sembawang	8 Dec 1949
HMS Triumph	4 Feb 1950
USS Boxer (Dt6)	6 Feb 1950
Kai Tak (Dts)	13 Mar 1950
to	10 Apr 1950
Iwakuni	15 Apr 1950
HMS Triumph	9 May 1950
Sqdn disbanded UK	10 Nov 1950
Ford	21 Aug 1951
HMS Eagle	4 Mar 1952
Ford	24 Mar 1952
HMS Eagle	7 Jun 1952
Ford	19 Jul 1952
HMS Eagle	4 Sep 1952
Ford	11 Oct 1952
HMS Eagle	7 Nov 1952
Ford	3 Dec 1952
HMS Eagle	26 Jan 1953
Ford	25 Mar 1953
HMS Eagle	16 Jun 1953
Ford	16 Jul 1953

Squadron bases

HMS Eagle	2 Sep 1953
Ford	26 Oct 1953
HMS Eagle	13 Nov 1953
Ford	30 Nov 1953
HMS Eagle	3 Feb 1954
Hal Far	15 Apr 1954
HMS Eagle	27 Apr 1954
Ford	26 May 1954
Squadron disbanded	11 Jun 1954
Brawdy	8 Nov 1954
HMS Bulwark (Dt)	8-23 Jun 1955
HMS Ark Royal	27 Sep 1955
Hal Far	24 Oct 1955
HMS Ark Royal	17 Feb 1956
Brawdy	26 Mar 1956
HMS Albion	15 Sep 1956
Brawdy	28 Oct 1956
HMS Albion	25 Jan 1957
Ford	6 Mar 1957
HMS Albion	16 Apr 1957
Hal Far	25 Apr 1957
HMS Albion	4 May 1957
Brawdy	15 May 1957
HMS Albion	16 Jun 1957
Brawdy	27 May 1957
HMS Albion	3 Oct 1957
Brawdy	29 Oct 1957
HMS Ark Royal	27 Jan 1958
Hal Far	9 Feb 1958
HMS Ark Royal	12 Feb 1958
Hal Far	19 Mar 1958
HMS Ark Royal	8 Apr 1958
Brawdy	5 Jul 1958
HMS Centaur	29 Nov 1958
Brawdy	2 Dec 1958
Valkenburg	13 Feb 1959
Brawdy	25 Feb 1959
Squadron disbanded	3 Mar 1959
Lossiemouth	1 Jul 1959
HMS Ark Royal	3 Mar 1960
Lossiemouth	30 Sep 1960
HMS Ark Royal	26 Oct 1960
Hal Far (Dt4)	4-24 Nov 1960
Lossiemouth	27 Feb 1961
HMS Ark Royal	13 Nov 1961
Hal Far (Dt6)	16 Dec 1961
to	2 Jan 1962
Lossiemouth	15 Jan 1962
HMS Ark Royal	10 Mar 1962
Tengah (Dt5)	28 Jun 1962
to	12 Jul 1962
Tengah (Dt6)	26 Jul 1962
to	6 Aug 1962
Pearce (Dt6)	19-30 Aug 1962
Tengah (Dt8)	13-28 Sep 1962
Lossiemouth	14 Dec 1962
HMS Ark Royal	19 Feb 1963
('A' Flight) to	16 Mar 1963
HMS Ark Royal	4 May 1963
Embakasi (Dt5)	7-19 Jun 1963
Tengah	10 Jul 1963
HMS Ark Royal	25 Jul 1963
Tengah (Dt7)	7-29 Aug 1963
Embakasi (Dt5)	18 Oct 1963
to	1 Nov 1963
Lossiemouth	31 Dec 1963
Squadron disbanded into 803 Sqdn	25 Feb 1964
Lossiemouth	18 Mar 1964
HMS Eagle	2 Dec 1964
Lossiemouth	21 May 1965
HMS Eagle	25 Aug 1965
Changi (Dt6)	11-20 Nov 1965
Changi (Dt4)	11-28 Feb 1965
Changi (Dt3)	9 May 1966
to	2 Jun 1966
Changi (Dt4)	1-12 Jul 1966
Lossiemouth	14 Aug 1966
HMS Eagle (Dt4)	7-12 Jun 1967
HMS Eagle	26 Jun 1967

Hawker Sea Hawk FGA.6 XE340 '-/O' of No.800 Squadron around 1955/6. (MAP)

Supermarine Scimitar F.1 XD322 '106/R' of No.800 Squadron in 1961. (MAP)

Squadron bases		Squadron bases		Squadron bases		Squadron bases	
Lossiemouth	18 Jul 1967	Yeovilton	31 Mar 1980	Stanley FOB	16 Jun 1982	Yeovilton	6 Jun 1985
HMS Eagle	15 Aug 1967	HMS Invincible		to	2 Jul 1982	HMS Illustrious	1 Aug 1985
Changi (Dt6)	5-24 Oct 1967	(Dt2)	20-27 May 1980	Yeovilton	19/21 Jul 1982	NAS Oceana	
Changi	21 Dec 1967	HMS Invincible		HMS Hermes (Dt3)	24 Nov 1982	(Dt4)	20-27 Aug 1985
HMS Eagle	23 Jan 1968	(Dt2)	20-30 Jun 1980	to	6 Dec 1982	Yeovilton	24 Sep 1985
Pearce (Dt6)	11-27 Feb 1968	HMS Invincible	9-12 Jul 1980	HMS Hermes	17 Jan 1983	HMS Illustrious	8 Oct 1985
Lossiemouth	18 Jun 1968	(Dt2)		Gutersloh (Dt3)	16-22 Feb 1983	Yeovilton	3 Dec 1985
HMS Eagle	28 Aug 1968	Farnborough (Dt4)	2-8 Sep 1980	Yeovilton	22 Mar 1983	HMS Illustrious	27 Jan 1986
Lossiemouth	2 Oct 1968	HMS Invincible	28 Sep 1980	HMS Hermes	7 Apr 1983	Yeovilton	18 Feb 1986
Luqa	7 Nov 1968	Gibraltar (Dt3/4)	6-23 Oct 1980	Cecil Field	28 Apr 1983	HMS Illustrious	2 Apr 1986
Lossiemouth	18 Nov 1968	Yeovilton	27 Oct 1980	HMS Hermes	16 May 1983	Yeovilton	3 Apr 1986
HMS Eagle	10 Apr 1969	HMS Invincible	18 Nov 1980	Oceana (Dt4)	18-26 May 1983	Culdrose (Dt3)	14-17 Apr 1986
Lossiemouth	28 Apr 1969	(daily dett) to	2 Dec 1980	Yeovilton	8 Jul 1983	HMS Ark Royal	
HMS Eagle	23 May 1969	HMS Invincible	4 Feb 1981	HMS Illustrious	1 Sep 1983	(Dt2)	15-18 Apr 1986
Lossiemouth	7 Jun 1969	Yeovilton	11 Feb 1981	Yeovilton	6 Sep 1983	Machrihanish	
HMS Eagle	13 Jun 1969	HMS Invincible	6 Mar 1981	HMS Illustrious		(Dt4)	21-25 Apr 1986
Lossiemouth	18 Jul 1969	Hyeres (Dt3)	13-19 Mar 1981	(Dt1)	6-14 Sep 1983	NAS Pensacola	
HMS Eagle	4 Sep 1969	Yeovilton	30 Mar 1981	HMS Illustrious	17 Sep 1983	(Dt2)	1-14 May 1986
Gibraltar (Dt4)	27 Sep 1969	Leeming (Dt2)	29-30 Apr 1981	Yeovilton	18 Nov 1983	Bodo (Dt2)	16-19 Jun 1986
to	11 Oct 1969	Lossiemouth (Dt4)	26 May 1981	Decimomannu	28 Nov 1983	HMS Illustrious	22 Jul 1986
Luqa (Dt6)	30 Oct 1969	to	3 Jun 1981	Yeovilton	9 Dec 1983	Paya Lebar(Dt3)	18-26 Aug 1986
to	18 Nov 1969	HMS Hermes (Dt2)		HMS Illustrious	19 Jan 1984	Yeovilton	15 Dec 1986
Lossiemouth	4 Dec 1969		10-11 Jun 1981	Oceana (Dt4)	10-16 Feb 1984	Decimomannu	2 Mar 1987
HMS Eagle	10 Jan 1970	HMS Hermes (Dt2)		Yeovilton	29 Mar 1984	Yeovilton	13 Mar 1987
Lossiemouth (Dt5)	27 Feb 1960		22-2 3 Jun 1981	HMS Illustrious	25 Apr 1984	HMS Illustrious	1 May 1987
to	10 Mar 1970	HMS Hermes	13 Jul 1981	Yeovilton	7 Jun 1984	Yeovilton (Dt3)	6-13 May 1987
Lossiemouth	23 Mar 1970	Culdrose (Dt4)	21-23 Jul 1981	HMS Illustrious	24 Jun 1984	Yeovilton	22 Jun 1987
HMS Eagle	2 Oct 1970	Yeovilton	24 Jul 1981	Yeovilton	19 Jul 1984	HMS Illustrious	24 Aug 1987
Lossiemouth	9 Dec 1970	HMS Hermes	2 Sep 1981	Decimomannu (Dt4)		Yeovilton	22 Sep 1987
HMS Eagle	17 Jan 1971	Cecil Field	16 Sep 1981		3-1 8 Sep 1984	Decimomannu	12 Oct 1987
Luqa (Dt6)	3-22 Mar 1971	Palm Beach(Dt2)	24-28 Sep 1981	HMS Illustrious	25 Sep 1984	Yeovilton	23 Oct 1987
Lossiemouth	31 Mar 1971	HMS Hermes	20 Oct 1981	Gibraltar (Dt4)	20-24 Oct 1984	HMS Ark Royal	2 Nov 1987
HMS Eagle	26 May 1971	Yeovilton	1 Dec 1981	Yeovilton	20 Nov 1984	Yeovilton	18 Nov 1987
Tengah	7 Jul 1971	HMS Hermes	22 Jan 1982	HMS Illustrious	26 Nov 1984	HMS Illustrious	19 Jan 1988
HMS Eagle	21 Jul 1971	Yeovilton	19 Feb 1982	Yeovilton	11 Dec 1984	Yeovilton	5 Mar 1988
Tengah (Dt6)	19 Sep 1971	HMS Hermes	11 Mar 1982	Decimomannu (Dt4)	21 Jan 1985	HMS Illustrious	6 Apr 1988
to	5 Oct 1971	Yeovilton	19 Mar 1982	to	1 Feb 1985	Gibraltar (Dt4)	18-21 Apr 1988
Kai Tak	14-29 Oct 1971	HMS Hermes	2/5 Apr 1982	Bitburg (Dt4)	15-22 Feb 1985	Yeovilton	19 May 1988
Lossiemouth	23 Jan 1972	San Carlos FOB	5-30 Jun 1982	Vaerlose (Dt4)	15-19 Mar 1985	HMS Illustrious	12 Jun 1988
Squadron disbanded	23 Feb 1972			HMS Illustrious	30 Apr 1985	Yeovilton	25 Jun 1988

Squadron bases

HMS Illustrious	30 Aug 1988
Yeovilton	23 Sep 1988
HMS Illustrious	3 Oct 1988
Cecil Field	17 Oct 1988
HMS Illustrious	7 Nov 1988
Yeovilton	15 Dec 1988
HMS Illustrious	27 Jan 1989
Yeovilton (Dt2)	16-22 Feb 1989
Yeovilton	22 Feb 1989
HMS Illustrious	28 Feb 1989
Yeovilton	23 Mar 1989
Decimomannu (Dt4)	24 Apr 1989
to	12 May 1989
HMS Invincible (daily dett)	1-13 Jun 1989
HMS Invincible (Dt3)	19-30 Jun 1989
HMS Invincible	12 Jul 1989
Yeovilton	2 Aug 1989
HMS Invincible (Dt5)	2-10 Aug 1989
HMS Invincible	16 Oct 1989
Cecil Field (Dt2)	1-8 Nov 1989
Cherry Point (Dt2)	1-8 Nov 1989
Cecil Field	7 Dec 1989
HMS Invincible	15 Jan 1990
Oceana (Dt5)	18- 24 Jan 1990
Yeovilton	22 Feb 1990
HMS Invincible	23 Apr 1990
Yeovilton	14 May 1990
HMS Invincible	24 Jun 1990
Yeovilton	28 Jun 1990
HMS Invincible	31 Aug 1990
Yeovilton	17 Sep 1990
Culdrose (Dt2)	2-5 Oct 1990
Leeuwarden (Dt5)	12-15 Nov 1990
Decimomannu (Dt6)	19-30 Nov 1990
HMS Invincible	19 Jan 1991
Yeovilton	24 Jan 1991
HMS Invincible	5 Feb 1991
Yeovilton	7 Feb 1991
HMS Invincible	12 Feb 1991
Yeovilton	18 Feb 1991
Coningsby (Dt4)	18-22 Feb 1991
HMS Invincible	26 Feb 1991
Yeovilton	23 May 1991
HMS Invincible (Dt4)	2-6 Jun 1991
Florennes (Dt6)	28 Jun 1991
to	5 Jul 1991
HMS Invincible	27 Aug 1991
Yeovilton	18 Nov 1991
Waddington (Dt4)	2-6 Dec 1991
Baden-Soellingen (Dt6)	9-16 Dec 1991
West Freugh (Dt5)	3-7 Feb 1992
HMS Invincible	21 Feb 1992
Yeovilton	21 Mar 1992
HMS Invincible	12 May 1992
Diego Garcia (Dt5)	29-30 Jun 1992
Paya Lebar	6 Sep 1992
HMS Invincible	17 Sep 1992
Akrotiri (Dt3)	10-11 Nov 1992
Yeovilton	26 Nov 1992
HMS Ark Royal	15 Jan 1993
(Dt2) to	19 Feb 1993
Waddington (Dt3)	25-29 Jan 1993
Leuchars (Dt3)	22 Feb 1993
to	5 Mar 1993
Leeming (Dt3)	26-28 Apr 1993
Lossiemouth (Dt2)	3-5 May 1993
HMS Invincible	11 May 1993
Yeovilton	24 May 1993
HMS Invincible (Dt6)	4 Jun 1993
Yeovilton	18 Jun 1993
Ramstein (Dt2)	20-24 Jun 1993
HMS Invincible	22 Jul 1993
Decimomannu (Dt5)	29 Nov 1993
to	17 Dec 1993
Grottaglie (Dt2)	19-25 Jan 1994
Yeovilton	7 Feb 1994
Florennes (Dt3)	29 Apr 1994
to	11 May 1994
Decimomannu (Dt3)	25 May 1994
to	14 Jun 1994
HMS Invincible	27 Jun 1994
(Dt3) to	8 Jul 1994
HMS Invincible	23 Aug 1994
Yeovilton	Mar 1995

Commanding Officers

L/C CJN Atkinson RN (Sq Ldr RAF)	3 Apr 1933
L/C JB Heath RN	1 Aug 1935
L/C HA Traill RN (Sq Ldr RAF)	17 Mar 1937
L/C BHM Kendall RN (Sq Ldr RAF)	18 Jul 1938
L/C GN Torry RN (Flt Lt RAF)	21 Nov 1938
Capt RT Partridge RM	3 Apr 1940
Lt EGD Finch-Noyes RN (temp)	5 May 1940
Lt RM Smeeton RN	16 Jun 1940
L/C JAD Wroughton DSC RN	12 May 1941
L/C JM Bruen DSC RN	16 Mar 1942
L/C H Muir-Mackenzie DSC RN	1 Dec 1942
L/C SJ Hall DSC RN	7 Jul 1943
L/C MF Fell DSC RN	24 Sep 1944
L/C(A) DB Law DSC RNVR	12 Dec 1944
L/C H de Wit RNethN	20 May 1945
Squadron disbanded	5 Dec 1945
L/C(A) DG Parker DSO DSC RN	15 Aug 1946
L/C M Hordern DSC RN (temp)	12 Feb 1948
L/C(A) JF Rankin DSC RN	Mar 1948
L/C R Pridham-Wippell RN	14 May 1948
L/C IM MacLachlen RN	24 Nov 1949
L/C TD Handley RN	29 Aug 1950
Squadron disbanded	10 Nov 1950
L/C GC Baldwin DSC & Bar RN	22 Aug 1951
L/C RW Kearsley	3 Dec 1952
L/C WI Campbell RN	23 Dec 1953
Squadron disbanded	11 Jun 1954
L/C RD Lygo RN	8 Nov 1954
L/C JD Russell RN	7 May 1955
L/C N Perrett RN	1 Nov 1957
L/C AA Fyfe RN	1 Dec 1958
Squadron disbanded	3 Mar 1959
L/C DP Norman AFC	1 Jul 1959
L/C A Mancais RN	2 Oct 1961
L/C DF Mills RN	17 Dec 1962
L/C PG Newman RN	5 Mar 1963
L/C JC Mather RN	18 Mar 1964
L/C CG Giles RN	26 Oct 1965
L/C JW Moore RN	1 Nov 1966
L/C SD Mather RN	1 Aug 1968
L/C JOFD Billingham RN	11 Dec 1969
L/C R Wren RN	11 Jan 1971
Squadron disbanded	23 Feb 1972
L/C TJH Gedge RN	31 Mar 1980
L/C AD Auld DSC RN	20 Jan 1982
L/C D Hamilton RN	13 Sep 1983
L/C R Frederikson RN	5 May 1985
L/C MW Watson RN	12 Jan 1988
L/C RC Hawkins RN	6 Jan 1990
L/C DD Braithwaite RN	20 Aug 1991
L/C CB Neave RN	23 Apr 1993
L/C JP Millward	20 Oct 1994

800B Flight

Squadron bases

Lossiemouth	9 Sep 1964
HMS Eagle	2 Dec 1964
Lossiemouth	7 May 1965
HMS Eagle	25 May 1965
Changi (Dt2)	11-20 Nov 1965
Changi (Dt2)	11-28 Feb 1966
Changi (Dt1)	1-12 Jul 1966
Yeovilton - disbanded	14 Aug 1966

Commanding Officers

Lt RC Dimmock RN	9 Sep 1964
L/C NG Grier-Rees RN	20 Oct 1965
Flight disbanded	14 Aug 1966

British Aerospace Sea Harrier FRS.1 ZD615 '124/N' of No.800 Squadron in 1990. (MAP)

No.801 Squadron

Badge: On a white field, a trident erect blue, winged proper
Motto: On les aura
(We'll get them)

No.801 Squadron was formed from No.401 Flight at Netheravon on 3 April 1933 as a Fleet Fighter squadron with three Flycatchers and six Nimrods, and embarked with these in HMS *Furious* for service in Home Waters and the Mediterranean Fleet. The Flycatchers gave way to Ospreys in early 1934, and the Nimrods were withdrawn in October 1936. Skuas and Sea Gladiators were received in early 1939 for service in HMS *Courageous* as a Deck Landing Training squadron, but on transfer of the Fleet Air Arm to Admiralty control on 24 May 1939 it was reclassified as a second line unit and renumbered 769 Squadron.

On 15 January 1940 No.801 reformed at Donibristle with 6 Skuas, taking part in Norwegian operations from HMS *Ark Royal* in April. Transferring to HMS *Furious*, the strength was increased by six Rocs in June, but these were soon replaced by further Skuas. However, after a spell ashore the squadron was redesignated No.800X Flight on 2 May 1941.

The squadron reformed at Yeovilton with 12 Sea Hurricanes on 1 August 1941, and later spent some time in defence of Scapa. In May 1942 it joined HMS *Argus* and sailed for the Mediterranean, where it transferred to HMS *Eagle* to see action in Malta convoys, but when that ship was torpedoed and sunk on 11 August the squadron ceased to exist. A few aircraft were in the air at the time, and landed on other ships, but the surviving crews were absorbed into other squadrons.

On 7 September 1942 No.801 formed up again at Stretton, temporarily equipped with 12 unmodified RAF Spitfire Va's and Vb's. These quickly gave way to 12 Seafire Ib's, No.801 being the second squadron to be equipped with this type, a few IIc's also being used for a time. In October the squadron embarked in HMS *Furious* for participation in the North African landings, after which the ship returned to join the Home Fleet based on Scapa Flow, No.801 carrying out operations in the North Sea, and also convoy escort. On 3 April 1944 cover was provided for a FAA bombing raid on the battleship *Tirpitz*, a similar role being undertaken the following month.

In May 1944 the squadron re-equipped with 12 Seafire L.IIIs, and with these it took part in further Tirpitz raids. Then in October it joined the 30th Naval Fighter Wing for service in HMS *Implacable*. After minelaying operations in December, the strength was increased to 24 aircraft before re-embarking in March 1945 for the Far East. Joining the British Pacific Fleet in May, the squadron became part of the 8th Carrier Air Group with which it escorted strikes on Truk and later shipping and other targets around the Japanese mainland. After VJ-day the squadron absorbed No.880 Squadron to reach a temporary peak strength of 48 aircraft before re-equipping with 18 Seafire XVs. These were discarded on sailing for the United Kingdom in April 1946, No.801 disbanding on arrival on 3 June 1946.

On 1 July 1947 the squadron reformed at Ford with six Sea Hornet F.20s, being brought up to a full strength of 12 in October when it joined the 1st CAG. Embarking in HMS *Implacable* in March 1948, the squadron saw service with the Home Fleet. In March 1951 No.801 re-equipped with 12 Sea Furies, with which it joined HMS *Indomitable* in September. A year later it transferred to HMS *Glory* with an increased strength of 16 (later 21) aircraft for service in Korean waters, later reverting to 12 aircraft to serve in the Mediterranean. From February 1954 it was shore based in the United Kingdom until it disbanded at Ford on 31 January 1955.

No.801 was reformed at Lossiemouth on 14 March 1955 with 12 Sea Hawk FGA.4s, with which it made a trip to Oslo in HMS *Bulwark* in May, followed in September by a visit to Trondheim and Copenhagen. In the New Year it joined HMS *Centaur* for a spell in the Mediterranean and Far East before returning home to disband at Lee-on-Solent on 16 May 1956.

The squadron next reformed at Brawdy on 4 May 1957, this time with 10 Sea Hawk FGA.6s. Joining HMS *Bulwark* in November, the ship sailed to the West Indies in the following January, later serving in the Mediterranean and Far East before assisting the RAF in Aden between July and September 1958. Returning home, the squadron transferred to HMS *Centaur* in January 1959 for further periods in the Mediterranean and Far East, and reached a peak strength of 16 aircraft before returning home to disband on arrival on 26 July 1960.

On 17 July 1962 No.801 reformed at Lossiemouth as a strike squadron with eight Buccaneer S.1s. After a spell in HMS *Ark Royal* in the Mediterranean it increased its strength to ten aircraft, embarking in HMS *Victorious* in August 1963 for the Far East. In February 1964 the squadron disembarked to Nairobi during a crisis in East Africa, later rejoining the ship for a further period in the Far East, including a visit to the Phillipines. Returning home, the squadron again disbanded on 27 July 1965.

12 Buccaneer S.2s were the equipment when No.801 next reformed at Lossiemouth on 14 October 1965, from a nucleus of No.700B Flight. Joining HMS *Victorious* for a spell in the Mediterranean, it returned home a year later. The squadron subsequently received the 1967 Boyd Trophy award for its efforts in bringing the Buccaneer S.2 into service. No.801 transferred to HMS *Hermes* in 1968 for a further spell in Eastern waters. In March 1969 the ship returned home to spend the next year in Home and Mediterranean waters, No.801 Squadron disbanding at Lossiemouth on 21 July 1970.

A Brewster Buffalo of No.801 Sqdn at Hatston in September 1940. (Capt R.H.P Carver)

Hawker Sea Hurricane Ib Z7086 'T' and others of No.801 Squadron at Yeovilton in early 1942. (R. Pridham-Wippell)

Supermarine Seafire Ib MB366 'K' of No.801 Squadron on the lift of HMS Furious in late 1942. (via A.H Thomson)

No.801 reformed once more on 28 January 1981, this time with five Sea Harrier FRS.1s. With these it embarked in HMS *Invincible* in May, being subsequently awarded the 1981 Boyd Trophy for its efforts. The aircraft seeing action the following year with the Falklands Task Force. After returning home in September 1982, No.801 increased its strength to 8 aircraft before re-embarking in February 1983 for a Caribbean cruise. It joined HMS *Invincible* again in December 1983 for a spell in the Far East, returning early in March 1984 due to the ship having major mechanical problems.

After operating mainly in home waters during the remainder of 1984 and a deployment to the western Mediterranean in the autumn of 1985 the squadron transferred to HMS *Ark Royal* in Feb 1986 with Westlant deployments in summer 1986 and again in spring 1987. HMS *Ark Royal* deployed to the Far East and Australia for Exercise *Outback* in June to December 1988, including the Australian bi-Centenary. The squadron operated mainly in the eastern Atlantic during 1989, with a further Westlant deployment in spring 1990. January 1991 saw the squadron sailing onboard HMS *Ark Royal* to the eastern Mediterranean in support of Operation *Granby*. Further Westlant deployments took place in autumn 1991 and 1992, and the squadron operated in the Adriatic from January to August 1993 on Operation *Grapple*, during the crisis in the former Yugoslavia. During the Sarajevo crisis in early 1994, the ship was back in the area, and No.801 was flying up to 14 sorties a day, many in the photo reconnaissance role. In April one aircraft was lost to ground fire during attacks on Serb forces at Gorazde. The squadron transferred to HMS *Illustrious* from October 1994, when HMS *Ark Royal* was laid up prior to refit.

Aircraft Equipment	Period of Service	Example	
Flycatcher I	Apr 1933 - Jun 1934	N9928	(512)
Nimrod I	Apr 1933 - Oct 1936	K2828	(517)
Osprey	Feb 1934 - Mar 1939	K4333	(134)
Sea Gladiator	Feb 1939 - May 1939	N5502	(135)
Skua II	Mar 1939 - May 1939	L2927	
	Jan 1940 - May 1941	L2887	(6G)
Roc I	Jun 1940 - Jun 1940	L3161	(H)
Sea Hurricane Ia	Aug 1941 - Nov 1941	Z4922	
Sea Hurricane Ib	Aug 1941 - Aug 1942	V7077	(7H)
Spitfire Va, Vb	Sep 1942 - Oct 1942	P7964	
Spitfire Vb/hooked	Sep 1942 - Oct 1942	AD513	(M)
Seafire Ib	Sep 1942 - Jun 1944	MB348	(R)
Seafire IIc	Oct 1942 - May 1943	MB151	
Seafire L.IIc	Apr 1944 - Jun 1944	NF582	
Seafire L.III	May 1944 - Nov 1945	PP994	(P8Q)
Seafire F.XV	Sep 1945 - Feb 1946	SR596	(125/N)
Sea Hornet PR.22	Dec 1949 - Mar 1950	VZ658	(465)
Sea Hornet F.20	Jul 1947 - Apr 1951	VR839	(152/FD)
Sea Fury FB.11	Mar 1951 - Jan 1955	WE711	(162/A)
Sea Fury T.20	Dec 1951 - Jan 1955	VX284	
Sea Hawk FGA.4	Mar 1955 - May 1956	WV846	(154/C)
Sea Hawk FGA.6	May 1957 - Jul 1960	WV916	(120/C)
Buccaneer S.1	Jul 1962 - Jul 1965	XN932	(115/R)
Buccaneer S.2	Oct 1965 - Jul 1970	XT273	(242/V)
Sea Harrier FRS.1	Jan 1981 - Oct 1994	ZD609	(006/R)
Sea Harrier FA.2	Oct 1994 - to date	ZE690	

de Havilland Sea Hornet F.20 VZ708 '456/C' of No.801 Squadron from HMS Implacable flying over Gibraltar in March 1950.
(RAF Museum 6383-2)

Blackburn Buccaneer S.1 XN934 '117/V' of No.801 Squadron aboard HMS Victorious around 1963/4. (via Brian Lowe)

Identification Markings
Flycatcher *512-514*; Nimrod *516-521*, to *134-136* 1936; Osprey *234-235*, to *134-143* 1936; Sea Gladiator *134-143*; Skua uncoded at first, to *U6A+* 1.40, to *A7A+* 4.40, unknown from 5.40; Sea Hurricane single letters, to *7A+* 6.42; Spitfire single letters; Seafire single letters to early 1945, then *P6A+*, *P7A+* and *P8A+*, to *111-151/N* 6.45; Sea Hornet *150-161/FD*, to *450-462/AO:C* 3.48; Sea Fury *150-162/A*, to *150-170/R* 3.52; Sea Hawk *146-158/C*, to *116-127/C* 1.56; Buccaneer *115-124/R:V* to 7.65, *230-243/V:H:LM* from 10.65; Sea Harrier *000-008/N:R*.

Battle Honours
Norway	1940-44
Dunkirk	1940
Atlantic	1940
Malta Convoys	1942
North Africa	1942-43
Japan	1945
Korea	1952-53
Falkland Islands	1982

Squadron bases
Netheravon	3 Apr 1933
HMS Furious	8 May 1933
Sutton Bridge(3ATC)	20 Jul 1933
Netheravon	28 Jul 1933
HMS Furious	7 Sep 1933
Netheravon	17 Oct 1933
HMS Furious	5 Jan 1934
Netheravon	12 Apr 1934
HMS Furious	1 Jun 1934
Hal Far	9 Jun 1934
HMS Furious	26 Jun 1934
Tatoi	17 Jul 1934
HMS Furious	22 Jul 1934
Hal Far	15 Aug 1934
HMS Furious	28 Aug 1934
Upavon	23 Oct 1934
Gosport	31 Oct 1934
Upavon	3 Nov 1934
HMS Furious	5 Jan 1935
Hal Far	18 Jan 1935
HMS Furious	21 Jan 1935
Upavon	25 Mar 1935
HMS Furious	8 May 1935
Sutton Bridge(3ATC)	13 May 1935
HMS Furious	1 Jun 1935
Gosport	4 Jul 1935
Upavon	17 Jul 1935
Gosport	16 Aug 1935
HMS Furious	3 Sep 1935
Gosport	7 Oct 1935
HMS Furious	4 Nov 1935
Gosport (transit)	22 Nov 1935
Eastleigh	23 Nov 1935
HMS Furious	2 Jan 1936
Eastleigh	21 May 1936
HMS Furious	12 Jun 1936
Eastleigh	20 Jul 1936
Roborough (Dt4)	1-8 Aug 1936
HMS Furious	28 Sep 1936
Novar	5 Oct 1936
HMS Furious	9 Oct 1936
Southampton	23 Oct 1936
HMS Furious	20 Jan 1937
Aboukir	11 Feb 1937
HMS Furious	22 Feb 1937
Southampton	29 Mar 1937
HMS Furious	24 May 1937
Evanton	28 May 1937
HMS Furious	3 Jun 1937
Evanton	9 Jun 1937
HMS Furious	15 Jun 1937
Southampton	21 Jul 1937
Roborough	26 Jul 1937
Southampton	9 Aug 1937
HMS Furious	10 Sep 1937
Donibristle	25 Sep 1937
HMS Furious	4 Oct 1937
Leuchars	4 Oct 1937
Evanton	6 Oct 1937
HMS Furious	7 Oct 1937
Evanton	11 Oct 1937
HMS Furious	12 Oct 1937
Evanton	14 Oct 1937
HMS Furious	21 Oct 1937
Southampton	28 Oct 1937
Sutton Bridge(3ATC)	1 Jan 1938
Lee-on-Solent	29 Jan 1938
Donibristle	4 May 1938
HMS Furious	24 Sep 1938
Donibristle	15 Oct 1938
HMS Furious	14 Nov 1938
Donibristle	21 Nov 1938
HMS Courageous	18 Feb 1939
Donibristle	22 Feb 1939
HMS Courageous	3 Apr 1939
Donibristle	4 Apr 1939
Sqdn redesignated 769 Sqdn	24 May 1939
Donibristle	15 Jan 1940
Evanton	2 Feb 1940
Hatston	12 Apr 1940
HMS Ark Royal	22 Apr 1940
Hatston (Dt3)	15-25 May 1940
HMS Furious	25 May 1940
Abbotsinch	25 May 1940
Sealand (transit)	30 May 1940
Detling	31 May 1940
Hatston	23 Jun 1940
HMS Furious	7 Sep 1940
Hatston	8 Sep 1940
HMS Furious	12 Sep 1940
Hatston	22 Sep 1940
HMS Furious	11 Oct 1940
Hatston	19 Oct 1940
HMS Furious	9 Nov 1940
Hatston	14 Dec 1940
HMS Furious (Dt6)	19 Dec 1940
to	31 Dec 1940
HMS Furious (Dt2)	31 Dec 1940
to	5 Feb 1941
St Merryn	17 Jan 1941
Donibristle (Dt6)	18-26 Jan 1941
St Eval	31 Jan 1941
Hatston	6 Feb 1941
Donibristle	14 Feb 1941
West Freugh (transit)	18 Feb 1941
St Merryn	19 Feb 1941
Campbeltown	24 Mar 1941
Lee-on-Solent	7 Apr 1941
Sqdn redesignated 800X Flight	2 May 1941
Yeovilton	1 Aug 1941
St Merryn	6 Oct 1941
West Freugh (transit)	6 Nov 1941
Arbroath (transit)	7 Nov 1941
Skeabrae	8 Nov 1941
Tain	15 Feb 1942
Turnhouse	29 Apr 1942
Abbotsinch	27 May 1942
HMS Argus	27 May 1942
North Front (Dt6)	7-10 Jun 1942
HMS Eagle	10 Jun 1942
North Front	22 Jun 1942
HMS Eagle (Dt6)	12 Jul 1942
ship sunk	11 Aug 1942
HMS Victorious/HMS Indomitable (Dt6)	11-15 Aug 1942
Stretton	7 Sep 1942
Machrihanish	29 Sep 1942
HMS Furious	19 Oct 1942
North Front(Dt6)	25-30 Oct 1942

Squadron bases

North Front (Dt)	10-15Nov1942
North Front (Dt9)	5-30Jan 1943
Machrihanish	11 Mar 1943
HMS Furious	6 Apr 1943
Hatston (Dt3)	6-10Apr 1943
Hatston	10 Apr 1943
HMS Furious (Dt3)	27-30Apr 1943
HMS Furious	30 Apr 1943
Machrihanish	6 May 1943
HMS Furious	31 May 1943
Hatston	13 Jun 1943
HMS Furious	6 Jul 1943
Machrihanish (transit)	15 Jul 1943
Stretton	15 Jul 1943
Andover	9 Aug 1943
Machrihanish (transit)	15 Sep 1943
Skeabrae	16 Sep 1943
Machrihanish	15 Oct 1943
HMS Furious	29 Oct 1943
Hatston	6 Dec 1943
HMS Furious	10 Dec 1943
Hatston	14 Dec 1943
HMS Furious	26 Dec 1943
Hatston	3 Jan 1944
Skeabrae	10 Jan 1944
HMS Furious	8 Feb 1944
Skeabrae	14 Feb 1944
HMS Furious	24 Feb 1944
Skeabrae	29 Feb 1944
HMS Furious	17 Mar 1944
Skeabrae	21 Mar 1944
HMS Furious	28 Mar 1944
Skeabrae	7 Apr 1944
HMS Furious	20 Apr 1944
Skeabrae	28 Apr 1944
HMS Furious	3 May 1944
Skeabrae	7 May 1944
HMS Furious	11 May 1944
Skeabrae	18 May 1944
HMS Furious (Dt7)	28 May 1944 to 7 Jun 1944
HMS Furious	7 Jun 1944
Drem (Dt4)	11-17Jun 1944
Skeabrae	17 Jun 1944
HMS Furious	22 Jun 1944
Skeabrae	23 Jun 1944
HMS Furious	1 Aug 1944
Skeabrae	7 Aug 1944
HMS Furious	9 Aug 1944
Skeabrae (Dt4	28 Aug 1944 to 16 Sep 1944
Machrihanish	13 Sep 1944
Skeabrae	25 Oct 1944
HMS Implacable	8 Nov 1944
Skeabrae	29 Nov 1944
HMS Implacable	6 Dec 1944
Skeabrae	9 Dec 1944
Grimsetter	4 Jan 1945
HMS Implacable	15 Mar 1945
Jervis Bay	7 May 1945
HMS Implacable	25 May 1945
Schofields	9 Sep 1945
HMS Implacable	16 Jan 1946
Schofields	15 Mar 1946
HMS Implacable	29 Apr 1946
Sqdn disbanded UK	3 Jun 1946
Ford	1 Jul 1947
Tangmere	28 Jul 1947
Ford	23 Aug 1947
HMS Implacable (Dt4) (DLT)	19-23Nov 1947
Culdrose	8 Jan 1948
HMS Implacable	5 Mar 1948
Donibristle (transit)	19 Mar 1948
Culdrose	20 Mar 1948
Arbroath	30 Apr 1948

Squadron bases

Anthorn	21 May 1948
Bramcote (Dt7)	9-15Jun 1948
Culdrose	20 Oct 1948
HMS Implacable	27 Jan 1949
Lee-on-Solent	25 Mar 1949
HMS Implacable	3 May 1949
Lee-on-Solent	7 Jul 1949
HMS Implacable	5 Sep 1949
Lee-on-Solent	11 Sep 1949
HMS Implacable	24 Jan 1950
Lee-on-Solent	31 Mar 1950
HMS Implacable	11 May 1950
Lossiemouth	21 Jun 1950
HMS Implacable	3 Jul 1950
Lee-on-Solent	26 Jul 1950
Celle	21 Sep 1950
Lee-on-Solent	1 Oct 1950
Topcliffe	6 Oct 1950
Lee-on-Solent	15 Oct 1950
HMS Indomitable	24 Nov 1950
Lee-on-Solent	8 Dec 1950
HMS Implacable	18 Jan 1951
Lee-on-Solent	14 Mar 1951
HMS Vengeance	27 Jun 1951
Lee-on-Solent	26 Jul 1951
HMS Indomitable	7 Sep 1951
North Front(Dt5)	12-27Nov1951
Lee-on-Solent	5 Dec 1951
HMS Indomitable	17 Jan 1952
Lee-on-Solent	30 Mar 1952
Hal Far	24 Jun 1952
HMS Glory	2 Sep 1952
Lossiemouth	7 Jul 1953
HMS Illustrious (Dt4)	31 Aug 1953 to 2 Oct 1953
Lee-on-Solent	28 Sep 1953
HMS Glory	2 Oct 1953
Hal Far	12 Nov 1953
HMS Glory	18 Nov 1953
Hal Far	18 Dec 1953
HMS Glory	4 Jan 1954
Lee-on-Solent	28 Feb 1954
Ford	27 Jul 1954
Lossiemouth	15 Sep 1954
Vaernes (transit)	20 Sep 1954
Bardufoss	21 Sep 1954
Trondheim(transit)	30 Sep 1954
Ford	1 Oct 1954
HMS Illustrious (DLP)	4 Oct 1954
Ford	14 Oct 1954
Squadron disbanded	31 Jan 1955
Lossiemouth	14 Mar 1955
Ford	23 May 1955
HMS Bulwark	28 May 1955
Lossiemouth	7 Jun 1955
Vaernes	19 Sep 1955
HMS Albion	27 Sep 1955
Lossiemouth(Dt4)	13-23Oct 1955
Lossiemouth	29 Oct 1955
HMS Centaur	10 Jan 1956
Tengah	4 Apr 1956
HMS Centaur	19 Apr 1956
Lee-on-Solent	14 May 1956
Squadron disbanded	16 May 1956
Brawdy	4 May 1957
HMS Bulwark	13 Nov 1957
Brawdy	26 Nov 1957
HMS Bulwark	10 Jan 1958
Brawdy	5 Nov 1958
HMS Centaur	23 Jan 1959
Hal Far	25 Feb 1959
HMS Centaur	3 Mar 1959
Brawdy	23 Mar 1959
HMS Centaur	29 Apr 1959
Hal Far (Dt7)	13-21Jun 1959
Khormaksar (Dt6)	3-9Jul 1959
Drigh Road (Dt4)	31 Jul 1959 to 11 Aug 1959
Seletar	4 Sep 1959

Hawker Sea Hawk FGA.6s of No.801 Squadron from HMS Bulwark starting up at North Front, Gibraltar around 1958.

Squadron bases

Butterworth	18 Sep 1959
Seletar	24 Jul 1959
HMS Centaur	30 Sep 1959
Seletar	21 Jan 1960
HMS Centaur	4 Feb 1960
Brawdy	25 Apr 1960
HMS Centaur	14 Jun 1960
Sqdn disbanded UK	26 Jul 1960
Lossiemouth	17 Jul 1962
HMS Ark Royal	19 Feb 1963
Lossiemouth	14 Mar 1963
HMS Victorious	14 Aug 1963
Tengah	25 Sep 1963
HMS Victorious	17 Oct 1963
Tengah (Dt4)	17 Oct 1963 to 10 Dec 1963
Kai Tak (Dt4)	23 Oct 1963 to 7 Nov 1963
Tengah	10 Dec 1963
HMS Victorious	3 Jan 1964
Embakasi	7 Feb 1964
HMS Victorious	22 Feb 1964
Tengah	9 Mar 1964
HMS Victorious	3 Apr 1964
Kai Tak	23 Apr 1964
HMS Victorious	6 May 1964
Cubi Point	26 May 1964
HMS Victorious	9 Jun 1964
Tengah	13 Jun 1964
HMS Victorious	26 Aug 1964
Changi	21 Sep 1964
HMS Victorious	14 Dec 1964
Changi	23 Dec 1964
HMS Victorious	6 Jan 1965
Changi	24 May 1965
HMS Victorious	8 Jun 1965
Lossiemouth	22 Jul 1965
Squadron disbanded	27 Jul 1965
Lossiemouth	14 Oct 1965
HMS Victorious	14 May 1966
Lossiemouth	9 Jun 1966
HMS Victorious	8 Jul 1966
Changi	16 Aug 1966
HMS Victorious	5 Sep 1966
Changi	9 Dec 1966
HMS Victorious	5 Jan 1967
Changi	15 Feb 1967
HMS Victorious	3 Mar 1967
Lossiemouth	13 Jun 1967
El Adem (Dt)	18-26Apr 1968
HMS Hermes	31 May 1968
Lossiemouth	20 Jun 1968
HMS Hermes	9 Jul 1968
Changi (Dt5)	28 Aug 1968 to 16 Sep 1968
Changi	12 Dec 1968
HMS Hermes	13 Jan 1969
Lossiemouth	30 Mar 1969
HMS Hermes	25 Sep 1969

Squadron bases

Lossiemouth	27 Oct 1969
HMS Hermes	14 Nov 1969
Lossiemouth	4 Dec 1969
HMS Hermes	19 Jan 1970
Luqa	17 Feb 1970
HMS Hermes	6 Mar 1970
Luqa	13 Apr 1970
HMS Hermes	4 May 1970
Lossiemouth	17 Jun 1970
Squadron disbanded	21 Jul 1970
Yeovilton	28 Jan 1981
HMS Invincible	21 May 1981
Yeovilton	8 Jun 1981
HMS Invincible	22 Jun 1981
Norfolk (Dt4)	8-19Aug1981
Yeovilton	23 Sep 1981
HMS Invincible (Dt5)	16-21Nov 1981
Decimomannu (Dt5)	1-15Dec 1981
HMS Invincible	31 Jan 1982
(Dt1) to	4 Feb 1982
HMS Invincible (Dt3)	11-15Feb 1982
HMS Invincible	15 Feb 1982
Yeovilton	21 Mar 1982
HMS Invincible	4 Apr 1982
San Carlos FOB	5-19Jun 1982
Stanley FOB	2 Jul 1982 to 26 Aug 1982
Yeovilton	17 Sep 1982
Lossiemouth (Dt3)	29 Nov 1982 to 3 Dec 1982
HMS Invincible	31 Jan 1983
Cherry Point (Dt3)	17-22Feb 1983
Belize International (Dt3)	1-3 Mar 1983
Yeovilton	27 Apr 1983
HMS Invincible	23 May 1983
Yeovilton	20 Jun 1983
HMS Invincible (Dt2)	20-30Jun 1983
HMS Invincible	1 Sep 1983
Gibraltar (Dt2)	12- 15 Sep 1983
Whenuapai (Dt3)	29 Nov 1983 to 5 Dec 1983
Nowra (Dt 4)	8-28Dec 1983
Paya Lebar (Dt5)	9-23Jan 1984
Paya Lebar (Dt3)	23 Jan 1984 to 1 Feb 1984
Yeovilton	9 Mar 1984
Decimomannu (Dt3)	22 Jun 1984 to 6 Jul 1984
HMS Invincible	30 Jul 1984
Yeovilton	2 Aug 1984
HMS Invincible	2 Oct 1984
Culdrose	5 Oct 1984
HMS Invincible	12 Oct 1984

Squadron bases		Squadron bases		Squadron bases		Commanding Officers	
North Front		HMS Ark Royal		Yeovilton	25 Nov 1993	L/C JG Baldwin	
(Dt3)	16-19Oct 1984	(Dt4)	12-20Jun 1989	HMS Ark Royal	18 Jan 1994	DSC RN	21 Dec 1950
Yeovilton (Dt4)	5-12Nov 1984	HMS Ark Royal	20 Jun 1989	Decimomannu (Dt4)		L/C LT Summerfield	
Yeovilton (Dt2)	12-19Nov1984	Yeovilton	30 Jun 1989		9-23 Feb 1994	RN	8 Sep 1951
Yeovilton	22 Nov 1984	HMS Ark Royal	30 Jun 1989	Chania (Dt3)	13-17Jun 1994	L/C A Gordon	
HMS Invincible	19 Jan 1985	(Dt3)	to 6 Jul 1989	Yeovilton	30 Aug 1994	-Johnson RN	10 Dec 1951
Culdrose	28 Mar 1985	HMS Ark Royal	4 Sep 1989			L/C PB Stuart RN	1 May 1952
HMS Invincible	14 May 1985	Yeovilton	21 Sep 1989	**Commanding Officers**		L/C JHS Pearce	
Yeovilton (Dt2)	21-30Jun 1985	HMS Ark Royal	2 Oct 1989	Lt RR Graham RN	3 Apr 1933	DSC RN	1 Mar 1954
Yeovilton	1 Jul 1985	Yeovilton	13 Oct 1989	(Flt Lt RAF)		Squadron disbanded	31 Jan 1955
HMS Ark Royal		Leeds (Dt4)	17-20Nov1989	Sq Ldr CEW Foster		L/C LJ Baker RN	14 Mar 1955
(Dt2)	23 Jul 1985	Decimomannu (Dt4)	20 Nov 1989	RAF	9 May 1933	Lt JH Nethersole	
HMS Invincible	31 Aug 1985	to	4 Dec 1989	Sq Ldr SLG Pope		RN	17 Feb 1956
Yeovilton (Dt3)	22-26Sep 1985	Landivisiau(Dt3)	11-13Dec1989	DFC AFC RAF	13 Sep 1933	Squadron disbanded	16 May 1956
Yeovilton	3 Dec 1985	HMS Ark Royal	15-18Jan 1990	Sq Ldr BV Reynolds		Lt JH Nethersole	4 May 1957
HMS Ark Royal		(daily detts)		RAF	11 Jun 1936	L/C W Noble DSC	
(Dt2/3)	2-12Feb 1986	HMS Ark Royal	30 Jan 1990	Sq Ldr GK		RN	27 Mar 1958
HMS Ark Royal	24 Feb 1986	Yeovilton	16 Mar 1990	Fairtlough RAF	16 May 1938	L/C DT McKeown	
Portland (Dt2)	14-18Mar 1986	HMS Ark Royal	18 Apr 1990	L/C CA Kingsley		RN	4 Aug 1959
Yeovilton	25 Mar 1986	Cecil Field	18 May 1990	-Rowe RN	10 Mar 1939	Squadron disbanded	26 Jul 1960
HMS Ark Royal	8 Apr 1986	South Weymouth		(Sq Ldr RAF)		L/C ER Anson RN	17 Jul 1962
Yeovilton	25 Apr 1986	(Dt4)	19-26May 1990	Squadron disbanded	24 May 1939	L/C PH Perks RN	15 Apr 1964
HMS Ark Royal	17 Jun 1986	HMS Ark Royal	30 May 1990	L/C HP Bramwell		L/C JHFC de Winton	
Oceana (Dt4)	9-15Aug 1986	Yeovilton	4 Jul 1990	RN	15 Jan 1940	RN	29 Dec 1964
HMS Ark Royal	15 Aug 1986	HMS Ark Royal	3 Sep 1990	Lt CP Campbell		Squadron disbanded	27 Jul 1965
Yeovilton	26 Sep 1986	Yeovilton	25 Sep 1990	-Horsfall RN	17 Apr 1940	L/C JHFC de Winton	
HMS Ark Royal	13 Oct 1986	HMS Ark Royal	15 Oct 1990	Lt IR Sarel RN	28 Jun 1940	RN	14 Oct 1965
Gibraltar (Dt3)	23-27Oct 1986	Gibraltar (Dt4)	19-25Oct 1990	Squadron disbanded	2 May 1941	L/C MC Clapp RN	10 Dec 1965
Yeovilton (Dt2)	13-19Nov1986	Yeovilton	Nov 1990	L/C(A) RA Brabner		L/C GAI Johnston	
Yeovilton	19 Nov 1986	HMS Ark Royal	11 Jan 1991	MP RNVR	11 Aug 1941	RN	14 Jun 1967
HMS Ark Royal	13 Jan 1987	Yeovilton	9 Apr 1991	L/C FRA Turnbull		L/C MJA Hornblower	
Cecil Field	3 Mar 1987	HMS Ark Royal	10 Sep 1991	DSC RN (temp)	7 Sep 1942	RN	28 Mar 1968
HMS Ark Royal	22 Mar 1987	Yeovilton	15 Nov 1991	L/C(A) RMcD Hall		Cdr RC Dimmock	
Yeovilton	7 Apr 1987	HMS Ark Royal	3 Apr 1992	RN	10 Sep 1942	RN	1 Aug 1969
HMS Ark Royal	5 May 1987	Yeovilton	1 May 1992	L/C(A) HF Bromwich		Squadron disbanded	21 Jul 1970
Yeovilton	14 May 1987	HMS Ark Royal	2 Sep 1992	RN	3 Nov 1943	L/C ND Ward RN	28 Jan 1981
HMS Ark Royal		Oceana (Dt)	17-23Sep 1992	L/C(A) S Jewers		L/C ARW Ogilvy	
(Dt1)	4-18Jun 1987	Cecil Field (Dt)	2-13Oct 1992	RNVR	18 Jul 1944	AFC RN	29 Jul 1982
Dalcross (Dt5)	15-18Jun 1987	Yeovilton	4 Nov 1992	L/C RM Crosley		L/C MS Blissett	
HMS Ark Royal	18 Jun 1987	HMS Ark Royal	15 Jan 1993	DSC & Bar RNVR	1 Sep 1945	AFC RN	23 Jul 1984
Yeovilton	26 Jun 1987	Decimomannu		L/C(A) JR Routley		L/C WM Covington	
HMS Ark Royal	14 Sep 1987	(Dt5)	12-31Mar 1993	RNVR	7 Jan 1946	RN	28 Apr 1987
Decimomannu		Yeovilton	30 Jul 1993	Squadron disbanded	3 Jun 1946	L/C JA Siebert RN	6 Feb 1989
(Dt1)	20-28Sep 1987	HMS Ark Royal	21 Jul 1993	L/C DB Law DSC		L/C MW Watson RN	20Mar 1990
Yeovilton (Dt3)	22 Sep 1987	(Dt1)	to 10 Sep 1993	RN	1 Jul 1947	L/C TS Mannion RN	20Nov 1992
to	6 Oct 1987	Valley (Dt3)	4-7Oct 1993	L/C(A) DH Richards		L/C ME Robinson	
Yeovilton	23 Oct 1987	HMS Invincible	27 Oct 1993	RN	3 May 1948	RN	4 Jan 1994
HMS Ark Royal	3 Nov 1987	(Dt1)	to 12 Nov 1993	L/C K Lee-White			
Yeovilton	18 Nov 1987	HMS Ark Royal	15 Nov 1993	MBE RN	14 Jul 1949		
HMS Ark Royal							
(Dt3)	18-23Nov 1987						
HMS Ark Royal							
(Dt2)	28 Jan 1988						
HMS Ark Royal	5 Feb 1988						
Yeovilton	22 Mar 1988						
Decimommanu	11 Apr 1988						
Yeovilton	22 Apr 1988						
HMS Ark Royal	9 Jun 1988						
Paya Lebar (Dt5)	22 Jul 1988						
to	4 Aug 1988						
Cubi (Dt2)	12-17Aug 1988						
Amberley (Dt5)	20-25Sep 1988						
Richmond (Dt5)	26 Sep 1988						
to	1 Oct 1988						
Nowra (Dt2)	1-7Oct 1988						
Yeovilton	13 Dec 1988						
HMS Ark Royal	8 Feb 1989						
Yeovilton	16 Feb 1989						
Honington (Dt4)	27 Feb 1989						
to	1 Mar 1989						
Lossiemouth (Dt2)	3-6Mar 1989						
HMS Ark Royal	1 Apr 1989						
Yeovilton	4 May 1989						
HMS Ark Royal	10 May 1989						
Yeovilton	2 Jun 1989						
Rota (Dt4)	9-10Jun 1989						
SNS Principe de Asturias							
(Spanish carrier)(Dt4)							
	10-12Jun 1989						
Rota (Dt4)	12-15Jun 1989						

British Aerospace Sea Harrier FRS.1 XZ493 '001/N' of No.801 Squadron in early 1981.
(Nigel B.Thomas)

No.802 Squadron

Badge: On a blue field, issuant from water, in base barry wavy white and blue, an arm embowed gold, the hand grasping an arrow white winged gold
Motto: Primus ferire (First to strike)

No.802 Squadron was formed on 3 April 1933 from Nos.408 and 409 Flights as a Fleet Fighter squadron, embarked in HMS *Glorious* with the Mediterranean Fleet. Equipped with 9 Nimrods and 3 Ospreys, it returned to the United Kingdom when the ship was paid off for a refit in 1934. After short periods in HMS *Courageous*, the squadron rejoined HMS *Glorious* for further Mediterranean service, re-equipping with 12 Sea Gladiators in May 1939. In April 1940 the ship was recalled to participate in the defence of Norway, but on 8 June she was sunk by the German battlecruisers *Scharnhorst* and *Gneisenau* with all her aircraft. No.802 Squadron then ceased to exist.

On 21 November 1940 part of No.804 Squadron broke away to form a new No.802 Squadron at Hatston, with 12 Martlet Is. A small number of these were embarked in HMS *Audacity* during July 1941, and two in HMS *Argus* as No.802B Flight the following month, these latter transferring to HMS *Victorious*. In September the whole squadron embarked in HMS *Audacity* for service escorting Gibraltar convoys, during which four Fw 200s were shot down, but unfortunately the CO suffered a similar fate on 8 November. The squadron again went down with its ship and ceased to exist when HMS *Audacity* was sunk by the U-boat *U-741* on 21 December 1941.

The squadron next reformed at Yeovilton on 1 February 1942 with 6 Sea Hurricane Ib's, and after extensive work-up embarked in HMS *Avenger* in September for patrol duty whilst escorting North Russian convoy PQ18. In conjunction with No.883 Squadron, 5 enemy aircraft were shot down and 17 more damaged. On return to Hatston, No.802 re-equipped with 9 Sea Hurricane IIb's in September then re-embarked in HMS *Avenger*, the ship providing escort for a convoy destined for the invasion of North Africa. After providing fighter cover of the invasion beaches in Algeria, the ship sailed as escort for a UK bound convoy, but No.802 suffered the same fate as its two predecessors, when HMS *Avenger* was torpedoed on 15 November 1942 by *U-155*.

The number then lay dormant until 1 May 1945 when No.802 reformed at Arbroath as a single seat fighter unit with 24 Seafire L.IIIs. In August these were transferred to No.806 Squadron, and 12 Seafire XVs replaced them. After a short spell in HMS *Queen*, the squadron was to have left for the British Pacific Fleet as part of the 9th CAG, but VJ-day intervened, and instead it spent some time at Ayr, deck landing training being carried out in HMS *Premier*. In April 1946 the squadron personnel sailed for the Far East without their aircraft, being intended to relieve No.1850 Squadron in HMS *Vengeance*. However, on arrival 12 new Seafire XVs were received, and these were embarked instead in HMS *Venerable*. In March 1947 the ship sailed for home, and on return to Plymouth on 30 March 1947 No.802 Squadron disembarked to Eglinton.

Seafire XVs were again the equipment when the squadron regrouped with 12 aircraft at Eglinton on 1 May 1947 as part of the 15th CAG. Embarking in HMS *Vengeance* in September, the Group later sailed for the Mediterranean, but No.802 was shipped home in March 1948 to re-equip with 13 Sea Fury F.10s. These were soon exchanged for FB.11s, and the squadron re-embarked in HMS *Vengeance* in August for service in Home waters and the Atlantic. In September 1951 the aircraft joined HMS *Theseus*, transferring in April 1952 to HMS *Ocean* for service in Korean waters. Nearly 4,000 sorties were flown, and in August 1952 a Mig-15 was credited to a squadron pilot. Returning at the end of 1952, the squadron transferred to HMS *Theseus* at Malta, to disband on arrival at Lee-on-Solent on 10 December 1952. Its shared the Boyd Trophy with No.805 Squadron for its work during 1952.

On 2 February 1953 No.802 Squadron again reformed with Sea Furies, at Arbroath, embarking its 12 aircraft in HMS *Theseus* in April. After taking part in the Coronation Review flypast, the squadron re-embarked for a Mediterranean cruise, then returned to the United Kingdom prior to jet conversion at Lossiemouth. 12 Sea Hawk F.1s arrived in February 1954, being replaced successively by F.2s and FGA.4s before embarking in HMS *Eagle* in May 1955 for the Mediterranean. After taking part in a NATO exercise off the Norwegian coast, the squadron disbanded on 22 November 1955.

On 6 February 1956 No.802 reformed with 11 Sea Hawk FB.3s at Lossiemouth. After deck landing practice in HMS *Bulwark* in June, the squadron embarked in HMS *Albion* in September for the Mediterranean, taking part in the Suez War in November. On return to the United Kingdom the FB.3s were gradually replaced by FB.5s, the squadron transferring to HMS *Ark Royal* in May 1957. The ship then sailed for America, and the squadron carried out cross-operations with USS *Saratoga* whilst en route from Norfolk, Va to New York. After a trip to the Mediterranean in the New Year, the squadron transferred in September 1958 to HMS *Eagle* for further Mediterranean service. No.802 squadron disbanded at Lossiemouth on 10 April 1959. Plans to reform at Yeovilton in 1979 with 5 Sea Harriers failed to materialise.

Identification Markings
Nimrod *561-574*; Osprey *548-549, 560*; Sea Gladiator *G6A+*; Martlet single letters; Sea Hurricane unknown; Seafire single letters, to *131-145/V* 1.46; Sea Fury *101-123/Q:T*, to *171-182:Q:O:T* 2.53; Sea Hawk *171-182/J* 11.54 - 11.55, *131-142/O:Z:R:E* from 2.56.

Aircraft Equipment	Period of Service	Example	
Nimrod I,II	Apr 1933 - May 1939	S1623	(572)
Osprey	Apr 1933 - May 1939	K3916	(560)
Sea Gladiator	May 1939 - Jun 1940	N5519	(G6A)
Martlet I	Nov 1940 - Dec 1941	AL247	(B)
Martlet III	Jun 1941 - Dec 1941	AM963	
Sea Hurricane I	May 1941 - Jun 1941		
Sea Hurricane Ib	Feb 1942 - Sep 1942	P3877	
Sea Hurricane IIb	Sep 1942 - Nov 1942		
Seafire L.III	May 1945 - Aug 1945	RX345	
Seafire F.XV	Aug 1945 - Apr 1948	PR407	(102/Q)
Sea Fury F.10	Apr 1948 - Jun 1948	TF925	(111/Q)
Sea Fury FB.11	May 1948 - Dec 1952	VR930	(110/Q)
	Feb 1953 - Mar 1954	WE717	(108/T)
Sea Fury T.20	Jun 1950 - Feb 1954	WE825	
Sea Hawk F.1	Feb 1954 - Apr 1954	WF217	
Sea Hawk F.2	Apr 1954 - Jul 1955	WF253	
Sea Hawk FGA.4	Nov 1954 - Nov 1955	WV824	(179/J)
Sea Hawk FB.3	Feb 1956 - Jul 1957	WM971	(133/Z)
Sea Hawk FB.5	Mar 1957 - Mar 1959	WM998	(138/E)
Sea Vampire T.22	Dec 1958 - Jan 1959	XA121	

Hawker Nimrod I S1639 '574' of No.802 Squadron around 1935.

Battle Honours		Squadron bases		Squadron bases		Squadron bases	
Norway	1940	Hal Far	27 Jul 1936	Dekheila	15 Oct 1939	Arbroath	1 May 1945
Atlantic	1941	HMS Glorious	29 Sep 1936	Aboukir	17 Nov 1939	Twatt	21 Jun 1945
Arctic	1942	Hal Far	30 Oct 1936	Hal Far	2 Dec 1939	Ayr	18 Jul 1945
North Africa	1942	HMS Glorious	4 Jan 1937	HMS Glorious	15 Jan 1940	Abbotsinch	22 Jul 1945
Korea	1952	Hal Far	8 Jan 1937	Dekheila (Dt3)	15 Jan 1940	HMS Queen	10 Aug 1945
		HMS Glorious	30 Jan 1937		to 10 Apr 1940	Abbotsinch	24 Aug 1945
Squadron bases		Hal Far (Flt)	23 Mar 1937	Hal Far	17 Jan 1940	Ayr	3 Sep 1945
HMS Glorious	3 Apr 1933		to 23 Apr 1937	HMS Glorious	25 Mar 1940	HMS Premier (DLT)	23 Oct 1945
Hal Far	27 Apr 1933	Southampton	5 May 1937	Hal Far	28 Mar 1940	Ayr	29 Oct 1945
HMS Glorious	27 Jun 1933	HMS Glorious	23 Jun 1937	HMS Glorious	31 Mar 1940	HMS Premier	19 Nov 1945
Aboukir	23 Sep 1933	Hal Far	23 Aug 1937	Dekheila	2 Apr 1940	Ayr	30 Nov 1945
HMS Glorious	2 Oct 1933	HMS Glorious	18 Sep 1937	HMS Glorious	9 Apr 1940	Nutts Corner	10 Jan 1946
Hal Far	23 Oct 1933	Abingdon	4 Nov 1937	Ship sunk	8 Jun 1940	Burscough	26 Feb 1946
HMS Glorious	20 Nov 1933	HMS Glorious	17 Jan 1938	Hatston	21 Nov 1940	Yeovilton	27 Feb 1946
Hal Far	25 Jan 1934	Hal Far	7 Feb 1938	Donibristle	9 Dec 1940	HMS Berwick	14 Apr 1946
HMS Glorious	2 Mar 1934	HMS Glorious	3 Mar 1938	West Freugh (Dt)	11-12 Feb 1941	(passage)	
Hal Far	11 Apr 1934	Hal Far	27 Mar 1938	Machrihanish	22 Jun 1941	Trincomalee	13 May 1946
HMS Glorious	23 Apr 1934	HMS Glorious	16 May 1938	HMS Audacity (Dt)		HMS Venerable/	
Upavon	1 May 1934	Hal Far	31 May 1938		10-21 Jul 1941	HMS Glory	20 Sep 1946
Netheravon	24 Jul 1934	HMS Glorious	18 Jul 1938	HMS Argus (Dt2)	14 Aug 1941	Sembawang	26 Sep 1946
Sutton Bridge(3ATC)	13 Aug 1934	Hal Far	25 Aug 1938		to 8 Sep 1941	HMS Venerable	14 Nov 1946
Netheravon	30 Aug 1934	HMS Glorious	16 Sep 1938	HMS Victorious	8-18 Sep 1941	Kai Tak	27 Nov 1946
HMS Courageous	7 Sep 1934	Dekheila	28 Sep 1938	(Dt8)		HMS Venerable	12 Feb 1947
Leuchars	5 Oct 1934	HMS Glorious	1 Nov 1938	Twatt	25 Aug 1941	Eglinton	30 Mar 1947
Netheravon	28 Sep 1934	Hal Far	9 Nov 1938	HMS Audacity	10 Sep 1941	HMS Vengeance	24 Sep 1947
HMS Courageous	27 Oct 1934	HMS Glorious	23 Jan 1939	Donibristle	17 Oct 1941	Abbotsinch (Dt3)	6-24 Oct 1947
(Dt)	to 5 Nov 1934	Hal Far	20 Mar 1939	HMS Audacity	28 Oct 1941	Hal Far	11 Nov 1947
Netheravon	30 Oct 1934	HMS Glorious	11 Apr 1939	Ship sunk	21 Dec 1941	Ta Kali	24 Nov 1947
Sutton Bridge(3ATC)	13 May 1935	Hal Far	12 Apr 1939	Yeovilton	1 Feb 1942	HMS Otranto	16 Mar 1948
Netheravon	31 May 1935	HMS Glorious	25 Apr 1939	St Merryn	17 Apr 1942	(transit)	
Gosport	1 Jun 1935	Dekheila	1 May 1939	Peterhead	21 May 1942	Lee-on-Solent	22 Mar 1948
Biggin Hill	17 Jul 1935	Aboukir	5 Jul 1939	Donibristle	6 Jul 1942	Eglinton	7 May 1948
Netheravon	27 Jul 1935	Dekheila	20 Jul 1939	Machrihanish	13 Jul 1942	HMS Vengeance	18 Aug 1948
HMS Glorious	21 Aug 1935	Dekheila	4 Aug 1939	HMS Avenger	13 Jul 1942	Lossiemouth	1 Sep 1948
Hal Far	23 Dec 1935	Dekheila	15 Aug 1939	Machrihanish	15 Jul 1942	HMS Vengeance	14 Sep 1948
HMS Glorious	1 Jan 1936	HMS Glorious	11 Sep 1939	Hatston	17 Aug 1942	Brooklyn	17 Oct 1948
Dekheila (Dt6)	3 Jan 1936	Dekheila	16 Sep 1939	HMS Avenger	3 Sep 1942	HMS Vengeance	16 Nov 1948
	to 3 Feb 1936	HMS Glorious	29 Sep 1939	Hatston	25 Sep 1942	Yeovilton	12 Dec 1948
Hal Far	22 Apr 1936	Dekheila	4 Oct 1939	HMS Avenger	16 Oct 1942	HMS Vengeance	28 Jan 1949
HMS Glorious	1 May 1936	HMS Glorious	9 Oct 1939	Ship sunk	15 Nov 1942	Lossiemouth	7 Mar 1949

Gloster Sea Gladiator N5518 of No.802 Squadron at Dekheila in 1939. (RAF Museum P.20013)

Hawker Sea Fury FB.11 VW575 '110/Q' of No.802 Squadron in 1950. (Brian Lowe)

Squadron bases		Squadron bases		Squadron bases		Commanding Officers	
Culdrose	9 Mar 1949	Arbroath	2 Feb 1953	HMS Ark Royal	8 Apr 1958	Lt DCEF Gibson	
HMS Vengeance	12 Sep 1949	HMS Theseus	29 Apr 1953	Akrotiri	2 Jun 1958	DSC RN	8 Nov 1941
Anthorn	6 Oct 1949	Brawdy	12 May 1953	HMS Ark Royal	23 Jun 1958	Squadron disbanded 21 Dec 1941	
HMS Vengeance	31 Oct 1949	HMS Theseus	16 Jun 1953	Culdrose	25 Jun 1958	Lt DCEF Gibson	
Culdrose	11 Nov 1949	Hal Far	6 Aug 1953	Ford	26 Jun 1958	DSC RN	1 Feb 1942
HMS Vengeance	24 Jan 1950	HMS Theseus	27 Aug 1953	transit	17 Jul 1958	L/C EWT Taylour	
Culdrose	31 Mar 1950	Lee-on-Solent	29 Oct 1953	HMS Eagle	18 Jul 1958	DSC RN	7 Apr 1942
Yeovilton	24 Apr 1950	Lossiemouth	23 Nov 1953	Hal Far	23 Aug 1958	Lt DPZ Cox RN	26 Sep 1942
Stretton	1 May 1950	HMS Eagle	10 May 1955	Idris	25 Aug 1958	Squadron disbanded 15 Nov 1942	
Yeovilton	3 May 1950	Ford (Dt6)	17 May 1955	Hal Far	30 Aug 1958	L/C RE Hargreaves	
Lee-on-Solent (transit)	25 May 1950		to 7 Jun 1955	HMS Eagle	9 Sep 1958	DSC RN	1 May 1945
		Lossiemouth (Dt3)	28 May 1955	Hal Far	2 Oct 1958	L/C(A) BH Harriss	
Wunstorf	26 May 1950		to 1 Jun 1955	HMS Eagle	15 Oct 1958	RN	5 Jan 1946
Sylt	1 Jul 1950	Hal Far (Dt6)	24 Jun 1955	North Front	30 Oct 1958	L/C M Hordern	
Wunstorf	9 Jul 1950		to 18 Jul 1955	HMS Eagle	18 Nov 1958	DSC RN	18 May 1947
Yeovilton	26 Jul 1950	North Front (Dt4)	23 Aug 1955	Lee-on-Solent	2 Dec 1958	L/C(A) RW Kearsley	
Culdrose	31 Jul 1950		to 8 Sep 1955	Lossiemouth	9 Dec 1958	RN	22 Dec 1948
HMS Vengeance	7 Sep 1950	Sqdn disbanded UK 22 Nov 1955		Brawdy	13 Jan 1959	L/C PH Moss RN	7 Apr 1950
Culdrose	14 Nov 1950	Lossiemouth	6 Feb 1956	HMS Eagle	14 Jan 1959	L/C JM Henry RN	21 Aug 1950
Ford	9 Dec 1950	HMS Bulwark	21 Jun 1956	North Front	3 Feb 1959	L/C SFF Shotton	
Culdrose	11 Dec 1950	Lossiemouth	2 Jul 1956	Hal Far	6 Feb 1959	DSC RN	21 Jan 1951
Wattisham	15 Feb 1951	Ford	13 Sep 1956	HMS Eagle	20 Feb 1959	L/C DA Dick DSC	
Culdrose	14 Mar 1951	HMS Albion	15 Sep 1956	North Front (Dt2)	2-13 Mar 1959	RN	22 Jul 1952
HMS Vengeance (Dt)	25-26 Apr 1951	Hal Far (Dt4)	12-23 Oct 1956	Lossiemouth	23 Mar 1959	L/C PH London	
		Hal Far	25 Dec 1956	Squadron disbanded 10 Apr 1959		DSC RN	14 Aug 1952
HMS Indomitable (Dt - DLP)	8-10 May 1951	HMS Ark Royal	4 Feb 1957			Squadron disbanded 10 Dec 1952	
		North Front	9 Feb 1957	**Commanding Officers**		L/C DM Steer RN	2 Feb 1953
HMS Indomitable	9 Jun 1951	HMS Albion	28 Feb 1957	L/C EMC Abel Smith	3 Apr 1933	L/C IHF Martin	
Culdrose	5 Jul 1951	Lossiemouth	5 Mar 1957	RN (Sq Ldr RAF)		DSC RN	19 Aug 1954
HMS Illustrious	23 Jul 1951	HMS Ark Royal	6 May 1957	Sq Ldr WE Swann		Squadron disbanded 22 Nov 1955	
Culdrose	22 Aug 1951	Lossiemouth	18 Jul 1957	RAF	9 Jun 1933	L/C RL Eveleigh RN	6 Feb 1956
HMS Theseus (Dt)	19 Sep 1951	HMS Ark Royal	31 Aug 1957	Sq Ldr RH Hanmer		L/C PE Atherton RN	22 Jul 1957
HMS Theseus	11 Oct 1951	Culdrose	1 Nov 1957	MC RAF	15 Jan 1935	L/C WD Lang RN	8 Dec 1958
Culdrose	5 Dec 1951	HMS Ark Royal	13 Nov 1957	Sq Ldr FE Bond		Squadron disbanded 10 Apr 1959	
HMS Theseus	19 Jan 1952	Lossiemouth	25 Nov 1957	RAF	11 Jun 1936		
North Front	25 Jan 1952	Merryfield (transit)	27 Jan 1958	L/C JPG Bryant RN (Sq Ldr RAF)	11 Jan 1938		
HMS Theseus	31 Jan 1952						
Hal Far	4 Feb 1952	HMS Ark Royal	27 Jan 1958	Lt JF Marmont RN	1 Mar 1940		
HMS Ocean	4 Apr 1952	Hal Far	9 Feb 1958	Squadron disbanded 8 Jun 1940			
HMS Theseus	1 Dec 1952	Idris	24 Mar 1958	L/C JM Wintour RN	21 Nov 1940		
Sqdn disbanded UK 10 Dec 1952		Hal Far	28 Mar 1958				

No.803 Squadron

Badge: On a field barry wavy of eight white and blue, a hornet proper

Motto: Cave punctum (Beware of the sting)

No.803 Squadron first formed at Netheravon as a Fleet Fighter squadron on 3 April 1933 by expanding No.405 Flight to nine Ospreys. Later that month the aircraft embarked in HMS *Eagle* for the Far East, where Kai Tak was the main shore base. The squadron transferred to HMS *Hermes* in January 1935, but on 1 April 1937 it was disbanded, still in the Far East.

On 21 November 1938, No.803 reformed at Worthy Down out of No.800 Squadron's 'B' Flight, with six Ospreys and three Nimrods. The Ospreys were withdrawn the following month on the arrival of six Skuas, the Nimrods being also replaced later. In April 1939, three Rocs arrived, and shortly afterwards the squadron embarked in HMS *Ark Royal*. On the outbreak of war the ship sailed from Scapa Flow for patrols off Norway and anti-submarine operations in the North West Approaches, the squadron losing two Skuas on 14 September whilst attacking the U-boat *U-30*. On 26 September a Do 18 was destroyed, this being the first German machine to be shot down during the war by any British aircraft. After six months ashore in Scotland and the Orkneys, the Rocs were discarded and the squadron embarked in HMS *Glorious* in April for operations in defence of Norway. During the German invasion of Norway, shore based Skuas of Nos.800 and 803 Squadrons, operating from Hatston, successfully dived bombed the cruiser *Königsberg* at Bergen. No.803 then returned to HMS *Ark Royal* for further activity in that theatre, but only two aircraft survived an attack on the German battlecruiser *Scharnhorst* on 6 June.

Re-equipping in October 1940 with 12 Fulmars, the squadron embarked in HMS *Formidable* in November, for service in the Eastern Mediterranean. In early 1941 fighter cover was provided for Malta convoys, and during the Battle of Cape Matapan in March, two aircraft were shot down and two others damaged. In May 1941 the ship was damaged by the Luftwaffe whilst attempting to cover convoys escaping from Crete, and on its withdrawal for repairs No.803 disembarked to Dekheila, and re-equipped with RAF Hurricanes. In June it moved to Palestine and began shore-based operations against Syria, then in August became part of a combined unit operating in the Western Desert as the RN Fighter Squadron. After re-equipping in March 1942 with 12 Fulmar IIs, these were flown to Ceylon for defence against Japanese attacks. Embarking in HMS *Formidable* in April 1942, long range reconnaissance was carried out in the Indian Ocean before disembarking to East Africa where No.806 Squadron was absorbed on 18 January 1943. The squadron undertook army co-operation exercises before being disbanded at Tanga on 12 August 1943.

No.803 next reformed with 25 Seafire L.IIIs at Arbroath on 15 June 1945. It was to have joined the 19th CAG for service in an *Implacable*-class carrier, but VJ-Day intervened. Equipment was changed to 12 Seafire XVs in August 1945, but on 24 January 1946 the squadron transferred to the Royal Canadian Navy on the commissioning of HMCS *Warrior*. Becoming part of the 19th CAG when it eventually formed as a RCN formation in May 1947, No.803 re-equipped with Sea Furies and served in HMCS *Magnificent* before being renumbered as No.870 Squadron on 1 May 1951.

Reformed as a Royal Navy squadron at Ford on 26 November 1951, jets were received in the shape of eight Attacker F.1s for service in HMS *Eagle*, these being increased to twelve FB.2s when No.890 Squadron disbanded in December 1952. In August 1954 the Attackers were replaced by 12 Sea Hawk FB.3s with which No.803 embarked in HMS *Albion*, later transferring to HMS *Centaur* before disbanding on arrival at Portsmouth on 4 November 1955.

On 14 January 1957 the squadron reformed at Lossiemouth with ten Sea Hawk FGA.6s, and these embarked in HMS *Eagle* in August. After spending the early part of 1958 in the Mediterranean, the squadron returned home to disband at Lossiemouth on 31 March 1958.

No.803 next reformed on 3 June 1958 at Lossiemouth around a nucleus of No.700X Flight, with eight Scimitar F.1s, embarking in September in HMS *Victorious* as the first operational squadron on this type. After a spell in Home waters, the ship sailed in November 1959 for a few weeks in the Mediterranean. Most of 1960 was spent at Lossiemouth until re-embarking in October for a further period in the Mediterranean, on return from which the squadron prepared for ten months Far Eastern service. In May 1962 No.803 transferred to HMS *Hermes*, initially serving in the Mediterranean and later the Far East. In February 1964 strength was increased to 16 aircraft on the absorption of No.800 Squadron, that year being spent mainly at Lossiemouth. In January 1965 it joined HMS *Ark Royal*, most of 1965 and 1966 being spent in the Far East, ending in two spells on the Beira patrol before disbanding at Lossiemouth on 1 October 1966.

No.803 last reformed at Lossiemouth on 3 July 1967 as the Buccaneer Headquarters Squadron. Various weapon trials were undertaken, and a detachment of four aircraft flew out to join HMS *Hermes* in the Indian Ocean in August 1968. The squadron finally disbanded on 18 December 1969.

Battle Honours

North Sea	1939
Norway	1940
Libya	1940-41
Matapan	1941
Mediterranean	1941

Hawker Osprey I S1693 '293' of No.803 Squadron, HMS Hermes in the China Station around 1934/5.

Identification Markings
Osprey *285-295*; Skua *A7A+*, then briefly *S6A+* 4.40, *A7A+* & *A8A+* from 5.40; Fulmar *6A+* 10.40 - 6.41, then single letters from 3.42, later *7A+*; Hurricane single letters; Seafire single letters; Sea Fury *VG-BCA to VG-BCZ*; Attacker *111-118/J*, to *140-154/J* 1.53; Sea Hawk *141-152/C:J:E*; Scimitar *145-159*, to *015-034/V:H:R* 6.65; Buccaneer *610-617/LM*.

Aircraft Equipment	Period of Service	Example	
Osprey I	Apr 1933 - Apr 1937	K2785	(295)
Osprey III,IV	Nov 1938 - Dec 1938		
Nimrod I,II	Nov 1938 - Dec 1938	K5057	
Skua II	Dec 1938 - Oct 1940	L3046	(A7H)
Roc I	Apr 1939 - Apr 1940	L3080	
Fulmar I	Oct 1940 - Jun 1941	N2003	
Hurricane I	Jun 1941 - Mar 1942	Z4024	(K)
Sea Hurricane	Jun 1942 - Aug 1942		
Fulmar II	Mar 1942 - Aug 1943	BP828	
Seafire III	Jun 1945 - Dec 1945	NF605	(P)
Seafire F.XV	Aug 1945 - Jul 1947	PR470	(F)
Sea Fury F.10	Aug 1947 - Feb 1950	TF924	
Sea Fury FB.11	Feb 1948 - May 1951	TG113	(BCK)
Attacker F.1	Nov 1951 - Jan 1953	WA496	(117/J)
Attacker FB.2	Dec 1952 - Oct 1954	WP277	(154/J)
Sea Hawk FB.3	Aug 1954 - Nov 1955	WM981	(143/C)
Sea Hawk FGA.6	Jan 1957 - Mar 1958	XE368	(145/J)
Scimitar F.1	Jun 1958 - Oct 1966	XD323	(032/R)
Hunter T.8	May 1960 - Jul 1960	XF357	
Buccaneer S.1	Jul 1967 - Aug 1968	XN964	(613/LM)
Buccaneer S.2	Jan 1968 - Dec 1969	XV165	(610/LM)

Fairey Fulmar II X8565 and another of No.803 Squadron in 1942. (RAF Museum P.16673)

Squadron bases

Netheravon	3 Apr 1933	Wick	11 Jan 1940	Dartmouth	2 Jun 1948	Hyeres (Dt4)	24 Oct 1958
HMS Eagle	26 Apr 1933	Hatston	10 Feb 1940	HMCS Magnificent	Aug 1948		to 3 Nov 1958
Seletar	3 Jun 1933	HMS Glorious	22 Apr 1940	Dartmouth	Sep 1948	Hal Far	8 Nov 1958
HMS Eagle	6 Jun 1933	HMS Ark Royal	26 Apr 1940	Rivers	May 1949	HMS Victorious	10 Dec 1958
Kai Tak	11 Jun 1933	Hatston	28 Apr 1940	Dartmouth	Nov 1949	Lossiemouth	13 Jan 1959
HMS Eagle	16 Apr 1933	HMS Ark Royal	3 May 1940	HMCS Magnificent	13 Jan 1950	HMS Victorious	21 Feb 1959
Kai Tak	27 Oct 1933	Hatston	25 May 1940	Dartmouth	2 Feb 1950	Lossiemouth	23 Mar 1959
HMS Eagle	28 Dec 1933	HMS Ark Royal	31 May 1940	HMCS Magnificent	1950	Yeovilton	1 May 1959
Seletar (Dt3)	16 Jan 1934	Hatston	14 Jun 1940	Dartmouth	Jun 1950	HMS Victorious	4 May 1959
	to 1 Feb 1934	HMS Ark Royal	17 Jun 1940	HMCS Magnificent	22 Aug 1950	Lossiemouth	9 Aug 1959
Kuala Lumpur (Dt3)		Donibristle	8 Oct 1940	Eglinton	Aug 1950	Yeovilton	14 Sep 1959
	8-14 Feb 1934	HMS Formidable	27 Nov 1940	Lee-on-Solent	Aug 1950	HMS Victorious	15 Sep 1959
Kai Tak	16 Mar 1934	Youngs Field	22-25 Jan 1941	HMCS Magnificent	11 Sep 1950	Lossiemouth	30 Sep 1959
HMS Eagle	3 May 1934	(Dt9)		Dartmouth	25 Nov 1950	HMS Victorious	31 Oct 1959
Kai Tak (Dt3)	20 Oct 1934	Port Sudan	25 Feb 1941	Redes 870 Sqdn	1 May 1951	Lossiemouth	14 Dec 1959
	to 6 Jan 1935	HMS Formidable	6 Mar 1941	Ford	26 Nov 1951	HMS Victorious	2 Feb 1960
Seletar	1 Dec 1934	Aboukir (Dt)	11-15 Mar 1941	HMS Eagle	4 Jun 1952	Lossiemouth	28 Feb 1960
HMS Eagle	14 Dec 1934	Aboukir	24 Mar 1941	Ford	10 Jul 1952	HMS Hermes (Dt2)	27 Aug 1960
Seletar	16 Dec 1934	HMS Formidable	27 Mar 1941	HMS Eagle	3 Sep 1952		to 1 Oct 1960
HMS Hermes	30 Jan 1935	Aboukir	30 Mar 1941	Ford	9 Oct 1952	HMS Victorious	19 Oct 1960
Kai Tak	1 Feb 1935	HMS Formidable	18 Apr 1941	HMS Eagle	7 Nov 1952	Hal Far	5 Nov 1960
HMS Hermes	11 Mar 1935	Aboukir	12 May 1941	Ford	3 Dec 1952	HMS Victorious	15 Nov 1960
Kai Tak	14 Mar 1935	Dekheila	27 May 1941	HMS Eagle	26 Jan 1953	Lossiemouth	19 Dec 1960
HMS Hermes	13 May 1935	Ramat David	22 Jun 1941	Ford	25 Mar 1953	HMS Victorious	20 Jan 1961
Singapore	23 Sep 1935	LG.13 Sidi Haneish	18 Aug 1941	HMS Eagle	16 Jun 1953	Tengah	28 Mar 1961
HMS Hermes	5 Dec 1935	LG.109	14 Nov 1941	Ford	16 Jul 1953	HMS Victorious	12 Apr 1961
Singapore	26 Dec 1935	LG.123 Maddalena	19 Nov 1941	HMS Eagle	2 Sep 1953	Butterworth	8 May 1961
HMS Hermes	10 Feb 1936	LG.128 Maddalena	24 Nov 1941	Ford	23 Nov 1953	HMS Victorious	16 Jun 1961
Kai Tak	2 Mar 1936	LG.123 Maddalena	25 Nov 1941	HMS Eagle	3 Feb 1954	Tengah	14 Sep 1961
HMS Hermes	21 Apr 1936	Tobruch	12 Dec 1941	Hal Far	14 Apr 1954	HMS Victorious	5 Oct 1961
Kai Tak	3 Nov 1936	Sidi Haneish	3 Feb 1942	Idris (Dt8)	16-26 Jun 1954	Yeovilton	8 Dec 1961
HMS Hermes	4 Jan 1937	Dekheila	6 Feb 1942	Hyeres	13 Aug 1954	Lossiemouth	9 Dec 1961
Seletar	4 Feb 1937	transit	4 Mar 1942	Lee-on-Solent	17 Aug 1954	HMS Victorious	5 Feb 1962
Penang	19 Feb 1937	Ratmalana	24 Mar 1942	Hal Far	19 Aug 1954	Lossiemouth	30 Mar 1962
Seletar	22 Feb 1937	China Bay	9 Apr 1942	HMS Albion	11 Nov 1954	HMS Hermes	25 May 1962
HMS Hermes	15 Mar 1937	HMS Formidable	25 Apr 1942	Hal Far	12 Dec 1954	Hal Far (Dt7)	12-27 Jun 1962
Colombo	1 Apr 1937	Port Reitz	10 May 1942	HMS Albion	14 Feb 1955	North Front (Dt8)	27 Jul 1962
- Sqdn disbanded		HMS Formidable	25 May 1942	HMS Centaur	15 Mar 1955		to 9 Aug 1962
Worthy Down	21 Nov 1938	Port Reitz	22 Aug 1942	Ford	6 Jun 1955	Hal Far (Dt7)	5-18 Sep 1962
Sutton Bridge(3ATS)	5 Feb 1939	Tanga	29 Aug 1942	HMS Centaur	31 Aug 1955	Yeovilton (transit)	2 Oct 1962
Gosport	23 Feb 1939	HMS Illustrious	7 Dec 1942	Sqdn disbanded UK	4 Nov 1955	Lossiemouth	2 Oct 1962
Exeter	15 Mar 1939	Port Reitz	12 Dec 1942	Lossiemouth	14 Jan 1957	HMS Hermes	13 Nov 1962
Worthy Down	23 Mar 1939	Tanga	12 Jan 1943	HMS Eagle	5 Aug 1957	Tengah (Dt6)	20 Dec 1962
HMS Ark Royal	3 Apr 1939	Squadron disbanded	12 Aug 1943	Lossiemouth	30 Aug 1957		to 7 Jan 1963
Worthy Down	18 Apr 1939	Arbroath	15 Jun 1945	HMS Eagle	10 Sep 1957	Tengah (Dt7)	18 Mar 1963
HMS Ark Royal	30 Apr 1939	Nutts Corner	23 Sep 1945	Lossiemouth	30 Sep 1957		to 24 Apr 1963
Gosport	8 May 1939	Lee-on-Solent	28 Feb 1946	HMS Eagle	10 Oct 1957	Yeovilton (Dt5)	11-27 Sep 1963
HMS Ark Royal	10 May 1939	HMCS Warrior	23 Mar 1946	Lossiemouth	23 Nov 1957	Lossiemouth	22 Oct 1963
Ford	28 Jun 1939	Dartmouth	31 Mar 1946	HMS Eagle	29 Jan 1958	HMS Hermes	30 Nov 1963
Lympne	1 Jul 1939	HMCS Warrior	10 Jul 1946	Hal Far	13 Feb 1958	Lossiemouth	12 Dec 1963
HMS Ark Royal	29 Jul 1939	Dartmouth	1 Oct 1946	HMS Eagle	28 Feb 1958	HMS Hermes	16 Jan 1964
Evanton	22 Aug 1939	HMCS Warrior	Apr 1947	Lossiemouth	29 Mar 1958	Lossiemouth	23 Feb 1964
HMS Ark Royal	24 Aug 1939	Dartmouth	15 May 1947	Squadron disbanded	31 Mar 1958	Yeovilton	24 Jun 1964
Hatston	1 Oct 1939	HMCS Warrior	3 Aug 1947	Lossiemouth	3 Jun 1958	Lossiemouth	3 Jul 1964
Wick	31 Oct 1939	Eglinton	8 Aug 1947	HMS Victorious	25 Sep 1958	Yeovilton	30 Aug 1964
Hatston	8 Dec 1939	HMCS Magnificent	20 May 1948	Hal Far (Dt2)	18-22 Oct 1958	Lossiemouth	21 Sep 1964

Supermarine Attacker FB.2 WP303 '150/J' of No.803 Squadron on HMS Eagle at Gibraltar around 1953/4. (FAA Museum)

Squadron bases		Commanding Officers		Commanding Officers		Commanding Officers	
Yeovilton		Flt Lt L Young RAF	3 Apr 1933	L/C AJ Tanner		L/C GR Higgs RN	25 Sep 1958
(Dt2-DLP)	6-7 Nov 1964	L/C RR Graham RN	5 Dec 1933	RCNVR	16 Nov 1945	L/C AJ Leahy	
HMS Ark Royal	8 Dec 1964	(Sq Ldr RAF)		L/C CG Watson RCN	May 1946	MBE DSC RN	14 Dec 1959
Lossiemouth	11 Dec 1964	Cdr CW Byas RN	27 Dec 1934	L/C(A) HJG Bird		L/C TCS Leece RN	18 Dec 1960
HMS Ark Royal	23 Jan 1965	(Sq Ldr RAF)		RCN	May 1947	L/C NJP Mills RN	1 Aug 1962
Lossiemouth	16 Mar 1965	Squadron disbanded	1 Apr 1937	Lt JP Whitby RCN	Aug 1948	L/C PG Newman RN	
HMS Ark Royal	17 Jun 1965	L/C BHM Kendall		L/C VJ Wilgress RCN	Sep 1948		4 May 1964
Changi (Dt8)	19 Jul 1965	RN	21 Nov 1938	L/C N Cogdon RCN		L/C J Worth RN	14 Jun 1965
	to 7 Aug 1965	L/C DRF Cambell			14 May 1949	Squadron disbanded	1 Oct 1966
Changi	20 Oct 1965	RN	2 Mar 1939	Lt DD Peacocke		L/C MJA Hornblower	
Butterworth	10 Nov 1965	Lt WP Lucy RN	8 Feb 1940	RCN	15 Jan 1951	RN	3 Jul 1967
Changi	22 Nov 1965	L/C J Casson RN	23 May 1940	Squadron disbanded	1 May 1951	L/C GB Hoddinott	
HMS Ark Royal	7 Dec 1965	Lt JM Bruen RN	16 Jun 1940	L/C TD Handley RN		RN	26 Feb 1968
Changi	6 Jan 1966	L/C JM Wintour RN			26 Nov 1951	L/C R Wren RN	22 May 1969
HMS Ark Royal	27 Jan 1966		16 Oct 1940	L/C JM Glaser RN	12 Jan 1953	Squadron disbanded	18 Dec 1969
Changi	15 Mar 1966	Lt JM Bruen RN	4 Nov 1940	L/C WDD MacDonald			
HMS Ark Royal	24 Mar 1966	Lt DCEF Gibson RN		RN	19 May 1953		
Lossiemouth	12 Jun 1966		20 Jul 1941	L/C JS Bailey			
HMS Ark Royal	2 Aug 1966	Lt BS McEwen RN	by Sep 1941	OBE DSC RN	4 Jun 1953		
Lossiemouth	1 Oct 1966	Lt WL Irving RN	11 Aug 1942	L/C TG Innes AFC			
- Sqdn disbanded		L/C(A) BF Cox		RN	2 Jun 1954		
Lossiemouth	3 Jul 1967	RNVR	7 Oct 1942	Squadron disbanded	4 Nov 1955		
HMS Hermes (Dt4)	23 Aug 1968	Squadron disbanded	12 Aug 1943	Cdr JO Roberts RN	14 Jan 1957		
	to 1 Apr 1969	L/C(A) LD Wilkinson		Squadron disbanded	31 Mar 1958		
Squadron disbanded	18 Dec 1969	DSC RNVR	15 Jun 1945	Cdr JD Russell RN	3 Jun 1958		

Hawker Sea Fury FB.11 VX690 'VG-BCO' of No.803 Squadron, Royal Canadian Navy in 1951. (MAP)

Hawker Sea Hawk FB.3 WM989 '141/C' of No.803 Squadron at Ford in 1955. (John Rawlings)

Supermarine Scimitar F.1 XD225 '154/H' of No.803 Squadron taking off from the angled deck of HMS Hermes around 1964. (via Brian Lowe)

No.804 Squadron

Badge: On a blue field, a tiger's face proper holding in the mouth a dagger fessewise also proper pommel and hilt gold

Motto: Swift to kill

No.804 Squadron formed as a shore-based fighter squadron on 30 November 1939, from a nucleus of four Sea Gladiators of No.769 Squadron which had been detached to Hatston five days earlier to counter enemy air activity over Scapa. In April 1940 the squadron embarked in HMS *Glorious* to provide fighter patrols whilst the ship was ferrying the Gladiators of No.269 Squadron, RAF to Norway. From the following month various detachments embarked in HMS *Furious* until re-equipping with 12 Martlet Is in October 1940. Some of these broke away the following month to form the basis of No.802 Squadron. The Martlets in turn gave way to a number of Fulmar IIs and Sea Hurricanes from February 1941. In May 1941 the squadron changed its role to provide aircraft to operate from catapult armed merchant ships (CAM-ships), and on 3 August a Fw 200 was shot down by a Sea Hurricane catapulted from HMS *Maplin*. By May 1942 this task had been taken over by the RAFs Merchant Ship Fighter Unit, and No.804 Squadron was then shore based for several months until embarking in HMS *Argus* for a Gibraltar convoy in July 1942. After a brief spell ashore at North Front it returned in HMS *Furious*, which was then engaged in ferrying aircraft to Malta.

In October 1942 the squadron joined HMS *Dasher* with six new Sea Hurricanes IIc's to provide escort during the North African landings, the strength being later increased to nine aircraft. The Sea Hurricanes were discarded to No.835 Squadron at Eglinton in June 1943 when the squadron regrouped, though it was not until two months later that ten Hellcats Is were received. In October 1943 No.804 joined No.7 Naval Fighter Wing, and in December embarked in HMS *Emperor* for a USA-bound convoy. Activities during the next few months included escort for attacks on the German battleship *Tirpitz* and also operations against Norwegian coastal targets. Following action in the Western Approaches during May and June 1944, the squadron was absorbed into No.800 Squadron on 18 June 1944.

The squadron reformed at Wingfield, Cape Town on 1 September 1944 with 24 Hellcat IIs, with which it embarked in HMS *Ameer* in January 1945 to provide cover during the Ramree Island landings. This was followed by spotting, fighter cover, bombing and TacR missions over Malaya and Sumatra. In April the aircraft embarked in HMS *Empress* and HMS *Shah* for attacks on the Andaman Islands and the Burmese coast, then the squadron returned to HMS *Ameer* in June for bombing attacks on Sumatran airfields and also operations off Phuket Island. After the Japanese surrender, No.804 returned to the United Kingdom without its aircraft, disbanding on arrival on 18 November 1945.

On 1 October 1946 No.804 reformed with 12 Seafire XVs at Eglinton as part of the 14th Carrier Air Group. After work-up the squadron embarked in HMS *Theseus* in February 1947 for a Far Eastern cruise, during which New Zealand and Australia were both visited. 13 Seafire FR.47s were received in January 1948, and these

these embarked in HMS *Ocean* in August 1948 for service in the Mediterranean. 13 Sea Fury FB.11s arrived as replacement in July 1949, and these joined HMS *Glory* in December, remaining in the Mediterranean until sailing for Korean waters in March 1951 with an increased complement of 21 aircraft. After withdrawing to Singapore in October for new aircraft, a spell was spent in Australia, then the ship returned north for further Korean action.

Sailing home in HMS *Theseus* in May 1952, periods were subsequently spent in both that ship and HMS *Indomitable* before re-equipping at Lossiemouth in November 1953 with 12 Sea Hawk F.1s, these being replaced in December 1954 by FGA.4s. In May 1955 the squadron joined HMS *Eagle* for a Mediterranean cruise, followed in October by a Norwegian exercise. Then on 17 November 1955 the squadron disbanded on arrival at Devonport.

On 6 February 1956 No.804 reformed with 11 Sea Hawk FGA.6s, with which it embarked in HMS *Bulwark* in June. After a short period in Home Waters the ship sailed for the Mediterranean, where its squadrons participated in the Suez operations in November, attacks being made on Egyptian airfields and support being provided for ground troops. The aircraft were then flown back to the United Kingdom, where they joined HMS *Ark Royal* in February 1957. Transferring to HMS *Albion* in July 1958, the ship sailed to the Far East three months later, Australia being visited in February 1959. In May the ship sailed for home, and No.804 Squadron disbanded at Brawdy on 30 September 1959.

When the squadron next reformed, at Lossiemouth on 1 March 1960, it was equipped with six Scimitar F.1s, with which it embarked in HMS *Hermes* in July. The winter of 1960/61 was spent in the Far East, then the ship returned home and on 15 September 1961 No.804 disbanded at Lossiemouth.

Gloster Sea Gladiator N2276 'H' of No.804 Squadron flying from HMS Furious in Norway 1940. (FAA Museum)

Identification Markings

Sea Gladiator uncoded; Martlet *S7A+*; Fulmar single letters; Sea Hurricane *S7A+*; Hellcat single letters 8.43 - 2.44 later *1A+* and *2A+* from 9.44, to *6A+* 2.45, then *K6A+*; Seafire *130-142/O:T*; Sea Fury *100-121/R*, to *150-159/T* 7.52; Sea Hawk *186-199/J* to 11.55, *160-171/O:B:R:A* from 2.56; Scimitar *161-166/H*.

Battle Honours

Norway	1940-41
Atlantic	1941
North Africa	1942
Normandy	1944
Burma	1945
Korea	1951-52

Aircraft Equipment	Period of Service	Example	
Sea Gladiator	Nov 1939 - Jan 1941	N5573	
Buffalo I	Jul 1940 - Sep 1940	AS422	
	Jul 1941 - 1942	AS423	
Whitney Straight	Dec 1940 - Mar 1941	BS755	
Martlet I	Sep 1940 - Mar 1941	BJ569	(F)
Fulmar I,II	Feb 1941 - May 1942	N4098	
Sea Hurricane Ia	Feb 1941 - Sep 1941	V7048	
Sea Hurricane Ib	Feb 1941 - Sep 1941	L2039	
Sea Hurricane IIb	Sep 1941 - Oct 1942	Z7148	(S7D)
Sea Hurricane IIc	Oct 1942 - Jun 1943	BW886	
Hellcat I	Aug 1943 - Jun 1944	JV156	(M)
Hellcat II	Sep 1944 - Oct 1945	JW733	(K6L)
Seafire F.XV	Oct 1946 - Mar 1948	SW853	(133/T)
Seafire FR.47	Jan 1948 - Aug 1949	VP483	(139/O)
Firefly 5	Jun 1949 - Dec 1949		
Sea Fury FB.11	Jul 1949 - Jan 1954	VX708	(103/R)
Sea Hawk F.1	Nov 1953 - Jan 1955	WF208	(188)
Sea Hawk FGA.4	Dec 1954 - Nov 1955	WV827	(192/J)
Sea Hawk FGA.6	Feb 1956 - Sep 1959	XE407	(160/A)
Scimitar F.1	Mar 1960 - Sep 1961	XD274	(164/H)

Grumman Hellcat II '2A' of No.804 Squadron being accelerated from HMS Ameer in 1945.

Squadron bases		Squadron bases	
Hatston	30 Nov 1939	Belfast	28 Aug 1942
HMS Glorious	22 Apr 1940	transit	23 Oct 1942
Campbeltown(Dt3)	7-14May 1940	HMS Dasher	26 Oct 1942
HMS Furious	9 May 1940	Donibristle	19 Nov 1942
Hatston	23 May 1940	Machrihanish	11 Dec 1942
HMS Furious (Dt6)	5-8Sep 1940	transit	1 Jan 1943
HMS Furious		Ouston	3 Jan 1943
(Dt3)	20-23Sep 1940	Twatt	3 Feb 1943
HMS Furious		HMS Dasher	
(Dt4)	11-19Oct 1940	(Dt5)	16-26Feb 1943
Skeabrae	10 Oct 1940	Hatston	17 Feb 1943
Hatston	19 Oct 1940	Charlton Horethorne	
Skeabrae	28 Oct 1940		6 Apr 1943
Skitten	7 Jan 1941	Eglinton	20 Jun 1943
Yeovilton	10 Feb 1941	HMS Ravager	12 Oct 1943
HMS Pegasus (Dt2)	10 Feb 1941	Eglinton	28 Oct 1943
to	23 Jul 1941	HMS Emperor	5 Dec 1943
Belfast (Dt)	30 Mar 1941	Norfolk	25 Jan 1944
	27 May 1941	HMS Emperor	5 Feb 1944
Belfast	27 May 1941	Eglinton	18 Feb 1944
(and Yeovilton)		HMS Engadine	27 Feb 1944
HMS Ariguani (Dt2)	17 Apr 1941	Eglinton	2 Mar 1944
to	23 Sep 1941	HMS Emperor	6 Mar 1944
HMS Springbank	8 May 1941	Hatston	6 Apr 1944
(Dt1) (sunk)	to 27 Sep 1941	HMS Emperor	11 Apr 1944
HMS Maplin (Dt3)	9 May 1941	Hatston	28 Apr 1944
to	10 May 1942	HMS Emperor	6 May 1944
SS Michael E (Dt1)	28 May 1941	Belfast	5 Jun 1944
(sunk)	31 May 1941	HMS Emperor	7 Jun 1944
North Front (Dt6)	10 Sep 1941	Squadron disbanded	18 Jun 1944
to	23 Nov 1941	Wingfield	1 Sep 1944
'A' Flight:		HMS Ameer	6 Dec 1944
(CO Lt(A) BF Cox RNVR)		Colombo Racecourse	20 Dec 1944
passage	12 Sep 1941	Trincomalee	27 Dec 1944
North Front	18 Sep 1941	HMS Ameer	4 Jan 1945
HMS Eagle	14 Oct 1941	Trincomalee	3 Feb 1945
Yeovilton	26 Oct 1941	HMS Khedive	
Detachment:		(Dt8)	16-21Feb 1945
HMS Argus	30 Sep 1941	HMS Ameer	20 Feb 1945
North Front	8 Oct 1941	HMS Empress (Dt4)	20 Feb 1945
HMS Eagle(Dt1)	26-28Feb 1942	to	9 Mar 1945
dett closed	2 Jun 1942	Colombo Racecourse	10 Mar 1945
HMS Argus (Dt2)	1-18Nov 1941	Tambaram	21 Mar 1945
Yeovilton	14 May 1942	Trincomalee	19 Apr 1945
St Merryn	22 Jun 1942	HMS Hunter (Dt)	19-20Apr 1945
Machrihanish	25 Jul 1942	HMS Empress	22 Apr 1945
HMS Argus	27 Jul 1942	HMS Shah (Dt4)	25 Apr 1945
North Front	10 Aug 1942	to	9 May 1945
HMS Furious	13 Aug 1942	HMS Shah (Dt4)	11-19May 1945

Hawker Sea Fury FB.11 WZ632 '155' of No.804 Squadron. (via Brian Lowe)

Squadron bases		Squadron bases		Squadron bases		Squadron bases	
Trincomalee	9 May 1945	HMS Ocean	10 Apr 1949	HMS Theseus	27 Aug 1953	Lossiemouth	1 Jul 1956
HMS Ameer	14 May 1945	Hal Far	20 May 1949	Lee-on-Solent	29 Oct 1953	HMS Bulwark	6 Aug 1956
Tambaram	23 Jun 1945	HMS Ocean	13 Jun 1949	Lossiemouth	30 Oct 1953	Hal Far	25 Aug 1956
HMS Ameer	27 Jun 1945	Hal Far	18 Jul 1949	Ford	12 Jun 1954	HMS Bulwark	4 Sep 1956
Tambaram	12 Jul 1945	HMS Glory	20 Dec 1949	Lossiemouth	19 Jun 1954	Hal Far (Dt)	14-25 Sep 1956
HMS Ameer	19 Jul 1945	Hal Far	31 Mar 1950	Hal Far	7 Mar 1955	Hal Far	1 Dec 1956
Coimbatore	3 Oct 1945	Deversoir (Dt4)	17-23 Apr 1950	Cagliari	13 Mar 1955	HMS Ark Royal	4 Feb 1957
Trincomalee	15 Oct 1945	Nicosia (Dt2)	21 Apr 1950	Lossiemouth	21 Mar 1955	Lossiemouth	28 Feb 1957
HMS Ameer	30 Oct 1945	HMS Glory	16 May 1950	HMS Eagle	10 May 1955	HMS Ark Royal	6 May 1957
Squadron disbanded	18 Nov 1945	Hal Far	5 May 1950	Hal Far (Dt)	24 Jun 1955	Lossiemouth	18 Jul 1957
Maydown	1 Oct 1946	HMS Glory	12 Jun 1950	North Front (Dt)	23 Aug 1955	Hal Far	29 Jul 1957
Donibristle	12 Dec 1946	Hal Far	31 Jul 1950		to 8 Sep 1955	HMS Ark Royal	31 Aug 1957
Maydown	6 Jan 1947	HMS Glory	4 Sep 1950	Lossiemouth(Dt6)	14-17 Oct 1955	Lossiemouth	25 Nov 1957
HMS Theseus	7 Feb 1947	Hal Far	1 Oct 1950	Squadron disbanded	17 Nov 1955	HMS Ark Royal	27 Jan 1958
Abbotsinch	13 Feb 1947	Castel Benito (Dt8)	7 Nov 1950	Lossiemouth	6 Feb 1956	Hal Far	14 Feb 1958
HMS Theseus	19 Feb 1947	HMS Glory	8 Mar 1951	HMS Bulwark	23 Jun 1956	HMS Ark Royal	25 Feb 1958
Trincomalee	15 Mar 1947	Sembawang	8 Oct 1951				
HMS Theseus	12 May 1947	HMS Glory	11 Oct 1951				
Sembawang	7 Jun 1947	Nowra	22 Oct 1951				
HMS Theseus	21 Jun 1947	HMS Glory	2 Jan 1952				
Kai Tak	20 Oct 1947	Hal Far	26 May 1952				
HMS Theseus	4 Nov 1947	HMS Theseus	26 May 1952				
Ford	20 Dec 1947	Lee-on-Solent	6 Jun 1952				
Eglinton	20 Dec 1947	Culdrose	3 Jul 1952				
Ford	11 Jan 1948	HMS Theseus	21 Aug 1952				
Donibristle	6 Apr 1948	Culdrose	24 Sep 1952				
Ford	13 Apr 1948	HMS Illustrious	20 Oct 1952				
Eglinton	25 May 1948	Lee-on-Solent	24 Oct 1952				
HMS Ocean	24 Aug 1948	Culdrose	25 Oct 1952				
Hal Far	14 Sep 1948	Brawdy	17 Nov 1952				
HMS Ocean	28 Sep 1948	HMS Indomitable	16 Jan 1953				
Hal Far	9 Dec 1948	HMS Theseus	19-20 Jan 1953				
HMS Triumph	3 Jan 1949	Hal Far	18 Feb 1953				
Hal Far (Dt7)	6 Jan 1949	HMS Indomitable	27 Apr 1953				
to	1 Feb 1949	Brawdy	7 May 1953				
Castel Benito	28 Feb 1949	HMS Theseus	17 Jun 1953				
Hal Far	14 Mar 1949	Hal Far	6 Aug 1953				

Supermarine Seafire F.XV '139/T' of No.804 Squadron, HMS Theseus in 1947. (via R.Mackay/John Hamlin)

Hawker Sea Hawks of No.804 Sqdn starting up. (via Ray Williams)

Squadron bases

USS Saratoga	4 Mar 1958
HMS Ark Royal	4 Mar 1958
Ford	8 May 1958
HMS Albion	8 Jul 1958
Ford	19 Jul 1958
Hal Far	29 Jul 1958
HMS Albion	4 Aug 1958
Hal Far	16 Aug 1958
HMS Albion	21 Aug 1958
Lee-on-Solent	15 Sep 1958
HMS Albion	20 Oct 1958
Seletar	12 Dec 1958
Kai Tak (Dt6)	19 Dec 1958 to 5 Jan 1959
Nowra	13 Feb 1959
HMS Albion	24 Feb 1959
Seletar	25 Mar 1959

Squadron bases

HMS Albion	14 Apr 1959
Seletar	11 May 1959
HMS Albion	22 May 1959
Brawdy	17 Aug 1959
Squadron disbanded	30 Sep 1959
Lossiemouth	1 Mar 1960
HMS Hermes	6 Jul 1960
Lossiemouth	1 Oct 1960
North Front	28 Nov 1960
HMS Hermes	29 Nov 1960
Tengah	29 Dec 1960
HMS Hermes	12 Jan 1961
Lossiemouth	18 Apr 1961
HMS Hermes	29 May 1961
Lossiemouth	10 Sep 1961
Squadron disbanded	15 Sep 1961

Commanding Officers

Capt RT Partridge RM		30 Nov 1939
L/C JC Cockburn RN		11 Dec 1939
L/C BHM Kendall RN		18 Nov 1940
L/C PH Havers RN		5 Mar 1941
Capt AE Marsh RM		9 Feb 1942
L/C(A) AJ Sewell DSC RNVR		18 Oct 1942
Lt OR Oakes RM (Temp)		13 Jul 1943
L/C(A) JW Hedges RNVR		29 Jul 1943
L/C(A) SG Orr DSC RNVR		10 Aug 1943
Squadron disbanded		18 Jun 1944
L/C(A) GBC Sangster RNVR		1 Sep 1944
L/C(A) DB Law RNVR		20 May 1945
Squadron disbanded		18 Nov 1945
L/C(A) RF Bryant RN		1 Oct 1946

Commanding Officers

L/C(A) SFF Shotton DSC RN		11 Jun 1947
L/C(A) CF Hargreaves RN		6 Feb 1949
L/C JS Bailey OBE RN		1 Dec 1950
L/C JR Routley RN		23 Jul 1952
L/C EM Brown OBE DSC AFC RN		28 Nov 1953
L/C JO Rowbottom RN		14 Jul 1954
L/C DRO Price DFC RN		13 Sep 1954
Squadron disbanded		17 Nov 1955
L/C RvonTB Kettle RN		6 Feb 1956
L/C GB Newby AFC RN		5 Apr 1957
L/C AGH Perkins RN		5 May 1958
Squadron disbanded		30 Sep 1959
L/C TVG Binney RN		1 Mar 1960
Squadron disbanded		15 Sep 1961

Supermarine Scimitar F.1s XD323 '163/H' and XD325 '165/H' of No.804 Sqdn, HMS Hermes around 1960/1. (via Brian Lowe)

No.805 Squadron

Badge: On a field per fesse barry wavy of four white and blue and gold, two palm trees proper

Motto: Over sea and sand

No.805 Squadron originally formed as a fighter squadron at Donibristle on 4 May 1940, and was intended to have 18 Roc seaplanes for operations in Norwegian waters. After a Roc conversion course at Donibristle, the first crews moved to Lee-on-Solent to begin training with No.765 Squadron, which had a few Rocs fitted with floats, but a week later the plan was abandoned and the embryo squadron disbanded on 13 May 1940.

On 1 January 1941 No.805 reformed at Aboukir with 12 aircraft, being mainly Fulmar Is plus a few Buffaloes. Detachments embarked soon afterwards in HMS *Illustrious*. From March, operations were carried out in the defence of Crete, some Sea Gladiators being added temporarily to the strength. Returning to Egypt, three RAF Hurricanes were used for a time, but in July the squadron re-equipped with 12 Martlet Is to become part of the temporary RN Fighter Squadron in the Western Desert, serving successively with RAF Nos.264, 269 and 234 Wings. The joint unit broke up in February 1942, but No.805 Squadron continued in the Western Desert until moving to the Canal Zone in August 1942 for shipping protection. Shortly afterwards it went south to Kenya, but on 10 January 1943 it was disbanded to provide experienced fighter pilots for new squadrons then forming.

No.805 reformed on 1 July 1945 at Machrihanish initially equipped with 25 Seafire L.IIIs, but soon replaced these with 25 Seafire XVs for service with the 20th Carrier Air Group, the strength being reduced to 12 aircraft by January 1946. Embarking in HMS *Ocean* in June 1946, the squadron disembarked in August when Seafire XVs were banned from deck landing due to technical problems. As a temporary measure No.805 used 12 Firefly FR.Is as single seat fighters for further service in HMS *Ocean*. More appropriate equipment arrived in April 1947 in the shape of 12 Seafire F.17s, which it flew until disbanding at Eglinton on 1 July 1948.

On 28 August 1948 the squadron reformed at Eglinton as a Royal Australian Navy squadron, equipped with 13 Sea Fury FB.11s. In February 1949 it embarked in HMAS *Sydney* and sailed for Australia. During the winter of 1951/52 the ship was in Korean Waters, and in October 1952 took part in the Atomic bomb tests in the Monte Bello islands. Spells were spent in HMAS *Vengeance* during 1953/54, before returning to HMAS *Sydney*, eventually disbanding on 26 March 1958 at Nowra.

The squadron reformed on 31 March 1958 at Nowra as an all-weather fighter squadron with 6 Sea Venom FAW.53s, and these embarked in HMAS *Melbourne* in October 1958. It took over the similar task of No.808 Squadron when that unit disbanded on 1 December 1958. No.805 Squadron was absorbed into 724 Squadron on 30 June 1963.

No.805 Squadron reformed at Nowra on 10 January 1968 with Skyhawks, but the squadron again disbanded into VC-724, as it was by then known, on 2 July 1982. The unit number remains permanently allotted to the Royal Australian Navy.

Aircraft Equipment	Period of Service	Example
Roc I	May 1940 - May 1940	L3164
Fulmar I	Jan 1941 - Jul 1941	N4000
Sea Gladiator	Mar 1941 - Jun 1941	N5538
Buffalo I	Jan 1941 - Aug 1941	AX815
Hurricane I	May 1941 - Jun 1941	V7800
Martlet I	Jun 1941 - Dec 1942	BuAer3876 (H)
Martlet II	Sep 1942	AJ152
Martlet IV	Dec 1942 - Jan 1943	FN180
Seafire L.III	Jul 1945 - Aug 1945	RX162
Seafire F.XV	Aug 1945 - Aug 1946	SW846 (O5G)
Firefly FR.1	Aug 1946 - Apr 1947	PP470 (O5C)
Firefly NF.1	Nov 1946 - May 1947	PP617
Seafire F.17	Apr 1947 - Jun 1948	SX196 (117/O)
Sea Fury F.10	Aug 1948 - Feb 1949	TF925 (110/JR)
Sea Fury FB.11	Aug 1948 - Mar 1958	WZ643 (113/NW)
Sea Venom FAW.53	Mar 1958 - Jun 1963	WZ943 (805/M)
TA-4G Skyhawk	Jan 1968 - Dec 1968	N13-154911 (880)
A-4G Skyhawk	Jan 1968 - Jul 1982	N13-154908 (887)

A Brewster Buffalo of No.805 Squadron in the desert.
(via Geoff Wakeham)

Fairey Fulmar I N1944 of No.805 Squadron at Dekheila.
(RAF Museum P.8445)

Grumman Martlet I 'H' of No.805 Squadron still bearing US Navy number 3876, which would later have been changed to a British number, possibly AX746. (RAF Museum P.841)

Identification Markings
Fulmar believed single letters; Buffalo & Martlet single letters; Sea Gladiator *6A+*; Seafire XV *5A+* then *O5A+*; Firefly *O5A+*; Seafire XV *101-118/O*; Sea Fury *100-111/JR:K:NW*; Sea Venom *800-810/M*; Skyhawk *870-890*.

Battle Honours
Crete	1941
Libya	1941-42
Korea	1951-52

Squadron bases
Donibristle	4 May 1940
Lee-on-Solent	7 May 1940
Squadron disbanded	13 May 1940
Akrotiri	1 Jan 1941
Aboukir (Dt)	1 Jan 1941
	to 23 Jan 1941
HMS Illustrious (Dt)	2-4 Jan 1941
HMS Eagle (Dt4)	30 Jan 1941
Dekheila	5 Feb 1941
HMS Eagle	18 Feb 1941
Aboukir	23 Feb 1941
Dekheila	24 Feb 1941
Maleme (Dt3)	1-6 Mar 1941
Maleme	6 Mar 1941
Aboukir (Dt)	10 Mar 1941
HMS Formidable (Dt)	16 Mar 1941
Aboukir (Dt)	18 Mar 1941
HMS Formidable (Dt4)	21 Apr 1941
Dekheila	19 May 1941
Mersa Matruh (Dt3)	16-17 Jun 1941
Maaten Bagush	22 Jul 1941
Dekheila	2 Aug 1941
Sidi Haneish North	17 Aug 1941
LG.109	14 Nov 1941
LG.123 Maddalena	19 Nov 1941
LG.128 Maddalena	24 Nov 1941
LG.123 Maddalena	25 Nov 1941
Tobruch	12 Dec 1941
LG.05 Sidi Barrani	26 Jan 1942
Maaten Bagush Main	7 Jan 1942
Dekheila	14 Mar 1942
LG.14 Maaten Bagush	6 Apr 1942
LG.20 El Daba	31 May 1942
Dekheila	27 Jun 1942
El Gamil	29 Jun 1942
Fayid	4 Aug 1942
transit	22 Aug 1942
Eastleigh	27 Aug 1942
Squadron disbanded	10 Jan 1943
Machrihanish	1 Jul 1945
Lee-on-Solent	25 Mar 1946
HMS Ocean	19 Jun 1946
North Front (Dt)	15 Jul 1946
	to 1 Aug 1946
Hal Far	4 Aug 1946
HMS Ocean	18 Sep 1946
Hal Far	15 Nov 1946
HMS Ocean	27 Dec 1946
Hal Far	15 Mar 1947
HMS Ocean	5 Jun 1947
Hal Far	22 Aug 1947
HMS Ocean	2 Oct 1947
Hal Far	11 Nov 1947
HMS Ocean	15 Jan 1948
Hal Far	20 Apr 1948
HMS Ocean	7 May 1948
Hal Far	18 May 1948
HMS Ocean	14 Jun 1948
Eglinton	28 Jun 1948
Squadron disbanded	1 Jul 1948
Eglinton	28 Aug 1948
HMAS Sydney	8 Feb 1949
Nowra	25 May 1949
HMAS Sydney	25 Jun 1949
Nowra	8 Oct 1949
HMAS Sydney	13 Jan 1950
Nowra	4 Apr 1950
HMAS Sydney	27 Jan 1951
Nowra	4 Apr 1951
HMAS Sydney	15 Jul 1951
Nowra	3 Mar 1952
HMAS Sydney	4 Jun 1952
Nowra	17 Jun 1952
HMAS Sydney	11 Aug 1952
Nowra	11 Nov 1952
HMAS Sydney	12 Jan 1953
Nowra	18 Feb 1953
HMAS Sydney	21 Sep 1953
Nowra	10 Jun 1954
HMAS Sydney	26 Aug 1954
Nowra	1 Dec 1954
HMAS Sydney	8 Feb 1955
Nowra	22 Apr 1955
HMAS Sydney	13 Mar 1956
Nowra	30 Mar 1956
Squadron disbanded	26 Mar 1958
Nowra	31 Mar 1958
HMAS Melbourne	22 Oct 1958
Nowra	19 Nov 1958
HMAS Melbourne	10 Feb 1959
Amberley	11 Jun 1959
Nowra	16 Jun 1959
HMAS Melbourne	12 Oct 1959
Nowra	4 Dec 1959
HMAS Melbourne	15 Feb 1960
Nowra	6 Jul 1960
HMAS Melbourne	11 Aug 1960
Nowra	21 Sep 1960
HMAS Melbourne	31 Jan 1961
HMS Victorious (Dt2)	29 Apr 1961
	to 6 May 1961
Kai Tak (Dt6)	8-23 May 1961
Seletar	13 Jun 1961
HMAS Melbourne	14 Jul 1961
Nowra	22 Sep 1961
HMAS Melbourne	25 Jan 1962
Kai Tak (Dt4)	16-30 Mar 1962
Cubi Point (Dt10)	2 Apr 1962
	to 7 May 1962
Nowra	18 Jun 1962
HMAS Melbourne	31 Jul 1962
Nowra	17 Sep 1962
Richmond (Dt4)	22-23 Oct 1962
Hobart (Dt6)	25-26 Oct 1962
Richmond (Dt4)	
	to 2 Nov 1962

Fairey Firefly NF.I 'O5B' of No.805 Squadron in HMS Ocean in 1947. (Mrs P.J. Hutton)

Hawker Sea Fury FB.11s TF925 '110/JR', TF952 '106/JR' and VR950 '107/JR' of No.805 Squadron Royal Australian Navy flying over Northern Ireland while working up at Eglinton in 1948. (RAF Museum 6300-6)

Squadron bases		Commanding Officers		Commanding Officers		Commanding Officers	
Richmond (Dt4)	5-9 Nov 1962	Mjr RC Hay RM	4 May 1940	L/C GFS Brown		L/C JR da Costa	
HMAS Melbourne	23 Jan 1963	Squadron disbanded	13 May 1940	DFC RAN	21 Aug 1952	RAN	10 Jan 1968
Tengah	20 Apr 1963	L/C AF Black RN	1 Jan 1941	Lt NR Williams RAN	18 Apr 1953	L/C WE Callan RAN	2 Dec 1968
HMAS Melbourne	14 May 1963	L/C LA Harris RM	27 Jul 1941	L/C AJ Gould RAN	18 May 1953	L/C FT Lane RAN	
Nowra	6 Jun 1963	Lt EA Shaw RN	31 Aug 1941	L/C FT Sherborne		L/C JR Da Costa	
Disbanded into		L/C TP Coode DSC		RAN	26 Jun 1954	RAN	28 Jul 1969
724 Sqdn	30 Jun 1963	RN	5 May 1942	L/C RE Bourke RAN	3 May 1955	L/C CJ Patterson	
Nowra	10 Jan 1968	L/C(A) MF Fell RN	27 Aug 1942	L/C JGB Campbell		MBE RAN	20 Jul 1970
HMAS Melbourne	2 Apr 1969	Squadron disbanded	10 Jan 1943	DFC RAN	26 Nov 1956	L/C WE Callan RAN	5 Jun 1972
Nowra	7 Jul 1969	L/C(A) PJ Hutton		Lt BH Stock RN	28 Feb 1958	L/C GS King RAN	23 Jan 1974
HMAS Melbourne	9 Feb 1970	DSC RNVR	1 Jul 1945	Squadron disbanded	26 Mar 1958	L/C BJ Diamond	
Nowra	14 Jul 1970	L/C PEI Bailey RN	28 Sep 1947	L/C GA Beange		RAN	22 Jan 1976
HMAS Melbourne	26 Oct 1970	Squadron disbanded	1 Jul 1948	DSC RAN	31 Mar 1958	L/C D Collingridge	
Nowra	8 Dec 1970	L/C PEI Bailey RN	28 Aug 1948	L/C MWMcD Barron		RAN	16 Jan 1978
HMAS Melbourne	11 Sep 1971	L/C CJ Cunningham		RN	20 Jul 1959	L/C EM Kavanagh	
Nowra	7 Dec 1971	DSC RN	23 Jul 1949	L/C IK Josselyn		RAN	11 Dec 1978
HMAS Melbourne	24 Jan 1972	L/C WG Bowles		RAN	1 Nov 1960	L/C CC Blennerhassett	
Nowra	27 Apr 1972	RAN	23 Oct 1950	L/C FT Lane RAN	30 Oct 1961	RAN	14 Jan 1980
HMAS Melbourne	27 Jul 1972	L/C JRN Salthouse		Lt WIT Mulholland		L/C GW Northern	
Nowra	3 Aug 1972	RAN	9 Apr 1951	RAN	3 Sep 1962	RAN	19 Jan 1981
HMAS Melbourne	15 Aug 1972	Lt GMc Jude RAN	28 Jan 1952	Squadron disbanded	30 Jun 1963	Squadron disbanded	2 Jul 1982
Nowra	24 Nov 1972	L/C DR Hare RAN	8 Apr 1952				
HMAS Melbourne	20 Aug 1973						
Nowra	7 Dec 1973						
HMAS Melbourne	13 May 1974						
Nowra	18 Jun 1974						
HMAS Melbourne	28 Oct 1974						
Nowra	27 Nov 1974						
HMAS Melbourne	3 Feb 1975						
Nowra	11 Apr 1975						
HMAS Melbourne	4 Aug 1976						
Nowra	4 Nov 1976						
HMAS Melbourne	20 Jan 1977						
Nowra	5 Oct 1977						
HMAS Melbourne	27 Feb 1978						
Nowra	31 May 1978						
HMAS Melbourne	22 May 1979						
Nowra	30 May 1979						
HMAS Melbourne	18 Jul 1979						
Nowra	14 Nov 1979						
HMAS Melbourne	29 Jan 1980						
Nowra	16 Apr 1980						
HMAS Melbourne	17 Jul 1980						
Nowra	12 Dec 1980						
Disbanded into							
VC-724	2 Jul 1982						

Sea Venom FAW.53 WZ940 '809/M' of No.805 Sqdn, RAN on HMAS Melbourne in 1961. (MAP)

Hawker Sea Fury FB.11 WH589 '115' of No.805 Squadron at Bankstown in 1968. (via Chris Ashworth)

Douglas A-4G Skyhawk N-13 154905 '884' and others of VF-805. (via BARG)

No.806 Squadron

Badge: On a field per fesse wavy red and barry wavy of six white and blue, issuant therefrom a dexter cubit arm in armour proper grasping a flash of lightning gold

Motto: *Sursum in pugnam*
(Up! and into the fight)

No.806 Squadron was formed as a fighter squadron at Worthy Down on 1 February 1940 with eight Skuas and four Rocs. Moving to Scotland, the squadron took part during May in bombing operations against shipping and oil tanks at Bergen in Norway, then returned south to provide cover for the Dunkirk evacuation. The Rocs were replaced by Fulmars in June, before embarking in HMS *Illustrious* for Bermuda. On return the Skuas were replaced by further Fulmars, and the squadron then re-embarked for the Mediterranean, a few Sea Gladiators being also used at one stage. During the next few months over 20 enemy aircraft were shot down. In February 1941 defence was provided for the forces in Crete, then the squadron joined HMS *Formidable* and took part in a series of operations before disembarking in May when the ship was damaged by enemy bombing. RAF Hurricanes were then used, and in August 1941 No.806 became part of the RN Fighter Squadron in the Western Desert, Fulmars being also added in November 1941. The joint unit dispersed in February 1942, and No.806 re-equipped with 12 Fulmars for transfer to Ceylon.

In May 1942 'A' Flight received Martlet IIs for service in HMS *Indomitable*, whilst 'B' Flight retained Fulmars and served for a time in HMS *Illustrious*. On 12 August HMS *Indomitable* was damaged in a Malta convoy (Operation *Pedestal*), and on its return to the United Kingdom No.806A Squadron disbanded, No.806B Squadron becoming effectively No.806 Squadron, still in HMS *Illustrious*. Whilst ashore in East Africa, the squadron was absorbed into No.803 Squadron on 18 January 1943.

No.806 reformed at Machrihanish on 1 August 1945 with 12 Seafire L.IIIs, soon replaced by F.XVs, but left these behind on sailing to the Far East in April 1946. It was to have joined the 21st Carrier Air Group in a *Colossus*-class carrier, but this failed to materialise and instead it became part of the 16th CAG with 12 Seafire F.XVs, embarking in HMS *Glory* in September. After an Australian tour the ship returned home, the squadron disbanding on arrival on 6 October 1947.

No.806 Squadron next reformed on 3 May 1948 as the unique RN Aerobatic Team, equipped with two Sea Hornets, two Sea Furies and a Sea Vampire for an American tour, the Sea Hornets being borrowed from No.801 Squadron. Embarking in HMCS *Magnificent* the squadron went ashore to Dartmouth (Nova Scotia) before giving displays at Halifax, the opening of New York's Idlewild Airport (now John F.Kennedy Airport), followed by Toronto and Ottawa before being shipped home to disband on 25 September 1948.

On 2 March 1953 the squadron reformed at Brawdy with eight Sea Hawk F.1s, with which it embarked in HMS *Eagle* in February 1954 for a Mediterranean cruise. On return, it re-equipped in July with 12 Sea Hawk FB.3s and then joined HMS *Centaur* to return to the Mediterranean, during which commission it won the 1955 Boyd Trophy award for pioneering the Sea Hawk at sea, and for contributions to tactical investigation in the night strike role. FGA.4s arrived in March 1955, but on 4 November 1955 the squadron disbanded on disembarking.

No.806 Squadron again reformed at Lossiemouth on 14 January 1957 with ten Sea Hawk FB.5s, embarking in HMS *Eagle* in August. These were exchanged in April 1958 for FGA.6s, and the ship left on a Mediterranean cruise. In February 1960 the squadron transferred to HMS *Albion*, which then sailed for the Far East. The squadron disbanded on return on 15 December 1960.

Battle Honours

Norway	1940
Dunkirk	1940
Mediterranean	1940-41
Libya	1940-41
Matapan	1941
Diego Suarez	1942
Malta Convoys	1942

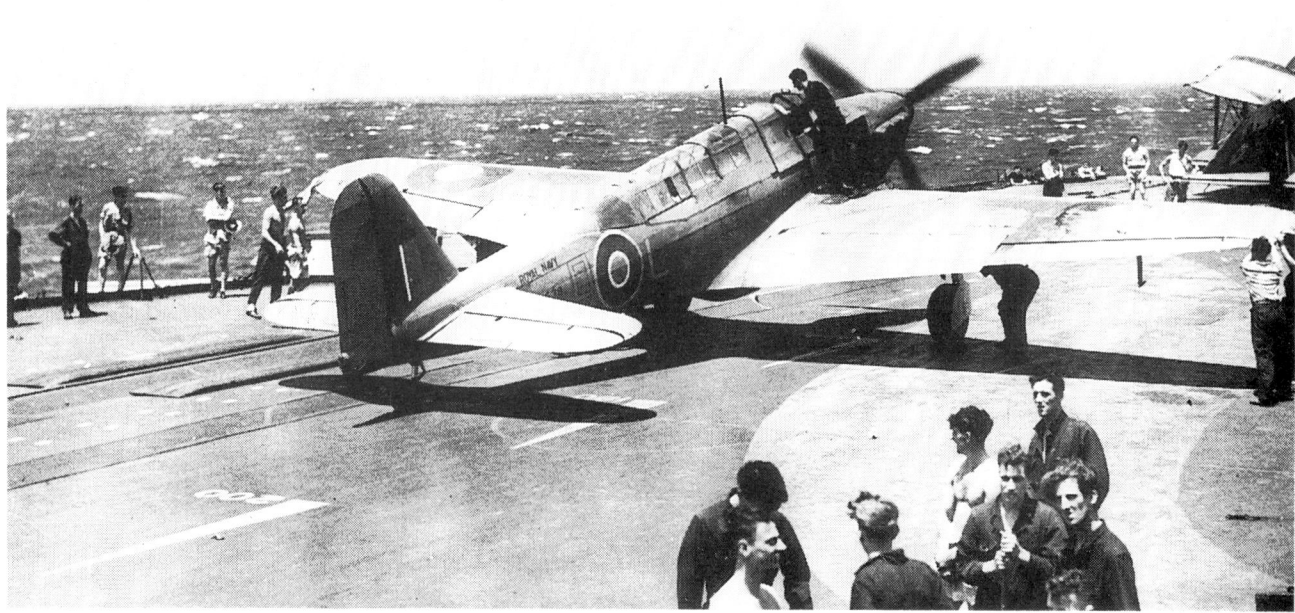

Fairey Fulmar II DR639 'O:L' of No.806B Squadron aboard HMS Illustrious around June 1942. (Charles N.Bates)

Supermarine Seafire XV '112/Y' of No.806 Squadron at Kai Tak in 1946. (via E.Abrams)

Sea Hornet FR.21 VR851 '450/C' of No.806 Squadron, on loan from No.801 Squadron for a Canadian visit in 1948.

Identification Markings
Skua & Roc *L6A+*; Fulmar & Sea Gladiator *6A+* 1940-41; Hurricane single letters; Fulmar *6A+* from 11.41, also 806B Sqdn *O:A+* on *Illustrious*; Martlet possibly *8A+*; Seafire *6A+*, to *111-123/Y:R* 8.46; Sea Hawk *161-174/C* 3.53 to 10.55, *175-190/J:E:A* from 1.57.

Aircraft Equipment	Period of Service	Example	
Skua II	Feb 1940 - Jul 1940	L3012	(L6K)
Roc I	Feb 1940 - Jul 1940	L3105	(L6R)
Fulmar I	Jun 1940 - May 1941	N1985	(R)
Sea Gladiator	Oct 1940 - May 1941	N5513	(6F)
Hurricane I	May 1941 - 1942	V7308	(C)
Fulmar II	Nov 1941 - Jan 1943	BP838	(OP)
Martlet I	May 1942 - Jun 1942	BJ559	
Martlet II	Aug 1942 - Dec 1942	AM997	
Seafire L.III	Aug 1945 - Sep 1945	NF578	
Seafire F.XV	Oct 1945 - Oct 1947	PR474	(116/Y)
Sea Fury FB.11	May 1948 - Sep 1948	TG116	
Sea Vampire F.20	May 1948 - Aug 1948	VF315	
Sea Hornet F.20	May 1948 - Aug 1948	VR851	(450/C)
Meteor T.7	Mar 1953 - Apr 1953	WA600	
Sea Hawk F.1	Mar 1953 - Jul 1954	WM902	(165)
Sea Hawk FB.3	Jul 1954 - May 1955	WM927	(167/C)
Sea Hawk FGA.4	Mar 1955 - Nov 1955	WV863	(163/C)
Sea Hawk FB.5	Jan 1957 - Apr 1958	WN119	(180/J)
Sea Hawk FGA.6	Apr 1958 - Dec 1960	XE403	(188/A)
Sea Vampire T.22	Apr 1958 - Sep 1959	XA162	(980/LM)

Squadron bases		Squadron bases	
Worthy Down	1 Feb 1940	Hal Far (Dt3)	1 Feb 1941
Hatston	28 Mar 1940		to 16 Mar 1941
West Freugh	31 Mar 1940	Maleme	15 Feb 1941
Hatston	1 May 1940	Aboukir (Dt) by	2 Mar 1941
Worthy Down	26 May 1940	HMS Formidable	4 Mar 1941
Detling (Dt9)	7-31 May 1940	Aboukir (Dt3)	16-27 Mar 1941
HMS Illustrious	11 Jun 1940	Dekheila	14 Mar 1941
Donibristle	24 Jul 1940	HMS Formidable	20 Mar 1941
HMS Illustrious	12 Aug 1940	Aboukir	24 Mar 1941
Donibristle (Dt10)	19-21 Aug 1940	HMS Formidable	27 Mar 1941
		Aboukir	30 Mar 1941
Dekheila	9 Aug 1940	HMS Formidable	18 Apr 1941
HMS Illustrious	15 Sep 1940	Aboukir (Dt)	23-29 Apr 1941
Dekheila	5 Oct 1940	Aboukir (Dt)	3-6 May 1941
HMS Illustrious	8 Oct 1940	Aboukir	12 May 1941
Dekheila	16 Oct 1940	Idku (Dt)	12-25 May 1941
HMS Illustrious	29 Oct 1940	HMS Formidable	25 May 1941
Dekheila	2 Nov 1940	Aboukir	27 May 1941
HMS Illustrious	6 Nov 1940	Mersa Matruh	16 Jun 1941
Aboukir	14 Nov 1940	Amriya	19 Jun 1941
HMS Illustrious	24 Nov 1940	Lydda	23 Jun 1941
Aboukir	1 Dec 1940	Ramat David	24 Jun 1941
HMS Illustrious	11 Dec 1940	Lakatamia (Dt5)	1-2 Jul 1941
Aboukir (Dt3)	12-16 Dec 1940	Dekheila	31 Jul 1941
Hal Far	11 Jan 1941	Sidi Haneish South	17 Aug 1941
Dekheila	1 Feb 1941	LG.109	14 Nov 1941

de Havilland Vampire F.20 VF315, Lt Cdr D.B.Law's aircraft for the visit of No.806 Squadron to Canada in 1948. (Howard Levy)

Squadron bases		Squadron bases		Squadron bases		Commanding Officers	
LG.123 Maddalena	19 Nov 1941	HMS Glory	6 Nov 1946	Hal Far	23 Feb 1955	L/C CLG Evans	
LG.128 Maddalena	24 Nov 1941	Sembawang	18 Nov 1946	HMS Centaur	26 Apr 1955	DSC RN	1 Feb 1940
LG.123 Maddalena	25 Nov 1941	HMS Glory	6 Dec 1946	Ford	27 May 1955	L/C JN Garnett RN	24 Jun 1941
El Gubbi	12 Dec 1941	Kai Tak	19 Dec 1946	HMS Centaur	31 Aug 1955	Lt RL Johnston RN	12 Aug 1942
LG.05 Sidi Barrani	26 Jan 1942	HMS Glory	14 Feb 1947	Squadron disbanded	4 Nov 1955	Squadron disbanded	18 Jan 1943
Dekheila	6 Feb 1942	Trincomalee	27 Feb 1947	Lossiemouth	14 Jan 1957	Lt AC Lindsay	
transit	3 Mar 1942	HMS Glory	2 Apr 1947	HMS Eagle	5 Aug 1957	DSC RN	1 Aug 1945
Ratmalana	27 Mar 1942	Sembawang	17 May 1947	Lossiemouth	31 Aug 1957	L/C(A) AW Bloomer	
Katukurunda	18 Apr 1942	HMS Glory	19 Jun 1947	HMS Eagle	10 Sep 1957	RN	1 Jan 1946
Ratmalana	22 Apr 1942	Squadron disbanded	6 Oct 1947	Lossiemouth	2 Nov 1957	L/C RP Thurston RN	1 Oct 1946
HMS Indomitable	23 Apr 1942	Eglinton	3 May 1948	HMS Eagle	29 Jan 1958	L/C WN Waller RN	1 Jun 1947
Port Reitz	23 May 1942	HMCS Magnificent	25 May 1948	Lossiemouth	29 Mar 1958	Squadron disbanded	6 Oct 1947
'A' Flight:		Dartmouth	2 Jun 1948	HMS Eagle	20 May 1958	L/C DB Law DSC	
HMS Indomitable	11 Jun 1942	transit	25 Jul 1948	Hal Far	4 Jul 1958	RN	3 May 1948
Tanga	20 Jun 1942	Idlewild	31 Jul 1948	HMS Eagle	15 Jul 1958	Squadron disbanded	25 Sep 1948
HMS Indomitable	8 Jul 1942	transit	8 Aug 1948	Hal Far	2 Oct 1958	L/C PCS Chilton RN	2 Mar 1953
Donibristle	27 Aug 1942	Dartmouth	11 Aug 1948	HMS Eagle	31 Oct 1958	L/C DPW Kelly RN	24 Feb 1955
- flight disbanded		Toronto	25 Aug 1948	Hal Far	5 Nov 1958	Squadron disbanded	4 Nov 1955
'B' Flight:		Ottawa	1 Sep 1948	HMS Eagle	20 Nov 1958	L/C WDD MacDonald	
HMS Illustrious	29 May 1942	Dartmouth	12 Sep 1948	Lossiemouth	2 Dec 1958	RN	14 Jan 1957
- became 806 Sqdn		SS Aquitania (no a/c)	Sep 1948	HMS Eagle	14 Jan 1959	L/C P Carmichael	
Stamford Hill	21 Sep 1942	Sqdn disbanded UK	25 Sep 1948	North Front	3 Feb 1959	RN	25 Apr 1958
HMS Illustrious	14 Oct 1942	Brawdy	2 Mar 1953	HMS Eagle	13 Feb 1959	L/C WW Illingworth	
Port Reitz	19 Oct 1942	Ford	12 Jun 1953	Lossiemouth	23 Mar 1959	RN	1 Oct 1959
Tanga	12 Jan 1943	Brawdy	16 Jun 1953	HMS Eagle	13 Apr 1959	Squadron disbanded	15 Dec 1960
Disbanded into		HMS Eagle	1 Feb 1954	Brawdy	29 Apr 1959		
803 Sqdn	18 Jan 1943	Hal Far	14 Apr 1954	HMS Albion	5 Feb 1960		
Machrihanish	1 Aug 1945	HMS Eagle	27 Apr 1954	Seletar	12 Apr 1960		
Yeovilton	28 Feb 1946	Yeovilton	4 Jun 1954	HMS Albion	29 Apr 1960		
HMS Cumberland/	24 Apr 1946	HMS Centaur	20 Jul 1954	Kai Tak (Dt4)	1-8 Jul 1960		
HMS Berwick (no a/c)		Hal Far	14 Oct 1954	Butterworth	12 Jul 1960		
Trincomalee	13 May 1946	HMS Centaur	15 Nov 1954	HMS Albion	29 Jul 1960		
HMS Glory	20 Sep 1946	Hal Far	14 Dec 1954	Changi	16 Sep 1960		
Kai Tak	1 Oct 1946	HMS Centaur	12 Jan 1955	HMS Albion	3 Oct 1960		
				Brawdy - disbanded	15 Dec 1960		

Hawker Sea Hawk FGA.6 XE362 '181/A' of No.806 Squadron in 1959. (Arthur Pearcy)

No.807 Squadron

Badge: On a field barry wavy of fourteen white and blue, seven daggers proper, pommels and hilts gold to the centre

Motto: *Quoquo versus ferituri* (Ready to strike in all directions)

No.807 Squadron formed at Worthy Down on 15 September 1940 as a fighter squadron with nine Fulmar Is, increasing later to 12 aircraft. Three of these embarked in HMS *Pegasus* in December for fighter catapult operations. After disembarking in February 1941, the whole squadron joined HMS *Furious* later for convoy escort duty. Re-equipping with 12 Fulmar IIs in April, No.807 joined HMS *Ark Royal* and shared the destruction of 15 enemy aircraft with No.806 Squadron during Malta convoy duties in July and September, another being probably destroyed and a further four damaged. When the ship was torpedoed on 13 November the four surviving aircraft flew to North Front, Gibraltar.

Fresh Fulmars were then issued, in addition to which two Sea Hurricanes were used briefly, and with these the squadron embarked in HMS *Argus* for further convoy duties. During June 1942, four aircraft each were embarked in HMS *Argus* and HMS *Eagle* for the defence of Operation Harpoon, a relief convoy to Malta, four Italian aircraft being shot down but five squadron Fulmars being unfortunately lost. The squadron then returned to the United Kingdom to become the first to receive Seafires, a few IB's being used for training whilst re-equipping with 12 IIc's. With these the squadron joined HMS *Furious* in August, and in November took part in the North African landings, shooting down two French aircraft and damaging two others, in addition to damaging two more on the ground.

Returning home in March 1943, the squadron undertook army support training and received new L.IIc's on 15 May, with which it embarked in HMS *Indomitable* two weeks later. During the Sicily landings the ship provided cover for the invasion fleets and possible interference by the Italian Fleet, but was damaged by an enemy torpedo on 16 July. Transferring to HMS *Battler*, No.807 then provided similar cover for the Salerno landings, aircraft of one flight operating from a beach-head airstrip for a time.

After returning home in HMS *Hunter*, No.807 trained in amphibious support and combined operations, tactical reconnaissance training being undertaken at Burscough and then Andover. Now part of the 4th Naval Fighter Wing, the strength was increased to 20 aircraft when it took over part of No.808 Squadron in February 1944. Returning to the Mediterranean in April, detachments were lent to the Desert Air Force in Italy for several weeks, some Seafire L.IIIs being received during June. The squadron was then reunited on board HMS *Hunter* to participate in the South of France landings in August. No.807 inflicted considerable damage to locomotives and motor transport during this operation, which was code-named Operation *Dragoon*. During September and October the squadron took part in army support operations in the Aegean, then disembarked to Dekheila to regroup whilst the ship was refitted.

Re-embarking in March 1945, HMS *Hunter* sailed to join the Eastern Fleet, and No.807 provided fighter support during April and May for the re-occupation of Rangoon, following which cover was given for anti-shipping strikes in the Andaman Sea. VJ-day forestalled the planned operations during the re-occupation of Penang, and the ship sailed for home. On return the squadron re-equipped with 12 Seafire XVIIs, and 1946 was mostly spent working up. In May 1947 they embarked in HMS *Vengeance* for a Norwegian cruise, prior to re-equipping in September with 12 Sea Fury F.10s. With these the squadron joined the 17th Carrier Air Group, and after exchanging them for FB.11s, embarked a year later in HMS *Theseus* for a visit to South Africa.

In September 1950 the ship reached the Far East, and here the squadron soon found itself involved in action in Korean waters, over 800 operational sorties being flown during the six months to April 1951, the Air Group being later awarded the 1950 Boyd Trophy for its achievements. On return to the United Kingdom, No.807 reformed on 4 July 1951 with eight new Sea Fury FB.11s

Snow-covered Hawker Sea Fury FB.11 '116/T' of No.807 Squadron on the flight deck of HMS Theseus in Korean waters. (via Fred Lynn)

at Arbroath. It joined the 17th Carrier Air Group in HMS *Ocean*, and sailed for the Mediterranean in July, transferring there to HMS *Theseus* in February 1952. Short spells were also spent in HMS *Glory* and HMS *Ocean* during that year, then in January 1953 the squadron was increased to 18 aircraft by absorbing No.898 Squadron. In April it sailed in HMS *Ocean* for a further five months spell in Korean waters, then returned home for re-equipment.

New aircraft in the shape of 12 Sea Hawk F.2s were received at Brawdy in May 1954, these being partially exchanged for FB.3s in November with a reduced strength of nine aircraft. Work-up ended with a two weeks spell aboard HMS *Bulwark* in February 1955, and the following month the last F.2 was withdrawn as FGA.4s began to arrive. No.807 embarked in HMS *Albion* in July and sailed for the Mediterranean, but after taking part in exercises it returned home to disband on arrival at Portsmouth on 4 November 1955.

On 1 October 1958, No.807 reformed at Lossiemouth with eight Scimitar F.1s, remaining ashore until March 1960 when it embarked in HMS *Ark Royal* for the Mediterranean. In April 1961 the squadron transferred to HMS *Centaur*, and after a further spell in the Mediterranean sailed to the Persian Gulf where the ship patrolled off Kuwait during a political crisis. In August the aircraft flew home from Malta, then in October the squadron embarked in HMS *Centaur* for the Far East. In March 1962 the ship spent a few weeks in the Mediterranean, but on return home No.807 disbanded on arrival at Lossiemouth on 15 May 1962.

Aircraft Equipment	Period of Service	Example	
Fulmar I	Sep 1940 - Apr 1941	N4006	
Fulmar II	Apr 1941 - Nov 1941	X8539	
	Nov 1941 - Jun 1942	DR651	
Sea Hurricane	Nov 1941 - Nov 1941		
Seafire Ib	Jun 1942 - Sep 1942	MB357	
Seafire L.IIc	Jun 1942 - Oct 1944	LR753	(HL)
Seafire L.III	Jun 1944 - Dec 1945	PP984	(D5P)
Seafire F.XVII	Dec 1945 - Sep 1947	SX129	(D)
Seafire III	Sep 1946 - Oct 1946	PX960	
Sea Fury F.10	Aug 1947 - Dec 1948	TF954	(125)
Sea Fury FB.11	Feb 1948 - May 1954	WF590	(135/O)
Sea Hawk F.2	May 1954 - Mar 1955	WF272	(125)
Sea Hawk F.1	Sep 1954 - Sep 1954	WF184	(122)
Sea Hawk FB.3	Nov 1954 - May 1955	WM996	(123)
Sea Hawk FGA.4	Mar 1955 - Nov 1955	WV917	(124/Z)
Scimitar F.1	Oct 1958 - May 1962	XD321	(196/R)

Identification Markings
Fulmar uncoded, later *6A+*; Seafire II/III single letters to 8.43, then *8A+* on *Battler*, then *H:A+* from 1.44 on *Hunter*, to *D5A+* 6.44; Seafire XVII single letters; Sea Fury *113-130/T*, to *131-151/O* 5.51, to *101-107* 12.54; Sea Hawk *121-130/Z*; Scimitar *190-199/R:C*.

Battle Honours
Atlantic	1940
Malta Convoys	1941-42
North Africa	1942-43
Sicily	1943
Salerno	1943
South France	1944
Aegean	1944
Burma	1945
Korea	1950-53

Squadron bases
Worthy Down	15 Sep 1940
St Merryn	18 Nov 1940
HMS Pegasus (Dt3)	1 Dec 1940
	to 10 Feb 1941
Yeovilton	9 Dec 1940
Prestwick	4 Feb 1941
Abbotsinch	7 Feb 1941
HMS Furious	5 Mar 1941
HMS Ark Royal	5 Apr 1941
North Front	15 Nov 1941
HMS Argus (Dt4)	16-27 Nov 1941
HMS Argus	27 Feb 1942
North Front	1 Apr 1942
HMS Argus	21 May 1942
North Front	7 Jun 1942
HMS Eagle	12 Jun 1942
North Front	17 Jun 1942
HMS Argus	18 Jun 1942
Lee-on-Solent	23 Jun 1942
Yeovilton	12 Jul 1942
Machrihanish	24 Aug 1942
HMS Furious	25 Aug 1942
Twatt	4 Sep 1942
HMS Furious	9 Sep 1942
Hatston	11 Sep 1942
HMS Furious	20 Sep 1942

Squadron bases
Machrihanish	22 Sep 1942
North Front	25 Oct 1942
HMS Furious	30 Oct 1942
Stretton	4 Feb 1943
Machrihanish	5 Feb 1943
Belfast	19 Mar 1943
HMS Indomitable	2 Jun 1943
Machrihanish	9 Jun 1943
HMS Indomitable	11 Jun 1943
North Front	23 Jun 1943
HMS Indomitable	10 Jul 1943
North Front	29 Jul 1943
HMS Battler	14 Aug 1943
Paestum (Dt)	12-17 Sep 1943
Burscough	9 Oct 1943
Andover	22 Nov 1943
Burscough	2 Dec 1943
HMS Hunter	20 Jan 1944
Turnhouse (Dt3)	20-21 Jan 1944
Grimsetter	5 Mar 1944
HMS Hunter	10 Mar 1944
Grimsetter	14 Mar 1944
Long Kesh	24 Mar 1944
HMS Hunter	30 Apr 1944
North Front (Dt7)	24 May 1944
	to 6 Jun 1944
North Front (Dt4)	6-12 Jun 1944
Blida (Dt8)	20 Jun 1944
	to 11 Jul 1944
La Senia (Dt4)	20-25 Jun 1944
Orvieto (Dt4)	25 Jun 1944
	to 4 Jul 1944
Fabrica (Dt4)	26 Jun 1944
	to 4 Jul 1944
North Front (Dt6)	27 Jun 1944
	to 21 Jul 1944

Supermarine Scimitar F.1 XD248 '195/R' of No.807 Squadron carrying out a practice rocket attack. (via Brian Lowe)

Squadron bases		Squadron bases		Squadron bases		Commanding Officers	
Castiglione(Dt4)	4-17Jul 1944	Culdrose	13 Mar 1948	Hal Far	15 Aug 1952	L/C(A) J Sholto	
Perugia (Dt4)	4-17Jul 1944	HMS Implacable	4 May 1948	HMS Theseus	15 Oct 1952	Douglas DSO RN	15 Sep 1940
North Front(Dt)	13-21Jul 1944	Donibristle	14 May 1948	Hal Far	28 Nov 1952	Lt AB Fraser Harris	
Blida (Dt8)	17 Jul 1944	HMS Theseus	14 Sep 1948	HMS Ocean	9 Dec 1952	DSC RN	15 Nov 1941
North Front(Dt8)	17-21Jul 1944	Lee-on-Solent	12 Dec 1948	Hal Far	16 Jan 1953	L/C(A) K Firth	
Dekheila (Dt6)	2-9Sep 1944	HMS Theseus	25 Jan 1949	HMS Ocean	10 Apr 1953	RNVR	1 Mar 1943
Dekheila (Dt6)	15-30Sep 1944	Hal Far	11 Feb 1949	Iwakuni	1 Jun 1953	L/C(A) GC Baldwin	
Dekheila (Dt7)	11-18Oct 1944	Ta Kali	18 Feb 1949	HMS Ocean	8 Jun 1953	DSC RN	25 Oct 1943
North Front (Dt3)	18 Oct 1944	HMS Theseus	23 Feb 1949	K.6 (Dt)	24-30Jul 1953	L/C(A) LGC Reece	
Dekheila	31 Oct 1944	Yeovilton	24 Mar 1949	Stretton	17 Dec 1953	RNZNVR	2 Jun 1944
HMS Hunter (Dt)	31 Oct 1944	HMS Theseus	3 May 1949	Anthorn	14 Jan 1954	L/C(A) EJ Clark	
to	9 Dec 1944	St Merryn (Dt6)	17-21May 1949	Brawdy	5 May 1954	RNVR	10 Nov 1944
HMS Hunter	6 Mar 1945	St Eval	20 Aug 1949	HMS Bulwark	19 Feb 1955	L/C(A) SJ Hall	
Katukurunda	20 Mar 1945	St Merryn	23 Aug 1949	Brawdy	3 Mar 1955	DSC RN	15 Mar 1946
Kyaukpyu (Dt4)	24 Mar 1945	Biggin Hill	21 Sep 1949	HMS Albion	18 Jul 1955	Lt(A) RJ Clark RN	27 Aug 1946
to	10 Apr 1945	St Merryn	27 Sep 1949	Sqdn disbanded UK	4 Nov 1955	(temp)	
HMS Hunter (Dt)	11-12Apr 1945	Wunstorf	1 Oct 1949	Lossiemouth	1 Oct 1958	L/C FRA Turnbull	
HMS Hunter	21 Apr 1945	St Merryn	15 Oct 1949	HMS Victorious	20-23Jan 1960	DSC & Bar RN	20 Sep 1946
Trincomalee (Dt6)	20 May 1945	HMS Theseus	19 Apr 1950	(DLP)		L/C SJ Hall RN	2 Feb 1947
to	1 Jun 1945	Culdrose	2 May 1950	HMS Ark Royal		L/C WN Waller RN	13 Apr 1948
Cochin	4 Jun 1945	Ford	15 Jun 1950	(Dt)	3-8Feb 1960	L/C(A) AJ Thomson	
Vizagapatam	23 Jun 1945	HMS Theseus	16 Aug 1950	HMS Ark Royal	3 Mar 1960	DSC RN	8 Jul 1948
HMS Hunter	26 Jun 1945	Hal Far	24 Aug 1950	Hal Far (Dt)	8-20Apr 1960	L/C MPG Smith	
Colombo Racecourse	30Jun 1945	HMS Theseus	25 Aug 1950	Hal Far (Dt)	1-23May 1960	DSC RN	25 Jul 1949
(Dt6)	to 17 Jul 1945	Sembawang	12 Sep 1950	North Front (Dt)	20 Jun 1960	L/C B Bevans RN	19 Apr 1950
Colombo Racecourse	17Jul 1945	HMS Theseus	20 Sep 1950	to	5 Jul 1960	L/C AJ Thomson	
Trincomalee	19 Jul 1945	Kai Tak	24 Sep 1950	Lossiemouth	30 Sep 1960	DSC RN	15 Jun 1951
HMS Hunter (Dt8)	4-15Aug 1945	HMS Theseus	29 Sep 1950	HMS Ark Royal	26 Oct 1960	L/C TLM Brander	
HMS Hunter	15 Aug 1945	Lee-on-Solent	28 May 1951	Hal Far	4 Nov 1960	DSC RN	1 Jan 1953
Trincomalee (Dt8)	13 Sep 1945	on leave	29 May 1951	HMS Ark Royal	24 Nov 1960	L/C PJ Hutton	
to	4 Oct 1945	Arbroath	15 Jun 1951	Lossiemouth	27 Feb 1961	DSC RN	14 Jan 1954
Belfast	30 Oct 1945	Lee-on-Solent	14-16Jul 1951	HMS Centaur	10 Apr 1961	Squadron disbanded	4 Nov 1955
Nutts Corner	31 Oct 1945	(Dt4)		Hal Far	29 Apr 1961	L/C KA Leppard RN	1 Oct 1958
Machrihanish	16 Feb 1946	HMS Ocean	24 Jul 1951	HMS Centaur	8 May 1961	L/C WA Tofts RN	19 Sep 1959
Maydown	19 Mar 1946	Hal Far	3 Aug 1951	Hal Far	31 Aug 1961	L/C GA Rowan	
Lee-on-Solent	18 May 1946	HMS Ocean	12 Sep 1951	Lossiemouth	1 Sep 1961	-Thomson RN	1 Mar 1961
HMS Implacable	28 Sep 1946	Hal Far	17 Oct 1951	HMS Centaur	20 Oct 1961	Squadron disbanded 15 May 1962	
Lee-on-Solent	24 Oct 1946	HMS Ocean	12 Nov 1951	Hal Far	15 Nov 1961		
Blenkensee	6 Nov 1946	HMS Theseus	26 Feb 1952	HMS Centaur	27 Nov 1961		
Lee-on-Solent	31 Jan 1947	Hal Far (Dt5)	15-22Mar 1952	Hal Far	18 Apr 1962		
Eglinton	12 Mar 1947	Hal Far	9 Apr 1952	Lossiemouth (Dt4)	26 Apr 1962		
HMS Vengeance	12 May 1947	HMS Theseus	21 Apr 1952	to	14 May 1962		
Stretton	27 Jun 1947	Hal Far	15 May 1952	HMS Centaur	30 Apr 1962		
HMS Vengeance	17 Jul 1947	Kasfareet	23 Jun 1952	Lossiemouth	14 May 1962		
Gosport	31 Jul 1947	HMS Glory	6 Jul 1952	Squadron disbanded 15 May 1962			
Culdrose	19 Aug 1947	Hal Far	8 Jul 1952				
Eglinton	29 Sep 1947	HMS Glory	21 Jul 1952				

Hawker Sea Hawk F.2s of No.807 Squadron WF254 '121' nearest, in 1954. (Mrs P.J.Hutton)

No.808 Squadron

Badge:
1. On an azure field, five rings, white, interlocked to form 808 interlaced with a trident gold
2. On an azure field, a trident or interlaced with five annulets linked to form the figures 808, argent (Australian)

Motto: Strength in unity

No.808 Squadron was formed at Worthy Down on 1 July 1940 as a Fleet Fighter squadron with 12 Fulmar Is (later Mk.IIs). After work-up it moved to the Isle of Man for land-based patrols over the Western Approaches and Irish Sea. In October it embarked in HMS *Ark Royal* to join Force H in the Mediterranean, with which it took part in a number of actions. Two enemy shadowers were shot down during an attack on Sardinia in November, and two more aircraft were destroyed whilst taking part in operations against Sicily in January 1941. Another success was scored during the defence of a Malta convoy in May, and 15 more were claimed jointly with No.807 Squadron in July and August. When HMS *Ark Royal* was sunk on 13 November the remnants of the squadron were put ashore to Gibraltar, where they were absorbed into No.807 Squadron.

On 1 January 1942 No.808 reformed at Donibristle with six Fulmar IIs, but after a brief period in HMS *Biter* during September it disembarked to Stretton where nine Seafire L.IIc's were received on 1 December. After work-up in HMS *Battler* during April and May 1943, the four aircraft of 'A' Flight re-embarked in June for Gibraltar convoy escort, a Fw 200 shadower being shot down on 22 June during the return convoy. The whole squadron joined the ship in July for the Mediterranean, where fighter cover was provided during the Salerno landings in September, a few aircraft going ashore to a beach-head airstrip. After this No.808 returned home in HMS *Hunter* for training at Burscough in close support, as part of the newly-formed 3rd Naval Fighter Wing. After re-embarking for exercises in the New Year, further training was undertaken for bombardment spotting and target reconnaissance. In May the squadron was attached to No.34 Recce Wing of the 2nd Tactical Air Force, RAF to put its training into practice during the Normandy invasion, by then re-equipped with 20 Seafire L.IIIs and based at Lee-on-Solent.

After completion of this task the squadron went to Ballyhalbert, where in October it re-equipped with 24 Hellcat Is and IIs. With these it joined HMS *Khedive* in January 1945 and sailed to join the East Indies Fleet. In April, air patrols, spotting and shipping attacks were undertaken during operations off Malaya and Sumatra, six aircraft being temporarily embarked in HMS *Emperor* for a strike. In May, air cover was provided during the re-occupation of Rangoon, then a similar task as well as photographic reconnaissance was performed during anti-shipping strikes in the Andaman Sea. This was followed in June by strikes against Sumatran airfields. After VJ-day, cover was provided during the occupation of Malaya, the aircraft being disembarked to Coimbatore and the personnel taking passage in HMS *Khedive* for the United Kingdom, where the squadron disbanded on arrival on 5 December 1945.

Fairey Fulmars of No.808 Squadron ranged on HMS Ark Royal in the Mediterranean in February 1941. (FAA Museum)

Grumman Hellcat II JZ796 'C7X' of No.808 Squadron. (MAP)

On 25 April 1950 the number was taken up again when No.808 reformed as a Royal Australian Navy squadron at St.Merryn. Equipped with 13 Sea Fury FB.11s, it embarked for Australia in HMAS *Sydney* in August as part of the 21st Carrier Air Group. In July 1951 the squadron transferred to the 20th CAG and rejoined HMAS *Sydney* for three months action in Korean waters. The squadron transferred to HMAS *Vengeance* in September 1953, eventually disbanding at RANAS Nowra on 5 October 1954.

No.808 reformed at Yeovilton, again as an RAN squadron, on 10 August 1955 with crews from No.891X Squadron, equipped with eight Sea Venom FAW.20s. Re-equipped with FAW.53s, it embarked in HMAS *Melbourne* on 29 February 1956 for passage to Australia, where Nowra was used as a shore base. After several periods of embarkation, the squadron disbanded at Nowra on 1 December 1958, its all-weather flying task being taken over by No.805 Squadron.

Identification Markings
Fulmar 7A+; Seafire 3A+; Spitfire 1A+; Hellcat K6A+ on *Khedive*, to C7A+ by 8.45; Sea Fury 100-139/K; Sea Venom FAW.20 261-269, FAW.53 200-211/Y.

Aircraft Equipment	Period of Service				Example	
Fulmar I	Jul	1940 -		1941	N1891	
Fulmar II		1941 -	Nov	1941	N4144	
	Jan	1942 -	Nov	1942	DR676	
Spitfire Vb/hooked	Dec	1942 -	Apr	1943	BM453	
Seafire L.IIc	Dec	1942 -	May	1944	MB312	(3D)
Spitfire PR.XIII	Mar	1944 -	Mar	1944	BM591	
Spitfire Vb	Feb	1944 -	May	1944	BL613	
Spitfire LF.Vb	May	1944 -	Jul	1944	EN964	(1H)
Seafire L.III	Jun	1944 -	Oct	1944	NN341	(3A)
Hellcat I	Oct	1944 -	Mar	1945	JV180	
Hellcat II	Oct	1944 -	Nov	1945	JX780	(K6A)
Sea Fury FB.11	Apr	1950 -	Oct	1954	VW663	(105/K)
Sea Vampire T.22	Aug	1955 -	Feb	1956	XG773	
Sea Venom FAW.20	Aug	1955 -	Feb	1956	WM512	(263)
Sea Venom FAW.53	Feb	1956 -	Dec	1958	WZ935	(210/Y)

Battle Honours
Spartivento	1940
'Bismarck'	1941
Malta Convoys	1941
Atlantic	1943
Salerno	1943
Normandy	1944
Burma	1945
Korea	1951-52

Squadron bases
Worthy Down	1 Jul 1940
Castletown	5 Sep 1940
Donibristle	2 Oct 1940
HMS Ark Royal	31 Oct 1940
Ship sunk	13 Nov 1941
Donibristle	1 Jan 1942
St Merryn	17 Mar 1942
Yeovilton	18 Apr 1942
Belfast	30 May 1942
HMS Biter	2 Sep 1942
Stretton	29 Sep 1942
Andreas (transit)	16 Oct 1942
Peterhead	20 Oct 1942
Machrihanish	24 Oct 1942
Stretton	20 Nov 1942
Charlton Horethorne	11 Dec 1942
St Merryn	8 Jan 1943
Machrihanish	9 Feb 1943
HMS Battler	10 Apr 1943
Donibristle	7 May 1943
HMS Battler(Dt3)	7-11 May 1943
Yeovilton	20 May 1943
HMS Battler(Dt4)	6-29 Jun 1943
Turnhouse	14 Jun 1943
Andover	20 Jul 1943
HMS Battler	30 Jul 1943
Machrihanish	29 Jul 1943
HMS Battler	30 Jul 1943
Paestum (Dt)	12-17 Sep 1943
HMS Hunter	17 Sep 1943
North Front	23 Sep 1943
HMS Hunter	1 Oct 1943
Burscough	6 Oct 1943
HMS Hunter	21 Jan 1944
Lee-on-Solent	25 Feb 1944
Henstridge	7 Mar 1944
St Merryn	31 Mar 1944
Henstridge	11 Apr 1944
Dundonald	22 Apr 1944
Ayr	6 May 1944
Lee-on-Solent	14 May 1944
Ayr	4 Aug 1944
Ballyhalbert	9 Aug 1944
Kirkistown (ADDLs)	21 Aug 1944
Hawarden	1 Sep 1944
Boulmer	25 Sep 1944
Eglinton	26 Sep 1944
Hawarden	28 Sep 1944
Ballyhalbert	12 Oct 1944
HMS Smiter (DLT)	4 Jan 1945
HMS Khedive	5 Jan 1945
Katukurunda	7 Feb 1945
HMS Khedive	16 Mar 1945
Trincomalee	5 Apr 1945
HMS Khedive	6 Apr 1945
HMS Emperor (Dt6)	4-20 Apr 1945
Colombo Racecourse	21 Apr 1945
HMS Khedive	23 Apr 1945
Colombo Racecourse	19 May 1945
HMS Khedive	14 Jun 1945
Trincomalee	23 Jun 1945
HMS Khedive	11 Jul 1945
Puttalam	21 Jul 1945
HMS Khedive	5 Aug 1945
Coimbatore	18 Sep 1945
HMS Khedive	8 Nov 1945
Sqdn disbanded UK	5 Dec 1945
St Merryn	25 Apr 1950
HMAS Sydney	29 Aug 1950
Nowra	6 Dec 1950
HMAS Sydney	24 Apr 1951
Nowra	18 May 1951
HMAS Sydney	15 Jul 1951
Nowra	3 Mar 1952
HMAS Sydney	14 Oct 1952
Nowra	29 Oct 1952
HMAS Sydney	12 Jan 1953
Nowra	18 Feb 1953
HMAS Vengeance	17 Sep 1953
Nowra	9 Nov 1953
HMAS Vengeance	11 Jan 1954
Nowra	4 Feb 1954
HMAS Vengeance	16 Feb 1954
Nowra	6 May 1954

Squadron bases
Squadron disbanded	5 Oct 1954
Yeovilton	10 Aug 1955
HMAS Melbourne	29 Feb 1956
Nowra	7 May 1956
HMAS Melbourne	6 Aug 1956
Nowra	18 Aug 1956
HMAS Melbourne	7 Sep 1956
Nowra	10 Dec 1956
HMAS Melbourne	5 Feb 1957
Nowra	14 Mar 1957
HMAS Melbourne	10 Oct 1957
Nowra	12 Dec 1957
HMAS Melbourne	12 Feb 1958
Nowra	20 Jul 1958
HMAS Melbourne	22 Oct 1958
Nowra	19 Nov 1958
Squadron disbanded	1 Dec 1958

Commanding Officers
Lt HER Torin RN	1 Jul 1940
L/C RC Tillard RN	20 Jul 1940
L/C EDG Lewin RN	31 May 1941
Squadron disbanded	13 Nov 1941
Lt CP Campbell-Horsfall RN	1 Jan 1942
L/C(A) AC Wallace RNVR	17 Mar 1943
L/C(A) JF Rankin DSC RN	25 Oct 1943
L/C(A) CF Wheatley RNVR	20 May 1945
L/C(A) RF Bryant RN	25 Jun 1945
Squadron disbanded	5 Dec 1945
L/C JL Appleby RAN	25 Apr 1950
L/C JHG Cavanagh RAN	20 Jul 1952
L/C GA Beange DSC RN	18 May 1953
Lt RG Owen RAN	16 May 1954
Lt AG Powell RAN	27 Sep 1954
Squadron disbanded	5 Oct 1954
Lt GM Jude RAN	10 Aug 1955
L/C PW Seed RAN	4 Nov 1956
L/C AG Cordell RAN	10 Jan 1957
L/C G Kable RAN	5 Aug 1957
L/C GHG Hanchard-Goodwin RAN	7 Mar 1958
Squadron disbanded	1 Dec 1958

Supermarine Seafire III NN342 '3B' of No.808 Squadron around September 1944. (FAA Museum)

No.809 Squadron

Badge: On a blue field, a Phoenix gold rising from flames proper
Motto: Immortal

No.809 Squadron first formed at Lee-on-Solent on 15 January 1941 as a single seater fighter squadron with 12 Fulmar IIs. Embarking with these in HMS *Victorious* in July, the squadron shot down four Bf 109s and Bf 110s for the loss of three of its own aircraft during an attack on the Arctic port of Petsamo. The squadron was in action several times during the next 12 months whilst the ship was escorting North Russian convoys, shipping strikes also being carried out on Bodø in Norway. On 9 March No.809 was the escort to the Albacores of Nos.817 and 832 Squadrons in an unsuccessful attack on the German battleship *Tirpitz* at sea. In July 1942 the ship sailed for the Mediterranean to take part in Operation *Pedestal*, an unlucky Malta convoy, during which No.809 Squadron accounted for 2 enemy aircraft for the loss of three of its own.

Returning home, the squadron undertook army co-operation training at Sawbridgeworth, being reduced to six aircraft when 'B' Flight broke away on 1 October 1942 to form the basis for No.879 Squadron. Re-embarking in HMS *Victorious* during October, No.809 carried out tactical reconnaissance during the North African landings, following which it returned home again to re-equip with ten Seafires IIc's, some Ib's also being used for a time. The latter were discarded in August 1943 when the squadron embarked in HMS *Unicorn* to provide cover the following month for the Salerno landings. On return from this trip the squadron joined the 4th Naval Fighter Wing at Andover, embarking at the end of the year in HMS *Stalker* for work-up. Disembarked to Dale in February, the strength was increased in March to 20 aircraft, including some LR.IIc's.

After a spell at Long Kesh working with the Army, No.809 re-embarked in HMS *Stalker* in May and sailed for the Mediterranean. The squadron then became split up for some weeks, detachments being ashore in both North Africa and with the Desert Air Force in Italy before reuniting and re-embarking at the end of July. During August the squadron provided support for the landings in the South of France, carrying out fighter patrols, spotting, bombing and tactical reconnaissance. During the next two months operations were carried out in the Aegean before returning home in November to be equipped entirely with Seafire L.IIIs.

At the end of November No.809 transferred to HMS *Attacker* for passage to Alexandria, where three months were spent ashore at Dekheila. In March 1945 it was reunited with HMS *Stalker*, in which it sailed for Ceylon to join the East Indies Fleet. During work-up, several pilots were attached to the RAF at Akyab in Burma, before re-embarking in May to provide fighter cover for the re-occupation of Rangoon. Bombing and fighter cover were provided during the photographic reconnaissance of Malaya and Sumatra in June, and after VJ-day the ship sailed to give cover for the re-occupation of Malaya. Returning home in October, the squadron re-equipped on arrival with 12 new Seafires, these being mainly F.XVIIs except for three F.XVs from No.805 Squadron. However, on 11 January 1946 the squadron disbanded at Nutts Corner.

No.809 next reformed at Culdrose on 20 January 1949 with four Sea Hornet NF.21s, later increasing to 8 aircraft and operating as a night fighter and strike squadron. In May 1950 the squadron embarked in HMS *Vengeance*, attached to the 15th Carrier Air Group, further short spells being spent in that carrier in July 1950 and May 1951. However, carrier operations with the twin-engined machines proved difficult, and three months were spent with the RAF at Coltishall from August 1951. In January 1952 the squadron flew out to Hal Far, returning home in March. In January 1953 No.809 joined HMS *Eagle* for work-up and the Spring cruise, returning home to participate in the Coronation Review flypast on 15 June. Further periods in HMS *Eagle* followed, then on 10 May 1954 the squadron disbanded at Culdrose.

The squadron reformed the same day at Yeovilton with nine Sea Venom FAW.20s, in the all-weather fighter role. A year later these were replaced by nine Sea Venom FAW.21s, with which deck landing practice was undertaken in HMS *Bulwark* during July 1955. The squadron was intended for HMS *Ark Royal*, in which it should have embarked in September, but problems with fractured deck

Fairey Fulmar '6Q' of No.809 Squadron ranged on the flight deck of HMS Victorious in late 1941.

de Havilland Sea Hornet NF.21s VX250 '486/Q' and VW962 '489/Q' of No.809 Squadron in 1951.

hooks prevented this, and instead it flew out to Malta during November, to take part in exercises in the Mediterranean. Four months later it flew home, to disband at Yeovilton on 20 March 1956.

On 7 May 1956 No.809 reformed at Yeovilton, again with nine Sea Venom FAW.21s, with which it practised deck landings in HMS *Bulwark* in July. In September it joined HMS *Albion* for the Mediterranean, and in November participated in the Suez operations. Attacks were made on Egyptian airfields as well as tanks and other military vehicles, 138 sorties being flown in all. In the New Year the squadron returned to the United Kingdom, disembarking to Merryfield in March 1957, the Yeovilton runways being then under repair. Various cruises were subsequently undertaken, and from July 1958 the squadron spent a period in the Mediterranean before re-embarking in October for the Far East, both New Zealand and Australia being visited in early 1959. In April 1959 cross-operations were carried out with USS *Yorktown* during a SEATO exercise before returning to Singapore. The ship then sailed home via Madagascar, South Africa and South America, No.809 Squadron being disbanded on arrival on 17 August 1959.

The squadron next reformed out of No.700Z Flight at Lossiemouth on 15 January 1963, as a strike squadron equipped with Buccaneer S.1s, eventually reaching a strength of 14 machines. It operated as the Operational Flying Training Squadron for all Buccaneer crew training, undertaking various trials and participating in several exercises. The squadron remained shore based, though one or two aircraft occasionally embarked in carriers for particular trials. No.809 lost its identity on 26 March 1965 when it was downgraded to second-line status and redesignated No.736 Squadron.

Six Buccaneer S.2s were the equipment when No.809 Squadron next reformed, at Lossiemouth on 27 January 1966, later increasing to 8 aircraft. After a year's work-up these embarked in HMS *Hermes* in January 1967 for the Mediterranean and Far East, returning home in September. Re-embarking in November, the ship again sailed east via the Ascension Isles and Capetown, and No.809 spent some time in the Aden area before the ship returned home in February 1968 by way of the Seychelles and Capetown. The squadron then remained largely shore-based until embarking in HMS *Ark Royal* in June 1970 for the Mediterranean. This was followed by a visit to the United States in June and July 1971,

returning to the Mediterranean in September. A further visit was paid to the United States in February 1972, after which the ship remained in Home waters, the squadron's shore base being changed to RAF Honington in October 1972.

In February 1973 HMS *Ark Royal* again sailed for the Mediterranean, making a further visit to the United States in June. The following month No.809 began to replace its Buccaneer S.2s with updated S.2c's and these were followed in October with similar S.2d's equipped with the Martel missile system. The squadron then flew out to Cyprus for an exercise. During 1974 three periods were spent afloat, including a trip to the Mediterranean in October, this pattern being continued in succeeding years, with trips to the United States being made in February-March 1975 and March-May 1976. From October 1976 the squadron was almost entirely shore-based, but again joined HMS *Ark Royal* in September 1977, further visits to the United States being made the following year. In November 1978 the aircraft were disembarked to St.Athan for disposal to the RAF, and the squadron officially disbanded at Lee-on-Solent on 15 December 1978.

No.809 next reformed on 8 April 1982 out of No.899 Squadron, for service with the Falklands Task Force. It officially recommissioned on 27 April at Yeovilton with 8 Sea Harrier FRS.1s, which then journeyed to Ascension Island, some making the 4,000 mile trip in a single flight, being refuelled en route by Victor tankers, the longest FAA flight on record. For the campaign they were shared between HMS *Hermes* and HMS *Invincible*. After the cessation of hostilities, the aircraft returned home, only to make a further voyage to the South Atlantic in HMS *Illustrious* in August. Returning home again at the end of the year, the squadron disbanded at Yeovilton on 17 December 1982, its aircraft being dispersed amongst Nos.800, 801 and 899 Squadrons. The commanding officer later received the 1982 Boyd Trophy Award for his efforts in the campaign.

Identification Markings
Fulmar *6A+* on *Victorious*; Seafire *S:A+* on *Stalker*, then *D6A+* from 3.45; Sea Hornet *481-494/CW:Q:A:J*; Sea Venom *226-235/O* to *220-229/O:Z:A* 1.56; Buccaneer *220-233/LM:R* to 3.65, then *320-327/LM:H* from 1.66, to *020-036/R* 1.70; Sea Harrier *250-257*.

Aircraft Equipment	Period of Service	Example	Squadron bases		Squadron bases	
Fulmar II	Jan 1941 - Mar 1943	DR641 (6B)	HMS Stalker	29 Dec 1943	HMS Vengeance	10 May 1951
Spitfire Va	Mar 1943 - Jun 1943	L1096	Dale	18 Feb 1944	Culdrose	22 May 1951
Seafire Ib	Apr 1943 - Aug 1943	NX919	Long Kesh	20 Mar 1944	Coltishall	31 Aug 1951
Seafire L.IIc	Mar 1943 - Feb 1945	MB133 (SS)	HMS Attacker (DLT)	7 Apr 1944	Culdrose	10 Dec 1951
Seafire L.III	Jul 1944 - Dec 1945	PP972 (D6M)	Long Kesh	7 Apr 1944	Hal Far	18 Jan 1952
Seafire F.XV	Nov 1945 - Dec 1945		HMS Stalker	2 May 1944	transit	19 Mar 1952
Seafire F.XVII	Nov 1945 - Jan 1946	SX138	North Front (Dt)	24 May 1944	Culdrose	24 Mar 1952
Sea Hornet F.20	Jan 1949 - May 1952	VR855	to	5 Jun 1944	HMS Indomitable	17 Jun 1952
Sea Hornet NF.21	Jan 1949 - May 1954	VZ672 (481/Q)	Blida (Dt)	5-21 Jun 1944	Culdrose	3 Jul 1952
Sea Hornet PR.22	Jul 1949 - May 1952	VZ655	Orvieto (Dt12)	25 Jun 1944	Leuchars	8 Sep 1952
Anson I	Aug 1950 - Sep 1950	MG863	to	4 Jul 1944	Culdrose	13 Oct 1952
Sea Fury T.20	Nov 1951 - Jan 1952	VZ346 (999)	Fabrica (Dt7)	25 Jun 1944	HMS Eagle	20 Jan 1953
Sea Vampire T.22	Jun 1954 - Oct 1954	XA154	to	5 Jul 1944	Culdrose	25 Mar 1953
Sea Venom FAW.20	May 1954 - Aug 1955	WM545 (228)	Foiano (Dt8)	4-16 Jul 1944	HMS Eagle	18 Jun 1953
Sea Venom FAW.21	May 1955 - Mar 1956	WW199 (235/O)	Perugia (Dt7)	5-16 Jul 1944	Culdrose	16 Jul 1953
	May 1956 - Aug 1959	XG670 (223/Z)	Castiglione (Dt4)	4-16 Jul 1944	HMS Eagle	2 Sep 1953
Buccaneer S.1	Jan 1963 - Mar 1965	XN960 (225/LM)	Blida (Dt12)	16-17 Jul 1944	Culdrose	30 Nov 1953
Buccaneer S.2	Jan 1966 - Dec 1973	XV152 (024/R)	North Front (Dt12)	17-21 Jul 1944	HMS Eagle	26 Jan 1954
Buccaneer S.2c	Jul 1973 - Dec 1978	XN982 (024/R)			North Front	20 Feb 1954
Buccaneer S.2d	Oct 1973 - Dec 1978	XV868 (025/R)	Perugia (Dt2)	21 Jul 1944	Culdrose	28 Mar 1954
Sea Harrier FRS.1	Apr 1982 - Dec 1982	ZA193 (254)	to	5 Aug 1944	Squadron disbanded	10 May 1954
			HMS Stalker	21 Jul 1944	Yeovilton	10 May 1954
			Dekheila (Dt)	2-19 Sep 1944	Ford	1 Feb 1955
			Dekheila (Dt4)	30 Sep 1944	Yeovilton	25 Feb 1955
			to	6 Oct 1944	HMS Bulwark (Dt6)	4-8 Jul 1955
			Dekheila (Dt)	11-15 Oct 1944	Capodichino (transit)	14 Nov 1955
			HMS Stalker	1 Nov 1944		
			HMS Attacker	28 Nov 1944	Ta Kali	15 Nov 1955

Battle Honours
Arctic	1941
Malta Convoys	1942
North Africa	1942
Salerno	1943
South France	1944
Aegean	1944
Burma	1945
Falkland Islands	1982

Squadron bases
Lee-on-Solent	15 Jan 1941
Gosport	10 Mar 1941
St Merryn	29 Mar 1941
Hatston	10 Jun 1941
HMS Victorious	2 Jul 1941
Hatston (Dts)	7-21 Aug 1941
HMS Victorious	21 Aug 1941
Hatston (Dt)	3-23 Sep 1941
Twatt	26 Oct 1941
HMS Victorious (Dt6)	3-30 Nov 1941
HMS Victorious	24 Dec 1941
Twatt (Dt6)	2-17 Jan 1942
HMS Victorious	4 Mar 1942
Twatt	10 Mar 1942
HMS Victorious	22 Mar 1942

Squadron bases
Twatt	28 Mar 1942
HMS Victorious	12 Apr 1942
Twatt	18 Apr 1942
HMS Victorious	16 May 1942
Twatt	16 Jun 1942
HMS Victorious	29 Jun 1942
Twatt	10 Jul 1942
HMS Victorious	22 Jul 1942
St Merryn	21 Aug 1942
Sawbridgeworth (Dt)	22 Aug 1942 to 8 Sep 1942
St Merryn	8 Sep 1942
Sawbridgeworth	1 Oct 1942
Machrihanish	11 Oct 1942
HMS Victorious	19 Oct 1942
Machrihanish	23 Nov 1942
Charlton Horethorne	26 Nov 1942
Doncaster	9 Dec 1942
Clifton Park	28 Dec 1942
Stretton	22 Mar 1943
Andover	13 Jul 1943
Machrihanish	28 Jul 1943
HMS Unicorn	7 Aug 1943
Paestum (Dt)	12-20 Sep 1943
Andover	12 Oct 1943
Burscough	19 Dec 1943

(continued)
Dekheila	11 Dec 1944	Hal Far	17 Nov 1955
HMS Stalker	7 Mar 1945	HMS Ark Royal	25 Nov 1955
Katukurunda	20 Mar 1945	Hyeres	2 Dec 1955
HMS Stalker	21 Apr 1945	HMS Ark Royal	6 Dec 1955
Trincomalee	31 May 1945	Hal Far	10 Feb 1956
HMS Stalker	5 Jun 1945	L'Artique	6 Mar 1956
Trincomalee	18 Jul 1945	Yeovilton	12 Mar 1956
HMS Stalker	1 Aug 1945	Squadron disbanded	20 Mar 1956
Trincomalee (Dt9)	28 Aug 1945 to 4 Sep 1945	Yeovilton	7 May 1956
Nutts Corner	21 Oct 1945	HMS Bulwark (DLP)	21 Jul 1956
Squadron disbanded	11 Jan 1946	Yeovilton	29 Jul 1956
Culdrose	20 Jan 1949	HMS Albion	15 Sep 1956
HMS Illustrious (Dt3 - DLT)	16-21 Jan 1950	Hal Far	28 Nov 1956
		HMS Albion	11 Dec 1956
HMS Vengence	12 May 1950	Hal Far	24 Dec 1956
Arbroath	18 Jun 1950	HMS Albion	8 Jan 1957
HMS Vengeance	5 Jul 1950	Merryfield	5 Mar 1957
Culdrose	27 Jul 1950	HMS Albion	16 Jun 1957
North Front	19 Sep 1950	Merryfield	19 Jul 1957
Culdrose	16 Oct 1950	HMS Albion	22 Jul 1957
		Merryfield	26 Jul 1957

de Havilland Sea Venom FAW.21 XG663 '227/Z' of No.809 Squadron in HMS Albion around 1957/8.

Blackburn Buccaneer S.2 XT281 '326/H' of No.809 Squadron, HMS Hermes in 1967. (via Brian Lowe)

Squadron bases

HMS Albion	3 Sep	1957
Merryfield (Dt4)	30 Sep	1957
	to 11 Oct	1957
Merryfield	28 Oct	1957
Yeovilton	28 Jan	1958
Lossiemouth (Dt5)	4-8 Mar	1958
HMS Albion	7 Jul	1958
Yeovilton	14 Jul	1958
Hal Far	28 Jul	1958
HMS Albion	4 Aug	1958
Hal Far (Dt5)	16-21 Aug	1958
Yeovilton	15 Sep	1958
HMS Albion	20 Oct	1958
Seletar (Dt6)	29 Nov	1958
	to 12 Dec	1958
Kai Tak (Dt5)	19 Dec	1958
	to 5 Jan	1959
Nowra (Dt5)	13-24 Feb	1959
Seletar (Dt5)	25 Mar	1959
	to 14 Apr	1959
Seletar (Dt5)	13-22 May	1959
Yeovilton	17 Aug	1959
Squadron disbanded	17 Aug	1959
Lossiemouth	15 Jan	1963
HMS Victorious	30 Jul	1963
(Dt2)	to 9 Aug	1963
HMS Eagle (Dt1)	14-18 Jul	1964
Redes 736 Sqdn	26 Mar	1965
Lossiemouth	27 Jan	1966
HMS Victorious	14 May	1966
Lossiemouth	9 Jun	1966
HMS Hermes (Dt3)	3-9 Sep	1966
HMS Hermes	18 Jan	1967
Gibraltar (Dt3)	5-19 Feb	1967
Hal Far	15 Mar	1967
HMS Hermes	31 Mar	1967
Changi	24 Jun	1967
HMS Hermes	17 Jul	1967
Lossiemouth	29 Sep	1967
HMS Hermes	4 Nov	1967
Lossiemouth	18 Feb	1968
Yeovilton	2 Sep	1968
Lossiemouth	23 Sep	1968
HMS Ark Royal (Dt4)	4-11 May	1970
Karup (Dt4)	4-11 May	1970
HMS Ark Royal	14 Jun	1970
Yeovilton	9 Jul	1970
Lossiemouth	25 Jul	1970
HMS Ark Royal	6 Sep	1970
Lossiemouth	26 Sep	1970
	to 11 Oct	1970
Luqa (Dt3)	19-29 Oct	1970
Luqa (Dt3)	14-22 Nov	1970
Lossiemouth	15 Dec	1970
HMS Ark Royal	15 Apr	1971
Lossiemouth (Dt7)	19 May	1971
	to 2 Jun	1971
Cecil Field (Dt3)	21 Jun	1971
	to 7 Jul	1971
Lossiemouth	4 Aug	1971
HMS Ark Royal	15 Sep	1971
Lossiemouth	8 Oct	1971
HMS Ark Royal	29 Oct	1971
Lossiemouth	6 Dec	1971
HMS Ark Royal	19 Jan	1972
Lossiemouth	8 Mar	1972
HMS Ark Royal	12 Jun	1972
Lossiemouth	17 Jul	1972
HMS Ark Royal	4 Sep	1972
Honington	18 Oct	1972
HMS Ark Royal	7 Nov	1972
Honington	11 Dec	1972
HMS Ark Royal	9 Feb	1973
Luqa (Dt7)	22 Feb	1973
	to 6 Mar	1973
Honington	14 Mar	1973
HMS Ark Royal	2 May	1973
Fort Lauderdale	7 Jun	1973
HMS Ark Royal	14 Jun	1973
Cecil Field (Dt8)	19-30 Jun	1973
Honington	24 Jul	1973
Landivisiau (Dt5)	Sep	1973
Lossiemouth	30 Sep	1973
Honington	5 Oct	1973
Akrotiri	13 Nov	1973
Honington	30 Nov	1973
Lossiemouth (Dt7)	7-11 Mar	1974
HMS Ark Royal	6 Jun	1974
Honington	17 Jun	1974
HMS Ark Royal	3 Jul	1974
Honington	25 Jul	1974
HMS Ark Royal	5 Sep	1974
Luqa (Dt4)	4-16 Oct	1974
Honington	3 Nov	1974
HMS Ark Royal	8 Jan	1975
Cecil Field (Dt8)	18 Feb	1975
	to 7 Mar	1975
Oceana (Dt9)	3-21 Apr	1975
HMS Ark Royal	21 Apr	1975
Honington	9 Jun	1975
HMS Ark Royal	6 Oct	1975
Honington	20 Nov	1975
HMS Ark Royal	6 Feb	1976
Cecil Field (Dt8)	22 Mar	1976
	to 13 Apr	1976
Oceana	19 Apr	1976
HMS Ark Royal	6 May	1976
Oceana (Dt8)	3-11 Jun	1976
Honington	14 Jul	1976
HMS Ark Royal	4 Sep	1976
Honington	18 Oct	1976
Gibraltar (Dt6)	18-28 Feb	1977
Schleswig (Dt8)	18-28 Mar	1977
HMS Ark Royal	30 Jun	1977
(Dt3)	to 7 Jul	1977
HMS Ark Royal	5 Sep	1977
Honington	12 Dec	1977
HMS Ark Royal	23 Feb	1978
Honington	5 Mar	1978
HMS Ark Royal	6 Apr	1978
Roosevelt Roads (Dt6)	27 Apr	1978
	to 7 May	1978
Cecil Field	21 Jun	1978
HMS Ark Royal	8 Aug	1978
Oceana (Dt4)	14-21 Aug	1978
Lee-on-Solent - disbanded	15 Dec	1978
Yeovilton	8 Apr	1982
Wideawake (8 a/c)	2 May	1982
HMS Hermes (Dt4)	18 May	1982
HMS Invincible (Dt4)	19 May	1982
Sqdn then integrated into 800/801 Sqdns		
Yeovilton	5 Jul	1982
HMS Illustrious (Daily detts)	5-16 Jul	1982
HMS Illustrious (Dt2)	16-26 Jul	1982
HMS Illustrious	2 Aug	1982
Stanley FOB	28 Aug	1982
	to 20 Oct	1982
Roosevelt Roads (Dt4)	4-11 Nov	1982
Yeovilton	6 Dec	1982
Squadron disbanded	17 Dec	1982

Commanding Officers

L/C SWD Colls RN	15 Jan	1941
L/C VC Grenfell DSO RN	3 Jul	1941
L/C EG Savage DSC RN	16 Oct	1941
Capt RC Hay DSC RM	24 Aug	1942
Mjr AJ Wright RM	1 Jun	1943
L/C(A) HDB Eadon RNVR	20 Apr	1944
L/C(A) NH Lester RNVR	10 Nov	1944
L/C AW Bloomer RN	17 Apr	1945
Mjr JO Armour RM	20 Jan	1949
L/C DH Richards RN	1 Aug	1950
L/C EM Frazer RN	21 Apr	1952
L/C MW Henley DSC RN	18 Jan	1954
Squadron disbanded	27 Mar	1954
L/C SA Mearns DSC RN	10 May	1954
Squadron disbanded	20 Mar	1956
L/C RA Shilcock RN	7 May	1956
L/C AA Knight RN	28 Oct	1957
Squadron disbanded	17 Aug	1959
L/C AJ Leahy MBE DSC RN	15 Jan	1963
L/C FD Stanley RN	18 Apr	1963
L/C LE Middleton RN	7 Oct	1963
L/C JFHC de Winton RN	12 Dec	1963
L/C WHC Watson RN	4 Jan	1965
Squadron disbanded	27 Mar	1965
L/C LE Middleton RN	27 Jan	1966
L/C AJ White RN	10 May	1967
L/C JDHB Howard RN	4 Dec	1968
L/C DP Mears RN	23 Jan	1970
L/C CCN Davis RN	30 Mar	1971
L/C AMD de Labilliere RN	10 Jul	1972
Cdr M Bickley RN	22 Nov	1973
L/C A Morton RN	21 Apr	1975
L/C M Bickley RN	24 Jun	1975
L/C EK Somerville -Jones RN	4 Nov	1975
L/C A Morton RN	27 Apr	1977
Squadron disbanded	15 Dec	1978
L/C TJH Gedge RN	8 Apr	1982
Squadron disbanded	17 Dec	1982

British Aerospace Sea Harrier FRS.1 ZA176 '250' of No.809 Sqdn at Yeovilton in July 1982. (MAP)

No.810 Squadron

Badge: On a field blue, over a base barry wavy white and blue, issuing from clouds white, a ray of lightning, gold
Motto: Ut fulmina de caelo
(Like a thunderbolt from heaven)

No.810 Squadron first formed with 12 Darts at Gosport on 3 April 1933 by combining Nos.463 and 464 Flights as a Torpedo Bomber squadron, being later redesignated a Fleet Torpedo Bomber unit. These embarked in HMS *Courageous* with the Home Fleet the following month, six of the Darts being replaced in September by Ripons. In July 1934 Baffins began to arrive, and by November the squadron was wholly equipped with that type. In August 1935 the ship sailed to the Mediterranean during the Abyssinian crisis, returning home in February 1936. The squadron received 12 Shark IIs in April 1937, these being flown during the Coronation Review flypast at Spithead on 20 June, but giving way to 12 Swordfish I in September 1937.

In October 1938, No.810 was allocated to the new carrier HMS *Ark Royal*, in which it embarked the following January. On the outbreak of war, anti-submarine searches were carried out in the Western Approaches, one U-boat being attacked on 14 September without success. Transfer to the Mediterranean in March 1940 was abruptly terminated when the Germans invaded Norway, where No.810 took part in several operations including a bombing attack on Vaernes aerodrome on 28 April.

After the Norwegian surrender, the ship sailed for Gibraltar and in July took part in operations against the French Fleet at Oran. On 3 July No.810 made an abortive strike against the battleship *Strasbourg*, and four days later participated in an attack on the battleship *Dunkerque* which lay aground in Oran harbour after having been damaged by surface ships in the earlier attack. Bombing attacks were made in August and early September against Cagliari in Sardinia, and these were followed in late September by attacks on the Vichy French Fleet at Dakar, including an unsuccessful attack on the battleship *Richelieu*. Then in late November the squadron provide anti-submarine patrols and searches during a convoy operation and an action against the Italian Fleet off Cape Spartivento.

On 2 February 1941 a bombing attack was made on the Tirso Dam in northern Sardinia but this had little effect. It was followed by bombing attacks on Leghorn and La Spezia in Italy. In May the ship participated in an Atlantic search for the *Bismarck*, and after two torpedo hits on 26 May by a striking force from HMS *Ark Royal* the Fleet was able to intercept and sink the German battleship. Next came a Malta reinforcement operation and further attacks on Sardinia, then in September the squadron reduced to six aircraft and embarked in HMS *Furious* for convoy escort to Jamaica. After a well-earned rest, No.810 joined HMS *Illustrious* in December, transferring to HMS *Formidable* at Norfolk, Va for the journey home.

Returning to 12 aircraft in January 1942, three were discarded on embarking in HMS *Illustrious* in March to take part in the Madagascar operation two months later. In the initial assault the squadron bombed ships and shore objectives at Diego Suarez, and in the final campaign at the end of September provided air support for the attacking forces. Following this it disembarked to Durban where it absorbed No.829 Squadron to increase the strength to a peak of 15 aircraft, including some Swordfish IIs, with which it returned to the United Kingdom in February 1943.

In April 1943 No.810 re-equipped at Lee-on-Solent with 12 Barracuda IIs to become a torpedo bomber reconnaissance squadron. After work-up ashore and in HMS *Illustrious*, operations were carried out off the Norwegian coast in July before sailing to provide support for the Salerno landings. Returning to the United Kingdom, the squadron regrouped as part of the 21st Naval TBR Wing in October, embarking the following month for the Far East.

Fairey Swordfish I L9784 'A2F' and others of No.810 Squadron flying from HMS Ark Royal in 1939. (RAF Museum)

Hawker Hurricane JS310 of No.810 Squadron in Operation Torch markings on HMS Biter, 8 November 1942. (J.M.Bruen)

After joining the Eastern Fleet, reconnaissance sweeps were carried out in the Bay of Bengal during March 1944. In April bombing attacks were made on oil tanks and docks at Sabang in Northern Sumatra, and similar operations was carried out during June on objectives in the Andaman Islands. In that month No.847 Squadron was absorbed, to bring the strength up to 21 aircraft, after which the squadron re-embarked for passage to Capetown where the crews had a rest whilst the ship was refitting. No.810 re-embarked for Ceylon in October for further operations, but instead it was replaced by an Avenger squadron and after leaving the aircraft in storage at Coimbatore returned home in HMS *Activity* to regroup.

Barracuda IIs were again received as temporary equipment at Burscough during December 1944, but these were superseded at Stretton in February 1945 by ten new Barracuda IIIs fitted with ASV Mk.XI radar. Two more arrived the following month, after which No.810 moved south to Thorney Island to try out the new equipment on anti-shipping patrols in the English Channel with RAF Coastal Command. In April it moved to the East Coast to search for midget submarines in the Schelde area, based at Beccles and still with Coastal Command. Following this it moved north to Scotland, disbanding at Machrihanish on 22 August 1945.

On 1 October 1947 No.810 reformed at Eglinton as a fighter squadron with 12 Firefly FR.4s for service with the 17th CAG. These embarked in HMS *Implacable* for an exercise during May 1948, then three months were spent ashore at Donibristle before joining HMS *Theseus* in August for a cruise to South Africa. Further cruises took place in 1949, first in the Mediterranean and later in Home waters, as well as participating in Army exercises in Germany in October. Then on 16 October 1949 the squadron disbanded at St.Merryn.

This was only a paper disbandment, as No.810 reformed as an anti-submarine squadron at the same station the following day, equipped with 12 Firefly AS.5s, some FR.4s being temporarily retained during work-up. The unit, which still formed part of the 17th CAG, discarded the remaining FR.4s in June 1950 to become a wholly strike squadron. Two months later it re-embarked to participate in the Korean War. Before being withdrawn in April 1951, the Air Group had carried out a total of 3446 sorties, the 1950 Boyd Trophy being awarded for its activities in Korea. A Sea Otter was attached to the squadron at this period for air-sea rescue work.

Fairefy Firefly WB415 '232/T' of No.810 Squadron on HMS Theseus in Korean waters around 1950. (via Fred Lynn)

The squadron regrouped at Arbroath on 29 June 1951 with 12 Firefly AS.5s, embarking in HMS *Ocean* in July, again as part of the 17th CAG. A short period was spent in HMS *Glory* in May and June, returning to HMS *Theseus* in October, then back to HMS *Ocean* on its return from Korea in December. In April 1953 the ship sailed for the Far East and the Air Group spent its second six-month period in Korean waters, the squadron being disbanded when the ship arrived home at Plymouth on 17 December 1953.

No.810 next reformed as a fighter squadron, equipped with 12 Sea Fury FB.11s at Ford on 1 March 1954, embarking in July in HMS *Centaur* for the Mediterranean. The aircraft flew home from Hal Far on 22 March 1955, the squadron disbanding on arrival.

On 4 July 1955 the squadron reformed at Lossiemouth as a ground attack fighter squadron equipped with 10 Sea Hawk FGA.4s. Embarking in HMS *Albion* in January 1956 it sailed for the Far East. On return home in May the squadron was to have disbanded, but this was postponed owing to the political situation in the Middle East. Instead it sailed in HMS *Bulwark* in August for the Mediterranean, where in November it participated in the Suez operations, attacks being made on airfields and other targets. On return home No.810 disbanded at Lee-on-Solent on 18 December 1956.

Next reformed at Culdrose as an anti-submarine squadron on 20 April 1959, it worked up with six Gannet AS.4s before flying out to Gibraltar in June. Here it joined HMS *Centaur* and sailed for the Mediterranean and then the Far East, including a visit to Australia. Returning home via the Suez Canal in April 1960, it re-embarked in June for exercises and a visit to Stockholm before disbanding on board on arrival home on 12 July 1960, the aircraft being afterwards flown ashore to Culdrose.

No.810 next reformed at Culdrose on 15 February 1983 with ten Sea King HAS.5s, being commissioned on 3 March. Formed as an offshoot of No.737 Squadron, the squadron took over the task of providing Advanced Flying Training (AFT) for anti-submarine warfare observers and aircrewmen, and Operational Flying Training (OFT) for ASW pilots, observers and aircrewmen. As part of this training, detachments were made to RFA *Engadine* for up to seven months each year. The AFT task was handed back to No.706 Squadron on 21 October 1985.

The squadron continues to operate from Culdrose with detachments to the Aviation Training Ship (RFA *Engadine* until 1989, then RFA *Argus*), for up to seven months of the year. The Sea King HAS.6 OEU was transferred to No.810 Squadron in July 1993 when No.826 Squadron disbanded, the OEU being based at Boscombe Down.

Identification Markings
Dart & Ripon *01-09, 1-3*; Baffin *01-09, 1-3* to 7.36, then *523-537*; Shark *523-537*; Swordfish *523-537*, to *A2A+* 5.39, later *2A+*; Barracuda *2A+*, to *N6A+* 2.45; Firefly *231-240/T*, to *230-238/O:R:T* 6.51; Sea Fury *100-112/C*; Sea Hawk *170-170/Z*, to *230-239/Z:B* 1.56; Gannet *230-236/C*; Sea King *501-510/CU*.

Aircraft Equipment	Period of Service	Example
Dart	Apr 1933 - Nov 1934	N9823 (2)
Ripon IIc	Sep 1933 - Nov 1934	S1658 (04)
Baffin	Jul 1934 - Apr 1937	S1650 (530)
Shark II	Apr 1937 - Sep 1937	K8486 (531)
Swordfish I	Sep 1937 - Mar 1943	P4271 (A2M)
Swordfish II	Mar 1942 - Mar 1943	HS164 (2F)
Albacore I	Jan 1943 - Jan 1943	BF715
Barracuda II	Apr 1943 - Nov 1944	P9981 (2X)
	Dec 1944 - Jul 1945	PM767 (Q)
Barracuda TR.III	Feb 1945 - Aug 1945	ME226 (N6A)
Firefly FR.4	Oct 1947 - Jun 1950	VG991 (236/T)
Firefly AS.5	Jan 1949 - Jun 1951	WB255 (235/T)
Firefly FR.5	Jun 1951 - Nov 1953	WB403 (233/O)
Sea Otter I	Jan 1951 - May 1951	JN196
Sea Fury FB.11	Mar 1954 - Mar 1955	WG601 (103/C)
Sea Hawk FGA.4	Jul 1955 - Dec 1956	WV922 (172/Z)
Sea Hawk FGA.6	Nov 1955 - Dec 1956	XE403 (178/Z)
Gannet AS.4	Apr 1959 - Jul 1960	XG797 (232/C)
Sea King HAS.5	Mar 1983 - Feb 1990	ZA103 (503/CU)
Sea King HAS.6	Oct 1989 - to date	ZA126 (509/CU)

Hawker Sea Fury FB.11 WE693 '106/C' of No.810 Squadron, HMS Centaur in 1954. (MAP)

Battle Honours

Norway	1940
Mediterranean	1940-41
Spartivento	1940
Atlantic	1941
'Bismarck'	1941
Diego Suarez	1942
Salerno	1943
Korea	1951-53

Squadron bases

Gosport	3 Apr 1933
HMS Courageous	8 May 1933
Gosport	17 Jul 1933
HMS Courageous	18 Sep 1933
Gosport	25 Sep 1933
Leuchars (Dt5)	10 Oct 1933
to	7 Nov 1933
HMS Courageous	20 Feb 1934
Gosport	13 Apr 1934
Leuchars	14 May 1934
HMS Courageous	25 Jun 1934
Gosport	11 Jul 1934
HMS Courageous	1 Aug 1934
Gosport	15 Aug 1934
HMS Courageous	4 Sep 1934
Leuchars	15 Sep 1934
HMS Courageous	8 Oct 1934
Gosport	6 Nov 1934
HMS Courageous	5 Jan 1935
Upavon	25 Mar 1935
HMS Courageous	7 May 1935
Gosport	13 Jun 1935
North Coates Fitties	16 Jun 1935
Gosport	6 Jul 1935
HMS Courageous	29 Aug 1935
Aboukir	16 Sep 1935
HMS Courageous	18 Sep 1935
Aboukir (Dt3)	2-10 Oct 1935
Hal Far	15 Dec 1935
HMS Courageous	21 Dec 1935
Aboukir	17 Jan 1936
HMS Courageous	20 Feb 1936
Gosport	28 Feb 1936

Squadron bases

Catfoss (1ATC)	23 May 1936
Gosport	20 Jun 1936
HMS Courageous	13 Jul 1936
Gosport	17 Nov 1936
HMS Courageous	19 Jan 1937
Gosport	22 Mar 1937
HMS Courageous	28 May 1937
Evanton (APC)	6 Jun 1937
Gosport	1 Jul 1937
HMS Courageous	7 Jul 1937
Gosport	9 Jul 1937
Southampton	13 Jul 1937
Gosport	27 Jul 1937
North Coates Fitties	20 Aug 1937
Gosport	1 Sep 1937
Evanton	17 Sep 1937
HMS Courageous	30 Sep 1937
Gosport	1 Nov 1937
HMS Courageous	10 Jan 1938
Southampton	29 Mar 1938
HMS Courageous	10 May 1938
Evanton	13 May 1938
Southampton	9 Jul 1938
HMS Courageous	18 Jul 1938
Southampton	23 Jul 1938
Roborough	26 Jul 1938
Southampton	6 Aug 1938
HMS Courageous	6 Sep 1938
Old Sarum	17 Sep 1938
Southampton	27 Oct 1938
HMS Ark Royal	11 Jan 1939
Dekheila	30 Jan 1939
Aboukir	14 Feb 1939
HMS Ark Royal	16 Feb 1939
Southampton	24 Mar 1939
HMS Ark Royal	27 Apr 1939
Lee-on-Solent	2 Jun 1939
Warmwell	15 Jun 1939
Old Sarum	3 Jul 1939
Lee-on-Solent	30 Jul 1939
HMS Ark Royal	30 Jul 1939
Hatston (Dt)	11-13 Sep 1939
Hatston	27 Sep 1939

Squadron bases

HMS Ark Royal	2 Oct 1939
Wingfield	3 Dec 1939
HMS Ark Royal	4 Dec 1939
Lee-on-Solent	15 Feb 1940
Gosport	1 Mar 1940
HMS Ark Royal	20 Mar 1940
Dekheila	2 Apr 1940
HMS Ark Royal	10 Apr 1940
Arbroath	8 Oct 1940
HMS Ark Royal	29 Oct 1940
North Front (Dt4)	28 Apr 1940
to	5 May 1941
HMS Furious	10 Sep 1941
Palisadoes	1 Oct 1941
HMS Illustrious	2 Dec 1941
Norfolk	8 Dec 1941
HMS Formidable	13 Dec 1941
Lee-on-Solent	21 Dec 1941
High Ercall	25 Feb 1942
Campbeltown	26 Feb 1942
Machrihanish	9 Mar 1942
HMS Illustrious	10 Mar 1942
Stamford Hill	22 Apr 1942
HMS Illustrious	28 Apr 1942
Port Reitz(Dt3)	26-29 May 1942
Kilindini	1 Jul 1942
HMS Illustrious	15 Jul 1942
Tanga	18 Aug 1942
Port Reitz (Dt)	25 Aug 1942
to	6 Sep 1942
HMS Illustrious	29 Aug 1942
Stamford Hill	31 Sep 1942
HMS Illustrious	13 Oct 1942
Tanga	21 Oct 1942
HMS Illustrious	8 Dec 1942
Machrihanish	4 Feb 1943
HMS Illustrious	5 Feb 1943
Stretton	18 Feb 1943
Machrihanish	20 Mar 1943
Errol	2 Apr 1943
Lee-on-Solent	4 Apr 1943
Machrihanish	21 May 1943
HMS Illustrious	8 Jun 1943
Ta Kali	22 Aug 1943

Squadron bases

HMS Illustrious	28 Aug 1943
Bizerta (Dt8)	15-16 Sep 1943
Crail	18 Oct 1943
Machrihanish	4 Nov 1943
HMS Illustrious	28 Nov 1943
China Bay	28 Jan 1944
HMS Illustrious	22 Feb 1944
China Bay	12 Mar 1944
HMS Illustrious	21 Mar 1944
China Bay	24 May 1944
HMS Illustrious	30 May 1944
Minneriya (Dt)	18 Jun 1944
to	8 Jul 1944
Minneriya	8 Jul 1944
HMS Illustrious	27 Jul 1944
Wingfield	11 Aug 1944
HMS Illustrious	13 Oct 1944
Coimbatore	2 Nov 1944
HMS Activity (no a/c)	3 Nov 1944
on leave	30 Nov 1944
Burscough	16 Dec 1944
Thorney Island	1 Feb 1945
Beccles	8 Apr 1945
Machrihanish	3 Jun 1945
HMS Queen (no a/c)	24 Jul 1945
Macrihanish	8 Aug 1945
HMS Queen	12 Aug 1945
Machrihanish	21 Aug 1945
Squadron disbanded	22 Aug 1945
Eglinton	1 Oct 1947
HMS Implacable	4 May 1948
Donibristle	14 May 1948
HMS Theseus	20 Aug 1948
Lee-on-Solent	14 Dec 1948
HMS Theseus	24 Jan 1949
Hal Far	11 Feb 1949
Ta Kali	18 Feb 1949
HMS Theseus	23 Feb 1949
Yeovilton	24 Mar 1949
HMS Theseus	3 May 1949
St Merryn (Dt6)	17-21 May 1949
St Merryn	20 Aug 1949
Wunstorf	1 Oct 1949

Squadron bases		Squadron bases		Squadron bases		Squadron bases	
St Merryn	15 Oct 1949	Lossiemouth	4 Jul 1955	Portland (Dt2)	13-24Feb1984	RFA Engadine (Dt3)	25 Oct 1985 to 15 Nov 1985
Squadron disbanded	16 Oct 1949	HMS Albion	10 Jan 1956	HMS Illustrious (Dt3)	5-24Mar 1984	Portland (Dt2)	4-15Nov 1985
St Merryn	17 Oct 1949	Hal Far	27 Jan 1956	RFA Engadine (Dt3)	3-18Apr 1984	RFA Engadine (Dt3)	22 Nov 1985 to 3 Dec 1985
Eglinton	5 Jan 1950	HMS Albion	6 Feb 1956	Benbecula (Dt2)	17-26Apr1984	Portland (Dt3)	27-30Jan 1986
St Merryn	17 Feb 1950	Lossiemouth	14 May 1956	RFA Engadine (Dt3)	1-14May1984	RFA Engadine (Dt3)	18-27Feb 1986
HMS Theseus	19 Apr 1950	HMS Bulwark	6 Aug 1956	RFA Engadine (Dt3)	11 Jun 1984 to 14 Jul 1984	RFA Engadine (Dt3)	7-25Apr 1986
Ford	15 Jun 1950	Hal Far	25 Aug 1956	RFA Blue Rover	29 Jun 1984	Portland (Dt3)	14-18Apr1986
HMS Theseus	16 Aug 1950	HMS Bulwark	4 Sep 1956	(Dt1) - joined RFA Engadine		RFA Engadine(Dt)	2-15May1986
Arbroath	29 May 1951	Lee-on-Solent	17 Dec 1956	Portland (Dt2)	9-20Jul 1984	Jersey (Dt2)	2-5May1986
HMS Ocean	25 Jul 1951	Squadron disbanded	18 Dec 1956	RFA Engadine (Dt3)	5 Sep 1984 to 10 Oct 1984	De Kooy (Dt3)	19-24Jun 1986
Hal Far	3 Aug 1951	Culdrose	20 Apr 1959	Portland (Dt2)	14-23Oct 1984	RFA Engadine(Dt3)	22 Jun 1986 to 3 Jul 1986
HMS Ocean	12 Sep 1951	North Front	6 Jun 1959	RFA Engadine (Dt3)	4-16Nov 1984	Portland (Dt3)	30 Jun 1986 to 3 Jul 1986
Hal Far	16 Oct 1951	HMS Centaur	8 Jun 1959	RFA Engadine (Dt3)	25 Nov 1984 to 5 Dec 1984	RFA Engadine (Dt3	22 Sep 1986 to 3 Oct 1986
HMS Ocean	12 Nov 1951	Hal Far	13 Jun 1959	Portland (Dt2)	4-15Feb 1985	RFA Engadine (Dt3)	11 Oct 1986 to 8 Nov 1986
Hal Far	9 Apr 1952	HMS Centaur	21 Jun 1959	Portland (Dt2)	24-28Feb1985	Portland (Dt3)	17-20Nov1986
HMS Glory	21 May 1952	Khormaksar	2 Jul 1959	Portland (Dt2)	4-7Mar 1985	RFA Engadine (Dt3)	29 Nov 1986 to 18 Dec 1986
Kasfareet	23 Jun 1952	HMS Centaur	9 Jul 1959	RFA Engadine (Dt3)	25 Mar 1985 to 4 Apr 1985	Portland (Dt3)	8-11Dec 1986
HMS Glory	6 Jul 1952	Drigh Road	30 Jul 1959	Portland (Dt2)	25-28Mar1985	Ronaldsway (Dt2)	9-10Jan 1987
Hal Far	14 Aug 1952	HMS Centaur	11 Aug 1959	RFA Engadine (Dt3)	10-18Apr 1985	RFA Engadine (Dt3)	23 Jan 1987 to 6 Feb 1987
HMS Theseus	15 Oct 1952	Seletar	4 Sep 1959	Portland (Dt2)	1-4May 1985	RFA Fort Grange (Dt4)	13-16Feb 1987
Hal Far	28 Nov 1952	HMS Centaur	30 Sep 1959	RFA Engadine (Dt3)	4-18May1985	RFA Engadine (Dt3)	27 Feb 1987 to 18 Mar 1987
HMS Ocean	9 Dec 1952	Seletar (Dt4)	21 Jan 1960 to 4 Feb 1960	RFA Engadine (Dt3)	8-22Jun 1985	Portland (Dt3)	16-23Mar1987
Hal Far	16 Jan 1953	Culdrose	26 Apr 1960	Portland (Dt2)	1-10Jul 1985	RFA Engadine (Dt3)	28 Mar 1987 to 10 Apr 1987
HMS Ocean	8 Apr 1953	HMS Centaur	13 Jun 1960	Portland (Dt2)	29 Jul 1985 to 2 Aug 1985	Nordholz (Dt3)	13-18May1987
K6 (Dt)	24-30Jul 1953	Culdrose-disbanded	12 Jul 1960	Jersey (Dt)	20-22Sep 1985	RFA Engadine (Dt)	16 May 1987 to 5 Jun 1987
K6 and K16	29 Aug 1953	Culdrose	15 Feb 1983	RFA Engadine (Dt3)	22 Sep 1985 to 3 Oct 1985		
HMS Ocean	9 Sep 1953	RFA Engadine (Dt3)	18-25Feb 1983	Portland (Dt2)	14-18Oct 1985	Portland (Dt3)	1-4Jun 1987
Sqdn disbanded UK	17 Dec 1953	RFA Engadine (Dt3)	14 Mar 1983 to 22 Apr 1983				
Ford	1 Mar 1954	Portland (Dt3)	3-6May 1983				
HMS Centaur	20 Jul 1954	RFA Engadine (Dt3)	14-19Jun 1983				
Hal Far	3 Aug 1954	RFA Engadine (Dt3)	22 Aug 1983 to 21 Sep 1983				
HMS Centaur	23 Aug 1954	RFA Engadine (Dt3)	31 Oct 1983 to 27 Nov 1983				
Hal Far	14 Oct 1954	Prestwick (Dt3)	13 Feb 1984 to 1 Mar 1984				
HMS Centaur	15 Nov 1954						
Hal Far	15 Dec 1954						
HMS Centaur	12 Jan 1955						
Hal Far	23 Feb 1955						
Bizerta	9 Mar 1955						
Hal Far	17 Mar 1955						
Sqdn disbanded UK	22 Mar 1955						

Hawker Sea Hawk FGA.6 XE408 '237/Z' of No.810 Squadron, HMS Albion in 1956. (via S.M. Coates)

Squadron bases
RFA Engadine
  (Dt3)   12-26Jun 1987
Guernsey (Dt2)   4-5Jul 1987
Plockton (Dt2)   13-21Jul 1987
RFA Engadine (Dt3)17 Jul 1987
    to   6 Aug 1987
Inskip (Dt)   24-31Jul 1987
Portland (Dt3)   3-8Aug1987
Portland (Dt3) 14-21Sep1987
RFA Engadine (Dt3)25 Sep 1987
    to   9 Oct 1987
Bitburg (Dt2)   16-21Oct 1987
Portland (Dt3)   26 Oct 1987
    to   9 Nov 1987
RFA Engadine (Dt3)31 Oct 1987
    to   5 Dec 1987
Plockton (Dt2)   9-18Nov1987
RFA Engadine (Dt3)21 Nov 1987
    to   5 Dec 1987
RFA Engadine (Dt3)15 Jan 1988
    to   4 Feb 1988
RFA Engadine (Dt3)19 Feb 1988
    to   3 Mar 1988
RFA Engadine (Dt3)
    17-29Apr 1988
RFA Engadine (Dt3)
    6-24 May 1988
RFA Engadine (Dt3)
    6-24 Jun 1988
RFA Fort Austin
  (Dt2)   1-6Jul 1988
RFA Engadine (Dt3)
    1-14 Jul 1988
RFA Argus (Dt1) 18 Jul 1988
    to   9 Aug 1988
Plockton (Dt2)   1-8Sep 1988
RFA Engadine
  (Dt3)   13-28Oct 1988
RFA Engadine
  (Dt3)   7-27Sep 1988

Squadron bases
RFA Engadine(Dt3) 19 Nov 1988
    to   8 Dec 1988
RFA Engadine
  (Dt3)   13-22Jan 1989
RFA Fort Grange 9 Feb 1989
  (Dt3)   to 9 Mar 1989
RFA Argus (Dt3) 29 Mar 1989
    to 10 Apr 1989
RFA Argus (Dt3) 26 Apr 1989
    to   4 May 1989
RFA Argus (Dt6) 4-18May1989
RFA Fort Austin
  (Dt3)   9-27Jul 1989
RFA Fort Austin
  (Dt3)   1-20Sep 1989
RFA Fort Austin
  (Dt3)   9-21Oct 1989
Portland (Dt3)   30 Oct 1989
    to   3 Nov 1989
RFA Argus (Dt3) 17 Nov 1989
    to   1 Dec 1989
RFA Argus (Dt3) 13 Jan 1990
    to   1 Feb 1990
Prestwick (Dt4) 30 Jan 1990
    to   3 Feb 1990
RFA Argus (Dt4) 3-8Feb 1990
HMS Ark Royal
  (Dt3)   12-15Feb 1990
RFA Argus (Dt3) 1-22Mar1990
RFA Argus (Dt3) 14-24May1990
RFA Fort Austin Jun 1990
  (Dt3)   to 6 Jul 1990
RFA Argus (Dt3) 20-31Jul 1990
RFA Argus (Dt3) 28 Sep 1990
    to   3 Oct 1990
RFA Tidespring
  (Dt2)   1-18Nov 1990
RFA Tidespring(Dt2) Mar 1991
RFA Olmeda (Dt2) 19 Apr 1991
    to 30 May 1991

Squadron bases
RFA Argus (Dt3) 3-13Jun 1991
RFA Argus (Dt3) 28 Jun 1991
    to   Jul 1991
RFA Argus (Dt3) 10-28Sep 1991
RFA Fort Austin(Dt3) Nov 1991
    to   Dec 1991
[details for 1992-93
  not available]
RFA Argus (Dt3) 24 Jan 1994
    to 18 Feb 1994
RFA Argus (Dt3) 22 Apr 1994
    to 20 May 1994

**810 Sqdn Sea King HAS.6 OEU
transferred from 826 Sqdn**
Boscombe Down 27 Jul 1993
RFA Olmeda   6 Sep 1993
Boscombe Down 17 Sep 1993
AUTEC   8 Nov 1993
Boscombe Down 14 Dec 1993
BUTEC Plockton 21 Feb 1994
Boscombe Down 4 Mar 1994

Commanding Officers
Cdr EW Anstice RN 3 Apr 1933
  (Sq Ldr RAF)
Sq Ldr TA Warne-
  Browne DSC RAF 10 Oct 1933
Sq Ldr GH Boyce
  AFC RAF 7 Feb 1934
Sq Ldr HM Mellor
  MVO RN 5 May 1936
Capt NRM Skene 9 Dec 1938
  RM (Sq Ldr RAF)
Capt AC Newsom
  RN 16 Jun 1940
L/C M Johnstone
  DSC RN 16 Jul 1940

Commanding Officers
Lt JV Hartley RN 11 Sep 1941
L/C RN Everett RN 29 Dec 1941
L/C WE Waters RN 31 Jan 1943
L/C(A) AJB Forde
  RN 18 Mar 1943
L/C(A) AG McWilliam
  RNVR 27 Feb 1944
L/C(A) A JB Forde
  DSC RN 1 Jul 1944
L/C(A) PC Heath
  RN 16 Dec 1944
Squadron disbanded 22 Aug 1945
L/C(A) LR Tivy RN 1 Oct 1947
L/C F Stovin
  -Bradford DSC RN25 Mar 1949
Squadron disbanded 16 Oct 1949
L/C KS Pattisson
  DSC RN 17 Oct 1949
L/C GR Coy RN 4 Jan 1951
L/C DE Johnson RN29Jun 1951
L/C AW Bloomer
  RN 28 Jun 1952
Squadron disbanded 17 Dec 1953
L/C HJ Abraham RN 1 Mar 1954
Squadron disbanded 22 Mar 1955
L/C PM Lamb
  DSC AFC RN 4 Jul 1955
Squadron disbanded 18 Dec 1956
L/C AMcK Sinclair
  RN 20 Apr 1959
Squadron disbanded 12 Jul 1960
L/C MS Tennant RN15Feb 1983
L/C DP Baudains RN20Jan 1984
L/C MS Burnett RN 10 Dec 1985
L/C DR Lamour RN 7 Dec 1987
L/C AGH Underwood
  RN 24 Jul 1989
L/C TR Forrester
  RN 10 Dec 1991
L/C RE Snook RN 30 Jul 1993

Westland Sea King HAS.5 ZA920 '510' of No.810 Squadron in 1984. (MAP)

Fairey Swordfish I V4559 '1C' of No.811 Squadron flying from Arbroath around March 1942. (Lord Kilbracken)

No.811 Squadron

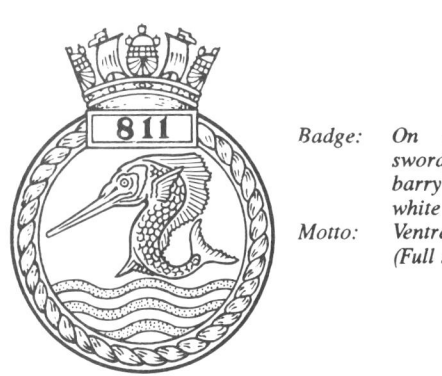

Badge: On a white field, a swordfish over a base barry wavy of six blue and white

Motto: Ventre a mer
(Full speed)

No.811 Squadron was originally formed on 3 April 1933 for Fleet Torpedo Bomber duties, from Nos.465 and 466 Flights at Gosport. Initial equipment was 12 Ripons, and these embarked in HMS *Furious* the following month for duty with the Home Fleet. In January 1935 the squadron re-equipped with 12 Baffins, spending a few weeks in the Mediterranean before returning to Home waters. The Baffins in turn gave way in October 1936 to 12 Swordfish, and the role was changed to torpedo spotter reconnaissance. On 20 May 1937 the squadron took part in the Coronation Review flypast at Spithead. When HMS *Furious* was paid off in December 1938, No.811 was reallocated for deck landing training duties. In January 1939 the aircraft embarked in HMS *Courageous* for this task, but when the Fleet Air Arm transferred from RAF to RN charge on 24 May 1939 the unit was redesignated No.767 Squadron.

In the meantime, a new sub-unit had formed on 15 May 1939 at Southampton, being initially known as No.811A Squadron. When the original No.811 Squadron was redesignated, this sub-flight took over its title. On the outbreak of war it transferred to HMS *Courageous*, but ceased to exist when that ship was sunk on 17 September 1939.

No.811 next reformed at Lee-on-Solent on 15 July 1941 as a torpedo bomber reconnaissance squadron, intended for service in an escort carrier. Equipment was 14 Chesapeakes and 2 Sea Hurricanes, but the take off run of the former proved too long for escort carrier work, and they gave way in November to 6 Swordfish IIs. With these No.811 undertook night operations from Bircham Newton from August 1942, under the control of RAF Coastal Command. Anti-shipping strikes and mine-laying were carried out in the English Channel before the squadron was withdrawn in December to Hatston, where it absorbed No.812 Squadron.

In January 1943, three Wildcats IVs were added, and with these the squadron embarked in HMS *Biter* in February, for escort duties. On 25 April *U-203* was attacked and damaged, and on 12 May a similar attack was made on *U-89*, both being later sunk by surface vessels. Six later such attacks were unsuccessful, but the Wildcats shot down a Ju 290B and its attached glider bomb on 16 February 1944. Further operations were carried out under Coastal Command during 1944, mainly from Limavady, then in September the squadron embarked in HMS *Vindex* with 12 Swordfish and 4 Wildcats to escort a North Russian convoy. The squadron disbanded on return from this on 9 December 1944.

No.811 reformed at Ford on 15 September 1945 equipped with 15 Mosquito FB.VIs, three of which were soon withdrawn. 12 Sea Mosquito TR.33s arrived from April 1946, but half of these were withdrawn when the squadron moved to Brawdy at the end of the year. The squadron was disbanded on 1 July 1947.

Reformed at Arbroath on 17 August 1953, the squadron initially had 9 Sea Fury FB.11s, being later increased to 12. These embarked in HMS *Warrior* in February 1954 for the Mediterranean, two further machines being added by the time the squadron sailed through the Suez Canal two months later, en route for Aden and Singapore. A peak strength of 19 was reached in September, when the ship sailed home via South Africa, No.811 disbanding at Lee-on-Solent on 30 December 1954.

Next reformed at Lossiemouth on 16 March 1955 with eight Sea Hawk FB.3's, No.811 soon increased its strength to ten aircraft. It was initially intended for HMS *Centaur*, but instead embarked in HMS *Bulwark* in June for a visit to Sweden. During October the aircraft spent a period in HMS *Albion* for an exercise, then in January 1956 at last joined HMS *Centaur*, sailing to the Far East via the Suez Canal. Returning in April, the squadron disbanded on arrival at Lossiemouth on 16 May 1956.

Chesapeakes of No.811 Sqdn in 1941. (RAF Museum P.17814)

Aircraft Equipment	Period of Service	Example
Ripon IIc	Apr 1933 - Jan 1935	S1562 (12)
Baffin	Nov 1934 - Nov 1936	S1554 (603)
Swordfish I	Oct 1936 - Sep 1939	K8374 (612)
Tutor	Jan 1937 - May 1937	K3339
Sea Hurricane	Jul 1941 - Sep 1941	
Chesapeake I	Jul 1941 - Nov 1941	AL918 (F)
Avro 652	Jul 1941 - Mar 1942	DG655
Swordfish II	Nov 1941 - Dec 1944	HS362 (K)
Swordfish III	Jul 1944 - Dec 1944	NR935 (B)
Wildcat IV	Jan 1943 - Apr 1944	FN212 (P)
Wildcat V	Mar 1944 - Sep 1944	JV670
Wildcat VI	Sep 1944 - Dec 1944	JV709
Mosquito FB.VI	Sep 1945 - Aug 1946	TE721 (FD4C)
Sea Mosquito TR.33	Apr 1946 - Jul 1947	TW268 (FD4G)
Sea Fury FB.11	Aug 1953 - Dec 1954	VW543 (102/J)
Sea Hawk FB.3	Mar 1955 - May 1956	WM997 (240/C)
Sea Hawk FGA.4	Mar 1955 - May 1955	WV841

Identification Markings
Ripon *4-16*; Baffin *4-16* to *601-614* 1.35; Swordfish *601-614*, to *U4A+* 5.39; Chesapeake single letters; Swordfish from 11.41 single letters, later *1A+*; Wildcat single letters; Mosquito *FD4A+*; Sea Fury *100-116/J*; Sea Hawk *158-169/C*, to *240-251/C* 1.56.

Battle Honours
English Channel	1942
North Sea	1942
Atlantic	1943-44
Arctic	1944

Squadron bases
Gosport	3 Apr 1933
HMS Furious	8 May 1933
North Coates Fitties	16 Jun 1933
HMS Furious	22 Jun 1933
Gosport	20 Jul 1933
Donibristle	18 Sep 1933
HMS Furious	23 Sep 1933
Donibristle (transit)	10 Oct 1933
Gosport	10 Oct 1933
Leuchars	15 Oct 1933
Gosport	27 Oct 1933
HMS Furious	5 Jan 1934
Gosport	13 Apr 1934
North Coates Fitties	16 Jun 1934
HMS Courageous	7 Jul 1934
Gosport	25 Jul 1934
HMS Furious	4 Jan 1935
Hal Far (Dt6)	18-21 Jan 1935
Hal Far (Dt6)	25 Jan 1935 to 4 Feb 1935
Gosport	25 Mar 1935
HMS Furious	8 May 1935
Gosport	13 Jun 1935
Leuchars (ATC)	15 Jun 1935
Gosport	6 Jul 1935
HMS Furious	3 Sep 1935
Gosport	7 Oct 1935
HMS Furious	4 Nov 1935
Gosport	22 Nov 1935
HMS Furious	2 Jan 1936
Gosport	21 May 1936
HMS Furious	12 Jun 1936
Gosport	20 Jul 1936
HMS Furious	28 Sep 1936
Donibristle	13 Oct 1936
HMS Furious	20 Oct 1936
Gosport	26 Oct 1936
HMS Furious	19 Jan 1937
Aboukir (Dt)	11-22 Feb 1937
Gosport	29 Mar 1937
HMS Furious	24 May 1937
Evanton	29 Jun 1937
HMS Furious	5 Jul 1937
Gosport	21 Jul 1937
HMS Furious	3 Aug 1937
Gosport	8 Sep 1937
HMS Furious	10 Sep 1937
Donibristle	16 Sep 1937
HMS Furious (Dt6)	23 Sep 1937 to 5 Oct 1937
HMS Furious	5 Oct 1937
Gosport	28 Oct 1937
Lee-on-Solent	11 Jan 1938
Gosport	29 Mar 1938
Donibristle	4 May 1938
Gosport	25 May 1938
HMS Furious	29 Jun 1938
Donibristle	22 Jul 1938
HMS Furious	24 Sep 1938
Donibristle	15 Oct 1938
HMS Courageous	31 Jan 1939
Donibristle	7 Feb 1939
HMS Courageous	3 Apr 1939
Donibristle	4 Apr 1939
Redesignated 767 Squadron	24 May 1939
811A Sqdn: Southampton	15 May 1939
Redesignated 811 Sqdn	24 May 1939
Southampton	1 Jul 1939
HMS Courageous	12 Aug 1939
Ship sunk	17 Sep 1939
Lee-on-Solent	15 Jul 1941
Arbroath	1 Nov 1941
Machrihanish	16 Mar 1942
Bircham Newton	6 Aug 1942
Thorney Island	29 Oct 1942
Hatston	18 Dec 1942
HMS Biter	21 Feb 1943
Ballykelly	27 Mar 1943
HMS Biter	6 Apr 1943
Machrihanish	18 May 1943
HMS Biter	2 Jun 1943
Belfast	9 Jul 1943
HMS Biter	19 Jul 1943
Machrihanish	26 Jul 1943
Belfast	6 Sep 1943
HMS Biter	24 Sep 1943
Donibristle	25 Nov 1943
Inskip	12 Dec 1943
HMS Biter	12 Jan 1944
North Front (Dt2)	26 Feb 1944 to 2 Mar 1944
Limavady (15 Gp)	10 Jun 1944
HMS Biter	14 Jul 1944
Limavady (15 Gp)	25 Aug 1944
HMS Vindex	30 Sep 1944
Fighter Flight:	
Crail	25 Nov 1943
Stretton	10 Dec 1943
HMS Biter	12 Jan 1944
North Front	25 Feb 1944
HMS Biter	2 Mar 1944
Eglinton	21 Apr 1944
HMS Biter	28 Apr 1944
Eglinton	10 Jun 1944
HMS Vindex	6 Oct 1944
Eglinton	15 Oct 1944
HMS Vindex	23 Nov 1944
Squadron disbanded	9 Dec 1944
Ford	15 Sep 1945
Brawdy	6 Dec 1946
Eglinton	31 Mar 1947
Squadron disbanded	1 Jul 1947
Arbroath	17 Aug 1953
Leuchars	19 Aug 1953
Lee-on-Solent	2 Feb 1954
HMS Warrior	17 Feb 1954
Hal Far	5 Mar 1954
HMS Warrior	23 Mar 1954
Hal Far	2 Apr 1954
HMS Warrior	17 Apr 1954
Sembawang	12 May 1954
HMS Warrior	2 Jun 1954
Kure	16 Jun 1954
HMS Warrior	22 Jun 1954
Kure	4 Jul 1954
HMS Warrior	11 Jul 1954
Kure	27 Jul 1954
HMS Warrior	9 Aug 1954
Sembawang	9 Aug 1954
HMS Warrior	23 Sep 1954
Lee-on-Solent	13 Dec 1954
Squadron disbanded	30 Dec 1954
Lossiemouth	16 Mar 1955
Ford	20 May 1955
HMS Bulwark	8 Jun 1955
Lossiemouth	23 Jun 1955
Yeovilton (Dt7)	15-17 Jul 1955
Yeovilton	16 Aug 1955
Ford	1 Sep 1955
Lossiemouth	14 Oct 1955
HMS Albion	23 Oct 1955
Lossiemouth	29 Oct 1955
HMS Centaur	10 Jan 1956
Tengah	4 Apr 1956
HMS Centaur	19 Apr 1956
Lossiemouth	16 May 1956
Squadron disbanded	16 May 1956

Commanding Officers
Sq Ldr TA Warne-Browne DSC RAF	3 Apr 1933
L/C FWH Clarke RN	2 Oct 1933
(Sq Ldr RAF)	
Cdr RR Graham RN	23 Sep 1935
(Sq Ldr RAF)	
L/C LIG Richardson RN (Sq Ldr RAF)	27 Feb 1936
Sq Ldr JAS Brown RAF	12 Dec 1937
L/C EOF Price RN (Sq Ldr RAF)	21 Jan 1938
Squadron disbanded	24 May 1939
L/C EOF Price RN	24 May 1939
L/C S Borrett RN	1 Jul 1939
Squadron disbanded	17 Sep 1939
L/C RD Wall RN	15 Jul 1941
L/C WJ Lucas RN	29 Oct 1941
L/C HS Hayes DSC RN	27 Feb 1942
Lt JG Baldwin RN	28 Jan 1943
Lt AS Kennard DSC RN	12 Apr 1943
L/C EB Morgan RANVR	29 Nov 1943
L/C(A) EEG Emsley RNVR	27 Jul 1944
Squadron disbanded	9 Dec 1944
L/C(A) SMP Walsh DSO DSC & Bar RNVR	15 Sep 1945
L/C(A) EW Lockwood RN	24 Jun 1946
Lt FMM Lewis RN (temp)	24 Apr 1947
L/C(A) DH Richards RN	1 May 1947
Squadron disbanded	1 Jul 1947
L/C LG Morris RN	17 Aug 1953
Squadron disbanded	30 Dec 1954
L/C RH Reynolds DSC AFC RN	16 Mar 1955
Squadron disbanded	16 May 1956

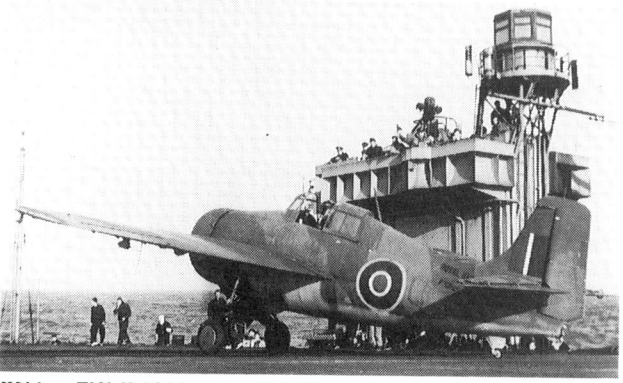
Wildcat FN168 'Q' landing HMS Biter after shooting down a Ju290, possibly on 16 February 1944. (Wellham/FAA Museum)

No.812 Squadron

Badge: On a blue field, over water, wavy green, a flying fish, gold
Motto: Dex aie
(God aid)

No.812 Squadron first formed on 3 April 1933 as a Fleet Torpedo Bomber unit, by combining Nos.461 and 462 Flights aboard HMS *Glorious*, then serving in the Mediterranean. Initial equipment was 12 Ripons, but these gave way in January 1934 to 12 Baffins. When HMS *Glorious* returned home for a refit, the squadron transferred first to HMS *Furious* in June 1934, then to HMS *Eagle* in February 1935. Following this it remained shore based at Hal Far until HMS *Glorious* returned in September. In December 1936 it again re-equipped, this time with 12 Swordfish, for further service in HMS *Glorious* in the Mediterranean, apart from a few weeks at home in May 1937 to take part in the Coronation Review flypast at Spithead.

On the outbreak of war, HMS *Glorious* sailed for the Indian Ocean to search for merchant ships and enemy raiders, but after completing a refit at Malta from January 1940 the ship was called home on the German invasion of Norway. On arrival No.812 Squadron disembarked and joined RAF Coastal Command for minelaying and bombing operations in coastal areas of Holland, Belgium and France. Leaving Coastal Command in March 1941, six aircraft embarked in HMS *Argus* to provide anti-submarine protection for a convoy ferrying RAF fighters to Malta. In July the whole squadron embarked in HMS *Furious* with a reduced strength of nine aircraft to participate in an attack on the Arctic port of Petsamo. This was followed by further Malta convoy escort duty, initially in HMS *Furious*, before transferring to HMS *Ark Royal* in September. When that ship was torpedoed on 13 November, No.812 had sufficient aircraft in the air to be able to regroup subsequently at Gibraltar.

At North Front new machines were received, equipped with ASV radar, and on 21 December this was used to good advantage when the first night sinking of a U-boat was achieved, this being the *U-451*. Brief spells were spent in HMS *Argus*, and during this period shore based aircraft damaged five U-boats on the surface during anti-submarine searches before returning to the United Kingdom in USS *Wasp* in April 1942. Reducing to six aircraft, No.812 rejoined Coastal Command in September for night operations in the English Channel, before amalgamating with No.811 Squadron on 18 December 1942.

No.812 reformed at Stretton on 1 June 1944 as a torpedo bomber reconnaissance squadron with 12 Barracuda IIs, increasing shortly afterwards to 16. In December the squadron reached its full strength of 18, and the following month embarked in HMS *Vengeance*. The ship sailed to the Mediterranean in February 1945, where No.812 continued its work-up, then in May sailed on to the Far East to join the British Pacific Fleet in July. However, the squadron saw no action in that theatre before the Japanese surrender. In October the squadron disembarked in Hong Kong, re-embarking at the end of the year for Australia, where it re-equipped in January 1946 with 12 Firefly FR.Is. It remained in the Far East until the ship returned home, disbanding at Lee-on-Solent on arrival on 12 August 1946.

On 1 October 1946, No.812 reformed at Eglinton with 12 Firefly FR.Is as part of the 14th Carrier Air Group. Embarking in HMS *Theseus* in February 1947, the ship sailed on a lengthy Far Eastern cruise, eventually returning home in November. The squadron regrouped on 15 January 1948, and re-equipped with 12 Firefly FR.4s in March, only to replace these with 12 Mk.5s in July.

After embarking in HMS *Ocean* in August 1948 the squadron sailed to the Mediterranean, where Hal Far was used as a shore base. Four Firefly NF.1s were taken over from No.816 Squadron at

Fairey Swordfish I K8867 'G3P' of No.812 Squadron from HMS Glorious ashore at Dekheila in late 1939. (Cdr R.N.Everett)

this time, and these were known as Black Flight, being transferred to No.827 Squadron in June 1949. In September 1949 the squadron flew home to Culham, where it re-equipped with updated Mk.5s, with which it returned to Hal Far later in the month.

No.812 transferred to HMS *Glory* in November 1949, still as part of the 14th CAG, and Black Flight was reformed, again with four Firefly NF.1s. The squadron participated in several cruises and exercises during that year, landings being made on USS *Midway* during October. In February, Black Flight disbanded, and in March 1951 the ship sailed for Korean waters. During six months of operations the squadron flew 852 sorties which included bombing, RP attacks, strafing and bombardment target spotting. During this period three aircraft were lost and several others damaged by flak. On 27 September 1949 the ship arrived at Kure, and all squadron aircraft were handed over to HMAS *Sydney* for No.817 Squadron. The ship then sailed to Singapore and on to Australia, where the Air Group had a well-earned rest, a number of Firefly 6's being loaned from the Royal Australian Navy during this period. Returning to the war zone in January 1952, No.812 flew a further 689 sorties, of which 104 were carried out in one day. Leaving the area in May, the squadron transferred its aircraft to HMS *Ocean*, and the crews sailed home in HMS *Theseus* from Malta.

In June 1952, No.812 re-equipped with eight Firefly AS.6s at Anthorn, and in September these embarked in HMS *Eagle* for an exercise and a visit to Oslo. In January 1953 the squadron joined HMS *Theseus* for a Spring cruise, and returning to HMS *Eagle* in June participated in exercises off northern Scotland, after which it disbanded at Eglinton on 20 October 1953.

No.812 next reformed at Eglinton on 7 November 1955 as an anti-submarine squadron with eight Gannet AS.1s and a T.2. In April 1956 it sailed for the Mediterranean in HMS *Eagle*, taking part in Fleet visits and exercises before flying home from Malta to disband on arrival at Lee-on-Solent on 13 December 1956.

Identification Markings
Ripon, Baffin & Swordfish *60-65, 70-75, 81-83*; Swordfish *G3A+* from 5.39, to *3A+* by 10.40, also *A2A+* and *R2A+* in 1942; Barracuda *N1A+*, to *370-381/A* 10.45; Firefly *V4A+*, to *270-281/M:N* 3.46, later *287-298/T* from 10.46, to *200-211/O:R* 2.48; Gannet *440-447/J*, to *255, 260-267/J:GN* 1.56.

Aircraft Equipment	Period of Service	Example	
Ripon IIc	Apr 1933 - Jan 1934	S1265	(75)
Baffin	Jan 1934 - Dec 1936	K3554	(60)
Swordfish I	Dec 1936 - Dec 1942	K5979	(74)
Swordfish II	Oct 1942 - Dec 1942	HS215	(L)
Barracuda II	Jun 1944 - Jan 1946	PM837	(N1M)
Firefly FR.1	Jan 1946 - Aug 1946	MB458	(V4K)
	Oct 1946 - Feb 1948	MB749	(289/T)
Firefly NF.1	Jul 1948 - Feb 1951	PP555	(213/O)
Firefly FR.4	Feb 1948 - Jul 1948	VH127	(208)
Firefly 5	Jul 1948 - Sep 1951	WB410	(213/O)
Firefly T.1	Oct 1950 - Jan 1951	DK489	
Firefly AS.6	Oct 1951 - Jan 1952	WD930	
	Jun 1952 - Oct 1953	WB426	(212)
Gannet AS.1	Nov 1955 - Dec 1956	WN400	(260/J)
Gannet T.2	Nov 1955 - Mar 1956	XA520	(255/GN)

A Barracuda II of No.812 Squadron landing on HMS Vengeance on 23 December 1945. (via C.H. Wood)

Battle Honours
North Sea	1940
English Channel	1940-42
Mediterranean	1941
Malta Convoys	1941
Korea	1951-52

Squadron bases
HMS Glorious	3 Apr 1933
Hal Far	24 Apr 1933
HMS Glorious	31 May 1933
Hal Far	6 Jun 1933
HMS Glorious	26 Jun 1933
Aboukir	13 Sep 1933
HMS Glorious	23 Sep 1933
Hal Far	23 Oct 1933
HMS Glorious	20 Nov 1933
Hal Far	25 Jan 1934
HMS Glorious	2 Mar 1934
Hal Far	11 Apr 1934
HMS Furious	26 Jun 1934
Hal Far	15 Aug 1934
HMS Furious	28 Aug 1934
Hal Far	13 Oct 1934
HMS Eagle	11 Feb 1935
Hal Far	22 Mar 1935
HMS Glorious	2 Sep 1935
Aboukir	16 Sep 1935
HMS Glorious	18 Sep 1935
Aboukir	30 Nov 1935
HMS Glorious	16 Dec 1935
Hal Far	23 Dec 1935
HMS Glorious	1 Jan 1936
Aboukir	18 Jun 1936
HMS Glorious	23 Jul 1936
Hal Far	27 Jul 1936
HMS Glorious	29 Sep 1936
Hal Far	30 Oct 1936
HMS Glorious	23 Apr 1937
Gosport	5 May 1937
HMS Courageous (Dt3)	28-31 May 1937
HMS Glorious	23 Jun 1937
Hal Far	20 Jul 1937
HMS Glorious	23 Aug 1937
'B' Flight:	
HMS Malaya	15 Sep 1937
Absorbed by 701 Sq	4 Oct 1937
Hal Far (Dt4)	1-19 Oct 1937
Hal Far	19 Oct 1937
HMS Glorious	7 Feb 1938
Hal Far	28 Mar 1938
HMS Glorious	16 May 1938
Hal Far	31 May 1938
HMS Glorious	18 Jul 1938
Hal Far	25 Aug 1938
HMS Glorious	9 Sep 1938
Dekheila	22 Oct 1938
HMS Glorious	1 Nov 1938
Hal Far	9 Nov 1938
HMS Glorious	23 Jan 1939
Hal Far	20 Feb 1939
HMS Glorious	23 Feb 1939
Hal Far	20 Mar 1939
HMS Glorious	11 Apr 1939
Hal Far	12 Apr 1939
HMS Glorious	13 Apr 1939
Hal Far	18 Apr 1939
HMS Glorious	25 Apr 1939
Hal Far	14 May 1939
HMS Glorious	6 Jun 1939
Dekheila	19 Jun 1939
HMS Glorious (Dt6)	4 Jul 1939
to	4 Aug 1939
HMS Glorious	4 Aug 1939
Dekheila	15 Aug 1939
HMS Glorious	11 Sep 1939
Dekheila (Dt2)	24 Oct 1939
to	8 Nov 1939
Hal Far	17 Jan 1940
HMS Glorious (Dt6)	25 Mar 1940

Squadron bases
HMS Glorious	28 Mar 1940
Manston	18 Apr 1940
Prestwick	21 Apr 1940
Ford	24 Apr 1940
North Coates	11 May 1940
Bircham Newton	28 May 1940
North Coates	29 May 1940
Ford	15 Jun 1940
Bircham Newton	19 Jun 1940
North Coates	19 Jun 1940
Detling (Dt7)	27-28 Aug 1940
Thorney Island	11 Sep 1940
North Coates	27 Sep 1940
Thorney Island	1 Oct 1940
North Coates	10 Oct 1940
St Eval (Dt6)	2-10 Nov 1940
North Coates (Dt)	22 Nov 1940
to	8 Dec 1940
Thorney Island (Dt6)	8-10 Dec 1940
North Coates(Dt)	11-27 Dec 1940
St Eval (Dt6)	10-15 Dec 1940
Detling (Dt2)	27 Dec 1940
to	12 Mar 1941
Thorney Island (Dt6)	27 Dec 1940 to 12 Jan 1941
Crail (Dt3)	16 Jan 1941
to	2 Mar 1941
Topcliffe(transit)	18 Mar 1941
Campbeltown	19 Mar 1941
HMS Argus (Dt6)	10 Apr 1941
to	16 May 1941
Hatston by	21 Apr 1941
Twatt	25 Jun 1941
HMS Furious	16 Jul 1941
Hatston	12 Aug 1941
HMS Furious	24 Aug 1941
North Front	7 Sep 1941
HMS Ark Royal	10 Sep 1941
North Front	1 Oct 1941
HMS Ark Royal	10 Nov 1941
North Front	15 Nov 1941
HMS Argus	16 Nov 1941
North Front	27 Nov 1941
HMS Argus	27 Jan 1942
USS Wasp	21 Apr 1942
Machrihanish	25 Apr 1942
Lee-on-Solent	7 May 1942
Machrihanish	29 Jun 1942
Docking (16 Gp)	7 Sep 1942
Bircham Newton	9 Oct 1942
Hatston	3 Nov 1942
Squadron disbanded	18 Dec 1942
Stretton	1 Jun 1944
Crail	28 Jun 1944
Burscough	7 Sep 1944
Fearn	10 Nov 1944
Ballyhalbert	5 Jan 1945
HMS Vengeance	26 Jan 1945
Ayr (Dt5)	2-10 Feb 1945
Ayr	10 Feb 1945
HMS Vengeance	27 Feb 1945
Hal Far	20 Mar 1945
HMS Vengeance	23 Apr 1945
Katukurunda	8 Jun 1945
HMS Vengeance	4 Jul 1945
Jervis Bay	22 Jul 1945
HMS Vengeance	13 Aug 1945
Ponam (Dt6)	28-30 Aug 1945
Kai Tak	8 Oct 1945
HMS Vengeance	20 Dec 1945
Schofields	12 Jan 1946
HMS Vengence	19 Mar 1946
Katukurunda	7 Apr 1946
HMS Vengeance	15 Jul 1946
Lee-on-Solent	12 Aug 1946
Squadron disbanded	12 Aug 1946
Eglinton	1 Oct 1946
HMS Theseus	7 Feb 1947
Trincomalee	17 Mar 1947

Squadron bases		Squadron bases		Squadron bases		Commanding Officers	
HMS Theseus	29 Apr 1947	HMS Glory	11 Nov 1949	HMS Bulwark	13 Feb 1956	L/C NGR Crawford	
Butterworth	24 May 1947	Hal Far	28 Nov 1949	Eglinton	23 Feb 1956	RN	22 Apr 1940
HMS Theseus	28 May 1947	HMS Glory	19 Dec 1949	HMS Eagle	17 Apr 1956	L/C WE Waters	
Sembawang	10 Jun 1947	Hal Far	31 Mar 1950	Hal Far	30 Apr 1956	DFC RN	6 Sep 1940
HMS Theseus	21 Jun 1947	HMS Glory	12 May 1950	HMS Eagle	2 Jun 1956	L/C GAL Woods RN	16 Nov 1941
Point Cook	11 Jul 1947	Hal Far	6 Jun 1950	Hal Far	29 Jun 1956	L/C BJ Prendergast	
HMS Theseus	15 Jul 1947	HMS Glory	12 Jun 1950	HMS Eagle	17 Jul 1956	RN	30 May 1942
Kai Tak	20 Oct 1947	Hal Far	31 Jul 1950	Hal Far	3 Aug 1956	Squadron disbanded	18 Dec 1942
HMS Theseus	4 Nov 1947	HMS Glory	17 Aug 1950	HMS Bulwark	9 Dec 1956	L/C(A) CRJ Coxon	
Ford	20 Dec 1947	Hal Far	1 Oct 1950	Lee-on-Solent	13 Dec 1956	RN	5 Jun 1944
Donibristle	6 Apr 1948	HMS Glory	10 Oct 1950	Squadron disbanded	13 Dec 1956	L/C(A) DMR Wynne	
Ford	13 Apr 1948	Castel Benito	8 Nov 1950			-Roberts RN	25 Jan 1946
Eglinton	26 May 1948	HMS Glory	22 Nov 1950	**Commanding Officers**		Squadron disbanded	12 Aug 1946
HMS Ocean (DLP)	19 Aug 1948	Hal Far	2 Feb 1951	Flt Lt FE Vernon		L/C(A) DMR Roberts	
Culdrose	19 Aug 1948	HMS Glory	8 Mar 1951	RAF	3 Apr 1933	RN	1 Oct 1946
Belfast (transit)	24 Aug 1948	Nowra	12 Nov 1951	Sq Ldr GH Boyce		L/C FGB Sheffield	
HMS Ocean	24 Aug 1948	HMS Glory	10 Jan 1952	AFC RAF	12 Jun 1933	DSC RN	15 Jan 1948
Hal Far	14 Sep 1948	HMS Theseus	26 May 1952	L/C CAN Hooper		L/C RM Fell RN	6 Mar 1949
HMS Ocean	28 Sep 1948	Anthorn	4 Jun 1952	RN	15 Jan 1934	L/C RG Hunt RN	17 Jul 1950
Hal Far	9 Dec 1948	Lee-on-Solent	3 Jul 1952	Sq Ldr BB Caswell		L/C FA Swanton	
HMS Triumph (Dt)	3-6 Jan 1949	HMS Eagle	3 Sep 1952	RAF	29 Jan 1934	DSC RN	1 Mar 1951
HMS Ocean	10 Apr 1949	Eglinton	4 Oct 1952	L/C CAN Hooper		L/C JM Culbertson	
Hal Far	2 Jun 1949	Ford	17 Jan 1953	RN	11 Nov 1936	RN	18 Dec 1951
HMS Ocean	13 Jun 1949	HMS Theseus	21 Jan 1953	Sq Ldr NAP		Squadron disbanded	20 Oct 1953
Hal Far	20 Jun 1949	Eglinton	15 Mar 1953	Pritchett RAF	23 Nov 1936	L/C GD Luff DFC	
Castel Benito (Dt)	23-27 Jul 1949	HMS Eagle	29 Jun 1953	Sq Ldr JH		RN	7 Nov 1955
Culham	12 Sep 1949	Eglinton	16 Jul 1953	Hutchinson RAF	26 Apr 1937	Squadron disbanded	13 Dec 1956
transit	26 Sep 1949	HMS Eagle	4 Sep 1953	L/C JDC Little RN	1 Nov 1938		
Hal Far	28 Sep 1949	Eglinton	3 Oct 1953	(Sq Ldr RAF)			
Castel Benito (Dt6)	24 Oct 1949	Squadron disbanded	20 Oct 1953	L/C AS Bolt RN	16 Jun 1939		
to	9 Nov 1949	Eglinton	7 Nov 1955				

Fairey Firefly NF.1 PP470 '214/R' of Black Flight, No.812 Squadron, HMS Glory flying over Malta in 1950. (FAA Museum)

No.813 Squadron

Badge: On a white field, over water in base barry wavy blue and white an eagle displayed reversed black
Motto: Full sails

No.813 Squadron first formed at Gosport on 18 January 1937 as a torpedo spotter reconnaissance squadron with nine Swordfish I. The following month it joined HMS *Eagle* for service in the China Station, a few days being spent at Hal Far when passing through the Mediterranean. The squadron was mainly based at Seletar whilst ashore, then on the outbreak of war the ship sailed to undertake convoy duty and search for enemy raiders in the Indian Ocean, based on Ceylon. She returned to Singapore in March 1940, but after a refit sailed for the Mediterranean, where four Sea Gladiators were added to the squadron strength in June.

The Gladiators quickly opened their score by destroying two Italian bombers, several more being shot down over the next few months. The Swordfish were equally successful, and in a shore based attack on Tobruk on 5 July they sank a destroyer and a merchant ship, and damaged another destroyer and two merchant ships. Three days later a further destroyer was sunk in a ship-based attack on Port Augusta in Sicily, and the squadron participated in numerous actions during the remainder of 1940. These included the successful attack on the Italian Fleet at Taranto on 11 November, in which four squadron aircraft operated from HMS *Illustrious*.

In March 1941 the Sea Gladiators were withdrawn, and No.813 was sent with No.824 Squadron to Port Sudan to cover local troop activities. Whilst there it disposed of five Italian destroyers sighted north of Massawa, two being sunk, two beached and the other later scuttled. Rejoining the carrier, No.813 sailed via Capetown for a period in the Atlantic. Here it found and sank the U-boat supply ship *Elbe* on 6 June, and then forced the tanker *Lothringen* to surrender. In October the squadron returned home for the first time in nearly five years to re-equip with nine new Swordfish Is and two Sea Hurricane Ib's. Two Buffaloes were also used briefly in December.

In January 1942 No.813 re-embarked and sailed with HMS *Eagle* for Gibraltar and the Mediterranean, taking part in several operations to deliver RAF Spitfires to Malta. The squadron reduced temporarily to six aircraft, and was fortunately ashore at Gibraltar when HMS *Eagle* was sunk on 11 August 1942, though the Sea Hurricanes, now four in number, were lost.

Increased to 12 aircraft on 22 August, the squadron carried out anti-submarine patrols from Gibraltar and was in action during the North African landings, part of the squadron moving to Algeria for a time. In November the squadron re-equipped with 12 Swordfish IIs, operating entirely from North Africa until part of the squadron returned to Gibraltar in March 1943. In October 1943 it took passage to the United Kingdom, disbanding on arrival on 18 October 1943.

No.813 reformed at Donibristle on 1 November with 9 new Swordfish II. In March 1944, 3 Fulmars night fighters were attached from No.784 Squadron, and these embarked with the Swordfish in HMS *Campania* in April for Atlantic and North Russian convoy escort. Also added to the squadron at this time was a flight of 4 Wildcat Vs, formerly 'F' flight of 1832 Squadron. On 30 September the Swordfish succeeded in sinking the U-boat *U-921*, and this was followed on 13 December by a similar success with *U-365*. In addition, 4 enemy aircraft were shot down by the Wildcats.

In January 1945 part of the squadron re-embarked for anti-submarine operations during a sweep off the Norwegian coast, cover being also provided for an attack on shore targets. From June 1944 the squadron had begun to receive Swordfish IIIs, some fitted with Sonar Buoy equipment, and by March 1945 it had a full complement of 12 fitted with this. New Wildcat VIs began to replace the Vs in September 1944, and eight of the two versions were on strength by November 1944. The Fulmars were withdrawn in March 1945. In April the squadron embarked in HMS *Vindex* for a final North Russian convoy, and on return it disbanded on 15 May 1945.

No.813 next reformed on 1 September 1945 out of No.708 Squadron at Ford as a torpedo fighter squadron with 15 Firebrand TF.IV's. Due to serviceability problems, three were withdrawn two months later. The squadron disbanded on 30 September 1946.

More successful were the 12 Firebrand TF.5s with which the squadron reformed at Ford on 1 May 1947. These too gave initial problems, and the squadron was only able to undertake short periods afloat in HMS *Illustrious* and HMS *Implacable* during the next 18 months. Eventually the aircraft were able to join HMS *Implacable* in January 1949 as part of the 1st Carrier Air Group, participating in several cruises and exercises before transferring to HMS *Indomitable* two years later. From December 1951 the squadron was again shore-based, though comparatively little flying took place.

In February 1953 No.813 moved to Ford, and here it began to re-equip in May with 12 Wyvern S.4s. The last of the Firebrands departed in August, but teething troubles were again experienced, and it was not until September 1954 that the new aircraft were able to join HMS *Albion* for a spell in the Mediterranean. The squadron sailed home again in March 1955, to join HMS *Eagle* in June for visits to the Mediterranean and Norway before disbanding on arrival at Devonport on 21 November 1955.

Wyvern S.4s were again the equipment when the squadron reformed with 9 aircraft at Ford on 26 November 1956. Embarking in HMS *Eagle* in August 1957, exercises were undertaken, including a spell in the Mediterranean in early 1958, but on 22 April 1958 the squadron disbanded at Ford.

Battle Honours
Calabria	1940
Mediterranean	1940-41
Taranto	1940
Libya	1940-41
Malta Convoys	1942
Atlantic	1942-44
Arctic	1944-45

Identification Markings
Swordfish *580-590*, to *E4A+* 13.7.39, later to *4A+*, single letters by 8.43, to *G:A* on *Campania* by 9.44; Sea Gladiator *6A+*; Wildcat *Z:1-Z:8* on *Campania* then single letters on *Vindex*; Firebrand TF.4 *FD1A+*, TF.5 *100-123/FD:C:A*; Wyvern *181-192/Z*, to *121-129/J* 5.55, *300 & 301/J* briefly 11.56, then *270-279/J:E*.

Aircraft Equipment	Period of Service	Example	
Swordfish I	Jan 1937 - Mar 1943	P4159	(E4G)
Sea Gladiator	Jun 1940 - Mar 1941	N5517	
Buffalo I	Dec 1941 - Dec 1941		
Sea Hurricane Ib	Jan 1942 - Aug 1942	Z4937	
Swordfish II	Nov 1942 - Sep 1943	HS212	(4C)
	Nov 1943 - Jul 1944	LS394	
Swordfish III	Jun 1944 - May 1945	NR993	(GP)
Wildcat V	Apr 1944 - Feb 1945	JV573	(Z7)
Wildcat VI	Sep 1944 - May 1945	JV755	(Z2)
Firebrand TF.IV	Sep 1945 - Sep 1946	EK729	(FD1N)
Firebrand TF.5	Apr 1947 - Aug 1953	EK768	(111/C)
Firefly FR.1	May 1952 - Aug 1953	PP392	(292/J)
Meteor T.7	Mar 1953 - Dec 1953	WS103	
Wyvern S.4	May 1953 - Nov 1955	VX780	(121/J)
	Nov 1956 - Apr 1958	VZ790	(301/J)

Fairey Swordfish '4A' of No.813 Squadron from Gibraltar over Curnero Point in 1942. (Cdr F.W.Baring)

Squadron bases		Squadron bases		Squadron bases		Squadron bases	
Gosport	18 Jan 1937	Kai Tak	17 Nov 1938	HMS Eagle	19 Apr 1941	HMS Vindex	8 Apr 1945
HMS Eagle	23 Feb 1937	HMS Eagle	5 Dec 1938	Machrihanish	26 Oct 1941	Wildcat Flight:	
Hal Far	6 Mar 1937	Kai Tak	7 Dec 1938	Lee-on-Solent	28 Oct 1941	HMS Campania	
HMS Eagle	12 Mar 1937	HMS Eagle	12 Mar 1939	Machrihanish	6 Dec 1941	Eglinton	22 Apr 1944
Seletar	9 Apr 1937	Seletar	17 Mar 1939	HMS Eagle	20 Jan 1942	HMS Campania	26 Apr 1944
HMS Eagle	30 Apr 1937	HMS Eagle	4 Apr 1939	North Front	8 Mar 1942	Eglinton	6 Sep 1944
Kai Tak	6 May 1937	Seletar	24 Apr 1939	HMS Eagle	17 May 1942	HMS Campania	12 Sep 1944
HMS Eagle	28 May 1937	HMS Eagle	19 May 1939	North Front	16 Jun 1942	Hatston	2 Dec 1944
Wei-Hai-Wei (Dt)	3 Jun 1937	Kai Tak	25 May 1939	Tafaroui (Dt6)	10 Nov 1942	HMS Campania	21 Jan 1945
to	22 Jul 1937	HMS Eagle	29 May 1939	to	13 Nov 1942	Hatston	24 Feb 1945
Wei-Hai-Wei (Dt)	6 Sep 1937	Wei-Hai-Wei (Dt)	3 Jun 1939	Blida (Dt6)	13 Nov 1942	Machrihanish	20 Mar 1945
to	7 Oct 1937	to	26 Jul 1939	to	6 Mar 1943	HMS Vindex	8 Apr 1945
Kai Tak	19 Oct 1937	Kai Tak	31 Jul 1939	Bone (Dt6)	12 Dec 1942	Hatston (Dt4)	8 Apr 1945
HMS Eagle	4 Nov 1937	HMS Eagle	12 Aug 1939	to	5 Mar 1943	Grimsetter (Dt4)	18 Apr 1945
Kai Tak	5 Nov 1937	Seletar	18 Aug 1939	HMS Hunter (Dt)	28 Mar 1943	Squadron disbanded	15 May 1945
HMS Eagle	30 Nov 1937	HMS Eagle	28 Aug 1939	to	11 Apr 1943	Ford	1 Sep 1945
Kai Tak	1 Dec 1937	Seletar	1 Nov 1939	Tafaroui (Dt6)	8 May 1943	Squadron disbanded	30 Sep 1946
HMS Eagle	8 Jan 1938	HMS Eagle	8 Nov 1939	to	10 Jul 1943	Ford	1 May 1947
Seletar	14 Jan 1938	Kallang	16 Mar 1940	HMS Illustrious/		St Merryn	8 Sep 1947
HMS Eagle	31 Jan 1938	Sembawang	17 Mar 1940	SS Lancashire		Ford	15 Sep 1947
Seletar	5 Feb 1938	HMS Eagle	8 May 1940	(no a/c)	4 Oct 1943	HMS Illustrious	22 Sep 1947
HMS Eagle	26 Feb 1938	Dekheila	4 Sep 1940	Sqdn disbanded UK	18 Oct 1943	(DLT)	
Penang	4 Mar 1938	HMS Illustrious (Dt4)		Donibristle	1 Nov 1943	Ford	24 Sep 1947
HMS Eagle	7 Mar 1938		6-13 Sep 1940	Dunino	13 Dec 1943	HMS Implacable	14 Oct 1947
Seletar	9 Mar 1938	Maaten Bagush	17-29 Sep 1940	Inskip	20 Jan 1944	Lossiemouth	11 Dec 1947
HMS Eagle	16 Mar 1938	(Dt3)		Burscough	15 Feb 1944	(transit)	
Kai Tak	14 Apr 1938	HMS Eagle	23 Sep 1940	Machrihanish	26 Feb 1944	Culdrose	15 Dec 1947
HMS Eagle	4 Jun 1938	Dekheila	29 Sep 1940	Maydown	26 Mar 1944	HMS Implacable	5 Mar 1948
Wei-Hai-Wei (Dt)	12-19 Jul 1938	HMS Illustrious	6-13 Nov 1940	HMS Campania	26 Apr 1944	Culdrose	20 Mar 1948
Wei-Hai-Wei (Dt)	27 Jul 1938	(Dt4)		Abbotsinch (Dt3)	21 Jul 1944	Arbroath	26 Apr 1948
to	3 Aug 1938	HMS Eagle	16 Nov 1940	to	3 Aug 1944	Anthorn	21 May 1948
Seletar	17 Sep 1938	Dekheila	29 Nov 1940	Belfast	18 Aug 1944	Bramcote	9 Jun 1948
HMS Eagle	27 Sep 1938	Fuka (Dt3)	3-20 Dec 1940	Machrihanish(Dt)	5-11 Nov 1944	Anthorn	12 Jun 1948
Wei-Hai-Wei (Dt)	8-10 Oct 1938	Fuka (Dt6)	5-9 Jan 1941	Machrihanish	11 Nov 1944	Culdrose	23 Oct 1948
Kai Tak	19 Oct 1938	HMS Eagle	11 Jan 1941	Burscough	20 Nov 1944	HMS Implacable	27 Jan 1949
HMS Eagle	1 Nov 1938	Dekheila	14 Feb 1941	HMS Campania	30 Nov 1944	Lee-on-Solent	25 Mar 1949
Kai Tak	3 Nov 1938	transit	25 Mar 1941	Hatston (Dt6)	19-24 Jan 1945	HMS Implacable	3 May 1949
HMS Eagle	15 Nov 1938	Port Sudan	28 Mar 1941	Machrihanish	1 Mar 1945	Lee-on-Solent	7 Jul 1949

Blackburn Firebrand TF.5 EK632 of No.813 Squadron, HMS Implacable at Eglinton in 1948. (Tony Hughes)

Westland Wyvern S.4s of No.813 Squadron in line abreast in 1953. (RAF Museum 6519-6)

Squadron bases
HMS Implacable	5 Sep 1949
Lee-on-Solent	11 Nov 1949
HMS Implacable	24 Jan 1950
Lee-on-Solent	31 Mar 1950
Bramcote	9 Jun 1950
Eglinton	10 Jun 1950
Culham	14 Jun 1950
Lee-on-Solent	15 Jun 1950
Lossiemouth	30 Jun 1950
HMS Implacable	3 Jul 1950
Lee-on-Solent	26 Jul 1950
Celle	21 Sep 1950
Lee-on-Solent	1 Oct 1950
Topcliffe	6 Oct 1950
Lee-on-Solent	15 Oct 1950
HMS Indomitable	24 Nov 1950
Lee-on-Solent	8 Dec 1950
HMS Indomitable	16 Jan 1951
Lee-on-Solent	14 Mar 1951
HMS Indomitable	25 Apr 1951
Arbroath	14 May 1951

Squadron bases
HMS Indomitable	26 May 1951
Stretton	25 Jul 1951
Lee-on-Solent	27 Jul 1951
HMS Indomitable	7 Sep 1951
Lee-on-Solent	6 Dec 1951
Ford	18 Feb 1953
HMS Albion	24 Sep 1954
Hal Far	16 Oct 1954
Karouba	9 Mar 1955
HMS Albion	22 Mar 1955
Ford	31 Mar 1955
HMS Eagle	4 Jun 1955
Hal Far (Dt4)	24 Jun 1955
	to 18 Jul 1955
North Front(Dt2)	23-24 Aug 1955
Ford	17 Nov 1955
Squadron disbanded	21 Nov 1955
Ford	26 Nov 1956
'X' Flight:	
Ford	18 Feb 1957
Brawdy	18 Mar 1957

Squadron bases
Ford	5 Apr 1957
Brawdy	20 Mar 1957
HMS Eagle	5 Aug 1957
Ford	30 Sep 1957
HMS Eagle	17 Oct 1957
Ford	27 Nov 1957
HMS Eagle	29 Jan 1958
Ford	22 Apr 1958
Squadron disbanded	22 Apr 1958

Commanding Officers
L/C CRV Pugh RN (Sq Ldr RAF)	18 Jan 1937
L/C N Kennedy DSC RN (Sq Ldr RAF)	1 Sep 1938
L/C DH Elles RN	9 Jan 1941
L/C AV Lyle RN	25 Nov 1941
L/C C Hutchinson RN	25 Mar 1942
L/C DAP Weatherall RN	Feb 1943
Lt JH Ree RN	27 Jun 1943
L/C DAP Weatherall RN	1 Aug 1943
Squadron disbanded	18 Oct 1943
L/C(A) JR Parish DSC RNVR	1 Nov 1943
L/C(A) CA Allen RNVR	2 Sep 1944
L/C(A) SG Cooke RNVR	12 Oct 1944
Squadron disbanded	15 May 1945
L/C K Lee-White RN	1 Sep 1945
Lt(A) W Orr RN (temp)	27 Aug 1946
Squadron disbanded	30 Sep 1946
L/C(A) AWR Turney RN	1 May 1947
L/C(A) CRJ Coxon RN	22 Oct 1947
L/C CK Roberts RN	1 Sep 1948
L/C JM Henry RN	5 Apr 1949
L/C DRS Abbott RN	21 Aug 1950
L/C JS Barnes RN	1 Oct 1950
L/C LWA Barrington RN	19 Mar 1951
L/C AD Corkhill DSC RN	12 Feb 1952
L/C SS Laurie RN	3 Mar 1953
L/C CE Price AFC RN	18 May 1953
L/C RM Crossley DSC & Bar RN	15 Dec 1954
Squadron disbanded	21 Nov 1955
L/C RW Halliday AFC RN	26 Nov 1956
L/C RWT Abraham RN	9 Dec 1957
Squadron disbanded	22 Apr 1958

Westland Wyvern S.4 VZ765 '270/E' of No.813 Squadron landing on HMS Eagle in 1957. (Mrs Castellano via John Hamlin)

No.814 Squadron

Badge: 2. On a blue field, base barry wavy of two white and blue, a tiger's mask proper winged white

Motto: In hoc signo vinces
(In this sign you will conquer)

No.814 Squadron first formed at Southampton on 1 December 1938 as a torpedo spotter reconnaissance unit with 6 Swordfish I. It embarked in HMS *Ark Royal* in January 1939, but transferred to HMS *Hermes* on the outbreak of war, with an increased complement of 9 aircraft. In October the ship sailed for West Africa, to join French ships operating out of Dakar and Freetown, an unsuccessful search being made for the German battleship *Graf Spee*. After the French surrender the squadron had the unhappy task of attacking the former Allies, considerable damage being caused to the battleship *Richelieu* at Dakar on 8 July 1940.

In December 1940 HMS *Hermes* sailed for the Indian Ocean, to undertake searches and convoy protection off East Africa. Support was provided in February 1941 for advancing land forces in British Somaliland, squadron aircraft enabling the capture of 5 enemy merchant ship by the cruiser HMS *Hawkins*, another being bombed when it failed to surrender. In May support was given to the RAF in Iraq, following which No.814 re-embarked for further trade protection duties in the Indian Ocean, disembarking to Ceylon in November 1941. Re-embarking in February 1942 to help search for a Japanese carrier force, No.814 was ashore on 5 April when HMS *Hermes* was sunk by Japanese aircraft four days later. It remained ashore on patrol duty and other tasks until being disbanded at Katukurunda on 31 December 1942.

No.814 reformed at Stretton on 1 July 1944 as a torpedo bomber reconnaissance unit with 16 Barracuda IIs, increasing to 18 at the end of the year. In March 1945 these embarked in HMS *Venerable*, and after working up in the Mediterranean sailed for the Far East, where the squadron reduced to 12 aircraft in June 1945, becoming part of the 15th Carrier Air Group. It saw no action in that theatre before the Japanese surrender. In December 1945 it began to re-equip with 12 Firefly FR.1s at Schofields, and re-embarked with these in March 1946. After further service in the Far East it returned home and disembarked to Eglinton in March 1947.

In September 1947 the squadron re-embarked for the Mediterranean, remaining ashore at Ta Kali from November 1947 until March 1948 when it took passage home, leaving its aircraft behind. In April eight Firefly FR.4s were received at Eglinton, and these embarked in HMS *Vengeance* in August, a visit being made to South Africa before returning home for Christmas. In the New Year the ship sailed for the Arctic Circle for cold weather trials. The first Mk.5s were received around this time, the squadron being completely re-equipped by the time it re-embarked in September. In early 1950 it spent 2 months in the Mediterranean, and in July paid a visit to Norway. In September the squadron re-embarked in HMS *Vengeance*, but on 19 November 1950 it disbanded at Culdrose.

No.814 reformed on 22 November 1950 at Culdrose, using Firefly FR.1s until its eight Firefly AS.6s arrived at the end of January 1951. With No.809 Squadron formed the 7th Night Air Group, this being the first all-weather group. It embarked in HMS *Vengeance* for work-up in May 1951, for its work with the Group, during which it completed 927 hours of night training, it received the annual award of the Boyd Trophy. It transferred to the 15th CAG in HMS *Theseus* in September, but after this was disbanded in January 1952 the squadron was shore based until embarking in HMS *Eagle* in June 1952, making two trips to the Arctic before the end of that year. 1953 was spent mainly on exercises, first in the Mediterranean and the remainder in Home Waters. On 15 March 1954 it re-equipped with eight Avenger AS.5s, which flew out to Malta in February 1955, embarking there in HMS *Centaur*. Returning later to Home waters, the squadron disbanded on 4 November 1955, its aircraft going into store at Abbotsinch.

On 14 January 1957, No.814 reformed at Culdrose as an anti-submarine unit with 8 Gannet AS.4s, embarking in HMS *Eagle* in August to take part in an exercise in Norwegian waters the following month. A trip to the Mediterranean was made in January 1958 and another in July, following which the squadron returned

Fairey Swordfish I of No.814 Squadron flying near HMS Ark Royal in 1939. (RAF Museum)

Fairey Swordfish I L2811 'F' and L9723 'H' of No.814 Squadron, believed at Ouakam, early in 1940. (Cdr J.H.Dundas)

home at the end of the year. After a further Mediterranean exercise early in 1959, followed by a visit to Brest, the squadron disembarked to Culdrose, where it disbanded on 30 September 1959.

No.814 became a helicopter squadron for the first time when it next reformed, at Culdrose on 1 April 1960 with eight Whirlwind HAS.7s for anti-submarine duties, being commissioned on 2 May. Embarking in HMS *Hermes* in July for an exercise with the US 6th Fleet, this was followed in September by a NATO exercise in Home waters. The next commission took it to the Far East in December 1960, returning home in April 1961, to disband at Culdrose on 14 September 1961.

Eight Wessex HAS.1s were the equipment when the squadron next reformed, at Culdrose on 28 November 1961, embarking in HMS *Hermes* in May 1962 for the Mediterranean. After returning home in October, it re-embarked the following month for the Far East, spending a brief period in HMAS *Melbourne* in April 1963 before transferring from HMS *Hermes* to HMS *Victorious* in August. Early in 1964 the aircraft were fitted out for Commando use, transferring in February to HMS *Albion* in readiness for possible use in East Africa, but this proved unnecessary and the aircraft returned to HMS *Victorious* and reconverted to the A/S role. After further service in the Far East, the squadron eventually returned home in July 1965. A year later it re-embarked for a further period in the Far East, returning home in June 1967.

In August 1967 the first Wessex HAS.3s arrived, and in October the squadron regrouped with six aircraft around a nucleus of No.700H Flight. Two of these embarked in RFA *Olwen* in November for exercises at Gibraltar, where they transferred to RFA *Tidepool*. In February 1968, three aircraft joined RFA *Olmeda* for exercises, and the next month four machines similarly embarked in RFA *Engadine*. From May 1968 the whole squadron was embarked in HMS *Hermes*, which in July sailed for the Far East, making a visit to Australia in September. For that year's activities No.814 received the annual Boyd Trophy Award. The journey home in February and March 1969 was made via Fremantle and Capetown, after which further voyages were made in HMS *Hermes* as well as various Royal Fleet Auxiliaries, before disbanding at Culdrose on 14 July 1970.

No.814 reformed at Prestwick on 30 March 1973 in the anti-submarine and commando role, with four Sea King HAS.1s. These embarked in HMS *Hermes* in August, and in 1974 the squadron was awarded the Australia Shield. In July 1975 a few weeks were spent in HMS *Tiger*, but it returned to HMS *Hermes* in September. In November 1977, Sea King HAS.2s were received, with which the strength gradually increased to ten, partial re-equipment with HAS.2A's taking place in 1979.

The squadron transferred to HMS *Bulwark* in January 1980, making a visit to the United States, followed by further periods in Home waters, until becoming mainly shore based in March 1981. At the time of the Falklands dispute, the squadron was preparing to re-equip with Sea King HAS.5s, and these embarked in HMS *Illustrious* in August 1982 for a spell in the South Atlantic. Returning home in December, it embarked in HMS *Hermes* with nine aircraft in January 1983. After a trip to the USA it returned home, re-embarking in HMS *Illustrious* in September 1983.

No.814 Squadron operated from HMS *Illustrious* until 1989, deploying to Westlant in autumn 1985, around the world on Exercise *Global 86* between July and December 1986, a Mediterranean cruise in the spring of 1988 and again to Westlant in the late autumn of 1988. The squadron transferred to HMS *Invincible* in June 1989, deploying back to Westlant between October 1989 to and February 1990. Operating mainly in home waters during 1991 they deployed to the Far East on Exercise *Orient 92* from May to November 1992. The Squadron converted to Sea King Mk.6s with improved Sonar processing equipment in 1992. However, with the change in world politics the emphasis of tasking has changed from passive ASW towards active ASW and the utility role. After a workup in home waters during the first half of 1993, *Invincible* relieved *Ark Royal* on patrol in the Adriatic from August, two aircraft being detached to RFA *Fort Grange* where the sonar equipment was removed to improve internal load carrying capability. The Squadron returned to the UK in February 1994, and deployed to the Adriatic again until March 1995.

Battle Honours
Atlantic   1940

Identification Markings
Swordfish *701-710*, to *A3A+* 5.39, to *H3A+* 9.39; Barracuda single letters, to *B1A+* 2.45, to *R1A+* 6.45, to *370-381/B* 7.43; Firefly *270-281/T:N*, to *285/V-296/V* 11.46, to *200-211/Q* 9.47, to *213-224/Q:T* 1952, to *255-263/J:GN* 7.52; Avenger *381-388/GN:C*; Gannet *280-287/J:E:CU*; Whirlwind *281-288/H*; Wessex *340-347/H:V*, to *270-277/V:H* 6.54; Sea King *264-275/H:B:N*.

Aircraft Equipment	Period of Service	Example
Swordfish I	Dec 1938 - Dec 1942	L9775 (705)
Barracuda II	Jul 1944 - Jul 1945	PM714 (B1H)
	Jul 1945 - Jan 1946	PM832
Firefly FR.1	Dec 1945 - Apr 1948	MB632 (281/T)
Firefly FR.4	Apr 1948 - Aug 1949	TW724 (218/Q)
Firefly 5	Feb 1949 - Nov 1950	WB256 (219/Q)
Firefly FR.1	Nov 1950 - Jul 1951	MB735
Firefly AS.6	Jan 1951 - Mar 1954	WH629 (261/J)
Avenger AS.4	Mar 1954 - May 1954	XB306
Avenger AS.5	Mar 1954 - Nov 1955	XB380 (388/C)
Gannet AS.4	Jan 1957 - Sep 1959	XG793 (282/CU)
Gannet T.2	Jan 1957 - Feb 1957	XG879
Whirlwind HAS.7	Apr 1960 - Sep 1961	XN308 (287/H)
Wessex HAS.1	Nov 1961 - Oct 1967	XM926 (276/V)
Wessex HAS.3	Aug 1967 - Jul 1970	XP147 (274/H)
Sea King HAS.1	Mar 1973 - Dec 1977	XV700 (272/H)
Sea King HAS.2/2a	Nov 1977 - Jun 1982	XV713 (267/H)
Sea King HAS.5	Jun 1982 - Oct 1992	ZA167 (273/H)
Sea King HAS.6	Oct 1992 - to date	XZ580 (267/N)

Fairey Firefly FR.1 DV117 '286/V' of No.814 Squadron near the edge of HMS Venerable's flight deck in late 1946. (via Peter Arnold)

Grumman Avenger TBM-3E XB443 '384/C' of No.814 Squadron, HMS Centaur in 1955. (John Rawlings)

Squadron bases		Squadron bases		Squadron bases		Squadron bases	
Southampton	1 Dec 1938	Shaibah	4 May 1941	Trincomalee	29 Oct 1945	HMS Vengeance	18 May 1950
HMS Ark Royal	11 Jan 1939	HMS Hermes	31 May 1941	HMS Venerable	13 Dec 1945	Donibristle	17 Jun 1950
Southampton	24 Mar 1939	Ratmalana	13 Jun 1941	Nowra	31 Dec 1945	HMS Vengeance	4 Jul 1950
Warmwell	2 Jun 1939	China Bay	18 Jun 1941	Schofields	22 Jan 1946	Culdrose	27 Jul 1950
Worthy Down	29 Jun 1939	HMS Hermes	1 Jul 1941	HMS Venerable	13 Mar 1946	HMS Vengeance	9 Sep 1950
HMS Ark Royal	29 Jul 1939	Port Reitz (Dt5)	9-14 Oct 1941	Katukurunda	26 Apr 1946	Culdrose	15 Nov 1950
Roborough	28 Aug 1939	Nairobi (Dt5)	14-15 Oct 1941	Trincomalee	27 May 1946	Squadron disbanded	19 Nov 1950
HMS Hermes	1 Sep 1939	Port Reitz	15 Oct 1941	HMS Venerable	28 May 1946	Culdrose	22 Nov 1950
Roborough	20 Sep 1939	HMS Hermes	19 Oct 1941	Trincomalee	1 Jun 1946	HMS Vengeance	10 May 1951
HMS Hermes	3 Oct 1939	Ratmalana	2 Nov 1941	HMS Venerable		Culdrose	26 Jun 1951
Hastings	29 Oct 1939	China Bay	9 Nov 1941	(Dt)	3-30 Jun 1946	HMS Illustrious	
HMS Hermes	7 Nov 1939	HMS Hermes	19 Feb 1942	HMS Venerable	20 Sep 1946	(Dt4 - DLP)	5-6 Sep 1951
Worthy Down	9 Jan 1940	China Bay	25 Feb 1942	Sembawang	26 Oct 1946	HMS Theseus	1 Oct 1951
Roborough	25 Jan 1940	Kokkolei	9 Apr 1942	HMS Venerable	14 Nov 1946	Culdrose	5 Dec 1951
HMS Hermes	10 Feb 1940	China Bay	13 Apr 1942	Kai Tak	27 Nov 1946	Eglinton	15 Jan 1952
Ouakam	19 Feb 1940	Colombo Racecourse		HMS Venerable	2 Jan 1947	Machrihanish	25 Mar 1952
HMS Hermes	27 Feb 1940	(Dt6)	3-5 Aug 1942	HMS Glory	14 Feb 1947	Lee-on-Solent	6 May 1952
Ouakam (Dt)	5-9 Mar 1940	Katukurunda	6 Nov 1942	Eglinton	26 Mar 1947	Ford	8 May 1952
Ouakam	27 Mar 1940	Squadron disbanded	31 Dec 1942	HMS Vengeance	23 Sep 1947	Machrihanish	14 May 1952
HMS Hermes	24 Apr 1940	Stretton	1 Jul 1944	Hal Far	11 Nov 1947	HMS Eagle	9 Jun 1952
Ouakam	18 May 1940	Arbroath (transit)	8 Aug 1944	SS Otranto(no a/c)	16 Mar 1948	Machrihanish	3 Jul 1952
HMS Hermes	28 May 1940	Hatston	9 Aug 1944	Lee-on-Solent	8 Apr 1948	Lee-on-Solent	2 Sep 1952
Ouakam (Dt)	20-26 Jun 1940	Fearn	8 Nov 1944	Eglinton	10 May 1948	transit	3 Sep 1952
'X' Flight:		Machrihanish	29 Nov 1944	HMS Vengeance	16 Aug 1948	HMS Eagle	6 Sep 1952
Young's Field	17 Aug 1940	Fearn	13 Jan 1945	Lossiemouth	13 Sep 1948	Lossiemouth	4 Oct 1952
HMS Hermes	18 Nov 1940	Machrihanish	28 Jan 1945	HMS Vengeance	14 Sep 1948	HMS Eagle	20 Oct 1952
Wellington	29 Nov 1940	HMS Venerable	8 Mar 1945	Brooklyn	18 Oct 1948	Lee-on-Solent	4 Dec 1952
'Y' Flight:		Hal Far	20 Mar 1945	HMS Vengeance	1 Nov 1948	HMS Eagle	27 Jan 1953
Wellington	15 Jul 1940	HMS Venerable	15 Apr 1945	Yeovilton	12 Dec 1948	Lee-on-Solent	26 Mar 1953
HMS Ark Royal	21 Sep 1940	Hal Far	21 Apr 1945	HMS Vengeance	28 Jan 1949	Eglinton (Dt4)	28 Apr 1953
Wellington	29 Sep 1940	HMS Venerable	21 May 1945	Culdrose	9 Mar 1949	to	22 May 1953
HMS Hermes	2 Dec 1940	Katukurunda	7 Jun 1945	HMS Vengeance	12 Sep 1949	HMS Eagle	16 Jun 1953
Wynberg (Dt8)	5-16 Jan 1941	HMS Venerable	5 Jul 1945	Eglinton	6 Oct 1949	Lee-on-Solent	23 Jul 1953
Stamford Hill	20-29 Jan 1941	Schofields	21 Jul 1945	HMS Vengeance	31 Oct 1949	HMS Eagle	2 Sep 1953
(Dt3)		HMS Venerable	13 Aug 1945	Culdrose	11 Nov 1949	Lossiemouth (Dt4)	7-20 Oct 1953
China Bay	9 Mar 1941	Kai Tak	3 Sep 1945	HMS Vengeance	24 Jan 1950	Lee-on-Solent	30 Nov 1953
HMS Hermes	16 Mar 1941	HMS Venerable	13 Oct 1945	Culdrose	31 Mar 1950	Eglinton	26 Jan 1954

Squadron bases		Squadron bases		Squadron bases		Squadron bases		Squadron bases	
Hal Far	7 Feb 1955	Culdrose	15 Oct 1960	HMS Albion	9 Feb 1964	RFA Tidespring (Dt3)/			
HMS Centaur	14 Feb 1955	HMS Hermes	7 Nov 1960	HMS Victorious	22 Feb 1964	RFA Tidepool(Dt2)			
Hal Far	7 Apr 1955	North Front	15 Nov 1960	Sembawang	23 Mar 1964		16-28 Oct 1966		
HMS Centaur	26 Apr 1955	HMS Hermes	29 Nov 1960	HMS Victorious	8 Apr 1964	RFA Olynthus (Dt4)	25 Nov 1966		
Lee-on-Solent	6 Jun 1955	Sembawang	31 Dec 1960	RFA Tidespring	19-22 May 1964		to 2 Dec 1966		
HMS Centaur	30 Aug 1955	HMS Hermes	12 Jan 1961	(Dt2)		Sembawang	9 Dec 1966		
Sqdn disbanded UK	4 Nov 1955	Sembawang	7 Feb 1961	Sembawang	12 Jun 1964	Sembawang(Dt2)	10-16 Dec 1966		
Culdrose	14 Jan 1957	HMS Hermes	18 Feb 1961	RFA Tidespring		HMS Victorious	10 Jan 1967		
HMS Eagle	5 Aug 1957	Hal Far	27 Mar 1961	(Dt2)	30 Jul 1964	RFA Olynthus (Dt4)	30 Jan 1967		
Culdrose	30 Sep 1957	HMS Hermes	6 Apr 1961	HMS Victorious	17 Aug 1964		to 3 Feb 1967		
HMS Eagle	12 Oct 1957	Culdrose	18 Apr 1961	Sembawang	23 Sep 1964	RFA Olynthus			
Eglinton	23 Nov 1957	HMS Hermes	10 Jun 1961	Labis (Dt)	26 Sep 1964	(Dt4)	6-15 Feb 1967		
HMS Eagle	28 Jan 1958	Portland	8 Aug 1961		to 31 Oct 1964	Sembawang	15 Feb 1967		
Eglinton	31 Mar 1958	HMS Hermes	8 Aug 1961	HMS Victorious	21 Nov 1964	HMS Victorious	6 Mar 1967		
HMS Eagle	20 May 1958	(Dt2-SAR)	to 11 Sep 1961	Sembawang	1 Mar 1965	Cubi Point (Dt3)	13-20 Apr 1967		
Hal Far	26 Aug 1958	Culdrose	14 Aug 1961	HMS Victorious	14 Mar 1965	Sembawang	24 Apr 1967		
HMS Eagle	29 Sep 1958	Squadron disbanded	14 Sep 1961	Culdrose	26 Jul 1965	HMS Victorious	2 May 1967		
Hal Far (Dt4)	3-14 Oct 1958	Culdrose	28 Nov 1961	Ballykelly (Dt3)	4 Aug 1965	Culdrose	19 Jun 1967		
Hal Far	31 Oct 1958	Portland (Dt6)	6 Mar 1962		to 19 Nov 1965	RFA Olwen (Dt2)	2-11 Nov 1967		
Eglinton	2 Dec 1958		to 11 Apr 1962	Portland (Dt4)	6-10 Dec 1965	RFA Tidepool	11-18 Nov 1967		
HMS Eagle	14 Jan 1959	HMS Hermes	26 May 1962	Portland (Dt3)	17-21 Jan 1966	(Dt2)			
North Front	3 Feb 1959	Hal Far (Dt4)	5-18 Sep 1962	HMS Victorious	12 Apr 1966	RFA Tidepool	18-24 Nov 1967		
HMS Eagle	13 Feb 1959	Culdrose	4 Oct 1962	Culdrose	2 May 1966	(Dt2)			
Culdrose	23 Mar 1959	HMS Hermes	12 Nov 1962	HMS Victorious	12 May 1966	RFA Olmeda(Dt3)	7-23 Feb 1968		
HMS Eagle	13 Apr 1959	Sembawang	21 Dec 1962	Culdrose	9 Jun 1966	RFA Engadine			
Culdrose	29 Apr 1959	HMS Hermes	5 Jan 1963	HMS Victorious	8 Jul 1966	(Dt4)	4-22 Mar 1968		
Squadron disbanded	30 Sep 1959	Sembawang	25 Feb 1963	Gan	4 Aug 1966	Tirstrup (Dt4)	1-15 May 1968		
Culdrose	1 Apr 1960	HMAS Melbourne	20 Apr 1963	HMS Victorious	6 Aug 1966	HMS Hermes	27 May 1968		
Portland	7 May 1960	HMS Hermes	8 May 1963	Sembawang	10 Aug 1966	RFA Olmeda (Dt3)	4-13 Jun 1968		
Culdrose	9 Sep 1960	Sembawang	13 Jun 1963	Sempang (Dt2)	22-26 Aug 1966	Culdrose	20 Jun 1968		
HMS Hermes	6 Jul 1960	HMS Hermes	28 Jun 1963	HMS Victorious	5 Sep 1966	HMS Hermes	9 Jul 1968		
Hal Far	11 Jul 1960	Khormaksar	15 Aug 1963	RFA Tidespring	5-8 Sep 1966	RFA Olna (Dt4)	22-25 Aug 1968		
HMS Hermes	21 Jul 1960	HMS Victorious	26 Aug 1963	(Dt2)		Sembawang	30 Aug 1968		
Hal Far	29 Jul 1960	Sembawang	25 Sep 1963	RFA Tidespring	6-9 Oct 1966	HMS Hermes	16 Sep 1968		
HMS Hermes	9 Aug 1960	HMS Victorious	16 Oct 1963	(Dt3)		Sembawang	12 Dec 1968		
Lossiemouth	1 Sep 1960	Sembawang	8 Nov 1963	RFA Olna (Dt4)	22-29 Nov 1968	HMS Hermes	13 Jan 1969		
HMS Hermes	9 Sep 1960	HMS Victorious	14 Jan 1964			Culdrose	30 Mar 1969		

Fairey Gannet XG783 '281/J' of No.814 Squadron on HMS Eagle around 1958/9. (via Brian Lowe)

Westland Sea King HAS.6 XZ580 '267/N' of No.814 Squadron on HMS Invincible in 1993. (MAP)

Squadron bases

RFA Engadine (Dt4)	12-31May1969
HMS Hermes	16 Sep 1969
Culdrose	28 Oct 1969
Lee-on-Solent(Dt2)	28 Oct 1969 to 13 Nov 1969
HMS Hermes	14 Nov 1969
RFA Olwen (Dt3)	23-28Nov1969
Culdrose	4 Dec 1969
HMS Hermes	14 Jan 1970
RFA Regent(Dt2)	28-30Jan 1970
RFA Olwen (Dt3)	9-18Feb 1970
Luqa (Dt3)	26 Feb 1970 to 5 Mar 1970
RFA Olna (Dt3)	5-20Apr 1970
RFA Olwen (Dt2)	26 Apr 1970 to 4 May 1970
Culdrose	22 Jun 1970
Squadron disbanded	14 Jul 1970
Prestwick	30 Mar 1973
HMS Bulwark	30 Jun 1973
Prestwick	13 Jul 1973
St Mawgan	26 Aug 1973
HMS Hermes	27 Aug 1973
Prestwick	17 Oct 1973
HMS Hermes	5 Nov 1973
Prestwick	2 Dec 1973
HMS Hermes	17 Jan 1974
Prestwick	25 Jan 1974
HMS Hermes	7 Feb 1974
Luqa	2 Apr 1974
HMS Hermes	22 Apr 1974
Dartmouth (Dt2)	5-14Jun 1974
Prestwick	6 Aug 1974
HMS Hermes	12 Sep 1974
Portland (Dt2)	11-21Oct 1974
Prestwick	29 Nov 1974
HMS Hermes (Dt-SAR)	3 Dec 1974

Squadron bases

Benbecula (Dts)	5 May 1975 to 19 Jun 1975
HMS Tiger	7 Jul 1975
Prestwick	5 Aug 1975
HMS Hermes	3 Sep 1975
Hal Far	7 Oct 1975
HMS Hermes	21 Oct 1975
Prestwick	27 Oct 1975
HMS Hermes	3 Nov 1975
Prestwick	24 Nov 1975
HMS Hermes	13 Jan 1976
Culdrose	9 Apr 1976
Stornoway	9 Jul 1976
Culdrose	2 Aug 1976
RFA Tidespring (Dt2)	8-25Oct 1976
Stornoway (Dt3)	9-25Oct 1976
RFA Engadine (Dt3)	10-15Dec 1976
HMS Hermes (Dt2)	13-17Dec 1976
HMS Hermes	11 Jan 1977
Culdrose	22 Jan 1977
HMS Hermes	3 Feb 1977
Culdrose	17 Feb 1977
HMS Hermes	21 Feb 1977
Luqa (Dt3)	5-19Apr 1977
Culdrose	25 May 1977
Yeovilton	21 Jun 1977
Culdrose	28 Jun 1977
HMS Hermes	29 Jun 1977
Culdrose	19 Jul 1977
HMS Hermes	30 Aug 1977
Mayport	15 Sep 1977
HMS Hermes	19 Sep 1977
Norfolk	24 Sep 1977
HMS Hermes	30 Sep 1977
Culdrose	29 Oct 1977
HMS Hermes	16 Jan 1978

Squadron bases

Mayport (Dt5)	28 Mar 1978 to 17 Apr 1978
Culdrose	15 May 1978
RFA Olna (Dt3)	10-19Jul 1978
HMS Hermes	14 Aug 1978
Culdrose	29 Sep 1978
HMS Hermes	9 Oct 1978
Culdrose	20 Nov 1978
HMS Hermes	12 Jan 1979
Fort Lauderdale (Dt)	30 Jul 1979 to 21 Aug 1979
Culdrose	10 Oct 1979
HMS Bulwark	5 Jan 1980
Jacksonville	18 Jan 1980
HMS Bulwark	19 Feb 1980
Culdrose	1 Apr 1980
RFA Fort Austin (Dt)	19 May 1980 to 5 Jun 1980
RFA Olmeda (Dt2)	19 May 1980 to 5 Jun 1980
Cameri (Dt2))	8-17Jun 1980
HMS Bulwark	15 Aug 1980
Leuchars (transit)	23 Sep 1980
Culdrose	24 Sep 1980
HMS Bulwark	13 Oct 1980
Culdrose	7 Nov 1980
HMS Bulwark	15 Jan 1981
Gibraltar (Dt4)	12-20Feb1981
Montijo (Dt2)	23-25Feb 1981
Culdrose	22 Mar 1981
Portland (Dt2)	11-14May1981
RFA Tidepool (Dt2)	2-21Jun 1981
HNLMS Zuiderkruis (Dt2)	9-19Jun 1981
Prestwick (Dt2)	11 Jun 1981 to 3 Jul 1981
Leuchars (Dt1)	22-26Jun 1981

Squadron bases

RFA Fort Grange (Dt4)	14 Jul 1981 to 23 Sep 1981
RFA Fort Austin (Dt4)	27 Jul 1981 to 21 Sep 1981
Norfolk (Dt2)	8-18Aug1981
Stornoway (Dt5)	5-12Nov1981
HMS Hermes (Dt6)	22 Jan 1982 to 19 Feb 1982
RFA Engadine (Dt3)	16 Mar 1982 to 6 Apr 1982
HMS Illustrious	2 Aug 1982
RFA Fort Austin (Dt3)	16 Oct 1982 to 16 Dec 1982
Fort Lauderdale	12 Nov 1982
HMS Hermes	23 Nov 1982
Culdrose	7 Dec 1982
HMS Hermes	21 Jan 1983
Culdrose	22 Mar 1983
HMS Hermes	6 Apr 1983
Jacksonville	29 Apr 1983
HMS Hermes	16 May 1983
Culdrose	17 Jun 1983
HMS Illustrious	18 Sep 1983
Culdrose	30 Nov 1983
HMS Illustrious	20 Jan 1984
Culdrose	29 Mar 1984
HMS Illustrious	25 Apr 1984
Culdrose	7 Jun 1984
HMS Illustrious (Dt1)	18-21Jun 1984
HMS Illustrious	25 Jun 1984
Culdrose (Dt1)	12-20Jul 1984
Culdrose	20 Jul 1984
HMS Illustrious	25 Sep 1984
HMS Invincible	22 Nov 1984
Culdrose	29 Nov 1984
HMS Invincible (Dt4)	29 Nov 1984 to 3 Dec 1984 (trapped by broken lift)

Squadron bases		Squadron bases		Squadron bases		Commanding Officers	
HMS Illustrious		HMS Illustrious		Culdrose	22 May 1991	L/C AC Lindsay	
(Dt2)	4-11 Dec 1984	(Dt2)	18-25 Aug 1988	Lee-on-Solent		DSC RN	27 Apr 1940
(Dt4)	to 23 Dec 1984	Lee-on-Solent		(Dt3)	3-7 Jun 1991	Squadron disbanded 19 Nov 1950	
Culdrose (Dt2)	2-4 Feb 1985	(Dt2)	25-30 Aug 1988	HMS Invincible		L/C AC Lindsay	
HMS Invincible		HMS Illustrious	30 Aug 1988	(Dt1)	3-7 Jun 1991	DSC RN	22 Nov 1950
(Dt4)	4-27 Feb 1985	Culdrose (Dt5)	23 Sep 1988	HMS Invincible	29 Aug 1991	L/C JA McColgan	
Bitburg (USAF)	18-22 Feb 1985		to 3 Oct 1988	Culdroe	17 Nov 1991	RN	6 Feb 1952
HMS Invincible	27 Feb 1985	RFA Olmeda (Dt1)	31 Oct 1988	HMS Invincible	21 Feb 1992	L/C WVE Andon	
	to 25 Mar 1985		to 1 Dec 1988	Culdrose	21 Mar 1992	RN	12 Sep 1952
RFA Tidespring	22 Apr 1985	Culdrose	14 Dec 1988	HMS Invincible	12 May 1992	L/C SW Birse	
(Dt2)	to 7 May 1985	HMS Illustrious		Culdrose	26 Nov 1992	OBE DSC	6 Oct 1952
HMS Illustrious	30 Apr 1985	(Dt2)	24 Jan 1989	HMS Invincible		L/C PR Elias DSC	13 Mar 1954
Culdrose (Dt2)	25-30 May 1985	Kaufbeuren(Dt2)	16-21 Feb 1989		19-29 Apr 1993	Squadron disbanded 4 Nov 1955	
Culdrose	6 Jun 1985	Lee-on-Solent		Lee-on-Solent	29 Apr 1993	L/C R Fulton RN	14 Jan 1957
HMS Illustrious	1 Aug 1985	(Dt4)	21-28 Feb 1989	(Dt2)	to 10 May 1993	L/C JJ Philips RN	4 Jan 1958
Jacksonville		HMS Illustrious	28 Feb 1989	HMS Invincible	11 May 1993	L/C GDH Sample	
(Dt2)	12-26 Aug 1985	Gutersloh (Dt2)	17-21 Mar 1989	Portland (Dt2)	31 May 1993	DSC RN	12 Sep 1958
Norfolk (Dt4)	20-26 Aug 1985	Culdrose	22 Mar 1989		to 4 Jun 1993	L/C DC Eve RN	1 May 1959
Culdrose	25 Sep 1985	Prestwick (Dt2)	2-24 May 1989	Culdrose	18 Jun 1993	Squadron disbanded 30 Sep 1959	
HMS Illustrious	7 Oct 1985	HMS Invincible		HMS Invincible	20 Jul 1993	L/C PE Bailey RN	1 Apr 1960
Culdrose (Dt2)	27 Nov 1985	(Dt2)	2-12 May 1989	RFA Fort Grange	30 Jul 1993	L/C JG Brigham RN	8 Aug 1961
	to 4 Dec 1985	Portland (Dt2)	15-19 May 1989	(Dt2)	to 9 Dec 1993	Squadron disbanded 14 Sep 1961	
Culdrose	4 Dec 1985	HMS Invincible	1 Jun 1989	RFA Fort Austin		L/C LJB Reynolds	
HMS Illustrious	27 Jan 1986	Culdrose	9 Jun 1989	(Dt2)	7-19 Jan 1994	RN	28 Nov 1961
Culdrose	18 Feb 1986	HMS Invincible	10 Jul 1989	Culdrose	10 Feb 1994	L/C JG Brigham RN	17 Dec 1962
HMS Illustrious	2 Apr 1986	Culdrose (Dt3)	2-9 Aug 1989	HMS Invincible		L/C JG Beyfus RN	3 Oct 1963
(major fire overnight)		Culdrose	9 Aug 1989	(Dt)	20-30 May 1994	L/C PJ Lynn RN	22 Sep 1964
Culdrose	3 Apr 1986	Linton-on-Ouse		Aarhus (Dt2)	20 May 1994	L/C NKL Whitwam	
RFA Fort Grange	13 Apr 1986	(Dt2)	19-30 Aug 1989		to 8 Jun 1994	RN	26 Nov 1965
(Dt3)	to Aug 1986	Lee-on-Solent		HMS Invincible	23 Aug 1994	L/C MCS Apps RN	17 Jan 1966
HMS Illustrious	14 Jul 1986	(Dt3)	24-29 Aug 1989	RFA Fort Austin (Dt3)		L/C JP Gunning RN	2 Oct 1967
Culdrose	17 Dec 1986	HMS Invincible	16 Oct 1989		6-1 4 Sep 1994	L/C MJ Harvey RN	14 Oct 1968
Portland (Dt2)	9-13 Feb 1987	Pensacola (Dt2)	2-10 Nov 1989			Squadron disbanded 14 Jul 1970	
Portland (Dt2)	25-26 Mar 1987	Jacksonville	2 Jan 1990	**Commanding Officers**		L/C CJ Horscroft	
HMS Illustrious		HMS Invincible	15 Jan 1990	L/C NS Luard DSC	1 Dec 1938	RN	30 Mar 1973
(Dt2)	2-8 Apr 1987	Culdrose	22 Feb 1990	RN (Sq Ldr RAF)		L/C EC Ashton	
RFA Olna (A Flt)	13 Apr 1987	RFA Olmeda (Dt2)	1-21 Mar 1990	Mjr WHN Martin		-Johnston RN	29 Jul 1974
	to 13 May 1987	RFA Fort Austin		RM	27 Dec 1940	L/C CLL Quarrie	
HMS Illustrious	27 Apr 1987	(Dt2)	1-21 Mar 1990	Lt AF Paterson RN	25 Sep 1942	RN	15 Apr 1976
(Dt3)	to 6 May 1987	HMS Invincible	23 Apr 1990	Squadron disbanded 31 Dec 1942		L/C RE Ward RN	17 Dec 1976
Portland (Dt3)	6-8 May 1987	Culdrose	17 May 1990	L/C JSL Crabbe RN	1 Jul 1944	L/C K Hindle RN	10 Aug 1978
HMS Illustrious	12 May 1987	HMS Invincible		L/C(A) GR Coy		L/C AR Welton RN	21 Jul 1980
Valkenburg (Dt3)	15-21 Jun 1987	(Dt1)	4-18 Jun 1990	DSC RN	28 Nov 1944	L/C R StJ Bishop RN	5 Jan 1982
HMS Ark Royal		HMS Invincible		L/C(A) AD Corkhill		L/C RM Turner RN	17 May 1982
(Dt2)	16-18 Jun 1987	(Dt1)	25-27 Aug 1990	DSC RN	1 Feb 1946	L/C AG Rogers RN	25 May 1983
Montijo (Dt2)	22-30 Jun 1987	HMS Invincible	31 Aug 1990	L/C(A) GR Humphries		L/C JRB Bullock RN	18 Nov 1984
Lee-on-Solent		Culdrose	17 Sep 1990	RN	14 Nov 1946	L/C NJ Cowley RN	14 Dec 1986
(Dt2)	22-25 Jun 1987	HMS Invincible	24 Sep 1990	L/C FA Swanton DSO		L/C DC Goodall RN	20 Oct 1988
Culdrose	26 Jun 1987	(Dt2)	to 3 Oct 1990	DSC & Bar RN	17 Apr 1947	L/C MR Pepper RN	14 Jan 1990
Colonsay (Dt2)	6-9 Jul 1987	HMS Invincible		Lt JS Barnes RN	18 Dec 1948	L/C MMD Mason RN	8 May 1992
HMS Illustrious	25 Aug 1987	(Dt3)	18-25 Jan 1991	L/C LD Empson RN	24 Mar 1949	L/C ACV Prince RN	8 Apr 1993
Culdrose	22 Sep 1987	HMS Invincible	12 Feb 1991			L/C IH Beamish RN	7 Oct 1994
HMS Illustrious							
(Dt3)	6-22 Oct 1987						
Linton-on-Ouse							
(Dt3)	7-13 Oct 1987						
RFA Fort Austin							
(Dt3)	7-13 Oct 1987						
Portland (Dt3)	20-23 Oct 1987						
HMS Illustrious							
(Dt4)	4-16 Nov 1987						
RFA Olmeda(Dt2)	4-18 Nov 1987						
HMS Illustrious	16 Nov 1987						
Culdrose	18 Nov 1987						
HMS Illustrious	19 Jan 1988						
Prestwick (Dt3)	23 Feb 1988						
	to 2 Mar 1988						
Culdrose (Dt3)	2-4 Mar 1988						
Culdrose	4 Mar 1988						
HMS Illustrious	7 Apr 1988						
Culdrose	19 May 1988						
HMS Illustrious							
(Dt4)	19-26 May 1988						
HMS Illustrious							
(Dt5)	7-9 Jun 1988						
Turnhouse (Dt3)	9-13 Jun 1988						
HMS Illustrious							
(Dt2)	9-13 Jun 1988						
HMS Illustrious	13 Jun 1988						
Culdrose	24 Jun 1988						

Westland Sea King HAS.5 XV675 '274' of No.814 Squadron at Lossiemouth on 3 May 1985. (A.S.Thomas)

No.815 Squadron

Badge: On a field barry wavy of six white and blue, a harpoon winged gold
Motto: Strike deep

No.815 Squadron formed at Worthy Down on 9 October 1939 from survivors of Nos.811 and 822 Squadron who had been embarked in HMS *Courageous* when she was sunk on 17 September 1939. Equipped with 12 Swordfish I, it undertook torpedo and armament training, and was intended to move to Hatston on 15 January 1940, but instead disbanded on 10 November 1939 and merged into No.774 Squadron.

On 23 November 1939 No.815 reformed under the same CO with 9 Swordfish I, being initially a spare squadron, not allocated at that stage to a carrier. In February 1940 it moved to Cardiff, then in April to Bircham Newton where it was attached to Coastal Command, giving support for the Dunkirk evacuation in May. The squadron embarked in HMS *Illustrious* in June, sailing for the Mediterranean in August. Attacks were made on Rhodes and Benghazi, then in October a further attack was made on Rhodes followed by minelaying in Tobruk harbour. On 11 November the whole squadron participated in the successful attack on the Italian Fleet at Taranto, the only loss being the CO's aircraft, he and his crew being taken prisoner. Further activity in the central and eastern Mediterranean included sinking two Italian ships in a convoy off Sicily in December, but on 11 January 1941 the carrier was badly damaged in a dive-bombing attack.

Five aircraft which were in the air at the time of the attack flew to Malta, and on 14 January 1941 these combined with No.821X Flight and the remnants of No.819 Squadron from HMS *Illustrious* to form what was essentially a new No.815 under the same CO, with 12 Swordfish I. The aircraft made their way to Dekheila where No.815 was officially reformed on 21 January 1941, then at the end of the month transferred to Crete for shore based operations. Here it carried out attacks on shipping as well minelaying, and some aircraft were based in Greece. In April it was evacuated back to Dekheila, then in May the squadron went to Cyprus, from where attacks were made on Vichy French shipping and other objectives in Syria, one destroyer being sunk and another damaged.

In August 1941 No.815 returned to Dekheila, and after re-equipping with 12 Albacores and two ASV-equipped Swordfish, was sent to the Western Desert to support the 8th Army. Operating from forward bases it carried out night attacks on enemy aerodromes and armoured formations, the two Swordfish carrying out night anti-submarine patrols from Fuka. Anti-submarine patrols were also carried out by a detachment based in Cyprus. Re-equipping with ASV-equipped Swordfish, support was provided for the advance into Libya early in 1942. Many attacks were also made on submarines, *U-652* being shared by aircraft V4707 'L' with an RAF Blenheim of 203 Sqdn on 2 June. Shore based operations continued throughout the year, and on 2 March 1943 a special flight of three Albacores was formed for Fleet bombardment spotting. The squadron disbanded at Mersa Matruh on 24 July 1943.

No.815 reformed at Lee-on-Solent on 1 October 1943 as a torpedo bomber reconnaissance unit with 12 Barracuda IIs. Forming part of the 52nd Naval TBR Wing for a time, the aircraft were embarked in HMS *Begum* in February 1944 for passage to India. On arrival it joined the 12th Naval TBR Wing, which embarked in HMS *Indomitable* in July for operations with the Eastern Fleet. The following month it took part in an attack on the Sumatran port of Emmahaven, followed in September by a similar attack on Sigli, and in October by a strike on the Nicobar Islands. However, following a decision to replace Barracuda squadrons by Avengers in the Pacific theatre, the squadron took passage home in HMS *Activity* in November without its aircraft.

Fairey Swordfish I L7648 'X' of No.814 Squadron at Heliopolis in 1942. (RAF Museum P.845)

A Fairey Albacore of No.815 Squadron in Cyprus, 1941. (Dennis Phillips)

During December, No.815 re-equipped with 12 Barracudas IIs at Machrihanish for anti-submarine work, these being replaced by 12 Barracuda IIIs from January 1945. In April a fighter flight was added by transferring No.825X Flight, and the following month the squadron embarked in HMS *Campania* for deck landing training. The Wildcats were soon withdrawn, as were the Barracudas before the squadron joined HMS *Smiter* for return to the Far East. However, before it could go into action VJ-day intervened, and it returned home in HMS *Fencer* in September. Twelve new Barracuda IIIs were received at Fearn in October, but the squadron disbanded at Rattray on 11 January 1946.

The squadron next reformed on 1 December 1947 at Eglinton as an anti-submarine squadron by renumbering No.744 Squadron. Equipped with 12 Barracuda IIIs, it operated as the Naval Joint Anti-Submarine Squadron in co-operation with the Joint Anti-Submarine School at Londonderry. The squadron was largely shore based, but occasionally embarked in carriers for exercises. In December 1951 it reduced to ten aircraft, then in May 1953 re-equipped with eight Avenger TBM-3Es, these being successively replaced by AS.4 and then AS.5 variants. In January 1954 it embarked in HMS *Eagle* for a Mediterranean cruise, and later in the year had a spell in HMS *Illustrious* in Home waters. A further period was spent in the Mediterranean from July 1955, this time in HMS *Albion*, but on 13 October 1955 the squadron disbanded on disembarking at Rosyth, the aircraft going to Abbotsinch.

On 6 February 1956 No.815 reformed at Eglinton as an anti-submarine squadron with eight Gannet AS.1s plus a T.2 for shore training. The former embarked in HMS *Ark Royal* in January 1957, making a 3-week visit to America in May. Cross operations were carried out with USS *Saratoga* before returning home. Re-equipping with AS.4s in December, further trips were made, to both northern and Mediterranean waters, before disbanding at Culdrose on 15 July 1958.

No.815 next became a helicopter unit, reforming at Eglinton on 1 October 1958 with 12 Whirlwind HAS.7s, to operate as the Naval Air Anti-Submarine School (Rotary Wing). Engine defects caused the HAS.7s to be grounded and withdrawn in March 1959. They were replaced by HAR.3s, and these moved in April to Portland. Here the squadron disbanded on 28 August 1959, when it adopted second line status to become No.737 Squadron.

On 8 September 1959 No.815 reformed at Culdrose as an anti-submarine unit with eight Whirlwind HAS.7s. After work-up these embarked in HMS *Albion* in January 1960 for the Mediterranean and later the Far East. Returning to the United Kingdom, the squadron disbanded on 16 December 1960 on arrival, the aircraft going to RNAY Fleetlands.

Eight Wessex HAS.1s were the equipment when No.815 next reformed at Culdrose on 4 July 1961. In November it embarked in HMS *Ark Royal* for the Mediterranean, but engine defects necessitated a return from Malta in HMS *Victorious* in December for modifications. By March 1962 the aircraft were able to return to the Mediterranean in HMS *Ark Royal*, continuing from there to the Far East. Returning home in December, it was later awarded the annual Boyd Trophy for pioneering the Wessex HAS.1 into service.

A further trip to the Far East in HMS *Ark Royal* was made in 1963, disembarking to Aden at the end of the year to help with tribal disturbances. It joined HMS *Centaur* in January 1964 to put No.45 RM Cdo ashore in Tanganyika where British assistance had been requested in dealing with an uprising. After returning to Aden in May, it re-embarked and by July was back in Singapore, returning home in December. In June 1965 the squadron joined HMS *Ark Royal* for a further spell in the Far East, a visit being made paid to Australia in December, returning home again in June 1966. After a further period embarked in HMS *Ark Royal* in Home Waters, the squadron disbanded at Culdrose on 7 October 1966.

Plans to reform No.815 at Culdrose in mid 1971 with Sea Kings, for embarkation in HMS *Tiger* in June of that year, failed to materialise. Instead the squadron next reformed at Yeovilton on 1 January 1981 as the headquarters squadron for embarked Lynx flights, which it took over from No.702 Squadron. It moved to Portland in July 1982, continuing with this task.

Embarked flights deployed throughout the world and were involved in all Naval operations during the 1980s, including the 1982 Falklands campaign, relief operations off Lebanon in 1983 and Aden in 1986 and in hurricane relief in the Caribbean. Flights were regularly deployed on the Armilla Gulf patrol from 1980 and the squadron was awarded the Boyd Trophy jointly with No.829 Squadron in 1988 for their operational contribution to the Royal Naval presence in the Persian Gulf.

Some Lynx Flights were transferred to No.829 Squadron in

Fairey Barracuda Mk.III ME261 '305/JR' of No.815 Squadron, Eglinton aboard HMS Illustrious around 1958. (via Midland Air Museum)

September 1986 with further flights in April 1988 when the Wasp was phased out of service. Parenting of Lynx flights was shared by the two squadrons until April 1993, when all front line Lynx were absorbed back into Nos.815 and 829 was disbanded. In July 1992, No.815 also absorbed No.700L Squadron, which became an Operational Evaluation Unit. Between August 1990 and February 1991 several flights were involved in offensive operations in the northern Persian Gulf, for which the Flight Commanders of HMS *Gloucester* and *Cardiff* were both awarded DSCs. Lynx flights continue to be involved in the standing naval patrols in the Gulf, Adriatic, West Indies and South Atlantic.

Identification Markings

Swordfish *U3A+*, to *L4A+* 1.40; Albacore *S7A+*; Swordfish 1942/3 single letters; Fulmar believed single letters; Wildcat unknown; Barracuda *4A+*, to *I7A+* 10.45, *300-312/JR:GN* from 12.47; Avenger *351-361/GN:FD*, to *381-389/Z:CU* 11.54; Gannet *290-299/O:R*; Whirlwind *300-311/A*; Wessex *300-307/R:C*, to *050-057/R* 6.65; Lynx various small ship codes.

Aircraft Equipment	Period of Service	Example	
Swordfish I	Oct 1939 - Nov 1939	P4087	
	Nov 1939 - Feb 1943	P3992	(H)
Swordfish II	Mar 1943 - Jul 1943	HS220	
Albacore I	Oct 1941 - Aug 1943	X9158	(J)
Fulmar I	Mar 1943 - Jul 1943	N4084	
Fulmar II	Sep 1942 - Jul 1943	X8636	
Barracuda II	Oct 1943 - Oct 1944	P9918	
	Nov 1944 - Apr 1945	MD737	
Barracuda TR.3	Jan 1945 - Jan 1946	ME248	(I7K)
Wildcat VI	Apr 1945 - May 1945	JV823	
Barracuda TR.3	Dec 1947 - May 1953	RJ790	(311/GN)
Firefly T.	Aug 1952 - May 1953	?	(240)
Avenger TBM-3E	May 1953 - Jan 1954	XB448	(355/GN)
Avenger AS.4	Jan 1954 - Jul 1954	XB356	(362)
Avenger AS.5	Jul 1954 - Oct 1955	XB309	(387/CU)
Gannet AS.1	Feb 1956 - Nov 1957	XA321	(293/O)
Gannet T.2	Feb 1956 - Sep 1956	XA515	
Gannet AS.4	Dec 1957 - Jul 1958	XA425	(296/R)
Whirlwind HAR.3	Jan 1959 - Aug 1959	XG577	(301)
Whirlwind HAS.7	Oct 1958 - Mar 1959	XK933	(310)
	Sep 1959 - Dec 1960	XL883	(308/A)
Wessex HAS.1	Jul 1961 - Oct 1966	XP104	(053/R)
Lynx HAS.2	Jan 1981 - Sep 1988	XZ723	(454/PN)
Lynx HAS.3	Nov 1982 - to date	ZD259	(323/AB)
Lynx HAS.3(CTS)	Jul 1990 - to date	XZ697	(341/AG)
Lynx HAS.8	Jul 1994 - to date	ZD266	

Grumman Avenger TBM-3E XB311 '360/GN' of No.815 Squadron, Eglinton in 1953. (MAP)

Westland/Aerospatiale Lynx HAS.2 XZ733 '420/EX' of Exeter Flight/No.239 Flight, No.815 Squadron at Culdrose on 22 July 1981. (MAP)

Battle Honours
Mediterranean	1940-41
Taranto	1940
Libya	1940-41
Matapan	1941
Burma	1944
Falkland Islands	1982
Kuwait	1991

Squadron bases
Worthy Down	9 Oct 1939
Squadron disbanded	10 Nov 1939
Worthy Down	23 Nov 1939
Cardiff	5 Feb 1940
Bircham Newton	8 Apr 1940
Ford	16 May 1940
Bircham Newton	20 May 1940
Ford	23 May 1940
Detling	27 May 1940
Bircham Newton	2 Jun 1940
Ford	5 Jun 1940
Bircham Newton	6 Jun 1940
HMS Illustrious	11 Jun 1940
Roborough	12 Jun 1940
HMS Illustrious	21 Jun 1940
Campbeltown	23 Jul 1940
HMS Illustrious	11 Aug 1940
Dekheila	5 Sep 1940
HMS Illustrious	11 Sep 1940
Aboukir	12 Sep 1940
HMS Illustrious	15 Sep 1940
Aboukir	19 Sep 1940
HMS Illustrious	29 Sep 1940
Dekheila	22 Oct 1940
Fuka satt (Dt6)	22-24 Oct 1940
HMS Illustrious	29 Oct 1940
Dekheila	14 Nov 1940
HMS Illustrious	21 Nov 1940
Heraklion (Dt)	29 Nov 1940 to 7 Jan 1941
Dekheila	30 Nov 1940
HMS Illustrious	16 Dec 1940
Dekheila	27 Dec 1940
HMS Illustrious	7 Jan 1941
Hal Far	10 Jan 1941
Heraklion (transit)	17 Jan 1941
Dekheila	19 Jan 1941
Monastir (Dt3)	23 Jan 1941 to 16 Feb 1941
Detached flight (6 a/c):	
Maleme	30 Jan 1941
Heraklion (Dt)	10-14 Feb 1941
Eleusis (transit)	11 Mar 1941
Paramythia	12 Mar 1941
Eleusis	17 Apr 1941
transit	18 Apr 1941
Maleme	20 Apr 1941
transit	22 Apr 1941
Nicosia	29 May 1941
Dekheila (Dt4)	25 Jun 1941 to 2 Jul 1941
Lakatamia	7 Jul 1941
Dekheila	13 Aug 1941
Lakatamia (Dt)	13 Aug 1941 to 17 Nov 1941
LG.75 Maaten	13 Nov 1941
Bagush satt (Dts)	to 8 Dec 1941
Fuka satt (Dt2)	28 Nov 1941 to Dec 1941
St.Jean D'Acre (Dt3)	19-24 Feb 1942
Nicosia (Dt3)	24-27 Feb 1942
LG.14 Maaten	19 Jan 1942
Bagush (Dt)	to 5 Feb 1942
LG.86 Amriya (Dt)	by 16 Feb 1942
LG.14 Maaten Bagush (Dt)	by 2 Mar 1942

Squadron bases
LG.121 Sidi Barrani (Dts)	15-29 Apr 1942
LG.14 Maaten	17 May 1942
Bagush (Dt)	to 27 Jun 1942
Gamil (Dt)	30 Jun 1942 to 6 Sep 1942
Gaza (Dt)	4 Sep 1942 to 13 Oct 1942
Mersah Matruh (Dt8)	25 Nov 1942 to 5 Dec 1942
LG.139	2 Dec 1942 to 1 Mar 1943
LG.08 Mersa Matruh (Dt)	23 Dec 1942 4 Jan 1943
LG.08 Mersa Matruh	4 Jan 1943
Dekheila (Dt)	9-27 Feb 1943

Squadron bases
Special Bombardment Flight:	
Berka No.3 (Dt)	3-28 Mar 1943
El Magrun	28 Mar 1943
Misurata	7 Apr 1943
Dekheila	18 May 1943
Ta Kali	2 Jul 1943
Fayid (Dt)	19-22 Jun 1943
Dekheila	18 Jul 1943
Squadron disbanded	24 Jul 1943
Lee-on-Solent	1 Oct 1943
transit	3 Dec 1943
Tain	7 Dec 1943
Belfast (transit)	27 Feb 1944
HMS Begum	27 Feb 1944

Westland/Aerospatiale Lynx HAS.2 XZ698 '424/MV' of Minerva Flight/No.210 Flight, No.815 Squadron at Culdrose on 22 July 1983. (MAP)

Squadron bases

SS Strathnaver/ SS Aronda (crews)	3 Mar 1944
St Thomas Mount	10 Apr 1944
Ulunderpet	14 Apr 1944
Katukurunda	14 Jun 1944
HMS Indomitable	23 Jul 1944
Katukurunda	27 Sep 1944
HMS Indomitable	8 Oct 1944
Coimbatore	28 Oct 1944
HMS Activity (no a/c)	4 Nov 1944
Machrihanish	30 Nov 1944
Ayr	22 Dec 1944
Mullaghmore	26 Jan 1945
Machrihanish	15 Mar 1945
HMS Campania (DLT)	18 Apr 1945
Machrihanish	20 Apr 1945
Stretton	21-22 Apr 1945
(Fighter Flt)	
HMS Campania (Fighter Flt)	6-21 May 1945
Belfast	25 Jun 1945
HMS Smiter	1 Jul 1945
Cochin	27 Jul 1945
Katukurunda	29 Jul 1945
HMS Smiter	11 Aug 1945
Sulur (no a/c)	18 Aug 1945
HMS Fencer (no a/c)	3 Sep 1945
Fearn	26 Sep 1945
Rattray	26 Oct 1945
Squadron disbanded	11 Jan 1946
Eglinton	1 Dec 1947
Lossiemouth (Dt6)	23-29 Apr 1948
HMS Implacable (Dt6)	4-14 May 1948
Arbroath (Dt6)	14 May 1948 to 4 Oct 1948
HMS Illustrious (DLT)	18 Nov 1948
Eglinton	15 Dec 1948
HMS Implacable	15 May 1950
Eglinton	17 Jun 1950
Lee-on-Solent (Dt8)	19-21 Apr 1951
HMS Indomitable	27 Apr 1951
Arbroath	14 May 1951
HMS Indomitable	28 May 1951
Eglinton	24 Jun 1951
Ford	16 Jun 1952
Eglinton	26 Jun 1952
Lee-on-Solent	9 Jun 1953
Eglinton	16 Jun 1953
HMS Illustrious	31 Aug 1953
Eglinton	2 Oct 1953
Culdrose	22 Jan 1954
HMS Eagle	26 Jan 1954
North Front (Dt4)	19-22 Mar 1954
L'Artique (Dt4)	22-26 Mar 1954
North Front (Dt4)	26-29 Mar 1954
Hal Far	15 Apr 1954
HMS Eagle	1 May 1954
Lee-on-Solent	26 May 1954
Ford	3 Jun 1954
Eglinton	5 Jul 1954
Bramcote	9 Jul 1954
Eglinton	12 Jul 1954
Ballykelly	26 Jul 1954
Ford	30 Jul 1954
HMS Illustrious	17 Sep 1954
Watton	14 Oct 1954
Ford	23 Oct 1954
Culdrose	8 Nov 1954
North Front (Dt4)	23 Aug 1955 to 8 Sep 1955
HMS Albion	19 Jul 1955
Sqdn disbanded UK	13 Oct 1955
Eglinton	6 Feb 1956
HMS Bulwark (DLP)	8 May 1956
Eglinton	20 Jun 1956
Culdrose	19 Nov 1956
HMS Ark Royal (Dt4) (DLP)	4-5 Dec 1956
HMS Ark Royal	14 Jan 1957
Culdrose	25 Feb 1957
HMS Ark Royal	6 May 1957
Culdrose	18 Jul 1957
HMS Ark Royal	28 Aug 1957
Culdrose (Dt3)	1-13 Nov 1957
Culdrose	25 Nov 1957
HMS Ark Royal	27 Jan 1958
Hal Far (Dt7)	15-25 Feb 1958
Hal Far (Dt6)	20 Mar 1958 to 8 Apr 1958
Culdrose	25 Jun 1958
Squadron disbanded	15 Jul 1958
Eglinton	1 Oct 1958
Portland	14 Apr 1959
Squadron redes 737 Sqdn	28 Aug 1959
Culdrose	8 Sep 1959
Portland	8 Oct 1959
Culdrose	21 Nov 1959
HMS Albion	15 Jan 1960
Hal Far (Dt5)	15-19 Feb 1960
Hal Far (Dt5)	4-9 Mar 1960
Hal Far	11 Mar 1960
HMS Albion	21 Mar 1960
Sembawang	13 Apr 1960
HMS Albion (Dt3)	28 Apr 1960 to 16 May 1960
HMS Albion	16 May 1960
Sembawang	13 Jul 1960
HMS Albion	28 Jul 1960
Sembawang	17 Sep 1960
HMS Albion	3 Oct 1960
Fleetlands	16 Dec 1960
Squadron disbanded	16 Dec 1960
Culdrose	4 Jul 1961
HMS Ark Royal	13 Nov 1961
HMS Victorious	10 Dec 1961
Lee-on-Solent	18 Dec 1961
Culdrose	12 Jan 1962
HMS Ark Royal	9 Mar 1962
Sembawang	12 Apr 1962
HMS Ark Royal	23 Apr 1962
Sembawang	27 Jun 1962
HMS Ark Royal	11 Jul 1962
Sembawang	26 Jul 1962
HMS Ark Royal	6 Aug 1962
Sembawang	4 Sep 1962
HMS Ark Royal	29 Sep 1962
Culdrose	14 Dec 1962
HMS Ark Royal	19 Feb 1963
North Front	19 Mar 1963
HMS Ark Royal	2 May 1963
Sembawang	11 Jul 1963
HMS Ark Royal	24 Jul 1963
HMS Albion (Dt6)	5-14 Aug 1963
Sembawang	14 Aug 1963
HMS Ark Royal	26 Aug 1963
Khormaksar	19 Dec 1963
HMS Centaur	15 Jan 1964
Sembawang	12 Feb 1964
HMS Centaur	1 Mar 1964
Sembawang	30 Apr 1964
HMS Centaur	14 May 1964
Radfan	22 May 1964
HMS Centaur	12 Jun 1964
Sembawang	15 Jul 1964
HMS Centaur	24 Jul 1964
Sembawang	15 Aug 1964
HMS Centaur	31 Aug 1964
Sembawang	16 Nov 1964
HMS Centaur	25 Nov 1964
Culdrose	20 Dec 1964
RFA Lofoten	4 Mar 1965
Culdrose	12 Mar 1965
HMS Ark Royal	15 Jun 1965
Sembawang	15 Jul 1965
HMS Ark Royal	3 Aug 1965
Sembawang	4 Sep 1965
Kuala Lumpur (Dt2)	7-15 Sep 1965
HMS Ark Royal	17 Sep 1965
RFA Tidespring (Dt2)	5-14 Oct 1965
Sembawang	20 Oct 1965
RFA Tidespring (Dt2)	5 Nov 1965 to 27 Dec 1965
HMS Ark Royal	6 Dec 1965
Sembawang	8 Jan 1966
HMS Ark Royal	27 Jan 1966
Sembawang	15 Mar 1966
HMS Ark Royal	24 Mar 1966
Sembawang	1 Apr 1966
HMS Ark Royal	13 Apr 1966
Culdrose	13 Jun 1966
HMS Ark Royal	29 Jun 1966
Culdrose	25 Aug 1966
Predannack	6 Sep 1966
HMS Ark Royal	8 Sep 1966
Dishforth	25 Sep 1966
Keevil	29 Sep 1966
Culdrose	1 Oct 1966
Squadron disbanded	7 Oct 1966
Yeovilton	1 Jan 1981
Portland	19 Jul 1982
Prestwick (Dt1)	18 May 1990 to 1 Jun 1990

Commanding Officers

L/C S Borrett RN	9 Oct 1939
Squadron disbanded	10 Nov 1939
L/C S Borrett RN	23 Nov 1939
L/C RA Kilroy DFC RN	17 Apr 1940
L/C K Williamson RN	3 Aug 1940
L/C JdeF Jago RN	16 Nov 1940
L/C FMA Torrens-Spence RN	15 Mar 1941
L/C TP Coode RN	27 Oct 1941
L/C PD Gick RN	14 Dec 1941
L/C AR Hallett RN (temp)	29 Sep 1942
L/C AR Hallett RN	5 Nov 1942
L/C(A) JWG Wellham DSC RN	7 Dec 1942
Squadron disbanded	24 Jul 1943
L/C(A) RG Lawson RNVR	1 Oct 1943
L/C D Norcock RN	23 Dec 1944
L/C(A) JS Bailey OBE RN	5 Jan 1945
L/C(A) MH Meredith DSC RNVR	18 Apr 1945
Squadron disbanded	11 Jan 1946
L/C KS Pattisson DSC RN	1 Dec 1947
L/C(A) DMR Wynne-Roberts RN	1 Apr 1949
Lt DW Pennick RN (acting)	1 Sep 1949
L/C C Murray RN	15 Jan 1950
L/C SS Laurie RN	22 Sep 1950
L/C CRJ Coxon RN	12 Mar 1951
L/C LP Dunne DSC RN	1 Apr 1952
L/C CW Rusbridger RN	18 Jun 1953
L/C F Bromilow RN	30 Oct 1954
Squadron disbanded	13 Oct 1955
L/C JP David RN	6 Feb 1956
L/C JK Mortimer RN	20 Jul 1957
Squadron disbanded	15 Jul 1958
L/C HMA Hayes RN	1 Oct 1958
Squadron disbanded	28 Aug 1959
L/C AG Cornabe RN	8 Sep 1959
Squadron disbanded	16 Dec 1960
L/C ALL Skinner RN	4 Jul 1961
L/C JRT Bluett RN	1 Oct 1962
L/C GA Bagnall RN	30 Apr 1964
L/C JE Kelly RN	9 Apr 1965
Squadron disbanded	7 Oct 1966
L/C DHN Yates RN	6 Jan 1981
L/C RI Money RN	23 Jun 1982
L/C MGB Manning RN	16 Dec 1983
L/C RA Goddard AFC RN	18 Mar 1986
Cdr RA Goddard AFC RN	30 Dec 1986
L/C RK O'Neill RN	24 Apr 1987
L/C TNE Williams RN	2 Mar 1989
L/C AA Rich RN	30 Aug 1989
L/C SJ Isacke RN	13 Mar 1990
L/C CGT Wilson RN	6 Sep 1991
L/C PA McKay RN	26 Apr 1993
L/C RL Bourne RN	9 Nov 1993

Westland/Aerospatiale Lynx HAS.3 '304/PO' of No.815 Headquarters Flight, Portland at Culdrose on 25 July 1984. (MAP)

No.816 Squadron

Badge:
1. On a blue field, the head of an Indian tiger affronte proper
2. On a sable field, a Bengal tiger's face, proper

Motto: Imitate the action of the tiger

No.816 Squadron formed aboard HMS *Furious* on 3 October 1939 with nine Swordfish Is for anti-submarine, search and strike duties providing cover later in the month for a Canadian convoy. In April 1940 the ship took part in operations during the defence of Norway, making the first airborne torpedo attack of the war. Returning home it began to convert to floats in May, but with the evacuation of France this plan was changed and it returned to wheels, operating briefly from Jersey for a few days. In June it re-embarked in HMS *Furious*, and on 5 September sailed for an attempted attack on the German battleship *Scharnhorst*. Five aircraft were lost in an attack on shipping at Trondheim on 22 September, and on 16 October a night bombing attack was made on fuel storage tanks at Tromso.

In March 1941 the squadron joined RAF Coastal Command, to carry out operations off the Dutch coast and later against French ports in the Channel. Three aircraft were detached in April to Detling as No.816X Squadron, being enlarged on 1 July 1941 to become No.821 Squadron. After further operations with Coastal Command, No.816 re-embarked in HMS *Furious* in June to act as escort whilst RAF aircraft were being ferried to Malta. It transferred to HMS *Ark Royal* during the return voyage, remaining in that carrier until she was torpedoed on 13 November. The remnants of No.816 were merged into No.812 Squadron, and it ceased to exist.

The squadron reformed at Palisadoes, Jamaica on 1 February 1942 with four Swordfish Is for torpedo bomber reconnaissance duties. In May these embarked in HMS *Avenger* to provide anti-submarine protection and reconnaissance with a convoy bound from USA to the United Kingdom, but two aircraft were lost en route. After re-equipping with six Swordfish IIs and working up, night operations were undertaken in the English Channel between September and December, under the control of Coastal Command. In February 1943 the squadron joined HMS *Dasher* for North Russian convoy duty, but on 27 March 1943 the ship blew up in the Clyde with heavy loss of life.

No.816 regrouped at Machrihanish with six new Swordfish IIs, and in May carried out attacks against E-boats in the English Channel. In June it moved north to Fearn and took over half of No.895 Squadron to form a fighter flight with six Seafire L.IIc's. In August the latter were withdrawn to re-arm No.897 Squadron, and

Fairey Swordfish I '5C' of No.816 Squadron after taking off from HMS Ark Royal in 1941. (via Chaz Bowyer)

six Seafire Ib's were received as replacements. At about the same time the Swordfish strength was increased to nine, and the squadron embarked in HMS *Tracker* for Atlantic convoy duty. After two such convoys the Seafires were withdrawn as unsuitable for this task, being replaced in January 1944 by six Wildcat IVs from No.878 Squadron. The squadron joined HMS *Chaser* that month for North Russian convoy escort. On 4 March aircraft 'B' helped HMS *Onslaught* to sink *U-472*, and on the next two successive days *U-366* and *U-973* were sunk by aircraft 'F' and 'X' respectively. The Wildcats were withdrawn in April to help form No.833 Squadron, the Swordfish strength being increased to 12. With these it carried out Channel operations with Coastal Command before and during the Normandy invasion, until disbanding at Perranporth on 1 August 1944, the aircrew being transferred to No.836 Squadron.

No.816 next reformed at Lee-on-Solent on 1 February 1945 as a torpedo bomber reconnaissance unit with 18 Barracuda IIs. It was intended to join a *Colossus*-class carrier with a reduced strength of 12 aircraft, as part of a planned 20th Carrier Air Group. Instead it re-equipped on 1 July 1945 with 12 Firefly FR.Is. In May 1946, a Night Fighter Flight was added with 4 Firefly NF.Is, and the following month the squadron embarked in HMS *Ocean* for the Mediterranean as part of the 20th CAG. On 1 November 1946 the Night Fighter Flight was transferred within the air group to No.805 Squadron, but returned to No.816 in May 1947. HMS *Ocean* returned home at the end of June 1948, and No.816 disbanded at Lee-on-Solent on 1 July 1948.

On 28 August 1948 No.816 reformed at Eglinton as a Royal Australian Navy squadron, initially under a British CO. Equipment was 12 Firefly FR.4s, and these embarked in HMAS *Sydney* in February 1949 as part of the 20th CAG, for passage to Australia, where Nowra was its shore base. Partial re-equipment with Firefly 5s began in March 1949, and a few Mk.6s were issued in July 1951, but it was not until October 1951 that the last of the FR.4s departed. In October 1952 it participated in the Monte Bello Islands atomic bomb tests, and from June 1953 spent a few days in HMAS *Vengeance* before returning to HMAS *Sydney* in September for a spell in Korean waters. The squadron was wholly equipped with Firefly 6s by that time, but in November withdrew to Sembawang to exchange these for Mk.5s, only to revert to Mk.6s in May 1954. The squadron eventually disbanded at Nowra on 27 April 1955.

On 15 August 1955 No.816 reformed at Culdrose, again as an Australian squadron, equipped with seven Gannet AS.1s for anti-submarine work. Strength was reduced to six aircraft in November, and in February 1956 the squadron embarked in HMAS *Melbourne* for passage to Australia. Again using Nowra as its shore base, the squadron was expanded in July 1964 by taking over some No.724 Squadron Sea Venom FAW.53s as 'B' Flight. No.816 disbanded at Nowra on 25 August 1967.

On 10 January 1968 No.816 once more reformed as an Australian squadron, this time at Nowra with 14 S-2E Trackers. In 1969 it adopted the American style nomenclature VS-816, but on 4 December 1976 a hangar fire at Nowra destroyed ten squadron aircraft and seriously damaged two more. These were replaced in March 1977 when new S-2G Trackers were embarked in HMAS *Melbourne* at San Diego, these shortly afterwards being re-embarked for the United Kingdom, where the ship participated in the Silver Jubilee Review. In January 1978 a detachment went to Darwin for fishery surveillance and to give early warning of Vietnam refugee vessels, this task being taken over by civil aircraft in December 1980. The squadron also undertook oil rig surveillance in the Bass Strait before being disbanded at Nowra on 2 July 1982 into VC-851.

No.816 reformed at Nowra on 9 February 1984 as a Wessex squadron, taking over the aircraft and troop transport commitment of No.723 Squadron. It had responsibility for ships flights using either Lynx or Seahawk helicopters when these are delivered. During 1986 personnel and aircraft from the squadron were designated for ship's flights for HMAS *Stalwart* and HMAS *Success*. The Wessexes were returned to No.723 Squadron when No.816 disbanded on 30 June 1987. No.816 was expected to reform with the Sikorsky S-70B Seahawk in 1988, but this did not happen.

Identification Markings

Swordfish *U4A +*, later *4A +* then *5A +* to 11.41, believed single letters from 2.42; Wildcat & Barracuda single letters; Firefly single letters, then *O6A +*, to *200-215/O* 1947 to 6.48, *220-238/JR:K* from 8.48; Gannet *421-426/B*, to *300-307/Y* 2.56, to *824-833/M* 1958, to *810-819/M* 1963, to *841-860/NW* 1966; Sea Venom *817-818/M+*; Tracker *840-853*; Wessex *810-834*.

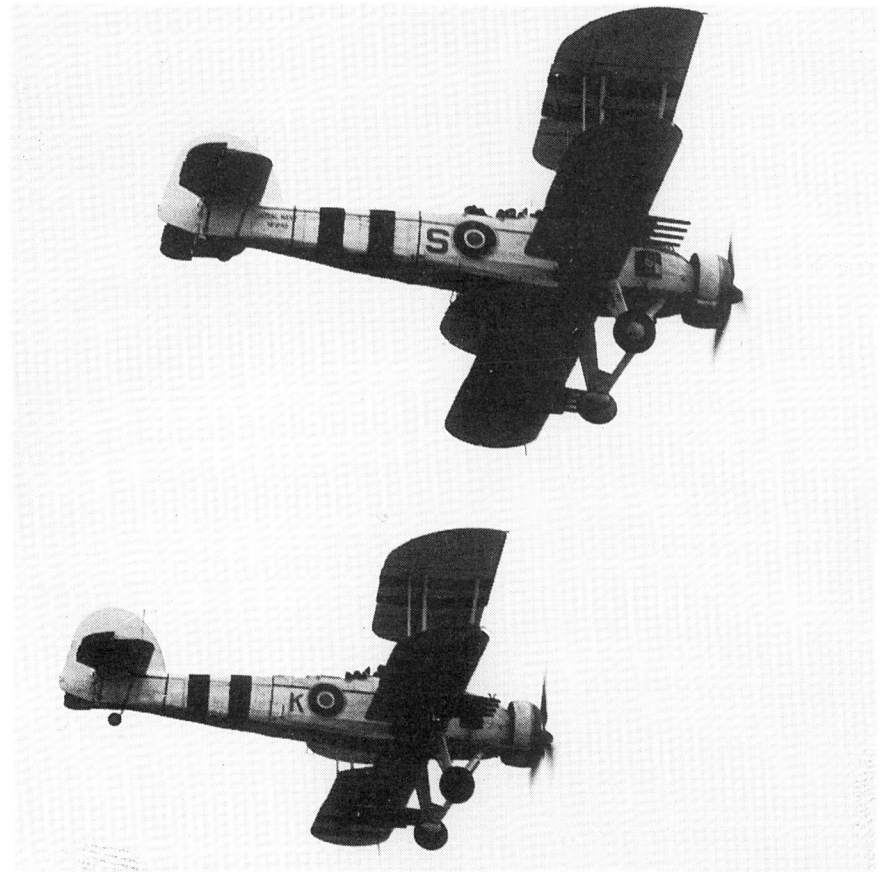

Battle Honours

Norway	1940
Malta Convoys	1941
Mediterranean	1941
Atlantic	1943
Arctic	1944
Normandy	1944
Kuwait	1991
(assumed)	

Fairey Swordfish II NF243 'S' with 'K' of No.816 Squadron, fitted with rocket launching rails, at St.Merryn in July 1944. (via P Snow)

Fairey Firefly FR.4s of No.816 Squadron, Royal Australian Navy aboard HMAS Sydney around 1948/9. (RAF Museum 6313-1)

Aircraft Equipment	Period of Service	Example
Swordfish I	Oct 1939 - Nov 1941	P4167 (U4B)
	Feb 1942 - Oct 1942	W5925
Swordfish II	Jun 1942 - Mar 1943	DK770
	Apr 1943 - Aug 1944	LS231
Seafire L.IIc	Jun 1943 - Aug 1943	
Seafire Ib	Aug 1943 - Dec 1943	NX988
Wildcat V	Jan 1944 - Apr 1944	JV419 (T)
Barracuda II	Feb 1945 - Jul 1945	PM739
Firefly FR.1	Jul 1945 - Jun 1948	PP588 (O6K)
Firefly NF.1	May 1946 - Nov 1946	
	May 1947 - Jun 1948	PP617
Firefly FR.4	Aug 1948 - Oct 1951	TW730 (231/JR)
Firefly 5	Mar 1949 - May 1954	WB379 (230/K)
Firefly 6	Jul 1951 - Apr 1955	WJ109 (238)
Gannet AS.1	Aug 1955 - Aug 1967	XG787 (818/M)
Gannet T.2	Mar 1959 - Oct 1963	XA517 (855/NW)
Sea Venom FAW.53	Jul 1964 - Aug 1967	WZ946 (817/M)
S-2E Tracker	Jan 1968 - Mar 1977	N12-153598 (843)
S-2G Tracker	Mar 1977 - Jul 1982	N12-153601 (846)
Wessex HAS.31b	Feb 1984 - 1991	N7-202 (812)
S-70B Sea Hawk	Jun 1991 - to date	

Commanding Officers
Lt J Dalyell-Stead
    RN (temp) 13 Oct 1939
L/C HH Gardner RN 19 Oct 1939
L/C TGC Jameson
    RN 6 May 1940
Squadron disbanded 13 Nov 1941
Capt O Patch RM 1 Feb 1942
Lt RCB Stallard
    -Penoyre RN 15 Oct 1942
Lt PF Pryor RN 22 Apr 1943
    (temp)
L/C(A) FC Nottingham
    DSC RNVR 12 Jul 1943
L/C P Snow RN 3 May 1944
Squadron disbanded 1 Aug 1944

Commanding Officers
L/C The Hon WAC
    Keppel DSC RN 1 Feb 1945
L/C JSL Crabbe RN 26 Jun 1945
L/C(A) S Hook RN 6 Jan 1947
Squadron disbanded 1 Jul 1948
L/C(A) CRJ Coxon
    RN 28 Aug 1948
L/C AJ Gould RAN 2 Sep 1950
L/C D Buchanan
    RAN 27 Sep 1951
L/C WG Herbert
    RAN 21 Oct 1952
L/C DJ Robertson
    RAN 27 Jul 1954
Squadron disbanded 27 Apr 1955

Commanding Officers
L/C BG O'Connell
    RAN 15 Aug 1955
L/C P Goldrick RAN Mar 1957
L/C J Griffin
    MVO RAN 5 Aug 1957
L/C DC Johns RAN 12 Jan 1959
L/C BG Hill RAN 11 Jan 1960
Cdr KM Barnett
    RAN 16 Jun 1961
L/C AE Payne RAN 22 Jun 1962
L/C TA Dadswell
    RAN 29 Jun 1963
L/C MJ Astbury
    RAN 1 Nov 1966
Squadron disbanded 25 Aug 1967
L/C KA Douglas
    RAN 10 Jan 1968
L/C R McKenzie
    RAN 21 Jul 1969
L/C E Wilson RAN 26 Jan 1970
L/C RV Morritt
    RAN 24 Apr 1971
L/C JLK Clarke
    RAN 15 Jan 1973
L/C GDW Bessel
    -Browne RAN 11 Feb 1974
L/C RN Partington
    RN 23 Aug 1976
L/C PO Hamon RAN 4 Apr 1977
L/C PK Coulson
    RAN 6 Jul 1978
L/C RJ Godfrey
    RAN 10 Dec 1979
L/C TL Ford RAN 22 Dec 1980
Squadron disbanded 2 Jul 1982
L/C C Mayo RAN 9 Feb 1984

Commanding Officers
L/C KJ Alderman
    RAN 6 Dec 1985
Squadron disbanded 30 Jun 1987
Cdr BM Dowsing
    RAN 23 Jul 1993
Cdr MJ Wright RAN May 1994

Squadron bases
HMS Furious 3 Oct 1939
HMS Ark Royal 13 Oct 1939
Hatston 17 Oct 1939
HMS Furious 18 Oct 1939
Abbotsinch 17 Dec 1939
HMS Furious 25 Dec 1939
Abbotsinch 4 Jan 1940
Campbeltown 19 Feb 1940
HMS Furious 9 Apr 1940
Campbeltown 28 Apr 1940
Donibristle 3 May 1940
Campbeltown 17 May 1940
Ternhill (transit) 30 May 1940
Ford 31 May 1940
Jersey 4 Jun 1940
Ford 11 Jun 1940
HMS Furious 14 Jun 1940
Prestwick (Dt) 11-13 Sep 1940
Bircham Newton 1-6 Jul 1940
    (Dt3)
Hatston 13 Sep 1940
HMS Furious 20 Sep 1940
Hatston 25 Sep 1940
HMS Furious 28 Sep 1940
Evanton (Dt6) 25 Oct 1940
    to 7 Nov 1940
Hatston (transit) 6 Nov 1940
Campbeltown 7 Nov 1940
North Coates (16 Gp) 15 Mar 1941

Gannet AS.1 XA331 '859/M' of No.816 Sqdn, RAN in 1965. (MAP)

Squadron bases

Detling (Dt2)	12 Mar 1941 to 4 Apr 1941
St Eval (Dt9)	5-15 Apr 1941
Campbeltown (Dt9)	15-18 Apr 1941
Detling (Dt2)	11-16 Apr 1941
'X' Flight: Detling	23 Apr 1941
Redes 821 Sqdn	1 Jul 1941
Thorney Island	2 May 1941
St Eval (19 Gp)	9 May 1941
Thorney Island	11 May 1941
Eastleigh	4 Jun 1941
Abbotsinch	14 Jun 1941
HMS Furious	21 Jun 1941
HMS Ark Royal	1 Jul 1941
Ship sunk	13 Nov 1941
Palisadoes	1 Feb 1942
Norfolk	22 Mar 1942
HMS Avenger	3 May 1942
Lee-on-Solent	11 May 1942
Machrihanish	29 Jun 1942
Thorney Island (16Gp)	7 Sep 1942
Machrihanish	30 Dec 1942
HMS Dasher	2 Feb 1943
Hatston	26 Feb 1943
Machrihanish (transit)	21 Mar 1943
HMS Dasher	21 Mar 1943
Machrihanish	27 Mar 1943
Lee-on-Solent	20 Apr 1943
Exeter (10 Gp)	20 May 1943
Fearn	25 Jun 1943
Machrihanish	8 Jul 1943
Maydown	1 Aug 1943
HMS Tracker	13 Aug 1943
Machrihanish	6 Oct 1943
HMS Tracker	17 Oct 1943
Argenta Field	14 Nov 1943
HMS Tracker	22 Nov 1943
Donibristle	28 Dec 1943
HMS Chaser	19 Jan 1944
Hatston	12 Feb 1944
HMS Chaser	16 Feb 1944
Donibristle	10 Mar 1944
Fighter Flight: HMS Chaser	10 Mar 1944
Renfrew	18 Mar 1944
Donibristle	21 Mar 1944
Machrihanish	31 Mar 1944
Crail	17 Apr 1944
Perranporth(19 Gp) (base-St Merryn)	20 Apr 1944
Squadron disbanded	1 Aug 1944
Lee-on-Solent	1 Feb 1945
Fearn	13 Mar 1945
Machrihanish (Dt3)	10-18 May 1945
Woodvale	1 Jul 1945
Inskip	11 Aug 1945
Machrihanish	11 Oct 1945
HMS Nairana (DLT)	23 Nov 1945
Machrihanish	16 Dec 1945
Lee-on-Solent (transit)	9 Feb 1946
HMS Theseus	11 Feb 1946
Lee-on-Solent	13 Feb 1946
HMS Theseus	25 Apr 1946
Lee-on-Solent	2 May 1946
HMS Ocean	19 Jun 1946
Hal Far	4 Aug 1946
HMS Ocean	18 Sep 1946
Hal Far	15 Nov 1946
HMS Ocean	27 Dec 1946
Hal Far	15 Mar 1947
HMS Ocean	5 Jun 1947
Hal Far	22 Aug 1947
HMS Ocean	2 Oct 1947
Hal Far	11 Nov 1947
HMS Ocean	15 Jan 1948
Hal Far	20 Apr 1948
HMS Ocean	7 May 1948
Hal Far	18 May 1948
HMS Ocean	14 Jun 1948
Lee-on-Solent	28 Jun 1948
Squadron disbanded	1 Jul 1948
Eglinton	28 Aug 1948
HMAS Sydney	8 Feb 1949
Nowra	25 May 1949
HMAS Sydney	25 Jun 1949
Nowra	11 Nov 1949
HMAS Sydney	13 Jan 1950
Nowra	4 Apr 1950
HMAS Sydney	23 Jan 1951

Squadron bases

Nowra	4 Apr 1951
HMAS Sydney	11 Aug 1952
Nowra	11 Nov 1952
HMAS Sydney	12 Jan 1953
Nowra	18 Feb 1953
HMAS Vengeance	23 Jun 1953
Nowra	9 Aug 1953
HMAS Sydney	21 Sep 1953
Sembawang	2 Nov 1953
HMAS Sydney	5 Nov 1953
Kai Tak	31 Dec 1953
HMAS Sydney	11 Jan 1954
Nowra	10 Jun 1954
HMAS Sydney	26 Aug 1954
Nowra	1 Dec 1954
HMAS Sydney	8 Feb 1955
Nowra	22 Apr 1955
Squadron disbanded	27 Apr 1955
Culdrose	15 Aug 1955
HMAS Melbourne	29 Feb 1956
Nowra	7 May 1956
HMAS Melbourne	6 Aug 1956
Nowra	10 Dec 1956
HMAS Melbourne	5 Feb 1957
Nowra	10 Jul 1957
HMAS Melbourne	4 Oct 1957
Nowra	12 Dec 1957
HMAS Melbourne	12 Feb 1958
Nowra	20 Jul 1958
HMAS Melbourne	22 Oct 1958
Nowra	19 Nov 1958
HMAS Melbourne	10 Feb 1959
Nowra	11 Jun 1959
HMAS Melbourne	12 Oct 1959
Nowra	4 Dec 1959
HMAS Melbourne	15 Feb 1960
Nowra	6 Jul 1960
HMAS Melbourne	11 Aug 1960
Nowra	21 Sep 1960
HMAS Melbourne	31 Jan 1961
Seletar	13 Jun 1961
HMAS Melbourne	14 Jul 1961
Nowra	20 Sep 1961
HMAS Melbourne	25 Jan 1962
Nowra	20 Jun 1962
HMAS Melbourne	31 Jul 1962
Nowra	17 Sep 1962
HMAS Melbourne	23 Jan 1963
Nowra	5 Jun 1963
HMAS Melbourne	21 May 1964
Nowra	5 Jun 1964
HMAS Melbourne	13 Jun 1964
Nowra	8 Nov 1964
HMAS Melbourne	14 Jan 1965
Nowra	21 Jun 1965
HMAS Melbourne	6 Aug 1965
Nowra	4 Oct 1965

Squadron bases

HMAS Melbourne	19 Feb 1966
Nowra	30 Jun 1966
HMAS Melbourne	15 Aug 1966
Nowra	27 Oct 1966
HMAS Melbourne	6 Apr 1967
Nowra	17 Aug 1967
Squadron disbanded	25 Aug 1967
Nowra	10 Jan 1968
HMAS Melbourne	1 Apr 1969
Nowra	14 Jul 1969
HMAS Melbourne	9 Feb 1970
Nowra	14 Feb 1970
HMAS Melbourne	26 Feb 1970
Nowra	8 Dec 1970
HMAS Melbourne	11 Sep 1971
Nowra	7 Dec 1971
HMAS Melbourne	24 Jan 1972
Nowra	27 Apr 1972
HMAS Melbourne	27 Jul 1972
Nowra	3 Aug 1972
HMAS Melbourne	15 Aug 1972
Nowra	24 Nov 1972
HMAS Melbourne	20 Aug 1973
Nowra	7 Dec 1973
HMAS Melbourne	13 May 1974
Nowra	18 Jun 1974
HMAS Melbourne	28 Oct 1974
Nowra	27 Nov 1974
HMAS Melbourne	3 Feb 1975
Nowra	11 Apr 1975
Broome (Dt4)	May 1975 to Dec 1975
HMAS Melbourne	4 Aug 1976
Nowra	4 Nov 1976
HMAS Melbourne	20 Jan 1977
Nowra	1977
HMAS Melbourne	27 Apr 1977
Nowra	5 Oct 1977
Darwin (Dt3)	20 Jan 1978 to 14 Dec 1980
HMAS Melbourne	27 Feb 1978
Nowra	31 May 1978
HMAS Melbourne	22 May 1979
Nowra	30 May 1979
HMAS Melbourne	18 Jul 1979
Nowra	14 Nov 1979
HMAS Melbourne	29 Jan 1980
Nowra	16 Apr 1980
HMAS Melbourne	17 Jul 1980
Nowra	12 Dec 1980
HMAS Melbourne	Apr 1981
Nowra	23 Jul 1981
HMAS Melbourne	Oct 1981
Nowra	10 Nov 1981
Disb into VC-851	2 Jul 1982
Nowra	9 Feb 1984

Grumman S-2E 153599 '844' of No.816 Squadron in 1968. (MAP)

No.817 Squadron

Badge: On an azure field, a sharkhaurient embowed proper pierced by an arrow in bend sinister gules flighted or

Motto: 1. Facere animo
(To act with spirit or courage)
2. Aude facere
(Dare to act)

No.817 Squadron formed at Crail on 15 March 1941 for torpedo spotter reconnaissance work with 9 Albacore Is. Embarking in HMS *Furious* in July, the ship sailed for an attack on the Arctic port of Petsamo. The following month the squadron joined HMS *Victorious* for operations in the Barents Sea area, followed in September and October by attacks on shipping in Vest Fjord. On 9 March 1942 a torpedo attack was made on the German battleship *Tirpitz* off northern Norway without success, and in July operations were carried out in the Bear Island area. In October the squadron embarked again in HMS *Victorious* to take part in the North African landings, during which a bombing attack was made on a fort at Algiers on 8 November. On 21 November one of the squadron's aircraft attacked and sank the *U-517* in the North Atlantic.

After returning home No.817 embarked in HMS *Furious* at Scapa in February 1943, transferring to HMS *Indomitable* the next month. On completion of work-up it sailed for the Mediterranean to provide cover for landings in Sicily, with an increased strength of 15 aircraft, but on 16 July the ship was badly damaged in a torpedo attack. HMS *Indomitable* then sailed to the United States for repair, but most of No.817 were put ashore to Gibraltar, leaving only 'Z' Flight aboard. The latter eventually disembarked ashore to Norfolk, Va and their aircraft went to Trinidad for No.750 Squadron at Piarco, whilst the Gibraltar party was dispersed. The squadron was declared non-operational with effect from 1 September 1943.

On 1 December 1943 No.817 regrouped at Lee-on-Solent under the same CO as a torpedo bomber reconnaissance unit with 12 Barracuda IIs. Initially attached to the 52nd Naval TBR Wing, it transferred to the 12th Naval TBR Wing in January 1944, embarking in HMS *Begum* for passage to Ceylon. In July the Wing joined HMS *Indomitable*, now repaired, and next month carried out a bombing attack on Sumatra, followed by another in September and operations in the Nicobar area in October. In November No.817 transferred to HMS *Unicorn* and sailed for South Africa, returning to southern India after a few weeks ashore. A few days after arrival in January 1945, however, the squadron lost its aircraft and re-embarked in HMS *Unicorn* for passage home, where it disbanded on arrival on 21 February 1945.

No.817 reformed at Rattray on 1 April 1945, again as a torpedo bomber reconnaissance unit. It was equipped with 18 Barracuda IIs fitted with AN/APS-04, the American version of ASV. The squadron moved to Fearn in that month, where it worked up to join the 21st Carrier Air Group in a *Colossus*-class carrier, for which it reduced its strength to 12 aircraft in August, but it was no longer required after VJ-day, and on 23 August 1945 disbanded at Fearn.

On 25 April 1950 No.817 reformed at St.Merryn as a Royal Australian Navy squadron for anti-submarine duties. Equipped with 12 Firefly 5s, these embarked in HMAS *Sydney* in August as part of the 21st CAG, for passage to Australia, where some AS.6s were received. The squadron left this group in October 1951 to sail for three months in Korean waters, and in October 1952 it took part in Atomic bomb tests in the Monte Bello Islands. The ship sailed for the United Kingdom in March 1953, and No.817 took part in the Coronation Review flypast at Spithead on 15 June from its shore base at Gosport. In September the squadron transferred to HMAS *Vengeance*, returning to HMAS *Sydney* in August 1954. No.817 disbanded at Nowra on 27 April 1955.

No.817 reformed, again as RAN squadron, at Culdrose on 4 August 1955 for anti-submarine duties with seven Gannet AS.1s. The strength was reduced to six in November, and these embarked in HMAS *Melbourne* in February 1956 for passage to Australia. After participating in many exercises and seeing much of the Far East, the squadron disbanded at Nowra on 18 August 1958.

On 18 July 1963 the squadron reformed at Nowra as an anti-submarine helicopter squadron, equipped with eight Wessex HAS.31As, which embarked in HMAS *Melbourne* the following month. They were modified in early 1969 to HAS.31B standard, and in that same year the unit changed its style to adopt the American type designation HS-817. In February 1976 the squadron re-equipped with ten Sea King HAS.50s with which it is still equipped, having taken part in numerous exercises. During 1986 one aircraft was painted with a special colour scheme to mark the 75th anniversary of the RAN.

Battle Honours
Norway	1941
North Africa	1942
Biscay	1942
Sicily	1943
Korea	1951-52

Identification Markings
Albacore *5A+*; Barracuda *5A+*, to *3A+* in *Indomitable* 7.44, to *7A+* 4.45; Firefly *200-208/K+*; Gannet *431-436/B*, to *310-316/Y* 2.56; Wessex *810-836*; Sea King *(8)01-10*.

Fairey Albacore BF632 '5M' and others of No.817 Squadron in 1942. (MAP)

Aircraft Equipment	Period of Service	Example
Albacore I	Mar 1941 - Aug 1943	BF612 (5A)
Barracuda II	Dec 1943 - Jan 1945	BV954 (3L)
Barracuda II(ASH)	Apr 1945 - Aug 1945	MX724
Firefly FR(AS).5	Apr 1950 - Jan 1952	WB354 (208/K)
Firefly AS.6	Dec 1950 - Apr 1955	WD837 (208/K)
Gannet AS.1	Aug 1955 - Aug 1958	XA350 (316/Y)
Wessex HAS.31a/31b	Jul 1963 - Feb 1976	N7-209 (819)
Sea King HAS.50/50a	Feb 1976 - to date	N16-125(10)

Fairey Firefly AS.6 VX386 '204/K' of No.817 Squadron picks up a wire landing on HMAS Sydney around 1952. (J.H.Stenning)

Squadron bases

Crail	15 Mar 1941	HMT Queen Elizabeth	9 Oct 1943	HMAS Sydney	11 Aug 1952	HMAS Melbourne	21 May 1964
HMS Furious	15 Jul 1941	(transit)		Nowra	11 Nov 1952	Nowra	8 Nov 1964
HMS Victorious	5 Aug 1941	Lee-on-Solent	6 Nov 1943	HMAS Sydney	12 Jan 1953	HMAS Melbourne	22 Feb 1965
Hatston	7 Aug 1941	Machrihanish	14 Jan 1944	Nowra	18 Feb 1953	Sembawang	Mar 1965
HMS Victorious	14 Aug 1941	Tain	8 Feb 1944	HMAS Sydney	21 Mar 1953	HMAS Melbourne	1965
Twatt (Dt6)	20-23 Sep 1941	HMS Begum	26 Feb 1944	Nowra	4 May 1953	Nowra	22 Jun 1965
Donibristle	13 Oct 1941	SS Strathnever/	3 Mar 1944	HMAS Sydney	17 May 1953	HMAS Melbourne	6 Aug 1965
HMS Victorious	19-26 Oct 1941	SS Aronda (crews)		Gosport	15 Jun 1953	Nowra	4 Oct 1965
(Dt4)		St Thomas Mount	10 Apr 1944	HMAS Sydney	18 Jun 1953	HMAS Melbourne	19 Feb 1966
Hatston	26 Oct 1941	Ulunderpet	14 Apr 1944	Nowra	13 Aug 1953	Nowra	30 Jun 1966
HMS Victorious	3 Nov 1941	China Bay	1 Jun 1944	HMAS Vengeance	17 Sep 1953	HMAS Melbourne	20 Aug 1966
Hatston	30 Nov 1941	Katukurunda	15 Jun 1944	Nowra	9 Nov 1953	Nowra	28 Oct 1966
HMS Victorious	23 Dec 1941	HMS Indomitable	23 Jul 1944	HMAS Vengeance	11 Jan 1954	HMAS Melbourne	6 Apr 1967
Hatston	2 Jan 1942	Katukurunda	27 Sep 1944	Nowra	4 Feb 1954	Nowra	17 Aug 1967
HMS Victorious	17 Jan 1942	HMS Indomitable	8 Oct 1944	HMAS Vengeance	16 Feb 1954	HMAS Melbourne	20 Sep 1967
Hatston	23 Feb 1942	Trincomalee	20 Oct 1944	Nowra	6 May 1954	Nowra	21 Nov 1967
HMS Victorious	4 Mar 1942	HMS Unicorn	7 Nov 1944	HMAS Sydney	27 Aug 1954	HMAS Melbourne	9 Apr 1969
Hatston	16 Jun 1942	Stamford Hill	18 Nov 1944	Nowra	1 Dec 1954	Sembawang	Jun 1969
HMS Victorious	29 Jun 1942	HMS Unicorn	1 Jan 1945	HMAS Sydney	8 Feb 1955	HMAS Melbourne	Jun 1969
Hatston	10 Jul 1942	Sulur	13 Jan 1945	Nowra	10 Feb 1955	Nowra	9 Jul 1969
HMS Victorious	30 Jul 1942	HMS Unicorn (crews)	19 Jan 1945	HMAS Sydney	14 Feb 1955	HMAS Melbourne	9 Feb 1970
(Dt2)	to 23 Aug 1942	Sqdn disbanded UK	21 Feb 1945	Nowra	22 Apr 1955	Nowra	14 Jul 1970
HMS Victorious	8 Oct 1942	Rattray	1 Apr 1945	Squadron disbanded	27 Apr 1955	HMAS Melbourne	26 Oct 1970
Machrihanish	23 Nov 1942	Fearn	27 Apr 1945	Culdrose	18 Aug 1955	Nowra	8 Dec 1970
HMS Furious	11 Dec 1942	HMS Pretoria Castle		HMAS Melbourne	29 Feb 1956	HMAS Melbourne	11 Sep 1971
Hatston	14 Dec 1942	(Dt7)	19-23 Aug 1945	Nowra	7 May 1956	Nowra	9 Dec 1971
HMS Furious	12 Feb 1943	Squadron disbanded	23 Aug 1945	HMAS Melbourne	6 Aug 1956	HMAS Melbourne	24 Jan 1972
HMS Indomitable	11 Mar 1943	St Merryn	25 Apr 1950	Nowra	10 Dec 1956	Nowra	27 Apr 1972
Machrihanish	17 Mar 1943	Eglinton	19 Jun 1950	HMAS Melbourne	5 Feb 1957	HMAS Melbourne	27 Jul 1972
HMS Indomitable	21 Mar 1943	St Merryn	29 Jul 1950	Nowra	10 Jul 1957	Nowra	31 Jul 1972
North Front	29 Jul 1943	HMAS Sydney	29 Aug 1950	HMAS Melbourne	4 Oct 1957	HMAS Melbourne	15 Aug 1972
HMS Indomitable	29 Jul 1943	Nowra	6 Dec 1950	Nowra	12 Dec 1957	Nowra	26 Nov 1972
('Z' Flight)	to 20 Aug 1943	HMAS Sydney	24 Apr 1951	HMAS Melbourne	12 Feb 1958	HMAS Melbourne	20 Aug 1973
Norfolk	31 Aug 1943	Nowra	18 May 1951	Nowra	20 Jul 1958	Nowra	7 Dec 1973
transit	1 Sep 1943	HMAS Sydney	14 Jul 1951	Squadron disbanded	18 Aug 1958	HMAS Melbourne	13 May 1974
Piarco	21 Sep 1943	Nowra	3 Mar 1952	Nowra	18 Jul 1963	Nowra	19 Jun 1974
transit	27 Sep 1943	HMAS Sydney	3 Jun 1952	HMAS Melbourne	1 Aug 1963	RFA Tidespring (Dt2)	Sep 1974
Norfolk	30 Sep 1943	Nowra	17 Jun 1952	Nowra	4 Sep 1963	to	Dec 1974

Westland Wessex HAS.31 N7-200 '(8)10' of HS-817 lowers a crewman at Darwin during relief work following Cyclone Tracy. (Royal Australian Navy)

Squadron bases
HMAS Melbourne	28 Oct 1974
Nowra	27 Nov 1974
HMAS Melbourne	26 Dec 1974
Nowra	23 Jan 1975
HMAS Melbourne	3 Feb 1975
Nowra	11 Apr 1975
HMAS Melbourne	4 Aug 1976
Nowra	4 Nov 1976
HMAS Melbourne	20 Jan 1977
Nowra	5 Oct 1977
HMAS Melbourne	27 Feb 1978
Nowra	31 May 1978
HMAS Melbourne	22 May 1979
Nowra	30 May 1979
HMAS Melbourne	18 Jul 1979
Nowra	14 Nov 1979
HMAS Melbourne	29 Jan 1980
Nowra	16 Apr 1980
HMAS Melbourne	17 Aug 1980
Nowra	12 Dec 1980
HMAS Melbourne	Sep 1981
Nowra	10 Nov 1981

Commanding Officers
L/C D Sanderson
  DSC RN   15 Mar 1941
L/C PG Sugden RN 23 Feb 1942
Lt LED Walthall
  DSC RN   30 Jun 1942
L/C NR Corbet
  -Milward RN   5 Jul 1942
L/C(A) TW May
  SANF(V)   7 Aug 1943
Squadron disbanded 21 Feb 1945
L/C(A) MA Lacayo
  RN   1 Apr 1945
Squadron disbanded 23 Aug 1945
L/C RB Lunberg
  DFC RN   25 Apr 1950
L/C AL Oakley
  DFC RAN   14 Jul 1952
L/C DS Harvey RAN 15 Aug 1953
L/C JD Goble RAN 13 Aug 1953 (sic)
Squadron disbanded 27 Apr 1955
L/C JA Gledhill
  DSC RAN   4 Aug 1955
L/C JS Hickson RAN 9 Nov 1956
L/C HE Bailey
  DSC RAN   7 Jan 1957
Squadron disbanded 18 Aug 1958
Cdr GM Jude RAN 18 Jul 1963
L/C RJ Simmonds
  RAN   19 Sep 1963
L/C DJ Orr RAN   4 Oct 1965
L/C F Hillier RAN 7 Jun 1966
L/C AAH Evans
  RAN   26 Jul 1966

Commanding Officers
L/C RA Waddell-Wood
  RAN   23 Oct 1967
L/C DN Rodgers
  RAN   15 Jan 1968
L/C GA Thomas
  RAN   1 Jul 1968
L/C DS Ferry RAN 28 Nov 1968

Commanding Officers
L/C DN Rodgers
  RAN   16 Mar 1969
L/C AG Whitton
  RAN   5 Jan 1970
L/C DC McLaren
  RAN   31 May 1971
L/C DG Debus RAN 26 Jul 1972
L/C TSJ Pennington
  RAN   28 Jun 1974
L/C IM Speedy RAN 9 Jun 1975
Cdr ES Bell RAN   2 Feb 1976
L/C RK Waldron
  RAN   8 Feb 1976
L/C JW Firth RAN 12 Apr 1977
L/C AH Craig RAN 29 May 1978
L/C KB Englesman
  RAN   4 May 1979
L/C WM Kimpton
  RAN   3 Apr 1980
L/C JWJ Nicoll RAN 30 Mar 1981
L/C HE Campey
  RAN   21 Jan 1983
L/C KW Eames RAN 6 Jul 1984
L/C RJ Cooper RAN 21 Dec 1984
L/C LN Phillips
  RAN   5 Dec 1986
L/C AF Wright RAN 1 Jul 1988
L/C T Gorman RAN 8 Dec 1989
L/C JH Edwards
  RAN   6 Dec 1991
L/C PR Lea RAN   9 Dec 1993
L/C RJ Smith RAN 5 Apr 1994

Westland Sea King HAS.50 N16-118 '07' of HS-817. (Trevor Boughton)

No.818 Squadron

Badge: A splayed red hand on a black swastika
(Design not approved)
Motto: Sin mora
(Without delay)

No.818 Squadron was originally planned to form at Lee-on-Solent on 1 October 1939 with 12 Swordfish I for torpedo spotter reconnaissance duties in HMS *Hermes*. The approach of war resulted in these plans being advanced, and instead it came into existence at Evanton on 24 August 1939 with nine of this type, embarking the next day in HMS *Ark Royal* at Scapa. After carrying out a shipping search off Norway, three aircraft were detached to HMS *Furious* in October, the remainder of the squadron remaining ashore. In April 1940 the whole squadron embarked in HMS *Furious* to take part in the defence of Norway, two German destroyers being attacked in Trondheim Fjord on 11 April.

In 1940 June the squadron carried out operations in the English Channel under the control of RAF Coastal Command, then embarked in HMS *Ark Royal* for the Mediterranean. Here attacks were made on the Vichy French Fleet at Oran, an unsuccessful strike being made on the battleship *Strasbourg*. Operations were then carried out against targets in Sardinia, including an unsuccessful strike on the Italian battleship *Littorio* on 27 November. The carrier then provided escort for Malta convoys, No.818 giving anti-submarine protection. In February 1941 bombing attacks were made on Leghorn, Genoa and Pisa, whilst mines were laid at La Spezia naval dockyard.

Towards the end of May 1941, HMS *Ark Royal* moved out into the North Atlantic to help search for the German battleship *Bismarck*. After sighting her, an attack involving No.818 secured two torpedo hits, enabling naval forces to sink her later with gunfire. Following further Malta escort duties the squadron returned home in July in HMS *Furious*, to rearm on 1 November with 9 Albacore Is. Embarking with these in HMS *Formidable* in February 1942, it sailed to join the Eastern Fleet, carrying out searches en route. In April it disembarked to Ceylon to augment the local forces against Japanese attacks, but as this danger had by then receded the squadron disbanded on 24 June 1942, its aircraft forming the basis of No.796 Squadron, and the crews eventually returned home in HMS *Unicorn*.

On 19 October 1942 No.818 reformed at Lee-on-Solent with six Swordfish II for torpedo bomber reconnaissance duties, increasing to nine shortly before embarking in HMS *Unicorn* in March 1943 for Gibraltar escort during May and June. In July it took part in a search for ships operating from ports in the Bay of Biscay, and six aircraft were disembarked to Gibraltar in August for duty during the invasion of Sicily. On 1 November part of the squadron broke away to form the basis for No.838 Squadron, and later in the month the remaining four aircraft sailed in HMS *Unicorn* to join the Eastern Fleet. Arriving in Ceylon in February 1944 they assisted carriers working up in the area until disbanding at Cochin on 14 October 1944.

No.818 next reformed at Rattray on 1 May 1945 as a torpedo bomber reconnaissance unit with 18 Barracuda IIs. Moving to Fearn in June to continue work-up, it was intended for the 22nd CAG in a Colossus-class carrier, but shortly after moving back to Rattray at the beginning of September it was retrospectively disbanded with effect from VJ-day, 15th August 1945.

Battle Honours
Norway   1940
English Channel   1940
Spartivento   1940
Mediterranean   1940-41
Atlantic   1941
'Bismarck'   1941

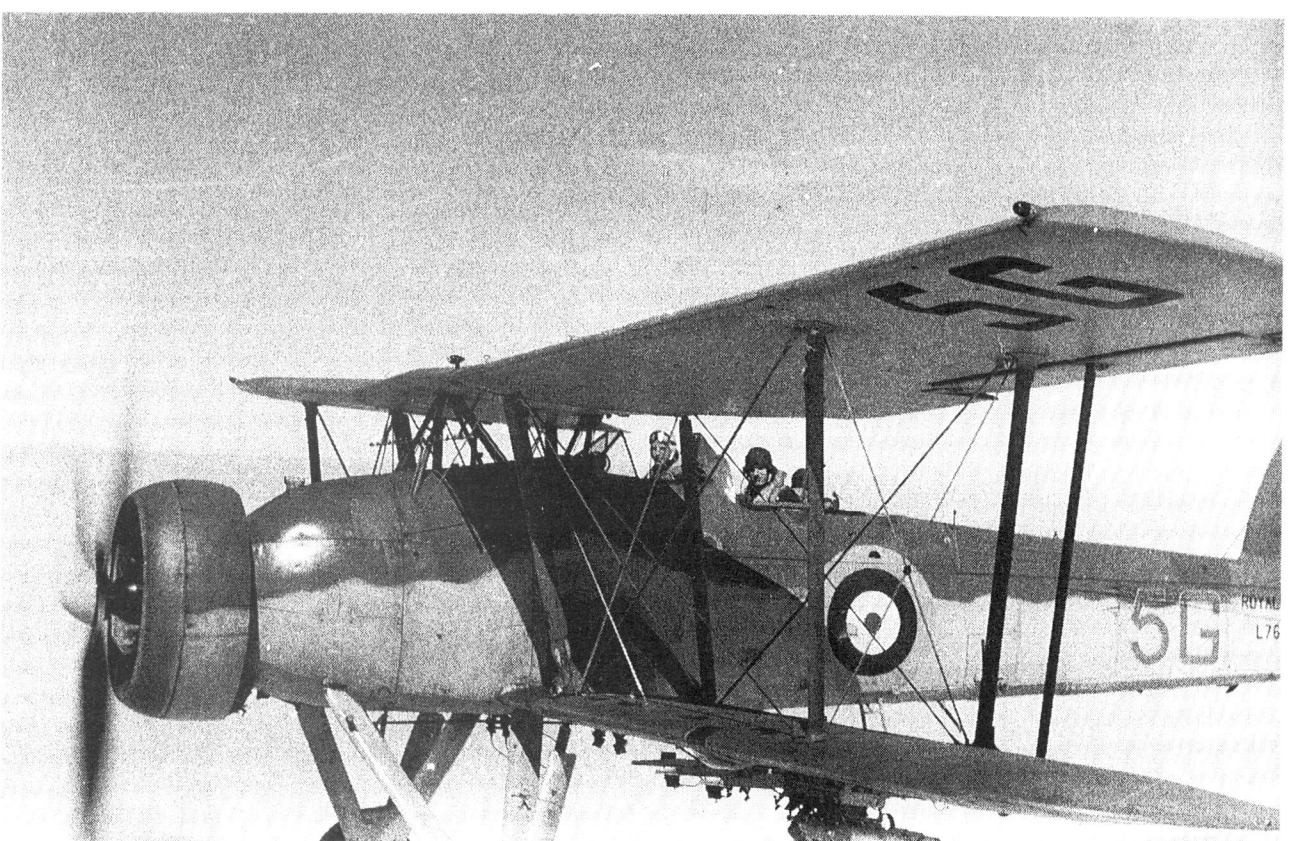

Fairey Swordfish I L7678 '5G' of No.818 Squadron from HMS Ark Royal in 1940 carries smoke floats under the wings. (Cdr R.N.Everett)

Fairey Swordfish II LS274 '1F' of No.818 Squadron over Ceylon in 1944. (Charles N.Bates)

Aircraft Equipment	Period of Service	Example
Swordfish I	Aug 1939 - Nov 1941	P4219 (5A)
Albacore I	Nov 1941 - Jun 1942	X9084
Swordfish II	Oct 1942 - Oct 1944	LS271 (1F)
Barracuda II	May 1945 - Aug 1945	DR256 (8N)

Identification Markings
Swordfish U3A+, to A5A 6.40, later 5A+; Albacore 4A+; Swordfish 1A+ from 10.42; Barracuda 8A+.

Squadron bases
Donibristle	24 Aug 1939
Evanton	30 Aug 1939
HMS Ark Royal	31 Aug 1939
Hatston	21 Sep 1939
HMS Ark Royal	23 Sep 1939
Hatston	1 Oct 1939
HMS Furious (Dt3)	23 Oct 1939
	to 17 Dec 1939
Abbotsinch	17 Dec 1939
HMS Furious	25 Dec 1939
Campbeltown	16 Feb 1940
HMS Furious	4 Apr 1940
Hatston	27 Apr 1940
HMS Furious (Dt9)	12-26 May 1940
Campbeltown	26 May 1940
Sealand (transit)	28 May 1940
Ford (transit)	29 May 1940
Thorney Island	30 May 1940
Carew Cheriton	14 Jun 1940
Aldergove (transit)	18 Jun 1940

Squadron bases
HMS Ark Royal	18 Jun 1940
Campbeltown	7 Oct 1940
HMS Ark Royal	29 Oct 1940
North Front	17 Jan 1941
HMS Ark Royal	28 Jan 1941
HMS Furious	1 Jul 1941
Arbroath	12 Jul 1941
Twatt	28 Jul 1941
Machrihanish	12 Aug 1941
HMS Argus (Dt2)	25 Sep 1941
	to 26 Oct 1941
HMS Argus (Dt2)	29 Oct 1941
	to 15 Nov 1941
Hatston	18 Jan 1942
Machrihanish	28 Jan 1942
HMS Formidable	4 Feb 1942
Juhu	13 Apr 1942
HMS Formidable	20 Apr 1942
Ratmalana	28 Apr 1942
Katukurunda	9 May 1942
Squadron disbanded	24 Jun 1942
Lee-on-Solent	19 Oct 1942
Machrihanish	17 Nov 1942
Kirkistown	2 Dec 1942
Machrihanish	18 Dec 1942
HMS Unicorn	24 Mar 1943
Belfast (Dt4)	28 Jun 1943
	to 11 Jul 1943

Squadron bases
North Front (Dt6)	28 Aug 1943
('Z' Flight)	to 30 Aug 1943
Belfast	13 Oct 1943
Machrihanish	20 Nov 1943
HMS Unicorn	22 Nov 1943
China Bay	5 Feb 1944
Juhu (Dt2)	20 Mar 1944
	to 6 Apr 1944
HMS Unicorn	29 Apr 1944
Juhu (Dt2)	7-19 May 1944
HMS Atheling	23 Aug 1944
Wingfield	12 Sep 1944
HMS Atheling	18 Sep 1944
Cochin	6 Oct 1944
Squadron disbanded	14 Oct 1944
Rattray	1 May 1945
Fearn	26 Jun 1945
Squadron disbanded	15 Aug 1945

Commanding Officers
L/C JE Fenton RN	30 Aug 1939
L/C PGO Sydney-Turner RN	19 Mar 1940
L/C TP Coode RN	24 Oct 1940
L/C TWB Shaw DSC RN	28 Jul 1941
Squadron disbanded	24 Jun 1942
L/C AH Abrams DSC RN	22 Oct 1942
L/C(A) WH Lloyd RNVR	7 Jul 1943
Squadron disbanded	14 Oct 1944
L/C(A) BW Vigrass RNVR	1 May 1945
Squadron disbanded	15 Aug 1945

No.819 Squadron

Badge: On a blue field, a foot in a sandal gold, pierced through the heel by an arrow white
Motto (1): *Redem feri claudum*
(Strike the foot that limps)
Motto (2): *Partem infirmissimam petito*
(Strike at the weakest point) [from 1991]

No.819 Squadron formed at Ford on 15 January 1940 with crews from HMS *Ark Royal* and HMS *Glorious*, equipped with 12 Swordfish Is for torpedo spotter reconnaissance duties. Part of the squadron detached to Detling during May to search for U-boats off the Belgian coast, then the following month the whole squadron joined HMS *Illustrious* for the North Atlantic, work-up being continued in Bermuda. In August the ship sailed with a Malta convoy, then joined the Mediterranean Fleet, using Dekheila as a shore base. On 4 September the squadron took part in a dive bombing attack on Calato airfield, Rhodes, this being the first of a series of attacks on enemy harbours and other targets around the Eastern Mediterranean.

Next came participation in the successful night attack on the Italian Fleet at Taranto during the night of 11-12 November, in which considerable damage was inflicted on shore targets and warships, including the sinking of the battleship *Conte Di Cavour*. Further attacks were made during the next two months, but on 10 January 1941 the carrier was badly damaged off Malta by Ju 87s and Ju 88s, several No.819 Squadron aircrew being killed and aircraft destroyed. Some squadron aircraft were in the air at the time, and these flew to Hal Far. The remnants were absorbed into No.815 Squadron on 14 January 1941, and the squadron ceased to exist.

Plans were made to reform No.819 at Lee-on-Solent on 1 September 1941 with 12 Swordfish and 2 Sea Hurricanes, for service in the second escort carrier conversion. Instead, however, it reformed there on 1 October 1941 as a torpedo bomber reconnaissance unit with only nine Swordfish Is and no fighters. After work-up ashore, and partial re-equipment with Swordfish IIs, it did in fact embark in June 1942 in what by then had become HMS *Avenger*, but only for trials. The following month the squadron was loaned to RAF Coastal Command for three months of night operations, including minelaying in the North Sea, and later the English Channel. Moving north to Scotland, it joined HMS *Archer* for trials and exercises, and later North Atlantic escort duty. On 23 May 1943, aircraft 'B' successfully attacked *U-752*, this being the first such success using rocket projectiles.

In August 1943, three Wildcats were added from No.892 Squadron, and the squadron joined HMS *Activity* for further escort duty. ASV Mk.X was fitted to the Swordfish in September 1943, and in March 1944 the fighter flight added five Wildcat Vs and VIs. Whilst escorting a North Russian convoy, aircraft 'C' claimed *U-288* jointly with No.846 Squadron on 3 April 1944, the Wildcats shooting down four enemy aircraft on this trip. In April the squadron disembarked to begin night patrols in the North Sea under Coastal Command, the Wildcats being withdrawn to help form No.833 Squadron. These continued for several months during the invasion period, initially from East Coast airfields and later from Belgium, No.819 forming part of No.155 Wing and later No.157 Wing, RAF. The squadron returned to the United Kingdom early in 1945, disbanding at Bircham Newton on 10 March 1945.

On 5 October 1961, No.819 reformed at Eglinton by renumbering No.719 Squadron. Equipped initially with 4 Wessex HAS.1s, it operated as the Wessex headquarters squadron. Numerous exercises were carried out in conjunction with the Joint Anti-Submarine School at Londonderry, the squadron moving to nearby Ballykelly when Eglinton closed in February 1963. Aircraft were embarked from time to time in NATO carriers such as USS *Essex*, HrMs *Karel Doorman* and HMS *Centaur*. Squadron strength varied, a peak of 7 aircraft being attained briefly in October 1963, and the HAS.1s were replaced by HAS.3s in April 1968. Some aircraft embarked at times in Royal Fleet Auxiliaries, but on 29 January 1971 the squadron disbanded when Ballykelly closed down.

The Wessex was by now obsolescent, and when the squadron next reformed, on 9 February 1971 at Culdrose, it received six Sea King HAS.1s for anti-submarine work. These moved to Prestwick Airport in October 1971, to undertake support for Clyde-based submarines and take part in exercises. Sea King HAS.2s were received in December 1977, and later HAS.2As, the strength gradually increasing to 9 aircraft. The squadron was re-equipped with Sea King HAS.5s from early 1985, and Sea King HAS.6s from April 1989, with aircraft numbers fluctuating between six and eleven. No.819 Squadron absorbed the remaining two aircraft of No.824 Squadron in late 1989. A, B, C & D Flts transferred from No.826 Squadron in July 1993, each flight consisting of one aircraft, along with air and ground crew, equipped to operate independently from Type 22 frigates or RFAs.

The Squadron remains based at Prestwick with the roles of support for the Clyde submarine flotilla, SAR for the west of Scotland and the provision of Sea King flights to embark in RFAs and Type 22 frigates. Occasionally flights are combined or augmented from the squadron headquarters for deployments.

Battle Honours

Mediterranean	1940-41
Libya	1940
Taranto	1940
English Channel	1942
*Atlantic	1943
Normandy	1944
Arctic	1944

Identification Markings
Swordfish *L5A*+ to 1.41, single letters from 10.41; Wildcat single letters; Wessex *320-325/H:R:CU*, to *530-533* 7.65; Sea King *300-310/CU:PW* to *700-708/PW* 16.2.81.

Aircraft Equipment	Period of Service	Example	
Swordfish I	Jan 1940 - Jan 1941	P4075	(L5Q)
	Oct 1941 - Jun 1943	W5916	(A)
Swordfish II	Apr 1942 - Mar 1945	NF134	(Z)
Swordfish III	Aug 1944 - Mar 1945	NF322	
Wildcat IV	Aug 1943 - Apr 1944	FN136	(T)
Wildcat V	Mar 1944 - Apr 1944	JV345	(T)
Wildcat VI	Mar 1944 - Apr 1944	JV601	(Z)
Whirlwind HAS.7	Oct 1961 - Jul 1962	XN359	
Wessex HAS.1	Oct 1961 - Apr 1968	XM872	(320/R)
Wessex HAS.3	Apr 1968 - Jan 1971	XP105	(532)
Sea King HAS.1	Feb 1971 - Jul 1978	XV655	(304/PW)
Sea King HAS.2/2a	Dec 1977 - Dec 1985	XV674	(306/PW)
Sea King HAS.5	Feb 1985 - Nov 1993	ZD634	(702/PW)
Sea King HAS.6	Apr 1989 - to date	XZ581	(704/PW)

Fairey Swordfish P4221 '5L' of No.819 Squadron in 1940.

A Fairey Swordfish of No.819 Squadron catches a wire as it lands on HMS Archer in 1943. (W.N.Preston)

Squadron bases
Ford	15 Jan 1940
West Freugh (4BGS)	9 Mar 1940
Ford	30 Mar 1940
Detling (Dt6)	21-23 May 1940
Roborough	27 May 1940
HMS Illustrious	11 Jun 1940
Roborough (Dt7)	16-21 Jun 1940
Bermuda	28 Jun 1940
Abbotsinch	23 Jul 1940
HMS Illustrious	11 Aug 1940
Dekheila	18 Sep 1940
HMS Illustrious	29 Sep 1940
Dekheila	3 Oct 1940
HMS Illustrious	5 Oct 1940
Fuka satt	22 Oct 1940
Dekheila	24 Oct 1940
HMS Illustrious	29 Oct 1940
Dekheila	14 Nov 1940
HMS Illustrious	25 Nov 1940
Heraklion (Dt6)	29 Nov 1940 to 6 Dec 1940
Dekheila	30 Nov 1940
HMS Illustrious	10 Dec 1940
Hal Far	10 Jan 1941
Squadron disbanded	14 Jan 1941
Lee-on-Solent	1 Oct 1941
Crail	8 Dec 1941
Twatt	27 Jan 1942
Hatston	22 Feb 1942
Donibristle	26 Mar 1942
Machrihanish	16 Apr 1942
HMS Avenger	8 Jun 1942
Machrihanish	13 Jul 1942
Langham (16 Gp)	17 Jul 1942
Bircham Newton (16Gp)	6 Aug 1942
Thorney Island	23 Sep 1942
Hatston	28 Oct 1942
Fearn	16 Dec 1942
Machrihanish	21 Jan 1943
HMS Archer	28 Feb 1943
Machrihanish	8 Apr 1943
Ballykelly	9 Apr 1943
Belfast (transit)	24 Apr 1943
HMS Archer	24 Apr 1943
Machrihanish (Dt4)	24-27 Apr 1943
Kaldadarnes	5 May 1943
HMS Archer	6 May 1943
Machrihanish	25 May 1943
Abbotsinch	27 May 1943
Ballykelly	10 Jun 1943
Abbotsinch	11 Jun 1943
HMS Archer	15 Jun 1943
St Merryn	1 Aug 1943
HMS Archer	2 Aug 1943
Machrihanish	6 Aug 1943

Squadron bases
Maydown	10 Aug 1943
Ayr (Dt4)	18-22 Aug 1943
Eglinton	22 Aug 1943
HMS Activity	30 Aug 1943
Inskip	27 Sep 1943
Belfast	15 Oct 1943
HMS Activity	12 Jan 1944
Donibristle (Dt3)	21 Feb 1944 to 25 Mar 1944
Machrihanish (Dt5)	25 Mar 1944 to 13 Apr 1944
Hatston (transit)	13 Apr 1944
Lee-on-Solent	13 Apr 1944
Manston	18 Apr 1944
Limavady	1 Aug 1944
Lee-on-Solent	1 Aug 1944
Swingfield (16 Gp)	7 Aug 1944
Biggin Hill (Dt)	29-30 Sep 1944
Bircham Newton	1 Oct 1944
Detached flight (6 a/c):	
B.63 St Croix	29 Oct 1944
B.65 Maldeghem	11 Nov 1944
B.83 Knocke-le-Zoute	14 Dec 1944
B.83 Knocke-le-Zoute	24 Jan 1945
Bircham Newton	26 Feb 1945
Squadron disbanded	10 Mar 1945

Squadron bases
Eglinton	5 Oct 1961
Culdrose	27 Oct 1961
Eglinton	10 Nov 1961
USS Essex	20 Nov 1961
Eglinton	30 Nov 1961
Machrihanish (Dt2)	2-4 Jun 1962
Belfast (Dt2)	29-30 Oct 1962
Brawdy	12 Nov 1962
Eglinton	16 Nov 1962
Machrihanish(Dt2)	3-11 Dec 1962
HMS Centaur	4 Feb 1963
Ballykelly	7 Feb 1963
Ballycastle(Dt)	25-28 Mar 1963
Ballycastle(Dt)	1-3 Apr 1963
HrMs Karel Doorman	16 Jun 1963
Ballykelly	28 Jun 1963
HMS Victorious (Dt2)	29 Jul 1963 to 29 Aug 1963
Portland	29 Aug 1963
HMS Hermes	5 Sep 1963
Portland	12 Sep 1963
HMS Hermes	26 Sep 1963
Ballykelly	22 Oct 1963
HMS Hermes	2 Dec 1963
Ballykelly	12 Dec 1963
Culdrose	6 Jan 1964
HMS Hermes	15 Jan 1964
Portland	30 Jan 1964
HMS Hermes	14 Feb 1964
Ballykelly	24 Feb 1964
RFA Tidepool (Dt2)	7-10 Apr 1964
Yeovilton (Dt2)	21-29 May 1964
RFA Tidepool (Dt2)	8-14 Jun 1964
Machrihanish(Dt2)	22-23 Jul 1964
HMS Lofoten (Dt2)	12-22 Oct 1964
HMS Lofoten (Dt2)	9-12 Nov 1964
HMS Lofoten (Dt2)	28-30 Nov 1964
HMS Ark Royal	16 Jan 1965
Ballykelly (Dt2)	12-24 Feb 1965
Ballykelly	16 Mar 1965
RFA Tidepool (Dt2)	15-18 Nov 1965
RFA Tidepool(Dt2)	30 Nov 1965 to 8 Dec 1965

Squadron bases
RFA Olynthus (Dt2)	26 Jan 1966 to 1 Feb 1966
RFA Olynthus (Dt2)	19 May 1966 to 14 Jun 1966
RFA Olynthus (Dt2)	27-30 Jun 1966
HMS Bulwark(Dt2)	4-5 Jul 1966
RFA Oleander(Dt2)	1-6 Oct 1966
HMS Lofoten(Dt2)	5-11 Nov 1966
HMCS Assiniboine (Dt1)	6-18 Nov 1966
RFA Olna (Dt2)	9-13 Dec 1966
RFA Tidespring (Dt2)	1-9 Feb 1967
RFA Tidespring (Dt2)	14-17 May 1967
Lossiemouth	14 Jun 1967
Ballykelly	16 Jun 1967
Belfast	18 Jun 1967
Ballykelly	26 Jun 1967
RFA Tidepool (Dt2)	4-17 May 1967
Arbroath (Dt2)	21-23 Jul 1967
RFA Tidepool (Dt2)	13-17 Aug 1967
RFA Tidepool (Dt2)	12-28 Sep 1967
Lossiemouth (Dt2)	7-12 Sep 1967
RFA Olwen	16 Oct 1967
Ballykelly	19 Oct 1967
RFA Engadine (Dt2)	26 May 1968 to 7 Jun 1968
RFA Tidepool (Dt2)	1-11 Jul 1968
Arbroath (Dt1)	20-21 Jul 1968
RFA Engadine (Dt2)	13-29 Aug 1968
RFA Engadine	21 Sep 1968
Ballykelly	5 Nov 1968
Prestwick	4 Dec 1968
RFA Tidepool	7 Dec 1968
Ballykelly	17 Dec 1968
RFA Engadine	28 Jan 1969
Ballykelly	6 Feb 1969
RFA Tidepool	1 Mar 1969
Ballykelly	10 Mar 1969
RFA Engadine	16 Apr 1969
Ballykelly	14 May 1969
Tiree	8 Jun 1969
Ballykelly	8 Jun 1969
RFA Olmeda	13 Aug 1969

Lt B.H.Beeston in the cockpit of Grumman Wildcat V JV 522 of No.819 Squadron's fighter flight in HMS Activity during March 1944. (FAA Museum)

Westland Wessex HAS.1 XS149 '530' of No.819 Squadron in 1967. (MAP)

Squadron bases		Squadron bases		Squadron bases		Squadron bases	
Ballykelly	10 Sep 1969	HMS Hermes	28 Sep 1973	Marham (Dt3)	9-12Jun 1980	RFA Engadine (Dt3)	29 Apr 1983
Linton-on-Ouse	4-6Jul 1969	Prestwick	17 Oct 1973	RFA Fort Austin	30 Jun 1980		to 20 May 1983
(Dt3)		RFA Engadine		(Dt3)	to 11 Jul 1980	Leconfield(Dt2)	23-27May1983
Bishops Court	30 Sep 1969	(Dt2)	4-7Nov 1973	Arbroath/RFA Fort		HMS Hermes (Dt2)	27 Jun 1983
Ballykelly	2 Oct 1969	RFA Olmeda (Dt1)	4-9Nov 1973	Austin (Dt2)	14-18Jul 1980		to 1 Jul 1983
RFA Olna (Dt2)	5-9Oct 1969	Sumburgh (Dt2)	9-16Nov1973	Culdrose (Dt2)	16-23Sep 1980	Stornoway (Dt3)	14-16Jul 1983
RFA Engadine		Aalborg	25 Apr 1974	Scampton (Dt2)	13-16Oct 1980	Stornoway (Dt3)	20-22Jul 1983
(Dt3)	7-15Dec 1969	Prestwick	15 May 1974	Kinloss (Dt2)	3-6Feb 1981	Culdrose (Dt2)	19-22Sep 1983
Prestwick (Dt2)	17-19Feb 1970	HMS Hermes (Dt3)	28 Sep 1974	Coltishall (Dt2)	6-10Apr1981	Otterburn (Dt)	11-13Oct 1983
RFA Olmeda	26 Feb 1970		to 17 Oct 1974	Tirstrup (Dt3)	24 Apr 1981	Benbecula (Dt)	25,28Oct 1983
RFA Engadine	19 Mar 1970	RFA Tidespring	19-28Feb 1975		to 16 May 1981	Coltishall (Dt2)	24-28Oct 1983
Ballykelly	23 Mar 1970	(Dt1)		Arbroath/	24-28May1981	Otterburn (Dt)	28-30Nov1983
Skrydstrup	19 Apr 1970	Sola (Dt4)	14-28 Apr 1975	Kinloss (Dt2)		Arbroath (Dt)	12-13Dec1983
Ballykelly	11 May 1970	Tirstrup (Dt4)	28 Apr 1975	RFA Olmeda (Dt3)	8-19Jun 1981	Andros Island,	
RFA Tidepool	27 Jul 1970		to 12 May 1975	RFA Olmeda		Bahamas (Dt2)	29 Mar 1984
Ballykelly	4 Aug 1970	Coltishall(Dt2)	10-13Jun 1975	(Dt3)	22-26Jun 1981		to 25 Apr 1984
RFA Tidepool (Dt3)	8 Aug 1970	Florennes (Dt1)	19-22Jun 1975	Binbrook (Dt2)	12-15Oct 1981	Wattisham (Dt1)	2-4Apr1984
to	3 Sep 1970	RFA Engadine (Dt3)	25 Jun 1975	Stornoway (Dt4)	6-13Nov1981	Coltishall (Dt1)	30 Apr 1984
RFA Engadine	12 Oct 1970		to 4 Jul 1975	West Freugh			to 4 May 1984
Ballykelly	21 Oct 1970	Valley (Dt1)	4-6Aug1975	(Dt2)	10-11Nov 1981	Scatsa (Dt2)	28 May 1984
RFA Grey Rover/		HMS Hermes		Arbroath (Dt2)	7-11Dec 1981		to 1 Jun 1984
RFA Tidepool	7 Dec 1970	(Dt3)	3-21Nov 1975	Kinloss (Dt2)	1-5Feb 1982	HrMs Poolster	
Ballykelly	13 Dec 1970	Sola (Dt4)	4-18May1976	Coltishall(Dt2)	15-19Mar1982	(Dt2)	17-29Jun 1984
Squadron disbanded	29 Jan 1971	Tirstrup (Dt4)	18-25May1976	Kinloss (Dt2)	3-7May1982	HMS Illustrious	
Culdrose	9 Feb 1971	Newcastle (Dt2)	10 Jan 1977	Leconfield (Dt2)	28 Jun 1982	(Dt2)	23-27Jul 1984
RFA Engadine	29 Mar 1971		to 20 Feb 1977		to 2 Jul 1982	Kinloss (Dt1)	1-5Oct 1984
Culdrose	5 Apr 1971	Tirstrup (Dt3)	13 May 1977	Benbecula (Dt2)	31 Jul 1982	RFA Fort George	
Tirstrup	27 Apr 1971		to 3 Jun 1977		to 4 Aug 1982	(Dt2)	4-16Nov 1984
Valkenberg	13 May 1971	HMS Hermes (Dt2)	30 Aug 1977	Leuchars (Dt2)	27 Sep 1982	Coltishall(Dt2)	10-14Dec1984
Culdrose	17 May 1971		to 1 Nov 1977		to 1 Oct 1982	Plockton (Dt1)	16-18Jan 1985
Boscombe Down	4 Jul 1971	Tirstrup (Dt4)	17 Apr 1978	HrMs Zuiderkruis	8-18Nov1982	RFA Fort Grange	1-15Feb 1985
RFA Engadine	21 Jul 1971		to 5 May 1978	(Dt2)		(Dt2)	
Culdrose	23 Sep 1971	HMS Hermes	1 Jul 1979	Arbroath (Dt2)	6-10Dec1982	Coltishall (Dt2)	1-4Apr1985
Prestwick	27 Oct 1971	Prestwick	13 Jul 1979	HrMs Zuiderkruis	27 Jan 1983	Aalborg (Dt3)	6-18May1985
RFA Olwen (Dt2)	22 May 1973	Marham (Dt3)	22-25Oct 1979	(Dt2)	to 11 Feb 1983	Culdrose (Dt2)	20-23May1985
to 20 Jun 1973		RFA Olwen (Dt)	4 Nov 1979	Coltishall (Dt2)	7-11Mar 1983	HrMs Poolster	
Stornoway (Dt3)	13-15Jul 1973	Tirstrup (Dt3)	18 Apr 1980	Sola (Dt2)	18-29Apr 1983	(Dt2)	9-21Jun 1985
Dounreay (Dt1)	16-21Jul 1973		to 12 May 1980			Scatsa (Dt2)	22-26Jul 1985

Westland Sea King HAS.1 XV695 '303/PW' of No.819 Squadron, Prestwick in 1973. (MAP)

Squadron bases
Waddington (Dt2) 21-24 Oct 1985
HMS Illustrious
  (Dt2) 4-9 Nov 1985
RFA Fort Austin
  (Dt2) 9-13 Nov 1985
Waddington (Dt2) 25-28 Nov 1985
RFA Olmeda (Dt2) 2-22 Feb 1986
Coltishall (Dt2) 24-27 Mar 1986
Sola (Dt2) 5-16 May 1986
Yeovilton (Dt2) 22 Jun 1986
  to 4 Jul 1986
Valley (Dt2) 29 Sep 1986
  to 7 Oct 1986
Machrihanish
  (Dt2) 13-16 Oct 1986
RFA Tidespring
  (Dt2) 1-11 Nov 1986
Coltishall (Dt2)
  24-28 Nov 1986
Arbroath (Dt2) 26-29 Jan 1987
Arbroath (Dt2) 21-24 Apr 1987

Squadron bases
Lista (Norway)
  (Dt3) 4-16 May 1987
Machrihanish
  (Dt1) 3-10 Jun 1987
Lossiemouth
  (Dt1) 15-17 Jun 1987
RFA Olwen (Dt2) 15-26 Jun 1987
Coltishall (Dt2) 14-17 Sep 1987
Waddington (Dt2) 5-14 Oct 1987
HMS Illustrious
  (Dt2) 19-23 Oct 1987
HMS Leeds Castle
  (Dt1) 23-29 Oct 1987
Waddington (Dt2) 2-5 Nov 1987
HrMs Poolster 28 Feb 1989
  (Dt2) to 17 Mar 1989
Kjevik (Dt2) 1-7 Jun 1989
RFA Fort Austin
  (Dt2) 8-20 Jun 1989
Portland (Dt2) 23-30 Sep 1989
FORACS (Dt2) 2-8 Nov 1989

Squadron bases
Stavanger (Dt2) 25 May 1991
  to 1 Jun 1991
A to D Flights from
826 Sqdn 30 Jul 1993
HrMs Poolster 6 Sep 1993
  (C Flt) to 18 Oct 1993
HrMs Poolster 1 Oct 1993
  (D Flt) to 19 Oct 1993
HrMs Poolster 25 Oct 1993
  (C Flt) to 19 Nov 1993
RFA Olna (C Flt) 18 Feb 1994
  to 7 Mar 1994
HrMs Poolster 1-24 Mar 1994
  (D Flt)
FORACS (C Flt) 28 Mar 1994
  to 4 Apr 1994
RFA Olna 13 Jun 1994
  (C & D Flts) to 5 Aug 1994
HrMs Zuiderkruis (Dt2)
  12-2 2 Sep 1994
HMS Illustrious (Dt2)
  26-30 Sep 1994

Commanding Officers
L/C JW Hale DSO
  RN 12 Feb 1940
Squadron disbanded 14 Jan 1941
L/C DG Goodwin
  DSC RN 25 Oct 1941
Lt HSMcN Davenport
  RN 10 Apr 1942
Lt(A) OAG Oxley
  RN 23 Jan 1943
L/C(A) PDT Stevens
  RNVR 20 Apr 1944
Squadron disbanded 10 Mar 1945
L/C JRT Bluett RN 5 Oct 1961
L/C PJ Lynn RN 7 Sep 1962
L/C P Burton RN 26 Aug 1964
L/C MA Botten RN 3 May 1965
L/C AG Claridge RN 9 Feb 1966
L/C PHG Rogers RN 30 May 1967
L/C DB Bathurst RN 7 Feb 1969
L/C DW Shrubb RN 30 Oct 1969
Squadron disbanded 29 Jan 1971
L/C DW Shrubb RN 9 Feb 1971
L/C JDW Husband
  RN 8 Nov 1971
L/C DT Ancona RN 28 Feb 1973
L/C M Hope RN 9 Oct 1974
L/C M Maddox RN 15 Oct 1976
L/C AF Hutchinson
  RN 10 Mar 1978
L/C A Finnes RN 8 Jan 1980
L/C PF Southon RN 1 Jul 1981
L/C MJ Priestley
  RN 14 Apr 1983
L/C JJ Carter RN 3 Apr 1985
L/C CJ Denny RN 20 Mar 1987
L/C IG Milne RN 1 Nov 1989
L/C CA Sutton RN 18 Jun 1991
L/C C Riley RN 3 Jul 1993
L/C DM Searle RN 2 Jun 1994

Westland Sea King HAS.6 ZD637 '700/N' of No.819 Squadron in 1993. (MAP)

No.820 Squadron

Badge: On a white field, over two bars wavy in base, a flying fish, blue
Motto: Tutamen et ultor (Safeguard and avenger)

No.820 Squadron formed at Gosport on 3 April 1933 from No.450 Flight and half of No.445 Flight, as a Fleet Spotter Reconnaissance squadron equipped with nine Fairey IIIFs. These embarked in HMS *Courageous* in May, 'B' Flight being detached to HMS *Furious* in January 1934 for passage to Gibraltar. In June six of the IIIFs were withdrawn and replaced by Seals, both types giving way to 12 Shark Is in December 1934. Problems with the Sharks' engines led to 'A' Flight being re-equipped with six Baffins in August 1935, when the ship sailed to the Mediterranean, where its squadrons were on standby in the Canal Zone during the Abyssinian crisis. The Baffins were withdrawn on return home in February 1936, and 12 Shark IIs arrived in December of that year.

On 20 May 1937 the squadron took part in the Coronation Review flypast at Spithead, then in September re-equipped with 12 Swordfish Is to become a torpedo spotter reconnaissance squadron. In November 1938 the squadron transferred to the then new HMS *Ark Royal*, becoming the first squadron to land aboard in January 1939. Shortly after the outbreak of war the ship sailed for the South Atlantic, No.820 having a reduced strength of 9 aircraft. These were involved in searches for enemy merchant ships, this task being continued when the ship moved into the Indian Ocean. After a spell in the Mediterranean, the ship was recalled to participate in the Norwegian operations, and No.820 carried out a number of patrols and bombing attacks on shore targets.

After the surrender of France, the ship sailed to North Africa, and torpedo attacks were carried out on French battleships and other warships at Oran, mines also being laid. This was followed by attacks on Cagliari, and a further attack on French ships off Dakar in September. An unsuccessful torpedo attack was made on the battleship *Littorio* with the Italian Fleet off Sardinia in November, followed by several searches, patrols and bombing attacks in both the Mediterranean and Atlantic. These culminated in May 1941 with participation in the torpedo attack on the German battleship *Bismarck*, which enabled it to be caught and sunk.

After a Malta reinforcement operation in June 1941, No.820 transferred to HMS *Victorious* for convoy protection, before disembarking to re-equip with 12 Albacores Is. With these it sailed to Iceland in November, transferring to HMS *Formidable* in February 1942 for duties in the Indian Ocean. From April it participated in the Madagascar operations, returning home in the autumn prior to taking part in the North African landings, during which *U-331* was sunk by a squadron aircraft on 17 November after an earlier attack by RAF Hudsons. During the early months of 1943 the squadron operated mainly in the Western Mediterranean. In July it provided cover for the Sicily landings, and in September for the landings at Salerno. After a trip to Iceland No.820 disbanded on arrival home on 13 November 1943, its aircraft going into storage at Donibristle.

On 1 January 1944 the squadron reformed at Lee-on-Solent as a torpedo bomber reconnaissance unit with 12 Barracuda IIs. These embarked in HMS *Indefatigable* in June, to take part in unsuccessful attacks on the German battleship *Tirpitz* in Norway. Disembarking in September, it re-equipped with 21 Avenger Is, these being exchanged for IIs before re-embarking in November for the Far East.

Blackburn Shark I K4352 '740' of No.820 Squadron, HMS Courageous in 1935. (MAP)

Fairey Swordfish I K8880 '647' and others of No.820 Squadron off the south coast around 1937/8. (A.T.Goodman)

On arrival in Ceylon No.820 joined No.2 Strike Wing, re-embarking in January 1945 to take part in a highly successful attack on oil refineries at Palembang, Sumatra. During March and April over 100 sorties were flown during strikes on airfields in the Sakashima Gunto group of islands in the East China Seas, returning to the same objectives in May. In June 1945 the squadron became part of the 7th Carrier Air Group, and shortly before VJ-day struck at targets in the Tokyo area on the Japanese mainland. After reducing to 12 aircraft in Australia it re-embarked for a trip to New Zealand, eventually disbanding on the ship's return to the United Kingdom on 16 March 1946.

No.820 next reformed at Eglinton on 3 July 1951 as an anti-submarine unit equipped with eight Firefly AS.5s. These were exchanged for eight Firefly AS.6s in December, and the squadron joined HMS Indomitable in January 1952 for a Mediterranean cruise, followed by an exercise. Transferring in August to HMS Theseus for a further exercise, it carried out intensive night flying work in the Mediterranean in October, flying home from Malta at the end of that year. A month later it returned to the Mediterranean in HMS Indomitable, but came home again in May to participate in the Coronation Review flypast at Spithead on 15 June 1953. Following this it rejoined HMS Theseus and once more returned to the Mediterranean. No.820 again sailed home in October 1953, to re-equip with eight Avenger AS.4s at Eglinton in February 1954. In July it was once again Mediterranean-bound, this time in HMS Centaur. In February 1955 the aircraft flew home in stages from Hal Far via Cagliari, Cuers and Bordeaux to Lee-on-Solent, thence to Eglinton.

On 7 March 1955 the squadron re-equipped at Eglinton with 9 Gannet AS.1s, with which it embarked in HMS Bulwark in September for an exercise. After completion of work up it joined HMS Centaur in January 1956 for a spell in the Mediterranean before sailing through the Suez Canal for service in the Far East, during which it visited India, Pakistan and Malaya. Returning through the Mediterranean, the squadron disbanded on arrival on 15 May 1956, the aircraft going into store at Donibristle.

No.820 next reformed on 30 July 1956 at Eglinton, again as an anti-submarine unit, with eight Gannet AS.1s. It was not until June 1957 that these embarked in HMS Bulwark, taking part in two exercises and a visit to Rotterdam before disbanding at Ford on 2 December 1957.

The squadron became the second anti-submarine helicopter unit when it next reformed at Eglinton on 21 January 1958 with 8 Whirlwind HAS.7s. These were reduced to six before joining HMS Eagle in May 1958, transferring direct to HMS Ark Royal the following month for a spell in the Mediterranean. Shortly after joining HMS Albion in August 1958 the aircraft engines began to suffer from overheating problems, and later the squadron was forbidden to fly over the sea due to losses of aircraft. At the end of the year the ship sailed to the Far East, and whilst at Hong Kong new engines were fitted. Early in 1959 visits were made to New Zealand and Australia before returning to Singapore, where the squadron disbanded at Sembawang on 8 May 1959.

Six Whirlwind HAS.7s were again the equipment when the squadron reformed on 3 November 1959 at Culdrose, and with these it embarked in HMS Ark Royal in March 1950 for the Mediterranean. In August the ship returned home to take part in exercises in Home waters, before disembarking No.820 to Culdrose, where it disbanded on arrival on 3 October 1960.

On 23 September 1964 the squadron reformed at Culdrose with 8 Wessex HAS.1s, again for anti-submarine work. These embarked in HMS Eagle in December, sailing for the Indian Ocean and then Singapore before returning home in May 1965. In August it re-embarked to return to the Far East, but in December rejoined hurriedly to sail for activities in Aden, returning to Singapore in February 1966. Returning home through the Suez Canal in August, squadron aircraft embarked for short periods in HMS Lofoten and RFA Olna before transferring to HMS Eagle in April 1967. In August the ship sailed for the Far East via Ascension Island and Cape Town, returning home in June 1968.

Disembarking to Culdrose in October 1968, the aircraft were exchanged for four Wessex HAS.3s in May 1969, and these embarked in the cruiser HMS Blake the following month. In February 1970 it sailed for the Far East, and on to Australia in May, where two aircraft were attached to RFA Olmeda. Returning home in December, aircraft were attached at various times during 1971 to Royal Fleet Auxiliaries before rejoining HMS Blake in July for a visit to the United States. After visits to Barbados, Tenerife and Gibraltar in November, the ship sailed to the Mediterranean for a few weeks before returning in January 1972. After further periods of embarkation, No.820 re-equipped in December 1972 with four Sea King HAS.1s, with which it rejoined HMS Blake in September 1973. A visit was paid in January 1974 to Bermuda, the United States and the Virgin Islands, returning home in April to visit Sweden and Germany. In September the squadron sailed for the Far East, eventually returning home in June 1975.

No.820 then participated in several exercises, before visiting Holland and Germany in the summer of 1976. It was mainly shore based from July 1976, apart from small detachments in various ships. In January 1977 it re-equipped with four Sea King HAS.2s, and these embarked in HMS Blake in September for a three months cruise. Sea King HAS.2As began to arrive in January 1979, and several periods were spent afloat that year. The squadron transferred to HMS Hermes in January 1980, disembarking to Culdrose in March, where it re-equipped with Sea King HAS.5s in November 1980 to work up for HMS Invincible. The whole squadron embarked in this new carrier in February 1981, and in April 1982 sailed in her as part of the Falklands Task Force, strength being increased to a peak of nine aircraft. The squadron joined HMS Invincible again in December 1983 for a spell in the Far East, returning early in Mar 1984 due to the ship having major mechanical problems.

After operating mainly in home waters during the remainder of 1984, and a deployment to the western Mediterranean in the autumn of 1985, the squadron transferred to HMS Ark Royal in February 1986, with Westlant deployments in summer 1986 and again in spring 1987. Ark Royal deployed to the Far East and Australia for Outback 1988, including the Australian bi-centenary. After operating in the eastern Atlantic during 1989 and the Mediterranean in spring 1991, No.820 took part in Ocean Safari during the summer. Westlant deployments in the autumn of 1991 and 1992 were punctuated by Shop Window in the Mediterranean in summer 1992.

In January 1993 the squadron deployed to the Adriatic in RFAs Fort Grange and Olwen along with the Ark Royal task group as part of Operation Grapple in support of troops ashore in the former Yugoslavia. The Squadron returned to the UK in August 1993 and deployed again to the Adriatic from January until June 1994. The squadron transferred to HMS Illustrious from October 1994 when Ark Royal was laid up prior to refit.

Identification Markings

IIIF, Seal & Shark *738-750*; Shark *645-659* from 12.35; Baffin *40-46*; Swordfish *645-659*, to *A4A+* 5.39, later *4A+*; Albacore *5A+*, also *ØA+*; Barracuda *3A+*, to *18A+* 10.44; Avenger *1A+*, later *370-389/S*; Firefly *236-243*, to *221-229/J:T* 12.51; Avenger from 3.54 - *371-378/GN:C*; Gannet *320-328/B*; Whirlwind *320-327/GN:A* to 5.59, *290-295/R* from 11.59; Wessex HAS.1 *290-297/E*, to *060-067/E* 7.65, HAS.3 *410/-414/BL*; Sea King *410-413/BL*, to *360-362/N* 11.80, to *010-020/N:R* 2.81.

Battle Honours

Norway	1940-44	Sicily	1943
Spartivento	1940	Salerno	1943
Mediterranean	1940	Palembang	1945
'Bismarck'	1941	Okinawa	1945
Atlantic	1941	Japan	1945
Malta Convoys	1941	Falkland Islands	1982
North Africa	1942-43		

Aircraft Equipment	Period of Service	Example
Fairey IIIF	Apr 1933 - Nov 1934	S1546 (741)
Seal	Jun 1934 - Dec 1934	K3521 (750)
Shark I	Dec 1934 - Dec 1936	K4361 (650)
Baffin	Aug 1935 - Feb 1936	S1553 (45)
Shark II	Dec 1936 - Sep 1937	L8474 (648)
Swordfish I	Sep 1937 - Jun 1941	P4127 (A4F)
Battle	Apr 1939 - Apr 1939	N2082
Albacore I	Jul 1941 - Nov 1943	X8968 (5G)
Barracuda II	Jan 1944 - Oct 1944	MD807 (H)
Avenger I	Oct 1944 - Nov 1944	JZ181
Avenger II	Oct 1944 - Mar 1946	JZ614 (1P)
Firefly AS.5	Jul 1951 - Dec 1951	VT373 (243)
Firefly AS.6	Dec 1951 - Feb 1954	VT401 (222/J)
Avenger AS.4	Feb 1954 - Mar 1955	XB306 (374/C)
Gannet AS.1	Mar 1955 - May 1956	XA340 (404/C)
	Jul 1956 - Nov 1957	XA396 (322/B)
Gannet T.2	Jul 1956 - Nov 1957	XA524 (320/GN)
Whirlwind HAS.7	Jan 1958 - May 1959	XL841 (323/A'V')
	Nov 1959 - Oct 1960	XL844 (295/R)
Wessex HAS.1	Sep 1964 - May 1969	XS122 (290/E)
Wessex HAS.3	May 1969 - Dec 1972	XM838 (412/BL)
Sea King HAS.1	Dec 1972 - Jan 1977	XV708 (410/BL)
Sea King HAS.2/2a	Jan 1977 - Nov 1980	XZ575 (410/BL)
Sea King HAS.5	Nov 1980 - Jan 1990	XZ918 (016/N)
Sea King HAS.6	Dec 1989 - to date	ZA135 (015/R)

Albacore BF653 ØL of No.820 Squadron being loaded up on HMS Formidable in November 1942 with six 250-lb bombs to be dropped on Fort D'Estrees, Algiers in Operation Torch. Of 36 bombs dropped by the squadron, 30 scored direct hits.
(Frank Hunter via Jack Bryant)

Squadron bases

Gosport	3 Apr 1933	HMS Courageous	3 Sep 1937			
HMS Courageous	5 May 1933	Evanton (8ATC)	1 Oct 1937			
Novar	12 May 1933	HMS Courageous	9 Oct 1937			
HMS Courageous	31 May 1933	Eastleigh	1 Nov 1937	La Senia	17 Dec 1942	HMS Indomitable	17 Jan 1952
Novar	30 Aug 1933	HMS Courageous	10 Jan 1938	HMS Formidable	23 Dec 1942	St Merryn	31 Mar 1952
transit	1 Nov 1933	Southampton	29 Mar 1938	North Front	12 Feb 1943	HMS Indomitable	16 May 1952
Gosport	2 Nov 1933	Evanton (8ATS)	2 May 1938	La Senia	16 Feb 1943	St Merryn	10 Jul 1952
Manston	6 Nov 1933	HMS Courageous	4 Jun 1938	Affreville	18 Feb 1943	HMS Theseus	21 Aug 1952
Gosport	8 Jan 1934	Southampton	23 Jul 1938	Blida	19 Feb 1943	Hal Far	8 Oct 1952
'B' Flight:		Evanton (8ATS)	9 Sep 1938	HMS Formidable	28 Feb 1943	HMS Theseus	18 Nov 1952
HMS Furious	9 Jan 1934	HMS Courageous	24 Sep 1938	Tafaroui	7 Apr 1943	Hal Far	28 Nov 1952
Gibraltar	15 Jan 1934	Southampton	27 Oct 1938	HMS Formidable	14 Apr 1943	St Merryn	11 Dec 1952
HMS Courageous	20 Feb 1934	HMS Ark Royal	11 Jan 1939	Tafaroui ('Z' Flt)	18 Apr 1943	HMS Indomitable	20 Jan 1953
Gosport (Dt5)	13 Apr 1934	Hal Far (Dt)	20-23 Feb 1939	to	26 May 1943	Hal Far	4 Feb 1953
to	16 May 1934	Southampton	24 Mar 1939	Ta Kali	11 Aug 1943	HMS Indomitable	17 Feb 1953
Novar	26 Jun 1934	HMS Ark Royal	27 Apr 1939	HMS Formidable	17 Aug 1943	Hal Far	19 Feb 1953
HMS Courageous	5 Jul 1934	Lee-on-Solent	28 Jun 1939	Dekheila	23 Aug 1943	HMS Indomitable	1 Mar 1953
Catfoss (1ATC)	7 Jul 1934	Gosport	29 Jun 1939	HMS Formidable	27 Aug 1943	Hal Far	31 Mar 1953
Upavon	28 Jul 1934	Ford	28 Jul 1939	Hatston	9 Nov 1943	HMS Indomitable	23 Apr 1953
Gosport	20 Aug 1934	HMS Ark Royal	30 Jul 1939	HMS Formidable	11 Nov 1943	Lee-on-Solent	8 May 1953
HMS Courageous	5 Sep 1934	Donibristle	9 Aug 1939	Squadron disbanded	13 Nov 1943	HMS Theseus	17 Jun 1953
Gosport (Dt4)	11-30 Oct 1934	HMS Ark Royal	11 Aug 1939	Lee-on-Solent	1 Jan 1944	Hal Far	6 Aug 1953
Gosport	14 Nov 1934	Evanton	22 Aug 1939	Arbroath	10 Jan 1944	HMS Theseus	27 Aug 1953
HMS Courageous	1 Jan 1935	HMS Ark Royal	1 Sep 1939	Lee-on-Solent	1 Feb 1944	Lee-on-Solent	31 Oct 1953
Gosport	25 Mar 1935	Lee-on-Solent	15 Feb 1940	transit	22 Feb 1944	Eglinton	12 Jan 1954
North Coates (2ATC)	15 Apr 1935	Ford	1 Mar 1940	Crail	24 Feb 1944	Lee-on-Solent	14 Jun 1954
Gosport	4 May 1935	HMS Ark Royal	20 Mar 1940	HMS Indefatigable	10 Jun 1944	HMS Centaur	16 Jul 1954
'A' Flight:		Dekheila	2 Apr 1940	HMS Formidable	26 Jun 1944	Hal Far	14 Oct 1954
HMS Courageous	29 Aug 1935	HMS Ark Royal	10 Apr 1940	(Dt6) to	2 Jul 1944	HMS Centaur	15 Nov 1954
Aboukir	3 Oct 1935	Hatston	30 Apr 1940	Hatston	5 Jul 1944	Hal Far	2 Feb 1955
HMS Courageous	9 Oct 1935	HMS Ark Royal	4 May 1940	HMS Indefatigable	10 Jul 1944	Cuers (transit)	7 Feb 1955
Aboukir	22 Nov 1935	Evanton (Dt3)	1-3 May 1940	Machrihanish	26 Sep 1944	Lee-on-Solent	9 Feb 1955
HMS Courageous	12 Dec 1935	Donibristle	8 Oct 1940	Dunino (transit)	18 Oct 1944	Eglinton	10 Feb 1955
Hal Far	15 Dec 1935	Campbeltown	23 Oct 1940	Lee-on-Solent	19 Oct 1944	HMS Bulwark	16 Sep 1955
HMS Courageous	21 Dec 1935	HMS Ark Royal	31 Oct 1940	St Eval	11 Nov 1944	Eglinton	4 Oct 1955
Aboukir	20 Feb 1936	North Front	16 Apr 1941	Upottery	18 Nov 1944	HMS Centaur	8 Jan 1956
troopship Neuralia		HMS Ark Royal	28 Apr 1941	HMS Indefatigable	21 Nov 1944	Sembawang	4 Apr 1956
transit UK	1-9 Aug 1936	HMS Victorious	17 Jun 1941	Katukurunda	10 Dec 1944	HMS Centaur	20 Apr 1956
'B' Flight:		Lee-on-Solent	27 Jun 1941	HMS Indefatgiable	1 Jan 1945	Sqdn disbanded UK	15 May 1956
HMS Courageous	13 Jul 1936	Crail	26 Sep 1941	Katukurunda	7 Jan 1945	Eglinton	30 Jul 1956
Eastleigh	20 Jul 1936	Hatston	1 Nov 1941	HMS Indefatigable	9 Jan 1945	Ford	28 Mar 1957
Eastleigh - squadron		HMS Victorious	3-30 Nov 1941	Nowra	10 Feb 1945	HMS Bulwark	25 Jun 1957
recombined		(Dt6)		HMS Indefatigable	27 Feb 1945	Ford	5 Aug 1957
HMS Courageous	16 Nov 1936	HMS Victorious	4-22 Dec 1941	Schofields	5 Jun 1945	HMS Bulwark	28 Aug 1957
Eastleigh	17 Nov 1936	(Dt)		HMS Indefatigable	1 Jul 1945	Ford	4 Nov 1957
HMS Courageous	19 Jan 1937	HMS Victorious	24 Dec 1941	Nowra	18 Sep 1945	Squadron disbanded	2 Dec 1957
Eastleigh	22 Mar 1937	Hatston	1 Jan 1942	HMS Indefatigable	23 Nov 1945	Eglinton	21 Jan 1958
West Freugh (4ATC)	24 May 1937	Machrihanish	20 Jan 1942	Schofields	31 Dec 1945	HMS Eagle	16 May 1958
Eastleigh	19 Jun 1937	HMS Formidable	3 Feb 1942	HMS Indefatigable	31 Jan 1946	HMS Ark Royal	15 Jun 1958
HMS Courageous	25 Jun 1937	Machrihanish	18 Sep 1942	Sqdn disbanded UK	16 Mar 1946	Hal Far	17 Jun 1958
Eastleigh	22 Jul 1937	Twatt	2 Oct 1942	Eglinton	3 Jul 1951	HMS Albion	2 Aug 1958
Eastchurch (AAS)	26 Jul 1937	Hatston	10 Oct 1942	St Merryn	3 Dec 1951	Hal Far	18 Aug 1958
Southampton	7 Aug 1937	HMS Formidable	21 Oct 1942				

Fairey Firefly AS.6 WD908 '226/T' of No.820 Squadron from HMS Theseus at Hal Far in 1953. (via Brian Lowe)

Squadron bases

HMS Albion	21 Aug 1958	Valley (Dt2)	5-9 Dec 1966	Prestwick	10 May 1971	RFA Olna (Dt2)	7-10 Feb 1975
Lee-on-Solent	16 Sep 1958	RFA Lofoten	30 Jan 1967	Culdrose	21 May 1971	RFA Olna (Dt1)	20-22 Feb 1975
HMS Albion	20 Oct 1958	RFA Tidespring (Dt2)	6-10 Feb 1967	HMS Blake (Dt2)	7-11 Jun 1971	Tengah	17 Mar 1975
Sembawang (Dt5)	1-11 Dec 1958			HMS Blake (Dt2)	28 Jun 1971	HMS Blake	2 Apr 1975
Kai Tak (Dt3)	19 Dec 1958	Culdrose	10 Feb 1967		to 2 Jul 1971	RFA Olna (Dt2)	5-8 May 1975
	to 5 Jan 1959	HMS Lofoten(Dt2)	1-20 Mar 1967	HMS Blake	19 Jul 1971	Culdrose	10 Jun 1975
Wigram (Dt3)	31 Jan 1959	HMS Eagle	7 Apr 1967	Crissy Field(Dt3)	1-9 Oct 1971	HMS Blake	4 Sep 1975
	to 1 Feb 1959	Culdrose	13 Apr 1967	North Front	17 Nov 1971	Culdrose (Dt2)	3-17 Oct 1975
Nowra (Dt2)	13-24 Feb 1959	Arbroath (Dt4)	15 May 1967	HMS Blake	16 Dec 1971	Culdrose	1 Dec 1975
Sembawang	26 Mar 1959	HMS Eagle	26 May 1967	Luqa (Dt)	21-31 Dec 1971	HMS Blake	13 Jan 1976
Squadron disbanded	8 May 1959	Culdrose	14 Jun 1967	Culdrose	27 Jan 1972	Culdrose	4 Mar 1976
Culdrose	3 Nov 1959	HMS Eagle	23 Jun 1967	HMS Blake	6 Mar 1972	HMS Blake (Dt3)	31 Mar 1976
Portland	26 Nov 1959	Culdrose	18 Jul 1967	Culdrose (Dt2)	22-29 Mar 1972		to 5 Apr 1976
Culdrose	29 Jan 1960	HMS Eagle	14 Aug 1967	Culdrose	29 Mar 1972	HMS Blake (Dt2)	13-14 Apr 1976
HMS Ark Royal	2 Mar 1960	Changi	6 Oct 1967	HMS Blake	19 Apr 1972	HMS Blake	21 Apr 1976
Hal Far	13 Mar 1960	HMS Eagle	23 Oct 1967	Luqa	23 May 1972	North Front (Dt2)	3-6 May 1976
HMS Ark Royal	19 Apr 1960	Changi	22 Dec 1967	HMS Blake	29 May 1972	Valkenburg (Dt2)	17-26 May 1976
Hal Far	23 Apr 1960	HMS Eagle	22 Jan 1968	RFA Olna (Dt3)	11-16 Jun 1972	Holstenan (Dt2)	21-24 Jun 1976
HMS Ark Royal	22 May 1960	Culdrose	18 Jun 1968	RFA Regent(Dt1)	12-15 Jun 1972	Culdrose	30 Jun 1976
St Mandrier	11 Jun 1960	HMS Eagle	22 Aug 1968	Culdrose	16 Jun 1972	Newcastle (Dt2)	12-23 Jul 1976
HMS Ark Royal	13 Jun 1960	Culdrose	3 Oct 1968	HMS Blake	26 Jun 1972	Arbroath (Dt2)	12-23 Jul 1976
Ta Kali (Dt5)	29 Jul 1960	RFA Olmeda (Dt3)	21 Oct 1968	Culdrose	17 Jul 1972	HrMs Poolster (Dt1)	6-25 Sep 1976
	to 8 Aug 1960	RFA Tidepool (Dt2)	25 Oct 1968	HMS Blake	25 Aug 1972		
Culdrose	3 Oct 1960	Culdrose (reunited)	5 Dec 1968	Portland	13 Oct 1972	RFA Tidepool(Dt1)	8-24 Sep 1976
Squadron disbanded	3 Oct 1960	HMS Blake	30 Jun 1969	HMS Blake	24 Oct 1972	RFA Tidepool(Dt1)	9-19 Nov 1976
Culdrose	23 Sep 1964	Culdrose	21 Jul 1969	Culdrose	16 Nov 1972	HrMs Zuiderkruis (Dt2)	9-19 Nov 1976
HMS Eagle	1 Dec 1964	HMS Blake	3 Sep 1969	HMS Blake	28 Nov 1972		
Sembawang	14 Jan 1965	Culdrose	12 Dec 1969	Culdrose	6 Dec 1972	RFA Olna (Dt2)	15-25 Feb 1977
HMS Eagle	26 Jan 1965	HMS Blake	19 Feb 1970	HMS Blake (Dt)	29 Jun 1973	RFA Olna (Dt2)	26 Apr 1977
Sembawang	6 Apr 1965	Detachment (2 a/c):			to 13 Jul 1973		to 6 May 1977
HMS Eagle	20 Apr 1965	Nowra	30 Apr 1970	HMS Blake (Dt2)	7-10 Aug 1973	Prestwick (Dt2)	24 May 1977
Culdrose	24 May 1965	RFA Olmeda	6 May 1970	HMS Blake	10 Sep 1973		to 3 Jun 1977
HMS Eagle	24 Aug 1965	Sembawang	15 May 1970	Culdrose	27 Sep 1973	RFA Engadine (Dt3)	4-15 Jul 1977
Sembawang	12 Oct 1965	Sembawang(Dt2)	11-15 May 1970	HMS Blake	22 Oct 1973		
HMS Eagle	19 Oct 1965	RFA Olmeda (Dt2)	25 May 1970	Culdrose	22 Nov 1973	HMS Blake	23 Sep 1977
Sembawang	12 Feb 1966		to 8 Jun 1970	HMS Blake	11 Jan 1974	Culdrose	15 Dec 1977
HMS Eagle	28 Feb 1966	RFA Olmeda (2)/		Culdrose	16 Apr 1974	HMS Hermes	23 Jan 1978
Sembawang	10 May 1966	RFA Tidespring(2)	15 Jun 1970	HMS Blake	15 May 1974	HMS Blake	27 Jan 1978
HMS Eagle	2 Jun 1966	Sembawang	27 Jun 1970	Luqa (Dt2)	3 Jun 1974	Culdrose	10 Mar 1978
Sembawang	1 Jul 1966	HMS Blake	16 Jul 1970		to 2 Jul 1974	HMS Blake	2 May 1978
HMS Eagle	11 Jul 1966	Culdrose	26 Oct 1970	Culdrose	8 Jul 1974	Culdrose	11 Dec 1978
Culdrose	22 Aug 1966	RFA Tidepool	18 Jan 1971	HMS Blake	16 Sep 1974	HMS Blake	25 Jan 1979
RFA Olna (Dt1)	3-11 Oct 1966	Culdrose	1 Feb 1971	RFA Olna (Dt2)	8-11 Oct 1974	Culdrose	15 Feb 1979
RFA Lofoten(Dt2)	10-13 Oct 1966	RFA Engadine (Dt3)	13-17 Feb 1971	RFA Olna (Dt2)	14-17 Nov 1974	HMS Blake	15 Mar 1979
HMCS Margaree (Dt1)	29 Oct 1966			Tengah (Dt1)	12-24 Dec 1974	HMS Bulwark (Dt2)	29 Jun 1979
	to 17 Nov 1966	RFA Olmeda	12 Mar 1971	Kai Tak	21 Dec 1974		to 13 Jul 1979
RFA Olna (Dt2)	4-17 Nov 1966	Culdrose	26 Mar 1971	HMS Blake	10 Jan 1975	HMS Blake	17 Sep 1979

Fairey Gannet AS.1 XA402 '327/B' and others of No.820 Squadron, HMS Bulwark around 1956/7. (FAA Museum)

Squadron bases
North Front	12 Oct 1979
HMS Blake	22 Oct 1979
Culdrose	6 Dec 1979
HMS Hermes	14 Jan 1980
Culdrose	19 Mar 1980
RFA Olmeda (Dt2)	9-15 May 1980
HMS Invincible (Dt2)	20-27 May 1980
HMS Invincible (Dt2)	9-10 Jun 1980
HMS Invincible (Dt2)	16-20 Jun 1980
RFA Gold Rover (Dt2)	27-28 Jul 1980
HMS Invincible (Dt2)	18 Nov 1980 to 2 Dec 1980
RFA Olwen (Dt2)	26-28 Jan 1981
HMS Invincible	2 Feb 1981
Culdrose	11 Feb 1981
HMS Invincible	6 Mar 1981
Culdrose	30 Mar 1981
HMS Invincible (Dt6)	6-8 Jun 1981
HMS Invincible	18 Jun 1981
Culdrose	25 Sep 1981
RFA Engadine	22-29 Oct 1981
HMS Invincible	13 Nov 1981
Culdrose	22 Nov 1981
HMS Invincible	21 Jan 1982
Culdrose	26 Feb 1982
HMS Invincible	4 Apr 1982
San Carlos (Dt2)	10-17 Jun 1982
Culdrose	17 Sep 1982
HMS Invincible (Dt2)	11-19 Jan 1983
HMS Invincible	1 Feb 1983
North Front (Dt2)	13-25 Apr 1983
Culdrose	27 Apr 1983

Squadron bases
HMS Illustrious	23 May 1983
Culdrose	17 Jun 1983
HMS Invincible (Dt2)	17-28 Jun 1983
HMS Invincible	1 Sep 1983
Hobsonville (Dt3)	30 Nov 1983 to 5 Dec 1983
Nowra (Dt4)	8-22 Dec 1983
Sembawang (Dt4)	9-31 Jan 1984
Culdrose	19 Mar 1984
Prestwick/(Dt2)	30 Apr 1984
Benbecula FOB	to 2 May 1984
RFA Olwen (Dt2)	26 May 1984 to 27 Jun 1984
Prestwick (Dt4)	4 Jul 1984 to 1984
HMS Invincible (Dt2)	11-13 Jul 1984
RFA Tidespring (Dt2)	16-27 Jul 1984
HMS Invincible (Dt2)	20-23 Jul 1984
HMS Invincible (Dt2)	30 Jul 1984 to 3 Aug 1984
HMS Invincible	2 Oct 1984
RFA Fort Grange (Dt4)	7-11 Oct 1984
HMS Illustrious (Dt2)	18-19 Oct 1984
Culdrose	12?-29 Nov 1984
HMS Invincible	17 Jan 1985
Culdrose	28 Mar 1985
HMS Invincible	15 May 1985
Culdrose	3 Jul 1985
HMS Invincible	31 Jul 1985
HMS Illustrious (Dt4)	1 Aug 1985 to 25 Sep 1985
Norfolk (Dt2)	20-? Aug 1985

Squadron bases
HMS Invincible (Dt4)	31 Aug 1985 to 22 Sep 1985
Prestwick (Dt4)	22 Sep 1985 to 1 Oct 1985
HMS Invincible (Dt4)	25 Sep 1985 to 1 Oct 1985
HMS Invincible	1 Oct 1985
Culdrose	4 Dec 1985
HMS Ark Royal (Dt2)	3-12 Feb 1986
HMS Ark Royal	24 Feb 1986
Culdrose	26 Mar 1986
HMS Ark Royal	9 Apr 1986
Culdrose	24 Apr 1986
HMS Ark Royal	17 Jun 1986
Norfolk (Dt3)	Aug 1986
Jacksonville (Dt2)	Aug 1986
Culdrose	27 Sep 1986
HMS Ark Royal	13 Oct 1986
Culdrose	19 Oct 1986
HMS Ark Royal	15 Jan 1987
Culdrose	17 Apr 1987
HMS Ark Royal	5 May 1987
Culdrose	15 May 1987
HMS Ark Royal (Dt5)	25-29 May 1987
HMS Ark Royal (Dt3)	29 May 1987 to 8 Jun 1987
Manston (Dt2)	1-8 Jun 1987
HMS Ark Royal	8 Jun 1987
Culdrose	25 Jun 1987
HMS Ark Royal (Dt2)	1-14 Sep 1987
HMS Ark Royal	14 Sep 1987
Portland (Dt2)	23-25 Sep 1987
Castlemartin (Dt2) (Pembs)	28 Sep 1987
Culdrose	24 Oct 1987

Squadron bases
Guernsey (Dt2)	13-16 Nov 1987
HMS Ark Royal	25 Jan 1988
Culdrose (Dt1)	26 Feb 1988 to 10 Mar 1988
Culdrose	10 Mar 1988
HMS Ark Royal (Dt3)	10-23 Mar 1988
HMS Ark Royal (Dt3)	7-9 Jun 1988
HMS Ark Royal	9 Jun 1988
RFA Fort Grange	26 Jun 1988
(Dt2)	to 8 Jul 1988
Kuantan (Dt2)	25-29 Jul 1988
Sembawang (Dt2)	1-3 Aug 1988
RFA Fort Grange (Dt2)	8-19 Aug 1988
RFA Olwen (Dt2)	28 Aug 1988 to 12 Sep 1988
RFA Fort Grange (Dt2)	7-18 Oct 1988
Culdrose	15 Dec 1988
HMS Fearless (Dt1)	31 Jan 1989 to 1 Feb 1989
HMS Ark Royal (Dt6)	6-17 Feb 1989
HMS Ark Royal	30 Mar 1989
Culdrose (Dt4)	26 Apr 1989 to 2 May 1989
Culdrose	2 May 1989
HMS Ark Royal (Dt3)	2-9 May 1989
Valkenburg (Dt3)	9-11 May 1989
HMS Ark Royal (Dt3)	10-11 May 1989
HMS Ark Royal	11 May 1989
Culdrose	3 Jun 1989
HMS Ark Royal (Dt1)	3-16 Jun 1989

Westland Whirlwind HAS.7 XL847 '327/A: Z' of No.820 Squadron, HMS Albion in 1959. (MAP)

Sea King HAS.1 XV714 '413/BL' of No.820 Sqdn in 1974. (MAP)

Squadron bases

HMS Ark Royal	19 Jun 1989
Culdrose	29 Jun 1989
HMS Ark Royal	29 Jun 1989
HMS Ark Royal (Dt2)	to 7 Jul 1989
HMS Ark Royal (Dt2)	21-27 Aug 1989
HMS Ark Royal	4 Sep 1989
Culdrose	22 Sep 1989
HMS Ark Royal (Dt4)	2-12 Oct 1989
HMS Ark Royal (Dt2)	12-14 Oct 1989
HMS Ark Royal (Dt5)	22 Feb 1990 to 2 Mar 1990
HMS Ark Royal	2 Mar 1990
Culdrose	16 Mar 1990
HMS Ark Royal	18 Apr 1990
Jacksonville (Dt5)	18-30 May 1990
Culdrose	4 Jul 1990
HMS Ark Royal	21 Aug 1990
Culdrose	26 Sep 1990
HMS Ark Royal	15 Oct 1990
Culdrose	2 Nov 1990
HMS Ark Royal (Dt2)	6-16 Nov 1990
HMS Ark Royal	10 Jan 1991
Culdrose	11 Apr 1991
HMS Ark Royal	30 May 1991
Culdrose	1 Jul 1991
HMS Ark Royal	2 Sep 1991

Squadron bases

Mayport (Dt3)	10-23 Oct 1991
Culdrose	11 Nov 1991
HMS Ark Royal (Dt2)	12-17 Jan 1992
HMS Ark Royal (Dt2)	4-20 Mar 1992
HMS Ark Royal	20 Mar 1992
Portland (Dt2)	2-10 Apr 1992
Culdrose	1 May 1992
HMS Ark Royal (Dt3)	1-17 Jun 1992
HMS Ark Royal (Dt1)	17-24 Jun 1992
HMS Ark Royal (Dt3)	26-31 Aug 1992
HMS Ark Royal	2 Sep 1992
Jacksonville	2 Oct 1992
HMS Ark Royal	13 Oct 1992
Culdrose	4 Nov 1992
Portland (Dt2)	23-26 Nov 1992
Portland (Dt2)	7-8 Dec 1992
RFA Olwen (Dt2)	13 Jan 1993 to 4 Aug 1993
RFA Fort Grange	17 Jan 1993
HMS Ark Royal	19 Mar 1993
Culdrose	4 Aug 1993
Portland (Dt2)	Oct 1993
HMS Ark Royal	18 Jan 1994
RFA Fort Austin (Dt2)	Feb 1994
Culdrose	Sep 1994

Sea King HAS.2 XZ576 '411/BL' of No.820 Sqdn in 1979. (MAP)

Commanding Officers

L/C AP Colthurst RN 2 May 1933 (Sq Ldr RAF)
L/C MS Slattery RN 9 Aug 1934 (Sq Ldr RAF)
L/C RG Poole RN 15 Apr 1935 (Sq Ldr RAF)
L/C CAN Hooper 1 Apr 1937 RN (Sq Ldr RAF)
L/C ACG Ermen RN 19 Aug 1937 (Sq Ldr RAF)
L/C GB Hodgkinson RN 7 Jan 1939
L/C A Yeoman RN 29 Aug 1940
L/C JA Stewart-Moore RN 27 Oct 1940
L/C W Elliott RN 18 Jul 1941
L/C JCN Shrubsole RN 4 Jun 1943
Squadron disbanded 13 Nov 1943
L/C(A) WR Nowell RN 1 Jan 1944
L/C(A) SP Luke RN 23 Oct 1944
L/C(A) FL Jones 18 May 1945 DSC & Bar RNVR
L/C JP Camp DSC & Bar RN 14 Jun 1945
Squadron disbanded 16 Mar 1946
L/C PS Cole RN 3 Jul 1951
L/C GC Hathway RN 21 Oct 1951
L/C WL Hughes RN 22 Jul 1953
L/C AD Cassidi RN 19 Feb 1955
L/C AH Smith RN 18 May 1955
Squadron disbanded 15 May 1956
L/C DO'D Newbery RN 30 Jul 1956

Commanding Officers

Squadron disbanded 2 Dec 1957
L/C FW Wilcox RN 21 Jan 1958
Squadron disbanded 8 May 1959
L/C WW Threlfall RNN 3 Nov 1959
Squadron disbanded 3 Oct 1960
L/C DC Smith RN 23 Sep 1964
L/C P Burton RN 23 Feb 1966
L/C A Casdagli RN 7 May 1967
L/C JBA Hawkins RN 26 Feb 1969
L/C PR Lloyd RN 28 Oct 1970
L/C DP Edwards RN 13 Apr 1972
L/C GEG Brown RN 14 Jan 1974
L/C CA Robertson RN 9 Jul 1975
L/C JS Turton RN 3 Nov 1976
L/C JD StJ Ainslie RN 17 Mar 1978
L/C CP Young RN 5 Nov 1979
L/C RJS Wykes-Sneyd AFC RN 12 Jun 1980
L/C GC Hunt RN 16 Mar 1983
L/C AJM Hogg AFC RN 7 Sep 1984
Cdr AJM Hogg AFC RN 30 Jun 1985
L/C CP Robinson RN 5 Oct 1985
L/C JM Knowles RN 7 Feb 1987
L/C NJK Deadman RN 28 Feb 1989
L/C MD Piggott RN 26 Mar 1991
L/C PA Barber RN Jun 1992
L/C CF Douglas RN 14 Jun 1994

Westland Sea King HAS.1 XV654 '050/R' of No.820 Squadron in 1970. (MAP)

No.821 Squadron

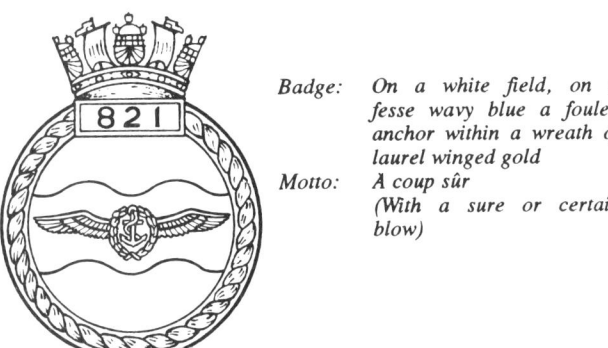

Badge: On a white field, on a fesse wavy blue a fouled anchor within a wreath of laurel winged gold
Motto: A coup sûr
(With a sure or certain blow)

No.821 Squadron formed at Gosport on 3 April 1933 as a Spotter Reconnaissance unit from No.446 Flight and half of No.445 Flight. Initial equipment was nine Fairey IIIFs, but almost immediately it began to re-equip with Seals, the last IIIF leaving in October. The squadron embarked in HMS *Courageous* in May for service in the Home Station, but in August 1935 the ship sailed to join the Mediterranean Fleet for the Abyssinian crisis. Squadron strength was now 12 aircraft, but soon after returning home the Seals were passed to No.822 Squadron in March 1936, to be replaced by 12 Shark IIs, and No.821 then became a torpedo spotter reconnaissance unit. The Sharks in turn gave way in September 1937 to 12 Swordfish Is. In November 1938 it transferred to HMS *Ark Royal*, embarking for the first time in January 1939 for a Spring Cruise in the Mediterranean.

Shortly after the outbreak of war, the squadron attacked the U-39 in the North West Approaches. The ship then sailed to search for enemy warships in the South Atlantic and Indian Ocean. After returning home in February 1940 for a refit the ship sailed to the Mediterranean, but was quickly recalled when the Germans invaded Norway. No.821 carried out attacks on enemy targets in that country, then disembarked to Hatston to make room for extra fighters. Anti-submarine patrols were carried out off the Norwegian coast, and on 21 June an unsuccessful daylight torpedo attack was made on the German battleship Scharnhorst. On 2 December the main squadron disbanded, and 'X' Flight broke away with six aircraft to take passage for Gibraltar in HMS *Argus*, then continued to Malta in HMS *Ark Royal*. Here it was soon absorbed into No.815 Squadron, which was then regrouping.

On 1 July 1941, the squadron reformed from 'X' Flight of No.816 Squadron at Detling with six Swordfish Is. After anti-submarine and reconnaissance patrols from Hatston and Sumburgh, the squadron personnel took passage for Egypt in November, operations being carried out in the Western Desert before re-equipping on 1 March 1942 with 6 Albacores. Moving to Cyprus with these, it provided assistance in the bombardment of Rhodes before returning to Egypt. Here it increased to 12 aircraft for further operations in support of the ground forces in the Western Desert, including minelaying, flare dropping and bombing attacks. In November it moved to Malta for attacks on enemy shipping taking supplies to North Africa, one flight moving in March 1943 to Castel Benito, a captured Italian aerodrome near Tripoli, to provide night illumination for RAF bombers carrying out attacks in that area. The whole squadron moved to the Tunis area in June for anti-submarine patrols and escort duty along the North African coast, after which it returned to the United Kingdom without aircraft and disbanded on 10 October 1943 on arrival.

No.821 reformed at Stretton on 1 May 1944 for torpedo bomber reconnaissance duties with 12 Barracuda IIs, embarking in HMS *Puncher* in November 1944. Re-equipment with Barracuda IIIs began in January 1945, minelaying operations being carried out off Norway in February. In April, six Wildcat VIs were transferred from No.835 Squadron, only to be withdrawn after VE-Day. In July the squadron embarked in HMS *Trumpeter* for passage to the Far East, but VJ-day intervened before she could join the Eastern Fleet. The squadron sailed home in HMS *Fencer* in September without aircraft, and the squadron disembarking to Rattray where it received new Barracuda IIIs before disbanding on 1 February 1946.

Fairey Seal floatplane K3479 '734' and two others of No.821 Squadron en route from Portsmouth to Pembroke Dock via Mount Batten on 3 May 1934. (via G.T.Smith)

Fairey Swordfish I L2768 'A5H' on HMS Ark Royal in 1939. (A.M.McKinnon)

On 18 September 1951, No.821 reformed at Arbroath as an anti-submarine unit with eight Firefly AS.6s. After training in this work and night flying, six of the aircraft undertook deck landing training in HMS *Illustrious*. In May 1952, however, the role was changed to that of a strike squadron, and it re-equipped with ten Firefly FR.5s. These flew out to Malta in June, the ground crews and stores being embarked in HMS *Vengeance*. In September the squadron joined HMS *Glory* for work up, but by November the ship was in Korean waters, where the strength was increased to 12 aircraft. During the next six months the squadron flew 1721 operational sorties, before sailing for Hong Kong, where it disbanded on 25 May 1953.

Battle Honours

Norway	1940
Libya	1942
Mediterranean	1942-43
Korea	1952-53

Identification Markings

IIIF & Seal *721-735*; Shark *678-691*; Swordfish *678-685*, to *A5A*+ 5.39, later *5A*+ to 7.41, then single letters; Albacore *S5A*+ later single letters; Barracuda *N:A*+ on Puncher, later single letters; Wildcat unknown; Firefly *241-248/MA*, to *200-209/R* 6.52.

Aircraft Equipment	Period of Service	Example	
Fairey IIIF	Apr 1933 - Oct 1933	S1189	(726)
Seal	Apr 1933 - Mar 1936	K3540	(725)
Shark II	Mar 1936 - Sep 1937	K5625	(680)
Swordfish I	Sep 1937 - Jan 1941	P4144	(A5G)
	Jul 1941 - Nov 1941	P4199	
Albacore I	Mar 1942 - Oct 1943	T9207	(S5L)
Barracuda II	May 1944 - Apr 1945	DR219	(X)
Barracuda TR.III	Jan 1945 - Oct 1945	MD836	
	Oct 1945 - Feb 1946	RJ785	
Wildcat VI	Apr 1945 - May 1945	JV712	
Firefly AS.6	Sep 1951 - May 1952	WJ117	(247/MA)
Firefly FR.5	May 1952 - May 1953	VT368	(207/R)

Squadron bases

Gosport	3 Apr 1933
HMS Courageous	5 May 1933
Manston	20 Jul 1933
Catfoss	7 Sep 1933
Novar	24 Sep 1933
Manston	27 Oct 1933
Gosport	8 Jan 1934
HMS Courageous	20 Feb 1934
Portland (4)/	
Pembroke Dock (4)	3 May 1934
HMS Courageous	31 May 1934
Catfoss (1ATC)	18 Jun 1934
HMS Courageous	7 Jul 1934
Upavon	14 Jul 1934
Gosport	15 Jul 1934
Upavon	25 Jul 1934
HMS Courageous	5 Sep 1934
Gosport	8 Nov 1934
Upavon	9 Dec 1934
Gosport	13 Dec 1934
Upavon	28 Dec 1934
HMS Courageous	3 Jan 1935
Hal Far	31 Jan 1935
HMS Courageous	9 Feb 1935
Upavon	25 Mar 1935
HMS Courageous	7 May 1935
Gosport	2 Jul 1935
Catfoss (1ATC)	22 Jul 1935
Upavon	Aug 1935
HMS Courageous	29 Aug 1935
Hal Far	15 Dec 1935
HMS Courageous	21 Dec 1935
Aboukir	23 Dec 1935
HMS Courageous	2 Jan 1936
Aboukir	19 Feb 1936
HMS Courageous	20 Feb 1936
Gosport	28 Feb 1936
HMS Courageous	13 Jul 1936
HMS Courageous	1 Sep 1936
Southampton	4 Nov 1936
Gosport (Dt)	4-19 Jan 1937
Lee-on-Solent (Dt)	6-19 Jan 1937
HMS Courageous	19 Jan 1937
Gibraltar (Dt6)	28 Jan 1937
	to 17 Mar 1937
Southampton	22 Mar 1937
Lee-on-Solent (Dt)	4-28 May 1937
HMS Courageous	28 May 1937
Portland (Dt)	25 May 1937
	to 12 Jul 1937
Gosport	16 Jul 1937
North Coates (ATC)	26 Jul 1937
Southampton	20 Aug 1937
HMS Courageous	23 Aug 1937
(Dt)	to 2 Sep 1937
Lee-on-Solent (Dt)	2-3 Sep 1937
Evanton (Dt)	4 Sep 1937
	to 11 Oct 1937
Gosport	7 Oct 1937
Lee-on-Solent (Dt)	12-27 Oct 1937
Southampton	27 Oct 1937
Portland (Dt)	29 Oct 1937
	to 15 Nov 1937
Lee-on-Solent (Dt)	29 Oct 1937
	to 19 Dec 1937
HMS Courageous	10 Jan 1938
Southampton	29 Mar 1938
Evanton (8ATS)	2 May 1938
HMS Courageous	4 Jun 1938
Southampton	23 Jul 1938
Eastchurch	29 Jul 1938
Southampton	8 Aug 1938
HMS Courageous	6 Sep 1938
Evanton (8ATS)	6 Oct 1938
HMS Courageous	11 Nov 1938
Southampton	17 Nov 1938
HMS Ark Royal	11 Jan 1939
Dekheila (Dt)	10-13 Feb 1939
Southampton	24 Mar 1939
HMS Ark Royal	29 Apr 1939
Southampton	28 Jun 1939
HMS Ark Royal	29 Jul 1939
Hatston	27 Sep 1939
HMS Ark Royal	29 Sep 1939
Ouakam	5 Jan 1940
HMS Ark Royal	8 Jan 1940
Lee-on-Solent	15 Feb 1940
Ford	18 Mar 1940
HMS Ark Royal	20 Mar 1940
Dekheila	2 Apr 1940
HMS Ark Royal	10 Apr 1940
Evanton	23 Apr 1940
Hatston	1 Jun 1940
Sqdn disbanded and replaced by	
X Flight	2 Dec 1940
Eastleigh	20 Jul 1936
821X Flight:	
Donibristle	2 Dec 1940
Prestwick	15 Dec 1940
Donibristle	17 Dec 1940
HMS Argus	19 Dec 1940
North Front	29 Dec 1940
HMS Ark Royal	31 Dec 1940
Hal Far	8 Jan 1941
Candia	17 Jan 1941
Dekheila	19 Jan 1941
Flight disbanded into 815 Sqdn	21 Jan 1941
Detling	1 Jul 1941
Donibristle	14 Jul 1941
(transit)	
Hatston	15 Jul 1941
Twatt	12 Aug 1941
Machrihanish	25 Oct 1941
Twatt	28 Oct 1941
Sumburgh	5 Nov 1941
Arbroath	10 Nov 1941
HMS Royal Sovereign/ HMT Niew Amsterdam/ HMT Highland Prince/ SS Ile de France	
(no a/c)	12 Nov 1941
Dekheila	9 Jan 1942
Nicosia Main	13 Mar 1942
Fayid (Dt)	18 Mar 1942
	to 7 Apr 1942
Dekheila	1 Apr 1942
Maaten Bagush satt	14 Apr 1942
Gambut (Dt2)	25 May 1942
	to 14 Jun 1942
LG.104 Daba	27 Jun 1942
Dekheila	28 Jun 1942
Nicosia	13 Aug 1942
Dekheila	6 Sep 1942
LG.21 Daba	7 Nov 1942
Dekheila	9 Nov 1942
Berka (transit)	27 Nov 1942
Hal Far	30 Nov 1942
Castel Benito (Dt4)	14 Mar 1943
	to 13 Apr 1943
Monastir	5 Jun 1943
El Haouaria	3 Aug 1943
transit to UK	28 Sep 1943
Sqdn disbanded UK	10 Oct 1943
Stretton	1 May 1944
Machrihanish	28 May 1944
Maydown	4 Nov 1944
HMS Puncher (DLT)	26 Nov 1944
Machrihanish	1 Dec 1944
HMS Puncher	30 Dec 1944
Abbotsinch (Dt6)	13-15 Jan 1945
Hatston (Dt4)	5-10 Feb 1945
Hatston	12 Feb 1945
HMS Puncher	17 Feb 1945
Hatston	25 Feb 1945

Fairey Albacore BF710 'S5L' and others of No.821 Squadron. (Lt Col A. Newson)

Fairey Albacore T9153 'S5M' of No.821 Squadron at El Madu landing ground, Sfax, Tunisia in April 1943. (FAA Museum)

Squadron bases

HMS Puncher (Dt4)	15-16 Mar 1945
HMS Puncher	23 Mar 1945
Hatston	29 Mar 1945
Fearn	1 Apr 1945
HMS Campania (Dt)	5-13 Apr 1945
HMS Puncher (Dt)	5-12 Apr 1945
Hatston	13 Apr 1945
HMS Trumpeter (Fighter Flight)	27 Apr 1945 to 10 May 1945
HMS Searcher (Dt)	1-10 May 1945
HMS Campania (Dt)	10-14 May 1945
Ayr	24 May 1945
Machrihanish	29 May 1945
Abbotsinch	23 Jun 1945
HMS Trumpeter	3 Jul 1945
Cochin	26 Jul 1945
Katukurunda	31 Jul 1945
HMS Trumpeter (DLT)	6 Aug 1945
Katukurunda	11 Aug 1945
Coimbatore	27 Aug 1945
Sulur (no a/c)	2 Sep 1945
HMS Fencer (no a/c)	4 Sep 1945
Rattray	26 Sep 1945
Squadron disbanded	1 Feb 1946
Arbroath	18 Sep 1951
Eglinton	8 Nov 1951
Machrihanish	15 Jan 1952
Lee-on-Solent	15 Mar 1952
HMS Illustrious (DLP)	17 Mar 1952
Lee-on-Solent	20 Mar 1952
Machrihanish	21 Mar 1952
Ford	20 Jun 1952
Lee-on-Solent (transit)	23 Jun 1952

Squadron bases

Istres (transit)	23 Jun 1952
Hal Far	26 Jun 1952
HMS Glory	2 Sep 1952
Hal Far (Dt6)	22-29 Sep 1952
Hong Kong - disb	25 May 1953

Commanding Officers

Lt RA Peyton RN (Flt Lt RAF)	3 Apr 1933
Sq Ldr BE Harrison AFC RAF	6 May 1933
L/C CB Tidd RN (Sq Ldr RAF)	5 Sep 1934
Sq Ldr FCB Saville RAF	4 Jan 1935
Sq Ldr HN Hampton DFC RAF	8 May 1935
Sq Ldr GRM Clifford RAF	21 Sep 1936
Sq Ldr NE Morrison RAF	Sep 1938
L/C JAD Wroughton RN (Sq Ldr RAF)	29 Mar 1939
L/C GM Duncan RN	24 May 1939
L/C JAD Wroughton RN	14 Sep 1939
Mjr WHN Martin RM	29 May 1940
L/C RR Wood RN	27 Dec 1940
Squadron disbanded	21 Jan 1941
Lt CWB Smith RN	15 Jul 1941
Mjr AC Newsom RM	12 Mar 1942
L/C CHC O'Rorke RN	24 Mar 1943
Squadron disbanded	10 Oct 1943
L/C(A) M Thorpe RN	1 May 1944
L/C(A) D Brooks DSC & Bar RNVR	14 Jun 1945

Commanding Officers

L/C(A) HP Dawson RN	15 Jan 1946
Squadron disbanded	1 Feb 1946
L/C BH Notley RN	18 Sep 1951
L/C JRN Gardner RN	12 May 1952
Squadron disbanded	25 May 1953

Fairey Firefly FR.5 of No.821 Squadron taking off from HMS Glory in Korean waters. (Capt E.D.G.Lewin)

No.822 Squadron

Badge: On a white field, an eagle displayed black beaked and legged red crowned with a Naval crown gold holding in the dexter claw a thunderbolt and in the sinister claw a grenade white both inflamed proper

Motto: None

No.822 Squadron formed on 3 April 1933 at Netheravon from Nos.442 and 449 Flights with 12 Fairey IIIFs for Spotter Reconnaissance duties. These embarked in HMS *Furious* later in the month for service with the Home Fleet. In June 1936 the squadron temporarily re-equipped with 12 Seals, discarded by No.821 Squadron, pending the arrival in November of 12 Shark IIs. These latter were flown at the Coronation Review flypast at Spithead on 20 May 1937, but 3 months later were discarded when 12 Swordfish Is arrived. In February 1939, No.822 was allocated for deck landing training duties, embarking in this role in HMS *Courageous* in February 1939. It was earmarked to become No.768 Squadron on 24 May 1939, but instead was absorbed into No.767 Squadron.

Meanwhile part of the squadron had broken away as No.822A Squadron at Eastleigh on 15 May 1939, and on 1 July this became the new No.822 Squadron. The following month the squadron transferred to HMS *Courageous*, and on the outbreak of war carried out anti-submarine patrols in the South West Approaches. On 17 September the ship was torpedoed and sunk by *U-29*, all squadron aircraft being lost and there was heavy loss of life. The remaining personnel were absorbed by No.767 Squadron, and No.822 ceased to exist.

On 15 October 1941, No.822 reformed as a torpedo bomber reconnaissance unit with 9 Swordfish I. These were intended for HMS *Biter*, but before she arrived from the USA the squadron had re-equipped in March 1942 with 9 Albacore Is. These embarked in HMS *Furious* in July, later taking part in convoy escort duty. In November the ship participated in the North African landings, and No.822 joined with Sea Hurricanes in an attack on La Senia aerodrome, 47 enemy aircraft being destroyed on the ground. Unfortunately the squadron lost four of the eight aircraft that took part, including that of the CO. The remainder disembarked to Gibraltar to make good the losses, and in January 1943 anti-submarine operations were carried out off the Algerian coast before rejoining HMS *Furious* in the Home Fleet for Arctic convoy duty.

In July 1943 the squadron re-equipped with 12 Barracuda IIs, and in October these joined the 45th Naval TBR Wing for service in the Eastern Fleet. Squadron personnel took passage whilst their aircraft were shipped in HMS *Atheling*, being reunited in southern July No.823 Squadron was absorbed to bring the strength up to 21 aircraft, and these embarked in HMS *Victorious* for a dive bombing attack on the rail centre at Sigli in northern Sumatra on 18 September. Poor performance by Barracudas in the tropical climate led to the squadron returning home the next month in HMS *Rajah* without its aircraft.

On 1 January 1945 the squadron regrouped at Lee-on-Solent with 12 Barracuda IIIs for intended duty in an escort carrier, but instead carried out anti-submarine operations in the English Channel with RAF Coastal Command. In June the original aircraft went to No.860 Squadron, and No.822 received 12 Barracuda IIs fitted with ASH radar, with which the squadron was to have joined a Colossus-class carrier in August as part of the 18th Carrier Air Group, for service with the British Pacific Fleet. VJ-day intervened, and instead the squadron re-equipped in September with 12 Firefly FR.1s, only to disband at Machrihanish on 19 February 1946.

The squadron has not since been reformed, but the number was used unofficially in July 1979 by Nos.819 and 824 Squadrons when they temporarily combined in HMS *Hermes* for Exercise *Highwood*.

Fairey IIIF S1331 '713' of No.822 Squadron, HMS Furious around 1933/4. (N.H.Hemming)

Swordfish I V4438 'B' and others of 822 Sqdn at Hatston in 1942.

Identification Markings
IIIF 701-714, to 901-921 9.35; Seal, Shark & Swordfish 901-912; Swordfish USA 5.39-11.39, single letters from 10.41; Albacore 4A+; Barracuda & Firefly single letters.

Aircraft Equipment	Period of Service	Example
Fairey IIIF	Apr 1933 - Jul 1936	S1342 (708)
Seal	Jun 1936 - Nov 1936	K4780 (907)
Shark II	Nov 1936 - Aug 1937	K8501
Swordfish I	Aug 1937 - May 1939	K6009 (912)
	May 1939 - Sep 1939	L2737
Swordfish II	Oct 1941 - Mar 1942	DK790 (A)
Albacore I	Apr 1942 - Aug 1943	BF603 (4A)
Fulmar	Oct 1942 - Nov 1942	N4108
Barracuda II	Jul 1943 - Oct 1944	DP933 (P)
Barracuda TR.III	Jan 1945 - Jun 1945	MD958 (A)
Barracuda II(ASH)	Jun 1945 - Sep 1945	PM876
Firefly FR.I	Sep 1945 - Feb 1946	MB698 (F)

Battle Honours
*Atlantic 1942
North Africa 1942-43
Arctic 1943

Squadron bases
Netheravon	3 Apr 1933
HMS Furious	21 Apr 1933
Netheravon (Dt)	4-8 May 1933
Manston	20 Jul 1933
Catfoss (1ATC)	28 Aug 1933
HMS Furious	7 Sep 1933
Netheravon(transit)	11 Oct 1933
Leuchars	12 Oct 1933
Netheravon	27 Oct 1933
HMS Furious	5 Jan 1934
Netheravon	13 Apr 1934
HMS Glorious (Dt6)	5-11 Apr 1934
Hal Far (Dt6)	11 Apr 1934 to 9 Jun 1934
HMS Furious	1 Jun 1934
Hal Far	9 Jun 1934
HMS Furious	26 Jun 1934
Hal Far	15 Aug 1934
HMS Furious	28 Aug 1934
Manston	23 Oct 1934
Gosport	16 Dec 1934
HMS Furious	5 Jan 1935
Hal Far	18 Jan 1935
HMS Furious	21 Jan 1935
Manston	25 Mar 1935
Catfoss (1ATC)	4 May 1935
HMS Furious	22 May 1935
Manston	17 Jul 1935
HMS Furious	20 Jul 1935
Manston	3 Aug 1935
HMS Furious	17 Aug 1935
Manston	20 Aug 1935
'B' Flight:	
HMS Courageous	28 Aug 1935
HMS Glorious	17 Sep 1935
HMS Courageous	18 Oct 1935 to 28 Feb 1936
HMS Furious	3 Sep 1935
Gosport	7 Oct 1935
HMS Furious	4 Nov 1935
Gosport	22 Nov 1935
HMS Furious	2 Jan 1936
Gibraltar (Dt)	26 Feb 1936 to 16 Jul 1936
Eastleigh	21 May 1936
HMS Furious	17 Jun 1936
Southampton	20 Jul 1936
HMS Furious	28 Sep 1936
Donibristle	20 Oct 1936
Southampton	23 Oct 1936
HMS Furious	23 Jan 1937
Aboukir	8 Feb 1937
HMS Furious	22 Feb 1937
Gosport	29 Mar 1937
HMS Furious	24 May 1937
Evanton	7 Jun 1937
HMS Furious	29 Jun 1937
Gosport	21 Jul 1937
HMS Furious	10 Sep 1937
Evanton (Dt6)	4-10 Oct 1937
Gosport	28 Oct 1937
Manston	9 Apr 1938
Donibristle	4 May 1938
HMS Furious	5 Jul 1938
Donibristle	8 Jul 1938
HMS Furious	18 Jul 1938
Donibristle	22 Jul 1938
HMS Furious	24 Sep 1938
Donibristle	15 Oct 1938
HMS Courageous	8 Feb 1939
Donibristle	14 Feb 1939
HMS Courageous	20 Mar 1939
Donibristle	4 Apr 1939
Squadron disbanded into 767 Sqdn	24 May 1939
822A Sqdn: Southampton	15 May 1939
Redesignated 822 Sqdn	1 Jul 1939
Southampton	1 Jul 1939
Donibristle	3 Jul 1939
Southampton	12 Jul 1939
HMS Courageous	12 Aug 1939
Ship sunk	17 Sep 1939
Lee-on-Solent	15 Oct 1941
Gosport	25 Nov 1941
Millom (transit)	25 Jan 1942
Hatston	27 Jan 1942
Crail	20 Mar 1942
Donibristle	2 May 1942
Machrihanish	6 Jun 1942
HMS Furious	15 Jul 1942
Machrihanish	29 Jul 1942
HMS Furious	30 Aug 1942
Hatston	11 Sep 1942
Machrihanish	23 Sep 1942
Twatt	27 Sep 1942
Machrihanish	16 Oct 1942
HMS Furious	18 Oct 1942
North Front(Dt)	25-30 Oct 1942
North Front	11 Nov 1942
HMS Furious	14 Nov 1942
North Front	6 Dec 1942
HMS Furious	2 Jan 1943
Hatston	11 Feb 1943
HMS Furious	3 Mar 1943
Hatston (Dt6)	10-27 Apr 1943
Lee-on-Solent	15 Jul 1943
Croft (transit)	9 Nov 1943
Tain	10 Nov 1943
Fearn	16 Jan 1944
Crail	1 Feb 1944
Burscough	18 Feb 1944
HMS Atheling (a/c)	26 Feb 1944
HMT Strathnaver/ HMT Aronda (crews)	2 Mar 1944
St Thomas Mount	11 Apr 1944
Ulunderpet	12 Apr 1944
China Bay	9 May 1944
Ulunderpet	18 May 1944
Katukurunda	19 Jun 1944
HMS Atheling (DLT)	15 Aug 1944
Katukurunda	21 Aug 1944
HMS Victorious (Dt9)	11-20 Sep 1944
HMS Rajah (no a/c)	11 Oct 1944
Ronaldsway	15 Nov 1944
Lee-on-Solent	18 Nov 1944
Thorney Island	19 Jan 1945
Manston (16 Gp)	14 Apr 1945
Maydown	3 Jun 1945
Belfast	26 Jul 1945
Woodvale	28 Aug 1945
Burscough	4 Oct 1945
Machrihanish	17 Dec 1945
Squadron disbanded	19 Feb 1946
HMS Hermes	6 Jul 1979
Temp sqdn disbanded	13 Jul 1979

Commanding Officers
L/C HL StJ Fancourt RN	3 Apr 1933
L/C EOF Price RN	1 Jun 1934
L/C EB Carnduff RN	21 Jun 1934
L/C AP Colthurst RN (Sq Ldr RAF)	18 Aug 1934
L/C AM Rundle RN (Sq Ldr RAF)	14 Mar 1936
L/C JB Buckley RN (Sq Ldr RAF)	21 Apr 1938
L/C K Williamson RN (Sq Ldr RAF)	28 Jul 1938
Squadron disbanded	24 May 1939
L/C WHG Saunt RN (Sq Ldr RAF)	15 May 1939
L/C HL McCulloch RN	1 Jun 1939
L/C PW Humphreys RN	1 Jul 1939
Squadron disbanded	17 Sep 1939
Mjr AR Burch DSC RM	15 Oct 1941
Lt(A) JGA McI Nares RN	6 Aug 1942
Lt HAL Tibbetts RCNVR	10 Nov 1942
Lt JW Collett RN	10 Feb 1943
L/C(A) PF King RN	3 Mar 1943
L/C BE Boulding DSC RN	10 Aug 1943
L/C(A) GA Woods RNVR	1 Dec 1943
L/C(A) LC Watson DSC RNVR	13 Jul 1944
L/C(A) DA Davies DSC RNVR	4 Apr 1945
L/C(A) JM Brown DSC RNVR	10 Jan 1946
Squadron disbanded	19 Feb 1946

Fairey Albacore BF609 '4L' of No.822 Squadron at Crail in 1942. (FAA Museum)

No.823 Squadron

Badge: On a white field, per fesse, and barry wavy of four blue and white in chief an eagle volant to the sinister black and in base a Maltese Cross party per pale white and red

Motto: *Vigueur de dessus* (Strength from above)

No.823 Squadron formed in HMS *Glorious* from Nos.441 and 448 Flights on 3 April 1933 as a spotter reconnaissance squadron with 12 Fairey IIIFs. Then serving with the Mediterranean Fleet, the ship returned home in May 1934 for a refit, and the squadron temporarily transferred to HMS *Courageous*. In December it re-equipped with six Seals from No.820 Squadron, increasing to the full strength of 12 when it sailed with with six each in HMS *Glorious* and HMS *Courageous* for the Mediterranean in August 1935. In October 1935 the whole squadron joined HMS *Glorious*, and in November 1936 re-equipped with 12 Swordfish Is to become a torpedo spotter reconnaissance squadron. It returned home briefly to take part in the Coronation Review flypast at Spithead on 20 May 1937, then returned to the Mediterranean.

On the outbreak of war, HMS *Glorious* sailed into the Red Sea to cover trade protection routes in the Indian Ocean. In January 1940 she returned to the Mediterranean, and No.823 undertook reconnaissance patrols, but in April the carrier was hurriedly recalled when the Germans invaded Norway. On 8 June she was sunk by the German battlecruisers *Scharnhorst* and *Gneisenau* en route from Norway to Scotland, half of No.823 being aboard at the time. The squadron then operated at a reduced strength of 9 aircraft, and on 21 June six aircraft of Nos.821 and 823 Squadron operating from Hatston made an unsuccessful daylight torpedo attack on the *Scharnhorst*, one squadron aircraft being lost. A torpedo attack was carried out against enemy destroyers and transport off Norway on 24 July, following which the squadron undertook routine anti-submarine patrols in the Scapa area until being disbanded at Hatston on 3 December 1940.

On 1 November 1941 the squadron reformed at Crail as a torpedo bomber reconnaissance unit, again with nine Swordfish Is. These gave way in April 1942 to nine Albacores, which embarked in HMS *Furious* in August for convoy escort duty, disembarking the following month for anti-submarine patrols in the English Channel with RAF Coastal Command. In June 1943 it re-equipped with four Barracuda IIs, increasing to 12 in September shortly before being allocated to the 45th Naval TBR Wing for intended service in HMS *Indefatigable*. Instead, the aircraft were loaded in HMS *Atheling* in February 1944 for passage east, and on arrival in southern India recommenced flying and work-up with the 11th TBR Wing. On 6 July 1944, however, the squadron disbanded at Katukurunda to enlarge No.822 Squadron.

Battle Honours
Norway   1940

Identification Markings
IIIF *801-806, 820-834*; Seal *801-814*; Swordfish *801- 814*, to *G4A*+ 5.39, later *4A*+ to 12.40, single letters 11.41 - 3.42; Albacore & Barracuda single letters.

Aircraft Equipment	Period of Service	Example	
Fairey IIIF	Apr 1933 - Dec 1934	S1356	(820)
Seal	Dec 1934 - Dec 1936	K3544	(803)
Swordfish I	Nov 1936 - Dec 1940	K8378	(807)
	Nov 1941 - Mar 1942	W5849	
Swordfish II	Feb 1942 - Mar 1942	DK695	
Albacore I	Mar 1942 - May 1943	BF631	(L)
Barracuda II	Jun 1943 - Jul 1944	BV703	(L)

Fairey IIIF S1346 '831' of No.825 Squadron, HMS Glorious at Alexandria in 1935. (RAF Museum P.13883)

Squadron bases		Squadron bases		Squadron bases		Squadron bases	
HMS Glorious	3 Apr 1933	'A' Flight:		Hal Far	27 Mar 1938	Lee-on-Solent	12 Mar 1942
Hal Far	27 Apr 1933	Aboukir	22 Nov 1935	HMS Glorious	16 May 1938	Machrihanish	4 May 1942
HMS Glorious	26 Jun 1933	HMS Glorious	4 Dec 1935	Hal Far	31 May 1938	HMS Furious	15 Jul 1942
Hal Far	17 Aug 1933	Amriya	18 Dec 1935	HMS Glorious	18 Jul 1938	Machrihanish	23 Jul 1942
HMS Glorious	30 Aug 1933	HMS Glorious	7 Jan 1935	Hal Far	9 Sep 1938	HMS Furious(Dt4)	3-30 Aug 1942
Aboukir (Dt4)	13-23 Sep 1933	'B' Flight:		Hal Far	9 Nov 1938	HMS Furious	30 Aug 1942
Hal Far	23 Oct 1933	HMS Glorious	5 Nov 1935	Dekheila	23 Jan 1939	Hatston	11 Sep 1942
HMS Glorious	20 Nov 1933	Aboukir	6 Dec 1935	HMS Glorious	30 Jan 1939	Tangmere (16 Gp)	25 Sep 1942
Hal Far	25 Jan 1934	HMS Glorious	16 Dec 1935	Hal Far	14 Feb 1939	Manston (16 Gp)	1 Jan 1943
HMS Glorious	2 Mar 1934	Amriya	18 Dec 1935	HMS Glorious	20 Feb 1939	Tangmere (16 Gp)	22 Mar 1943
Hal Far	11 Apr 1934	HMS Glorious	21 Dec 1936	Hal Far	23 Feb 1939	Lee-on-Solent	1 Jun 1943
HMS Glorious	23 Apr 1934	Hal Far (Dt)	24 Dec 1935	HMS Glorious	20 Mar 1939	Fearn	19 Aug 1943
Upavon	1 May 1934		to 1 Jan 1936	Hal Far	11 Apr 1939	Burscough	9 Jan 1944
Donibristle	2 May 1934	Aboukir	27 Feb 1936	HMS Glorious	12 Apr 1939	Renfrew (transit)	25 Feb 1944
HMS Courageous	Jul 1934	(recombined)		Hal Far	13 Apr 1939	HMS Atheling	26 Feb 1944
Upavon	25 Jul 1934	HMS Glorious	10 Mar 1936	HMS Glorious	18 Apr 1939	Ulunderpet	12 Apr 1944
Donibristle	26 Jul 1934	Aboukir	19 Mar 1936	Hal Far	25 Apr 1939	Katukurunda	19 Jun 1944
Leuchars	11 Aug 1934	HMS Glorious	31 Mar 1936	HMS Glorious	14 May 1939	Sqdn disbanded into	
Novar	3 Sep 1934	Amriya	3 Apr 1936	Hal Far	6 Jun 1939	822 Sqdn	6 Jul 1944
HMS Courageous	26 Oct 1934	HMS Glorious	15 Apr 1936	Dekheila	15 Aug 1939		
Donibristle	5 Nov 1934	Aboukir	8 May 1936	HMS Glorious	11 Sep 1939	**Commanding Officers**	
HMS Courageous	7 Jan 1935	HMS Glorious	18 Jun 1936	Dekheila	16 Sep 1939	L/C CB Tidd RN	18 Aug 1933
Gosport (transit)	25 Mar 1935	Hal Far (Dt6)	27 Jul 1936	HMS Glorious	14 Oct 1939	(Sq Ldr RAF)	
Donibristle	26 Mar 1935	Hal Far (remainder)	27 Jul 1936	Hal Far	17 Jan 1940	Flt Lt MM Freehill	
HMS Courageous	7 May 1935	HMS Glorious	29 Sep 1936	HMS Glorious	25 Mar 1940	RAF	Sep 1934
Gosport	2 Jul 1935	Hal Far	30 Oct 1936	Hatston	18 Apr 1940	L/C GC Dickens RN	30 Aug 1935
'A' Flight:		HMS Glorious	30 Jan 1937	Evanton	22 Apr 1940	(Sq Ldr RAF)	
HMS Courageous	29 Aug 1935	Hal Far	23 Mar 1937	HMS Glorious	30 Apr 1940	L/C DW MacKendrick	
Aboukir	2 Oct 1935	HMS Glorious	23 Apr 1937	Evanton	3 May 1940	RN (Sq Ldr RAF)	21 May 1937
HMS Courageous	10 Oct 1935	Gosport	5 May 1937	HMS Glorious		L/C RA Kilroy RN	1 Feb 1938
HMS Glorious	17 Oct 1935	HMS Glorious	24 Jun 1937	(Dt6)	3-12 May 1940	(Sq Ldr RAF)	
'B' Flight:		Hal Far	15 Jul 1937	Hatston	14 May 1940	L/C RD Watkins RN	24 May 1939
HMS Glorious	21 Aug 1935	HMS Glorious	18 Jul 1937	HMS Glorious		L/C CJT Stephens	
Hal Far	28 Aug 1935	Hal Far	23 Aug 1937	(Dt6)	3-8 Jun 1940	RN	27 May 1940
HMS Glorious	2 Sep 1935	Aboukir	2 Sep 1937	Squadron disbanded	3 Dec 1940	L/C DH Elles RN	3 Jul 1940
Aboukir	5 Sep 1935	HMS Glorious	9 Sep 1937	Crail	1 Nov 1941	L/C(A) AJD Harding	
HMS Glorious		Hal Far	19 Oct 1937	Fraserburgh	6 Dec 1941	DSC RN	1 Nov 1941
(recombined)	17 Oct 1935	HMS Glorious	7 Feb 1938	Machrihanish	30 Jan 1942	L/C JW Collett RN	1 Aug 1942
						Lt RW Spackman RN	24 Nov 1942
						L/C G Douglas RNR	22 Mar 1943
						L/C(A) LC Watson	
						DSC RNVR	1 Dec 1943
						Squadron disbanded	6 Jul 1944

Fairey Seal K3543 '802' of No.823 Squadron around 1935/6. (RAF Museum P.17001)

No.824 Squadron

Badge: 1. On a blue field, over water in barry wavy white and blue, a great white heron flying to the sinister proper
2. Revised badge with an eagle carrying a torpedo (details of heraldic description lacking)

Motto: *Spectat ubique spiritus* (The wind everywhere looks on)

No.824 Squadron formed at Gosport on 3 April 1933 from No.460 Flight as a spotter reconnaissance squadron equipped with nine Fairey IIIFs. Later in the month these embarked in HMS *Eagle* for the China Station, and on arrival at Hong Kong the squadron also absorbed No.440 Flight to bring the strength up to 12 aircraft. No.824 lost its identity when it was renumbered to become No.825 Squadron on 8 October 1934.

On the same day a new No.824 was formed at Upavon with nine Seals for spotter reconnaissance duties. These joined HMS *Hermes* the following month, and sailed for the China Station through the Mediterranean. In January 1937, a nucleus of nine new Swordfish Is and their crews embarked at Portsmouth in HMS *Eagle*, and when these arrived in the China Station in April they replaced the former No.824 and its aircraft. The squadron then changed its task to torpedo spotter reconnaissance.

On the outbreak of war the ship changed its base from Singapore to Trincomalee and began searching for enemy shipping in the Indian Ocean. In May it was transferred to the Mediterranean, where No.824's activities included Malta convoy escort duty. In August it spotted for a gunnery bombardment of Bardia by battleships, and later in the month provided cover for the passage of HMS *Illustrious* to the Eastern Mediterranean. On 4 September a dawn bombing attack was made on Maritza airfield on the island of Rhodes. Two aircraft temporarily joined HMS *Illustrious* for the Taranto attack on 11 November, then later in the month the squadron flew from HMS *Eagle* to attack docks at Tripoli.

Early in 1941 the squadron was split for a time, half being embarked in HMS *Eagle* for search and anti-submarine duties with convoys, whilst the remainder performed a similar task from Dekheila. In March the whole squadron flew to Port Sudan to provide support for land forces in the Red Sea area, and on 3 April attacked enemy destroyers off Massawa in Eritrea, two being sunk and two driven ashore. No.824 then re-embarked to sail round the Cape for the South Atlantic to help search for the German battleship *Bismarck*. The U-boat supply ship Elbe was sighted and successfully bombed in mid-Atlantic on 6 June, then nine days later squadron aircraft forced the German tanker *Lothringen* to surrender. In October the ship sailed home for a refit.

Fairey IIIF S1821 '83' of No.824 Squadron about to be hooked on to the crane of HMS Eagle after helping to rescue British nationals from a pirate sampan in Chinese waters in June 1934. (Cdr John Casson)

Fairey Seal K4215 '890' of No.824 Squadron, HMS Hermes at Kai Tak in 1935. (via TAG Association)

Re-embarking in January 1942, escort was provided for a Gibraltar convoy the following month. After carrying out anti-submarine patrols during a Malta convoy in March, the squadron spent the next few months mainly ashore in Gibraltar, taking it in turn with No.813 Squadron to provide aircraft for HMS *Eagle* as required. When that ship was sunk on 11 August during a Malta convoy, No.824 ceased to exist, its remnants being transferred to No.813 Squadron.

A new No.824 assembled at Lee-on-Solent on 22 August 1942, but it was not until 1 October that it officially reformed, with six Swordfish Is. These were soon exchanged for Mk.IIs, which embarked in HMS *Unicorn* in March 1943 for work up and anti-submarine operations. Increasing to nine aircraft in June, it re-embarked for a sweep off northern Norway the following month. In August, 6 Sea Hurricanes were added, and with these the squadron joined HMS *Striker* in October for convoy escort operations on the North Atlantic and Gibraltar routes.

In May 1944 a further three Swordfish were added, and the following month the fighter flight re-equipped with six Wildcat Vs, No.824 then re-embarking to provide anti-submarine defence and fighter protection during an offensive sweep against enemy shipping off Norway. Four more Wildcats were received in August for similar duties on North Russian convoy escort. A Bv 138 was shot down on 22 August, and the Swordfish made several unsuccessful attacks on U-boats. After a similar task in September, the squadron returned home to disband at Abbotsinch on 16 October 1944.

On 2 July 1945 No.824 reformed at Katukurunda, Ceylon as a torpedo bomber reconnaissance squadron with 12 Barracuda IIs, of which 10 were taken over from No.812 Squadron. These were intended to join the 17th Carrier Air Group in a *Colossus*-class carrier with the British Pacific Fleet, but VJ-day intervened and instead it discarded its aircraft and took passage home in HMS *Activity* to re-equip at Ayr the following month with 12 Firefly FR.Is. However, on 4 January 1946 it disbanded at Burscough.

No.824 next reformed at Eglinton on 18 February 1952 as an anti-submarine squadron with eight Firefly AS.6s. These embarked in HMS *Illustrious* in June for the first of a series of exercises, then transferred to HMS *Theseus* in January 1953 for a spell in the Mediterranean before rejoining the Home Fleet to participate in the Coronation Review flypast at Spithead on 15 June. Following this it rejoined HMS *Illustrious* for further exercises before disembarking to Lee-on-Solent to re-equip in July with unmodified Avenger TBM-3Es. After exchanging these for British-standard Avenger AS.4s in January 1954 the squadron moved to Culdrose, the first of a number of shore bases from which it operated with these aircraft. In February 1955 No.824 re-equipped with 8 Gannet AS.1s, and these embarked in HMS *Ark Royal* in October to sail for the Mediterranean. The ship returned home in April 1956, and the squadron disbanded at Ford on 17 April 1956.

The squadron next reformed at Culdrose on 7 May 1956, being commissioned on 15 May as an anti-submarine squadron, again equipped with eight Gannet AS.1s. These were replaced in October by nine Gannet AS.4s, and in January 1957 it sailed for the Mediterranean in HMS *Ark Royal*, transferring to HMS *Albion* off Malta on 22 January before going ashore to Gibraltar the following month. It re-embarked from Malta in April, to return home in May. After a series of exercises in HMS *Albion* from early September, the aircraft flew ashore to Culdrose where the squadron disbanded on 1 November 1957.

No.824 next reformed on 21 April 1958 at Eglinton as a helicopter squadron, equipped with eight Whirlwind HAS.7s for anti-submarine duties. These embarked in HMS *Victorious* in August 1958, but engine defects led to the loan of six Whirlwind HAS.22s from No.848 Squadron in November. When the ship returned home in January 1959 its own aircraft were lightered aboard, being transferred to HMS *Eagle* in February for an exercise. However, the aircraft were grounded in March, the faults being never satisfactorily rectified, and the squadron disbanded at Culdrose on 20 April 1959.

On 3 November 1959 No.824 reformed at Culdrose, again with eight Whirlwind HAS.7s. These embarked in HMS *Ark Royal* in March 1960 for the Mediterranean, taking part in a number of exercises and visits to various ports around the northern Mediterranean. Returning home, four aircraft joined HMS *Hermes* in October for an exercise before re-embarking in HMS *Ark Royal* for a further spell in the Mediterranean. In the New Year came a trip to the Artic for cold weather trials, and in February 1961 they visited New York. In April the squadron transferred to HMS *Centaur* for further Mediterranean exercises, but in July the ship sailed through the Suez Canal for the Persian Gulf, owing to events in Kuwait. The following month the ship returned home, and No.824 spent a few weeks ashore before re-embarking in October for the Far East.

In early December 1961, part of the squadron was put ashore in Mombasa for flood relief work in Kenya, using No.825 Squadron's aircraft. Continuing to the Far East, No.824 disembarked to Singapore in February 1962, then re-embarked to sail home, arriving back at Culdrose in May. The next few months were spent in exercises and visits to various ports in the northen Mediterranean, then in January 1963 assistance was provided after a heavy snowfall in South Wales. After a visit to the Indian Ocean commencing in February, the squadron disbanded on 21 May 1963.

No.824 became a Sea King HAS.1 unit when it next reformed at Culdrose on 24 February 1970, equipped with six aircraft for anti-submarine duties. These embarked in HMS *Ark Royal* in June for exercises, followed by a visit to Oslo in September. In January 1972, a visit was made to the United States. On return, several further periods were spent in the ship before transferring to HMS *Hermes* in September 1973. From November 1973 various detachments operated from Royal Fleet Auxiliaries on trials, before rejoining HMS *Ark Royal* in July 1974. In November the squadron was briefly attached to HMS *Hermes*, but had returned to HMS *Ark Royal* by January 1975 for another visit to the United States. In 1976 further visits were made to the United States, and in November the squadron flew direct from Culdrose to Brest.

In March 1977 No.824 re-equipped with seven Sea King HAS.2s, and these joined HMS *Ark Royal* in September. The last trip in this ship commenced in April 1978 and included another visit to the United States. Disembarking in December the HAS.2s were discarded in favour of eight Sea King HAS.2A's on becoming the parent unit for the new RFA Sea King flights, each of two aircraft. 'A' Flight was the first to embark, in RFA *Fort Grange* in January 1979. The squadron participated in an exercise from HMS *Bulwark* in May, then 'A' Flight rejoined RFA Fort *Grange* in June for a visit to Borneo, returning home for Christmas. At about the time they departed, the remainder of the squadron joined with No.819 Squadron in HMS *Hermes* to operate temporarily as "No.822 Squadron" before sailing for a visit to America.

Fairey Swordfish I K8390 '946' of No.824 Squadron on floats aboard HMS Eagle in the China Station around 1938. (H.Liddle)

Fairey Swordfish I K8419 '5B' of No.824 Squadron, piloted by John Wellham, this aircraft participated in numerous operations between November 1939 and January 1941, including helping to sink the Italian submarine Iride on 22 August 1940.
(Wellham collection/FAA Museum)

In January 1980, 'C' Flight embarked in RFA *Olmeda*, and 'D' Flight in RFA *Fort Grange*, and the following month RFA *Fort Austin* sailed with 'B' Flight to Gibraltar. By early April all aircraft were back at Culdrose, but in that month 'C' Flight joined RFA *Olna* for a few weeks, returning in late May, by which time 'D' Flight had embarked in RFA *Olwen*. In July, 'A' Flight joined RFA *Tidepool* for a few days, transferring to RFA *Fort Austin* soon after returning to Culdrose, for a visit to the United States. In September, 'A' Flight returned, and 'B' and 'C' Flights embarked in RFA *Olna* and RFA *Fort Grange* respectively. The following month 'C' Flight joined HMS *Invincible*, and in November RFAs *Fort Austin* and *Olmeda* sailed to the Middle East with 'A' and 'B' Flights respectively. In early December, 'D' Flight disbanded without having re-embarked, and the squadron strength was reduced to six aircraft.

The pattern for 1981 was fairly similar, with 'A' Flight spending periods in RFAs *Fort Austin* and *Fort Grange*, 'B' Flight in RFAs *Olwen* and *Olmeda,* and 'C' Flight in RFAs *Olwen, Fort Grange* and *Fort Austin*. In May 1982 the squadron participated in the Falklands Task Force, 'A' and 'C' Flights being embarked in RFAs *Olmeda* and *Fort Grange* respectively. At the same time, 'B' Flight was reactivated to evaluate the Sea King HAS.5 for RFA use, operating from RFA *Olna*. 'D' Flight reformed in June with 2 Sea King HAS.2s fitted with Searchwater radar, this being a hasty conversion after the lack of this facility in the Falklands, the aircraft being embarked in HMS *Illustrious* in August. In January 1983, 'B' Flight re-embarked in RFA *Olwen*, and shortly afterwards 'A' and 'C' Flights were transferred to No.826 Squadron. 'D' Flight had a spell in HMS *Illustrious* from March, then 'B' Flight joined her early in 1984.

'D' Flt reformed as 849 Sqdn in November 1984, leaving 824 Sqdn with one flight of two aircraft. In spring 1985 the squadron deployed to the USN AUTEC range on Andros Island for ASW trials and in the summer into the Barents Sea embarked on an RFA, this deployment was repeated in summer 1986. In Jul 1987 the squadron moved to Prestwick to become the Sea King Mk.6 IFTU, carrying out trials between April 1988 and April 1989 when the Mk.6 aircraft were transferred to 819 Sqdn. There was another deployment to AUTEC in autumn 1988 and to the Barents Sea in summer 1989 with the two remaining Mk.5 aircraft, after which the squadron disbanded in August on being absorbed into No.819 Sqdn.

'D Flt reformed as No.849 Squadron in Nov 1984, leaving No.824 Squadron with one flight of two aircraft. In spring 1985 the Squadron deployed to the USN AUTEC range on Andros Island for ASW trials and in the summer into the Barents Sea embarked on an RFA, this deployment was repeated in summer 1986. In July 1987 the Squadron moved to Prestwick to become the Sea King Mk.6 IFTU, carrying out trials between April 1988 and April 1989 when the Mk.6 aircraft were transferred to No.819 Squadron. There was another deployment to AUTEC in autumn 1988 and to the Barents Sea in summer 1989 with the two remaining Mk.5 aircraft, after which the Squadron disbanded in August, being absorbed into No.819 Squadron.

Aircraft Equipment	Period of Service	Example	
Fairey IIIF	Apr 1933 - Oct 1934	S1821	(83)
Seal	Oct 1934 - Apr 1937	K4224	(879)
Swordfish I	Apr 1937 - Aug 1942	K8414	(E5G)
	Oct 1942 - Jan 1943	V4645	
Swordfish II	Nov 1942 - Oct 1944	HS224	(2A)
Sea Hurricane IIc	Aug 1943 - Jun 1944	NF694	(U)
Wildcat V	Jun 1944 - Oct 1944	JV476	(R)
Barracuda II	Jul 1945 - Sep 1945	MX723	
Firefly FR.1	Oct 1945 - Jan 1946	MB399	
Firefly AS.6	Feb 1952 - Jul 1953	VT392	(288)
Avenger TBM-3E	Jul 1953 - Jan 1954	XB318	(309)
Avenger AS.4	Jan 1954 - Feb 1955	XB307	(398)
Gannet AS.1	Feb 1955 - Apr 1956	WN419	(332/O)
	May 1956 - Oct 1956	WN394	(335/Z)
Gannet T.2	Apr 1956 - Dec 1956	XG879	
Gannet AS.4	Oct 1956 - Nov 1957	XA418	(332/Z)
Whirlwind HAS.7	Apr 1958 - Apr 1959	XL851	(335/V)
	Nov 1959 - May 1963	XM667	(332/R)
Sea King HAS.1	Feb 1970 - Sep 1977	XV703	(050/R)
Sea King HAS.2/2a	Mar 1977 - Apr 1983	XV659	(053/R)
Sea King HAS.2(AEW)	Aug 1982 - Nov 1984	XV704	(361)
Sea King HAS.5	Jun 1982 - Aug 1989	ZE420	(354/CU)
Sea King HAS.6	Apr 1988 - Apr 1989	XZ581	(254)

Identification Markings

IIIF *71-75, 81-86*; Seal *870-891*; Swordfish *945-954*, to *E5A+* 5.39, later *5A+* to 8.42, *1A+* from 10.42, then *2A+* later single letters; Sea Hurricane & Wildcat single letters; Barracuda single letters; Firefly single letters *1945/6*, to *281-288* 2.52; Avenger *214-217* in error initially, changed to *301-310*, to *391-398* 2.54; Gannet *411-419/GN:CU:O*, to *331-339/O:Z:A* 1.56. Whirlwind *330-338/V:R:C*, also initially carried individual letters *J,U,M,P,C,A,T,S* for obvious reasons; Sea King *050-056/R*, to *575-584/CU* 1.2.79, to *530-538/CU* 3.80, to *350-355/CU* 3.81, to *251-255* 9.85, also D Flt *361-362* 1982/3.

Battle Honours

Calabria	1940
Mediterranean	1940
Taranto	1940
Libya	1940-41
Malta Convoys	1942
Atlantic	1942
Arctic	1944
Falkland Islands	1982

Squadron bases

Gosport	3 Apr 1933
HMS Eagle	26 Apr 1933
Kai Tak	11 Jun 1933
HMS Eagle	16 Jun 1933
Kai Tak	27 Oct 1933
HMS Eagle	28 Dec 1933
Singapore (Dt4)	16 Jan 1934
to	1 Feb 1934
Kai Tak	16 Mar 1934
HMS Eagle	3 May 1934
Redesignated 825 Sqdn	8 Oct 1934
Upavon	8 Oct 1934
HMS Hermes	8 Nov 1934
Hal Far (Dt4)	27-30 Nov 1934
Kai Tak	6 Jan 1935
HMS Hermes	13 May 1935
Singapore	19 Sep 1935
HMS Hermes	10 Dec 1935
Seletar	19 Dec 1935
HMS Hermes	25 Feb 1936
Kai Tak	2 Mar 1936
HMS Hermes	21 Apr 1936
Wei-hai-Wei	27 May 1936
HMS Hermes	24 Jul 1936
Kai Tak	3 Nov 1936
HMS Hermes	4 Jan 1937
Seletar	4 Feb 1937
HMS Hermes	15 Mar 1937
Gosport	3 May 1937
Replacement Sqdn:	
Gosport	18 Jan 1937
HMS Eagle	23 Feb 1937
Hal Far	5 Mar 1937
HMS Eagle	12 Mar 1937
Seletar	9 Apr 1937
HMS Eagle	30 Apr 1937
Kai Tak	6 May 1937
HMS Eagle	28 May 1937
Kai Tak	19 Oct 1937
HMS Eagle	4 Nov 1937
Kai Tak	5 Nov 1937
HMS Eagle	8 Jan 1938
Seletar	14 Jan 1938
Penang (Dt3)	21-27 Jan 1938
HMS Eagle	31 Jan 1938
Seletar	5 Feb 1938
HMS Eagle	26 Feb 1938
Penang	4 Mar 1938
HMS Eagle	7 Mar 1938
Seletar	9 Mar 1938
HMS Eagle	16 Mar 1938
Kai Tak	14 Apr 1938
HMS Eagle	4 Jun 1938
Seletar	17 Sep 1938
HMS Eagle	27 Sep 1938
Kai Tak	19 Oct 1938
HMS Eagle	1 Nov 1938
Kai Tak	3 Nov 1938
HMS Eagle	15 Nov 1938
Kai Tak	17 Nov 1938
HMS Eagle	5 Dec 1938
Kai Tak	7 Dec 1938
HMS Eagle	11 Mar 1939
Seletar	17 Mar 1939
HMS Eagle	4 Apr 1939
Seletar	24 Apr 1939
HMS Eagle	19 May 1939
Kai Tak	25 May 1939
HMS Eagle	29 May 1939
Kai Tak	31 Jul 1939
HMS Eagle	12 Aug 1939
Seletar	18 Aug 1939
HMS Eagle	29 Aug 1939
Seletar	1 Nov 1939
HMS Eagle	8 Nov 1939
China Bay (Dt6)	16-29 Jan 1940
China Bay (Dt6)	6-12 Mar 1940
Kallang (transit)	16 Mar 1940
Sembawang	17 Mar 1940
HMS Eagle	8 May 1940
Dekheila	28 May 1940
HMS Eagle	29 Jun 1940
Dekheila	1 Jul 1940
HMS Eagle	8 Jul 1940
Dekheila	22 Jul 1940
HMS Eagle	28 Jul 1940
Dekheila	3 Aug 1940
Maaten Bagush (Dt3)	22-29 Aug 1940
HMS Eagle	30 Aug 1940
Dekheila	4 Oct 1940
Maaten Bagush (Dt3)	17-29 Sep 1940
HMS Eagle	3 Oct 1940
Dekheila	6 Oct 1940
HMS Eagle	10 Oct 1940
Dekheila	15 Oct 1940
Fuka satt (Dt4)	21-24 Oct 1940
HMS Eagle	25 Oct 1940
HMS Illustrious (Dt)	7-20 Nov 1940
Dekheila (and Fuka satt)	28 Nov 1940
HMS Eagle (Dt)	11-18 Jan 1941
HMS Eagle (Dt)	20-24 Jan 1941
Dekheila	25 Jan 1941
HMS Eagle (Dt)	1-4 Feb 1941
HMS Eagle	19 Feb 1941
Dekheila	10 Mar 1941
Port Sudan (operate from LGs)	25 Mar 1941
HMS Eagle	19 Apr 1941
Port Reitz	26 Apr 1941
HMS Eagle	28 Apr 1941
Machrihanish	26 Oct 1941
HMS Eagle	20 Jan 1942
North Front	24 Feb 1942
HMS Argus (Dt4)	23 May 1942
to	17 Jun 1942

Rocket-armed Fairey Gannet AS.1 XA420 '333/Z' of No.824 Squadron aboard HMS Albion in 1957. (FAA Museum)

Westland Sea King HAS.1 XV659 '055/R' of No.824 Squadron around 1971. (via Brian Lowe)

Squadron bases							
HMS Eagle (Dt6)	22 Jun 1942	Hatston	25 Jun 1944	Lossiemouth	14 Sep 1954	HMS Eagle	14 Feb 1959
to	8 Jul 1942	HMS Striker	11 Jul 1944	Eglinton	21 Sep 1954	North Front	13 Mar 1959
North Front	11 Jul 1942	Machrihanish	6 Oct 1944	Brawdy (Dt)	25-26 Oct 1954	Culdrose	20 Mar 1959
HMS Eagle (Dt4)	20 Jul 1942	Abbotsinch	7 Oct 1944	HMS Bulwark (DLP)	7 Jun 1955	Squadron disbanded	20 Apr 1959
to	5 Aug 1942	Lee-on-Solent	11 Oct 1944	Brawdy	7 Jun 1955	Culdrose	3 Nov 1959
Ship sunk - squadron		Squadron disbanded	16 Oct 1944	Marham	1 Jul 1955	Portland	26 Nov 1959
disbanded into 813		Katukurunda	2 Jul 1945	Eglinton	23 Jul 1955	Culdrose	1 Feb 1960
Squadron	11 Aug 1942	Sulur	27 Aug 1945	HMS Ark Royal	5 Oct 1955	HMS Ark Royal	2 Mar 1960
Lee-on-Solent	22 Aug 1942	Katukurunda	11 Sep 1945	Hal Far (Dt4)	29 Oct 1955	Hal Far	13 Mar 1960
Machrihanish	2 Nov 1942	HMS Activity	26 Sep 1945	to	8 Nov 1955	HMS Ark Royal	24 Mar 1960
Abbotsinch	23 Dec 1942	Ayr	20 Oct 1945	Hal Far (Dt4)	18-29 Nov 1955	Hal Far	7 Apr 1960
HMS Activity (DLT)	5 Jan 1943	Burscough	18 Dec 1945	Hal Far (Dt4)	14 Dec 1955	HMS Ark Royal	19 Apr 1960
Machrihanish	5 Jan 1943	Squadron disbanded	4 Jan 1946	to	17 Feb 1956	Hal Far	24 Apr 1960
Fearn	23 Jan 1943	Eglinton	18 Feb 1952	Ford	5 Apr 1956	HMS Ark Royal	22 May 1960
Machrihanish	11 Mar 1943	HMS Illustrious	4 Jun 1952	Squadron disbanded	17 Apr 1956	St Mandrier	11 Jun 1960
Dunino	16 Mar 1943	Eglinton	24 Jun 1952	Culdrose	7 May 1956	HMS Ark Royal	13 Jun 1960
Machrihanish	23 Mar 1943	HMS Illustrious	3 Sep 1952	HMS Bulwark (DLP)	23 Jul 1956	North Front (Dt4)	22 Jun 1960
HMS Unicorn	24 Mar 1943	Eglinton	23 Sep 1952	Culdrose	29 Jul 1956	to	4 Jul 1960
Machrihanish	13 May 1943	HMS Illustrious	17 Oct 1952	Lossiemouth	25 Sep 1956	Ta Kali (Dt6)	29 Jul 1960
HMS Unicorn	8 Jun 1943	Eglinton	25 Oct 1952	Culdrose	12 Oct 1956	to	8 Aug 1960
Donibristle	31 Jul 1943	HMS Theseus	17 Jan 1953	HMS Ark Royal	9 Jan 1957	Culdrose	26 Aug 1960
Machrihanish	18 Aug 1943	Eglinton	15 Mar 1953	HMS Albion	22 Jan 1957	Dartmouth (Dt6)	18-23 Sep 1960
Maydown	11 Sep 1943	Lee-on-Solent	16 Apr 1953	North Front	26 Feb 1957	HMS Hermes (Dt4)	4-15 Oct 1960
Ayr	14-27 Sep 1943	HMS Theseus	28 Apr 1953	Hal Far	12 Mar 1957	Portland (Dt)	17-21 Oct 1960
(Fighter Flt)		HMS Illustrious	27 May 1953	HMS Albion (Dt)	22 Apr 1957	HMS Ark Royal	25 Oct 1960
St Angelo	28 Sep 1943	Lee-on-Solent	29 May 1953	to	4 May 1957	HMS Victorious	15-17 Nov 1960
HMS Striker	27 Oct 1943	HMS Illustrious	17 Jun 1953	HMS Albion	4 May 1957	(Dt3)	
Donibristle	19 Feb 1944	Lee-on-Solent	24 Jun 1953	Culdrose	1 Jun 1957	Hal Far (Dt3)	17 Nov 1960
HMS Striker	29 Feb 1944	Culdrose	27 Jan 1954	HMS Albion	18 Jun 1957	to	19 Dec 1960
Grimsetter	12 Apr 1944	Topcliffe	12 Mar 1954	Culdrose	26 Jul 1957	Hal Far	19 Dec 1960
HMS Striker	5 May 1944	Lee-on-Solent	25 Mar 1954	HMS Albion	3 Sep 1957	HMS Ark Royal	23 Dec 1960
Hatston	9 May 1944	North Front	19 May 1954	Culdrose	28 Oct 1957	Hal Far	27 Dec 1960
HMS Striker	12 May 1944	Lee-on-Solent	19 Jun 1954	Squadron disbanded	1 Nov 1957	HMS Ark Royal	5 Jan 1961
Hatston (Dt8)	17-31 May 1944	Ford	9 Jul 1954	Eglinton	21 Apr 1958	Culdrose	28 Feb 1961
Grimsetter (Dt 13)	1-2 Jun 1944	Eglinton	13 Jul 1954	HMS Victorious	27 Aug 1958	HMS Centaur (Dt2)	17 Mar 1961
Hatston	14 Jun 1944	Anthorn	17 Jul 1954	Hal Far	23 Nov 1958	to	9 Apr 1961
HMS Striker	19 Jun 1944	Eglinton	18 Jul 1954	HMS Victorious	9 Dec 1958	HMS Centaur	10 Apr 1961
Eglinton (Fighter	30 Jun 1944	Anthorn	23 Jul 1954	Culdrose	9 Jan 1959	Hal Far	26 Apr 1961
Flight)	to 10 Jul 1944	Eglinton	28 Jul 1954	HMS Victorious	18 Jan 1959	HMS Centaur	8 May 1961

Westland Sea King HAS.2 XZ578 '055/R' of No.824 Squadron in 1978. (MAP)

Squadron bases

North Front	14 Jun 1961
HMS Centaur	29 Jun 1961
Culdrose	1 Sep 1961
Portland	25 Sep 1961
Culdrose	29 Sep 1961
HMS Centaur	19 Oct 1961
Hal Far	13 Nov 1961
HMS Centaur	25 Nov 1961
Port Reitz (Dt2)/ Malindi (Dt4)/ Lamu Beach (Dt2)/ HMS Centaur (Dt2)	8 Dec 1961
HMS Centaur	27 Dec 1961
Sembawang	1 Feb 1962
HMS Centaur	15 Feb 1962
Hal Far	17 Apr 1962
HMS Centaur	2 May 1962
Culdrose	14 May 1962
HMS Centaur	19 Jun 1962
Portland	5 Jul 1962
HMS Centaur	20 Jul 1962
North Front	29 Aug 1962
HMS Centaur	19 Sep 1962
Portland (Dt5)	26 Oct 1962 to 7 Nov 1962
Culdrose	21 Nov 1962
Portland	15 Jan 1963
HMS Centaur	21 Jan 1963
Culdrose	14 Feb 1963
HMS Centaur	21 Feb 1963
Sqdn disbanded UK	21 May 1963
Culdrose	24 Feb 1970
RFA Engadine (Dt2)	13-16 Apr 1970
Lossiemouth (Dt4)	3-6 May 1970
Ballykelly	8 May 1970
RFA Engadine (Dt3)	25-27 May 1970
Culdrose	29 May 1970
HMS Ark Royal	12 Jun 1970
Culdrose	30 Jul 1970
HMS Ark Royal	3 Sep 1970
RFA Olna (Dt2)	22-24 Sep 1970
Luqa (Dt3)	19 Oct 1970 to 3 Nov 1970
RFA Olna (Dt2)	4-13 Nov 1970
Luqa (Dt3)	14-29 Nov 1970
Culdrose	14 Dec 1970
HMS Ark Royal	15 Apr 1971
Culdrose	18 May 1971
HMS Ark Royal	2 Jun 1971
Culdrose	6 Aug 1971
HMS Ark Royal	15 Sep 1971
Culdrose	9 Oct 1971
HMS Ark Royal	29 Oct 1971
Culdrose	8 Dec 1971
HMS Ark Royal	19 Jan 1972
Key West (Dt3)	30 Jan 1972 to 7 Feb 1972
RFA Olmeda (Dt2)	31 Jan 1972 to 7 Feb 1972
Culdrose	8 Mar 1972
Manston (Dt3)	1-5 May 1972
HMS Ark Royal (Dt2)	6-8 Jun 1972
HMS Ark Royal	9 Jun 1972
Culdrose	17 Jul 1972
HMS Ark Royal	31 Aug 1972
Culdrose	19 Oct 1972
HMS Ark Royal	13 Nov 1972
HMS Bulwark (Dt3)	24-26 Nov 1972
Culdrose	11 Dec 1972
HMS Ark Royal	25 Jan 1973
Luqa	23 Feb 1973
HMS Ark Royal	6 Mar 1973
Culdrose	15 Mar 1973
HMS Ark Royal	1 May 1973
Roosevelt Roads	11 May 1973
HMS Ark Royal	25 May 1973
Mayport (Dt4)	14-24 Jun 1973
Culdrose	26 Jul 1973
HMS Hermes	22 Sep 1973
Culdrose	17 Oct 1973
HMS Hermes (Dt3)	19 Oct 1973 to 5 Nov 1973
RFA Olna (Dt2)	2-16 Nov 1973
Lanveoc (Dt2)	2-16 Nov 1973
RFA Engadine (Dt2)	5 Dec 1973 (trials unit) to 27 Apr 1974
RFA Olna (Dt2)	21 Feb 1974 to 8 Mar 1974
HMS Ark Royal (Dt2)	18-29 Apr 1974
HMS Ark Royal (Dt4)	7-10 Jun 1974
HMS Ark Royal (Dt2)	12-14 Jun 1974
HMS Ark Royal	3 Apr 1974
Culdrose	27 Jul 1974
HMS Ark Royal	4 Sep 1974
Culdrose	4 Nov 1974
HMS Ark Royal	5 Nov 1974
HMS Hermes	18 Nov 1974
Culdrose	29 Nov 1974
HMS Ark Royal	7 Jan 1975
Mayport (Dt4)	18 Feb 1975 to 6 Mar 1975
Culdrose	11 Jun 1975
Portland (Dt2 - SAR)	1 Sep 1975 to 30 Nov 1975
Culdrose	27 Nov 1975
HMS Ark Royal	4 Feb 1976
Mayport (Dt3)	23-30 Mar 1976
Mayport	1 Apr 1976
HMS Ark Royal	9 Apr 1976
Norfolk (Dt4)	19 Apr 1976 to 6 May 1976
RFA Olmeda (Dt2)	23 Apr 1976 to 6 May 1976
Roosevelt Roads (Dt3)	21-29 May 1976
Norfolk (Dt5)	4-10 Jun 1976
Culdrose	15 Jul 1976
HMS Ark Royal	2 Sep 1976
Culdrose	25 Oct 1976
Lanveoc	12 Nov 1976
Culdrose	20 Nov 1976
RFA Olna	17 Jan 1977
North Front (Dt1)	9-29 Jan 1977
Culdrose	10 Feb 1977
HMS Ark Royal (Dt3)	13-17 Jun 1977
RFA Olna (Dt2)	31 May 1977 to 1 Jul 1977
RFA Engadine (Dt3)	25 Apr 1977 to 6 May 1977
HMS Ark Royal	1 Sep 1977
RFA Olmeda (Dt2)	2-15 Oct 1977
Culdrose	13 Dec 1977
HMS Ark Royal	21 Feb 1978
Culdrose	8 Mar 1978
HMS Ark Royal	5 Apr 1978
Roosevelt Roads (Dt3)	27 Apr 1978 to 7 May 1978
RFA Olmeda (Dt2)	15-29 May 1978
RFA Fort Grange (Dt3)	17-23 Jun 1978
Jacksonville	22 Jun 1978
HMS Ark Royal	7 Aug 1978
RFA Olwen (Dt2)	21-25 Oct 1978
RFA Olwen (Dt2)	25-28 Nov 1978
Culdrose	3 Dec 1978
de Kooy (Dt2)	Mar 1979
HMS Bulwark	4 May 1979
Culdrose	1 Jun 1979
HMS Hermes	28 Jun 1979
Jacksonville (Dt4)	30 Jul 1979 to 21 Aug 1979
Culdrose	9 Oct 1979
- then operated as A,B,C,D Flights	
Culdrose	14 Dec 1984
(824D Flt only remaining flight became Sqdn)	
Felixstowe Docks	20 Feb 1985
MV Dart Continent (passage UK-USA)	22 Feb 1985
Charleston	9 Mar 1985
Patrick AFB	10 Mar 1985
AUTEC Andros Is	16 Mar 1985
Patrick AFB	27 Apr 1985
MV Dart Americana (passage USA-UK)	29 Apr 1985
Culdrose	15 May 1985
RFA Olmeda	17 Jun 1985
Culdrose	6 Aug 1985
Plockton, (Dt1)	30 Sep 1985
Lochalsh to	4 Oct 1985
Prestwick (Dt1)	4-11 Oct 1985
HMS Invincible (Dt1) to	1 Nov 1985
	4 Dec 1985
RFA Olmeda	24 Feb 1986

215

Westland Sea King HAS.5 ZA130 '353' of No.824 Squadron, Culdrose in 1984. (MAP)

Squadron bases
Base	Date
Culdrose	5 Mar 1986
RFA Olwen	17 Jun 1986
Culdrose	4 Aug 1986
RFA Olwen	17 Oct 1986
Culdrose	21 Nov 1986
RFA Tidespring	22 Jan 1987
Culdrose	22 Feb 1987
RFA Fort Austin	19 May 1987
Culdrose	22 Jun 1987
Koksijde (Dt1)	8-12 Jul 1987
Prestwick	20 Jul 1987
Machrihanish (Dt1)	12-15 Sep 1987
Benbecula	27 Sep 1987
Prestwick	1 Oct 1987
Plockton (Dt1)	23 Nov 1987 to 4 Dec 1987
RFA Fort Austin (Dt1)	6 May 1988 to 4 Jun 1988
HrMs Poolster (Dt2)	12-24 Jun 1988
RFA Olmeda (Dt2)	1-15 Aug 1988
Benbecula	22 Aug 1988
Prestwick	29 Aug 1988
RFA Olmeda (Dt2)	29 Sep 1988 to 19 Oct 1988
HMS Illustrious (Dt2)	29 Sep 1988 to 19 Oct 1988
AUTEC Andros Is	19 Oct 1988
Patrick AFB (Dt3)	29 Oct 1988 to 3 Nov 1988
RFA Olmeda (Dt3)	19 Nov 1988 to 13 Dec 1988
HMS Illustrious (Dt1)	19 Nov 1988 to 13 Dec 1988
RFA Olmeda	13 Dec 1988
Prestwick	14 Dec 1988
RFA Olwen (Dt2)	16-31 Jan 1989
RFA Olwen	11 May 1989
Prestwick	Jul 1989
Squadron disbanded	Aug 1989

824A Flight

Flight bases
Base	Date
Culdrose	
RFA Fort Grange	1 Jan 1979
Sek Kong (Dt2)	28 Jun 1979 to Oct 1979
Culdrose	13 Dec 1979
RFA Olwen	19 Mar 1980
Culdrose	7 May 1980
RFA Fort Austin (Dt1)	23-27 Jun 1980
RFA Tidepool	14 Jul 1980
Culdrose	18 Jul 1980
RFA Fort Austin	29 Jul 1980
Jacksonville	14 Aug 1980
RFA Fort Austin	21 Aug 1980
Culdrose	25 Sep 1980
RFA Fort Austin	14 Nov 1980
Culdrose	22 Apr 1981
Lee-on-Solent (Dt1)	7-11 Sep 1981
RFA Fort Grange	9 Oct 1981
Culdrose	15 Oct 1981
RFA Tidepool	26 Oct 1981
Culdrose	13 Nov 1981
Arbroath	6 Dec 1981
Culdrose	9 Dec 1981
RFA Olmeda	15 Jan 1982
Prestwick	26 Feb 1982
Culdrose	30 Mar 1982
RFA Olmeda	4 Apr 1982
Culdrose	10 Jul 1982
RFA Fort Austin	4 Sep 1982
RFA Olmeda	27 Sep 1982
Lively Island	9 Oct 1982
RFA Olmeda	22 Oct 1982
Lively Island	20 Nov 1982
RFA Olmeda	22 Nov 1982
Culdrose	19 Dec 1982
Flight transferred to No.826 Sqdn	1 Feb 1983

824B Flight

Flight bases
Base	Date
Culdrose	Dec 1979
RFA Fort Austin	11 Feb 1980
Gibraltar	21 Mar 1980
RFA Fort Austin	28 Mar 1980
Culdrose	15 May 1980
RFA Olna	3 Sep 1980
Culdrose	3 Oct 1980
RFA Olmeda	14 Nov 1980
Culdrose	18 Mar 1981
RFA Olwen	11 May 1981
Culdrose	17 Jun 1981
RFA Olmeda	10 Jul 1981
Culdrose	24 Nov 1981
RFA Olna	19 Feb 1982
Gibraltar	26 Feb 1982
RFA Fort Austin	26 Mar 1982
RFA Olwen	7 Jun 1982
Culdrose	10 Jun 1982
Brawdy	1 Jul 1982
Culdrose	5 Jul 1982
Aberporth	25 Jul 1982
Culdrose	27 Jul 1982
Prestwick (Dt1)	14-20 Oct 1982
RFA Olna	3 Nov 1982
Culdrose	1 Dec 1982
RFA Olwen	28 Jan 1983
AUTEC Andros Island	Feb 1983
RFA Olwen	28 Mar 1983
Gibraltar	12 Apr 1983
RFA Olna	23 Apr 1983

Squadron bases
Base	Date
Culdrose	27 Apr 1983
RFA Olmeda	19 Jun 1983
Culdrose	10 Aug 1983
HMS Illustrious	20 Jan 1984
Patrick AFB	5 Feb 1984
AUTEC Andros Is	1 Mar 1984
Charleston	22-23 Apr 1984
Dart line container ship (passage USA-UK)	25 Apr 1984
Lee-on-Solent	8 May 1984
Culdrose	24 May 1984
Portland	16 Jun 1984
RFA Olmeda	17 Jun 1984
Culdrose	6 Aug 1984
RFA Olna	12 Nov 1984
Culdrose	14 Dec 1984
only remaining Flt - became Sqn	

824C Flight

Flight bases
Base	Date
Culdrose	
RFA Olmeda	14 Jan 1980
Culdrose	1 Apr 1980
RFA Olna	20 Apr 1980
Culdrose	27 May 1980
RFA Fort Grange	25 Sep 1980
Culdrose	17 Oct 1980
HMS Invincible	29 Oct 1980
Culdrose	2 Dec 1980
RFA Olwen	12 Jan 1981
Culdrose	21 Jan 1981
RFA Fort Grange	6 Mar 1981
Culdrose	24 Jun 1981
RFA Fort Austin	19 Oct 1981
RFA Olwen	23 Nov 1981
Culdrose	16 Dec 1981
Prestwick	11 Jan 1982
Culdrose	26 Feb 1982
RFA Fort Grange	6 May 1982
Culdrose	1 Oct 1982
Flight transferred to No.826 Sqdn	1 Feb 1983

824D Flight

Flight bases
Base	Date
Culdrose	
RFA Fort Grange	17 Jan 1980
Culdrose	2 Apr 1980
RFA Olwen	19 May 1980
Sek Kong	1 Aug 1980
RFA Olwen	15 Aug 1980
Culdrose-disbanded	7 Dec 1980
Culdrose	14 Jun 1982
HMS Illustrious	2 Aug 1982
Culdrose	7 Dec 1982
HMS Illustrious	3 May 1983
Culdrose	13 May 1983
Paris Air Show (Dt1)	2-6 Jun 1983
Geilenkirchen (Dt1)	1-5 Dec 1983
Redes 849 Sqdn	1 Nov 1984

Commanding Officers
Sq Ldr HH Down RAF	25 Apr 1933
Squadron disbanded	8 Oct 1934
Sq Ldr WAK Dalzell RAF	28 Oct 1934
Sq Ldr FL Pearce RAF	26 Oct 1935
Sq Ldr AB Woodhall RAF	18 Jan 1937
Sq Ldr RG Forbes RAF	27 Apr 1938
L/C H Gardner RN	24 May 1939
L/C AJ Debenham DSC RN	15 Jun 1939
Capt FW Brown RM	11 Aug 1941
Squadron disbanded	11 Aug 1942
Lt JA Ievers RN	1 Oct 1942
L/C(A) EL Russell DSC RNVR	12 Mar 1943
L/C GC Edwards RCNVR	2 Mar 1944
Squadron disbanded	16 Oct 1944
Lt(A) GR Clarke RNVR	2 Jul 1945
L/C(A) S Brilliant RNVR	10 Jul 1945
Squadron disbanded	4 Jan 1946
L/C OGW Hutchinson RN	18 Feb 1952
L/C NC Manley-Cooper DSC RN	28 Jul 1953
L/C JD Honywill RN	11 Jan 1955
Squadron disbanded	17 Apr 1956
L/C LD Urry RN	7 May 1956
Squadron disbanded	1 Nov 1957
L/C J Trevis RN	21 Apr 1958
Squadron disbanded	20 Apr 1959
L/C FK Steel RN	3 Nov 1959
L/C RGD Williams RN	20 Aug 1961
Squadron disbanded	21 May 1963
L/C L Hallett RN	24 Feb 1970
L/C DW Shrubb RN	26 Nov 1971
L/C HA Pawsey RN	19 Sep 1973
L/C AN Wigley RN	14 Oct 1974
L/C D Anderson RN	18 Apr 1975
L/C PS Buckley RN	28 Mar 1977
L/C CP West RN	12 Apr 1979
L/C I Thorpe RN	30 Oct 1980
L/C DJD Acland RN	5 May 1982
L/C M Bishop-Bailey RN	12 Jan 1984
L/C PN Dickinson RN	1 Nov 1984
L/C M Llewellyn-Jones RN	30 May 1986
Squadron disbanded	Aug 1989

824A Flight
Capt AD Schultz CF	7 Jan 1980
L/C RB Lambert USN	13 May 1980
L/C IS McKenzie MBE RN	6 Jul 1981
L/C NJ Cowley RN	26 Nov 1982
Flt trans to 826 Sqdn	1 Feb 1983

824B Flight
?	1 Jan 1980
L/C GJP Wingate RN	15 Oct 1980
L/C BG Hodge RN	6 Jan 1982
L/C DLW Sim RN	30 Jul 1982
L/C PN Dickinson RN	1983
Flight disbanded	14 Dec 1984

824C Flight
Lt L Mathews RN	1 Jan 1980
L/C RC Harrison RN	8 Dec 1981
L/C RC Green RN	6 Dec 1982
Flight trans to 826 Sqdn	1 Feb 1983

824D Flight
?	1 Jan 1980
Flight disbanded	10 Dec 1980
L/C PM Flutter AFC RN	14 Jun 1982
Flight reformed as 849 Sqdn	1 Nov 1984

No.825 Squadron

Badge: On a blue field, a Maltese Cross, each arm per pale red and white surmounted by an eagle rising proper
Motto: Nihil obstat (Nothing stops us)

No.825 Squadron formed on 8 October 1934 as a spotter reconnaissance squadron with 12 Fairey IIIFs by renumbering No.824 Squadron in HMS *Eagle*. Initially in the China Station, the ship transferred to the Mediterranean Fleet in January 1935, No.825 and reduced to six aircraft. In March the ship disembarked its aircraft to Hal Far, then sailed home for a refit. No.825 reverted to 12 aircraft, then joined HMS *Glorious* in September for further service in the Mediterranean. In July 1936 it re-equipped with 12 Swordfish Is and became a torpedo spotter reconnaissance squadron. The ship returned home briefly for the Coronation Review at Spithead on 20 May 1937, its aircraft taking part in the flypast.

On the outbreak of war in September 1939, HMS *Glorious* sailed to the Indian Ocean for trade protection based on Aden, returning to the Mediterranean in January 1940. She rushed home in April when Germany invaded Norway, and No.825 disembarked to carry out operations in the English Channel against U-boats, E-boats and enemy transport in the Calais area during the Dunkirk evacuation. Eight aircraft were lost at this time, including five which failed to return from a bombing raid on 31 May. Re-equipping with a reduced complement of nine aircraft, the squadron joined HMS *Furious* in July, and in September took part in operations off Norway, including night attacks on Trondheim and Tromsø. In February 1941 it re-embarked for escort duty with a convoy ferrying aircraft to the Gold Coast.

In May 1941 No.825 joined HMS *Victorious* for operations during a successful search for the German battleship *Bismarck*, which culminated in her being sunk on 26 May by surface forces after damage by aircraft. The squadron transferred to HMS *Ark Royal* in June to provide anti-submarine defence for Malta convoys, targets in Sardinia, Sicily and Pantellaria being attacked in September, but on 13 November the ship was torpedoed 50 miles from Gibraltar by *U-81* and sank the next day. Some aircraft of No.825 Squadron were airborne at the time, and these flew to Gibraltar, where they were taken over by No.812 Squadron.

No.825 reformed at Lee-on-Solent on 1 January 1942 with nine Swordfish Is for torpedo bomber reconnaissance duties. In early February, six aircraft were detached to Manston to be on standby for a possible breakout of the German battlecruisers *Scharnhorst* and *Gneisenau* and the cruiser *Prinz Eugen*, then at Brest. When this materialised on 12 February, the squadron took off and despite lack of real fighter cover made a torpedo attack, but no hits were obtained and all the aircraft were lost. A posthumous Victoria Cross was awarded to Lieutenant Commander Esmonde, the CO, and five surviving crew members were all decorated.

On 2 March 1942, No.825 regrouped at Lee-on-Solent, receiving Swordfish IIs as replacements for the lost machines. Three aircraft embarked in HMS *Avenger* in September for anti-submarine patrols during a North Russian convoy, 16 U-boats being sighted of which only six could be attacked. *U-589* was shared with HMS *Onslow* on 14 September, when a Swordfish reported its position. Operations were then carried out in the English Channel under RAF Coastal Command until February 1943. The squadron joined HMS *Furious* the following month for anti-submarine operations during convoy escort from Scapa and Iceland.

In July 1943 an offensive sweep was made off the Norwegian coast, following which the squadron was shore based for a time. Six Sea Hurricane IICs were added to the complement in August, and the squadron joined HMS *Vindex* in December to provide anti-submarine protection for Atlantic convoys. Terrible weather failed to prevent intensive flying, and the squadron shared with surface forces the sinking of *U-653* on 15 March 1944 and U-765 on 6 May. During April 1944, three Fulmars of No.784 Squadron were briefly attached to the squadron in HMS *Vindex*.

In June 1944 the squadron was re-equipped with 12 Swordfish IIIs. Further successes occurred in a North Russian convoy two months later, Swordfish 'C' sinking *U-354* on 22 August and claiming a possible the following day. Another U-boat was damaged by a Sea Hurricane on 22 August, and joint successes with surface forces were the sinking of *U-344* on 24 August and *U-394* by aircraft 'A' on 2 September. The Sea Hurricanes were then withdrawn, but in November the fighter flight was restored when 8 Wildcat VIs arrived. Another North Russian convoy was undertaken in December but severe weather prevented operations by either side. In March 1945 a similar trip was made in HMS *Campania*, after which the squadron disembarked to Machrihanish where it was retrospectively disbanded into No.815 Squadron with effect from 3 April 1945. The Wildcats continued separately as No.825X Squadron until being also absorbed into No.815 Squadron on 23 May 1945.

No.825 next reformed at Rattray on 1 July 1945 as a Canadian-manned unit earmarked for the 19th Carrier Air Group in a *Colossus*-class carrier. Equipped with 12 ASH radar-equipped Barracuda IIs for torpedo bomber reconnaissance duties, these were replaced in November by 12 Firefly FR.Is. The squadron was transferred to the Royal Canadian Navy on 24 January 1946, when HMCS *Warrior* commissioned, embarking in her in March for Canada, where the 19th CAG officially formed in May 1947, Dartmouth being used as the shore base. In August the squadron handed over its aircraft to No.826 Squadron and sailed in HMCS *Warrior* to the United Kingdom, where it re-equipped with 9 Firefly FR.4s. On completion of work-up these embarked in HMCS *Magnificent* in May, the squadron transferring to the 18th CAG in November. In February 1949 the ship returned to the United Kingdom and the squadron re-equipped with 11 Firefly AS.5s. It then transferred to the 18th CAG. In January 1951 it returned to the 19th Support Air Group, as it had by then become, only to be redesignated No.880 Squadron on 1 May 1951.

No.825 reformed on 12 June 1951 as a Royal Navy squadron at Eglinton, equipped with eight Firefly AS.5s for anti-submarine duties, being briefly part of the 15th CAG. In November the role was changed to interdiction, and Firefly FR.5s were received. In January 1952 the strength was increased to ten, and the aircraft embarked in HMS *Theseus* for the Mediterranean, transferring in February to HMS *Ocean* before continuing to the Far East. The strength was further increased to 12 in April, and in May operations commenced in Korean waters. 1907 sorties were flown by November, when the strength was reduced to eight, but these were also soon withdrawn. The ship then left the area for the Mediterranean, where No.825 personnel transferred to HMS *Theseus* for the remainder of the voyage home, to disband on arrival on 10 December 1952. It was later awarded the 1952 Boyd Trophy jointly with No.802 Squadron for its activities in Korea.

Fairey IIIF S1803 '834' of No.825 Squadron, HMS Glorious in 1935. (RAF Museum P.18104)

Fairey Swordfish P3992 'G5K' of No.825 Squadron aboard HMS Glorious shortly before the outbreak of war. (RAF Museum P.12203)

On 2 March 1953 No.825 reformed at Lee-on-Solent for anti-submarine duties with eight Firefly AS.5s. After taking part in the Coronation Review flypast at Spithead on 15 June it joined HMS *Eagle* for the first of two spells afloat that year for exercises. At the end of 1953 the strength was increased to 10 and then 12, but in February 1954 it joined HMS *Warrior* with eight aircraft for passage to the Far East, where in May 16 R/P sorties were made against Malayan terrorists in the jungle of central Johore. The squadron returned home at the end of the year to disband at Lee-on-Solent on 30 December 1954.

No.825 next reformed at Culdrose on 4 July 1955 with eight Gannet AS.1s as an anti-submarine squadron, embarking in HMS *Albion* in January 1956 for the Mediterranean and then the Far East. It returned to the United Kingdom in May, taking part in several exercises before disbanding at Lee-on-Solent on 7 August 1956.

The squadron next reformed at Culdrose on 6 May 1957, again as an anti-submarine squadron, with nine Gannet AS.4s which, after participating in several exercises flew out to Malta in January 1958. After a further exercise it flew home to disband at Culdrose on 29 April 1958.

No.825 became a helicopter squadron when it next reformed at Culdrose on 16 August 1960 with eight Whirlwind HAS.7s. These joined HMS *Victorious* in October for a period in the Mediterranean, where they participated in an exercise. Returning home in December, they re-embarked early in the New Year for the Far East, but in June 1961 sailed for a few weeks in the Persian Gulf owing to a crisis in Kuwait. Flood relief was provided in East Africa towards the end of the year, most of the squadron aircraft being handed over to No.824 Squadron. Returning home in HMS *Victorious*, it took part in two further exercises before being disbanded on disembarkation on 2 April 1962, the aircraft going to Fleetlands.

On 7 May 1982 No.825 was reformed at Culdrose from a nucleus of No.706 Squadron for service with the Falklands Task Force in the trooping and heavy lift role. Equipped with ten Sea King HAS.2As, eight of these joined SS *Atlantic Causeway*, whilst two embarked in SS *Queen Elizabeth II*. The squadron saw action, a detachment being put ashore to Port San Carlos in June. Returning in July, it disbanded at Culdrose on 17 September 1982.

Identification Markings
IIIF *71-76, 81-86*, to *830-843* 1.35; Swordfish *967-981* to *G5A*+ 5.39, later *5A*+, single letters from 1.42; Sea Hurricane *2A*+; Wildcat, Barracuda and Firefly FR.1 single letters; Firefly 4/5 (RCN) *VG-BDA to VG-BDZ*; Firefly from 6.51 *280-291/J:G:/O*; Gannet *410-417/CU*, to *340-347/CU/Z* 1.56; Whirlwind *310-318/V*.

Aircraft Equipment	Period of Service	Example	
Fairey IIIF	Oct 1934 - Jul 1936	S1803	(834)
Swordfish I	Jul 1936 - Nov 1941	P3992	(G5K)
	Jan 1942 - Jun 1944	W5904	(H)
Swordfish II	Mar 1942 - Jun 1944	HS223	(L)
Swordfish III	Jun 1944 - Apr 1945	NR915	
Sea Hurricane IIc	Aug 1943 - Sep 1944	NF668	
Wildcat VI	Nov 1944 - Apr 1945	JV723	(R)
Barracuda II(ASH)	Jul 1945 - Nov 1945	MX856	
Firefly FR.1	Nov 1945 - Jan 1946	MB662	(M)
	Jan 1947 - Aug 1947	PP431	(N)
	Oct 1948 - May 1950	MB579	
Firefly FR.4	Aug 1947 - Feb 1949	VG966	(BDG)
Firefly AS.5	Feb 1949 - May 1951	VH139	(BDF)
Firefly AS.5/FR.5	Jun 1951 - Nov 1952	WB362	(283/GN)
Firefly AS.5	Mar 1953 - Dec 1954	VX436	(281/J)
Gannet AS.1	Jul 1955 - Aug 1956	WN404	(341/Z)
Gannet T.2	Oct 1955 - Dec 1955	XA516	
	May 1957 - Apr 1958	XG869	(325)
Gannet AS.4	May 1957 - Apr 1958	XG790	(340/CU)
Whirlwind HAS.7	Aug 1960 - Apr 1962	XN381	(314/V)
Sea King HAS.2/2a	May 1982 - Sep 1982	XV700	

Battle Honours
Dunkirk	1940
English Channel	1940-42
Norway	1940
'Bismarck'	1941
Malta Convoys	1941
Arctic	1942-45
Atlantic	1944
Korea	1952
Falkland Islands	1982

Squadron bases
HMS Eagle	8 Oct 1934
Kai Tak	20 Oct 1934
HMS Eagle	5 Nov 1934
Hal Far	31 Jan 1935
HMS Eagle	20 Feb 1935
Hal Far	22 Mar 1935
HMS Glorious	2 Sep 1935
Hal Far	23 Dec 1935
Aboukir	5 Feb 1936
Amriya	27 Feb 1936
HMS Glorious	31 Mar 1936
Amriya (Dt)	21 May 1936
	to 27 Jul 1936
Hal Far	27 Jul 1936
HMS Glorious	30 Oct 1936
Hal Far	9 Nov 1936
HMS Glorious	4 Jan 1937
Hal Far	23 Mar 1937
HMS Glorious	23 Apr 1937
Gosport	5 May 1937
HMS Glorious	23 Jun 1937
Hal Far	16 Jul 1937
HMS Glorious	23 Aug 1937

Fairey Firefly FR.5 WB409 '292/O' of No.825 Squadron, HMS Ocean over Korea in 1952. (MAP)

Squadron bases

Base	Date
Hal Far	19 Oct 1937
Part of squadron:	
HMS Glorious (Dt)	25 Oct 1937
Gosport	3 Nov 1937
Abingdon	3 Nov 1937
Southampton	17 Jan 1938
HMS Glorious	17 Jan 1938
Hal Far	25 Jan 1938
HMS Glorious	7 Feb 1938
Hal Far	27 Mar 1938
HMS Glorious	16 May 1938
Hal Far	31 May 1938
HMS Glorious	18 Jul 1938
Hal Far	25 Aug 1938
HMS Glorious	9 Sep 1938
Aboukir (Dt6)	24 Sep 1938
to	1 Oct 1938
Dekheila (Dt6)	28 Sep 1938
to	1 Oct 1938
Dekheila	1 Oct 1938
HMS Glorious	23 Oct 1938
Hal Far	9 Nov 1938
HMS Glorious	23 Jan 1939
Hal Far	20 Feb 1939
HMS Glorious	23 Feb 1939
Hal Far	20 Mar 1939
HMS Glorious	11 Apr 1939
Hal Far	12 Apr 1939
HMS Glorious	13 Apr 1939
Hal Far	18 Apr 1939
HMS Glorious	25 Apr 1939
Aboukir (Dt6)	28 Apr 1939
to	1 May 1939
Dekheila	1 May 1939
HMS Glorious	19 Jun 1939
Dekheila	16 Sep 1939
HMS Glorious	28 Sep 1939
Dekheila	4 Oct 1939
HMS Glorious	9 Oct 1939
Hal Far	17 Jan 1940
HMS Glorious (Dt6)	25 Mar 1940
HMS Glorious	28 Mar 1940
Prestwick	21 Apr 1940
transit	1 May 1940
Worthy Down	4 May 1940
Detling	18 May 1940
Worthy Down	28 May 1940
Thorney Island	16 Jun 1940
Carew Cheriton	20 Jun 1940
Worthy Down	27 Jun 1940
Detling (16Gp)	1 Jul 1940
Worthy Down	5 Jul 1940
Prestwick	11 Jul 1940
HMS Furious	14 Jul 1940
Hatston	26 Jul 1940
HMS Furious	31 Jul 1940
Hatston	23 Aug 1940
HMS Furious	5 Sep 1940
Prestwick (Dt)	11-13 Sep 1940
Hatston	24 Sep 1940
Evanton	1 Oct 1940
HMS Furious	11 Oct 1940
Donibristle(transit)	6 Nov 1940
Lee-on-Solent	7 Nov 1940
Evanton (Dt5)	9 Dec 1940
to	31 Jan 1941
Arbroath	11 Dec 1940
Detachment (2 a/c):	
HMS Argus	19 Dec 1940
HMS Furious	25 Dec 1940
HMS Argus	27 Dec 1940
Castletown (transit)	14 Jan 1941
Evanton	14 Jan 1941
Abbotsinch (Dt5)	31 Jan 1941
HMS Furious (Dt6)	26 Feb 1941
to	12 Apr 1941
Donibristle (Dt6)	6 Mar 1941
Campbeltown	11 Apr 1941
Hatston	17 May 1941
HMS Victorious	19 May 1941
HMS Ark Royal	11 Jun 1941
Ship sunk	13 Nov 1941
Lee-on-Solent	1 Jan 1942
Manston	4 Feb 1942
Machrihanish(Dt3)	4-12 Feb 1942
Lee-on-Solent	13 Feb 1942
Andreas	1 Apr 1942
Lee-on-Solent	8 Apr 1942
Machrihanish	29 Apr 1942
Hatston	5 Jun 1942
HMS Avenger	22 Jul 1942
Hatston	4 Aug 1942
HMS Avenger	28 Aug 1942
Hatston	26 Sep 1942
Fearn	30 Sep 1942
transit	9 Dec 1942
Thorney Island (16 Gp)	14 Dec 1942
Exeter (Dt4)	30 Dec 1942
to	1 Feb 1943
transit	31 Jan 1943
Worthy Down	2 Feb 1943
Dunino	3 Feb 1943
Machrihanish	9 Mar 1943
HMS Furious	11 Mar 1943
Hatston	13 Jun 1943
Stornoway	4 Jul 1943
Hatston	5 Jul 1943
HMS Furious(Dt4)	6-15 Jul 1943
Stornoway(transit)	13 Jul 1943
Donibristle (transit)	14 Jul 1943
Stretton	15 Jul 1943
Lee-on-Solent	15 Jul 1943
Yeovilton	7 Sep 1943
Lee-on-Solent	11 Sep 1943
Yeovilton (Hurricane) & Hooton Park (Swordfish)	
-transit	13 Sep 1943
Machrihanish	14 Sep 1943
Maydown	10 Oct 1943
Ayr (Dt-fighters)	10-23 Oct 1943
Belfast (transit)	23 Oct 1943
HMS Pretoria Castle	25 Oct 1943
Kaldadarnes	29 Oct 1943
HMS Pretoria Castle	30 Oct 1943
Belfast (transit)	4 Nov 1943
Donibristle	5 Nov 1943
Inskip	14 Nov 1943
HMS Vindex	18 Dec 1943
HMS Vindex	23 Apr 1944
Stornoway (15 Gp)	8 Aug 1944
HMS Vindex	10 Aug 1944
Machrihanish	7 Sep 1944
Limavady (15 Gp)	29 Sep 1944
Mullaghmore(15 Gp)	7 Nov 1944

Fairey Gannet AS.4s of No.825 flying near Malta on their arrival from HMS Eagle in 1958. (via Brian Lowe)

Fairey Gannet AS.1 WN349 '341/Z' of No.825 Squadron at Baginton in 1956. (MAP)

Squadron bases
HMS Vindex	11 Dec 1944
Machrihanish	27 Jan 1945
HMS Trouncer(DLP)	23 Feb 1945
Machrihanish	24 Feb 1945
HMS Campania	9 Mar 1945
Machrihanish	7 Apr 1945
Squadron disbanded	12 Apr 1945

Wildcat Flight:
Stretton	
Machrihanish	1 Dec 1944
HMS Vindex	15 Dec 1944
Machrihanish	10 Feb 1945
HMS Campania	9 Mar 1945
Grimsetter	30 Mar 1945
HMS Puncher	3 Apr 1945
Grimsetter	13 Apr 1945
(as 825X Squadron)	
Stretton	21 Apr 1945
To 815 Sqdn	23 Apr 1945
Rattray Head	1 Jul 1945
Fearn	31 Aug 1945
Burscough	6 Nov 1945
Lee-on-Solent	28 Feb 1946
HMCS Warrior	23 Mar 1946
Dartmouth	31 Mar 1946
HMCS Warrior	Jul 1946
Dartmouth	Jul 1946
HMCS Warrior	5 Nov 1946
Dartmouth	Dec 1946
Patricia Bay	Jan 1947
HMCS Warrior	Feb 1947
Dartmouth	27 Mar 1947
HMCS Warrior	May 1947
Dartmouth	15 May 1947
HMCS Warrior	3 Aug 1947
Eglinton	8 Aug 1947
HMCS Magnificent	22 May 1948
Dartmouth	2 Jun 1948
HMCS Magnificent	Aug 1948
Dartmouth	Sep 1948
HMCS Magnificent	Jan 1949
Dartmouth	25 Feb 1949
HMCS Magnificent	Mar 1949
Dartmouth	7 Apr 1949
Quonset Point	1949
Dartmouth	Sep 1949
HMCS Magnificent	17 Nov 1949
Dartmouth	16 Dec 1949
HMCS Magnificent	13 Jan 1950
Dartmouth	2 Feb 1950
HMCS Magnificent	13 Feb 1950
Dartmouth	14 Apr 1950
HMCS Magnificent	22 Aug 1950

Squadron bases
Eglinton	Aug 1950
HMCS Magnificent	11 Sep 1950
Dartmouth	27 Nov 1950
Sqdn redesignated 880 Sqdn	1 May 1951
Eglinton	12 Jun 1951
St Merryn	5 Nov 1951
HMS Theseus	19 Jan 1952
Hal Far	4 Feb 1952
HMS Ocean	18 Feb 1952
Hal Far	10 Mar 1952
HMS Ocean	5 Apr 1952
HMS Theseus	1 Dec 1952
Sqdn disbanded UK	10 Dec 1952
Lee-on-Solent	2 Mar 1953
Eglinton	23 Apr 1953
Lee-on-Solent	14 May 1953
HMS Eagle	16 Jun 1953
Lee-on-Solent	25 Jul 1953
HMS Eagle	2 Sep 1953
Lee-on-Solent	23 Oct 1953
HMS Warrior	16 Feb 1954
Hal Far	5 Mar 1954
HMS Warrior	23 Mar 1954
Hal Far	2 Apr 1954
HMS Warrior	17 Apr 1954
Sembawang	12 May 1954
Tengah	16 Aug 1954
HMS Warrior	23 Sep 1954
Lee-on-Solent	13 Dec 1954
Squadron disbanded	30 Dec 1954
Culdrose	4 Jul 1955
HMS Albion	10 Jan 1956
Sembawang (Dt4)	10-15 Mar 1956
Culdrose	14 May 1956
Squadron disbanded	7 Aug 1956
Culdrose	6 May 1957
Ford	23 Aug 1957
Culdrose	9 Sep 1957
Hal Far	15 Jan 1958
Culdrose	21 Apr 1958
Squadron disbanded	29 Apr 1958
Culdrose	16 Aug 1960
Portland	9 Sep 1960
HMS Victorious	18 Oct 1960
Hal Far	31 Oct 1960
HMS Victorious	19 Nov 1960
Portland	9 Jan 1961
HMS Victorious	27 Jan 1961
Sembawang	29 Mar 1961
HMS Victorious	11 Apr 1961
HMS Bulwark (Dt5)	19-21 Apr 1961

Squadron bases
HMAS Melbourne	29 Apr 1961
(Dt)	to 31 May 1961
Sembawang	9 May 1961
HMS Victorious	14 Jun 1961
Sembawang	15 Sep 1961
HMS Victorious	4 Oct 1961
Mombasa detachment:	
Port Reitz	22 Nov 1961
Malindi (Dt2)/ Lamu (Dt2)	23 Nov 1961
A/c to 824 Sqdn	8 Dec 1961
Sqdn on leave UK	20 Dec 1961
Squadron disbanded	2 Apr 1962
Culdrose	3 May 1982
SS Queen Elizabeth II (Dt2)	12-27 May 1982
SS Atlantic Causeway (Dt8)	13-29 May 1982
SS Canberra (Dt2)	27 May 1982 to 2 Jun 1982
Port San Carlos (Dt4)	31 May 1982 to 1 Jun 1982
(Dt8)	1-2 Jun 1982
(10)	2 Jun 1982
San Carlos FOB	3 Jun 1982
RFA Engadine (Dt1)	7-30 Jul 1982
SS Atlantic Causeway	13 Jul 1982
Culdrose	27 Jul 1982
Squadron disbanded	17 Sep 1982

Commanding Officers
Sq Ldr HH Down RAF	8 Oct 1934
Cdr RR Graham RN	25 Dec 1934
(Sq Ldr RAF)	
L/C JI Robertson RN (Sq Ldr RAF)	8 Jun 1935
L/C A Brock RN (Sq Ldr RAF)	11 Sep 1937
L/C JW Hale RN	19 Aug 1938
L/C JB Buckley RN	22 Jan 1940
L/C(A) E Esmonde DSO RN	31 May 1940
Squadron disbanded	13 Nov 1941
L/C(A) E Esmonde VC DSO RN	1 Jan 1942
L/C(A) S Keane RN	23 Feb 1942
L/C(A) SG Cooper RN	15 Dec 1942
L/C(A) AHD Gough RN	29 Feb 1944
L/C(A) FGB Sheffield DSC RNVR	5 May 1944
L/C P Snow RN	25 Feb 1945
Squadron disbanded	12 Apr 1945
L/C(A) F Stovin-Bradford DSC RN	1 Jul 1945
L/C DW Tattersall DSC RN	21 Dec 1945
L/C RE Bartlett RCN	5 Feb 1947
Lt DD Peacocke RCN	20 Aug 1948
L/C JA Stokes RCN	10 Nov 1948
L/C DW Knox RCN	27 Apr 1950
Squadron disbanded	1 May 1951
L/C CK Roberts RN	12 Jun 1951
Squadron disbanded	10 Dec 1952
L/C RP Keogh RN	2 Mar 1953
L/C JL Wallace-Thompson RN	12 Oct 1953
Squadron disbanded	30 Dec 1954
L/C JRC Johnston RN	4 Jul 1955
Squadron disbanded	7 Aug 1956
L/C RC Ashworth RN	6 May 1957
L/C R Leonard MBE DFC RN	23 Feb 1958
Squadron disbanded	29 Apr 1958
L/C J Ashton RN	16 Aug 1960
Squadron disbanded	2 Apr 1962
L/C HS Clark DSC RN	7 May 1982
Squadron disbanded	17 Sep 1982

Westland Sea King HAS.2s of No.825 Squadron in the Falklands in 1982. (RAF Museum P.21369)

No.826 Squadron

Badge: On a blue field, a sea horse white grasping a trident the point in base gold

Motto: *Latet anguis in aqua* (A snake lies concealed in the water)

No.826 Squadron was originally to have formed at Lee-on-Solent on 1 January 1940 as a spare squadron, but instead came into existence at Ford on 15 March 1940 as a torpedo spotter reconnaissance squadron with 12 Albacores. During the Dunkirk evacuation these provided cover from Detling, and on 31 May bombed rail and road communications at Westende, and attacked E-boats off Zeebrugge. For the next five months they operated from Bircham Newton under RAF Coastal Command, Swordfish being used during July whilst the Albacore's engines were being modified. In this period with the RAF, 22 night attacks were made against coastal targets in Holland, Belgium and France. The aircraft dropped 7 tons of mines and 56 tons of bombs, destroyed or damaged five enemy aircraft and escorted 92 convoys, 57 of them during September.

In November 1940 the squadron embarked in HMS *Formidable*, which sailed the following month to escort a convoy via Capetown to Egypt, after which she proceeded to the Red Sea. In February 1941, attacks were made on targets at Mogadishu in Somalia and later Massawa in Eritrea before sailing through the Suez Canal to join the Mediterranean Fleet. From March, six Swordfish were used for 6 months to keep the squadron up to strength. After escorting a Malta convoy, the ship took part in the Battle of Matapan at the end of March, during which No.826 was involved in a torpedo attack which damaged the Italian battleship *Vittorio Veneto*. The following month anti-submarine patrols, flare-dropping and bombardment spotting were carried out during fleet gunnery attacks on Tripoli and Bardia. During the evacuation of Crete, a successful raid was carried out on an airfield on the island of Scarpanto on 26 May, but in a subsequent retaliatory raid the ship was severely damaged and had to retire for repairs.

No.826 then became shore-based, operating first in the Eastern Mediterranean and later the Western Desert. In July 1941, attacks were carried out from Cyprus against Vichy French ships at Beirut, before moving to Maaten Bagush to support the 8th Army. Illumination was provided for night bombardment of coastal targets by the 7th Cruiser Squadron, and this proved so successful that it was asked to give a similar service to both the Army and the Desert Air Force. In the 4 months prior to the Battle of El Alamein in October 1942, the squadron dropped 12,000 flares, as well as attacking harbour installations and carrying out anti-shipping strikes.

In December 1942, half the squadron flew to Malta, where they were attached to No.821 Squadron for attacks on supply convoys sailing between Sicily and Tunis. In January 1943 the squadron was reunited for a brief respite at Dekheila before flying to Algeria to carry out local patrols and shipping strikes for several months. In June it moved to Malta to provide anti-submarine support for the invasion of Sicily, following which it disbanded at Ta Kali on 16 October 1943.

No.826 next reformed with 12 Barracuda IIs at Lee-on-Solent on 1 December 1943 as a torpedo bomber reconnaissance unit, later joining the 9th Naval TBR Wing. It embarked in HMS *Indefatigable* in June 1944, for an unsuccessful attack on the German battleship *Tirpitz*, followed by anti-submarine patrols off Norway in August. Leaving the Wing, it joined HMS *Formidable* for an equally unsuccessful *Tirpitz* attack, followed by strikes against shore targets and enemy shipping. After briefly rejoining the Wing in HMS *Indefatigable*, the squadron disbanded into No.820 Squadron at Machrihanish on 23 October 1944.

On 15 August 1945, No.826 reformed at East Haven as a Canadian-manned torpedo bomber reconnaissance squadron, equipped with 12 Barracuda IIs fitted with ASH radar. It moved to Fearn in October, re-equipping in January 1946 with 12 Firefly FR.Is, only to disband on 28 February 1946.

The number having been reserved for the Royal Canadian Navy, it was taken up as such when the squadron next reformed, at Dartmouth, Nova Scotia on 15 May 1947. Equipped with 12 Firefly FR.1s, it formed part of the 18th Carrier Air Group which embarked in HMCS *Warrior* in November 1947. Transferred to HMCS *Magnificent* in March 1949 with a reduced complement of ten aircraft, No.826 re-equipped with 12 Avenger TBM-3Es in October 1950. Under a reorganisation of RCN air units, they were renumbered on 1 May 1951 to become No.880 Squadron.

Having become available again for Royal Navy use, the number

Fairey Albacore N4319 '4F' of No.826 Squadron with engine running ready for operations, left with six 250-lb bombs, and right with four 25-lb depth charges. (both Mike Langman)

Fairey Albacore L7097 '5C' of No.826 Squadron, piloted by Sub-Lt A.H. Blacow, after being attacked by Messerschmitt Bf109s while bombing German invasion barges off Calais on 11 September 1940. (A.M.Tuke)

was very quickly taken up when No.826 reformed at Ford on 15 May 1951 as a strike and anti-submarine unit with 8 Firefly AS.6s. It initially formed part of the 13th CAG, being originally intended for HMS *Eagle*. In October, however, the squadron joined HMS *Illustrious* for an autumn cruise in the Mediterranean, transferring to HMS *Indomitable* for the Spring and Summer cruises of 1952, the former being again in the Mediterranean but the latter took place off Portugal. The autumn cruise of 1952 was spent in HMS *Theseus*, but the squadron returned to HMS *Indomitable* early in 1953 for passage to the Malta area when trouble broke out in Egypt. An explosion and fire aboard ship resulted in disembarkation to Hal Far, but they soon re-embarked, returning to Lee-on-Solent in May 1953 to participate in the Coronation Review flypast at Spithead on 20 May.

After a further short spell in HMS *Illustrious*, the squadron transferred in November 1953 to HMS *Glory* for a further 4 months in the Mediterranean, after which it returned home pending re-equipment. Eight Gannet AS.1s arrived in January 1955, and these embarked in HMS *Eagle* in June to spend the summer in the Mediterranean, the squadron returning overland in August. Following a Scandinavian cruise in the autumn, No.826 disbanded on arrival at Lee-on-Solent on 22 November 1955.

When No.826 next reformed, at Culdrose on 18 March 1966, it became a helicopter unit with 8 Wessex HAS.1s for anti-submarine duties. These joined HMS *Hermes* in September, and after a visit to Hamburg took part in exercises off the Channel Isles. In March 1967 further exercises were undertaken in the Mediterranean, later sailing for the Indian Ocean and the Far East. Continuing to Australia, the ship eventually returned home in September, and No.826 disembarked to Culdrose. It soon re-embarked, and sailed via Cape Town to the Persian Gulf, returning by the same route in February 1968. Reduced to 4 aircraft, detachments embarked during the year in RFAs *Olmeda* and *Olna*, then in October it re-equipped with 6 Wessex HAS.3s, plus an SAR Flight of two Wessex HAS.1s.

No.826 again became a carrier based squadron when in April 1969 it embarked in HMS *Eagle*, a trip to Scottish waters being followed by a visit to the eastern seaboard of the United States in June and July. After returning home, the ship sailed in September for the Mediterranean, a further spell being spent there early in 1970 after taking Christmas leave. The squadron disbanded on disembarking to Culdrose on 25 March 1970.

The number was not dormant for long, and on 2 June 1970 a new No.826 formed at Culdrose with 4 Sea King HAS.1s, being commissioned on 8 June for anti-submarine work. By the time it embarked in HMS *Eagle* in November the strength had increased to 6 aircraft. Several periods were spent afloat in 1971, including trips to the Mediterranean and later the Far East and Australia. The squadron received the 1971 Boyd Trophy for a rescue from HMS *Eagle* during the year. In March 1972 the squadron was transferred to RFA *Engadine*, and at the end of that year joined the cruiser HMS *Tiger* with a reduction to 4 aircraft. Numerous trips were made in her during the next three years, then in October 1975 the squadron joined HMS *Hermes* for a month. By the end of 1976 it had re-equipped with 4 Sea King HAS.2s, and these joined HMS

Fairey Firefly AS.6 WB438 '274/A' of No.826 Squadron in 1953. (MAP)

Fairey Firefly VT406 '278/R' of No.826 Squadron in 1953.
(via Brian Lowe)

Tiger in September 1977 for a trip to the Far East and Australia.

No.826 was equipped with Sea King HAS.2As by January 1979, and the following month these embarked in HMS *Bulwark* when the squadron again became carrier based. A visit was paid to the United States in January 1980, then in March 1981 No.826 received Sea King HAS.5s, which embarked in HMS *Hermes* in September 1981. The squadron re-embarked in this carrier in April 1982 when she sailed to joined the Falklands Task Force, 4 of the aircraft being in RFA *Fort Austin*. On return in July the squadron again ceased to be carrier based, being split into 3 flights for RFA operation.

No.826 Squadron took over No.824 Squadron A & C Flts on 1 February 1983 and then operated as three autonomous flights on rotation in the South Atlantic, mainly embarked in RFAs. The deployment initially consisted of five aircraft, reducing gradually to three, until the task completed in August 1986. With the demise of the South Atlantic rotation the Squadron reduced to three less autonomous Flts of two aircraft each with one HQ, deploying from Culdrose in support of towed array patrols in the North Atlantic, Clyde submarine operations, the Barents Sea, and trials and exercises, including a number of deployments to Dutch oilers. The Squadron carried out embarked trials in Type 22 frigates in 1987 and thereafter regularly deployed flights operating in the Atlantic, Caribbean, Mediterranean and the Gulf. A detached Flt of No.826 Squadron operated from HrMs *Zuiderkruis* and RFA *Fort Grange* during the Gulf War in 1990-91, deploying further east from March to July 1991 for hurricane relief work off Bangladesh.

No.826 Squadron E Flt formed as the Sea King HAS.6 Operational Evaluation Unit, at Culdrose in June 1991, moving in turn to Farnborough and Boscombe Down. From June 1991 the remainder of the Squadron operated as four single aircraft flights. No.826 Squadron disbanded in July 1993, four flights being transferred to No.819 Squadron at Prestwick and E Flightt remaining at Boscombe Down and becoming No.810 Squadron Sea King HAS.6 OEU.

Identification Markings

Albacore *L4A+* initially, then *4A+*, later *S4A+*; Swordfish *4A+*; Barracuda *4A+*, single letters from 8.45; Firefly & Avenger (RCN) *VG-ABA* to *VG-ABZ*; Firefly from 5.51 *271-279/J:A:R:FD*; Gannet *343-350/J*; Wessex *340-347/H:CU*, to *140-145/E* 10.68; Sea King *140-147/E:TG:B:H*, to *520-539* 1983, to *127-139* 10.85.

Battle Honours

Dunkirk	1940
North Sea	1940-44
Atlantic	1940
Matapan	1941
Mediterranean	1941-43
Libya	1941-42
Falkland Islands	1982
Kuwait	1991

Squadron bases

Ford	15 Mar 1940	LG.201 (Dt)	1-3 Feb 1942
Bircham Newton	7 May 1940	Maaten Bagush	3 Feb 1942
Jersey	21 May 1940	LG.86 Amrya (Dt)	c16-17 Feb 1942
Bircham Newton	29 May 1940	St Jean D'Acre (Dt)	19-25 Feb 1942
Detling	31 May 1940	Dekheila	25 Feb 1942
Bircham Newton	1 Jun 1940	Maaten Bagush	1 Mar 1942
St Merryn	7 Oct 1940	Gasr-el-Arid (Dt3)	11-12 Mar 1942
Campbeltown	4 Nov 1940	Sidi Barrani (Dt3)	11 Mar 1942
Belfast (Dt3)	12-21 Nov 1940	Gambut (Dt3)	12-23 Mar 1942
HMS Formidable	26 Nov 1940	Dekheila	23 Mar 1942
Wynberg (Dt3)	22-25 Jan 1941	Maaten Bagush (Dt)	27 Mar 1942 to 17 Apr 1942
Sheikh Othman	15-18 Feb 1941	Maaten Bagush	10 May 1942
Dekheila	10 Mar 1941	El Adem (Dt2)	22-27 May 1942
HMS Formidable	15 Mar 1941	Bu Amud	23 May 1942
Dekheila	19 Mar 1941	Maaten Bagush	24 May 1942
HMS Formidable	26 Mar 1941	LG.05 Sidi Barrani (Dt8)	27 May 1942 to 1 Jun 1942
Dekheila	30 Mar 1941	LG.05 Sidi Barrani (Dt8)	15 Jun 1942 to 21 Jun 1942
HMS Formidable	18 Apr 1941	Daba (Dt)	25-29 Jun 1942
Dekheila	23 Apr 1941	Dekheila	1 Jul 1942
HMS Formidable	28 Apr 1941	El Birwa	1 Oct 1942
Dekheila (Dt)	13-25 May 1941	Gamil	19 Oct 1942
Dekheila	27 May 1941	Dekheila	22 Oct 1942
Fuka (Dt)	1-2 Jun 1941	Berka satt (Dt6)	2-6 Dec 1942
Fuka (Dt6)	7-28 Jun 1941	Berka satt	6 Dec 1942
Maaten Bagush satt	14 Jun 1941	Benghazi (Dt6)	4-6 Dec 1942
Dekheila	21 Jun 1941	Hal Far (Dt6)	6-11 Dec 1942
Nicosia	1 Jul 1941	Hal Far	11 Dec 1942
Dekheila	15 Jul 1941	Berka 2	16 Dec 1942
Maaten Bagush satt (Dt6)	31 Jul 1941 to 27 Aug 1941	Wadi Tamet(Dt4)	12-17 Jan 1943
		Dekheila	22 Jan 1943
Maaten Bagush	27 Aug 1941	Blida (transit)	11 Feb 1943
Bu Amud	18 Dec 1941	Misurata (transit)	15 Feb 1943
Berka Main	4 Jan 1942	Hal Far	19 Feb 1943
Bu Amud	6 Jan 1942	Bone (transit)	21 Feb 1943
Benina	16 Jan 1942	Blida	24 Feb 1943
Bu Amud	19 Jan 1942	Bone	8 Mar 1943
Berka satt	21 Jan 1942	Tafaroui	30 May 1943
Bu Amud	24 Jan 1942	HMS Formidable (Dt5 - DLT)	12-13 Jun 1943
Martuba (Dt)	Jan 1942 to 1 Feb 1942	transit	28 Jun 1943
		Ta Kali	10 Jul 1943
		Squadron disbanded	16 Oct 1943
		Lee-on-Solent	1 Dec 1943
		Crail	3 Feb 1944

Aircraft Equipment	Period of Service	Example	
Albacore I	Mar 1940 - Aug 1943	N4319	(4F)
Swordfish I	Jul 1940 - Aug 1940	K8883	
	Mar 1941 - Sep 1941	L2739	
Barracuda II	Dec 1943 - Oct 1944	MD622	(4X)
Barracuda II(ASH)	Aug 1945 - Jan 1946	MX861	
Firefly FR.1	Jan 1946 - Feb 1946	MB581	
	May 1947 - Oct 1950	PP412	(ABK)
Firefly T.1	Dec 1948 - Jan 1949	MB433	
Avenger TBM-3E	Oct 1950 - May 1951	53545	(ABZ)
Firefly AS.6	May 1951 - Jan 1955	WJ105	(276/J)
Gannet AS.1	Jan 1955 - Nov 1955	WN418	(345/J)
Wessex HAS.1	Mar 1966 - Oct 1968	XS881	(344/H)
Wessex HAS.3	Oct 1968 - Mar 1970	XP116	(145/E)
Sea King HAS.1	Jun 1970 - Dec 1976	XV647	(144/TG)
Sea King HAS.2/2a	Nov 1976 - May 1983	XZ573	(141/TG)
Sea King HAS.5	Mar 1981 - May 1993	XZ577	(142/H)
Sea King HAS.6	Apr 1988 - Jul 1993	ZA136	(251)

Westland Wessex HAS.1 XS880 '343/H' of No.826 Squadron in 1966. (MAP)

Squadron bases

HMS Indefatigable	10 Jun 1944
Hatston	5 Jul 1944
HMS Indefatigable	10 Jul 1944
Grimsetter	7 Aug 1944
HMS Formidable	15 Aug 1944
Grimsetter	2 Sep 1944
HMS Indefatigable	17 Sep 1944
Machrihanish	26 Sep 1944
Squadron disbanded	23 Oct 1944
East Haven	15 Aug 1945
Fearn	11 Oct 1945
Squadron disbanded	28 Feb 1946
Dartmouth	15 May 1947
HMCS Warrior	Nov 1947
Dartmouth	21 Nov 1947
Rivers	Aug 1948
Dartmouth	Sep 1948
HMCS Magnificent	5 Mar 1949
Dartmouth	7 Apr 1949
HMCS Magnificent	May 1949
Dartmouth	Jun 1949
Quonset Point	Jul 1949
Dartmouth	Sep 1949
HMCS Magnificent	17 Nov 1949
Dartmouth	6 Dec 1949
HMCS Magnificent	13 Jan 1950
Dartmouth	2 Feb 1950
HMCS Magnificent	13 Feb 1950
Dartmouth	14 Apr 1950
Quonset Point	Feb 1951
HMCS Magnificent	5 Feb 1951
Dartmouth	Mar 1951
HMCS Magnificent	Mar 1951
Dartmouth	27 Apr 1951
Redes 881 Sqdn	1 May 1951
Ford	15 May 1951
HMS Illustrious	1 Oct 1951
Ford	24 Oct 1951
HMS Indomitable	17 Jan 1952
North Front	7 Feb 1952
HMS Indomitable	3 Mar 1952
Machrihanish	17 Apr 1952
Lee-on-Solent	14 May 1952
HMS Indomitable	16 May 1952
Lee-on-Solent	10 Jul 1952
HMS Theseus	20 Aug 1952
Hal Far	9 Oct 1952
HMS Theseus	17 Nov 1952
Hal Far	28 Nov 1952
Istres (transit)	3 Dec 1952
Lee-on-Solent	3 Dec 1952
HMS Indomitable	20 Jan 1953
Hal Far	18 Feb 1953
HMS Indomitable	1 Mar 1953
North Front	12 Mar 1953
Hal Far	30 Mar 1953
HMS Indomitable	21 Apr 1953
Lee-on-Solent	7 May 1953
HMS Illustrious	31 Aug 1953
Lee-on-Solent	2 Oct 1953
HMS Glory	2 Nov 1953
Hal Far	12 Nov 1953
HMS Glory	18 Nov 1953
Hal Far	18 Dec 1953
HMS Glory	4 Jan 1954
Lee-on-Solent	28 Feb 1954
HMS Eagle(Dt4)	10-17 May 1955
HMS Eagle	4 Jun 1955
Hal Far (Dt4)	24 Jun 1955
	to 18 Jul 1955
Hal Far	19 Aug 1955
North Front	22 Aug 1955
Le Bourget(transit)	9 Sep 1955
Lee-on-Solent	12 Sep 1955
HMS Eagle	15 Sep 1955
Lee-on-Solent	22 Nov 1955
- disbanded on arrival	
Culdrose	18 Mar 1966
Arbroath (Dt4)	4-11 Jul 1966
RFA Lofoten(Dt)	11-15 Jul 1966

Westland Sea King HAS.1 XV663 '141/E' of No.826 Squadron, HMS Eagle at practice.

Squadron bases

HMS Hermes	22 Sep 1966
Arbroath	13 Oct 1966
HMS Hermes	5 Nov 1966
Culdrose	15 Nov 1966
HMS Hermes	16 Jan 1967
Gibraltar	6 Feb 1967
HMS Hermes	20 Feb 1967
Hal Far	16 Mar 1967
HMS Hermes	30 Mar 1967
Sembawang	7 Jul 1967
HMS Hermes	14 Jul 1967
Culdrose	30 Sep 1967
HMS Hermes	31 Oct 1967
Culdrose	18 Feb 1968
RFA Olmeda (Dt3)	18 Apr 1968
	to 27 May 1968
RFA Olmeda (Dt2)	17-30 Jun 1968
RFA Olna (Dt3)	1-11 Jul 1968
RFA Olmeda(Dt2)	9-24 Sep 1968
HMS Eagle	1 Apr 1969
Culdrose	1 May 1969
HMS Eagle	23 May 1969

Squadron bases

Hal Far (Dt5)	31 Oct 1969
	to 12 Nov 1969
Culdrose	12 Dec 1969
HMS Eagle	15 Jan 1970
St Mandrier (Dt3)	30 Jan 1970
	to 6 Feb 1970
Culdrose-disbanded	25 Mar 1970
Culdrose	2 Jun 1970
Bergen	17 Aug 1970
RFA Olna	24 Aug 1970
Aalborg	27 Aug 1970
Culdrose	29 Aug 1970
HMS Eagle	6 Nov 1970
Culdrose	10 Dec 1970
HMS Eagle	19 Jan 1971
Luqa	3 Mar 1971
HMS Eagle	22 Mar 1971
Culdrose	6 Apr 1971
HMS Eagle	28 May 1971
Nowra(Dt4)	3-6 Aug 1971
Sembawang	20 Sep 1971
HMS Eagle	5 Oct 1971
Culdrose	24 Jan 1972

Squadron bases

RFA Engadine	6 Mar 1972
Culdrose	22 Mar 1972
RFA Engadine	15 May 1972
Culdrose	18 May 1972
RFA Engadine	12 Jun 1972
Culdrose	17 Jun 1972
HMS Tiger(Dt3)	22-24 Aug 1972
HMS Albion(Dt3)	10-29 Sep 1972
RFA Olna (Dt3)	11-26 Oct 1972
HMS Tiger	5 Dec 1972
Culdrose	13 Dec 1972
HMS Tiger	22 Jan 1973
Culdrose	21 Feb 1973
HMS Tiger	13 Mar 1973
Culdrose	17 Apr 1973
HMS Tiger	5 Jun 1973
Tengah	1 Aug 1973
HMS Tiger	13 Aug 1973
Tengah	5 Oct 1973
HMS Tiger	19 Oct 1973
Culdrose	20 Dec 1973
HMS Tiger	28 Jan 1974
Culdrose	9 Apr 1974

Westland Sea King HAS.1 XV667 '145/E' of No.826 Squadron landing on HMS Eagle on 17 November 1970. (via Fred Motley)

Squadron bases
Prestwick (Dt)	1-9 May 1974
HMS Tiger	28 Jun 1974
Culdrose	7 Aug 1974
HMS Tiger	9 Aug 1974
Culdrose	7 Nov 1974
HMS Tiger	9 Dec 1974
Culdrose	13 Mar 1975
HMS Tiger	21 Apr 1975
Culdrose	6 Jun 1975
HMS Tiger	17 Jun 1975
Culdrose	1 Jul 1975
HMS Hermes	28 Oct 1975
Culdrose	22 Nov 1975
Valley (Dt3)	16-23 Feb 1976
Portland (Dt3)	5-8 Apr 1976
Lossiemouth	13 May 1976
RFA Engadine	21 May 1976

Squadron bases
Gibraltar (Dt3)	14-18 Jun 1976
Culdrose	22 Jun 1976
HMS Tiger	22 Sep 1976
Culdrose	16 Dec 1976
HMS Tiger	25 Jan 1977
Culdrose	23 May 1977
HMS Tiger	7 Sep 1977
Amberley (Dt2)	4-31 Jan 1978
Cubi Point (Dt2)	16-20 Feb 1978
Tengah	2 Mar 1978
HMS Tiger	13 Mar 1978
Culdrose	19 Apr 1978
Lee-on-Solent (Dt2)	19-23 Jun 1978
HrMs Poolster (Dt2)	15-24 Aug 1978
HMS Hermes(Dt3)	1-19 Sep 1978

Squadron bases
Otterburn	11-22 Nov 1978
HrMs Poolster (Dt2)	5-16 Feb 1979
HMS Bulwark	20 Feb 1979
Lee-on-Solent	14 Mar 1979
HMS Bulwark	18 Apr 1979
Sennybridge(Dt3)	27-30 Apr 1979
Culdrose (Dt3)	1-4 Jun 1979
Culdrose	16 Jul 1979
HMS Bulwark	17 Sep 1979
RFA Olna (Dt2)	20 Sep 1979 to 10 Oct 1979
Culdrose	21 Nov 1979
HMS Bulwark	5 Jan 1980
Jacksonville	18 Jan 1980
HMS Bulwark	19 Feb 1980
Culdrose	1 Apr 1980
HMS Bulwark	24 Apr 1980
Culdrose	20 May 1980
HMS Bulwark	15 Aug 1980
Culdrose	23 Sep 1980
HMS Hermes (Dt2)	18-21 May 1981
HMS Hermes (Dt4)	8-30 Jun 1981
HMS Hermes	3 Sep 1981
Jacksonville (Dt5)	16 Sep 1981 to 20 Oct 1981
Culdrose	2 Dec 1981
Prestwick (C Flt)	11 Jan 1982 to 26 Feb 1982
HMS Hermes	22 Jan 1982
Culdrose	19 Feb 1982
Prestwick (A Flt)	28 Mar 1982 to 31 Mar 1982
HMS Hermes	11 Mar 1982
Culdrose	18 Mar 1982
HMS Hermes	3 Apr 1982

Squadron bases
RFA Fort Austin (Dt4)	17 May 1982 to 3 Jun 1982
San Carlos (Dt4)	3-6 Jun 1982
San Carlos (Dt2)	17-23 Jun 1982
Culdrose	22 Jul 1982
Prestwick (Dt2)	5-29 Sep 1982
RFA Tidespring(Dt1)	8 Nov 1982 to 9 Dec 1982
RFA Fort Grange (Dt1)	21 Nov 1982 to 9 Dec 1982
(Early 1983 took over A & C Flights of 824 Sqdn, and then operated as A, B & C Flights)	
RFA Fort Austin (Dt2)	10 May 1991 to 19 Aug 1991
HrMs Poolster (Dt2)	1992 to 10 Nov 1992
HrMS Zuiderkruis	10 May 1993
De Kooy	14 May 1993
HrMS Poolster	24 May 1993
Culdrose	25 May 1993
Portland (Dt1)	7-25 Jun 1993
De Kooy (Dt1)	8-12 Jun 1993
Squadron disbanded	27 Jul 1993

826A Flight

Flight bases
RFA Fort Grange	1 Feb 1983
RFA Tidespring (Dt1)	1 Feb 1983
Relieved by B Flt sea/air passage to UK	Mar 1983
Culdrose (detts Portland)	Mar 1983
Main Party:	
Brize Norton	31 Jul 1983
Wideawake	31 Jul 1983

Westland Sea King HAS.1 XV665 '143/E' and others of No.826 Sqdn, HMS Eagle in a flypast for the Commander-in-Chief Far East at Singapore on 31 October 1971. (via Fred Motley)

Westland Sea King HAS.2 XZ573 '141/TG' of No.826 Sqdn in 1977. (MAP)

Squadron bases
SS Uganda	1 Aug 1983
RFA Fort Austin	13 Aug 1983
(San Carlos Water)	
(relieved C Flt)	
RFA Olwen (Dt1)	16 Aug 1983
	to 24 Sep 1983
Kelly's Garden	8-10 Sep 1983
(Dt2)	
Kelly's Garden	24-27 Sep 1983
(Dt1)	
Stanley (Dt1)	27-30 Sep 1983
RFA Olwen (Dt1)	30 Sep 1983
	to 18 Oct 1983
HMS Bristol (Dt1)	18 Oct 1983
RFA Olwen (Dt2)	18-31 Oct 1983
Navy Point (Dt1)	18-31 Oct 1983
RFA Olwen (Dt1)	31 Oct 1983
	to 17 Nov 1983
Navy Point (Dt1)	17-19 Nov 1983
Relieved by B Flt	19 Nov 1983
sea/air passage to UK	
Air Party to UK	29 Nov 1983
Sea Party arrive	
UK in RFA Fort	
Austin	9 Dec 1983
Culdrose	Jan 1984
RFA Olmeda (Dt2)	3-8 Apr 1984
RFA Olna (Dt2)	30 Apr 1984
	to 10 May 1984
RFA Fort Grange	26 May 1984
passage to Falklands	
Relieved C Flt	8 Jun 1984
Relieved by B Flt	16 Aug 1984
Detachment:	
RFA Olwen	11 Aug 1984
RFA Reliant	16 Oct 1984
RFA Invincible	22 Nov 1984
RFA Olmeda	7 Dec 1984
Culdrose	Sep 1984
Brize Norton	24 Jan 1985
Wideawake/	
SS Uganda	25 Jan 1985
(air/sea passage to UK)	
RFA Reliant	7 Feb 1985
(relieved C Flt)	
RFA Olna (Dt2)	12-27 Feb 1985
RFA Olna (Dt2)	5-10 Mar 1985
Navy Point (Dt2)	20-27 Mar 1985
RFA Olna (Dt2)	3-17 Apr 1985
RFA Olna (Dt2)	3 May 1985
(passage to UK)	to Jun 1985
MV Keren	10 May 1985
(relieved by B Flt,	
sea/air passage to Falklands)	
Culdrose	30 May 1985
HMS Ark Royal	29 Jul 1985
(Dt2)	to 2 Aug 1985

Squadron bases
HMS Ark Royal	
(Dt1)	5-9 Aug 1985
Valley (Dt1)	12-16 Aug 1985
Guernsey Airport	
	19-21 Aug 1985
HrMs Poolster	
(Dt2)	6-19 Sep 1985
Portland (Dt2)	7-9 Oct 1985
Brize Norton	18 Nov 1985
air passage to Falklands	
RFA Reliant/	
Port Stanley	19 Nov 1985
(relieved C Flt)	
Kelly's Garden	
(Dt2)	21-24 Dec 1985
Kelly's Garden	
(Dt2)	24-26 Jan 1986
air passage to UK	21 Feb 1986
(relieved by B Flt)	
Culdrose	26 Feb 1986
Valley (Dt2)	2-5 Jun 1986
RFA Tidespring	23 Jun 1986
(Dt2)	to 4 Jul 1986
Erding (Dt2)	15-22 Jul 1986
RFA Tidespring	17 Sep 1986
(Dt2)	to 6 Oct 1986
Prestwick (Dt2)	10-21 Nov 1986
HrMs Zuiderkruis	1 Feb 1987
(Dt2)	to 28 May 1987
Prestwick (Dt2)	14-18 Sep 1987
HMS London (Dt1)	2-9 Oct 1987
RFA Olmeda (Dt)	5-10 Oct 1987
HMS Brave (Dt1)	17-28 Oct 1987
RFA Olna (Dt2)	27 Nov 1987
	to 7 Dec 1987
Portland	25-28 Jan 1988
RFA Fort Austin	14 Feb 1988
(Dt3)	to 26 Mar 1988
(including 1 810 Sqdn a/c)	
Prestwick	30 May 1988
	to 9 Jun 1988
Portland	11-15 Jul 1988
HMS Brave (Dt1)	30 Aug 1988
	to 2 Oct 1988
RFA Olmeda (Dt1)	30 Aug 1988
	to 23 Sep 1988
RFA Tidespring	23 Sep 1988
(Dt1)	to 2 Oct 1988
RFA Resource	14-26 Oct 1988
(Dt1)	
Portland	7-10 Oct 1988
HMS Invincible	28 Nov 1988
	to 4 Dec 1988
HMS Invincible	12-19 Dec 1988
HMS Invincible	29 Jan 1989
	to 10 Feb 1989

Squadron bases
HMS London (Dt1)	29 Jan 1989
	to 25 Apr 1989
RFA Fort Austin	19 May 1989
	to 5 Jun 1989
Prestwick	7-15 Aug 1989
HMS London	
(Dt1)	4-22 Sep 1989
RFA Fort Austin	8-24 Nov 1989
1990-1993 -	
see Ships Flights section	
Became A Flt	
819 Sqdn	30 Jul 1993

826B Flight

Flight bases
Formed from A & C	
Flts 824 Sqdn	
Culdrose	1 Feb 1983
air/sea passage to	
Falklands	Mar 1983
RFA Fort Grange	Mar 1983
(relieved A Flt)	
RFA Olwen (Dt1)	Mar 1983
	to May 1983
Relieved by C Flt	21 May 1983
air/sea passage to UK	
Culdrose	Jun 1983
air/sea passage to	
Falklands	Nov 1983
Stanley	19 Nov 1983
RFA Fort Grange	19 Nov 1983
(relieved A Flt)	
RFA Olna (Dt1)	22 Nov 1983
	to 21 Jan 1984
Navy Point (Dt1)	21-27 Jan 1984
RFA Olna (Dt1)	27 Jan 1984
	to 18 Feb 1984
Navy Point (Dt1)	18-21 Feb 1984
SS Uganda	21 Feb 1984
(relieved by C Flt)	
(sea/air passage to UK)	
Culdrose	24 Apr 1984
RFA Fort Grange	14-26 May 1984
(Dt2)	
RFA Fort Austin	1-16 Aug 1984
passage UK to Ascension	
Wideawake	16 Aug 1984
(air passage from UK)	
RFA Fort Austin	16 Aug 1984
Relieved A Flt	23 Aug 1984
RFA Olwen (Dt1)	23 Aug 1984
	to 22 Sep 1984
Navy Point (Dt1)	22-29 Sep 1984
RFA Olwen (Dt1)	29 Sep 1984
	to 8 Nov 1984
Navy Point (Dt1)	8-12 Nov 1984

Squadron bases
SS Uganda	12 Nov 1984
releived by C Flt	
Sea/air passage to UK	
Culdrose	27 Nov 1984
Wideawake/	
MV Keren	9 May 1985
air/sea passage to Falklands	
RFA Reliant	10 May 1985
relieved A Flt	
Air passage to UK	16 Aug 1985
(relieved by C Flt)	
Culdrose	Oct 1985
Air passage to	20 Feb 1986
Falklands	
RFA Reliant	21 Feb 1986
(relieved A Flt)	
Air passage to UK	24 May 1986
(relieved by C Flt)	
Culdrose	Jun 1986
Prestwick	25 Aug 1986
Culdrose	24 Sep 1986
RFA Olna	1 Feb 1987
Culdrose	4 Feb 1987
Portland	23 Feb 1987
Culdrose	26 Feb 1987
RFA Olmeda	30 Jun 1987
Culdrose	3 Jul 1987
HrMs Zuiderkruis	25 Aug 1987
Culdrose	24 Sep 1987
HMS Ark Royal	2 Nov 1987
Culdrose	24 Nov 1987
RFA Tidespring/	11 Apr 1988
Olna	
Culdrose	16 Jan 1989
HMS Invincible	13 Feb 1989
Culdrose	16 Feb 1989
RFA Argus	27 Feb 1989
Culdrose	3 Mar 1989
HMS Invincible	6 Mar 1989
Culdrose	9 Mar 1989
RFA Tidespring	7 Apr 1989
Culdrose	23 Apr 1989
RFA Tidespring	15 May 1989
Culdrose	4 Jun 1989
RFA Tidespring	15 Jun 1989
Culdrose	20 Jul 1989
Prestwick (Dt)	25 Aug 1989
	to 20 Sep 1989
RFA Tidespring	2 Oct 1989
Culdrose	2 Nov 1989
Portland	23 Jan 1990
Culdrose	27 Jan 1990
Linton-on-Ouse	5 Mar 1990
Culdrose	7 Mar 1990
RFA Tidespring	4 Apr 1990
Culdrose	28 Apr 1990
HMS Coventry	13 May 1990

Westland Sea King HAS.2A XV655 '142/B' of No.826 Squadron in 1979. (MAP)

Squadron bases
Culdrose	21 Feb 1991
HMS Fearless	15 May 1991
Culdrose	11 Jul 1991
HMS Cornwall	12 Sep 1991
Culdrose	16 Dec 1991
HMS Cornwall	3 Feb 1992
Culdrose	24 Feb 1992
HMS Cornwall	8 Oct 1992
Culdrose	20 Nov 1992
Portland	22 Feb 1993
Culdrose	25 Feb 1993
HMS Chatham	26 Apr 1993
Culdrose	27 Apr 1993
HMS Chatham	5 May 1993
Culdrose	22 Jul 1993
Prestwick	29 Jul 1993
Became B Flt 819 Sqdn	30 Jul 1993

826C Flight

Culdrose	12 Apr 1983
RFA Fort Austin (Dt2)	21-22 Apr 1983
Brize Norton	9 May 1983
Wideawake	10 May 1983
RFA Fort Austin (crews only)	11 May 1983
RFA Fort Austin (aircraft embarked in Port William Sound, relieved B Flt)	21 May 1983
Kelly's Garden (Dt1)	21-28 May 1983
RFA Tidespring (Dt1)	28 May 1983 to 17 Jun 1983
Kelly's Garden (Dt1)	17-30 Jun 1983
RFA Tidespring (Dt1)	30 Jun 1983 to 26 Aug 1983
SS Uganda relieved by A Flt sea/air passage to UK	13 Aug 1983
Culdrose	30 Aug 1983
RFA Engadine (Dt3)	25-28 Oct 1983
Portland (Dt3)	9-12 Jan 1984
Wideawake/ SS Uganda air/sea passage to Falklands	7 Feb 1984
RFA Fort Grange (relieved B Flt)	21 Feb 1984
RFA Tidespring (Dt1)	21 Feb 1984 to 13 May 1984
RFA Fort Austin	6 Mar 1984
Navy Point(Dt1)	13-22 May 1984
Wideawake (air passage to Brize Norton) relieved by A Flt	14 Jun 1984
Culdrose	17 Jul 1984
Lee-on-Solent	24-27 Aug 1984
Guernsey Airport (Dt2)	29 Sep 1984 to 1 Oct 1984
Wideawake/ SS Uganda air/sea passage to Falklands	1 Nov 1984
RFA Fort Austin (relieved B Flt)	12 Nov 1984
Navy Point (Dt1)	12-15 Nov 1984
RFA Tidespring (Dt1)	15 Nov 1984 to 17 Jan 1985
RFA Reliant	26 Nov 1984
RFA Tidespring (Dt2)	17-29 Jan 1985
RFA Tidespring (Dt1)	29 Jan 1985 to 7 Feb 1985
RFA Tidespring (Dt2) (passage to UK)	7 Feb 1985 to Feb 1985
SS Uganda	7 Feb 1985

Squadron bases
Relieved by A Flt -sea/air passage to UK	
Culdrose	28 Feb 1985
AUTEC Andros(Dt1)	9 Mar 1985 to 15 May 1985
Hildesheim (Dt2)	13-17 May 1985
HMS Invincible (Dt2)	7 Jun 1985 to 5 Jul 1985
MV Singelgaracht (Dt1)	16 Jul 1985 to 21 Aug 1985
(passage to Falklands)	
Air passage to Falklands	15 Aug 1985
RFA Reliant (relieved B Flt)	16 Aug 1985
Stanley (Dt2)	1-10 Nov 1985
air passage to UK (relieved by A Flt)	19 Nov 1985
Culdrose	6 Jan 1986
Valkenburg(Dt2)	27-31 Jan 1986
Portland (Dt2)	3-5 Feb 1986
Plockton (Dt2)	4-10 Mar 1986
Air passage to Falklands	23 May 1986
RFA Fort Austin (relieved B Flt)	24 May 1986
MV Asifi (Dt2) (passage to UK)	20 Aug 1986
Culdrose	1 Oct 1986
RFA Olna	28 Oct 1986
Culdrose	9 Dec 1986
RFA Olna	27 Feb 1987
Culdrose	27 Mar 1987
HMS Ark Royal	6 May 1987
Culdrose	15 May 1987
RFA Olmeda	31 Jul 1987
Culdrose	18 Sep 1987
Portland	16 Nov 1987
Culdrose	20 Nov 1987
HrMs Poolster	27 Jan 1988
Culdrose	28 Mar 1988
RFA Olmeda	16 May 1988
Culdrose	1 Aug 1988
Benbecula	2 Sep 1988
Culdrose	22 Sep 1988
RFA Fort Austin	13 Feb 1989
Culdrose	16 Mar 1989
RFA Fort Austin	29 Mar 1989
Culdrose	27 Apr 1989
Prestwick	24 May 1989
Culdrose	21 Jul 1989
HMS Ark Royal	4 Sep 1989
Culdrose	22 Sep 1989
HrMs Zuiderkruis	10 Nov 1989
Culdrose	24 Nov 1989
RFA Olmeda	28 Mar 1990
Culdrose	1 Jun 1990
RFA Olmeda	31 Aug 1990
Culdrose	19 Sep 1990
air passage to Gulf	12 Dec 1990
HrMs Zuiderkruis (relieved D Flt)	13 Dec 1990
RFA Argus	26 Jan 1991
RFA Sir Galahad FOB	Jan 1991 to Mar 1991
RFA Fort Grange	16 Mar 1991
Relieved by D Flt (air passage to UK)	30 Mar 1991
Culdrose	Apr 1991
Portland (Dt2)	16-21 Sep 1991
RFA Tidespring (Dt2)	14-21 Oct 1991
Prestwick (Dt1)	21 Oct 1991 to 29 Nov 1991
Portland (Dt2)	8-15 Nov 1991
RFA Olna (Dt2)	1 Jun 1992 to 20 Aug 1992
HrMs Zuiderkruis (Dt2)	8 Feb 1993 to 10 Mar 1993

Sea King HAS.5 ZA133 '139' of No.826 Squadron in 1942. (MAP)

Squadron bases
HrMs Zuiderkruis (Dt2)	14 Apr 1993 to 10 May 1993
Portland	7 Jun 1993
Culdrose	25 Jun 1993
Prestwick	12 Jul 1993
Culdrose	16 Jul 1993
Prestwick became 819 Sqn	29 Jul 1993
C Flt	30 Jul 1993

826D Flight

RFA Olna	18 Aug 1990
HrMs Zuiderkruis	Oct 1990
air passage to UK (relieved by C Flt)	14 Dec 1990
Culdrose	Dec 1990
air passage to Gulf	Mar 1991
RFA Fort Grange (relieved C Flt)	30 Mar 1991
RFA Fort Austin	7 Jun 1991
Culdrose	19 Aug 1991
HrMs Poolster	25 Oct 1991
Culdrose	22 Nov 1991
HrMs Poolster	14 Sep 1992
Culdrose	10 Nov 1992
HrMs Zuiderkruis	8 Feb 1993
Culdrose	10 Mar 1993
HrMs Zuiderkruis	14 Apr 1993
De Kooy	13 May 1993
HrMs Poolster	24 May 1993
Culdrose	25 May 1993
Prestwick	29 Jul 1993
became 819D Flt	30 Jul 1993

No.826E Flight
(Sea King HAS.6 OEU)

Culdrose	Jun 1991
Farnborough	Oct 1991
RFA Tidespring (FORACS)	22 Oct 1991 to 18 Dec 1991
Boscombe Down	Jul 1992
RFA Olmeda (AUTEC)	1 Sep 1992
Boscombe Down	Nov 1992
Plockton BUTEC	15 Feb 993
Boscombe Down	22 Feb 1993
FORACS	26 Mar 1993
Boscombe Down	Apr 1993
Plockton BUTEC	22 Jun 1993
Boscombe Down	30 Jun 1993
Became 810 Sqdn OEU	27 Jul 1993

Commanding Officers

Lt FHE Hopkins RN	15 Mar 1940
L/C CJT Stephens RN	7 Apr 1940
L/C WHG Saunt DSC RN	27 May 1940
L/C JWS Corbett RN	24 Jun 1941
Lt CWB Smith DFC RN	23 Jan 1942
Lt PW Compton RN	5 Mar 1942
Lt VGH Ramsey -Fairfax RN	22 Aug 1942
L/C(A) RE Bradshaw DSC RN	1 May 1943
Squadron disbanded	25 Aug 1943
L/C(A) AJI Temple -West RN	1 Dec 1943
L/C(A) SP Luke RN	26 Jan 1944
Squadron disbanded	23 Oct 1944
L/C ES Carver DSC RN	15 Aug 1945
L/C CG Watson RCN(R)	20 Feb 1946
Squadron disbanded	28 Feb 1946
L/C JB Fotheringham RCN	15 May 1947
L/C RIW Goddard DSC RCN	Jan 1948
L/C JW Roberts RCN	Oct 1948
L/C JN Donaldson RCN	20 Apr 1950
Squadron disbanded	1 May 1951
L/C PC Heath RN	15 May 1951
L/C JW Powell DSC RN	4 Dec 1952
L/C R Fulton RN	10 Sep 1954
L/C GF Birch RN	17 Jan 1955
Squadron disbanded	22 Nov 1955
L/C RA Duxbury RN	18 Mar 1966
L/C JG Kemp RN	3 Oct 1967
L/C N Usworth RN	3 Nov 1969
Squadron disbanded	25 Mar 1970
L/C RE Van der Plank RN	2 Jun 1970
L/C KF Harding RN	1 Sep 1972
L/C JM Neville -Rolfe RN	7 May 1974
L/C MJ Lehan RN	4 Jul 1975
L/C CJS Craig RN	1 Dec 1975
L/C GNI Harvey RN	1 Apr 1976
L/C AW English RN	15 Oct 1977
L/C TPH Richardson RN	29 May 1979
L/C DJS Squier AFC RN	1 Dec 1980
L/C DA Raines RN	3 Sep 1982
L/C K Dudley RN	5 Jun 1984
L/C JR Skinner RN	28 Jan 1986
L/C PA Shaw MVO RN	16 Feb 1988
Cdr PA Shaw MVO RN	1 Oct 1989
L/C MW Butcher RN	13 Jun 1990
L/C AK Grant RN	23 Aug 1991
Cdr AK Grant RN	30 Jun 1993
Squadron disbanded	27 Jul 1993

No.827 Squadron

Badge: On a field per fesse wavy white and barry wavy of six blue and white, a rod caduceas and a trident in satire gold in chief a winged cap red
[On the right is an earlier unapproved version]
Motto: Ya-mansur-amit (O! Conqueror fight desperately

No.827 Squadron originally formed at Yeovilton on 15 September 1940 as a torpedo spotter reconnaissance squadron with 12 Albacores. After work up in Scotland these carried out anti-submarine patrols and convoy escorts under RAF Coastal Command before moving south in May 1941 to stand by for attacks on the German battlecruisers *Scharnhorst* and *Gneisenau*, during which period they undertook seven night minelaying operations off Brest and Cherbourg. In July the squadron joined HMS *Victorious* to take part in an attack on 30 July on Kirkenes harbour in northern Norway, but lost six of its aircraft, though one pilot managed to destroy a Ju 87 with his front gun.

The remains of the squadron regrouped at Hatston, and in October embarked in HMS *Indomitable* to sail via Jamaica and the USA to Capetown before arriving in Aden in January 1942. Here local patrols were carried out, and the ship later operated in the Indian Ocean. In May the squadron carried out anti-submarine patrols and bombing attacks at a reduced strength of nine aircraft during the invasion of Madagascar. Then after further patrols in the Indian Ocean, the ship sailed for Gibraltar. During Operation *Pedestal*, a fast reinforcement convoy to Malta in August 1942, five squadron officers were killed in attacks on the ship. After temporary repairs HMS *Indomitable* returned home, and No.827 disembarked to regroup.

In January 1943, No.827 rearmed at Stretton with 12 Barracuda IIs to become a torpedo bomber reconnaissance squadron. Reducing to 9 aircraft in September, it joined the 8th Naval TBR Wing the following month for service with the Home Fleet in HMS *Furious*. In March 1944 it temporarily transferred to HMS *Victorious* for a successful dive bombing attack on the German battleship *Tirpitz* in Kaa Fjord on 3 April, during which it shared ten hits with No.830 Squadron. Returning to HMS *Furious*, No.827 carried out successful attacks on enemy shipping around Norway in atrocious weather in April and May, but a proposed further strike on *Tirpitz* had to be cancelled. For another attempt in July the squadron joined HMS *Formidable*, but a smoke screen enabled the enemy ship to avoid being hit. A final attempt was made from HMS *Furious* in August, and this time two hits were obtained in one attack, despite another smoke screen.

Fairey Albacores of No.827 Sqdn, HMS Indomitable over Eastern waters. (RAF Museum P.17823)

Fairey Barracudas of No.827 Squadron from HMS Colossus.
(J.Burn)

In October 1944, No.827 absorbed No.830 Squadron and the strength consequently increased to 18 aircraft. These were then based in East Anglia for an attack on shipping off the Dutch coast in support of the invasion forces. In January 1945 the squadron joined HMS *Colossus*, and in March sailed to join the British Pacific Fleet, being reduced to 12 aircraft whilst temporarily disembarked at Dekheila en route. By the time they arrived the war in the Far East was virtually over, and the squadron disembarked in Ceylon to become part of the 14th Carrier Air Group. In December it re-embarked for a visit to Cape Town then, after a brief return to Ceylon, the ship finally sailed for home and the squadron disbanded at Lee-on-Solent on 24 July 1946.

On 15 August 1946 No.827 reformed at Eglinton with 12 Firefly FR.1s as a fighter reconnaissance squadron. In October it became part of the 13th CAG, which embarked in HMS *Triumph* in January for two years in the Mediterranean. Returning home in March 1949, 12 new machines of the same type were received, and these embarked the following month to return to the Mediterranean.

Four Firefly NF.1s were attached from No.812 Squadron in June 1949 as Black Flight, and four of the FR.1s were consequently withdrawn. In August the squadron lost Black Flight and sailed for the Far East, where operations were carried out from October against Malayan bandits. When the Korean war broke out in June 1950, Black Flight was returned to No.812 Squadron, and No.827 sailed with 12 Firefly FR.1s for that theatre to carry out anti-submarine patrols and attacks on shore targets. In September the ship sailed home via Singapore, and No.827 disbanded at Ford on 22 November 1950.

No.827 next reformed at Ford on 13 December 1950 as a single seater torpedo strike squadron, equipped with 12 Firebrand TF.5s, one of the only two first line squadrons to receive this type. The concept was not a great success, but the squadron flew to Malta in May 1951, where it joined HMS *Illustrious* in October to return to the United Kingdom. In June 1952 it embarked in HMS *Eagle* for a summer cruise, and in September participated in a NATO exercise off Norway. After Arctic trials by the ship in November, the squadron disbanded on disembarking to Ford on 3 December 1952.

On 1 November 1954, No.827 reformed at Ford from a nucleus of No.703W Flight, equipped with 9 Wyvern S.4s for torpedo strike duties. These embarked in HMS *Eagle* in May 1955, and in June participated in combined exercises with the US Navy in the Mediterranean. In September they took part in a NATO exercise off Norway, but after a further exercise in the Moray Firth in October, the squadron disembarked to Ford on 19 November and disbanded.

Battle Honours

Diego Suarez	1942
Malta Convoys	1942
Norway	1944
Korea	1950

Identification Markings

Albacore *4A+* on *Victorious*, to *5A+* on *Indomitable* 10.41; Barracuda *4A+*, to *U1A+* by 4.45, later *A1A+* briefly, to *370-379/D:C* 9.45; Firefly single letters initially, then *271-282/P*; Firebrand *120-129/J:FD*; Wyvern *131-139/J*.

Fairey Firefly NF.1 '280/P' of No.827 Squadron's Black Flight. (via Brian Lowe)

Aircraft Equipment	Period of Service
Albacore I	Sep 1940 - Jan 1943
Barracuda I	Jan 1943 - Jul 1943
Barracuda II	Mar 1943 - Jul 1946
Fulmar II	Nov 1942 - Dec 1942
Firefly FR.1	Aug 1946 - Nov 1950
Firefly NF.1	Jun 1949 - Jun 1950
Firebrand TF.5	Dec 1950 - Dec 1952
Firefly FR.1	1951 - May 1952
Wyvern S.4	Nov 1954 - Dec 1955

Example	
T9206	(5C)
P9658	
BV727	(4H)
BP824	
PP488	(272/P)
PP660	(279/P)
EK745	(129/J)
PP392	
WL882	(137/J)

Squadron bases

Yeovilton	15 Sep 1940
Crail	2 Nov 1940
HMS Argus (DLT)	9 Mar 1941
Crail	10 Mar 1941
Stornoway (18 Gp)	14 Mar 1941
Thorney Island	1 May 1941
St Eval	11 May 1941
Machrihanish	4 Jun 1941
Donibristle	5 Jun 1941
Machrihanish	27 Jun 1941
Hatston	1 Jul 1941
HMS Victorious	2 Jul 1941
Hatston	8 Aug 1941
Machrihanish	10 Oct 1941
HMS Indomitable	13 Oct 1941
Norfolk	10 Nov 1941
HMS Indomitable	22 Nov 1941
Wynberg	2 Jan 1942
HMS Indomitable	7 Jan 1942
Khormaksar	11 Jan 1942
HMS Indomitable	23 Feb 1942
Juhu	14 Apr 1942
HMS Indomitable	20 Apr 1942
Port Reitz	26 May 1942
HMS Indomitable	9 Jul 1942
Stamford Hill (Dt4)	13-18 Jul 1942
Machrihanish	27 Aug 1942
Lee-on-Solent	23 Sep 1942
Stretton	15 Dec 1942
Machrihanish	12 Feb 1943
Lee-on-Solent	2 Apr 1943
Dunino	24 Apr 1943
Machrihanish	12 Aug 1943
HMS Furious	11 Oct 1943
Hatston	6 Dec 1943
HMS Furious	10 Dec 1943
Hatston	14 Dec 1943
HMS Furious	26 Dec 1943
Hatston	3 Jan 1944
HMS Furious	8 Feb 1944
Hatston	14 Feb 1944
HMS Furious	24 Feb 1944
Hatston	29 Feb 1944
HMS Furious	17 Mar 1944
Hatston	22 Mar 1944
HMS Victorious	30 Mar 1944
HMS Furious	6 Apr 1944
Donibristle	7 Apr 1944
HMS Victorious	20 Apr 1944
HMS Furious	25 Apr 1944
Hatston	28 Apr 1944
HMS Furious	3 May 1944
Hatston	18 May 1944
HMS Furious	28 May 1944
Hatston	17 Jun 1944
HMS Furious	22 Jun 1944
Hatston	23 Jun 1944
HMS Formidable	11 Jul 1944
Hatston	11 Jul 1944
HMS Formidable	14 Jul 1944
Hatston	19 Jul 1944
HMS Furious (Dt5)	9 Aug 1944 to 9 Sep 1944
HMS Furious	11 Sep 1944
Hatston	13 Sep 1944
HMS Furious	11 Oct 1944
Beccles (16 Gp)	15 Oct 1944
Langham (16 Gp)	28 Oct 1944

Squadron bases

Machrihanish	14 Dec 1944
HMS Colossus	13 Jan 1945
Ballyhalbert (Dt)	23-27 Jan 1945
Ballyhalbert	28 Jan 1945
HMS Colossus	20 Feb 1945
Dekheila	22 Mar 1945
HMS Colossus	4 May 1945
Katukurunda	12 Jun 1945
HMS Colossus	3 Jul 1945
Jervis Bay	22 Jul 1945
HMS Colossus	13 Aug 1945
Kai Tak (Dt6)	15-18 Oct 1945
Katukurunda	26 Oct 1945
HMS Colossus	30 Dec 1945
Wingfield	17 Jan 1946
HMS Colossus	8 Apr 1946
Katukurunda	27 Apr 1946
HMS Colossus	17 May 1946
Lee-on-Solent	22 Jul 1946
Squadron disbanded	24 Jul 1946
Lee-on-Solent	15 Aug 1946
Eglinton	17 Sep 1946
Belfast (transit)	13 Jan 1947
HMS Triumph	13 Jan 1947
Hal Far	22 Feb 1947
HMS Triumph	10 Mar 1947
Hal Far	24 Mar 1947
HMS Triumph	14 Apr 1947
Hal Far	15 May 1947
HMS Triumph	24 Jun 1947
Hal Far	4 Jul 1947
HMS Triumph	15 Jul 1947
Hal Far	22 Aug 1947
HMS Triumph	15 Sep 1947

Squadron bases

Hal Far	16 Oct 1947
Castel Benito	5 Nov 1947
Hal Far	28 Nov 1947
HMS Triumph	16 Dec 1947
Hal Far	19 Dec 1947
HMS Triumph	12 Jan 1948
Hal Far	21 Apr 1948
HMS Triumph	3 Jun 1948
Hal Far	28 Jul 1948
HMS Triumph	18 Aug 1948
Hal Far	28 Sep 1948
Castel Benito	12 Oct 1948
Hal Far	16 Oct 1948
HMS Triumph	20 Dec 1948
Hal Far	5 Feb 1949
HMS Triumph	22 Feb 1949
Donibristle	16 Mar 1949
HMS Triumph	25 Apr 1949
Hal Far	6 May 1949
Sembawang (Dt6)	25-29 Jun 1949
HMS Triumph	30 Jun 1949
Kai Tak	15 Sep 1949
HMS Triumph	27 Sep 1949
Sembawang	3 Oct 1949
HMS Triumph	1 Nov 1949
Kai Tak	5 Nov 1949
HMS Triumph	3 Dec 1949
Sembawang	8 Dec 1949
HMS Triumph	4 Feb 1950
Iwakuni	15 Apr 1950
HMS Triumph	9 May 1950
Ford	15 Nov 1950
Squadron disbanded	22 Nov 1950
Ford	13 Dec 1950
transit	21 May 1951
Hal Far	25 May 1951
HMS Illustrious	12 Oct 1951
Ford	24 Oct 1951
HMS Eagle	4 Mar 1952
Ford	24 Mar 1952
HMS Eagle	3 Jun 1952
Ford	7 Jul 1952
HMS Eagle	3 Sep 1952
Lossiemouth	4 Oct 1952
HMS Eagle	20 Oct 1952

Squadron bases

Ford	3 Dec 1952
Ford	1 Nov 1954
HMS Eagle	10 May 1955
Hal Far (Dt)	24 Jun 1955 to 18 Jul 1955
Hal Far (Dt3)	2-3 Aug 1955
North Front (Dt)	23 Aug 1955 to 8 Sep 1955
Ford	19 Nov 1955
Squadron disbanded	19 Nov 1955

Commanding Officers

Officer	Date
L/C WGC Stokes RN	15 Sep 1940
L/C JA Stewart-Moore RN	18 Jul 1941
L/C PGO Sydney-Turner RN	22 Aug 1941
L/C DK Buchanan-Dunlop RN	15 May 1942
Lt RW Little RN	7 Sep 1942
L/C(A) JS Bailey RN	12 Feb 1943
L/C(A) RS Baker-Falkner DSC RN	12 Aug 1943
L/C(A) KH Gibney DSC RN	25 Oct 1943
L/C(A) GR Woolston RN	30 Jun 1944
L/C(A) GR Clarke RN	6 Jul 1945
L/C(A) LR Tivy RN	16 Dec 1945
Squadron disbanded	24 Jul 1946
L/C PC Heath RN	15 Aug 1946
L/C PB Jackson RN	18 Apr 1949
L/C N Matthews DSC RN	24 Oct 1949
L/C BC Lyons RN	11 Dec 1949
Squadron disbanded	22 Nov 1950
L/C RD Henderson RN	13 Dec 1950
L/C LG Morris RN	11 Jul 1952
Squadron disbanded	3 Dec 1952
L/C SJA Richardson RN	1 Nov 1954
Squadron disbanded	19 Nov 1955

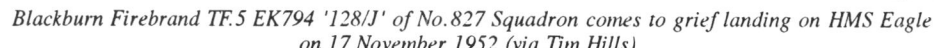

Blackburn Firebrand TF.5 EK794 '128/J' of No.827 Squadron comes to grief landing on HMS Eagle on 17 November 1952 (via Tim Hills)

No.828 Squadron

No.828 Squadron first formed at Lee-on-Solent on 15 September 1940 as a torpedo spotter reconnaissance squadron with nine Albacores. After moving to Scotland for work-up, it carried out anti-submarine operations and local patrols under RAF Coastal Command. In July 1941 it embarked in HMS *Victorious* for operations off northern Norway, including an attack on Kirkenes in which 5 aircraft were lost. After regrouping it joined HMS *Argus* in September for passage to Gibraltar, transferring there to HMS *Ark Royal* for Malta, where it spent the next 18 months.

Based at Hal Far from October 1941, attacks were carried out on enemy shipping sailing to supply their forces in Libya. Numerous attacks were also carried out on shore targets, initially in Sicily and later also in Libya. From 26 March 1942, Nos.828 and 830 Squadrons were combined for operational purposes for the remainder of that year, being known as the Naval Air Squadron Malta, though retaining their separate identities. No.828 started these operations with 14 aircraft, but despite replacements only two of these were serviceable at one stage. Nevertheless, considerable damage was inflicted on enemy merchant vessels and warships.

By December 1942, No.828 was again in a parlous state, and consequently absorbed some aircraft of No.826 Squadron and the remnants of No.830 Squadron, to bring its own strength up to nine aircraft. In May 1943 it joined forces with No.821 Squadron for shipping attacks, as well as providing illumination for a bombardment of the island of Pantellaria. By the time it completed the anti-shipping task it had accounted, in conjunction with No.830 Squadron, for 30 enemy ships sunk and 50 damaged. No.828 was then withdrawn to Tunisia to carry out anti-submarine coastal patrols during the invasion of Sicily, being disbanded at Monastir on 1 September 1943, eight days before the Italian surrender.

No.828 reformed at Lee-on-Solent on 1 March 1944 as a TBR squadron with 12 Barracuda IIs. Allocated to the 2nd Naval TBR Wing, it embarked in HMS *Implacable* in August for duty with the Home Fleet, being temporarily detached to HMS *Formidable* later that month for strikes against the German battleship *Tirpitz* in Operation Goodwood. From October it was involved in a series of shipping strikes off the Norwegian coast, during which the strength was increased to 21 aircraft by absorbing No.841 Squadron, the Wing then ceasing to exist.

In January 1945 it re-equipped with 21 Avenger Is and IIs, which embarked the following month to join the British Pacific Fleet. In June the squadron reduced to 15 aircraft on becoming part of the 8th Carrier Air Group, and was then involved in attacks on Truk in the Caroline Isles. The following month a series of strikes was made on targets on the Japanese mainland. After VJ-day the ship withdrew to Australia, where No.828 reduced to 12 Avenger Is and IIIs in November. The squadron remained ashore until May 1946 when it discarded its aircraft and re-embarked for the journey home, disbanding on arrival at Devonport on 3 June 1946.

Aircraft Equipment	Period of Service	Example
Albacore I	Sep 1940 - Sep 1943	X8943 (5C)
Swordfish I	Oct 1941 - Nov 1941	
Barracuda II	Mar 1944 - Feb 1945	MD642
Avenger I	Jan 1945 - Sep 1945	JZ278
Avenger II	Feb 1945 - Sep 1945	JZ547
Avenger III	Aug 1945 - May 1946	JZ718

Identification Markings
Albacore 5A+, later S5A+; Barracuda and Avenger single letters.

Battle Honours
Mediterranean	1941-43
Norway	1944
Japan	1945

Commanding Officers
Lt EA Greenwood RN	15 Sep 1940
L/C(A) LA Cubitt RN	26 Sep 1940
L/C DE Langmore DSC RN	6 May 1941
L/C GM Haynes RAN	19 Dec 1941
L/C ME Lashmore DSC RN	30 Nov 1942
L/C A Gregory RN	28 Feb 1943
Lt HH Britton RN	12 Mar 1943
L/C(A) JF Turner RNVR	8 May 1943
Squadron disbanded	1 Sep 1943
L/C(A) FA Swanton DSC RN	1 Mar 1944
L/C(A) RE Bradshaw DSC & Bar RN	31 Aug 1945
Squadron disbanded	3 Jun 1946

Squadron bases
Lee-on-Solent	15 Sep 1940
St Merryn	25 Oct 1940
Campbeltown	18 Nov 1940
Crail (Dt)	21 Jan 1941
	to 23 Mar 1941
Donibristle	17 Mar 1941
Hatston	21 Mar 1941
Sumburgh	23 May 1941
Hatston	24 May 1941
HMS Victorious	2 Jul 1941
Crail	8 Aug 1941
HMS Argus	26 Sep 1941
HMS Ark Royal	16 Oct 1941
Hal Far	18 Oct 1941
Ta Kali	8 Jun 1943
Monastir	28 Jun 1943
Hal Far	8 Jul 1943
Squadron disbanded	1 Sep 1943
Lee-on-Solent	1 Mar 1944
Fearn	14 Apr 1944
Machrihanish	5 Jul 1944
HMS Implacable	8 Aug 1944
HMS Formidable	18 Aug 1944
Donibristle	2 Sep 1944
Machrihanish	13 Sep 1944
HMS Implacable	23 Sep 1944
Hatston	21 Oct 1944
HMS Implacable	24 Oct 1944
Hatston	31 Oct 1944
HMS Implacable	29 Nov 1944
Hatston	9 Dec 1944
HMS Trumpeter (Dt)	24-27 Jan 1945
Fearn	5 Feb 1945
Inskip	10 Feb 1945
Fearn	5 Mar 1945
Hatston	12 Mar 1945
HMS Implacable	13 Mar 1945
Trincomalee	9 Apr 1945
HMS Implacable	22 Apr 1945
Jervis Bay	7 May 1945
HMS Implacable	24 May 1945
Ponam	29 May 1945
HMS Implacable	9 Jun 1945
Ponam (Dt9)	9-12 Jun 1945
HMS Implacable	12 Jun 1945
Nowra	24 Aug 1945
HMS Implacable	5 May 1946
Sqdn disbanded UK	3 Jun 1946

Fairey Albacore X8942 '5B' of No.828 Squadron at Hal Far in 1942. (W.N.Jones)

No.829 Squadron

Badge: On a field blue base barry wavy white and blue, a kingfisher hovering proper
Motto: Non effugient
(They shall not escape)

No.829 Squadron first formed on 15 June 1940 at Ford with nine Albacores for torpedo spotter reconnaissance work. In October it began nightly bombing attacks from St.Eval on shipping and docks at Brest, the CO being lost on 9 October. Next month it joined HMS *Formidable*, which then sailed to escort a convoy to West Africa and Cape Town. Part of the convoy contacted the German cruiser *Admiral Hipper*, but squadron aircraft failed to sight her. Leaving Cape Town in January 1941, the ship sailed for the Red Sea, where her aircraft carried out attacks on Mogadishu and Massawa in February. After passage through the Suez Canal, the squadron had to partially re-equip with Swordfish due to losses.

During the Battle of Matapan, late in March, one of the squadron's Albacores scored a hit on the Italian battleship *Vittorio Veneto*, the CO being unfortunately shot down and killed. Further activities in the Mediterranean involved an attack on the airfield on Scarpanto Island at the end of May, after which the aircraft operated from Lydda for a time, attacking Vichy French shipping during the invasion of Syria, but the ship was badly damaged on 26 May. After a spell ashore in Cyprus the Albacores were withdrawn, and the squadron re-embarked in July to provide anti-submarine patrols with six Swordfish whilst the ship was en route for repairs in the USA, by way of Cape Town.

After being put ashore for a spell in Jamaica, No.829 joined HMS *Illustrious* for passage to Norfolk, Va before rejoining the repaired HMS *Formidable* to return home. Here it re-equipped with 12 new ASV-equipped Swordfish IIs, with which it rejoined HMS *Illustrious* in March. Sailing by way of Cape Town, it participated in an attack on Diego Suarez during the invasion of Madagascar. Successful attacks were carried out on the Vichy French submarines *Bévéziers* and *Le Héros*, and also a sloop and an escort ship, for the loss of five aircraft. Airborne support was provided in September for attacks on the remaining Vichy troops in south Madagascar. Following this the ship sailed to Durban for a refit, and whilst there No.829 was amalgamated with No.810 Squadron at Stamford Hill on 7 October 1942.

On 1 October 1943, No.829 reformed as a torpedo bomber reconnaissance squadron at Lee-on-Solent with 12 Barracuda IIs as part of the 52nd Naval TBR Wing. These embarked in HMS *Victorious* in February 1944, and on 3 April carried out a successful attack on the German battleship *Tirpitz* in Kaa Fjord for the loss of two aircraft. After an abortive attempt to carry out a similar attack in May, attacks were made on shipping off Norway, but on 9 July 1944 No.829 was amalgamated with No.831 Squadron in HMS *Victorious* and ceased to exist.

No.829 next reformed at Culdrose on 4 March 1964 from a nucleus of No.700W Flight, the Wasp IFTU, from which it took over the Wasp commitment. Its task was to provide aircraft flights to operate from small ships and survey vessels, the Wasp performing in the role of medium range anti-submarine torpedo-carrying helicopter. The first four such flights were allocated to the frigates HMS *Leander, Dido, Mohawk* and *Penelope*.

The squadron also took over responsibility for Wessex HAS.1s operating from County Class destroyers, gradual replacement by HAS.3s commencing in 1969. In December 1964 the squadron handed over the task of Wasp conversion to No.706 Squadron, and then moved to Portland. In January 1965 it took over the Whirlwind task of the disbanding No.771 Squadron, returning it when that squadron reformed in June 1967. In 1966 No.829 received two Wessex HU.5s for operation from RFA's *Regent* and *Resource*. Responsibility for the ice patrol ship HMS *Protector* was also

Fairey Swordfish W5848 '3B' of No.829 Squadron picks up a wire landing on HMS Illustrious in 1942. (RAF Museum P.105803)

Westland Wasp HAS.1 XT779 '452' taking off from HMS Galatea during NATO exercises in the Mediterranean in 1971. (via Brian Lowe)

taken over in 1966, initially using Whirlwind HAR.1s, but soon replaced by HAR.9s, which transferred to HMS *Endurance* in 1968, eventually giving way in 1976 to Wasps. In June 1970 responsibility for small ships' Wessexes was transferred to No.737 Squadron at Portland.

A further restructuring took place in January 1972 when No.703 Squadron formed at Portland to take over the Wasp conversion and operational flying training role. In January 1981 the No.703 Squadron task was reabsorbed, and in August 1982 the residual task of parenting Wessex HAS.3 ship's flights was returned by No.737 Squadron. Squadron aircraft participated in the Falklands Task Force, being embarked in HMS *Active*, HMS *Endurance*, HMS *Plymouth*, HMS *Yarmouth*, *MV Contender Bezant* and survey ships.

From Sep 1986 No.829 parented a number of Lynx flights transferred from No.815 Squadron, with more flights transferring in 1987 and 1988, and eventually the squadron had up to 30 Lynx. Flights were regularly deployed on the Armilla patrol and the Squadron was awarded the Boyd Trophy jointly with No.815 Squadron in 1988 for their operational contribution to the Royal Naval presence in the Persian Gulf. Wasp parenting continued until the aircraft was phased out of service in Mar 1988. Between August 1990 and February 1991 several flights were involved in offensive operations in the northern Persian Gulf. The squadron disbanded on 26 March 1993, when parenting of all Lynx flights was absorbed back into No.815 Squadron.

Aircraft Equipment	Period of Service	Example	
Albacore I	Jun 1940 - Aug 1941	L7127	
Swordfish I	Jul 1940 - Sep 1940	L2770	
	Mar 1941 - Dec 1941	W5891	
Swordfish II(ASV)	Dec 1941 - Oct 1942	DK785	
Barracuda II	Oct 1943 - Jul 1944	LS580	(4Q)
Whirlwind HAR.1	Dec 1964 - May 1966	XA868	(449)
Whirlwind HAS.7	Jan 1965 - Jun 1967	XL873	(514)
Whirlwind HAR.9	Jul 1967 - Aug 1976	XL880	(448/ED)
Wasp HAS.1	Mar 1964 - May 1988	XV626	(472/AM)
Wessex HAS.1	Mar 1964 - Jun 1970	XP115	(401/KE)
Wessex HAS.3	Jun 1969 - Jun 1970	XS149	(403/FF)
	Aug 1982 - Jan 1984	XM837	(400/GL)
Wessex HU.5	Oct 1966 - Oct 1976	XT484	(469/RS)
Lynx HAS.2	Sep 1986 - Sep 1988	XZ254	(328/BA)
Lynx HAS.3	Sep 1986 - Mar 1993	ZD567	(365/AY)
Lynx HAS.3 (CTS)	Feb 1991 - Aug 1991	ZF557	(374/VB)

Battle Honours
*Atlantic	1940
Matapan	1941
Mediterranean	1941
Diego Suarez	1942
Norway	1944
Falkland Islands	1982
Kuwait	1991

Westland Wasp HAS.1 XS531 '419' of No.829 Squadron Hydra Flight around 1969/70. (via Brian Lowe)

Identification Markings
Albacore *4A+*; Swordfish *3A+*; Barracuda *4A+*; Whirlwind *511-519/PO* & *448-449/ED:PR*; Wessex, Wasp and Lynx small ship codes.

Westland Wasp HAS.1 XT442 '456' of No.829 Squadron Yarmouth Flight in 1972. (via Brian Lowe)

Squadron bases

Ford	15 Jun 1940		Tanga (daily	18 Aug 1942
Campbeltown (Dt6)	14 Jul 1940		detachments to	
	to 10 Aug 1940		Port Reitz)	
Campbeltown	23 Aug 1940		HMS Illustrious	29 Aug 1942
St Merryn	14 Sep 1940		Stamford Hill	21 Sep 1942
St Eval	7 Oct 1940		Squadron disbanded	7 Oct 1942
Crail	3 Nov 1940		Lee-on-Solent	1 Oct 1943
HMS Formidable	15 Nov 1940		Tain	25 Nov 1943
Dekheila	11 Mar 1941		Machrihanish	8 Feb 1944
HMS Formidable	15 Mar 1941		HMS Victorious	
Dekheila	30 Mar 1941		(DLT)	12 Feb 1944
HMS Formidable	18 Apr 1941		Machrihanish	15 Feb 1944
Dekheila	23 Apr 1941		HMS Victorious	8 Mar 1944
HMS Formidable	25 May 1941		Machrihanish	11 Apr 1944
Dekheila	27 May 1941		HMS Victorious	17 Apr 1944
Lydda	17 Jun 1941		Hatston	3 May 1944
Nicosia	1 Jul 1941		HMS Victorious	3-12 May 1944
HMS Formidable	24 Jul 1941		(Dt3)	
Palisadoes	23 Aug 1941		Burscough	20 May 1944
HMS Illustrious	2 Dec 1941		HMS Victorious	26 May 1944
Norfolk	8 Dec 1941		Hatston (Dt5)	27 May 1944
HMS Formidable	10 Dec 1941			to 9 Jun 1944
Eastleigh	21 Dec 1941		Squadron disbanded	9 Jul 1944
Lee-on-Solent	30 Jan 1942		Culdrose	4 Mar 1964
Speke	19 Feb 1942		Portland	1 Dec 1964
Ternhill (transit)	24 Feb 1942		(see Appendix	
Machrihanish	25 Feb 1942		for Ship's Flights)	
HMS Illustrious	7 Mar 1942		Squadron disbanded	26 Mar 1993

Westland Wasp HAS.1 XT439 '442/ZU' of No.829 Squadron Zulu Flight in 1979. (MAP)

Commanding Officers

L/C OS Stevinson RN		15 Jun 1940
L/C J Dalyell-Stead RN		12 Oct 1940
L/C LCB Ashburner RN		29 Mar 1941
L/C FM Griffiths RN		24 Dec 1941
Squadron disbanded		7 Oct 1942
L/C(A) GPC Williams DSC RN		1 Oct 1943
L/C(A) DW Phillips RN		3 Mar 1944
Squadron disbanded		9 Jul 1944
L/C KM Mitchell DFC RN		4 Mar 1964
L/C JRJ Rutherford RN		1 Dec 1964
L/C JM Shrives RN		13 Sep 1965
L/C N Usworth RN		14 Dec 1967
L/C M Forrest RN		19 Sep 1969
L/C BG Skinner RN		26 Jul 1971
L/C NCH James RN		26 Feb 1973
L/C MW Attrill RN		17 Jul 1974
L/C DA Scott RN		12 Mar 1976
L/C AL Horton RN		12 Dec 1977
L/C NPM Whinney RN		18 May 1979
L/C CJ Clay RN		17 Dec 1980
L/C MJ Mullane RN		1 Sep 1981
L/C GC Kent RN		7 Dec 1983
L/C WA Pollock RN		12 Feb 1985
L/C JPS Greenop RN		7 Apr 1987
L/C MR Legg RN		20 Jul 1989
L/C BS Leyshon RN		26 Jun 1990
L/C PA McKay RN		20 May 1992
Squadron disbanded		26 Mar 1993

Westland Wasp HAS.1 XS545 '182/GA' of No.829 Squadron Galatea Flight in 1964. (MAP)

Westland/Aerospatiale Lyncx HAS.3 XZ228 '-/LN' of No.829 Sqdn London Flight in 1989. (MAP)

Westland/Aerospatiale Lynx HAS.3 XZ696 '336/CV' of No.829 Squadron Coventry Flight in 1989. (MAP)

No.830 Squadron

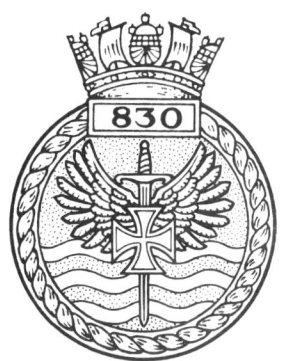

Badge: On a field per fesse wavy blue and barry wavy of six white and blue, a sword erect point downward, proper winged gold surmounted by a Maltese Cross white

Motto: In via gloriae
(In the way of glory)

No.830 Squadron first formed on 1 July 1940 out of No.767 deck landing training squadron on the arrival at Malta of 12 Swordfish, for shore-based operations. A dive bombing attack was made on oil storage tanks in Sicily in August, and during the remainder of the year operations were carried out against targets in Sicily and Libya as well as a bombing attack on a U-boat on 19 July. Similar activities continued throughout 1941, including minelaying, bombing and torpedo attacks. The range of the Swordfish was increased in this, as in other squadrons, by replacing the third crew member by a 50 gallon saddle tank fitted in the rear cockpit, and in May 1941 the leader aircraft were fitted with ASV radar. Most operations were carried out by night, being joined in these by No.828 Squadron in October 1941.

By March 1942 strength was down to three serviceable aircraft, and consequently it amalgamated with No.828 to operate as the Naval Air Squadron Malta, though retaining its separate identity. Its few remaining aircraft acted in conjunction with the Albacores of No.828 for which they provided target illumination. The arrival of two final replacement Swordfish in May enabled the squadron to continue its role, but by the end of the year strength was at such a low ebb that the remaining aircraft were used to bring No.828 up to full strength, and No.830 then only existed on paper, officially disbanding on 31 March 1943. During its period in Malta the squadron, together with No.828, had accounted for 30 enemy ships sunk and another 50 damaged.

On 15 May 1943, No.830 reformed at Lee-on-Solent as a torpedo bomber reconnaissance squadron equipped with 12 Barracuda IIs, most of the aircrew being New Zealanders. Joining No.8 Naval TBR Wing in October it embarked in HMS *Furious* with a reduced strength of nine aircraft for operations with the Home Fleet off Norway. In Operation *Tungsten*, it carried out a surprise diving attack with No.827 Squadron against the German battleship *Tirpitz* in Kaa Fjord on 3 April 1944, ten bomb hits were scored for the loss of only one squadron aircraft. Further similar attacks in May had to be cancelled owing to bad weather. A final attack, Operation *Goodwood*, was mounted on 17 July, the squadron being temporarily embarked in HMS *Formidable*, but surprise was lost and a thick smoke screen prevented any bombs reaching their target. The squadron rejoined HMS *Furious* in August for a Norwegian strike, but on 3 October 1944 it was disbanded into No.827 Squadron at Hatston.

No.830 next reformed at Ford on 21 November 1955 as a torpedo strike squadron with nine Wyvern S.4s, with which it embarked in HMS *Eagle* in April 1956 for an exercise in the Mediterranean. In November 1956 it was active during the Suez War, making 82 sorties in which it attacked airfields and other targets in the Canal Zone. The ship returned home at the end of the year, and No.830 disbanded on arrival on 5 January 1957.

Identification Markings
Swordfish single letters; Barracuda *5A+*; Wyvern *124-128/J* to 2.56, then *370-379/J*.

Aircraft Equipment	Period of Service	Example
Swordfish I	Jul 1940 - Mar 1943	K8866 (S)
Skua II	Oct 1940 - Nov 1940	
Albacore I	Sep 1940 - Jul 1942	T9232
Barracuda II	May 1943 - Oct 1944	BV937 (5H)
Wyvern S.4	Nov 1955 - Jan 1957	WP338 (377/J)

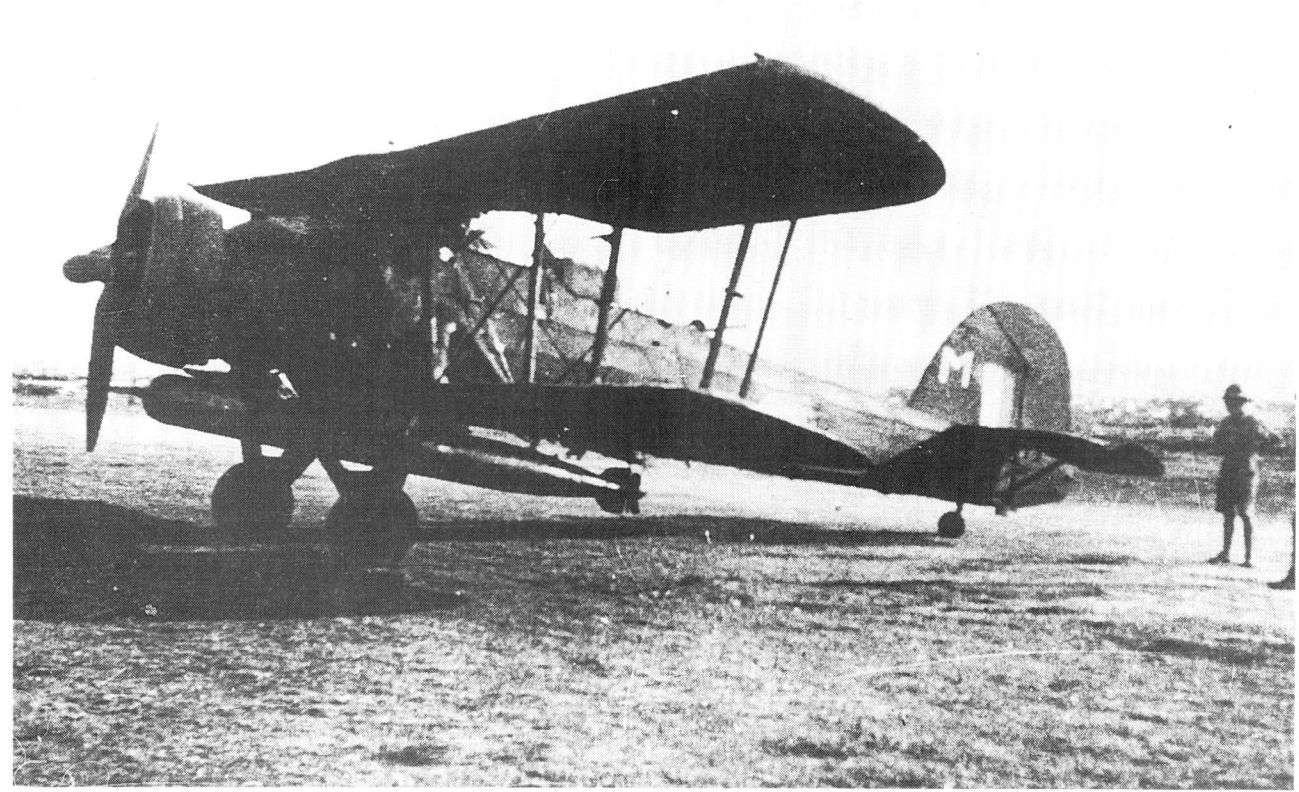

Fairey Swordfish 'M' of No.830 Squadron, Hal Far visiting Ta Kali. (J.Alton/Malta National War Museum)

Battle Honours		Squadron bases	
Mediterranean	1940-42	HMS Furious	9 Aug 1944
Norway	1944	Hatston	13 Sep 1944
		Squadron disbanded	3 Oct 1944
Squadron bases		Ford	21 Nov 1955
Hal Far	1 Jul 1940	HMS Eagle	16 Apr 1956
Squadron disbanded	31 Mar 1943	Hal Far (Dt6)	7-22 May 1956
Lee-on-Solent	15 May 1943	Hal Far	29 Jun 1956
Hatston	18 Jun 1943	HMS Eagle	16 Jul 1956
Machrihanish	16 Aug 1943	Hal Far (Dt6)	3-14 Aug 1956
HMS Furious	9 Oct 1943	Hal Far (Dt4)	23 Aug 1956
Hatston	6 Dec 1943		to 4 Sep 1956
HMS Furious	10 Dec 1943	Hal Far (Dt4)	5-9 Oct 1956
Hatston	14 Dec 1943	North Front(Dt3)	13-20 Oct 1956
HMS Furious	26 Dec 1943	Hal Far (Dt6)	30 Nov 1956
Hatston	3 Jan 1944		to 11 Dec 1956
HMS Furious	8 Feb 1944	Sqdn disbanded UK	5 Jan 1957
Hatston	14 Feb 1944		
HMS Furious	24 Feb 1944	**Commanding Officers**	
Hatston	29 Feb 1944	L/C FD Howie	
HMS Furious	17 Mar 1944	DSO RN	1 Jul 1940
Hatston	22 Mar 1944	Lt HEH Pain RN	1 Aug 1940
HMS Furious	28 Mar 1944	L/C JG Hunt RN	1 Sep 1941
Donibristle	7 Apr 1944	L/C FHE Hopkins RN	6 Dec 1941
HMS Furious	20 Apr 1944	L/C AJT Roe RN	7 Jun 1942
Hatston	28 Apr 1944	Lt A Gregory RN	23 Feb 1943
HMS Furious	3 May 1944	Squadron disbanded	31 Mar 1943
Hatston	18 May 1944	L/C(A) FH Fox RN	24 May 1943
HMS Furious	28 May 1944	L/C(A) RD Kingdon	
Hatston	17 Jun 1944	DSC RNVR	21 Jan 1944
HMS Furious	22 Jun 1944	Squadron disbanded	3 Oct 1944
Hatston	23 Jun 1944	L/C CV Howard RN	21 Nov 1955
HMS Formidable	9 Jul 1944	Squadron disbanded	5 Jan 1957
Hatston	19 Jul 1944		

Westland Wyvern S.4 WP337 '378/J' of No.830 Squadron landing at Stretton in 1957. (via Ray Williams)

No.831 Squadron

Badge: On a white field, issuant from water wavy in base blue and white a clenched gauntlet proper upon which is perched an eagle black

Motto: *Aquila non capit muscas* (Eagles don't catch flies)

No.831 Squadron first formed at Crail on 1 April 1941 as a torpedo spotter reconnaissance squadron with 12 Albacores. These embarked in October in HMS *Indomitable*, which then sailed for Jamaica to work up. At the end of the year the ship crossed the South Atlantic to Cape Town, continuing in January 1942 to Port Sudan and then across the Indian Ocean to Java to ferry 50 RAF Hurricanes. During all this period and the later voyage to Aden via Colombo and Addu Atoll, No.831 carried out anti-submarine patrols, but sighted nothing. After a spell ashore at Khormaksar for local patrol duties, the squadron re-embarked for the Indian Ocean. During the invasion of Madagascar in June they carried out dive bombing attacks, anti-submarine patrols and close support. After sailing around the Cape to Gibraltar, the ship was damaged during a replenishment convoy to Malta in August, disembarking her squadrons at home before sailing on to the United States for repairs. The squadron was temporarily reduced to nine aircraft at this time, a few Barracuda Is being briefly on strength.

No.831 re-embarked in March 1943, but went ashore in May to re-equip with 12 Barracuda IIs. With these it joined the No.52 Naval TBR Wing in November, embarking in HMS *Victorious* in February 1944 for deck landing training. The following month it joined HMS *Furious* for an attack on the German battleship *Tirpitz* on 3 April in which several hits were scored. In May it returned to HMS *Victorious* for another attempt, but bad weather intervened. After strikes against shipping off Norway the ship returned home.

HMS *Victorious* sailed to join the Eastern Fleet, and on 9 July No.831 absorbed No.829 Squadron to increase its strength to 21 aircraft, the Wing then ceasing to exist. Later in the month No.831 dive bombed installations and oil storage tanks in Sabang harbour, Sumatra, and also attacked two airfields in the area. A similar raid was carried out in August on Emmahaven, near Padang. The aircraft had their limitations in tropical climates, and it was decided to replace them with Avengers. Consequently No.831 discarded its machines in November and returned home in HMS *Battler* and HMS *Thane*, to disband at Lee-on-Solent on 6 December 1944.

On 21 November 1955 No.831 reformed at Ford as a torpedo strike squadron with 9 Wyverns. It was not until January 1957 that these embarked in HMS *Ark Royal* for a brief visit to Gibraltar and Malta. In May 1957 they re-embarked for a Royal Review in the Moray Firth, then the ship sailed for America, where they participated in cross-operations and exercises with USS *Saratoga*, returning home in July. After two further period embarked in Home waters, the squadron disbanded at Ford on 10 December 1957.

No.831 reformed at Culdrose on 1 May 1958 as an Electronic Warfare squadron by renumbering No.751 Squadron, initially with four Avenger AS.6s and four Sea Venom 21ECMs, operated respectively by 'A' and 'B' Flights. These participated in numerous exercises, embarking from time to time in Fleet carriers. 'B' Flight re-equipped with five Sea Venom 22ECMs from April 1960, though 21s were still in service in 1964. 'A' Flight had two Gannet AS.1s for a time, then in February 1959 it began to replace its Avengers with Gannet ECM.6s. In 1960 the squadron received the annual Boyd Trophy award for efficiency in training with the Fleet. A Sea Prince was added in 1962, and in July 1963 the squadron headquarters moved to Watton for better liaison with its RAF counterpart. On 16 May 1966 the squadron was paid off when the remaining personnel transferred to No.360 Squadron, RAF for joint RAF/RN trials and training in ECM work. No.831 officially disbanded on 26 August 1966.

Battle Honours
Diego Suarez 1942
Malta Convoys 1942
Norway 1944
Sabang 1944

Identification Markings
Albacore *4A+*; Barracuda *5A+*; Wyvern *143-149/J* in error initially but probably not carried, then *380-388/J:O:FD*; Avenger *380-383*, to *265-268* 3.59; Gannet/Sea Venom/Sea Vampire/Sea Prince *270-279*, to *381-398/CU* 3.62.

Aircraft Equipment	Period of Service	Example
Albacore I	Apr 1941 - Jun 1943	BF661 (4B)
Swordfish I	Jan 1942 - May 1942	K8400 (Y)
Barracuda I	Dec 1942 - Jan 1943	P9657
Barracuda II	Jun 1943 - Nov 1944	LS637 (5R)
Wyvern S.4	Nov 1955 - Dec 1957	WP337 (384/O)
Avenger AS.6	May 1958 - Jun 1959	XB446 (268/CU)
Gannet AS.1	May 1958 - 1958	XA340 (279)
Gannet ECM.4	Feb 1959 - Feb 1961	WN464 (275)
Gannet ECM.6	Feb 1961 - May 1966	XG831 (396/CU)
Sea Venom 21ECM	May 1958 - Oct 1964	XG608 (272)
Sea Venom 22ECM	Apr 1960 - May 1966	WW292 (381)
Sea Vampire T.22	Nov 1958 - May 1964	XA155 (279)
Sea Prince T.1	May 1962 - May 1966	WF122 (390)

Squadron bases

Crail	1 Apr 1941
Machrihanish	26 Aug 1941
HMS Indomitable	15 Oct 1941
Norfolk	10 Nov 1941
HMS Indomitable	22 Nov 1941
Wynberg	31 Dec 1941
HMS Indomitable	2 Jan 1942
China Bay	2 Feb 1942
Ratmalana	5 Feb 1942
China Bay	6 Feb 1942
Ratmalana	10 Feb 1942
China Bay	11 Feb 1942
HMS Indomitable	16 Feb 1942
Khormaksar	23 Feb 1942
HMS Indomitable	16 Mar 1942
Mackinnon Road	23 May 1942
HMS Indomitable	9 Jul 1942
Crail	27 Aug 1942

Squadron bases

Lee-on-Solent	27 Dec 1942
Hatston	1 Jan 1943
Machrihanish	22 Feb 1943
HMS Indomitable	3 Mar 1943
Lee-on-Solent	19 May 1943
Machrihanish	9 Aug 1943
Maydown	23 Oct 1943
Machrihanish	6 Nov 1943
Hatston	11 Jan 1944
Machrihanish	11 Feb 1944
HMS Victorious (DLT)	12 Feb 1944
Machrihanish	15 Feb 1944
HMS Victorious	8 Mar 1944
HMS Furious	28 Mar 1944
HMS Victorious	8 Apr 1944
HMS Furious	20 Apr 1944
Hatston	3 May 1944

Squadron bases

HMS Victorious	11 May 1944
Burscough	20 May 1944
HMS Victorious	26 May 1944
Katukurunda	7 Jul 1944
HMS Victorious	19 Jul 1944
Minneriya	27 Jul 1944
HMS Victorious	4 Aug 1944
Katukurunda	28 Aug 1944
Minneriya	10 Oct 1944
HMS Battler (crews)	7 Nov 1944
HMS Thane (crews)	22 Nov 1944
Lee-on-Solent	6 Dec 1944
Squadron disbanded	6 Dec 1944
Ford	21 Nov 1955
HMS Eagle (DLT)	16 Apr 1956
Ford	18 Apr 1956
Lossiemouth	18 Jun 1956
Ford	8 Jul 1956
Lossiemouth	6 Oct 1956
Ford	26 Oct 1956
HMS Ark Royal	9 Jan 1957
Hal Far	24 Jan 1957
HMS Ark Royal	6 Feb 1957
Ford	25 Feb 1957
HMS Ark Royal	3 May 1957
Ford	18 Jul 1957
HMS Ark Royal	28 Aug 1957
Ford	2 Sep 1957
Culdrose	28 Oct 1957
Ford	2 Nov 1957
HMS Ark Royal	13 Nov 1957
Lossiemouth	25 Nov 1957
Ford	10 Dec 1957
Squadron disbanded	10 Dec 1957
Culdrose	1 May 1958
Watton	26 Jul 1963
Squadron disbanded	16 May 1966
Sqdn operated as A & B Flights	

831A Flight - (Avenger/Gannet):

Squadron bases

Culdrose	1 May 1958
Watton	15 Oct 1958
Culdrose	20 Oct 1958
Abbotsinch (Dt2)	4-11 May 1959
Lossiemouth	25 May 1959
Sola	8 Jun 1959
Culdrose	12 Jun 1959
El Adem	17 Jun 1959
Culdrose	27 Jun 1959
Lossiemouth (Dt2)	21 Sep 1959
Andoya (Dt2)	21-24 Sep 1959
Hal Far	4 Nov 1959
Hyeres	2 Dec 1959
Culdrose	8 Dec 1959
HMS Victorious (Dt2)	27 Jan 1960 to 22 Feb 1960
Hal Far	29 Feb 1960
North Front (Dt2)	14-29 Mar 1960
Culdrose	7 Apr 1960
Hal Far (Dt2)	2-13 May 1960
Valkenburg	18 May 1960
Culdrose	23 May 1960
Decimomannu (Dt2)	14-15 Jun 1960
Hal Far	15 Jun 1960
Culdrose	22 Aug 1960
Lossiemouth (Dt2)	26-30 Aug 1960
Bodö	23 Sep 1960
Culdrose	3 Oct 1960
Valkenburg (Dt2)	19-20 Oct 1960
HMS Ark Royal	26 Oct 1960
Culdrose	30 Oct 1960
HMS Ark Royal	27 Nov 1960
Hal Far	2 Dec 1960
Culdrose	14 Dec 1960
Hal Far	17 Dec 1960

Westland Wyvern S.4 WN324 '380/J' of No.831 Sqdn, HMS Eagle in 1956.

Fairey Gannet ECM.6 XA459 '394/CU' of No.831 Squadron, Culdrose in 1963. (MAP)

Squadron bases
Culdrose	10 Feb 1961
HMS Ark Royal	12 Mar 1961
Hal Far	28 Apr 1961
HMS Hermes (Dt2-DLP)	15 May 1961
Culdrose	20 May 1961
HMS Hermes(Dt2)	7-14 Jun 1961
HMS Hermes	14 Jun 1961
Hal Far (Dt2)	29 Jun 1961
to	15 Jul 1961
Culdrose	17 Jul 1961
Hal Far	24 Aug 1961
to	12 Sep 1961
Lossiemouth	13 Oct 1961
Culdrose	27 Oct 1961
Hal Far (Dt2)	23 Nov 1961
to	13 Dec 1961
North Front (Dt2)	8 Mar 1962
to	2 Apr 1962
Detachment of 2 a/c:	
HMS Ark Royal	10 Mar 1962
Seletar	12 Apr 1962
HMS Ark Royal	24 Apr 1962
Seletar	13 Sep 1962
HMS Ark Royal	28 Sep 1962
Culdrose	14 Dec 1962
Hal Far (Dt1)	1-7 May 1962
Lossiemouth(Dt3)	13-25 Jun 1962
Sola (Dt3)	25-28 Jun 1962
Hal Far (Dt2)	19-25 Sep 1962
Orange (Dt2)	25 Sep 1962
to	3 Oct 1962
Ballykelly (Dt2)	22-28 Nov 1962
Ballykelly (Dt2)	14-22 Jan 1963
Lann-Bihoue (Dt2)	21 Feb 1963
to	8 Mar 1963
Ballykelly (Dt2)	26 Mar 1963
to	2 Apr 1963
Ballykelly (Dt2)	11-13 Jun 1963
Lossiemouth(Dt2)	4-25 Oct 1963
Culdrose (Dt2)	17-30 Jan 1964
North Front (Dt3)	20 Feb 1964
to	13 Mar 1964
Sola (Dt2)	1-4 May 1964
Hal Far (Dt2)	9-22 Jul 1964
Lossiemouth(Dt2)	18-21 Sep 1964
Lossiemouth (Dt2)	4-8 Oct 1964
Brawdy (Dt2)	16-19 Nov 1964

Squadron bases
Lossiemouth (Dt3)	20 Feb 1965
to	6 Mar 1965
Akrotiri (Dt3)	5-15 Jun 1965
Hal Far (Dt3)	19-26 Jul 1965
Rygge (Dt3)	7-10 Sep 1965
Lossiemouth(Dt2)	14-16 Sep 1965
Ballykelly (Dt2)	20-22 Sep 1965
Hal Far (Dt2)	5-12 Oct 1965
Yeovilton (Dt3)	18-21 Oct 1965
Ballykelly (Dt2)	9-11 Nov 1965
North Front (Dt3)	10 Feb 1966
to	3 Mar 1966
Squadron disbanded	16 May 1966

831B Flight (Sea Venom):

Squadron bases
Culdrose	1 May 1958
HMS Eagle	22 May 1958
Hal Far	4 Jul 1958
Culdrose	6 Nov 1958
HMS Victorious	19 Nov 1958
Culdrose	8 Dec 1958
Hal Far	9 Feb 1959
Culdrose	7 Mar 1959
Lossiemouth	25 May 1959
Sola	8 Jun 1959

Squadron bases
Culdrose	12 Jun 1959
El Adem	17 Jun 1959
Culdrose	23 Jun 1959
HMS Victorious	15 Sep 1959
Culdrose	2 Oct 1959
HMS Victorious	30 Oct 1959
Culdrose	14 Dec 1959
Valkenburg(Dt2)	18-23 May 1960
Hal Far	14 Jun 1960
Culdrose	4 Jul 1960
Lossiemouth (Dt2)	26 Aug 1960
to	1 Sep 1960

de Havilland Sea Venom 22ECM WW221 '381/CU of No.831 Squadron, Culdrose in 1963. (MAP)

Grumman Avenger AS.6 XB375 '382' of No.831 Squadron, Watton, with 'Champagne Charlie' motif on the nose, in 1958. (MAP)

Squadron bases

Bodö (Dt2)	23 Sep 1960
	to 3 Oct 1960
Valkenburg (Dt2)	19-20 Oct 1960
Hal Far	11 Nov 1960
HMS Ark Royal	27 Nov 1960
Hal Far	2 Dec 1960
Culdrose	13 Dec 1960
Valkenburg	12 May 1961
Culdrose	15 May 1961
Lossiemouth	7 Jun 1961
Sola	20 Jun 1961
Culdrose	22 Jun 1961
Hal Far (Dt2)	24 Aug 1961
	to 11 Sep 1961
Lossiemouth	23 Oct 1961
Culdrose	27 Oct 1961
Hal Far (Dt2)	23 Nov 1961
	to 13 Dec 1961
North Front	8 Mar 1962
Culdrose	2 Apr 1962
Hal Far (Dt2)	1-7 May 1962
Lossiemouth (Dt2)	13-25 Jun 1962
Sola (Dt2)	25-28 Jun 1962
Hal Far	13 Jul 1962
North Front	20 Jul 1962
Culdrose	27 Jul 1962
Hal Far	19 Sep 1962
Orange (transit)	25 Sep 1962
Culdrose	27 Sep 1962
Valkenburg	29 Sep 1962
Culdrose	1 Oct 1962
Ballykelly	22 Nov 1962
Culdrose	28 Nov 1962
Ballykelly (Dt2)	14-22 Jan 1963
Hal Far	10 Jan 1963
Culdrose	1 Feb 1963
Lann-Bihoue	22 Feb 1963
Culdrose	8 Mar 1963
Ballykelly (Dt2)	26 Mar 1963
	to 2 Apr 1963
Ballykelly (Dt2)	11-13 Jun 1963
Watton	26 Jul 1963
Lossiemouth	7 Oct 1963
Watton	11 Oct 1963
Lossiemouth	15 Oct 1963
Watton	28 Oct 1963
Ballykelly (Dt2)	2-3 Dec 1963
Culdrose	18 Jan 1964
Watton	31 Jan 1964
North Front	21 Feb 1964
Watton	10 Mar 1964
Hal Far	12 Oct 1964
Watton	19 Oct 1964
Brawdy	16 Nov 1964
Watton	19 Nov 1964
Lossiemouth	20 Feb 1965
Watton	6 Mar 1965
Valkenburg	20 May 1965
Watton	3 Jun 1965
Yeovilton (Dt2)	20-28 Oct 1965
Sola (Dt2)	2-13 May 1966
Squadron disbanded	16 May 1966

Commanding Officers

L/C PL Mortimer RN 1 Apr 1941
L/C AG Leatham RN 1 Jul 1942
L/C(A) DEC Eyres
    RN 8 May 1943
L/C EM Britton RN 15 Sep 1943
L/C V Rance RN 4 Jan 1944
L/C(A) D Brooks
    DSC RNVR 13 Feb 1944
L/C(A) JL Fisher
    RNVR 6 May 1944
Squadron disbanded 6 Dec 1944
L/C SC Farquhar RN 21 Nov 1955
Squadron disbanded 10 Dec 1957
L/C WJ Hanks RN 1 May 1958
L/C BJ Williams RN 16 Jul 1959
L/C DK Blair RN 16 May 1961
L/C JG Grindle RN 30 May 1963
L/C MJ Bateman RN 9 Apr 1964
L/C H Ellis RN 11 Jun 1965
Squadron disbanded 16 May 1966

Percival Sea Prince T.1 WF122 '390', ECM classroom conversion of No.831 Squadron at Le Bourget airport in June 1963. (MAP)

No.832 Squadron

No.832 Squadron formed at Lee-on-Solent on 1 April 1941 as a torpedo spotter reconnaissance squadron with 12 Albacores. These embarked in HMS *Victorious* in August 1941, which then sailed for Northern waters. On 12 September attacks were carried out on shipping off the Lofoten Islands and the following month similar activities were carried out in the Bödo area. In November the ship sailed to Iceland, returning to that area in February 1942, in which month the CO was lost whilst searching for enemy naval units in bad weather off Norway. After escorting a North Russian convoy in March, the squadron participated in an unsuccessful attack on the German battleship *Tirpitz*, then returned to North Russian convoy duty. This task ended in July when the ship sailed to escort a fast Malta convoy in Operation Pedestal.

In October 1942 the squadron re-embarked to take part in the North African landings. During this period No.832 attacked forts at Algiers and carried out anti-submarine patrols before returning to be reunited with a sub-flight which had remained at Manston for minelaying and anti-shipping strikes. In December the squadron re-embarked for the United States, where it rearmed in January 1943 with 12 US Navy Avenger TBF-1s before sailing through the Panama Canal for the Pacific. In May the ship made a sweep in the Coral Sea area, No.832 transferring the following month to USS *Saratoga* for operations in support of landings in the Mid Solomons. Rejoining HMS *Victorious*, it sailed home via Pearl Harbour, and on arrival re-equipped with 12 Avenger Is at Hatston in September for operations against enemy shipping.

In January 1944, four Wildcat Vs of No.1832 Squadron's 'C' Flight were added to the squadron, which embarked the following month in HMS *Athene* and HMS *Engadine* for passage to Ceylon. Disembarking in April, it joined HMS *Illustrious* for a bombing attack on Sourabaya on 17 May. No.832 then transferred to HMS *Begum* and for the next six months carried out trade protection in the Indian Ocean, the strength being reduced to nine in October. The ship sailed for the United Kingdom in the New Year and the squadron disbanded on arrival on 21 February 1945.

Identification Markings
Albacore & Avenger 4A+; Wildcat believed single letters.

Aircraft Equipment	Period of Service	Example
Albacore I	Apr 1941 - Dec 1942	X9116 (4A)
Avenger TBF-1	Jan 1943 - Nov 1943	BuAer06002
Avenger I	Sep 1943 - Jan 1945	JZ180 (4B)
Wildcat V	Jan 1944 - Jan 1945	JV459 (Y)

Battle Honours
Malta Convoys	1942
North Africa	1942
Arctic	1942

Squadron bases
Lee-on-Solent	1 Apr 1941
Campbeltown	29 May 1941
Strabane	16 Jun 1941
Hatston (transit)	14 Aug 1941
HMS Victorious	14 Aug 1941
Twatt (Dt6)	20-23 Sep 1941
Hatston	26 Oct 1941
HMS Victorious	3 Nov 1941
Hatston (Dt6)	3-22 Dec 1941
HMS Victorious	23 Dec 1941
Hatston	23 Feb 1942
HMS Victorious	4 Mar 1942
Hatston	11 Mar 1942
HMS Victorious	19 Mar 1942
Hatston	9 Apr 1942
HMS Victorious	12 Apr 1942
Hatston	18 Apr 1942
HMS Victorious	21 Apr 1942
Hatston	6 May 1942
HMS Victorious	12 May 1942
Reykjavik	8 Jun 1942
HMS Victorious	14 Jun 1942
Hatston	16 Jun 1942
HMS Victorious	29 Jun 1942
Hatston	7 Jul 1942
HMS Victorious	30 Jul 1942
Crail	21 Aug 1942
Machrihanish	10 Sep 1942
Crail	20 Sep 1942
Manston (Dt3)	23 Sep 1942 to 22 Nov 1942
Machrihanish	24 Sep 1942
HMS Victorious	19 Oct 1942
Crail	22 Nov 1942
Machrihanish	8 Dec 1942
HMS Victorious	11 Dec 1942
Norfolk	1 Jan 1943
HMS Victorious	3 Feb 1943
Ford Island	6 Mar 1943
HMS Victorious	7 May 1943
Tontouta Field	3 Jun 1943
HMS Victorious	16 Jun 1943
Tontouta Field	20 Jun 1943
USS Saratoga	27 Jun 1943
HMS Victorious	24 Jul 1943
Hatston	26 Sep 1943
Machrihanish	4 Dec 1943
Maydown	2 Jan 1944
Machrihanish	9 Jan 1944
HMS Ravager (DLT)	8 Feb 1944
Machrihanish	8 Feb 1944
Abbotsinch	12 Feb 1944
HMS Athene/HMS Engadine (crews)	27 Feb 1944
Katukurunda	15 Apr 1944
HMS Unicorn(DLT)	29 Apr 1944
Katukurunda	29 Apr 1944
HMS Illustrious	3 May 1944
Katukurunda (Dt - Fighter Flt)	3-25 May 1944
Katukurunda	25 May 1944
HMS Begum	26 May 1944
China Bay	8 Jun 1944
HMS Begum	14 Jun 1944
Colombo Racecourse	2 Jul 1944
HMS Begum	23 Jul 1944
Katukurunda	30 Jul 1944
HMS Begum	3 Aug 1944
Katukurunda	12 Oct 1944
HMS Begum	21 Oct 1944
Colombo Racecourse	22 Dec 1944
HMS Begum	15 Jan 1945
Sqdn disbanded UK	21 Feb 1945

Commanding Officers
L/C AJP Plugge RN	1 Apr 1941
L/C WJ Lucas RN	27 Feb 1942
L/C(A) FKA Low RN	24 Nov 1942
L/C(A) J Randall RNVR	14 Oct 1944
Squadron disbanded	21 Feb 1945

Fairey Albacore X9034 '4L' of No.832 Squadron at Kaldadarnes, Iceland in 1942. (RAF Museum P.11814)

No.833 Squadron

No.833 Squadron formed at Lee-on-Solent on 8 December 1941 as a torpedo bomber reconnaissance squadron with nine Swordfish Is. Originally intended for the ill-fated HMS *Dasher*, the squadron reduced to six aircraft in May 1942, eventually joining HMS *Biter* instead, in September. In October it sailed to take part in the North African landings, 'A' Flight being in HMS *Biter* and 'B' Flight in HMS *Avenger*, each with three Swordfish IIs. The squadron disembarked to Gibraltar in November, and carried out anti-submarine patrols before returning home in HMS *Argus* at the end of the year.

In February 1943 No.833 was attached to RAF Coastal Command. Moving to Thorney Island it took over the aircraft of No.825 Squadron to carry out night patrols, minelaying and shipping attacks in the English Channel. In April it flew north to Scotland where it increased to nine aircraft, a fighter flight of six Seafire L.IICs being added in June. The following month six Swordfish and six Seafires embarked for Gibraltar in HMS *Stalker*, but on arrival the Seafires transferred to No.880 Squadron and the Swordfish then operated as No.833Z Squadron. After returning to the United Kingdom the squadron strength was restored to nine Swordfish IIs, moving to Maydown in December for MAC-ship operations, but under a change of policy this activity was centralised, and it disbanded on 7 January 1944 to become part of No.836 Squadron.

On 26 April 1944, No.833 reformed aboard HMS *Activity* with three Swordfish IIs detached from No.836 Squadron 'F' Flight, and a fighter flight of 7 Wildcat Vs from Nos.816 and 819 Squadrons. Anti-submarine patrols and fighter protection were then provided during a North Russian convoy, a similar task being performed in May and June for an Atlantic convoy. After carrying out the same duties to Gibraltar and return in July and August, the squadron returned home to disband at Eglinton on 13 September 1944.

Battle Honours
North Africa	1942
Atlantic	1944
Arctic	1944

Identification Markings
Swordfish single letters, to 5A+ 6.43; Seafire 5A+; Wildcat unknown.

Aircraft Equipment
Aircraft	Period of Service	Example
Swordfish I	Dec 1941 - Nov 1942	V4455 (C)
Swordfish II	May 1942 - Jan 1944	DK701 (5B)
Seafire L.IIc	Jun 1943 - Sep 1943	NM946 (5Y)
Swordfish II	Apr 1944 - Sep 1944	LS280
Wildcat V	Apr 1944 - Sep 1944	JV356

Squadron bases
Lee-on-Solent	8 Dec 1941
Gosport	29 Dec 1941
Lee-on-Solent	5 Jan 1942
Crail	5 Feb 1942
Hatston	21 Mar 1942
Machrihanish	2 Apr 1942
HMS Biter	2 Sep 1942
Stretton	30 Sep 1942
Machrihanish	22 Oct 1942
HMS Biter (A Flt)/ HMS Avenger(B Flt)	23 Oct 1942
North Front	11 Nov 1942
HMS Argus	25 Dec 1942
Stretton	31 Dec 1942
Thorney Island(16Gp)	1 Feb 1943
St Eval (19 Gp)	11 Mar 1943
Machrihanish	15 Apr 1943
Ballykelly	30 May 1943
Machrihanish	15 Jun 1943
HMS Stalker	7 Jul 1943
Machrihanish (Dt3)	29 Jul 1943 to 13 Aug 1943
North Front (Z Flt - Swordfish)	9 Aug 1943 to 21 Sep 1943
Machrihanish	5 Oct 1943
Dunino	6 Oct 1943
Maydown	15 Dec 1943
Squadron disbanded	7 Jan 1944
HMS Activity	26 Apr 1944
Machrihanish	10 Jun 1944
HMS Activity	16 Jun 1944
Maydown	8 Sep 1944
Eglinton (Fighter Flight)	7 Sep 1944
Squadron disbanded	13 Sep 1944

Commanding Officers
L/C RJH Stephens RN	8 Dec 1941
Capt WGS Aston RM	14 Jan 1943
L/C JRC Callander	17 May 1943
Squadron disbanded	7 Jan 1944
L/C(A) JG Large RNVR	26 Apr 1944
Squadron disbanded	13 Sep 1944

Fairey Swordfish I W5889 'M' of No.833 Squadron, Crail early in 1942. (H.Barclay/FAA Museum)

No.834 Squadron

Badge: On a blue field in base water barry wavy white and blue, two gauntlets conjoined winged gold, the upper grasping an axe, and the lower a trident, also gold
Motto: Una feriendo delemus (By striking together we destroy)

The personnel for No.834 Squadron assembled at Eastleigh on 12 November 1941, and after taking passage to Jamaica officially formed at Palisadoes on 10 December 1941. Equipped with four Swordfish Is for torpedo bomber reconnaissance work, these joined HMS *Archer*, the first of the American-built escort carriers (CVEs) in March 1942 in the United States, and then sailed for Freetown and Cape Town. Returning to the USA in July, anti-submarine cover was provided en route for a westbound convoy, similar duties being undertaken in October for a Gibraltar convoy, some Swordfish IIs having been received by then. In January 1943 the strength was increased to six aircraft, and these joined RAF Coastal Command for night patrols and shipping attacks in the English Channel.

In April, three more Swordfish were received, and in June a fighter flight of six Seafire L.IICs was added. All except three Swordfish embarked in HMS *Hunter* in July for Gibraltar, where the Swordfish element disembarked to operate as No.834Z Squadron, the other three being meanwhile absorbed into No.836 Squadron. During the Salerno landings in September, the Seafires operated with No.899 Squadron to provide fighter protection, a few aircraft operating from a beach airstrip. The whole squadron then transferred to HMS *Battler* with nine Swordfish and six Seafires to sail for Aden. After providing anti-submarine patrols in that area, they re-embarked for Bombay, to give support to convoys in the Indian Ocean. In February 1944 a further three aircraft were added, and on 12 March the German tanker *Brake* was located in the Mauritius area, being then sunk by HMS *Roebuck*. Two U-boats were also sighted, one being claimed as probably damaged by rocket projectiles.

In April, whilst the squadron was shore based at Durban, a fighter flight of six Wildcat Vs was formed in southern India. The remainder of the squadron embarked in HMS *Battler* in June, to join the Wildcats in Ceylon the following month, the Seafires being withdrawn. The squadron then provided trade protection in the Indian Ocean until disembarking in September. In November it discarded its aircraft and took passage home in HMS *Battler* and HMS *Thane* to disband on arrival on 6 December 1944.

Plans to reform at Culdrose in 1994/95 as a special operations squadron failed to materialise. Squadron number 834 was allocated to New Zealand in March 1994, and a new No.834 Squadron is expected to form at Auckland with helicopters for small ships, possibly in 1997.

Battle Honours
*Atlantic   1942
Salerno   1943

Identification Markings
Swordfish single letters, to 4A+ 9.43; Seafire individual letters; Wildcat unknown.

Aircraft Equipment	Period of Service	Example
Swordfish I	Dec 1941 - Apr 1943	V4653 (A)
Swordfish II	Sep 1942 - Nov 1944	HS559 (4H)
Seafire L.IIc	Jun 1943 - Aug 1944	NM972 (Q)
Wildcat V	Apr 1944 - Nov 1944	JV514

Fairey Swordfish of No.834 Squadron ranged aboard HMS Battler in 1943. (via D.K.Davies)

*Fairey Swordfish II HS669 'H' of No.834 Squadron, HMS Battler during compass swinging at Kinjo Park, Durban in 1944.
(via D.K.Davies)*

Squadron bases
Palisadoes	10 Dec 1941
HMS Archer	19 Mar 1942
Floyd Bennett Fd	16 Jul 1942
HMS Archer	31 Oct 1942
Crail	2 Dec 1942
Exeter (19 Gp)	9 Feb 1943
Harrowbeer (Dt3)	14-15 Apr 1943
Machrihanish	21 Apr 1943
Eglinton	30 May 1943
Ballykelly	30 May 1943
Machrihanish	15 Jun 1943
HMS Hunter	8 Jul 1943
Machrihanish(Dt3)	7-13 Aug 1943
North Front (Z Flt	9 Aug 1943
- 6 Swordfish)	to 1 Oct 1943
Paestum (Dt)	12-16 Sep 1943
HMS Battler	7 Sep 1943
Rbiyan (nr Lurkulla)	3 Oct 1943
HMS Battler	17 Oct 1943
Santa Cruz (Dt4	17 Nov 1943
- Seafire)	to 26 Dec 1943
Stamford Hill	4 Feb 1944
HMS Battler	13 Feb 1944
Stamford Hill	21 Mar 1944
Puttalam (Fighter	14 Apr 1944
Flight)	to 25 Jul 1944
HMS Battler	24 Jun 1944
Katukurunda	25 Jul 1944
HMS Battler	11 Aug 1944
Coimbatore	19 Sep 1944
Cochin	27 Sep 1944
HMS Battler	28 Sep 1944
Trincomalee	7 Oct 1944
Vavuniya	18 Oct 1944
HMS Battler (crews)	7 Nov 1944
HMS Thane	22 Nov 1944
Sqdn disbanded UK	6 Dec 1944
Auckland (to form)	

Commanding Officers
L/C LCB Ashburner RN	12 Nov 1941
Lt LG Wilson RN	20 Nov 1941
L/C(A) ED Child RN	21 Jan 1943
L/C(A) DW Phillips DSC RN	12 Aug 1944
Squadron disbanded	6 Dec 1944

*Supermarine Seafire L.IIc LR755 and others of No.834 Squadron's fighter flight around 1943/4.
(via Bryan Philpott)*

No.835 Squadron

Badge: The word JOE (to reflect the squadron's feeling that they were always given the dirty and unglamorous tasks)

Motto: Semper miseri sumus (Always in trouble?) [Unofficial badge]

Identification Markings
Swordfish single letters, to 5A+ 4.43, to Y:A+ on *Nairana* 7.44, to Z:A on *Nairana* early 1945; Sea Hurricane 7A+; Wildcat Y:A on *Nairana*.

Aircraft Equipment	Period of Service	Example
Swordfish I	Feb 1942 - Feb 1943	V4719 (K)
Swordfish II	Oct 1942 - Jul 1944	HS227 (5A)
Swordfish III	Jul 1944 - Mar 1945	NR939 (YC)
Sea Hurricane IIc	Jun 1943 - Sep 1944	NF698 (7D)
Wildcat VI	Sep 1944 - Mar 1945	JV718 (YW)

Battle Honours
Atlantic 1943-44
Arctic 1944-45

No.835 Squadron assembled at Eastleigh on 15 January 1942, and after passage to Jamaica officially formed at Palisadoes on 15 February 1942 for torpedo bomber reconnaissance duties with four Swordfish Is. After flying north to Norfolk,Va these joined HMS *Furious* in April for the United Kingdom, where it increased in May to six aircraft. By November these had been replaced by Mk.IIs, which joined HMS *Activity* for deck landing training. In April 1943 the squadron embarked in HMS *Battler* for convoy escort work, and shortly afterwards the strength was again increased. Three further Swordfish were received, and a fighter flight was formed from six Sea Hurricanes IICs taken over from No.804 Squadron. In November the squadron embarked in HMS *Chaser*, transferring at the end of the year to HMS *Nairana*.

During January and February 1944 several enemy aircraft were encountered whilst escorting an Atlantic convoy. Three Fulmars of No.784 Squadron were attached briefly in March and April, then in May the Swordfish strength was brought up to 12. Two Ju 290s were claimed whilst engaged in Atlantic convoy escort in May and June, and in July Swordfish IIIs were received before undertaking further North Atlantic convoy duty. On return the Sea Hurricanes were exchanged for four Wildcat VIs, and the squadron switched to North Russian convoy escort, two U-boats being attacked and four enemy aircraft shot down. After operations in March 1945 at Rovda in the Trondheim area, the squadron returned to Hatston and disbanded on 31 March 1945, its fighter component going to No.821 Squadron.

Squadron bases

Palisadoes	15 Feb 1942
Norfolk	22 Mar 1942
HMS Furious	3 Apr 1942
Lee-on-Solent	15 Apr 1942
Hatston	10 Jun 1942
Stretton	22 Sep 1942
Machrihanish	25 Oct 1942
HMS Activity (daily DLT)	27 Oct 1942 to 3 Nov 1942
HMS Activity (DLT)	13 Nov 1942
Machrihanish (transit)	18 Dec 1942
Kirkistown	18 Dec 1942
Ballyhalbert(Dt4)	7 - 8 Jan 1943
Machrihanish	29 Jan 1943
HMS Battler	10 Apr 1943
Machrihanish(Dt3)	7-14 May 1943
Ballykelly	16 May 1943
Eglinton	30 May 1943
Sydenham (Dt5)	4-5 Jun 1943
HMS Battler (Dt5)	5-28 Jun 1943
Machrihanish	4-8 Jul 1943
HMS Battler	13 Jul 1943
Ayr	30 Jul 1943
Evanton (Fighter Flight)	8-16 Sep 1943
HMS Argus	20 Sep 1943
HMS Ravager (Fighter Flt)	28 Sep 1943 to 12 Oct 1943
Eglinton	12 Oct 1943
Machrihanish (Dt7)	25-27 Oct 1943
HMS Chaser	6 Nov 1943
HMS Chaser (Fighter Flight)	6 Nov 1943
Abbotsinch (Fighter Flt)	11-18 Dec 1943
Eglinton	20 Dec 1943
HMS Nairana	30 Dec 1943
Burscough	4 Jul 1944
HMS Nairana	13 Aug 1944
Machrihanish	29 Sep 1944
HMS Nairana	4 Oct 1944
Machrihanish (Fighter Flight)	10-24 Nov 1944
Machrihanish	23 Nov 1944
HMS Nairana	24 Nov 1944

Fairey Swordfish I V4719 'K' of No.835 Squadron, Lee-on-Solent in June 1944.

Squadron bases

Hatston	25 Nov 1944
HMS Nairana	29 Nov 1944
Hatston	28 Dec 1944
HMS Nairana	31 Dec 1944
Hatston (Fighter Flight)	5 Jan 1945
Machrihanish	9 Jan 1945
HMS Nairana	22 Jan 1945
Hatston	1 Feb 1945
HMS Nairana	Feb 1945
Hatston	5 Mar 1945
HMS Nairana	8 Mar 1945
Hatston	16 Mar 1945
HMS Nairana	22 Mar 1945
Hatston	29 Mar 1945
Squadron disbanded	31 Mar 1945

Fighter Flight:

Yeovilton	22 Sep 1944
Abbotsinch	30 Sep 1944
HMS Nairana	4 Oct 1944
Hatston	25 Nov 1944
HMS Nairana	29 Nov 1944
Hatston	28 Dec 1944

Squadron bases

HMS Nairana	1 Jan 1945
Machrihanish	9 Jan 1945
HMS Nairana	27 Jan 1945
Hatston	31 Jan 1945
HMS Nairana	4 Feb 1945
Hatston	15 Mar 1945
HMS Nairana	23 Mar 1945
Hatston	29 Mar 1945
Squadron disbanded	31 Mar 1945

Commanding Officers

L/C M Johnstone DSC RN	15 Feb 1942
L/C JR Lang RN	28 Apr 1942
L/C WN Waller RN	15 Sep 1943
L/C(A) TT Miller RN	2 Dec 1943
L/C EE Barringer RNVR	17 Feb 1944
L/C FV Jones RNVR	12 Aug 1944
L/C(A) JR Godley RNVR	15 Jan 1945
Squadron disbanded	31 Mar 1945

Hawker Sea Hurricane IIc '7N' of No.835 Squadron taking off from HMS Nairana. (Ken Atkinson)

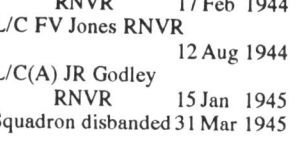

The three Fairey Swordfish of No.836R Flight, MV Empire MacAndrew in 1944. (via Tony Hill/Peter Green)

No.836 Squadron

Badge: On a field barry wavy of ten white and blue, a winged lion rampant, red
Motto: *Mari coeloque*
(By sea and sky)

No.836 Squadron assembled at Eastleigh on 1 February 1942, and after passage to Jamaica officially formed at Palisadoes on 1 March 1942 with six Swordfish Is for torpedo bomber reconnaissance work. Sailing to the United Kingdom in June in HMS *Biter*, it continued work-up until being attached to RAF Coastal Command in January 1943 for night operations in the English Channel. In March the squadron re-equipped with Swordfish IIs and moved to Machrihanish. Here its role was changed to become an Operational Pool for Swordfish aircraft operating from merchant aircraft carriers (MAC-ships) in protection of North Atlantic convoys. The headquarters was moved to Maydown in June. The squadron's activities proved a successful deterrent to U-boats, and on 13 August the strength was increased to 27 Swordfish and two Walruses by absorbing Nos.838 and 840 Squadrons, No.700W Flight, and detachments of Nos.833 and 834 Squadrons then based at Machrihanish. The Walruses were soon discarded, and the squadron was given primary responsibility for all MAC-ship flights, each of which consisted of either three or four Swordfish.

In January 1944 the remainder of No.833 Squadron was absorbed, and with No.860 Netherlands Squadron they then controlled 83 aircraft, operating from 19 MAC-ships. Whilst ashore in Canada the aircraft used the western base at Dartmouth, Nova Scotia. The aircraft did not go ashore on New York runs. As the U-boat menace decreased the squadron strength was run down, and by February 1945 only 30 aircraft were left. Around this time Swordfish IIIs began to appear, but the squadron task was superfluous after VE-day, and its aircraft were flown to Barton for breaking up. One aircraft which succeeded in avoiding this fate is LS326, once coded 'L2' with 'L' Flight in MV *Rapana*, and now with the Fleet Air Arm Historic Flight at Yeovilton. The squadron officially disbanded at Maydown on 29 July 1945.

Battle Honours
Atlantic 1943-45

Identification Markings
Swordfish single letters, to *Flight letter/individual number* 10.43, to *M1-M4/flight letter* 10.44.

Aircraft Equipment	Period of Service	Example
Swordfish I	Mar 1942 - Feb 1943	V4364 (G)
Swordfish II	Mar 1943 - Jun 1945	LS387 (D1)
Swordfish III	Dec 1944 - May 1945	NS151 (M3V)
Walrus	Aug 1943 - 1943	

Squadron bases	
Palisadoes	1 Mar 1942
transit	13 May 1942
Floyd Bennett Field	18 May 1942
HMS Biter	2 Jun 1942
Lee-on-Solent	27 Jun 1942
Machrihanish	9 Aug 1942
Crail	24 Sep 1942
Machrihanish	28 Oct 1942
St Merryn	26 Nov 1942
Thorney Island	30 Dec 1942
Machrihanish	16 Mar 1943
Ballykelly	27 Mar 1943
Machrihanish (detachment)	6-14 Mar 1943
Machrihanish	5 May 1943
MV Empire MacAlpine (flying trials)	7-10 May 1943
MV Empire MacAlpine	14 May 1943
Dartmouth	10 Jun 1943
MV Empire MacAlpine	19 Jun 1943
Maydown	5 Jul 1943
Belfast	6 Jul 1943
Maydown	18 Jul 1943
Squadron disbanded	29 Jul 1945

Fairey Swordfish II LS384 'M3' of No.836M Flight, MV Empire Mackendrick in 1944. (via Tony Hill/Peter Green)

The four Fairey Swordfish II of No.836U Flight over Dartmouth, Nova Scotia. (Reg Singleton)

836A Flight

Squadron bases

Maydown (formed)	Nov 1943
MV Empire MacColl	28 Nov 1943
Dartmouth	3 Jan 1944
MV Empire MacColl	6 Jan 1944
Maydown	21 Jan 1944
MV Empire MacColl	26 Jan 1944
Maydown	16 Mar 1944
MV Empire MacColl	30 Mar 1944
Dartmouth	22 Apr 1944
MV Empire MacColl	27 Apr 1944
Maydown	13 May 1944
MV Empire MacColl	22 May 1944
Dartmouth	5 Jun 1944
MV Empire MacColl	12 Jun 1944
Maydown	24 Jun 1944
MV Empire MacColl	30 Jun 1944

836A Flight

Squadron bases

Dartmouth	16 Jul 1944
MV Empire MacColl	27 Jul 1944
Maydown	7 Aug 1944
MV Empire MacCabe	12 Sep 1944
Dartmouth	3 Oct 1944
MV Empire MacCabe	6 Oct 1944
Maydown	19 Oct 1944
MV Empire MacCabe	18 Nov 1944
Dartmouth	7 Dec 1944
MV Empire MacCabe	11 Dec 1944
Ronaldsway	23 Dec 1944
Maydown	26 Dec 1944

836A Flight

Squadron bases

MV Empire MacCabe	10 Jan 1945
Dartmouth	30 Jan 1945
MV Empire MacCabe	4 Feb 1945
Maydown	16 Feb 1945
MV Empire MacCabe	22 Feb 1945
Dartmouth	15 Mar 1945
MV Empire MacCabe	27 Mar 1945
Maydown	9 Apr 1945
Flight disbanded	1 May 1945

836B Flight

Squadron bases

Maydown (formed)	Jul 1943
MV Empire MacAlpine	21 Jul 1943
Dartmouth	8 Aug 1943
MV Empire MacAlpine	14 Aug 1943
Maydown	3 Sep 1943
MV Empire MacAlpine	10 Sep 1943
Dartmouth	29 Sep 1943
MV Empire MacAlpine	4 Oct 1943
Maydown	18 Oct 1943
MV Empire MacAlpine	29 Oct 1943
Dartmouth	13 Nov 1943
MV Empire MacAlpine	19 Dec 1943
Maydown	1 Jan 1944
MV Empire MacAlpine	6 Feb 1944
Dartmouth	22 Feb 1944
MV Empire MacAlpine	27 Feb 1944
Maydown	14 Mar 1944
Machrihanish	26 Mar 1944
Maydown	12 Apr 1944
MV Empire MacMahon	26 Apr 1944
Dartmouth	15 May 1944
MV Empire MacMahon	21 May 1944
Maydown	1 Jun 1944
MV Empire MacMahon	8 Jun 1944
Dartmouth	25 Jun 1944
MV Empire MacMahon	5 Jul 1944
Maydown	17 Jul 1944
MV Empire MacMahon	23 Jul 1944
Dartmouth	6 Aug 1944
MV Empire MacMahon	13 Aug 1944
Maydown	25 Aug 1944
MV Empire MacMahon	30 Aug 1944
Dartmouth	16 Sep 1944
MV Empire MacMahon	18 Sep 1944
Maydown	2 Oct 1944
MV Empire MacAndrew	4 Nov 1944
Dartmouth	22 Nov 1944
MV Empire MacAndrew	24 Nov 1944
Maydown	16 Dec 1944
MV Empire MacAndrew	24 Dec 1944
Dartmouth	16 Jan 1945
MV Empire MacAndrew	24 Jan 1945
Maydown	6 Feb 1945
MV Empire MacDermott	11 Apr 1945
Dartmouth	30 Apr 1945
MV Empire MacDermott	7 May 1945
Maydown	26 May 1945
- Flight disbanded	

Fairey Swordfish II LS155 'Q2' of No.836Q Flight after breaking an oleo while landing on MV Alexia on 26 October 1944. (Len Jeyes)

836C Flight

Squadron bases

Maydown (formed)	Sep 1943
MV Empire MacRae	1 Oct 1943
Dartmouth	5 Nov 1943
MV Empire MacRae	14 Nov 1943
Maydown	26 Nov 1943
MV Empire MacRae	16 Dec 1943
Dartmouth	3 Jan 1944
MV Empire MacRae	6 Jan 1944
Maydown	21 Jan 1944
MV Empire MacRae	30 Jan 1944
Dartmouth	14 Feb 1944
MV Empire MacRae	22 Feb 1944
Maydown	8 Mar 1944
MV Empire MacRae	6 Apr 1944
Dartmouth	22 Apr 1944
MV Empire MacRae	26 Apr 1944
Maydown	13 May 1944
MV Amastra	15 Jul 1944
Dartmouth	30 Jul 1944
MV Amastra	5 Aug 1944
Dartmouth	10 Aug 1944
MV Amastra	15 Aug 1944
Maydown	26 Aug 1944
Flight disbanded	4 Sep 1944

836D Flight

Squadron bases

Maydown (formed)	Sep 1943
MV Empire MacKay	11 Oct 1943
Dartmouth	21 Nov 1943
MV Empire MacKay	28 Nov 1943
Maydown	10 Dec 1943
MV Empire MacKay	24 Dec 1943
Dartmouth	8 Jan 1944
MV Empire MacKay	15 Jan 1944
Maydown	27 Jan 1944
MV Empire MacKay	13 Feb 1944
Maydown	20 Mar 1944
MV Empire MacKay	9 Apr 1944
Dartmouth	28 Apr 1944
MV Empire MacKay	5 May 1944
Maydown	18 May 1944
MV Empire MacKay	24 May 1944
Dartmouth	6 Jun 1944
MV Empire MacKay	21 Jun 1944
Maydown	2 Jul 1944
MV Ancylus	18 Aug 1944
Dartmouth	5 Sep 1944
MV Ancylus	18 Sep 1944
Maydown	2 Oct 1944
MV Empire MacAlpine	22 Oct 1944
Dartmouth	8 Nov 1944
MV Empire MacAlpine	9 Nov 1944
Maydown	30 Nov 1944
MV Empire MacAlpine	8 Dec 1944
Dartmouth	27 Dec 1944
MV Empire MacAlpine	30 Dec 1944
Maydown	23 Jan 1945
MV Empire MacRae	17 Mar 1945
Dartmouth	12 Apr 1945
MV Empire MacRae	15 Apr 1945
Maydown	28 Apr 1945
MV Empire MacRae	7 May 1945
Dartmouth	25 May 1945
MV Empire MacRae	30 May 1945
Maydown-disbanded	12 Jun 1945

836E Flight

Squadron bases

Maydown (formed)	Sep 1943
MV Amastra	13 Oct 1943
Dartmouth	21 Nov 1943
MV Amastra	2 Dec 1943
Maydown	15 Dec 1943
MV Amastra	28 Dec 1943
Dartmouth	18 Jan 1944
MV Amastra	24 Jan 1944
Maydown	6 Feb 1944
MV Amastra	13 Feb 1944
Maydown	30 Mar 1944
MV Amastra	9 Apr 1944
Dartmouth	27 Apr 1944
MV Amastra	7 May 1944
Maydown	18 May 1944
MV Amastra	2 Jun 1944
Dartmouth	19 Jun 1944
MV Amastra	26 Jun 1944
Maydown	10 Jul 1944
MV Empire MacColl	13 Aug 1944
Dartmouth	31 Aug 1944
MV Empire MacColl	2 Sep 1944
Maydown	16 Sep 1944
MV Empire MacColl	20 Sep 1944
Dartmouth	10 Oct 1944
MV Empire MacColl	18 Oct 1944
Maydown	1 Nov 1944
- became 'V' Flight	

836F Flight

Squadron bases

Maydown (formed)	Sep 1943
MV Acavus	23 Oct 1943
Dartmouth	3 Dec 1943
MV Acavus	13 Dec 1943
Maydown	28 Dec 1943
MV Alexia	16 Jan 1944
Maydown	7 Apr 1944
HMS Activity (became Swordfish element of No.833 Squadron)	17 Apr 1944
Maydown (returned)	8 Sep 1944
- flight disbanded	

836G Flight

Squadron bases

Maydown (formed)	27 Sep 1943
MV Ancylus	2 Nov 1943
Dartmouth	17 Dec 1943
MV Ancylus	27 Dec 1943
Maydown	13 Jan 1944
MV Ancylus	26 Jan 1944
Maydown	16 Mar 1944
MV Ancylus	27 Mar 1944
Dartmouth	14 Apr 1944
MV Ancylus	20 Apr 1944
Maydown	3 May 1944
MV Ancylus	15 May 1944
Dartmouth	31 May 1944
MV Adula	11 Jul 1944
Maydown	23 Jul 1944
MV Adula	29 Jul 1944
Dartmouth	13 Aug 1944
MV Adula	19 Aug 1944
Maydown	30 Aug 1944
- Flight disbanded	
Maydown (reformed)	25 Sep 1944
MV Empire MacMahon	11 Oct 1944
Dartmouth	30 Oct 1944
MV Empire MacMahon	2 Nov 1944
Maydown	16 Nov 1944
MV Empire MacMahon	9 Dec 1944

A Fairey Swordfish II of No.836 Squadron being hauled back on board after nearly going over the side of a Mac-ship.
(Reg Singleton)

836G Flight

Squadron bases

Dartmouth	2 Jan 1945
MV Empire MacMahon	15 Jan 1945
Maydown	28 Jan 1945
MV Empire MacMahon	2 Feb 1945
Dartmouth	25 Feb 1945
MV Empire MacMahon	1 Mar 1945
Maydown	15 Mar 1945
Flight disbanded	6 Apr 1945

836H Flight

Squadron bases

Maydown (formed)	27 Sep 1943
Machrihanish	10 Oct 1943
MV Empire MacAndrew	11 Nov 1943
Dartmouth	26 Nov 1943
MV Empire MacAndrew	5 Dec 1943
Maydown	15 Dec 1943
MV Empire MacAndrew	30 Dec 1944
Dartmouth	15 Jan 1944
MV Empire MacAndrew	20 Jan 1944
Maydown	6 Feb 1944
MV Empire MacAndrew	17 Feb 1944
Maydown	28 Mar 1944
MV Empire MacAndrew	9 Apr 1944
Dartmouth	27 Apr 1944
MV Empire MacAndrew	5 May 1944
Maydown	18 May 1944
MV Miralda	30 Aug 1944
Dartmouth	20 Sep 1944
MV Miralda	23 Sep 1944
Maydown	6 Oct 1944
MV Miralda	2 Nov 1944
Dartmouth	19 Nov 1944
MV Miralda	26 Nov 1944
Maydown	8 Dec 1944
MV Miralda	19 Dec 1944
Dartmouth	6 Jan 1945
MV Miralda	16 Jan 1945
Maydown	30 Jan 1945
MV Empire MacCabe	10 May 1945
Dartmouth	31 May 1945
MV Empire MacCabe	2 Jun 1945
Maydown	12 Jun 1945
- Flight disbanded	

836J Flight

Squadron bases

Maydown (formed)	Nov 1943
MV Empire MacMahon	24 Dec 1943
Maydown	30 Dec 1943
MV Empire MacMahon	13 Jan 1944
Dartmouth	28 Jan 1944
MV Empire MacMahon	5 Feb 1944
Maydown	19 Feb 1944
MV Empire MacMahon	27 Feb 1944
Maydown	5 Apr 1944
MV Alexia	7 May 1944
Dartmouth	25 May 1944
MV Alexia	2 Jun 1944
Maydown	18 Jun 1944
MV Alexia	3 Jul 1944
Dartmouth	22 Jul 1944
MV Empire MacColl	27 Jul 1944
Maydown	7 Aug 1944
MV Empire MacColl	15 Aug 1944
Dartmouth	31 Aug 1944
MV Empire MacColl	2 Sep 1944
Maydown	16 Sep 1944
Flight disbanded	9 Oct 1944

836K Flight

Squadron bases

Maydown (formed)	Dec 1943
MV Empire MacCallum	24 Jan 1944
Dartmouth	8 Feb 1944
MV Empire MacCallum	12 Feb 1944
Maydown	28 Feb 1944
MV Empire MacDermott	8 Apr 1944
Dartmouth	9 May 1944
MV Empire MacDermott	24 May 1944
Maydown	8 Jun 1944
MV Empire MacDermott	22 Jun 1944
Dartmouth	9 Jul 1944
MV Empire MacDermott	12 Jul 1944
Maydown	23 Jul 1944
MV Empire MacDermott	31 Jul 1944
Dartmouth	14 Aug 1944
MV Empire MacDermott	24 Aug 1944
Maydown	8 Sep 1944

836K Flight

Squadron bases
MV Empire
   MacDermott   19 Sep 1944
Dartmouth   7 Oct 1944
MV Empire
   MacDermott   14 Oct 1944
Maydown   29 Oct 1944
MV Empire MacCallum
   1 Mar 1945
Dartmouth   22 Mar 1945
MV Empire MacCallum
   31 Mar 1945
Maydown   14 Apr 1945
MV Empire MacCallum
   22 Apr 1945
Dartmouth   9 May 1945
MV Empire MacCallum
   15 May 1945
Maydown   29 May 1945
- Flight disbanded

836L Flight

Squadron bases
MV Rapana   13 Aug 1943
(formed ex 'L' Flt)
Maydown   28 Aug 1943
MV Rapana   31 Aug 1943
Dartmouth   11 Sep 1943
MV Rapana   26 Sep 1943
Maydown   12 Oct 1943
MV Rapana   29 Oct 1943
Dartmouth   13 Nov 1943
MV Rapana   17 Nov 1943
Maydown   3 Dec 1943
Machrihanish   15 Dec 1943
MV Rapana   16 Dec 1943
Dartmouth   3 Jan 1944
MV Rapana   6 Jan 1944
Maydown   27 Jan 1944
MV Rapana   8 Feb 1944
Maydown   20 Feb 1944
MV Empire MacRae 21 May 1944
Dartmouth   6 Jun 1944
MV Empire MacRae 19 Jun 1944
Maydown   2 Jul 1944
MV Empire MacRae 9 Jul 1944
Dartmouth   22 Jul 1944
MV Empire MacRae 5 Aug 1944
Maydown   16 Aug 1944
MV Empire MacRae 22 Aug 1944
Dartmouth   5 Sep 1944
MV Empire MacRae 15 Sep 1944
Maydown   28 Sep 1944
MV Empire MacRae 10 Oct 1944
Dartmouth   1 Nov 1944
MV Empire MacRae 6 Nov 1944
Maydown   19 Nov 1944
MV Empire
   MacKendrick   8 Jan 1945
Dartmouth   28 Jan 1945
MV Empire
   MacKendrick   Feb 1945

836L Flight

Squadron bases
Maydown   12 Feb 1945
- Redes 'V' Flight
Maydown (reformed) 6 Apr 1945
MV Alexia   28 Apr 1945
Dartmouth   16 May 1945
MV Alexia   18 May 1945
Maydown   8 Jun 1945
Flight disbanded   13 Jun 1945

836M Flight

Squadron bases
MV Empire MacAndrew
   13 Aug 1943
(formed ex 'M' Flt)
Maydown   4 Sep 1943
MV Empire MacAndrew
   24 Sep 1943
Dartmouth   15 Oct 1943
MV Empire MacAndrew
   18 Oct 1943
Maydown   22 Oct 1943
MV Empire
   MacKendrick   16 Jan 1944
Dartmouth   28 Feb 1944
MV Empire
   MacKendrick   7 Mar 1944
Maydown   20 Mar 1944
MV Empire
   MacKendrick   29 Mar 1944
Dartmouth   14 Apr 1944
MV Empire
   MacKendrick   21 Apr 1944
Maydown   3 May 1944
MV Empire
   MacKendrick   14 May 1944
Dartmouth   6 Jun 1944
MV Empire
   MacKendrick   12 Jun 1944
Maydown   24 Jun 1944
MV Empire
   MacKendrick   6 Jul 1944
Dartmouth   22 Jul 1944
MV Empire
   MacKendrick   27 Jul 1944
Maydown   7 Aug 1944
MV Empire
   MacKendrick   14 Aug 1944
Dartmouth   1 Sep 1944
MV Empire
   MacKendrick   6 Sep 1944
Maydown   19 Sep 1944
HMS Campania   19 Oct 1944
Hatston   28 Oct 1944
HMS Campania   31 Oct 1944
Belfast   16 Nov 1944
Maydown   19 Nov 1944
MV Adula   18 Dec 1944
Dartmouth   6 Jan 1945
MV Adula   16 Jan 1945
Maydown   30 Jan 1945
MV Adula   18 Feb 1945
Dartmouth   7 Mar 1945
MV Adula   17 Mar 1945
Maydown   30 Mar 1945
MV Adula   8 Apr 1945
Dartmouth   28 Apr 1945
MV Adula   7 May 1945
Maydown   21 May 1945
- Flight disbanded

836N Flight

Squadron bases
Maydown (formed)   Dec 1944
MV Empire MacCabe
   15 Jan 1944
Dartmouth   31 Jan 1944
MV Empire MacCabe
   11 Feb 1944
Maydown   29 Feb 1944
MV Empire MacCabe 7 Mar 1944
Dartmouth   22 Mar 1944
MV Empire MacCabe
   28 Mar 1944
Maydown   14 Apr 1944
MV Empire MacCabe
   29 Apr 1944

Fairey Swordfish II HS380 'A' of No.836 Squadron in formation in 1943. (Reg Singleton)

836N Flight

Squadron bases
Dartmouth   16 May 1944
MV Empire MacCabe
   21 May 1944
Maydown   1 Jun 1944
MV Empire MacCabe 7 Jun 1944
Dartmouth   25 Jun 1944
MV Empire MacCabe 5 Jul 1944
Maydown   17 Jul 1944
MV Empire MacCabe 1 Aug 1944
Dartmouth   17 Aug 1944
MV Empire MacCabe
   27 Aug 1944
Maydown   8 Sep 1944
MV Empire
   MacDermott   8 Nov 1944
Dartmouth   3 Dec 1944
MV Empire
   MacDermott   4 Dec 1944
Maydown   18 Dec 1944
MV Empire
   MacDermott   26 Dec 1944
Dartmouth   11 Jan 1945
MV Empire
   MacDermott   19 Jan 1945
Maydown   1 Feb 1945
MV Empire
   MacDermott   13 Feb 1945
Dartmouth   8 Mar 1945
MV Empire
   MacDermott   15 Mar 1945
Maydown   28 Mar 1945
Flight disbanded   18 Apr 1945

836P Flight

Squadron bases
Maydown (formed)   Jan 1944
MV Adula   9 Mar 1944
Maydown   22 Apr 1944
MV Adula   1 May 1944
Dartmouth   15 May 1944
MV Adula   21 May 1944
Maydown   1 Jun 1944
MV Adula   14 Jun 1944
Dartmouth   29 Jun 1944
MV Adula   13 Jul 1944
Maydown   23 Jul 1944
- Flight disbanded
Maydown (reformed) 21 Aug 1944
MV Adula   11 Sep 1944
Dartmouth   26 Sep 1944
MV Adula   4 Oct 1944
Maydown   18 Oct 1944
MV Adula   26 Oct 1944

836P Flight

Squadron bases
Dartmouth   15 Nov 1944
MV Adula   21 Nov 1944
Maydown   6 Dec 1944
MV Miralda   14 Feb 1945
Dartmouth   6 Mar 1945
MV Miralda   11 Mar 1945
Maydown   24 Mar 1945
MV Miralda   4 Apr 1945
Dartmouth   22 Apr 1945
MV Miralda   28 Apr 1945
Maydown   13 May 1945
- Flight disbanded

836Q Flight

Squadron bases
Maydown (formed)   Jan 1944
MV Miralda   10 Feb 1944
Maydown   13 Apr 1944
MV Miralda   20 Apr 1944
Dartmouth   8 May 1944
MV Miralda   12 May 1944
Maydown   25 May 1944
MV Miralda   7 Jun 1944
Dartmouth   25 Jun 1944
MV Miralda   5 Jul 1944
Maydown   17 Jul 1944
MV Miralda   28 Jul 1944
Dartmouth   6 Aug 1944
MV Miralda   12 Aug 1944
Maydown   25 Aug 1944
MV Alexia   25 Sep 1944
Dartmouth   14 Oct 1944
MV Alexia   20 Oct 1944
Maydown   3 Nov 1944
MV Alexia   15 Nov 1944
Dartmouth   21 Dec 1944
MV Alexia   29 Dec 1944
Maydown   17 Jan 1945
MV Empire MacColl 25 Mar 1945
Dartmouth   20 Apr 1945
MV Empire MacColl 25 Apr 1945
Maydown   8 May 1945
Flight disbanded   26 May 1945

836R Flight

Squadron bases
Maydown (formed) 19 Feb 1944
MV Empire MacCallum
   21 Mar 1944
Dartmouth   18 Apr 1944
MV Empire MacCallum
   26 Apr 1944

836R Flight

Squadron bases
Maydown	13 May	1944
MV Empire MacAndrew	2 Jun	1944
Dartmouth	19 Jun	1944
MV Empire MacAndrew	26 Jun	1944
Maydown	10 Jul	1944
MV Empire MacAndrew	22 Jul	1944
Dartmouth	7 Aug	1944
MV Empire MacAndrew	16 Aug	1944
Maydown	30 Aug	1944
- Flight disbanded		
Maydown	3 Sep	1944
(Reformed ex 'V' Flt)		
MV Empire MacAndrew	10 Sep	1944
Dartmouth	7 Oct	1944
MV Empire MacAndrew	11 Oct	1944
Maydown	24 Oct	1944
MV Empire MacKay	2 Dec	1944
Dartmouth	26 Dec	1944
MV Empire MacKay	31 Dec	1944
Maydown	13 Jan	1945
MV Empire MacKay	21 Jan	1945
Dartmouth	7 Feb	1945
MV Empire MacKay	9 Feb	1945
Maydown	21 Feb	1945
MV Empire MacKay	22 Mar	1945
Dartmouth	12 Apr	1945
MV Empire MacKay	1 Jun	1945
Maydown	24 Jun	1945
- Flight disbanded		

836T Flight

Squadron bases
Maydown (formed)	Jun	1944
- Dutch manned		
MV Empire MacCallum	26 Jun	1944
Dartmouth	16 Jul	1944
MV Empire MacCallum	19 Jul	1944
Maydown	1 Aug	1944
MV Empire MacCallum	7 Aug	1944
Maydown	16 Sep	1944
Flight disbanded	20 Sep	1944

836U Flight

Squadron bases
Maydown (formed)	Jan	1944
MV Empire MacAlpine	Feb	1944
Maydown	14 Mar	1944
MV Empire MacAlpine	24 Mar	1944
Dartmouth	14 Apr	1944
MV Empire MacAlpine	19 Apr	1944
Maydown	30 Apr	1944
MV Empire MacAlpine	9 May	1944
Dartmouth	25 May	1944
MV Empire MacAlpine	7 Jun	1944
Maydown	8 Jun	1944
MV Empire MacAlpine	11 Jul	1944
Dartmouth	31 Jul	1944
MV Empire MacAlpine	5 Aug	1944
Maydown	25 Aug	1944

836U Flight

Squadron bases
MV Empire MacAlpine	6 Sep	1944
Dartmouth	20 Sep	1944
MV Empire MacAlpine	Sep	1944
Maydown	12 Oct	1944
MV Empire MacRae	28 Nov	1944
Dartmouth	20 Dec	1945
MV Empire MacRae	5 Jan	1945
Ronaldsway	16 Jan	1945
Maydown	17 Jan	1945
MV Empire MacRae	28 Jan	1945
Dartmouth	19 Feb	1945
MV Empire MacRae	25 Feb	1945
Maydown	10 Mar	1945
Flight disbanded	6 Apr	1945

836V Flight

Squadron bases
Maydown (formed)	13 Mar	1944
MV Acavus	17 Apr	1944
Dartmouth	6 May	1944
MV Acavus	11 May	1944
Maydown	25 May	1944
MV Acavus	12 Jun	1944
Dartmouth	29 Jun	1944
MV Acavus	13 Jul	1944
Maydown	23 Jul	1944
Redes 'R' Flight	3 Sep	1944
Maydown (reformed)	Nov	1944
- ex 'E' Flight		
MV Empire MacColl	29 Nov	1944
Dartmouth	20 Dec	1944
MV Empire MacColl	26 Dec	1944
Maydown	8 Jan	1945
Flight disbanded	1 Feb	1945
Maydown (reformed	Feb	1945
- ex 'L' Flight		
MV Empire MacKendrick	4 Mar	1945
Dartmouth	27 Mar	1945
MV Empire MacKendrick	4 Apr	1945
Maydown	20 Apr	1945
MV Empire MacKendrick	28 Apr	1945
Dartmouth	16 May	1945
MV Empire MacKendrick	19 May	1945
Maydown	1 Jun	1945
- Flight disbanded		

836W Flight

Squadron bases
Maydown (formed)	14 Mar	1944
HMS Vindex	13 Apr	1944
- became No.825 Sqdn		
Swordfish element		
Maydown (reformed)	24 Apr	1944
MV Empire MacKay	16 Jul	1944
Dartmouth	31 Jul	1944
MV Empire MacKay	5 Aug	1944
Maydown	16 Aug	1944
MV Empire MacKay	22 Aug	1944
Dartmouth	5 Sep	1944
MV Empire MacKay	15 Sep	1944
Maydown	28 Sep	1944
MV Empire MacKay	22 Oct	1944
Dartmouth	7 Nov	1944
MV Empire MacKay	11 Nov	1944
Maydown	25 Nov	1944
MV Empire MacMahon	25 Mar	1945
Dartmouth	18 Apr	1945
MV Empire MacMahon	20 Apr	1945

836W Flight

Squadron bases
Maydown	3 May	1945
MV Empire MacMahon	12 May	1945
Dartmouth	31 May	1945
MV Empire MacMahon	2 Jun	1945
Maydown	14 Jun	1945
- Flight disbanded		

836X Flight

Squadron bases
Maydown (formed)	Mar	1944
MV Rapana	9 Apr	1944
Dartmouth	Apr	1944
MV Rapana	26 May	1944
Maydown	8 Jun	1944
MV Rapana	22 Jun	1944
Dartmouth	9 Jul	1944
MV Rapana	18 Jul	1944
Maydown	1 Aug	1944
MV Rapana	7 Aug	1944
Dartmouth	27 Aug	1944
MV Rapana	28 Aug	1944
Maydown	19 Sep	1944
Flight disbanded	13 Oct	1944

836Y Flight

Squadron bases
Maydown (formed?)	21 Aug	1944
MV Empire MacCallum	23 Sep	1944
Dartmouth	14 Oct	1944
MV Empire MacCallum	27 Oct	1944
Maydown	8 Nov	1944
MV Empire MacCallum	20 Nov	1944
Dartmouth	7 Dec	1944
MV Empire MacCallum	16 Dec	1944
Maydown	27 Dec	1944
MV Empire MacCallum	5 Jan	1945
Dartmouth	21 Jan	1945
MV Empire MacCallum	30 Jan	1945

836Y Flight

Squadron bases
Maydown	10 Feb	1945
MV Empire MacAlpine	4 Apr	1945
Dartmouth	29 Apr	1945
MV Empire MacAlpine	4 May	1945
Maydown	18 May	1945
- Flight disbanded		

836Z Flight

Squadron bases
Maydown (formed)	4 Sep	1944
MV Empire MacKendrick	30 Sep	1944
Dartmouth	27 Oct	1944
MV Empire MacKendrick	31 Oct	1944
Maydown	12 Nov	1944
MV Empire MacKendrick	23 Nov	1944
Dartmouth	11 Dec	1944
MV Empire MacKendrick	14 Dec	1944
Maydown	30 Dec	1944
MV Empire MacKendrick	18 Feb	1945
Dartmouth	11 Mar	1945
MV Empire MacAndrew	27 Mar	1945
Maydown	7 Apr	1945
MV Empire MacAndrew	18 Apr	1945
Dartmouth	6 May	1945
MV Empire MacAndrew	14 May	1945
Maydown	26 May	1945
- Flight disbanded		

Commanding Officers
L/C JA Crawford RN	1 Mar	1942
L/C RW Slater OBE DSC RN	9 Jul	1942
L/C JRC Callander RN	29 Jun	1944
L/C(A) FGB Sheffield DSC RNVR	5 Mar	1945
Squadron disbanded	29 Jul	1945

Fairey Swordfish IIs NF193 'M1B' and NE941 'M2B' of No.836B Flight, MV Empire MacAndrew in December 1944.

No.837 Squadron

Badge: On a field red in base water barry wavy of four white and blue, a Chinese dragon regardant gold in the dexter claw three rays of lightning also gold and in chief a sun in splendour also gold surmounted by a decrescent white

Motto: None

No.837 Squadron personnel assembled at Eastleigh and Worthy Down on 15 March 1942, and sailed on 3 April for Jamaica, to officially form at Palisadoes on 1 May as a torpedo bomber reconnaissance squadron with four Swordfish Is. These flew north two months later, to embark in HMS *Dasher* from Floyd Bennett Field, New York. The ship sailed on 24 August for the United Kingdom, and No.837 carried out anti-submarine patrols en route. On arrival the complement was increased to six aircraft, including some Mk.IIs, though in actual fact they were down to only two aircraft by September.

After working up in Scotland, the squadron was split in January 1943, three aircraft joining HMS *Argus* as No.837A Flight, for anti-submarine duties on a Gibraltar convoy. The other three rejoined HMS *Dasher* for a trip to Iceland as No.837D Flight, being fortunate not to be aboard when that ship blew up on 27 March off the Isle of Arran. The squadron reassembled at Dunino in late March and early April, undertaking deck landing training in HMS *Argus* in the latter month. After further training it disbanded at Eglinton on 15 June 1943, to become 'Z' Flight of No.886 Squadron at Machrihanish.

On 1 August 1944. No.837 reformed at Stretton as a torpedo bomber reconnaissance squadron with 16 Barracuda IIs, though it was not until 4 September that the first two aircraft arrived, at Lee-on-Solent. In November it moved to Fearn, to increase to 18 aircraft on 1 December. In April 1945 these joined HMS *Glory* for service with the British Pacific Fleet. Strength was temporarily reduced to nine new aircraft before the ship sailed in May, three more being received at Dekheila on 27 May before the squadron re-embarked for Ceylon as part of the 16th Carrier Air Group. The war ended before the squadron could see action, and instead it sailed for Rabaul to be available for possible trouble during the Japanese surrender. In October it re-equipped in Australia with 12 Firefly FR.Is, and with these re-embarked in HMS *Glory* in January 1946 for service in the East Indies Fleet and the Far East. In June 1947 the squadron re-embarked at Singapore for the last time, and after an Australian tour sailed home to disband on arrival on 6 October 1947.

Battle Honours
Atlantic   1943

Identification Markings
Swordfish single letters; Barracuda single letters, to Y1A + 4.45, to 370-381/Y 9.45; Firefly 270-283/Y/R.

Aircraft Equipment	Period of Service	Example
Swordfish I	May 1942 - Jun 1943	W5858 (A)
Swordfish II	Jun 1942 - Jun 1943	HS439
Barracuda II	Sep 1944 - Oct 1945	PM714 (J)
Firefly F.1, FR.1	Oct 1945 - Oct 1947	MB552 (279/Y)

Squadron bases		Squadron bases	
Palisadoes	1 May 1942	Machrihanish	28 Apr 1943
in transit	7 Jul 1942	Ballykelly	16 May 1943
Floyd Bennett Fd	10 Jul 1942	Eglinton	30 May 1943
HMS Dasher	25 Jul 1942	Machrihanish -	15 Jun 1943
Campbeltown	10 Sep 1942	disbanded into 886	
transit	11 Sep 1942	Squadron as 'Z' Flt	
Lee-on-Solent	13 Sep 1942	Stretton	1 Aug 1944
St Merryn	19 Oct 1942	Lee-on-Solent	31 Aug 1944
in transit	16 Nov 1942	Fearn	5 Nov 1944
Hatston	17 Nov 1942	Ayr	2 Apr 1945
Crail	30 Dec 1942	HMS Glory	4 Apr 1945
837A Flight (6 a/c):		Ayr	18 Apr 1945
HMS Argus	15 Jan 1943	HMS Glory	11 May 1945
North Front	31 Jan 1943	Dekheila	24 May 1945
HMS Argus	4 Feb 1943	HMS Glory	25 Jun 1945
Crail	9 Feb 1943	Katukurunda	15 Jul 1945
Dunino	25 Feb 1943	HMS Glory	27 Jul 1945
837D Flight (3 a/c):		Schofields	16 Aug 1945
HMS Dasher	22 Jan 1943	HMS Glory	1 Sep 1945
Hatston	26 Feb 1943	Jervis Bay	11 Sep 1945
Dunino	29 Mar 1943	Nowra	29 Oct 1945
Dunino (reunited)	29 Mar 1943	HMS Glory	14 Jan 1946
Machrihanish	14 Apr 1943	Williamtown	15 Feb 1946
HMS Argus (DLT)	15 Apr 1943	HMS Glory	10 Jun 1946
		Trincomalee	9 Aug 1946
		HMS Glory	20 Sep 1946
		Kai Tak	1 Oct 1946
		HMS Glory	4 Nov 1946
		Sembawang	18 Nov 1946
		HMS Glory	9 Dec 1946
		Kai Tak	19 Dec 1946
		HMS Glory	14 Feb 1947
		Trincomalee	27 Feb 1947
		HMS Glory	15 Apr 1947
		Trincomalee (Dt7)	30 Apr 1947
		to	12 May 1947
		Sembawang	17 May 1947
		HMS Glory	19 Jun 1947
		Sqdn disbanded UK	6 Oct 1947

Commanding Officers
L/C AS Whitworth DSC RN	15 Mar 1942
Squadron disbanded	15 Jun 1943
L/C(A) RB Martin RNVR	1 Aug 1944
L/C(A) W Siddall-Simpson RNVR	14 Dec 1945
L/C GH Bates RN	25 Jan 1946
L/C RH Hain RN	7 Mar 1947
Squadron disbanded	6 Oct 1947

Fairey Barracuda II MX570 'P' of No.837 Squadron at Fearn in 1945.

No.838 Squadron

The nucleus of No.838 Squadron assembled at Eastleigh on 10 April 1942, and sailed in the troop transport Banfora for Halifax, Nova Scotia, where they disembarked to Dartmouth on 15 May. Here No.838 officially formed as a torpedo bomber reconnaissance squadron with four Swordfish Is for service in an escort carrier. In August these flew to California, and continued work-up at USNAS Alameda Island, then in December embarked in HMS *Attacker*. After sailing through the Panama Canal, the squadron disembarked on New Years Day to Quonset Point, re-embarking two months later to provide air cover for an eastbound convoy from Curacao. Disembarking to Machrihanish in April, it was reallocated for MAC-ship service and given new machines. These joined HMS *Argus* in July for deck landing training, and then spent a few days in HMS *Activity* before embarking the following month in the MAC-ship *Rapana* for trials. Owing to a change of policy, the squadron merged into No.836 Squadron on 13 August 1943 as 'L' Flight.

On 1 November 1943, No.838 reformed at Belfast from part of No.818 Squadron as a torpedo bomber reconnaissance squadron with 4 Swordfish IIs. A month was spent working up in HMS *Nairana* in the Clyde, after which it increased to 9 aircraft at Inskip on 14 February 1944, and to 12 aircraft at Machrihanish on 1 April. Later that month No.838 moved south to join No.156 GR Wing, RAF Coastal Command at Harrowbeer for anti-submarine operations in the English Channel with 12 Swordfish IIs and IIIs equipped with ASV Mk.XI. When the invasion bridgehead had been established it withdrew to Northern Ireland, and then rejoined Coastal Command in Scotland. A fighter flight was formed at Eglinton on 27 October with four Wildcat VIs, but this was soon transferred to No.856 Squadron. No.838 moved south to Thorney Island in November, to disband there on 3 February 1945.

Aircraft Equipment	Period of Service	Example	
Swordfish I	May 1942 – Apr 1943	V4387	(2C)
Swordfish II	Apr 1943 – Aug 1943	HS214	
	Nov 1943 – Feb 1945	NE946	(K)
Swordfish III	May 1944 – Feb 1945	NS118	(F)
Wildcat VI	Oct 1944 – Nov 1944	JV763	(W)

Battle Honours
Atlantic   1943
Normandy   1944

Identification Markings
Swordfish 2A+, to single letters 4.43; Wildcat single letters.

Squadron bases
Dartmouth	15 May 1942
Alameda Island	6 Aug 1942
HMS Attacker	12 Dec 1942
Quonset Point	1 Jan 1943
HMS Attacker	2 Mar 1943
Machrihanish	2 Apr 1943
Maydown	13 Jun 1943
HMS Argus (DLT)	9 Jul 1943
HMS Activity	18 Jul 1943
Belfast	30 Jul 1943
MV Rapana	2 Aug 1943
Redes 'L' Flt	
836 Sqdn	13 Aug 1943

Squadron bases
Belfast	1 Nov 1943
HMS Nairana	17 Dec 1943
Dunino	16 Jan 1944
Inskip	6 Feb 1944
Machrihanish	18 Mar 1944
Harrowbeer (156 Wg)	20 Apr 1944
Worthy Down	8 Aug 1944
Long Kesh	9 Aug 1944
Maydown	27 Aug 1944
Long Kesh	10 Sep 1944
Benbecula	12 Sep 1944
Dallachy	28 Sep 1944
Fraserburgh	22 Oct 1944
Benbecula (Dt)	1-2 Nov 1944
Eglinton (Fighter Flight-6 Wildcat)	27 Oct 1944
– to 856 Sqdn	29 Nov 1944
Thorney Island	15 Nov 1944
Squadron disbanded	3 Feb 1945

Commanding Officers
L/C JRC Callandar RN	15 May 1942
Lt(A) RG Large RNVR	7 Jun 1943
Squadron disbanded	13 Aug 1943
L/C(A) JM Brown DSC RNVR	1 Nov 1943
L/C P Snow RN	19 Aug 1944
Squadron disbanded	3 Feb 1945

Fairey Swordfish Is '2A', '2C' and '2P' of No.838 Squadron flying near San Francisco in 1942. (A.M.McKinnon)

No.840 Squadron

The nucleus of No.840 Squadron assembled at Eastleigh on 4 May 1942 and sailed for Jamaica, where it officially formed at Palisadoes on 1 June. Equipped with six Swordfish Is for torpedo bomber reconnaissance duties in an escort carrier, these soon gave way to six Mk.IIs. After working up in Miami from September, it embarked in HMS *Battler* in December for passage to New York, and No.840 disembarked to Quonset Point to continue work-up. In March 1943 it joined HMS *Attacker* for passage to the United Kingdom, anti-submarine patrols being carried out en route. Disembarking to Stretton, No.840 was reallocated for MAC-ship duty the following month at Hatston, embarking in MV *Empire MacAndrew* in July. Owing to a change of policy which saw the centralisation of this task in No.836 Squadron, No.840 disbanded on 13 August 1943 to become 'M' Flight of that squadron.

Aircraft Equipment	Period of Service	Example
Swordfish I	Jun 1942 - Mar 1943	V4577
Swordfish II	Sep 1942 - Aug 1943	HS609

Battle Honours
Atlantic   1943

Identification Markings
Swordfish single letters.

Squadron bases
Palisadoes	1 Jun 1942
Miami	25 Sep 1942
HMS Battler	12 Dec 1942
Quonset Point	26 Dec 1942
HMS Attacker	2 Mar 1943
Stretton (transit)	2 Apr 1943
Machrihanish	2 Apr 1943
Hatston	3 May 1943

Squadron bases
HMS Activity (DLT)	25 May 1943
Hatston	28 May 1943
Machrihanish	8 Jun 1943
Maydown	27 Jun 1943
MV Empire MacAndrew	12 Jul 1943
Redes 'M' Flight 836 Sqdn	13 Aug 1943

Commanding Officers
Lt(A) LR Tivy RN	1 Jun 1942
Lt(A) CMT Hallewell RN	21 Apr 1943
Squadron disbanded 13 Aug 1943	

No.841 Squadron

Badge: *On a blue field, a barn owl affronté white, perched upon a beam, also white*
Motto: *Lucemus nocte* (We shine by night)

No.841 Squadron formed at Lee-on-Solent on 1 July 1942 as a torpedo bomber reconnaissance squadron for special service with two Albacores, these being increased to four the following month. It was attached to RAF Fighter Command for most of its career, initially at Middle Wallop, then from late August at Manston. Here it operated at night against enemy shipping and E-boats in the Dover Straits and the English Channel, making 99 such attacks in all. On 31 May 1943 it took over the similar task of No.823 Squadron at Tangmere, and other detachments were operated from Coltishall and Exeter. The Albacore strength gradually increased to a peak of 16 in October, and three Swordfish were also attached, but on 1 December 1943 No.841 disbanded at Manston, its aircraft and task being transferred to No.415 (RCAF) Squadron.

On 1 February 1944 No.841 reformed at Lee-on-Solent as a torpedo bomber reconnaissance squadron with 12 Barracuda IIs. These moved to Scotland for work-up, where the squadron was allocated to the 2nd Naval TBR Wing. Embarking briefly in HMS *Formidable* in August, it transferred later that month to HMS *Implacable*, and in October carried out anti-submarine patrols and anti-shipping strikes off the coast of Norway. No.841 disbanded into No.828 Squadron at Hatston on 28 November 1944.

Battle Honours
English Channel   1943
Norway   1944

Identification Markings
Albacore uncoded initially, then 5A+; Swordfish unknown; Barracuda single letters.

Aircraft Equipment	Period of Service	Example	
Albacore I	Jul 1942 - Nov 1943	X9290	(5D)
Swordfish I	Jan 1943 - Apr 1943	V4646	
Swordfish II	Jan 1943 - Apr 1943	HS433	
Barracuda II	Feb 1944 - Nov 1944	BV790	(M)

Squadron bases
Lee-on-Solent	1 Jul 1942
Machrihanish	25 Jul 1942
Lee-on-Solent	6 Aug 1942
Middle Wallop	17 Aug 1942
Manston	23 Aug 1942
Coltishall (Dt3)	7 Feb 1943
	to 23 Jun 1943
Tangmere (Dt4)	31 May 1943
	to 7 Oct 1943
Exeter (Dt3)	9 Jul 1943
	to 5 Oct 1943
Exeter (Dt3)	18 Oct 1943
	to 25 Nov 1943
Squadron disbanded	1 Dec 1943
Lee-on-Solent	1 Feb 1944
Arbroath (transit)	28 Feb 1944
Fearn	29 Dec 1944
Machrihanish	28 Jun 1944
HMS Formidable	8 Aug 1944
Grimsetter	14 Aug 1944
Machrihanish	20 Aug 1944
HMS Implacable	30 Aug 1944
Machrihanish	31 Aug 1944
HMS Implacable	22 Sep 1944
Hatston	31 Oct 1944
Skeabrae (Dt4)	15-16 Oct 1944
Skeabrae (Dt4)	21-22 Oct 1944
Skeabrae (Dt4)	3-4 Nov 1944
Skeabrae (Dt4)	7-8 Nov 1944
Squadron disbanded 28 Nov 1944	

Commanding Officers
Lt RL Williamson DSC RN	1 Jul 1942
Lt(A) LJ Kiggell DSC RN	15 Oct 1942
L/C(A) WFC Garthwaite DSC RNVR	28 Dec 1942
L/C(A) SMP Walsh DSC RNVR	2 Jul 1943
Squadron disbanded	1 Dec 1943
L/C(A) RJ Fisher RNZNVR	1 Feb 1944
L/C(A) EFL Montgomery RNZNVR	1 Jun 1944
Squadron disbanded 28 Nov 1944	

No.842 Squadron

Badge: On a blue field, over water barry wavy in base white and blue, a winged anchor white, suspended therefrom by a riband gold, a bugle horn also proper
Motto: Tantivy

No.842 Squadron was originally planned to form at Lee-on-Solent on 1 September 1942, but in the event it came into existence there on 1 March 1943, as a torpedo bomber reconnaissance squadron with six Swordfish IIs. In April these moved to Scotland for work-up, where in early July a fighter flight of six Seafire L.IIc's from the disbanding No.895 Squadron was added, three further Swordfish also being received. The Seafires soon departed to No.897 Squadron, to be replaced by six Seafire Ib's. In August the squadron embarked in HMS *Fencer*, and during October and November the Swordfish were involved in anti-submarine operations during the occupation of the Azores. From 17 November 1943, 'A' Flight of No.1832 Squadron was attached to the squadron, its four Wildcat Vs operating as 'Q' Flight, and for some time the squadron was operating three different types of aircraft. One of the Wildcats succeeded in shooting down an enemy aircraft on 1 December, whilst the ship was escorting a Gibraltar convoy.

In January 1944 the Seafire strength was reduced to three, two further Wildcats being added the following month. On 10 February, a squadron aircraft sank *U-666*, and on 17 March the Seafires departed, to be replaced by four more Wildcats from 'E' Flight of No.1832 Squadron. During April the squadron Swordfish carried out anti-submarine patrols during an attack on the German battleship *Tirpitz*. On 1 May the Swordfish strength was increased to 12 before re-embarking, the ship acting as escort for a North Russian convoy. During this, attacks were made on 11 U-boats, of which 3 were sunk, being *U-277* on 1 May, and *U-674* and *U-959* the following day.

During July 1944 the squadron temporarily split up, six Swordfish joining HMS *Indefatigable* and three others joining HMS *Furious* for anti-submarine duties during an attack on the German battleship *Tirpitz*; whilst six Swordfish and five Wildcats re-embarked in HMS *Fencer* for a Gibraltar convoy. In September the Swordfish element was attached to RAF Coastal Command for anti-submarine patrols in Scottish waters, whilst the Wildcat element was reduced to four aircraft, these re-embarking in HMS *Fencer* for operations off Norway, transferring to HMS *Campania* in October. The remaining Wildcats were transferred to No.813 Squadron on disembarking in November, shortly after the Swordfish had moved south to continue operations from Thorney Island, where it disbanded on 15 January 1945.

Aircraft Equipment	Period of Service	Example
Swordfish II	Feb 1943 - Jan 1945	HS625 (G)
Seafire L.IIc	Jul 1943 - Jul 1943	NM921
Seafire Ib	Jul 1943 - Mar 1944	PA120 (D)
Wildcat V	Nov 1943 - Mar 1944	JV394 (X)
	Mar 1944 - Nov 1944	JV573 (Y)

Identification Markings
Swordfish single letters, later *F:A*+ on *Fencer*; Seafire & Wildcat individual letters.

Battle Honours
Atlantic 1943-44
Norway 1944
Arctic 1944

Commanding Officers
L/C(A) CB Lamb DSO DSC RN 1 Mar 1943
L/C(A) LR Tivy RN 21 Apr 1943
L/C(A) GFS Hodson RNR 27 Mar 1944
L/C(A) LA Edwards RN 2 Aug 1944
Squadron disbanded 15 Jan 1945

Fairey Swordfish IIs HS329 'F' and HS315 'G' of No.842 Sqdn from HMS Fencer in 1943. (via Harry Wragg)

Fairey Swordfish II LS191 'A' of No.842 Squadron crashed on the lift of HMS Fencer during a Gibraltar convoy after returning from an attack on a U-boat (via Bill Penlington)

Squadron bases

Lee-on-Solent	1 Mar 1943
Machrihanish	1 Apr 1943
Hatston	3 May 1943
Machrihanish	27 Jun 1943
Maydown	18 Jul 1943
Machrihanish	30 Jul 1943
Belfast	31 Jul 1943
HMS Fencer	5 Aug 1943
Lagens	6 Oct 1943
HMS Fencer	24 Oct 1943
Grimsetter	6 Apr 1944
Hatston	11 Apr 1944
HMS Fencer	18 Apr 1944
Machrihanish	7 May 1944
HMS Fencer	10 Jun 1944
Grimsetter (half)	26 Jun 1944
Grimsetter (rest)	30 Jun 1944
HMS Fencer (Dt6)	5 Jul 1944 to 10 Aug 1944
HMS Furious(Dt3)	5-19 Jul 1944
HMS Indefatigable (Dt6)	6-21 Jul 1944
Hatston	19 Jul 1944
Stornoway	8 Aug 1944
HMS Fencer	16 Aug 1944
Stornoway	22 Aug 1944
Benbecula	10 Sep 1944
Mullaghmore (Dt6)	1-2 Nov 1944
Machrihanish	8 Nov 1944
Thorney Island	10 Nov 1944

'Q' Flight (Wildcats):

HMS Fencer	20 Nov 1943
Hatston	22 Mar 1944
HMS Fencer	27 Mar 1944
Hatston	11 Apr 1944
HMS Fencer	18 Apr 1944
Machrihanish	7 May 1944
HMS Fencer	10 Jun 1944
Hatston	10 Aug 1944
HMS Furious (Dt2)	14-28 Aug 1944
HMS Fencer	27 Sep 1944
HMS Campania	19 Oct 1944
Flight disbanded	28 Nov 1944
Squadron disbanded	15 Jan 1945

Fairey Swordfish of No.842 Squadron ashore in the Azores in October 1943. (via Bill Penlington)

A Grumman Wildcat of No.842 Squadron's fighter flight landing on HMS Fencer. (via Gordon Pickard)

No.845 Squadron

Badge: On a field barry wavy of eight white and blue, a dragonfly flying in bend proper
Motto: Audio hostem (I hear the enemy)

No.845 Squadron personnel assembled at Lee-on-Solent on 1 January 1943, and took passage in HMT *Queen Elizabeth* on 19 January for the United States, disembarking a week later to Astbury Park transit camp, New York. They arrived at Quonset Point on 29 January, and officially formed there on 1 February as a torpedo bomber reconnaissance squadron with 12 Avenger Is. After working up these embarked in HMS *Chaser* in June for passage to the United Kingdom, anti-submarine patrols being carried out en route. Disembarking to Hatston in July, No.845 reduced to nine aircraft in September, but restored to 12 in November. It moved to Machrihanish in January 1944 where it was allocated to the 31st Naval TBR Wing for intended service in HMS *Victorious*, but this failed to materialise. Instead, four Wildcats from No.1832 Squadron were added at Eglinton on 18 February, and soon afterwards the squadron was shipped in HMS *Atheling*, HMS *Engadine*, and SS *Strathnaver* to arrive in Ceylon in April. Here, owing to a change of policy the fighter flight disbanded, the Wildcats going to No.890 Squadron.

In May 1944 No.845 joined HMS *Illustrious*, and later in the month took part in a dive bombing attack on the oil refinery and harbour installations at Sourabaya, Java. In July the squadron embarked in the escort carrier HMS *Ameer* for three months fruitless trade protection anti-submarine escort patrols in the Indian Ocean. A fighter flight of four Wildcat Vs was again added on 16 August, but the Avenger strength was reduced to eight aircraft on disembarking in October. In February 1945 No.845 again lost its Wildcats, by now increased to six, and joined HMS *Empress* to provide anti-submarine patrols whilst the Hellcats of Nos.804 and 888 Squadrons carried out photo reconnaissance operations over Malaya and northern Sumatra during Operation Stacey. In April it rejoined HMS *Empress* for a similar mission, transferring to HMS *Khedive* for the return trip to Ceylon.

In June, four of the Avengers sailed in HMS *Shah* for anti-submarine duties whilst that ship's own aircraft carried out strikes in northern Sumatra, then in July these were joined by the remainder of the squadron to work up for an intended invasion. The dropping of the first atomic bomb led to the cancellation of an intended strike on Penang, and the ship returned to Trincomalee. Plans to regroup in Australia with 15 Avengers for the 12th Carrier Air Group were abandoned. The aircraft were left behind when No.845 re-embarked in September for passage home in HMS *Shah*, the squadron disembarking on arrival at Gourock on 7 October 1945.

No.845 reformed on 15 March 1954 at Gosport as a helicopter anti-submarine squadron with 8 Whirlwind HAS.22s, being formed around a nucleus from the disbanded No.706 Squadron. Its main role was to perfect the use of sonar equipment, and evaluate the navigational reliability of the Whirlwind. The squadron embarked in HMS *Perseus* in April for passage to Malta, where it soon re-embarked in HMS *Eagle* to provide assistance for earthquake victims in Greece, but this proved unnecessary, and it returned to Hal Far. In October the squadron joined HMS *Centaur* for exercises, followed by periods in HMS *Triumph*, HMS *Albion*, and HMS *Centaur* again, for a similar purpose. In January 1955, HMS *Centaur* and HMS *Albion* each embarked four aircraft for a visit to Toulon, after which the squadron operated from Hal Far until joining HMS *Eagle* in August to sail to Gibraltar for a further

Grumman Avenger '5Q' of No.845 Squadron taking off.

Westland Whirlwind HAS.7 XK945 'J' and others of No.845 Squadron flying over Aden around 1958. (via Andy Thomas)

exercise. In September it continued home in HMS *Eagle*, transferring briefly to HMS *Bulwark* for an exercise before disbanding at Lee-on-Solent on 10 October 1955.

On 14 November 1955, No.845 reformed at Lee-on-Solent, again as a helicopter anti-submarine squadron with eight Whirlwind HAS.22s, two HAR.3s being also operated. In April 1956 the squadron moved to Eglinton for JASS exercises, and in June to Lossiemouth from where 4 aircraft embarked in HMS *Ocean* for a visit to Hamburg, and the remainder in HMS *Theseus* for a visit to Kristiansund. In July it participated in a Royal Flypast at Spithead, then returned to Eglinton in September from where the squadron joined HMS *Ocean* briefly before transferring to HMS *Theseus* to sail to the Mediterranean to work up with the Royal Marine Commandos. This training stood them in good stead when in March they were called upon to ferry the Commandos from HMS *Theseus* to the beach in Port Said during the Suez Crisis. After carrying out casualty evacuation the ship returned to Malta, and No.845 disembarked, a further short spell being spent in HMS *Theseus* from late November.

During the early part of 1957 periods were spent in HMS *Albion*, including visits home in March and May. During the latter, the squadron re-equipped with eight Whirlwind HAS.7s, with which it joined HMS *Bulwark* in August, taking part in two exercises before returning to Lee-on-Solent in October for night hovering and sonar dunking trials. The squadron rejoined HMS *Bulwark* in January 1958 for a spring cruise to the West Indies and Canada before sailing for the Far East via Gibraltar and the Suez Canal. In June the ship paid a goodwill visit to East Africa, but a deteriorating situation in the Middle East caused the ship to leave for Aden with 300 troops, and No.845 then performed various troop lifts. In September the squadron was very active during salvage operations after two tankers collided in the Persian Gulf, and for this they were later awarded the 1958 Boyd Trophy. Returning home in November, the squadron transferred to HMS *Centaur* which they joined in January 1959 for a Mediterranean trip, but engine trouble caused the aircraft to be grounded and No.845 returned home to disband at Culdrose on 20 April 1959.

No.845 Squadron next reformed at Culdrose on 10 April 1962, as a Commando squadron with 12 Wessex HAS.1s. These embarked in HMS *Albion* in September, sailing in her to the Far East in November. On arrival the squadron was quickly involved in action against Indonesian guerillas operating in Brunei, a task which it was to perform for the next two and a half years, transferring to HMS *Bulwark* when HMS *Albion* sailed home in February 1964. Three Hiller HT.2s were added in April 1964, and the occasional Whirlwind HAS.7 was also flown, but these had all been withdrawn by the time the squadron sailed home to the United Kingdom in September 1965, to be presented with the 1964 Boyd Trophy award for outstanding defence work in Malaysia. The squadron re-equipped in January 1966 with 16 Wessex HU.5s, and these embarked in 1966 in HMS *Bulwark*, sailing in August for the Far East, where a Wasp HAS.1 was added for liaison with the Royal Marines. The ship sailed home in April 1968, and later in the year No.845 re-embarked for an exercise off Norway, after which it was mainly ashore until rejoining HMS *Bulwark* in April 1969 for the Mediterranean, returning home in July. After excercises in the Mediterranean and northern Norway, the squadron transferred to HMS *Albion* in May 1970 with 14 Wessex HU.5s and a Wasp HAS.1, sailing to Cyprus in September. The ship returned home in November, and the squadron spent the next nine months operating in Home waters until embarking in HMS *Bulwark* in September 1971 for exercises in the Mediterranean, returning at the end of that year.

In January 1972 a detachment sailed in HMS *Bulwark* to assist in the withdrawal from Malta, returning home in April. In September the squadron joined HMS *Albion* for an exercise in Canada, and a year later was attached to HMS *Hermes*. In early 1974 an exercise was undertaken in northern Norway, and in March the ship sailed for the Mediterranean. In May a visit was made to Canada, and in January 1975 it participated in a further exercise in northern Norway. HMS *Hermes* sailed in March for the Western Atlantic and the East Indies, following which No.845 spent 3 weeks ashore at New Brunswick before re-embarking to return home in June. This pattern continued with exercises in northern Norway at the beginning of each year, and occasional periods of embarkation in HMS *Hermes*, including a Mediterranean tour in September 1975. Strength was reduced to eight aircraft in April 1976.

From 1977 the squadron was mainly shore based, No.846 Squadron being absorbed in September 1977. Aircraft were embarked from time to time in HMS *Bulwark* and HMS *Hermes*. From Oct 1977 there was a permanent detachment in Northern Ireland, this being recalled in May 1982 when the squadron joined the South Atlantic Task Force with 12 aircraft. During the campaign aircraft were embarked in fourteen different ships at various times and at one stage most of the squadron was based ashore. 'D' Flt, with up to three aircraft, remained at Ascension Island from April 1982 until July 1985. The remainder of the squadron returned to the UK by July 1982. A detachment deployed to the Falklands again in September 1982 to take over the assets of No.847 Squadron, returning eventually to the UK in December 1982.

The major role of No.845 Squadron during the 1980s was in support of No.3 Commando Brigade on the NATO northern flank. Training for this involved deployments to Norway each winter. During the remainder of the year the squadron deployed detachments far and wide in the UK, Europe and at sea, along with spring and autumn exercises and a major squadron training period. In 1986 the squadron converted from Wessex to Sea King helicopters. From December 1990 to April 1991 the squadron deployed into the Saudi Arabian desert to provide Casevac services during Operation *Desert Storm*, for which they were awarded the 1991 Boyd Trophy. Later in 1991 No.845 provided men and aircraft to No.846 Squadron in Turkey in support of UN assistance to the Kurds in northern Iraq.

No.845 returned to northern Norway in Jan 1992 and participated in deployments and exercises later in the year then in Nov 1992 deployed a four aircraft detachment to Split, Croatia in support of UN forces providing humanitarian aid in the former Yugoslavia. This deployment continues, there being a regular rotation of personnel, and aircraft are routinely returned to Yeovilton for base maintenance, flying overland across France and Italy. The squadron was awarded the 1993 Boyd Trophy for its work in support of United Nations forces.

Battle Honours

Falkland Islands	1982
Kuwait	1991

Westland Whirlwind HAS.7 XL834 '391' 'B' of No.845 Squadron at Kai Tak in 1958. (A.Straw via Peter Gosden)

Westland Wessex HU.5 XS516 'X/H' of No.845 Squadron, HMS Hermes lifting supplies from RFA Retainer in March 1975. (via Brian Lowe)

Identification Markings
Avenger single letters, to 5A+ 5.44, to H1A+ 2.45; Wildcat unknown; Whirlwind/Hiller/Wasp/Wessex single letters, later with fin letter B:A:H:VL; from 1979 Wessex/Sea King (Y)A-(Y)i.

Aircraft Equipment	Period of Service	Example
Avenger I	Feb 1943 - Sep 1945	FN932 (H1A)
Wildcat V	Feb 1944 - Apr 1944	
	Aug 1944 - Feb 1945	JV462
Whirlwind HAS.22	Mar 1954 - Oct 1955	WV204 (P)
	Nov 1955 - Aug 1957	WV199 (T)
Whirlwind HAR.3	Nov 1955 - Aug 1957	XG585 (T)
Whirlwind HAS.7	Jun 1957 - Apr 1959	XL837 (392 'B')
Wessex HAS.1	Apr 1962 - Aug 1965	XS115 (A/A)
Hiller HT.2	Apr 1964 - Aug 1965	XS164 (X)
Wasp HAS.1	Nov 1966 - Jan 1973	XS537 (O/B)
Whirlwind HAS.7	Dec 1964 - Jun 1965	XL841 (P)
Wessex HU.5	Jan 1966 - Oct 1986	XT468 (YD)
Sea King HC.4	Jun 1984 - to date	ZA425 (A)

Squadron bases
Quonset Point	1 Feb 1943
HMS Tracker (DLT)	25 Apr 1943
Quonset Point	25 Apr 1943
Norfolk	27 May 1943
USS Charger (DLT)	27 May 1943
Norfolk	29 May 1943
HMS Chaser	1 Jun 1943
Machrihanish	6 Jul 1943
Hatston	6 Jul 1943
Machrihanish	3 Jan 1944
Maydown	29 Jan 1944
Eglinton	11 Feb 1944
HMS Ravager (DLT)	16 Feb 1944
Eglinton	17 Feb 1944
SS Strathnaver/ HMS Atheling/ HMS Engadine	1 Mar 1944
Katukurunda	5 Apr 1944

Squadron bases
HMS Illustrious	3 May 1944
Katukurunda	27 May 1944
HMS Ameer	26 Jul 1944
Katukurunda	23 Aug 1944
Colombo Racecrse	20 Oct 1944
Vavuniya	19 Nov 1944
HMS Ameer	24 Dec 1944
HMS Begum	29 Dec 1944
Colombo Racecrse	30 Dec 1944
HMS Empress	3 Feb 1945
Colombo Racecrse	9 Mar 1945
HMS Empress	29 Mar 1945
Trincomalee	30 Mar 1945
HMS Emperor	8 Apr 1945
HMS Khedive	18 Apr 1945
Colombo Racecrse	20 Apr 1945
HMS Empress	13 May 1945
Trincomalee	22 May 1945
HMS Empress	10 Jun 1945
Trincomalee	13 Jun 1945
HMS Shah (DLP)	15 Jun 1945
Colombo Racecrse	16 Jun 1945
HMS Shah (Dt4)	27 Jun 1945
to	17 Jul 1945
HMS Shah	17 Jul 1945
Katukurunda	1 Sep 1945
HMS Shah (crews)	9 Sep 1945
Sqdn disbanded UK	7 Oct 1945
Gosport	15 Mar 1954
HMS Perseus	21 Apr 1954
Hal Far	28 Apr 1954
HMS Eagle	1 May 1954
Hal Far	3 May 1954
HMS Centaur	1 Oct 1954
Hal Far	4 Oct 1954
HMS Triumph	26 Oct 1954
Hal Far	27 Oct 1954
HMS Centaur (Dt3)	18-20 Nov 1954
HMS Albion (Dt3)	23 Nov 1954
to	2 Dec 1954
HMS Albion/Centaur	18 Jan 1955
Hal Far	1 Feb 1955
HMS Albion/Centaur	7 Mar 1955
Hal Far	14 Mar 1955
HMS Eagle	19 Aug 1955
North Front	24 Aug 1955
HMS Eagle	8 Sep 1955
HMS Bulwark	17 Sep 1955
Lee-on-Solent	3 Oct 1955
Squadron disbanded	10 Oct 1955
Lee-on-Solent	14 Nov 1955
Gosport (Dt)	21 Nov 1955
to	10 Jan 1956
Portland (Dt)	10 Jan 1956
to	23 Apr 1956
Eglinton	20 Apr 1956
Lossiemouth	7 Jun 1956
HMS Ocean/Theseus	19 Jun 1956
Lee-on-Solent	6 Jul 1956
Eglinton	4 Sep 1956
Tiree	10 Sep 1956
Eglinton	12 Sep 1956
Lee-on-Solent	21 Sep 1956
HMS Ocean	29 Sep 1956
HMS Theseus	18 Oct 1956
Hal Far	26 Oct 1956
Ta Kali	29 Oct 1956
HMS Theseus	1 Nov 1956
Ta Kali	10 Nov 1956
HMS Theseus	22 Nov 1956
Ta Kali	5 Dec 1956
HMS Albion	19 Jan 1957
Lee-on-Solent	6 Mar 1957
HMS Albion	16 Apr 1957
Hal Far	22 Apr 1957
HMS Albion	4 May 1957
Lee-on-Solent	15 May 1957
HMS Bulwark	27 Aug 1957

Squadron bases		Squadron bases		Squadron bases		Squadron bases	
Lee-on-Solent	21 Oct 1957	HMS Fearless	23 Jan 1967	Luqa	17 Jul 1969	Manston	25 Jan 1974
HMS Bulwark	10 Jan 1958	('B' Flight)	to 20 Feb 1967	HMS Bulwark	30 Jul 1969	Lossiemouth (Dt2)	25 Jan 1974
Culdrose	4 Nov 1958	Sek Kong	18 Feb 1967	Culdrose	13 Aug 1969		to 6 Feb 1974
HMS Centaur	22 Jan 1959	HMS Bulwark	22 Feb 1967	Yeovilton (Dt4)	2-8 Sep 1969	Yeovilton	12 Mar 1974
Hal Far	20 Feb 1959	Sembawang	4 Mar 1967	Yeovilton	8 Sep 1969	HMS Hermes	19 Mar 1974
HMS Centaur	10 Mar 1959	HMS Bulwark	9 Mar 1967	HMS Bulwark	19 Sep 1969	Luqa (Dt7)	2-22 Apr 1974
Culdrose	25 Mar 1959	Sembawang	17 Mar 1967	Culdrose	23 Oct 1969	HMS Fearless (Dt2)	11 May 1974
Squadron disbanded	20 Apr 1959	Mersing (Dt)	3-8 Apr 1967	HMS Albion	15 May 1970		to 20 Jul 1974
Culdrose	10 Apr 1962	Terrendak (Dt)	18-22 Apr 1967	Culdrose	23 Nov 1970	Luqa (Dt10)	13-22 May 1974
Yeovilton	28 May 1962	Kluang	24-25 Apr 1967	HMS Albion	29 Jan 1971	Gagetown (Dt8)	3-28 Jun 1974
Culdrose	8 Jun 1962	Mersing	2-8 May 1967	Culdrose	17 Feb 1971	Akrotiri (Dt)	24-27 Jul 1974
Plasterdown Camp,	30 Jul 1962	HMS Bulwark	14 May 1967	HMS Bulwark	27 Apr 1971	Yeovilton	6 Aug 1974
Dartmoor (Dt8)	to 2 Aug 1962	Sembawang	20-30 Jun 1967	Culdrose	28 May 1971	HMS Hermes	12 Sep 1974
HMS Albion	18 Sep 1962	('C' Flight)		HMS Bulwark	10 Jun 1971	HMS Fearless (Dt2)	27 Sep 1974
Culdrose	24 Sep 1962	Sembawang	1-12 Jul 1967	Culdrose	17 Jun 1971		to 1 Nov 1974
HMS Albion	2 Nov 1962	('B' Flight)		HMS Bulwark	30 Jun 1971	Yeovilton (Dt6)	10 Oct 1974
Kuching	14 Dec 1962	Thailand	1-13 Jul 1967	Culdrose	8 Jul 1971		to 6 Nov 1974
HMS Albion	7 Jan 1963	('A','C' and		HMS Bulwark	12 Aug 1971	Yeovilton	6 Nov 1974
Sembawang (Dt)	10 Jan 1963	'D' Flights)		HMS Fearless	6-24 Sep 1971	Arbroath (Dt4)	29 Nov 1974
	to 12 Feb 1963	Kuantan	21 Jul 1967	(Dt4)			to 5 Dec 1974
Sembawang	12 Feb 1963	Sembawang	27 Jul 1967	Akrotiri	14 Sep 1971	Valley (Dt2)	18-22 Nov 1974
Kuching (Dt)	9 Apr 1963	Terrendak	13 Sep 1967	HMS Bulwark	24 Sep 1971	RFA Sir Galahad/	31 Dec 1974
	to 27 Jul 1963	Sembawang	20 Sep 1967	Culdrose	8 Dec 1971	Bardufoss	to 28 Feb 1975
HMS Albion	17 Apr 1963	HMS Bulwark	29 Sep 1967	HMS Fearless(Dt4)	3 Jan 1972	HMS Fearless (Dt2)	9 Jan 1975
Labuan (Dt)	18 Aug 1963	Sembawang	23 Oct 1967	- to Bardufoss			to 27 Mar 1975
	to 30 Sep 1963	HMS Bulwark	6-17 Nov 1967	Detachment (6):		HMS Hermes (Dt6)	25 Feb 1975
Sibu (Dt)	19 Aug 1963	('A' & 'B' Flights)		HMS Bulwark	11 Jan 1972		to 6 Mar 1975
	to 8 Sep 1963	HMS Bulwark	10-17 Nov 1967	Hal Far	18 Jan 1972	HMS Hermes	6 Mar 1975
Sibu (Dt)	26 Sep 1963	('C' Flight)		HMS Bulwark	30 Mar 1972	Blissville	7 May 1975
	to 23 Jun 1965	Sembawang	6-17 Nov 1967	Culdrose	4 Apr 1972	HMS Hermes	28 May 1975
Kuching (Dt)	30 Sep 1963	('D' Flight)		HMS Fearless (Dt4)	2 Mar 1972	St Hubert (Dt4)	3-13 Jun 1975
	to 15 Dec 1963	Sembawang	17 Nov 1967	to	14 Mar 1972	Yeovilton	26 Jun 1975
Belaga (Dt)	1 Oct 1963	HMS Bulwark	27 Nov 1967	Tirstrup (Dt3)	24 Apr 1972	RFA Olna (Dt2)	6 Jul 1975
	to 1 Nov 1963	HMS Eagle (Dt2)	9-11 Dec 1967	to	10 May 1972		to 7 Aug 1975
Nanga Gaat (Dt)	1 Nov 1963	HMS Hermes		HMS Bulwark	17 May 1972	Bassingbourne	8-12 Jul 1975
	to 23 Jun 1965	(Dt2)	14-2 3 Dec 1967	Culdrose	17 Jul 1972	(Dt2)	
HMS Albion	29 Jan 1964	HMS Hermes		Lee-on-Solent	25 Aug 1972	HMS Hermes	1 Sep 1975
Sembawang (Dt4)	7-17 Mar 1965	(Dt2)	2-15 Jan 1968	Culdrose	29 Aug 1972	HMS Intrepid (Dt2)	30 Sep 1975
Semangyang (Dt)	10 Mar 1964	Sembawang	2 Feb 1968	HMS Albion	6 Sep 1972		to 1 Dec 1975
	to 4 Jun 1964	Changi	9 Feb 1968	Yeovilton	28 Sep 1972	Hal Far (Dt8)	7-20 Oct 1975
HMS Bulwark	23 Jun 1965	HMS Bulwark	17 Feb 1968	HMS Albion	10 Oct 1972	Yeovilton	27 Oct 1975
Culdrose	3 Sep 1965	Culdrose	20 Apr 1968	Gagetown	19-30 Oct 1972	HMS Hermes (Dt4)	27 Oct 1975
HMS Bulwark(Dt6)	2-6 May 1966	HMS Bulwark	30 May 1968	(Pekersville Camp -			to 24 Nov 1975
HMS Bulwark (Dt6)	19 May 1966	Culdrose (Dt9)	21 Jun 1968	'A' & 'D' Flights)		Arbroath (Dt4)	24-29 Nov 1975
	to 10 Jun 1966		to 3 Jul 1968	Dartmouth (Dt7)	21 Oct 1972	RFA Sir Geraint	28 Dec 1975
HMS Bulwark (Dt6)	17 Jun 1966	Valkenburg (Dt6)	4-9 Jul 1968		to 2 Nov 1972	(Dt4)	to 3 Jan 1976
	to 7 Nov 1966	Culdrose	2 Aug 1968	Yeovilton	23 Nov 1972	Bardufoss (Dt4)	30 Jan 1976
HMS Bulwark	13 Aug 1966	Farnborough	6 Sep 1968	HMS Intrepid (Dt2)	8 Jan 1973		to 10 Feb 1976
Sembawang	16 Sep 1966	Culdrose	23 Sep 1968		to 28 Mar 1973	HMS Hermes	12 Jan 1976
HMS Bulwark	3 Oct 1966	HMS Fearless	23-26 Sep 1968	Bardufoss (Dt4)	11 Jan 1973	Yeovilton	10 Feb 1976
Sembawang (Dt)	25 Nov 1966	(Dt3)			to 16 Mar 1973	HMS Hermes	18 Feb 1976
	to 3 Dec 1966	HMS Fearless	19-26 Oct 1968	Prestwick (Dt3)	5 Feb 1973	Elvergardsmoen	29 Feb 1976
Gemas	6 Dec 1966	(Dt8)			to 21 Feb 1973		to 15 Mar 1976
HMS Bulwark	12 Dec 1966	HMS Bulwark	17 Apr 1969	Castlemartin	2-6 Apr 1973	Yeovilton	6 Apr 1976
Sembawang	13 Jan 1967	Akrotiri (Dt8)	2-17 May 1969	('C' & 'D' Flts)		Barry Buddon, nr	11 Jun 1976
HMS Bulwark	3 Feb 1967	Dekhelia (Dt6)	28-29 May 1969	Barry Buddon Range	29 May 1973	Arbroath	
Jason's Bay	22-28 Feb 1967	St Mandrier	20 Jun 1969	(Dt9)	to 7 Jun 1973	HMS Intrepid	12-14 Jun 1976
('A' Flight)		HMS Bulwark	4 Jul 1969	Valley (Dt2)	11-13 Jun 1973	('D' Flight)	
				Castlemartin	14-20 Jun 1973	Yeovilton	26 Jun 1976
				Range (Dt4)		HMS Fearless	
				Sennybridge(Dt4)	17-20 Jun 1973	(Dt2)	5-19 Sep 1976
				Culdrose (Dt3)	19-21 Jun 1973	RFA Sir Tristram	5-19 Sep 1976
				Okehampton	2 Jul 1973	(Dt4)	
				Yeovilton	6 Jul 1973	Otterøy Island	18-28 Sep 1976
				Davidstowe Moor	16 Jul 1973	(Dt6)	
				Yeovilton	20 Jul 1973	RFA Sir	
				HMS Hermes (Dt8)	19 Aug 1973	Tristram (Dt6)	24-28 Sep 1976
					to 6 Sep 1972	HMS Hermes	11 Jan 1977
				HMS Hermes (Dt4)	24 Sep 1973	Yeovilton	21 Jan 1977
					to 19 Oct 1973	HMS Hermes	2 Feb 1977
				Otterburn	4 Oct 1973	Yeovilton	17 Feb 1977
				Yeovilton	8 Oct 1973	Valkenburg(Dt4)	21-24 Feb 1977
				Prestwick (Dt2)	24-26 Oct 1973	Bardufoss (Dt4)	24 Feb 1977
				HMS Hermes	5 Nov 1973		to 7 Mar 1977
				Arbroath (Dt3)	29 Nov 1973	HMS Hermes (Dt4)	21 Feb 1977
					to 8 Dec 1973	Narvik/RFA Sir	30 Mar 1977
				Yeovilton	4 Dec 1973	Galahad (Dt3)	to 4 Apr 1977
				Bardufoss (Dt4)	3 Jan 1974	HMS Hermes (sqdn)	4 Apr 1977
					to 11 Feb 1974	Yeovilton	25 May 1977
				HMS Hermes	9 Jan 1974	HMS Hermes	29 Jun 1977

Wessex HU.5 XT470 'L/H' of No.845 Sqn HMS Hermes 1976 (MAP)

Westland Sea King HU.5 ZF118 'H' of No.845 Squadron in 1988

Squadron bases
Yeovilton 5 Jul 1977
HMS Hermes (Dt4) 30 Aug 1977
  to 29 Oct 1977
Norfolk 24-29Sep 1977
Aldergrove (Dt4) 10 Oct 1977
  to 10 May 1982
Seaton Barracks
  (Dt2) 24-27Oct 1977
Bardufoss (Dt4) 18 Nov 1977
  to 21 Mar 1978
Saetermoen FOB 13-16Dec 1977
Gardermoen 30 Jan 1978
  to 24 Feb 1978
Lyngen Fjord 28 Feb 1978
  to 6 Mar 1978
Elvergardsmoen 13-16Mar1978
HMS Fearless(Dt2) 2-4May1978
Salisbury Plain
  (Dt2) 8-12May1978
Barry Budden (Dt8) 23 May 1978
  to 2 Jun 1978
HMS Fearless
  (Dt4) 5-12Jun 1978
Balmarca FAB
  (Dt4) 12-15Jun 1978
HMS Fearless
  (Dt2) 4-14Jul 1978
Arbroath (Dt3) 24-28Jul 1978
Prestwick (Dt1) 24 Jul 1978
  to 7 Aug 1978
HMS Hermes(Dt6)
  21-30Aug 1978
HMS Hermes (Dt8) 30 Aug 1978
  to 28 Sep 1978
HMS Fearless
  (Dt4) 4-12Sep 1978
Scatsta FAB(Dt4) 4-12Sep 1978
Avendal FAB 19-26Sep 1978
Castlemartin
  (Dt2) 9-11Oct 1978
Arbroath (Dt2) 6-10Nov1978
HMS Hermes
  (Dt2) 11-17Nov 1978
Castlemartin
  (Dt4) 14-17Feb 1979
HMS Hermes
  (Dt2) 11-28Mar 1979
Asegarden FAB 18-22Mar1979

Squadron bases
HMS Intrepid
  (Dt2) 1-11Apr 1979
Alderney (Dt2) 2-5Apr 1979
Alderney (Dt2) 25-27Apr1979
HMS Intrepid (Dt2) 11 May 1979
  to 25 Jun 1979
Lee-on-Solent
  (Dt2) 18-22Jun 1979
HMS Hermes (Dt2) 27 Jun 1979
  to 13 Jul 1979
Blankenheim
  (Dt2) 13-26Jul 1979
RFA Tidepool (Dt1) 29 Jul 1979
  to 1 Aug 1979
Cape Wrath (Dt1) 29 Jul 1979
  to 2 Aug 1979
HMS Intrepid (Dt2) 4 Sep 1979
  to 16 Nov 1979
Gibraltar 20 Sep 1979
  to 3 Oct 1979
RFA Olna 17-18Oct 1979
HMS Bulwark 18-23Oct 1979
RFA Olna 23-24Oct 1979
Arbroath (Dt2) Oct 1979
Castlemartin(Dt4) 3-7Dec1979
HMS Intrepid (Dt2) 7 Jan 1980
  to 24 Mar 1980
Leek (Dt1) 8-11Feb 1980
Aviemore (Dt1) 14-28Feb 1980
Castlemartin
  (Dt2) 18-20Feb 1980
HMS Intrepid (Dt2) 29 Apr 1980
  to 25 Jun 1980
Gibraltar 8-12May1980
RFA Sir Geraint
  DLT (Dt3) 8-9May1980
Alderney (Dt2) 12-13Jun 1980
Alderney (Dt2) 19-20Jun 1980
Otterburn (Dt4) 10-15Jul 1980
Blankenheim (Dt2) 18 Jul 1980
  to 1 Aug 1980
USS Saipan (Dt4) Sep 1980
Norway FAB (Dt4) Oct 1980
HMS Bulwark (Dt4) Oct 1980
HMS Intrepid (Dt2) 29 Sep 1980
  to 28 Nov 1980
Gibraltar Oct 1980

Squadron bases
HMS Bulwark (Dt2) 13 Oct 1980
  to 6 Nov 1980
Castlemartir
  (Dt3) 8-12Dec 1980
HMS Intrepid (Dt2) 6 Jan 1981
  to 6 Mar 1981
HMS Bulwark
  (Dt2) 6-23Mar 1981
Catterick (Dt1) 25 Feb 1981
  to 2 Mar 1981
HMS Intrepid (Dt2) 29 Apr 1981
  to 18 May 1981
HMS Hermes
  (Dt2) 11-21May1981
Saillagouse (Dt3) 1-7Jun 1981
Salisbury Plain Jun 1981
  (Dt) to Jul 1981
Castlemartin
  (Dt) 24-28Jul 1981
HMS Hermes
  (Dt4) 13-24Jul 1981
HMS Hermes (Dt2) 2 Sep 1981
  to 2 Dec 1981
Jacksonville Sep 1981
Jersey (Dt2) 7-11Sep 1981
HMS Intrepid
  (Dt2) 8-28Sep 1981
HMS Intrepid(Dt2) 28 Sep 1981
  to Dec 1981
Gibraltar 2-10Nov1981
Machrihanish
  (Dt2) 12-15Oct 1981
Arbroath (Dt2) 19-22Oct 1981
HMS Fearless (Dt2) 17 Oct 1981
  to 2 Dec 1981
HMS Invincible
  (Dt7) 4-10Dec 1981
RFA Sir Geraint (Dt4) Dec 1981
(passage UK-Norway)
  to 2 Jan 1982
Bardufoss (Dt4) 2 Jan 1982
  to 12 Mar 1982
HMS Fearless (Dt2) 6 Jan 1982
  to 5 Mar 1982
HMS Hermes (Dt1) 22 Jan 1982
  to 14 Feb 1982
HMS Hermes
  (Dt7) 16-27Feb 1982

Squadron bases
HMS Fearless
  (Dt2) 4-12Mar 1982
RFA Olmeda (Dt2) 7-12Mar1982
Gardermoen
  FAB (Dt8) 12-13Mar 1982
Gratanganfjord FOB
  (Dt8) 13-17Mar 1982
HMS Invincib2 5 Jun 1979
Lee-on-Solent
  (Dt2) 18-22Jun 1979
HMS Hermes (Dt2) 27 Jun 1979
  to 13 Jul 1979
Blankenheim
  (Dt2) 13-26Jul 1979
RFA Tidepool (Dt1) 29 Jul 1979
  to 1 Aug 1979
Cape Wrath (Dt1) 29 Jul 1979
  to 2 Aug 1979
HMS Intrepid (Dt2) 4 Sep 1979
  to 16 Nov 1979
Gibraltar 20 Sep 1979
  to 3 Oct 1979
RFA Olna 17-18Oct 1979
HMS Bulwark 18-23Oct 1979
RFA Olna 23-24Oct 1979
Arbroath (Dt2) Oct 1979
Castlemartin(Dt4) 3-7Dec1979
HMS Intrepid (Dt2) 7 Jan 1980
  to 24 Mar 1980
Leek (Dt1) 8-11Feb 1980
Aviemore (Dt1) 14-28Feb 1980
Castlemartin
  (Dt2) 18-20Feb 1980
HMS Intrepid (Dt2) 29 Apr 1980
  to 25 Jun 1980
Gibraltar 8-12May1980
RFA Sir Geraint
  DLT (Dt3) 8-9May1980
Alderney (Dt2) 12-13Jun 1980
Alderney (Dt2) 19-20Jun 1980
Otterburn (Dt4) 10-15Jul 1980
Blankenheim (Dt2) 18 Jul 1980
  to 1 Aug 1980
USS Saipan (Dt4) Sep 1980
Norway FAB (Dt4) Oct 1980
HMS Bulwark (Dt4) Oct 1980
HMS Intrepid (Dt2) 29 Sep 1980
  to 28 Nov 1980
Gibraltar Oct 1980
HMS Bulwark (Dt2) 13 Oct 1980
  to 6 Nov 1980
Castlemartin
  (Dt3) 8-12Dec 1980
HMS Intrepid (Dt2) 6 Jan 1981
  to 6 Mar 1981
HMS Bulwark
  (Dt2) 6-23Mar 1981
Catterick (Dt1) 25 Feb 1981
  to 2 Mar 1981
HMS Intrepid (Dt2) 29 Apr 1981
  to 18 May 1981
HMS Hermes
  (Dt2) 11-21May1981
Saillagouse (Dt3) 1-7Jun 1981
Salisbury Plain
  (Dt) to Jul 1981
Castlemartin
  (Dt) 24-28Jul 1981
HMS Hermes
  (Dt4) 13-24Jul 1981
HMS Hermes (Dt2) 2 Sep 1981
  to 2 Dec 1981
Jacksonville Sep 1981
Jersey (Dt2) 7-11Sep 1981
HMS Intrepid
  (Dt2) 8-28Sep 1981
HMS Intrepid(Dt2) 28 Sep 1981
  to Dec 1981
Gibraltar 2-10Nov1981

Squadron bases
Machrihanish
  (Dt2) 12-15Oct 1981
Arbroath (Dt2) 19-22Oct 1981
HMS Fearless (Dt2) 17 Oct 1981
  to 2 Dec 1981
HMS Invincible
  (Dt7) 4-10Dec 1981
RFA Sir Geraint (Dt4) Dec 1981
  (passage UK-Norway)
  to 2 Jan 1982
Bardufoss (Dt4) 2 Jan 1982
  to 12 Mar 1982
HMS Fearless (Dt2) 6 Jan 1982
  to 5 Mar 1982
HMS Hermes (Dt1) 22 Jan 1982
  to 14 Feb 1982
HMS Hermes
  (Dt7) 16-27Feb 1982
HMS Fearless
  (Dt2) 4-12Mar 1982
RFA Olmeda (Dt2) 7-12Mar1982
Gardesmoen
  FAB (Dt8) 12-13Mar 1982
Gratanganfjord FOB
  (Dt8) 13-17Mar 1982
HMS Invincible
  (Dt8) 17-22Mar 1982
Operation CORPORATE -
  South Atlantic:
'A' Flt (Dt3):
RFA Resource 3 Apr 1982
HMS Glamorgan
  (Dt1) 29-30Apr 1982
San Carlos 23 May 1982
Port San Carlos 30 May 1982
  Fitzroy FOB 11-15Jun 1982
  Port Stanley FOB
  15-24Jun 1982
RFA Resource 24 Jun 1982

Squadron bases
Yeovilton 19 Jul 1982
'B' Flt (Dt3):
Ascension 5 Apr 1982
RFA Fort Austin 8 Apr 1982
HMS Invincible
  (Dt1) 9-22May1982
HMS Hermes
  (Dt1) 17-20May 1982
MV Atlantic Conveyor
  (Dt2) 20-25May1982
  (ship sunk 25 May, 1 a/c
  abandoned, other to HMS Hermes)
RFA Stromness
  (Dt1) 22-26May 1982
HMS Hermes
  (Dt1) 25-26May 1982
San Carlos 26 May 1982
  (flight disbanded - aircraft
  to 847 Sqdn, Atlantic Conveyor
  survivors retd UK 7Jun)
'C' Flt (Dt2):
Ascension 10 Apr 1982
RFA Tidespring 11 Apr 1982
  (both a/c destroyed in S Georgia
  22 Apr, replacement aircraft
  embarked Ascension 14 May)
Port San Carlos 10 Jun 1982
HMS Hermes 3 Jul 1982
Yeovilton 22 Jul 1982
'D' Flt (Dt2):
Ascension 10 Apr 1982
  (Wideawake) to17 Sep 1982
'E' Flt (Dt2):
HMS Intrepid 26 Apr 1982
RFA Tidepool 8 May 1982
HMS Antrim
  (Dt1) 19-21May 1982
SS Canberra
  (Dt1) 21-24May 1982

Squadron bases
San Carlos 26 May 1982
Port San Carlos 30 May 1982
MV Atlantic Causeway
  13 Jul 1982
  (passage Falklands-UK)
Yeovilton Aug 1982
Sqdn take over 847 Sqdn assets
  in Falklands:
Port San Carlos
  (Dt11) 14 Sep 1982
HMS Illustrious (Dt2, passage
  Falklands-UK)
  (Dt2) 19 Oct 1982
  to 7 Dec 1982
Roosevelt Roads 5-9Nov1982
MV Astronomer(Dt9) 30Oct1982
  (passage Falklands-UK)
  to 3 Dec 1982
Yeovilton 3/7Dec 1982
RFA Olmeda (Dt1) 7-17Sep 1982
  (passage UK-Ascension)
Ascension (Dt3) 17 Sep 1982
  to 11 Jul 1984
HMS Fearless (Dt1) 28 Sep 1982
  to 27 Nov 1982
SS Transfjell Dt4) 30 Oct 1982
  (passage UK-Norway)
  to 11 Nov 1982
Aberporth (Dt1) 8-12Nov1982
Bardufoss (Dt4) 11 Nov 1982
  to 13 Mar 1983
HMS Hermes (Dt1) 24 Nov 1982
  to 6 Dec 1982
HMS Fearless (Dt2) 3 Jan 1983
  to 4 Mar 1983
RFA Resource (Dt1) 6 Jan 1983
  to 27 Apr 1983
Stanford (Dt1) 7-12Jan 1983

Squadron bases
HMS Hermes
  (Dt1) 17-28Jan 1983
RFA Regent (Dt1) 31 Jan 1983
  to 12 Apr 1983
Elvergardsmoen
  (Dt2) 7-25Feb 1983
Leeming (Dt1) 9-12Mar1983
HMS Illustrious
  (Dt1) 11-16Mar 1983
HMS Fearless
  (Dt2) 17-21Mar 1983
Asegarden FOB
  (Dt4) 10-13Mar 1983
  (Dt6) 13-17Mar 1983
HMS Fearless
  (Dt2) 17-21Mar 1983
HMS Hermes
  (Dt4) 17-22Mar 1983
Lanveoc-Poulmic
  (Dt3) 5-7 Apr 1983
HMS Invincible 23 Apr 1983
  (Dt3) to 16 May 1983
HMS Fearless
  (Dt2) 3-23May1983
HMS Invincible 23 May 1983
  (Dt3) to 10 Jun 1983
Salisbury Plain
  FOB (Dt5) 10-16Jun 1983
Ronaldsway
  (Dt1) 19-24Jun 1983
Sennybridge
  (Dt2) 22-28Jun 1983
HMS Hermes
  (Dt2) 8-21Jul 1983
Fremlington
  (Dt1) 21-24Jun 1983
Sennybridge
  (Dt2) 22-28Jun 1983

Westland Sea King HC.4 ZA298 '(Y)G' of No.845 Squadron in United Nations colours for Operation Grapple in 1992.
(845 Sqdn/Kevin Prece)

Squadron bases
Greenham Common
 (Dt) 20-25Jul 1983
Culdrose (Dt6) 25-28Jul 1983
RFA Regent (Dt1) 30 Aug 1983
  to 17 Apr 1984
RFA Resource (Dt1) 1 Sep 1983
  to Nov 1983
HMS Fearless
 (Dt4) 7-27Sep 1983
 (Dt1) 27 Sep 1983
  to Nov 1983
HMS Hermes (Dt3) 14 Sep 1983
  to 22 Nov 1983
Akrotiri 24-27Oct 1983
El Hamman FOB
  1-3 Nov 1983
MV Transfjell
 (Dt4) 20-28Oct 1983
 (passage UK-Norway)
Bardufoss (Dt4) 28 Oct 1983
  to 17 Mar 1984
Saetermoen FOB
 (Dt2) 30 Jan 1984
  to 3 Feb 1984
Saetermoen FOB
 (Dt2) 28 Feb 1984
  to 3 Mar 1984
Saillagouse (Dt3) 29 Nov 1984
  to 3 Dec 1984
RFA Resource (Dt1)19 Jan 1984
  to Mar 1984
HMS Fearless (Dt3) Feb 1984
  to 17 Mar 1984
Ballsfjorden
 FOB (Dt7) 17-22Mar1984
Bardufoss (Dt7) 22-23 Mar 1984
HMS Hermes
 (Dt1) 9-12Apr 1984
RFA Resource (Dt1)26 Apr 1984
  to Jun 1984
HMS Fearless(Dt2) 2-6May1984
Arbroath (12) 14-25 May 1984
Arbroath (Dt3) 25-31 May 1984
RFA Fort Grange
 (Dt1) 19-26May1984
 (passage UK-Ascension)
RFA Fort Austin
 (Dt1) 13-22Jun 1984
 (passage Ascension-UK)
RFA Resource
 (Dt1) 16-29Jun 1984
Middle Wallop
 (Dt2) 3-8 Jul 1984
RFA Olwen (Dt1) 11-25Jul 1984
 (passage UK-Ascension)
Ascension (Dt2) 11 Jul 1984
  to 5 Sep 1984
Culdrose (Dt6) 23-26Jul 1984
RFA Olmeda (Dt3) 3-9Sep1984
RFA Resource(Dt1) 3-9Sep1984
Vaerlose (Dt4) 9-10Sep 1984
 (Dt6) 10-12Sep 1984
RFA Olmeda
 (Dt2) 12-16Sep 1984
RFA Resource
 (Dt2) 12-16Sep 1984
RFA Sir Bedivere
 (Dt1) 12-19Sep 1984
RFA Sir Percivale
 (Dt1) 12-19Sep 1984
Zeeland FOB
 (Dt4) 16-20Sep 1984
Bad Lippspringe
 (Dt2) 18-20Sep 1984
Bad Tolz (Dt4) 20 Sep 1984
  to 1 Oct 1984
RFA name unknown
 (Dt1) 5-17Sep 1984
 (passage Ascension-UK)

Westland Sea King HC.4 ZG820 '(Y)F' of No.845 Squadron dropping a small vehicle into a landing ground at Split, Croatia during Operation Grapple, 1993. (845 Sqdn/Kevin Preece)

Squadron bases
Ascension (Dt1) 5 Sep 1984
  to 25 Jul 1985
HMS Fearless (Dt2)28 Sep 1984
  to 21 Nov 1984
Hellenikon 15-20 Oct 1984
Dhekalia 25-28Oct 1984
Arbroath (Dt3) 8-12Oct 1984
RFA Olmeda (Dt1) 8-26Oct 1984
RFA Fort Grange 12-23Oct 1984
Newcastle (Dt1) 11 Oct 1984
  to 6 Nov 1984
RFA (LSL) (Dt3) 31 Oct 1984
 (passage UK-Norway)
  to 5 Nov 1984
HMS Invincible
 (Dt1) 9-22Nov 1984
Bardufoss (Dt3) 5 Nov 1984
  to 15 Mar 1985

Squadron bases
HMS Fearless (Dt2) 7 Jan 1985
  to 7 Mar 1985
RFA Green Rover
  16-18Jan 1985
Roosevelt Roads 5-7Feb 1985
Mayport 13-16Feb 1985
Saillagouse(Dt3) 4-12Feb1985
RFA Olwen (Dt3) 8-15Mar 1985
Lyngen FOB
 (Dt6) 15-21Mar 1985
RFA Olwen (Dt3) 21-25Mar1985
HMS Invincible
 (Dt3) 21-28Mar 1985
Aberporth (Dt1) 9-18Apr1985
HMS Fearless (Dt1)29 Apr 1985
  to 27 May 1985
Arbroath (10) 7-17May1985
Otterburn (Dt2) 17-1 9 May1985

Squadron bases
HMS Illustrious (Dt) May 1985
HMS Intrepid (Dt) May 1985
Scillies (Dt1) May 1985
De Kooy (Dt2) Jun 1985
HMS Ark Royal (Dt) Jun 1985
RFA Fort Grange
 (Dt1) 25-31Jul 1985
 (passage Ascension-UK,
  det started Apr 1982)
Stornoway (Dt2) Jul 1985
Sennybridge (Dt2) Jul 1985
HMS Ark Royal
 (Dt2) 16-31Jul 1985
RFA Olna (Dt2) 1-2Aug1985
RFA Fort Austin
 (Dt2) 2-6Aug 1985
RFA Olna 6 Aug 1985
  to 23 Sep 1985

Squadron bases
HMS Invincible (Dt3) 9-24Sep 1985
RFA Olmeda (Dt3) 9-24Sep 1985
Plockton FOB 12-15Sep 1985
Cape Wrath FOB 17-21Sep 1985
HMS Intrepid (Dt1) 24 Sep 1985 to 4 Oct 1985
Hamstede (Dt6) 28 Sep 1985 to 1 Oct 1985
Prisenbozn (Dt6) 1-4Oct 1985
HMS Intrepid(Dt3) 4-8Oct 1985
GAF Landsberg (Dt4) 4-21Oct 1985
RFA Fort Austin (Dt1) 10-29Oct 1985
HMS Ark Royal (Dt2) 4 Nov 1985 to 16 Dec 1985
Bardufoss (Dt3) 29 Oct 1985 to 5 Mar 1986
HMS Invincible (Dt3) 13 Jan 1986 to 16 Mar 1986
HMS Ark Royal (Dt1) 27 Jan 1986 to 13 Feb 1986
RFA Fort Austin (Dt2) 20 Feb 1986 to 5 Mar 1986
(Dt1) 5-12Mar 1986
Tovil FOB (Dt4) 5-12Mar 1986
RFA Sir Percivale (Dt1) 12-17Mar 1986

Squadron bases
HMS Intrepid (Dt3) 12-18Mar 1986
RFA Sir Lancelot (Dt1) 12-19Mar 1986
HMS Intrepid (Dt1) 21 Apr 1986 to 20 Jun 1986
Mayport 2-12May 1986
Arbroath 6 May 1986
Yeovilton 22 May 1986
Lee-on-Solent (Dt3) 8-13Jun 1986
Arbroath (Dt2) 7-10Jul 1986
Sennybridge 15-18Jul 1986
RFA Fort Grange (Dt2) 22 Jul 1986 to 15 Dec 1986
RFA Olwen (Dt3) 29 Aug 1986 to 29 Sep 1986
Larvik FOB (Dt2) 9-15Sep 1986
Porsgrunn (Dt2) 5-16Sep 1986
Elkernforde(Dt2) 16-26 Sep 1986
Gutersloh (Dt2) 26 Sep 1986 to 2 Oct 1986
Landsberg (Dt2) 2-10Oct 1986
Valley (Dt2) 29 Sep 1986 to 3 Oct 1986
Otterburn (Dt2) 14-17Oct 1986
Coltishall(Dt3) 17-24Oct 1986
Arbroath (Dt2) 29 Oct 1986 to 7 Nov 1986
HMS Ark Royal (Dt6) 5-7Nov 1986
HMS Ark Royal (8) 7 Nov 1986
Yeovilton 20 Nov 1986
Coltishall (Dt4) 24-28Nov 1986

Squadron bases
Bardufoss (Dt3) 10 Jan 1987 to 10 Feb 1987
(Dt5) 10 Feb 1987 to 28 Mar 1987
Mo-I-Rana FOB (Dt2) 24 Feb 1987 to 6 Mar 1987
Arbroath (Dt2) 27 Apr 1987 to 1 May 1987
Prestwick (Dt2) 27 Apr 1987 to 1 May 1987
Salisbury Plain (Dt2) 21-26May 1987
Lee-on-Solent (Dt2) 25-29May 1987
Detmold (Dt6) 29 May 1987 to 16 Jun 1987
Otterburn B Flt (Dt3) 13-29Jul 1987
Dunkeswell (Dt1) 1-14Aug 1987
HMS Intrepid (Dt1) 14 Sep 1987 to 5 Oct 1987
(Dt3) 5-8 Oct 1987
Bastia (Dt3) 19 Sep 1987 to 4 Oct 1987
Coltishall(Dt2) 14-18Sep 1987
Arbroath (Dt1) 11-23Oct 1987
Bickleigh (Dt2) 12-15Oct 1987
HMS Ark Royal (Dt1) 12-24Oct 1987
HMS Illustrious (Dt5) 4-11Nov 1987
HMS Intrepid (Dt2) 4-11Nov 1987
Loch Ryan FOB (Dt7) 11-13Nov 1987
(Dt5) 13-16Nov 1987

Squadron bases
HMS Intrepid (Dt2) 13-16Nov 1987
West Freugh (Dt2) 16-19Oct 1987
Bardufoss (Dt3) 4 Jan 1988 to 12 Mar 1988
Mo-I-Rana (Dt2) 26 Feb 1988 to 9 Mar 1988
HMS Intrepid (Dt1) 19-23Jan 1988
HMS Illustrious (Dt1) 3-16Feb 1988
Kinloss (Dt3) 18-23Apr 1988
Dortmund (Dt6) 3-20May 1988
(Dt3) 20-24 May 1988
HMS Fearless (Dt2) 20-30Jun 1988
HMS Ark Royal 20 Jun 1988
(Dt2) to 14 Dec 1988
RFA Fort Grange 20 Nov 1988
(Dt2) to 4 Dec 1988
HMS Illustrious (Dt1) 30 Aug 1988 to 24 Sep 1988
Bardufoss (Dt4) 10-24Sep 1988
Rolla FOB 15-21Sep 1988
Okehampton(Dt2) 11-15Oct 1988
Sennybridge(Dt2) 17-25Oct 1988
Bardufoss (Dt2) 7 Nov 1988 to 4 Jan 1989
Arbroath (Dt1) 5-8Dec 1989
Bardufoss (Dt3) 4 Jan 1989 to 4 Feb 1989
RFA Fort Grange (Dt1) 19-30Jan 1989
Bardufoss (Dt6) 4 Feb 1989 to 3 Mar 1989

Westland Sea King HC.4 ZA298 (Y)G of No.845 Squadron in UN colours flying in mountainous coutnry during Operation Grapple, while based at Split, Croatia in 1993. (845 Sqdn/Kevin Preece)

Squadron bases

Mo-I-Rana FOB	
(Dt2)	7-12 Feb 1989
(Dt4)	12-23 Feb 1989
Evenes FOB	
(Dt2)	11-16 Feb 1989
Harstad FOB	
(Dt2)	24-28 Feb 1989
HMS Ark Royal	23 Feb 1989
(Dt1)	to 3 Mar 1989
(Dt7)	3-17 Mar 1989
(Dt1)	1-10 Apr 1989
HMS Invincible	
(Dt1)	2-10 May 1989
Dortmund (Dt6)	26 May 1989 to 12 Jun 1989
De Kooy (Dt2)	12-23 Jun 1989
Arbroath (Dt1)	5-13 Jul 1989
HMS Invincible	19 Jul 1989
(Dt1)	to 2 Aug 1989
Keevil	4 Sep 1989
Yeovilton	21 Sep 1989
Kinloss (Dt3)	1-10 Oct 1989
Tancos Portugal	
(Dt1)	5-24 Oct 1989
Capel Curig	
(Dt1)	16-20 Oct 1989
HMS Invincible	16 Oct 1989
(Dt1)	to 23 Feb 1990
Jacksonville	9 Dec 1989 to 15 Jan 1990
Sennybridge (Dt3)	13-16 Nov 1989
Okehampton (Dt2)	22-26 Nov 1989
Machrihanish (Dt2)	26 Nov 1989 to 1 Dec 1989
Bardufoss (Dt3)	5-16 Jan 1990
(Dt4)	16 Jan 1990 to 10 Mar 1990
Gardermoen	
(Dt3)	18-23 Feb 1990
HMS Intrepid	
(Dt1)	22-26 Jan 1990
Mo-I-Rana (Dt2)	9 Feb 1990 to 10 Mar 1990
HMS Invincible	
(Dt6)	10-23 Mar 1990
HMS Intrepid (Dt1)	24 Apr 1990 to 18 May 1990

Squadron bases

Deelen (Dt6)	11-25 May 1990
Arbroath (Dt2)	4-7 Jun 1990
Leuchars (Dt3)	11-15 Jun 1990
Lossiemouth (Dt1)	19-29 Jun 1990
Plockton (Dt2)	14-20 Jul 1990
HMS Intrepid (Dt3)	8-23 Sep 1990
RFA Argus (Dt4)	8-24 Sep 1990
Namsos FOB	15-19 Sep 1990
Lee-on-Solent (Dt4)	29 Sep 1990 to 4 Oct 1990
HMS Ark Royal	
(Dt3)	15-30 Oct 1990
Coltishall (Dt2)	22-26 Oct 1990
Tancos (Dt1)	2-20 Nov 1990
Operation GRANBY	
Persian Gulf:	
SS Atlantic Conveyor	21 Dec 1990
(passage UK-Gulf)	
Al Jubayl	5 Jan 1991
(aka NAS Flip Flop)	
Strawberry Fields MOB	23 Jan 1991
(Saudi Arabian desert)	
Trumpton MOB	6 Mar 1991
Al Jubayl (Dt3)	26 Mar 1991
(6)	31 Mar 1991
Alamo MOB (Dt3)	6-29 Apr 1991
(Doha, Kuwait City)	
(Dt1)	29 Apr 1991 to 9 May 1991
SS Baltic Eagle	
(Dt3)	6-21 Apr 1991
(passage Gulf-UK, diverted to Turkey)	
Incirlik (Dt3/1)	22 Apr 1991 to 12 May 1991
(2 a/c absorbed into 846 Sqdn 30 May 1991)	
SS Mercand Duke	
(Dt1)	12-31 May 1991
(passage Turkey-UK)	
Al Jubayl (Dt3)	29 Apr 1991
(Dt2)	9 Apr 1991 to 12 Apr 1991
(Dt1)	9-10 May 1991
SS Baltic Eider	
(Dt2)	12-23 May 1991
(passage Gulf-UK)	

Squadron bases

Yeovilton	23 May 1991
HMS Fearless 'C' Flt	
(Dt2)	14-24 Sep 1991
Altcar (Dt4)	5-16 Oct 1991
Valley (Dt2)	13-16 Jan 1992
RFA Fort Grange	
(Dt1)	22 Jan 1992 to 3 Feb 1992
Bardufoss (Dt3)	8-18 Feb 1992
(Dt5)	18 Feb 1992 to 25 Mar 1992
RFA Fort Grange	
(Dt4)	25-27 Mar 1992
HMS Fearless 'B' Flt	
(Dt3)	29 Apr 1992 to 18 May 1992
(Dt2)	18 May 1992 to 5 Jul 1992
(Dt3)	5-10 Jul 1992
Akrotori	24-29 May 1992
RFA Fort Austin	
(Dt2)	11 May 1992 to 26 Nov 1992
Sek Kong	13-21 Aug 1992
HMS Invincible	4-17 Sep 1992
HMS Ark Royal	27 Jun 1992
(Dt1)	to 5 Jul 1992
Sennybridge (Dt2)	Sep 1992
Keevil (Dt5)	11-30 Sep 1992
Prestwick (Dt1)	14-20 Oct 1992
RFA Argus B Flt	11 Nov 1992
(Dt4) to	14 Dec 1992
Split (Dt4)	14 Dec 1992
(NAS Banana) B Flt to date	
Gorni Vakuf FOB	7 Jun 1994 to date
Deelen (Dt1)	10-14 Jun 1993
De Kooy (Dt1)	6-10 Sep 1993
Soesterberg (Dt1)	1-3 Jun 1994

Commanding Officers

L/C WH Crawford RN		1 Feb 1943
L/C(A) JF Arnold RN		25 Oct 1943
L/C(A) DS Watts RNVR		15 May 1945

Commanding Officers

Squadron disbanded		7 Oct 1945
L/C H Phillips RN		15 Mar 1954
Squadron disbanded		10 Oct 1955
L/C JC Jacob RN		14 Nov 1955
L/C PJ Pritchett RN		24 Nov 1956
L/C HMA Hayes RN		3 Jun 1957
L/C CMA Wheatley RAN		19 Aug 1958
L/C AG Cornabe RN		4 Nov 1958
Squadron disbanded		20 Apr 1959
L/C AA Hensher RN		10 Apr 1962
L/C GJ Sherman RN		2 Oct 1963
L/C AD Levy RN		12 Feb 1965
L/C JHS Jervis RN		1 Nov 1966
L/C BC Sarginson MBE RN		23 Oct 1967
L/C DJ Lickfold MBE RN		3 Nov 1969
L/C JT Rawlins MBE RN		26 Dec 1970
L/C NS Foster RN		22 Mar 1972
L/C GS Clarke RN		18 Sep 1973
L/C WM Berry RN		8 Feb 1975
L/C RAY Bridges RN		24 Jan 1977
L/C AC Gratton-Cooper RN		31 Jul 1978
L/C TJ Stanning RN		14 Jul 1980
L/C RJ Warden RN		22 Feb 1982
L/C CJ de Mowbray RN		23 Nov 1983
L/C DG Widgery RN		25 Oct 1985
Capt PS Belding AFC RM		5 Feb 1987
L/C PS Belding AFC RN		1 Nov 1988
L/C HJ Ledingham RN		9 May 1989
Cdr HJ Ledingham RN		30 Jun 1989
L/C MD Salter RN		16 Oct 1990
L/C GWA Wallace AFC RN		22 Jun 1992
L/C PS Doyne-Ditmas RN		14 Feb 1994

Westland Sea King HC.4 ZG821 '(Y)D' of No.845 Squadron being painted in UN colours for Operation Grapple, 1993. (MAP)

No.846 Squadron

Badge: On a blue field, out of water barry wavy in base white and blue, a man proper, helmeted red, holding in his sinister hand a sword, gold, and riding on a Pegasus, white, attacking a sea serpent proper

Motto: Semper instans
(Always threatening)

[On the right is the unofficial badge of No.846 Squadron's fighter flight, with the motto 'Veniant Omnes']

No.846 Squadron personnel assembled at Lee-on-Solent on 1 March 1943 for passage to the United States, sailing from Gourock in HMT *Queen Elizabeth* on 17 March. Arriving at Halifax, Nova Scotia on 25 March they staged through New York to arrive at Quonset Point on 30 March. Here No.846 officially formed on 1 April as a torpedo bomber reconnaissance squadron with 12 Avenger Is for escort carrier service. These embarked in HMS *Ravager* in July for passage to the United Kingdom, anti-submarine patrols being carried out en route. The squadron worked up in Scotland, a fighter flight of four Wildcat Vs being added on 20 December from 'B' Flight of No.1832 Squadron. No.846 embarked in HMS *Tracker* in January 1944 to provide anti-submarine patrols for Gibraltar convoys. During a similar task on a convoy to Kola Inlet in March and April the Avengers sighted and attacked six U-boats, a further two being sighted on the return voyage. Further brief periods were spent in the ship in April and June, but on 3 June she was damaged in a collision whilst patrolling in the South West Approaches, and the squadron was disembarked.

The Wildcat strength was then briefly increased to a peak of ten but reduced to six before No.846 transferred to HMS *Trumpeter* in July for operations off the Norwegian coast. The Wildcat Vs were withdrawn in September, to be replaced by eight Wildcat VIs from No.852 Squadron. Minelaying operations were carried out off Norway in September, and in December four Avengers were detached to HMS *Premier* for operations. These activities continued into 1945, anti-submarine escort also being provided in March for a North Russian convoy. After VE-day the fighter flight was disbanded, and the remainder of the squadron stayed ashore. Plans to join HMS *Illustrious* as part of the 4th Carrier Air Group in the British Pacific Fleet were abandoned, and instead it became a trials unit, being consequently renumbered as No.751 Squadron at Machrihanish on 22 September 1945.

On 8 May 1962 No.846 reformed at Culdrose as a Commando squadron with six Whirlwind HAS.7s, these embarking in HMS *Albion* in September. In November it sailed for the Middle East, later continuing through the Suez Canal to Aden and then Mombasa.

Grumman Avenger I FN908 '4M' of No.846 Squadron, Machrihanish in December 1943. (RAF Museum 5988-11)

Grumman Avenger I FN814 'A' of No.846 Squadron, HMS Tracker approaching Gibraltar early in 1944. (Cdr J.W.Powell)

The ship was ordered to Brunei in December to assist in operations against terrorists, a task with which the squadron continued until October 1964 when it embarked in HMS *Bulwark* and sailed for Singapore. Here the squadron disbanded at Seletar on arrival on 19 October, being awarded the 1963 Boyd Trophy for its activities in Borneo.

No.846 reformed at Culdrose on 29 July 1968 as the Commando headquarters squadron with four Wessex HU.5s. In October it embarked in HMS *Fearless* during the Gibraltar talks on the future of Rhodesia, and in February 1969 went to Norway in RFA *Engadine* for cold weather trials, similar detachments being sent the following two winters. In September 1971 a detachment went to Lossiemouth for evasion trials against fixed wing aircraft, and in February 1972 four aircraft were in HMS *Bulwark* during the British withdrawal from Malta. In May 1972 No.846 moved to Yeovilton to become the Wessex HU.5 headquarters and trials squadron. Further detachments were sent to Norway each winter, and in addition the squadron took over the parentage of the three aircraft in RFAs *Regent*, *Resource* and *Tidespring*. No.846 disbanded at Yeovilton on 17 December 1975.

On 1 April 1976 No.846 reformed at Yeovilton from the remnants of the disbanded No.848 Squadron as a Commando squadron with eight Wessex HU.5s, being commissioned four days later. Various detachments took place during the year, including four aircraft to the Mediterranean in HMS *Fearless* in October. Aircraft went to northern Norway for exercises early in 1977, the squadron being embarked in both RFA *Sir Galahad* and RFA *Sir Tristram* before joining HMS *Hermes* in June for two exercises. The squadron ceased to exist as a separate entity on 5 September 1977 when it was pooled with No.845 Squadron at Yeovilton.

No.846 reformed at Yeovilton on 6 September 1977 as a non-flying deep maintenance unit. Known as 846 Naval Aircraft Squadron Support Unit (NACSSU), it lost its squadron number in November 1977, becoming the Naval Air Commando Squadron Support Unit.

On 4 October 1978 No.846 reformed at Yeovilton as a Commando squadron with 12 Wessex HU.5s. On 12 January 1979 it was allocated to HMS *Hermes*, but the following month the first of several detachments was embarked in HMS *Bulwark*. The squadron eventually joined HMS *Hermes* in June, but was soon reallocated to HMS *Bulwark*, and in December began a gradual re-equipment with Sea King HC.4s. In April 1980 the whole squadron embarked in HMS *Bulwark* for an exercise, and in September part went to northern Norway for an exercise, followed by a visit to Hamburg. The squadron was awarded the Australia Shield for its work in 1980. Further visits were made to northern Norway in early 1981, and to Denmark in September, the last of the Wessexes leaving in October. In April 1982 it embarked in HMS *Hermes* as part of the Falkland Task Force, elements being also in HMS *Fearless*, HMS *Intrepid*, SS *Canberra* and MV *Norland*. It returned to Yeovilton in July. During 1983 detachments embarked in HMS *Hermes* and HMS *Invincible*, and towards the end of the year three aircraft joined HMS *Fearless* for duty off Lebanon.

The major role of No.846 during the 1980s was in support of 3 Commando Brigade on the northern flank of NATO, training for this involved deployments to Norway each winter from 1984 to 1990. During the remainder of the year the squadron deployed detachments far and wide in the UK, Europe and at sea along with squadron training periods in the early summer and major NATO or amphibious exercises in the early autumn. The squadron was awarded the 1984 Boyd Trophy for operations in Lebanon. From October 1990 to April 1991 the squadron deployed in the Persian Gulf aboard RFAs *Fort Grange*, *Olna* and *Argus* for the Gulf War. Immediately on return they were again deployed this time to Silopi in southern Turkey in support of UN assistance to the Kurds in northern Iraq, returning to the UK in June 1991. The squadron returned to Norway again in January 1992 but the 1993 deployment was recalled after only three days and the squadron embarked in HMS *Ark Royal* from January to August 1993 deployed in the Adriatic ready to support UN forces ashore in Yugoslavia. Half the squadron returned in March, the remainder recovered overland to Yeovilton in July. Four aircraft deployed to Norway during the 1993-94 winter and No.846 Squadron relieved No.707 Squadron Z Flt at Aldergrove in April 1994 with four aircraft in support of internal security operations; this deployment continues, with a regular rotation of aircraft and personnel to and from Yeovilton.

Battle Honours

Atlantic	1944
Arctic	1944-45
Norway	1944-45
Normandy	1944
Falkland Islands	1982
Kuwait	1991

Identification Markings

Avenger 4A+, then J:A+ on *Trumpeter* by 9.44; Wildcat single letters, then J:A+ by 9.44; Whirlwind single letter with fin letter A; Wessex single letter with fin letter CU/VL; From 4.64 Wessex & Sea King VA+/VL:B:H (individual letters S,Q,U,A,D,R,O,N used on Wessex 1977/8, then P,O,L,A,R,C,U,B,S 1978/81).

Aircraft Equipment	Period of Service	Example	
Avenger I	Apr 1943 - Jun 1945	FN903	(JQ)
Avenger II	Jun 1945 - Sep 1945	JZ590	(JF)
Wildcat V	Dec 1943 - Sep 1944	JV352	(H)
Wildcat VI	Sep 1944 - May 1945	JV665	(JF)
Whirlwind HAS.7	May 1962 - Oct 1964	XN298	(X/A)
Wessex HU.5	Jul 1968 - Dec 1975	XT461	(XD/VL)
	Apr 1976 - Sep 1977	XT465	(VR/VL)
	Oct 1978 - Oct 1981	XT451	(VL/VL)
Sea King HC.4	Dec 1979 - to date	ZA294	(VT/B)

Squadron bases		Squadron bases	
Quonset Point	1 Apr 1943	HMS Tracker	4 Jan 1944
Norfolk	27 May 1943	Machrihanish	12 Feb 1944
Brunswick	1 Jun 1943	HMS Tracker	13 Feb 1944
Quonset Point	30 Jun 1943	North Front	25 Feb 1944
Norfolk (transit)	1 Jul 1943	HMS Tracker	2 Mar 1944
HMS Ravager	2 Jul 1943	Machrihanish(Dt)	14-25 Mar 1944
Machrihanish	27 Jul 1943	(Fighter Flight)	
Hatston	28 Jul 1943	Hatston	14 Apr 1944
Grimsetter	25 Sep 1943	Machrihanish	17 Apr 1944
Machrihanish	13 Oct 1943	Burscough	20 Apr 1944
Maydown	6 Nov 1943	HMS Tracker	28 Apr 1944
Machrihanish	4 Dec 1943	Machrihanish	15 May 1944

Grumman Wildcat VI JV699 'JF' of No.846 Squadron's fighter flight being manhandled after a deck landing accident on HMS Trumpeter in late 1944.

Westland Wessex HU.5s XS492 'VW/A' and XT459 'VB/A' of No.846 Squadron in 1972. (MAP)

Squadron bases
HMS Tracker	3 Jun 1944
Limavady (15 Gp)	11 Jun 1944
HMS Trumpeter	5 Jul 1944
Hatston	16 Sep 1944
HMS Trumpeter	23 Sep 1944
Hatston (Dt8)	6-12 Oct 1944
Hatston (Dt3)	18-21 Oct 1944
Ayr	15 Nov 1944
Machrihanish	15 Nov 1944
HMS Trumpeter	23 Nov 1944
HMS Premier (Dt4)	5-8 Dec 1944
Hatston	19 Dec 1944
HMS Trumpeter	19 Dec 1944
(Fighter Flight) to	5 Jan 1945
HMS Trumpeter	1 Feb 1945
Hatston	6 Mar 1945
HMS Trumpeter	11 Mar 1945
Hatston	30 Mar 1945
HMS Trumpeter	5 Apr 1945
Hatston	13 Apr 1945
HMS Trumpeter	27 Apr 1945
Ayr	15 May 1945
Stretton	23 May 1945
(Fighter Flight - disbanded)	
Hatston	19 Jun 1945
Twatt	20 Jul 1945
Crail	1 Aug 1945
Machrihanish	21 Sep 1945
Sqdn redes No.751 Sqdn	22 Sep 1945
Culdrose	8 May 1962
HMS Albion	17 Sep 1962
Culdrose	22 Sep 1962
HMS Albion	2 Nov 1962
AAC Falaise, Aden (Dt4)	20-23 Nov 1962
Melindiana (Dt4)	1-5 Dec 1962
Kuching	15 Dec 1962
HMS Albion	5 Jan 1963
Labuan (Dt6)	7-8 Jan 1963
Sembawang	10 Jan 1963
HMS Albion	1 Feb 1963
Labuan	7 Feb 1963
HMS Albion	20 Feb 1963
Brunei Airport	19 Mar 1963
Kuching	13 Apr 1963
Sembawang	18 May 1963

Squadron bases
Kuching	1 Jun 1963
HMS Albion	30 Jun 1963
Kuching	19 Aug 1963
HMS Albion	10 Nov 1963
Kai Tak	22 Dec 1963
Tawau	12 Jan 1964
HMS Bulwark	12 Oct 1964
Sembawang - disbanded	19 Oct 1964
Culdrose	29 Jul 1968
Doniford Camp (Dt8)	12-13 Sep 1968
Okehampton Dt2)	12-13 Sep 1968
Culdrose	13 Sep 1968
HMS Fearless	17 Sep 1968
Culdrose	19 Sep 1968
HMS Fearless	4 Oct 1968
Gibraltar	8 Oct 1968
HMS Fearless	13 Oct 1968
Culdrose	17 Oct 1968
Old Sarum (Dt2)	18-29 Nov 1968
Old Sarum	10-12 Dec 1968
RFA Engadine	9 Feb 1969
Bardufoss	14 Feb 1969
RFA Engadine	16 Mar 1969
Culdrose	20 Mar 1969
Arbroath	9 May 1969
Culdrose	22 May 1969
HMS Bulwark (Dt3)	15-19 Sep 1969
HMS Fearless (Dt3)	8-11 Mar 1971
RFA Engadine (Dt2)	7-25 Jun 1971
Yeovilton	15 Jul 1971
Culdrose	19 Jul 1971
Lossiemouth (Dt5)	24 Sep 1971
to	8 Oct 1971
Bardufoss (Dt2)	3 Jan 1971
to	19 Mar 1972
HMS Bulwark (Dt4)	11 Jan 1972
to	4 Apr 1972
Yeovilton	15 May 1972
Aalborg (Dt2)	24 Apr 1974
to	15 May 1974
Sola (Dt4)	16-30 Apr 1975
Tirstrup (Dt4)	30 Apr 1975
to	13 May 1975

Squadron bases
Squadron parented the flights in RFA Regent, RFA Resource and RFA, Tidespring	
Squadron disbanded	17 Dec 1975
Yeovilton	1 Apr 1976
Sola (Dt4)	6-19 May 1976
Tirstrup (Dt4)	19-31 May 1976
Otterburn (Dt6)	7-16 Jun 1976
Castlemartin Range ('B' Flight)	28 Jun 1976
Valley (Dt3)	28 Jun 1976
to	2 Jul 1976
USS Austin (Dt6)	13-21 Sep 1976
Otterøy Island (Dt6)	21-24 Sep 1976
RFA Sir Tristram (Dt6)	24-28 Sep 1976
HMS Fearless (Dt4)	1 Oct 1976
(shore base to Hal Far)	19 Nov 1976
HMS Fearless (Dt2)	26 Nov 1976
to	2 Dec 1976
RFA Sir Galahad (Dt4) to	22 Dec 1976 4 Jan 1976
Bardufoss (Dt)	4-28 Jan 1977
Bardufoss (Dt)	4-25 Feb 1977
Bardufoss	1 Mar 1977
RFA Sir Tristram	16 Mar 1977
Yeovilton	21 Mar 1977
Sennybridge Range	16 May 1977
Yeovilton	27 May 1977
HMS Hermes	29 Jun 1977
Yeovilton	5 May 1977
HMS Hermes	16 Jul 1977
Yeovilton	20 Jul 1977
Squadron disbanded	5 Sep 1977
Yeovilton	6 Sep 1977
Redes Naval Air Commando Squadron Support Unit	Nov 1977
Yeovilton	4 Oct 1978
Okehampton (Dt8)	20-27 Nov 1978
Lilstock (Dt2)	25-29 Nov 1978
Bardufoss (Dt4/6)	4 Jan 1979
to	27 Mar 1979

Squadron bases
HMS Bulwark	21 Feb 1979
(Dt6/4) to	16 Mar 1979
(Dt3)	18 Apr 1979
to	4 May 1979
Arbroath (Dt2)	29 Apr 1979
to	3 May 1979
HMS Bulwark (Dt4)	18 May 1979
to	11 Jun 1979
Vaerlose (Dt4)	6-11 Jun 1979
HMS Bulwark (Dt8)	11-19 Jun 1979
(12)	20 Jun 1979
HMS Hermes	21 Jun 1979
Yeovilton (12)	13 Jul 1979
Culdrose (Dt8)	23-26 Jul 1979
HMS Bulwark (Dt6)	17 Sep 1979
to	22 Nov 1979
Sennybridge (Dt2)	24-27 Sep 1979
HMS Hermes (Dt2)	22 Oct 1979
to	8 Nov 1979
Arbroath (Dt3)	19-23 Nov 1979
Yeovilton (12)	23 Nov 1979
Bardufoss (Dt4)	28 Dec 1979
to	19 Mar 1980
HMS Bulwark (Dt2)	4 Jan 1980
to	1 Apr 1980
Jacksonville	18 Jan 1980
to	22 Feb 1980
HMS Hermes (Dt2)	15 Jan 1980
to	21 Mar 1980
Bardufoss (Dt3)	4 Feb 1980
to	21 Mar 1980
HMS Bulwark (Dt7)	24 Apr 1980
to	22 May 1980
Castlemartin (Dt3)	10-13 Jun 1980
Salisbury Plain (Dt)	21 Jun 1980
to	2 Jul 1980
Yeovilton (14)	15 Jul 1980
HMS Bulwark (Dt8)	5 Sep 1980
to	6 Oct 1980
(Dt6)	13-21 Oct 1980
(Dt2)	21 Oct 1980
to	7 Nov 1980
Kristiansund (4SK)	8-24 Sep 1980
HMS Intrepid (4Wx)	4-13 Sep 1980
Yeovilton (14)	20 Nov 1980
Bardufoss (Dt5)	5 Nov 1980
to	2 Feb 1981
HMS Bulwark (Dt2)	7 Jan 1981
to	23 Mar 1981
Bardufoss (Dt9)	2 Feb 1981
to	23 Mar 1981
Vaernes (Dt3)	3-16 Feb 1981
Vaernes (Dt1)	16 Feb 1981
to	8 Mar 1981
Andalasnes (Dt2)	16-25 Feb 1981
Mosfjellstue (Dt3)	2-9 Mar 1981
Andalesnes (Dt)	8-9 Mar 1981
Yeovilton (11)	3 Apr 1981
Coltishall (Dt3)	6-9 Apr 1981
Netheravon (Dt4)	18-20 May 1981
HMS Invincible (Dt2)	20 May 1981
to	9 Jun 1981
HMS Hermes (Dt2)	4 Jun 1981
to	2 Jul 1981
Kinloss (Dt1)	7-19 Jun 1981
RFA Olmeda (Dt2)	22-26 Jun 1981
Salisbury Plain	25 Jun 1981
to	1 Jul 1981
(Dt2)	12-14 Jul 1981
Yeovilton (9)	14 Jul 1981
Mjulfjell (Dt1)	20 Jul 1981
Norway to	10 Aug 1981

Squadron bases

HMS Intrepid	
(Dt2)	25-27Aug 1981
HMS Hermes (Dt2)	2 Sep 1981
	to 2 Dec 1981
Jacksonville	16 Sep 1981
	to 13 Oct 1981
New River	13-23Oct 1981
Tortola	4-15 Nov 1981
HMS Intrepid	
(Dt2)	8-16Sep 1981
Vaerlose (Dt4)	11-16Sep 1981
Vordinborg	
(Dt4)	16-21Sep 1981
HMS Intrepid	
(Dt2)	16-21Sep 1981
Kalundgorg FOB	
(Dt6)	21-25Sep 1981
Nordholtz (Dt4)	22-24Sep 1981
HMS Intrepid	
(Dt2)	25-28Sep 1981
Yeovilton (8)	14 Oct 1981
Binbrook (Dt2)	12-15Oct 1981
Arbroath (Dt2)	19-23Oct 1981
Kinloss (Dt1)	31 Oct 1981
	to 16 Nov 1981
Salisbury Plain	
(Dt4)	7-19Nov 1981
HMS Fearless	
(Dt1)	16-26Nov 1981
Yeovilton (10)	30 Nov 1981
HMS Invincible	
(Dt4)	4-9Dec 1981
Prestwick (Dt2)	7-10Dec 1981
Boulmer (Dt1)	11-29Jan 1982
Bardufoss (Dt4)	11 Jan 1982
	to 8 Mar 1982
Trondheim (Dt1)	9 Feb 1982
	to 8 Mar 1982
HMS Hermes	
(Dt4)	16-25Feb 1982
Arbroath (Dt2)	1-5 Mar 1982
HMS Invincible	
(Dt2)	1-8Mar 1982
(Dt5)	8-13Mar 1982
(Dt6)	16-20Mar 1982
HMS Fearless	
(Dt1)	8-16Mar 1982
Elversgardsmoen FOB	
	13-16Mar 1982
Coltishall	
(Dt2)	15-19Mar 1982
Yeovilton (12)	9 Mar 1982
(14)	2 Apr 1982
Operation CORPORATE	
South Atlantic:	
HMS Hermes	
(Dt9)	3-18Apr 1982
HMS Fearless (Dt3)	6 Apr 1982
	to 19 May 1982

Squadron bases

Ascension Is	
(Dt1)	8-18Apr 1982
(Dt5)	18 Apr 1982
	to 7 May 1982
HMS Hermes (Dt5)	18 Apr 1982
	to 19 May 1982
HMS Intrepid (Dt1)	26 Apr 1982
	to 8 May 1982
MV Elk (Dt3)	7-19May 1982
SS Canberra(Dt1)	7-19 May 1982
HMS Intrepid	
(Dt2)	8-19May1982
SS Canberra	
(Dt2)	19-23May 1982
MV Norland	
(Dt1)	19-23May 1982
HMS Fearless	
(Dt4)	19-29May 1982
HMS Intrepid	
(Dt4)	19-27May 1982
San Carlos(Dt3)	23-27May 1982
(Dt7)	27-29May 1982
San Carlos (11)	29 May 1982
	to 16 Jun 1982
(Dt3)	16-18Jun 1982
HMS Fearless (Dt4)	16 Jun 1982
	to 13 Jul 1982
HMS Intrepid (Dt4)	16 Jun 1982
	to 13 Jul 1982
Port Stanley (Racecourse)	
(Dt3)	18-23Jun 1982
(Dt2)	23 Jun 1982
	to 3 Jul 1982
SS Canberra (Dt1)	23 Jun 1982
	to 11 Jul 1982
HMS Hermes	
(Dt2)	3-21Jul 1982
Yeovilton (Dt1)	11-13Jul 1982
(Dt9)	13-21Jul 1982
Yeovilton (11)	21 Jul 1982
Otterburn (Dt3)	25-28Oct 1982
Arbroath (Dt3)	5-10Dec 1982
Bardufoss (Dt2)	3 Jan 1983
	to 10 Mar 1983
Gardermoen (Dt4)	25 Jan 1983
	to 8 Feb 1983
(Dt3)	8 Feb 1983
	to 6 Mar 1983
Mo-I-Rana (Dt1)	8 Feb 1983
	to 7 Mar 1983
HMS Hermes	
(Dt4)	7-17Mar 1983
(Dt6)	17-21Mar 1983
Scatsta (Dt3)	24 Apr 1983
	to 4 May 1983
HMS Illustrious	
(Dt2)	3-20May1983
HMS Invincible	
(Dt4)	23-26May 1983

Squadron bases

(Dt3)	26-31May 1983
(Dt5)	31 May 1983
	to 3 Jun 1983
(Dt6)	3- 16Jun 1983
HMS Hermes (Dt2)	27 Jun 1983
	to 8 Jul 1983
Arbroath (Dt2)	11-15Jul 1983
HMS Hermes (Dt4)	14 Sep 1983
	to 22 Nov 1983
Tirstrup (Dt4)	15-25Sep 1983
Yeovilton (8)	21 Oct 1983
HMS Fearless (Dt3)	20 Nov 1983
	to 11 Jan 1984
RFA Reliant (Dt1)	2-11Jan 1984
HMS Fearless	
(Dt1)	11-19Jan 1984
RFA Reliant (Dt3)	11 Jan 1984
	to 5 Apr 1984
Dekhelia	26-31Jan 1984
Akrotiri	24-27Feb 1984
Dekhelia	8-12Mar 1984
Dekhelia	16-19Mar 1984
Coltishall(Dt4)	24-28Oct 1983
Prestwick (Dt3)	27 Nov 1983
	to 2 Dec 1983
Bardufoss (Dt2)	2-19Jan 1984
(Dt1)	19 Jan 1984
	to 25 Mar 1984
Gardermoen (Dt2)	19 Jan 1984
	to 1 Feb 1984
(Dt3)	1 Feb 1984
	to 11 Mar 1984
Vaernes (Dt3)	11-24Mar 1984
Wattisham (Dt2)	2-6Apr 1984
Coltishail (Dt3)	30 Apr 1984
	to 4 May 1984
Lee-on-Solent	
(Dt2)	8-11May1984
Yeovilton (9)	25 May 1984
Lossiemouth (Dt2)	27 May 1984
	to 1 Jun 1984
Lee-on-Solent	
(Dt3)	4-7Jun 1984
Saillagouse	
(Dt4)	10-17Jun 1984
HMS Fearless	
(Dt2)	20-24Jun 1984
(Dt1)	24 Jun 1984
	to 6 Jul 1984
Sennybridge(Dt2)	9-12Jul 1984
HMS Illustrious	
(Dt1)	12-23Jul 1984
(Dt4)	23-27Jul 1984
HMS Fearless (Dt1)	30 Aug 1984
	to 3 Sep 1984
(Dt3)	3-8Sep 1984
Vaerlose (Dt7)	8-20Sep 1984
HMS Fearless	
(Dt1)	20-23Sep 1984
Bad Lippspringe	
(Dt4)	20-27Sep 1984
Yeovilton (10)	28 Sep 1984
Kinloss (Dt2)	1-5Oct 1984
Otterburn (Dt3)	14-17Oct 1984
Kinloss (Dt1)	4-16Nov1984
HMS Illustrious	
(Dt1)	8-31Nov 1984
(Dt8)	26 Nov 1984
	to 2 Dec 1984
(Dt6)	2-5Dec 1984
(Dt4)	5-12Dec 1984
Coltishall (Dt2)	10-14Dec1984
Yeovilton	14 Dec 1984
Bardufoss (Dt3)	3-25Jan 1985
(Dt2)	25 Jan 1985
	to 14 Mar 1985
Gardermoen (Dt4)	25 Jan 1985
	to 10 Mar 1985
HMS Fearless	
(Dt2)	7-14Mar 1985

Squadron bases

(Dt4)	14-15Mar 1985
HMS Invincible	
(Dt2)	10-15Mar 1985
RFA Fort Grange	
(Dt2)	10-15Mar 1985
Gardermoen FOB	
(8)	15-21Mar1985
RFA Fort Grange	
(Dt4)	21-24Mar 1985
HMS Invincible	
(Dt2)	21-26Mar 1985
HMS Fearless	
(Dt2)	21-26Mar 1985
Yeovilton	26 Mar 1985
Coltishall (Dt2)	1-4Apr1985
Saillagouse	
(Dt3)	12-19May 1985
Otterburn	27 May 1985
Yeovilton	7 Jun 1985
Kinloss (Dt1)	7-21Jun 1985
De Kooy (Dt2)	6-19Jul 1985
Stornoway (Dt2)	21-25Jul 1985
RFA Fort Austin	
(Dt1)	2 Aug 1985
	to 23 Sep 1985
HMS Invincible	
(Dt2)	9-24Sep 1985
HMS Intrepid	
(Dt3)	9-24Sep 1985
Plockton FOB	12-14Sep 1985
Loch Eriboll FOB	
	17-21Sep 1985
Dartmoor FOB	24-28Sep 1985
Arbroath (Dt1)	4-12Sep 1985
Yeovilton	28 Sep 1985
HMS Invincible	
(Dt1)	2-23Oct 1985
RFA Fort Austin	
(Dt1)	23-29Oct 1985
Arbroath (Dt2)	18-25Oct 1985
Waddington(Dt2)	21-25Oct 1985
Arbroath (Dt2)	4 15Nov 1985
Waddington(Dt3)	25-28Nov1985
Arbroath (Dt2)	1-6Dec 1985
Yeovilton	6 Dec 1985
Bardufoss (Dt2/3)	28 Jan 1986
	to 5 Mar 1986
Gardermoen (Dt3/4)	8 Jan 1986
	to 2 Mar 1986
HMS Intrepid	
(Dt1)	15-23Jan 1986
HMS Illustrious	
(Dt1)	3-19Feb 1986
RFA Fort Austin	
(Dt3)	2-13Mar 1986
HMS Intrepid	
(Dt3)	5-13Mar 1986
Yeovilton	15 Mar 1986
Coltishall(Dt2)	24-26Mar1986
HMS Ark Royal	
(Dt1)	7-10Apr 1986
Bad Tölz (Dt3)	24 May 1986
	to 19 Jun 1986
Doorn (Dt2)	26-30 May 1986
Baumholder (Dt3)	1-19Jun 1986
HMS Intrepid (Dt)	26 Jun 1986
	to 4 Jul 1986
Yeovilton (8)	30 Jun 1986
Brawdy (Dt2)	14-18Jul 1986
HMS Intrepid	
(Dt3)	29 Aug 1986
	to 27 Sep 1986
Porsgrunn (Dt3)	4-27Sep 1986
Otterburn (Dt3)	6-10Oct 1986
Machrihanish	
(Dt2)	13-17Oct 1986
HMS Intrepid	
(Dt2)	23 Oct 1986
	to 18 Dec 1986
Bardufoss (Dt3)	3 Nov 1986
	to 10 Dec 1986

Westland Wessex HU.5 'XC/CU' of No.846 Squadron, Culdrose in 1971. (MAP)

Westland Sea King HC.4 ZA292 'VH/B' of No.846 Squadron.

Squadron bases
Bardufoss (Dt1)	10 Dec 1986
	to 9 Feb 1987
Tretten (Dt2)	21 Jan 1987
(Dt4)	2 Feb 1987
(Dt5)	9 Feb 1987
	to 14 Mar 1987
HMS Intrepid	
(Dt3)	14-21Mar 1987
RFA Fort Grange	
(Dt2)	14-21Mar 1987
Norway - field	
(Dt5)	21-25Mar 1987
Bardufoss (Dt5)	25-27Mar 1987
Hemer (8)	9 May 1987
Yeovilton (8)	26 May 1987
HMS Illustrious	
(Dt2)	28 May 1987
	to 21 Jun 1987
Lossiemouth (Dt2)	31 May 1987
	to 5 Jun 1987
Thetford (Dt2)	8-12Jun 1987
Salisbury Plain	
(Dt4)	21-28Jun 1987
HMS Intrepid (Dt2)	29 Jun 1987
	to 9 Jul 1987
Koksijde (Dt1)	8-12Jul 1987
HMS Intrepid(Dt1)	1-9Sep1987
Tancos (Dt2)	9-17Sep 1987
Thetford (Dt2)	5-10Oct 1987
Waddington (Dt2)	5-9Oct 1987
RFA Tidespring	
(Dt1)	15 Oct 1987
(to Olna) to	Feb 1988
HMS Illustrious	
(Dt3)	19-23Oct 1987
(Dt7)	4-19Nov 1987
Bardufoss (Dt2)	4 Jan 1988
	to 15 Feb 1988

Squadron bases
Tretten (Dt3)	7 Jan 1988
	to 15 Feb 1988
(Dt5)	15-28Feb 1988
RFA Olna (Dt1)	Feb 1988
(ex Tidespring) to	9 Jun 1988
HMS Intrepid (Dt2)	28 Feb 1988
	to 8 Mar 1988
Dortmund (Dt1)	12-15Apr 1988
HMS Intrepid (Dt2)	20 Apr 1988
	to 25 May 1988
Castlemartin	
(Dt2)	25-28Apr 1988
Dortmund (Dt6)	27 May 1988
	to 13 Jun 1988
De Kooy (Dt2)	13-26Jun 1988
Yeovilton (8)	26 Jun 1988
Stromness (Dt1)	11-26Jul 1988
Brawdy (Dt2)	18-22Jul 1988
HMS Intrepid	
(Dt3)	5-26Sep 1988
Bardufoss (Dt3)	8-24Sep 1988
HMS Illustrious	
(Dt1)	2 Oct 1988
	to 15 Dec 1988
HMS Intrepid (Dt1)	2 Oct 1988
	to 29 Nov 1988
IAF Cameri (Dt2)	6-14Oct 1988
Tancos (Dt1)	7-2 5 Nov 1988
Bardufoss (Dt2)	7 Nov 1988
	to 6 Feb 1989
Tretten (Dt6)	6 Feb 1989
	to 1 Mar 1989
HMS Ark Royal	24 Feb 1989
(Dt1)	to 1 Mar 1989
(Dt7)	1-16Mar 1989
Castlemartin	
(Dt5)	10-21Apr 1989

Squadron bases
HMS Intrepid	
(Dt3)	12-24Apr 1989
(Dt2)	24 Apr 1989
	to 12 Jul 1989
Jacksonville	19-22 May 1989
Aruba	27-3 0 May 1989
Aruba	10-1 4 Jun 1989
Valley (Dt3)	21-24Apr 1989
Dortmund (Dt6)	5-20May1989
(Dt2)	20-22May 1989
De Kooy (Dt2)	22 May 1989
	to 2 Jun 1989
Brawdy (Dt3)	17-20Jul 1989
Lee-on-Solent	
(Dt6)	5-17Jul 1989
Stornoway (Dt6)	24-27Jul 1989
HMS Intrepid (Dt1)	2 Oct 1989
	to 23 Nov 1989
Machrihanish (Dt2)	17 Oct 1989
	to 2 Nov 1989
Bardufoss (Dt4)	27 Oct 1989
	to 8 Jan 1990
Tretten (Dt4)	8-12Jan 1990
(Dt6)	12 Jan 1990
	to 30 Mar 1990
HMS Ark Royal	
(Dt1)	17 Apr 1990
	to 5 Jul 1990
HMS Intrepid (Dt2)	24 Apr 1990
	to 12 Jun 1990
Castlemartin (Dt3)	30 Apr 1990
	to 4 May 1990
Deelan (Dt4)	25 May 1990
	to 8 Jun 1990
RFA Fort Grange	
(Dt2)	21 Aug 1990
	to 16 Mar 1991

Squadron bases
HMS Intrepid	
(Dt1)	29-30Aug 1990
Huynes (Dt3)	7-1 4 Sep 1990
(Dt4)	14-22Sep 1990
Guernsey (Dt1)	8-15Sep 1990
RFA Tidespring	
(Dt1)	12-24Sep 1990
RFA Argus (Dt4)	28 Oct 1990
	to 26 Mar 1991
RFA Olna (Dt2)	16-26Mar 1991
RFA Fort Grange	
(Dt1)	16 Mar 1991
	to 3 Jul 1991
Doha Kuwait	5-9Apr 1991
Doha Kuwait	29 Apr 1991
	to 10 May 1991
Yeovilton	3 Apr 1991
RFA Argus (8)	20-30Apr 1991
(passage UK-Turkey)	
Silopi (10)	30 Apr 1991
	to 29 May 1991
Silopi (Dt6)	29 May 1991
	to 22 Jun 1991
Incirlik	22 Jun 1991
	to 5 Jul 1991
SS Baltic Eagle	
(Dt4)	30 May 1991
(passage Turkey-UK)	
	to 11 Jun 1991
SS Arcadian Queen	
(Dt6)	5 Jul 1991
(passage Turkey-UK)	
Yeovilton	16 Jul 1991
Salisbury Plain	
(Dt2)	14-26Oct 1991
Kinlochleven (Dt2)	27 Oct 1991
	to 9 Nov 1991

Westland Sea King HC.4 'VG/B' of No.846 Squadron at Farnborough in September 1980. (MAP)

Squadron bases
Oberammergau
  (Dt2) 26-28Nov 1991
Bardufoss (Dt5) 2 Jan 1992
  to 8 Feb 1992
  (Dt3) 8-15Feb 1992
HMS Fearless (Dt3) 25 Feb 1992
  to 2 Mar 1992
RFA Fort Grange
  (Dt3) 2-30Mar 1992
Deelan (Dt4) 6-1 5May 1992
HMS Ark Royal
  (Dt5) 29 May 1992
  to 17 Jun 1992
  (Dt2) 17-25Jun 1992
  (Dt2) 27 Jun 1992
  to 13 Jul 1992
  (Dt1) 1 Sep 1992
  to 20 Oct 1992
Keevil (Dt5) 11-30Sep 1992
Tancos (Dt2) 2-20Oct 1992
Garelochhead (Dt2) 27 Oct 1992
  to 16 Nov 1992
Arbroath (Dt2) 16-27Oct 1992
Valley (Dt2) 27-30Oct 1992
Bardufoss (Dt2) 27 Nov 1992
  to 5 Jan 1993
Bardufoss (Dt4) 5-11Jan 1993

Squadron bases
Yeovilton (8) 13 Jan 1993
HMS Ark Royal (8) 15 Jan 1993
RFA Fort Austin 19 Mar 1993
  to 25 Mar 1993
HMS Ark Royal(Dt4)19Mar1993
  to 21 Jul 1993
Yeovilton 25 Mar 1993
HMS Fearless
  (Dt3) 6-10May1993
  (Dt2) 5-10Sep 1993
  (Dt2) 11-15Oct 1993
Otterburn 15 Oct 1993
Yeovilton 22 Oct 1993
HMS Fearless
  (Dt2) 15-25Nov 1993
Garelochhead (Dt3) 17 Nov 1993
  to 10 Dec 1993
Bardufoss (Dt2) 28 Nov 1993
  to 8 Jan 1994
Bardufoss (Dt4) 8 Jan 1994
  to 8 Mar 1994
HMS Fearless (Dt2) 7 Feb 1994
  to 7 Mar 1994
Aldergrove (Dt3) 1 Apr 1994
  to date
HMS Fearless (Dt2) 25 Apr 1994
  to 25 May 1994

Squadron bases
Lee-on-Solent (Dt2) 2-6Jun 1994
HMS Fearless (Dt2) 8 Jun 1994
  to 15 Aug 1994
Prestwick (Dt2) 12-17Jun 1994
Deelen (Dt1) 22 Jun 1994
  to 8 Jul 1994
Bardufoss (Dt2) 23-28Jun 1994

Commanding Officers
L/C(A) RD Head
  DSC RN 1 Mar 1943
L/C CLF Webb RN 7 Oct 1944
L/C JSL Crabbe RN 9 May 1945
L/C(A) DJ Bunyan
  RNVR 16 Jun 1945
Squadron disbanded 22 Sep 1945
L/C DF Burke MBE
  RN 8 May 1962
L/C AA Hensher RN 25Sep 1962
L/C JHS Jervis RN 7 Apr 1964
Squadron disbanded 19 Oct 1964
L/C DJ Lickfold
  MBE RN 29 Jul 1968
L/C BC Sarginson
  MBE RN 3 Nov 1969
L/C NS Foster RN 16 Sep 1969

Commanding Officers
L/C JS Kelly
  MBE RN 10 Mar 1972
L/C JJD Knapp RN 21 Aug 1973
Cdr BG Skinner RN 6 Jan 1975
Squadron disbanded 17 Dec 1975
L/C JJD Knapp RN 1 Apr 1976
L/C DA Goodenough
  -Bayly RN 14 Oct 1976
Squadron disbanded 5 Sep 1977
L/C RP Seymour
  AFC RN 4 Sep 1978
L/C TJ Yarker RN 5 Jun 1980
L/C SC Thornewill
  DSC RN 15 Dec 1981
L/C N McMillan RN29Oct 1982
L/C NGT Harris RN19 Jun 1984
L/C JPK Rooke RN 4 Dec 1985
L/C TJ Eltringham RN
  22 Jun 1987
L/C LA Port MBE
  RN 7 Jul 1989
L/C NJ North
  DSC RN 10 Apr 1992
L/C FW Robertson
  RN 15 Mar 1994

Westland Sea King HC.4 ZD479 'VJ' of No.846 Squadron. (MAP)

No.847 Squadron

Badge: On a blue field, a sea lion winged gold
Motto: Ex alto concutimus
(We shake them from on high)

No.847 Squadron formed at Lee-on-Solent on 1 June 1943 as a torpedo bomber reconnaissance squadron with 12 Barracuda IIs. After moving north to Scotland to work up, it was reduced to nine aircraft in November and allocated to the 21st Naval TBR Wing. This embarked in HMS *Illustrious* and sailed for the Indian Ocean at the end of the year. In March 1944 the ship made an abortive sweep for three Japanese cruisers sighted off the Cocos Islands, then in April the squadron took part in a dive-bombing attack on harbour installations and oil storage tanks at Sabang in northern Sumatra. The strength was restored to 12 aircraft for a minor attack in June on Port Blair in the Andamans, but on 30 June 1944 the squadron was absorbed into No.810 Squadron at Trincomalee.

On 17 March 1956 No.847 reformed at Eglinton from part of No.812 Squadron, with three Gannet AS.1s for service in Cyprus. These flew out to Nicosia on 5 April, arriving three days later. The squadron's task was to maintain daily patrols looking for ships attempting to infiltrate arms into the troubled island, the Gannets AS.1s being replaced by three AS.4s in June 1958. These eventually flew home, and the squadron disbanded on arrival at Yeovilton on 1 December 1959.

No.847 next reformed at Culdrose on 7 May 1963 as a Commando squadron, by splitting No.848 Squadron. It commissioned nine days later with 12 Whirlwind HAS.7s and trained pilots for intensive operations in Indonesia. From March 1964, 'B' Flight spent a period in HMS *Bulwark* exercising with the Royal Marines in the Far East. In May the squadron took part in the Fleet Air Arm's 30th Anniversary flypast before the Duke of Edinburgh at Yeovilton, and in June a Hiller HT.2 was attached for three weeks. The squadron disbanded on 2 December 1964, its task being taken over by No.707 Squadron.

On 14 March 1969 No.847 reformed at Sembawang from part of No.848 Squadron as a helicopter support unit with 10 Wessex HU.5s. In May the squadron joined HMS *Albion* for an exercise, and aircraft were later embarked from time to time in HMS *Fearless* and RFA *Sir Galahad*. From February 1970 short periods were spent in HMS *Bulwark*, as well as embarking in support ships at various times during the remainder of the year. In November the squadron embarked in HMS *Intrepid* and HMS *Triumph* for flood relief work in East Pakistan, and in January 1971 performed a similar task in West Malaysia. On 22 May 1971 the squadron disbanded at Sembawang, it aircraft being transferred to No.848 Squadron.

No.847 next reformed hurriedly at Culdrose on 7 May 1982 from Nos.771 and 772 Squadron as a Commando squadron with 21 Wessex HU.5s. These embarked within less than a week in RFA *Engadine* and SS *Atlantic Causeway*, to sail with the South Atlantic Task Force. They disembarked to Port San Carlos on 1 June, transferring later in the month to Port Stanley, where the squadron disbanded in September 1982, its task going to No.845 Squadron.

Battle Honours
Falkland Islands   1982

Identification Markings
Barracuda *3A+*; Gannet *086-088/HF*; Whirlwind & Wessex single letter with fin letter *CU:A*; Wessex from 1982 *XA+*.

Fairey Gannet AS.1 XA335 '086/HF' of No. 847 Squadron, Nicosia after being returned to storage in the UK in 1958. (MAP)

Westland Wessex XT761 'J' of No.847 Squadron during flood relief work in East Pakistan (now Bangladesh) in late 1970.

Aircraft Equipment	Period of Service	Example
Barracuda II	Jun 1943 - Jun 1944	LS467 (B)
Gannet AS.1	Mar 1956 - Jun 1958	XA335 (086/HF)
Gannet AS.4	Jun 1958 - Nov 1959	XA462 (086)
Whirlwind HAS.7	May 1963 - Dec 1964	XN304 (F/CU)
Wessex HU.5	Mar 1969 - May 1971	XT755 (D/S)
	May 1982 - Sep 1982	XT755 (XX)

Squadron bases

Lee-on-Solent	1 Jun 1943
Fearn (Dt2)	8-13 Jul 1943
Fearn	13 Jul 1943
Machrihanish	14 Aug 1943
HMS Illustrious	28 Nov 1943
HMS Unicorn (Dt8)	5-26 Jan 1944
Katukurunda	27 Jan 1944
HMS Illustrious	10 Feb 1944
China Bay	14 Feb 1944
HMS Illustrious	22 Feb 1944
China Bay/ Katukurunda	8 Mar 1944
HMS Illustrious	21 Mar 1944
China Bay	8 May 1944
HMS Illustrious	16 Apr 1944
Katukurunda	3 May 1944
China Bay	24 May 1944
HMS Illustrious	10 Jun 1944
China Bay (transit)	18 Jun 1944
Minneriya	19 Jun 1944
Disb into 810 Sq	30 Jun 1944
Eglinton	17 Mar 1956
in transit	5 Apr 1956
Nicosia	8 Apr 1956
Yeovilton-disbanded	1 Dec 1959
Culdrose	7 May 1963
'B' Flight:	
HMS Bulwark	5 Mar 1964
Sembawang	Apr 1964
Squadron disbanded	2 Dec 1964
Sembawang	14 Mar 1969
HMS Albion	16 May 1969
Sembawang	28 May 1969
HMS Fearless(5)/ RFA Sir Galahad(3)	14 Jul 1969
Sembawang	19 Jul 1969
HMS Fearless (Dt3)	13-25 Aug 1969
RFA Sir Galahad (Dt4)	15-21 Oct 1969

Squadron bases

HMS Fearless (Dt4)	21 Oct 1969 to 8 Nov 1969
HMS Fearless(5)/ RFA Sir Galahad(3)	4 Dec 1969
Gemas	10 Dec 1969
Sembawang	15 Dec 1969
HMS Fearless (Dt3)	9-12 Jan 1970
HMS Fearless (Dt1)	19 Jan 1970 to 5 Feb 1970
HMS Fearless	26 Feb 1970
HMS Bulwark	1 Mar 1970
Sembawang	9 Mar 1970
HMS Bulwark	4 Apr 1970
Sembawang	11 Apr 1970
HMS Bulwark	11 Jun 1970
RFA Stromness (Dt1)	3 Jun 1970 to 15 Aug 1970
Sembawang	29 Jun 1970
HMS Intrepid (Dt1)	7-15 Aug 1970
HMS Intrepid (Dt5)	31 Aug 1970 to 12 Sep 1970
RFA Sir Galahad (Dt3)	4 Sep 1970 to 12 Sep 1970
HMS Triumph (Dt3)	23-28 Sep 1970
Kai Tak	28 Sep 1970
HMS Intrepid (Dt5)	9-15 Oct 1970
HMS Intrepid	19 Oct 1970
Sembawang	23 Oct 1970
HMS Triumph(3)/ HMS Intrepid(5)	20-28 Nov 1970
Patwakhal (Dt6)	28 Nov 1970 to 8 Dec 1970
HMS Intrepid	8 Dec 1970
Sembawang	15 Dec 1970
HMS Intrepid (Dt2)	25 Jan 1971 to 19 Feb 1971
RFA Stromness (Dt1)	17-18 Feb 1971

Squadron bases

RFA Sir Galahad	10-13 Mar 1971
HMS Intrepid (Dt3)	10-14 Mar 1971
HMS Intrepid/ RFA Sir Galahad	22 Mar 1971
Sembawang	12 Apr 1971
Asahan (Dt4)	15-18 Apr 1971
Squadron disbanded into 848 Sqdn	22 May 1971
Culdrose	7 May 1982
'A' Flight:	
RFA Engadine	13 May 1982
Port San Carlos	9 Jun 1982
'B' Flight:	
SS Atlantic Causeway	13 May 1982
Port San Carlos	1 Jun 1982
Navy Point, Port Stanley (Sqdn)	25 Jun 1982
Squadron disbanded	17 Sep 1982

Commanding Officers

L/C(A) PC Whitfield R N	1 Jun 1943
L/C(A) JL Cullen RN	20 Jul 1943
Squadron disbanded	30 Jun 1944
L/C WC Martin RN	6 Apr 1956
L/C WD Lawrence RN	22 Mar 1957
L/C RWR Hawkesworth DSC RN	19 May 1958
Squadron disbanded	1 Dec 1959
L/C GA Andrews RN	7 May 1963
L/C DJ Lickfold RN	18 Jun 1964
Squadron disbanded	2 Dec 1964
L/C PJ Williams RN	14 Mar 1969
L/C JS Kelly MBE RN	4 Jul 1970
Squadron disbanded	22 May 1971
L/C MD Booth DSC RN	7 May 1982
Squadron disbanded	17 Sep 1982

Westland Wessex HU.5 XT755 'XX' of No.847 Squadron at Yeovilton on 31 July 1982. (via Andy Thomas)

No.848 Squadron

Badge: 1. On a red field, a plate charged with a hawk volant proper releasing a torpedo also proper, into water barry wavy in base blue and white
2. Revised badge without torpedo
(unofficial - from 1979)
Motto: Accipe hoc
(Take that)

No.848 Squadron personnel assembled at Lee-on-Solent on 1 May 1943 for passage to the United States, where it officially formed at Quonset Point on 1 June 1943 for torpedo bomber reconnaissance duties with 12 Avenger Is. These embarked in HMS *Trumpeter* in September 1943, and No.848 provided anti-submarine patrols during her voyage to the Clyde. In April 1944 the squadron was allocated to RAF Coastal Command, carrying out anti-shipping patrols in the English Channel from Manston and later Thorney Island during the invasion period.

In September the squadron increased to 21 aircraft and embarked in HMS *Formidable* for the Far East, anti-submarine patrols being carried out en route to Gibraltar, where the ship was held up for three months due to propellor shaft troubles. No.848 then flew to Dekheila, where it remained ashore until re-embarking in January 1945 to continue for the British Pacific Fleet. Arriving in Australia in March, the ship joined the Fleet in the Phillipines and in April the squadron took part in operations against airfields and shore installations in the Sakishima Gunto Islands in the East China Seas, these being continued for over a month as well as similar attacks on Formosa. Kamikaze attacks on the ship caused damage to the flight deck, and several squadron aircraft were destroyed in these and a subsequent hangar fire. The ship withdrew to Australia in early June, and No.848 joined the 2nd Carrier Air Group with a reduced complement of 15 aircraft. These embarked in July for further strikes, this time against the Japanese mainland, before VJ-Day intervened. Returning to Australia, strength was increased to 16 aircraft, including some Mk.IIs, but these were left in Australia when the squadron personnel sailed home in HMS *Victorious*, to disband on arrival at Devonport on 31 October 1945.

On 29 October 1952 No.848 reformed at Gosport as a helicopter squadron with ten American built Whirlwind HAS.21s for anti-terrorist duties in Malaya. These embarked in the ferry carrier HMS *Perseus* in December, disembarking to Sembawang in January 1953, to come under the administrative control of No.303 Wing, RAF. By early February the squadron was fully operational and flying from an advanced base at Kuala Lumpur. For their activities during the year they were awarded the 1953 Boyd Trophy. In October 1954, five Whirlwind HAR.1s were added for search and rescue duties, these being withdrawn in June 1955. Operations continued until 18 December 1956, when the squadron disbanded at Sembawang.

On 14 October 1958 No.848 reformed at Hal Far from 728 Squadron 'C' Flight as the Amphibious Warfare Trials Unit. Equipped with five Whirlwind HAS.22s, it became the first Royal Marine Commando helicopter squadron, serving in Cyprus with 45 Commando, with which it was known as 45 Heliforce. In November 1959 it re-equipped at Worthy Down with 16 Whirlwind HAS.7s, still in the Commando role. In March 1960 these embarked in HMS *Bulwark*, and after a spell in the Mediterranean sailed for the Far East. Visits were paid to the Persian Gulf in February and July 1961, and in January 1962 the ship went to Australia. After returning to Singapore, the ship sailed home in September, and the

Grumman Avengers of No.848 Squadron, HMS Formidable on the way to bomb a Kamikaze airfield in 1945.

Westland Whirlwind HAS.7s of No.848 Squadron, HMS Bulwark during cross-operations with USS Leyte in the Persian Gulf in 1961. (via Roy Hawkridge)

squadron disembarked to Culdrose at the end of the year. Part of the squadron broke away in May 1963 to form No.847 Squadron, and No.848 disbanded at Culdrose on 30 July 1963.

No.848 next reformed at Culdrose on 7 May 1964 as a Commando helicopter squadron with 18 Wessex HU.5s. These spent a period in HMS *Albion* in January 1965, two Whirlwind HAS.7s being attached at that time, then in March the ship sailed for Aden, where hot weather trials were carried out. After a visit to Mombasa, the ship then continued to Singapore, where No.848 divided into a Headquarters flight and four sub-flights, operating as required from jungle airstrips. It was not until August 1966 that these were reunited and the complete squadron then embarked in HMS *Albion* for passage home. In August 1967 a Wasp HAS.1 was attached for Royal Marines liaison, and in March of that year the squadron was involved in anti-pollution work after the giant tanker SS *Torrey Canyon* went aground off the Scilly Isles, and spent periods in HMS *Albion* before joining that ship in December to return to Singapore. Various further periods were spent in HMS *Albion* before she returned to the United Kingdom in June 1969, the strength having been reduced to ten aircraft when eight were used to form No.847 Squadron in March 1969. In January 1970 No.848 joined HMS *Bulwark* to return once more to the Far East, returning home to Culdrose in August.

In March 1971 No.848 joined HMS *Albion* with 12 aircraft for a further spell in the Far East. On arrival it increased to 22 aircraft by taking over the 10 discarded machines of the disbanded No.847 Squadron. Detached flights spent periods in HMS *Intrepid* before the whole squadron returned home in HMS *Albion* at the end of the year. In April 1972 it re-embarked for a spell in the Mediterranean, and later in the year flights were embarked in HMS *Fearless* and HMS *Intrepid*, the other two flights joining HMS *Bulwark*. In January 1973 the whole squadron embarked in HMS *Bulwark* for a visit to the West Indies, returning in March. From August the squadron was attached to HMS *Bulwark* until disembarking to Yeovilton for twelve months in March 1974. Further periods were spent in HMS *Bulwark* with a strength of 16 aircraft during 1975, and in January 1976 a visit was made to the Caribbean. On return home the squadron disbanded at Yeovilton on 31 March 1976.

On 17 April 1982 No.848 was hastily reformed at Yeovilton from elements of Nos.707 and No.772 Squadron for service in the South Atlantic. The squadron deployed in four flights embarked in SS *Atlantic Conveyor* and RFAs *Olna, Olwen and Regent*. A and B Flights returned to the UK in September and C Flight by air in October having been relieved by No.845 Squadron. D Flight aircraft were lost when *Atlantic Conveyor* was sunk on 25 May, the survivors returning to the UK by air in early June. No.848 disbanded again at Yeovilton on 30 November 1982.

The squadron was again reformed at Yeovilton on 16 November 1990 with six Sea King HC4s from Nos.845, 846 and 707 squadrons, for service in the Gulf after the Iraqi invasion of Kuwait. The aircraft deployed to the Gulf onboard the new *Atlantic Conveyor*, and after service in the desert returned home to disband at Yeovilton on 19 April 1991.

No.848 Squadron will form at Yeovilton on 9 February 1995 when No.707 Squadron is to be renumbered. Squadron roles are to be aircrew and maintainer training and Royal Marines support. The Squadron will also take over from No.772 Squadron the task of deployments on exercises in support of security contingency plans.

Aircraft Equipment	Period of Service	Example
Avenger I	Jun 1943 - Sep 1945	JZ114 (376/X)
Avenger II	Aug 1945 - Sep 1945	JZ466 (380/X)
Swordfish I	Aug 1944 - Aug 1944	W5841
Whirlwind HAR.21	Oct 1952 - Dec 1956	WV195 (G)
Whirlwind HAR.1	Oct 1954 - Jun 1955	XA870
Whirlwind HAS.22	Oct 1958 - Oct 1959	WV220
Whirlwind HAS.7	Nov 1959 - Jul 1963	XN297 (G/B)
Wasp HAS.1	Aug 1967 - Apr 1973	XT422 (Z/A)
Whirlwind HAS.7	Jan 1965 - Apr 1966	XN299
Wessex HU.5	May 1964 - Mar 1976	XT449 (VS/B)
	Apr 1982 - Nov 1982	XT482 (WL)
Sea King HC.4	Nov 1990 - Apr 1991	ZA298 (WA)
Sea King HC.4	Feb 1995	

Westland Whirlwind HAS.7s XN300 'L/B' and XN301 'M/B' of No.848 Squadron flying above HMS Bulwark in 1960. (RAF Museum 6823-14)

Identification Markings
Avenger *4A+*, to *370-391/X* 10.45; Whirlwind single letters 1952/6, *351-355/B* 1959/63; Wessex single letters with fin letter *A/B*, to *VA+/A/B/VL* 1971; Sea King *WA+*.

Battle Honours
Normandy	1944
Okinawa	1945
Japan	1945
Falkland Islands	1982
Kuwait	1991

Squadron bases
Quonset Point	1 Jun 1943
Brunswick	15 Jul 1943
Squantum	31 Jul 1943
Norfolk (Dt)	7 Aug 1943
(DLT USS Charger)	
HMS Trumpeter	4 Sep 1943
Belfast	1 Nov 1943
Ayr	3 Nov 1943
Grimsetter	6 Nov 1943
Hatston	24 Nov 1943
Gosport	by 31 Dec 1943
(Dt3-ATDU)	to 3 Feb 1944
Machrihanish	29 Jan 1944
Maydown	26 Feb 1944

Westland Wessex HU.5 XS483 'E/A' of No.848 Squadron during jungle operations in 1964. (via Brian Lowe)

Squadron bases

Eglinton	16 Mar 1944
Machrihanish (Dt2)	25 Mar 1944
	to 22 Apr 1944
Manston (16Gp)	20 Apr 1944
Thorney Island	14 Jun 1944
Lee-on-Solent	24 Aug 1944
Turnhouse (Dt)	6-16 Sep 1944
HMS Formidable	16 Sep 1944
Dekheila	23 Oct 1944
HMS Formidable	27 Jan 1945
Colombo Racecourse	13 Feb 1945
Jervis Bay	1 Jun 1945
HMS Formidable	22 Jun 1945
Nowra	24 Aug 1945
HMS Victorious	25 Sep 1945
Sqdn disbanded UK	31 Oct 1945
Gosport	29 Oct 1952
HMS Perseus	10 Dec 1952
Sembawang	8 Jan 1953
Kuala Lumpur (Dt3)	21 Jan 1953
(Tiger Flight)	to 20 May 1953
Kuala Lumpur	20 May 1953
(Anchor Flt also)	
Kluang(3)/	
Sembawang(4)	26 Mar 1956
Kluang(2)/Kuala	
Lumpur(2)/	
Sembawang(3)	14 May 1956
Kluang(3)/	
Sembawang(4)	31 May 1956
Squadron disbanded	18 Dec 1956
Hal Far	14 Oct 1958
Worthy Down	9 Nov 1959
HMS Bulwark	10 Mar 1960
Hal Far (Dt8)	24-28 Mar 1960
Hal Far	2 May 1960

Squadron bases

HMS Bulwark	12 May 1960
Sembawang	7 Jun 1960
HMS Bulwark	15 Jul 1960
Sembawang	15 Sep 1960
HMS Bulwark	3 Oct 1960
Sembawang	22 Oct 1960
HMS Bulwark	29 Oct 1960
Sek Kong (Dt)	9-21 Nov 1960
Kai Tak (Dt)	9-21 Nov 1960
Sembawang	2 Dec 1960
HMS Bulwark	3 Jan 1961
Sumail (Dt4)	6-11 Feb 1961
Dhal (Dt4)	19-21 Feb 1961
Sembawang	22 Mar 1961
HMS Bulwark	18 Apr 1961
Sembawang (Dt4)	8 May 1961
	to 12 Jun 1961
Sembawang	12 Jun 1961
HMS Bulwark	20 Jun 1961
Oasis near Kuwait	
Town	13 Jul 1961
HMS Bulwark	17 Jul 1961
Sembawang	31 Jul 1961
HMS Bulwark	10 Nov 1961
Pearce (Dt8)	16-25 Jan 1962
Sembawang	22 Mar 1962
HMS Bulwark	16 Apr 1962
Sembawang	19 May 1962
HMS Bulwark	10 Jul 1962
Sembawang	4 Sep 1962
HMS Bulwark	12 Sep 1962
Culdrose	19 Dec 1962
Squadron disbanded	30 Jul 1963
Culdrose	7 May 1964
HMS Albion('D'Flt)	30 Nov 1964
	to 13 Dec 1964
HMS Albion(Dt6)	10-20 Jan 1965

Squadron bases

HMS Albion	20 Jan 1965
Culdrose	15 Feb 1965
HMS Albion	12 Mar 1965
Sembawang	28 Apr 1965
'A' Flight:	
Radfan Area (Dt)	27 Mar 1965
Khormaksar/Radfan	5 Apr 1965
RFA Sir Lancelot	9 Jun 1965
Sembawang	19 Jun 1965
Flights detached in	
succession:	
Sibu	23 May 1965
	to 18 Sep 1965
Nanga Gaat	23 May 1965
	to 15 Sep 1965
Bario	12 Jul 1965
	to 5 Aug 1966
Labuan	20 Sep 1965
	5 Aug 1966
Falaise, Aden	10-24 Nov 1965
('C' Flight	
via HMS Albion)	
Kota Balud (Dt2)	
	14-16 Apr 1966
Sepulot (Dt2)	13 Jul 1966
	to 5 Aug 1966
HMS Albion	5 Aug 1966
Culdrose	7 Sep 1966
HMS Albion	1 May 1967
Culdrose	5 Jul 1967
HMS Albion	8 Sep 1967
Sembawang	16 Dec 1967
HMS Albion	19 Jan 1968
Mersing/Jason's Bay	
('A' & 'D' Flts)	5 Feb 1968
	to 4 Apr 1968
Sembawang	27 May 1968

Squadron bases

HMS Albion	3 Jun 1968
Sembawang	21 Jun 1968
HMS Intrepid	
('B' & 'C' Flts)	23 Jun 1968
	to 5 Jul 1968
HMS Albion	2 Jul 1968
Sembawang	5 Aug 1968
HMS Albion	29 Aug 1968
('B' & 'C' Flights)	
HMS Albion (rest)	18 Sep 1968
Sembawang	5 Nov 1968
HMS Albion	26 Nov 1968
Sembawang	13-17 Jan 1969
('A' Flt)	
Sembawang	12 Feb 1969
HMS Albion	14 Mar 1969
Culdrose	29 Jul 1969
HMS Bulwark	
(Dt6)	15-19 Sep 1969
HMS Bulwark	13 Jan 1970
Sembawang	9 Mar 1970
HMS Bulwark	4 Apr 1970
Sembawang	16 May 1970
HMS Bulwark	10 Jun 1970
Culdrose	19 Aug 1970
HMS Albion	29 Mar 1971
Sembawang	22 May 1971
HMS Albion	24 Jun 1971
(less 'B' Flt	
until 28 Jul)	
Sembawang	23 Aug 1971
HMS Intrepid	27 Aug 1971
('A' Flight)	to 1 Oct 1971
HMS Albion	17 Sep 1971
HMS Intrepid	1 Dec 1971
('D' Flight)	to 9 Jan 1972
Culdrose	20 Jan 1972

Squadron bases		Squadron bases		Squadron bases		Commanding Officers	
HMS Albion	12 Apr 1972	HMS Bulwark	10 Mar 1975	Yeovilton	22 Oct 1982	L/C SH Suthers	
Culdrose	26 May 1972	Yeovilton	3 Jul 1975	'D' Flight (6 a/c):		DSC DFC	29 Oct 1952
HMS Albion	9 Jun 1972	HMS Bulwark	1 Sep 1975	Yeovilton	20 Apr 1982	L/C B Paterson MBE	18 Jan 1954
Culdrose	5 Jul 1972	Turkey	25-27 Sep 1975	SS Atlantic		L/C MW Wotherspoon	
Bardufoss (Dt4)	14 Sep 1972	('A' & 'D' Flts)		Conveyor	25 Apr 1982	RN	1 Mar 1955
to	4 Oct 1972	Yeovilton	21 Oct 1975	Ship sunk	25 May 1982	L/C DTJ Stanley	
HMS Fearless	11 Oct 1972	HMS Bulwark	10 Nov 1975	(a/c lost)		MBE DFC RN	8 Jul 1955
('B' Flight)	to 29 Nov 1972	Yeovilton	13 Nov 1975	Sea/air passage to UK		Squadron disbanded 18 Dec 1956	
HMS Intrepid	13-29 Nov 1972	HMS Bulwark	7 Jan 1976		26 May 1982	L/C GCJ Knight RN	14 Oct 1958
('C' Flight)		Aruba ('A' Flt)	27-28 Jan 1976	Yeovilton	7 Jun 1982	L/C BM Tobey RN	4 Mar 1959
HMS Bulwark	17 Nov 1972	Vieques ('D' Flt)	26-27 Feb 1976	Squadron disbanded 30 Nov 1982		L/C TJ Kinna RN	15 Nov 1960
('A' & 'D' Flts)		Portland	23 Mar 1976	Yeovilton	16 Nov 1990	L/C K Mitchell	
Others joined	29 Nov 1972	Yeovilton	26 Mar 1976	SS Atlantic		DFC RN	20 Jan 1961
Yeovilton	4 Dec 1972	Squadron disbanded 31 Mar 1976		Conveyor	21 Dec 1990	L/C BC Sarginson	
HMS Bulwark	16 Jan 1973	Yeovilton	17 Apr 1982	(passage UK-Gulf)		RN	19 Feb 1962
Yeovilton	21 Mar 1973	'A' Flight (2 a/c):		Al Jubayl	5 Jan 1991	L/C CJ Isacke RN	16 Jan 1963
HMS Bulwark	19 Apr 1973	Yeovilton	17 Apr 1982	Strawberry Fields		Squadron disbanded 30 Jul 1963	
Nicosia	7-25 May 1973	RFA Regent	19 Apr 1982	MOB	23 Jan 1991	L/C GA Andrews	
('B' & 'D' Flts)		RFA Endurance	17-24 Jun 1982	Helter Skelter MOB	28 Feb 1991	RN	24 Jun 1964
Luqa	7-25 May 1973	(Dt1)		Revolver MOB	2 Mar 1991	L/C PJ Craig RN	15 Mar 1966
('A' & 'C' Flts)		SS Atlantic Causeway		Al Jubayl	14 Mar 1991	L/C PJ Williams RN	14 Sep 1967
Yeovilton	29 Jun 1973	(Dt1)	10-27 Jul 1982	RFA Argus	18 Mar 1991	Capt MJ Reece RM	14 Feb 1969
('A' & 'C' Flts)	to 17 Jul 1973	Yeovilton	12 Sep 1982	(passage Gulf-UK)		L/C BB Hartwell RN	21 Oct 1970
Kirkwall (Dt12)	9-17 Jul 1973	'B' Flight (2 a/c):		Yeovilton	2 Apr 1991	L/C RE Smith MBE	
Yeovilton	26 Jul 1973	Yeovilton	19 Apr 1982	Squadron disbanded 19 Apr 1991		RN	6 Mar 1972
HMS Bulwark	31 Aug 1973	RFA Olna	22 Apr 1982	Yeovilton	9 Feb 1995	L/C BG Skinner RN	11 Apr 1973
Yeovilton	15 Oct 1973	Yeovilton	16 Sep 1982			L/C RN Woodward	
Valkenburg (Dt4)	31 Oct 1973	'C' Flight (2 a/c):				RN	14 Oct 1974
to	9 Nov 1973	Yeovilton	19 Apr 1982			L/C JJD Knapp RN	14 Apr 1975
HMS Bulwark	5 Nov 1973	RFA Olwen	16 Jun 1982			Squadron disbanded 31 Mar 1976	
Yeovilton	14 Dec 1973	Navy Point	7 Aug 1982	Commanding Officers		L/C DEP Baston	
HMS Bulwark	12 Jan 1974	RFA Olwen	10 Aug 1982	L/C(A) RG Hunt RN 1 Jun 1943		AFC RN	19 Apr 1982
RNIAS Hato (Dt6)	25 Jan 1974	Navy Point	9 Sep 1982	L/C AP Boddam		Squadron disbanded 30 Nov 1982	
to	7 Feb 1974	RFA Olwen	16 Sep 1982	-Whetham RN 29 May 1944		L/C NJ North	
Yeovilton	9 Mar 1974	RFA Fort Austin	27 Sep 1982	L/C TGV Percy RN 21 Aug 1944		DSC RN	16 Nov 1990
Aalborg (Dt2)	24 Apr 1974	HMS Illustrious	16 Oct 1982	L/C(A) AWR Turney		Squadron disbanded 19 Apr 1991	
to	15 May 1974	(flight disbanded)		RN	8 Jun 1945	L/C DA Lord MBE	
Lossiemouth (Dt3)	9-16 Sep 1974	Air passage to UK	17 Oct 1982	Squadron disbanded 31 Oct 1945		RN	9 Feb 1995

Westland Wessex HU.5 XS491 'L/A' of No.848 Squadron disembarking Royal Marines aboard HMS Albion around 1968. (via Brian Lowe)

No.849 Squadron

Badge: On a field blue in base two bars wavy white, a streak of lightning winged in bend sinister gold and charged with an eye proper
Motto: *Primus video* (*The first to see*)

The nucleus of No.849 Squadron assembled at Townhill Camp on 1 July 1943, and took passage for the USA. It officially formed at Quonset Point on 1 August 1943 as a torpedo bomber reconnaissance squadron equipped with 12 Avenger Is. After work-up these joined HMS *Khedive* in November for the UK, the squadron spending a period at Grimsetter, followed by a two weeks anti-submarine course at Maydown and then five further weeks training in this task at Eglinton. In April 1944 No.849 moved to Perranporth where, operating alongside Nos.816 Swordfish and 850 Avenger squadrons, it carried out anti-submarine patrols and anti-shipping strikes during the invasion period, under the control of RAF Coastal Command.

In September 1944 the squadron embarked in HMS *Rajah* and sailed for Ceylon, where the strength was increased to 21 aircraft, being mainly Mk.IIs by then. On 10 December it joined No.820 Squadron in No.2 Naval Strike Wing, embarking in HMS *Victorious* to carry out bombing attacks on Sumatran oil refineries at Pangkalan Brandon and Palembang during January 1945. Strength was reduced to 14 aircraft in February, then from March No.849 participated in a series of strikes on shore targets in the Sakishima Islands in the East China Seas, and later on Formosa, before sailing for Australia at the end of May. In the month before VJ-Day, a series of similar attacks was carried out on the Japanese mainland, in the Tokyo area. Returning to Australia, the aircraft were flown to Mascot, and the crews rejoined HMS *Victorious* to return home, disbanding on arrival on 31 October 1945.

No.849 reformed at Brawdy on 7 July 1952 as an Airborne Early Warning squadron, by redesignating No.778 Squadron. The squadron was equipped with Skyraider AEW.1s, fitted with powerful radar to provide early warning to the Fleet of attacks by ships and low-flying aircraft. Its headquarters flight trained crew members before they joined its operational flights, which embarked from time to time in the major fixed-wing carriers. Both A and B Flights formed in November 1952, though aircraft were in short supply at that stage. A Flight was the first to embark, in HMS *Eagle* during January 1953. B Flight went out to Hal Far in January, and in June the newly-formed C Flight joined A Flight in HMS *Eagle*, disembarking in October to sail in HMS *Glory* to Malta, where it relieved B Flight. D Flight formed in August 1953, and spent two weeks in HMS *Eagle* during November. In January 1954, 'E' Flight formed, and B Flight embarked in HMS *Eagle*, only to disband in July to reinforce A and C Flights'. It was immediately replaced when C Flight became the new B Flight, and at the same time D Flight became a new C Flight, joining HMS *Ark Royal* in August 1954. To complete this complicated series of changes, a new D Flight formed in October 1954.

In May 1955, C Flight was briefly in HMS *Bulwark*, and in October B Flight embarked in HMS *Ark Royal*. In January 1956 D Flight joined HMS *Albion*, leaving again in May, and in June C Flight spent another short period in HMS *Albion*. D Flight next embarked in June 1957, when it joined HMS *Bulwark*. During 1958, B Flight transferred from HMS *Ark Royal* to HMS *Victorious*, whilst B Flight left HMS *Bulwark*. In 1959, A Flight disembarked from HMS *Eagle*, C Flight left HMS *Albion*, and D Flight spent a few months in HMS *Centaur*.

A major change occurred in 1960, when the first Gannet AEW.3s arrived, the squadron completely re-equipping with these between February and the end of the year. No.849 continued to operate in flights, and A Flight embarked in HMS *Eagle* in March with the new type, followed by C Flight in HMS *Hermes* in July. D Flight was the last to operate Skyraiders, disbanding on leaving HMS *Albion* in December. The pattern then continued much as before, though seldom with all four flights in commission. D Flight reformed in September 1964, and at the end of that year the squadron headquarters moved to Brawdy. B Flight disbanded in September 1965, after disembarking from HMS *Centaur*, a new B Flight forming for HMS *Hermes* in April 1966, only to disband again in February 1968. C Flight disbanded, in October 1966, and never reformed, being subsequently awarded the 1966 Boyd Trophy for outstanding performance in HMS *Ark Royal* during Mozambique patrol. B Flight reformed for HMS *Ark Royal* in January 1970, but A Flight disbanded for the last time in July 1970.

The squadron headquarters moved again in November 1970, this time to Lossiemouth, but it now controlled only two flights. No attempt was made to fill the alphabetical gaps in these, and D Flight remained with HMS *Eagle* until disbanding in January 1972. Finally, B Flight disembarked from HMS *Ark Royal* in November 1978, and both it and the squadron headquarters ceased to exist on 15 December 1978. During its existence, No.849 had been on the scene of numerous international incidents, including participation by A Flight in the Suez operation, whilst embarked in HMS *Eagle*. Squadron aircrew had frequently been exchanged with their US Navy counterparts.

The Falklands campaign highlighted the need for the Royal Navy to have a continued airborne early warning capability. As a temporary expedient this was fulfilled by the formation of No.824 Squadron D Flight, equipped with AEW Sea Kings. A new No.849 Squadron formed from 824D Flight, commissioning on 8 Nov 1984 at Culdrose. The squadron eventually consisted of eight AEW Sea King helicopters, HQ and two Flts of three aircraft each (A Flight from Mar 1985, and B Flight from Mar 1986). AEW training is carried out by the squadron headquarters, the flights embarking on the carriers, transferring with the air group each time one of the carriers enters refit. The squadron was awarded the Boyd Trophy for 1986 for the "timely, efficient and enthusiastic manner" in which they re-introduced the role of AEW to the Fleet.

The squadron continues to operate from Culdrose, with A Flt deploying to HMS *Invincible* and B Flt to HMS *Illustrious*.

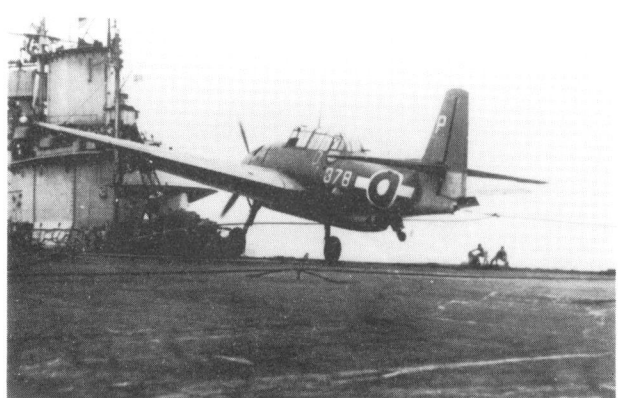

Grumman Avenger II JZ616 '378/P' of No.849 Squadron catches a wire landing on HMS Indomitable in 1945. (R.A.Bartholomew)

Identification Markings
Avenger single letters, to *P1A+* by 1.45, to *370-385/P* 6.45; Skyraider *301-326/CW:J:Z:O*, to *410-429/CU:E:R:B:A:V* 1.56; Gannet *410-454/CU:BY:R:V:H:E:CU*, to *760-777/BY:LM, 260-264/V:H, 330-333/H:BY, 070-074/E & 034-040/R* 1.65; Sea King *363-370*, to *180-187/CU:B:N* 9.85.

Aircraft Equipment	Period of Service	Example
Avenger I	Aug 1943 - Aug 1945	FN858 (P1U)
Avenger II	Sep 1944 - Aug 1945	JZ538 (376/P)
Skyraider AEW.1	Jul 1952 - Dec 1960	WV183 (419/R)
Gannet AEW.3	Feb 1960 - Dec 1978	XP225 (261/H)
Gannet AS.4	Sep 1959 - May 1966	XG783 (445/CU)
Gannet COD.4	Sep 1961 - Sep 1974	XG786 (074/E)
Gannet T.5	Sep 1961 - Jan 1976	XT752 (772/BY)
Sea King AEW.2/2A	Nov 1984 - to date	XV664 (185/CU)

Douglas Skyraider AEW.1 WT944 of No.849 HQ Squadron, Culdrose. (via Brian Lowe)

Battle Honours
Normandy	1944
Palembang	1945
Okinawa	1945
Japan	1945

Squadron bases
Quonset Point	1 Aug 1943
Squantum	24 Aug 1943
Norfolk (transit)	1 Nov 1943
HMS Khedive	1 Nov 1943
Speke	17 Nov 1943
Grimsetter	25 Nov 1943
Maydown	14 Feb 1944
Eglinton	26 Feb 1944
Machrihanish	25 Mar 1944
Perranporth	20 Apr 1944
St Eval	9 Aug 1944
Lee-on-Solent	26 Aug 1944
Belfast	6 Sep 1944
HMS Rajah	9 Sep 1944
Cochin (transit)	9 Oct 1944
Coimbatore	9 Oct 1944
Katukurunda	11 Oct 1944
HMS Battler(Dt3)	4 Nov 1944
[DLT] to	6 Nov 1944
HMS Victorious	19 Dec 1944
Nowra	10 Feb 1945
HMS Victorious	27 Feb 1945
Nowra	6 Jun 1945
HMS Victorious	24 Jun 1945
Maryborough	23 Aug 1945
Mascot	24 Aug 1945
HMS Victorious (no aircraft)	24 Aug 1945
Sqdn disbanded UK	31 Oct 1945
Culdrose	7 Jul 1952
HMS Eagle (Dt2)	2-29 Sep 1952
HMS Hermes (Dt3)	30 Nov 1963 to 12 Dec 1963
Brawdy	15 Dec 1964
Valkenburg (Dt)	2-10 May 1966
HMS Hermes (Dt)	25 Aug 1966 to 5 Sep 1966

Squadron bases
Ballykelly (Dt)	28 Sep 1966 to 5 Oct 1966
Valkenburg (Dt)	24-30 May 1967
Aalborg	1-4 Dec 1967
Ballykelly	24 Apr 1968
Brawdy	26 Apr 1968
Binbrook (Dt3)	5-8 Oct 1970
Lossiemouth	19 Nov 1970
Karup (Dt4)	29 Apr 1971 to 13 May 1971
Karup (Dt2)	15-16 Jun 1971
Binrook (Dt3)	22-25 Jun 1971
Lann-Bihoue (Dt)	9-17 Sep 1971
Coltishall (Dt)	27-30 Sep 1971
Squadron disbanded	15 Dec 1978
Culdrose	9 Nov 1984
HMS Illustrious	31 Jul 1985
Lann-Bihoue (Dt2)	16-19 May 1986
Aalborg	5-17 Jun 1986
Lann-Bihoue(Dt4)	6-9 Mar 1987
Wildenrath (Dt1)	29 May 1987 to 2 Jun 1987
Wildenrath(Dt2)	26-30 Nov 1987
Rheims (Dt2)	16-19 Jun 1989 to 4 Dec 1989
Wildenrath (Dt2)	30 Jun 1989 to 3 Jul 1989
Lann-Bihoue (Dt2)	15-18 Jul 1989
Leeuwarden (Dt2)	8-11 Jun 1990
Coningsby (Dt1)	26-28 Jun 1990
Rheims (Dt2)	30 Nov 1990 to 4 Dec 1990
Coningsby (Dt1)	14-18 Jan 1991
Wattisham (Dt1)	11-14 Mar 1991
Lann Bihoue(Dt2)	10-13 May 1991
Coningsby (Dt1)	10-14 Jun 1991
Yeovilton (Dt3)	25-27 Jun 1991
Aalborg (Dt2)	22 Oct 1991 to 1 Nov 1991
Leeming (Dt1)	25-28 Feb 1992
Brawdy (Dt1)	9-13 Mar 1992

Squadron bases
Bruggen (Dt1)	13-1 6 Mar 1992
Koksijde (Dt1)	3-6 Jul 1992
Dugny(Dt2)	23-2 6 Oct 1992
Coningsby (Dt1)	22-27 Nov 1992
Coningsby (Dt1)	24-29 Jan 1993
St.Mawgan (Dt1)	3-12 Mar 1993
Cognac (Dt1)	14-17 May 1993
Lakenheath (Dt2)	3- 7 May 1993
Coningsby (Dt2)	20-25 Jun 1993
Koksijde (Dt1)	2-5 Jul 1993

849A

Squadron bases
Culdrose	3 Nov 1952
HMS Eagle	29 Jan 1953
Culdrose	25 Mar 1953
HMS Eagle	18 Jun 1953
Culdrose	23 Jul 1953
HMS Eagle	2 Sep 1953
Culdrose	29 Nov 1953
HMS Eagle	26 Jan 1954
North Front(Dt3)	19-29 Mar 1954
Hal Far (Dt2)	14-27 Apr 1954
Culdrose	to 25 May 1954
North Front (Dt2)	1-8 Nov 1954
HMS Eagle	6 May 1955
Culdrose	17 May 1955
HMS Eagle	7 Jun 1955
Hal Far (Dt)	24 Jun 1955 to 23 Aug 1955
North Front (Dt)	23 Aug 1955 to 8 Sep 1955
Culdrose (Dt2)	11-12 Sep 1955
Culdrose	3 Nov 1955
HMS Bulwark(DLP)	13 Feb 1956
Culdrose	23 Feb 1956
HMS Eagle	16 Apr 1956
Hal Far	29 Jun 1956
HMS Eagle	17 Jul 1956
Culdrose	3 Jan 1957
Lossiemouth(Dt)	13-22 May 1957
HMS Eagle	5 Aug 1957

Squadron bases
Culdrose	2 Nov 1957
HMS Eagle	14 Nov 1957
Culdrose	27 Nov 1957
HMS Eagle	28 Jan 1958
Culdrose	29 Mar 1958
HMS Eagle	20 May 1958
Culdrose	2 Dec 1958
HMS Eagle	14 Jan 1959
North Front	3 Feb 1959
HMS Eagle	13 Feb 1959
Culdrose	23 Mar 1959
HMS Eagle	13 Apr 1959
Culdrose	29 Apr 1959
HMS Ark Royal	3 Mar 1960
Hal Far	1 May 1960
HMS Ark Royal	22 May 1960
Culdrose	30 Sep 1960
HMS Ark Royal	26 Oct 1960
Hal Far	18 Dec 1960
HMS Ark Royal	6 Jan 1961
Culdrose	27 Feb 1961
HMS Centaur	10 Apr 1961
Hal Far	28 Apr 1961
HMS Centaur	8 May 1961
Culdrose	1 Sep 1961
HMS Centaur	20 Oct 1961
Tengah	1 Feb 1962
HMS Centaur	Feb 1962
Culdrose	14 May 1962
HMS Centaur	21 Jun 1962
Culdrose	5 Jul 1962
HMS Centaur	12 Jul 1962
Culdrose	25 Oct 1962
HMS Centaur	22 Jan 1963
Culdrose	12 Feb 1963
HMS Centaur	21 Feb 1963
Khormaksar	5 Mar 1963
HMS Centaur	18 Mar 1963
Embakasi (Dt3)	7-23 Apr 1963
Culdrose	20 May 1963
HMS Centaur	25 May 1963
Culdrose	6 Jun 1963
HMS Victorious	14 Aug 1963

*Fairey Gannet AS.4 XG790 '040/R' of No.849B Flight aboard HMS Ark Royal around 1971.
(via Brian Lowe)*

Squadron bases

Tengah	1 Dec 1963
HMS Victorious	8 Jan 1964
Embakasi (Dt2)	7-22 Feb 1964
Seletar	23 Mar 1964
HMS Victorious	8 Apr 1964
Seletar	12 Jun 1964
HMS Victorious	19 Aug 1964
Seletar	21 Sep 1964
HMS Victorious	7 Dec 1964
Brawdy	22 Jul 1965
Squadron disbanded	27 Jul 1965
Brawdy	20 Jan 1966
HMS Victorious	14 May 1966
Brawdy	9 Jun 1966
HMS Victorious	8 Jul 1966
Changi	15 Aug 1966
HMS Victorious	4 Sep 1966
Changi	8 Dec 1966
HMS Victorious	4 Jan 1967
Changi	16 Feb 1967
HMS Victorious	3 Mar 1967
Brawdy	19 Jun 1967
HMS Hermes	29 May 1968
Brawdy	20 Jun 1968
HMS Hermes	9 Jul 1968
Changi	29 Aug 1968
HMS Hermes	16 Sep 1968
Changi	12 Dec 1968
HMS Hermes	13 Jan 1969
Brawdy	31 Mar 1969
HMS Hermes	25 Sep 1969
Brawdy	28 Oct 1969
HMS Hermes	14 Nov 1969
Brawdy	4 Dec 1969
HMS Hermes	14 Jan 1970
Luqa	16 Feb 1970
HMS Hermes	6 Mar 1970
Luqa	13 Apr 1970
HMS Hermes	4 May 1970
Brawdy	22 Jun 1970
Flight disbanded	14 Jul 1970
Culdrose	18 Mar 1985
HMS Illustrious	1 Aug 1985
Norfolk (Dt3)	20-26 Aug 1985
Culdrose	25 Sep 1985
HMS Illustrious	9 Oct 1985
Culdrose	4 Dec 1985
HMS Illustrious	27 Jan 1986
Culdrose	19 Feb 1986
HMS Illustrious	2 Apr 1986
Culdrose	4 Apr 1986
Lann-Bihoue (Dt2)	16-19 May 1986
HMS Illustrious	21 Jul 1986
Culdrose	17 Dec 1986
Coningsby (Dt2)	22-26 Feb 1987
Binbrook (Dt2)	29 Mar 1987 to 3 Apr 1987
HMS Illustrious	26 Apr 1987
Culdrose	22 Jun 1987
HMS Illustrious	24 Aug 1987
Culdrose	25 Sep 1987
HMS Illustrious	6 Oct 1987
Aalborg	14 Oct 1987
Culdrose	28 Oct 1987
HMS Ark Royal (Dt1)	2-19 Nov 1987
Binbrook (Dt2)	16 Nov 1987 to 20 Nov 1987
HMS Illustrious	19 Jan 1988
Culdrose	3 Mar 1988
HMS Illustrious	6 Apr 1988
Culdrose	20 May 1988
HMS Illustrious	12 Jun 1988
Culdrose	26 Jun 1988
HMS Illustrious	29 Aug 1988
Culdrose	24 Sep 1988
HMS Illustrious	3 Oct 1988
Culdrose	15 Dec 1988
HMS Illustrious	27 Jan 1989
Culdrose	22 Feb 1989
HMS Illustrious	28 Feb 1989
Culdrose	22 Mar 1989
HMS Invincible	23 May 1989
Culdrose	1 Jun 1989
HMS Invincible	12 Jul 1989
Culdrose	9 Aug 1989
HMS Invincible	16 Sep 1989
Jacksonville	2 Nov 1989
HMS Invincible	16 Nov 1989
Culdrose	22 Feb 1990
Aalborg	7 Mar 1990
Culdrose	20 Mar 1990
HMS Invincible	24 Apr 1990
Culdrose	14 May 1990
HMS Invincible	4 Jun 1990
Culdrose	7 Jun 1990
Waddington (Dt2)	11-15 Jun 1990
HMS Invincible	26 Jun 1990
Culdrose	13 Jul 1990
HMS Invincible	1 Sep 1990
Culdrose	17 Sep 1990
Aalborg	21 Oct 1990
Culdrose	2 Nov 1990
Waddington	19 Nov 1990
Culdrose	30 Nov 1990
HMS Invincible	18 Jan 1991
Culdrose	23 Jan 1991
HMS Invincible	5 Feb 1991
Culdrose	18 Feb 1991
Coningsby (Dt2)	18-22 Feb 1991
HMS Invincible	26 Feb 1991
Culdrose	22 Mar 1991
HMS Invincible	15 Apr 1991
Culdrose	22 May 1991
HMS Invincible (Dt2)	3-6 Jun 1991
HMS Invincible	29 Aug 1991
Culdrose	17 Nov 1991
HMS Invincible	21 Feb 1992
Culdrose	23 Mar 1992
HMS Invincible	11 May 1992
Sembawang	7 Sep 1992
HMS Invincible	17 Sep 1992
Al Bateen (Dt1)	21-25 Oct 1992
Culdrose	25 Nov 1992
HMS Invincible	11 May 1993
Culdrose	24 May 1993
HMS Invincible	4 Jun 1993
Culdrose	19 Jun 1993
HMS Invincible	22 Jul 1993

Fairey Gannet AEW.3 XP226 '422/V' of No.849A Flight, HMS Victorious having difficulty landing in 1963. (via Brian Lowe)

Westland Sea King AEW.2 XV704 '363 of No.849 Squadron at Yeovilton in 1985.

Squadron bases
ITS Guiseppe Garibaldi (Dt2)	2-18 Nov 1993
Grottaglie (Dt1)	19-25 Jan 1994
Culdrose	10 Feb 1994
Bulmer (Dt2)	20-25 Mar 1994
Cristiansand (Dt2)	25 Apr 1994 to 9 May 1994
HMS Invincible (Dt2)	20-30 May 1994
HMS Invincible	27 Jun 1994 to 6 Jul 1994
HMS Invincible	23 Aug 1994

849B

Squadron bases
Culdrose	25 Nov 1952
Hal Far	19 Jan 1953
Culdrose	2 Nov 1953
HMS Eagle	26 Jan 1954
Hal Far (Dt)	14-27 Apr 1954
Culdrose	25 May 1954
Flight disbanded	5 Jul 1954
Culdrose	5 Jul 1954
Kinloss	13 Sep 1954
Culdrose	21 Sep 1954
Hal Far	11 Oct 1954
Karouba	26 Mar 1955
Culdrose	4 Apr 1955
Yeovilton	27 Jun 1955
Culdrose	30 Jun 1955
HMS Ark Royal	5 Oct 1955
Hal Far	20 Jan 1956
HMS Ark Royal	31 Jan 1956
Culdrose	5 Apr 1956
HMS Ark Royal	9 Jan 1957
Culdrose	25 Feb 1957
HMS Ark Royal	6 May 1957
Culdrose	18 Jul 1957
HMS Ark Royal	30 Aug 1957
Culdrose	25 Nov 1957
HMS Ark Royal	27 Jan 1958
Culdrose	25 Jun 1958
HMS Victorious	26 Sep 1958
Culdrose	13 Jan 1959
HMS Victorious	21 Feb 1959
HMS Eagle	14 Feb 1959
HMS Victorious	16 Feb 1959
Culdrose	23 Mar 1959
HMS Victorious	5 May 1959
Culdrose	9 Aug 1959
HMS Victorious	15 Sep 1959
Culdrose	6 Oct 1959
HMS Victorious	30 Oct 1959
Culdrose	14 Dec 1959
HMS Victorious	25 Jan 1960
Culdrose	22 Feb 1960

Squadron bases
HMS Victorious	18 Oct 1960
Hal Far	5 Nov 1960
HMS Victorious	15 Nov 1960
Culdrose	19 Dec 1960
HMS Victorious	26 Jan 1961
Tengah (Dt2)	28 Mar 1961 to 12 Apr 1961
Seletar	8 May 1961
HMS Victorious	15 Jun 1961
Tengah	14 Sep 1961
HMS Victorious	6 Oct 1961
Culdrose	17 Dec 1961
HMS Victorious	5 Feb 1962
North Front (Dt2)	28 Feb 1962 to 13 Mar 1962
Culdrose	30 Mar 1962
HMS Hermes	16 May 1962
Culdrose	23 May 1962
HMS Hermes	26 May 1962
Hal Far (Dt2)	12-27 Jun 1962
North Front (Dt2)	27 Jul 1962 to 9 Aug 1962
Hal Far	5 Sep 1962
HMS Hermes	18 Sep 1962
Culdrose	2 Oct 1962
HMS Hermes	14 Nov 1962
Seletar	20 Dec 1962
HMS Hermes	7 Jan 1963
Seletar	18 Mar 1963
HMS Hermes	24 Apr 1963
Seletar	12 Jun 1963
HMS Hermes	28 Jun 1963
Culdrose	11 Sep 1963
HMS Hermes	27 Sep 1963
Culdrose	18 Oct 1963
HMS Centaur	22 Dec 1963
Seletar	11 Feb 1964
HMS Centaur	3 Mar 1964
Kai Tak	28 Mar 1964
HMS Centaur	13 Apr 1964
Seletar	30 Apr 1964
HMS Centaur	14 May 1964
Embakasi	29 May 1964
HMS Centaur	12 Jun 1964
Seletar	14 Aug 1964
HMS Centaur	1 Sep 1964
Seletar	14 Sep 1964
HMS Centaur	17 Sep 1964
Kai Tak	25 Sep 1964
HMS Centaur	14 Oct 1964
Brawdy	20 Dec 1964
HMS Centaur	8 Apr 1965
Hal Far (Dt2)	23 Apr 1965 to 11 May 1965
HMS Centaur	11 May 1965
North Front (Dt2)	10-26 Jun 1965
North Front (Dt3)	5-19 Jul 1965
Brawdy	27 Jul 1965

Squadron bases
Flight disbanded	12 Sep 1965
Brawdy	18 Apr 1966
Ballykelly	9 May 1966
Yeovilton	13 May 1966
Brawdy	16 May 1966
Yeovilton	30 Aug 1966
Brawdy	12 Sep 1966
HMS Hermes	22 Sep 1966
Brawdy	20 Oct 1966
HMS Hermes	8 Jan 1966
Brawdy	17 Nov 1966
HMS Hermes	18 Jan 1967
Gibraltar	6 Feb 1967
HMS Hermes	20 Feb 1967
Hal Far	15 Mar 1967
HMS Hermes	31 Mar 1967
Changi	21 Jun 1967
HMS Hermes	17 Jul 1967
Brawdy	30 Sep 1967
HMS Hermes	1 Nov 1967
Brawdy	18 Feb 1968
Flight disbanded	28 Feb 1968
Brawdy	5 Jan 1970
HMS Ark Royal	4 May 1970
Brawdy	5 May 1970
Lossiemouth	12 Jun 1970
HMS Ark Royal	14 Jun 1970
Brawdy	9 Jul 1970
HMS Ark Royal	20 Jul 1970
Brawdy	30 Jul 1970
HMS Ark Royal	3 Sep 1970
Brawdy	26 Sep 1970
Yeovilton (transit)	9 Oct 1970
HMS Ark Royal	10 Oct 1970
Luqa	18 Oct 1970
HMS Ark Royal	29 Oct 1970
Lossiemouth	16 Dec 1970
HMS Ark Royal	19 Apr 1971
Lossiemouth	29 Apr 1971
Lossiemouth	15 May 1971
Lossiemouth	19 May 1971
HMS Ark Royal	2 Jun 1971
Lossiemouth	29 Jul 1971
HMS Ark Royal	16 Aug 1971
Lossiemouth	7 Oct 1971
HMS Ark Royal	29 Oct 1971
Lossiemouth	6 Dec 1971
HMS Ark Royal	19 Jan 1972
Lossiemouth	8 Mar 1972
Kastrup (Dt2)	28 Apr 1972 to 12 May 1972
Binbrook	22 May 1972
Lossiemouth	25 May 1972
HMS Ark Royal	12 Jun 1972
Lossiemouth	17 Jul 1972
HMS Ark Royal	4 Sep 1972
Lossiemouth	18 Oct 1972
HMS Ark Royal	4 Nov 1972
Lossiemouth	11 Dec 1972

Squadron bases
HMS Ark Royal	25 Jan 1973
Luqa (Dt2)	22 Feb 1973 to 6 Mar 1973
Lossiemouth	14 Mar 1973
HMS Ark Royal	2 May 1973
Dett (2 a/c)	
Mayport	19 May 1973
Norfolk	21 Jun 1973
Mayport	25 Jun 1973
Cecil Field	29 Jun 1973
returned ship	30 Jun 1973
Lossiemouth	24 Jul 1973
Yeovilton (Dt2)	23-28 Aug 1973
HMS Ark Royal	8 Jul 1974
Lossiemouth	26 Jul 1974
HMS Ark Royal	5 Sep 1974
Luqa (Dt2)	4-16 Oct 1974
Lossiemouth	4 Nov 1974
Yeovilton (transit)	7 Jan 1975
HMS Ark Royal	8 Jan 1975
Mayport	18 Feb 1975
Pensacola (Dt2)	24-26 Feb 1975
Norfolk (Dt2)	3-4 Mar 1975
HMS Ark Royal	7 Mar 1975
Norfolk	4 Apr 1975
HMS Ark Royal	21 Apr 1975
Lossiemouth	10 Jun 1975
HMS Ark Royal (Dt2)	19-24 Sep 1975
HMS Ark Royal	6 Oct 1975
Lossiemouth	21 Nov 1975
Culdrose (transit)	5 Feb 1976
HMS Ark Royal	6 Feb 1976
Mayport	22 Mar 1976
HMS Ark Royal	13 Apr 1976
Norfolk	18 Apr 1976
HMS Ark Royal	6 May 1976
Norfolk	3 Jun 1976
HMS Ark Royal	14 Jun 1976
Lossiemouth	14 Jul 1976
HMS Ark Royal	4 Sep 1976
Lossiemouth	19 Oct 1976
Eggebek	11 Mar 1977
Lossiemouth	21 Mar 1977
HMS Ark Royal	5 Sep 1977
Lossiemouth	12 Dec 1977
HMS Ark Royal	22 Feb 1978
Lossiemouth	5 Mar 1978
HMS Ark Royal	5 Apr 1978
Jacksonville	21 Jun 1978
HMS Ark Royal	8 Aug 1978
Yeovilton (transit)	27 Nov 1978
Lossiemouth	28 Nov 1978
Flight disbanded	15 Dec 1978
Culdrose	3 Mar 1986
HMS Ark Royal	17 Jun 1986
Oceana	9 Aug 1986
HMS Ark Royal	14 Aug 1986
Culdrose	27 Sep 1986

Westland Sea King AEW.2A XV656 '186/N' of No.849 Squadron in 1990. (MAP)

Squadron bases

HMS Ark Royal	13 Oct 1986
Culdrose	20 Nov 1986
HMS Ark Royal	15 Jan 1987
Culdrose	7 Apr 1987
HMS Ark Royal	5 May 1987
Culdrose	15 May 1987
HMS Ark Royal	2 Jun 1987
Culdrose	26 Jun 1987
HMS Ark Royal	3 Sep 1987
Culdrose	24 Oct 1987
HMS Ark Royal	2 Nov 1987
Culdrose	19 Nov 1987
HMS Ark Royal	25 Jan 1988
HMS Ark Royal	9 Jun 1988
Culdrose	15 Dec 1988
Coningsby (Dt2)	Feb 1989
	to 2 Mar 1989
HMS Ark Royal	31 Mar 1989
Culdrose	2 May 1989
HMS Ark Royal	10 May 1989
Culdrose	3 Jun 1989
HMS Ark Royal	12 Jun 1989
Culdrose	6 Jul 1989
HMS Ark Royal	4 Sep 1989
Culdrose	21 Sep 1989
HMS Ark Royal	2 Oct 1989
Culdrose	13 Oct 1989
HMS Ark Royal	18 Jan 1990
Culdrose	24 Jan 1990
HMS Ark Royal	30 Jan 1990
Culdrose	16 Mar 1990
HMS Ark Royal	18 Apr 1990
RFA Olna (Dt1)	1-4 May 1990
Culdrose	4 Jul 1990
HMS Ark Royal (Dt1)	21-28 Aug 1990
Lee-on-Solent (Dt1)	24-27 Aug 1990
HMS Ark Royal	3 Sep 1990
Culdrose	26 Sep 1990
HMS Ark Royal	15 Oct 1990
Gibraltar (Dt2)	19-25 Oct 1990
Culdrose	1 Nov 1990
HMS Ark Royal	11 Jan 1991
Culdrose	10 Apr 1991
HMS Ark Royal	30 May 1991
Culdrose	27 Jun 1991
HMS Ark Royal	30 Aug 1991
HMS Ark Royal (Dt1)	to 10 Sep 1991
Lee-on-Solent (Dt1)	1-5 Sep 1991
HMS Ark Royal	10 Sep 1991
Culdrose	15 Nov 1991
HMS Ark Royal	20 Mar 1992
Culdrose	1 May 1992
HMS Ark Royal	2 Sep 1992
Culdrose	4 Nov 1992
HMS Ark Royal	15 Jan 1993
Culdrose	5 Aug 1993
Aalborg	8 Nov 1993
HMS Ark Royal	19 Nov 1993
Culdrose	25 Nov 1993
HMS Ark Royal	18 Jan 1994
Culdrose	3 Sep 1994
HMS Illustrious	Nov 1994

849C

Squadron bases

Culdrose	1 Jun 1953
HMS Eagle	18 Jun 1953
Culdrose	23 Jul 1953
HMS Eagle	2 Sep 1953
Culdrose	3 Oct 1953
transit	21 Oct 1953
Hal Far	23 Oct 1953
HMS Glory	30 Nov 1953
Hal Far	16 Dec 1953
Culdrose	8 Apr 1954
Redesignated 'B' Flight	5 Jul 1954
Culdrose	5 Jul 1954
HMS Albion	23 Aug 1954
Culdrose	26 Aug 1954
HMS Albion	17 Sep 1954
Hal Far	12 Dec 1954
HMS Albion	16 Dec 1954
Culdrose	31 Mar 1955
HMS Bulwark	12 May 1955
Culdrose	27 May 1955
HMS Albion	19 Jul 1955
Culdrose	2 Nov 1955
Eglinton	21 Jan 1956
Culdrose	10 Feb 1956
HMS Bulwark	8 Jun 1956
Culdrose	20 Jun 1956
HMS Albion	15 Sep 1956
Culdrose	6 Mar 1957
HMS Albion	16 Apr 1957
Hal Far	25 Apr 1957
HMS Albion	3 May 1957
Culdrose	1 Jun 1957
HMS Albion	18 Jun 1957
Culdrose	10 Jul 1957
HMS Albion	3 Sep 1957
Culdrose	28 Oct 1957
HMS Albion	8 Jul 1958
Culdrose	19 Jul 1958
Hal Far	28 Jul 1958
HMS Albion	4 Aug 1958
Culdrose	15 Sep 1958
HMS Albion	20 Oct 1958
Seletar (Dt2)	28 Nov 1958
	to 15 Dec 1958
Nowra	13 Feb 1959
HMS Albion	24 Feb 1959
Laverton (Dt2)	2-8 Mar 1959
Seletar	25 Mar 1959
	to 14 Apr 1959
Culdrose	18 Aug 1959
HMS Hermes	5 Jul 1960
Lossiemouth	28 Aug 1960
HMS Hermes	22 Sep 1960
Culdrose	15 Oct 1960
HMS Hermes	7 Nov 1960
Culdrose	18 Apr 1961
HMS Hermes	29 May 1961
Culdrose	28 Jul 1961
HMS Hermes	9 Aug 1961
Culdrose	10 Sep 1961
HMS Ark Royal	13 Nov 1961
Hal Far (Dt2)	15 Dec 1961
	to 2 Jan 1962
Culdrose	14 Jan 1962
HMS Ark Royal	10 Mar 1962
Tengah	28 Jun 1962
HMS Ark Royal	12 Jul 1962
Tengah	26 Jul 1962
HMS Ark Royal	10 Aug 1962
Seletar (Dt2)	13-28 Sep 1962
Culdrose	1 Jan 1963
HMS Ark Royal	20 Feb 1963
North Front	21 Mar 1963
HMS Ark Royal	4 May 1963
Embakasi (Dt2)	7-19 Jun 1963
Seletar	10 Jul 1963
HMS Ark Royal	26 Jul 1963
Seletar (Dt2)	6-29 Aug 1963
Embakasi (Dt2)	18 Oct 1963
	to 1 Nov 1963
Culdrose	30 Dec 1963
HMS Hermes	16 Jan 1964
Culdrose	30 Jan 1964
HMS Hermes	14 Feb 1964
Lossiemouth (transit)	23 Feb 1964
Culdrose	24 Feb 1964
Brawdy	18 Dec 1964
HMS Ark Royal	14 Jan 1965
Lossiemouth	13 Feb 1965
HMS Ark Royal	25 Feb 1965
Brawdy	16 Mar 1965
HMS Ark Royal	8 May 1965
Brawdy	25 May 1965
HMS Ark Royal	17 Jun 1965
Seletar	19 Jul 1965
HMS Ark Royal	4 Aug 1965
Changi	3 Sep 1965
HMS Ark Royal	18 Sep 1965
Changi	19 Oct 1965
Butterworth	10 Nov 1965
Changi	19 Nov 1965
HMS Ark Royal	7 Dec 1965
Changi	7 Jan 1966
HMS Ark Royal	27 Jan 1966
Changi	25 Mar 1966
HMS Ark Royal	27 Apr 1966
Brawdy	12 Jun 1966
HMS Ark Royal	2 Aug 1966
Brawdy	1 Oct 1966
Squadron disbanded	5 Oct 1966

Westland Sea King AEW.2A XV671 '181/CU' of No.849 Squadron, Culdrose in 1991. (MAP)

849D

Squadron bases

Culdrose	17 Aug 1953
HMS Eagle	16 Nov 1953
Culdrose	30 Nov 1953
Eglinton	12 Mar 1954
Culdrose	5 Jul 1954
- redesignated 'C' Flight	
Culdrose	15 Oct 1954
HMS Bulwark (Dt2)	14-25 Feb 1955
transit	28 Mar 1955
Hal Far	30 Mar 1955
transit	9 Oct 1955
Culdrose	10 Oct 1955
HMS Albion (Dt2)	21-25 Nov 1955
Yeovilton	5 Dec 1955
Culdrose	9 Dec 1955
HMS Albion	10 Jan 1956
Culdrose	14 May 1956
HMS Bulwark	25 Jun 1957
Culdrose	5 Aug 1957
HMS Bulwark	28 Aug 1957
Culdrose	2 Nov 1957
HMS Bulwark	14 Nov 1957
Culdrose	27 Nov 1957
HMS Bulwark	11 Jan 1958
North Front	26 Mar 1958
HMS Bulwark	7 Apr 1958
Kilindindi (Dt2)	8-17 Jul 1958
Khormaksar (Dt2)	11 Aug 1958 to 9 Sep 1958
Culdrose	5 Nov 1958
HMS Centaur	23 Jan 1959
North Front	14 Mar 1959
Culdrose	23 Mar 1959
HMS Centaur	29 Apr 1959
North Front	5 Jun 1959
transit	6 Jun 1959
Culdrose	8 Jun 1959
Hyeres (transit)	21 Aug 1959
Hal Far	22 Aug 1959
Grottaglie (Dt)	14-17 Sep 1959
transit	23 Sep 1959
Culdrose	25 Sep 1959
HMS Albion	5 Feb 1960
Hal Far	11 Mar 1960
HMS Albion	21 Mar 1960
Seletar	12 Apr 1960
HMS Albion	29 Apr 1960
Seletar	13 Jul 1960
HMS Albion	5 Feb 1960
Culdrose-disbanded	15 Dec 1960
Culdrose	3 Sep 1964
Lossiemouth	19 Sep 1964
Culdrose	22 Sep 1964
HMS Eagle	2 Dec 1964
Seletar	13 Jan 1965
Kai Tak	23 Feb 1965
HMS Eagle	11 Mar 1965
Seletar	6 Apr 1965
HMS Eagle	20 Apr 1965
Brawdy	24 May 1965
HMS Eagle	25 Aug 1965
Changi	12 Nov 1965
HMS Eagle	20 Nov 1965
Changi	11 Feb 1966
HMS Eagle	28 Feb 1966
Changi	9 May 1966
HMS Eagle	3 Jun 1966
Changi	26 Jun 1966
HMS Eagle	12 Jul 1966
Brawdy	21 Aug 1966
HMS Eagle	6 Jun 1967
Brawdy	10 Jun 1967
HMS Eagle	26 Jun 1967
Brawdy	17 Jul 1967
HMS Eagle	14 Aug 1967
Changi	5 Oct 1967
HMS Eagle	24 Oct 1967
Changi	21 Dec 1967
HMS Eagle	23 Jan 1968
Pearce	11 Feb 1968
HMS Eagle	27 Feb 1968
Kai Tak	23 Mar 1968
HMS Eagle	4 Apr 1968
Brawdy	17 Jun 1968
HMS Eagle	24 Aug 1968
Brawdy	2 Oct 1968
transit	6 Nov 1968
Decimomannu transit	7 Nov 1968 19 Nov 1968
Brawdy	20 Nov 1968
HMS Eagle	3 Apr 1969
Brawdy	29 Apr 1969
HMS Eagle	23 May 1969
Brawdy	2 Jun 1969
HMS Eagle	16 Jun 1969
Brawdy	19 Jul 1969
HMS Eagle	4 Sep 1969
Gibraltar (Dt1)	27 Sep 1969 to 11 Oct 1969
Luqa	30 Oct 1969
HMS Eagle	13 Nov 1969
Brawdy	4 Dec 1969
HMS Eagle	12 Jan 1970
Brawdy	26 Feb 1970
Lossiemouth	9 Jun 1970
Brawdy	12 Jun 1970
HMS Eagle	5 Oct 1970
Lossiemouth	9 Dec 1970
HMS Eagle	19 Jan 1971
Luqa	3 Mar 1971
HMS Eagle	22 Mar 1971
Lossiemouth	6 Apr 1971
HMS Eagle	26 May 1971
Tengah	7 Jul 1971
HMS Eagle	21 Jul 1971
Tengah	19 Sep 1971
HMS Eagle	5 Oct 1971
Kai Tak (Dt2)	19 Sep 1971 to 5 Oct 1971
Yeovilton	24 Jan 1972
Lossiemouth	26 Jan 1972
Squadron disbanded	26 Jan 1972

849E

Squadron bases

Culdrose	29 Jan 1954
Hal Far	7 Apr 1954
transit	16 Sep 1954
Culdrose	17 Sep 1954
Redesignated 'D' Flight	15 Oct 1954

Commanding Officers

L/C(A) KG Sharp RN 1 Aug 1943
L/C(A) DR Foster DSO DSC RNVR 5 Sep 1944
L/C AJ Griffith DSC RNVR 14 Jun 1945
Squadron disbanded 31 Oct 1945
L/C JD Treacher RN 7 Jul 1952
L/C MJ Baring RN 20 Jul 1953
L/C CB Armstrong RN 18 Dec 1954
L/C DH Frazer RN 1 May 1956
L/C F Bromilow RN 13 May 1957
L/C AGB Phillip RN 9 Apr 1959
L/C W Hawley RN 8 Dec 1960

Commanding Officers

L/C JF McGrail RN 7 Feb 1962
L/C WH Barnard RN 17 May 1963
L/C MJF Rawlinson RN 4 Jan 1965
L/C AW Roberts RN 1 Aug 1966
L/C B Prideaux RN 7 Feb 1968
L/C RM Scott RN 2 May 1969
L/C JE Nash RN 4 Sep 1970
L/C T Goetz RN 11 Sep 1972
L/C AJ Light RN 17 Apr 1974
L/C GJL Holman RN 21 Aug 1974
Cdr TG Maltby BA RN 20 Aug 1976
Squadron disbanded 15 Dec 1978
L/C PM Flutter AFC RN 1 Nov 1984
L/C PJ Howarth RN 9 Apr 1987
L/C NAM Butler RN 19 Jul 1989
L/C SB Phillips RN 30 Mar 1990
L/C MD Wells RN 5 Jun 1992
L/C JN Saunders MBE RN 21 Oct 1994

849A

Commanding Officers

Lt W Holdridge RN 20 Jan 1953
Lt MWP Betts RN 6 Jan 1954
L/C GP Sabin RN 5 Jul 1954
L/C CB Armstrong RN 31 Aug 1954
L/C GE Legg RN 4 Jan 1955
L/C AD Hooper RN 4 Jan 1956
L/C RHS Menzies RN 5 Sep 1956
L/C BJ Williams RN 10 Sep 1956
L/C CR Mellor RN 17 Apr 1958
Lt KWC Readings RN 17 Aug 1959
L/C W Handley RN 1 Feb 1960
L/C WH Barnard RN 1 Aug 1960
Lt AW Roberts RN 27 Aug 1960
L/C W Hawley RN 14 Sep 1960
L/C MP Smith RN 1 Oct 1960
L/C MJF Rawlinson RN 16 Aug 1962
L/C B Prideaux RN 16 Dec 1963
L/C JE Nash RN 18 Nov 1964
Flight disbanded 27 Jul 1965
L/C JE Nash RN 20 Jan 1966
L/C WM Forbes RN 28 Oct 1966
L/C RM Scott RN 4 Dec 1967
L/C AT Kennedy RN 1 May 1969
Flight disbanded 14 Jul 1970
L/C PJ Howarth RN 26 Mar 1985
L/C RJ Pharoah RN 18 Mar 1987
L/C L Mathews RN 5 May 1989
L/C NK Bennett RN 7 Jan 1991
L/C A McKie RN by Nov 1992
L/C NC Funnell RN 5 Mar 1993
L/C A McKie RN 13 Apr 1992
L/C RM Tuppen RN 16 Sep 1994

849B

Commanding Officers

Lt AW Sabey DSM RN 25 Nov 1952
L/C GP Sabin RN 7 Jan 1954
L/C RM Shave RN 5 Jul 1954
L/C RC Ashworth RN 7 May 1955
L/C RFG Hubbard RN 2 May 1956
L/C JW Wickham RN 1 Apr 1957

Commanding Officers

L/C BH Stock RN 23 Jul 1958
L/C CR Mellor RN 27 Aug 1959
L/C D Levy RN 29 Feb 1960
L/C AR Robinson RN 10 Apr 1962
Lt MH Mumford RN 22 Apr 1963
L/C ESE Taylor RN 21 Sep 1964
L/C RB Cobb RN 18 Apr 1966
L/C PJG Wilkins RN 3 Oct 1967
Flight disbanded 28 Feb 1968
L/C TG Maltby RN 5 Jan 1970
L/C GJL Holman RN 1 Mar 1971
L/C MI Neale RN 4 Oct 1972
L/C KA Harris RN 8 Jul 1974
L/C PM Jones RN 28 Nov 1975
L/C M Rotheram RN 1 Jul 1977
Flight disbanded 15 Dec 1978
L/C JL Irving RN 3 Mar 1986
L/C NAM Butler RN 6 Jun 1988
L/C JN Saunders MBE RN 8 Jul 1989
L/C GP Cass RN 11 Jan 1991
L/C M Roper RN 18 Dec 1992
L/C JG Rich RN 27 Aug 1994

849C

Commanding Officers

Lt HGL Nash RN 1 Jun 1953
L/C DW Winterton RN 19 Oct 1953
L/C HGL Nash RN 25 Jan 1954
L/C RM Shave RN 16 Jun 1954
Lt DT Andrews RN 5 Jul 1954
L/C DA Fuller RN 4 Dec 1955
L/C NGT Taylor RN 5 Apr 1957
L/C PA Woollings RN 18 Aug 1959
L/C TJ Penfold RN 25 Sep 1962
L/C AA Reid RN 17 Nov 1963
L/C JM Barbour RN 1 Nov 1965
Flight disbanded 5 Oct 1966

849D

Commanding Officers

L/C DT Andrews RN 7 Sep 1953
Squadron disbanded 5 Jul 1954
L/C N Ovenden RN 15 Oct 1954
L/C A Baillie RN 5 Jan 1955
L/C WL Shepherd RN 6 Jun 1956
L/C PGW Morris RN 7 Oct 1957
L/C TG Butler RN 6 Dec 1958
Flight disbanded 15 Dec 1960
L/C DW Besley RN 3 Sep 1964
L/C JL Coward RN 15 Dec 1965
L/C J Burton RN 14 Dec 1966
L/C T Goetz RN 23 Feb 1968
L/C AJ Light RN 1 Aug 1969
Flight disbanded 26 Jan 1972

849E

L/C N Ovenden RN 29 Jan 1954
Flight disbanded 15 Oct 1954

No.850 Squadron

Badge: On an azure field, a dexter arm issuant from the sea, proper grasping an inflamed sword with for a guard wings, or and to the sinister the Southern Cross, argent

Motto: *Vincit omnia virtus* (Courage conquers all)

Aircraft Equipment	Period of Service	Example
Seamew	Jan 1943 - Jan 1943	Not received
Avenger I	Sep 1943 - Dec 1944	FN912 (4L)
Wildcat V	Aug 1944 - Sep 1944	JV396 (Q)
Wildcat VI	Aug 1944 - Dec 1944	JV674
Sea Fury FB.11	Jan 1953 - Aug 1954	WJ246 (168/K)

Battle Honours
Normandy 1944
Atlantic 1944

Identification Markings
Avenger single letters, to 4A+ 12.43; Wildcat single letters; Sea Fury *160-171/K*.

Squadron bases
Quonset Point	1 Jan 1943
Squadron disbanded	30 Jan 1943
Squantum	1 Sep 1943
USS Charger (DLT)	9 Nov 1943
Squantum	10 Nov 1943
in transit	1 Dec 1943
Sea Island	12 Dec 1943
HMS Empress(DLT)	20 Jan 1944
HMS Empress	17 Feb 1944
Lee-on-Solent	10 Apr 1944
Perranporth	23 Apr 1944
Limavady	1 Aug 1944
Maydown	13 Aug 1944
Limavady	26 Aug 1944
Mullaghmore	6 Nov 1944
Squadron disbanded	24 Dec 1944
Fighter Flight:	
Eglinton	30 Jul 1944
HMS Fencer	26 Sep 1944
HMS Campania	18 Oct 1944
Machrihanish	16 Nov 1944
Burscough	29 Nov 1944
Yeovilton	30 Nov 1944
Flight disbanded	3 Dec 1944
Nowra	12 Jan 1953
HMAS Vengeance	2 Jul 1953
Nowra	9 Aug 1953
HMAS Sydney	21 Sep 1953
Kai Tak (Dt6)	2-4 Nov 1953
Iwakuni (Dt6)	19-25 Nov 1953
Kai Tak (Dt4)	31 Dec 1953 to 31 Jan 1954
Nowra	10 Jun 1954
Squadron disbanded	3 Aug 1954

Commanding Officers
Lt JH Dundas DSC RN	1 Jan 1943
Squadron disbanded	30 Jan 1943
L/C AP Boddam-Whetham DSC RN	1 Sep 1943
L/C(A) B White DSC RNVR	28 May 1944
L/C(A) FS Martin RNVR	18 Dec 1944
Squadron disbanded	24 Dec 1944
L/C RA Wilde DFC RN	12 Jan 1953
L/C PM Austin RN	18 May 1953
Squadron disbanded	3 Aug 1954

No.850 Squadron formed at Quonset Point on 1 January 1943 for long range duties, and was intended to be equipped with 12 Seamews for service in HMS *Pursuer*. It existed only on paper, and was disbanded on 30 January 1943.

On 1 September 1943, No.850 reformed at Squantum as a Torpedo Bomber Reconnaissance squadron with 12 Avenger Is, and after work-up embarked in HMS *Empress* in February 1944, carrying out U-boat patrols en route to the UK. From April, operations were undertaken in the English Channel with RAF Coastal Command, one merchant ship being destroyed and another damaged off St.Peter Port, Guernsey on 24 July. Moving to Northern Ireland early in August, a flight of four Wildcats was added, but after further anti-submarine patrols with Coastal Command, the squadron disbanded on 24 December 1944.

The squadron existed briefly postwar as a Royal Australian Navy unit, being reformed at Nowra on 12 January 1953 with 12 Sea Furies. Following a spell in HMAS *Sydney* in Korean waters, No.850 disbanded on 3 August 1954.

Grumman Avenger I FN912 '4L' of No.850 Squadron over the Rockies. (F.S.Martin)

No.851 Squadron

Badge: On a sable field, a spiked mace, argent, winged or
Motto: Be forthright
[Also depicted is the proposed wartime badge, which was never approved - see also text]

No.851 Squadron formed at Squantum on 1 October 1943 for Torpedo Bomber Reconnaissance work with 12 Avenger Is, embarking in HMS *Shah* in January 1944 for service in the Indian Ocean. A Wildcat flight was added in April, and during August three U-boats were attacked. In February 1945 the ship had a refit at Durban, and then the squadron went ashore to Stamford Hill, where the Wildcats were withdrawn. During April and May strikes were made against coastal and shore targets in Burma, and on 15 May a Japanese cruiser and destroyer were attacked whilst the squadron was temporarily embarked in HMS *Emperor*. After VJ-Day, No.851 sailed to the UK in HMS *Shah*, disbanding on arrival at Gourock on 7 October 1945.

The wartime unit submitted the motto *'Oderint Modo Metuant'*, but there is no record that it was ever approved. This was the Emperor Caligula's favourite saying, and translates as "Let them hate so long as they fear us".

The squadron number was allocated for postwar use by the Royal Australian Navy, and No.851 Squadron reformed at Nowra on 3 August 1954 for anti-submarine training on Firefly AS.6s, disbanding on 13 January 1958.

No.851 reformed on 2 September 1968, again as a RAN unit, for a miscellany of duties which included anti-submarine training, fleet requirements, VIP and communications work, using Trackers, C-47s and HS.748s. The American-style designation VC-851 was adopted in 1969. From 1974 detachments were sent periodically to Broome for coastal surveillance and fishery surveillance. Following a hangar fire, the squadron re-equipped with S-2G Trackers, and from February 1981 oil rig protection patrols were undertaken in the Bass Strait. On 2 July 1982 the squadron absorbed VC-816, and continued in service with six S-2G Trackers and two HS-748s. The squadron disbanded on 31 August 1984.

Lt-Cdr A.M.Tuke, the CO of No.851 Squadron, makes the first catapult trial launch from HMS Shah in Trincomalee harbour in Grumman Avenger I JZ116 '1A' in early 1944. (Lt-Cdr A.M.Tuke)

Battle Honours
Malaya   1945
Burma   1945

Identification Markings
Avenger *1A+.* to *SA+* 28.7.45 ; Wildcat single letters; Firefly *260-272*; C-47 *VJ-ORA & ORB/NW, later 800-801/NW*; HS738 *800-801*; Tracker *840-859*.

Aircraft Equipment	Period of Service	Example
Avenger I	Oct 1943 - Sep 1945	JZ185 (SF)
Wildcat V	Apr 1944 - Feb 1945	JV513 (Y)
Firefly T.5	Aug 1954 - Feb 1957	VX373 (263)
Firefly AS.6	Aug 1954 - Jan 1958	WD887 (260)
C-47B	Aug 1954 - Jan 1958	A65-43 (VJ-ORA/NW)
	Sep 1968 - Jun 1973	N2-43 (800/NW)
S-2E Tracker	Sep 1968 - May 1977	N12-153607 (852)
HS748	Jun 1973 - Jun 1984	N15-709(800)
S-2G Tracker	May 1977 - Jun 1984	N12-153566 (854)

Douglas C-47B N2-23 '801/NW' of No.851 Squadron RAN seen at Llanherne in December 1968. (via Chris Ashworth)

Squadron bases

Squantum	1 Oct 1943
Norfolk/USS Charger (DLT)	14-16 Dec 1943
in transit	2 Jan 1944
HMS Shah	14 Jan 1944
Cochin	23 Feb 1944
HMS Shah	6 Mar 1944
Colombo Racecourse	21 Mar 1944
Katukurunda	1 Apr 1944
HMS Unicorn (DLT)	1 May 1944
Katukurunda	1 May 1944
HMS Shah	13 May 1944
Colombo Racecourse	30 Jun 1944
HMS Shah	26 Jul 1944
Port Reitz (Dt10)	21 Sep 1944
to	5 Oct 1944
Ratmalana	19 Oct 1944
Vavuyina	18 Nov 1944
Minneriya	20 Nov 1944
Colombo Racecourse	19 Dec 1944

Squadron bases

HMS Shah	10 Jan 1945
Trincomalee	23 Jan 1945
HMS Shah	8 Feb 1945
Stamford Hill	23 Feb 1945
HMS Shah	5 Apr 1945
Port Reitz (Dt4)	13-15 Apr 1945
HMS Emperor	11 May 1945
Katukurunda	19 May 1945
Colombo Racecourse	7 Jun 1945
HMS Shah	27 Jun 1945
Trincomalee	6 Jul 1945
HMS Shah (Dt5)	7 Aug 1945
to	1 Sep 1945
HMS Shah (crews)	3 Sep 1945
Sqdn disbanded UK	7 Oct 1945
Nowra	3 Aug 1954
HMAS Sydney	13 Mar 1956
Nowra	30 Mar 1956
Squadron disbanded	13 Jan 1958
Nowra	2 Sep 1968

Commanding Officers
L/C(A) AM Tuke DSC RN 1 Oct 1943
L/C(A) MT Fuller DSC RNVR 15 Sep 1944
Squadron disbanded 7 Oct 1945
L/C DC Johns DFC RAN 3 Aug 1954
L/C ME Scott RAN 3 Aug 1956
L/C JM Wade-Brown RAN 12 Aug 1957
Squadron disbanded 13 Jan 1958
L/C RRM Lea RAN 2 Sep 1968
L/C HCD Findlay RAN 20 Apr 1970

Squadron bases
Broome (Dt) 1974
Broome (Dts) 3 Mar 1975
    to May 1975
Broome (Dt) 1976
Darwin (Dt) Nov 1977

Commanding Officers
L/C JL Clarke RAN 9 Dec 1971
L/C RV Morritt RAN 15 Jan 1973
L/C JD Campbell RAN 19 Apr 1973
L/C TA Burdorf RAN 15 Jan 1975
L/C CW Talbot AFC RAN 19 Jul 1976
L/C PO Hamon RAN 4 Oct 1976
L/C REN Geale MBE RAN 20 Feb 1978
L/C CW Talbot RAN 20 Jan 1980
L/C TA Peck RAN 13 Jul 1981
L/C JW Dalgleish RAN 14 Jan 1983
L/C DRA Scott RAN 8 Apr 1984
L/C RP Scovell RAN 4 Jun 1984
Squadron disbanded 31 Aug 1984

Grumman S-2E Tracker N12-153601 '846' of No.851 Squadron RAN at Nowra on 4 November 1968. (Joe Barr)

No.852 Squadron

No.852 Squadron formed at Squantum on 1 November 1943 for Torpedo Bomber Reconnaissance work with 12 Avenger Is, embarking in HMS *Nabob* in February 1944. A fighter flight of four Wildcat Vs was added in May 1944, and in June the squadron re-embarked for anti-shipping strikes and minelaying off the Norwegian coast. However, on 22 August the ship was torpedoed by *U-354*, though it managed to limp home to Scapa Flow. No.852 then transferred to HMS *Trumpeter*, the fighter flight re-equipping with Wildcat VIs, but on 17 October 1944 the squadron was disbanded, the Wildcats going to No.846 Squadron.

A proposal to reform the squadron in July 1945 for service in the East Indies Fleet never materialised.

Battle Honours
Norway   1944

Identification Markings
Avenger 2*A*+; Wildcat single letters, later 2*A*+.

Grumman Avengers of No.852 Squadron as viewed from a hangar roof at Squantum in December 1943. (via C.Bristow)

Aircraft Equipment	Period of Service	Example
Avenger I	Nov 1943 - Oct 1944	FN891 (2B)
Wildcat V	May 1944 - Sep 1944	JV536 (S)
Wildcat VI	Sep 1944 - Oct 1944	JV739 (2G)

Squadron bases		Squadron bases		Squadron bases	
Squantum	1 Nov 1943	Hatston	27 Aug 1944	Squadron disbanded 17 Oct 1944	
in transit	2 Feb 1944	HMS Trumpeter	10 Sep 1944	Fighter Flight:	
HMS Nabob	11 Feb 1944	Hatston	13 Sep 1944	Eglinton	3 Feb 1944
Machrihanish	6 Apr 1944	HMS Trumpeter	23 Sep 1944	HMS Nabob	26 Jun 1944
Maydown	7 May 1944	(Dt4) to	8 Oct 1944	Hatston	1 Sep 1944
Machrihanish	20 May 1944	HMS Fencer (Dt4)	27 Sep 1944	HMS Fencer	27 Sep 1944
HMS Nabob	26 Jun 1944	to	7 Oct 1944	Hatston	7 Oct 1944
Abbotsinch	8 Jul 1944	HMS Trumpeter	12-17 Oct 1944	HMS Fencer	10 Oct 1944
Machrihanish	12 Jul 1944	(Dt3)		Hatston	17 Oct 1944
HMS Nabob	14 Jul 1944	HMS Fencer(Dt4)	10-17 Oct 1944	Flight disbanded	17 Oct 1944

Commanding Officer
L/C(A) RE Bradshaw
    DSC RN   1 Nov 1943
Squadron disbanded 17 Oct 1944

Grumman Avenger I JZ165 '2P' of No.852 Squadron. (via C.Bristow)

No.853 Squadron

Badge: On a blue field, a Greek warrior with spear, riding on a Pegasus all gold
Motto: Defend, avenge

Grumman Avenger I JZ410 '3Q' of No.853 Squadron, Squantum in December 1943. (FAA Museum)

No.853 Squadron formed at Squantum on 1 December 1943 as a Torpedo Bomber Reconnaissance squadron with 12 Avenger IIs. It sailed for the UK in HMS *Arbiter* in May 1944, a fighter flight with 4 Wildcat Vs being formed in the meantime at Eglinton. The latter disbanded after a short period in HMS *Formidable*, but a new fighter flight formed with four Wildcat VIs in September. The whole squadron joined HMS *Tracker* in that month, and in October anti-submarine patrols were undertaken whilst the ship was escorting a North Russian convoy, two U-boats being sighted. In January 1945 the squadron transferred to HMS *Queen*, carrying out several anti-shipping and anti-submarine strikes off the Norwegian coast, in addition to minelaying. On completion of further escort duties with North Russian convoys, the squadron disbanded on 30 May 1945.

Battle Honours
Arctic 1944-45
Norway 1945

Aircraft Equipment	Period of Service	Example
Avenger II	Dec 1943 - May 1945	JZ456 (QK)
Wildcat V	May 1944 - Sep 1944	
Wildcat VI	Sep 1944 - May 1945	JV706 (QT)

Identification Markings
Avenger 3A+, to T:A+ on *Tracker* 30.9.44, to Q:A on *Queen* 16.1.45; Wildcat T:A+, to Q:A+ 16.1.45.

Squadron bases	
Squantum	1 Dec 1943
HMS Arbiter	31 May 1944
Machrihanish	19 Jun 1944
Fighter Flight:	
HMS Formidable	14-24 Jun 1944
Maydown	11 Jul 1944
Machrihanish	29 Jul 1944
Fighter Flight:	
Eglinton	28 Aug 1944
HMS Tracker	12 Sep 1944
Machrihanish	5 Oct 1944
HMS Tracker	14 Oct 1944
Machrihanish	29 Nov 1944
Hatston	1 Dec 1944
Fighter Flight	
HMS Premier (Dt4)	11 Dec 1944 to 18 Dec 1944

Squadron bases	
Ayr	25 Jan 1945
HMS Queen	27 Jan 1945
Hatston	29 Mar 1945
HMS Queen	3 Apr 1945
Hatston	13 Apr 1945
HMS Queen	27 Apr 1945
Squadron disbanded	30 May 1945

Commanding Officers
L/C(A) NG Haigh RNVR 1 Nov 1943
L/C(A) JM Glaser RN 20 Dec 1944
Squadron disbanded 30 May 1945

Lt B.H.Beeston in Grumman Wildcat VI JV735 of No.853 Squdron on HMS Queen on 20 March 1945. (FAA Museum)

No.854 Squadron

Badge: On a blue field, a base barry wavy of four white and blue, in front of a sword in pale point downwards proper hilted white a lion passant regardant winged gold

Motto: *Audentes fortuna juvat* (Fortune helps the daring)

Battle Honours
Normandy 1944
Palembang 1945
Okinawa 1945

Identification Markings
Avenger 4A+, later J4A+, to Q4A+ 12.44.

Aircraft Equipment	**Period of Service**	**Example**
Avenger II	Jan 1944 - Sep 1944	JZ512 (4M)
Avenger I	Oct 1944 - May 1945	FN861 (Q4Y)
Avenger III	Jul 1945 - Oct 1945	JZ688

Squadron bases
Squantum 1 Jan 1944
HMS Indomitable 10 Apr 1944
Machrihanish 1 May 1944
Hawkinge 23 May 1944
Thorney Island 7 Aug 1944
Lee-on-Solent 27 Aug 1944
HMS Activity 7 Sep 1944
Cochin 7 Oct 1944
Katukurunda 11 Oct 1944
Trincomalee 30 Nov 1944
HMS Illustrious 1 Dec 1944
Katukurunda 22 Dec 1944
HMS Illustrious 28 Dec 1944
Nowra 11 Feb 1945
HMS Illustrious 6 Mar 1945
Nowra 18 May 1945
SS Stratheden 20 Oct 1945
   (no a/c)
Sqdn disbanded UK 8 Dec 1945

Commanding Officers
L/C WJ Mainprice
   DSC RN 1 Jan 1944
L/C(A) FC Nottingham
   DSC RNVR 30 Jan 1945
L/C RE Jess
   DSC RCNVR 28 Mar 1945
None 28 Jun 1945
Squadron disbanded 8 Dec 1945

No.854 Squadron personnel assembled at Townhill Camp on 15 November 1943, and after passage to the United States officially formed at Squantum on 1 January 1944. Equipped with 12 Avenger IIs, they embarked in HMS *Indomitable* in April for the United Kingdom. From May, anti-shipping patrols were carried out in the English Channel from Hawkinge, the squadron being temporarily part of No.157 Wing, RAF Coastal Command. The aircraft were left behind when the personnel embarked in HMS *Activity* in September for the Far East, re-equipping on arrival with Avenger Is on which they worked-up at Katukurunda. No.854 joined HMS *Illustrious* in December, taking part in Sumatran operations at Belawan Deli and Palembang in December 1944 and January 1945. In March and April attacks were made on airfields and other shore targets in the Sakishima Gunto group of islands in the East China Seas, but in May No.854 disembarked to become a spare squadron, without aircraft. Avenger IIIs were received in July, and No.854 joined the the 3rd Carrier Air Group shortly afterwards, but the aircraft were again withdrawn in September, and the crews sailed home in the SS *Stratheden*, to disband on arrival on 8 December 1945.

Grumman Avenger II JZ456 of No.854 Squadron, Hawkinge in D-Day invasion stripes. FAA Museum)

No.855 Squadron

Badge: (Heraldic description lacking)
Motto: *Delere ut protegemu* (Annihilate in order to protect)

Grumman Avengers of No.855 Squadron at Hawkinge in June 1944. (via J.Lees-Jones)

No.855 Squadron formed at Squantum on 1 February 1944 for Torpedo Bomber Reconnaissance work with 12 Avenger IIs. Embarking in May in HMS *Queen* for passage to the United Kingdom, the squadron spent the next three months on anti-shipping patrols in the English Channel with RAF Coastal Command, as part of No.157 Wing. Once the Normandy invasion had been consolidated, No.855's services were no longer required, and on 19 October 1944 it disbanded.

Battle Honours
Normandy 1944

Identification Markings
Avenger *5BA+*, to *5A+* 5.44.

Aircraft Equipment	Period of Service	Example
Avenger II	Feb 1944 - Oct 1944	JZ500 (5BR)

Squadron bases		Squadron bases	
Squantum	1 Feb 1944	Machrihanish	13 Oct 1944
Norfolk	1 May 1944	Squadron disbanded	19 Oct 1944
HMS Queen	6 May 1944		
Hawkinge	31 May 1944	**Commanding Officers**	
Thorney Island	3 Aug 1944	L/C JB Harrowar	
Docking	7 Aug 1944	RNR	1 Feb 1944
Lee-on-Solent	17 Aug 1944	Squadron disbanded	19 Oct 1944
Bircham Newton	7 Sep 1944		
Docking	14 Sep 1944		

Grumman Avenger IIs JZ496 '5M' and '5L' of No.855 Squadron while working up at Squantum in 1944.

No.856 Squadron

No.856 Squadron formed at Squantum on 1 March 1944 as a Torpedo Bomber Reconnaissance squadron equipped with 12 Avenger IIs. These embarked in HMS *Smiter* in June, and after passage to the United Kingdom the squadron undertook anti-submarine training before joining HMS *Premier* in September for operations. A fighter flight of four Wildcat VIs formed on 10 September, a further four being later transferred from No.838 Squadron, and during the next six months the squadron engaged mainly in minelaying operations off the Norwegian coast. In April and May 1945 the ship escorted a North Russian convoy, and No.856 flew anti-submarine patrols, but by the time it returned home the war in Europe was over. Plans for it to be transferred to the British Pacific Fleet as part of the 10th Carrier Air Group were cancelled, and No.856 disbanded on 15 June 1945.

Identification Markings
Avenger *6A+*, to *P:A+* on *Premier* late 1944; Wildcat - *P:S-P:Z* on *Premier*.

Wildcat VI JV750 'PS' of No.856 Squadron on 9 December 1944 after missing all wires on a fast approach to HMS Premier, the pilot, Sub-Lt B.J.C.Dibben, being luckily unhurt. (via Dick Yeo)

Aircraft Equipment	Period of Service	Example
Avenger II	Mar 1944 - Jun 1945	JZ508 (PB)
Wildcat V	Sep 1944 - Dec 1944	JV402 (PS)
Wildcat VI	Sep 1944 - May 1945	JV742 (PV)

Squadron bases		Squadron bases		Squadron bases		Commanding Officers	
Squantum	1 Mar 1944	HMS Trumpeter	13 Aug 1944	Hatston	13 Jan 1945	L/C(A) SMP Walsh	
USS Charger (DLT)	17 Apr 1944	(Dt3)	to 29 Aug 1944	HMS Premier	17 Jan 1945	DSC RNVR	1 Mar 1944
Squantum	22 Apr 1944	HMS Premier	13 Sep 1944	(Fighter Flight) to	13 Feb 1945	Lt PS Foulds RNVR	31 Dec 1944
HMS Smiter	1 Jun 1944	Hatston	27 Nov 1944	HMS Premier	22 Jan 1945	(temp)	
Speke	21 Jun 1944	HMS Trumpeter(Dt)	5-8 Dec 1944	Hatston	30 Jan 1945	L/C HCK Housser	
Machrihanish	22 Jun 1944	(Fighter Flight)		HMS Premier (Dt)	5-13 Feb 1945	RCNVR	15 Jan 1945
Maydown	30 Jul 1944	HMS Premier	8 Dec 1944	HMS Premier	17 Feb 1945	Squadron disbanded	15 Jun 1945
Eglinton	12 Aug 1944	HMS Premier	20 Dec 1944	Hatston	23 Feb 1945		
Hatston (Dt6)	12-30 Aug 1944	(Fighter Flight) to	14 Jan 1945	HMS Premier	6 Mar 1945	**Battle Honours**	
HMS Nabob(Dt3)		Hatston	23 Dec 1944	Hatston	19 May 1945	Norway	1944-45
	18-31 Aug 1944	HMS Premier	11 Jan 1945	Squadron disbanded	15 Jun 1945	Arctic	1945

Grumman Avengers of No.856 Squadron on 2 April 1944 while working up at Squantum. (FAA Museum)

No.857 Squadron

Badge: On a blue field, a hand proper issuing from water barry wavy in base white and blue, grasping a sword erect, white pommel and hilt gold

Motto: Animis opibusque parati (Prepared in minds and resources)

Battle Honours
Palembang 1945
Okinawa 1945

Identification Markings
Avenger 7A+, to W7A+ 11.44, W1A+ 1.45, 370-386/W 8.45.

Aircraft Equipment	Period of Service	Example
Avenger II	Apr 1944 - Oct 1945	JZ614 (372/W)
Avenger I	Sep 1944 - Jun 1945	FN915 (382/W)

Squadron bases
Squantum	1 Apr 1944
HMS Rajah	29 Jun 1944
Belfast	13 Jul 1944
Machrihanish	14 Aug 1944
Belfast	8 Sep 1944
HMS Rajah	9 Sep 1944
Coimbatore	11 Oct 1944
Katukurunda	19 Nov 1944
HMS Indomitable	27 Nov 1944
Nowra	10 Feb 1945
HMS Indomitable	28 Feb 1945
Nowra	5 Jun 1945
HMS Indomitable	2 Aug 1945
Kai Tak	30 Aug 1945
HMS Indomitable	28 Sep 1945
Nowra	11 Oct 1945
HMS Indomitable	22 Oct 1945
Squadron disbanded	30 Nov 1945

Commanding Officers
L/C(A) W Stuart DSC & 2 Bars RNVR — 1 Apr 1944
Squadron disbanded 30 Nov 1945

No.857 Squadron personnel assembled at Townhill Camp on 23 February 1944 for transit to the USA, where it officially formed at Squantum on 1 April 1944 as a Torpedo Bomber Reconnaissance squadron with 12 Avengers, being mainly Mk.IIs. These embarked in HMS *Rajah* in June, and the strength increased to 21 aircraft after disembarking to Belfast. Following an anti-submarine course at Machrihanish, No.857 rejoined HMS *Rajah* for passage to Ceylon. After further work-up it transferred to HMS *Indomitable* in November, attacking Sumatran targets at Belawan Deli, Pangkalan Brandan and Palembang during the next two months. No.857 then regrouped in Australia before re-embarking in February 1945 for two months continuous attacks on the Sakishima Gunto group of islands in the East China Seas, and later Formosa. The squadron then reduced to 15 aircraft, but VJ-Day intervened before further operations could be undertaken, the ship sailing instead for Hong Kong where the squadron was active against Japanese suicide boats on 31 August and 1 September. The aircraft were left in Australia when the squadron returned home to disband on arrival on 30 November 1945.

Lt Cdr A.Stuart, the CO of No.857 Squadron, HMS Indomitable at around 12,000ft in Grumman Avenger II JZ594 'W1A', about to lead the attack on Belawan Deli oil refinery, which had just been hit by rockets from the fighters. (Joe Clayton)

No.860 Squadron

Badge:
Silver winged gauntlet; three gold lightning flashes; and a demi-fountain
Motto:
Arcens affligo
(Warding off, I afflict)

Fairey Swordfish II of No.860 Squadron at Maydown. (Royal Netherlands Navy)

No.860 Squadron formed at Donibristle on 15 June 1943 as a Royal Netherlands Navy-manned Torpedo Bomber Reconnaissance squadron with six Swordfish Is. After weapon training at Machrihanish in November, the squadron moved to Maydown, by then equipped with 12 Swordfish IIs, being earmarked to operate from MAC-ships, under the umbrella of the MAC-ship Wing, which mainly comprised No.836 Squadron. It was divided into 'O' and 'S' Flights for operational purposes, and by February 1944 these were embarked in MV Acavus and MV *Gadila* respectively. 'S' Flight remained with MV Gadila for the remainder of the war, but 'O' Flight transferred to MV *Macoma* in June 1944, being renamed 'F' Flight in October 1944, possibly because its abbreviated title of 860O Flight proved too confusing.

After VE-Day the squadron lost its MAC-ship role, and re-equipped with 12 Barracuda IIIs which it took over from No.822 Squadron on 30 June 1945. Deck landing training was undertaken with these in HMS *Nairana* during October, and in January 1946 No.860 re-equipped with 12 Dutch-serialled Fireflies. These embarked from St.Merryn aboard HMS *Nairana* in September, this ship having in the meantime become HrMs *Karel Doorman,* and the squadron then ceased to be attached to the Royal Navy. The squadron continued after the war, retaining its Royal Navy-sequence number, and operating from time to time from Royal Navy ships and shore bases. During 1947 it was involved in operations against Indonesian separatist forces, eventually disbanding on 18 March 1950.

On 15 July 1950 it reformed, again as a Dutch squadron, at Valkenburg with Sea Fury Mk.50s, by redesignating the Gevechtsvliegopleiding, or fighter pilot combat school. It operated regularly from HrMs *Karel Doorman* until disbanding on 15 June 1956, its aircraft being transferred to No.3 Dutch Navy Squadron.

No.860 next reformed on 18 September 1957, at Valkenburg with Sea Hawk Mk.50s, following crew training at Anthorn. It again operated from HrMs *Karel Doorman* until disbanding on 30 October 1964.

On 4 October 1966 the squadron became a helicopter unit when it reformed at de Kooy with Wasps. The first Lynx arrived in September 1979, the last of the Wasps departing in December 1980. The squadron continues to be based at de Kooy, its 17 Lynxes being flown from Royal Netherlands Navy frigates.

Identification Markings
Swordfish single letters initially, then *flight letter/individual letter*, to *M1-M4/flight letter* 10.44; Barracuda single letter.

Hawker Sea Fury FB.50 6-2 of No.860 Squadron, Royal Dutch Navy aboard the carrier Karel Doorman. (MAP)

Hawker Sea Hawk 50 6-50 of No.860 Squadron, Royal Netherlands Navy. (MAP)

Aircraft Equipment

Type	Period of Service	Example	
Swordfish I	Jun 1943 - Nov 1943	V4431	
Swordfish II	Nov 1943 - Jun 1945	LS437	(S2)
Swordfish III	Mar 1945 - Jun 1945	NS187	
Barracuda III	Jun 1945 - Jan 1946	RJ773	
Firefly I	Jan 1946 - Mar 1950	6-27	
Sea Fury FB.50	Jul 1950 - Jun 1956	6-33	
Sea Hawk 50	Sep 1957 - Oct 1964	6-71	
Wasp HAS.1	Oct 1966 - Dec 1980	240	(-/EV)
SH-14B Lynx HAS.27	Oct 1978 - to date	270	(-/KN)
SH-14C Lynx Mk.81	Oct 1980 - to date	277	

Battle Honours
Atlantic   1944-45

Squadron bases
Donibristle	15 Jun 1943
Hatston	19 Jul 1943
Dunino	15 Aug 1943
Machrihanish	3 Nov 1943
Maydown	4 Dec 1943
Machrihanish (Dt4)	14-21 May 1944
Ayr	3 Sep 1945
HMS Nairana	30 Oct 1945

Squadron bases
Ayr	15 Nov 1945
Fearn	19 Apr 1946
St Merryn	7 May 1946
HrMs Karel Doorman	27 Jul 1946
(Transferred to RNN)	
Morokrembangan	Oct 1946
Squadron disbanded	18 Mar 1950
Valkenburg	15 Jul 1950

Squadron bases
St.Merryn	17 Jan 1951
HMS Illustrious	19 Jun 1951
HMS Indomitable	5 Jul 1951
St.Merryn	18 Jul 1951
HMS Indomitable	7 Sep 1951
Valkenburg	4 Dec 1951
HrMs Karel Doorman	17 Jan 1952
Valkenburg	20 Aug 1952
HMS Illustrious	30 Aug 1952
Valkenburg	24 Sep 1952
(regularly operated from HrMs Karel Doorman)	
Squadron disbanded	15 Jun 1956
Valkenburg	18 Sep 1957
(regularly operated from HrMs Karel Doorman)	
HrMs Karel Doorman	4 Nov 1958
Valkenburg	1 Dec 1958
HrMs Karel Doorman	13 Jan 1959
Valkenburg	29 Jun 1959
HrMs Karel Doorman	Sep 1959
Valkenburg	1959
HrMs Karel Doorman	31 May 1960
Valkenburg	14 Jul 1961
Lossiemouth	6 May 1963
Valkenburg	15 May 1963
Squadron disbanded	30 Oct 1964
de Kooy	4 Oct 1966
Portland	14-21 Jun 1974
(HrMs Van Speijk Flt)	
Portland	13-24 Sep 1974
(HrMs Van Nes Flt)	
Portland	4-14 Oct 1974
(HrMs Van Nes Flt)	
Portland (HrMs Van Galen Flt)	30 Oct 1974 to 1 Nov 1974
Portland	7-17 Feb 1975
(HrMs Evertsen Flt)	
[see Ships and Flights section]	

860F Flight

Flight bases
Maydown(ex 'O' Flt)	Oct 1944
MV Macoma	26 Oct 1944
Dartmouth	15 Nov 1944
MV Macoma	17 Nov 1944
Maydown	3 Dec 1944
MV Macoma	10 Dec 1944
Dartmouth	1 Jan 1945
MV Macoma	10 Jan 1945
Maydown	22 Jan 1945
MV Macoma	29 Jan 1945
Dartmouth	17 Feb 1945
MV Macoma	25 Feb 1945
Maydown	12 Mar 1945
MV Macoma	3 Apr 1945
Dartmouth	30 Apr 1945
MV Macoma	7 May 1945
Maydown	21 May 1945
- Flight disbanded	

860O Flight

Maydown (formed)	Jan 1944
MV Acavus	Jan 1944
Dartmouth	25 Jan 1944
MV Acavus	28 Jan 1944
Maydown	13 Feb 1944
MV Acavus	27 Feb 1944
Maydown	Apr 1944
MV Macoma	2 Jun 1944
Dartmouth	9 Jul 1944
MV Macoma	19 Jul 1944
Maydown	1 Aug 1944
MV Macoma	7 Aug 1944
Dartmouth	25 Aug 1944
MV Macoma	27 Aug 1944
Maydown	8 Sep 1944
MV Macoma	16 Sep 1944
Dartmouth	2 Oct 1944
MV Macoma	7 Oct 1944
Maydown	19 Oct 1944
- Redes 'F' Flight	

860S Flight

Maydown (formed)	Feb 1944
MV Gadila	27 Feb 1944
Dartmouth	4 Apr 1944
MV Gadila	11 Apr 1944
Maydown	1 May 1944
MV Gadila	8 May 1944
Dartmouth	25 May 1944
MV Gadila	29 May 1944
Maydown	8 Jun 1944
MV Gadila	15 Jun 1944
Dartmouth	30 Jun 1944
MV Gadila	13 Jul 1944
Maydown	23 Jul 1944
MV Gadila	7 Aug 1944
Dartmouth	31 Aug 1944
MV Gadila	2 Sep 1944
Maydown	16 Sep 1944
MV Gadila	10 Oct 1944
Dartmouth	12 Nov 1944
MV Gadila	17 Nov 1944
Maydown	3 Dec 1944
MV Gadila	15 Dec 1944
Dartmouth	2 Jan 1945
MV Gadila	20 Jan 1945
Maydown	2 Feb 1945
MV Gadila	10 Feb 1945
Dartmouth	8 Feb 1945
MV Gadila	7 Mar 1945
Maydown	20 Mar 1945
MV Gadila	3 Apr 1945
Dartmouth	22 Apr 1945
MV Gadila	1 May 1945
Maydown	15 May 1945
- Flight disbanded	

Westland Wasp AH-12A 243 '-/K' of No.860 Squadron, Royal Netherlands Navy. (via Eric Myall)

Westland/Aerospatiale Lynx SH-14B 274 of No.860 Squadron, Royal Netherlands Navy in 1986. (MAP)

Commanding Officers			
LTZ J van der Tooren RNIN 15 Jun 1943	LTZV2 L Oldhof RNIN 27 Nov 1954	LTZ1 JDW van Renesse RNIN 13 Jun 1969	KLTZ HW Krijns RNIN 1 Oct 1985
LTZV1 B Sjerp RNIN 14 Feb 1946	Squadron disbanded 15 Jun 1956	LTZ1 JE Kaasschieter RNIN 17 Apr 1970	LTZ1 FMP 't Hart RNIN 21 Dec 1986
Transferred to Royal Netherlands Navy Sep 1946	LTZV1 BJ Idzerda RNIN 18 Sep 1957	LTZ1 GA 'd Ancona RNIN 3 Dec 1971	KLTZ FMP 't Hart RNIN 1987
LTZV G Volkers RNIN 20 Jun 1948	LTZV2 oc AHM Hagdorn RNIN 1 Jul 1958	LTZ1 oc A Veentjer RNIN 19 Oct 1973	KLTZ WFC Muilwijk RNIN 11 Nov 1988
LTZV2 A Bruinsma RNIN 11 Mar 1949	LTZV1 WF van der Heuvel RNIN 29 Jun 1959	LTZ1 NHA Ostendorp RNIN 21 May 1976	KLTZ A Stoel RNIN 14 Jun 1991
Squadron disbanded 15 Mar 1950	LTZV2 oc L Haanraadts RNIN 14 Jul 1961	LTZ1 HW den Ouden RNIN 22 Sep 1978	KLTZ LGJM van Esdonk RNIN 25 Mar 1994
LTZV2 A Bruinsma RNIN 15 Jul 1950	LTZV2 oc CK Krijger RNIN 20 Sep 1962	LTZSD1 K Baaker IR RNIN 19 Dec 1980	
LTZV2 KA La Bree RNIN 7 Jan 1952	LTZV2 oc JAC den Hartogh RNIN 11 Sep 1963	KLTZ A Veentjer RNIN 17 Dec 1982	
LTZV1 A Bruinsma RNIN 20 Aug 1952	Squadron disbanded 30 Jan 1964	LTZ1 HW Krijns RNIN 20 Jul 1984	
LTZV1 BJ Idzerda RNIN 18 Feb 1953	LTZ1 CE van der Minne RNIN 4 Oct 1966		

No.861 Squadron

No.861 Squadron formed at Dale on 16 September 1946 as a Royal Netherlands Navy squadron attached to the Royal Navy for work-up. Equipped initially with 4 Dutch Fireflies, it embarked in February 1947 in HrMs *Karel Doorman*, but disbanded shortly after disembarking.

Identification Markings
Firefly *F1+*.

Aircraft Equipment	Period of Service	Example
Firefly I	Sep 1946 - 1947	F10

Squadron bases		Commanding Officers	
Dale	16 Sep 1946	Lt GH Greve RNIN	16 Sep 1946
HrMs Karel Doorman	22 Feb 1947	Lt GJ Zegers de Beijl DSC RNIN	12 Dec 1946
Netherlands	Feb 1947	Squadron to	
Squadron disbanded	1947	R Netherlands Navy	Feb 1947

Royal Navy Fireflies with Dutch orange triangles, believed of No.861 Squadron. (via Hendrik Cazemier)

No.870 Squadron

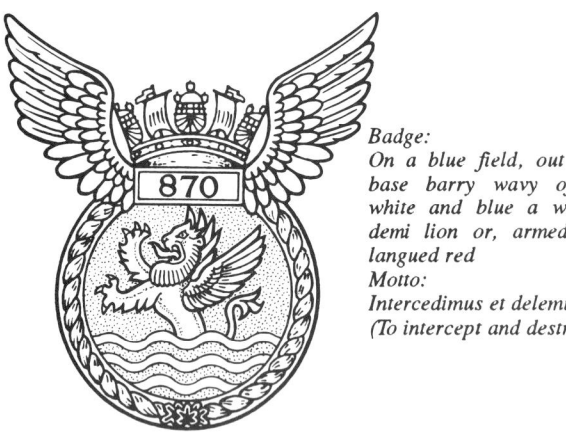

Badge:
On a blue field, out of a base barry wavy of six white and blue a winged demi lion or, armed and langued red
Motto:
Intercedimus et delemus
(To intercept and destroy)

Aircraft Equipment	Period of Service	Example
Sea Fury FB.11	May 1951 - Jun 1954	VX686 (127)
F2H-3 Banshee	Nov 1955 - Sep 1962	126347 (105)

Identification Markings
Sea Fury believed *100+*; Banshee *100+*,

Squadron bases		Squadron bases	
Dartmouth	1 May 1951	Dartmouth	7 Oct 1960
HMCS Magnificent	Dec 1952	HMCS Bonaventure	14 Nov 1960
Dartmouth	Dec 1952	Dartmouth	16 Dec 1960
Scoudouc	18 Jun 1953	HMCS Bonaventure	19 Apr 1961
Summerside	24 Sep 1953	Dartmouth	28 Apr 1961
HMCS Magnificent	Jan 1954	Cecil Field	8 Feb 1962
Summerside	9 Mar 1954	Dartmouth	16 Mar 1962
Squadron disbanded	30 Mar 1954	HMCS Bonaventure	9 Apr 1962
Summerside	1 Nov 1955	Dartmouth	29 Jun 1962
Dartmouth	May 1956	Squadron disbanded	7 Sep 1962
Key West	Feb 1957		
Dartmouth	2 Mar 1957		
HMCS Bonaventure	3 Sep 1957	**Commanding Officers**	
Belfast (Dts)	30 Oct 1957	L/C DD Peacocke	
	to 16 Nov 1957	RCN	1 May 1951
Dartmouth	27 Nov 1957	L/C DM McLeod	
Rivers (CJATC)	15 Oct 1958	RCN	9 Feb 1953
Dartmouth	31 Oct 1958	Squadron disbanded	30 Mar 1954
Key West	15 Jan 1959	L/C RH Falls CD	
HMCS Bonaventure	7 Sep 1959	RCN	1 Nov 1955
Dartmouth	13 Dec 1959	L/C WJ Walton RCN	14 Jan 1958
Key West	19 Feb 1960	Lt KS Nicolson	
Dartmouth	6 Apr 1960	CD RCN	30 Jun 1960
Rivers	by 6 Sep 1960	Squadron disbanded	7 Sep 1962

In 1951, squadron numbers in the 870 series were reserved within a unified Commonwealth numbering sequence for use by the Royal Canadian Navy. No.870 was taken up on 1 May 1951 when No.803 Squadron at Dartmouth, a fighter squadron equipped with nine Sea Fury FB.11s, was renumbered, becoming VF-870 when US Navy-style numbering was adopted in November 1952. The unit was part of the 31st Support Air Group, and spent periods in HMCS *Magificent* before disbanding at Summerside on 30 March 1954.

On 1 November 1955 it reformed, again as VF-870, with eight McDonnell F2H-3 Banshees at Summerside. These joined HMCS *Bonaventure* when she came into service in 1957, a visit being paid in October to Northern Ireland. In 1958, Sidewinder air-to-air missiles were added to their armament, but the squadron disbanded at Dartmouth on 7 September 1962.

No.871 Squadron

Badge: On a blue field, a base barry wavy of four white and blue, over all a winged centaur white reguardent and arresting, holding in the position to shoot to the sinister a bow and arrow red, the latter flighted and barbed white and bow stringed of the same, a quiver red filled with arrows and issuing from the dexter side of the centaur, being suspended by a strap yellow from the sinister shoulder, the centaur winged, maned and unguled yellow
Motto: *Pugnandum surgimus*
(We rise to fight)

Identification Markings
Sea Fury *c.110+* also *VG-AAA+*; Banshee *c.140+*,

Aircraft Equipment	Period of Service	Example
Sea Fury FB.11	May 1951 - Aug 1956	TG118 (AAB)
F2H-3 Banshee	Aug 1956 - Mar 1959	126392 (146)

Squadron bases			
Dartmouth	1 May 1951		
HMCS Magnificent	Oct 1951		
Dartmouth	Dec 1952		
HMCS Magnificent	17 Aug 1953		
Dartmouth	1953		
HMCS Magnificent	4 Apr 1955	**Commanding Officers**	
Dartmouth	7 Jun 1955	L/C WD Munro	
HMCS Magnificent	Sep 1955	RCN	1 May 1951
Dartmouth	7 Dec 1955	L/C DHP Ryan RCN	Nov 1951
HMCS Bonaventure	15 Feb 1958	L/C R Heath RCN	Jul 1952
Key West	29 Apr 1958	L/C M Wasteneys	
Dartmouth	15 Jun 1958	RCN	23 Mar 1953
Rivers (CJATC)	13 Oct 1958	L/C JW Logan RCN	2 Jul 1954
Dartmouth	10 Nov 1958	L/C RA Laidler	
HMCS Bonaventure	15 Jan 1959	RCN	13 Jan 1956
Dartmouth	27 Feb 1959	L/C JJ Harvie	
Squadron disbanded	16 Mar 1959	CD RCN	22 Jul 1957
into VF870		Squadron disbanded	16 Mar 1959

No.871 Squadron formed within the Commonwealth Navies numbering sequence as a Royal Canadian Navy squadron, by renumbering No.883 Squadron at Dartmouth on 1 May 1951. Equipped with ten Sea Fury FB.11s, it formed part of the 30th Carrier Air Group, spending periods afloat in HMCS *Magnificent*. The unit became VF-871 when American-style numbering was adopted in November 1952, re-equipping in August 1956 with eight McDonnell F2H-3 Banshees. In 1958 the aircraft were fitted with Sidewinder air-to-air missiles, and in the same year the squadron embarked in HMCS *Bonaventure*. VF-871 disbanded into VF-870 at Dartmouth on 16 March 1959.

Hawker Sea Fury FB.11 VW231 '120' of No.871 Squadron, Royal Canadian Navy. (via Brian Lowe)

No.877 Squadron

No.877 Squadron formed at Tanga, East Africa, on 1 April 1943 as a Fleet Fighter unit for local defence duties. Its equipment comprised nine borrowed RAF Hurricane IIBs, these being fitted with long-range tanks. Moving to Port Reitz in July, it was planned to fly the aircraft across the Indian Ocean for the defence of Ceylon, but this never materialised, and the squadron instead disbanded at Port Reitz on 30 December 1943.

Identification Markings
Hurricane possibly single letters.

Aircraft Equipment	Period of Service	Example
Hurricane IIb	Apr 1943 - Dec 1943	BP694

Squadron bases
Tanga   1 Apr 1943
Port Reitz   6 Jul 1943
Squadron disbanded 30 Dec 1943

Commanding Officers
Capt PP Nelson
  -Gracie RM   1 Apr 1943
Squadron disbanded 30 Dec 1943

Hawker Sea Fury TG129 '114' of No.871 Squadron, Royal Canadian Navy in 1953. (MAP)

No.878 Squadron

Badge: On a black field, a wildcat's face, white
Motto: *Feles non pusilla* (A cat but no weakling)

Battle Honours
Salerno 1943

Identification Markings
Martlet unknown.

Aircraft Equipment	Period of Service	Example
Martlet IV	Mar 1943 - Oct 1943	FN288
Wildcat V	Oct 1943 - Jan 1944	JV390

Squadron bases
Lee-on-Solent	1 Mar 1943
Hatston	10 Apr 1943
Machrihanish	8 Jun 1943
HMS Illustrious	8 Jun 1943
Port Ellen	18 Oct 1943
Eglinton	13 Dec 1943
Squadron disbanded	25 Jan 1944

No.878 Squadron formed at Lee-on-Solent on 1 March 1943 as a Fleet Fighter unit equipped with 12 Martlet IVs. After working-up in Scotland, the squadron embarked in HMS *Illustrious* in June, undertaking operations in the Iceland area the following month. In August the ship sailed for the Mediterranean, where No.878 was in action over the Salerno beachhead. Returning home, it re-equipped in October with 10 Martlet Vs, these being shared between Nos.816 and 1832 Squadrons when No.878 disbanded at Eglinton on 25 January 1944.

Commanding Officers
L/C(A) MF Fell RN 1 Mar 1943
L/C(A) DK Evans
      RNZNVR 30 Oct 1943
Squadron disbanded 25 Jan 1944

Grumman Martlets of No.878 Squadron ranged on the flight deck of HMS Illustrious in 1943. (FAA Museum)

No.879 Squadron

Badge: *On a white field, a peregrine falcon proper perched upon a portcullis sable*

Motto: *Si vis defendere oppugna (Attack is the best defence)*

Aircraft Equipment	Period of Service	Example
Fulmar II	Oct 1942 - Mar 1943	DR739
Spitfire Va	Mar 1943 - Mar 1943	P7694
Spitfire Vb/hooked	Mar 1943 - Mar 1943	W3846
Seafire Ib	Mar 1943 - Jun 1943	NX889
Seafire L.IIc/LR.IIc	Jun 1943 - Nov 1945	MB317 (AE)
Seafire L.III	Mar 1944 - Nov 1945	PR292 (D4Y)
Seafire F.XVII	Nov 1945 - Jan 1946	SX363

Battle Honours
Salerno	1943
South France	1944
Aegean	1944

Identification Markings
Fulmar unknown; Seafire *A:A+*, later *D4A+*.

Squadron bases
St Merryn	1 Oct 1942
Charlton Horethorne	10 Oct 1942
Old Sarum	18 Nov 1942
Stretton	22 Mar 1943
Dundonald	26 Apr 1943
Stretton	1 May 1943
Andover	17 Jun 1943
Machrihanish	8 Jul 1943
HMS Attacker	29 Jul 1943
Machrihanish	6 Oct 1943
Andover	7 Oct 1943
Burscough	29 Nov 1943
Andover	9 Dec 1943
Burscough	19 Dec 1943
HMS Attacker	29 Dec 1943
Burscough	6 Feb 1944
HMS Attacker	16 Mar 1944
Long Kesh	24 Mar 1944
HMS Attacker	30 Apr 1944
North Front (Dts)	24 May 1944 to 5 Jun 1944
Blida (half sqdn)	17 Jun 1944 to 22 Jul 1944
Pomigliano (Dt12)	22-25 Jun 1944

Battle Honours
Capodichino (Dt)	22-26 Jun 1944
Orvieto (Dts)	25 Jun 1944 to 19 Jul 1944
Castiglione (Dts)	5-18 Jul 1944
HMS Attacker	23 Jul 1944
Mitylene	26 Oct 1944
HMS Attacker	29 Oct 1944
Dekheila	11 Dec 1944
Helwan	5 Feb 1945
Dekheila	9 Feb 1945
HMS Attacker	14 Apr 1945
Katukurunda	29 Apr 1945
HMS Attacker	10 Jun 1945
Katukurunda	7 Jul 1945
HMS Attacker	10 Jul 1945
Trincomalee	19 Jul 1945
HMS Attacker	10 Jul 1945
Trincomalee	19 Jul 1945
HMS Hunter (Dt-DLT)	2-16 Aug 1945
HMS Attacker	9 Aug 1945
Trincomalee	19 Sep 1945
HMS Attacker	10 Oct 1945
Nutts Corner	10 Nov 1945
Squadron disbanded	7 Jan 1946

Commanding Officers
Lt SFF Shotton RNR	30 Sep 1942
L/C(A) RJH Grose RNVR	14 Jan 1943
L/C PEI Bailey RN	9 Nov 1944
L/C(A) BH Harriss RN	14 Apr 1945
Squadron disbanded	7 Jan 1946

No.879 Squadron formed at St.Merryn on 1 October 1942 from 'B' Flight of No.809 Squadron as a Fleet Fighter unit. Equipped initially with six Fulmar Is, four months were spent at Old Sarum on Army Support training before moving in March 1943 to Stretton to re-equip with ten Seafire IBs. Following a combined operations course at Dundonald, No.879 moved to RAF Andover for army co-operation training with No.36 (AC) Wing on 10 new Seafire L.IICs. The squadron then sailed in July for the Mediterranean in HMS *Attacker*, 75 patrols being flown during the Salerno landings and two of the aircraft being disembarked for anti-submarine work. On return to the UK, No.879 joined the 4th Naval Fighter Wing, absorbing the aircraft and some crews of No.886 Squadron on 24 February 1944 to bring the strength up to 20 aircraft.

After replacing some aircraft with L.IIIs, and undertaking further army training at Long Kesh, the squadron rejoined HMS *Attacker* in late April to return to the Mediterranean. The squadron was then split up for a time, various detachments being based on Gibraltar and Blida, whilst others were attached to Desert Air Force fighter squadrons in Italy, undertaking close support of the Army, bombing and tactical reconnaissance work. Re-embarking in late July, they supported the landings in the south of France, and later undertook several operations in the Aegean. No.879 disembarked in December to Dekheila, where it remained, equipped with 24 Seafire L.IICs and L.IIIs, until re-embarking in April 1945 for Ceylon.

Shortly VJ-Day, the squadron undertook operations against the Malay Peninsula, followed on 5-6 September by photographic reconnaissance and tactical reconnaissance sorties over Singapore. The ship then sailed home, and No.879 re-equipped at Nutts Corner with 12 Seafire XVIIs, only to disband on 7 January 1946.

Supermarine Seafires of No.879 Squadron in a flypast over Athens in October 1944. (Capt P.E.I. Bailey)

No.880 Squadron

Badge (RCN): On a yellow field, in base three barulets wavy blue, and issuing therefrom a demi-opinicus black armed and langued red and holding in the dexter paw a maple leaf of the last

Motto: Repérer et détruire (To seek out and destroy)

[Also depicted is the unapproved wartime badge apparently depicting a fish-tailed pegasus rising from the water, the motto being 'Surgentes vim aquiramus']

No.880 Squadron formed at Arbroath on 15 January 1941 as a Fleet Fighter squadron. Equipped initially with three Martlet Is, it was destined for HMS *Indomitable*, which was then still under construction. In the meantime it borrowed three Sea Gladiators, and later 9 Sea Hurricane IAs arrived, being replaced in July by IBs. 'A' Flight joined HMS *Furious* in July for an attack on the Arctic port of Petsamo during which the CO shot down a Do 18. Sea Hurricane IBs arrived at the end of July, and these joined the now-completed HMS *Indomitable* in October, sailing for the West Indies and then Cape Town before joining the Eastern Fleet. The squadron participated in the Madagascar landings in May 1942, during which attacks were made on the Vichy French sloop *D'Entrecasteaux*, Diego Suarez airfield, and various shore targets, as well as carrying out air patrols.

Returning via the Cape to Gibraltar, the ship then provided escort to a Malta convoy in Operation *Pedestal*, during which No.880 destroyed eight enemy aircraft and damaged three others, but unfortunately lost three of its own, the ship being badly damaged on 12 August. Disembarking in August to Stretton, the squadron worked up on Spitfires before re-equipping in September with 12 Seafire IICs. These joined HMS *Argus* in October, and the next month provided support for the North African landings. Rejoining the now-repaired HMS *Indomitable* in March 1943, this sailed for Gibraltar and the Mediterranean in June, and No.880 provided fighter patrols for the Fleet during the landings in Sicily in July, performing a similar task in September at Salerno during which the pilots totalled 120 hours flying hours.

Transferring to HMS *Furious* in February 1944, operations were carried out off Norway before re-equipping on 16 March with 12 Seafire F.IIIs. With these, numerous Norwegian attacks were carried out in the next six months, including providing CAP for four attacks on the German battleship *Tirpitz*. A composite squadron of four Seafires each from Nos.801 and 880 Squadrons became operational at Drem on 11 June, for local defence under RAF control, dispersing to their respective squadrons in August. In October, No.880 joined the 30th Naval Fighter Wing, which embarked in HMS *Implacable* the following month for an anti-shipping strike off Norway.

Hawker Hurricane IBs of No.880 Squadron, Arbroath around March-April 1941. (Cdr R.N.Everett)

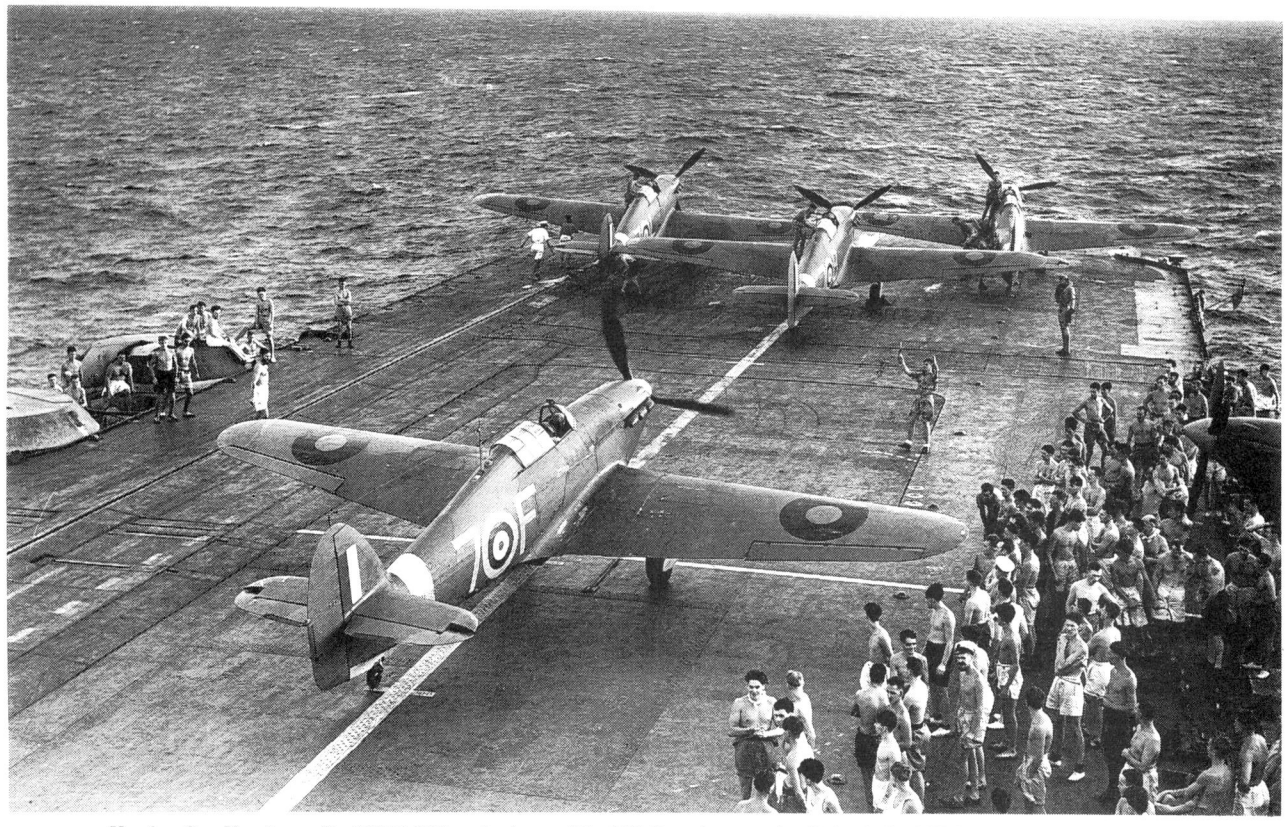

Hawker Sea Hurricane Ib AF966 '7F' and others of No.880 Squadron on the flight deck of HMS Indomitable in late 1941.

In January 1945 the squadron increased to 24 aircraft, then in March re-embarked in HMS *Implacable* to join the British Pacific Fleet. In June No.880 provided air patrols, fighter escort and bombardment spotting during attacks on the island of Truk, as well as dive bombing oil tanks, then at the end of that month the Wing was merged into the newly-formed 8th Carrier Air Group. During the last month of the war, a series of attacks was made on targets on the Japanese mainland, during which considerable damage was inflicted including the destruction of many enemy aircraft. After VJ-Day the squadron disembarked in Australia, where it disbanded at Schofields on 11 September 1945, being absorbed by No.801 Squadron.

In 1951 the squadron number was allocated for use by the Royal Canadian Navy within a standard Commonwealth sequence. No.880 accordingly reformed at Dartmouth on 1 May 1951 by renumbering No.825 Squadron, which formed part of the 31st Air Support Group. Equipped with 12 Firefly 5s, these gave way in November 1951 to seven Avengers, for service in HMCS *Magnificent*. The unit US Navy-style designation VS-880 was adopted in November 1952, and in October 1957 the squadron began to re-equip with ten CS2F-1 Trackers for service aboard the new carrier HMCS *Bonaventure*. In January 1960 they were replaced by 12 CS2F-2s incorporating improved radio and electronic devices. By the time CS2F-3s arrived early in 1970, VS-880 had ceased to be a carrier squadron, its parent carrier having been taken out of service, and its subsequent history is therefore outside the scope of this book.

Battle Honours

Diego Suarez	1942
North Africa	1942
Sicily	1943
Salerno	1943
Norway	1944
Japan	1945

Identification Markings

Martlet & Sea Gladiator probably uncoded; Sea Hurricane initially uncoded, then *7A+* from 10.41; Seafire *7A+*, to *P7A+* on *Implacable* 3.45, to *111-122/N* 9.45; Avenger (RCN) *VG-BDA* to *VG-BDZ*, later *300+*.

Aircraft Equipment	Period of Service	Example	
Martlet I	Jan 1941 - Feb 1941	AX824	
Sea Gladiator	Feb 1941 - Jun 1941	N5503	
Sea Hurricane Ia	Mar 1941 - Jul 1941	V6881	
Sea Hurricane Ib	Jul 1941 - Aug 1942	AR969	(7D)
Spitfire Vb	Aug 1942 - Feb 1943	W3756	
Seafire IIc	Sep 1942 - Aug 1943	MB240	(7B)
Seafire L.IIc	Aug 1943 - Mar 1944	LR691	
Spitfire I	Nov 1943 - Jan 1944	R6716	
Seafire F.III	Mar 1944 - Feb 1945	LR858	
Seafire L.III	Feb 1945 - Sep 1945	NN621	(115/N)
Firefly AS.5	May 1951 - Nov 1951	VX414	
Avenger TBM-3E	Nov 1951 - Dec 1957	85597	(381)
CS2F-1 Tracker	Oct 1957 - Feb 1960	1513	(6/B)
CS2F-2 Tracker	Jan 1960 - Dec 1969	1583	

Squadron bases		Squadron bases	
Arbroath	15 Jan 1941	Palisadoes (Dt2)	6-13 Dec 1941
in transit	29 Jun 1941	Khormaksar	11 Jan 1942
St Merryn	1 Jul 1941	HMS Indomitable	12 Jan 1942
Yeovilton	17 Jul 1941	Port Sudan	14 Jan 1942
4 a/c detached as 880A Sqdn:		HMS Indomitable	15 Jan 1942
Twatt	20 Jul 1941	Ratmalana	10 Feb 1942
HMS Furious	21 Jul 1941	HMS Indomitable	16 Feb 1942
North Front	18 Sep 1941	Khormaksar(Dt2)	22-23 Feb 1942
in transit	1 Oct 1941	China Bay	6 Mar 1942
Yeovilton	5 Oct 1941	HMS Indomitable	10 Mar 1942
HMS Indomitable	10 Oct 1941	Juhu	13 Apr 1942
St Merryn	24 Jul 1941	HMS Indomitable	20 Apr 1942
Twatt	14 Aug 1941	Port Reitz	22 May 1942
Sumburgh	15 Sep 1941	HMS Indomitable	10 Jun 1942
HMS Indomitable 7-11 Oct 1941 (Dt7)		Port Reitz	16 Jun 1942
		HMS Indomitable	9 Jul 1942
Machrihanish	11 Oct 1941	North Front	8 Aug 1942
HMS Indomitable	11 Oct 1941	HMS Indomitable	9 Aug 1942
Palisadoes (Dt4)	4-7 Nov 1941	North Front	8 Aug 1942
Norfolk	11 Nov 1941	HMS Indomitable	9 Aug 1942
HMS Indomitable	22 Nov 1941	North Front	14 Aug 1942
Palisadoes (Dt3)	28 Nov 1941	HMS Indomitable	24 Aug 1942
	to 3 Dec 1941	Machrihanish	27 Aug 1942

*Supermarine Seafire IIc '7F' of No.880 Squadron, HMS Indomitable goes round again in 1943.
(RAF Museum 5958-15)*

Squadron bases
Stretton	28 Aug 1942
Machrihanish	21 Sep 1942
HMS Argus	16 Oct 1942
North Front	3 Nov 1942
HMS Argus	14 Nov 1942
Hatston	20 Nov 1942
Machrihanish	22 Feb 1943
HMS Indomitable	3 Mar 1943
Machrihanish (Dts)	1 May 1943
to	8 Jun 1943
HMS Indomitable	8 Jun 1943
North Front	10 Jul 1943
HMS Indomitable	13 Jul 1943
North Front	29 Jul 1943
HMS Stalker	11 Aug 1943
Ballyhalbert	7 Oct 1943
Skeabrae	6 Feb 1944
HMS Furious	8 Feb 1944
Skeabrae	14 Feb 1944
HMS Furious	24 Feb 1944
Skeabrae	29 Feb 1944
HMS Furious	17 Mar 1944
Skeabrae	21 Mar 1944
HMS Furious	28 Mar 1944
Skeabrae	7 Apr 1944
HMS Furious	20 Apr 1944
Skeabrae	28 Apr 1944
HMS Furious	3 May 1944
Skeabrae	7 May 1944
HMS Furious	11 May 1944
Skeabrae	18 May 1944
HMS Furious	28 May 1944
Drem (Dt8)	11-17 Jun 1944
Skeabrae	17 Jun 1944
HMS Furious	22 Jun 1944
Skeabrae	23 Jun 1944
HMS Furious	22 Jun 1944
Skeabrae	23 Jun 1944
HMS Furious	10 Jul 1944
Skeabrae	19 Jul 1944
HMS Furious	1 Aug 1944
Drem (Dt8)	1-7 Aug 1944
Skeabrae	7 Aug 1944
HMS Furious	14 Aug 1944

Squadron bases
Skeabrae	27 Aug 1944
HMS Furious	11 Sep 1944
Skeabrae	13 Sep 1944
Machrihanish	16 Sep 1944
Skeabrae	27 Oct 1944
HMS Implacable	8 Nov 1944
Skeabrae	29 Nov 1944
Grimsetter	15 Jan 1945
HMS Implacable	15 Mar 1945
Jervis Bay	7 May 1945
HMS Implacable	25 May 1945
Ponam	28 Jul 1945
HMS Implacable	31 Jul 1945
Schofields	25 Aug 1945
Squadron disbanded	11 Sep 1945
Dartmouth	1 May 1951
HMCS Magnificent	1951
Dartmouth	Oct 1951
HMCS Magnificent	2 Dec 1952
Dartmouth	30 Dec 1952
Scoudouc	18 Jun 1953
Summerside	24 Sep 1953
HMCS Magnificent	Jan 1954
Summerside	9 Mar 1954
Kindley AFB	Apr 1954
Summerside	6 May 1954
Kindley AFB	Nov 1954
Summerside	12 Dec 1954
HMCS Magnificent	4 Apr 1955
Dartmouth	7 Jun 1955
HMCS Magnificent	Sep 1955
Summerside	7 Dec 1955
Dartmouth	22 Mar 1956
Summerside (Dt)	22 Mar 1956
to	14 May 1956
HMCS Magnificent	25 Sep 1956
Dartmouth	12 Oct 1956
HMCS Bonaventure	3 Sep 1957
Dartmouth	27 Nov 1957
HMCS Bonaventure	15 Jan 1959
Dartmouth	27 Feb 1959
HMCS Bonaventure	4 Mar 1959
Dartmouth	10 Apr 1959
HMCS Bonaventure	1 May 1959

Squadron bases
Kindley AFB	May 1959
HMCS Bonaventure	May 1959
Dartmouth	2 Jul 1959
HMCS Bonaventure	4 Nov 1959
Dartmouth	Dec 1959
HMCS Bonaventure	18 Jan 1960
Dartmouth	29 Feb 1960
HMCS Bonaventure	29 Apr 1960
Dartmouth	14 Jul 1960
HMCS Bonaventure	14 Nov 1960
Dartmouth	16 Dec 1960
HMCS Bonaventure	9 Jan 1961
Dartmouth	1 May 1961
HMCS Bonaventure	22 May 1961
Dartmouth	29 Jul 1961
HMCS Bonaventure	21 Sep 1961
Dartmouth	14 Dec 1961
HMCS Bonaventure	22 Jan 1962
Dartmouth	16 Mar 1962

Squadron bases
HMCS Bonaventure	9 Apr 1962
Dartmouth	30 Jul 1962
HMCS Bonaventure	17 Sep 1962
Dartmouth	5 Nov 1962
HMCS Bonaventure (Dt12)	by 2 Jul 1963
HMCS Bonaventure (Dt14)	1-13 Dec 1963
HMCS Bonaventure	13 Jan 1964
(Dt14)	to 31 Mar 1964
HMCS Bonaventure	18 Apr 1964
(Dt12)	to 8 May 1964
HMCS Bonaventure	13 Jan 1965
(Dt)	to 31 Mar 1965
HMCS Bonaventure	4 May 1965
(Dt)	to 9 Jul 1965
HMCS Bonaventure	by 5 Oct 1965
(Dt)	to 19 Nov 1965
HMCS Bonaventure	12 Jan 1966
(Dt)	to 25 Mar 1966
HMCS Bonaventure	Feb 1968
(Dt12)	Mar 1968
HMCS Bonaventure	1969
(Dt)	to 12 Dec 1969

Commanding Officers
L/C FEC Judd RN	15 Jan 1941
L/C RJ Cork DSO DFC	12 Aug 1942
L/C(A) WH Martyn DSC RNVR	7 Sep 1942
L/C(A) RM Crosley DSC & Bar RNVR	5 Aug 1944
Squadron disbanded	11 Sep 1945
L/C DW Knox RCN	1 May 1951
L/C EM Davis RCN	21 Nov 1951
L/C FG Townsend RCN	17 Apr 1954
L/C P Lewry CD RCN	17 Jan 1956
Cdr HD Buchanan CD RCN	26 Aug 1957
Cdr WJ Walton CD RCN	10 Nov 1960
Cdr DM MacLeod RCN	7 Aug 1961
Cdr RC MacLean RCN	3 Jun 1963
Cdr RA Laidler CD RCN	Aug 1965
Cdr RL Hughes RCN	Dec 1967
Cdr D Tate RCN	Jul 1969
Ceased to be carrier squadron	

Grumman CS-2F-2 Tracker 1534 of No.880 Squadron, Royal Canadian Navy in 1965. (MAP)

No.881 Squadron

Badge:
1. On a blue field, in base water barry wavy white and blue, a sword in pale, point downwards, white winged, gold
2. On a blue field, in base two barulets wavy white, over all a sword in pale point downwards of the second, pommel and hilt yellow, enfiling a coronet of Canada of the last, and issuing in the base from behind the sword blade wings conjoined white (Canadian)

Motto: Ense constanter alato (Steadfastly with winged sword)

No.881 Squadron formed at Lee-on-Solent on 1 June 1941 as a Fleet Fighter squadron with six Martlet Is and IIs, being intended for HMS *Ark Royal*. Before it could embark, the ship was sunk on 13 November, and the squadron was reallocated to HMS *Illustrious*. It had increased to nine aircraft by the time it embarked for the Indian Ocean in March 1942, a further three being added for the Madagascar operations in May, when it joined with No.882 in carrying out patrols, strike escort and tactical reconnaissance in support of the capture of Diego Suarez, the two squadrons jointly shooting down 7 enemy aircraft. On 19 May No.882 Squadron was absorbed into No.881. Returning home early in 1943, part of the squadron embarked in HMS *Furious* in July for operations during a simulated invasion of Norway, one enemy aircraft being shot down.

The squadron re-equipped in August with 12 Wildcat Vs, and in November 1943 joined the 7th Naval Fighter Wing, embarking in HMS *Pursuer*. In February 1944 it provided fighter cover for a Gibraltar-bound convoy, during which it shot down two enemy aircraft and damaged another. During April it participated in an attack on the German battleship *Tirpitz*, another enemy aircraft being claimed whilst on escort duty in June. Later in that month, by then equipped with 20 Wildcat VIs, including some from the disbanding No.896 Squadron, it embarked temporarily in HMS *Fencer* during an anti-shipping operation off northern Norway.

Rejoining HMS *Pursuer* to sail for the Mediterranean, 180 sorties were flown during the landings in the south of France in August, and the following month the squadron was in action in the

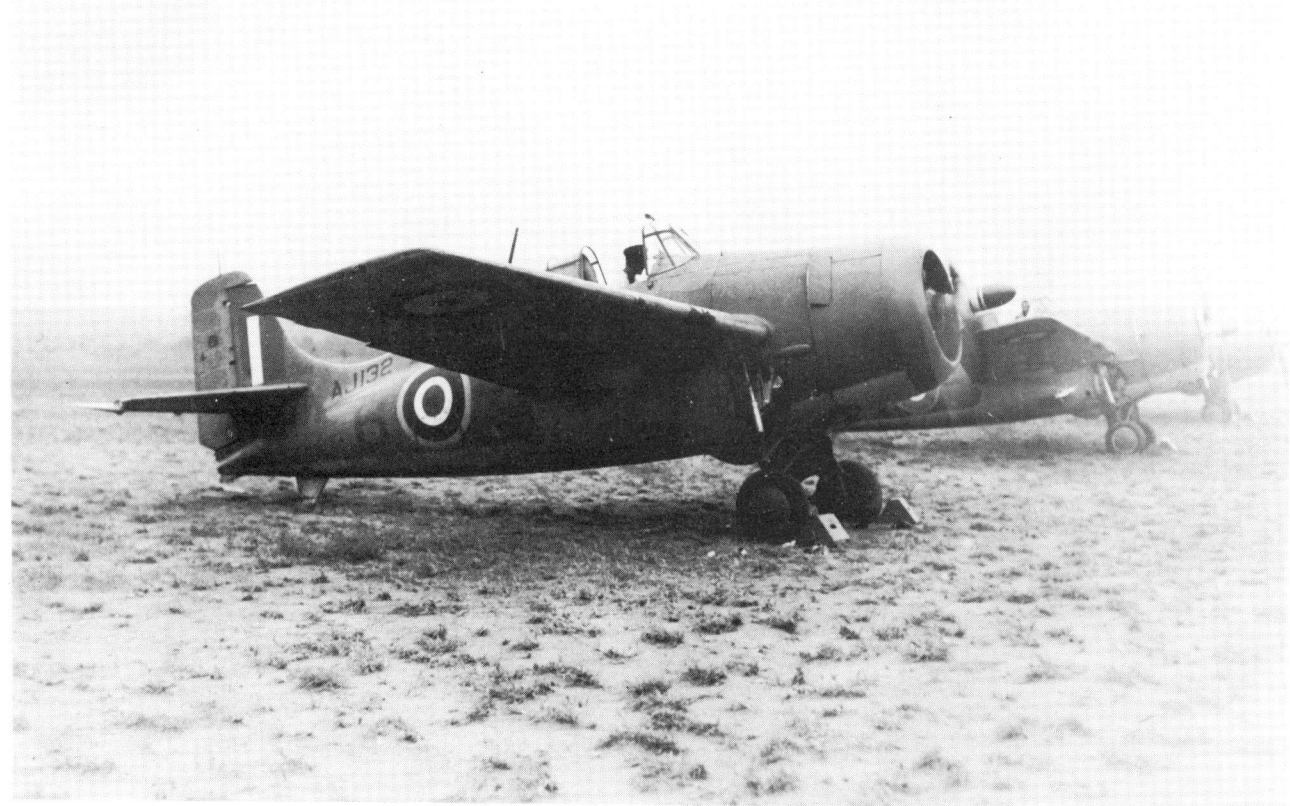

Grumman Martlet II AJ132 'BA' and others of No.881 Squadron at Mackinnon Road in late 1942, after the Madagascar operations. (FAA Museum)

Grumman Martlet II AM968 of No.881 Squadron being lowered from the flight deck to the hangar of HMS Illustrious in 1942. (RAF Museum 5923-1)

Aegean. Returning home, it spent three months in further Norwegian operations, aircraft being embarked at various times in HMS *Pursuer*, HMS *Trumpeter* and HMS *Premier*. In March 1945 the squadron rejoined HMS *Pursuer* for Capetown, where it re-equipped with 30 Hellcat IIs. It should have left South Africa in September, after working-up on these, as part of the 12th Carrier Air Group with the British Pacific Fleet, but VJ-Day intervened, and instead the crews took passage home to disband on arrival on 27 October 1945.

In 1951 the squadron number was allocated to the Royal Canadian Navy within a standard Commonwealth sequence, and on 1 May 1951 it reformed at Dartmouth by renumbering No.826 Squadron. Equipped with 15 Avengers, it formed part of the 30th Carrier Air Group, embarking later in the year in HMCS *Magnificent*. In November 1952 it adopted the US Navy-style designation VS-881, and in June 1953 participated in the Coronation Review flypast at Spithead. In March 1955 a flight of four AEW Avengers was added to provide the Royal Canadian Navy with an airborne early warning capability, but in February 1957 the Avengers were phased out on the arrival of CS2F-1 Trackers. These embarked later in the year in the new carrier HMCS *Bonaventure* for a visit to Northern Ireland. However, on 7 July 1959 the squadron was amalgamated into VS-880 at Dartmouth.

Aircraft Equipment

Aircraft	Period of Service	Example
Martlet I	Jun 1941 - Dec 1941	AX829
Martlet II	Jun 1941 - Aug 1943	AM974 (BJ)
Fulmar	Mar 1942 - Apr 1942	X8806
Martlet IV	Oct 1942 - Aug 1943	FN249
Wildcat V	Aug 1943 - Jun 1944	JV392 (5H)
Wildcat VI	Jun 1944 - Mar 1945	JV715 (UG)
Hellcat II	Apr 1945 - Aug 1945	JX981
Avenger TBM-3E	May 1951 - Mar 1957	53503 (ABS)
Avenger AEW	Mar 1955 - Mar 1957	
CS2F-1 Tracker	Feb 1957 - Jul 1959	1502

Identification Markings
Martlet single letters, then *B:A+*; Wildcat *5A+*, to *U:A+* on *Pursuer* 7.44; Hellcat *2A+* & *3A+*; Avenger (RCN) *VG-ABA* to *VG-ABZ*.

Battle Honours
Diego Suarez	1942
Norway	1944
Aegean	1944
South France	1944
Normandy	1944
Atlantic	1944

Squadron bases

Lee-on-Solent	1 Jun 1941
Machrihanish	13 Feb 1942
HMS Illustrious	15 Mar 1942
Port Reitz (Dt2)	26-29 May 1942
Mackinnon Road	19 Aug 1942
HMS Illustrious	6 Sep 1942
Stamford Hill	21 Sep 1942
HMS Illustrious	14 Oct 1942
Mackinnon Road 'B' Flt	20 Oct 1942
Donibristle	26 Oct 1942
Kirkistown	19 Nov 1942
Donibristle	19 Dec 1942
Kirkistown	30 Dec 1942
Donibristle	4 Jan 1943
Disbanded into 890 Sqdn	8 Jan 1943
HMS Illustrious	7 Dec 1942
Machrihanish	4 Feb 1943
HMS Illustrious	5 Feb 1943
Lee-on-Solent	18 Feb 1943
West Freugh (trans)	26 Mar 1943
Hatston	27 Mar 1943
HMS Furious (Dt7)	6-9 Jul 1943
HMS Unicorn	26 Jul 1943
Hatston	29 Jul 1943
Eglinton	15 Aug 1943
Stretton	20 Sep 1943
Hatston	9 Nov 1943
HMS Formidable	10 Nov 1943
Hatston	12 Nov 1943
Stretton	12 Nov 1943
Belfast	25 Nov 1943
HMS Pursuer	26 Nov 1943
Burscough	1 May 1944
HMS Furious (Dt5)	11-18 May 1944
HMS Furious (Dt5)	28 May 1944 to 2 Jun 1944
HMS Pursuer	2 Jun 1944
Drem (Dt8)	11-16 Jun 1944
Skeabrae (Dt8)	16-20 Jun 1944
HMS Fencer	20 Jun 1944
Eglinton	23 Jun 1944
HMS Pursuer	4 Jul 1944
Ta Kali	25 Jul 1944
HMS Pursuer	1 Aug 1944
Dekheila (Dt6)	3-10 Sep 1944
Long Kesh	12 Oct 1944
HMS Pursuer	27 Oct 1944
Grimsetter	30 Oct 1944
HMS Pursuer	5 Nov 1944
Grimsetter	27 Nov 1944
HMS Trumpeter (Dt2)	4-12 Dec 1944
HMS Implacable (Dt10)	5-9 Dec 1944
Grimsetter	9 Dec 1944
HMS Premier (Dt2)	11-16 Dec 1944
HMS Trumpeter (Dt5)	12-18 Dec 1944
HMS Trumpeter (Dt7)	20-24 Dec 1944
HMS Trumpeter (Dt10)	31 Dec 1944 to 5 Jan 1945
HMS Trumpeter (Dt4)	9-14 Jan 1945
HMS Premier (Dt14)	9 Jan 1945 to 5 Feb 1945
Skeabrae	28 Jan 1945
HMS Puncher	9 Feb 1945
Skeabrae	14 Feb 1945
HMS Puncher	17 Feb 1945
HMS Premier (Dt3)	17-23 Feb 1945
Skeabrae	25 Feb 1945
Hatston	2 Mar 1945
HMS Pursuer	23 Mar 1945
Wingfield	26 Apr 1945
MV Reino del Pacifico (no a/c)	10 Oct 1945
Sqdn disbanded UK	27 Oct 1945
Dartmouth (for HMCS Magnificent)	1 May 1951
HMCS Magnificent	1952
Dartmouth	2 Dec 1952
HMCS Magnificent	16 Apr 1955
(AEW Flight) to	7 Jun 1955
HMCS Magnificent	Sep 1955
(AEW Flight) to	7 Dec 1955
Bermuda	27 Oct 1955
Dartmouth	12 Dec 1955
HMCS Magnificent	27 Feb 1956
Dartmouth	9 Jun 1956
HMCS Magnificent	20 Aug 1956
Dartmouth	30 Aug 1956
HMCS Magnificent	8 Sep 1956
Dartmouth	18 Sep 1956
HMCS Bonaventure	3 Sep 1957
Dartmouth	27 Nov 1957
HMCS Bonaventure	21 Jan 1958
Dartmouth	9 May 1958
HMCS Bonaventure	8 Oct 1958
Dartmouth	15 Dec 1958
HMCS Bonaventure	15 Jan 1959
Dartmouth	27 Feb 1959
Squadron disbanded into 880 Sqdn	7 Jul 1959

Commanding Officers

L/C JC Cockburn RN	1 Jun 1941
L/C RA Bird RN	1 Mar 1943
L/C DRB Cosh RCNVR	27 Nov 1943
L/C(A) LA Hordern DSC RNVR	25 Jun 1944
L/C(A) C Ballard RNVR	23 Oct 1944
Squadron disbanded	1 Sep 1945
L/C JN Donaldson RCN	1 May 1951
L/C WHI Atkinson DSC RCN	4 Mar 1953
L/C MHE Page RCN	13 Aug 1953
L/C RWJ Cocks RCN	30 Aug 1954
L/C NJ Geary CD RCN	26 May 1955
L/C VM Langman DSC RCN	Jun 1956
L/C HJG Bird CD RCN	27 Nov 1956
Cdr WH Fearon CD RCN	Apr 1959
Squadron disbanded	7 Jul 1959

Grumman TBM-3E Avenger 53732 '316' of No.881 Squadron at Lee-on-Solent on 13 June 1953. (John Rawlings)

No.882 Squadron

No.882 Squadron formed at Donibristle on 15 July 1941 as a Fleet Fighter squadron with nine Martlet Is, being originally intended for service in an escort carrier. Some Sea Hurricanes were also flown briefly. In February 1942 it went to Turnhouse for ground attack training, following which it embarked in HMS *Illustrious*, providing support during the Madagascar operations in May. On 19 May it merged with No.881 Squadron, though apparently regarded as a separate sub-unit until September. A detachment had joined HMS *Archer* in April 1942, and this continued in existence, disembarking to Floyd Bennett Field, New York in July to carry out anti-submarine patrols on Swordfish until this too disbanded on 30 September 1942.

A new No.882 had meanwhile formed at Donibristle on 7 September 1942 with 12 Martlet IVs, joining HMS *Victorious* in October for participation in the North African landings. After returning home, the ship sailed to America, and then through the Panama Canal into the Pacific, where it carried out a sweep in the Coral Sea area during May 1943, followed in June by operations in support of American landings in the Middle Solomon Islands, a few US Navy F4F-4s being flown by the squadron. Returning home by the same route, No.882 was disembarked to Eglinton in September, where it re-equipped with ten Martlet Vs on joining the 7th Naval Fighter Wing. In December it embarked in HMS *Searcher* for a US convoy, then in February 1944 the ship joined the Home Fleet for a series of Norwegian operations including a strike on the German battleship *Tirpitz*.

No.882 increased to 24 aircraft on 5 July 1944, when it absorbed No.898 Squadron. HMS *Searcher* then sailed for the Mediterranean, where No.882 flew 167 sorties in support of the landings in the south of France, carrying out bombing attacks and reconnaissance in support of the US Army. In September, a further 90 sorties were flown during operations in the Aegean. After a spell of training in Northern Ireland, during which No.882 re-equipped with 20 Wildcat VIs, HMS *Searcher* was rejoined in February 1945 for operations off Norway which culminated in May with a successful strike on the U-boat base at Kilbotn. During this phase two Firefly night fighters were attached from No.746 Squadron. In June the ship sailed for Ceylon, but arrived too late to participate actively in the Pacific War, and No.882 disbanded on arrival home on 9 October 1945, plans to re-equip the squadron in Ceylon for service with a new 6th Carrier Air Group in an *Illustrious*-class carrier having been abandoned.

Battle Honours

Diego Suarez	1942
North Africa	1942
Atlantic	1943-44
South France	1944
Norway	1944-45
Arctic	1945

Identification Markings
Martlet/Wildcat individual letters, to 7A+ on *Victorious* by 6.43, to 6A+ on *Searcher* by 6.44, to S:A+ in *Searcher* by 3.45.

Aircraft Equipment	Period of Service	Example
Sea Hurricane Ib	Jul 1941 - Apr 1942	AF971
Martlet I	Jul 1941 - Sep 1942	AX828 (A)
Martlet II	Apr 1942 - Dec 1942	AJ122
Martlet IV	Sep 1942 - Jul 1943	FN299
Wildcat F4F-4	Jun 1943 - Jul 1943	BuAer11922
Wildcat V	Sep 1943 - Jan 1945	JV445 (6Q)
Wildcat VI	Jan 1945 - Sep 1945	JV768 (SX)
Firefly INF	Feb 1945 - May 1945	MB492

Grumman Wildcat Vs of No.882 Squadron ready for take-off from HMS Searcher in 1944. (RAF Museum 275-31)

*Grumman Martlet II AM964 'F' of No.882 Squadron awaiting take-off from HMS Illustrious in 1942.
(FAA Museum)*

Squadron bases

Dekheila (Dt4)	21 Sep 1944
to	1 Oct 1944
Ballyhalbert	12 Oct 1944
Long Kesh	29 Oct 1944
Ayr	2 Dec 1944
Long Kesh	9 Dec 1944
HMS Searcher	9 Feb 1945
Grimsetter	29 Mar 1945
HMS Searcher	5 Apr 1945
Grimsetter	13 Apr 1945
HMS Searcher	17 Apr 1945
HMS Vindex (Dt4)	17 Apr 1945
to	6 May 1945
Grimsetter	19 Apr 1945
HMS Searcher	27 Apr 1945
HMS Campania	10 May 1945
Machrihanish	21 May 1945
Ayr	27 May 1945
Belfast (transit)	25 Jun 1945
HMS Searcher	25 Jun 1945
Cochin	20 Jul 1945
HMS Searcher	8 Aug 1945
Katukurunda	20 Aug 1945
HMS Searcher	19 Sep 1945
Sqdn disbanded UK	9 Oct 1945

Commanding Officers

L/C ON Bailey RN	15 Jul 1941
Lt FC Furlong RNVR (temp)	10 Aug 1941
L/C HJF Lane RN	9 Sep 1941
Lt(A) ILF Lowe DSC RN	7 Sep 1942
L/C EA Shaw RN	3 Dec 1942
L/C(A) J Cooper DSC RNVR	25 Oct 1943
L/C(A) GR Henderson DSC RNVR	5 Jul 1944
L/C RA Bird RN	18 Nov 1944
L/C(A) GAM Flood RNVR	5 Jun 1945
Squadron disbanded	9 Oct 1945

Squadron bases

Donibristle	15 Jul 1941
St Merryn	3 Nov 1941
Yeovilton	1 Dec 1941
Gosport	15 Dec 1941
Turnhouse (13 Gp)	13 Feb 1942
Machrihanish	17 Mar 1942
HMS Illustrious	22 Mar 1942
Detached flight (2 a/c)	
HMS Archer	9 Apr 1942
Floyd Bennett Fld	Jul 1942
Flight disbanded	30 Sep 1942
Mackinnon Road	19 Aug 1942
HMS Illustrious	5 Sep 1942
(merged into 881 Sqdn)	
Donibristle	7 Sep 1942
Lossiemouth(trans)	29 Sep 1942
Skeabrae (14 Gp)	1 Oct 1942
HMS Victorious	6 Oct 1942
Machrihanish	22 Nov 1942
Hatston	23 Nov 1942
Machrihanish	14 Dec 1942
HMS Victorious	20 Dec 1942
Norfolk	1 Jan 1943
HMS Victorious	1 Feb 1943
Barbers Point	4 Mar 1943
HMS Victorious	7 May 1943
Tontouta	17 May 1943
HMS Victorious	24 May 1943
Tontouta	3 Jun 1943
HMS Victorious	16 Jun 1943
Tontouta	20 Jun 1943
HMS Victorious	27 Jun 1943
Tontouta	25 Jul 1943
HMS Victorious	31 Jul 1943
Barbers Point	9 Aug 1943
HMS Victorious	12 Aug 1943
Willow Grove	1 Sep 1943
Norfolk	11 Sep 1943
HMS Victorious	14 Sep 1943
Eglinton	26 Sep 1943
HMS Searcher	9 Dec 1943

Squadron bases

Brunswick	10 Jan 1944
Norfolk	4 Feb 1944
HMS Searcher	8 Feb 1944
Eglinton	28 Feb 1944
HMS Searcher	2 Mar 1944
Hatston	6 Apr 1944
HMS Fencer	11 Apr 1944
Hatston	15 Apr 1944
HMS Searcher	18 Apr 1944

Squadron bases

Hatston (Dt7)	11 May 1944
to	2 Jun 1944
HMS Furious (Dt4)	28 May 1944
to	2 Jun 1944
Hatston	2 Jun 1944
HMS Searcher	7 Jun 1944
Ta Kali (Dt10)	25 Jul 1944
to	7 Aug 1944
Dekheila (Dt6)	1-9 Sep 1944

*Grumman Wildcat V JV338 'SX' of No.882 Squadron on HMS Searcher in late 1944.
(via E.V.Morton)*

No.883 Squadron

(Heraldic description lacking)

No.883 Squadron formed at Yeovilton on 10 October 1941 as a Fleet Fighter squadron equipped with 6 Sea Hurricane IBs. Fighter defence duties in Scotland under RAF No.14 Group were followed by embarkation in HMS *Avenger*, and whilst escorting North Russian convoy PQ18 in September 1942, No.883 joined with No.802 Squadron in shooting down 5 German aircraft and damaging 17 others. In November the ship took part in the North African landings, during which No.883 provided fighter protection, but on 15 November HMS *Avenger* was torpedoed and blew up while returning to the UK. No.883 then ceased to exist.

In 1945 the number was allocated for Royal Canadian Navy use, and a new No.883 formed with this intention at Arbroath on 18 September 1945 with 16 Seafire IIIs, being 13 taken over from No.805 Squadron and the remainder from No.803. The squadron had already been earmarked for a new 10th Carrier Air Group with the British Pacific Fleet, but by the time it formed was no longer required as such. It moved in November to Nutts Corner, where it re-equipped with 18 Seafire XVs, but manning difficulties prevented it joining the RCN, and on 23 February 1946 it disbanded at Machrihanish.

A second attempt proved more successful, No.883 reforming as an RCN squadron at Dartmouth on 15 May 1947, equipped with 12 Seafire XVs for service in HMCS *Warrior*, as part of the 18th Carrier Air Group. The squadron re-equipped in September 1948 with 8 Sea Fury FB.11s, and under a reorganisation in November 1948 transferred to the 19th CAG, with which it later embarked in HMCS *Magnificent*. In a reversal of policy it reverted to the 18th CAG in January 1951, but on 1 May 1951, was redesignated to become No.871 Squadron.

Battle Honours
North Africa 1942
Arctic 1942

Identification Markings
Sea Hurricane unknown; Seafire individual letters; Seafire & Sea Fury (RCN) *VG-AAA* to *VG-AAZ*.

Aircraft Equipment	Period of Service	Example
Sea Hurricane Ib	Oct 1941 - Sep 1942	Z7050
Sea Hurricane IIb	Sep 1942 - Nov 1942	
Seafire III	Sep 1945 - Dec 1945	NN602 (J)
Seafire XV	Nov 1945 - Feb 1946	SW872
	May 1947 - Sep 1948	SW869 (AAH)
Sea Fury FB.11	Sep 1948 - May 1951	VR918 (AAY)

Supermarine Seafire F.XV PR479 AA-B of No.883 Squadron, Dartmouth in 1947. (MAP)

Squadron bases		Squadron bases	
Yeovilton	10 Oct 1941	Eglinton	Aug 1950
St Merryn	5 Dec 1941	HMCS Magnificent	Sep 1950
Yeovilton	19 Dec 1941	Dartmouth	27 Nov 1950
Fraserburgh(14 Gp)	28 Jan 1942	HMCS Magnificent	5 Feb 1951
Peterhead (14 Gp)	15 Feb 1942	Dartmouth	Mar 1951
Machrihanish	11 May 1942	HMCS Magnificent	Mar 1951
HMS Avenger	16 Jun 1942	Dartmouth	27 Apr 1951
Hatston	27 Aug 1942	Redes 871 Sqdn	1 May 1951
HMS Avenger	3 Sep 1942		
Hatston	25 Sep 1942	**Commanding Officers**	
HMS Avenger	16 Oct 1942	Capt WHC Manson	
ceased to exist	15 Nov 1942	RM	10 Oct 1941
Arbroath	18 Sep 1945	Lt(A) PWV Massey	
Nutts Corner	7 Nov 1945	DSC RN	10 Apr 1942
Machrihanish	21 Feb 1946	Squadron disbanded	15 Nov 1942
Squadron disbanded	23 Feb 1946	L/C(A) TJA King	
Dartmouth	15 May 1947	-Joyce RN	18 Sep 1945
HMCS Warrior	Nov 1947	Squadron disbanded	23 Feb 1946
Dartmouth	21 Nov 1947	L/C RA Monks RCN	15 May 1947
Rivers	Aug 1948	L/C JB Fotheringham	
Dartmouth	Sep 1948	RCN	Jan 1948
HMCS Magnificent	Jan 1950	L/C RAB Creery	
Dartmouth	Feb 1950	RCN	1 Dec 1948
HMCS Magnificent	1950	Lt WD Munro RCN	Apr 1950
Dartmouth	Jun 1950	Squadron disbanded	1 May 1951
HMCS Magnificent	22 Aug 1950		

The CO's Supermarine Seafire F.XV of No.883 Squadron after a landing accident at Nutts Corner on 15 February 1946.
(George Standley)

No.884 Squadron

Badge: On a blue field, issuant from water barry wavy in base white and blue a cubit arm in bend grasping in the gauntlet an axe proper, the arm winged gold
Motto: None?

No.884 Squadron formed at Donibristle on 1 November 1941 as a Fleet Fighter squadron. It was equipped with 6 Fulmar IIs, and was originally intended for HMS *Biter*. After spending some time at Turnhouse attached to RAF No.14 Group, it embarked instead in HMS *Victorious* in July 1942 to help provide fighter cover for a Malta convoy. After returning to the UK, the ship sailed to participate in the North African invasion, during which No.884 afforded fighter protection. It then returned to fighter defence at Turnhouse, before disbanding at Machrihanish on 20 July 1943. A proposal to reform the squadron in late 1945 with 21 Seafires for service with a new 22nd Carrier Air Group in the British Pacific Fleet ended with the cessation of hostilities in that theatre.

Battle Honours
Malta Convoys 1942
North Africa 1942

Identification Markings
Fulmar and Spitfire possibly uncoded; Seafire believed 8A+.

Aircraft Equipment	Period of Service	Example
Fulmar II	Nov 1941 - Sep 1942	DR665
Spitfire Va	Sep 1942 - Oct 1942	P8246
Spitfire Vb	Sep 1942 - Oct 1942	AA866
Spitfire Vb/hooked	Sep 1942 - Oct 1942	BL253
Seafire IIc	Sep 1942 - Jul 1943	MB237

Squadron bases	
Donibristle	1 Nov 1941
St Merryn	1 Jan 1942
Yeovilton	7 Feb 1942
Turnhouse (13 Gp)	22 Mar 1942
Peterhead (13 Gp)	6 Jul 1942
Turnhouse (13 Gp)	11 Jul 1942
Hatston	21 Jul 1942
HMS Victorious	23 Jul 1942
Lee-on-Solent	21 Aug 1942
Skeabrae (14 Gp)	25 Sep 1942
HMS Victorious	22 Oct 1942
Twatt	23 Nov 1942
Skeabrae (14 Gp)	25 Sep 1942
HMS Victorious	22 Oct 1942
Twatt	23 Nov 1942
Skeabrae (14 Gp)	25 Nov 1942
Turnhouse (13 Gp)	14 Dec 1942
Machrihanish (13Gp)	24 Mar 1942
HMS Argus (DLT)	25 Mar 1942
Drem (13 Gp)	10 Apr 1943
Grimsetter	by 5 May 1943
Turnhouse (13 Gp)	11 May 1943
Machrihanish	16 Jul 1943
Squadron disbanded	20 Jul 1943

Commanding Officers
L/C NG Hallett
RN 1 Nov 1941
L/C TB Winstanley
RN 20 Mar 1943
Squadron disbanded 20 Jul 1943

No.885 Squadron

Badge: (1) Heraldic description lacking
(2) On a blue field, issuant from water barry engrailed white and blue, flames proper therein a cat affronté black
Motto: Celerrime
(Very quickly)

No.885 Squadron formed at Dekheila on 1 March 1941 as a Fleet Fighter squadron with six Sea Gladiators and three Buffaloes. Two days later these embarked in HMS *Eagle* for a week before returning to Dekheila as a shore based squadron, only to disband on 1 May 1941. In October the number was temporarily allocated to No.775 Squadron Fighter Unit, but was withdrawn before the end of that month and instead that sub-unit became the RN Fighter Flight, which eventually formed the basis of No.889 Squadron.

Reformed at Yeovilton on 1 December 1941, No.885 was again a Fleet Fighter squadron, equipped with six Sea Hurricane IBs and intended for the escort carrier HMS *Charger*. In the event the latter was retained by the US Navy to provide deck landing training to British squadrons forming up in America, and instead No.885 joined HMS *Victorious* in June 1942, covering Russian convoys PQ17 and QP13 in July. In August the ship sailed for the Mediterranean, and No.885 provided air cover for a Malta convoy. In September the squadron moved to Machrihanish to train for the North African landings, temporarily using Spitfire Vs until these were replaced by six Seafires IBs and IICs. It then joined HMS *Formidable* for this operation, during which it provided air cover, afterwards remaining in the Mediterranean theatre for the Sicily and Salerno landings, returning returning to the UK in October 1943. It was to have taken passage to the United States, to rearm in December at Brunswick with ten Corsairs, but instead disbanded at Lee-on-Solent on 15 November 1943.

No.885 next reformed on 15 February 1944, as part of the 3rd Naval Fighter Wing at Lee-on-Solent, equipped with 12 Seafire F.IIIs and L.IIIs. For several weeks from D-Day it formed part of

Supermarine Seafire IIc 'Ø6B' of No.885 Squadron taking off from HMS Formidable soon after the North African landings. (via Ron Porter)

Hawker Hurricanes of No.885 Squadron at Hutton Cranswick in April 1942. (Capt R.H.P.Carver)

the Air Spotting Pool of No.34 Reconnaissance Wing, 2nd Tactical Air Force, providing bombardment spotting, escort for the invasion fleet and subsequent ship movements, offensive sweeps and anti-submarine patrols, equipped now with 20 Seafire L.IIIs. In July it absorbed the remnants of Nos.886 and 897 Squadrons. Then in November No.885 handed over its Seafires to Nos.709 and 715 Squadrons at St. Merryn, to re-equip with 24 Hellcat Is and IIs, with which it embarked the following month in HMS *Ruler* to join the British Pacific Fleet. From May 1945, fighter cover was provided in the Fleet replenishment area, a few Corsairs being attached whilst the squadron was ashore at Ponam. A TBR flight was also added in May, equipped with Avengers. The Hellcats were fitted to carry rocket projectiles in July, but saw no action before VJ-Day. After a visit to Tokyo, the ship sailed for Australia, but plans for No.885 to join a new 12th Carrier Air Group were abandoned, and instead it disbanded at Schofields on 27 September 1945.

Battle Honours

Malta Convoys	1942
North Africa	1942
Sicily	1943
Normandy	1944
Okinawa	1945

Squadron bases

Dekheila	1 Mar 1941
HMS Eagle	3 Mar 1941
Dekheila	10 Mar 1941
Squadron disbanded	1 May 1941
Yeovilton	1 Dec 1941
St Merryn	6 Feb 1942
Yeovilton	10 Mar 1942
Sherburn-in-Elmet	14 Mar 1942
Hutton Cranswick	22 Mar 1942
Machrihanish	16 Jun 1942
Hatston	23 Jun 1942
HMS Victorious	29 Jun 1942
Hatston	10 Jul 1942
HMS Victorious	31 Jul 1942
Arbroath (transit)	21 Aug 1942
Lee-on-Solent	22 Aug 1942
Machrihanish	16 Sep 1942
HMS Formidable	28 Oct 1942
North Front	7 Dec 1943
HMS Formidable	5 Jan 1943
La Senia	15 Jan 1943
HMS Formidable	26 Jan 1943
La Senia	2 Feb 1943
HMS Formidable	7 Feb 1943
North Front	8 Feb 1943
HMS Formidable	10 Mar 1943
Tafaroui	15 Mar 1943
HMS Formidable	25 Mar 1943
North Front	26 Mar 1943
HMS Formidable	31 Mar 1943
Tafaroui	9 Apr 1943
HMS Formidable	14 Apr 1943
North Front	16 Apr 1943
HMS Formidable	19 Apr 1943
Tafaroui	1 May 1943
HMS Formidable	4 May 1943
North Front	7 May 1943
HMS Formidable	28 May 1943
Tafaroui	2 Jun 1943
HMS Formidable	14 Jun 1943
Ta Kali	31 Jul 1943
HMS Formidable	21 Aug 1943
Dekheila	24 Aug 1943
HMS Formidable	28 Aug 1943
Ta Kali	30 Aug 1943
HMS Formidable	5 Sep 1943
Paestum (Dt2)	7-11 Sep 1943
HMS Unicorn (Dt2)	11 Sep 1943 to 10 Oct 1943
Ta Kali	12 Sep 1943
Sidi Ahmed	15 Sep 1943
Ta Kali	16 Sep 1943
HMS Formidable	20 Sep 1943
North Front	22 Sep 1943
HMS Formidable	5 Oct 1943
Lee-on-Solent	18 Oct 1943
Squadron disbanded	15 Nov 1943
Lee-on-Solent	15 Feb 1944
St Merryn	19 Feb 1944
Henstridge	31 Mar 1944
Dundonald	22 Apr 1944
Ayr	6 May 1944
Lee-on-Solent	13 May 1944
Ballyhalbert	4 Aug 1944
Kirkistown (Dt-ADDLs)	21 Aug 1944
Hawarden (Dt6)	1 Sep 1944 to 13 Oct 1944

Identification Markings

Sea Gladiator and Buffalo unknown; Sea Hurricane single letters, to *7A+* on *Victorious* 6.42; Seafire *Ø6A+* on *Formidable* for Op Torch, later *D6A+*, to *2A+* by 6.44; Hellcat single letters, to *K8A+* 2.45; Corsair single letters, later *100+*.

Aircraft Equipment	Period of Service	Example	
Sea Gladiator	Mar 1941 - May 1941		
Buffalo I	Mar 1941 - May 1941		
Sea Hurricane Ib	Dec 1941 - Aug 1942	V7506	(7T)
Spitfire Va	Sep 1942 - Oct 1942	R6722	
Spitfire Vb/hooked	Sep 1942 - Oct 1942	BL343	
Seafire Ib	Oct 1942 - Aug 1943	MB345	(K)
Seafire IIc	Sep 1942 - Nov 1943	MB318	(Ø6L)
Seafire L.III	Feb 1944 - Nov 1944	NF426	(2A)
Seafire F.III	Feb 1944 - Nov 1944	LR853	
Seafire L.IIc	Aug 1944 - Nov 1944	MB257	
Hellcat I	Oct 1944 - May 1945	JV235	
Hellcat II	Oct 1944 - Sep 1945	JW740	(K8B)
Avenger I	May 1945 - Sep 1945	JZ266	
Corsair II	Jun 1945 - Aug 1945	JT382	
Corsair IV	Jun 1945 - Aug 1945	KD531	(122)

Squadron bases

Belfast (transit)	15 Dec 1944
HMS Ruler (DLT)	16 Dec 1944
Ayr	19 Dec 1944
HMS Ruler (DLT)	22 Dec 1944
Ayr	23 Dec 1944
HMS Ruler	30 Dec 1944
Schofields	20 Mar 1945
HMS Ruler	4 Apr 1945
Schofields	5 Apr 1945
HMS Ruler	14 Apr 1945
Ponam	31 May 1945
HMS Ruler	17 Jun 1945
Ponam (Dt12)	19-28 Jun 1945
HMS Indefatigable	5 Sep 1945
Schofields	18 Sep 1945
Squadron disbanded	27 Sep 1945

Commanding Officers

L/C JN Garnett RN	1 Mar 1941
Squadron disbanded	1 May 1941
Lt EDG Lewin RN	1 Dec 1941
L/C(A) RHP Carver DSC RN	2 Feb 1942
Squadron disbanded	15 Nov 1943
L/C(A) SL Devonald RN	15 Feb 1944
L/C(A) JR Routley RNVR	7 Nov 1944
Squadron disbanded	27 Sep 1945

Supermarine Seafire L.IIc LR734 '2H' of No.885 Squadron, Ballyhalbert. (R.E.Goadsby)

No.886 Squadron

Badge: On a white field, a Chinese dragon, green
Motto: Vires acquirit eundo (It gains strength as it goes)

Aircraft Equipment	Period of Service	Example	
Fulmar II	Mar 1942 - Mar 1943	X8809	
Huricane I	Mar 1942	P2972	
Spitfire Vb/hooked	Feb 1943 - Mar 1943	AB190	
Seafire L.IIc	Mar 1943 - Feb 1944	LR641	(B)
Swordfish II	Jun 1943 - Oct 1943	HS547	(L)
Spitfire Vb/hooked	Feb 1944 - Mar 1944	AA964	
Seafire L.III	Mar 1944 - Jul 1944	NF537	

Battle Honours
Salerno 1943
Normandy 1944

Squadron bases
Donibristle	15 Mar 1942
St Merryn	23 May 1942
Yeovilton	22 Jun 1942
Charlton Horethorne	10 Jul 1942
Turnhouse (13 Gp)	11 Aug 1942
Peterhead (14 Gp)	13 Aug 1942
Stretton	7 Oct 1942
Machrihanish	24 Oct 1942
Belfast	5 Dec 1942
Turnhouse	1 Jan 1943
Eglinton	1-15 Jun 1943
(Dt - 'B' Flt)	
Machrihanish	15 Jun 1943
HMS Attacker	19 Jun 1943
Machrihanish	21 Jun 1943
HMS Attacker	12 Jul 1943
North Front	9 Aug 1943
HMS Attacker	31 Aug 1943
Paestum (Dt 2)	12-26 Sep 1943
North Front	9 Aug 1943
(Dt - 'Z' Flt) to	1 Oct 1943
Machrihanish	6 Oct 1943
Burscough	7 Oct 1943
HMS Ravager (DLT)	4 Dec 1943
Burscough	8 Dec 1943
HMS Attacker	29 Dec 1943
Andreas (transit)	6 Feb 1944
Burscough	7 Feb 1944
Lee-on-Solent	25 Feb 1944
Henstridge	11 Mar 1944
St Merryn	25 Apr 1944
Henstridge	4 May 1944
Ayr	6 May 1944
Dundonald	13 May 1944
Lee-on-Solent	20 May 1944
Squadron disbanded	19 Jul 1944

Commanding Officers
Lt JCM Harman RN 15 Mar 1942
L/C(A) RHHL Oliphant RN 27 Jul 1942
L/C PEI Bailey RN 28 Oct 1943
Squadron disbanded 19 Jul 1944

No.886 Squadron formed at Donibristle on 15 March 1942 as a Fleet Fighter squadron equipped with six Fulmar IIs. It was initially categorised as a supernumerary unit, spending a period with RAF Fighter Command before re-equipping in March 1943 with nine Seafire L.IICs. In June a Swordfish element of six aircraft was added when a new 'Z' Flight formed from the disbanding No.837 Squadron. No.886 then embarked in HMS *Attacker*, and after sailing for the Mediterranean provided cover in September for the Salerno landings, two aircraft being put ashore at Paestum for anti-submarine patrols. During this period the Swordfish undertook anti-submarine patrols from Gibraltar. The Swordfish were discarded on returning to the UK in October, and the squadron then joined the 3rd Naval Fighter Wing. In February 1944 special training was received in spotting and reconnaissance, at Lee-on-Solent, using Spitfires until 10 new Seafire L.IIIs arrived in March. From D-Day No.885 operated as part of the Air Spotting Pool of No.34 Reconnaissance Wing, 2nd Tactical Air Force, undertaking bombardment spotting, offensive sweeps, escort and anti-submarine patrols. On 19 July 1944 it was absorbed into No.885 Squadron.

Identification Markings
Fulmar believed uncoded; Seafire single letters, to 2A+ by 6.44; Spitfire 3A+; Swordfish single letters.

A lucky escape during the Salerno landings in July 1943. Sub-Lt J.A.Luke in Swordfish II HS547 '1L' of No.886 Squadron bounced over the barrier in a semi-stalled condition, missing by six inches another Swordfish which had landed half a minute earlier. (via Ray Williams)

No.887 Squadron

Badge: On a blue field, over a base barry wavy of eight white and blue in front of a sword pointing downwards gold a globe white winged also gold
Motto: Believed none

Supermarine Seafire III 'H5S' of No.887 Squadron pulls a wire out during deck landing practice on HMS Ravager on 30 May 1945.

No.887 Squadron formed at Lee-on-Solent on 1 May 1942 as a Fleet Fighter squadron. Equipped with six Fulmar IIs, it was earmarked for service in an escort carrier, being re-equipped in December with six Spitfire Vs pending the arrival of Seafires. After using IBs for a short period, nine Seafire IICs arrived in March 1943, and with these No.887 embarked in HMS *Unicorn* the following month, sailing with a Malta convoy in May. In August the ship sailed again, for the Mediterranean, where the squadron provided fighter cover for the Salerno landings in September, two aircraft operating ashore for a time. In October No.887 became part of the 24th Naval Fighter Wing, joining HMS *Indefatigable* in July 1944 for action off Norway, including fighter cover during operations against the German battleship *Tirpitz*.

After a brief spell in HMS *Implacable*, the squadron rejoined HMS *Indefatigable* and sailed for Ceylon. Joining the British Pacific Fleet, attacks were made in January 1945 on Sumatra, and in March and April on the Sakishima Group of islands in the East China Seas, and also on Formosa. Shortly before VJ-Day it was in action over the Japanese mainland. Then followed a cruise to New Zealand in November, and after a few weeks in Australia the ship sailed home in January via the Cape, No.887 disbanding at Gosport on arrival on 15 March 1946.

Identification Markings
Fulmar unknown; Seafire *1A+* and *2A+*, to *P5A+* by 6.44, to *H5A+* by 12.44, to *111/S+* by 8.45.

Aircraft Equipment	Period of Service	Example
Fulmar I	Jun 1942	N1982
Fulmar II	May 1942 - Dec 1942	BP821
Spitfire Va	Dec 1942 - Apr 1943	P7964
Seafire IIc	Jan 1943 - Dec 1943	NM917 (2A)
Seafire F.III	Dec 1943 - Mar 1946	LR817 (P5H)
Seafire L.III	Dec 1943 - Mar 1946	PR295 (127/S)

Battle Honours
Atlantic	1943
Salerno	1943
Norway	1944
Palembang	1945
Okinawa	1945
Japan	1945

Squadron bases
Lee-on-Solent	1 May 1942
Yeovilton	1 Jun 1942
Charlton Horethorne	10 Jul 1942
St Merryn	25 Jul 1942
Dyce (14 Gp)	28 Jul 1942
Belfast	15 Oct 1942
Ballyhalbert	19 Oct 1942
Kirkistown	4 Nov 1942
Lee-on-Solent	19 Dec 1942
Machrihanish	21 Feb 1943
St Merryn	3 Mar 1943
Hatston	22 Mar 1943
Machrihanish	9 Apr 1943
HMS Unicorn	19 Apr 1943
Belfast	18 Jun 1943
HMS Unicorn	11 Jul 1943
Paestum (Dt)	12-15 Sep 1943
Andover (transit)	11 Oct 1943
Machrihanish	12 Oct 1943
Henstridge	13 Dec 1943
Burscough	8 Jan 1943
Ballyhalbert	6 Feb 1944
Eglinton	21 Mar 1944
Culmhead	18 Apr 1944
Ballyhalbert	15 May 1944
HMS Indefatigable (DLT)	23 May 1944
Eglinton	29 May 1944
Wick (transit)	4 Jul 1944
Skeabrae (transit)	6 Jul 1944
HMS Indefatigable	6 Jul 1944
Skeabrae (13 Gp)	24 Sep 1944
Grimsetter (transit)	16 Oct 1944
HMS Implacable	16 Oct 1944
Lee-on-Solent	30 Oct 1944
HMS Indefatigable	21 Nov 1944
Katukurunda	10 Dec 1944
HMS Indefatigable	24 Dec 1944
Schofields	10 Feb 1945
HMS Indefatigable	27 Feb 1945
Schofields	5 Jun 1945
HMS Indefatigable	7 Jul 1945
Schofields	18 Sep 1945
HMS Indefatigable	15 Nov 1945
Schofields	22 Dec 1945
HMS Indefatigable	31 Jan 1946
Gosport	15 Mar 1946
Squadron disbanded	15 Mar 1946

Commanding Officers
Lt GR Callingham RN	1 May 1942
L/C DW Kirke RN	29 Aug 1942
L/C(A) BF Wiggington DSC RNVR	4 Jan 1944
L/C(A) AJ Thomson DSC RNVR	19 Aug 1944
L/C NG Hallett DSC & Bar RN	14 May 1945
L/C(A) G Dennison RNVR	27 Sep 1945
Squadron disbanded	15 Mar 1946

Supermarine Seafire III NN212 '112/S' of No.887 Squadron pecks the deck after entering the barrier of HMS Indefatigable on 22 January 1946. (FAA Museum)

No.888 Squadron

Badge: On a blue field, a martlet white flying over water in base barry wavy, white and blue

Motto: Sine missione (No quarter)
[An earlier unapproved version has the martlet holding a vertical bomb in its claws, with the motto 'Nullo missio']

No.888 Squadron formed at Lee-on-Solent on 1 November 1941 as a Fleet Fighter squadron with six Martlet Is, having re-equipped with 12 Martlet IIs by the New Year. Embarking in HMS *Formidable* in February 1942 it sailed for the Indian Ocean, where it provided cover in May for the Madagascar invasion forces, later undertaking reconnaissance of the outlying outlands for possible Japanese forces. Returning home in August, Martlet IVs began to arrive as partial replacement in October. The ship then sailed with the North African invasion forces, No.888 shooting down two enemy aircraft during the operation. Most of the next year was spent in the Mediterranean, including providing cover for the landings in Sicily in July and those at Salerno in September. Returning to the UK, the squadron disbanded on 16 November 1943 at Yeovilton.

On 10 June 1944 the squadron reformed as a single seater fighter unit at Burscough, equipped with six Hellcat II(PR)s. In September these were transported in HMS *Rajah* to Ceylon, where No.888 undertook photographic reconnaissance training sorties. At the end of the year it joined HMS *Indefatigable* for operations early in 1945 over Sumatra, then in February transferred to HMS *Empress* for PR sorties over the Kra Isthmus, Penang, Phuket Island and northern Sumatra at heights of between 30,000 and 42,000 feet. Similar work was carried out over southern Malaya in April from HMS *Emperor*, and in the same areas from HMS *Ameer* in June. After VJ-Day, the squadron retained its basic role, being employed on air survey work under the control of Air Command South East Asia, taking passage home in June 1946 to disband on arrival in August.

Battle Honours
North Africa 1942
Sicily 1943
Salerno 1943

Identification Markings
Martlet single letters, to Ø7A+ on *Formidable* for Operation *Torch* 10.42, later 7A+.

Aircraft Equipment	Period of Service	Example
Martlet I	Nov 1941 - Jan 1942	BJ522
Martlet II	Dec 1941 - Sep 1943	AJ148 (Ø7A)
Martlet IV	Oct 1942 - Nov 1943	FN229 (7B)
Hellcat II(PR)	Jun 1944 - Jun 1946	JX876

Squadron bases		Squadron bases	
HMS Formidable	11 Mar 1943	Ratmalana (Dt)	23-24 Apr 1942
Tafaroui (Dt3)	12-25 Mar 1943	Port Reitz	10-29 May 1942
Lee-on-Solent	1 Nov 1941	Port Reitz (Dt)	1-15 Jul 1942
Machrihanish (Dt3)	15 Dec 1941	Ratmalana (Dt)	28-30 Jul 1942
	to 11 Jan 1942	Port Reitz	11 Aug 1942
St Merryn	29 Dec 1941	HMS Formidable	24 Aug 1942
Lee-on-Solent	12 Jan 1942	Donibristle	21 Sep 1942
Machrihanish	25 Jan 1942	Hatston	8 Oct 1942
HMS Formidable	4 Feb 1942	HMS Formidable	20 Oct 1942
Wynberg (Dt)	10-12 Mar 1942	North Front (Dt)	6-10 Dec 1942
China Bay (Dt)	24-30 Mar 1942	La Senia (Dt)	11-24 Dec 1942

Grumman Martlet II AJ104 'P' of No.888 Squadron landing on HMS Formidable in the Indian Ocean during 1942. (via Pat Chambers)

A formation of Grumman Hellcat II(PR)s of No.888 Squadron flying over the jungle. (via Brian MacCaw)

Squadron bases

North Front (Dt)	5-12 Jan 1943
La Senia	14 Jan 1943
HMS Formidable	7 Feb 1943
North Front	8 Feb 1943
North Front (Dt2)	26 Mar 1943 to 4 Apr 1943
Tafaroui (Dt)	8-14 Apr 1943
North Front (Dt)	15-19 Apr 1943
North Front (Dt)	20-29 Apr 1943
Tafaroui (Dt)	30 Apr 1943 to 3 May 1943
North Front (Dt)	7-28 May 1943
Tafaroui	3 Jun 1943
HMS Formidable	14 Jun 1943
North Front	15-28 Jun 1943
(Dt - 'Black Flight')	
Ta Kali (Dt8)	17 Jul 1943 to 21 Aug 1943
Dekheila	22 Aug 1943
HMS Formidable	28 Aug 1943
Ta Kali	30 Aug 1943
HMS Formidable	5 Sep 1943
HMS Unicorn (Dt)	11-12 Sep 1943
Ta Kali	12 Sep 1943
HMS Formidable	20 Sep 1943
Machrihanish	18 Oct 1943
HMS Formidable	8 Nov 1943
Hatston (Dt)	8-12 Nov 1943
Machrihanish	13 Nov 1943
Yeovilton	14 Nov 1943
Squadron disbanded	16 Nov 1943
Burscough	10 Jun 1944
Belfast	7 Sep 1944
HMS Rajah	9 Sep 1944
China Bay	11 Oct 1944
Cochin	19 Oct 1944
Colombo Racecourse	23 Oct 1944
HMS Indefatigable	24 Dec 1944
Colombo Racecourse	7 Jan 1945
HMS Empress	7 Feb 1945
Colombo Racecourse	6 Mar 1945
HMS Khedive	1 Apr 1945
Colombo Racecourse	5 Apr 1945
HMS Emperor	8 Apr 1945
Colombo Racecourse	20 Apr 1945
HMS Shah	25 Apr 1945
Colombo Racecourse	9 May 1945
HMS Empress	31 May 1945
Colombo Racecourse	4 Jun 1945
HMS Ameer	13 Jun 1945
Colombo Racecourse	25 Jun 1945
Katukurunda	7 Sep 1945
HMS Smiter	16 Dec 1945
Sembawang	27 Dec 1945
passage to UK	29 Jun 1946
Sqdn disbanded UK	Aug 1946

Commanding Officers

Capt FDG Bird RM	1 Nov 1941
L/C M Hordern RN	22 Oct 1943
Squadron disbanded	16 Nov 1943
L/C(A) L Mann RNVR	10 Jun 1944
L/C(A) BA MacCaw DSC RNVR	20 Mar 1945
L/C(A) JA Young RNVR	28 Oct 1945
None	29 Jun 1946
Squadron disbanded	Aug 1946

Grumman Hellcat II(PR)s of No.888 Squadron being manhandled on the deck of HMS Indefatigable before the attack on oil refineries at Pangkalan Brandan, Sumatra on 4 January 1945. (FAA Museum)

No.889 Squadron

No.889 Squadron formed from the RN Fighter Flight at Fuka South on 16 March 1942. Equipped with 12 Fulmar IIs, it carried out shipping protection and Canal Zone defence, including night fighting. For the latter, each squadron engaged in this work was allocated to one of a series of ground beacons along the North African coast, the theory being that any aircraft seen during an alert must be an enemy and should therefore be attacked, though No.889 had no such success. Operations were carried out under the control of RAF No.234 Wing, until transferring to No.252 Wing in June, shortly before the squadron moved to Fayid. Two flights went to Syria to operate with No.250 Wing, returning in October and November to partially re-equip with seven borrowed RAF Hurricane IICs. Operations were then carried out in the Western Desert until disbanding at El Daba on 28 February 1943.

On 1 April 1944, No.889 reformed at Colombo Racecourse as a Fighter squadron equipped with 10 Seafire L.IICs and F.IIIs. In May it embarked in HMS *Atheling* for an offensive sweep in the Bay of Bengal, but having lost several of its pilots in accidents, including the original CO, it disbanded at Puttalam on 11 July 1944.

Reformed on 1 June 1945 at Woodvale with six Hellcat Is and II(PR)s, it was intended for the British Pacific Fleet, embarking in HMS *Trouncer* on 10 September 1945, but orders were changed, and it disembarked to Ayr the following day and immediately disbanded.

Identification Markings
Fulmar and Hurricane believed uncoded; Seafire single letters; Hellcat, believed single letters.

A Fairey Fulmar of No.889 Squadron. (Stuart Jewers)

Aircraft Equipment	Period of Service	Example
Fulmar II	Mar 1942 - Feb 1943	DR705
Hurricane IIc	Oct 1942 - Feb 1943	HL767
Seafire L.IIc	Apr 1944 - Jul 1944	MB179
Seafire LR.IIc	Apr 1944 - Jul 1944	LR699
Seafire F.III	Apr 1944 - Jul 1944	LR807
Hellcat I	Jun 1945 - Sep 1945	FN377
Hellcat II(PR)	Jun 1945 - Sep 1945	JZ897

Squadron bases
Fuka Satt (LG.16) 16 Mar 1942
Dekheila 21 Jun 1942
Fayid 1 Jul 1942
Hurghada ('A' Flt) 5 Jul 1942
  to 24 Nov 1942
Abu Zenima ('B'Flt) 8 Jul 1942
  to 15 Oct 1942
Ras Gharib('B'Flt) 15 Oct 1942
  to 24 Nov 1942
Rayak (Base Party) 17 Jul 1942
  to 31 Aug 1942
LG.20 (Nr El Daba) 25 Nov 1942
LG.104 (El Daba) 18 Dec 1942
Squadron disbanded 28 Feb 1943
Colombo Racecourse 1 Apr 1944
HMS Atheling 13 May 1944
Puttalam 30 Jun 1944
Squadron disbanded 11 Jul 1944
Woodvale 1 Jun 1945
HMS Ravager (DLT) 10 Aug 1945
Belfast 12 Aug 1945
Woodvale 28 Aug 1945
HMS Trouncer 10 Sep 1945
Ayr - disbanded 11 Sep 1945

Commanding Officers
L/C(A) AR Ramsey
  DSC RNVR 16 Mar 1942
L/C(A) RE Gardner
  DSC RNVR 18 Jul 1942
Squadron disbanded 28 Feb 1943
L/C(A) FAJ
  Pennington RNZNVR 1 Apr 1944
L/C JB Edmundson
  RN 24 Apr 1944
L/C DAE Holbrook
  RN 11 Jun 1944
Squadron disbanded 11 Jul 1944
Lt(A) ND Fisher
  RNVR 1 Jun 1945
Squadron disbanded 11 Sep 1945

Hawker Hurricane IIb BN688 of No.889 Squadron, on loan from the RAF, at readiness in the desert in 1942. (Sir Edward Singleton)

No.890 Squadron

Badge: On a white field, issuant from water barry wavy in base blue and white, a knight in armour to the sinister holding in his hands a broom proper; a chief wavy blue

Motto: *Caelum verrimus*
(We sweep the sky)

No.890 Squadron assembled on 20 May 1942 at Eastleigh, Southampton for passage, officially forming at Dartmouth, Nova Scotia as a single seater fighter squadron on 15 June. Moving to Norfolk, Va the squadron initially received a number of US Navy F4F-3s, known to the Royal Navy as Martlet IIIs. In September these gave way to six Martlet IVs, which after work-up embarked in HMS *Battler* for the UK, where 'A' Flight of No.881 Squadron was absorbed. After further training the squadron joined HMS *Illustrious* in June 1943, carrying out patrols off Iceland and Norway. This was followed in August by a spell in the Mediterranean with Force H, support being provided in September for the Salerno landings. After returning home, No.890 re-equipped with ten Wildcat Vs, the personnel then joining HMS *London* in February for Ceylon, only to disband at Puttalam on 1 August 1944.

On 30 January 1952 the squadron reformed at Ford as a fighter squadron, but it was not until 22 April that it commissioned with eight Attacker F.1s, its main task being to act as a pool to provide pilots and aircraft as required to Nos.800 and 803 Squadron. In October 1952 it embarked in HMS *Eagle*, but disbanded aboard her on 3 December 1952, the aircraft being dispersed amongst the other two squadrons.

The number was next taken up when No.890 reformed at Yeovilton on 20 March 1954 as an All-Weather Fighter squadron. Equipped with nine Sea Venom FAW.20s, it embarked in HMS *Albion* in July 1955, but was relegated to second-line status on 18 October 1955, becoming No.766 Squadron.

No.890 next reformed at Yeovilton on 1 February 1956, again as an All-Weather Fighter squadron, equipped this time with six Sea Venom FAW.21s. It disbanded into No.893 Squadron on 25 June 1956 after losing two of its crews in accidents, including the CO.

The squadron again reformed at Yeovilton on 1 February 1960 in the All-Weather Fighter capacity, this time with ten Sea Vixen FAW.1s. These joined HMS *Hermes* in July, being initially in the Mediterranean before sailing on the Far East. Returning in May 1961, the squadron transferred in November to HMS *Ark Royal* for a further spell in the Mediterranean. Returning home early in 1962, it rejoined her in March and sailed by way of the Mediterranean to the Far East, visiting Australia in August, to arrive back at Yeovilton for Christmas.

A third voyage in HMS *Ark Royal* during 1963 included some weeks in the Indian Ocean, with visits to Aden and Mombasa, as well as a detachment to Nairobi before sailing on to the Far East. Again returning at the end of the year, most of 1964 was spent ashore, apart from brief periods in HMS *Hermes* and HMS *Eagle*. A detachment rejoined HMS *Ark Royal* when she recommissioned in November 1965, for catapult and arrester wire trials, then after a brief spell in Home waters No.890 joined the ship on the Beira patrol off the coast of Mozambique before she sailed on once again to the Far East. Several more spells were spent on the Beira patrol in 1966, but No.890 disbanded at Yeovilton on 7 October 1966.

On 14 August 1967 the squadron again reformed at Yeovilton as an All-Weather Fighter squadron, with six Sea Vixen FAW.2s for operational trials and operational training on this type. From December 1969 its aircraft were maintained by Airwork, then on 10 December 1970 its Fleet Requirements Unit and tanking tasks were handed over to the locally based Airwork FRU, which also took over the Sea Vixens in replacement for its own ageing Sea Venoms. No.890 then absorbed the aircraft of No.766 Squadron to operate for a time as the Sea Vixen FAW.2 Headquarters squadron, but on 6 August 1971 it disbanded at Yeovilton.

Battle Honours
Salerno   1943

Grumman F4F-3 F-25 of the US Navy on loan to No.890 Squadron at Norfolk in 1942. (C.S.Nell)

Supermarine Attacker FB.2 WK320 '151/J' of No.890 Squadron after a belly landing at Milltown on 22 October 1952. (R.G.Dennison)

Identification Markings
Martlet/Wildcat individual letters; Attacker *105-119, 141-147/J*; Sea Venom FAW.20 *200-208/VL:Z*, FAW.21 *350-356/O*; Sea Vixen *240-254/H:R*, to *001-104/R* 6.65, *750-755/VL* from 8.67, to *701-706/VL* 1.71.

Aircraft Equipment	Period of Service	Example
F4F-3	Jun 1942 - Sep 1942	BuAer3856
Martlet IV	Sep 1942 - Oct 1943	FN228 (C)
Wildcat V	Oct 1943 - Jul 1944	JV435 (S)
Attacker F.1	Apr 1952 - Oct 1952	WA513 (118/J)
Attacker FB.1	Jul 1925 - Oct 1952	WA532 (106)
Attacker FB.2	Jul 1952 - Dec 1952	WK326 (146/J)
Sea Venom FAW.20	Mar 1954 - Oct 1955	WM513 (204/VL)
Sea Vampire T.22	Aug 1954 - May 1955	XA158
Sea Venom FAW.21	Feb 1956 - Jun 1956	WW224 (355/O)
Sea Vixen FAW.1	Feb 1960 - Oct 1966	XN654 (250/R)
	Aug 1967 - Jul 1969	XN704 (750/VL)
Sea Vixen FAW.2	Aug 1967 - Jan 1971	XN658 (750/VL)
	Jan 1971 - Aug 1971	XP919 (706/VL)

Squadron bases		Squadron bases	
Dartmouth	15 Jun 1942	HMS Hermes	6 Jul 1960
Norfolk	26 Jun 1942	Hal Far	30 Jul 1960
USS Charger(Dt)	20-23 Aug 1942	HMS Hermes	9 Aug 1960
HMS Battler	8 Dec 1942	Lossiemouth	24 Aug 1960
Machrihanish (transit)	8 Jan 1943	HMS Hermes	11 Nov 1960
		Tengah	31 Dec 1960
Donibristle	8 Jan 1943	HMS Hermes	12 Jan 1961
Machrihanish	4 Mar 1943	Tengah (Dt3)	1-9 Feb 1961
HMS Argus (DLT)	5 Mar 1943	Yeovilton	8 May 1961
Donibristle	25 Mar 1943	HMS Hermes	29 May 1961
Hatston	28 Mar 1943	Yeovilton	23 Jun 1961
Machrihanish	8 Jun 1943	HMS Hermes	30 Jun 1961
HMS Illustrious	14 Jun 1943	Yeovilton	10 Sep 1961
Port Ellen (15 Gp)	18 Oct 1943	HMS Ark Royal	13 Nov 1961
Eglinton	13 Dec 1943	Hal Far (Dt6)	16 Dec 1961
Donibristle	29 Jan 1944		to 2 Jan 1962
HMS London(transit)	17 Feb 1944	Yeovilton	13 Jan 1962
Puttalam	14 Mar 1944	HMS Ark Royal	10 Mar 1962
HMS Atheling	13 May 1944	Tengah (Dt4)	28 Jun 1962
Puttalam	11 Jul 1944		to 12 Jul 1962
Squadron disbanded	1 Aug 1944	Tengah (Dt6)	26 Jul 1962
Ford	30 Jan 1952		to 6 Aug 1962
HMS Illustrious (DLP)	9 Jul 1952	Pearce	18 Aug 1962
		HMS Ark Royal	30 Aug 1962
Ford	12 Jul 1952	Tengah (Dt5)	13-28 Sep 1962
Culdrose	9 Sep 1952	Yeovilton	14 Dec 1962
Ford	1 Sep 1952	HMS Ark Royal	19 Feb 1963
Milltown	27 Oct 1952	Yeovilton	14 Mar 1963
HMS Eagle	29 Oct 1952	HMS Ark Royal	4 May 1963
Squadron disbanded	3 Dec 1952	Embakasi (Dt6)	7-19 Jun 1963
Yeovilton	20 Mar 1954	Tengah	10 Jul 1963
HMS Bulwark (DLP)	15 May 1955	HMS Ark Royal	25 Jul 1963
Yeovilton	26 May 1955	Tengah (Dt6)	6-27 Aug 1963
HMS Albion	19 Jul 1955	Embakasi (Dt6)	18 Oct 1963
Yeovilton	12 Sep 1955		to 1 Nov 1963
Redes 766 Sqdn	18 Oct 1955	Yeovilton	28 Dec 1963
Yeovilton	1 Feb 1956	HMS Hermes	16 Jan 1964
Lossiemouth	23 Apr 1956	Yeovilton	30 Jan 1964
Yeovilton	11 May 1956	HMS Eagle (DLP)	6-7 Nov 1964
HMS Bulwark (DLP)	30 May 1956	HMS Ark Royal	12 Jan 1965
Yeovilton	6 Jun 1956	Lossiemouth (Dt5)	13 Feb 1965
Squadron disbanded	25 Jun 1956	Yeovilton	18 Mar 1965
Yeovilton	1 Feb 1960	HMS Ark Royal	14 May 1965

de Havilland Sea Venom FAW.21 WW223 '356/O' of No.890 Squadron displays the squadron's black witch-on-a-broomstick motif on the nose in 1953. (via Brain Lowe)

de Havilland Sea Venom FAW.21s of No.890 Squadron in 1956 have black and yellow chequered wing tanks and black fin bullets in addition to the black witch nose motif. (via Brian Lowe)

Commanding Officers
L/C JW Sleigh
    DSC RN   15 Jun 1942
L/C NA Bartlett RN 4 Nov 1943
Squadron disbanded 1 Aug 1944
L/C RW Kearsley
    RN   30 Jan 1952
Squadron disbanded 3 Dec 1952
L/C A Gordon
    -Johnson RN 20 Mar 1954
Squadron disbanded 18 Oct 1955
L/C PS Brewer RN   1 Feb 1956
Squadron disbanded 25 Jun 1956
L/C WR Hart AFC
    RN   1 Feb 1960
L/C D Monsell RN 11 Sep 1961
Lt RGM Campbell
    RN   15 Jul 1963
L/C AMG Pearson
    RN   15 Apr 1965
Squadron disbanded 7 Oct 1966
L/C MF Kennett RN 14 Aug 1967
L/C WR Patterson
    RN   2 Feb 1968
L/C MJ Bateman RN 6 Jan 1969
L/C F Milner RN   23 Jan 1970
L/C PR Sheppard RN 14 Jan 1971
Squadron disbanded 6 Aug 1971

Squadron bases
Yeovilton	27 May 1965
HMS Ark Royal	15 Jun 1965
Changi	19 Jul 1965
HMS Ark Royal	4 Aug 1965
Changi	3 Sep 1965
HMS Ark Royal	18 Sep 1965
Changi	20 Oct 1965
Butterworth	10 Nov 1965
HMS Ark Royal	7 Dec 1965
Changi	7 Jan 1966
HMS Ark Royal	27 Jan 1966
Changi	15 Mar 1966
HMS Ark Royal	24 Mar 1966
Changi	23 Apr 1966
HMS Ark Royal	26 Apr 1966
Yeovilton	12 Jun 1966
HMS Ark Royal	2 Aug 1966
Yeovilton	1 Oct 1966
Squadron disbanded	7 Oct 1966
Yeovilton	14 Aug 1967
Akrotiri	16 Apr 1968
Yeovilton	29 Apr 1968
Lossiemouth	17 Mar 1971
Yeovilton	26 Mar 1971
Karup (13 days)	3 May 1971
Yeovilton	13 May 1971
Squadron disbanded	6 Aug 1971

de Havilland Sea Vixen FAW.2 XJ604 '755' of No.890 Squadron in 1970. (MAP)

No.891 Squadron

Badge: On a white field, in base three bars wavy blue, a reproduction of the Polynesian god Kon Tiki, red and gold

Motto: Venamur ut necemus
(We search (hunt) in order that we may kill)

No.891 Squadron formed at Lee-on-Solent on 1 July 1942 as a single seater fighter squadron equipped with six Sea Hurricane IBs. Initially intended for HMS *Stalker*, this was not available by the time the squadron was needed for the North African landings, and so instead the squadron embarked in October in HMS *Dasher*, with six Sea Hurricane IICs, to provide fighter patrols over the invasion beaches. Strength was increased to nine aircraft in December, and in February 1943 the ship joined the Home Fleet. No.891 then sailed with her to Iceland, but a further trip by three squadron aircraft two months later ended in disaster when the carrier blew up in the Clyde on 27 March with heavy loss of life. As a consequence the squadron disbanded on 5 April 1943.

On 1 June 1945 No.891 reformed at Eglinton, as a single seater night fighter squadron with 16 Hellcat II(NF)s, only to disband at Nutts Corner on 24 September 1945.

The squadron reformed at Yeovilton on 8 November 1954, this time as an all-weather fighter squadron with initial equipment of two Sea Venom FAW.20s and four Sea Vampire T.22s. Sea Venom strength was up to nine by the New Year, and 'X' Flight formed on 1 March 1955 to train Royal Australian Navy crews on the type pending formation of No.808 RAN Squadron on 10 August 1955. No.891 spent a few weeks in HMS *Ark Royal* in the Mediterranean early in 1956, but disbanded at Yeovilton on 17 April 1956.

On 3 September 1956 No.891 reformed as an FAW squadron at Yeovilton with eight Sea Venom FAW.21s. From November, Merryfield was used as the shore base due to reconstruction of Yeovilton's runways. Embarking in HMS *Bulwark* in March 1957 the squadron spent several periods afloat in Home waters, then in April 1958 sailed for a spell in the Far East, returning via Aden. Transferring to HMS *Centaur*, it sailed again for the Far East in June 1959, visiting Australia in November. Arriving home again in April 1960, it was based mostly at Yeovilton, apart from a Norwegian visit in September 1960, until disbanding there on 27 July 1961.

Battle Honours
North Africa   1942

Identification Markings
Sea Hurricane unknown; Hellcat uncoded; Sea Venom *281-283*, to *435-444/O* 9.56; Sea Venom FAW.20 *221-233?*, FAW.21/2 *435-444/B:C*.

Aircraft Equipment	Period of Service	Example
Sea Hurricane Ib	Jul 1942 - Oct 1942	V6555
Sea Hurricane IIc	Oct 1942 - Apr 1943	JS318
Hellcat I	Jun 1945 - Aug 1945	JV196
Hellcat IINF	Aug 1945 - Sep 1945	JZ912
Sea Vampire T.22	Nov 1954 - Jan 1955	XA162
Sea Venom FAW.20	Nov 1954 - Jun 1955	WM552
Sea Venom FAW.21	Jun 1955 - Apr 1956	WW137 (437/O)
	Sep 1956 - Dec 1957	XG624 (439/B)
Sea Venom FAW.22	Dec 1957 - Jul 1961	XG691 (436/C)

891X

Aircraft Equipment	Period of Service	Example
Sea Venom FAW.20	Mar 1955 - Aug 1955	WM500 (200)
Vampire FB.5	Mar 1955 - May 1955	VZ192

Hellcat II(NF) JZ912 of No.891 Sqdn after its port oleo collapsed while landing at Nutts Corner on 3 September 1945. (George Standley)

de Havilland Sea Venom FAW.22 WW296 '444' of No.891 Squadron, seen here in 1956, was a conversion from an FAW.21. (via Brian Lowe)

Squadron bases

Lee-on-Solent	1 Jul 1942
Charlton Horethorne	11 Aug 1942
St Merryn	9 Sep 1942
Belfast	8 Oct 1942
HMS Argus	12 Oct 1942
HMS Dasher	15 Oct 1942
Donibristle	18 Nov 1942
Machrihanish	10 Dec 1942
HMS Dasher	25 Jan 1943
Hatston	26 Feb 1943
Machrihanish	22 Mar 1943
HMS Dasher (Dt3)	22-27 Mar 1943
Squadron disbanded	5 Apr 1943
Eglinton	1 Jun 1945
Nutts Corner	11 Aug 1945
Squadron disbanded	24 Sep 1945
Yeovilton	8 Nov 1954
(891X Flt formed	1 Mar 1955)
HMS Ark Royal (DLP)	14 Jul 1955
Yeovilton	5 Jul 1955
Hal Far	5 Jan 1956
HMS Ark Royal	7 Jan 1956
Hal Far	10 Jan 1956
Yeovilton	26 Mar 1956
Squadron disbanded	17 Apr 1956
Yeovilton	3 Sep 1956
Lossiemouth	19 Nov 1956
Merryfield	30 Nov 1956
Brawdy	2 Mar 1957
Merryfield	14 Mar 1957
Lossiemouth	21 May 1957
Merryfield	28 May 1957
HMS Bulwark	25 Jun 1957
Merryfield	19 Aug 1957
HMS Bulwark	28 Aug 1957
Merryfield	2 Nov 1957
HMS Bulwark	14 Nov 1957
Merryfield	27 Nov 1957
HMS Bulwark	12 Jan 1958
North Front	26 Mar 1958
HMS Bulwark	7 Apr 1958
Kai Tak	17 May 1958
HMS Bulwark	3 Jun 1958
Khormaksar	31 Jul 1958
HMS Bulwark	4 Aug 1958
Khormaksar	10 Aug 1958
HMS Bulwark	20 Aug 1958
Khormaksar (Dt)	28 Aug 1958 to 8 Sep 1958
Hal Far	24 Oct 1958
Orange (transit)	27 Oct 1958
Yeovilton	28 Oct 1958
HMS Centaur	23 Jan 1959
Hal Far	20 Mar 1959
HMS Centaur	3 Mar 1959
Yeovilton	23 Mar 1959
HMS Centaur	29 Apr 1959
Hal Far	13 Jun 1959
HMS Centaur	21 Jun 1959
Khormaksar (Dt2)	3-9 Sep 1959
Drigh Road	31 Jul 1959
HMS Centaur	11 Aug 1959
Seletar	5 Sep 1959
HMS Centaur	30 Oct 1959
Seletar (Dt4)	21 Jan 1960 to 4 Feb 1960
Yeovilton	25 Apr 1960
HMS Centaur (Dt for radar jamming trials) to	31 May 1960 2 Jun 1960
HMS Centaur	12 Jun 1960
Yeovilton	22 Jul 1960
Lossiemouth (Dt6)	8-9 Sep 1960
Bodø	24 Sep 1960
Sola	1 Oct 1960
Yeovilton	3 Oct 1960
Lossiemouth	27 Jan 1961
Yeovilton	25 Feb 1961
Culdrose	21 Mar 1961
Yeovilton	24 Mar 1961
Squadron disbanded	27 Jul 1961

Commanding Officers

Lt(A) MJS Newman RN	1 Jul 1942
Lt(A) BHStAH Hurle-Hobbs RN	12 Mar 1943
Lt ON Bailey RN	19 Mar 1943
Squadron disbanded	5 Apr 1943
L/C N Perrett RNZNVR	1 Jun 1945
Squadron disbanded	24 Sep 1945
L/C MA Birrell DSC RN	8 Nov 1954
Squadron disbanded	17 Apr 1956
L/C IJ Brown RN	3 Sep 1956
L/C WGB Black RN	5 Dec 1957
L/C JF Blunden RN	9 Dec 1957
L/C LA Jeyes RN	1 Sep 1958
L/C JB Robathan RN	21 Jan 1960
L/C ML Brown RN	29 Aug 1960
Squadron disbanded	27 Jul 1961

891X

L/C GM Jude RAN	1 Mar 1955
Flight disbanded	10 Aug 1955

de Havilland Sea Venom FAW.22s of No.891 Squadron aboard HMS Centaur in 1960. (MAP)

No.892 Squadron

Badge: On a black field, above waves white and black in front of a flash of lightning an eye proper conjoined with two wings displayed gold

Motto: Strike unseen

No.892 Squadron formed at Norfolk, Va as a single seater fighter squadron on 15 July 1942. Equipped with six Martlet IVs, it was earmarked for HMS *Tracker*, but instead joined HMS *Battler* in December and sailed for the UK. In February 1943 it undertook convoy escort duties in HMS *Archer*, reducing to three aircraft in June, these being transferred to No.819 Squadron when No.892 disbanded aboard HMS *Archer* on 11 August 1943.

The squadron reformed at Eglinton on 1 April 1945 with 16 Hellcat IINFs, and after night fighter training at Drem joined HMS *Ocean* in December. On return from a spell in the Mediterranean it disbanded at Gosport on 19 April 1946.

On 4 July 1955 No.892 reformed at Yeovilton as an all-weather fighter squadron equipped with eight Sea Venom FAW.21s. Embarking in HMS *Albion* in January 1956 for the Mediterranean and Far East, the ship returned home in May. In July the squadron flew out to Malta, to join HMS *Eagle* the following month, attacking Egyptian airfields during the Suez operations. On 26 December 1956 it was absorbed by No.893 Squadron aboard HMS *Eagle*.

The squadron reformed at Yeovilton on 1 July 1959 out of No.700Y Flight with 12 Sea Vixen FAW.1s. Four of these broke away as a separate 'B' Flight in November 1959, to act as an Intensive Flying Trials Unit for the evaluation of Firestreak missiles. 'A' Flight embarked in HMS *Ark Royal* in March 1960 for an exercise in the Mediterranean, where it was joined in August by 'B' Flight to be reunited. Returning home, No.892 transferred in October to HMS *Victorious* for the remainder of this lengthy exercise, then in New Year sailed for the Far East, returning home in December 1961. Transferred to HMS *Hermes* in May 1962 for a further spell in the Far East, the squadron again returned home briefly, then sailed back to the Eastern waters in HMS *Centaur* in December 1963. From July 1965, No.892 was shore based at Yeovilton for almost a year, gradually re-equipping from December with 12 Sea Vixen FAW.2s. It joined HMS *Hermes* with these in September 1966, making a further trip to the Far East the following year. It disbanded at Yeovilton on 4 October 1968.

On 31 March 1969, No.892 reformed at Yeovilton from a nucleus of No.700P Squadron with Phantom FG.1s. Numerous periods were spent afloat in HMS *Ark Royal*, including a trip to the Mediterranean during 1972-1973, and visits to the Caribbean and the USA in 1975, 1976 and 1978. It finally disbanded on 15 December 1978.

Battle Honours
Atlantic 1943

Identification Markings
Martlet single letters; Hellcat *O5A+* later *5A+*; Sea Venom *251-258/Z*, to *445-452/J* 1.56; Sea Vixen *207-219/R:V:H:C*, later *301-314/H*; Phantom *001-017/H*

Aircraft Equipment	Period of Service	Example
F4F-3	Jul 1942 - Sep 1942	BuAer3868
Martlet IV	Sep 1942 - Aug 1943	FN246 (A)
Hellcat I	Apr 1945 - Jul 1945	JV213
Hellcat IINF	May 1945 - Apr 1946	JW879
Sea Venom FAW.21	Jul 1955 - Dec 1956	WW190 (258/Z)
Sea Vampire T.22	Sep 1955 - Feb 1956	XA130
Sea Vixen FAW.1	Jul 1959 - Dec 1965	XN695 (215/H)
Sea Vixen FAW.2	Dec 1965 - Oct 1968	XS588 (306/H)
Phantom FG.1	Mar 1969 - Dec 1978	XV566 (010/R)

Grumman Wildcat IV FN296 'A' of No.892 Squadron being catapulted from HMS Archer in 1943. (Dick Yeo)

de Havilland Sea Venom WW150 '253' of No.892 Squadron in 1956. (via Brian Lowe)

Squadron bases		Squadron bases		Squadron bases		Squadron bases	
Norfolk	15 Jul 1942	'A' Flight:		Kai Tak	1 Apr 1964	HMS Hermes	5-12 Jul 1966
HMS Battler	8 Dec 1942	HMS Ark Royal	3 Mar 1960	HMS Centaur	13 Apr 1964	(Dt3-DLP)	
Machrihanish	8 Jan 1943	Hal Far	1 May 1960	Tengah	30 Apr 1964	HMS Hermes	22 Sep 1966
HMS Archer	19 Feb 1943	HMS Ark Royal	23 May 1960	HMS Centaur	14 May 1964	Yeovilton	20 Oct 1966
Ballykelly	9 Apr 1943	HMS Ark Royal	1 Jul 1960	Embakasi	30 May 1964	HMS Hermes	8 Nov 1966
Machrihanish	23 Apr 1943	(remainder)		HMS Centaur	12 Jun 1964	Yeovilton	30 Nov 1966
'A' Flight (3 a/c):		Yeovilton	30 Sep 1960	Tengah	14 Jul 1964	HMS Hermes	19 Jan 1967
HMS Archer	28 Apr 1943	HMS Victorious	22 Oct 1960	HMS Centaur	24 Jul 1964	Hal Far	17 Mar 1967
Kaldadarnes	5 May 1943	Hal Far	5 Nov 1960	Tengah	14 Aug 1964	HMS Hermes	30 Mar 1967
HMS Archer	6 May 1943	HMS Victorious	15 Nov 1960	HMS Centaur	1 Sep 1964	Changi	24 Jun 1967
Machrihanish	26 May 1943	Lossiemouth	18 Dec 1960	Kai Tak	19 Sep 1964	HMS Hermes	17 Jul 1967
Abbotsinch (Sqdn)	12 Jun 1943	(transit)		HMS Centaur	14 Oct 1964	Yeovilton	29 Sep 1967
HMS Archer	15 Jun 1943	Yeovilton	19 Dec 1960	Yeovilton	19 Dec 1964	HMS Hermes	30 Oct 1967
Squadron disbanded	11 Aug 1943	HMS Victorious	21 Jan 1961	HMS Centaur	8 Apr 1965	Yeovilton	18 Feb 1968
Eglinton	1 Apr 1945	Tengah	29 Mar 1961	Hal Far	26 Apr 1965	Squadron disbanded	4 Oct 1968
HMS Premier	3 Jul 1945	HMS Victorious	12 Apr 1961	HMS Centaur	5 May 1965	Yeovilton	31 Mar 1969
Drem	6 Jul 1945	Tengah	8 May 1961	North Front	11 Jun 1965	USS Saratoga	18 Oct 1969
Machrihanish	2 Nov 1945	HMS Victorious	15 Jun 1961	HMS Centaur	26 Jun 1965	Yeovilton	24 Oct 1969
HMS Ocean	22 Nov 1945	Tengah (Dt4)	14 Sep 1961	Yeovilton	27 Jul 1965	HMS Ark Royal	30 Apr 1969
Lee-on-Solent	29 Nov 1945		to 6 Oct 1961	Brawdy (Exercise)	21 Aug 1965	(Dt3) to	15 May 1970
HMS Ocean	7 Dec 1945	Yeovilton	8 Dec 1961	Yeovilton	9 Sep 1965	HMS Ark Royal	14 Jun 1970
Hal Far	4 Jan 1946	HMS Victorious	9 Feb 1962				
HMS Ocean	18 Feb 1946	Yeovilton	30 Mar 1962				
Donibristle	16 Apr 1946	HMS Hermes	18 May 1962				
Gosport	19 Apr 1946	Hal Far (Dt5)	12-27 Jun 1962				
Squadron disbanded	19 Apr 1946	North Front	27 Jul 1962				
Yeovilton	4 Jul 1955		to 9 Aug 1962				
HMS Albion	10 Jan 1956	Hal Far	6 Sep 1962				
Yeovilton	14 May 1956	HMS Hermes	18 Sep 1962				
Hal Far	9 Jul 1956	Yeovilton	1 Oct 1962				
HMS Eagle	14 Aug 1956	HMS Hermes	13 Nov 1962				
Hal Far	24 Aug 1956	Tengah	20 Dec 1962				
HMS Eagle	4 Sep 1956	HMS Hermes	7 Jan 1963				
Hal Far	16 Sep 1956	Tengah	18 Mar 1963				
HMS Eagle	25 Sep 1956	HMS Hermes	24 Apr 1963				
Hal Far	30 Nov 1956	Tengah	12 Jun 1963				
HMS Eagle	11 Dec 1956	HMS Hermes	27 Jun 1963				
Squadron disbanded	26 Dec 1956	Yeovilton	11 Sep 1963				
Yeovilton	1 Jul 1959	HMS Hermes	27 Sep 1963				
HMS Victorious	13-23 Oct 1959	Yeovilton (Dt)	12 Oct 1963				
(Dt3 - DLT)		Yeovilton	21 Oct 1963				
'B' Flight (4 a/c)		HMS Centaur	21 Dec 1963				
- broke away as		Tengah	11 Feb 1964				
Firestreak IFTU	2 Nov 1959	HMS Centaur	8 Mar 1964				

de Havilland Sea Vixen FAW.2 XS589 '305/H' of No.892 Squadron landing on HMS Hermes in 1966. (via Brian Lowe)

McDonnell Douglas Phantom FG.1 XV592 '004/R' of No.892 Squadron aboard HMS Ark Royal around 1971. (via Brian Lowe)

Squadron bases			Squadron bases		Commanding Officers		Commanding Officers	
Yeovilton (Dt9)	9-20 Jul	1970	Leuchars	4 Nov 1974	Lt(A) RG French		L/C EJ Trounsen RN	17 Aug 1964
Yeovilton	30 Jul	1970	HMS Ark Royal	8 Jan 1975	RNVR	15 Jul 1942	L/C BG Young RN	24 Aug 1964
HMS Ark Royal	3 Sep	1970	Cecil Field	19 Feb 1975	Lt(A) K Firth RNVR	13 Dec 1942	L/C JNS Anderdon	
Yeovilton (Dt5)	25 Sep	1970	HMS Ark Royal	7 Mar 1975	Lt(A) JG Large		RN	8 Nov 1965
	to 10 Oct	1970	Cecil Field	3 Apr 1975	RNVR	1 Mar 1943	L/C S Idiens RN	19 May 1967
Yeovilton	15 Dec	1970	HMS Ark Royal	21 Apr 1975	Squadron disbanded 11 Aug 1943		Squadron disbanded	4 Oct 1968
HMS Ark Royal	20 Apr	1971	Lossiemouth	9 Jun 1975	Mjr JO Armour RM	1 Apr 1945	L/C B Davies	
Yeovilton	18 May	1971	Leuchars	24 Jul 1975	Squadron disbanded 19 Apr 1946		AFC RN	31 Mar 1969
HMS Ark Royal	2 Jun	1971	HMS Ark Royal	14-23 Sep 1975	L/C MHJ Petrie RN	4 Jul 1955	L/C NH Kerr RN	2 Oct 1970
Yeovilton	6 Aug	1971	(Dt4)		L/C WAM Ferguson		L/C CR Hunneyball	
HMS Ark Royal	15 Sep	1971	HMS Ark Royal	6 Oct 1975	RN	27 Nov 1956	RN	7 Jul 1972
Yeovilton	9 Oct	1971	Leuchars	25 Oct 1975	Squadron disbanded 26 Dec 1956		L/C WLT Peppe RN	7 Jan 1974
HMS Ark Royal	29 Oct	1971	HMS Ark Royal	27 Oct 1975	Cdr MHJ Petrie RN	1 Jul 1959	L/C HS Drake RN	10 Dec 1975
Yeovilton	6 Dec	1971	Leuchars	20 Nov 1975	L/C DMAH Hamilton		L/C NR Harris RN	31 Mar 1977
HMS Ark Royal	19 Jan	1972	HMS Ark Royal	6 Feb 1976	RN	18 Apr 1960	L/C JE Ellis RN	4 Oct 1977
Yeovilton	19 Mar	1972	Cecil Field	22 Mar 1976	L/C A Gray RN	1 Jun 1961	Squadron disbanded 15 Dec 1978	
Schleswig	28 Apr	1972	Point Mugu	8 Apr 1976	L/C IF Blake RN	8 Apr 1963		
Yeovilton	11 May	1972	Oceana	18 Apr 1976				
HMS Ark Royal	11 Jun	1972	HMS Ark Royal	6 May 1976				
Yeovilton	29 Jun	1972	Oceana	3 Jun 1976				
Leuchars	17 Jul	1972	HMS Ark Royal	14 Jun 1976				
HMS Ark Royal	3 Sep	1972	Leuchars	14 Jul 1976				
Leuchars	18 Oct	1972	HMS Ark Royal	4 Sep 1976				
HMS Ark Royal	7 Nov	1972	Leuchars	18 Oct 1976				
Leuchars	11 Dec	1972	Ramstein (Dt6)	18 Mar 1977				
HMS Ark Royal	25 Jan	1973		to 8 Apr 1977				
Luqa	23 Feb	1973	HMS Ark Royal	5 Sep 1977				
HMS Ark Royal	6 Mar	1973	Leuchars	7 Oct 1977				
Leuchars	14 Mar	1973	HMS Ark Royal	14 Oct 1977				
HMS Ark Royal	2 May	1973	Leuchars	12 Dec 1977				
Cecil Field	6 May	1973	HMS Ark Royal	22 Feb 1978				
HMS Ark Royal	30 Jun	1973	Leuchars	9 Mar 1978				
Leuchars	24 Jul	1973	HMS Ark Royal	4 Apr 1978				
HMS Ark Royal (Dt2)	18-29 Apr	1974	Roosevelt Roads (Dt6)	16-20 Apr 1978				
Leuchars	6 Jun	1974	Cecil Field	21 Jun 1978				
Leuchars	18 Jun	1974	HMS Ark Royal	8 Aug 1978				
HMS Ark Royal	4 Jul	1974	Oceana (Dt7)	13-20 Aug 1978				
Leuchars	26 Jul	1974	Sqdn disbanded UK 15 Dec 1978					
HMS Ark Royal	5 Sep	1974						

McDonnell Douglas Phantom FG.1s '003/R' and '007/R of No.892 Squadron taking off (via Brian Lowe)

No.893 Squadron

Badge: On a field per pale wavy blue and black, over water barry wavy in base white and blue a ray of lightning white winged gold issuant in bend sinister

Motto: *Saepe feriendum* (Strike often)

No.893 Squadron formed at Donibristle on 15 June 1942 as a single seater fighter squadron. Equipped with six Martlet Is, and also a small number of Fulmars as a temporary measure, it was intended for service in HMS *Archer*, but in the event joined HMS *Formidable* with ten Martlet IVs in October to provide fighter patrols during the North African landings, assisting in an attack on a U-boat during this period. Remaining in the area, patrols were carried out over the Mediterranean during the next few months, and in July 1943 patrols were carried out over the Sicily landings, a similar task being performed at Salerno in September. Shortly afterwards a change of climate saw No.893 assisting in the defence of a North Russian convoy, but on 16 November 1943 it disbanded on arrival back in the UK. Plans to reform with ten Corsairs at Brunswick on 1 February 1944 were abortive, as was a later proposal to reform with 16 Hellcat IINFs at Eglinton on 15 August 1945.

No.893 reformed as an all-weather fighter squadron at Yeovilton on 6 February 1956 with six Sea Venom FAW.21s intended for HMS *Ark Royal*. However, the Suez crisis brought a change of plan, and No.893 increased in June to nine aircraft by absorbing No.890 Squadron, taking part in operations from HMS *Eagle*. It was further increased in December by absorbing No.892 Squadron. Transferring to HMS *Ark Royal* in February 1957 in the Mediterranean, periods were also spent in Home waters and the Atlantic before transfer to HMS *Victorious* in the Mediterranean in September 1958. The squadron became the first with Sea Venoms equipped with Firestreak guided missiles, re-equipping in January 1959 with FAW.22s. It disbanded at Yeovilton on 29 February 1960.

On 9 September 1960, No.893 reformed at Yeovilton with six Sea Vixen FAW.1s, with which it flew out to join HMS *Ark Royal* in the Mediterranean two months later. By the time of the 1961 Kuwait crisis it was in HMS *Centaur*, later spending periods in both the Far East and the Mediterranean before transferring to HMS *Victorious* in August 1963 for a trip to the Far East and Australia. After return to the UK it disbanded at Yeovilton on 29 July 1965.

Equipped with 11 Sea Vixen FAW.2s, the squadron reformed at Yeovilton on 4 November 1965, embarking six months later in HMS *Victorious*. After a spell in the Far East the squadron returned home, and in May 1968 joined HMS *Hermes* for a further eastern trip. Periods were subsequently spent in the Mediterranean, but on 14 July 1970 No.893 disbanded.

Battle Honours
North Africa	1942-43
Sicily	1943
Salerno	1943
Arctic	1943

Identification Markings
Martlet *09A+* on *Formidable* for Operation *Torch*, later *9A+*; Sea Venom *090-099/O*, to *457-469/O:V:A:R* 9.57, to *255-259/V* 1960; Sea Vixen FAW.*1 455-464/C:V:R*, FAW.2 *244-257//H:V*.

Grumman Martlet IV FN121 '09Z' of No.893 Squadron in Operation Torch markings taking off from HMS Formidable in late 1942. (via Col F.D.G.Bird)

Grumman Martlet IV FN114 'Ø9F' of No.893 Squadron taking off from HMS Formidable in the Western Mediterranean around March-April 1943. (FAA Museum)

Aircraft Equipment	Period of Service	Example
Fulmar I	Jun 1942 - Sep 1942	X8713
Martlet I	Jun 1942 - Oct 1942	BJ515
Martlet II	Sep 1942 - Oct 1942	AM956
Martlet IV	Oct 1942 - Nov 1943	FN148 (Ø9C)
Sea Vampire T.22	Feb 1956 - Jul 1957	XA167 (944)
Sea Venom FAW.21	Feb 1956 - Jan 1959	WW218 (459/O)
Sea Venom FAW.22	Jan 1959 - Feb 1960	XG685 (259/V)
Sea Vixen FAW.1	Sep 1960 - Jul 1965	XN650 (456/C)
Sea Vixen FAW.2	Nov 1965 - Jul 1970	XN702 (242/H)

Squadron bases

Donibristle	15 Jun 1942
HMS Archer (Dt2)	1-13 Jul 1942
St Merryn	23 Aug 1942
Charlton Horethorne	9 Sep 1942
Hatston	6 Oct 1942
HMS Formidable	21 Oct 1942
North Front (Dt5)	5-12 Jan 1943
La Senia (Dt3)	14-21 Jan 1943
La Senia (Dt3)	3-7 Feb 1943
North Front (Dt3)	8 Feb 1943
to	12 Mar 1943
North Front (Dt3)	15-19 Apr 1943
Tafaroui (Dt)	6-14 Jun 1943
Dekheila	23 Aug 1943
HMS Formidable	28 Aug 1943
HMS Unicorn (Dt)	11-12 Sep 1943
Machrihanish	18 Oct 1943
HMS Formidable	29 Oct 1943
Machrihanish - Stretton-Yeovilton	13 Nov 1943
Squadron disbanded	16 Nov 1943-
Yeovilton	6 Feb 1956
HMS Bulwark	8 Jun 1956
Yeovilton	20 Jun 1956
Ciampino (transit)	10 Aug 1956
Hal Far	11 Aug 1956

Squadron bases

HMS Eagle	17 Aug 1956
Hal Far	24 Aug 1956
HMS Eagle	11 Sep 1956
Hal Far	14 Sep 1956
HMS Eagle	25 Sep 1956
North Front	13 Oct 1956
HMS Eagle	20 Oct 1956
Hal Far	30 Nov 1956
HMS Eagle	2 Dec 1956
Hal Far	24 Dec 1956
HMS Ark Royal	5 Feb 1957
Merryfield	25 Feb 1957
HMS Ark Royal	28 Aug 1957
Merryfield	26 Oct 1957
HMS Ark Royal	27 Jan 1958
Yeovilton	24 Jun 1958
HMS Victorious	25 Sep 1958
Hal Far	28 Nov 1958
HMS Victorious	9 Dec 1958
Yeovilton	13 Jan 1959
HMS Victorious	21 Feb 1959
Yeovilton	23 Mar 1959
HMS Victorious	5 May 1959
Yeovilton	9 Aug 1959
HMS Victorious	15 Sep 1959
Yeovilton	1 Oct 1959
Brawdy	6 Oct 1959

Squadron bases

Yeovilton	24 Oct 1959
HMS Victorious	30 Oct 1959
Yeovilton	14 Dec 1959
HMS Victorious	27 Jan 1960
Yeovilton	25 Feb 1960
Squadron disbanded	29 Feb 1960
Yeovilton	9 Sep 1960
HMS Victorious (Dt3)	27-29 Sep 1960
Hal Far	24 Nov 1960
HMS Ark Royal	25 Nov 1960
Hal Far (Dt3)	18 Dec 1960
to	6 Jan 1961
Yeovilton	28 Feb 1961
HMS Centaur	1 Apr 1961
Hal Far	29 Apr 1961
HMS Centaur	8 May 1961
North Front (Dt3)	14-30 Jun 1961
Khormaksar	12 Jul 1961
HMS Centaur	20 Jul 1961
Hal Far (Dt5)	27-29 Aug 1961
(to Yeovilton)	
Yeovilton	1 Sep 1961
HMS Centaur	20 Oct 1961
Hal Far	8 Nov 1961
HMS Centaur	27 Nov 1961
Tengah	2 Feb 1962
HMS Centaur	18 Feb 1962
Khormaksar (Dt4)	23-31 Mar 1962
Hal Far (Dt7)	17 Apr 1962
to	3 May 1962
Yeovilton	14 May 1962
HMS Centaur	22 Jun 1962
Yeovilton	5 Jul 1962
HMS Centaur	12 Jul 1962
North Front (Dt4)	29 Jul 1962
to	2 Aug 1962
Farnborough	27 Aug 1962

Squadron bases

Hal Far	20 Sep 1962
HMS Centaur	22 Sep 1962
Yeovilton	25 Oct 1962
Culdrose	13 Jan 1963
HMS Centaur	22 Jan 1963
Yeovilton	14 Feb 1963
HMS Centaur	21 Feb 1963
Khormaksar (Dt7)	5-18 Mar 1963
Embakasi (Dt6)	6-23 Apr 1963
Yeovilton	15 May 1963
HMS Victorious	14 Aug 1963
Tengah	25 Sep 1963
HMS Victorious	22 Oct 1963
Kai Tak (Dt4)	23 Oct 1963
to	7 Nov 1963
Tengah	16 Dec 1963
HMS Victorious	8 Jan 1964
Embakasi (Dt6)	7-22 Feb 1964
Tengah	18 Mar 1964
HMS Victorious	8 Apr 1964
Tengah	12 Jun 1964
HMS Victorious	19 Aug 1964
Tengah	21 Sep 1964
HMS Victorious	7 Dec 1964
Changi (Dt2)	26-27 May 1965
Yeovilton	22 Jul 1965
Sqdn disbanded UK	29 Jul 1965
Yeovilton	4 Nov 1965
HMS Victorious	14 May 1966
Yeovilton	9 Jun 1966
HMS Victorious	8 Jul 1966
Changi	15 Aug 1966
HMS Victorious	6 Sep 1966
Changi	9 Dec 1966
HMS Victorious	4 Jan 1967
Changi	15 Feb 1967
HMS Victorious	3 Mar 1967
Culdrose	13 Jun 1967

de Havilland Sea Venom FAW.21 WW139 '463/O of No.893 Squadron from HMS Ark Royal landing on USS Saratoga during cross-operating in October 1957. (via Brian Lowe)

Squadron bases

Boscombe Down	30 Jun 1967
Yeovilton	24 Aug 1967
Akrotiri	18 Apr 1968
Yeovilton	30 Apr 1968
HMS Hermes	31 May 1968
Yeovilton	20 Jun 1968
HMS Hermes	8 Jul 1968
Changi	29 Aug 1968
HMS Hermes	13 Jan 1969
Yeovilton	1 Apr 1969
HMS Hermes	25 Sep 1969
Yeovilton	27 Oct 1969
HMS Hermes	14 Nov 1969
Yeovilton	3 Dec 1969
HMS Hermes	14 Jan 1970
Luqa	16 Feb 1970
HMS Hermes	6 Mar 1970
Luqa	13 Apr 1970
HMS Hermes	4 May 1970
transit	17 Jun 1970
Yeovilton	22 Jun 1970
Squadron disbanded	14 Jul 1970

Commanding Officers

Lt(A) RG French RNVR	15 Jun 1942
L/C(A) RB Pearson RN	12 Sep 1943
L/C DRB Cosh RCNVR	11 Nov 1943
Squadron disbanded	16 Nov 1943
L/C MW Henley DSC RN	6 Feb 1956
L/C GJR Elgar RN	13 May 1957
L/C EVH Manuel RN	9 Jun 1958
Squadron disbanded	29 Feb 1960
L/C FD Stanley RN	9 Sep 1960
L/C KE Kemp RN	18 Dec 1962
L/C D Melhuish RN	1 Jul 1964
L/C JA Sanderson RN	26 Nov 1964
L/C R King RN	23 Jan 1965
Squadron disbanded	29 Jul 1965
L/C GP Carne RN	4 Nov 1965
L/C R McQueen RN	28 Sep 1967
L/C RC Sturgeon RN	31 May 1968
L/C TJ Bolt RN	2 Apr 1969
Squadron disbanded	14 Jul 1970

Snow covered Sea Vixen FAW.1 '466' of No.893 Squadron during a visit to Liverpool. (via Brian Lowe)

No.894 Squadron

Badge: On a blue field, a sea horse winged white
Motto: Omnium capax ubique (Capable of anything anywhere)

No.894 Squadron personnel assembled at Stretton 15 July 1942 and were shipped to the USA where they formed up at Norfolk on 15 August as a single seater fighter squadron. Equipped with six Martlet IVs, the squadron sailed for the UK in December in HMS *Battler*, re-equipping at Hatston in March 1943 with nine Seafire IICs.

In July 1943 No.894 joined HMS *Illustrious* for a trip to Iceland, followed by an operation off the Norwegian coast. Taking passage to Malta in August, the squadron was engaged the next month in support of the Salerno landings, some aircraft operating from a captured airstrip. On returning home the squadron became part of the 24th Naval Fighter Wing at Henstridge, re-equipping with 12 Seafire F.IIIs in November. In April 1944, these accompanied RAF Typhoons carrying out anti-shipping attacks in the English Channel. Embarking in HMS *Indefatigable* in July, operations were carried out over Norway, including providing cover for two attacks on the German battleship *Tirpitz*, two enemy aircraft being shot down on 22 August. In November the squadron re-equipped with 24 Seafire L.IIIs, then sailed for Ceylon to provide cover in January for attacks on Sumatran oil installations. Similar cover was provided in March and April for attacks on the Sakishima Gunto group of islands in the South China Seas, and shortly before VJ-Day attacks was made on the Japanese mainland. Some time was then spent in Australia, followed by a visit to New Zealand in November. Returning home in the New Year, No.894 disbanded at Gosport on arrival on 15 March 1946.

Reformed at Merryfield on 14 January 1957 as an all-weather fighter squadron, No.894 received 12 Sea Venom FAW.22s, though some FAW.21s were used at first until the full complement arrived. It embarked in HMS *Eagle* in August, spending much of 1958 in the Mediterranean. Most of 1959 was spent at Yeovilton, but in February 1960 the squadron joined HMS *Albion* for a spell in the Far East before returning home to disband at Yeovilton on 17 December 1960.

Battle Honours
Salerno	1943
Norway	1944
Palembang	1945
Okinawa	1945

Supermarine Seafire F.III 'P6D' of No.894 Squadron crashes on the deck of HMS Indefatigable in late 1944. (via Gregor Lamb)

Supermarine Seafire NN460 'H6Z' of No.894 Squadron, HMS Indefatigable being manhandled on deck during Sumatran operations in early 1945. (FAA Museum)

Identification Markings
Martlet unknown; Seafire single letters, to 1A+ on *Indefatigable* 7.44, to P6+ 10.44, to H6A+ 12.44, to 130-154/S 1945; Sea Venom 485-499/J:E:A.

Aircraft Equipment	Period of Service	Example
Martlet IV	Aug 1942 - Feb 1943	FN128
Seafire Ib	Feb 1943 - Apr 1943	MB358
Seafire IIc	Mar 1943 - Nov 1943	MB204 (P)
Seafire L.IIc	Mar 1943 - Nov 1943	MB306
Seafire F.III	Nov 1943 - Nov 1944	LR859 (1G)
Seafire L.III	Nov 1944 - Mar 1946	NN460 (H6Z)
Sea Venom FAW.21	Jan 1957 - Mar 1957	WW298
Sea Venom FAW.22	Jan 1957 - Dec 1960	XG700 (493/A)

Squadron bases

Base	Date	Base	Date
Norfolk	15 Aug 1942	HMS Implacable	21 Nov 1944
USS Wolverine (DLT)	12 Oct 1942	Katukurunda	10 Dec 1944
Norfolk	19 Oct 1942	HMS Indefatigable	24 Dec 1944
Quonset Point	2 Nov 1942	Schofields	10 Feb 1945
HMS Battler	8 Dec 1942	HMS Indefatigable	27 Feb 1945
Machrihanish	8 Jan 1943	Schofields	5 Jun 1945
Hatston	18 Feb 1943	HMS Indefatigable	7 Jul 1945
Machrihanish	8 Jun 1943	Schofields	18 Sep 1945
HMS Illustrious (Dt6)	2 Jul 1943	HMS Indefatigable	23 Nov 1945
HMS Illustrious	24 Jul 1943	Schofields	22 Dec 1945
Ta Kali (Dt)	24 Aug 1943	HMS Indefatigable	31 Jan 1946
	to 2 Sep 1943	Gosport-disbanded	15 Mar 1946
HMS Unicorn	11 Sep 1943	Merryfield	14 Jan 1957
Paestum (Dt)	12-15 Sep 1943	HMS Eagle	5 Aug 1957
Sidi Ahmed (Dt7) (transit)	15 Sep 1943	Lossiemouth	30 Aug 1957
Ta Kali	16 Sep 1943	HMS Eagle	10 Sep 1957
HMS Illustrious	20 Sep 1943	Merryfield	30 Sep 1957
North Front	22 Sep 1943	HMS Eagle	10 Oct 1957
HMS Illustrious	29 Sep 1943	Merryfield	2 Nov 1957
Machrihanish(trans)	18 Oct 1943	HMS Eagle	14 Nov 1957
Henstridge	19 Oct 1943	Merryfield	27 Nov 1957
Burscough	8 Jan 1944	HMS Eagle	28 Jan 1958
Ballyhalbert	8 Feb 1944	Yeovilton	31 Mar 1958
Culmhead	28 Apr 1944	HMS Eagle	20 May 1958
Ballyhalbert	15 May 1944	Hal Far	4 Jul 1958
HMS Indefatigable (DLT)	23 May 1944	HMS Eagle	15 Jul 1958
Eglinton	30 May 1944	Hal Far	23 Aug 1958
Grimsetter	18 Jul 1944	HMS Eagle	9 Sep 1958
HMS Indefatigable	24 Jul 1944	Hal Far (Dt4)	2-14 Oct 1958
Skeabrae	24 Sep 1944	Hal Far (Dt5)	14-31 Oct 1958
Grimsetter(transit)	16 Oct 1944	Culdrose (transit)	2 Dec 1958
HMS Implacable	16 Oct 1944	Yeovilton	3 Dec 1958
Lee-on-Solent	30 Oct 1944	HMS Eagle	14 Jan 1959
		North Front	3 Feb 1959
		Hal Far (Dt6)	6-20 Feb 1959
		HMS Victorious (Dt10)	14-16 Feb 1959

Squadron bases

HMS Eagle	13 Mar 1959
Yeovilton	29 Apr 1959
HMS Victorious (Dt6)	9-2 2 Jun 1959
HMS Victorious (Dt6) to	30 Jun 1959 9 Aug 1959
Yeovilton	18 Sep 1959
HMS Albion	1 Feb 1960
Hal Far (Dt4)	16-17 Feb 1960
Hal Far (Dt6)	11-21 Mar 1960
Seletar	12 Apr 1960
HMS Albion	29 Apr 1960
Kai Tak (4 a/c)	1-8 Jul 1960
Seletar	12 Jul 1960
HMS Albion	29 Jul 1960
Seletar	30 Sep 1960
HMS Albion	3 Oct 1960
Yeovilton	15 Dec 1960
Squadron disbanded	17 Dec 1960

Commanding Officers

L/C(A) DA Van Epps RNVR	15 Aug 1942
L/C FRA Turnbull DSC RN	17 Jun 1943
L/C(A) C Walker RN	17 Jan 1944
L/C(A) J Crossman DSO RNVR	22 Nov 1944
L/C(A) JR Routley RNVR	24 Oct 1945
L/C(A) RM Crosley DSC RNVR	7 Jan 1946
Squadron disbanded	15 Mar 1946
L/C PG Young RN	14 Jan 1957
L/C WGB Black RN	17 Apr 1958
L/C HER Bain RN	27 Aug 1959
Squadron disbanded	17 Dec 1960

de Havilland Sea Venom FAW.22 XG724 '485/E' of No.894 Squadron on HMS Eagle around 1957/8. (MAP)

de Havilland Sea Venom FAW.22 XG693 '492/A' of No.894 Squadron from HMS Albion lined up around 1959/60. (via Brian Lowe)

No.895 Squadron

Badge: On a field per fesse white and barry wavy of six blue and white, in front of two swords points upwards in saltire proper winged hilts gold, a hawk proper perched on a cubit arm, sleeved and gauntletted also gold

Motto: *Sicut falco expeditus* (Ready like the hawk)

No.895 Squadron formed at Stretton on 15 November 1942 as a single seater fighter squadron equipped with 6 Sea Hurricane IBs. It was to have embarked in an escort carrier, but in March 1943 it re-equipped with 9 Seafire IICs before disbanding at Turnhouse on 30 June 1943, forming the basis for the fighter flights of Nos.816 and 842 Squadrons.

On 23 April 1956 No.895 reformed at Brawdy with 12 Sea Hawk FGA.4s and FGA.6s, embarking in HMS *Bulwark* in August. For the Suez campaign, it exchanged aircraft on 12 October with No.897 Squadron, from which it acquired 12 Sea Hawk FB.3s, these retaining their former codes. No 895 disembarked to Lee-on-Solent towards the end of the year, disbanding there on 19 December 1956.

Identification Markings
Sea Hurricane & Seafire unknown; Sea Hawk *190-201/J:A:B*, to *454-466/B* 10.56.

Aircraft Equipment	Period of Service	Example
Sea Hurricane Ib	Nov 1942 - May 1943	
Seafire IIc	Mar 1943 - Jun 1943	MB316
Sea Hawk FGA.4	Apr 1956 - Sep 1956	WV835 (199/J)
Sea Hawk FGA.6	Apr 1956 - Oct 1956	XE439 (200/B)
Sea Hawk FB.3	Oct 1956 - Dec 1956	WM962 (465/B)

Squadron bases
Stretton	15 Nov 1942
Charlton Horethorne	31 Dec 1942
Lee-on-Solent	23 Feb 1942
St Merryn	22 Mar 1943
Machrihanish	3 May 1943
Turnhouse	15 Jun 1943
Squadron disbanded	30 Jun 1943
Brawdy	23 Apr 1956
HMS Bulwark (half squadron) to	25 Jun 1956 2 Jul 1956
Ford	1 Aug 1956
HMS Bulwark	3 Aug 1956
Hal Far	18 Aug 1956
HMS Bulwark	25 Aug 1956
Lee-on-Solent	17 Dec 1956
Squadron disbanded	19 Dec 1956

Commanding Officers
L/C(A) JW Hedges RNVR	15 Nov 1942
Squadron disbanded	30 Jun 1943
L/C JM Jones RN	23 Apr 1956
Squadron disbanded	19 Dec 1956

Hawker Sea Hawk FGA.6s of No.895 Squadron on HMS Bulwark in 1956. (via M.Burrow)

No.896 Squadron

No.896 Squadron personnel assembled at Stretton on 15 August 1942 and, after crossing the Atlantic in HMT *Queen Mary*, officially formed at Norfolk on 15 September as a single seater fighter squadron equipped with six Martlet IVs. Joining HMS *Victorious* in February 1943, the ship sailed through the Panama Canal for operations with the US Pacific Fleet. In May patrols and sweeps were carried out in the Coral Sea, and the following month support was provided for landings by US Marines in the Middle Solomons. Returning to the UK in September, No.896 re-equipped with ten Wildcat Vs, then joined the 7th Naval Fighter Wing in November, sailing in HMS *Pursuer* with a Gibraltar convoy in February 1944, during which it carried out fighter patrols. The squadron participated in an attack on the German battleship *Tirpitz* in April, but on 12 June 1944 it was disbanded aboard HMS *Pursuer*, being absorbed by No.881 Squadron.

Personnel for a new No.896 Squadron embarked in a troopship at Liverpool on 5 November 1944, arriving at Wingfield, Cape Town on 5 January 1945. Four days later it reformed as a single seat fighter squadron equipped with 24 Hellcat FB.IIs, sailing for Ceylon in HMS *Ameer* in April. In July fighter cover and bombing were undertaken during operations in the Car Nicobar area, then No.896 transferred to HMS *Empress* to provide fighter patrols during minesweeping operations off Phuket Island later in the same month. Following VJ-Day, support was provided in early September during occupation of the Malayan Peninsula, then the ship returned home and the squadron disbanded on arrival on 19 December 1945.

The squadron number was taken up again briefly when on 1 September 1978 two Sea King HAS.2s of No.819 Squadron and three from No.826 in HMS *Hermes* were detached as "No.896 Squadron" to the Royal Netherlands Navy base at De Kooy for Exercise *Northern Wedding*. Later in the month they returned to their respective squadrons.

Aircraft Equipment

Aircraft	Period of Service	Example
Martlet IV	Sep 1942 - Sep 1943	FN261
Wildcat V	Sep 1943 - Jun 1944	JV421
Hellcat IIFB	Jan 1945 - Nov 1945	JX688 (B8H)
Sea King HAS.2	Sep 1978 - Sep 1978	XV655 ("142/TG")

Identification Markings
Martlet/Wildcat single letters, to *8A+* on *Pursuer* by 2.44; Hellcat *2A+* on *Ameer*, to *B7+* & *B8+* 6.45.

Battle Honours
Norway	1944
Atlantic	1944
Normandy	1944
Burma	1945

Squadron bases
Norfolk	15 Sep 1942
Quonset Point	2 Nov 1942
Norfolk	6 Jan 1943
(DLT in USS Charger)	
HMS Victorious	1 Feb 1943
Barbers Point	4 Mar 1943
HMS Victorious	7 May 1943
Tontouta	3 Jun 1943
HMS Victorious	16 Jun 1943
Tontouta	20 Jun 1943
HMS Victorious	27 Jun 1943
Tontouta	25 Jul 1943
HMS Victorious	31 Jul 1943
Norfolk	1 Sep 1943
Willow Grove	2 Sep 1943
Norfolk	11 Sep 1943
HMS Victorious	16 Sep 1943
Eglinton	26 Sep 1943
Ayr (Dt4)	27 Oct 1943
	to 6 Nov 1943
HMS Pursuer	26 Nov 1943
Hatston	6 Apr 1944
HMS Pursuer	11 Apr 1944
Burscough	1 May 1944
HMS Pursuer	2 Jun 1944
Squadron disbanded	12 Jun 1944
Wingfield	9 Jan 1945

Squadron bases
Durban	22 Apr 1945
HMS Ameer	24 Apr 1945
Tambaram	12 May 1945
Trincomalee	30 May 1945
Tambaram	5 Jun 1945
HMS Empress	10 Jun 1945
HMS Emperor(DLT)	20 Jun 1945
HMS Ameer	24 Jun 1945
Trincomalee	16 Jul 1945
HMS Empress	17 Jul 1945
Trincomalee	30 Jul 1945
HMS Empress (Dt)	8 Aug 1945
	to 13 Sep 1945
HMS Empress (no a/c)	
	27 Nov 1945
Sqdn disbanded UK	19 Dec 1945

Commanding Officers
Lt(A) SG Orr DSC RNVR		15 Sep 1942
L/C(A) BHC Nation RN		28 Mar 1943
L/C(A) LA Hordern DSC RNVR		25 Oct 1943
Squadron disbanded		12 Jun 1944
L/C(A) RM Norris RNVR		9 Jan 1945
L/C(A) GJ Zegers de Beijl DSC RNethN		14 Jul 1945
L/C(A) MF Turner RNVR		12 Oct 1945
Squadron disbanded		19 Dec 1945

No.896 Squadron under inspection at Wingfield in early 1946 by the Commander-in-Chief South Africa, Hellcat JX890 FB.II '2AB' can be seen. (via R.A.Shilcock)

No.897 Squadron

Badge: On a blue field, a roseate tern proper
Motto: Quam possumus optime (The very best we can)

Aircraft Equipment	Period of Service	Example
Seafire IIc	Aug 1942 - Sep 1942	MA981
Fulmar II	Aug 1942 - Sep 1942	BP823
Sea Hurricane Ib	Dec 1942 - Mar 1943	Z4504
Spitfire Ib	Mar 1943 - Mar 1943	X4337
Seafire Ib	Mar 1943 - Jul 1943	NX892
Spitfire Vb/hooked	Mar 1943 - Dec 1943	EP762
Seafire L.IIc	Aug 1943 - May 1944	MA982
Spitfire L.Vb	Mar 1944 - Jul 1944	BL895
Sea Hawk FB.3	Nov 1955 - Oct 1956	WM913 (456/J)
Sea Hawk FGA.6	Oct 1956 - Jan 1957	XE379 (197/J)

No.897 Squadron formed at Stretton on 1 August 1942 as a single seater fighter squadron with three Seafire IICs and three Fulmar IIs, but on 3 September 1942 it was disbanded into No.801 and 880 Squadrons.

The squadron reformed at Stretton on 1 December 1942, again as a single seat fighter squadron, with six Sea Hurricane IBs. These were replaced in March 1943 by ten Seafire IBs, which in turn gave way in August to ten L.IICs with which No.897 joined HMS *Unicorn* to provide cover the following month for the Salerno landings, two aircraft operating ashore from Paestum. Returning home, the squadron joined the 3rd Naval Fighter Wing, training in tactical reconnaissance and bombardment spotting work. Changing to Spitfire LF.VBs, or L.VBs as the Navy preferred to call them, cover was provided for the Normandy invasion forces, one Bf 109 being shot down and a midget submarine damaged. This task completed, No.897 was amalgamated with No.885 at Lee-on-Solent on 15 July 1944.

Reformed at Brawdy on 7 November 1955 as a fighter unit with 12 Sea Hawk FB.3s, it embarked five months later in HMS *Eagle* for the Mediterranean. On 12 October 1956 its aircraft were exchanged for the FGA.6s of No.895 Squadron for operations during the Suez crisis, in which they bombed Egyptian airfields. The squadron then returned home to disband on 5 January 1957.

Identification Markings
Sea Hurricane unknown; Seafire unknown initially, *4A+* by 6.44; Sea Hawk *455-466/J:B*, to *190-201/J* 10.56.

Battle Honours
Salerno	1943
Normandy	1944

Squadron bases
Stretton	1 Aug 1942
Squadron disbanded	3 Sep 1942
Stretton	1 Dec 1942
Charlton Horethorne	11 Jan 1943
Lee-on-Solent	22 Mar 1943
St Merryn	5 May 1943
Machrihanish	12 Jul 1943
HMS Unicorn	4 Aug 1943
North Front(Dt)	17-20 Aug 1943
Paestum (Dt2)	12-20 Sep 1943
Burscough	10 Oct 1943
HMS Stalker	29 Dec 1943
Dale	18 Feb 1944
Lee-on-Solent	26 Feb 1944
Henstridge	2 Mar 1944
St Merryn	11 Apr 1944
Henstridge	22 Apr 1944
Dundonald	6 May 1944
Lee-on-Solent	21 May 1944
Squadron disbanded	15 Jul 1944
Brawdy	7 Nov 1955
Ford (transit)	30 Jan 1956
HMS Bulwark (DLT)	31 Jan 1956

Squadron bases
Brawdy	6 Feb 1956
HMS Eagle	16 Apr 1956
Hal Far	7 May 1956
HMS Eagle	22 May 1956
Hal Far	29 Jun 1956
HMS Eagle	17 Jul 1956
Hal Far	31 Jul 1956
HMS Eagle	14 Aug 1956
Hal Far	23 Aug 1956
HMS Eagle	4 Sep 1956
Hal Far	14 Sep 1956
HMS Eagle	25 Sep 1956
Hal Far (Dt4)	30 Nov 1956
	to 11 Dec 1956
Lee-on-Solent	1 Jan 1957
Squadron disbanded	5 Jan 1957

Commanding Officers
Capt RC Hay DSC RM	1 Aug 1942
Squadron disbanded	3 Sep 1942
L/C(A) WC Simpson DSC RN	1 Dec 1942
Squadron disbanded	15 Jul 1944
L/C AR Rawbone AFC RN	7 Nov 1955
Squadron disbanded	5 Jan 1957

The Caspian Tern's head motif of No.897 Squadron can be seen on these Sea Hawks of No.897 Squadron in 1956. In the background can be seen a French carrier with Corsairs on deck.

No.898 Squadron

Badge: On a blue field, a sun in splendour, gold, charged with a flying fish, black
Motto: Far and wide

No.898 Squadron personnel assembled at Lee-on-Solent on 17 September 1942, and sailed in HMT *Queen Mary* to officially form at Norfolk on 15 October 1942 as a single seater fighter squadron. Equipped with six Martlet IVs, the squadron joined HMS *Victorious* in February 1943, sailing through the Panama Canal to join the US Pacific Fleet. Six months were spent in that theatre, including a sweep in the Coral Sea area in May, followed in June by support for landings by US troops in the Middle Solomons. The ship then sailed to the UK by way of Pearl Harbour and the Panama Canal, and on arrival at Eglinton in September No.898 re-equipped with ten Wildcat Vs and joined the 7th Naval Fighter Wing. In December it joined HMS *Searcher* for convoy escort duties in the North Atlantic, and in April 1944 participated in an attack on the German battleship *Tirpitz* in Alten Fjord. During the next two months numerous shipping strikes were made off Norway, during which four Bv 138s and a Fw 200 were shot down. After escorting a Gibraltar convoy in June, the squadron amalgamated with No.882 on 5 July 1944.

Reformed at Wingfield, Cape Town on 1 January 1945 as a single seater fighter squadron with 24 Hellcat IIs, it embarked in HMS *Attacker* for Ceylon in June. The aircraft were fitted with rocket projectiles in July, but the squadron failed to see action before VJ-Day, and the pilots were shipped home in HMS *Pursuer* without their aircraft, to disband on arrival, on 12 December 1945.

No.898 Squadron reformed at Arbroath on 4 July 1951 with 8 Sea Fury FB.11s, as part of the 17th Carrier Air Group and joined HMS *Ocean* for six months of intensive flying in the Mediterranean. In February 1952 the squadron transferred in the Mediterranean to HMS *Theseus*, and then in July to HMS *Glory* and back to HMS *Theseus* in October. Rejoining HMS *Ocean* in December it was amalgamated into No.807 Squadron on 1 January 1953, having spent almost the whole of its existence overseas.

On 24 August 1953 the squadron reformed at Brawdy with 12 Sea Hawks F.1s, exchanging these for 12 Sea Hawk FB.3s in July 1954. No.898 remained ashore until embarking in HMS *Albion* in September 1954 for six months in the Mediterranean. In May 1955 it joined HMS *Bulwark* briefly for a visit to Oslo, re-equipping on return with 12 Sea Hawk FGA.6s, then in September embarked in HMS *Ark Royal* for a further six months spell in the Mediterranean, disbanding at Brawdy on 19 April 1956.

No.898 next reformed at Brawdy on 30 July 1956 with 12 Sea Hawk FGA.4s, these being gradually replaced by FGA.6s from January 1957, in which month it joined HMS *Ark Royal*. In June it transferred to HMS *Bulwark*, returning to HMS *Ark Royal* in September, then back to HMS *Bulwark* in November. The squadron joined HMS *Eagle* in May 1958 for six months in the Mediterranean, having a further spell in her in early 1959, before being disbanded at Brawdy on 30 April 1959.

Aircraft Equipment

Aircraft	Period of Service	Example
Martlet IV	Oct 1942 - Sep 1943	FN307
Wildcat V	Sep 1943 - Jul 1944	JV425 (7Q)
Hellcat II	Jan 1945 - Nov 1945	JX995 (B9R)
Sea Fury FB.11	Jul 1951 - Jan 1953	WF615 (146/O)
Sea Hawk F.1	Aug 1953 - Aug 1954	WF192 (110/BY)
Sea Hawk FB.3	Jul 1954 - Jun 1955	WM967 (109/Z)
Sea Hawk FGA.6	Jun 1955 - Apr 1956	XE440 (140/O)
Sea Hawk FGA.4	Nov 1955 - Feb 1956	WV919 (482/O)
	Jul 1956 - Jul 1957	WV807 (476/O)
Sea Hawk FGA.6	Jan 1957 - Apr 1959	XE378 (471/B)

Identification Markings
Martlet/Wildcat *7A+* by 7.55; Hellcat *3A+*, to *B9A+* & *B0A+* by 7.45; Sea Fury *143-149/O:T*; Sea Hawk *100-112/Z*, to *130-141/O:Z* 6.55, to *470-483/O:B:E* 1.56.

Battle Honours
Norway	1944
Atlantic	1944

Squadron bases

Norfolk	15 Oct 1942
Quonset Point	4 Nov 1942
Brunswick (DLT - USS Charger)	10 Jan 1943
Quonset Point	Jan 1943
HMS Victorious	3 Feb 1943
Barbers Point	6 Mar 1943
HMS Victorious	19 Apr 1943
Barbers Point	24 Apr 1943
HMS Victorious	7 May 1943
Tontouta	3 Jun 1943
HMS Victorious	16 Jun 1943
Tontouta	25 Jul 1943
HMS Victorious	31 Jul 1943
Eglinton	26 Sep 1943
HMS Searcher	9 Dec 1943
Brunswick	4 Jan 1944
HMS Searcher	8 Feb 1944
Eglinton	28 Feb 1944
HMS Searcher	2 Mar 1944
Hatston	7 Apr 1944
HMS Fencer	11 Apr 1944
Hatston	15 Apr 1944
HMS Searcher	18 Apr 1944
Hatston	28 Apr 1944
HMS Searcher	3 May 1944
Hatston	1 Jun 1944
HMS Searcher	8 Jun 1944
Squadron disbanded	5 Jul 1944
Wingfield	1 Jan 1945
HMS Attacker	23 Jun 1945
Colombo Racecourse	Jul 1945
Katukurunda	19 Jul 1945
HMS Pursuer	29 Jul 1945
Trincomalee	1 Aug 1945
HMS Pursuer	6 Aug 1945
Puttalam	18 Aug 1945
Katukurunda	14 Sep 1945
HMS Pursuer (no a/c)	20 Nov 1945
Sqdn disbanded UK	12 Dec 1945
Arbroath	4 Jul 1951
HMS Ocean	24 Jul 1951
Hal Far	3 Aug 1951
HMS Ocean	12 Sep 1951
Hal Far	17 Oct 1951
HMS Ocean	12 Nov 1951
HMS Theseus	26 Feb 1952
Hal Far	9 Apr 1952
HMS Theseus	21 Apr 1952
Hal Far	15 May 1952
Kasfareet	23 Jun 1952
HMS Glory	6 Jul 1952
Hal Far	8 Jul 1952
HMS Glory	21 Jul 1952
Hal Far	15 Aug 1952
HMS Theseus	15 Oct 1952
Hal Far	28 Nov 1952
HMS Ocean	9 Dec 1952
Squadron disbanded	1 Jan 1953
Brawdy	24 Aug 1953
HMS Albion	19 Sep 1954
Hal Far	13 Dec 1954
HMS Albion	22 Mar 1955
Stretton	31 Mar 1955
HMS Bulwark	23 May 1955
Stretton	4 Jun 1955
HMS Ark Royal	28 Sep 1955
Brawdy	6 Mar 1956
Squadron disbanded	19 Apr 1956
Brawdy	30 Jul 1956
HMS Ark Royal	9 Jan 1957
Brawdy	25 Feb 1957
HMS Ark Royal	6 May 1957
HMS Bulwark	28 Jun 1957
Brawdy	4 Aug 1957
HMS Ark Royal	5 Sep 1957
HMS Bulwark	1 Nov 1957
Brawdy	25 Nov 1957
HMS Eagle	20 May 1958
Brawdy	2 Dec 1958
HMS Eagle	14 Jan 1959
North Front (Dt3)	2-13 Mar 1959
Brawdy	29 Apr 1959
Squadron disbanded	30 Apr 1959

Commanding Officers
Capt AJ Wright RM	15 Oct 1942
L/C(A) ILF Lowe DSC RN	24 Nov 1942
L/C(A) GR Henderson DSC RNVR	20 Oct 1943
Squadron disbanded	5 Jul 1944
L/C(A) RW Kearsley RN	1 Jan 1945
Squadron disbanded	12 Dec 1945

Grumman Hellcat II JX696 of No.898 Squadron going down on HMS Pursuer's lift in 1945.

Commanding Officers
L/C TLM Brander
  DSC RN 4 Jul 1951
Squadron disbanded 1 Jan 1953
L/C DG Parker
  DSO DSC DFC RN 24 Aug 1953
L/C WI Campbell RN 9 Jul 1954
L/C JHS Pearce
  DSC RN 22 Aug 1955
Squadron disbanded 19 Apr 1956
L/C DB Morison RN 30 Jul 1956
L/C PL Keighly
  -Peach DSO RN 5 Nov 1957
L/C WH Cowling RN 2 Dec 1957
Squadron disbanded 30 Apr 1959

Hawker Sea Hawk FGA.6 WV860 '473/E' and two others of No.898 Squadron, HMS Eagle in 1959. (via Brian Lowe)

No.899 Squadron

Badge: On a blue field upon water barry and wavy in base white and blue, a winged gauntlet proper in chief five clouds white
Motto: Strike and defend

No.899 Squadron formed at Hatston on 15 December 1942 as a single seater fighter squadron from surplus personnel and aircraft of No.880 Squadron, which was reduced in size that day. Equipped with 12 Seafire IICs, it embarked in HMS *Indomitable* in March 1943, sailing for the Mediterranean in June. The following month the squadron helped to provide fighter cover for the Sicily landings, but the ship was damaged by a torpedo, and No.899 disembarked to Gibraltar. Transferring to HMS *Hunter*, cover was given for the landings at Salerno, a few aircraft going ashore for a short period. Returning to the UK, the squadron was at first earmarked for the 30th Naval Fighter Wing in HMS *Implacable*, then under construction, but this plan was changed, and in December 1943 they received 20 Spitfire VBs prior to re-equipping in February 1944 with 20 Seafire L.IIIs.

The squadron embarked in HMS *Khedive* in April 1944, sailing in July for the Mediterranean, where 201 sorties were flown during landings in the South of France in August. The following month attacks were made on shore targets and shipping in Crete and Rhodes, then after a further period of training in the UK, including a bombardment course at Ayr, the squadron joined HMS *Chaser* in January 1945 with an increased strength of 24 aircraft. Sailing for Ceylon in February, No.899 saw no action, being disembarked to Schofields, Australia in April as a Seafire Pool, most of its pilots being gradually posted away to other squadrons.

No.899 then became an Operational Training Unit, with the task of initiating into naval flying a number of RAAF operational fighter pilots who had voluntarily transferred to the Royal Australian Navy to form a nucleus for what was to become the Australian Fleet Air Arm. Each had considerable operational experience, a number of them on Spitfires, in a variety of theatres, but needed to be taught the art of decklanding. Two courses each of 12 pilots undertook deck landings off the Queensland coast, the first in HMS *Indomitable* and the second in HMS *Arbiter*. The Pacific war ended during the second course, but this was completed before the squadron disbanded at Schofields on 18 September 1945, plans for it to join a new 9th Carrier Air Group in November being cancelled.

On 7 November 1955, the squadron reformed at Brawdy with 12 Sea Hawk FGA.6s, embarking in HMS *Bulwark* in January 1956 for carrier work up. In April No.899 joined HMS *Eagle* and left for the Mediterranean, where in November it participated in Suez operations, making attacks on airfields and carrying out other tasks. The squadron then returned home to disband at Brawdy on 5 January 1957.

No.899 reformed at Yeovilton on 1 February 1961 as the Sea Vixen FAW.1 Headquarters squadron. It was mainly shore-based, though detachments occasionally embarked in HMS *Centaur* and HMS *Hermes*. On 15 June 1964 it was recommissioned as the Sea Vixen FAW.2 Intensive Flying Trials Unit and given first-line status, embarking in December for the Far East. The squadron remained attached to HMS *Eagle*, spending periods in both Home and Far Eastern waters, including visits to Australia in 1968 and 1971, before disbanding at Yeovilton on 26 January 1972.

On 31 March 1980, No.899 reformed at Yeovilton from No.700A Flight, the Sea Harrier Intensive Flying Trials Unit, as the Sea Harrier Headquarters Squadron. In April 1982 several aircraft were embarked in HMS *Hermes* and saw action with the South Atlantic Task Force, a detachment operating from HMS *Invincible*. The squadron then returned home, three aircraft being detached to HMS *Illustrious* in April 1983, and five in March 1984.

No.899 Squadron continues to operate from Yeovilton as the Sea Harrier Training Squadron. Regular detachments are made to the North Sea and Decimomannu Air Combat Manoeuvering Instrumentation (ACMI) ranges, and occasional detachments are made to CVSGs for student deck landing practice.

The No.899 Squadron Sea Harrier FRS2 Operational Evaluation Unit formed at Boscombe Down in June 1993 and the squadron re-equipped with FRS.2 from January 1994.

Identification Markings
Seafire 6A+, to 2A+ by early 1944, to K:A+ on *Khedive* 5.44, to C:A+ on *Chaser* 1.45; Sea Hawk 485-496/J; Sea Vixen 485-494/VL, to 121-137/E 1.65; Sea Harrier/Hunter 100-106/VL, to 710-722/VL 10.7.81.

Supermarine Seafire F.III LR856 '2W' of No.899 Squadron bites the deck of HMS Khedive in early 1944. (via Andy Thomas)

Aircraft Equipment	Period of Service	Example
Seafire IIc	Dec 1942 - Jan 1944	MB244 (6Q)
Spitfire Vb	Dec 1943 - Mar 1944	AB867
Spitfire Vb/hooked	Dec 1943 - Mar 1944	AD187
Seafire L.III	Feb 1944 - Sep 1945	NN599 (KP)
Sea Hawk FGA.6	Nov 1955 - Jan 1957	XE401 (492/J)
Sea Vixen FAW.1	Feb 1961 - Sep 1964	XN467 (490/VL)
Sea Vixen FAW.2	Feb 1964 - Jan 1972	XS576 (125/E)
Sea Harrier FRS.1	Mar 1980 - Jan 1994	XZ452 (101/VL)
Hunter T.8M	Aug 1981 - Oct 1993	XL580 (717/VL)
Harrier T.4N	Sep 1983 - Apr 1995	ZB604 (717)
Harrier T.4A	Jul 1987 - Apr 1995	XZ445 (727)
Sea Harrier FRS.2	Jun 1993 - to date	XZ495 (713/OEU)
Harrier T.8	Jan 1995 - to date	ZB605

Battle Honours
Sicily 1943
Salerno 1943
Aegean 1944
South France 1944
Falkland Islands 1982

Squadron bases
Hatston 15 Dec 1942
Machrihanish 22 Feb 1943
HMS Indomitable 11 Mar 1943
Machrihanish(Dt) 22-27 Apr 1943
Machrihanish(Dt) 12-15 May 1943
Machrihanish(Dt) 29 May 1943
 to 9 Jun 1943
North Front 29 Jul 1943
HMS Hunter 28 Aug 1943
Paestum (Dt) 12-16 Sep 1943
Ballyhalbert 13 Oct 1943
Belfast 17 Jan 1944
HMS Argus (DLT) 15 Mar 1944
Belfast 18 Mar 1944
HMS Khedive 1 Apr 1944
Long Kesh 27 Apr 1944
HMS Khedive 12 May 1944
Hatston (Dt3) 14 May 1944
Grimsetter (Dt4) 16 May 1944
Peterhead (13 Gp) 31 May 1944
HMS Khedive 5 Jul 1944
Hal Far 27 Jul 1944
HMS Khedive 1 Aug 1944
Dekheila (Dt6) 2-9 Sep 1944
 (DLT HMS Stalker)
Ballyhalbert(trans) 12 Oct 1944
Long Kesh 12 Oct 1944
Ayr 23 Nov 1944
Long Kesh 30 Nov 1944
HMS Chaser 25 Jan 1945
Long Kesh (Dt3) 25 Jan 1945
 to 23 Feb 1945
Belfast 29 Jan 1945
HMS Ravager
 (Dt10) (DLT) 5-9 Feb 1945
HMS Chaser 25 Feb 1945

Squadron bases
Schofields 23 Apr 1945
HMS Indomitable 24-27 Jul 1945
 - DLT from Maryborough
HMS Arbiter (DLT) 15 Aug 1945
 - from Maryborough
Point Cook (Dt2) 30 Aug 1945
 to 4 Sep 1945
HMS Arbiter
 (DLT) 10-13 Sep 1945
 - from Maryborough
Squadron disbanded 18 Sep 1945

Squadron bases
Brawdy 7 Nov 1955
HMS Bulwark 31 Jan 1956
Brawdy 10 Feb 1956
HMS Eagle 16 Apr 1956
Hal Far 29 Jun 1956
HMS Eagle 17 Jul 1956
Hal Far 31 Jul 1956
HMS Eagle 14 Aug 1956
Hal Far 23 Aug 1956
HMS Eagle 4 Sep 1956
Hal Far 14 Sep 1956
HMS Eagle 25 Sep 1956
Hal Far 30 Nov 1956
HMS Eagle 11 Dec 1956
Brawdy 3 Jan 1957
Squadron disbanded 5 Jan 1957
Yeovilton 1 Feb 1961
HMS Ark Royal 18-24 Oct 1961
 (DLT)
HMS Hermes (Dt4) 2-8 May 1962
HMS Centaur
 (Dt4) 22-28 Jun 1962
HMS Centaur
 (Dt4) 15-26 Nov 1962
HMS Eagle (Dt2) 14-20 Jul 1963
HMS Victorious(Dt) 1-8 Aug 1963
HMS Hermes (Dt4) 27 Sep 1963
 to 12 Oct 1963
HMS Centaur(Dt) 22-28 Nov 1963
HMS Eagle 2 Dec 1964
Yeovilton (Dt4) 15 May 1965
Yeovilton (Sqdn) 24 Jun 1965
HMS Eagle 25 Aug 1965
Changi (Dt8) 11-20 Nov 1965
Changi (Dt6) 11-28 Feb 1966
Changi (Dt4) 9 May 1966
 to 2 Jun 1966
Changi (Dt6) 1-12 Jul 1966
Yeovilton 15 Aug 1966
Boscombe Down 24 May 1967
HMS Eagle 24 Jun 1967
Boscombe Down 18 Jul 1967
HMS Eagle 15 Aug 1967
Changi (Dt6) 5-24 Oct 1967
Changi 21 Dec 1967
HMS Eagle 23 Jan 1968
Pearce (Dt6) 11-27 Feb 1968
Yeovilton 19 Jun 1968

Squadron bases
HMS Eagle 24 Aug 1968
Yeovilton (Dt4) 27 Sep 1968
Yeovilton (Sqdn) 2 Oct 1968
Decimomannu 7 Nov 1968
Yeovilton 18 Nov 1968
HMS Eagle 3 Apr 1969
Yeovilton 29 Apr 1969
HMS Eagle 16 Jun 1969
Yeovilton 18 Jul 1969
HMS Eagle 4 Sep 1969
Gibraltar (Dt4) 27 Sep 1969
 to 11 Oct 1969
Luqa (Dt6) 30 Oct 1969
 to 13 Nov 1969
Yeovilton 3 Dec 1969
HMS Eagle 12 Jan 1970
Yeovilton 23 Mar 1970
HMS Eagle 2 Oct 1970
Yeovilton 9 Dec 1970
HMS Eagle 19 Jan 1971
Luqa (Dt5) 3-22 Mar 1971
Yeovilton 5 Apr 1971
HMS Eagle 26 May 1971
Tengah 7 Jul 1971
HMS Eagle 21 Jul 1971
Tengah (Dt6) 19 Sep 1971
 to 5 Oct 1971
Yeovilton 23 Jan 1972
Squadron disbanded 26 Jan 1972
Yeovilton 31 Mar 1980
Gutersloh (Dt5) 12-16 Jun 1980
Alconbury (Dt3) 4-6 Aug 1980
HMS Invincible
 (Dt4) 6-10 Nov 1980
HMS Hermes
 (Half sqdn) 5 Apr 1982
HMS Invincible
 (Half sqdn) 5 Apr 1982
 (Falklands)
Yeovilton 21 Jul 1982
Farnborough(Dt4) 4-23 Sep 1982
HMS Illustrious May 1983
 (Dt3)
Decimomannu (Dt6) 27 Jun 1983
 to 4 Jul 1983
HMS Illustrious 5-23 Mar 1984
 (Dt5)

de Havilland Sea Vixen FAW.XS579 '130/E' of No.899 Squadron, HMS Eagle around 1967/8. (via Brian Lowe)

Hunter T.8M XL603 '720/OEU' of No.899 Squadron Operational Evaluation Unit at Yeovilton in 1985

Hawker Sea Harrier FRS.2 ZE695 '711' of No.899 Squadron in 1993. (MAP)

Squadron bases
Decimomannu
  (Dt6) 4-18Jun 1984
Decimomannu (Dt5) Sep 1984
Decimomannu (Dt5) May 1985
Paris Air Show 28 May 1985
  (Dt1) to 10 Jun 1985
Decimomannu
  (Dt1) 7-18Oct 1985
Decimomannu
  (Dt7) 7-15Jan 1986
Decimomannu
  (Dt6) 2-16Jun 1986
Decimomannu 27 Oct 1986
  (Dt4) to 5 Nov 1986
Lossiemouth
  (Dt2) 2-5Dec 1986
Lossiemouth
  (Dt3) 2-9Mar 1987
Decimomannu
  (Dt5) 1-15Jun 1987
Decimomannu
  (Dt4) 21-28Sep 1987
HMS Illustrious
  (Dt4) 28-29Oct 1987
Decimomannu
  (Dt7) 14-25Mar 1988
Farnborough (Dt6) 30 Aug 1988
  to 8 Sep 1988
Decimomannu (Dt6) Nov 1988
Wittering (Dt3) Feb 1989
  to Mar 1989
Decimomannu
  (Dt4) 13-27Mar 1989
Decomomannu (Dt7) Oct 1989
Lossiemouth
  (Dt4) 13-16Nov 1989
Waddington (Dt6) Sep 1990
Decimomannu
  (Dt6) 10-22Jun 1991
Decimomannu Jan 1992
  (Dt4) to Feb 1992
HMS Ark Royal
  (Dt2) Mar 1992
Decimomannu (Dt5) Mar 1992
Lossiemouth (Dt5) May 1992
Decimomannu
  (Dt6) 12-26Jun 1992
Decimomannu (Dt6) Nov 1992
Waddington (Dt5) Dec 1992
Waddington (Dt6) 4-14May 1993
Akrotiri (Dt8) 1-14Jun 1993
Decimomannu
  (Dt5) 2-15Jul 1993
Akrotiri (Dt6) 6-22Sep 1993
Leuchars (Dt5) 11-22Oct 1993
Waddington (Dt4) 29 Nov 1993
  to 10 Dec 1993

Squadron bases
HMS Invincible
  (Dt1) 6-25Jan 1994
Florennes (Dt2) 2-11Feb 1994
Waddington (Dt4) 28 Feb 1994
  to 4 Mar 1994
Florennes (Dt3) 14-25Mar 1994
Florennes (Dt2) 2-11May 1994
Wittering (Dt4) 9-20May 1994
Florennes (Dt2) 29 Jun 1994
  to 8Jul 1994
Waddington (Dt5) 25 Jul 1994
  to 5 Aug 1994
HMS Ark Royal 16 Sep 1994
  (Dt2) to 19 Sep 1994
Decimomannu (Dt6)24 Oct 1994
  to 7 Nov 1994

899 SEA HARRIER FRS.2 OEU
Boscombe Down 1 Jun 1993
Akrotiri (Dt2) 6-20Sep 1993
Yeovilton 30 Sep 1993
Florennes(Dt2) 13-21Oct 1993
HMS Ark Royal
  (Dt2) 7-14Nov 1993

OEU bases
Waddington (Dt3) 29 Nov 1993
  to 10 Dec 1993
HMS Invincible 27 Jun 1994
Yeovilton 8 Jul 1994
HMS Invincible 23 Aug 1994
Yeovilton 12 Sep 1994

Commanding Officers
L/C(A) RF Walker
  RNVR 15 Dec 1942
L/C(A) RB Howarth
  RNVR 2 Aug 1943
L/C(A) G Dennison
  RNVR 1 Nov 1944
Squadron disbanded 18 Sep 1945
L/C ABB Clark RN 7 Nov 1955
Squadron disbanded 5 Jan 1957
L/C WJ Carter RN 1 Feb 1961
L/C DMAH Hamilton
  RN 5 Mar 1962
L/C JA Sanderson
  RN 2 Sep 1963
L/C DC Matthews
  RN 18 Apr 1964
L/C TEM Kirby RN 25 Aug 1965

Commanding Officers
L/C GD Varley RN 1 Sep 1966
L/C RD McCulloch
  RN 2 Jan 1967
L/C GWG Hunt RN 20 May 1968
L/C DJ Dunbar
  -Dempsey RN 1 Aug 1969
L/C MHG Layard
  RN 16 Feb 1970
L/C F Milner RN 4 Mar 1971
Squadron disbanded 26 Jan 1972
L/C N Ward RN 31 Mar 1980
L/C NW Thomas
  DSC RN 19 Jan 1981
L/C DJ Thornton RN 3 Feb 1983
L/C HGB Slade RN 26 Jun 1985
Cdr HGB Slade RN 30 Jun 1987
L/C S Lidbetter RN 9 Nov 1987
Cdr S Lidbetter RN 31 Dec 1987
L/C WM Covington
  RN 14 Mar 1989
Cdr WM Covington
  RN 30 Jun 1989
L/C IRM Bradshaw
  RN 5 Apr 1990
L/C SN Hargreaves
  RN 7 Sep 1992

British Aerospace Harrier T.4N ZB603 '718' of No.899 Squadron with special D-Day anniversary markings in 1994. (MAP)

No.1700 Squadron

Badge: On a blue field, issuant from a base barry wavy white and blue two cubit arms proper grasping a stockless anchor erect gold winged white

Motto: *Ex mari messis*
(*Our harvest is from the sea*)

Identification Markings
Sea Otter & Walrus believed uncoded.

Aircraft Equipment	Period of Service	Example
Sea Otter I	Nov 1944 - Jun 1946	JM750
Walrus	Feb 1945 - Jun 1946	X9493
Reliant I	Nov 1945 - Jan 1946	FB615
Tiger Moth II	Nov 1945 - Jan 1946	NL750
Avenger II	Dec 1945 - Jan 1946	JZ509
Seafire IIc	Dec 1945 - Jan 1946	LR699
Swordfish II	Jan 1946 - Jun 1946	LS331

No.1700 Squadron formed at Lee-on-Solent on 1 November 1944 as a amphibian bomber reconnaissance squadron with six Sea Otters for service in the Pacific. Embarking in HMS *Khedive* in January 1945, the squadron sailed for southern India, disembarking to Sulur in February where Walruses were also received, as the Sea Otter had not been cleared for deck landing at that time. Moving to Ceylon, aircraft were embarked in small numbers in various escort carriers for air sea rescue and minesweeping operations. Some were embarked in HMS *Hunter* and HMS *Stalker* during an anti-shipping sweep in the Andaman Sea during June, and another detachment was in HMS *Emperor* during operations at Car Nicobar in July. Further detachments were in HMS *Ameer* and HMS *Emperor* later that month during minesweeping operations off Phuket Island, Thailand. After VJ-Day the squadron was largely based ashore, 'A' Flight operating six Sea Otters at Trincomalee from November, whilst 'B' Flight had six Walruses at Katukurunda. 'C' Flight operated at times from Sembawang, and a small number of Swordfish were also flown at this stage. On 3 June 1946 No.1700 was absorbed in No.733 Squadron at Trincomalee.

Battle Honours
Burma 1945

Squadron bases
Lee-on-Solent	1 Nov 1944
HMS Khedive	8 Jan 1945
Sulur	8 Feb 1945
Koggala	4 Apr 1945
HMS Stalker (Dt)	14 Apr 1945
to	24 Jun 1945
HMS Hunter (Dt)	23 Apr 1945
to	12 Jun 1945
Trincomalee	26 May 1945
HMS Khedive (Dt1)	12 Jun 1945
to	18 Sep 1945
HMS Emperor (Dt)	2-13 Jul 1945
HMS Emperor (Dt1)	17-30 Oct 1945
HMS Ameer (Dt1)	19 Jul 1945
to	20 Jul 1945
HMS Attacker (Dt1)	16 Aug 1945
to	21 Sep 1945
HMS Shah (Dt)	8-26 Aug 1945
HMS Hunter (Dt)	16 Aug 1945
to	18 Sep 1945

'A' Flight:
Trincomalee 17 Nov 1945
'B' Flight:
Katukurunda 24 Nov 1945
'C' Flight:
Sembawang 8 Nov 1945
Katukurunda 20 Nov 1945
Sembawang 15 Dec 1945
Trans 791 Sqdn 26 Jan 1946
Squadron disbanded 3 Jun 1946

Commanding Officers
Lt(A) AB Edgar RNVR 1 Nov 1944
Lt(A) JA Gossett RNVR 25 Jan 1946
Squadron disbanded 3 Jun 1946

A Supermarine Walrus, believed of No.1700 Squadron, aboard HMS Shah. (J.H.W.Puttock/FAA Museum)

No.1701 Squadron

No.1701 formed at Lee-on-Solent on 1 February 1945 as an amphibian bomber reconnaissance squadron with 6 Sea Otters for service in the Pacific. Embarking in HMS *Begum* in April, it sailed for the Far East to be attached to Mobile Naval Air Bases for air sea rescue duties. 'B' Flight joined MONAB No.4 at Ponam in May, whilst 'A' Flight was disembarked in June to MONAB No.6 at Maryborough. After VJ-Day the squadron reverted to second line duties, being based at Kai Tak from November 1945, where a Tiger Moth was added, and also an Oxford flight. No.1701 disbanded at Kai Tak on 27 August 1946.

Supermarine Sea Otters of No.1701 Squadron at Kai Tak in 1946. (Ken Chambers)

Squadron bases		Squadron bases	
Lee-on-Solent	1 Feb 1945	'B' Flight:	
HMS Begum	17 Apr 1945	Ponam	28 May 1945
'A' Flight:		HMS Reaper	3 Oct 1945
transit	14 Jun 1945	Kai Tak	13 Oct 1945
Maryborough	17 Jun 1945	Kai Tak	1 Nov 1945
Bankstown	24 Jul 1945	HMS Chaser	
Maryborough	7 Aug 1945	(Dt1)	17-31 Dec 1945
Bankstown	15 Oct 1945	Squadron disbanded 27 Aug 1946	
Maryborough	21 Oct 1945		
Archerfield	1 Nov 1945	**Commanding Officers**	
HMS Striker	4 Nov 1945	Lt(A) LF Plant	
Kai Tak	16 Nov 1945	RNVR	1 Feb 1945
		Lt(A) PH Woodham	
Identification Markings		DSC RNVR	19 Oct 1945
Sea Otter possibly *P3A+* at Ponam		Squadron disbanded 27 Aug 1946	

Aircraft Equipment	Period of Service	Example
Sea Otter I	Feb 1945 - Aug 1946	JN105
Oxford	Apr 1946 - Aug 1946	
Tiger Moth II	Jul 1946 - Aug 1946	A17-84

No.1702 Squadron

No.1702 formed at Lee-on-Solent on 1 June 1945 as a special service squadron with 6 Sea Otters for intended service in the Pacific, but VE-Day intervened. It sailed in September for the Mediterranean in HMS *Trouncer*, and spent a short period on ASR duties at Hal Far before leaving for Greece to hunt for mines in the Eastern Mediterranean, continuing this duty in Tunisia from May 1946, No.1702 returning to Malta two months later. When the squadron disbanded at Ta Kali on 12 September 1946, a detachment of three aircraft in HMS *Ocean* became its Ships Flight.

Identification Markings: Sea Otter *O2A+* on *Ocean*.

Aircraft Equipment	Period of Service	Example
Sea Otter I	Jun 1945 - Sep 1946	JN249 (O2B)

Squadron bases		Squadron bases	
Lee-on-Solent	1 Jun 1945	El Aouina (Dt)	5-19 Jul 1946
Abbotsinch	5 Sep 1945	Ta Kali	19 Jul 1946
HMS Trouncer	13 Sep 1945	HMS Ocean (Dt3)	25 Jul 1946
Hal Far	22 Sep 1945		to 12 Sep 1946
Hassani	27 Oct 1945	Squadron disbanded 12 Sep 1946	
Calato (Dt)	5 Mar 1946		
	to 23 May 1946	**Commanding Officers**	
Hal Far (Dt)	23-25 May 1946	Lt(A) OGW Hutchinson	
Araxos (Dt)	17 Apr 1946	RNVR	1 Jun 1945
	to 27 May 1946	Lt(A) RH Kilburn	
El Aouina	25 May 1946	RNVR	15 Jan 1946
Bizerta (Dt)	28 May 1946	Squadron disbanded 12 Sep 1946	

Supermarine Sea Otter 'O2C' of No.1702 Squadron around 1945/6.

No.1703 Squadron

Badge: An elephant's head (Unofficial)
Motto: Elephanti Albi! (White elephant!)

No.1703 Squadron formed at Lee-on-Solent on 1 August 1945 with 6 Sea Otters for intended service in the Pacific. It experienced considerable trouble with its aircraft, including corroded bolts which made the tails liable to drop off, and also unexplained engine failure. There were consequently mixed feelings when it was ordered to disband on 18 September 1945.

A Supermarine Sea Otter of No.1703 Squadron at Lee-on-Solent in 1945. (Donald Payne)

Identification Markings
Sea Otter uncoded.

Aircraft Equipment	Period of Service	Example
Sea Otter I	Aug 1945 - Sep 1945	JN182

Squadron bases	
Lee-on-Solent	1 Aug 1945
Squadron disbanded	18 Sep 1945

Commanding Officers	
Lt(A) KA Chare RNVR	1 Aug 1945
Squadron disbanded	18 Sep 1945

No.1770 Squadron

Badge: On a blue field, issuant from water in base barry wavy of four blue and white a trident, gold, on the middle prong thereof a firefly lambent proper
Motto: Videre est vincere (To see is to conquer)

No.1770 Squadron formed at Yeovilton on 10 September 1943 as a two seater fighter squadron equipped with 12 Firefly Is. In May 1944 it joined HMS *Indefatigable*, taking part in July in operations against the German battleship *Tirpitz*, during which it attacked gun positions and two auxiliary vessels. During the next month cover was provided for minelaying operations in Norwegian waters, and this was followed by further Tirpitz operations including bombing attacks and photography. In November the ship sailed for the Far East, and in January 1945 the ship was involved in attacks on oil refineries in Sumatra. On joining the British Pacific Fleet, strikes were made between March and May on the Sakishima Gunto group of islands in the East China Seas, and later against Formosa. In June, No.1770 disembarked to Australia, where it became part of the 7th Carrier Air Group, but it disbanded at Maryborough on 30 September 1945 without re-embarking.

Battle Honours
Norway	1944
Palembang	1945
Okinawa	1945

Identification Markings
Firefly 4A+, to 270-281/S 3.45, to single letters 8.45.

Aircraft Equipment	Period of Service	Example
Firefly I	Sep 1943 - Sep 1945	DT941 (276/S)

Squadron bases	
Yeovilton	10 Sep 1943
Grimsetter	14 Dec 1943
Hatston	15 Feb 1944
HMS Indefatigable	18 May 1944
Ayr	29 May 1944
HMS Indefatigable	10 Jun 1944
Grimsetter	5 Jul 1944
HMS Indefatigable	9 Jul 1944
Hatston (transit)	25 Jul 1944
Donibristle	25 Jul 1944
Burscough	27 Jul 1944
Ayr	30 Jul 1944
Donibristle	31 Jul 1944
Kinloss	1 Aug 1944
Hatston	2 Aug 1944
HMS Indefatigable	7 Aug 1944
Grimsetter (Dt5)	6-17 Sep 1944
Ayr	26 Sep 1944

Squadron bases	
Dale	16 Nov 1944
HMS Indefatigable	21 Nov 1944
Puttalam	10 Dec 1944
HMS Indefatigable	24 Dec 1944
Schofields	10 Feb 1945
HMS Indefatigable	27 Feb 1945
Schofields	5 Jun 1945
Maryborough	29 Aug 1945
Squadron disbanded	30 Sep 1945

Commanding Officers
L/C(A) IP Godfrey RNVR	10 Sep 1943
Mjr VBG Cheesman DSO MBE DSC RM	5 Feb 1944
L/C(A) DJ Holmes RN	22 Jun 1945
Squadron disbanded	30 Sep 1945

Fairey Firefly FR.1s of No.1770 Squadron, HMS Indefatigable. (via Val Bennett)

No.1771 Squadron

Badge: On a blue field, an eagle, gold, in combat with a sea monster black rising from water barry wavy in base, blue and white
Motto: Undaunted

Fairey Firefly I Z1888 'T' of No.1771 Squadron aboard HMS Ravager on 16 August 1944. (L.I.Loch)

No.1771 Squadron formed at Yeovilton on 1 February 1944 as a two seater fighter squadron. Equipped with 12 Firefly Is, it embarked in September in HMS *Implacable*, carrying out a reconnaissance the following month of the Tromso area and of the anchorage in which the German battleship *Tirpitz* was lying. This was followed by anti-shipping strikes off the Norwegian coast, and in late November by further strikes in the same area, one troopship being destroyed and four other ships damaged. In March 1945 the ship sailed to join the British Pacific Fleet, taking part in attacks on Truk in the Caroline Islands in June. During the last few weeks of the war No.1771 operated against the Japanese mainland, a part of the 8th CAG disembarking after VJ-Day to Australia, where it disbanded at Nowra on 16 October 1945.

Battle Honours
Norway 1944
Japan 1945

Identification Markings
Firefly single letters, to 4A+ 19.9.44, to *270-281/N* 19.7.45.

Aircraft Equipment	Period of Service	Example
Firefly I	Feb 1944 - Sep 1945	DV130 (4L)

Squadron bases
Yeovilton	1 Feb 1944
Burscough	3 Mar 1944
HMS Trumpeter (Dt4 - DLT)	29 Jun 1944 to 1 Jul 1944
Machrihanish	7 Aug 1944
HMS Ravager (Dt4 - DLT)	16-17 Aug 1944
HMS Implacable	22 Sep 1944
Hatston	7 Nov 1944
HMS Implacable	16 Nov 1944
Hatston	29 Nov 1944
HMS Implacable	5 Dec 1944
Hatston	9 Dec 1944
Mullaghmore	8 Jan 1945
Ayr	7 Feb 1945
HMS Pretoria Castle (Dt6) - DLT	6 Mar 1945
Arbroath	10 Mar 1945
HMS Implacable	12 Mar 1945
Jervis Bay	7 May 1945
HMS Implacable	24 May 1945
Ponam (Dt7)	9-12 Jun 1945
Nowra	13 Sep 1945
Squadron disbanded	16 Oct 1945

Commanding Officers
L/C(A) HM Ellis DFC DSC RN	1 Feb 1944
L/C(A) WJR MacWhirter DSC RN	9 Mar 1945
Squadron disbanded	16 Oct 1945

No.1772 Squadron

Badge: On a field per fess red and blue, a bow white, string with an arrow white winged and flighted gold
Motto: Tenax proposite (Steadfast of purpose)

Aircraft Equipment	Period of Service	Example
Firefly I	May 1944 - Mar 1946	DK551 (276/S)

Battle Honours
Japan 1945

Squadron bases
Burscough	1 May 1944
HMS Empress (DLT)	25 Nov 1944
Burscough	27 Nov 1944
Belfast	16 Jan 1945
HMS Ruler	20 Jan 1945
Schofields	18 Mar 1945
HMS Indefatigable	7 Jul 1945
Schofields	18 Sep 1945
HMS Indefatigable	18 Nov 1945
Schofields	22 Dec 1945
HMS Indefatigable	31 Jan 1946
Squadron disbanded	10 Mar 1946

Commanding Officers
L/C(A) AHD Gough RN	1 May 1944
L/C(A) LC Wort DSC RNVR	3 Nov 1945
L/C(A) DJ Holmes RNVR	24 Sep 1945
Squadron disbanded	10 Mar 1946

No.1772 Squadron formed at Burscough on 1 May 1944 as a two seater fighter squadron equipped with 12 Firefly Is. On completion of deck landing training aboard HMS *Empress* in November, the original aircraft were handed over to No.766 Squadron, and new aircraft were issued fitted with long range tanks. These embarked in HMS *Ruler* in January 1945, and sailed to join the British Pacific Fleet. Disembarking to Australia in March, the squadron joined HMS *Indefatigable* in July for strikes against the Japanese mainland. After VJ-Day supplies were dropped on Prisoner of War camps in Japan, then the ship sailed south to Australia. Joining the 7th CAG, the squadron re-embarked for a visit to New Zealand. In January 1946 the ship sailed for the UK, and No.1772 disbanded on arrival at Portsmouth on 10 March 1946.

Identification Markings
Firefly single letters, to 4A+ 10.44; to *270-281/S* 6.45.

Fairey Firefly I Z1977 'S' of No.1772 Squadron in 1944. (via Harry Holmes)

Nos. 1773 to 1775 Squadrons

Three other squadrons were to have formed in the 1770 series, for service with the British Pacific Fleet, but they proved unnecessary. No.1773 Squadron would have formed at Woodvale on 1 July 1945 with Barracudas, this being changed later to Fireflies, which should have embarked in a light Fleet carrier in November 1945 for the 9th Carrier Group. Nos.1774 and 1775 were to have been Firefly squadrons with the 12th and 10th Carrier Air Groups respectively. None of these materialised.

No.1790 Squadron

No.1790 Squadron formed at Burscough on 1 January 1945 as a night fighter squadron equipped initially with 12 Firefly Is. These gave way by May to Firefly INFs fitted with ASH radar, which embarked in HMS *Vindex* the following month for passage to Australia, but by the time the ship arrived the war against the Japanese had ended. In April 1946 No.1790 embarked in HMS *Implacable* for passage to the UK, a New Zealand Walrus being loaned ASR duties en route, the squadron disbanding on arrival at Devonport on 3 June 1946.

Aircraft Equipment	Period of Service	Example
Firefly I	Jan 1945 - May 1945	DK476 (4A)
Firefly INF	Jan 1945 - Apr 1946	MB617 (295)
Walrus (ASR)	Mar 1946 - Jun 1946	NZ151

Identification Markings
Firefly *4A+*, later *282-298*.

Squadron bases
Burscough	1 Jan 1945
HMS Puncher (DLP)	25 May 1945
Burscough	5 Jun 1945
Belfast (transit)	24 Jun 1945
HMS Vindex	24 Jun 1945
Schofields	13 Aug 1945
HMS Implacable	16 Jan 1946
Schofields	28 Mar 1946
HMS Implacable	29 Apr 1946
Sqdn disbanded UK	3 Jun 1946

Commanding Officers
L/C(A) JH Kneale RNVR	1 Jan 1945
L/C(A) BC Lyons RNVR	9 Nov 1945
Squadron disbanded	3 Jun 1946

Fairey Firefly FR.I MB476 '4Z' of No.1790 Squadron, HMS Puncher in May 1945. (J.H.Kneale)

No.1791 Squadron

Badge: A Red Indian's head (Unapproved)

No.1791 Squadron formed at Lee-on-Solent on 15 March 1945 as a night fighter squadron equipped with 12 Firefly INFs. These embarked in HMS *Puncher* in June for deck landing practice, but the squadron was no longer required after VJ-Day, and it disbanded at Burscough on 23 September 1945.

Identification Markings
Firefly single letters.

Aircraft Equipment	Period of Service	Example
Firefly INF	Mar 1945 - Sep 1945	MB641 (X)
Firefly FR.1	May 1945 - Sep 1945	DK461 (N)

Squadron bases
Lee-on-Solent	15 Mar 1945
Inskip	19 Apr 1945
HMS Puncher (Dt6 - DLT)	11-13 Jun 1945
Drem	18 Jun 1945
Burscough	18 Aug 1945
Squadron disbanded	23 Sep 1945

Commanding Officers
L/C HJ Hunter RCNVR	15 Mar 1945
Squadron disbanded	23 Sep 1945

No.1792 Squadron

Badge: On a field per fess wavy black and barry wavy white and black, a sword in pale point downwards white pommel and hilt gold winged white

Motto: *Nocte vincimus*
(We conquer by night)

Fairey Firefly INFs of No.1792 Squadron awaiting take-off from HMS Ocean in 1946.

No.1792 Squadron formed at Lee-on-Solent on 15 May 1945 as a night fighter squadron equipped with 12 Firefly INFs. In December it embarked in HMS *Ocean* for a spell in the Mediterranean, but on return to the UK it disbanded on arrival on 17 April 1946.

Squadron bases		Squadron bases	
Lee-on-Solent	15 May 1945	HMS Ocean	18 Feb 1946
Inskip	15 Jun 1945	Sqdn disbanded UK	17 Apr 1946
Drem	29 Aug 1945		
Machrihanish	27 Nov 1945	**Commanding Officers**	
HMS Ocean	11 Dec 1945	L/C(A) S Dixon	
Hal Far	4 Jan 1946	-Child RNVR	15 May 1945
		Squadron disbanded	17 Apr 1946

Identification Markings
Firefly single letters, to *O4A+* on *Ocean* 12.45.

Aircraft Equipment	Period of Service	Example
Firefly INF	May 1945 - Apr 1946	MB575 (O4S)

No.1820 Squadron

Badge: (Heraldic description lacking)

Curtiss Helldiver JW104 '4L' taking off. (FAA Museum)

No.1820 Squadron formed at Brunswick on 1 April 1944 as a dive bomber squadron equipped with 9 Helldivers. After work-up these embarked in HMS *Arbiter* in July for passage to the UK, but the type was found unsatisfactory for its intended purpose, the squadron losing several aircraft and crews through accidents, including three aircraft which failed to pull out of vertical dives. No.1820 was therefore disbanded at Burscough on 16 December 1944.

Identification Markings
Helldiver *4A+*, also *1A+*.

Aircraft Equipment	Period of Service	Example
Helldiver I	Apr 1944 - Dec 1944	JW104 (4L)

Squadron bases		Squadron bases	
Brunswick	1 Apr 1944	Hatston	31 Oct 1944
Squantum	1 May 1944	Donibristle	1 Dec 1944
Norfolk (transit)	5 Jul 1944	Burscough	4 Dec 1944
HMS Arbiter	5 Jul 1944	Squadron disbanded	16 Dec 1944
Speke	24 Jul 1944		
Burscough	11 Aug 1944	**Commanding Officers**	
Donibristle	23 Oct 1944	L/C(A) HIA Swayne	
HMS Speaker (DLT)	29 Oct 1944	DSC RN	1 Apr 1944
Donibristle	30 Oct 1944	Squadron disbanded	16 Dec 1944

No.1830 Squadron

Badge: *On a blue field, barry wavy in base white and blue, two torches in saltire gold, inflamed proper*

Motto: *Force on*

Firefly FR.1 PP404 of No.1830 Sqdn, Donibristle in 1950.
(Ray Williams)

No.1830 Squadron personnel assembled at Lee-on-Solent on 1 April 1943 and embarked for the USA, disembarking to Quonset Point on 7 May, where it officially formed on 1 June as a single seater fighter squadron. Equipped with ten Corsair Is for work-up, these gave way in August to ten Corsair IIs, which in October embarked in HMS *Slinger* for passage to the UK. In December the strength was increased to fourteen aircraft by absorbing part of No.1831 Squadron, and No.1830 then became part of the 15th Naval Fighter Wing. The following month it joined HMS *Illustrious* for work-up in the Clyde, sailing in late January 1944 for Ceylon, from where as part of the Eastern Fleet a three day sweep was carried out in the Bay of Bengal in March. In April attacks were made on shore installations and shipping at Sabang, and the next month similar operations were carried out at Sourabaya. The Andaman Islands were attacked in June, followed by further operations at Sabang in July.

In August the ship sailed to Durban to refit, and No.1830 increased its strength to 18 aircraft. By December the ship was back in action, and No.1830 participated in attacks on oil refineries in Sumatra in December 1944 and January 1945, following which the ship joined the British Pacific Fleet. Intensive operations were carried out in March and April against the Sakishima Gunto group of islands in the East China Seas but, after being damaged from a near miss by a Kamikaze, the ship pulled out of the line on 14 April and returned with No.1830 to the UK. Here the squadron was to have regrouped with new Corsairs before returning to the British Pacific Fleet as part of the 6th Carrier Air Group, but instead it disbanded on arrival in the UK on 28 July 1945.

No.1830 reformed at Abbotsinch on 15 August 1947 as a fighter/anti-submarine squadron in the RN Volunteer Reserve, equipped initially with three Seafire F.XVIIs and three Firefly Is. In May 1948 the fighter role was dropped and No.1830 standardised on Fireflies. During August and September 1949 these joined HMS *Illustrious* for the squadron's first period of embarkation during annual training, and it subsequently received the annual Boyd Trophy award for completing 205 accident-free deck landings. The squadron moved temporarily to Donibristle in December 1950 to enable the Abbotsinch runways to be reconstructed. Firefly AS.6s arrived in 1951, and on 1 June 1952 the Scottish Air Division was formed to control No.1830 and its offshoot No.1830A which later became No.1843 Squadron. Returning to Abbotsinch on 1 November 1952, some Firefly FR.5s were received in 1953, but in November 1955 the squadron re-equipped with Avengers, only to disband on 10 March 1957 as part of the defence cuts that year.

Grumman Avenger AS.5 XB437 '800/AC' of No.1830 Squadron, Abbotsinch around 1956. (MAP)

Identification Markings
Corsair 7A+, to A7A+ 12.44, to *111-128/Q* 3.45; Firefly/Harvard *201-261/AC/DO*; Avenger *320-322/AC*, to *800-807/AC* 1.56.

Aircraft Equipment	Period of Service	Example	
Corsair I	Jun 1943 - Aug 1943	JT116	(7H)
Corsair II	Aug 1943 - May 1945	JT352	(117/Q)
Defiant TT.I	Mar 1944 - Apr 1944		
Seafire F.XVII	Aug 1947 - May 1948	SX245	
Harvard T.2b	Jan 1950 - Oct 1954	KF517	(239/DO)
Harvard T.3	Jan 1950 - Mar 1955	EZ272	(202/AC)
Firefly FR.1	Aug 1947 - Oct 1951	MB738	(221/AC)
Firefly T.1	Jun 1948 - Nov 1949	MB465	
Firefly T.2	Oct 1950 - Nov 1955	DK489	(236/O)
Firefly T.3	Oct 1950 - Oct 1951	PP610	(210/DO)
Firefly FR.5	Aug 1953 - Nov 1955	VT470	(226/AC)
Firefly AS.6	Oct 1951 - Nov 1955	VX392	(222/AC)
Sea Fury T.20	Oct 1952 - Oct 1954	VZ366	(234/AC)
Anson 1	Apr 1953 - Jul 1953		
Sea Prince T.1	Jul 1953 - May 1956	WP312	(888/AC)
Oxford	Sep 1953 - Jan 1955	PH408	(601/AC)
Sea Balliol T.21	Oct 1954 - Mar 1957	WP325	(204/AC)
Avenger AS.5	Nov 1955 - Mar 1957	XB443	(806/AC)

Battle Honours
Sabang	1944
Palembang	1945
Okinawa	1945

Squadron bases
Quonset Point	1 Jun 1943
Brunswick	21 Sep 1943
Sanford	22 Sep 1943
Norfolk (transit)	9 Oct 1943
HMS Slinger	9 Oct 1943
Belfast	1 Nov 1943
Stretton	3 Nov 1943
HMS Illustrious	9 Dec 1943
Machrihanish (Dt10)	20-23 Dec 1943
China Bay	28 Jan 1944
HMS Illustrious	10 Feb 1944
China Bay	14 Feb 1944
HMS Illustrious	22 Feb 1944
China Bay	12 Mar 1944
HMS Illustrious	21 Mar 1944
China Bay	31 Mar 1944
HMS Illustrious	13 Apr 1944
Wingfield	11 Aug 1944
HMS Illustrious	13 Oct 1944
Colombo Racecourse	2 Nov 1944
Puttalam	17 Nov 1944
China Bay (Dt8)	21-25 Nov 1944
Katukurunda	27 Nov 1944
HMS Illustrious	29 Nov 1944
Trincomalee (Dt7)	22 Dec 1944 to 12 Jan 1945
Nowra	9 Feb 1945
HMS Illustrious	7 Mar 1945
Bankstown	14 May 1945
HMS Illustrious	24 May 1945
Sqdn disbanded UK	28 Jul 1945
Abbotsinch	15 Aug 1947
Donibristle	2 Dec 1950
Abbotsinch	1 Nov 1952
Culham	12 Jun 1953
Abbotsinch	15 Jun 1953
Annual training:	
Eglinton	16-30 Aug 1948
HMS Illustrious	27 Aug 1949 to 10 Sep 1949
Hal Far	30 Jul 1950 to 10 Aug 1950
HMS Vengeance	2-13 Jul 1951
Eglinton	13-26 Jul 1952
Hal Far	24 Aug 1953 to 5 Sep 1953
Culdrose	10-24 Jul 1954
Hal Far	8-21 May 1955
Squadron disbanded	10 Mar 1957

1830A
Donibristle	1 Oct 1952
Abbotsinch	1 Nov 1952
Redes 1843 Sqdn	28 Mar 1953

Commanding Officers
L/C D BM Fiddes DSO RN	1 Jun 1943
L/C(A) AM Tritton DSC RNVR	18 Dec 1943
Squadron disbanded	28 Jul 1945
L/C(A) JD Murricane DSC RNVR	15 Aug 1947
L/C(A) RC Read RNVR	1 Jun 1952
Squadron disbanded	10 Mar 1957

No.1831 Squadron

Badge: On a field per fess wavy blue and white, in base two bars wavy also blue and white, a winged greyhound, courant gold
Motto: Nec temere nec timide (Neither rashly nor timidly)

No.1831 Squadron formed at Quonset Point on 1 July 1943 as a single seater fighter squadron equipped with 10 Corsair Is. After work-up it embarked in HMS *Trumpeter* in October, and joined the 15th Naval Fighter Wing on disembarking in the UK, but it disbanded at Stretton on 10 December 1943, being split up between Nos.1830 and 1833 Squadrons in that Wing.

Reformed at Brunswick on 1 November 1944, again as a single seater fighter squadron, it received 18 Corsair IVs, sailing to the UK in HMS *Pursuer* in February 1945. In May it increased to 21 aircraft then joined HMS *Glory* for British Pacific Fleet attacks on Japanese islands, becoming part of the 16th Carrier Air Group in June. However, by the time the ship arrived in Ceylon the war was almost over, and it saw no action. Intended as part of the 11th Aircraft Carrier Squadron in support of operations in Borneo and South East Asia, she and her squadrons were operational when escorting invasion forces to Rabaul after the Japanese surrender, in case of opposition. Some time was then spent in Australia before re-embarking in January 1946 for a cruise to New Zealand and Japan. Returning to Australian waters, the squadron discarded its aircraft and transferred to HMS *Vengeance* at Trincomalee for passage home, disbanding on arrival on 13 August 1946.

No.1831 reformed at Stretton on 1 June 1947 as an RNVR Fighter squadron, equipped with six Seafire XVs and XVIIs. These were replaced in August 1951 by nine Sea Fury FB.11s, and on 1 June 1952 the squadron joined the Northern Air Division. No.1831 squadron re-equipped in May 1955 with seven Attacker FB.2s, but was disbanded on 10 March 1957 in the defence cuts of that year.

On 3 April 1980, No.1831 reformed at Lee-on-Solent as a Royal Naval Reserve squadron, with the task of giving annual training to former helicopter aircrew officers and fixed-wing pilots who had retired from the Royal Navy more than three years previous to joining the RNR Air Branch. Flying experience was provided on aircraft of RN air squadrons, though a Chipmunk was originally attached to No.781 Squadron for the use of No.1831. When No.781 disbanded at Lee-on-Solent on 31 March 1981, No.1831 transferred to Yeovilton, but the concept soon lapsed, and members of the RNR Air Branch instead became attached for their 2-3 weeks annual training to any squadron with the aircraft type for which they were qualified.

Auster 5 TJ704 was flown by No.1831 Squadron for a time in 1953/4. (FAA Musuem)

Aircraft Equipment	Period of Service	Example
Corsair I	Jul 1943 - Dec 1943	JT137
Corsair IV	Nov 1944 - Aug 1946	KD905 (123/Y)
Seafire F.15	Jun 1947 - Aug 1951	SW800 (109/JA)
Seafire F.17	Jun 1947 - Aug 1951	SX168 (108/JA)
Firefly T.1	Jun 1948 - Dec 1948	MB465
Auster V	Jan 1949 - Mar 1954	TJ704
Harvard T.2b	May 1950 - Nov 1954	KF507 (205/JA)
Harvard T.3	Jun 1947 - Jul 1950	EZ408 (202/JA)
Sea Fury T.20	Oct 1950 - Jun 1955	VZ350 (213/ST)
Sea Fury FB.11	Aug 1951 - Jun 1955	WM489 (109/ST)
Firefly T.3	May 1952 - Aug 1952	PP617 (280/ST)
Sea Balliol T.21	Oct 1954 - Feb 1957	WP326 (202/ST)
Sea Vampire T.22	May 1955 - Mar 1957	XA161 (818/ST)
Attacker FB.2	May 1955 - Mar 1957	WZ283 (170/ST)

Squadron bases		Squadron bases	
Quonset Point	1 Jul 1943	St Merryn	7-20 Jul 1951
Brunswick	23 Aug 1943	Hal Far	19-30 May 1952
Norfolk	4 Oct 1943	St Merryn	22 Jun 1953
HMS Trumpeter	6 Oct 1943	(DLT in HMS	to 4 Jul 1953
Belfast	1 Nov 1943	Illustrious)	
Stretton	3 Nov 1943	Valkenburg	12-13 Sep 1953
Squadron disbanded	10 Dec 1943	Hal Far	20 Aug 1954
Brunswick	1 Nov 1944		to 3 Sep 1954
Bar Harbour	2 Dec 1944	Valkenburg	12-13 Apr 1956
Brunswick	8 Dec 1944	Brawdy	28 Jul 1956
Norfolk	20 Dec 1944		to 10 Aug 1956
Brunswick	28 Dec 1944	Squadron disbanded	10 Mar 1957
Norfolk (transit)	31 Jan 1945	Lee-on-Solent	3 Apr 1980
HMS Pursuer	1 Feb 1945	Yeovilton	1 Apr 1981
Eglinton	18 Feb 1945	Concept lapsed	
Renfrew (transit)	9 May 1945		
HMS Glory	11 May 1945	**Commanding Officers**	
Hal Far	22 May 1945	L/C HP Allingham	
HMS Glory	26 May 1945	RNR	1 Jul 1943
Dekheila	18 Jun 1945	Squadron disbanded	10 Dec 1943
HMS Glory	2 Jul 1945	L/C(A) RWM Walsh	
Katukurunda	15 Jul 1945	RN	1 Nov 1944
HMS Glory	27 Jul 1945	Lt(A) RWH Boyns RNVR	
Schofields	16 Aug 1945		2 Aug 1945
HMS Glory	1 Sep 1945	L/C(A) RT Leggott	
Jacquinot Bay (Dt)	5-30 Sep 1945	MBE RN	28 Mar 1946
Jervis Bay	11 Sep 1945	Squadron disbanded	12 Aug 1946
Nowra	29 Oct 1945	L/C(A) NG Mitchell	
HMS Glory	19 Jan 1946	DSC RNVR	1 Jun 1947
Williamtown	15 Feb 1946	L/C(A) RI Gilchrist	
HMS Glory	10 Jun 1946	MBE RNVR	26 May 1948
Trincomalee	15 Jul 1946	L/C(A) KH Tickle	
HMS Vengeance	16 Jul 1946	RNVR	1 Jun 1952
Squadron disbanded	13 Aug 1946	L/C(A) WA Storey	
Stretton	1 Jun 1947	RNVR	18 Aug 1952
Annual training:		L/C(A) F Morrell	
Culdrose	4-17 Sep 1948	RNVR	1954
HMS Illustrious	21 Sep 1949	L/C(A) PLV Rougier	
	to 1 Oct 1949	RNVR	23 Apr 1955
HMS Illustrious	29 Aug 1950	Squadron disbanded	10 Mar 1957
	to 9 Sep 1950		

Hawker Sea Fury FB.11 VR947 '104/JA' of No.1831 Squadron, Stretton in 1951. (Jim Palmer)

Identification Markings

Corsair *1V7+*, later *Y8A*, then *112/Y+*; Seafire & Sea Fury *101-113/JA:ST*; Harvard *201-205/JA*; Sea Fury T.20 *201/JA:ST*, later *210-213/ST*; Sea Balliol *202-203/ST*, to *867-868/ST* 1.56; Attacker *170-176/ST*, to *810-816/ST* 1.56; Sea Vampire *260-263/ST*, to *818/ST*.

No.1832 Squadron

Badge: On a field barry wavy of six white and blue, in front of a sword point downwards red a dove volant white in the beak a sprig of olive proper

Motto: *Robur in pace*
(Strong in peace)

Wildcat V 'D' of No.1832 Squadron, Eglinton 1943. (Mick Burrow)

No.1832 Squadron formed at Eglinton on 15 August 1943 as a single seater fighter squadron equipped mainly with ten Wildcat Vs. It soon moved to Stretton, where its task was to form fighter flights of four aircraft each, for attachment to TBR squadrons serving in escort carriers. The first such flight formed in November for HMS *Fencer*, and eventually ten flights formed, most being merged into the squadron to which they were attached. Returning to Eglinton in February 1944 it absorbed the remains of No.878 Squadron, but was itself disbanded on 1 June 1944. Plans to reform in November 1945 with 15 Corsairs for a 5th Carrier Air Group were cancelled when the war against the Japanese ended.

On 1 July 1947 No.1832 reformed at Culham as a fighter quadron in the RN Volunteer Reserve, drawing its pilots mainly from the London and Oxford areas. Equipped initially with four Seafire IIIs, these soon gave way to six Seafire FR.46s, plus some F.17s from June 1948. F.15s began to replace the FR.46s in April 1949 and by January 1950 the strength was 14 Seafire F.15s and F.17s. In August 1951 No.1832 began to re-equip with nine Sea Fury FB.11s, and on 1 June 1952 the Southern Air Division was formed to control No.1832 and its two offshoots, Nos.1832A and 1832B Squadrons, which formed on 1 October 1952, becoming respectively Nos.1836 and 1835 Squadrons in April 1953.

In July 1953 the three squadrons moved to RAF Benson, where they operated their aircraft on a pooled basis, a peak of 27 Sea Furies, 4 Harvards and 2 Sea Balliols being on strength by 1955. In August 1955 No.1832 re-equipped with eight Attacker FB.2s, the other two squadrons continuing to operate Sea Furies for a time. By April 1956 the three squadrons were back to being pooled, and now had 8 Attackers, 2 Sea Vampire T.22s, 2 Sea Hawk F.1s and 2 Sea Fury T.20s. By the end of that year the Attackers had gone and equipment was 2 Sea Vampires and 13 Sea Hawks. The squadron disbanded on 10 March 1957 as part of the defence cuts.

On 3 April 1980, No.1832 reformed at Yeovilton as a Royal Naval Reserve squadron, with the task of giving annual training to former helicopter aircrew officers retired from the Royal Navy less than three years previous to joining the RNR Air Branch. Flying experience was to be provided on aircraft of RN air squadrons. However, this concept soon lapsed, and members of the RNR Air Branch instead became attached for their 2-3 weeks annual training to any squadron with the aircraft type for which they were qualified.

Supermarine Seafire F.15 SW794 '134/CH' of No.1832 Squadron in 1950. (via Brian Lowe)

Aircraft Equipment	Period of Service	Example	
Martlet I	Aug 1943 - Dec 1943	BJ567	
Martlet II	Aug 1943 - Dec 1943	AJ127	
Martlet IV	Aug 1943 - Dec 1943	FN143	
Wildcat V	Aug 1943 - Jun 1944	JV579	(F)
Seafire III	Jul 1947 - Nov 1947	RX158	
Seafire FR.46	Aug 1947 - Jan 1950	LA555	(105/CH)
Seafire F.17	Jun 1948 - May 1953	SX198	(101/CH)
Seafire F.15	Apr 1949 - Aug 1951	SW856	(116/CH)
Harvard T.2b	Jul 1947 - Apr 1955	KF500	(203/CH)
Harvard T.3	Jan 1948 - Feb 1951	EZ318	(205/CH)
Anson 1	Jan 1949 - Mar 1950	NK762	
Auster 5	Jan 1950 - Jul 1952	TJ688	
Sea Fury T.20	Oct 1950 - Jun 1956	VZ355	(201/CH)
Sea Fury FB.11	Aug 1951 - Aug 1955	VX693	(104)
Dominie 1	Jul 1953 - Nov 1955	NF867	(905/CH)
Sea Balliol T.21	Mar 1955 - Nov 1955	WP325	(276)
Sea Vampire T.22	Jul 1955 - Mar 1957	XA159	(854)
Attacker FB.2	Aug 1955 - Nov 1956	WP275	(827)
Sea Hawk F.1	Jan 1956 - Mar 1957	WF222	(850)

Sea Furies of No.1832 Squadron, Culham. (M.R.H.Shippey)

Identification Markings
Wildcat single letters; Seafire *101-134/CH*; Harvard *201-206/CH*, later *276-279*; Sea Fury FB.11 *151-160/CH*, to *101+* 7.53; Sea Fury T.20 *100-203/CH*, to *272-273* 7.53 later *851-852*; Attacker *101-108*, to *820-834* 1.56; Sea Balliol *275-276*; Sea Hawk *820-824, 845-852*; Sea Vampire *278-279*, to *853-854* 1.56.

Battle Honours
Norway	1944
Atlantic	1944
Arctic	1944

Squadron bases
Eglinton	15 Aug 1943
Speke	20 Sep 1943
Stretton	9 Dec 1943
Eglinton	2 Feb 1944

'A' Flight:
Maydown	6 Nov 1943
HMS Argus (DLT)	15 Nov 1943
Machrihanish	19 Nov 1943
HMS Fencer	20 Nov 1943

Squadron bases
To 842 Sqdn as 'Q' Flight

'B' Flight:
| Machrihanish | 20 Dec 1943 |
(for HMS Tracker)
To 846 Sqdn

'C' Flight:
| Stretton | 9 Dec 1943 |
| Machrihanish | 30 Jan 1944 |
- to 832 Sqdn

'D' Flight:
| Eglinton | 3 Feb 1944 |
| HMS Engadine | 18 Feb 1944 |
- to 845 Sqdn

'E' Flight:
| Eglinton | 3 Feb 1944 |
| HMS Fencer | 17 Mar 1944 |

'F' Flight:
| Eglinton | 3 Feb 1944 |
| HMS Campania | 5 Apr 1944 |
- to 813 Sqdn
(was to have gone to 848 Sqdn HMS Ameer)

'G' Flight:
| Eglinton | 3 Feb 1944 |
- to 852 Sqdn

'H' Flight:
| Eglinton | 26 Mar 1944 |

Squadron bases
'I' Flight:
| Eglinton | 26 Mar 1944 |

'J' Flight:
| Eglinton | 16 Mar 1944 |

'L' Flight:
| Machrihanish | 13 May 1944 |
| HMS Tracker | 3 Jun 1944 |
- to 846 Sqdn

Squadron disbanded	1 Jun 1944
Culham	1 Jul 1947
Benson	18 Jul 1953

Annual training:
Culdrose	29 May 1948
	to 12 Jun 1948
Culdrose	19 Jun 1948
	to 3 Jul 1948
HMS Implacable	9-23 Jul 1949
HMS Theseus	17-30 Jun 1950
St Merryn	23 Jun 1950
	to 8 Jul 1951
Hal Far	7-12 Jun 1952
Culdrose	4-18 Jul 1953
Schleswigland	10-24 Jul 1954
Ford/HMS Bulwark	23 Jun 1956
	to 7 Jul 1956
Squadron disbanded	10 Mar 1957
Yeovilton	3 Apr 1980

1832A

Squadron bases
| Culham | 1 Oct 1952 |
| Redes 1836 Sqdn | 28 Mar 1953 |

1832B
| Culham | 1 Oct 1952 |
| Redes 1835 Sqdn | 28 Mar 1953 |

Commanding Officers
L/C(A) TW Harrington RN 15 Aug 1943
L/C M Hordern RN 15 Dec 1943
Squadron disbanded 1 Jun 1944
L/C(A) P Godfrey OBE RNVR 1 Jul 1947
L/C(A) GM Rutherford MBE DSC RNVR 7 Dec 1948
L/C(A) GR Willcocks DSC RNVR 1 Jun 1952
L/C(A) MRH Shippey RNVR 27 Nov 1953
L/C(A) TC Fletcher RNVR 30 Sep 1955
L/C(A) AJ Austin RNVR 12 Jul 1956
Squadron disbanded 10 Mar 1957

Supermarine Attacker FB.2 WP289 '826' of No.1832 Squadron in 1957. (via Brian Lowe)

No.1833 Squadron

Badge: On a blue field, above a base barry wavy of four white and blue an eagle volant gold
Motto: In caelo regimus (We rule the skies)

Hawker Sea Fury FB.11s of No.1833 Squadron, Bramcote around 1954/5. (B.W.Vigrass)

No.1833 Squadron personnel assembled at Donibristle and Townhill Camp on 15 June 1943, and after being shipped to the USA formed officially at Quonset Point on 15 July 1943 as a single seater fighter squadron. Equipped with ten Corsair Is, these soon gave way to Mk.IIs, which after work-up embarked in HMS *Trumpeter* in October for the UK. Here the strength was increased to 14 aircraft by absorbing part of No.1831 Squadron, and No.1833 joined the 15th Naval Fighter Wing, embarking in HMS *Illustrious* in December to join the Eastern Fleet. Arriving in Ceylon, a three day sweep was carried out in the Bay of Bengal in March 1944, and during April shore and shipping objectives were attacked at Sabang. Similar attacks were carried out the next month on Sourabaya, and on the Andaman Islands in June and Sabang again in July.

The ship sailed to Durban in August for a refit, and No.1833 increased its strength to 18 aircraft. Returning to action, the squadron took part in attacks on Sumatran oil refineries in December 1944 and January 1945. These were followed in March and April by extensive operations against targets in the Sakishima Gunto group of islands in the East China Seas. During one of these the ship was damaged by a near-miss from a Kamikaze, and retired on 14 April to Australia. Here No.1833 discarded its aircraft and the pilots returned to the UK to disband on arrival on 28 July 1945. Plans to re-equip with 24 Seafires and return as part of a 10th Carrier Air Group were cancelled after VJ-Day.

On 15 August 1947 No.1833 reformed at Bramcote as an RNVR fighter squadron. Equipped initially with six Seafire F.17s, these were supplemented in July 1949 by Seafire F.15s, a peak strength of 11 aircraft being reached by October 1951. In June 1952 the squadron re-equipped with ten Seafire FR.47s, and on 1 July 1953 the Midland Air Division was formed to control the Bramcote units. The Seafires were replaced in February 1954 by nine Sea Fury FB.11s, and these in turn gave way in October 1955 to seven Attacker FB.2s, the arrival of jet aircraft necessitating a move to RAF Honiley where there were hard runways. The squadron disbanded on 10 March 1957 as part of that year's defence cuts.

Chance Vought Corsair II JT228 '6A' of No.1833 Squadron, Machrihanish on 9 December 1943. (RAF Museum 5989-5)

Supermarine Seafire F.15 SP352 '163/BR' of No.1833 Squadron, Bramcote in 1959. (Brian Lowe)

Identification Markings
Corsair *6A+*, to *A6A+* to 12.44; to *129-147/Q* 3.45; Seafire *151-168/BR*; Harvard *251-258/BR*; Sea Fury T.30 *254-255/BR*, to *271-273/BR* 2.54; Firefly *251-256/BR*; Sea Fury FB.11 *151-162/BR*; Attacker *160-166/ST*, to *833-841* 1.56.

Aircraft Equipment

Aircraft	Period of Service	Example
Corsair I	Jul 1943 - Sep 1943	JT166 (6F)
Corsair II	Jul 1943 - May 1945	JT528 (143/Q)
Seafire F.17	Aug 1947 - Jul 1952	SX279 (156/BR)
Seafire F.15	Jul 1949 - Aug 1951	SW786 (164/BR)
Harvard T.2b	Aug 1947 - Sep 1950	KF521 (257/BR)
Harvard T.3	Jan 1949 - Jan 1955	EZ438 (253/BR)
Anson 1	Dec 1949 - Jul 1954	LT417 (901/BR)
Sea Fury T.20	Oct 1950 - Oct 1955	VZ346 (273/BR)
Sea Hornet PR.22	Jun 1951 - Feb 1952	VW931
Seafire FR.47	Jun 1952 - May 1954	VP474 (156/BR)
Firefly T.2	Sep 1952 - Oct 1952	MB752 (251/BR)
Firefly T.3	Nov 1952 - Jul 1954	PP485 (255/BR)
Tiger Moth T.2	Jul 1953 - Sep 1953	A17-84
Sea Fury FB.11	Feb 1954 - Jul 1955	WE711 (157/BR)
Attacker FB.2	Oct 1955 - Mar 1957	WZ301 (837)

Battle Honours
Sabang 1944
Palembang 1945
Okinawa 1945

Squadron bases
Quonset Point	15 Jul 1943	Annual training:
Brunswick	25 Aug 1943	Culdrose 15-29 Aug 1948
Floyd Bennett Fd	14 Oct 1943	HMS Illustrious 17-29 Sep 1949
Norfolk (transit)	17 Oct 1943	HMS Illustrious 29 Aug 1950
HMS Trumpeter	17 Oct 1943	St Merryn 7-20 Jul 1951
Belfast	1 Nov 1943	HMS Triumph 9-20 Jun 1952
Stretton	3 Nov 1943	St Merryn 11-26 Jul 1953
Machrihanish	8 Dec 1943	Hal Far 4-18 Sep 1954
HMS Ravager (Dt-DLT)	20 Dec 1943	Ford 3-17 Aug 1956
HMS Illustrious	22 Dec 1943	Squadron disbanded 10 Mar 1957
China Bay	28 Jan 1944	
HMS Illustrious	22 Feb 1944	**Commanding Officers**
China Bay	12 Mar 1944	L/C(A) HA Monk
HMS Illustriousa	21 Mar 1944	DSM & Bar RN 15 Jul 1943
China Bay	31 Mar 1944	L/C(A) NS Hanson
HMS Illustrious	13 Apr 1944	DSC RNVR 20 Mar 1944
Wingfield	11 Aug 1944	Squadron disbanded 28 Jul 1945
HMS Illustrious	13 Oct 1944	L/C(A) LF Auckland
Koggala	2 Nov 1944	DSC RNVR 15 Aug 1947
Trincomalee(trans)	28 Nov 1944	L/C(A) RIM Scott
HMS Illustrious	29 Nov 1944	OBE RNVR 16 Mar 1948
Trincomalee (Dt)	22 Dec 1944	L/C(A) RF Hallam
to	16 Jan 1945	RNVR 1 Feb 1950
Nowra (Dt6)	9 Feb 1945	L/C(A) BW Vigrass
to	7 Mar 1945	RNVR 1 Apr 1952
Bankstown(transit)	14 May 1945	L/C(A) DG Jenkins
HMS Illustrious	14 May 1945	DFC RNVR 28 Jun 1953
Squadron disbanded	28 Jul 1945	Squadron disbanded 10 Mar 1957
Bramcote	15 Aug 1947	
Honiley	23 Oct 1955	

Hawker Sea Fury FB.11 VW656 '151/BR' of No.1833 Squadron, Bramcote in 1954.

No.1834 Squadron

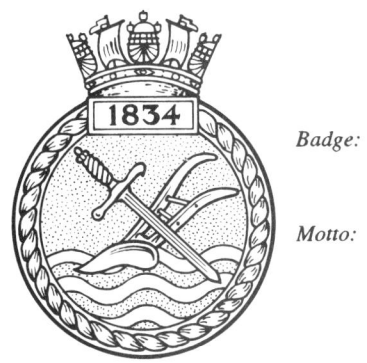

Badge: (Heraldic description lacking)

Motto: *Cleaving earth and sky*

Aircraft Equipment	Period of Service	Example
Corsair I	Jul 1943 - Oct 1943	JT158 (9L)
Corsair II	Oct 1943 - Aug 1945	JT311 (T7B)
Corsair IV	Apr 1945 - Aug 1945	KD171 (113/P)
Sea Fury FB.11	Oct 1953 - Apr 1955	VW542 (150/VL)
Sea Fury T.20	Oct 1953 - Apr 1955	WG653 (261/VL)
Harvard T.2b	Oct 1953 - Apr 1955	KF559 (265/VL)
Sea Balliol T.21	Oct 1954 - Apr 1955	WP325 (266/VL)

Battle Honours
Norway	1944
Sabang	1944
Palembang	1945
Okinawa	1945
Japan	1945

Squadron bases
Quonset Point	15 Jul 1943
Brunswick	27 Aug 1943
Norfolk	14 Oct 1943
USS Charger (DLT)	16 Oct 1943
Brunswick	17 Oct 1943
Floyd Bennett Field (transit)	30 Oct 1943
Norfolk (transit)	31 Oct 1943
HMS Khedive	1 Nov 1943
Maydown	16 Nov 1943
Speke	19 Nov 1943
Maydown	22 Nov 1943
Stretton	20 Dec 1943
Machrihanish	1 Feb 1944
HMS Ravager (DLT)	7 Feb 1944
Machrihanish	11 Feb 1944
HMS Victorious	12 Feb 1944
Machrihanish	15 Feb 1944
HMS Victorious	8 Mar 1944
Machrihanish	20 Mar 1944
Grimsetter	24 Mar 1944
HMS Victorious	30 Mar 1944
Colombo Racecourse	7 Jul 1944
HMS Victorious	19 Jul 1944
Minneriya	27 Jul 1944
HMS Victorious	10 Aug 1944
Colombo Racecourse	28 Aug 1944
HMS Victorious	14 Sep 1944
Puttalam	25 Sep 1944
HMS Victorious	11 Oct 1944
Colombo Racecourse	28 Oct 1944
HMS Victorious	19 Dec 1944
Nowra	10 Feb 1945
HMS Victorious	27 Feb 1945
Schofields	5 Jun 1945
HMS Victorious	26 Jun 1945
Bankstown/Maryborough	23 Aug 1945
HMS Victorious	25 Sep 1945
Sqdn disbanded UK	31 Oct 1945
Benson	10 Oct 1953
Yeovilton	16 Jan 1954
Squadron disbanded	May 1955

Commanding Officers
L/C(A) AM Tritton DSC RNVR	15 Jul 1943
L/C(A) PN Charlton DFC RN	23 Dec 1943
L/C(A) RDB Hopkins RN	10 Oct 1944
L/C JG Baldwin DSC RN	26 Apr 1945
Squadron disbanded	31 Oct 1945
L/C(A) ACB Ford VRD DSC RNVR	10 Oct 1953
Squadron disbanded	30 Apr 1955

No.1834 Squadron personnel assembled at Donibristle and Townhill Camp on 15 June 1943 for passage to the USA, where it officially formed at Quonset Point on 15 July as a single seater fighter squadron. Equipped with ten Corsair Is, these gave way to Corsair IIs before embarking in HMS *Khedive* in November for the UK. In January 1944 it joined the 47th Naval Fighter Wing with an increased strength of 14 aircraft, and in April embarked in HMS *Victorious* to help provide top cover for attacks during the next two months on the German battleship *Tirpitz* which was anchored in a Norwegian fjord. In June the ship sailed for the Far East, where No.1834 took part in a series of attacks on targets in Sumatra between July 1944 and January 1945. The ship then joined the British Pacific Fleet, and between March and May 1945 operations were carried out against the Sakishima Group of islands. In June the squadron joined the 1st CAG, and just before VJ-Day strikes were made against the Tokyo area, the ship then retiring to Australia. The Corsairs were discarded there, and No.1834 returned to the UK in HMS *Victorious*, disbanding on arrival on 31 October 1945.

On 10 October 1953, No.1834 reformed as a fighter unit in the Southern Air Division of the RNVR at Benson. Equipped with Sea Furies, it moved on 16 January 1954 to Yeovilton, where it was disbanded on 30 April 1955.

Identification Markings
Corsair *9A+* to 10.43, later *7A+* by 4.44, to *T7A+* 1.45, to *111-128/P* 3.45; Sea Fury FB.11 *150-156/VL*, T.20 *260-261/VL*; Sea Balliol *265-266/VL*, to *275-276* 3.55.

Hawker Sea Fury FB.11 VW653 '154', formerly of No.1834 Squadron, in store at Abbotsinch in 1957. (MAP)

No.1835 Squadron

No.1835 Squadron personnel assembled at Townhill Camp on 1 July 1943, and after passage to the USA officially formed at Quonset Point on 15 August 1943 as a single seater fighter squadron. Equipped with 10 Corsair Is, these gave way in October to Corsair IIs, with which it was to have become part of the 47th Naval Fighter Wing. However, it instead disbanded on 23 November 1943 to form the basis of No.732 Squadron.

On 1 December 1944 No.1835 reformed at Brunswick, again as a single seater fighter squadron, equipped with 18 Corsair IVs. These were left behind on taking passage to the UK, and 18 new Corsair IIIs were received at Eglinton. These were passed on to No.1837 Squadron in June, and 21 Corsair IVs replaced them. It was intended that after work-up the squadron would join the 17th Carrier Air Group in the British Pacific Fleet, but VJ-Day intervened and instead it disbanded at Nutts Corner on 3 September 1945.

On 1 October 1952 No.1832B Squadron formed at Culham as an RNVR fighter squadron in the Southern Air Division, becoming No.1835 Squadron in March 1953. Aircraft were shared with Nos.1832 and 1836 Squadrons, and details will be found under the former. The Air Division moved in July 1953 to RAF Benson, where No.1835 disbanded on 10 March 1957 under defence cuts.

Chance Vought Corsair IV KD283 'Q' of No.1835 Squadron aboard HMS Premier in the Irish Sea in July 1945. (J.D.Buchanan)

Identification Markings
Corsair *5A+* 1943, *1V11+* from 12.44, to single letters 4.45

Aircraft Equipment	Period of Service	Example
Corsair I	Aug 1943 - Nov 1943	JT168 (5K)
Corsair II	Oct 1943 - Nov 1943	JT275 (5A)
Corsair IV	Dec 1944 - Mar 1945	KD748 (4V11)
Corsair III	Apr 1945 - Jun 1945	JS771 (S)
Corsair IV	Jun 1945 - Aug 1945	KD423 (U)
Widgeon 1	Dec 1944 - Mar 1945	FP457

Commanding Officers		Squadron bases	
L/C(A) MS Godson RN	15 Aug 1943	Quonset Point	15 Aug 1943
		Brunswick	30 Aug 1943
Squadron disbanded	23 Nov 1943	Squadron disbanded	23 Nov 1943
L/C(A) TJA King -Joyce RN	1 Dec 1944	Brunswick	1 Dec 1944
		passage to UK	20 Mar 1945
Squadron disbanded	3 Sep 1945	arrived (no a/c)	4 Apr 1945
L/C(A) ACB Ford DSC RNVR	1 Nov 1952	Eglinton	21 Apr 1945
		Belfast	29 Jun 1945
L/C(A) PJ Robins RNVR	31 Oct 1953	HMS Premier (DLT)	25 Jul 1945
		Belfast	2 Aug 1945
L/C(A) NJ Cook RNVR	20 Jun 1956	Nutts Corner	23 Aug 1945
		Squadron disbanded	3 Sep 1945
Squadron disbanded	10 Mar 1957	Culham	28 Mar 1953
		Benson	18 Jul 1953
		Squadron disbanded	10 Mar 1957

No.1836 Squadron

No.1836 Squadron personnel assembled at Townhill Camp on 1 July 1943, and after taking passage to the USA officially formed at Quonset Point on 15 August as a single seater fighter squadron. Equipped with 10 Corsair Is, it exchanged these for for 18 Corsair IIs in November, embarking in HMS *Atheling* in January 1944 for the UK. On arrival it joined the 47th Naval Fighter Wing and reduced to 14 aircraft, embarking in HMS *Victorious* in March to help provide top cover during attacks during the next two months on the German battleship *Tirpitz*, then anchored in a Norwegian fjord. Sailing in June to join the Eastern Fleet, attacks were made between July 1944 and January 1945 on oil refineries in Sumatra. By March the ship had joined the British Pacific Fleet, and its attentions turned to targets in the Sakishima Gunto group of islands in the East China Seas, some Corsair IVs being received by No.1836 about that time. In June it became part of the 1st CAG, and just before VJ-Day, attacks were made on targets in the Tokyo area. Leaving its aircraft in Australia, the squadron then sailed for home, disbanding on arrival on 31 October 1945.

On 1 October 1952 No.1832A Squadron formed at Culham as an RNVR fighter squadron in the Southern Air Division, becoming No.1836 Squadron in March 1953. The Air Division moved in July 1953 to RAF Benson, where aircraft were used on a pooled basis by Nos.1832, 1835 and 1836 Squadrons. Details will be found under the first of these. No.1836 disbanded on 10 March 1957 as part of defence cuts.

Aircraft Equipment	Period of Service	Example
Corsair I	Aug 1943 - Nov 1943	JT192 (3Q)
Corsair II	Nov 1943 - Oct 1945	JT413 (133/P)
Corsair IV	Apr 1945 - Oct 1945	KD368 (135/P)

Identification Markings
Corsair *3A+*, to *8A+* by 4.44, to *T8A+* 1.45, to *131-150/P* 3.45.

A Chance Vought Corsair II of No.1836 Squadron on HMS Atheling in January 1944. (Cdr P.Carmichael)

Battle Honours		Squadron bases	
Norway	1944	Norfolk (DLT)	12 Nov 1943
Sabang	1944	Brunswick	17 Nov 1943
Palembang	1945	Norfolk (transit)	18 Dec 1943
Okinawa	1945	HMS Atheling	18 Dec 1943
Japan	1945	Belfast (transit)	9 Jan 1944
		Burscough	10 Jan 1944
Squadron bases		Stretton	3 Feb 1944
Quonset Point	15 Aug 1943	Machrihanish	14 Feb 1944
Brunswick	1 Sep 1943	HMS Victorious	8 Mar 1944

No.1836 Squadron continued

Squadron bases		Squadron bases		Commanding Officers		Commanding Officers	
Colombo Racecourse	7 Jul 1944	Nowra	10 Feb 1945	L/C(A) CC Tomkinson		L/C(A) TO Adkin	
HMS Victorious	19 Jul 1944	HMS Victorious	27 Feb 1945	RNVR	18 Aug 1943	RNVR	14 Feb 1953
Minneriya	27 Jul 1944	Schofields	5 Jun 1945	L/C JB Edmundson		L/C(A) WLE Brewer	
HMS Victorious	4 Aug 1944	HMS Victorious	26 Jun 1945	DSC RN	27 Mar 1945	RNZNVR	23 Jul 1956
Colombo Racecourse	28 Aug 1944	Bankstown/	23 Aug 1945	L/C JG Baldwin RN	21 May 1945	Squadron disbanded 10 Mar 1957	
HMS Victorious	14 Sep 1944	Maryborough		L/C(A) DK Evans			
Colombo Racecourse	25 Sep 1944	HMS Victorious	23 Aug 1945	RNZNVR	14 Jun 1945		
HMS Victorious	11 Oct 1944	(no a/c)		Lt(A) DT Chute			
Colombo Racecourse	23 Oct 1944	Sqdn disbanded UK 31 Oct 1945		RNVR	27 Aug 1945		
Puttalam	10 Nov 1944	Culham	28 Mar 1953	Squadron disbanded 31 Oct 1945			
Colombo Racecourse	17 Nov 1944	Benson	18 Jul 1953				
HMS Victorious	20 Dec 1944	Squadron disbanded 10 Mar 1957					

No.1837 Squadron

No.1837 Squadron formed at Quonset Point on 1 September 1943 as a single seater fighter squadron. Equipped with ten Corsair Is, these had been exchanged for 14 Corsair IIs by the time it embarked in HMS *Begum* in January 1944 for the UK. After a brief sojourn at Burscough, the squadron took leave and then embarked for Ceylon in HMS *Atheling* as the only squadron in the 6th Naval Fighter Wing. Joining HMS *Illustrious* in June, No.1837 helped to provide fighter defence for the Fleet, and participated in attacks on shore targets during action against the Andaman Islands. In July it provided fighter defence during a bombardment of Sabang in Sumatra. In August No.1837 transferred to the 47th Fighter Wing in HMS *Victorious*, only to be disbanded on 9 September 1944 to enable Nos.1834 and 1836 Squadrons to be expanded.

On 1 July 1945 No.1837 reformed as a single seater fighter squadron at Eglinton. Equipped with 22 Corsair IIIs, mainly from No.1835 Squadron, it was earmarked for the 4th Carrier Air Group in HMS *Illustrious* with the British Pacific Fleet. With the ending of hostilities against Japan it was no longer required, and on 18 August 1945 it disbanded at Nutts Corner, its aircraft going to No.1 Naval Air Fighter School at Yeovilton.

A Corsair I of No.1837 Squadron in November 1943. (R. Pridham-Wippell)

Battle Honours
Sabang   1944

Identification Markings
Corsair 7A+ 1943/5, single letters 1945.

Aircraft Equipment	Period of Service	Example	
Corsair I	Sep 1943 - Jan 1944	JT214	(7A)
Corsair II	Jan 1944 - Sep 1944	JT322	(7A)
Corsair III	Jul 1945 - Aug 1945	JS496	(H)

Squadron bases		Squadron bases	
Quonset Point	1 Sep 1943	Squadron disbanded	9 Sep 1944
Brunswick	1 Oct 1943	Eglinton	1 Jul 1945
Norfolk (DLT)	8 Jan 1944	Nutts Corner	31 Jul 1945
HMS Begum	19 Jan 1944	Squadron disbanded 18 Aug 1945	
Burscough	1 Feb 1944		
Stretton	12 Feb 1944	**Commanding Officers**	
HMS Atheling	26 Feb 1944	L/C(A) AJ Sewell	
Minneriya	13 Apr 1944	DSC RNVR	1 Sep 1943
HMS Unicorn	5 Jun 1944	L/C R Pridham	
Minneriya (DLT)	7 Jun 1944	-Wippell RN	17 Oct 1943
HMS Illustrious	19 Jun 1944	Squadron disbanded 9 Sep 1944	
Colombo Racecourse	23 Jun 1944	L/C(A) R Tebble	
Minneriya	26 Jun 1944	RNVR	1 Jul 1945
HMS Illustrious	8 Jul 1944	Squadron disbanded 18 Aug 1945	
Colombo Racecourse	27 Jul 1944		
HMS Victorious	14 Aug 1944		
Colombo Racecourse	28 Aug 1944		

No.1838 Squadron

No.1838 Squadron formed at Brunswick on 1 October 1943 as a single seater fighter squadron. Equipped with 10 Corsair Is, these gave way to Corsair IIs before embarking in HMS *Begum* in January 1944 for the UK. After a brief stay at Burscough, followed by some leave, the pilots joined HMS *Atheling* and sailed for Ceylon. In July the squadron was briefly lent to HMS *Victorious* for an attack on Sabang, then in August it rejoined HMS *Atheling* and sailed for Cape Town, but after arriving at Wingfield on 12 September, it disbanded the following day to enable Nos.1830 and 1833 Squadrons to enlarge. It was planned to reform in November 1945 with 15 Corsairs for a 5th Carrier Air Group in the British Pacific Fleet, but this was cancelled after VJ-Day.

Aircraft Equipment	Period of Service	Example
Corsair I	Oct 1943 - Jan 1944	JT184
Corsair II	Jan 1944 - Sep 1944	JT294

Squadron bases		Battle Honours	
Brunswick	1 Oct 1943	Sabang	1944
Norfolk (DLT)	8 Jan 1944		
HMS Begum	19 Jan 1944	**Identification Markings**	
Machrihanish	31 Jan 1944	Corsair unknown.	
Burscough	1 Feb 1944		
HMS Atheling	26 Feb 1944	**Commanding Officers**	
Minneriya	13 Apr 1944	L/C(A) FBP Sanderson	
HMS Unicorn (DLT)		RNVR	1 Oct 1943
	6 Jun 1944	L/C(A) MS Godson	
Minneriya	8 Jun 1944	RN	28 Jun 1944
HMS Victorious	23 Jul 1944	Squadron disbanded 13 Sep 1944	
Colombo Racecourse	27 Jul 1944		
HMS Atheling	25 Aug 1944		
Wingfield	12 Sep 1944		
Squadron disbanded 13 Sep 1944			

No.1839 Squadron

Badge: On a red field, an Indian tiger's head couped at the neck proper
Motto: Believed none

No.1839 Squadron formed at Eglinton on 15 November 1943 as a single seater fighter squadron. Equipped with 10 Hellcat Is, it sailed for southern India in HMS *Begum* in February 1944 as part of the 5th Naval Fighter Wing. In July it embarked in HMS *Indomitable*, and the following month provided fighter cover and photography during attacks on shore targets in Sumatra. In December 1944 and January 1945 the squadron was in action during raids on Sumatran oil refineries and other targets, then the ship joined the British Pacific Fleet and transferred its attentions to targets in the Sakishima Gunto group of islands in the East China Seas. No.1839 was enlarged in April 1945 by absorbing No.1840 Squadron. The 5th Wing was disbanded into the 11th Carrier Air Group in June, and after a spell in Australia during which the strength was increased to 18 aircraft, including some Mk.IIs, No.1839 re-embarked in early August for further operations. VJ-Day prevented this and instead the ship sailed to Hong Kong. Returning to Australia in October, the aircraft were withdrawn and the ship then sailed for the UK, disbanding on arrival on 30 November 1945.

Identification Markings
Hellcat single letters, to 5A+ by 8.44, to R5A+ 1.44, to 111-126/W 3.45.

Aircraft Equipment	Period of Service	Example
Hellcat I	Nov 1943 - Oct 1945	FN434 (R5K)
Hellcat II	Mar 1945 - Oct 1945	JW859 (112/W)

Grumman Hellcat I FN373 'J' of No.1839 Squadron, Eglinton in 1943. (via M.J.Burrow)

Battle Honours
Palembang 1945
Okinawa 1945

Squadron bases
Eglinton	15 Nov 1943
HMS Begum	26 Feb 1944
Ulunderpet	7 Apr 1944
Colombo Racecourse	23 Jun 1944
HMS Indomitable	25 Jul 1944
China Bay	21 Oct 1944
HMS Indomitable	1 Dec 1944
China Bay	3 Dec 1944
HMS Indomitable	17 Dec 1944
Nowra	10 Feb 1945
HMS Indomitable	27 Feb 1945
Nowra	4 Jun 1945
HMS Indomitable	3 Aug 1945
Nowra	11 Oct 1945
HMS Indomitable (no a/c)	22 Oct 1945
Sqdn disbanded UK	30 Nov 1945

Commanding Officers
L/C(A) DM Jeram RN 15 Nov 1943
L/C SFF Shotton DSC RNR 8 Sep 1944
L/C(A) BHC Nation RN 26 Apr 1945
Squadron disbanded 30 Nov 1945

No.1840 Squadron

Badge: On a white field, a wild cat winged, issuing from flames proper
Motto: Allied and avenging

No.1840 Squadron was originally to have formed at Eglinton on 15 October 1943 as a single seater fighter squadron with 10 Wildcat Vs. This was cancelled, and instead it came into existence at Burscough on 1 March 1944 with 10 Hellcat Is. After a brief work-up in HMS *Indefatigable* in June, with an increased strength of 20 aircraft, the squadron embarked the following month in HMS *Furious* to participate in an attack on the German battleship *Tirpitz* in a Norwegian fjord. After a further work-up, this time in HMS *Formidable*, No.1840 returned to HMS *Indefatigable* for a further raid on *Tirpitz*, some Hellcat IIs being now on strength. It then joined the 3rd Naval Fighter Wing at Eglinton, sailing at the end of the year with 24 aircraft in HMS *Speaker* for the Pacific. During March and April 1945 the squadron provided fighter coverage of the British Pacific Fleet train, but on 27 April 1945 was disbanded aboard HMS *Speaker* to enlarge No.1839 Squadron.

Grumman Hellcat II JX750 'K7P' of No.1840 Squadron on HMS Speaker on 14 February 1945. (FAA Museum)

On 14 April 1951, No.1840 reformed in the RN Volunteer Reserve as an anti-submarine squadron at Culham. Equipped with six Firefly FR.4s and two Harvards, it moved in June to Ford, where nine Firefly AS.6s replaced the FR.4s. On 1 June 1952 the Channel Air Division was formed to control the Ford units, and on 1 October 1952 No.1840A Squadron came into existence as an offshoot, becoming No.1842 Squadron in March 1953. Aircraft were then pooled, the Firefly strength having increased to 15, including trainers, by the time these were replaced by 11 Gannet AS.1s from February 1956. No.1840 Squadron disbanded on 10 March 1957 as part of that year's defence cuts.

Battle Honours
Norway 1944
Okinawa 1945

1840
Identification Markings
Hellcat single letters, to *K7A+* by 3.45; Firefly *201-212/FD*, to *855-864, 875-882/FD*; Harvard *217-221/FD*; Gannet *855-864/FD*.

Aircraft Equipment	Period of Service	Example	
Hellcat I	Mar 1944 - Dec 1944	FN403	
Hellcat II	Aug 1944 - May 1945	JX750	(K7P)
Firefly FR.4	Apr 1951 - Jul 1951	VG982	
Firefly AS.6	Jul 1951 - May 1956	WH628	(220/FD)
Firefly T.2	Jul 1951 - Jun 1956	MB725	(884/FD)
Harvard T.2b	Apr 1951 - Dec 1954	KF514	(219/FD)
Harvard T.3	Jul 1952 - Feb 1954	EZ372	(221)
Anson 1	Oct 1951 - Jul 1953	MG673	(601/FD)
Sea Prince T.1	Jun 1953 - Mar 1956	WF133	(881/FD)
Sea Balliol T.21	Mar 1954 - Sep 1955	WL719	(223/FD)
Firefly T.7	Mar 1956 - Nov 1956	WM764	(861)
Gannet AS.1	Feb 1956 - Mar 1957	XA387	(877/FD)
Gannet T.2	Feb 1956 - Mar 1957	XA525	(864/FD)

Fairey Firefly AS.6 WB428 '208/FD' of No.1840 Squadron, Ford visiting Filton in 1955. (Dave Watkins)

Squadron bases
Burscough	1 Mar 1944
Stretton	13 Mar 1944
Eglinton	13 Apr 1944
Ballyhalbert	30 May 1944
HMS Trumpeter (Dt8 - DLT)	15-25 Jun 1944
HMS Indefatigable	25 Jun 1944
Machrihanish - transit via Stornoway-Tiree	2 Jul 1944
Hatston	6 Jul 1944
HMS Furious	9 Jul 1944
Hatston	19 Jul 1944
HMS Formidable	31 Jul 1944
Hatston	5 Aug 1944
HMS Indefatigable	7 Aug 1944
Hatston	14 Aug 1944
Eglinton (Dt9)	14-17 Aug 1944
HMS Indefatigable	15 Aug 1944
Grimsetter	1 Sep 1944
Eglinton	2 Sep 1944
Ballyhalbert	24 Oct 1944
Ayr	9 Nov 1944
Ballyhalbert	16 Nov 1944
HMS Speaker	16 Dec 1944
Abbotsinch	23 Dec 1944
Ayr (re-equip)	31 Dec 1944
HMS Speaker	31 Dec 1944
Schofields	23 Feb 1945
HMS Speaker	9 Mar 1945
Squadron disbanded	27 Apr 1945
Culham	14 Apr 1951
Ford	30 Jun 1951
Annual training:	
HMS Triumph	9-21 Jun 1952
Eglinton(A Flt)	16-30 May 1953
Eglinton(B Flt)	22 Aug 1953 to 5 Sep 1953
Hal Far	9-23 May 1954
HMS Illustrious	3-11 Oct 1954
Eglinton	20 Aug 1955 to 3 Sep 1955
Squadron disbanded	10 Mar 1957

1840A
Squadron bases
| Ford | 1 Oct 1952 |
| Redes 1842 Sqdn | 28 Mar 1953 |

Commanding Officers
L/C(A) AR Richardson RNZNVR 1 Mar 1944
L/C(A) BHC Nation RN 12 Sep 1944
Squadron disbanded 27 Apr 1945
L/C(A) NH Bovey DSC RNVR 14 Apr 1951
L/C(A) APD Simms RNVR 1 Jun 1952
Squadron disbanded 10 Mar 1957

Fairey Firefly AS.6 WD918 '204/FD' of No.1840 Squadron, Channel Air Division around 1953/4.

No.1841 Squadron

Badge: On a blue field, above a base barry wavy of four white and blue an eagle volant gold holding in its claws a dolphin, green

Motto: *Aquila moras nescit* (The eagle knows no obstacles)

Corsair IV KD560 of No.1841 Squadron fom HMS Formidable on the catapult of HMS Arbiter in August 1945. (Alex Hodgins)

No.1841 Squadron formed at Brunswick on 1 March 1944 as a single seater fighter squadron equipped with 18 Corsair Is, IIs and IIIs. These were replaced in June by Mk.IIs with which the squadron embarked in HMS *Smiter* for passage to the UK. After a period working up in the Clyde in HMS *Formidable*, the squadron helped to provide escort in July and August for bombing attacks on the German battleship *Tirpitz*, then lying in a Norwegian fjord. In September No.1841 became part of the 6th Naval Fighter Wing, and the following month the ship sailed for the Far East. Intended operations in Crete en route were cancelled, and the squadron spent periods at Gibraltar and Dekheila before continuing with the ship in January 1945 to Ceylon.

The squadron went ashore in southern India, and after re-equipping with 18 Corsair IVs saw action against targets in the Sakishima Gunto group of islands in the East China Seas in April and May 1945. In June the Wing was merged into the 2nd Carrier Air Group, and shortly before VJ-Day strikes were carried out in the Tokyo area. During one of these, Lt R.H.Gray, DSC, RCNVR lost his life whilst making an attack on a Japanese destroyer on 9 August, being subsequently awarded a posthumous Victoria Cross. The ship sailed for Australia after VJ-Day, where the squadron aircraft were withdrawn. The pilots then embarked in HMS *Victorious* for passage to the UK, disbanding on arrival on 31 October 1945.

No.1841 reformed at Stretton on 18 August 1952 as an Anti-Submarine squadron in the Northern Air Division of the RN Volunteer Reserve. Equipment was five Firefly FR.1s, these being replaced in March 1955 by eight Firefly AS.6s, which in turn gave way in December 1955 to six Avenger AS.5s. No.1841 disbanded on 10 March 1957 as part of that year's defence cuts.

Identification Markings
Corsair *7A+*, to *111-128/X* 3.45; Firefly *205-211*, *280-289/ST*; Avenger *309/ST*, to *869-874/ST* 1.56.

Squadron bases
Brunswick	1 Mar 1944
Bar Harbour/ADDLs	12 May 1944
Brunswick	12 May 1944
Norfolk (transit)	2 Jun 1944
HMS Smiter	5 Jun 1944
Speke (Dt6)	21-22 Jun 1944
Ayr	22 Jun 1944
HMS Formidable	26 Jun 1944
Hatston	5 Jul 1944
HMS Formidable	10 Jul 1944
Hatston (transit)	19 Jul 1944
Eglinton	20 Jul 1944
HMS Formidable	7 Aug 1944
Skeabrae (Dt4)	14-18 Aug 1944
Donibristle	2 Sep 1944
HMS Formidable	16 Sep 1944
North Front (half)	21 Sep 1944
	to 14 Jan 1945
Colombo (Dt) left	
Gibraltar overland	15 Oct 1944
Dekheila (Dt9)	3 Nov 1944
	to 27 Jan 1945
HMS Formidable	27 Jan 1945
Puttalam	8 Feb 1945

Squadron bases
HMS Formidable	22 Feb 1945
Jervis Bay	1 Jun 1945
HMS Formidable	22 Jun 1945
Ponam	18 Aug 1945
HMS Formidable	19 Aug 1945
Nowra	23 Aug 1945

Aircraft Equipment
Aircraft	Period of Service	Example
Corsair I	Mar 1944 - Apr 1944	JT142 (7M)
Corsair II	Mar 1944 - Apr 1944	JT325 (7H)
Corsair III	Apr 1944 - Jul 1944	JS661 (7X)
Corsair II	Jun 1944 - Jul 1945	JT650 (125/X)
Corsair IV	Feb 1945 - Oct 1945	KD560 (119/X)
Firefly FR.1	Aug 1952 - Jun 1954	DK566 (286/ST)
Firefly T.2	Jan 1952 - Oct 1955	MB747 (205/ST)
Firefly T.3	Aug 1952 - May 1953	PP491 (282/ST)
Harvard T.2b	Aug 1952 - Jan 1955	KF500 (203/ST)
Harvard T.3	Jul 1952 - Feb 1954	EZ353 (204)
Anson 1	Aug 1953 - Nov 1953	NK209 (-/ST)
Sea Prince T.1	Nov 1953 - Apr 1956	WF132 (409/ST)
Firefly AS.6	Mar 1955 - Dec 1955	WD913 (283/ST)
Avenger AS.5	Dec 1955 - Mar 1957	XB377 (874/ST)

Squadron bases
HMS Victorious	25 Sep 1945
Squadron disbanded	31 Oct 1945
Stretton	18 Aug 1952
Annual training:	
Eglinton	20 Jun 1953
	to 4 Jul 1953
Valkenburg	12-13 Sep 1953
Ford	26-27 Sep 1953
Hal Far	22 Aug 1954
	to 5 Sep 1954
Hal Far	31 May 1955
	to 10 Jun 1955
Valkenburg	28-29 Apr 1956
Hal Far	22 Jun 1956
	to 6 Jul 1956
Squadron disbanded	10 Mar 1957

Commanding Officers
L/C(A) RL Bigg-Wither	
DSC & Bar RN	1 Mar 1944
Squadron disbanded	31 Oct 1945
L/C(A) KH Tickle	
RNVR	18 Aug 1952
L/C(A) F Morrell	
RNVR	22 Jul 1955
L/C(A) AE Frost	
RNVR	1 Oct 1956
Squadron disbanded	10 Mar 1957

Battle Honours
Norway	1944
Okinawa	1945
Japan	1945

Fairey Firefly AS.6 WB260 '284' of No.1841 Squadron, Stretton in 1954. (MAP)

No.1842 Squadron

No.1842 Squadron assembled at Townhill Camp in February 1944, and after taking passage to the USA officially formed at Brunswick on 1 April 1944 as a single seater fighter squadron. Equipped with 18 Corsairs IIIs, these gave way to Corsair IIs after arrival in the United Kingdom in HMS *Rajah* in June. In September, No.1842 joined the 6th Naval Fighter Wing in HMS *Formidable*, and during August lost several aircraft during attacks on the German battleship *Tirpitz*, then lying in an Norwegian fjord. The ship then sailed for the Far East, but was delayed in the Mediterranean, and the squadron spent a period ashore, being split between Gibraltar and Dekheila.

Continuing east in January 1945, it re-equipped in March with 18 Corsair IVs, with which it participated in operations against the Sakishima Gunto group of islands in the East China Seas during April and May. The Wing was merged into the 2nd CAG in June. During the last few weeks of the war strikes were carried out in the Tokyo area, two pilots being fortunate to be picked up by a US submarine when on 28 July they had to ditch inside a Japanese harbour. HMS *Formidable* then withdrew to Australia, where No.1841 left its aircraft, and the pilots returned in HMS *Victorious* to the UK, where the squadron disbanded on arrival on 31 October 1945.

On 1 October 1952, No.1840A Squadron formed at Ford as an Anti-Submarine squadron in the Channel Air Division of the RN Volunteer Reserve, becoming No.1842 Squadron on 28 March 1953. Aircraft were pooled with No.1840, under which details of these can be found. The squadron disbanded at Ford on 10 March 1957 in the defence cuts of that year.

Corsair IIs of No.1842 Squadron ranged for Operation Goodwood.

Aircraft Equipment	Period of Service	Example
Corsair III	Apr 1944 - Jun 1944	JS573 (Q)
Corsair II	Jul 1944 - Feb 1945	JT687 (141/X)
Corsair IV	Feb 1945 - Oct 1945	KD572 (138/X)

Commanding Officers
L/C(A) A McD Garland RNVR 1 Apr 1944
L/C(A) DG Parker DSC RNVR 27 Apr 1945
Squadron disbanded 31 Oct 1945
L/C(A) RA Jameson RNVR 28 Mar 1953
Squadron disbanded 10 Mar 1957

Battle Honours
Norway 1944
Okinawa 1945
Japan 1945

Identification Markings
Corsair single letters, to single numbers 5.44, to *129-146/X* 3.45.

Squadron bases
Brunswick	1 Apr 1944
Bar Harbour/ADDLs	23 May 1944
Brunswick	31 May 1944
USS Charger (Dt)	1-7 Jun 1944
Norfolk (transit)	27 Jun 1944
HMS Rajah	29 Jun 1944
Stretton	13 Jul 1944
Eglinton	21 Jul 1944
HMS Formidable	7 Aug 1944
Hatston	14 Aug 1944
HMS Formidable	18 Aug 1944
Donibristle	2 Sep 1944
HMS Formidable	16 Sep 1944
North Front (part)	21 Sep 1944
to	15 Jan 1945
Colombo (Dt) left overland	15 Oct 1944

Squadron bases
Dekheila (Dt9)	3 Nov 1944
to	1 Jan 1945
HMS Formidable	15 Jan 1945
Puttalam	8 Feb 1945
HMS Formidable	22 Feb 1945
Jervis Bay	1 Jun 1945
HMS Formidable	22 Jun 1945
Nowra	23 Aug 1945
HMS Victorious	25 Sep 1945
Squadron disbanded	31 Oct 1945
Ford	28 Mar 1953
Annual training:	
Eglinton	22 Aug 1953
to	5 Sep 1953
Hal Far	8-22 May 1954
Eglinton	20 Aug 1955
to	3 Sep 1955
Squadron disbanded	10 Mar 1957

Boulton Paul Sea Balliol T.21 WL716 '222' of No.1842 Squadron, Channel Air Division in 1954. (MAP)

No.1843 Squadron

No.1843 Squadron formed at Brunswick on 1 May 1944 as a single seater fighter squadron. Equipped with 18 Corsair IIIs, these were replaced by Mk.IIs before embarking in HMS *Trouncer* for the UK in August 1944. Joining the 10th Naval Fighter Wing, the squadron embarked in HMS *Arbiter* with 24 Corsair IVs in February 1945 and sailed to Australia, but saw no action before the war ended. In August it became part of the 3rd Carrier Air Group. The aircraft were withdrawn in September, and the squadron personnel sailed home in SS *Stratheden* to disband on arrival on 10 December 1945.

On 1 October 1952, No.1830A Squadron formed at Donibristle as an Anti-Submarine squadron of the Scottish Air Division of the RN Volunteer Reserve, moving shortly afterwards to Abbotsinch. It shared the aircraft of No.1830 Squadron, becoming No.1843 Squadron in March 1953. Avengers arrived in November 1955, but No.1843 disbanded on 10 March 1957 under the defence cuts of that year.

Corsair IV KD578 of No.1843 Squadron after wreaking havoc on the flight deck of HMS Arbiter on 13 March 1945. (via G.S.Leslie)

Identification Markings
Corsair *1V11+*, later single letters.

Aircraft Equipment	Period of Service	Example
Corsair III	May 1944 - Aug 1944	JS665 (3V11)
Corsair II	Jul 1944 - Feb 1945	JT693 (R)
Corsair IV	Feb 1945 - Sep 1945	KD747 (X)

Squadron bases		Squadron bases		Squadron bases		Commanding Officers	
Brunswick	1 May 1944	HMS Arbiter	13 Apr 1945	Abbotsinch	28 Mar 1953	L/C(A) DK Evans	
Bar Harbour/ADDLs	5 Jun 1944	Schofields	1 May 1945	Annual training:		RNZNVR	1 May 1944
Brunswick	9 Jun 1944	HMS Arbiter	20 May 1945	Hal Far	23 Aug 1953	L/C DFV Davis	
HMS Trouncer	2 Aug 1944	Ponam	31 May 1945		to 4 Sep 1953	RCNVR (temp)	20 Sep 1944
Eglinton	24 Aug 1944	HMS Arbiter	25 Jun 1945	Culdrose	10-24 Jul 1954	Mjr PP Nelson-Gracie	
Ayr	23 Oct 1944	Maryborough	4 Jul 1945	Hal Far	8-20 May 1955	RM	14 Oct 1944
Eglinton	15 Dec 1944	Jervis Bay	14 Jul 1945	Squadron disbanded 10 Mar 1957		L/C(A) PCS Chilton	
HMS Patroller (Dt8)		Nowra	22 Jul 1945			RN	11 Feb 1945
- DLT	21-23 Dec 1944	SS Stratheden	24 Oct 1945			Squadron disbanded 10 Dec 1945	
Belfast (transit)	13 Feb 1945	(no a/c)				L/C(A) M Ross	
HMS Arbiter	14 Feb 1945	Sqdn disbanded UK 10 Dec 1945				RNVR	1 Oct 1952
Colombo	4 Apr 1945					Squadron disbanded 10 Mar 1957	

Fairey Firefly AS.6 WD871 '244/AC' flown by No.1843 Squadron in the Scottish Air Division at Abbotsinch around 1953/4. (FAA Museum)

No.1844 Squadron

Badge: On a blue field and in base two bars wavy white, on a rock issuing from the sinister proper a black cat couchant also proper

Motto: Strength in reserve

Identification Markings
Hellcat *6A+*, to *R6A+* 10.44, to *131-146, 162-163/W* 3.45; Firefly *201-206, 252-264/BR*, to *891-896/BR*; Sea Balliol *257-258/BR*, to *897-898/BR* 1.56; Avenger *892-896/BR*.

Aircraft Equipment

Aircraft	Period of Service	Example
Hellcat I	Dec 1943 - May 1945	FN383 (R6F)
Hellcat II	Feb 1945 - Oct 1945	JX743 (143/W)
Firefly FR.5	Feb 1954 - Dec 1955	WB419 (255/BR)
Firefly AS.6	Dec 1955 - Jun 1956	WJ118 (896/BR)
Firefly T.2	Feb 1954 - Sep 1954	MB752 (251/BR)
Firefly T.3	Feb 1954 - Jul 1954	PP485 (255/BR)
Sea Balliol T.21	Jun 1954 - Mar 1957	WL728 (258/BR)
Sea Prince T.1	Jul 1954 - Oct 1956	WM740 (401/BR)
Dominie 1	Feb 1956 - Mar 1957	X7332 (890/BR)
Avenger AS.5	Mar 1956 - Mar 1957	XB391 (892/BR)

Battle Honours
Palembang 1945
Okinawa 1945

Squadron bases
Eglinton	15 Dec 1943
Belfast	25 Feb 1944
HMS Begum	26 Feb 1944
Ulunderpet	7 Apr 1944
Colombo Racecourse	7 Jun 1944
China Bay	12 Jun 1944
HMS Unicorn (DLT)	14-15 Jun 1944
Colombo Racecourse	18 Jun 1944
HMS Indomitable	25 Jul 1944
China Bay	21 Oct 1944
HMS Indomitable	1 Dec 1944
Trincomalee	9 Dec 1944
HMS Indomitable	14 Dec 1944
Nowra	10 Feb 1945
HMS Indomitable	27 Feb 1945
Nowra	5 Jun 1945
HMS Indomitable	3 Aug 1945
Nowra	11 Aug 1945
HMS Indomitable	16 Aug 1945
Nowra	10 Oct 1945
HMS Indomitable (no a/c)	22 Oct 1945
Sqdn disbanded UK	30 Nov 1945
Bramcote	15 Feb 1954
Annual training:	
Hal Far	4-17 Sep 1954
Hal Far	22 Aug 1955 to 2 Sep 1955
Hal Far	29 Jul 1956 to 10 Aug 1956
Squadron disbanded	10 Mar 1957

Commanding Officers
L/C(A) TW Harrington RN 15 Dec 1943
L/C(A) MS Godson RN 9 Sep 1944
L/C PJP Leckie RN 12 May 1945
Squadron disbanded 30 Nov 1945
L/C(A) D Woodhead RNVR 15 Feb 1954
Squadron disbanded 10 Mar 1957

No.1844 Squadron formed at Eglinton on 15 December 1943 as a single seater fighter squadron with ten Hellcat Is, as part of the 5th Naval Fighter Wing. In February 1944 it took passage in HMS *Begum* for the Far East, and after work-up in southern India embarked in HMS *Indomitable* in July to provide fighter cover and photographic reconnaissance during attacks the following month on Indaroeng and Emma Haven in Sumatra. Similar work was carried out in September during bombing attacks on Sigli, and in October fighter cover was given during attacks on Car Nicobar.

After a period ashore the squadron re-embarked for operations in December on oil installations at Belawan Deli in Sumatra. In January 1945 airfields and shore targets were attacked at Pangkalan Brandan, and later in the month oil refineries were attacked at Palembang. Sailing to Australia, where No.1844 received 18 Hellcat IIs, the ship then returned north for attacks on the Sakishima Gunto group of islands in the East China Seas, and also on Formosa. Further planned operations in August were cancelled following the Japanese surrender, and after discarding its aircraft in Australia the squadron sailed for the UK, where it disbanded on arrival on 30 November 1945.

On 15 February 1954, No.1844 reformed at Bramcote as an anti-submarine squadron in the Midland Air Division of the RN Volunteer Reserve. Equipped initially with 6 Firefly 5s, it exchanged these for six Firefly AS.6s in December 1955, but the latter soon gave way to Avenger AS.5s from March 1956. On 10 March 1957 No.1844 disbanded under that year's defence cuts.

Fairey Firefly T.2 MB752 '251/BR' of No.1844 Squadron, Bramcote in 1952. (MAP)

No.1845 Squadron

Badge: Two eagles flying over base barry wavy of five white and blue (Correct heraldic description lacking)
Motto: Pluribus optimum (The best out of many)

Chance Vought Corsair IV ('139') of No.1845 Squadron at Nowra in 1945. (R.J.H.Grose)

No.1845 Squadron personnel assembled at Donibristle in April 1944, and after passage to the USA officially formed at Brunswick on 1 June 1944 as a single seater fighter squadron. Equipped with 18 Corsair IIIs, these embarked in HMS *Puncher* in August for passage to the UK, where the squadron joined the 10th Naval Fighter Wing, re-equipping in November with 24 Corsair IVs. In December No.1845 embarked in HMS *Slinger* and sailed for the Far East. After a spell in Australia it re-embarked, and the ship sailed for the British Pacific Fleet replenishment area in March 1945. However, on 5 April 1945 the squadron disbanded, its pilots and aircraft being divided between squadrons in HMS *Formidable* and HMS *Victorious*.

On 1 June 1945, No.1845 reformed as a single seater fighter squadron at Archerfield, Australia. After a brief spell in HMS *Slinger*, it became a spare squadron in the 3rd Carrier Air Group at Nowra. On 24 October 1945 it disbanded there, its personnel sailing home in SS *Stratheden*.

Aircraft Equipment

Aircraft	Period of Service	Example
Corsair III	Jun 1944 - Nov 1944	JS834 (4V7)
Corsair IV	Nov 1944 - Apr 1945	KD246 (7G)
Corsair IV	May 1945 - Oct 1945	KD628
Corsair III	Jul 1945 - Oct 1945	JT671

Identification Markings
Corsair *1V7+*, later *7A+* by 12.44, to *139+*.

Battle Honours
Okinawa 1945

Squadron bases
Brunswick	1 Jun 1944
Bar Harbour/ADDLs	3 Jul 1944
Brunswick	7 Jul 1944
HMS Puncher	30 Aug 1944
Eglinton	18 Sep 1944
Ayr	23 Oct 1944
Eglinton	6 Nov 1944
HMS Slinger	19 Dec 1944
Schofields	25 Feb 1945
HMS Slinger	11 Mar 1945
Squadron disbanded	5 Apr 1945
Archerfield	1 Jun 1945
Maryborough	23 Jun 1945
Nowra	14 Jul 1945
Squadron disbanded	24 Oct 1945

Commanding Officers
L/C(A) DG Parker RNVR	1 Jun 1944
Squadron disbanded	5 Apr 1945
Not identified	15 May 1945
L/C(A) RJH Grose RNVR	24 Jun 1945
Squadron disbanded	24 Oct 1945

No.1846 Squadron

Badge: On a field blue a base barry wavy of four white and blue, a scimitar in pale point upwards white hilted gold winged white
Motto: To the swift the race

No.1846 Squadron personnel assembled at Donibristle and Townhill Camp in June 1944, and sailed for the USA where it officially formed on 1 July 1944 at Brunswick as a single seater fighter squadron. Equipped with 18 Corsair IIIs, these took passage in HMS *Ranee* for the UK in October, being expanded to 24 aircraft on taking over part of the disbanded No.1848 Squadron in November. Re-equipping with 24 Corsair IVs, it embarked in HMS *Colossus* for the Far East in February 1945, joining the 14th Carrier Air Group when it formed in June. The squadron saw no action, eventually returning home to disband on arrival at Gosport on 23 July 1946.

Identification Markings
Corsair *1V4+*, to *U5, U6 & U7* by 2.45, to *111-131/D:C* 7.45.

Aircraft Equipment

Aircraft	Period of Service	Example
Corsair III	Jul 1944 - Feb 1945	JS882 (4V4)
Corsair IV	Feb 1945 - Jul 1946	KD644 (U6K)

Squadron bases
Brunswick	1 Jul 1944
Norfolk	23 Aug 1944
Brunswick	25 Aug 1944
Norfolk (transit)	15 Oct 1944
HMS Ranee	18 Oct 1944
Eglinton	2 Nov 1944
Ayr	11 Dec 1944
Eglinton	18 Dec 1944
Ballyhalbert	13 Jan 1945
HMS Colossus (Dt12)	22-27 Jan 1945
HMS Colossus	20 Feb 1945
Dekheila	22 Mar 1945
HMS Colossus	4 May 1945
Tambaram	10 Jun 1945
HMS Colossus	5 Jul 1945
Nowra	21 Jul 1945
HMS Colossus	13 Aug 1945
Kai Tak (Dt)	12-18 Oct 1945
Katukurunda	26 Oct 1945
HMS Colossus	30 Dec 1945
Wingfield	17 Jan 1946
HMS Colossus	8 Apr 1946
Katukurunda	27 Apr 1946
HMS Colossus	17 May 1946
Gosport	23 Jul 1946
Squadron disbanded	23 Jul 1946

Commanding Officers
L/C(A) DG Brooker RNVR	1 Jul 1944
L/C(A) SL Devonald DFC RN	4 Apr 1945
L/C(A) DA Dick DSC RNVR	26 Feb 1946
Squadron disbanded	23 Jul 1946

Corsair IV '111/D' of No.1846 Squadron, HMS Colossus.

No.1847 Squadron

No.1847 Squadron formed at Eglinton on 1 February 1944 as a single seater fighter squadron. Equipped with 10 Hellcat Is, it had four British pilots and eight from the Royal Netherlands Navy. It was intended for service in an escort carrier, but instead was absorbed into No.1840 Squadron at Eglinton on 20 May 1944.

Identification Markings
Hellcat single letters.

Aircraft Equipment	Period of Service	Example
Hellcat I	Feb 1944 - May 1944	FN374 (E)

Squadron bases
Eglinton 1 Feb 1944
Squadron disbanded 20 May 1944

Commanding Officers
L/C(A) H Colville
 -Stewart RNVR 1 Feb 1944
Squadron disbanded 20 May 1944

No.1848 Squadron

No.1848 Squadron personnel assembled at Donibristle in May 1944, and after passage to the USA officially formed at Brunswick on 1 July as a single seater fighter squadron. Equipped with 12 Corsair Is and IIs, these were increased to 18 on taking passage home in HMS *Ranee* in October. However, soon after arrival No.1848 disbanded at Machrihanish on 21 November 1944, its aircraft and pilots being shared equally between Nos.1843, 1845 and 1846 Squadrons.

Aircraft Equipment	Period of Service	Example
Corsair I	Jul 1944 - Oct 1944	JT102 (16V9)
Corsair II	Jul 1944 - Nov 1944	JT704 (18V9)

Squadron bases
Brunswick 1 Jul 1944
Bar Harbour/ADDLs 30 Jul 1944
Brunswick 5 Aug 1944
Norfolk (transit) 15 Oct 1944
HMS Ranee 18 Oct 1944
Machrihanish 3 Nov 1944
Squadron disbanded 21 Nov 1944

Identification Markings
Corsair *1V9+*.

Commanding Officers
L/C(A) EJ Clark
 RNVR 1 Jul 1944
Squadron disbanded 21 Nov 1944

Corsair II JT601 '12V9' of No.1848 Squadron. (John Rawlings)

No.1849 Squadron

No.1849 Squadron personnel assembled at Townhill Camp in June 1944, then took passage to the USA where it officially formed at Brunswick on 1 August 1944 as a single seater fighter squadron. Equipped with eight Corsair IIIs, these were replaced by Corsair IVs shortly before embarking in HMS *Reaper* in November for the UK. Due to the high number of losses from accidents, it disbanded on arrival in the UK on 6 December 1944, being shared between Nos.1845 and 1850 Squadrons.

Aircraft Equipment	Period of Service	Example
Corsair III	Aug 1944 - Oct 1944	JS667 (19V11)
Corsair IV	Oct 1944 - Dec 1944	KD510 (C)
2-seater (SNJ?)	Sep 1944 - Oct 1944	? (9V11)

Squadron bases
Brunswick 1 Aug 1944
Bar Harbour/ADDLs 10 Sep 1944
Brunswick 19 Sep 1944
Floyd Bennett Fd 15 Nov 1944
Norfolk (transit) 17 Nov 1944
HMS Reaper 22 Nov 1944
Sqdn disbanded UK 6 Dec 1944

Identification Markings
Corsair *1V11+*, later individual letters.

Commanding Officers
L/C(A) PCS Chilton
 RN 1 Aug 1944
Squadron disbanded 6 Dec 1944

No.1850 Squadron

Badge: On a white field, a wyvern ramping red
Motto: None

No.1850 Squadron formed at Brunswick on 1 August 1944 as a single seater fighter squadron. Equipped with 18 Corsair IVs, it sailed for the UK in HMS *Reaper* in November, absorbing part of the disbanded No.1849 Squadron on arrival to increase the strength to 24 aircraft. After work-up and deck landing practice in HMS *Venerable* in February 1945, the squadron joined HMS *Vengeance* for the British Pacific Fleet. After weapon training and dive bombing practice in southern India, during which the squadron became part of the 13th Carrier Air Group, it re-embarked and the ship entered the war zone in August, but was too late to take an active part. No.1850 remained in the area for some time, reducing to 12 aircraft in October 1945, but in June 1946 returned to the UK, where it disbanded on arrival at Gosport on 12 August 1946. The number was earmarked in 1953 for a postwar RN Volunteer Reserve squadron, but this became No.1843 instead.

Identification Markings
Corsair single letters, to *N5A+* by 6.45, to *111-131/A* 10.45, to *V8A+* by 4.46.

Commanding Officers
L/C(A) M Hordern RN 1 Aug 1944
L/C WN Waller RN 2 Dec 1945
Squadron disbanded 12 Aug 1946

Chance Vought Corsair IV '120/A' of No.1850 Sqdn on HMS Vengeance on 23 December 1945. (via R.B.Phillips)

Squadron bases
Brunswick	1 Aug 1944	Tambaram	11 Jun 1945
Bar Harbour/ADDLs	Sep 1944	(and Coimbatore)	
Brunswick	Sep 1944	HMS Vengeance	1 Jul 1945
(DLT in USS Charger)		Jervis Bay	22 Jul 1945
Floyd Bennett Field	15 Nov 1944	HMS Vengeance	13 Aug 1945
Norfolk (transit)	23 Nov 1944	Ponam (Dt12)	23-30 Aug 1945
HMS Reaper	23 Nov 1944	Kai Tak	3 Oct 1945
Belfast	6 Dec 1944	HMS Vengeance	20 Dec 1945
Eglinton	27 Dec 1944	Schofields	12 Jan 1946
Ayr	13 Jan 1945	HMS Vengeance	19 Mar 1946
HMS Venerable		Katukurunda	5 Apr 1946
(DLT)	10 Feb 1945	HMS Vengeance	11 Jun 1946
HMS Vengeance	25 Feb 1945	Gosport	12 Aug 1946
Hal Far	19 Mar 1945	Squadron disbanded	12 Aug 1946
HMS Vengeance	23 Apr 1945		

Aircraft Equipment	Period of Service	Example
Corsair IV	Aug 1944 - Aug 1946	KD705 (V8D)

No.1851 Squadron

No.1851 Squadron personnel assembled at Townhill Camp on 25 July 1944, and after passage to the USA in HMT *Queen Mary* formed officially at Brunswick on 1 September 1944 as a single seater fighter squadron. Equipped with 18 Corsair IVs, it embarked in HMS *Thane* in December for the UK. The aircraft were disembarked to Belfast on 14 January 1945, which turned out to be rather fortunate, as the ship was torpedoed by *U-482* the following day off the Clyde Light Vessel, though it managed to make Greenock with the aid of a tow from a frigate. No.1851 joined HMS *Venerable* with 24 aircraft in March, and then spent some weeks in the Mediterranean before continuing to southern India, where it became part of the 15th Carrier Air Group. The Pacific war ended before it could see any action, but a detachment was operational ashore during the occupation of Hong Kong. Reducing in December 1945 to 12 aircraft, the squadron transferred in June 1946 to HMS *Vengeance*, but the following month this sailed for the UK, where No.1851 disbanded on arrival at Devonport on 13 August 1946.

Commanding Officers
L/C(A) DJ McDonald RN 1 Sep 1944
Lt(A) C Malins RNVR (temp) 12 Feb 1945
L/C(A) DJ McDonald RN 29 Apr 1945
Lt(A) MB Gerrish RNVR (acting) 30 May 1945
L/C(A) K Stilliard RNVR 29 Jun 1945
L/C(A) CF Hargreaves RN 6 Dec 1945
Squadron disbanded 13 Aug 1946

Identification Markings
Corsair *1V7+*, to *R6A+* by 7.45, to *111-131/B:T:Y* by 2.46.

Aircraft Equipment	Period of Service	Example
Corsair IV	Sep 1944 - Aug 1946	KD777 (117/T)

Squadron bases
Brunswick	1 Sep 1944	Nowra	30 Dec 1945
Bar Harbour/ADDLs	23 Oct 1944	Schofields	24 Jan 1946
Brunswick	1 Nov 1944	HMS Venerable	22 Feb 1946
Norfolk	7-10 Nov 1944	Katukurunda	26 Apr 1946
(DLT in USS Charger)		HMS Venerable	28 May 1946
Floyd Bennett Field	23 Dec 1944	Katukurunda	31 May 1946
Norfolk (transit)	28 Dec 1944	HMS Vengeance	11 Jun 1946
HMS Thane	28 Dec 1944	Katukurunda	15 Jun 1946
Belfast	14 Jan 1945	HMS Vengeance	18 Jul 1946
Eglinton	17 Jan 1945	Sqdn disbanded UK	13 Aug 1946
HMS Venerable	6 Mar 1945		
Hal Far	20 Mar 1945		
HMS Venerable	16 Apr 1945		
Hal Far	20 Apr 1945		
HMS Venerable	21 May 1945		
Tambaram	7 Jun 1945		
HMS Venerable	3 Jul 1945		
Schofields	21 Jul 1945		
HMS Venerable	13 Aug 1945		
Kai Tak (Dt8)	3 Sep 1945		
to 18 Oct 1945			
Trincomalee	28 Oct 1945		
HMS Venerable	13 Dec 1945		

Corsair IV KD206 'R6S' of No.1851 Sqdn. (M.R.H.Shippey)

No. 1852 Squadron

No.1852 Squadron formed at Brunswick on 1 February 1945 as a single seater fighter squadron. Equipped with 18 Corsair IVs, these embarked in HMS *Patroller* for the UK in May 1945. It continued work-up in Northern Ireland, at the same time converting the aircraft from a normal reflector gunsight to the GGS Mk.IID gyro gunsight, but plans for it to become part of the 18th Air Group in the British Pacific Fleet were cancelled after VJ-Day. It disbanded at Nutts Corner on 29 August 1945.

Aircraft Equipment	Period of Service	Example
Corsair IV	Feb 1945 - Aug 1945	KD822 (15V10)
Widgeon I	Mar 1945 - Apr 1945	FP466

Identification Markings
Corsair *1V10+*, to single letters 5.45.

Squadron bases
Brunswick	1 Feb 1945
Bar Harbour/ADDLs	24 Mar 1945
Brunswick	29 Mar 1945
Norfolk	3 Apr 1945
(DLT in USS Charger)	
Brunswick	8 Apr 1945
Norfolk (transit)	30 Apr 1945
HMS Patroller	4 May 1945
Belfast	25 May 1945
Eglinton	26 May 1945
Belfast	9 Aug 1945
Nutts Corner	29 Aug 1945
Squadron disbanded	29 Aug 1945

Commanding Officers
L/C(A) IF Voller RNVR   1 Feb 1945
Squadron disbanded 29 Aug 1945

Chance Vought Corsair IV KD785 '8V10' of No.1852 Squadron in 1945. (Bill Voller)

No. 1853 Squadron

No.1853 Squadron personnel assembled at Townhill Camp on 23 February 1945, and after passage to the USA formed officially at Brunswick on 1 April 1945 as a single seater fighter squadron. Equipped with 18 Corsair IVs it embarked in HMS *Rajah* for the UK in July 1945, but plans for it to join a 4th Carrier Air Group in HMS *Illustrious* were cancelled, and it disbanded at Machrihanish on VJ-Day, 15 August 1945.

Aircraft Equipment	Period of Service	Example
Corsair IV	Apr 1945 - Aug 1945	KD808 (11V11)
Widgeon I	Jun 1945 - Aug 1945	

Identification Markings
Corsair *1V11+*, to single letters 4.45.

Squadron bases
Brunswick	1 Apr 1945
Norfolk	30 Apr 1945
Bar Harbour/ADDLs	21 May 1945
Brunswick	2 Jun 1945
Norfolk	6 Jun 1945
USS Charger (DLT)	7 Jun 1945
Norfolk	8 Jun 1945
Brunswick	15 Jun 1945
Floyd Bennett Field	13 Jul 1945
Norfolk	14 Jul 1945
HMS Rajah	24 Jul 1945
Machrihanish	6 Aug 1945
Squadron disbanded	15 Aug 1945

Commanding Officers
L/C JR Schuiling RNethN   1 Apr 1945
Squadron disbanded 15 Aug 1945

Chance Vought Corsair IV KD748 '4V11' of No.1853 Squadron in January 1945. (J.D.Buchanan)

INDEX OF AIRCRAFT EQUIPMENT

AIRACOBRA I, Bell
778
ALBACORE I, Fairey
700, 733, 747, 750, 753, 754, 756, 763, 766, 767, 767, 768, 769, 771, 774, 775, 778, 781, 782, 783, 785, 786, 787, 788, 789, 791, 793, 796, 797, 799, 810, 815, 817, 818, 820, 821, 822, 823, 826, 827, 828, 829, 830, 831, 832, 841
ANSON I, Avro
700, 703, 707, 710, 711, 719, 720, 724, 725, 728, 732, 735, 737, 739, 740, 742, 744, 744, 745, 747, 749, 750, 751, 758, 762, 763, 766, 771, 772, 778, 782, 783, 784, 785, 786, 787, 787X, 789, 790, 792, 798, 799, 809, 1830, 1832, 1833, 1840, 1841
ANSON II, Avro
745
ANSON V, Avro
743
ANSON C.X, Avro
701
ANSON C.XII, Avro
773, 781, 782, 790, 799
ANSON C.XIX
781X
ATTACKER F.1, Supermarine
702, 703, 736, 767, 787, 800, 803, 890
ATTACKER FB.1, Supermarine
703, 767, 787, 800, 890
ATTACKER FB.2, Supermarine
700, 703, 718, 736, 767, 787, 800, 803, 890, 1831, 1832, 1833
AUDAX, Hawker
780
AUSTER I, Taylorcraft
730, 768, 778, 781, 790
AUSTER V, Taylorcraft
790, 790, 1831, 1832
AUTOCAR J/5G, Auster
723, 724, 725
AVENGER TBF-1, Grumman
721, 832
AVENGER TBM-3E, Grumman
703, 815, 824, 825, 826, 880, 881
AVENGER I, Grumman
700, 706, 711, 733, 738, 756, 763, 768, 778, 783, 785, 786, 787, 797, 820, 828, 832, 845, 846, 848, 849, 850, 851, 852, 854, 857
AVENGER II, Grumman
700, 703, 706, 711, 733, 736, 738, 744, 751, 756, 759, 763, 764, 768, 774, 778, 782, 783, 785, 787, 798, 820, 828, 832, 846, 848, 849, 853, 854, 855, 856, 857
AVENGER III, Grumman
702, 703, 706, 707, 738, 778, 787, 828, 854
AVENGER AS.4, Grumman
703, 751, 767, 814, 815, 820, 824
AVENGER AS.5, Grumman
700, 744, 814, 815, 1830, 1841, 1844
AVENGER TS.5, Grumman
745
AVENGER AS.6, Grumman
831
AVENGER AEW, Grumman
881
AVRO 652
781, 811
A.W.XVI, Armstrong Whitworth
800
BAFFIN, Blackburn
810, 811, 812, 820
BALTIMORE IV, Martin
728
BALTIMORE V, Martin
728
BANSHEE F2H-3, McDonnell
870, 871
BARRACUDA I, Fairey
747, 767, 768, 778, 785, 786, 787, 827, 831
BARRACUDA II, Fairey
700, 703, 706, 707, 710, 711, 713, 714, 717, 731, 733, 735, 736, 744, 747, 750, 753, 756, 764, 767, 768, 769, 774, 777, 778, 780, 781, 783, 785, 786, 787, 797, 798, 810, 812, 814, 815, 816, 817, 818, 820, 821, 822, 823, 824, 826, 827, 828, 830, 831, 837, 841, 847
BARRACUDA II(ASH), Fairey
817, 822, 825, 826
BARRACUDA III, Fairey
700, 703, 707, 703, 710, 713, 714, 719, 735, 737, 744, 747, 750, 756, 769, 778, 783, 785, 796, 798, 799, 810, 815, 821, 822, 860

BARRACUDA TR.V, Fairey
700, 778, 783
BATTLE, Fairey
820
BEAUFIGHTER II, Bristol
721, 726, 728, 733, 762, 775, 779, 781, 788, 789, 797, 798
BEAUFIGHTER X, Bristol
728, 736, 770, 772
BEAUFIGHTER TT.10, Bristol
728
BEAUFORT I, Bristol
728, 733, 762, 788, 798
BEAUFORT T.II, Bristol
762
BEECH AT-7
742
BLACKBURN YA.8
703
BLENHEIM I, Bristol
770, 771, 776, 780, 787
BLENHEIM IV, Bristol
748, 759, 762, 770, 771, 772, 775, 776, 787, 787, 788, 798
BOSTON III, Douglas
771, 772
BOTHA I, Blackburn
770
BUCCANEER S.1, Blackburn
700, 736, 800, 801, 803, 809
BUCCANEER S.2, Hawker Siddeley
700, 736, 800, 801, 803, 809
BUFFALO I, Brewster
759, 760, 804, 805, 813, 885
C-47B (DAKOTA), Douglas
723, 724, 725, 851
CANBERRA D.14, English Electric
728B
CHESAPEAKE I, Vought-Sikorsky
770, 771, 772, 776, 778, 781, 784, 786, 787, 811
CHIPMUNK T.10, de Havilland
771, 781
CORSAIR I, Chance Vought
700, 732, 738, 767, 1830, 1831, 1833, 1834, 1835, 1836, 1837, 1838, 1841, 1848
CORSAIR II, Chance Vought
703, 706, 723, 731, 732, 738, 748, 757, 759, 768, 771, 778, 787, 885, 1830, 1833, 1834, 1835, 1836, 1837, 1838, 1841, 1841, 1842, 1843, 1848
CORSAIR III, Chance Vought
700, 715, 718, 719, 721, 731, 736, 748, 757, 759, 760, 767, 768, 771, 778, 787, 794, 797, 1835, 1837, 1841, 1842, 1843, 1845, 1846, 1849
CORSAIR IV, Chance Vought
706, 715, 718, 721, 733, 748, 757, 759, 768, 778, 791, 794, 885, 1831, 1834, 1835, 1835, 1836, 1841, 1842, 1843, 1844, 1845, 1845, 1846, 1849, 1850, 1851, 1852, 1853
DH.86/DH.86b, de Havilland
781, 782, 783
DAKOTA, Douglas (see also C-47)
782, 789, 799
DART, Blackburn
810
DAUNTLESS I, Douglas
700, 787
DEFIANT TT.I, Boulton Paul
721, 726, 727, 728, 733, 766, 770, 771, 772, 775, 777, 788, 789, 794, 797, 1830
DEFIANT TT.III, Boulton Paul
774, 776, 779, 791, 792, 794
DOMINIE I, de Havilland
700Z, 701, 703, 736, 739, 740, 744, 767, 776, 778, 781, 782, 787, 790, 799, 1832, 1844
DRAGONFLY HR.1, Westland
700, 705
DRAGONFLY HR.3, Westland
705, 728, 744
DRAGONFLY HR.5, Westland
701, 705, 727, 771
EXPEDITER C.1, Beech
701, 730, 781, 782
EXPEDITER C.2, Beech
701, 723, 724, 728, 733, 742, 755, 781, 782, 791, 799
FAIREY IIIF
714, 718, 820, 821, 822, 823, 824, 825
FALCON, Miles
781
FIREBRAND F.I, Blackburn
778

FIREBRAND TF.I, Blackburn
764
FIREBRAND TF.II, Blackburn
708
FIREBRAND TF.III, Blackburn
700, 703, 708, 778
FIREBRAND TF.4, Blackburn
703, 736, 738, 778, 813
FIREBRAND TF.5/5a, Blackburn
700, 703, 759, 767, 778, 787, 799, 813, 827
FIREFLY F.I/FR.I, Fairey
700, 703, 706, 719, 730, 731, 736, 737, 741, 744, 748, 759, 764, 766, 767, 768, 771, 772, 778, 780, 781, 782, 783, 787, 790, 795, 796, 798, 799, 805, 812, 814, 816, 822, 824, 825, 826, 827, 837, 860, 861, 1770, 1771, 1772, 1790, 1791, 1830, 1841
FIREFLY NF.I, Fairey
732, 746, 784, 792, 794, 805, 812, 816, 827, 1790, 1791, 1792
FIREFLY T.1, Fairey
736, 737, 744, 764, 766, 767, 771, 778, 781, 782, 799, 812, 815, 826, 1830, 1831
FIREFLY NF.II, Fairey
746, 772
FIREFLY T.2, Fairey
737, 744, 764, 765, 766, 771, 781, 782, 799, 1830, 1833, 1840, 1841, 1844
FIREFLY T.3, Fairey
796, 1830, 1831, 1833, 1841, 1844
FIREFLY FR.4, Fairey
703, 727, 736, 767, 778, 781, 782, 787, 799, 810, 812, 814, 816, 825, 1840
FIREFLY TT.4, Fairey
700, 771
FIREFLY AS.5/FR.5, Fairey
703, 703A, 719, 737, 737X, 778, 781, 782, 796, 804, 810, 812, 814, 816, 817, 820, 821, 825, 880, 1830, 1844
FIREFLY Mk.5 T.2, Fairey
723
FIREFLY T.5, Fairey
724, 851
FIREFLY TT.5, Fairey
723, 725, 771
FIREFLY AS.6, Fairey
703, 703A, 719, 723, 724, 737, 737X, 744, 751, 767, 771, 782, 796, 812, 814, 816, 817, 820, 821, 824, 826, 851, 1830, 1840, 1841, 1844
FIREFLY TT.6, Fairey
724, 725
FIREFLY T.7, Fairey
719, 750, 765, 796, 1840
FIREFLY U.8, Fairey
728B
FIREFLY U.9, Fairey
728B
FLAMINGO, de Havilland
782
FLYCATCHER I
801
FOX MOTH, de Havilland
781
FULMAR I, Fairey
700, 740, 748, 759, 760, 761, 762, 766, 767, 768, 769, 772, 775, 778, 780, 781, 784, 787, 787Z, 790, 800, 803, 804, 805, 806, 807, 808, 815, 893
FULMAR II, Fairey
700, 726, 731, 733, 739, 748, 756, 757, 759, 760, 761, 762, 766, 767, 768, 769, 772, 775, 778, 779, 781, 782, 787, 787, 788, 789, 790, 792, 793, 794, 795, 798, 800, 803, 804, 806, 807, 808, 809, 815, 822, 827, 835, 879, 881, 884, 886, 887, 889, 897
FULMAR IINF, Fairey
746, 784
FULMAR IITT, Fairey
746
GANNET AS.1, Fairey
700, 703, 703X, 719, 724, 725, 737, 744, 796, 812, 814, 815, 816, 817, 820, 824, 825, 826, 831, 847, 1840
GANNET T.2, Fairey
700, 719, 724, 725, 728, 737, 796, 812, 816, 820, 824, 825, 1840
GANNET AEW.3, Fairey
700G, 849
GANNET AS.4, Fairey
700, 810, 814, 815, 824, 825, 847, 849
GANNET COD.4, Fairey
849

GANNET ECM.4, Fairey
831
GANNET T.5, Fairey
849
GANNET ECM.6, Fairey
831
GAZELLE HT.2, Westland/Aerospatiale
705
GIPSY MOTH, de Havilland
759, 780
GLADIATOR I, Gloster
800
GOOSE I, Grumman
749
HARRIER T.4A, British Aerospace
899
HARRIER T.4N, British Aerospace
899
HART, Hawker
781
HART TRAINER, Hawker
780
HARROW ('Sparrow' type), Handley Page
782
HARVARD I, North American
780
HARVARD IIa, North American
727, 757, 782, 789
HARVARD IIb, North American
702, 709, 715, 719, 727, 733, 736, 738, 743, 757, 758, 760, 766, 767, 771, 780, 781, 782, 791, 794, 798, 799, 1830, 1831, 1832, 1833, 1834, 1840, 1841
HARVARD III, North American
700, 701, 709, 715, 718, 721, 726, 727, 728, 729, 732, 741, 748, 750, 758, 759, 761, 766, 767, 768, 778, 780, 781, 782, 784, 789, 794, 797, 798, 799, 1830, 1831, 1832, 1833, 1840, 1841
HAVOC I, Douglas
771, 772, 778
HAWK T.1, British Aerospace
FRADU
HELLCAT I, Grumman
700, 703, 706, 709, 721, 723, 725, 735, 748, 756, 757, 760, 768, 771, 778, 787, 800, 804, 808, 885, 889, 891, 892, 1839, 1840, 1844, 1847
HELLCAT II, Grumman
700, 703, 706, 709, 721, 757, 759, 778, 781, 787, 787X, 800, 804, 808, 881, 885, 896, 898, 1839, 1840, 1844
HELLCAT IINF, Grumman
732, 746, 784, 787, 891, 892
HELLCAT II(PR), Grumman
888, 889
HELLDIVER I, Curtiss
700, 778, 1820
HENLEY III, Hawker
771
HERON C.2, de Havilland
728
HERON C.4, de Havilland
781
HERON CC.4, de Havilland
781
HILLER HT.1
705, 706
HILLER HT.2
705, 706B
HORNET MOTH, de Havilland
759, 780. 781
HOVERFLY I, Vought-Sikorsky
703, 705, 771
HOVERFLY II, Vought-Sikorsky
705, 771
HUDSON III, Lockheed
781
HUDSON IV, Lockheed
781, 782
HUDSON V, Lockheed
781
HUNTER T.8, Hawker
700B, 700Z, 736, 738, 759, 764, 803, 899
HUNTER GA.11/PR.11, Hawker
738, 764
HURRICANE I, Hawker
748, 760, 803, 805, 806
HURRICANE IIb, Hawker
788, 794, 877
HURRICANE IIc, Hawker
700, 727, 728, 770, 771, 772, 774, 775, 776, 779, 784, 889
HURRICANE IV, Hawker
787Z
IROQUOIS (UH-1B), Bell
723
JETSTREAM T.1, British Aerospace
750

JETSTREAM T.2, British Aerospace
750
JETSTREAM T.3, British Aerospace
750
KINGFISHER I, Vought-Sikorsky
700, 703, 726, 740, 764, 765, 778, 787, 789
KIOWA (206B-1), Bell
723
LANCASTER I, Avro
780
LEOPARD MOTH, de Havilland
759, 799
LYNX HAS.2, Westland/Aerospatiale
700L, 702, 815, 829
LYNX HAS.3, Westland/Aerospatiale
702, 815, 829
LYNX HAS.3(CTS), Westland/Aerospatiale
700L, 815, 815OEU, 829
LYNX HAS.8, Westland/Aerospatiale
815, 815OEU
LYNX HAS.27, Westland/Aerospatiale
860
LYNX Mk.81, Westland/Aerospatiale
860
LYSANDER III/IIIa, Westland
754, 755, 757
MACCHI MB.326H
724
MAGISTER, Miles
778, 780
MARTINET TT.1, Miles
718, 722, 723, 725, 726, 728, 733, 736, 740, 766, 770, 771, 772, 773, 775, 776, 779, 789, 792, 793, 794, 797
MARTLET I (WILDCAT), Grumman
738, 748, 759, 760, 762, 767, 768, 768, 778, 781, 787, 795, 802, 804, 805, 806, 880, 881, 882, 888, 893, 1832
MARTLET II (WILDCAT), Grumman
768, 778, 787, 795, 805, 806, 881, 882, 888, 893, 1832
MARTLET III (WILDCAT), Grumman
768, 795, 802
MARTLET IV, Grumman
- see WILDCAT IV
MARYLAND, Martin
771
MASTER I, Miles
740, 748, 759, 760, 761, 762, 780, 785, 792, 794, 798
MASTER II, Miles
700, 715, 718, 719, 736, 748, 759, 761, 766, 772, 780, 794, 798
METEOR F.3, Gloster
703
METEOR T.7, Gloster
700Z, 702, 703, 728, 736, 759, 764, 767, 771, 781, 806, 813
METEOR F.8, Gloster
703
METEOR U.15, Gloster
728B
METEOR U.16, Gloster
728B
METEOR TT.20, Gloster
700, 728
MOSQUITO, de Havilland
721
MOSQUITO T.3, de Havilland
704, 728, 762, 780
MOSQUITO FB.6, de Havilland
700, 703, 704, 751, 762, 771, 773, 778, 780, 787, 790, 811
MOSQUITO PR16, de Havilland
703, 728, 770, 771, 772, 778
MOSQUITO B.25, de Havilland
704, 728, 733, 762, 770, 771, 772, 777, 778, 790, 797
MOSQUITO PR.34, de Havilland
751, 771, 772
MOSQUITO TT.39, de Havilland
728, 771
MOTH, de Havilland
767, 769, 770, 782
NIMROD I, Hawker
753, 759, 800, 801, 802, 803
NIMROD II, Hawker
780, 781, 800, 801, 802, 803
OSPREY, Hawker
701, 711, 712, 713, 714, 715, 716, 718, 750, 755, 757, 758, 759, 780, 800, 801, 802, 803
OXFORD, Airspeed
700, 701, 702, 703, 720, 727, 728, 729, 730, 739, 740, 744, 750, 751, 758, 759, 760, 761, 762, 765, 766, 771, 775, 776, 778, 780, 781, 782, 787, 789, 790, 792, 798, 799, 1701, 1830
PHANTOM FG.1, McDonnell-Douglas
700, 767, 892

PROCTOR Ia, Percival
746, 752, 754, 755, 756, 758, 759, 761, 767, 778, 780, 781, 782, 784, 787, 794
PROCTOR II, Percival
752, 754, 755, 759, 770, 772, 781
PROCTOR IIa, Percival
752, 754, 755, 756, 758, 759, 778, 781
PERCIVAL III, Percival
755
PERCIVAL IV, Percival
755
Q.6 PETREL, Percival
730, 781, 782, 787
QUEEN BEE, de Havilland
775
QUEEN MARTINET TT.1
773
RELIANT I, Stinson
700, 703, 711, 712, 722, 725, 730, 733, 740, 742, 744, 746, 747, 748, 752, 753, 754, 758, 759, 770, 772, 781, 782, 784, 787, 794
RIPON IIc, Blackburn
810, 811, 812
ROC I, Blackburn
725, 758, 759, 760, 765, 769, 769, 770, 771, 772, 773, 774, 775, 776, 777, 778, 782, 787, 789, 791, 792, 793, 794, 800, 801, 803, 805, 806
SCIMITAR F.1, Supermarine
700, 700X, 736, 764, 764B, 800, 800B, 804, 807
SCOUT, Westland
723
SEA BALLIOL T.21, Boulton Paul
702, 703, 727, 765, 781, 796, 1831, 1832, 1834, 1840, 1844
SEA DEVON C.20, de Havilland
727, 750, 765, 771, 781
SEAFANG F.32, Supermarine
778
SEAFIRE Ib, Supermarine
700, 708, 715, 719, 731, 736, 748, 759, 761, 768, 778, 779, 781, 787, 787Y, 790, 798, 801, 807, 809, 816, 842, 879, 885, 887, 894, 897
SEAFIRE IIc, Supermarine
700, 708, 718, 719, 728, 731, 748, 757, 759, 761, 768, 770, 775, 776, 778, 787, 787Y, 790, 794, 798, 799, 801, 807, 808, 809, 816, 833, 834, 842, 879, 880, 884, 885, 886, 887, 889, 894, 895, 897, 899
SEAFIRE III, Supermarine
700, 706, 708, 709, 715, 718, 721, 728, 733, 736, 736B, 740, 744, 748, 757, 759, 760, 761, 766, 767, 768, 771, 772, 777, 778, 781, 782, 787, 787Y, 790, 794, 799, 801, 802, 803, 805, 806, 807, 808, 809, 879, 880, 883, 885, 886, 887, 889, 894, 899, 1832
SEAFIRE XV, Supermarine
700, 701, 706, 709, 715, 718, 721, 728, 733, 736, 736B, 737, 751, 759, 761, 766, 767, 768, 771, 773, 777, 778, 780, 781, 787, 790, 791, 799, 800, 801, 802, 803, 804, 805, 806, 809, 883, 1831, 1832, 1833
SEAFIRE F.17, Supermarine
701, 703, 727, 728, 736, 737, 738, 746, 759, 761, 764, 766, 778, 781, 782, 787, 799, 800, 805, 807, 809, 879, 1830, 1831, 1832, 1833
SEAFIRE F/FR.45, Supermarine
700, 703, 709, 771, 777, 778, 780, 787
SEAFIRE F.46, Supermarine
736, 738, 767, 771, 777, 778, 781, 787, 1832
SEAFIRE F.47, Supermarine
759, 777, 778, 787, 800, 804, 1833
SEAFOX I, Fairey
700, 702, 703, 713, 714, 716, 718, 754, 764, 765, 773
SEA FURY F.10, Hawker
700, 703, 736, 738, 778, 781, 787, 799, 802, 803, 805, 807
SEA FURY FB.11, Hawker
700, 703, 723, 724, 725, 736, 738, 739, 744, 751, 767, 773, 778, 781, 782, 787, 799, 801, 802, 803, 804, 805, 806, 807, 808, 811, 850, 870, 871, 883, 898, 1831, 1832, 1833, 1834
SEA FURY T.20, Hawker
703, 736, 738, 759, 771, 781, 782, 787, 799, 801, 802, 809, 1830, 1831, 1832, 1833, 1834
SEA FURY FB.50, Hawker
860
SEA GLADIATOR, Gloster
759, 760, 767, 769, 769, 770, 771, 775, 776, 778, 787, 791, 797, 801, 802, 804, 805, 806, 813, 880, 885
SEA HARRIER FRS.1, British Aerospace
700A, 800, 801, 809, 899
SEA HARRIER FRS.2/FA.2, British Aerospace
800, 801, 899, 899OEU

SEA HAWK F.1, Hawker
700, 736, 738, 764, 767, 787, 802, 804, 806, 807, 1832
SEA HAWK F.2, Hawker
700, 736, 738, 764, 767, 802, 807
SEA HAWK FB.3, Hawker
700, 703, 736, 738, 764, 767, 787, 800, 802, 803, 806, 807, 811, 895, 897
SEA HAWK FGA.4, Hawker
700, 736, 738, 764, 767, 800, 801, 802, 804, 806, 807, 810, 811, 895, 898
SEA HAWK FB.5, Hawker
700, 736, 802, 806
SEA HAWK FGA.6, Hawker
700, 736, 738, 764, 781, 800, 801, 803, 804, 806, 810, 895, 897, 898, 899
SEA HERON C.2, de Havilland
781
SEA HORNET F.20/FR.20, de Havilland
703, 728, 736, 738, 739, 759, 771, 778, 801, 806, 809
SEA HORNET NF.21, de Havilland
703, 759, 771, 792, 809
SEA HORNET PR.22, de Havilland
703, 738, 739, 759, 787, 801, 809, 1833
SEA HURRICANE, Hawker
803, 807, 811
SEA HURRICANE Ia, Hawker
762, 787, 787Z, 791, 792, 801, 802, 804, 880
SEA HURRICANE Ib, Hawker
702, 731, 748, 759, 760, 761, 762, 768, 769, 774, 776, 778, 779, 781, 787, 788, 789, 791, 794, 795, 800, 801, 802, 804, 813, 880, 882, 883, 885, 891, 895, 897
SEA HURRICANE IIb, Hawker
700, 759, 800, 802, 804, 883
SEA HURRICANE IIc, Hawker
748, 759, 760, 761, 766, 768, 776, 778, 781, 787, 787Z, 791, 800, 804, 824, 825, 835, 891
SEA KING HAS.1, Westland
700S, 706, 737, 814, 819, 820, 824, 826
SEA KING HAS.2/2a, Westland
706, 814, 819, 820, 824, 825, 826
SEA KING HAS.2(AEW), Westland
824D, 849
SEA KING AEW.2/2a, Westland
849, 849A, 849B
SEA KING HAR.3, Westland
706/SKTU
SEA KING HC.4, Westland
707, 772, 845, 846
SEA KING HAR.5, Westland
771
SEA KING HAS.5, Westland
706, 810, 814, 819, 820, 824, 826
SEA KING HAS.6, Westland
810, 810OEU, 814, 819, 820, 824, 826, 826OEU
SEA KING HAS.50/50a, Westland
817
SEAL, Fairey
701, 702, 753, 782, 820, 821, 822, 823, 824
SEAMEW I, Curtiss
700, 744, 745, 755, 850
SEAMEW AS.1, Short
700
SEA MOSQUITO TR.33, de Havilland
703, 739, 751, 762, 771, 778, 787, 790, 811
SEA MOSQUITO TR.37, de Havilland
703, 771
SEA OTTER, Supermarine
700, 712, 716, 721, 723, 728, 729, 733, 740, 742, 744, 771, 772, 778, 781, 799, 810, 1700, 1701, 1702, 1703
SEA PRINCE T.1, Hunting Percival
700, 702, 727, 744, 750, 781, 831, 1830, 1840, 1841, 1844
SEA PRINCE C.1, Hunting Percival
781
SEA PRINCE C.2, Hunting Percival
781
SEA VAMPIRE F.10, de Havilland
778
SEA VAMPIRE F.20, de Havilland
700, 702, 703, 728, 759, 764, 771, 787, 806
SEA VAMPIRE F.21, de Havilland
703, 764, 771
SEA VAMPIRE T.22, de Havilland
700, 700X, 702, 718, 724, 727, 736, 750, 759, 764, 766, 781, 802, 806, 808, 809, 831, 890, 891, 892, 893, 1831, 1832
SEA VENOM FAW.20, de Havilland
700, 766, 808, 809, 890, 891, 891X
SEA VENOM FAW.21, de Havilland
700, 736, 738, 750, 766, 787, 809, 890, 891, 892, 893, 894
SEA VENOM 21ECM, de Havilland
751, 831

SEA VENOM FAW.22, de Havilland
750, 891, 893, 894
SEA VENOM 22ECM, de Haviiland
831
SEA VENOM FAW.53, de Havilland
724, 805, 808, 816
SEA VIXEN FAW.1, de Havilland
700Y, 766, 890, 892, 893, 899
SEA VIXEN FAW.2, de Havilland
766, 890, 892, 893, 899
SHARK, Blackburn
701, 705, 750, 753, 755, 757, 758, 767, 774, 780, 785, 810, 820, 821, 823
SIKORSKY S-55
705
SKEETER 3, Saro
705
SKUA II, Blackburn
755, 757, 758, 759, 760, 767, 769, 770, 771, 772, 774, 776, 778, 779, 780, 782, 787, 788, 789, 791, 792, 794, 797, 800, 801, 803, 806
SKYHAWK A-4G, McDonnell-Douglas
724, 805
SKYHAWK TA-4G, McDonnell-Douglas
724, 805
SKYRAIDER AEW.1, Douglas
778, 849
SM.79, Savoia-Marchetti
788
SPITFIRE I, Supermarine
748, 759, 761, 762, 775, 791, 794, 880, 897
SPITFIRE II, Supermarine
759
SPITFIRE Va, Supermarine
736, 748, 759, 761, 794, 801, 809, 879, 884, 885, 887
SPITFIRE Vb, Supermarine
719, 748, 759, 761, 768, 770, 778, 787, 790, 791, 794, 798, 801, 808, 879, 880, 884, 885, 886, 897, 899
SPITFIRE Vc, Supermarine
775
SPITFIRE IX, Supermarine
778, 798
SPITFIRE XII, Supermarine
778
SPITFIRE PR.XIII, Supermarine
718, 761, 808, 886
SPITFIRE LF.XVI, Supermarine
761
SQUIRREL, Aerospatiale
723
STURGEON TT.2, Short
703, 728, 771
STURGEON TT.3, Short
728
SWORDFISH I, Fairey
700, 700W, 701, 702, 703, 705, 710, 726, 727, 728, 731, 733, 735, 739, 740, 741, 744, 747, 753, 759, 763, 764, 765, 766, 767, 768, 769, 770, 771, 772, 773, 774, 775, 777, 778, 779, 780, 781, 782, 783, 785, 786, 787, 787Y, 787Z, 788, 789, 791, 794, 796, 797, 810, 811, 812, 813, 814, 815, 816, 818, 819, 820, 821, 822, 823, 824, 825, 826, 828, 829, 830, 833, 834, 835, 836, 837, 838, 840, 841, 848, 860
SWORDFISH II, Fairey
700, 707, 710, 722, 727, 728, 730, 731, 733, 735, 737, 740, 741, 742, 743, 744, 745, 747, 754, 756, 759, 763, 766, 768, 769, 772, 774, 775, 776, 777, 778, 779, 780, 781, 783, 785, 786, 787Z, 788, 789, 791, 796, 810, 811, 812, 813, 815, 816, 818, 819, 822, 824, 825, 829, 833, 834, 835, 836, 837, 838, 840, 841, 842, 860, 886
SWORDFISH III, Fairey
700, 705, 707, 731, 740, 741, 744, 766, 767, 768, 781, 782, 811, 813, 819, 825, 835, 836, 838, 860
SYCAMORE HR.50, Bristol
723, 724
SYCAMORE HR.51, Bristol
723, 724
TIGER MOTH II, de Havilland
700, 701, 702, 721, 723, 727, 733, 752, 753, 755, 756, 758, 759, 762, 767, 768, 769, 775, 780, 781, 782, 785, 786, 788, 794, 796, 798, 799, 1833
TIGERCAT, Grumman
787
TRACKER CS2F-1, Grumman
880, 881
TRACKER CS2F-2, Grumman
880
TRACKER S-2E, Grumman
816, 851

TRACKER S-2G, Grumman
816, 851
TRAVELLER I, Beech
701, 712, 730, 740, 776, 778, 781, 782, 787, 799, 725
TUTOR, Avro
780, 811
TYPHOON Ib, Hawker
778
VAMPIRE F.1, de Havilland
703, 778, 787
VAMPIRE FB.5, de Havilland
702, 703, 787, 891
VAMPIRE T.11, de Havilland
759
VAMPIRE T.11/22, de Havilland
702, 781
VAMPIRE T.34/T.34A, de Havilland
723, 724
VEGA GULL, Percival
752, 754, 780, 781, 782
VENGEANCE TT.II, Vultee
733
VENGEANCE TT.IV, Vultee
721, 723, 791
WALRUS, Supermarine
700, 701, 702, 710, 711, 712, 714, 715, 716, 718, 720, 722, 728, 730, 733, 737, 740, 742, 743, 747, 749, 751, 754, 757, 763, 764, 765, 771, 772, 773, 777, 778, 781, 782, 783, 787, 788, 789, 796, 836, 1700
WASP P.531-O/N, Cierva/Westland
700, 771
WASP HAS.1, Westland
700W, 703, 705, 706, 771, 829, 845, 848, 860
WELLINGTON I, Vickers
783
WELLINGTON II, Vickers
783
WELLINGTON X, Vickers
765
WELLINGTON XI, Vickers
716, 736, 758, 762, 765
WELLINGTON XIV, Vickers
728
WESSEX HAS.1, Westland
700H, 706, 706B, 737, 771, 772, 814, 815, 819, 820, 826, 829, 845
WESSEX HAS.3, Westland
700H, 706, 737, 814, 819, 820, 826, 829
WESSEX HAS.31a/b, Westland
723, 725, 816, 817
WESSEX HU.5, Westland
700V, 707, 771, 772, 781, 829, 845, 846, 847, 848
WHIRLWIND HAR.1, Westland
700, 701, 705, 771, 781, 829, 848
WHIRLWIND HAR.3, Westland
700, 701, 705, 728, 737, 771, 781, 815, 845
WHIRLWIND HAR.9, Westland
829
WHIRLWIND HAR.21, Sikorsky
848
WHIRLWIND HAS.22, Sikorsky
701, 705, 706, 728, 728, 737, 771, 781, 845, 848
WHIRLWIND HAS.7, Westland
700, 700H, 701, 705, 719, 737, 771, 781, 814, 815, 819, 820, 824, 825, 829, 845, 846, 847, 848
WHITLEY VII, Armstrong-Whitworth
734
WHITNEY STRAIGHT, Miles
787, 792, 804
WIDGEON I, Grumman
738, 1835, 1852, 1853
WILDCAT F4F-3, Grumman
890, 892
WILDCAT F4F-4, Grumman
882
WILDCAT IV, Grumman
700, 719, 738, 748, 759, 768, 771, 772, 778, 787, 794, 795, 805, 811, 819, 878, 881, 882, 888, 890, 892, 893, 894, 896, 898, 1832
WILDCAT V, Grumman
700, 718, 733, 738, 748, 757, 759, 768, 771, 772, 778, 787, 790, 811, 813, 816, 819, 824, 832, 833, 834, 842, 845, 846, 850, 851, 852, 853, 878, 881, 882, 890, 896, 898, 1832
WILDCAT VI, Grumman
700, 722, 748, 757, 771, 787, 794, 811, 813, 815, 819, 821, 825, 835, 838, 846, 850, 852, 853, 856, 878, 881, 882
WIRRAWAY, Wackett
723, 724
WYVERN S.4, Westland
700, 703, 703W, 764, 787, 813, 827, 830, 831

INDEX OF UNITED KINGDOM LOCATIONS

ABBOTSINCH, Renfrew
(7 miles W of Glasgow)
730, 768, 771, 800, 801, 802, 804, 807, 813, 816, 818, 819, 821, 824, 825, 831, 832, 835, 852, 892, 1702, 1830, 1840, 1843
ABERPORTH, Dyfed
845
ABINGDON, Berkshire
(5 miles SSW of Oxford)
802, 825
ALDERGROVE, Co.Antrim
(10 miles W of Belfast)
702, 707Z, 774, 815, 818, 829, 845, 846
ALTCAR, Merseyside
(1m SE of Formby)
845
ANDOVER, Hampshire
(3 miles W of Andover)
801, 807, 808, 809, 879, 887
ANDREAS, Isle of Man
(15 miles N of Douglas)
772, 776, 808, 825
ANGLE, Pembrokeshire
(8 miles W of Pembroke)
759, 794
ANTHORN, Cumberland
(13 miles WNW of Carlisle)
772, 801, 802, 807, 812, 813, 824
ARBROATH, Angus
(15 miles N of Dundee)
703A, 735, 737, 740, 741, 751, 753, 754, 758, 767, 768, 769, 770, 771, 772, 778, 783, 787, 791, 800, 801, 802, 803, 807, 809, 810, 811, 813, 814, 815, 818, 819, 820, 821, 824, 825, 826, 841, 845, 846, 880, 883, 885, 898, 1771
AYR, Ayrshire
(1 mile NE of Ayr)
730, 740, 768, 770, 772, 800, 802, 808, 812, 815, 819, 821, 824, 825, 835, 837, 846, 848, 853, 860, 882, 885, 886, 889, 896, 899, 1770, 1771, 1840, 1841, 1843, 1845, 1846, 1850
BALLYCASTLE, Co.Antrim
(18 miles ENE of Coleraine)
819
BALLYHALBERT, Co.Down
(19 miles ESE of Belfast)
718, 725, 768, 784, 787, 800, 808, 812, 827, 835, 880, 882, 885, 887, 894, 899, 1840, 1846
BALLYKELLY, Co.Londonderry
(14 miles E of Londonderry)
744, 745, 772, 811, 814, 815, 819, 824, 831, 833, 834, 835, 836, 837, 849, 849B, 892
BARRY BUDDON, Tayside
(8 miles ENE of Dundee)
845
BECCLES, Suffolk
(7 miles WSW of Lowestoft)
810, 827
BELFAST, Co.Down (SYDENHAM)
(1 mile E of Belfast)
702, 706, 721, 800, 804, 807, 808, 811, 812, 813, 815, 818, 819, 822, 825, 826, 827, 835, 836, 836M, 838, 842, 845, 848, 849, 857, 870, 881, 882, 885, 886, 887, 888, 889, 891, 899, 1772, 1790, 1830, 1831, 1833, 1835, 1836, 1843, 1850, 1851, 1852
BENBECULA, Outer Hebrides
(On NW point of island)
810, 814, 819, 820, 824, 826, 838, 842
BENSON, Oxfordshire
(12 miles SSE of Oxford)
1832, 1834, 1835, 1836
BICKLEIGH, Devon
(Royal Marines Base, 4m NNE Plymouth)
845
BIGGIN HILL, Kent
(13 miles SSE of London)
802, 807, 819
BINBROOK, Lincolnshire
(10 miles SW of Grimsby)
819, 849, 849B,
BIRCHAM NEWTON, Norfolk
(14 miles NE of Kings Lynn)
811, 812, 815, 816, 819, 826, 855
BISHOPS COURT, Co.Down
(4 miles NE of Ardglass)
819

BOSCOMBE DOWN, Wilts
(7 miles NNE of Salisbury)
810OEU, 819, 826OEU, 893, 899, 899OEU
BOULMER, Northumberland
(5 miles E of Alnwick)
808
BRAMCOTE, Warwickshire
(7 miles NE of Coventry)
801, 813, 815, 1833, 1844
BRAWDY, Pembrokeshire
(8 miles NW of Haverfordwest)
727, 736, 738, 751, 759, 767, 773, 784, 800, 801, 802, 804, 806, 807, 811, 813, 824, 831, 846, 849, 849A, 849B, 849C, 849D, 891, 892, 893, 895, 897, 898, 1831
BRIZE NORTON, Oxfordshire
(14 miles W of Oxford)
826, 848
BURSCOUGH, Lancashire
(6 miles SE of Southport)
707, 735, 737, 758, 772, 776, 784, 787, 798, 802, 807, 808, 809, 810, 812, 813, 822, 823, 824, 825, 829, 831, 835, 846, 850, 879, 881, 886, 887, 888, 894, 896, 897, 1770, 1771, 1772, 1790, 1791, 1820, 1836, 1837, 1838, 1840
CAMPBELTOWN, Argyllshire
(3 miles W of Campbeltown)
766, 772, 804, 810, 812, 815, 816, 818, 820, 825, 826, 828, 829, 832, 837
CAPEL CURIG, Gwynnedd
(4m W of Betws-y-Coed)
845
CAPE WRATH, Highlands
845
CARDIFF, Glamorgan
(2 miles E of Cardiff)
815
CAREW CHERITON, Pembrokeshire
(5 miles E of Pembroke)
818, 825
CASTLEMARTIN, Pembrokeshire
(6 miles WSW of Pembroke)
702, 820, 845, 846
CASTLETOWN, Caithness
(7 miles E of Thurso)
808, 825
CATFOSS, Yorkshire
(12 miles NNE of Hull)
810, 820, 821, 822
CHARLTON HORETHORNE, Somerset
(5 miles NNE of Sherborne)
765, 780, 790, 794, 804, 808, 809, 879, 886, 887, 891, 893, 895, 897
CHARTER HALL, Berwickshire
(3 miles E of Greenlaw)
770, 772
CHICKERALL, Dorset
(2 miles NW of Weymouth)
705
CHIVENOR, Devon
(4 miles W of Barnstaple)
748
CLIFTON PARK, Yorkshire
(2 miles NW of York)
809
COLONSAY, Isle of, Strathclyde
814
COLTISHALL, Norfolk
(9 miles NNE of Norwich)
809, 819, 841, 845, 846, 849
CONINGSBY, Lincs
(8m SSW of Horncaastle)
800, 849A, 849B
COOKSWORTHY MOOR, Cornwall?
846
CRAIL, Fifeshire
(8 miles S of St.Andrews)
711, 747, 758, 770, 778, 780, 785, 786, 800, 810, 811, 812, 816, 817, 819, 820, 822, 823, 826, 827, 828, 829, 831, 832, 833, 834, 836, 837, 846
CRIMOND see RATTRAY
CROFT, Yorkshire
(5 miles S of Darlington)
822
CULDROSE, Cornwall,
(2 miles SE of Helston)
700G, 700H, 700S, 700V, 700W, 702, 705, 706, 706B, 707, 736, 738, 744, 745, 750,751, 759, 762, 765, 766, 771, 778, 780,
790, 792, 796, 801, 802, 804, 807, 809, 810, 812, 813, 814, 815, 816, 817, 819, 820, 824, 825, 826, 829, 831, 845, 846, 847, 848, 849, 849A, 849B, 849C, 849D, 849E, 890, 891, 893, 894, 1830, 1831, 1832, 1833, 1843
CULHAM, Oxfordshire
(5 miles S of Oxford)
739, 812, 1830, 1832, 1832A, 1832B, 1835, 1836, 1840
CULMHEAD, Somerset
(6 miles S of Taunton)
790, 887, 894
DALCROSS, Highlands
(8m NE of Inverness)
801
DALE, Pembrokeshire
(11 miles W of Pembroke)
748, 762, 784, 790, 794, 809, 861, 897, 1770
DALLACHY, Morayshire
(9 miles E of Elgin)
838
DARTMOUTH, Devon
(6 miles S of Paignton)
824
DAVIDSTOWE MOOR, Cornwall
(11 miles W of Launceston)
748, 845, 846
DETLING, Kent
(4 miles NE of Maidstone)
801, 806, 812, 815, 816, 819, 821, 825, 826
DISHFORTH, Yorkshire
(5 miles E of Ripon)
815
DOCKING, Norfolk
(14 miles NE of Kings Lynn)
812, 855
DONCASTER, Yorkshire
(1 miles SE of Doncaster)
809
DONIBRISTLE, Fifeshire
(5 miles SE of Dunfermline)
700, 701, 739, 758, 767, 769, 770, 772, 780, 782, 784, 800, 801, 802, 803, 804, 805, 806, 807, 808, 810, 811, 812, 813, 814, 816, 817, 818, 819, 820, 821, 822, 823, 824, 825, 827, 828, 830, 860, 881, 882, 884, 886, 888, 890, 891, 892, 893, 1770, 1820, 1830, 1830A, 1841, 1842
DONIFORD CAMP, Somerset
(2 miles E of Watchet)
846
DOUNREAY, Caithness
(8 miles WNW of Thurso)
819
DREM, East Lothian
(15 miles ENE of Edinburgh)
732, 770, 784, 801, 880, 881, 884, 892, 1791, 1792
DUNDEE, Angus
(2 miles of Dundee)
703, 751
DUNDONALD, Ayrshire
(8 miles N of Ayr)
808, 879, 885, 886, 897
DUNINO, Fifeshire
(6 miles SE of St.Andrews)
737, 770, 785, 786, 813, 820, 824, 825, 827, 833, 837, 838, 860
DUNKESWELL, Devon
(5m N of Honiton)
845
FELIXSTOWE DOCK, Suffolk
824
DUXFORD, Cambridgeshire
(8 miles S of Cambridge)
787
DYCE, Aberdeenshire
(6 miles NW of Aberdeen)
887
EASTCHURCH, Kent
(12 miles NW of Canterbury)
820, 821
EAST HAVEN, Angus
(3 miles SW of Arbroath)
731, 767, 768, 769, 826
EASTLEIGH, Hants (SOUTHAMPTON)
(3 miles NE of Southampton)
716, 758, 759, 760, 780, 800, 801, 802, 810, 811, 814, 816, 820, 821, 822, 825, 829

EGLINTON, Co.Londonderry
(6 miles NNE of Londonderry)
700W, 706, 718, 719, 725, 737, 737X, 744,
745, 758, 768, 782, 794, 795, 800, 802,
803, 804, 805, 806, 807, 808, 810, 811,
812, 813, 814, 815, 816, 817, 819, 820,
821, 824, 825, 827, 833, 834, 835, 837,
838, 845, 847, 848, 849, 849C, 849D, 850,
852, 853, 856, 878, 881, 882, 883, 886,
887, 890, 891, 892, 894, 896, 898, 1830,
1831, 1832, 1835, 1837, 1840, 1841, 1842,
1843, 1844, 1845, 1846, 1847, 1850, 1851,
1852
ERROL, Perthshire
(1 mile NE of Perth)
810
EVANTON (ex NOVAR), Ross & Cromarty
(13 miles N of Inverness)
771, 774, 800, 801, 803, 810, 811, 816,
818, 820, 821, 822, 823, 825, 835
EXETER, Devon
(5 miles E of Exeter)
803, 816, 825, 834, 841
FARNBOROUGH Hampshire
(2 miles N of Aldershot)
845, 893, 899
FEARN, Ross & Cromarty
(8 miles NE of Invergordon)
708, 714, 717, 719, 736B, 747, 812, 814,
815, 816, 817, 818, 819, 821, 822, 823,
824, 825, 826, 828, 837, 841, 847, 860
FORD, Sussex
(8 miles E of Chichester)
700, 700X, 702, 703, 703A, 703W, 703X,
708, 720, 745, 746, 750, 751, 752, 762,
764, 767, 771, 771, 778, 781, 782, 787,
793, 796, 800, 801, 802, 803, 803, 804,
806, 807, 809, 810, 811, 812, 813, 814,
815, 816, 818, 819, 820, 821, 824, 825,
826, 827, 829, 830, 831, 890, 895, 897,
1832, 1833, 1840, 1840A, 1841, 1842
FRASERBURGH, Aberdeenshire
(17 miles NW of Peterhead)
823, 838, 883
FREMINGTON, Devon
(3 miles W of Barnstaple)
845
GARELOCHHEAD, Strathclyde
846
GOSPORT, Hampshire
(3 miles W of Portsmouth)
705, 706, 707, 708, 720, 727, 764, 771,
778, 799, 800, 801, 802, 803, 807, 809,
810, 811, 812, 813, 820, 821, 822, 823,
824, 825, 833, 845, 848, 882, 887, 892,
894, 1846, 1850
GREENHAM COMMON, Berkshire
(2 miles SE of Newbury)
845
GRIMSETTER, Orkney Islands
(4 miles SE of Kirkwall)
800, 801, 807, 824, 825, 826, 841, 842,
846, 848, 849, 880, 881, 882, 884, 887,
894, 899, 1770, 1834, 1840
GUERNSEY AIRPORT, Channel Islands
810, 820, 826, 846
HALDON, Devon
(2 miles NW of Teignmouth)
759, 761, 794
HALESWORTH, Suffolk
(7 miles W of Southwold)
762, 798
HAMBLE, Hampshire
(5 miles SE of Southampton)
780
HARROWBEER, Devon
(8 miles N of Plymouth)
834, 838
HASLEMERE, Surrey
(9 miles SSE of Farnham)
705, 771
HATSTON, Orkney Islands
(2 miles NW of Kirkwall)
700, 701, 712, 746, 771, 800, 801, 802,
803, 804, 806, 807, 809, 810, 811, 812,
813, 814, 816, 817, 818, 819, 820, 821,
821, 822, 823, 824, 825, 826, 827, 828,
829, 830, 831, 832, 833, 835, 836M, 837,
840, 841, 842, 845, 846, 848, 852, 853,
856, 860, 878, 880, 881, 882, 883, 884,
885, 887, 888, 890, 891, 893, 894, 896,
898, 899, 1770, 1771, 1820, 1840, 1841,
1842
HAWARDEN, Flintshire
(4 miles W of Chester)
808, 885

HAWKINGE, Kent
(2 miles N of Folkestone)
854, 855
HEATH ROW, Middlesex
(3 miles NE of Staines)
781
HENSTRIDGE, Somerset
(10 miles NE of Yeovil)
718, 748, 760, 761, 767, 794, 799, 808,
885, 886, 887, 894, 897
HESTON, Middlesex
(11 miles W of London)
701
HIGH ERCALL, Shropshire
(8 miles ENE of Shrewsbury)
810
HINSTOCK, Shropshire
(4 miles S of Market Drayton)
702, 729, 734, 758, 780, 798
HONILEY, Warwickshire
(12 miles SE of Birmingham)
718, 1833
HONINGTON, Suffolk
(5 miles S of Thetford)
801, 809
HOOTON PARK, Cheshire
(7 miles S of Liverpool)
701, 825
HORNCHURCH, Essex
(12 miles W of London)
765
HUTTON CRANSWICK, Yorkshire
(15 miles N of Hull)
885
INSKIP, Lancashire
(2 miles NE of Kirkham)
735, 737, 747, 760, 762, 763, 766, 787,
810, 811, 813, 816, 819, 825, 828, 838,
1791, 1792
INVERNESS, Invernesshire
(1 mile N of Inverness)
782
JERSEY AIRPORT, Channel Islands
(4 miles WNW of St.Helier)
755, 763, 810, 816, 826, 846
JURBY, Isle of Man
(14 miles N of Douglas)
KEEVIL, Wiltshire
(10 miles ESE of Bath)
815, 845, 846
KINLOCHLEVEN, Highlands
846
KINLOSS, Morayshire
(9 miles W of Elgin)
702, 819, 845, 846, 849B, 1770
KIRKISTOWN, Co.Down
(20 miles SE of Belfast)
808, 818, 835, 881, 885, 887
LAKENHEATH, Suffolk
(9m W of Thetford)
849
LANGHAM, Norfolk
(14 miles W of Cromer)
819, 827
LAWRENNY FERRY, Pembrokeshire
(4 miles NE of Pembroke)
764
LECONFIELD, Yorkshire
(10 miles NNE of Hull)
819
LEEDS, Yorkshire
801
LEEMING, Yorkshire
(11 miles NNW of Hull)
800, 845, 849
LEE-ON-SOLENT, Hampshire
(11 miles SE of Southampton)
700H, 700W, 701, 702, 703, 705, 708, 710,
712, 716, 728C, 737X, 739, 746, 752, 753,
754, 760, 763, 764, 764B, 765, 770, 771,
772, 773, 776, 778, 780, 781, 782, 783,
784, 787, 793, 798, 799, 799, 800, 801,
802, 803, 804, 805, 807, 808, 809, 810,
811, 812, 813, 814, 815, 816, 817, 818,
819, 819, 820, 821, 823, 824, 825, 826,
827, 828, 829, 830, 831, 832, 833, 835,
836, 837, 841, 842, 845, 847, 848, 849,
849B, 850, 854, 855, 878, 881, 884, 885,
886, 887, 888, 891, 892, 894, 895, 897,
1700, 1701, 1702, 1703, 1791, 1792, 1831
LEUCHARS, Fifeshire
(4 miles NW of St.Andrews)
800, 801, 802, 809, 810, 811, 814, 819,
822, 845, 892

LIMAVADY, Co.Londonderry
(16 miles E of Londonderry)
737, 811, 819, 825, 846, 850
LINTON-ON-OUSE, Yorkshire
(9 miles NW of York)
814, 819
LLANBEDR, Merioneth
(7 miles NNW of Barmouth)
776
LOCH ERIBOLL, Highlands
845, 846
LONG KESH, Co.Down
(11 miles SW of Belfast)
800, 807, 809, 838, 879, 881, 882, 899
LOCH RYAN, Galloway
845
LOSSIEMOUTH, Morayshire
(4 miles N of Elgin)
700B, 700Z, 736, 738, 750, 751, 759, 764,
764B, 766, 771, 800, 800B, 801, 802, 803,
804, 806, 807, 809, 810, 811, 813, 814,
815, 819, 824, 831, 845, 846, 849, 849A,
849B, 849C, 849D, 860, 882, 890, 891,
892, 894
LYMPNE, Kent
(7 miles W of Folkestone)
800, 803
MACHRIHANISH, Argyllshire
(4 miles W of Campbeltown)
700W, 730, 740, 744, 751, 766, 768, 772,
784, 787, 790, 799, 800, 801, 802, 804,
805, 806, 807, 808, 809, 810, 811, 812,
813, 814, 815, 816, 817, 818, 819, 820,
821, 822, 823, 824, 825, 826, 827, 828,
829, 830, 831, 832, 833, 834, 835, 836,
837, 838, 840, 841, 842, 845, 846, 847,
848, 849, 850, 852, 853, 854, 855, 856,
857, 860, 878, 879, 880, 881, 882, 883,
884, 885, 886, 887, 888, 890, 891, 892,
893, 894, 895, 897, 899, 1771, 1792, 1830,
1832, 1833, 1834, 1836, 1838, 1840, 1848,
1853
MANSTON, Kent
(12 miles ENE of Canterbury)
765, 812, 816, 819, 820, 821, 822, 823,
824, 825, 832, 841, 845, 848
MARHAM, Norfolk
(9 miles SE of Kings Lynn)
819, 824
MAYDOWN, Londonderry
(4 miles NE of Londonderry)
744, 758, 794, 804, 807, 813, 816, 819,
821, 822, 824, 825, 831, 832, 833, 836,
838, 840, 842, 845, 846, 848, 849, 850,
852, 853, 856, 860, 1830, 1832, 1834
MERRYFIELD, Somerset
(7 miles SE of Taunton)
700, 766, 802, 809, 891, 893, 894
MIDDLE WALLOP, Hampshire
(5 miles SW of Andover)
700, 841, 845
MILLOM, Cumberland
(2 miles WSW of Millom)
776, 822
MILLTOWN, Morayshire
(4 miles NE of Elgin)
759, 764, 766, 767, 890
MOUNT BATTEN, Devon
(1 mile SE of Plymouth)
702, 710, 712, 716, 720, 771
MULLAGHMORE, Co.Londonderry
(6 miles SW of Ballymoney)
815, 825, 842, 850, 1771
NETHERAVON, Wiltshire
(13 miles W of Andover)
800, 801, 802, 803, 822
NEWCASTLE-UPON-TYNE, Tyne & Wear
(6 miles NW of Newcastle)
819, 820, 845
NORTH COATES FITTIES, Lincolnshire (10
miles SE of Grimsby)
810, 811, 812, 816, 820
NORTHOLT, Middlesex
(12 miles WNW of London)
800
NOVAR - see EVANTON
NUTTS CORNER, Co.Antrim
(8 miles W of Belfast)
772, 802, 803, 807, 809, 879, 883, 891,
1835, 1837, 1852
ODIHAM, Hampshire
(14 miles S of Reading)
787
OKEHAMPTON, Devon
845, 846

OLD SARUM, Wiltshire
(3 miles N of Salisbury)
810, 846, 879
OTTERBURN, Northumberland
(28 miles NW of Newcastle)
819, 826, 845, 846
OUSTON, Durham
(11 miles NW of Newcastle)
770, 804
PEMBROKE DOCK, Pembrokeshire
(2 miles NW of Pembroke)
764, 821
PEPLOW, Salop
(7 miles S of Market Drayton)
734, 758, 772, 780, 798
PERRANPORTH, Cornwall
(7 miles SW of Newquay)
816, 849, 850
PETERHEAD, Aberdeenshire
(4 miles W of Peterhead)
802, 808, 883, 884, 886, 899
PLASTERDOWN, Devon
(Dartmoor)
845
PLOCKTON, Kyle of Lochalsh
810, 810OEU, 824, 826, 845, 846
PORT ELLEN, Argyllshire
(4 miles NNW of Port Ellen)
878, 890
PORTLAND, Dorset
(2 miles S of Weymouth)
700L, 701, 702, 703, 705, 706B, 737, 771, 772, 801, 810, 814, 815, 815OEU, 819, 820, 821, 824, 825, 826, 829, 845, 848, 860
PREDANNACK, Cornwall
(12 miles SW of Falmouth)
705, 738, 815
PRESTWICK, Ayrshire
(3 miles N of Ayr)
702, 737, 800, 807, 810, 814, 815, 819, 820, 821, 824, 825, 826, 845
RATTRAY (ex CRIMOND),
(8 miles NNE of Peterhead)
708, 714, 717, 753, 766, 769, 774, 815, 817, 818, 821, 825
RENFREW, Renfrewshire
(6 miles W of Glasgow)
816, 823, 1831
ROBOROUGH, Devon
(8 miles N of Plymouth)
801, 810, 814, 815, 819
RONALDSWAY, Isle of Man
(1 mile NE of Castletown)
705, 710, 713, 725, 747, 772, 810, 822, 836A, 836U, 845
ST.ANGELO, Co.Fermanagh
(3 miles NE of Enniskillen)
824
ST.DAVIDS, Pembrokeshire
(2 miles NW of Pembroke)
787
ST.EVAL, Cornwall
(6 miles NNE of Newquay)
796, 801, 807, 812, 816, 820, 827, 829, 833, 849
ST.MAWGAN, Cornwall
(4 miles NE of Newquay)
702, 744, 814, 849
ST.MERRYN, Cornwall
(3 miles SW of Padstow)
709, 715, 719, 725, 736, 738, 741, 748, 750, 762, 774, 787, 792, 794, 796, 800, 801, 802, 804, 807, 808, 809, 810, 813, 817, 819, 820, 825, 826, 828, 829, 836, 837, 860, 879, 880, 882, 883, 884, 885, 886, 887, 888, 891, 893, 895, 897, 1831, 1832, 1833
SALISBURY PLAIN, Wilts
845, 846

SANDBANKS, Dorset
(Poole Harbour)
700W, 765
SAWBRIDGEWORTH, Hertfordshire
(4 miles N of Harlow)
809
SCAMPTON, Lincolnshire
(6 miles N of Lincoln)
819
SCATSA, Outer Henrides
819
SCILLIE ISLES
845
SEALAND, Flint
(4 miles WNW of Chester)
800, 801, 818
SENNYBRIDGE, Brecon
(7 miles W of Brecon)
826, 845, 846
SHERBURN-IN-ELMET, Yorkshire
(11 miles SSW of York)
885
SKEABRAE, Orkney Islands
(13 miles NW of Kirkwall)
801, 804, 841, 880, 881, 882, 884, 887, 894, 1841
SKITTEN, Caithness
(4 miles NNW of Wick)
804
SOUTHAMPTON see EASTLEIGH
SPEKE, Lancashire
(6 miles SE of Liverpool)
736B, 776, 787, 829, 849, 1820, 1832, 1834
STORNOWAY, Isle of Lewis
(2 miles E of Stornoway)
700, 701, 814, 819, 825, 827, 842, 845, 846, 1840
STRABANE see MACHRIHANISH
STRETTON, Cheshire
(3 miles S of Warrington)
718, 728B, 767, 798, 801, 802, 807, 808, 809, 810, 811, 812, 813, 814, 815, 821, 825, 827, 833, 835, 837, 840, 846, 879, 880, 881, 886, 893, 895, 897, 898, 1830, 1831, 1832, 1833, 1834, 1836, 1837, 1840, 1841, 1842
SULLOM VOE, Shetland Islands
(10 miles NNW of Lerwick)
700, 701
SUMBURGH, Shetland Islands
(21 miles S of Lerwick)
819, 821, 828, 880
SUTTON BRIDGE, Lincolnshire
(8 miles W of Kings Lynn)
800, 801, 802, 803
SWINGFIELD, Kent
(5 miles NW of Dover)
819
TAIN, Ross & Cromarty
(3 miles E of Tain)
801, 815, 817, 822, 829
TANGMERE, Sussex
(3 miles ENE of Chichester)
720, 771, 778, 787, 801, 823, 841
TERNHILL, Shropshire
(14 miles NE of Shrewsbury)
816, 829
THETFORD, Norfolk
814
THORNEY ISLAND, Sussex
(8 miles ENE of Portsmouth)
703, 704, 810, 811, 812, 816, 818, 819, 822, 825, 825, 827, 829, 833, 836, 838, 842, 848, 854, 855
THURLEIGH, Beds
703
TIREE, Argyllshire
(3 miles W of Scaranish)
819, 845, 1840

TOPCLIFFE, Yorkshire
(8 miles NE of Ripon)
801, 812, 813, 824
TRELIGGA, Cornwall
(2 miles W of Delabole)
787
TURNHOUSE, Midlothian
(6 miles W of Edinburgh)
801, 807, 808, 814, 848, 882, 884, 886, 895
TWATT, Orkney Islands
(9 miles N of Stromness)
700, 771, 802, 804, 807, 809, 812, 817, 818, 819, 820, 821, 822, 832, 846, 880, 884
UPAVON, Wiltshire
(14 miles NW of Andover)
800, 801, 802, 810, 820, 821, 823, 824
UPOTTERY, Devon
(5 miles NNE of Honiton)
820
USWORTH, Co.Durham
(7 miles SE of Newcastle)
776
VALLEY, Anglesey
(6 miles SE of Holyhead)
819, 820, 826, 845, 846
WADDINGTON, Lincolnshire
800, 819, 846, 849A
WALNEY ISLAND, Lancashire (BARROW)
(1 mile NW of Barrow-in-Furness)
776
WALTHAM, Lincolnshire
(5 miles S of Grimsby)
776
WARMWELL, Dorset
(5 miles WSW of Dorchester)
793, 794, 810, 814
WATTISHAM, Suffolk
(9 miles WNW of Ipswich)
802, 819, 849, 899
WATTON, Norfolk
(11 miles NNE of Thetford)
751, 815, 831
WEST FREUGH, Wigtownshire
(4 miles SSE of Stranraer)
800, 801, 806, 819, 820, 845, 881
WEST RAYNHAM, Norfolk
(14 miles NE of Kings Lynn)
746, 787
WESTHAMPNETT, Sussex
(2 miles NE of Chichester)
787
WICK, Caithness
(1 mile NE of Wick)
803, 887
WITTERING, Northamptonshire
(10 miles WNW of Peterborough)
746, 787, 899
WOODVALE, Lancashire
(12 miles NNW of Liverpool)
736B, 776, 816, 822, 889
WORTHY DOWN, Hampshire
(3 miles N of Winchester)
700, 734, 739, 755, 756, 757, 763, 774, 800, 803, 806, 807, 808, 814, 815, 825, 838, 848
YEOVILTON, Somerset
(3 miles E of Ilchester)
700, 700A, 700L, 700P, 700X, 700Y, 702, 707, 736, 748, 750, 751, 752, 759, 760, 761, 762, 764, 766, 767, 787, 790, 794, 799, 800, 800B, 801, 802, 803, 804, 806, 807, 808, 809, 810, 811, 814, 815, 819, 824, 825, 827, 831, 835, 845, 846, 847, 848, 849B, 849D, 850, 880, 882, 883, 884, 885, 886, 887, 888, 890, 891, 892, 893, 894, 899, 899OEU, 1770, 1771, 1831, 1834
ZEALS, Wiltshire
(8 miles NW of Shaftesbury)
704, 759, 760, 771, 834

INDEX OF OVERSEAS LOCATIONS

AALBORG, Denmark
819, 826, 846, 848, 849, 849A, 849B
AARHUS, Denmark
814
ABOUKIR, Egypt
700Med, 711, 775, 800, 801, 802, 803, 806, 810, 811, 812, 815, 820, 821, 822, 823, 823, 825
ABU ZENIMA, Egypt
889
AFFREVILLE, Algeria
820
AKROTIRI, Cyprus
800, 802, 805, 809, 831, 845, 890, 893, 899, 899OEU
ALAMEDA ISLAND, USA
838
ALAMO, Saudi Arabia
845
AL BATEEN, Abu Dhabi
849A
AL JUBAYL, Saudi Arabia
845, 848
AMBERLEY, Australia
801, 805, 826
AMRIYA, Egypt
806, 823, 825
AMRIYA (LG.86), Egypt
815, 826
ANDALESNES, Norway
846
ANDOYA, Norway
831
ANDROS ISLAND, Bahamas
700L, 810OEU, 815, 819, 820, 824, 826
ANTISARBE, Madagascar
795, 796
ARAXOS, Greece
1702
ARCHERFIELD, Australia
721, 1701, 1845
ARGENTA FIELD, Canada
816
ARUBA, Lesser Antilles
846, 848
ARZEU, Algeria
700Algiers
ASCENSION ISLAND - see WIDEAWAKE
ASAHAN, Malaya
847
ASEGARDEN, Norway
845
ATHENS AIRPORT - see ELEUSIS
AUCKLAND, New Zealand
720

BADEN-SOELLINGEN, Germany
800
BAD LIPPSPRING, Germany
845, 846
BAD TÖLZ, Germany
845, 846
BALLSFJORDEN, Norway
845
BANKSTOWN, Australia
723, 724, 1701, 1830, 1833, 1834, 1836
BARBERS POINT, Hawaii (Pearl Harbour)
882, 896, 898
BARDUFOSS, Norway
801, 845, 846, 848
BAR HARBOUR, USA
732, 738, 1831, 1841, 1842, 1843, 1845, 1848, 1849, 1850, 1851, 1852, 1853
BARIO, Borneo
848
BASTIA, Corsica
845
BATHURST, Gambia
710
BAUMHOLDER, Germany
846
BELAGA, Borneo
845
BELIZE INTERNATIONAL,
British Honduras
801
BENGHAZI, Libya
826
BENINA, Libya
826
BERGEN, Norway
826

BERKA MAIN, Libya
821, 826
BERKA No.2, Libya
826
BERKA NO.3, Libya
815
BERMUDA
718, 773, 819, 881
BITBURG, Germany
810, 814
BIZERTA, Tunisia
(see also KAROUBA, ex SIDI HAMED)
810, 1702
BLENKENSEE, Germany
807
BLIDA, Algeria
727, 779, 807, 807, 809, 813, 820, 826, 879
BLISSVILLE, USA
845
BODØ, Norway
800, 831, 891
BONE, Algeria
767, 813, 826
BROOKLYN, South Africa
814
BROOME, Australia
816, 851
BRUGGEN, Belgium
849
BRUNEI AIRPORT, Borneo
846
BRUNSWICK, USA
732, 738, 846, 848, 882, 898, 1820, 1830, 1831, 1833, 1834, 1835, 1836, 1837, 1838, 1841, 1842, 1843, 1845, 1846, 1848, 1849, 1850, 1851, 1852, 1853
BU AMUD, Egypt
826
BUTTERWORTH, Malaya
801, 803, 806, 812, 890

CAGLIARI, Sardinia
804
CALATO, Rhodes Island
1702
CALAFRANA, Malta (ex KALAFRANA)
701, 705, 711, 713
CAMERI, Italy
814, 846
CAMP BEARCAT, Vietnam
723 Heli
CAMP BLACKHORSE, Vietnam
723 Heli
CANDIA, Greece
821
CAPODICHINO, Italy
728, 809, 879
CASTEL BENITO, Libya (renamed IDRIS)
800, 802, 803, 804, 812, 821, 827,
CASTIGLIONE, Italy
807, 809, 879
CATANIA, Sicily
728
CECIL FIELD, USA
800, 801, 809, 849B, 870, 892
CELLE, Germany
801, 813
CHANGI, Singapore
800, 800B, 801, 803, 806, 809, 820, 845, 849B, 849C, 849D, 890, 892, 893, 899
CHANIA, Crete (Souda Bay)
801
CHARLESTON, USA
824
CHERRY POINT, Mayport, USA (see also MAYPORT)
800, 801
CHINA BAY, Ceylon (or TRINCOMALEE)
733, 788, 791, 800, 802, 803, 804, 806, 807, 808, 809, 810, 812, 814, 817, 818, 822, 824, 828, 830, 831, 832, 834, 837, 845, 847, 851, 854, 879, 880, 888, 896, 898, 1700, 1830, 1831, 1833, 1839, 1844, 1851
CIAMPINO, Italy
728, 893
COCOA BEACH, USA
700L
COCHIN, India
722, 800, 807, 815, 818, 821, 834, 848, 851, 854, 882, 888

COIMBATORE, India
729, 742, 800, 804, 808, 810, 815, 821, 834, 848, 857, 1850
COLOMBO RACECOURSE, Ceylon
742, 755, 756, 797, 800, 803, 804, 807, 808, 814, 832, 845, 848, 851, 888, 889, 898, 1830, 1834, 1836, 1837, 1838, 1839, 1841, 1842, 1843, 1844
CONAKRY, French Guinea
777
CRISSY FIELD, San Francisco, USA
820
CUBI POINT, Phillipines (SUBIC BAY)
801, 805, 814, 826
CUERS, France
820

DABA - see EL DABA
DAKAR, French West Africa
710
DARTMOUTH, Canada
743, 803, 806, 814, 824, 825, 826, 836 flights, 838, 845, 860 flights, 870, 871, 880, 881, 883, 890
DARWIN, Australia
816, 851
DECIMOMANNU, Italy
800, 801, 831, 849D, 899
DEELEN, Netherlands
845, 846
DEKHEILA, Egypt
700Med, 701, 728, 775, 800, 802, 803, 805, 806, 807, 809, 810, 812, 813, 815, 819, 820, 821, 823, 824, 825, 826, 827, 829, 837, 848, 879, 881, 882, 885, 888, 889, 893, 899, 1831, 1841, 1842, 1846
DEKHELIA, Cyprus
845, 848
DE KOOY, Netherlands
810, 826, 845, 846, 860
DETMOLD, Germany
845
DEVERSOIR, Egypt
804
DHALA, Aden
848
DIEGO GARCIA, Indian Ocean
800
DOHA, Kuwait
845, 846
DONG TAM, Vietnam
723 Heli
DOORN, Germany
846
DORTMUND, Germany
845, 846
DRIGH ROAD, India (KARACHI)
801, 810, 891
DUGNY, France
849
DURBAN - see STAMFORD HILL

EASTLEIGH, Kenya
(NAIROBI or EMBAKASI)
788, 796, 800, 805, 849A, 849B, 849C, 890, 892, 893
EGGEBEK, Germany
849B
EL ADEM, Libya
801, 826, 831
EL AOUINA, Tunisia
1702
EL BIRWA, Palestine
826
ELCKENFORDE, Germany
845
EL DABA (LG.20), Egypt
805, 826, 889
EL DABA (LG.21), Egypt
821
EL DABA (LG.104), Egypt
821, 889
ELEUSIS, Greece (ATHENS AIRPORT)
815
EL GAMIL, Egypt
805, 815, 826
EL GUBBI, Libya
806
EL HAMMAN, Egypt
845
EL HAOUARIA, Tunisia (Cape Bon)
821

EL MAGRUN, Libya
815
ELVERGARDSMOEN, Norway
845, 846
ERDING, Germany
826
EVENES, Norway
845

FABRICA, Italy
807, 809
FALAISE, Aden
846, 848
FAYID, Egypt
775, 805, 815, 820, 889
FITROY, Falkland Islands
845
FLORENNES, Belgium
702, 800, 801, 819, 899, 899OEU
FLOYD BENNETT FIELD
806, 834, 837, 882, 1833, 1834, 1849, 1850, 1851, 1853
FOIANO, Italy
809
FORD ISLAND, Hawaii
(PEARL HARBOUR)
832
FORT LAUDERDALE, USA
809, 814
FUHLSBUTTEL, Germany
781X
FUKA MAIN (LG.18), Egypt
813, 824, 826
FUKA satellite (LG.16), Egypt
815, 819, 824, 889

GAGETOWN (Pekersville Camp), Canada
845
GAMBUT, Libya
821, 826
GAMIL see EL GAMIL
GAN, Addu Atoll
814
GARDERMOEN, Norway
845, 846
GASR-EL-ARID, Libya
826
GAZA, Egypt
815
GEILENKIRCHEN, Germany
824
GEMAS, Malaya
845, 847
GIBRALTAR - see NORTH FRONT
GIBRALTAR RACECOURSE
800, 820, 821, 822
GRATANG FJORD, Norway
845
GROTTAGLIE, Italy
800, 849A, 849D
GUTERSLOH, Germany
800, 814, 845899

HAIFA, Palestine
815
HAL FAR, Malta
728, 728B, 728C, 736B, 744, 750, 751, 765, 767, 800, 801, 802, 803, 804, 805, 806, 807, 809, 810, 811, 812, 813, 814, 815, 816, 819, 820, 821, 821, 822, 823, 824, 825, 826, 827, 828, 830, 831, 845, 846, 848, 849A, 849B, 849C, 849D, 849E, 890, 891, 892, 893, 894, 895, 897, 898, 899, 1702, 1792, 1830, 1831, 1832, 1833, 1840, 1841, 1842, 1843, 1844, 1850, 1851
HAMSTEDE, Norway
845
HARSTAD, Norway
701, 845
HASSANI, Greece
1702
HASTINGS, Sierra Leone
710, 777, 814
HELLENIKON (ATHENS), Greece
845
HELTER SKELTER, Saudi Arabia
848
HELWAN, Egypt
879
HEMER, Germany
846
HERAKLION, Crete
815, 819
HILDESHEIM, Germany
826
HOBART, Australia
805

HOBSONVILLE, New Zealand
820
HOLSTENAN, Germany
820
HURGHADA, Egypt
889
HYERES LA PALYVESTRE, France
767, 770, 800, 803, 809, 831, 849D
HYNESS, Norway
846

IDKU, Egypt
806
IDRIS - see CASTEL BENITO
INCIRLIK, Turkey
845, 846
ISTRES, France
821, 826
IWAKUNI, Japan
800, 807, 827, 850

JACKSONVILLE, USA
814, 820, 824, 826, 845, 846, 849A, 849B
JACQUINOT BAY, Australia
1831
JASON'S BAY, Malaya
845, 848
JERVIS BAY, Australia
706, 723, 801, 812, 827, 828, 837, 848, 880, 1771, 1831, 1841, 1842, 1843, 1850
JUHU, India
722, 797, 818, 827, 880

K.6, South Korea
807, 810
K.16, South Korea
810
KAI TAK, Hong Kong
715, 721, 800, 801, 802, 803, 804, 805, 806, 809, 812, 812, 813, 814, 816, 820, 824, 825, 827, 837, 846, 847, 848, 849B, 849D, 850, 857, 891, 892, 893, 894, 1701, 1846, 1850, 1851
KALDADARNES, Iceland
819, 825, 892
KALLANG, Singapore
813, 824
KALUNDBORG, Denmark
846
KAROUBA (BIZERTA), Tunisia (ex SIDI HAMED)
813, 849B
KARUP, Denmark
809, 849, 890
KASFAREET, Egypt
807, 810, 898
KASTRUP, Denmark
849B
KATUKURUNDA, Ceylon
729, 742, 756, 757, 797, 800, 806, 807, 808, 809, 812, 814, 815, 817, 818, 820, 821, 822, 823, 824, 827, 831, 832, 834, 837, 845, 847, 849, 851, 854, 857, 879, 882, 887, 888, 894, 898, 1700, 1830, 1831, 1846, 1850, 1851
KAUFBEUREN, Germany
814
KEIL, Germany
815
KELLY'S GARDEN, Falklands
826
KEY WEST, USA
824, 870, 871
KHORMAKSAR, Aden
800, 801, 810, 814, 815, 827, 831, 848, 849A, 849D, 880, 891, 893
KIEL, Germany
705
KILINDINI, Kenya
710, 810, 849D
KINDLEY AFB, Bermuda
880
KJEVIK, Norway
819
KLUANG, Malaya
845, 848
KNOCKE-LE-ZOUTE (B.83), Belgium
819
KOGGALA, Ceylon
1700, 1833
KOKKOLEI, Ceylon
814
KOKSIJDE, Belgium
824, 846, 849
KOTA BALUD, Borneo
848

KRISTIANSUND, Norway
846
KUALA LUMPUR, Malaya
803, 815, 848
KUANTAN, Malaysia
820, 845
KUCHING, Sarawak
845, 846
KURE, Japan
811
KUWAIT TOWN, Kuwait
848
KYAUKPYU, Burma
807

LANDING GROUNDS IN THE WESTERN DESERT:
LG.05 see SIDI BARRANI
LG.08 see MERSA MATRUH
LG.13 see SIDI HANEISH
LG.14 see MERSA MATRUH
LG.16 see FUKA SATELLITE
LG.18 see FUKA MAIN
LG.20 see EL DABA
LG.21 see EL DABA
LG.75 see MAATEN BAGUSH
LG.104 see EL DABA
LG.109 803, 805, 806
LG.123 see MADDALENA
LG.128 see MADDALENA
LG.139 815
LG.201 826
LABIS, Malaya
814
LABUAN, Borneo
845, 846, 848
LAGENS, Azores
700W, 842
LAKATAMIA, Cyprus
806, 815
LAMU, Kenya
824, 825
LANN-BIHOUE (LORIENT), France
831, 849, 849A
LANDIVISIAU, France
801, 809
LANDSBERG, Germany
845
LANVEOC, France
824, 845
L'ARTIQUE, Algeria
809, 815
LARVIK, Norway
845
LA SENIA, Algeria
779, 807, 820, 885, 888, 893
LATAKIA, Syria
701
LAVERTON, Australia
849C
LE BOURGET, France
826
LEEUWARDEN, Netherlands
767, 800
LEWISTON, USA
738
LISTA, Norway
819
LIVELY ISLAND, Falklands
824
LUQA, Malta
728, 800, 801, 809, 814, 820, 824, 826, 845, 848, 849A, 849B, 849C, 849D, 892, 893, 899
LYDDA, Palestine
806, 829
LYNGEN, Norway
845

MAATEN BAGUSH, Egypt
813, 824, 826,
MAATEN BAGUSH (LG.14), Egypt
805, 815
MAATEN BAGUSH (LG.75), Egypt
815
MAATEN BAGUSH SATELLITE, Egypt
821, 826
MACKINNON ROAD, Kenya
795, 796, 831, 881, 882
MADDALENA (LG.123), Libya
803, 805, 806,
MADDALENA (LG.128), Libya
803, 805, 806
MAISON BLANCHE, Algeria
779
MAJUNGA, Madagascar
710, 795, 796

MALDEGHEM (B.65), Belgium
819
MALEME, Crete
805, 806, 815
MALINDI, Kenya
824, 825
MAPUTO, South Africa
710
MARYBOROUGH, Australia
706, 849, 899, 1701, 1770, 1834, 1836, 1843, 1845
MARYUT, Egypt
775
MASCOT, Australia
724, 849
MARTUBA, Libya
826
MAYOTTE, Comoro Islands
710
MAYPORT, USA (see also CHERRY POINT)
814, 820, 824, 845, 849B
MEDJAZ-EL-BAB, Algeria
767
MELINDIANA, Kenya
846
MERSA MATRUH, Egypt
805, 806, 815
MERSA MATRUH (LG.08), Egypt
815
MERSING, Malaya
845, 848
MIAMI, USA
840
MINNERIYA, Ceylon
733, 810, 831, 847, 851, 1834, 1836, 1837, 1838
MISURATA, Libya
815, 826
MITYLENE, Greece
879
MJULFJELL, Norway
846
MO-I-RANA, Norway
845
MOMBASA, Kenya
788
MONASTIR, Tunisia
815, 821, 828
MONROVIA, Liberia
777
MONTIJO, Portugal
814
MOROKREMBANGAN, Netherlands East Indies (SOURABAYA)
860
MOSFJELLSTUE, Norway
846

NAMSOA, Norway
845
NANGA GAAT, Borneo
845, 848
NARVIK, Norway
845
NAVY POINT, Falklands (PORT STANLEY)
826, 847, 848
NICOSIA, Cyprus
728C, 804, 815, 821, 826, 829, 847, 849D
NORDHOLTZ, Germany
810, 846
NORFOLK, Virginia, USA
738, 800, 804, 810, 814, 816, 817, 820, 824, 827, 829, 831, 832, 835, 845, 846, 848, 849, 849A, 849B, 851, 855, 880, 882, 890, 892, 894, 896, 898, 1820, 1830, 1831, 1833, 1834, 1836, 1837, 1838, 1841, 1842, 1846, 1848, 1849, 1850, 1851, 1852, 1853
NORTH FRONT, Gibraltar (named changed to RAF Gibraltar December 1966)
700Gib, 727, 728, 737X, 751, 773, 775, 779, 800, 801, 802, 803, 804, 805, 806, 807, 808, 809, 810, 811, 812, 813, 814, 815, 817, 818, 820, 821X, 822, 824, 826, 828, 830, 831, 833, 834, 837, 845, 846, 849A, 849B, 849C, 849D, 879, 880, 885, 886, 888, 891, 892, 893, 894, 897, 898, 899, 1841, 1842
NOWRA, Australia
706, 723, 725, 801, 804, 805, 808, 809, 812, 814, 816, 817, 820, 826, 828, 837, 848, 849, 849C, 850, 851, 854, 857, 1771, 1830, 1831, 1833, 1834, 1836, 1839, 1841, 1842, 1843, 1844, 1845, 1846, 1851

OBERAMMERGAU, Germany
846

OCEANA, USA
800, 801, 809, 849A, 892
ORANGE, France
831, 891
ORVIETO, Italy
807, 809, 879
OTTAWA, Canada
806
OTTERØY ISLAND, Norway
845, 846
OUJDA, French Morocco
728, 779
OUAKAM, French West Africa (DAKAR)
814, 821

PAESTUM, Italy
807, 808, 809, 834, 885, 886, 887, 894, 897, 899
PALISADOES, Jamaica
703, 800, 810, 816, 829, 834, 835, 836, 837, 840, 880
PALYVESTRE (see HYERES LA PALYVESTRE)
PARAMYTHIA, Greece
815
PATRICIA BAY, Canada
825
PATRICK AFB, USA
824
PATUAKHAL, East Pakistan
847
PAYA LEBAR, Singapore
800, 801
PEARCE, Australia
800, 848, 849D, 890, 899
PEARL HARBOUR - see FORD ISLAND
PEKERSVILLE CAMP - see GAGETOWN
PENANG, Malaya
803, 813, 824
PENSACOLA, USA
814, 849B
PERUGIA, Italy
807, 809
PIARCO, Trinidad
749, 750, 752, 793, 817
POINT COOK, AUSTRALIA
812, 899
POINT MUGU, USA
892
POMIGLIANO, Italy
728, 879
PONAM, Manus, Admiralty Islands
721, 812, 828, 880, 885, 1701, 1841, 1843, 1850
PORSGRUNN, Norway
845, 846
PORTLAND, USA
820
PORT REITZ, Kenya
710, 796, 800, 803, 806, 810, 814, 824, 825, 827, 829, 851, 877, 880, 881, 888
PORT SAN CARLOS, Falklands
825, 845, 847
PORT STANLEY, Falklands
(see also NAVY POINT)
710, 826, 845
PORT STANLEY RACECOURSE, Falklands
846
PORT SUDAN, Sudan
803, 813, 824, 880
PRISENBOZN, Netherlands
845
PUTTALAM, Ceylon
729, 757, 808, 834, 889, 890, 898, 1770, 1830, 1834, 1836, 1841, 1842

QUONSET POINT, USA
738, 825, 826, 838, 840, 845, 846, 848, 849, 850, 894, 896, 898, 1830, 1831, 1833, 1834, 1835, 1836, 1837

RADFAN, Aden
815, 848
RAMAT DAVID, Palestine
803, 806
RAMSTEIN, Germany
800, 892
RAS GHARIB, Egypt
889
RATMALANA, Ceylon
742, 800, 803, 806, 814, 818, 831, 851, 880, 888
RAYAK, Syria
700Levant, 700Med, 701, 889
RBIYÁN, Aden
834

REVOLVER, Kuwait
848
REYKJAVIK, Iceland
701, 832
RHEIMS, France
849
RICHMOND, Australia
801, 805
RIVERS, Canada
803, 826, 871, 883
ROLLA, Norway
845
ROOSEVELT ROADS, USA
809, 824, 845, 892
ROTA, Spain
801
RYGGE, Norway
831

SAETERMOEN, Norway
845
SAILLAGOUSE, France
845, 846
ST CROIX (B.63), Belgium
819
ST HUBERT, Canada
845
ST JEAN D'ACRE, Palestine
700Med, 701, 775, 826
ST MANDRIER, France (TOULON)
702, 820, 824, 826, 845
ST THOMAS MOUNT, India
815, 817, 822
SAN CARLOS, Falklands
820, 826, 845, 846
SAN CARLOS WATER, Falklands
846
SANFORD, USA
1830
SANTA CRUZ, India
710, 834
SCHLESWIG(LAND), Germany
809, 892, 1832
SCHOFIELDS, Australia
702, 706, 723, 724, 801, 812, 814, 820, 837, 880, 885, 887, 894, 899, 1770, 1772, 1790, 1831, 1834, 1836, 1840, 1843, 1845, 1850, 1851
SCOUDOUC, Canada
870, 880
SEA ISLAND, Canada
850
SEK KONG, Hong Kong
824, 845, 848
SELETAR, Singapore (ex SINGAPORE)
714, 801, 803, 804, 806, 809, 810, 813, 816, 824, 831, 849A, 849B, 849C, 849D, 891, 894
SEMANGYANG, Borneo
845
SEMBAWANG, Singapore
791, 800, 802, 804, 806, 807, 811, 812, 814, 815, 816, 817, 820, 824, 825, 826, 827, 837, 845, 846, 847, 848, 849A, 888, 1700
SEMPANG, Malaya
814
SENNELAGNER, Germany
846
SEPULOT, Borneo
848
SHAIBAH, Iraq
814
SHEIKH OTHMAN, Aden
826
SIBU, Borneo
845, 848
SIDI AHMED, Tunisia
885, 894
SIDI BARRANI (LG.05), Egypt
805, 806, 815, 826
SIDI HAMED - see KAROUBA
SIDI HANEISH (LG.13), Egypt
803
SIDI HANEISH NORTH, Egypt
805
SIDI HANEISH SOUTH, Egypt
806
SILOP, Turney
806
SIMONSTOWN, South Africa
716
SINGAPORE (and see SELETAR)
742, 824
SKRYDSTRUP, Denmark
819

SOLA, Norway
　819, 831, 846, 891
SOLLUR - see SULUR
SOUTH GEORGIA
　845
SOUTH WEYMOUTH, USA
　801
SPLIT, Croatia
　845, 845A
SQUANTUM, USA
　848, 850, 851, 852, 853, 854, 855, 856,
　857, 1820
STAMFORD HILL, South Africa (DURBAN)
　710, 726, 806, 810, 814, 817, 827, 829,
　834, 851, 881
STANFORD, USA
　845
STANLEY, Falklands
　809, 826
STAVANGER, Norway
　819
STRAWBERRY FIELDS, Saudi Arabia
　845, 848
SULUR (or SOLLUR), India
　742, 815, 817, 821, 824
SUMAIL, Muscat
　848
SUMMERSIDE, Canada
　870, 880
SYLT, Germany
　802

TAFAROUI, Algeria
　727, 728, 779, 813, 820, 826, 885, 888, 893
TA KALI, Malta
　727, 728, 800, 802, 807, 809, 810, 815,
　820, 824, 826, 828, 845, 881, 882, 885,
　888, 894, 1702
TAMBARAM, India
　722, 729, 742, 757, 804, 896, 1846, 1850,
　1851
TANCOS, Portugal
　845, 846
TANGA, Tanganyika
　788, 795, 796, 800, 803, 806, 810, 829, 877
TARANTO, Italy
　779

TARHUNA, Libya
　728C
TATOI, Greece
　801
TAWAU, Borneo
　846
TEAL ISLAND, Falklands
　845
TENGAH, Singapore
　800, 801, 803, 804, 805, 811, 820, 825,
　826, 849A, 849B, 849C, 849D, 890, 892,
　893, 899
TERRENDAK, Malaya
　845
TIRSTRUP, Denmark
　702, 814, 819, 845, 846
TOBRUCH, Libya
　803, 805
TONTOUTA FIELD, Noumea
　832, 882, 896, 898
TORONTO, Canada
　806
TOUSSUS, France
　781X
TOVIL, Norway
　845
TRETTEN, Norway
　846
TRINCOMALEE - see CHINA BAY
TRONDHEIM, Norway
　801
TRUMPTON, Saudi Arabia
　845
TURKEY
　848

ULUNDERPET, India
　815, 817, 822, 823, 1839, 1844

VAERLOSE, Denmark
　700L, 815, 829, 845, 846
VAERNES, Norway
　801, 846
VALKENBURG, Netherlands
　751, 800, 814, 819, 820, 826, 831, 845,
　848, 849, 860, 861, 1831, 1841

VAVUNIYA, Ceylon
　834, 845, 851
VIEQUES, ISLE DE, Puerto Rico
　848
VIZAGAPATAM, India
　722, 807
VORDINGBORG, Denmark
　846
VUNG TAU, Vietnam
　723 Heli

WADI TAMET, Libya
　826
WEI-HAI-WEI, China
　813, 824
WELLINGTON, Sierra Leone
　710, 814
WHENUAPAI, New Zealand
　801
WIDEAWAKE, Ascension Island
　809, 826, 845, 846
WIGRAM, New Zealand
　820
WILDENRATH, Germany
　849
WILLIAMTOWN, Australia
　837, 1831
WILLOW GROVE, USA
　882
WINGFIELD, South Africa
　789, 799, 804, 810, 818, 827, 881, 896,
　898, 1830, 1833, 1838, 1846
WUNSTORF, Germany
　781X, 799X, 802, 807, 810
WYNBERG, South Africa
　814, 826, 827, 831, 888

YARMOUTH, Canada
　743, 744, 745, 754
YOUNG'S FIELD, South Africa
　803, 814

ZEELAND, Netherlands
　845

The shape of things to come - Westland/EHI EH-101 Merlin ZF644 at Yeovil in 1994

INDEX OF SHIPS

MV ACAVUS
836F, 836V, 860O
HMS ACHILLES (1)
700, 720
HMS ACHILLES (2)
829
HMS ACTIVE
815, 829
HMS ACTIVITY
767, 768, 810, 815, 819, 824, 833, 835, 836F, 840, 854
HMAS ADELAIDE
723
MV ADULA
836G, 836M, 836P
HMS AJAX (1)
700, 718
HMS AJAX (2)
700W, 829
HMS ALACRITY
702, 815, 829
HMS ALBATROSS
710, 795, 796
HMS ALBION
701C, 745, 800, 801, 802, 803, 804, 806, 807, 809, 810, 813, 814, 815, 820, 824, 825, 826, 845, 846, 847, 848, 849C, 849D, 890, 892, 894, 898
HMS ALCANTARA
702
MV ALEXIA
836F, 836J, 836L, 836Q
MV AMASTRA
836C, 836E
HMS AMAZON
702, 815, 829
HMS AMBUSCADE
815, 829
HMS AMEER
804, 845, 888, 896, 1700
HMS AMPHION
716
MV ANCYLUS
836D, 836G
HMS ANDROMEDA
702, 815, 829
HMS ANSON
700
HMS ANTELOPE
702, 815, 829
USS ANTIETAN
703
HMS ANTRIM
737, 829, 845
HMS APOLLO (1)
718
HMS APOLLO (2)
829
HMS ARBITER
853, 899, 1820, 1843
SS ARCADIAN QUEEN
846
HMS ARCHER
819, 834, 882, 892, 893
HMS ARDENT
702, 815, 829
HMS ARETHUSA (1)
700, 713
HMS ARETHUSA (2)
829
HMS ARGONAUT
702, 815, 829
HMS ARGUS
701, 761, 767, 768, 769, 770, 771, 800, 801, 802, 804, 807, 812, 818, 821, 824, 825, 827, 828, 833, 835, 837, 838, 880, 884, 890, 891, 899, 1832
RFA ARGUS
700L, 702, 810, 826, 845, 846, 848
HMS ARGYLL
815, 815OEU, 829
HMS ARIADNE
829
MV ARIGUANI
804
HMS ARK ROYAL (1)
701, 767, 800, 801, 803, 807, 808, 810, 812, 814, 816, 818, 820, 821, 825, 828
HMS ARK ROYAL (2)
701B, 703, 728C, 800, 801, 802, 803, 804, 807, 809, 815, 819, 820, 824, 831, 846, 849A, 849B, 849C, 890, 891, 892, 893, 898, 899

HMS ARK ROYAL (3)
800, 801, 810, 814, 820, 826, 846, 849B, 899, 899OEU
HMS ARROW
815, 829
HMS ASHANTI
829
MV ASIFI
826
HMCS ASSINIBOINE
819
MV ASTRONOMER
845
HMS ASTURIAS
702
HMS ATHELING
756, 757, 818, 822, 823, 889, 890, 1836, 1837, 1838
HMS ATHENE
832
SS ATLANTIC CAUSEWAY
825
SS ATLANTIC CONVEYOR (1)
809, 845, 848
SS ATLANTIC CONVEYOR (2)
845, 848
HMS ATTACKER
756, 809, 838, 840, 879, 886, 898
HMS AUDACITY
802
HMS AURORA
829
USS AUSTIN
846
HMS AVENGER (1)
802, 816, 819, 825, 833, 883
HMS AVENGER (2)
702, 815

HMS BACCHANTE
829
SS BALTIC EAGLE
845, 846
SS BALTIC EIDER
845
HMS BARHAM
700, 701
HMS BATTLEAXE
815, 829
HMS BATTLER
757, 767, 768, 807, 808, 831, 834, 835, 840, 890, 892, 894
HMS BEAVER
815, 829
HMS BEGUM
721, 757, 815, 817, 832, 845, 1701, 1837, 1838, 1839, 1844
HMS BELFAST
700, 712
HMS BERMUDA
700
HMS BERWICK (1)
700, 715, 718
HMS BERWICK (2)
829
HMS BIRMINGHAM (1)
700, 715
HMS BIRMINGHAM (2)
700L, 702, 815
HMS BITER
768, 800, 808, 811, 833, 836
HMS BLAKE
820
RFA BLUE ROVER
810
HMCS BONAVENTURE
870, 871, 880, 881
HMS BOXER
700L, 815, 829
USS BOXER
800
HMS BRAVE
815, 826, 829
HMS BRAZEN
815, 829
HMS BRIGHTON
829
HMS BRILLIANT
815, 829
HMS BROADSWORD
702, 815, 829

HMS BULWARK
701D, 703, 706, 745, 751, 800, 801, 802, 804, 807, 809, 810, 812, 814, 815, 819, 820, 824, 825, 826, 845, 846, 847, 848, 849A, 849C, 849D, 890, 891, 893, 895, 897, 898, 899, 1832

HMS CAERNARVON CASTLE
702
HMS CAMPBELTOWN
815, 829
HMS CAMPANIA
784, 813, 815, 821, 825, 836M, 842, 850, 882, 1832
HMAS CANBERRA
723
SS CANBERRA
825, 845
HMS CANTON
702, 703
HMS CARDIFF
702, 815
HMS CENTAUR
703, 751, 800, 801, 803, 806, 807, 810, 814, 815, 819, 820, 824, 845, 849A, 849B, 849D, 891, 892, 893, 899
HMS CEYLON
700
USS CHARGER
848, 850, 851, 856, 890, 898, 1834, 1851, 1852, 1853
HMS CHARYBDIS
815, 829
HMS CHASER
816, 835, 845, 899
HMS CHATHAM
815OEU, 819, 826, 829
HMS CILICIA
703
HMS CLEOPATRA
702, 815, 829
HMS COLOSSUS
736, 827, 1846
HMS CORFU
703
HMS CORNWALL (1)
700, 712, 715
HMS CORNWALL (2)
815, 826, 829
HMS COURAGEOUS
800, 801, 802, 810, 811, 812, 820, 821, 822, 823
HMS COVENTRY (1)
702, 815
HMS COVENTRY (2)
815, 826, 829
HMS CUMBERLAND (1)
700, 712, 715
HMS CUMBERLAND (2)
815, 819, 826, 829

HMS DANAE
702, 815, 829
MV DART AMERICANA
824
MV DART CONTINENT
824
HMAS DARWIN
723
HMS DASHER
804, 816, 837, 891
HMS DEVONSHIRE (1)
700, 711
HMS DEVONSHIRE (2)
737, 829
HMS DIDO
700W, 829
HMS DIOMEDE
829
HMS DORSETSHIRE
700, 715
HMS DUKE OF YORK
700

HMS EAGLE (1)
801, 803, 804, 805, 807, 812, 813, 824, 825, 885
HMS EAGLE (2)
701A, 703, 728C, 751, 800, 802, 803, 804, 806, 809, 812, 813, 814, 815, 820, 825, 826, 827, 830, 831, 845, 849, 849A, 849B, 849C, 849D, 890, 892, 893, 894, 897, 898, 899

HMS EDINBURGH (1)
700, 712
HMS EDINBURGH (2)
815
HMS EFFINGHAM
700
HMS EMERALD
700, 702, 703, 712
HMS EMPEROR
800, 804, 808, 845, 851, 888, 896, 1700
MV EMPIRE MACALPINE
836, 836B, 836D, 836U, 836Y
MV EMPIRE MACANDREW
836B, 836H, 836M, 836R, 836Z, 840
MV EMPIRE MACCABE
836A, 836H, 836N
MV EMPIRE MACCALLUM
836K, 836R, 836T, 836Y
MV EMPIRE MACCOLL
836A, 836E, 836J, 836Q, 836V
MV EMPIRE MACDERMOTT
836B, 836K, 836N
MV EMPIRE MACKAY
836D, 836R, 836W
MV EMPIRE MACKENDRICK
836L, 836M, 836V, 836Z
MV EMPIRE MACMAHON
836B, 836G, 836W
MV EMPIRE MACRAE
836C, 836D, 836L, 836U
HMS EMPRESS
768, 804, 845, 850, 888, 896, 1772
HMS ENDURANCE (1)
829, 848
HMS ENDURANCE (2)
815, 829
HMS ENGADINE
702, 737, 804, 810, 815, 832, 845, 1832
RFA ENGADINE
814, 819, 820, 824, 825, 826, 846, 847
HMS ENTERPRISE
700, 703, 714
HMS ESKIMO
829
USS ESSEX
819
HMS EURYALUS
829
HrMS EVERTSON
860
HMS EXETER (1)
700, 718
HMS EXETER (2)
815

HMS FALMOUTH
829
HMS FEARLESS
820, 826, 845, 846, 847, 848
HMS FENCER
700W, 815, 821, 842, 850, 852, 881, 882, 898, 1832
HMS FIDELITY
703
HMS FIFE
737, 815, 829
HMS FIJI
700
HMS FORMIDABLE
803, 805, 806, 810, 818, 820, 826, 827, 828, 829, 830, 841, 848, 853, 881, 885, 888, 893, 1840, 1841, 1842
RFA FORT AUSTIN
702, 810, 814, 819, 820, 824, 826, 845, 846, 848
RFA FORT GEORGE
819
RFA FORT GRANGE
702, 810, 814, 820, 824, 826, 845, 846
HMS FURIOUS
767, 768, 769, 771, 800, 801, 804, 807, 810, 811, 812, 816, 817, 818, 820, 822, 823, 825, 827, 830, 831, 835, 842, 880, 881, 882, 1840

MV GADILA
860S
HMS GALATEA (1)
713
HMS GALATEA (2)
829
HMS GAMBIA
700
HMS GLAMORGAN
737, 815, 829, 845
HMS GLASGOW (1)
700, 712

HMS GLASGOW (2)
702, 815
HMS GLORIOUS
701, 802, 803, 804, 812, 822, 823, 825
HMS GLORY
801, 802, 804, 806, 807, 810, 812, 821, 826, 837, 849C, 898, 1831
HMS GLOUCESTER (1)
700
HMS GLOUCESTER (2)
815
RFA GOLD ROVER
820
RFA GREEN ROVER
845
RFA GREY ROVER
819
ITS GUISEPPE GARIBALDI
849A
HMS GURKHA
829

HMS HAMPSHIRE
737, 829
HMS HECATE
829
HMS HECLA
829
HMS HERALD
829
HMS HERMES (1)
710, 803, 814, 824
HMS HERMES (2)
719, 800, 801, 803, 804, 809, 814, 819, 820, 822, 824, 826, 831, 845, 846, 849, 849A, 849B, 849C, 890, 892, 893, 899
HMS HERMIONE
815, 829
HMAS HOBART
700
HMS HOWE
700
HMS HUNTER
757, 804, 807, 808, 813, 834, 899, 1700
HMS HYDRA
829

HMS ILLUSTRIOUS (1)
703, 738, 751, 767, 795, 796, 801, 802, 803, 804, 805, 806, 809, 810, 813, 814, 815, 819, 821, 824, 826, 827, 829, 832, 845, 847, 848, 854, 878, 881, 882, 890, 894, 1830, 1831, 1833, 1837, 1840
HMS ILLUSTRIOUS (2)
800, 801, 809, 810, 814, 819, 820, 824, 845, 848, 849, 849A, 899
HMS IMPLACABLE
702, 719, 767, 773, 794, 795, 801, 807, 810, 813, 815, 828, 841, 880, 881, 887, 894, 1771, 1790, 1832
HMS INDEFATIGABLE
737X, 799, 820, 826, 842, 885, 887, 888, 894, 1770, 1772, 1840
HMS INDOMITABLE
703, 796, 800, 801, 802, 804, 806, 807, 809, 810, 813, 815, 817, 820, 826, 827, 831, 854, 857, 880, 899, 1839, 1844
HMS INTREPID
845, 846, 847, 848
HMS INVINCIBLE
800, 801, 809, 814, 820, 824, 826, 845, 846, 849A, 899
HMS IRON DUKE
815

HMS JAMAICA
700
HMAS JERVIS BAY
723
HMS JUNO
829
HMS JUPITER
815, 829

HrMs KAREL DOORMAN
819, 860, 861
HMS KENT (1)
700, 715
HMS KENT (2)
737, 829
MV KEREN
826
HMS KENYA
700
HMS KHEDIVE
769, 800, 804, 808, 845, 849, 888, 899, 1700, 1834

HMS KING GEORGE V
700

HMS LANCASTER
815, 829
HMS LEANDER (1)
700, 712, 720
HMS LEANDER (2)
700W, 829
HMS LEEDS CASTLE
819
HMS LIVERPOOL (1)
700, 714
HMS LIVERPOOL (2)
815
TLC LOFOTEN
826, 815, 819
HMS LONDON (1)
700, 711
HMS LONDON (2)
737, 772C, 829
HMS LONDON (3)
700L, 815, 826, 829
HMS LONDONDERRY
829
HMS LOWESTOFT
829

MV MACOMA
860F, 860O
HMCS MAGNIFICENT
803, 806, 825, 826, 870, 871, 880, 881, 883
HMS MALAYA
700, 701, 812
HMS MANCHESTER (1)
700, 714
HMS MANCHESTER (2)
815
HMS MAPLIN
702, 804
HMS MARLBOROUGH
815, 829
HMS MAURITIUS
700
HMAS MELBOURNE
723H, 724B, 805, 808, 814, 816, 817, 825
SS MICHAEL E
804
NAeL MINAS GERAIS
700
HMS MINERVA
702, 815, 829
MV MIRALDA
836H, 836P, 836Q
HMS MOHAWK
700W, 829
HMS MONMOUTH
815
HMS MONTROSE
815
HMAS MORESBY
723

HMS NABOB
852, 856
HMS NAIAD
829
HMS NAIRANA
768, 784, 816, 835, 838, 860
HMS NELSON
702
HMS NEPTUNE
700, 712, 716
HMS NEWCASTLE (1)
700, 712
HMS NEWCASTLE (2)
702, 815
HMS NEWFOUNDLAND
700
HMS NIGERIA
700
HMS NORFOLK (1)
700, 712, 714
HMS NORFOLK (2)
737
HMS NORFOLK (3)
815, 829
HMS NORTHUMBERLAND
815
HMS NOTTINGHAM
815
HMS NUBIAN
829

HMS OCEAN
800, 802, 804, 805, 807, 810, 812, 816, 825, 845, 845, 892, 898, 1702, 1792

RFA OLEANDER
819
RFA OLMEDA
702, 810, 810OEU, 814, 819, 820, 824, 826, 845
RFA OLNA
702, 737, 772, 814, 819, 820, 824, 826, 845, 846, 848, 849B
RFA OLWEN
702, 737, 814, 819, 820, 824, 826, 845, 848
RFA OLYNTHUS
814, 819
HMS ORION
700, 712, 718

HMS PATROLLER
768, 1843, 1852
HMS PEGASUS
763, 764, 804, 807
HMS PENELOPE (1)
713
HMS PENELOPE (2)
700W, 815, 829
HMS PERSEUS
706, 845, 848
HMAS PERTH
700, 718
HMS PHOEBE
700L, 702, 815, 829
HMS PLYMOUTH
829
HMS POLAR CIRCLE
829
HrMs POOLSTER
819, 820, 824, 826
HMS PREMIER
746A, 767, 768, 802, 846, 856, 881, 892, 1835
HMS PRETORIA CASTLE
702, 703, 768, 777, 778, 817, 825, 1771
SNS PRINCIPE DE ASTURIAS
801
HMS PROTECTOR
701P, 771, 829
HMS PUNCHER
821, 825, 881, 1790, 1791, 1845
HMS PURSUER
881, 896, 898, 1831

HMS QUEEN
802, 810, 853, 855
HMS QUEEN ELIZABETH
700
SS QUEEN ELIZABETH II
825
HMS QUEEN OF BERMUDA
702

HMS RAJAH
767, 768, 769, 822, 849, 857, 888, 1842, 1853
HMS RAMILLIES
702
HMS RANEE
768, 769, 1846, 1848
HMS RANPURA
703
MV RAPANA
836L, 836X, 838
HMS RAVAGER
746A, 761, 767, 768, 769, 800, 804, 832, 835, 845, 846, 886, 889, 899, 1771, 1834
HMS REAPER
768, 1701, 1849, 1850
RFA REGENT
814, 820, 845, 848
RFA RELIANT
826, 846
HMS RENOWN
700
HMS REPULSE
700, 705
HMS RESOLUTION
700, 702
RFA RESOURCE
707, 772, 826, 845

HMS RHYL
829
HMS RICHMOND
815
HMS RODNEY
700, 702
HMS ROTHESAY
829
HMS ROYAL OAK
701, 702
HMS RULER
885, 1772

USS SARATOGA
804, 832, 892
HMS SCYLLA
815, 829
HMS SEARCHER
746A, 821, 882, 898
HMS SHAH
800, 804, 845, 851, 888, 1700
HMS SHEFFIELD (1)
700, 712
HMS SHEFFIELD (2)
702, 815, 829
HMS SHEFFIELD (3)
815, 829
HMS SHROPSHIRE
700, 711
MV SINGELGERACHT
826
RFA SIR BEDIVERE
845
RFA SIR GALAHAD
826, 845, 846, 847
RFA SIR GERAINT
845
HMS SIRIUS
702, 815, 829
RFA SIR PERCIVALE
845
RFA SIR TRISTRAM
845, 846
HMS SLINGER
768, 1830, 1845
HMS SMITER
746A, 767, 768, 769, 791, 808, 815, 856, 888, 1841
HMS SOUTHAMPTON (1)
700, 712
HMS SOUTHAMPTON (2)
815
HMS SPEAKER
721, 768, 1820, 1840,
HMS SPRINGBANK
804
HMS STALKER
757, 809, 833, 880, 897, 899, 1700
HMAS STALWART
723, 816, 817
HMS STRIKER
824
RFA STROMNESS
845, 847
HMAS SUCCESS
723, 816
HMS SUFFOLK
700, 712, 715
HMS SUSSEX
700, 711
HMS SUTHERLAND
815
HMAS SYDNEY (1)
700
HMAS SYDNEY (2)
723, 805, 808, 816, 817, 850, 851

HMS TARTAR
829
HMS TERROR
715
HMS THANE
831, 834, 1851
HMS THESEUS
702, 703, 744, 767, 773, 794, 802, 804, 807, 810, 812, 814, 816, 820, 824, 825, 826, 845, 898, 1832

RFA TIDEPOOL
737/Oscar, 772, 814, 819, 820, 824, 829, 845
RFA TIDESPRING
707, 737, 772, 810, 814, 815, 817, 819, 820, 824, 826, 845, 846
HMS TIGER
814, 826
HMAS TOBRUK
723, 816, 817
HMS TRACKER
768, 816, 845, 846, 853
SS TRANSFJELL
845
HMS TRINIDAD
700
HMS TRIUMPH
738, 767, 800, 804, 812, 827, 845, 847, 1833, 1840
HMS TROUNCER
768, 825, 889, 1702, 1843
HMS TRUMPETER
767, 821, 828, 846, 848, 852, 856, 881, 1771, 1831, 1833, 1840

HMS UGANDA
700
SS UGANDA
826
HMS UNICORN
721, 756, 800, 809, 817, 818, 824, 832, 847, 851, 881, 885, 887, 888, 893, 894, 897, 1837, 1838, 1844

HMS VALIANT
700, 701
HrMs VAN GALEN
860
HrMs VAN NES
860
HrMs VAN SPEIJK
860
HMS VENERABLE
802, 814, 1850, 1851
HMS VENGEANCE
703, 738, 767, 773, 801, 802, 807, 808, 809, 812, 814, 816, 850, 1830, 1831, 1850, 1851
HMS VICTORIOUS
701C, 756, 800, 801, 802, 803, 805, 807, 809, 814, 815, 817, 819, 820, 822, 824, 825, 827, 828, 829, 831, 832, 848, 849, 849A, 849B, 882, 884, 885, 892, 893, 894, 896, 898, 899, 1834, 1836, 1837, 1838, 1841, 1842
HMS VIDAL
701V, 829
HMS VINDEX
784, 811, 813, 825, 836W, 882, 1790

HMCS WARRIOR
703, 803, 811, 825, 826, 883
HMS WARSPITE
700, 701
USS WASP
812
HMS WESTMINSTER
815
USS WOLVERINE
894

HMS YARMOUTH
829
HMS YORK (1)
700, 718
HMS YORK (2)
815

HrMs ZUIDERKRUIS
814, 819, 820, 826, 860
HMS ZULU
829

INDEX OF COMMANDING OFFICERS NAMES

Abbott L/C DRS, 813
Abel Lt SC, 765
Abel Smith L/C EMC, 802
Abraham L/C HJ, 738, 810
Abraham L/C RWT, 813
Abrams L/C AH, 775, 785, 818, 20CAG
Acland L/C DJD, 824
Adams L/C AP, 851
Adams Lt SE, 796
Adkin L/C TO, 1836
Ainslie L/C JDStJ, 820
Allen L/C CA, 813
Allingham L/C HP, 750, 1831
Allison Lt JLWM, 765
Ancona L/C DT, 819
Anderson L/C D, 824
Anderson L/C JNS, 764, 892
Andon L/C WVE, 814
Andrews L/C DT, 849C, 849D
Andrews L/C GA, 847, 848
Angel L/C DH, 740, 751, 764
Ansell L/C JA, 733, 788
Anson L/C ER, 801
Anstice Cdr EW, 810
Appleby L/C JL, 719, 737, 794, 808
Apps L/C MCS, 814
Archer L/C TJ, 792
Armour Mjr JO, 784, 809, 892, 7CAG, 15CAG
Armour Cdr RSD, 701
Armstrong L/C CB, 849, 849A
Arnall-Culliford L/C ND, 772
Arnold L/C FGJ, 744
Arnold L/C JF, 710, 719, 785, 845
Ashburner L/C LCB, 829, 834
Ashton L/C J, 825
Ashton-Johnston L/C EC, 705, 814
Ashworth L/C RC, 825, 849B
Astbury L/C MJ, 724, 816
Aston Cpt WGS, 833
Atherton L/C PE, 802
Atkinson L/C CJN, 800
Atkinson L/C NC, 750
Atkinson L/C WHI, 881
Attrill L/C MW, 829
Auckland L/C LF, 1833
Auld L/C AD, 800
Austin L/C AJ, 1832
Austin L/C PM, 736, 850
Averill L/C FG, 758A, 758Y
Ayres L/C JW, 764
Ayres L/C KJMcK, 771

Baaker LTZSD1 IR, 860
Bagley L/C PCS, 728
Bagnall L/C GA, 705, 815
Bailey L/C HE, 817
Bailey L/C JS, 768, 803, 804, 815, 827
Bailey L/C ON, 882
Bailey L/C PE, 737, 814
Bailey L/C PEI, 787, 805, 879, 886
Bailey L/C ON, 759, 795, 891
Bailey L/C TL, 702
Baillie L/C A, 849D
Bain L/C HER, 727, 894
Baker L/C JD, 736
Baker L/C JI, 765
Baker L/C LJ, 767, 801
Baker-Falkner L/C RS, 767, 827, 8Wg
Baldwin L/C GC, 800, 807, 3Wg, 15CAG, 51TAG
Baldwin L/C JG, 736, 771, 801, 811, 1834, 1836
Ball L/C JN, 799, 15CAG, 50TAG

Ballard L/C C, 881
Barber L/C PA, 820
Barbour L/C JM, 849C
Baring L/C FW, 756, 757
Baring L/C MJ, 849
Barlass L/C GP, 782
Barnard L/C WH, 849, 849A
Barnes L/C JS, 813, 814
Barnett Cdr KM, 724, 725, 816
Barnes L/C JS, 781, 796
Barras L/C GW, 705, 706
Barringer L/C EE, 835
Barrington L/C LWA, 781, 813
Barrington L/C V, 782
Barron L/C MWMcD, 724, 805
Barsham L/C ES, 758A, 758C, 758D
Bartlett L/C NA, 703, 768, 890
Bartlett L/C RE, 825, 18CAG, 30CAG
Barton L/C P, 772
Bassett L/C TM, 747
Baston L/C DEP, 707, 848
Bateman L/C CR, 771
Bateman L/C JG, 51TAG
Bateman L/C MJ, 831, 890
Bates L/C GH, 787Z, 837
Bathurst L/C DB, 819
Battesse L/C VT, 723
Battison L/C DF, 764
Baudains L/C DP, 810
Beange L/C GA, 723, 805, 808
Beard L/C JW, 738
Beard L/C KW, 771, 772, 773
Beard L/C RA, 733
Beattie L/C J, 707
Beaumont L/C IH, 814
Bedells Lt JHB, 744
Belding L/C PS, 845
Bell Cdr ES, 725, 817
Bellamy L/C R, 736
Bender Lt AH, 729
Bennett L/C G, 705, 739, 769
Bennett L/C NK, 705, 849A
Berrill L/C DA, 719
Berry L/C WM, 845
Bertholdt L/C GT, 702, 758A
Besley L/C DW, 849D
Bessel-Browne L/C GDW, 816
Betts Lt MWP, 849A
Bevans L/C B, 807, 728, 764
Beyfus L/C JG, 814
Bibby L/C RE, 736B, 766, 787Y
Bickley Cdr M, 809
Bigg-Wither L/C RL, 1841, 6Wg
Billingham L/C JOFD, 800
Billson Lt RH, 701
Binney L/C TVG, 702, 804
Birch L/C GF, 799, 826
Bird Mjr FDG, 759, 888
Bird L/C HJG, 803, 881
Bird L/C RA, 794, 881, 882
Birrell L/C MA, 780, 891
Birse L/C SW, 781, 798, 814
Bishop L/C R StJ, 814
Bishop-Bailey L/C M, 702, 824
Black L/C AF, 805
Black L/C WGB, 891, 894
Blackwell Lt TWT, 718
Blair L/C DK, 831
Blake L/C IF, 892
Blake L/C RHW, 719, 744
Blake L/C WHC, 755, 756, 770
Blennerhassett L/C CC, 724, 805
Bloomer L/C AW, 766, 806, 809, 810
Bolt L/C AS, 812

Blissett L/C MS, 801
Bluett L/C JRT, 719, 815, 819
Blunden L/C JF, 766, 891
Blythe L/C DA, 703
Boddam-Whetham L/C AP, 848, 850
Boettcher L/C BJ, 723, 725
Boland L/C M, 700L
Bolt L/C TJ, 893
Bond S/L FE, 802
Booth L/C FC, 793
Booth L/C MD, 847
Borrett L/C S, 774, 811, 815
Borroman L/C DA, 767
Botten L/C MA, 819
Boulding L/C BE, 786, 822, 21Wg, 45Wg
Bourke L/C AD, 756
Bourke L/C RE, 787, 805
Bourne L/C RL, 815
Bovey L/C NH, 1840
Bowen L/C MF, 745, 750
Bowles L/C WG, 805
Boyce S/L GH, 810, 812
Brabner L/C RA, 801
Bracken Lt HH, 701
Bradley L/C OP, 758D
Bradley L/C WH, 18CAG
Bradshaw L/C IRM, 899
Bradshaw L/C RE, 706, 826, 828, 852
Braithwaite L/C DD, 800
Bramall L/C EK, 771
Bramwell L/C HP, 759, 778, 801
Brander L/C TLM, 807, 898
Bret L.V. AE, 781X
Brewer L/C PS, 764, 890
Brewer L/C WLE, 1836
Bricker L/C GW, 705
Bridger L/C DJA, 706
Bridges L/C RAY, 845
Brigham L/C JG, 814
Brilliant L/C S, 824
Britton L/C EM, 728, 778, 788, 831, 2Wg, 12Wg, 52Wg
Britton Lt HH, 828
Brock L/C A, 825
Brock L/C BM, 772
Bromilow L/C F, 815, 849
Bromwich L/C HF, 801
Brooker L/C DG, 1846
Brooks L/C D, 769, 821, 831
Brown Lt AL, 762
Brown L/C DM, 768, 783
Brown L/C EM, 804
Brown Cpt FW, 786, 824
Brown L/C GEG, 820
Brown L/C GFS, 805
Brown L/C GR, 765
Brown L/C IJ, 891
Brown S/L JAS, 811
Brown L/C JM, 719, 768, 795, 822, 838
Brown L/C ML, 891
Brown L/C RJG, 763
Brown L/C WLM, 701
Bruen L/C JM, 759, 800, 803
Bruinsma LTZV1 A, 860
Brunt L/C A, 717
Bryant L/C JPG, 713, 778, 802
Bryant L/C RF, 804, 808
Bryant L/B PJ, 702
Buchanan L/C D, 816
Buchanan Cdr HD, 880
Buchanan L/C J, 723
Buchanan-Dunlop L/C DK, 827
Buckland Lt PD, 714
Buckley L/C JB, 822, 825

Buckley L/C PS, 824
Bullivant L/C BE, 771
Bullivant L/C HAP, 723
Bullock L/C JRB, 814
Bunyan L/C DJ, 846
Burbury L/C NH, 772
Burch Mjr AR, 771, 822
Burdorf L/C TA, 851
Burgess L/C PM, 750
Burke L/C CC, 771
Burke L/C DF, 846
Burke L/C PG, 760
Burnett L/C MS, 810
Burroughs Cdr JHF, 750
Burrows L/C RG, 702
Burt L/C EJE, 754, 776, 781
Burton L/C J, 849D
Burton L/C P, 819, 820
Butcher L/C MW, 826
Butler L/C NAM, 849, 849B
Butler L/C TG, 849D
Byas Cdr CW, 803

Caddy L/C HH, 714
Caldwell L/C WB, 781
Callan L/C WE, 724, 805
Callander L/C JRC, 833, 836, 838
Callingham L/C GR, 799, 887, 13CAG, 14CAG
Cambell L/C DRF, 803
Camp L/C JP, 820
Campbell L/C JD, 851
Campbell L/C JGB, 723, 805
Campbell Lt RGM, 890
Campbell L/C WI, 787, 800, 898
Campbell-Horsfall Lt CP, 761, 801, 808, 30Wg
Campey L/C HE, 817
Cannell L/C PJ, 723
Cantrill L/C OH, 741
Cane L/C P, 750
Carlisle L/C DG, 715
Carmichael L/C P, 738, 766, 806
Carnduff L/C EB, 822
Carne L/C GP, 766, 893
Carne Lt P, 764
Carter Lt DR, 777
Carter L/C JJ, 819
Carter L/C WJ, 766, 899
Carver L/C ES, 735, 826
Carver L/C RHP, 761, 778, 885, 3Wg
Casdagli L/C A, 705, 820
Casperd L/C CS, 759
Cass L/C GP, 849A
Cassidi L/C AD, 820
Casson L/C J, 760, 803
Castlemaine L/C LRE, 700
Caswell S/L BB, 812
Cavalier L/C GA, 700L, 703
Cavanagh L/C JHG, 808
Champ Lt CE, 724
Chare Lt KA, 1703
Charlton L/C PN, 761, 1834
Cheesman Mjr VBG, 766, 788, 1770
Chester-Lawrence L/C LEA, 736
Child L/C ED, 834
Child Lt EHG, 783
Chilton L/C PCS, 748, 806, 1843, 1849
Chorley Lt PC, 701
Chute Lt DT, 1836
Clapp L/C MC, 801
Claridge L/C AG, 737, 819
Clark L/C ABB, 702, 899
Clark L/C EJ, 807, 1848
Clark L/C HS, 706, 825

Clark L/C MP, 706
Clark L/C PJG, 703
Clark L/C PL, 724
Clark Lt RJ, 807
Clarke L/C FWH, 811
Clarke L/C GR, 824, 827
Clarke L/C GS, 707, 845
Clarke L/C JLK, 816
Clay L/C CJ, 703, 829
Clayton L/C PF, 781
Clifford S/L G, 821
Coates Lt DH, 765
Coates L/C T, 755
Cobb L/C RB, 849B
Cockburn L/C JC, 718, 804, 881
Cockburn L/C RC, 734
Cocks L/C RWJ, 881
Cogdon L/C N, 803, 19CAG, 31SAG
Cole L/C PS, 739, 820
Colles Lt GH, 783
Collett L/C JW, 822, 823
Collingridge L/C D, 724, 805
Colls L/C SWD, 702, 809
Colthurst L/C AP, 820, 822
Colville-Stewart L/C H, 1847
Comins L/C CAM, 738
Compton L/C PW, 799, 826
Connolly L/C PJ, 772
Connor L/C DR, 710
Coode L/C TP, 720, 805, 815, 818
Cook L/C NJ, 1835
Cook L/C WG, 718
Cooke L/C SG, 767, 813
Cooper L/C GRFT, 752
Cooper L/C HS, 780
Cooper L/C J, 882
Cooper L/C SG, 741, 825
Cooper L/C WJ, 751
Cope L/C E, 764
Corbet-Milward L/C NR, 817, 21Wg
Corbett L/C JG, 728B
Corbett L/C JWS, 826
Cordell L/C AG, 724
Cork L/C RJ, 761, 880, 15Wg
Corkhill L/C AD, 723, 813, 814
Cornabe L/C AG, 700H, 815, 845
Cosh L/C DRB, 881, 893
Cotton Lt WE, 727, 780
Coulson L/C PK, 816
Courtier L/C SBE, 723
Covington L/C WM, 801, 899
Coward L/C JL, 849D
Cowley L/C NJ, 814, 824A
Cowling L/C WH, 898
Cowtan L/C FE, 703, 703X, 744
Cox L/C BF, 779, 803
Cox Lt DPZ, 802
Coxon L/C CRJ, 719, 795, 812, 813, 815, 816
Coy L/C GR, 810, 814
Crabbe L/C JSL, 814, 816, 846, 20CAG
Craig L/C AH, 817
Craig L/C CJS, 705, 826
Craig L/C PJ, 705, 707, 848
Crane L/C VR, 714
Crawford L/C BC, 723
Crawford L/C JA, 836
Crawford L/C NGR, 812
Crawford L/C WH, 769, 845
Creery L/C RAB, 883, 30CAG
Crighton L/C CA, 791
Crook L/C JH, 750
Crookston L/C TL, 794
Croome L/C WPT, 773
Crosley L/C RM, 718, 794, 801, 813, 880, 894
Crossman L/C J, 894
Cruttenden Lt PJWW, 728

Cubitt L/C LA, 753, 828
Culbertson L/C JM, 812
Cullen L/C JL, 738, 847
Cunningham L/C AB, 701
Cunningham L/C CJ, 805
Cureton L/C H, 781
Curgenven-Robinson L/C JB, 711
Curry L/C DR, 736
Curry L/C FP, 781

da Costa L/C JR, 724, 805
Dadswell L/C TA, 816
Daley L/C CF, 723
Dalgleish L/C JW, 851
Dallosso L/C PR, 724
Dalyell-Stead L/C J, 816, 829
Dalzell S/L WAK, 824
Daly L/C BJ, 724
d'Ancona LTZ1 GA, 860
Darlington L/C MI, 759
Darlow L/C FE, 750
Daubney Lt WLM, 783
Davenport Lt HSMcN, 819
David L/C JP, 815
Davies L/C B, 892
Davies L/C DA, 822
Davies Lt GH, 720
Davies L/C GLC, 746, 784
Davies L/C RO, 784
Davis Cdr CCN, 759, 809
Davis L/C DFV, 1843
Davis L/C EM, 880
Davis L/C KDR, 793
Davison Lt TG, 787Z
Dawson L/C HP, 821
Deadman L/C NJK, 820
Debenham L/C AJ, 824
Debus L/C DG, 817
de Hartog L/C NT, 772
de Labilliere L/C AMD, 809
Deller L/C PD, 707
de Mowbray L/C CJ, 845
Demuth L/C RP, 790
den Hartogh LTZV2 oc JAC, 860
Dennis L/C AM, 727, 796
Dennison L/C G, 794, 887, 899, 52TAG
Denny L/C CJ, 819
den Ouden LTZ1 HW, 860
Devonald L/C SL, 885, 1846
de Winton L/C JFHC, 801, 809
de Wit L/C H, 800
Diamond L/C BJ, 805
Dibell L/C ATJ, 750
Dick L/C DA, 1846
Dick Lt DG, 720
Dickens L/C GC, 823
Dickinson L/C PN, 824, 824B
Di Pietro L/C VEB, 723
Diggens L/C LF, 740
Dimmock Cdr RC, 801
Dimock Lt HR, 792
Dimsdale Lt JR, 737
DiPeitro L/C AFE, 723
Dismore L/C OMC, 706
Dixon-Child L/C S, 1792
Dobson L/C W, 771
Doe L/C CRV, 700H, 706
Dominey L/C IS, 771
Domoney L/C IC, 706
Donaghue Lt GA, 764
Donaldson L/C JN, 743, 826, 881
Douglas L/C CF, 820
Douglas L/C G, 823, 45Wg
Douglas L/C KA, 723, 724, 816
Doust L/C MJ, 767
Down S/L HH, 824, 825
Doyne-Ditmas L/C PS, 845
Drake L/C HS, 892
Draper L/C C, 777
Drummond L/C JAL, 767

Dudley L/C K, 826
Dunbar-Dempsey L/C DJ, 766, 899
Duncan L/C GM, 821
Dundas L/C JH, 703, 850
Dunn L/C WE, 754
Dunne L/C LP, 737, 815
Durrant L/C RW, 757
Dutch L/C BA, 724
Duxbury L/C RA, 706, 825
Dyas L/C MV, 727
Dykes L/C JJ, 755, 757

Eadon L/C HDB, 809
Eagle L/C JH, 750
Eagles L/C AJ, 705
Edgar Lt AB, 1700
Edmonds L/C RF, 702
Edmundson L/C JB, 889, 1836
Edwards L/C DP, 820
Edwards L/C GC, 769, 824
Edwards L/C LA, 842
Edwards L/C RW, 764
Elgar L/C GJR, 766, 893
Elias L/C PR, 814
Elles L/C DH, 813, 823
Elliott L/C W, 820
Ellis L/C H, 831
Ellis L/C HM, 1771
Ellis L/C JE, 892
Eltringham L/C TJ, 846
Empson L/C LD, 767, 814
Emsley L/C EEG, 811
Engelsman L/C KB, 817
English L/C AW, 826
Ermen L/C ACG, 701, 820
Esmonde L/C E, 754, 825
Evans L/C AAH, 817
Evans L/C CLG, 806
Evans L/C DK, 878, 1836, 1843
Evans Lt JHL, 724
Evans L/C JKN, 782
Evans L/C RM, 772
Eve L/C DC, 814
Eveleigh L/C RL, 802
Everall L/C RHS, 771
Everett L/C MA, 701, 772
Everett L/C RN, 810
Everett Lt RWH, 794
Eyres L/C DEC, 831

Fairtlough S/L GK, 801
Falls L/C RH, 870
Fancourt L/C HLStJ, 822
Farquhar L/C SC, 831
Farthing L/C DD, 723
Fearon Cdr WH, 881
Featherstone L/C NLC, 750
Fell L/C MF, 736, 800, 805, 878, 7Wg
Fell L/C RM, 812
Fenner L/C GE, 784
Fenton L/C JE, 818
Fenwick L/C CE, 710, 777
Ferbrache Cdr CD, 702
Ferguson L/C WAM, 766, 892
Ferry L/C DS, 817
Fiddes L/C DBM, 762, 1820
Filmer L/C CH, 772
Finch-Noyes Lt EGD, 800
Findlay L/C HCD, 851
Finnes L/C A, 819
Firth L/C JW, 817
Firth L/C K, 807, 892
Fish L/C PA, 771
Fisher L/C JL, 717, 767, 831
Fisher Lt ND, 889
Fisher L/C RJ, 786, 841
Fitzgerald L/C M, 737
Fleming L/C AHT, 700, 711
Fletcher L/C TC, 1832
Flood L/C GAM, 882

Flood L/C JP, 738
Flutter L/C PM, 824D, 849
Forbes S/L RG, 824
Forbes L/C WM, 849A
Ford L/C ACB, 1834, 1835
Ford L/C JAD, 736
Ford L/C T, 816
Forde L/C AJB, 810, 21Wg
Forrest L/C M, 829
Forrester L/C TR, 810
Forty Lt RFJ, 751
Forwood Cdr EAR, 759E
Foster S/L CEW, 801
Foster L/C DR, 849
Foster L/C GNN, 707
Foster L/C HC, 706
Foster L/C NS, 707, 845, 846
Fotheringham L/C JB, 826, 883, 31SAG
Foulds Lt PS, 856
Fowler L/C GCW, 773
Fox L/C FH, 830, 52Wg
Francklin Lt MBP, 764
Franklin L/C FH, 786
Fraser L/C CA, 706
Fraser Harris Lt AB, 807
Frazer L/C DH, 849
Frazer L/C EM, 809
Frederikson L/C RV, 800
Freehill F/L MM, 823
French L/C RG, 748, 892, 893
Frost L/C AE, 1841
Frudd L/C PH, 750
Fuller L/C DA, 849C
Fuller Lt GNC, 705
Fuller L/C MT, 851
Fulton L/C R, 744, 814, 826
Funnell L/C NC, 849A
Furlong Lt FC, 882
Fyfe L/C AA, 800

Gadsden L/C GRK, 771
Gairdner L/C WTD, 782
Gardner L/C DWH, 790
Gardner L/C FB, 750, 793
Gardner L/C H, 824
Gardner L/C HH, 816
Gardner L/C J, 703, 777, 821
Gardner L/C RE, 715, 736, 889
Garland L/C AMcD, 1842
Garnett L/C JN, 759, 806, 885
Garthwaite L/C WFC, 766, 841
Garvin L/C R, 781
Geale L/C REN, 851
Geary L/C NJ, 881
Gedge L/C TJH, 800, 809
Genge L/C ET, 750
George L/C C, 723
George L/C DR, 750, 771
Gerrish Lt MB, 1851
Gibbons L/C JH, 774
Gibbs L/C HJ, 777
Gibney L/C KH, 827
Gibson L/C DCEF, 758A, 780, 802, 803, 17CAG
Gick L/C PD, 736, 815, 15CAG
Gilbert L/C L, 733, 774, 779, 791
Gilchrist L/C RI, 1831
Giles L/C CG, 800
Gillett L/C R, 743
Gladish L/C GN, 720
Gladish Lt JM, 793
Glaser L/C JM, 703, 803, 853
Gledhill L/C JA, 723, 817
Goble L/C JD, 817
Goddard L/C NE, 771, 776
Goddard Cdr RA, 815
Goddard L/C RIW, 826, 18CAG
Godfrey L/C IP, 1770
Godfrey L/C P, 1832
Godfrey L/C RJ, 816

Godley L/C JR, 835
Godson L/C MS, 732, 1835, 1838, 1844
Goetz L/C T, 849, 849D
Goldrick L/C P, 725, 816
Goldsmith L/C LD, 765
Goodall L/C DC, 814
Goodenough-Bayly L/C DA, 846
Goodfellow L/C A, 782
Goodwin L/C DG, 819
Goodyear L/C J, 776, 780
Gordon-Johnson L/C A, 801, 890
Gossett Lt JA, 1700
Gough L/C AB, 737
Gough L/C AHD, 825, 1772
Gould L/C AJ, 805, 816
Graham Cdr RR, 801, 803, 811, 825,
Grant Cdr AK, 826
Gratton-Cooper L/C AC, 845
Gray L/C A, 892
Green L/C CR, 737
Green Lt ERG, 720
Green L/C RC, 824C
Greenop L/C JPS, 829
Greenwood Lt EA, 828
Gregory L/C A, 828, 830
Gregson L/C PG, 703
Grenfell L/C VC, 768, 809
Greve Lt GH, 861
Grier-Rees L/C NG, 738, 800B
Griffin L/C J, 816
Griffin L/C CRW, 750
Griffith L/C AJ, 849
Griffith L/C RJ, 755
Griffiths Lt ES, 784
Griffiths L/C FM, 829
Grindle L/C JG, 831
Grose L/C RJH, 879, 1845
Groves Lt JRW, 728, 763
Gunn Lt IHM, 772B
Gunning L/C JP, 814
Gunston L/C RE, 712

Haanraadts LTZV2 oc L, 860
Hagdorn LTZV2 oc AHM, 860
Haigh L/C NG, 763, 785, 853
Hain L/C RH, 837
Hale L/C DG, 705
Hale L/C DK, 705
Hale L/C JW, 819, 825
Hall L/C JF, 738
Hall L/C RMcD, 762, 801
Hall L/C SJ, 718, 800, 807, 3Wg, 14CAG
Hallam L/C RF, 1833
Hallam L/C RH, 728
Hallett L/C L, 824
Hallett L/C NG, 759, 768, 884, 887, 3Wg, 24Wg, 7CAG
Hallewell L/C CMT, 744, 791, 840
Halliday L/C DG, 700, 727
Halliday L/C RW, 813
Halton L/C HF, 702
Hamilton L/C D, 800
Hamilton L/C DMAH, 892, 899
Hamilton Lt J, 713
Hamilton L/C JM, 724
Hamon L/C PO, 816, 851
Hampton S/L HN, 821
Hanchard-Goodwin L/C GHG, 724, 808
Handley L/C TD, 800, 803
Handley L/C W, 849A
Hanks L/C WJ, 751, 831
Hanmer S/L RH, 802
Hanson L/C NS, 1833
Harding L/C AJD, 823
Harding L/C KF, 737, 826
Harding Lt HTT, 717
Hare L/C DR, 805

Hargreaves L/C CF, 804, 1851
Hargreaves L/C RE, 802
Hargreaves L/C RT, 758A, 758Rover
Hargreaves L/C SN, 899
Harley L/C FAH, 723, 745
Harman Lt JCM, 701, 768, 791, 886
Harrington L/C TW, 741, 766, 1832, 1844, 5Wg, 21CAG
Harris L/C KA, 849B
Harris Mjr LA, 746, 784
Harris Lt MJJ, 710
Harris L/C NGT, 846
Harris L/C NR, 892
Harris L/C TJ, 796, 799
Harrison S/L BE, 821
Harrison L/C RC, 824C
Harrison L/C RG, 706
Harriss L/C BH, 799, 802, 879
Harrowar L/C JB, 799, 855
Hart L/C WR, 890
Hartley Lt JV, 810
Hartwell L/C BB, 707, 848
Harvey L/C GNI, 826
Harvey L/C MJ, 706, 814
Harvie L/C JJ, 871
Haslam Lt A, 773
Hathway L/C GC, 820
Hatton L/C HF, 702
Havers L/C PH, 760, 804
Hawkes L/C GF, 700
Hawkesworth L/C RDR, 737
Hawkesworth L/C RWR, 847
Hawkins L/C JBA, 820
Hawkins L/C RC, 800
Hawley L/C SJ, 762
Hawley L/C W, 700G, 849, 849A
Hay Mjr RC, 761, 805, 809, 897, 6Wg, 47Wg
Hayes L/C HL, 710
Hayes L/C HMA, 737, 815, 845
Hayes L/C HS, 811
Hayes L/C RT, 735
Haynes L/C GM, 828
Head L/C RD, 721, 846
Heath L/C JB, 800
Heath L/C PC, 810, 826, 827
Heath L/C R, 871
Hedges L/C JW, 804, 895
Hefford L/C F, 738
Henderson L/C GR, 882, 898
Henderson L/C RD, 796, 827
Henley L/C MW, 809, 893
Hennell L/C NJ, 706
Henry L/C JM, 766, 802, 813
Hensher L/C AA, 845, 846
Herbert L/C WG, 816
Heron L/C G, 724
Hickling L/C AM, 724
Hickson L/C JS, 817
Hide L/C CG, 700
Higgs L/C GR, 803
Hill L/C AL, 794
Hill L/C CL, 772
Hill Lt DC, 767
Hill L/C RMcD, 3Wg
Hilliard L/C DG, 725
Hillier L/C F, 817
Hindle L/C K, 814
Hoare L/C JEM, 784
Hoddinott L/C GB, 803
Hodge L/C BG, 824B
Hodgkinson L/C GB, 820
Hodgson L/C CR, 757, 790
Hodson L/C GFS, 842
Hogg Cdr AJM, 820
Holbrook L/C DAE, 889
Holdridge Lt W, 849A
Holman L/C CR, 772, 779
Holman L/C GJL, 849, 849B
Holmes L/C DJ, 1770, 1772

Holmes L/C MJ, 737
Holt L/C JA, 772
Honywill L/C JD, 737, 824
Hood L/C FG, 726, 788
Hook L/C S, 816
Hooper L/C AD, 849A
Hooper L/C CAN, 812, 820
Hope L/C M, 819
Hopkins L/C FHE, 826, 830
Hopkins L/C RDB, 1834
Hordern L/C LA, 881, 896
Hordern L/C M, 800, 802, 888, 1832, 1850
Horn L/C EH, 728, 788
Hornblower L/C MJA, 801, 803
Horne Lt GH, 723
Horscroft L/C CJ, 814
Horsley L/C TB, 783
Horton L/C AL, 829
Horton L/C DA, 754
Horton L/C RI, 707
Hoskin Lt MC, 701
Housser L/C HCK, 856
Howard L/C CV, 830
Howard L/C JDHB, 736, 809
Howard Lt SM, 763
Howarth L/C PJ, 849, 849A
Howarth L/C RB, 899
Howell L/C MBW, 732
Howie L/C FD, 830
Hubbard L/C RFG, 849B
Hudson L/C PAM, 704
Hughes Cdr RL, 880
Hughes L/C WL, 796, 820
Humphreys L/C JS, 750
Humphreys L/C PN, 784
Humphreys L/C PW, 714, 822
Humphries L/C GR, 780, 814
Hunneyball L/C CR, 892
Hunt L/C GC, 820
Hunt L/C GWG, 764, 766, 899
Hunt L/C JG, 830
Hunt L/C RG, 812, 848
Hunter L/C HJ, 1791, 19CAG
Hurle-Hobbs Lt BHStAH, 891
Husband L/C JDW, 819
Hutchinson L/C AF, 819
Hutchinson L/C C, 813
Hutchinson Lt DLR, 708, 764
Hutchinson S/L JH, 812
Hutchinson L/C OGW, 824, 1702
Hutton L/C PJ, 796, 805, 807

Idiens L/C S, 892
Idzerda LTZV1 BJ, 860
Ievers L/C JA, 747, 824
Ignatieff L/C A, 723, 724
Illingworth Cdr PHC, 700
Illingworth L/C WW, 806
Innes Cdr TG, 700, 700X, 803
Irving L/C JL, 849B
Irving Lt WL, 803
Irwin L/C ACS, 781
Isacke L/C CJ, 700V, 848
Isacke L/C SJ, 815

Jackson L/C PB, 768, 827, 13CAG
Jacob L/C JC, 705, 845
Jago L/C JdeF, 815
James L/C DLG, 719
James L/C NCH, 829
James L/C WP, 723, 725
Jameson L/C RA, 1842
Jameson Cdr TGC, 816, 5Wg
Jane L/C T, 706
Jenkins L/C DG, 1833
Jennings L/C FDG, 768
Jeram L/C DM, 791, 1838
Jervis L/C JHS, 845, 846
Jess L/C RE, 854
Jewers L/C S, 801

Jeyes L/C L, 766
Jeyes L/C LA, 891
Johns L/C DC, 816, 851
Johnson L/C DE, 810
Johnson L/C ERA, 719
Johnson L/C K, 724
Johnson L/C KC, 722
Johnston L/C GAI, 801
Johnston L/C JRC, 825
Johnston L/C KC, 789
Johnston Lt RL, 806
Johnstone L/C M, 713, 762, 810, 835
Jones Lt BT, 767
Jones L/C FL, 820
Jones L/C FV, 737, 835
Jones L/C H, 751
Jones L/C JM, 895
Jones L/C PM, 849B
Jordan L/C PA, 750, 790
Josselyn L/C IK, 724, 805
Judd L/C DM, 711
Judd L/C FEC, 716, 764, 771, 880
Jude Lt G, 805
Jude Cdr GM, 808, 817, 891X
Just L/C RE, 750

Kaasschieter LTZ1 JE, 860
Kable L/C G, 808
Kavanagh L/C EM, 724, 805
Keane L/C S, 786, 825
Kearsley L/C RW, 800, 802, 890, 898
Keene-Miller L/C JM, 779, 781, 783
Keighly-Peach L/C PL, 727, 898
Kelly L/C DPW, 806
Kelly L/C JE, 706, 815
Kelly L/C JS, 846, 847
Kelsall Lt JD, 760
Kemp L/C JG, 826
Kemp Cdr KE, 766, 893
Kendall Cdr BHM, 759, 787, 800, 803, 804
Kennard Lt AS, 811
Kennedy L/C AT, 849A
Kennedy Lt JC, 730
Kennedy L/C N, 813
Kennett L/C JF, 736
Kennett L/C MF, 764, 890
Kent L/C GC, 829
Kenworthy L/C H, 738
Kenworthy L/C M, 707
Keogh L/C RP, 728, 825
Keppel L/C The Hon AC, 816
Kerby L/C WB, 705
Kerr L/C NH, 892
Kerrison L/C REF, 756
Kettle L/C RvonTB, 804
Kiggell Lt LJ, 841
Kilburn Lt RH, 1702
Kilroy Cdr RA, 778, 787, 823, 815
Kimpton L/C WM, 817
King L/C GS, 724, 805
King L/C NA, 772
King L/C PF, 822
King L/C R, 781, 893
Kingdon L/C RD, 747, 830
King-Joyce L/C TJA, 883, 1835
Kingsley-Rowe L/C CA, 750, 769, 788, 801
Kinna L/C TJ, 848
Kirby L/C TEM, 899
Kirby L/C WB, 705
Kirke L/C DW, 887, 16CAG
Knapp L/C JJD, 846, 848
Kneale L/C JH, 1790
Knight L/C AA, 728, 809
Knight L/C GCJ, 705, 728C, 848
Knowles L/C JM, 820
Knox L/C DW, 825, 880, 31 SAG
Koeller L/C TR, 762

Krijger LTZV2 oc CK, 860
Krijns KLTZ HW, 860

La Bree LTZV2 KA, 860
Lacayo L/C MA, 778, 817
Lachlan L/C I, 771
Laidler Cdr RA, 871, 880
Lamb L/C CB, 842
Lamb L/C PM, 700, 810
Lamb L/C R, 772
Lambert L/C RB, 824A
Lamour L/C DR, 810
Lane L/C FT, 805
Lane L/C HJF, 882
Lang L/C JR, 835
Lang L/C WD, 802
Langley Lt DC, 726
Langman L/C VM, 881
Langmore L/C DE, 828
Lane L/C HJF, 714, 778
Large L/C JG, 833, 892
Large Lt RG, 838
Larkins Lt WC, 772
Lashmore L/C ME, 828
Laurie L/C SS, 707, 719, 813, 815, 53TAG
Law L/C DB, 800, 801, 804, 806
Lawrence L/C MJ, 771
Lawrence L/C WD, 847
Lawson Lt EW, 770, 792
Lawson Lt J, 701
Lawson L/C RG, 815
Layard L/C MHG, 899
Law L/C AN, 737
Law L/C DB, 709, 736, 1CAG
Law L/C HR, 729, 758A
Lawrence L/C MJ, 750
Lea L/C R, 851
Leach L/C F, 751, 758
Leahy L/C AJ, 700Z, 738, 803, 809
Leatham L/C AG, 767, 831
Leak L/C JM, 723
Leckie L/C PJP, 736, 1844, 52TAG
Ledingham Cdr HJ, 845
Lee L/C EK, 750
Lee L/C NE, 724, 725
Lee L/C PG, 749, 752
Leece L/C TCS, 803
Lee-White L/C K, 801, 813
Legg L/C GE, 849A
Legg L/C MR, 829
Leggott L/C RT, 1831
Lehan L/C M, 723
Lehan L/C MJ, 826
Leonard L/C R, 737, 825
Leppard L/C KA, 807
Lester L/C NH, 809
Levy L/C AD, 845
Levy L/C D, 849B
Lewin L/C EDG, 759, 808, 885
Lewis Lt FMM, 811
Lewis L/C Sir Geo JE, 781
Lewry L/C P, 880
Leyshon L/C BS, 829
Lickfold L/C DJ, 707, 845, 846, 847
Lidbetter Cdr S, 899
Light L/C AJ, 849, 849D
Lindsay L/C AC, 718, 794, 806, 814
Linstead Lt AR, 772B
Little L/C JDC, 812
Little Lt RW, 827
LLewellyn-Jones L/C M, 824
Lloyd L/C PR, 820
Lloyd L/C WH, 818
Lockwood L/C EW, 811
Lockwood L/C JT, 705
Logan L/C BEW, 720
Logan L/C JW, 871
London L/C PH, 736, 802
Longsden L/C SMdeL, 703, 756
Lord L/C DA, 707, 848

Loughran L/C TW, 706
Lovell Lt WJ, 700
Low L/C FKA, 832
Lowe L/C ILF, 882, 898
Lowndes Lt PD, 703A
Luard L/C NS, 700, 814, 3CAG
Lucas L/C WJ, 811, 832
Lucy Lt WP, 803
Luff L/C GD, 812
Luke L/C SP, 736, 769, 780, 820, 826, 51TAG, 52TAG
Lunberg L/C RB, 727, 780, 785, 817
Luxton L/C R, 723
Lygo L/C RD, 759, 800
Lyle L/C AV, 813
Lynn L/C PJ, 814, 819
Lyons L/C BC, 792, 827, 1790

MacCaw L/C BA, 739, 888
MacDermott L/C R, 725, 742
MacDonald L/C WDD, 736, 759, 803, 806
MacGregor L/C CL, 771
Machin L/C PJ, 723
MacKendrick L/C DW, 705, 823
MacLachlen L/C IM, 800
Maclean L/C NG, 776, 792
MacLean Cdr RC, 880
MacLeod Cdr DM, 880
MacQueen Lt DG, 768
MacWhirter L/C WJR, 703, 764, 1771, 15CAG
Maddox L/C M, 819
Maddox L/C NPR, 707
Mainprice L/C WJ, 767, 854
Malcolm L/C JHMcI, 752
Malins Lt C, 1851
Malpas-Finlay Lt GW, 700
Maltby Cdr TG, 849, 849B
Mancais L/C A, 736, 800
Manley-Cooper L/C NC, 824
Mann L/C L, 888
Manning L/C CK, 750
Manning L/C MGB, 815
Mannion L/C TS, 801
Mansfield L/C JE, 764
Manson Capt WHC, 710, 883
Manthorpe L/C D, 770
Manuel L/C EVH, 893
Marmont Lt JF, 802
Marsh Capt AE, 804
Marshall L/C PC, 724, 767
Martin L/C FS, 850
Martin L/C IHF, 802
Martin L/C RB, 837
Martin L/C WC, 847
Martin Mjr WHN, 814, 821
Martyn L/C WH, 880
Mason L/C MMD, 814
Mason L/C RP, 783
Massey Lt PWV, 883
Mather L/C JC, 764, 800
Mather L/C SD, 800
Mathews L/C L, 750, 771, 824C, 849A
Matthews L/C DC, 899
Matthews L/C N, 827
Matthews L/C BF, 725
May L/C TW, 817
Mayne L/C JH, 735
McCandless L/C RJ, 738
McColgan L/C JA, 792, 814
McCulloch L/C HL, 764, 765, 775, 822
McCulloch L/C RD, 899
McDonald L/C DJ, 1851
McDonald L/C JDO, 750
McDowell L/C SJ, 725
McElroy Lt WA, 726
McEwen Lt BS, 803

McGrail L/C JF, 849
McKay L/C PA, 815, 829
McKenzie L/C I, 766
McKenzie L/C IS, 824A
McKenzie L/C R, 816
McKeown L/C DT, 764, 801
McKie L/C A, 849A
McLaren L/C DC, 817
McLean L/C R, 771
McLeod L/C DM, 870
McMillan L/C N, 846
McNair L/C EA, 772
McPhee L/C G, 723
McQueen L/C R, 893
McVey L/C T, 758C
McWilliam L/C AG, 713, 810
Meads L/C BAG, 752, 776
Mearns L/C SA, 738, 809
Mears L/C DP, 736, 809
Medd L/C PN, 769
Meiklejohn L/C EL, 727, 779
Melhuish L/C D, 893
Mellor L/C CR, 728, 750, 849A, 849B
Mellor S/L HM, 810
Menzies L/C RHS, 849A
Meredith L/C MH, 815
Mervik L/C CF, 702
Middleton L/C LE, 809
Miers L/C REP, 772
Miller L/C TT, 756, 767, 835
Mills L/C AC, 753, 772
Mills L/C DF, 800
Mills L/C J, 762
Mills Cdr NJP, 700B, 803
Millward L/C JP, 800
Milne L/C IG, 819
Milner L/C F, 890, 899
Milner-Barry Lt PJ, 715
Milnes L/C AH, 759
Mitchell L/C K, 700W, 848
Mitchell L/C KM, 829
Mitchell L/C NG, 1831
Mogridge Lt PH, 767
Molyneaux L/C HT, 770, 771
Money L/C RI, 815
Monk L/C HA, 701, 728, 1833
Monks L/C RA, 883
Monsell L/C D, 738, 890
Montgomery L/C EFL, 841
Moore Lt JC, 749
Moore L/C JL, 721, 725
Moore L/C JW, 738, 800
Morgan L/C EB, 766, 811
Morison L/C DB, 898
Morrell L/C F, 1831, 1841
Morris L/C LG, 722, 737, 811, 827
Morris L/C PGW, 781, 849D
Morrison L/C DB, 738
Morritt L/C RV, 816
Mortimer L/C JK, 815
Mortimer L/C PL, 763, 767, 774, 771, 831
Mortimore L/C HJ, 733
Morton L/C A, 809
Moss L/C PH, 802
Muilwijk KLTZ WFC, 860
Muir L/C FC, 777, 794
Muir-Mackenzie L/C H, 790, 800
Mulholland Lt WIT, 805
Mullane L/C MJ, 829
Mumford Lt MH, 849B
Munday L/C IV, 750
Munro L/C WD, 71, 883
Murray L/C AA, 711, 718
Murray L/C C, 815
Murray Lt WA, 720
Murricane L/C JD, 1820

Nares Lt JGAMcI, 822
Nash L/C HGL, 849C

Nash L/C JE, 849, 849A
Nation L/C BHC, 748, 787, 896, 1839, 1840, 3Wg
Neale L/C MI, 849B
Neave L/C CB, 800
Nelson-Gracie Mjr PP, 877, 1843, 3Wg, 10Wg, 2CAG, 8CAG
Nethersole Lt JH, 801
Neville-Rolfe L/C JM, 737, 826
Newbery L/C DO'D, 767, 820
Newby L/C GB, 767, 804
Newman L/C MJS, 762, 891
Newman L/C PG, 736, 800, 803
Newsom Capt AC, 753, 810, 821
Nicholas L/C JF, 716
Nicholl L/C GWR, 700, 720
Nichols L/C PJE, 748
Nicoll L/C JWJ, 817
Nicolls Lt OJR, 760
Nicolson Lt KS, 870
Nixon L/C MC, 705
Noble L/C W, 801
Norcock L/C D, 717, 786, 815
Norman L/C DP, 800
Norris L/C RM, 896
North L/C NJ, 846, 848
Northard L/C RJ, 764
Northern L/C G, 805
Notley L/C BH, 821
Nottingham L/C FC, 816, 854
Nowell L/C WH, 769
Nowell L/C WR, 820, 9Wg
Nunn L/C JD, 719, 799, 50TAG

Oakes Lt OR, 804
Oakley L/C AL, 817
O'Brien Lt PE, 702, 705
O'Connell L/C BG, 816
Oddy L/C GV, 792
O'Farrell L/C JA, 723
O'Flynn L/C GB, 758Y
Ogilvy L/C ARW, 801
Oldhof LTZV2 L, 860
Oliphant L/C RHHL, 886
O'Neil Lt NT, 796
O'Neill L/C RK, 815
O'Rorke L/C CHC, 767, 821
Orr L/C DJ, 723, 817
Orr L/C SG, 761, 787, 804, 896, 1CAG, 13CAG
Orr Lt W, 708, 813
Orr-Ewing Lt RM, 700
Osborn L/C GMT, 771
Osman L/C MR, 705
Ostendorp LTZ1 NHA, 860
O'Sullivan L/C JG, 755
O'Sullivan L/C MJA, 790
Ovenden L/C NJ, 796
Ovenden L/C N, 849D, 849E
Ovey L/C RH, 745, 755, 756
Oxley Lt OAG, 819

Page Lt FL, 797
Page L/C MHE, 881, 30CAG
Pain Lt HEH, 830
Palmer L/C CL, 702
Pardoe-Matthews L/C PP, 774
Parish L/C GW, 795
Parish L/C JR, 813
Park L/C DR, 767
Parker L/C DG, 800, 898, 1842, 1845
Parkes Lt RG, 734
Parrish L/C GW, 757
Parsons L/C PH, 742, 783
Partington L/C RN, 816
Partridge Capt RT, 800, 804
Patch Capt O, 785, 816
Paterson Lt AF, 814
Paterson L/C B, 848
Patterson L/C CJ, 805

Pattisson L/C KS, 810, 815
Patterson L/C WR, 890
Pawsey L/C HA, 703, 824
Payen L/C AFE, 722, 754, 770
Payne L/C AE, 724, 725, 816
Peacocke L/C DD, 803, 825, 870
Pearce S/L FL, 824
Pearce L/C JHS, 801, 898
Pearson Cdr AMG, 700P, 890
Pearson L/C RB, 893
Peck L/C TA, 851
Pendrich L/C SD, 705, 771
Penfold L/C TJ, 849C
Pennick L/C DW, 737, 815
Pennington L/C FAJ, 889
Pennington L/C TSJ, 817
Peppe L/C WLT, 892
Pepper L/C MR, 814
Percy L/C TGV, 848, 15CAG
Perkins L/C AGH, 804
Perks L/C PH, 801
Perrett L/C N, 702, 736, 800, 891
Perrott L/C MA, 723
Petrie Cdr MHJ, 700Y, 892
Peyton L/C RA, 755, 821
Pharoah L/C RJ, 849A
Philips L/C JJ, 814
Phillimore L/C RAB, 702
Phillip L/C AGB, 849
Phillips L/C AJ, 753, 758E
Phillips L/C DW, 744, 829, 834
Phillips L/C H, 706, 720, 845
Phillips L/C SB, 849
Pierssene L/C APT, 791
Piggott L/C MD, 820
Plant Lt LF, 1701
Plugge L/C AJP, 832
Pollock L/C WA, 829
Poole L/C RG, 820
Pope S/L SLG, 801
Port L/C LA, 846
Powell L/C JW, 826
Pratt L/C PB, 728
Prendergast L/C BF, 702
Prendergast L/C BJ, 812
Price L/C CE, 813
Price L/C DRO, 759, 804
Price L/C EOF, 715, 767, 811, 822
Prideaux L/C B, 849, 849A
Pridham L/C GK, 758C, 790
Pridham-Wippell L/C R, 731, 768, 771, 800, 1837
Priestley L/C MJ, 819
Prince L/C ACV, 814
Pritchard L/C EF, 710, 750, 766
Pritchard L/C HES, 754
Pritchett Sq Ldr NAP, 812
Pritchett L/C PJ, 845
Pryor Lt PF, 816
Pugh L/C CDW, 759
Pugh L/C CRV, 813
Pugh L/C JBW, 758

Quarrie L/C CLL, 814
Quill L/C NR, 799

Radley L/C S, 707
Raines L/C DA, 826
Ralph L/C N, 723, 725
Ramsey L/C AR, 889
Ramsey-Fairfax Lt VGH, 826
Ranald L/C HC, 765
Rance L/C V, 831, 52Wg
Randall L/C J, 832
Rankin L/C JF, 800, 808
Rawbone L/C AR, 736, 898
Rawlins L/C JT, 771, 845
Rawlinson L/C MJF, 849, 849A
Rayer L/C GHGS, 782
Read L/C RC, 1820
Readings Lt KWC, 849A

Ree Lt JH, 813
Reece Capt MJ, 848
Reece L/C LGC, 736B, 807
Reed L/C JC, 738
Reed Lt KM, 705
Rees L/C A, 750
Reid L/C AA, 719, 849C
Reid Lt JU, 712
Revett L/C SL, 735
Reynolds S/L BV, 801
Reynolds L/C LJB, 814
Reynolds L/C PB, 766
Reynolds L/C RH, 811
Rich L/C AA, 815
Richards L/C DH, 781, 801, 809, 811
Richards Lt JC, 712
Richardson L/C AR, 1840
Richardson L/C LIG, 811
Richardson L/C SJA, 703W, 827
Richardson L/C TPH, 826
Richmond L/C P, 773
Riley L/C C, 819
Riley L/C RJB, 705
Robathan L/C JB, 891
Roberts L/C AW, 849, 849A
Roberts L/C CK, 767, 813, 825
Roberts L/C DMR, 812
Roberts Cdr JO, 803
Roberts L/C JW, 826, 30CAG
Robertson L/C CA, 820
Robertson L/C DJ, 816
Robertson L/C FJ, 846
Robertson L/C IO, 733
Robertson L/C J, 738
Robertson L/C JI, 825
Robins L/C PJ, 1835
Robinson L/C AR, 849B
Robinson L/C CP, 820
Robinson L/C DV, 716
Robinson L/C LA, 724
Robinson L/C ME, 801
Robinson Lt PV, 725
Rock L/C FA, 705
Rodgers L/C DN, 817
Roe L/C AJT, 716, 830
Rogers L/C AG, 814
Rogers L/C PHG, 819
Rohrsheim L/C GR, 723, 725
Rooke L/C JPK, 846
Roper L/C M, 849B
Ross L/C M, 1843
Rotheram L/C M, 849B
Rougier L/C PLV, 1831
Rouse L/C DM, 781
Routley L/C JR, 801, 804, 885, 894
Rover L/C PB, 705
Rowan-Thomson L/C GA, 807
Rowbottom L/C JO, 804
Rudorf L/C MW, 771, 781, 785, 796
Rumble Lt HE, 765
Rundle L/C AM, 822
Rusbridger L/C CW, 815
Russell L/C EL, 824
Russell Cdr JD, 800, 803
Rutherford L/C GM, 1832
Rutherford L/C JRJ, 771, 829
Ryan L/C DHP, 871
Sabey L/C AW, 719, 849B
Sabin L/C GP, 849A, 849B
Salter L/C MD, 845
Salthouse L/C J, 723, 805
Sample L/C GDH, 814
Sanderson L/C D, 817
Sanderson L/C FBP, 1838
Sanderson L/C JA, 893, 899
Sangster L/C GBC, 804
Sarel Lt IR, 715, 801
Sargent L/C TE, 751, 781X, 782, 799

Sarginson L/C BC, 705, 845, 846, 848
Saunders L/C JN, 849, 849A
Saunt L/C WHG, 758, 822, 826
Savage L/C EG, 809
Saville S/L FCB, 821
Schonfield L/C PB, 778
Schuiling L/C JR, 1853
Schulz Capt AD, 824A
Scott L/C DA, 829
Scott L/C JMacD, 758A
Scott L/C ME, 851
Scott L/C RIM, 1833
Scott L/C RM, 849, 849A
Searle L/C DM, 819
Sears Cdr HP, 755, 5Wg, 6Wg
Searson L/C LDM, 796
Seed L/C PW, 808
Sender L/C JH, 751
Sewell L/C AJ, 804, 1837
Seymour L/C RP, 846
Seymour L/C TMB, 737
Sharp L/C KG, 785, 849
Shattock L/C EH, 712
Shave L/C RM, 849B, 849C
Shaw L/C AIR, 700, 771
Shaw Cdr EA, 787, 882
Shaw L/C GL, 766
Shaw L/C NB, 706, 771
Shaw Cdr PA, 826
Shaw L/C TWB, 818
Sheffield L/C FGB, 719, 772, 812, 825, 836
Shepherd L/C WL, 849D
Sheppard L/C PR, 890
Sherborne L/C FJ, 703
Sherborne L/C JT, 805
Shercliff L/C RF, 707
Sherman L/C GJ, 845
Shilbach Lt HE, 796
Shilcock L/C RA, 700, 781, 787, 791, 809
Shippey L/C MRH, 1832
Sholto Douglas L/C J, 807
Shotton L/C SFF, 738, 802, 804, 879, 1839
Shrives L/C JM, 829
Shrubb L/C DW, 819, 824
Shrubsole Cdr JCN, 703, 750, 820, 52Wg, 1CAG, 3CAG
Siddall-Simpson L/C W, 837
Siebert Cdr JA, 801
Sim L/C DLW, 750, 824B
Simmonds L/C RJ, 817
Simms L/C APD, 1840
Simpson L/C FA, 721
Simpson Cdr WC, 709, 737, 898, 13CAG, 52TAG
Simpson L/C WE, 767
Sinclair L/C AMcK, 781, 810
Sinclair L/C B, 789, 790
Sinclair L/C K, 750, 766, 766B
Sirett L/C VG, 700S, 706
Sjerp LTZV1 B, 860
Skene Cpt N, 810
Skinner L/C ALL, 815
Skinner Cdr BG, 829, 846, 848
Skinner L/C JR, 826
Slade Cdr HGB, 899
Slater L/C RW, 836
Slattery L/C MS, 820
Sleigh L/C JW, 759, 890, 15Wg, 14CAG
Smallwood L/C JE, 710
Smeeton Lt RM, 800
Smith L/C AH, 796, 820
Smith L/C AR, 772
Smith L/C CG, 743
Smith Lt CWB, 821, 826
Smith Cpt DBL, 764
Smith L/C DC, 820

Smith Lt G, 739
Smith L/C JF, 773
Smith L/C JG, 748
Smith L/C MP, 849A
Smith L/C MPG, 807, 17CAG
Smith L/C RE, 707, 848
Smith L/C RJ, 816
Snook L/C RE, 810
Snow L/C MCP, 796
Snow L/C P, 728, 772, 816, 825, 838
Somerset-Thomas L/C VJ, 757
Somerville-Jones L/C EK, 809
Southon L/C PF, 819
Spackman Lt RW, 823
Sparke Lt JO, 774
Spedding L/C HR, 705
Speedy L/C M, 817
Sproule L/C JS, 701
Spurway Lt KVV, 760
Squier L/C DJS, 826
Stack L/C TN, 742
Stallard-Penoyre Lt RCB, 786, 816
Stanley L/C DTJ, 848
Stanley L/C FD, 809, 893
Stanley L/C I, 706
Stanley Lt ME, 767
Stanning L/C TJ, 845
Staveley L/C GJ, 737
Steel L/C FK, 824
Steer L/C DM, 802
Steggall L/C FR, 753
Stenning Lt JH, 785
Stephens L/C CJT, 823, 826
Stephens Cdr RJH, 711, 787, 833
Stevens L/C PDT, 819
Stevens L/C PJW, 707
Stevens Lt WH, 718, 794
Stevinson L/C OS, 711, 712, 755, 829
Stewart L/C MN, 777
Stewart L/C RE, 753
Stewart-Moore L/C JA, 820, 827
Stilliard L/C K, 731, 1851
Stirling L/C DL, 781
Stock L/C B, 805
Stock L/C BH, 849B
Stock L/C GP, 737
Stock L/C RC, 781
Stoel KLTZ A, 860
Stokes L/C JA, 825
Stokes L/C WGC, 774, 827
Storey L/C WA, 1831
Stovin-Bradford L/C F, 735, 810, 825, 17CAG
Stratton L/C RMcA, 741
Stride L/C GF, 737
Stringer L/C GNP, 753
Stuart L/C PB, 736, 801
Stuart L/C W, 736, 857
Stubley L/C TG, 750, 780
Sturgeon L/C RC, 893
Sturges Lt RJ, 787X
Sugden L/C PG, 817
Summerfield L/C LT, 740, 801
Suthers L/C SH, 705, 848
Sutton L/C CA, 819
Swales L/C MR, 705
Swales L/C RC, 706
Swann S/L WE, 802
Swanton L/C FA, 747, 767, 812, 814, 828
Swayne L/C HIA, 1820
Sydney-Turner L/C PGO, FRU, 785, 818, 827
Syer L/C PG, 772

Talbot L/C CW, 851
Talbot Lt KG, 799
Tanner L/C AJ, 803
Tate Cdr D, 880

Tattersall L/C DW, 825
Taylor L/C ESE, 849B
Taylor L/C NGT, 849C
Taylor L/C PTS, 705
Taylor L/C RD, 787
Taylour L/C EWT, 759, 760, 802
Tebble L/C R, 760, 1837
Temple-West L/C AJI, 796, 826, 9Wg
Tennant L/C MS, 737, 810
't Hart KLTZ FMP, 860
Thomas L/C GA, 817
Thomas L/C NW, 899
Thompson L/C JLW, 737
Thomson L/C AJ, 807, 887, 24Wg
Thornewill L/C SC, 707, 846
Thornton L/C CC, 782
Thornton L/C CE, 700L
Thornton L/C DJ, 899
Thorne Lt RW, 785
Thorpe L/C I, 824
Thorpe L/C M, 785, 821
Threlfall L/C WW, 820
Thurston L/C RP, 806
Tibbetts Lt HAL, 822
Tibby L/C MA, 727
Tickle L/C KH, 1831, 1841
Tidd L/C CB, 821, 823
Tillard L/C AJ, 778
Tillard L/C RC, 808
Tilney L/C GA, 712
Tivy L/C LR, 796, 810, 827, 840, 842
Tobey L/C BM, 848
Tofts L/C WA, 807
Tomkinson L/C CC, 1836
Toner Lt JS, 767
Tonge L/C GM, 752
Torin Lt HER, 770, 792, 808
Torrens-Spence L/C FMA, 815
Torry L/C GN, 760, 800
Townsend L/C FG, 880
Traill L/C HA, 712, 800, 825
Treacher L/C JD, 778, 849
Trelawney L/C RCB, 728, 773
Trerise L/C EJ, 744, 745
Trevis L/C J, 824
Tritton L/C AM, 732, 1820, 1834, 15Wg
Trounsen L/C EJ, 892
Tuke L/C AM, 783, 851
Turnbull L/C A, 737, 53TAG
Turnbull L/C FRA, 715, 778, 801, 807, 894, 47Wg
Turnbull L/C RL, 701
Turner L/C JF, 828

Turner L/C MF, 896
Turner L/C RM, 814
Turney L/C AWR, 813, 848
Turpin L/C R, 700H
Turral L/C RW, 700, 771
Turton L/C JS, 820

Underwood L/C AGH, 810
Urry L/C LD, 824
Usworth L/C N, 826, 829

van der Heuvel LTZV1 WF, 860
van der Minne LTZ1 CE, 860
Van der Plank L/C RE, 826
van der Tooren LTZ J, 860
Van Epps L/C DA, 894
van Esdonk KLTZ LGJM, 860
Van Gelder L/C JP, 724
van Renesse LTZ1 JDW, 860
Varley L/C GD, 781, 899
Veentjer KLTZ A, 860
Vernon F/L FE, 812
Vigrass L/C BW, 767, 818, 1833
Volkersz LTZV G, 860
Voller L/C IF, 1852
Voute L/C PA, 707

Waddell L/C JM, 775, 783
Waddell-Wood L/C RA, 817
Wade-Brown L/C JM, 725, 851
Wain L/C RN, 702
Waldron L/C RK, 817
Walker L/C C, 894
Walker L/C RF, 899
Wall L/C RD, 811
Wallace L/C AC, 808, 3Wg
Wallace L/C GWA, 845
Wallace L/C IJ, 798
Wallace-Thompson L/C JL, 825
Waller L/C WN, 732, 788, 806, 807, 835, 1850
Walsh L/C RWM, 771, 1831
Walsh L/C SMP, 704, 811, 841, 856
Walthall Lt LED, 817
Walton Cdr WJ, 870, 880
Ward L/C B, 776
Ward L/C JE, 750
Ward L/C N, 899
Ward L/C ND, 700A, 801
Ward L/C RE, 814
Warden L/C RJ, 845
Warne-Browne S/L TA, 810, 811
Warren L/C DR, 706
Wasteneys L/C M, 871
Waters L/C WE, 810, 812
Watkins L/C RD, 823

Watson L/C CG, 803, 826
Watson L/C JCVK, 758
Watson L/C LC, 785, 786, 822, 823
Watson L/C MW, 800, 801
Watson L/C RJ, 743
Watson L/C WHC, 809
Watts L/C DS, 845
Weatherall L/C DAP, 813
Webb L/C AS, 714
Webb L/C CLF, 846
Wellham L/C JWG, 775, 815, 50TAG
Wells L/C MD, 849
Welply L/C JA, 771
Welton L/C AR, 814
West L/C CP, 771, 824
Whatley Lt EDJR, 764
Wheatley L/C CF, 808
Wheatley L/C CMA, 723, 724, 845
Wheeler L/C PRV, 784
Whinney L/C NPM, 829
Whitaker L/C H, 750, 782
Whitby Lt JP, 803
White L/C AJ, 809
White L/C B, 850
White L/C WTE, 789, 799
Whitehead Lt DJ, 720
Whitfield L/C PC, 847, 20CAG
Whitton L/C AC, 750
Whitton L/C AG, 725, 817
Whitwam L/C NKL, 814
Whitworth L/C AS, 837
White Lt C, 730
White Lt K, 708
White L/C MGW, 737
Wickham L/C JW, 849B
Widdows L/C WE, 743, 756
Widgery L/C DG, 845
Wiggington L/C BF, 887
Wigley L/C AN, 824
Wilcox L/C FW, 820
Wilde L/C RA, 850
Wilgress L/C VJ, 803, 19CAG
Wilkins L/C PJG, 849B
Wilkinson L/C LA, 736, 750, 803
Wilkinson L/C RE, 706
Willcocks L/C GR, 1832
Williams L/C BJ, 831, 849A
Williams L/C DJW, 768
Williams L/C GPC, 829
Williams L/C JGC, 700H
Williams L/C JT, 751
Williams Lt NR, 805
Williams L/C PJ, 847, 848
Williams L/C R, 790
Williams L/C RGD, 705, 824

Williams Lt RWM, 712
Williams L/C TNE, 815
Williamson L/C K, 815, 822
Williamson Lt RL, 841, 767
Wilson L/C CGT, 815
Wilson L/C E, 816
Wilson L/C JML, 770
Wilson L/C LB, 765
Wilson Lt LG, 834
Windsor Lt G, 730
Wingate L/C GJP, 824B
Winn L/C GH, 749
Winstanley L/C KC, 783, 797, 884
Winterton L/C DW, 765, 766, 849C
Winter L/C P, 751
Wintour L/C JM, 758, 802, 803
Wood L/C RR, 821
Woodard L/C RN, 771
Woodhall S/L AB, 824
Woodham Lt PH, 1701
Woodhead L/C D, 1844
Woods L/C GA, 822
Woods L/C GAL, 812
Woodward L/C RN, 848
Woodward L/C RV, 771
Woollings L/C PA, 849C
Woolston L/C GR, 751, 827
Worby L/C AE, 749
Wordsworth L/C JL, 775
Wort L/C LC, 1772
Worth L/C J, 736, 764B, 803
Wotherspoon L/C MW 848
Wreford L/C PJ, 728
Wren L/C R, 736, 800, 803
Wright Mjr AJ, 809, 898, 16CAG
Wright L/C H, FRU, 764, 773
Wright Lt JCS, 767
Wright Cdr MJ, 816
Wroughton L/C JAD, 800, 821
Wykes-Sneyd L/C RJS, 820
Wynne-Roberts L/C DMR, 706, 812, 815

Yarker L/C TJ, 846
Yates L/C DHN, 702, 815
Yeoman L/C A, 820
Young L/C BG, 766, 892
Young L/C CP, 820
Young L/C JA, 888
Young L/C JOB, 764
Young F/L L, 803
Young L/C PG, 894
Young L/C PJ, 766

Zegers de Beijl L/C GJ, 861, 896

FLEET AIR ARM FLAG OFFICERS

Flag Officer Home Air Command
RA R Bell-Davies VC CB DSO AFC	24 May 1939
RA C Moody CB	30 Sep 1941
RA CV Robinson CB	12 May 1943
RA Sir Cloudesley Robinson KCB	1 Jan 1945
VA Sir Dennis Boyd KCB CBE DSC	1 Jun 1945
RA GN Oliver CB DSO**	1 Apr 1946
RA Sir Thomas Troubridge KCB DSO	25 Sep 1946
VA Sir Thomas Troubridge KCB DSO	31 Jan 1947
VA RH Portal CB DSC	Nov 1947
VA Sir Reginald Portal KCB DSC	1 Jan 1949
Adm Sir Reginald Portal KCB DSC	4 Oct 1950
VA CE Lambe CB CVO	Mar 1951
VA Sir Charles Lambe KCB CVO	1 Jan 1953
VA JAS Eccles CB CBE	15 Jan 1953
VA Sir John Eccles KCVO CB CBE	16 Jul 1953
VA Sir John Eccles KCVO KCB CBE	1 Jan 1955
VA C John CB	1 Jun 1955
VA Sir Caspar John KCB	31 Mar 1956
Adm Sir Caspar John KCB	10 Jan 1957
VA WT Couchman CB CVO DSO OBE	5 Mar 1957
VA Sir Walter Couchman KCB CVO DSO OBE	12 Jun 1958
Adm Sir Walter Couchman KCB CVO DSO OBE	30 Apr 1959
VA Sir Deric Holland-Martin KCB DSO DSC	8 Jan 1960
VA DP Dreyer	15 May 1961
VA Sir John Hamilton KBE CB	2 Oct 1962
became:	

Flag Officer Naval Air Command
VA Sir Richard Smeeton KCB MBE	22 Jan 1964
RA DCEF Gibson CB DSC	28 Oct 1965
VA DCEF Gibson CB DSC	29 Sep 1967
VA Sir Donald Gibson KCB DSO	8 Jun 1968
VA HRB Janvrin CB DSC	Oct 1968
VA Sir Richard Janvrin KCB DSC	1 Jan 1969
VA MF Fell CB DSO DSC	1 Nov 1970
VA JD Treacher	Jun 1972
RA PM Austin	Aug 1973
VA PM Austin	19 Aug 1974
VA Sir Peter Austin KCB	12 Jun 1976
RA JO Roberts CB	Aug 1976
VA Sir Desmond Cassidi KCB	Jan 1978
RA ER Anson	Jul 1979
VA JMH Cox	May 1982
VA Sir John Cox KCB	12 Jun 1982
VA DR Reffell	Sep 1983
VA Sir Derek Reffell KCB	16 Jun 1984
RA LE Middleton CB DSO	Sep 1984
RA RC Dimmock CB	Feb 1987
RA MHG Layard CBE	Aug 1988
became:	

Flag Officer Naval Aviation
RA MHG Layard CBE	23 Mar 1990
RA CHD Cooke-Priest CB	4 Dec 1990
RA IDG Garnett	Feb 1993

Rear Admiral/Vice Admiral Aircraft Carriers
RA RGH Henderson CB	21 Sep 1931
RA Hon Sir Alexander Ramsey KCVO CB DSO	15 Sep 1933
RA NF Laurence CB DSO	4 Mar 1936
VA NF Laurence CB DSO	12 Jul 1936
VA GCC Royle CB CMG	27 Jul 1937
RA LV Wells CB DSO	26 Jul 1939
VA LV Wells CB DSO	31 Jul 1939
RA ALStG Lyster CVO DSO	19 Jul 1940
became:	

Flag Officer Mediterranean Aircraft Carriers
RA ALStG Lyster CVO DSO	1 Sep 1940
RA DW Boyd CBE DSC	18 Feb 1941
became:	

Rear Admiral Eastern Fleet Aircraft Carriers Feb 1942

Flag Officer Home Fleet Aircraft Carriers
RA ALStG Lyster CB CBE CVO DSO	11 Jul 1942
VA ALStG Lyster CB CBE CVO DSO	29 Oct 1942
RA C Moody CB	21 May 1943
transferred to:	
Eastern Fleet Aircraft Carriers	1 Dec 1943

Flag Officer 3rd Aircraft Carrier Sqn
RA MJ Mansergh CB CBE	Jul 1948
RA CE Lambe CB CVO	8 Sep 1949
RA C John	15 Jan 1951
became:	

Flag Officer Heavy Sqn Home Fleet
RA C John CB	Jan 1952
VA J Hughes Hallet CB DSO	11 Jul 1952
RA WT Couchman CB CVO DSO OBE	8 Dec 1953
became:	

Flag Officer Aircraft Carriers
RA WT Couchman CB CVO DSO OBE	1 Oct 1954
RA AR Pedder	21 Dec 1954
VA ML Power CB CBE DSO	15 May 1956
VA ANC Bingley CB OBE	6 Jan 1958
VA Sir Alexander Bingley KCB OBE	1 Jan 1959
RA CLG Evans CB CBE DSO DSC	13 Jan 1959
RA RM Smeeton CB MBE	1 Mar 1960
VA FHE Hopkins CB DSO DSC	22 Jan 1962
RA DCEF Gibson DSC	25 Jan 1963
RA HRB Janvrin CB DSC	1 Apr 1964
RA WD O'Brien	Feb 1966
RA LD Empson	Apr 1967
RA MF Fell DSO DSC	Jun 1968
became:	

Flag Officer Carriers and Amphibious Ships
RA MF Fell DSO DSC	1 Sep 1968
RA JD Treacher	Jul 1970
RA RD Lygo	May 1972
RA AD Cassidi	Jan 1974
RA JHF Eberle	May 1975
RA WDM Staveley	Mar 1977
RA PGM Herbert OBE	Jul 1978
became:	

Flag Officer Third Flotilla
RA PGM Herbert	1 Jan 1979
RA JMH Cox	Dec 1979
VA JMH Cox	4 Apr 1981
RA DR Reffell	Mar 1982
VA RGA Fitch	Aug 1983
RA JJR Oswald	Sep 1985
VA JJR Oswald	3 Jan 1986
VA Sir Julian Oswald KCB	1 Jan 1987
RA HM White CBE	Apr 1987
RA A Grose	Oct 1988
RA Hon Nicholas Hill-Norton	21 Feb 1989
VA Hon Nicholas Hill-Norton	3 Dec 1990
became:	
Flag Officer Surface Flotilla	Apr 1992

Rear Admiral Eastern Fleet Aircraft Carriers
RA DW Boyd CBE DSC	Feb 1942
RA C Moody CB	1 Dec 1943
became:	

Flag Officer (Air) East Indies
VA C Moody CB	13 Dec 1944
became:	

Flag Officer Aircraft Carriers and Naval Air Stations East Indies
RA ARM Bridge CBE	Dec 1945
became:	

Flag Officer Air Far East
RA GE Creasy CB CBE DSO MVO	8 Mar 1947
became:	

Flag Officer Second in Command Far East Fleet
(Commanding Carriers deployed East of Suez)

RA ACG Madden CB CBE	Sep 1948
VA ACG Madden CB CBE	5 Feb 1949
RA WG Andrews CB CBE DSO	17 Jan 1950
VA WG Andrews CB CBE DSO	1 Dec 1950
RA AK Scott-Moncrieff CB CBE DSO*	10 Apr 1951
RA EGA Clifford CB	23 Sep 1952
RA GV Gladstone CB	18 Nov 1953
VA GV Gladstone CB	1 Feb 1955
RA RF Elkins CB CVO OBE	18 Feb 1955
VA RF Elkins CB CVO OBE	13 Jun 1955
RA WK Edden CB OBE	2 Jun 1956
RA LG Durlacher CB OBE DSC	23 Aug 1957
VA LG Durlacher CB OBE DSC	7 Jul 1958
RA VC Begg CB DSO DSC	2 Dec 1958
VA VC Begg CB DSO DSC	21 May 1960
RA M LeFanu CB DSC	15 Jul 1960
RA JB Frewin CB	24 Jul 1961
VA JB Frewin CB	9 Aug 1962
RA JP Scatchard CB DSC**	11 Dec 1962
VA JP Scatchard CB DSC**	14 Aug 1963
RA PJ Hill-Norton CB	13 Jun 1964
VA PJ Hill-Norton CB	7 Aug 1965
VA CP Mills CB CBE DSC	Jan 1966
RA EB Ashmore CB DSC	Apr 1967
RA ATFG Griffin CB	Aug 1968
VA ATFG Griffin CB	13 Nov 1968
RA TT Lewin MVO DSC	Aug 1969
VA TT Lewin MVO DSC	7 Oct 1970
RA D Williams	Nov 1970
post disestablished	May 1971
(on withdrawal from Far East)	

Flag Officer Carrier Training and Administration

VA ALStG Lyster CB CBE CVO DSO	27 Apr 1943
VA Sir Lumley Lyster KCB CBE CVO DSO	2 Jun 1945
RA LD MacIntosh DSO DSC	19 Sep 1945
became:	

Flag Officer Flying Training

RA LD MacIntosh CB DSO DSC	Jun 1946
RA CE Lambe CB CVO	17 Sep 1947
RA EW Anstice	26 Aug 1949
RA WT Couchman DSO OBE	14 Aug 1951
RA G Willoughby	21 Jun 1953
RA CLG Evans CBE DSO DSC	21 Feb 1956
RA DRF Campbell DSC	15 Oct 1957
RA FHE Hopkins DSO DSC	20 Sep 1960
RA PD Gick OBE DSC	16 Oct 1961
became:	

Flag Officer Naval Flying Training

RA DCEF Gibson DSC	20 Jul 1964
RA DW Kirke CBE	28 Oct 1965
RA CK Roberts DSO	8 Feb 1968
post disestablished by	Jan 1971

Flag Officer Naval Air Stations Indian Ocean

RA HC Rawlings	30 Apr 1943
post disestablished	Dec 1945

Rear Admiral Escort Carriers

RA AWLaT Bisset	28 Oct 1943
Cdre GN Oliver CB DSO**	Jul 1944
became:	

21st Aircraft Carrier Squadron Eastern Fleet

Cdre GN Oliver CB DSO**	23 Feb 1945
RA GN Oliver CB DSO**	Jul 1945
subsumed by:	

Flag Officer Aircraft Carriers and Naval Air Stations East Indies

	Dec 1945

Flag Officer Naval Air Stations Australia and Pacific

RA RH Portal DSC	1944-1947

Flag Officer Aircraft Carriers British Pacific Fleet

RA Sir Philip Vian KCB KBE DSO**	15 Nov 1944
became:	

1st Aircraft Carrier Squadron - BPF

RA Sir Philip Vian KCB KBE DSO**	23 Feb 1945
VA Sir Philip Vian KCB KBE DSO**	8 May 1945
RA CHL Woodhouse CB early	May 1946
subsumed by:	
Flag Officer Air Far East	Mar 1947

11th Aircraft Carrier Squadron - BPF

RA CJJH Harcourt CB CBE	Mar-Sep 1945

30th Aircraft Carrier Squadron

Cdre WP Carne	Mar-Sep 1945

Flag Officer Force H

RA EN Syfret CB (Acting VA)	10 Jan 1942
VA Sir Neville Syfret KCB	8 Sep 1942
VA AU Willis CB DSO	24 Feb 1943
VA Sir Algernon Willis KCB DSO	2 Jun 1943

Flag Officer Force V - Salerno

RA PL Vian DSO**	Sep 1942

Naval Commander Operation TORCH

Cdre TH Troubridge DSO	Nov 1942

Flag Officer Air Mediterranean

VA Sir Cecil Harcourt KCB CBE	7 Jan 1947
VA Sir Thomas Troubridge KCB DSO	8 Jan 1948
VA CE Douglas Pennant CB CBE DSO DSC	15 Dec 1948
VA Hon Sir Cyril Douglas Pennant KCB CBE DSO DSC	2 Jan 1950
RA G Grantham CB CBE DSO	8 Apr 1950
RA RAB Edwards CB CBE	15 Aug 1951
VA RAB Edwards CB CBE	26 May 1952
VA WW Davis CB DSO	17 Dec 1952
VA JPL Reid CB CVO	11 Feb 1954
VA M Richmond CB DSO OBE	18 Aug 1955
VA LF Durnford-Slater CB	24 Oct 1956
VA Sir Robin Durnford-Slater KCB	13 Jun 1957
post disestablished by	Dec 1957

Flag Officer Ground Training

RA DH Everett CBE DSO	24 Jan 1949
RA CRL Parry DSO	May 1951
RA AD Torlesse CB DSO	15 May 1953
RA RL Fisher	19 Nov 1954
RA RA Ewing DSC	4 Jun 1958
post disestablished by	Jan 1960

Rear Admiral/Flag Officer Reserve Aircraft

RA LE Rebbeck CB	25 Feb 1952
RA JDN Ham CB	3 Oct 1955
RA AJ Tyndale-Biscoe OBE	8 Jul 1957
post disestablished by	Jan 1960

BATTLE HONOURS

After the Second World War the unofficial tradition of ships Battle Honours was formalised and a list of Naval Battle and Campaign Honours published. Thirty Battle Honours were awarded to Naval Air Squadrons for actions and campaigns during the Second World War, and four more since 1945.

ATLANTIC 1939-45
Ocean convoy escorts, or support forces that took part in a successful action, Equator to the Arctic Circle between 3 September 1939 and 8 May 1945. Awarded to Nos.700, 801, 802, 804, 807, 808, 810, 811, 813, 814, 816, 818, *819, 820, *822, 824, 825, 826, *829, 833, *834, 835, 836, 837, 838, 840, 842, 846, 850, 860, 881, 882, 892, 896, 898 and 1832 Squadrons.

ENGLISH CHANNEL 1939-45
Channel coastal convoy escorts, or other forces that took part in a successful action, English Channel and all waters on the South Coast between Southend and Bristol, east of a line Ushant to the Scilly Islands then to the north coast of Cornwall between 3 September 1939 and 8 May 1945. Awarded to Nos.811, 812, 818, 819, 825 and 841 Squadrons.

NORTH SEA 1939-45
Coastal convoy escorts, or other forces that took part in a successful action, North Sea and all waters to the eastward between Southend and the Shetland Islands, except coastal waters of Norway between 3 September 1939 and 8 May 1945. Awarded to Nos.803, 811, 812 and 826 Squadrons.

RIVER PLATE 1939
Pursuit of German Battleship *Graf Spee* in South Atlantic on 13 December 1939. Awarded to No.700 Squadron.

BISCAY 1940-5
Patrolling forces that took part in a successful action, Ushant to Cape Ortegal from 12°W to the coast of France, between January 1940 and May 1945. Awarded to No.817 Squadron.

MEDITERRANEAN 1940-5
Operations in the Mediterranean not covered by other Battle Honours in the theatre, between January 1940 and May 1945. Awarded to Nos.700, 767, 800, 803, 806, 810, 812, 813, 815, 816, 818, 819, 820, 821, 824, 826, 828, 829 and 830 Squadrons.

NORWAY 1940-5
Operations in coastal waters of Norway as far north as Tromso between 8 April and 8 June 1940, and successful actions in these waters at later date. Awarded to Nos.700, 701, 800, 801, 802, 803, 804, 806, 810, 816, 817, 818, 820, 821, 823, 825, 827, 828, 829, 830, 831, 841, 842, 846, 852, 853, 856, 880, 881, 882, 887, 894, 896, 898, 1770, 1771, 1832, 1834, 1836, 1840, 1841 and 1842 Squadrons.

DUNKIRK 1940
Operation DYNAMO, evacuation of British Expeditionary Force, 26 May to 4 June 1940. Awarded to Nos.801, 806, 825 and 826 Squadrons

CALABRIA 1940
Action against Italian fleet off Calabria, Italy on 9 July 1940. Awarded to Nos.813 and 824 Squadrons.

LIBYA 1940-42
Inshore operations between Port Said and Benghazi, and support of the Army in the Western Desert, September 1940 to June 1942. Awarded to Nos.803, 805, 806, 813, 815, 819, 821, 824 and 826 Squadrons.

TARANTO 1940
Night air strike on Italian fleet and harbour, 11 November 1940. Awarded to Nos.813, 815, 819 and 824 Squadrons.

SPARTIVENTO 1940
Action against Italian battleships and cruisers off Cape Spartivento, Sardinia, 27 November 1940. Awarded to Nos.700, 800, 808, 810, 818 and 820 Squadrons.

MALTA CONVOYS 1941-2
Operations to resupply aircraft and stores to Malta, January 1941 to December 1942. Awarded to Nos.800, 801, 806, 807, 808, 809, 812, 813, 816, 820, 824, 825, 827, 831, 832, 884 and 885 Squadrons.

ARCTIC 1941-5
Covering forces employed as escorts or in support of convoys running to and from North Russia within the Arctic Circle, January 1941 to May 1945. Awarded to Nos.802, 809, 811, 813, 816, 819, 822, 824, 825, 832, 833, 835, 842, 846, 853, 856, 882, 883, 893 and 1832 Squadrons.

MATAPAN 1941
Night action against Italian fleet off Greece, 28-29 March 1941. Awarded to Nos.700, 803, 806, 815, 826 and 829 Squadrons.

CRETE 1941
Defence and evacuation of Crete, 20 May to 1 June 1941. Awarded to No.805 Squadron.

"BISMARCK" 1941
Pursuit and destruction of German battleship *Bismarck* in North Atlantic, 23-27 May 1941. Awarded to Nos.800, 808, 810, 818, 820 and 825 Squadrons.

MALAYA 1942-45
Forces taking part in a successful action in Malacca Strait and waters adjacent to the Malay Peninsula and Sumatra between 7°N-7°S and 95°-108°E, January 1942 to August 1945. Awarded to No.851 Squadron.

DIEGO SUAREZ 1942
Operation IRONCLAD, support of landing forces in Madagascar, 5-7 May 1942. Awarded to Nos.800, 806, 810, 827, 829, 831, 880, 881 and 882 Squadrons.

NORTH AFRICA 1942-3
Operation TORCH, support of landing forces and of Army ashore in Algeria and Tunisia, 8 November 1942 to 20 February 1943. Awarded to Nos.700, 800, 801, 802, 804, 807, 809, 817, 820, 822, 832, 833, 880, 882, 883, 884, 885, 888, 891 and 893 Squadrons.

SICILY 1943
Operation HUSKY, support of landing forces in Sicily 10 July to 17 Aug 1943. Awarded to Nos.807, 817, 820, 880, 885, 888, 893 and 899 Squadrons.

AEGEAN 1943-4
Engagements with the enemy in all waters of the Aegean Archipeligo 35°-42°N, 22°-30°E, 7 September to 28 November 1943 and January to December 1944. Awarded to Nos.800, 807, 809, 879, 881 and 899 Squadrons.

SALERNO 1943
Operation AVALANCHE, support of landing forces at Salerno on mainland of Italy, 9 September to 6 October 1943. Awarded to Nos.807, 808, 809, 810, 820, 830, 834, 878, 879, 880, 886, 887, 888, 890, 893, 894, 897 and 899 Squadrons.

NORMANDY 1944
Operation NEPTUNE, covering and support forces in the Channel, Dover to Ushant, for landings in France, 6 June to 3 July 1944. Awarded in 1994 to Nos.700+, 800, 804, 808, 816, 819, 838, 846, 848, 849, 850, 854, 855, 881, 885, 886, 896 and 897 Squadrons.
[+ - in fact No.700 Squadron did not exist by that time]

SABANG 1944
Operation CRIMSON, air strikes and bombardment on harbour and oil installations North Sumatra, 25 July 1944. Awarded to Nos.831, 1830, 1833, 1834, 1836, 1837 and 1838 Squadrons.

SOUTH FRANCE 1944
Operation DRAGOON, support of landing forces on the South coast of France, 15-27 August 1944. Awarded to Nos.800, 807, 809, 879, 881, 882 and 899 Squadrons.

BURMA 1944-5
Operations over Burma, October 1944 to April 1945 and May to August 1945. Awarded to Nos.800, 804, 807, 808, 809, 815, 851, 896 and 1700 Squadrons.

PALEMBANG 1945
Operation MERIDIAN I, air strikes on oil refineries on Sumatra, 24 January 1945. Awarded to Nos.820, 849, 854, 857, 887, 894, 1770, 1830, 1833, 1834, 1836, 1839 and 1844 Squadrons.

OKINAWA 1945
Operation ICEBERG, attacks on airfields in the Sakishima Group of islands in the East China Sea up to and including the assault on Okinawa, 26 March to 25 May 1945. Awarded to Nos.820, 848, 849, 854, 857, 885, 887, 894, 1770, 1830, 1833, 1834, 1836, 1839, 1840, 1841, 1842, 1844 and 1845 Squadrons.

JAPAN 1945
Fleet Carriers and their Squadrons that took part in the final attacks on warships and mainland of Japan, 16 July to 11 August 1945. Awarded to Nos.801, 820, 828, 848, 849, 880, 887, 1771, 1772, 1834, 1836, 1841 and 1842 Squadrons.

KOREA 1950-3
Operations in support of United Nations forces ashore in Korea, 2 July 1950 to 27 June 1953. Awarded to Nos.800, 801, 802, 804, 805, 807, 808, 810, 812, 817, 821, 825 and 827 Squadrons.

VIETNAM 1965-72
Operations ashore in Vietnam 28 May 1965 to June 1972. Australian honour awarded to HS-723 only.

FALKLAND ISLANDS 1982
Operation CORPORATE, campaign to liberate the Falkland Islands, 2 April to 13 June 1982. Awarded to Nos.737, 800, 801, 809, 815, 820, 824, 825, 826, 829, 845, 846, 847, 848 and 899 Squadrons.

KUWAIT 1991
Operation GRANBY, operations against Iraqi forces or logistic support duties in central or northern Gulf, west of 51°E, 17 January to 28 Feb 1991. Awarded to Nos.723, 815, 816, 826, 829, 845, 846 and 848 Squadrons.

[Honours marked * appear to have been earned, but confirmation of an actual award is lacking at the time of writing]

BOYD TROPHY AWARD

The Boyd Trophy is a silver model of a Fairey Swordfish, presented in 1946 by the Fairey Aviation Company Limited in commemoration of the work for Naval Aviation of Admiral Sir Dennis Boyd, KCB, CBE, DSC. It is awarded annually to the Naval pilot(s) or aircrew(s) who in the opinion of the Flag Officer Naval Aviation has/have achieved the finest feat of aviation during the previous year. It is held by the ship, station or establishment in which the winner(s) was/were serving at the time the winning feat was achieved.

AWARD WINNERS

1946　Lt Cdr D.B.Law and Lt R.H.Reynolds DSC for formation aerobatic display in Seafires at St.Merryn.

1947　Lt Cdr H.J.Mortimore, CO of No.733 Squadron for leading a flight of three Expediters from Trincomalee to Lee-on-Solent in adverse weather conditions.

1948　Lt Cdr E.M.Brown, of RAE Farnborough, for trials with rubber deck.

1949　No.1830 Squadron, RNVR for 205 accident-free deck landings during embarked period in HMS *Illustrious*.

1950　17th Carrier Air Group, HMS *Theseus* for operations in Korea.

1951　No.814 Squadron for night flying in HMS *Vengeance*.

1952　Nos.802 and 825 Squadrons for operations in Korea.

1953　No.848 Squadron for operations in Malaya.

1954　Naval Test Squadron, Boscombe Down for improvements to Naval aircraft.

1955　No.806 Squadron for pioneering the Sea Hawk at sea, and for contributions to tactical investigation in night strike role.

1956　Search and Rescue Flight at Lossiemouth.

1957　Not awarded.

1958　No.845 Squadron for operations in the Persian Gulf and salvage of SS *Melika*.

1959　No.781 Squadron, Lee-on-Solent, for efficiency in communications flights.

1960　No.831 Squadron for efficiency in training with the Fleet.

1961　HMS *Protector*'s Ship's Flight for efficiency in Antarctica.

1962　No.815 Squadron for bringing the Wessex HAS.1 into service, pioneering night and all-weather ASW tactics and Wessex SAR procedures.

1963　No.846 Squadron for operations in Borneo.

1964　No.845 Squadron for services in the defence of Malaysia.

1965　No.759 Squadron for fine record in converting Jet Provost pilots to Hunter aircraft.

1966　No.849C Flight for outstanding performance in HMS *Ark Royal* during Mozambique patrol.

1967　No.801 Squadron for bringing the Buccaneer S.2 into service.

1968　No.814 Squadron for bringing the Wessex HAS.3 to a high state of operational effectiveness at sea.

1969　Lt Cdr P.C.Marshall, AFC for exceptional skill and personal courage in bringing a badly damaged Phantom safely back to base.

1970　Lt Cdr V.Sirrett for the work of No.700S Squadron, the Sea King IFTU.

1971　No.826 Squadron for *Steel Vendor* rescue from HMS *Eagle*.

1972　Lt Cdr C.C.N.Davis, Lt Cdr C.D.Walkinshaw, Lt A.S.Park and Lt M.P.Lucas for flying 2,600 miles from HMS *Ark Royal* to Belize.

1973　Not awarded.

1974　Lt I.McKechnie, HMS *Andromeda* Flight for evacuation of refugees from Cyprus.

1975　Not awarded.

1976　Lt Cdr K.M.C.Simmons, Lt T.J.MacMahon, Lt A.B.Ross and CPO ACM E.A.Butler, HMS *Antrim* Flight, for rescue off Iceland.

1977　No.700L Squadron, the Lynx IFTU, for introducing the Lynx into Naval service.

1978　Aircrews of Culdrose squadrons for the outstanding record of rescue, medical and humanitarian flights during the year.

1979　HMS *Fife*'s Ship's Flight for outstanding performance in Dominica following the devastation caused by Hurricane David.

1980　Not awarded.

1981　No.801 Squadron pilots for their outstanding achievements in operating the Sea Harrier embarked in HMS *Invincible*.

1982　Cdr T.J.H.Gedge for his leadership on the ground and in the air, perseverance, skill, professional knowledge and courage.

1983　No.705 Squadron for its excellent overall performance, training achievement, outstanding airmanship, and exceptional contribution to the prestige of Naval aviation.

1984　No.846 Squadron for its outstanding contribution to naval aviation in support of operations in Lebanon, January to March 1984.

1985　No.815 Squadron HMS *Beaver* Flight (No.244 Flight) for its outstanding long-range casualty rescue and subsequent evacuation sortie at night from the freighter *Reefer Dolphin* in the South West Approaches in October 1985.

1986　No.849 Squadron for the re-introduction of the role of AEW into the Fleet's operational capability in a timely, efficient and enthusiastic manner.

1987　Not awarded.

1988　Nos.815 and 829 Squadrons jointly for the operational contributions made by their flights in the undoubted success of the Royal Navy's Armilla Patrol in the Persian Gulf during 1988.

1989　No.815 Squadron's HMS *Alacrity* Flight (No.233 Flight) for providing immediate life-saving and disaster relief on the island of Monserrat in the wake of Hurricane Hugo in September 1989.

1990　No.829 Squadron's HMS *Sheffield* Flight (No.234 Flight) for excellent performance on patrol in the Barents Sea on Operation *Nickleby* in May 1990.

1991　No.845 Squadron for Casevac operations in Saudi Arabia, Iraq and Kuwait during operation *Desert Storm*, January to March 1991.

1992　No.771 Squadron for outstanding contribution to saving life at sea, night rescue off Guernsey in August 1992.

1993　No.845 Squadron for outstanding performance in support of United Nations Protection Force operations in the former Yugoslavia.

SHIPS NAMES OF FLEET AIR ARM STATIONS

Royal Navy shore establishments are generally given ships names, this custom being applied to Fleet Air Arm shore bases when the Admiralty took over their control on 24 May 1939, such names often being that of a bird for obvious reasons. Where a small base operates as a satellite of a larger one it may be given the title of the latter suffixed by the Roman numeral II or III. In some instances a shore base may not operate as a separate establishment, particularly for accounting purposes, and it is then regarded as being borne on the books of, or as a tender to, the larger establishment to which it is attached. The following list gives in alphabetical order the more important ships names relevant to FAA shore bases, more detailed information being given in the alphabetical lists of stations.

Ships Name	Base	Ships Name	Base
HMS Afrikander	Simonstown/Wingfield/Wynberg	HMS Malabar	Palisadoes
HMAS Albatross	Nowra	HMS Malabar II	Bermuda
HMS Ariel	Culcheth/Worthy Down/Lee-on-Solent	HMS Malabar III	Bermuda
HMS Ariel II	Worthy Down	HMS Malagas	Wingfield
HMS Asbury	Quonset Point	HMS Medina	Puckpool Camp
HMS Baidur	Huitanes/Kaldadarnes	HMS Mentor II	Stornoway
HMS Bambara	China Bay/Trincomalee/Clappenburg Bay	HMS Merganser	Rattray
HMS Bherunda	Colombo Racecourse	HMS Merlin	Donibristle/Campbeltown/Evanton/Fearn/Drem
HMS Blackcap	Stretton/Inskip/Speke		
HMS Buzzard	Lympne/Palisadoes	HMS Monara	Maharagama
HMS Canada	Halifax/Dartmouth/Yarmouth	HMS Moragai	Gan (Addu Atoll)
HMS Caroline	Belfast Dockyard/Sydenham	HMS Nabaron	MONAB 4 (Ponam/Pityilu)
HMS Chough	Culdrose	HMS Nabberley	MONAB 2 (Bankstown)
HMS Condor	Arbroath	HMS Nabbington	MONAB 1 (Nowra)
HMS Condor II	Dundee/East Haven	HMS Nabcatcher	MONAB 8 (Kai Tak)
HMS Cormorant II	North Front (Gibraltar)	HMS Nabhurst	MONAB 10
HMS Corncrake	Ballyhalbert	HMS Nabreekie	MONAB 7 (Archerfield)
HMS Corncrake II	Kirkistown	HMS Nabrock	MONAB 9 (Sembawang)
HMS Curlew	St Merryn	HMS Nabsford	TAMY 1 (Archerfield)
HMS Daedalus	Lee-on-Solent/Cowdray Park/Defford/Ford/Gosport/Heston/Manston/Portland/Tangmere/Thorney Island	HMS Nabstock	MONAB 6 (Maryborough/Schofields)
		HMS Nabswick	MONAB 5 (Jervis Bay/Nowra)
		HMS Nabthorpe	MONAB 3 (Schofields)
HMS Daedalus II	Lympne/Lawrenny Ferry/Sandbanks/Newcastle-under-Lyme	HMS Nighthawk	Drem/MacMerry
		HMS Nightjar	Inskip/Burscough
HMS Daedalus III	Bedhampton Camp	HMS Nile	Aboukir
HMS Dipper	Henstridge	HMS Nile II	Dekheila
HMS Dotterel	East Haven	HMAS Nirimba	Schofields
HMS Drake II	Roborough	HMS Nuthatch	Anthorn
HMS Dryad	Southwick	HMS Osprey	Portland
HMS Edinburgh Castle	Hastings (Freetown)	HMS Owl	Fearn/Evanton
HMS Europa II	Bungay	HMS Peewit	East Haven
HMS Falcon	Hal Far	HMS Pembroke II	Eastchurch
HMS Fieldfare	Evanton	HMS Peregrine	Ford
HMS Fledgling	Milreece	HMS Phoenix	Fayid
HMS Flycatcher	Ludham/Middle Wallop/Kai Tak	HMS Pintail	Nutts Corner
HMS Fulmar	Lossiemouth/Twatt	HMS Rajaliya	Puttalam
HMS Fulmar II	Milltown	HMS Rajawali	Penang
HMS Gadwall	Belfast (Sydenham)	HMS Raven	Eastleigh/Christchurch
HMS Gamecock	Bramcote	HMS Ringtail	Burscough
HMS Gannet	Eglinton/Maydown/Toome/Cluntoe	HMS Ringtail II	Woodvale
HMS Gannet II	Maydown	HMS Robin	Grimsetter
HMS Gannet III	Belfast (Sydenham)	HMS Rooke	North Front (Gibraltar)
HMS Garuda	Coimbatore	HMS St Vincent	Gosport
HMS Godwit	Hinstock/Bramcote/Bratton	HMS Saker	Halifax/Lewiston/Brunswick/Squantum/New York/Washington
HMS Godwit II	Weston Park/Peplow		
HMS Goldcrest	Angle/Dale/Kete/Brawdy	HMS Saker II	Quonset Point/Dartmouth/Lewiston
HMS Goldcrest II	Brawdy	HMS Sanderling	Abbotsinch/Machrihanish
HMS Goldfinch	Ta Kali	HMS Seaborn	Dartmouth/Yarmouth
HMS Goshawk	Piarco	HMS Sea Eagle	Eglinton
HMS Gosling	Risley	HMS Seahawk	Culdrose
HMS Grebe	Dekheila	HMS Sealion	Ballykelly
HMS Haitan	Gan (Addu Atoll)	HMS Seruwa	Ratmalana
HMS Harrier	Kete	HMS Sheba	Khormaksar
HMS Heron	Yeovilton/Merryfield/Duxford/Wittering/Tangmere	HMS Shrike	Maydown
		HMS Simbang	Sembawang
HMS Heron II	Haldon/Charlton Horethorne	HMS Siskin	Gosport
HMS Highflyer	China Bay	HMS Sparrowhawk	Hatston/Halesworth/Skeabrae/Sullom Voe
HMS Hornbill	Culham		
HMS Hornbill II	Beccles/Halesworth	HMS Spurwing	Hastings (Freetown)
HMS Humming Bird	Zeals	HMS Tamar	Kai Tak
HMS Jackdaw	Crail	HMS Tern	Twatt
HMS Jackdaw II	Dunino	HMS Tern II	Skeabrae/Dounreay/Hatston
HMS Kaluga	Cochin	HMS Turnstone	Watford/Fulham
HMS Kestrel	Worthy Down/Somerford/Thorney Island/Bush Barn/Haslemere	HMS Ukussa	Katukurunda/Puttalam
		HMS Urley	Ronaldsway
HMS Kilele	Tanga	HMS Vairi	Sulur
HMS Kipanga	Kilindini	HMS Valkyrie	Ronaldsway
HMS Kipanga II	Mackinnon Road/Port Reitz (Mombasa)/Voi	HMS Valluru	Tambaram
		HMS Vulture	St Merryn
HMS Kongoni	Durban	HMS Vulture II	Treligga
HMS Korongo	Nairobi	HMS Wagtail	Ayr
HMS Landrail	Campbeltown/Machrihanish	HMS Wara	Komendah
HMS Landrail II	Campbeltown	HMS Waxwing	Townhill Camp
HMS Lanka	Puttalam	HMS Woodpecker	Gosport
HMS Macaw	Bootle		

FLEET AIR ARM BASES IN THE UNITED KINGDOM

ABBOTSINCH
Used by the FAA from 1939, and commissioned on a lodger basis on 19 June 1940. Transferred from RAF No.17 Group on 11 August 1943, and commissioned as HMS *Sanderling* on 20 September 1943. Its main functions were Reserve Aircraft Storage and an RN Aircraft Maintenance Yard. Reconstructed between 1950 and November 1952. Paid off 31 October 1963 and transferred to Ministry of Civil Aviation.

ALDERGROVE
No.774 Squadron attached to No.3 Bombing & Gunnery School RAF December 1939 to July 1940. From October 1977 to April 1982 was the base for a detachment of Wessex HU.5 of No.845 Sqdn in support of internal security forces, and for occasional detachments of Lynx of Nos.702, 815 and 829 Sqdns from 1978. No.707Z Flight of Sea King HC.4, again in support of internal security forces, operated from October 1993, with the task being taken over by No.846 Sqdn in April 1994. All these deployments as lodger units with the RAF.

ANGLE
Transferred from RAF No.10 Group on 1 May 1943, and commissioned 15 May 1943 as HMS *Goldcrest*. HMS *Goldcrest* to Dale on 5 September 1943, and Angle returned to RAF on 7 September 1943 for No.19 Group.

ANTHORN
Commissioned on 7 September 1944 as HMS *Nuthatch*, for No.1 Aircraft Receipt and Despatch Unit. Paid off 28 February 1958, and reduced to Care and Maintenance basis 31 March 1958. Opened as a NATO radio station on 27 November 1964.

ARBROATH
Also known as Aberbrothock. Commissioned on 19 June 1940 as HMS *Condor*, as base for No.2 Observers School and Deck Landing Training School, and later Naval Air Signals School. It could accommodate up to 200 aircraft and for a time housed the Office of the Commodore Flying Training and later that of the Rear Admiral Reserve Aircraft. Flying ceased in 1954, but continued in use for ground training. Paid off 31 March 1971, and taken over by Royal Marines as Condor Barracks.

AYR
Occasional lodger facilities for FAA. Transferred on loan from RAF No.13 Group on 6 September 1944, and commissioned as HMS *Wagtail* on 20 October 1944. In addition to disembarked squadrons it housed an FRU, a Communications squadron, a Calibration Flight and the Bombardment Spotting School. It could accommodate up to 110 aircraft. Paid off 10 March 1946, and reduced to Care and Maintenance basis.

BALLYHALBERT
Lodger facilities from RAF Northern Ireland. Transferred on loan to Admiralty on 14 July 1945, and commissioned 17 July 1945 as HMS *Corncrake* for No.4 Naval Air Fighter School, with a maximuim capacity of 100 aircraft. Paid off 13 November 1945, and reduced to Care and Maintenance basis.

BALLYKELLY
Lodger facilities from RAF Northern Ireland. From 14 July 1945 the naval element was attached to HMS *Sea Eagle*, the Joint Anti-submarine School at Londonderry. Attachment ceased when No.819 Squadron disbanded in January 1971.

BANFF
Disused airfield loaned from 1 April 1947 for simulated bombing by Lossiemouth units.

BECCLES
Occasional lodger facilites from RAF No.16 Group. On books of HMS *Hornbill* and believed known as HMS *Hornbill II* for a time, with a satellite at Halesworth.

BEDHAMPTON CAMP
Non-airfield satellite of Lee-on-Solent used until at least 1946.

BELFAST
Also known as Sydenham. Lodger facilities from RAF, the accounts being borne in HMS *Caroline*. Transferred to Admiralty and commissioned 21 June 1943 as HMS *Gadwall*. In addition to disembarked squadrons it housed a RN Aircraft Maintenance Yard. It was responsible for overseas shipment of aircraft, and during the war had a berth alongside for escort carriers. When HMS *Gadwall* decommissioned on 30 April 1946, Belfast recommissioned as HMS *Gadwall III* from the following day. It reverted to the RAF when the latter closed on 2 July 1973.

BENBECULA
Lodger facilities from RAF No.15 Group.

BENSON
Lodger facilities from RAF Transport Command for postwar RNVR squadrons.

BIRCHAM NEWTON
Lodger facilities from RAF No.16 Group.

BOOTLE
FAA aircrew reception centre in Cumberland commissioned as HMS *Macaw*.

BRAMCOTE
Briefly attached to HMS *Godwit* until transferred from RAF No.4 Group on 1 December 1946, being commissioned 3 December 1946 as HMS *Gamecock*. Used for ground training and also by RNVR squadrons. Paid off 10 November 1958, and then to Army as Gamecock Barracks.

BRATTON
RAF No.21 Group station provided training facilities for RNAS Hinstock (HMS *Godwit*) during 1943-1944.

BRAWDY
Transferred from RAF No.19 Group on 1 January 1946 as HMS *Goldcrest II*, being initially a satellite to Dale. It recommissioned on 4 September 1952 as HMS *Goldcrest*. It was paid off on 1 April 1971 and reverted to RAF use.

BUNGAY
Also known as Flixton. Transferred from RAF No.42 Group and commissioned as HMS *Europa II* on 25 September 1945 as an intended satellite of Halesworth, under the control of HMS *Europa* at RN Lowestoft. Paid off 31 May 1946 and taken over by the Air Ministry.

BURSCOUGH
Commissioned on 1 September 1943 as HMS *Ringtail*. Undertook radar training and also housed squadrons disembarked or working up. Paid off 15 June 1946, and reduced to Care and Maintenance basis under the control of Stretton. On the books of HMS *Nightjar* at Inskip at one stage.

BUSH BARN
A Ministry of Aircraft Production satellite landing ground. Transferred to the Admiralty on 1 August 1944 for the storage of reserve aircraft under the control of Worthy Down, and later St.Merryn. Reduced to a Care and Maintenance basis after VE-Day.

CAMPBELTOWN
Civil aerodrome requisitioned by the Air Ministry on 12 February 1940 for Admiralty use. Taken over on 1 June 1940 and initially borne on the books of HMS *Merlin* at Donibristle. Commissioned 1 April 1941 as HMS *Landrail*, becoming HMS *Landrail II* on 15 June 1941, when Machrihanish became the parent station. Closed in mid-1945.

CHARLTON HORETHORNE
Lodger facilities on RAF station until transferred to Admiralty from No.10 Group, and commissioned on 1 January 1943 as HMS *Heron II*, a satellite to Yeovilton. Paid off 17 April 1945, and to RAF No.42 Group in exchange for Zeals.

CHRISTCHURCH
Lodger facilities for a Naval Air Section on an RAF aerodrome. Accounts in HMS *Raven*. Used by the Naval Air Radio Installation Unit until moving to Worthy Down after the war. Naval Air Section moved to Middle Wallop on 22 October 1945.

CLUNTOE
Loaned by the RAF as a reserve airfield from 1 April 1947, and used occasionally into the 1950's. On books of HMS *Gannet*.

COWDRAY PARK
Private aerodrome near Midhurst, requisitioned in June 1941 for storage of obsolescent naval aircraft under control of Lee-on-Solent. Paid off 30 September 1945 and reduced to a Care and Maintenance basis, being later de-requisitioned.

CRAIL
Commissioned on 1 October 1940 as HMS *Jackdaw* for torpedo training. HMS *Jackdaw* paid off 28 April 1947, and Crail ceased to be FAA, becoming HMS *Bruce* for ground training purposes.

CRIMOND
See Rattray

CULCHETH
Commissioned on 12 October 1942 as HMS *Ariel* for air radio maintenance training. Became Air Electrical School, moving to Worthy Down in June 1952.

CULDROSE
Commissioned 17 April 1947 as HMS *Seahawk*, though originally to have been HMS *Chough*. Used continuously until the present day by both first and second line units.

CULHAM
Commissioned on 1 November 1944 as HMS *Hornbill*. Used mainly by No.2 Aircraft Receipt and Despatch Unit, with some post-war use by RNVR squadrons. Paid off 30 September 1953.

CULMHEAD
Also known as Church Stanton. Occasional lodger facilities from RAF No.10 Group.

DALE
Transferred from RAF No.19 Group on 5 September 1943, and commissioned two days later as HMS *Goldcrest*, which moved there from Angle. HMS *Goldcrest* was primarily the RN Aircraft Direction Centre at nearby Kete, which used Dale as its air station, initially for twin-engine conversion. HMS *Goldcrest* paid off 31 January 1948.

DEFFORD
A RN Air Section was attached to the Telecommunications Flying Unit for trials purposes.

DETLING
Lodger facilities provided by RAF No.16 Group during 1940-1941.

DOCKING
Lodger facilities provided by RAF No.16 Group during 1942 - 1944.

DONIBRISTLE
First used as a naval air station in 1917. Commissioned on 24 May 1939 as HMS *Merlin*. Used by many units, including a Communications Squadron and a RN Aircraft Repair Yard. Towards the end of the war it housed the Office of the Flag Officer Carrier Training. It had a maximum capacity of 220 aircraft. Station paid off 23 October 1959, the RNARY being closed.

DOUNREAY
Built for RAF Coastal Command who never used it. Transferred to Admiralty on 15 May 1944 as HMS *Tern II*, a satellite of Twatt for up to 140 aircraft, but it was never officially commissioned and little use was made of it. Reduced to Care and Maintenance basis postwar, and transferred to the Air Ministry on 1 October 1954. Became site of a nuclear power station.

DREM
Lodger facilities provided by RAF No.13 Group until 21 April 1945, when it was loaned to the Admiralty as a satellite of Donibristle. Borne on the books of HMS *Merlin*, an RN Air Section operating the Night Fighter School and an FRU. Commissioned on own account as HMS *Nighthawk* on 1 June 1945, but paid off and returned to the RAF on 15 March 1946.

DUNDEE
Commissioned on 15 July 1941 as HMS *Condor II*, a satellite seaplane base of Arbroath. Paid off 15 June 1944.

DUNDONALD
Lodger facilities provided during 1944 by RAF No.105 Wing for squadrons of the 3rd Naval Fighter Wing.

DUNINO
Transferred from RAF on 1 December 1942, and commissioned on 15 December 1942 as HMS *Jackdaw II*, a satellite of Crail for Reserve Aircraft Storage with a maximum capacity of 180 aircraft. Reduced to a Care and Maintenance basis on 2 April 1946.

DUXFORD
Lodger facilities provided during 1941-1943 by RAF No.12 Group for a RN Air Section attached to the Air Fighting Development Unit. On books of HMS *Heron*.

EAST HAVEN
Was intended to be HMS *Dotterel*, but became HMS *Peewit* when it commissioned on 1 May 1943 as a TBR Deck Landing Training School. It also undertook Part II TBR training, DLCO training and Aircraft Handling training. Paid off 14 August 1946.

EASTLEIGH
RAF Eastleigh opened at Southampton Airport on 1 October 1935 in Coastal Area (later Coastal Command) to accommodate shore based naval squadrons. On 16 November took over responsibility for those squadrons which had used Upavon as a shore base until 1 September 1935, and which had been temporarily using Gosport. Renamed RAF Southampton on 1 August 1936. To RN and commissioned on 1 July 1939 as HMS *Raven*. Later housed the Safety Equipment School and the School of Air Medicine and undertook fire fighting training. Closed down on 21 May 1946, and station paid off 30 April 1947.

EGLINTON
From RAF No.82 Group on loan 1 May 1943, and commissioned 15 May 1943 as HMS *Gannet*. Used by first line squadrons working up, it also housed a series of second line squadrons as well as providing storage for second line aircraft. Transferred from RAF 4 March 1947. Paid off 31 May 1959, but reopened in 1960 as part of HMS *Sea Eagle*, for use by helicopters. Finally closed on 8 February 1963.

EVANTON
Used prewar by FAA squadrons, being known as Novar until 1937. The Admiralty had lodger facilities from RAF No.25 Group from 15 January 1940, being a satellite of Donibristle. It was loaned by No.29 Group on 1 September 1944 as Reserve Storage for Fearn, but commissioned in its own right on 9 October 1944 as an RN Aircraft Maintenance Yard. It had a maximum capacity of 500 aircraft. Transferred from RAF 1 December 1946. Paid off 24 March 1948 and reduced to a Care and Maintenance basis.

FEARN
Used briefly as a satellite for RAF Tain until transferred to Admiralty charge on 15 July 1942, commissioning on 1 August 1942 as a satellite to Donibristle. On 11 October 1942 it commissioned in its own right as HMS *Owl*, for first line TBR squadrons working up, with a capacity of 96 aircraft. Paid off on 2 July 1946.

FLEETLANDS
Opened in May 1940 as a civilian-manned RN Aircraft Repair Yard, and still in use as such, the title having been abbreviated to RN Aircraft Yard.

FORD
Transferred from RAF No.17 Group on 24 May 1939, and commissioned as HMS *Peregrine* for an Immediate Reserve Storage Unit, storing Albacores and Swordfish, also housing No.1 Observer School. It was transferred to No.11 Group on 30 September 1940, but the School of Naval Photography remained as a lodger, on the books of Lee-on-Solent. It returned to Admiralty charge on 1 August 1945, and recommissioned as HMS *Peregrine* on 15 August 1945, mainly for the formation of first line squadrons. With a capacity of 50 aircraft, it was paid off on 30 June 1948 to become a satellite of Lee-on-Solent. It again recommissioned as HMS *Peregrine* on 1 February 1950, being paid off for the last time on 13 November 1958.

FRASERBURGH
Occasional wartime lodging facilities on an RAF station.

GOSPORT
Used as a FAA station between the wars, under the control of Coastal Area (later Coastal Command). Lodger facilities during the war, under the control of Lee-on-Solent. A Fleet Arm Maintenance Unit was formed by renaming the station workshops on 1 May 1940, this becoming No.3502 Servicing Unit on 11 June 1942. Station transferred to Admiralty charge from RAF No.16 Group on 1 August 1945 and proposed to be HMS *Woodpecker*, but instead commissioned as HMS *Siskin*. Used by the Service Trials Unit, the Tactical Trials Unit and later other second line squadrons. Accounts in HMS *Daedalus* until 1 January 1947, then own accounts. Paid off 31 May 1956. The nearby camp, HMS *St.Vincent*, undertook post-entry training of flying crews.

GRIMSETTER
Transferred from RAF No.14 Group on 6 July 1943, initially as a satellite to Hatston, until being commissioned 15 August 1943 as HMS *Robin* with a capacity of 48 aircraft. Paid off 31 July 1945 and transferred to RAF No.13 Group.

HALDON
Transferred from RAF charge on 18 August 1941_1 and commissioned as HMS *Heron II*. Having only a grass surface, it operated as a satellite to Yeovilton until being reduced to a Care and Maintenance basis in May 1943, it ships name having been already transferred to Charlton Horethorne.

HALESWORTH
A wartime USAAF base taken over by the Admiralty from the RAF on 5 August 1945, and commissioned as HMS *Sparrowhawk*, the ships name formerly used by Hatston, for monoplane conversion. Reduced to a Care and Maintenance basis on 28 February 1946, and transferred to RAF No.12 Group on 15 March 1946. Was HMS *Hornbill II* for a time.

HARROWBEER
Lodger facilities provided by RAF No.10 Group during 1944.

HATSTON
Commissioned on 2 October 1939 as HMS *Sparrowhawk*, and used during the war by numerous first line squadrons from ships in Scapa Flow. Paid off 1 August 1945 as HMS *Sparrowhawk*, becoming HMS *Tern II* as a satellite of Twatt. Reduced to a Care and Maintenance basis on 15 September 1945, later becoming Kirkwall Airport for a time.

HEATH ROW
Lodger facilities from Fairey Aviation Ltd for a flight of No.781 Squadron during 1944-1945.

HENSTRIDGE
Commissioned on 1 April 1943 as HMS *Dipper*, for No.2 Naval Air Fighter School, with a maximum capacity of 120 aircraft. Paid off 11 October 1946, but taken over again in 1949 as a satellite of Yeovilton until again being paid off in March 1954.

HESTON
Lodger facilities from the Director General of Civil Aviation between April 1945 and January 1947 for No.701 Squadron.

HINSTOCK
Formerly Ollerton satellite landing ground. Transferred to Admiralty from Ministry of Aircraft Production on 23 July 1942 for use as a Beam Approach School, and name changed to Hinstock shortly afterwards. Commissioned on 14 June 1943 under the control of Stretton, becoming HMS *Godwit* in its own right on 1 April 1944. The resident unit became the Naval Advanced Instrument Flying School and operated up to 120 aircraft. Paid off 28 February 1947.

HONINGTON
Lodger facilities on RAF station for FAA Buccaneers from October 1972. Facility ceased when No.809 Squadron disbanded on 15 December 1978.

HURN
Used by Airwork Ltd from 1 September 1952 for the civilian operated Fleet Requirements Unit. Ceased to be used when this moved to Yeovilton on 16 October 1972.

INSKIP
Commissioned on 15 May 1943 as HMS *Nightjar* for No.1 Operational Training Unit, with a maximum capacity of 145 aircraft. Paid off 2 July 1946.

JERSEY
Facilities at Jersey Airport from 11 Mar 1940, under the control of Worthy Down. Aerodrome evacuated 31 May 1940.

KETE
Commissioned in 1945 as HMS *Harrier*, to operate in conjunction with Dale as an Aircraft Direction Centre.

KIRKISTOWN
Lodger facilities from RAF Northern Ireland during the war. Transferred to Admiralty charge 14 July 1945, and commissioned 17 July 1945 as HMS *Corncrake II*, a satellite of Ballyhalbert. Paid off 15 January 1946.

LANDS END
A civil aerodrome at St.Just, used briefly by the FAA in 1940.

LANGHAM
Lodger facilities from RAF No.16 Group during 1942-1944.

LAWRENNY FERRY
A FAA seaplane base controlled by Lee-on-Solent, and commissioned on 1 February 1942 as HMS *Daedalus II*. Reduced to a Care and Maintenance basis 24 October 1943.

LEE-ON-SOLENT
Used as a seaplane training station from 1917, an aerodrome being also opened in 1934. Commissioned as HMS *Daedalus* on 24 May 1939 and used continuously ever since. In addition to No.781 Communications Squadron it provided Reserve Aircraft Storage for a time, and many first line squadrons were formed there, its maximum capacity being originally 100 aircraft. During the war it also housed the Office of the Admiral (Air) and was the main depot for Naval Air Ratings. Seaplane facilities ceased postwar. Retitled HMS *Ariel* on becoming a ground training establishment on 31 October 1959, and HMS *Daedalus* became purely Wykeham Hall, the locally-based headquarters of Flag Officer Naval Air Command. Lee-on-Solent again became HMS *Daedalus* on 5 October 1965.

781 Sqdn disbanded in March 1981, leaving behind a helicopter SAR Flight of 772 Sqdn, which in turn handed over to a civilian SAR Flight in 1988. The airfield continued with Southampton University Air Squadron, Bristow's SAR Flight and the Hampshire Police helicopter unit until April 1993 when the UAS moved to Boscombe Down and routine Naval flying operations ceased apart from occasional activation for exercises. Air Engineering training is to continue until Christmas 1995 when the school is to transfer to HMS *Sultan*. Lee-on-Solent will finally close in April 1996.

LEUCHARS
RAF Base Leuchars trained FAA aircrew between the wars, continuing this task as No.1 Flying Training School from 1 April 1935 until moving to Netheravon on 26 March 1938. FAA units lodged on the station during that period. From July 1972 lodger facilities were provided by the RAF for No.892 Phantom squadron and the RN Phantom Support Unit, until the latter disbanded on 29 September 1978.

LIMAVADY
Lodger facilities from RAF No.15 Group during 1944. The station was transferred to Admiralty charge on 1 December 1945, but no naval use was made of it until 1950 when 737 Sqdn began using it regularly for ADDLs. Also used for refresher pilots re-establishing their deck landing qualifications and for new pilots undergoing operational training prior to entering first line service.

LONG KESH
Lodger facilities from RAF Northern Ireland during 1944-1945.

LOSSIEMOUTH
Transferred from RAF No.18 Group on 12 July 1946 and commissioned as HMS *Fulmar*. Returned to RAF control on 29 September 1972. Later used by an RN detachment until this disbanded on 9 February 1979.

LUDHAM
Transferred from RAF No.12 Group on 24 August 1944, and commissioned on 4 September 1944 as HMS *Flycatcher*. Acted as the headquarters of the Mobile Naval Airfield organisation until the airfield was returned to the RAF on 16 February in exchange for Middle Wallop, which then became HMS *Flycatcher*.

LYMPNE
Transferred from RAF No.22 Group on 1 July 1939 and commissioned as HMS *Buzzard*. Reduced to Care and Maintenance basis on 25 September 1939, but later reopened as HMS *Daedalus II* under the control of Lee-on-Solent. Transferred to No.11 Group on 23 May 1940.

MACHRIHANISH
Commissioned 15 June 1941 as HMS *Landrail*, which transferred from Campbeltown, having a capacity of 85 aircraft. Known as Strabane until August 1941. Used by numerous disembarked first line squadrons until paid off 16 April 1946, when it was reduced to a Care and Maintenance basis. Recommissioned as HMS *Landrail* on 1 December 1951, reverting to civil use when again paid off 30 September 1952. Later rebuilt as NATO standby airfield with US Navy facilities.

MACMERRY
Loaned by the RAF on 21 April 1945 for intended use by No.770 Squadron. Commissioned on 1 June 1945 as a satellite of Drem but never used as such. Reverted to the RAF on 15 March 1946, and later used for civil flying.

MANSTON
Used 1933-1935 as a shore base for FAA squadrons. Lodger facilities from RAF No.12 Group during WW2. Used by No.845 Squadron early 1974.

MAYDOWN
Transferred from RAF Northern Ireland on 1 May 1943, and commissioned on 13 May 1943 as a satellite of Eglinton. Commissioned on 1 January 1944 as HMS *Shrike* with a capacity of 105 aircraft. It housed the Anti U-boat School, provided refresher and conversion Naval Operational Training and was the headquarters for MAC-ship operations. Paid off 13 September 1945 and recommissioned as HMS *Gannet II*, a satellite to Eglinton. Little used as such and reduced to Care and Maintenance basis.

MERRYFIELD
Transferred from No.1 Bomber Group, RAF and commissioned 24 October 1956 as a satellite of Yeovilton. Reduced to a Care and Maintenance basis on 31 January 1958, but reopened in January 1960 as an overflow for Yeovilton, closing again in July 1961. Again reopened as a satellite to Yeovilton on 22 May 1972. It continues to the present day as a Helicopter Relief Landing Ground for Yeovilton and Portland.

MERSTON
Reported used by a few FAA Martinets during 1945-1946.

MIDDLE WALLOP
Transferred from RAF No.70 Group on 16 February 1945, and commissioned as HMS *Flycatcher* to become headquarters of the Mobile Naval Airfield organisation on transfer from Ludham. Naval Air Section moved from Christchurch 22.10.45. Also used by the Maintenance Test Pilots School and as Reserve Aircraft Storage for Worthy Down. Paid off 10 April 1946 and returned to the RAF (later Army Air Corps). Due to become to become multi-service helicopter training base.

MILLTOWN
Transferred from RAF No.25 Group on 2 July 1946 and commissioned as HMS *Fulmar II*, a satellite to Lossiemouth. Returned to RAF in September 1972.

MILMEECE
Commissioned as a camp and training school on 15 April 1943 as HMS *Fledgling* to train WRNS Air Mechanics. Borne on the books of HMS *Daedalus*, it was paid off after the war.

MOUNT BATTEN
FAA floatplane base transferred here from Lee-on-Solent on 4 June 1935, and used by catapult flights from ships based at Plymouth. The base reverted to Lee-on-Solent on 15 November 1937.

MULLAGHMORE
Lodger facilities from RAF No.15 Group in 1944-1945.

NETHERAVON
Used as shore base by FAA flights and squadrons 1931-1934.

NEWCASTLE-UNDER-LYME
Housed the RN Aircraft Training Establishment, which transferred from Lympne in May 1941. Operating under the control of Lee-on-Solent as HMS *Daedalus II*, it provided technical training for Air Apprentices, Air Fitters and Air Mechanics, and also W/T training for selected ratings. It was paid off after the war.

NORTH COATES
RAF practice camp used by FAA for armament training prewar. Lodger facilities from RAF No.16 Group 1940-1941.

NUTTS CORNER
Transferred from RAF Northern Ireland on 9 July 1945, and commissioned on 11 July 1945 as HMS *Pintail* for first line fighter squadrons, with capacity for up to 60 aircraft. Paid off 31 March 1946 and station to RAF Transport Command.

PEMBROKE DOCK
Lodger facilities from RAF No.15 Group in 1940-1941.

PEPLOW
Transferred from RAF No.21 Group on 28 February 1945 and commissioned as HMS *Godwit II*, a satellite to Hinstock. Paid off at the end of 1949.

PERRANPORTH
Lodger facilities from RAF No.19 Group in 1944, under the control of St Merryn.

PETERHEAD
Lodger facilities from RAF Nos.14 and 13 Groups in 1942-1944.

PORT ELLEN
Lodger facilities from RAF No.15 Group during 1943.

PORTLAND
Used as an occasional seaplane base prewar. Some wartime use, under control of Lee-on-Solent. Commissioned on 24 April 1959 for helicopter use as HMS *Osprey*, being the base for Wasp small ships flights between December 1964 and March 1988, and for Lynx small ships flights from July 1982. Due to close in 1999 and function transferred to Yeovilton.

PREDANNACK
Built 1940-41 and operated until 1946 as RAF Predannack Down with fighters, bombers and Coastal Command aircraft. Bought by RN in 1959 and operated since as a satellite to Culdrose for helicopter training.

PRESTWICK
Lodger facilities from RAF No.15 Group in 1940-1941. Naval element commissioned on 23 November 1971 as HMS *Gannet* on the international airport, and is presently the base for No.819 Sea King Squadron. The additional title of RNAS Prestwick was allocated in January 1994.

PUCKPOOL
At Ryde, Isle of Wight, it commissioned on 15 November 1939 as HMS *Medina* for new entry Fleet Air Arm ratings.

RATTRAY (or **RATTRAY HEAD**)
Known as Crimond when commissioned on 31 October 1944 as HMS *Merganser*, being renamed Rattray Head on 1 July 1945. It undertook TBR Training Part II and could house up to 130 aircraft. Paid off 30 September 1946, and reduced to Care and Maintenance basis.

RISLEY
A training establishment near Warrington, commissioned 1 July 1942 as HMS *Gosling* to give aerodrome defence training to naval airmen. Paid off 31 March 1947.

ROBOROUGH
Occasional prewar use of civil airfield during Navy Weeks. Used early in war by Admiralty as part of HMS *Drake* until transferred to Air Ministry on 1 May 1942. Postwar use as HMS *Drake II*, including the RNEC Manadon Flight. Home of the Dartmouth Flight, operated by Airwork.

ROCHESTER
Used by Shorts civilian-operated Ferry Flight and Admiralty Flight from November 1950 until 1962.

RONALDSWAY
Commissioned on 21 June 1944 as HMS *Urley*, for TBR training and Naval Operational Training Part III, with a capacity of 120 aircraft. Paid off 14 January 1946 and became a civil airport.

ST DAVIDS
A relief airfield for Brawdy, loaned from the RAF from 1 April 1947 on a Care and Maintenance basis. Brought into use on 5 January 1950 by the Airwork FRU, and used until this moved to Yeovilton in January 1961.

ST EVAL
Lodger facilities from RAF Nos.15 and 19 Groups in 1940-1944.

ST MAWGAN
Lodger facilities from RAF No.19 Group in 1954-1956 for No.744 Squadron, then working with the Air-Sea Warfare Development Unit there.

ST MERRYN
Commissioned 10 August 1940 as HMS *Vulture*, and used by many first and second line squadrons. It housed the School of Naval Air Warfare, and had a capacity of 145 aircraft. Recommissioned as HMS *Curlew* on 31 December 1952, becoming primarily a ground training base. Reduced to a Care and Maintenance basis in June 1955, and paid off 10 January 1956.

SANDBANKS
Seaplane base in Poole Harbour commissioned on 15 May 1940 as HMS *Daedalus II*, being a satellite to Lee-on-Solent. Reduced to a Care and Maintenance basis on 9 October 1943.

SKEABRAE
Lodger facilities from RAF Nos.14 and 13 Groups from 2 May 1940 whilst still under construction, and used extensively by squadrons ashore from carriers in Scapa Flow. A satellite of Hatston, becoming a postwar satellite of Twatt on a Care and Maintenance basis as HMS *Tern II*.

SKITTEN
Lodger facilities from RAF No.14 Group in 1940-1941.

SPEKE
Lodger facilities from RAF Nos.9 and 15 Groups 1942 - 1945. It housed a RN Air Section, which moved to Woodvale on 7 April 1945 with No.776 Squadron.

STORNOWAY
Seaplane base established November 1940 as HMS *Mentor II*, attached to HMS *Mentor* at RN Stornoway. It was reduced to a Care and Maintenance basis in June 1941. It then became an RAF station, and lodger facilities were granted in 1943-1944 by Nos.15 and 18 Groups.

STRETTON
Commissioned on 1 June 1942 as HMS *Blackcap*, and used by many first and second line squadrons. It operated as a RN Aircraft Maintenance Yard, and also provided Reserve Aircraft Storage, having a capacity of up to 180 aircraft. Mainly used postwar as an Aircraft Holding Unit and by RNVR squadrons, until paid off 4 November 1958.

SULLOM VOE
RN Air Section established in July 1940 under the control of Hatston, as a lodger from RAF No.18 Group. Operated mainly as a seaplane base for disembarked catapult flights until mid-1941.

SUMBURGH
Lodger facilities from RAF Nos.14 and 18 Groups in 1941-1942.

TAIN
Lodger facilities from RAF Nos.14 and 18 Groups in 1942-1944.

TANGMERE
Lodger facilities from RAF Nos.11 and 15 Groups in 1942-1950, controlled by Lee-on-Solent. On the books of HMS *Heron* at one stage, and for a time housed the Naval Air Fighting Development Unit.

TERNHILL
A RN Air Section was attached briefly until being withdrawn on 3 April 1946.

THORNEY ISLAND
Lodger facilities from RAF No.16 Group 1940-1948, under the control of Lee-on-Solent and later Worthy Down. Used for a time by the Naval Air Sea Warfare Development Unit.

TOOME
Transferred from RAF Maintenance Command on 1 April 1947 as a reserve station for Eglinton, until at least 1954, but never used.

TOWNHILL CAMP
Established as a Naval Air Depot on 1 Jul 1942 when it commissioned as HMS *Waxwing*. It provided accommodation for naval personnel awaiting draft, and many FAA squadrons assembled there before taking passage to the United States to equip and work up. To Care and Maintenance basis 31 August 1946.

TRELIGGA
Opened late in 1939 as a bombing and gunnery range. Under the control of St Merryn, it was named HMS *Vulture II* but had no flying facilities other than a wheels-up emergency landing strip. Closed in late 1955.

TURNHOUSE
Lodger facilities from RAF No.13 Group 1942-1944.

TWATT
Commissioned on 1 April 1941 as a satellite of Hatston, becoming an independent command as HMS *Tern* on 1 January 1941 with a capacity of 50 aircraft. Paid off 30 September 1946, but retained on a Care and Maintenance basis under control of Lossiemouth until January 1957.

UPAVON
Acted as shore base for FAA squadrons from 15 May 1934 under control of Coastal Area until 1 September 1935, when the station was taken over by the Central Flying School. The base for these squadrons was then transferred to Gosport.

WATFORD
RN Aircraft Training Establishment commissioned 1 January 1944 as HMS *Turnstone*, it provided accomodation for Air Fitters undergoing preliminary technical training. Paid off 18 August 1945.

WATTON
An RAF station, which provided lodger facilities for No.751 Sqdn and later No.831 Sqdn between 1947 and 1966.

WEST FREUGH
Lodger facilities from RAF No.25 Group 1940-1943.

WESTHAMPNETT
Lodger facilities for No.787 Squadron from RAF No.11 Group in 1945, as a satellite of Tangmere.

WESTON PARK
Used as a satellite landing ground of Hinstock in 1945, as HMS *Godwit II*.

WEST RAYNHAM
Lodger facilities from RAF No.11 Group in 1945-1956, for naval units attached to the Central Fighter Establishment.

WICK
Lodger facilities from RAF No.13 Group 1939-1940.

WITTERING
Lodger facilities from RAF No.12 Group 1943-1945, for naval units attached to the Air Fighting Development Unit. On the books of HMS *Heron*.

WOODVALE
Lodger facilities from RAF Nos.9 and 12 Groups 1942-1945. Transferred to Admiralty on 7 April 1945 as HMS *Ringtail II*, being a satellite of Burscough. It housed an FRU and also provided accommodation for first line squadrons. Returned to RAF 28 January 1946.

WORTHY DOWN
Lodger facilities from Nos.2 and 17 Groups in 1938-1939. Transferred to Admiralty on 24 May 1939 and commissioned as HMS *Kestrel*. With a capacity of 150 aircraft it housed No.1 Air Gunners School, the School of Aircraft Maintenance and the Engine Handling Unit. Reserve Aircraft Storage was also available. Reduced to a Care and Maintenance basis in late 1947, and paid off 9 January 1950. Reopened in June 1952 as HMS *Ariel II* for ground training, being paid off on 1 December 1960 and transferred to the Army.

WROUGHTON
RAF No.15 MU until RN Aircraft Yard opened 5 April 1972 as a satellite of Fleetlands for helicopter maintenance and storage. Operated as an integral part of the Naval Aircraft Repair Organisation. Closed in September 1992.

YEOVILTON
Officially opened on 1 June 1940, but some temporary earlier use by units from Ford. Commissioned 18 June 1940 as HMS *Heron*, being initially the home of the No.1 Naval Air Fighter School and later the Aircraft Direction Centre. Used continuously until the present time, and now houses the FAA Museum. Became headquarters of the FAA when the Office of the Flag Officer Naval Air Command (later Flag Officer Naval Aviation) moved from Lee-on-Solent on 12 November 1970. Currently the base for Sea Harrier fighters and Sea King utility helicopters as well as an increasing number of lodger units. To take over function of base for small ships helicopter flights from Portland by 1999.

ZEALS
Transferred from RAF on 14 April 1945, initially as a satellite to Yeovilton. Commissioned on 18 May 1945 as HMS *Humming Bird*, it housed an FRU for a time and also undertook fighter conversion. Paid off 1 January 1946 and reduced to a Care and Maintenance basis.

de Havilland Chipmunk T.10 WB671 '910' of Britannia Flight. (via Brian Lowe)

FLEET AIR ARM BASES OVERSEAS

ABOUKIR
An RAF station which became a FAA Base when HMS *Glorious* arrived at Alexandria on 5 Sep 1935 during the Abyssinian crisis. Ceased to be a FAA Base on 3 September 1936. Used by naval air squadrons at other times, being on the books of HMS *Nile* during 1941.

ANDRAKAKA
Lodger facilities on an airfield at Diego Suarez, Madagascar. On the books of HMS *Ironclad*.

ARCHERFIELD
Civil airfield near Brisbane, used from February 1945 by TAMY No.1 under the ships name HMS *Nabsford*, and later also shared by MONAB No.7. HMS *Nabsford* paid off 31 March 1946.

ARGENTIA
A RCAF station in Newfoundland used from 1942 by FAA squadrons disembarked from escort carriers.

BANKSTOWN
Loaned from the RAAF and commissioned as a Naval Air Station on 29 January 1945. Occupied by MONAB No.2 under the name HMS *Nabberley* until this paid off 31 March 1946.

BERMUDA
A prewar seaplane station used as a shore base for catapult aircraft in ships of the America and West Indies Station. A landing strip was later built, and the ships names HMS *Malabar II and III* were used for a time though these were discontinued in 1940. It had a capacity of 12 aircraft and housed a Fleet Requirements Unit equipped with seaplanes. Reduced to a Care and Maintenance basis in 1944.

BRUNSWICK
A US Navy base in Maine, loaned to the FAA from August 1943 for work-up of Corsair squadrons forming in the USA. Operated under the parentage of HMS *Saker* until station returned to the US Navy in August 1945. Due to overcrowding, ADDLs were carried out at satellite US Naval Air Stations at Rockland and Sanford, some 50-70 miles distant.

CHANGI
An RAF station at Singapore opened in April 1946 and used by a naval Aircraft Holding Unit until this closed in 1969.

CHINA BAY
Lodger facilities from 1 August 1940 on an RAF station in Ceylon, the air section being borne on the books of HMS *Lanka*, the local naval base. The FAA base moved to Mombasa after the Japanese strike on Ceylon on Easter Day 1942, but FAA squadrons continued to use the station, and these came under HMS *Highflyer* until 1 January 1944 when HMS *Bambara* commissioned to comprise the RN Air Section at China Bay and the RNAMY at Clappenburg Bay. On 1 November 1944 the name of the station was changed to RNAS Trincomalee, this being the name of the nearby port and naval base. The air station was transferred from RAF to naval charge on 15 November 1944, being eventually paid off on 31 December 1947.

CHOLAVARUM
Lodger facilities for an RN Air Section on an RAF Station near Madras in southern India. Had a capacity for two disembarked squadrons.

CLAPPENBURG BAY
An RN Aircraft Maintenance Yard at Trincomalee, Ceylon. Under the control of HMS *Bambara*.

COCHIN
Lodger facilities for an RN Air Section on an RAF station in southern India occupied primarily by a Maintenance Unit. The naval element commissioned on 1 February 1945 as HMS *Kalugu*, but was responsible to HMS *Garuda* at Coimbatore until 1 April 1946 when it became independent. Used for an Aircraft Erection Depot with a capacity of 130 aircraft per month, to serve Coimbatore. Could also take one disembarked squadron. Paid off 1 August 1946.

COIMBATORE
A RN Aircraft Repair Yard in southern India, with responsibility for erecting aircraft shipped from both the UK and USA. Commissioned on 1 October 1942 as HMS *Garuda* and provided Reserve Aircraft Storage for up to 250 aircraft. Paid off 1 April 1946.

COLOMBO RACECOURSE
Transferred from the RAF on 1 September 1943, and commissioned on 1 October 1943 as HMS *Bherunda*. Having a capacity of 90 aircraft, it housed a Fleet Requirements Unit and a communications squadron, and also had limited facilities for erecting aircraft. A number of disembarked squadrons also spent periods there. Sub-units in Colombo provided facilities for work on American-built aircraft, including a Shipping and Salvage Unit handling crashed and cased aircraft. The local Rowlands Garage was taken over to undertake limited repairs to engines and components, and to refabricate aircraft wings. Paid off 30 November 1945.

DARTMOUTH
A prewar RCAF station in Nova Scotia used from September 1940 by an RN Air Section to service Swordfish and Walruses, this being initially responsible to HMS *Seaborn*. On 1 October 1941 responsibility was transferred to HMS *Saker* then later to HMS *Canada*, the latter being renamed HMS *Seaborn* on 1 July 1944. Used from 1943 as a shore base for Swordfish aircraft disembarking from MAC-ships heading for Halifax. With a capacity of 32 aircraft, it also had limited facilities for aircraft repairs. HMS *Seaborn* paid off 28 January 1946, and Dartmouth was transferred back to the RCAF after the war. A RCN Air Section became operational on 31 March 1946, and on 1 December 1948 the station was transferred to the RCN and commissioned as HMCS Shearwater.

DEKHEILA
The prewar Alexandria airport used as a shore base for aircraft flown ashore from RN carriers using the naval base. Taken over by the Royal Egyptian Air Force on the outbreak of war, but continued to be used by the FAA as HMS *Nile II*, being attached to the naval base, otherwise HMS *Nile*. Loaned as a Naval Air Station from 16 September 1940 and commissioned as HMS *Grebe* with a capacity of 72 aircraft. Attached to HMS *Nile* until 1 April 1941 when it became self-accounting. Acted as the base for all FAA units operating in Egypt and the Western Desert, and also housed a Fleet Requirements Unit. Returned to control of HMS *Nile* on 1 April 1943, but retained the name HMS *Grebe*. Reduced to a Care and Maintenance basis on 31 January 1946, being returned to Egyptian control 18 March 1946.

DURBAN
SAAF station at Stamford Hill with lodger facilities for an RN Air Section. Housed a Fleet Requirements Unit, and could accommodate one disembarked squadron from an escort carrier. Loaned by Royal Navy from 31 March 1944 and commissioned as HMS *Kongoni*. Paid off 31 January 1946.

FAYID
An air station in the Canal Zone of Egypt, commissioned 15 May 1941 as HMS *Phoenix*. Used by a RN Aircraft Repair Yard and also provided Reserve Aircraft Storage for up to 130 aircraft. Paid off 28 February 1946 and reduced to a Care and Maintenance basis, being later taken over by the RAF.

GAN
An airstrip on Addu Atoll in the Indian Ocean. Used for anti-submarine work from 1942, being a secondary base for Trincomalee, Ceylon with a capacity of 24 aircraft. Borne on the books of HMS *Haitan*, which was renamed HMS *Moraga* on 1 February 1944. Paid off 20 March 1945 and reduced to a Care and Maintenance basis, providing only emergency facilities.

GIBRALTAR
See North Front

HAL FAR
Built soon after the first World War as a shore base for aircraft with the Mediterranean Fleet. Opened on 16 January 1923, and was initially attached to Calafrana. RAF Station Hal Far was officially formed on 31 March 1929, becoming a separate unit on 18 June 1929. Although used by a number of FAA squadrons it remained under RAF control until being transferred and commissioned as HMS *Falcon* on 15 April 1946. In addition to disembarked squadrons it housed a Fleet Requirements Unit. Paid off and returned to the RAF on 1 September 1965.

HALIFAX
RN Base in Nova Scotia, under the control of HMS *Saker*, becoming HMS *Canada* on 1 August 1942.

HASTINGS
Aerodrome near Freetown, Sierra Leone, first used by No.710 Squadron in January 1940, and later by other first and second line squadrons including a Fleet Requirements Unit. Became a RN Air Station on 1 April 1941, responsible at first to HMS *Edinburgh Castle*, the local headquarters ship in Freetown harbour. The station was transferred from the RAF on 16 March 1943, and it commissioned as HMS *Spurwing* on 22 March 1943 with a capacity of 84 aircraft. HMS *Spurwing* paid off 31 December 1944 and the station was reduced to a Care and Maintenance basis.

HUITANES
A RN Air Section was established during the war to provide shore facilities in Iceland for the Fleet Air Arm. It was responsible to HMS *Baidur*, the local naval base.

HYERES LA PALYVESTRE
Lodger facilities early in the war on a French naval air base near Toulon for deck landing training aircraft operating in the area from HMS *Argus*.

JERVIS BAY
A RAAF airstrip used by the FAA as a satellite to Nowra. It was taken over on 1 May 1945 by MONAB No.5, which operated as HMS *Nabswick*. Officially paid off on 15 November 1945 when MONAB No.5 moved to Nowra. Later used as a satellite field to HMAS Albatross (Nowra) by the RAN

KAI TAK
Aerodrome at Hong Kong, first used as a RAF base during the 1920's, mainly for FAA use. Occupied during the war by the Japanese. Used again by the FAA from September 1945 when MONAB No.8 arrived, as HMS *Nabcatcher*. The latter paid off 27 August 1946, and the station then operated under the control of HMS *Tamar*, the local naval base. On 1 April 1947 it recommissioned as a separate command and was renamed HMS *Flycatchger*.

KALAFRANA
Opened at Malta in 1917 as a RN Air Service seaplane station. Used between the wars as an RAF base for both shore based and ship based seaplanes, being known as Calafrana until reverting to the original spelling of Kalafrana in December 1936. Later used during and after World War 2 by the RAF as a flying boat base. Transferred from RAF as an RNAMY on 16 May 1946.

KALDADARNES
An aerodrome in Iceland with a RN Air Section during the war with shore facilities for FAA aircraft. Under the control of HMS *Baidur*, the local naval base.

KANTALAI
Airfield under construction in Ceylon during 1945 for up to 127 aircraft. Intended for use by disembarked first line squadrons and an ATTU but never completed.

KATUKURUNDA
Transferred from the RAF in Ceylon on 1 September 1942, and commissioned 15 October 1942 as HMS *Ukussa*. With accommodation for up to 144 aircraft, it housed an RN Aircraft Repair Yard and provided Reserve Aircraft Storage. Used by a number of first and second line FAA squadrons until paid off 27 September 1946, being returned to the RAF on 1 October 1946.

KHORMAKSAR
Opened in Aden during 1917 for the Royal Flying Corps, and used continuously from 1918 until 1967 by the RAF. Occasional lodger facilities for FAA squadrons, a RN Air Section being based there during the war under the control of HMS *Sheba*, the local naval base.

KOMENDA
FAA station at Takoradi, Gold Coast, commissioned 1 October 1942 as HMS *Wara*. Its task was to unpack and erect aircraft to be flown across Africa by the reinforcement route. It provided Reserve Aircraft Storage and housed up to 104 aircraft. Paid off 7 December 1943, and station reduced to a Care and Maintenance basis 16 December 1943.

LEWISTON
A US Navy base in Maine, commissioned in 1943 as part of HMS *Saker*, the accounting base at Washington, which had itself commissioned on 1 October 1941. Acted as the parent ship for all FAA facilities in the USA, and some responsibility at times for those in Canada. Commissioned as HMS *Saker II* as an independant command on 1 October 1942, but reverted to being part of HMS *Saker* on 1 November 1942. Lewiston was paid off in 1945, and HMS *Saker* on 29 February 1948.

MACKINNON ROAD
Wartime RAF station in East Africa. Lodger facilities for the FAA as part of HMS *Kipanga II*, being under the control of HMS *Kipanga* at Kilindini, the port base for Mombasa. With a capacity of 64 aircraft it housed disembarked squadrons and provided both Reserve Aircraft Storage and fighter training facilities. It was reduced to a Care and Maintenance basis at the end of the war.

MAHARAGAMA
The RN Aircraft Training Establishment, Ceylon, commissioned 1 December 1944 as HMS *Monara* to train Singalese recruits to the FAA. Paid off after the war.

MARYBOROUGH
A RAAF station, with lodger facilities for the FAA from 1 June 1945. Used by MONAB No.6 as HMS *Nabstock*, and paid off 15 November 1945 when this withdrew to Schofields.

MINNERIYA
An RAF station in Ceylon with lodger facilities for an RN Air Section able to take one disembarked squadron.

NAIROBI
A prewar civil airport in Kenya, also known as Eastleigh but generally referred to as Nairobi to avoid confusion with Southampton airport. An RAF station headquarters opened on 1 March 1938, and the FAA had facilities during the war, being commissioned on 1 September 1942 as HMS *Korongo*, for use mainly as a RN Aircraft Repair Yard. Also provided Reserve Aircraft Storage, with a capacity of 160 aircraft. Paid off 15 October 1944 and station reduced to a Care and Maintenance basis.

NAVY POINT
FAA base at Port San Carlos in the Falkland Islands, first occupied 25 June 1982.

NORFOLK
Facilities on a US Navy Base in Virginia from 1941 for disembarked squadrons and squadrons working up. Facility transferred to Quonset Point in November 1942.

NORTH FRONT
A RAF airstrip at Gibraltar which was eventually enlarged to a proper runway. Administration was transferred to the RN on 26 September 1940 as HMS *Cormorant II*, under the control of HMS *Cormorant*, the local naval base. Returned to the RAF 1 August 1941, but retained facilities for naval aircraft when required. Recommissioned as HMS *Cormorant II* on 1 January 1944, housing a RN Air Section with a capacity of 24 aircraft, and a Fleet Requirements Unit. Provided facilities for a limited number of disembarked aircraft. Paid off 1 November 1944. The naval base became HMS *Rooke* after the war, with lodger facilities for FAA aircraft at the RAF station. It was renamed RAF Gibraltar in December 1966. Ships helicopter flights often disembark when the parent ship is in the area. Home for Lynx flight of No.815 Sqdn 1982 to 1991.

NOWRA
RAAF station near Sydney loaned to the FAA on 2 January 1945 as one its main bases in Australia. Occupied by MONAB No.1 as HMS *Nabbington* until this was paid off on 15 November 1945, being then taken over by MONAB No.5 as HMS *Nabswick*. When this paid off on 18 March 1946 the station was handed over to the Royal Australian Navy as its primary aircraft shore base, being still in use as HMAS Albatross.

PALISADOES
Commissioned in Jamaica on 21 December 1940, being initially administered by HMS *Malabar*, the local naval base. Became independent on 1 August 1941 when it became HMS *Buzzard*. With a capacity of 60 aircraft it provided Reserve Aircraft Storage and could accommodate disembarked squadrons. Paid off 15 July 1943 and reduced the following day to a Care and Maintenance basis, being then administered by HMS *Moga*. The station was finally paid off 31 December 1944.

PIARCO
FAA station in Trinidad, commissioned 6 November 1940 as HMS *Goshawk* and operated mainly as No.1 Observer School. Could accommodate 162 aircraft including Reserve Aircraft Storage. Paid off 28 February 1946.

PITYILU
The base on the island of Manus in the Admiralty Islands for HMS *Pioneer*'s Test Flight Party, and eventually for R.N.F.A.P.1 (RN Forward Aircraft Pool No.1), opened by June 1945.

PLAISANCE
Airfield on Maurutius, on the books of HMS *Sambur*, the local naval base. Intended to house disembarked squadrons, but severely damaged in a cyclone and never completed.

PONAM
US Navy airstrip on the island of Manus in the Admiralty Islands. Handed over to the Royal Navy and opened on 2 April 1945 by MONAB No.4 as HMS *Nabaron*. This withdrew to Australia after VJ-Day.

PORT REITZ
Wartime facilities for an RN Air Section on a SAAF/RAF station near Mombasa. Operated as part of HMS *Kipanga II*, under the control of HMS *Kipanga* at Kilindini. Housed a TBR Pool and had aircraft erection facilities. Could also take two disembarked squadrons. Reduced to a Care and Maintenance basis by 1945.

PUTTALAM
Airstrip in Ceylon used from May 1942. Under the control of HMS *Lanka* until being commissioned 1 February 1943 as HMS *Rajaliya*. With a capacity of 104 aircraft, it provided accommodation for disembarked squadrons and also Reserve Aircraft Storage. Paid off 31 October 1945, and transferred to local civil authorities 12 December 1945.

QUONSET POINT
US Navy station on Rhode Island, New York used during the war by FAA squadrons forming in the USA. Initially commissioned on 1 October 1942 as HMS *Asbury*, which also had responsibility for escort carriers working up in the USA. Became HMS *Saker II* when HMS *Asbury* paid off on 31 March 1944.

RATMALANA
A RAF station in Ceylon with lodger facilities for FAA squadrons. Also used as a Personnel Transit Camp. Used the ships name HMS *Seruwa* around 1946.

ST THOMAS MOUNT
Lodger facilities for an RN Air Section on an RAF station near Madras in southern India. Could take up to 7 disembarked squadrons, though never called upon to do so.

SANTA CRUZ
Lodger facilities for an RN Air Section on an RAF station near Bombay, India. Capacity of up to 4 disembarked squadrons.

SCHOFIELDS
A RAAF station near Sydney, loaned to the FAA from February 1945 and used by MONAB No.3 as HMS *Nabthorpe*. This paid off on 15 November 1945 and the station was then taken over by MONAB No.6 as HMS *Nabstock*. The latter disbanded 8 June 1946 and the station was paid off, being then handed over to the Royal Australian Navy to become HMAS *Nirimba* as an apprentice training school.

SELETAR
Prewar RAF station at Singapore occupied during World War 2 by the Japanese, but returned to RAF use after VJ-Day. Lodger facilities for FAA squadrons.

SEMBAWANG
Aerodrome at Singapore used by the FAA from 1 October 1945 being initially occupied by MONAB No.9 as HMS *Nabrock*. Commissioned as HMS *Simbang* when the mobile base paid off 15 December 1945. HMS *Simbang* paid off 31 December 1947 and the station was temporarily reduced to a Care and Maintenance basis until being transferred to the RAF 16 January 1948. Recommissioned as HMS *Simbang* 28 January 1950, later reverting to RAF control. Again recommissioned as HMS *Simbang* on 1 July 1953, being paid off and reduced to a Care and Maintenance basis on 1 April 1957. Next recommissioned as HMS *Simbang* on 4 September 1962 and used by many visiting FAA squadrons. Transferred to Malaysian control 1971.

SIGRIYA
Lodger facilities for an RN Air Section on an RAF station in Ceylon. Able to take one disembarked squadron.

SPLIT
Former seaplane base at civil airport in Croatia, used as a base for Sea King flight of No.845 Sqdn from December 1992, operating in support of UN forces providing humanitarian aid in Bosnia.

SQUANTUM
US Navy Base used from September 1943 by newly formed torpedo squadrons. Returned to US Navy in July 1944.

SULUR
An RAF station in southern India, also known as Sollur, transferred to the FAA in June 1944 for development as an Aircraft Storage Depot. Commissioned 1 February 1945 under the ships name HMS *Vairi* as an RN Aircraft Yard, under the control of HMS *Garuda* at Coimbatore. Intended to have Reserve Aircraft Storage with a capacity of 300 aircraft. Paid off 1 April 1946.

TA KALI
Wartime RAF station in Malta with lodger facilities for the FAA under the control of HMS *St.Angelo*, the local naval base. Transferred to the FAA on 1 April 1945 and commissioned as HMS *Goldfinch* for use by a Fleet Requirements Unit. Returned to the RAF on 9 June 1953.

TAMBARAM
RN Air Station and Aircraft Maintenance Yard in southern India, commissioned on 1 July 1944 as HMS *Valluru*. With a capacity of 72 aircraft it housed a Fleet Requirements Unit and provided facilities for disembarked squadrons. It was also intended to house a RN Aircraft Repair Yard, but this was not completed before the end of the war. Paid off 1 December 1945 and handed over to RAF control as a transit camp.

TANGA
RN Air Station in Tanganyika, commissioned on 1 October 1942 as HMS *Kilele*. With facilities for up to 96 aircraft, it housed disembarked squadrons and also had limited facilities for erecting aircraft. Paid off on 31 May 1944 and reduced to a Care and Maintenance basis.

TENGAH
RAF station opened at Singapore in August 1939. Occupied by the Japanese from February 1942, but returned to RAF use after VJ-Day. Lodger facilities after the war for FAA squadrons, and a naval Aircraft Holding Unit was also based there for some years.

VAVUNIYA
Lodger facilities on an RAF station in Ceylon for an RN Air Section able to take one disembarked squadron.

VOI
RN Air Section in East Africa operating as part of HMS *Kipanga II* under the control of HMS *Kipanga* at Kilindini, the port base for Mombasa. Provided temporary accommodation for disembarked squadrons until being reduced to a Care and Maintenance basis.

WINGFIELD
SAAF station with lodger facilities for the FAA from 1941 under the control of HMS *Afrikander I*, the RN base at Simonstown. Commissioned on 15 March 1942 as HMS *Malagas*, as a RN Air Station and Aircraft Repair Yard. Took over the RN Air Section from Wynberg on 18 May 1942. Could accommodate up to 222 aircraft and towards the end of the war undertook the formation and work-up of Hellcat squadrons. Paid off 31 May 1946 and station reduced to a Care and Maintenance basis.

WYNBERG
Lodger facilities on a SAAF station for a RN Air Section from 1940, under the control of HMS *Afrikander III* until 2 June 1941 when transferred to the control of HMS *Afrikander I*, the RN base at Simonstown. The Air Section transferred to Wingfield on 18 May 1942.

YARMOUTH
RCAF station in Nova Scotia, transferred to the FAA on 1 January 1943 for use by No.2 Telegraphist Air Gunners School, though known by the Canadians as No.1 Naval Air Gunners School. With a capacity of 480 pupils, it came under the control of HMS *Canada* at Dartmouth, this becoming HMS *Seaborn* on 1 July 1944. The school was paid off on 30 March 1945.

RCAF Yarmouth, Nova Scotia in 1943. (via Bert Joss)

AIRCRAFT CARRIERS

This section contains brief histories of Aircraft Carriers, Seaplane Carriers, Maintenance Carriers and Aircraft Transports, with details of Flights (400 series), allocated 1923 to 1933 and Squadrons (700, 800, 1700 and 1800 series), embarked from 1933. For clarity embarkations purely for passage, with or without aircraft, and some short detachments post-war, have been omitted.

Current Ships:

HMS ARK ROYAL(4) R07
Invincible-class Light Aircraft Carrier. Built Wallsend 1978-85, commissioned 1 November 1985, laid up into reserve September 1994, due refit 1996/7, parent ship letter R.

801	Jul 1985-Oct 1994	Sea Harrier FRS.1
820	Feb 1986-Oct 1994	Sea King HAS.5/6
849B	Jun 1986-Oct 1994	Sea King AEW.2
846	Jan 1993-Jul 1993	Sea King HC.4

HMS ILLUSTRIOUS(2) R06
Invincible-class Light Aircraft Carrier. Built Wallsend 1976-82, commissioned 18 June 1982, laid up at Portsmouth 1989, refit 1991-94 including 12 degree ski ramp, returned to service October 1994, parent ship letter L.

809	Aug 1982-Dec 1982	Sea Harrier FRS.1
814	Aug 1982-Dec 1982	Sea King HAS.5
845 Dt2	Oct 1982-Dec 1982	Wessex HU.5
800	Sep 1983-Jun 1989	Sea Harrier FRS.1
814	Sep 1983-Jun 1989	Sea King HAS.5
849A	Mar 1985-May 1989	Sea King AEW.2
820	Oct 1994-to date	Sea King HAS.6
849B	Oct 1994-to date	Sea King AEW.2
801	Oct 1994-to date	Sea Harrier FRS.2

HMS INVINCIBLE R05
Invincible-class Light Aircraft Carrier. Built Barrow-in-Furness 1973-80, commissioned 11 July 1980, Falklands 1982, refit 1986-89 including 12 degree ski ramp, rededicated 18 May 1989, parent ship letter N.

820	May 1980-Nov 1980	Sea King HAS.2
820	Nov 1980-Jul 1985	Sea King HAS.5
801	Jan 1981-Jul 1985	Sea Harrier FRS.1
846	Dts 1981-to date	Sea King HC.4
809	Apr 1982-Jul 1982	Sea Harrier FRS.1
899	Apr 1982-Jul 1982	Sea Harrier FRS.1
815/231	May 1982-Jul 1982	Lynx HAS.2
849A	May 1989-to date	Sea King AEW.2
800	Jun 1989-to date	Sea Harrier FRS.1
814	Jun 1989-to date	Sea King HAS.5/6

HMS OCEAN(2) R14
Landing Platform Helicopter (LPH). Building Govan 1993-96, to be fitted out at Barrow-in-Furness, to commission August 1997, to operate Helicopters and Harriers, parent ship letter O.

* * * * * * * *

Other Carriers:

HMS ACTIVITY D94
Escort carrier. Built Dundee 1938-42, laid down as mercantile *Telemachus*, purchased on stocks and renamed *Empire Activity*, then HMS *Activity* (L946). Commissioned November 1942, war service Atlantic and Arctic, became merchantile *Breconshire* 1946, scrapped at Kobe 1967.

819	Aug 1943-Apr 1944	Swordfish II
833	Apr 1944-Sep 1944	Wildcat V
836F	Apr 1944-Sep 1944	Swordfish II

HMS AFRICA
Ark Royal-class Fleet Attack Carrier. Building Tyne, cancelled October 1945 and scrapped on slip.

HMAS/HMS ALBATROSS I22 (D22 from 1940)
Seaplane carrier. Built Sydney 1926-28, commissioned in RAN 1928, transferred to RN July 1938 in part payment for the Cruiser HMAS *Hobart*. Used mainly by No.710 Sqdn off West Africa but also Madagascar and in Indian Ocean. Fitted EIIIH catapult (ex HMS *Orion*) c.August 1941. Became a repair ship November 1943, Home Fleet 1944, reserve 1945, became mercantile *Hellenic Prince* 1946, scrapped 1954.

710	Aug 1939-Oct 1943	Walrus I

HMS ALBION 08 (R07 1947)
Hermes-class Fleet Carrier. Built Wallsend 1944-54, commissioned 27 May 1954, Suez 1956, converted to Commando carrier 1959, Malaysia and Borneo 1962-64. Parent ship letter Z 1954-57, then A 1958-72. Paid off 1 March 1973, sold October 1973 for North Sea use but broken up from November 1973.

815	Jul 1954-Oct 1954	Avenger AS.5
849C	Jul 1954-Aug 1959	Skyraider AEW.1
898	Aug 1954-Apr 1955	Seahawk FB.3
813	Sep 1954-Mar 1955	Wyvern S.4
803	Nov 1954-Mar 1955	Sea Hawk FB.3
845 Dt	Nov 1954-Mar 1955	Whirlwind HAS.22
811	Jun 1955	Sea Hawk FB.3
890	Jul 1955-Sep 1955	Sea Venom FAW.20
807	Jul 1955-Nov 1955	Sea Hawk FGA.4
801	Sep 1955-Oct 1955	Sea Hawk FGA.4
810	Jan 1956-May 1956	Sea Fury FGA.4/6
825	Jan 1956-May 1956	Firefly AS.5
849D	Jan 1956-May 1956	Skyraider AEW.1
892	Jan 1956-May 1956	Sea Venom FAW.21
802	Sep 1956-Dec 1956	Sea Hawk FB.3
800	Sep 1956-Oct 1957	Sea Hawk FGA.6
809	Sep 1956-Aug 1959	Sea Venom FAW.21
845	Jan 1957-May 1957	Whirlwind HAS.22/HAR.3
824	Jan 1957-Oct 1957	Gannet AS.4
802	Feb 1957-Mar 1957	Sea Hawk FB.3
701C	Jul 1958-Sep 1958	Whirlwind HAR1
804	Jul 1958-Aug 1959	Sea Hawk FGA.6
820	Aug 1958-Mar 1959	Whirlwind HAS.7
815	Jan 1960-Dec 1960	Whirlwind HAS.7
806	Feb 1960-Dec 1960	Sea Hawk FGA.6
849D	Feb 1960-Dec 1960	Sykraider AEW.1
894	Feb 1960-Dec 1960	Sea Venom FAW.22
846	Sep 1962-Jan 1964	Whirlwind HAS.7
845	Sep 1962-Jun 1965	Wessex HAS.1
848	Nov 1964-Jul 1969	Wessex HU.5
845	May 1970-Feb 1971	Wessex HU.5
848	Mar 1971-Jul 1972	Wessex HU.5
845	Sep 1972-Nov 1972	Wessex HU.5

HMS AMEER(1)
Escort Carrier. Was to be *Ameer* but retained by USN as USS *Alazon Bay* January 1943, later USS *Casablanca*.

HMS AMEER(2) D01
Ruler-class Assault/Fighter Carrier. Built Seattle-Tacoma 1942-43 and commissioned 28 June 1943 as USS *Baffins Bay* AVG-35. Transferred to RN 19 July 1943, war service East Indies and British Pacific Fleet, damaged in kamikaze attack 26 July 1945. Returned to USN 17 January 1946, became mercantile *Robin Kirk* 1948, scrapped at Kaohsiung 1969.

845	Jul 1944-Aug 1944	Wildcat V
804	Dec 1944-Mar 1945	Hellcat II
845	Dec 1944	Wildcat V
896	Apr 1945-Sep 1945	Hellcat IIFB
804	May 1945-Oct 1945	Hellcat II
888	Jun 1945	Hellcat II(PR)
1700 Dt	Jul 1945-Aug 1945	Walrus I

HMS ARBITER D31
Ruler-class Escort Carrier. Built Seattle-Tacoma from April 1943 as USS *St.Simon* ACV/CVE-51. Transferred to RN on completion 31 December 1943, war service Atlantic, mainly employed as ferry and transport. Returned to USN 3 March 1946, became mercantile *Coracero* 1948, *President Macapagal* 1964, *Lucky Two* 1971, scrapped at Kaohsiung 1972.

853	May 1944-Jun 1944	Avenger II
1820	Jun 1944	Helldiver I
1843	Feb 1945-Jul 1945	Corsair IV

HMS ARCHER D78
Archer-class Escort Carrier. Built Chester, Pennsylvania, laid down as mercantile *Mormacland*, launched 14 December 1939, converted to *BAVG-1*, first American built conversion to British order, commissioned on completion at Norfolk, Va 18 November 1941. War service in Atlantic, paid off March 1945, returned to

USN 18 January 1946, became mercantile *Empire Lagan* 1946, *Anna Salen* 1949, *Tasmania* 1955 and *Union Reliance* 1961, scrapped at New Orleans March 1962.

834	Mar 1942-Dec 1942	Swordfish I/II
882 Dt2	Apr 1942-Jul 1942	Martlet I
893 Dt2	Jul 1942	Martlet I
892	Feb 1943-Aug 1943	Martlet IV
819	May 1943-Aug 1943	Swordfish II

HMS ARGUS I49 (D49 1940)
Fleet Carrier. Built Clyde 1914-18, laid down as Italian Liner *Conte Rosso*, construction suspended 1914-16. Purchased August 1916 to be seaplane carrier, completed as carrier, commissioned September 1918. Refit 1925-26, to reserve July 1930, reconditioned 1937-38, recommissioned 9 August 1938 as parent ship for radio controlled aircraft. To deck landing training in September 1939, operational late 1940, war service Atlantic and Mediterranean, reverted to deck landing training September 1943, harbour service 1944, sold to scrap Inverkeithing in December 1946.

401	May 1923-Oct 1925	Nightjar/Flycatcher
442	May 1923-Oct 1924	Panther
441	Jul 1923-Oct 1923	Panther
423	May 1924-Sep 1925	Bison/Walrus
442	Jan 1925-Oct 1925	Fairey IIID
422	Jan 1927-May 1928	Fairey IIID
443A	Jan 1927-May 1928	Fairey IIID
404B	Feb 1927-May 1928	Flycatcher
441	Feb 1927-Mar 1930	Fairey IIID/IIIF
422	May 1928-Apr 1929	Blackburn
401	Jun 1928-Mar 1930	Flycatcher
450	Apr 1929-Mar 1930	Blackburn
701	Jun 1940-Oct 1940	Walrus I
821X	Dec 1940	Swordfish I
825 Dt2	Dec 1940-Jan 1941	Swordfish I
800Y	May 1941	Fulmar I
804B	Sep 1941-Oct 1941	Fulmar II
828	Sep 1941-Oct 1941	Albacore I/Swordfish I
818 Dt2	Sep 1941-Nov 1941	Swordfish I
812	Nov 1941-Apr 1942	Swordfish I
804 Dt2	Nov 1941	Fulmar II
807 Dt4	Nov 1941	Fulmar II
807	Feb 1942-Jun 1942	Fulmar II
801	May 1942-Jun 1942	Sea Hurricane Ib
824 Dt4	May 1942-Jun 1942	Swordfish I
804	Jul 1942-Aug 1942	Hurricane IIb
880	Oct 1942-Nov 1942	Spitfire Vb
837A Dt6	Jan 1943-Feb 1943	Swordfish I/II

HMS ARK ROYAL(1), I35 (D35 1940)
Seaplane Carrier. Built Blythe, laid down as collier but taken over during construction, commissioned December 1914, renamed HMS *Pegasus* December 1934, as name required for new Aircraft Carrier. Converted to catapult ship 1940, war service Atlantic, training ship 1941-44, to reserve 1 September 1944 and later relegated to accommodation ship, became mercantile *Anita I* October 1946, scrapped Greys Yard, Essex October 1950.

804 Dt2	Feb 1941-Jul 1941	Fulmar I/II

HMS ARK ROYAL(2) D91
Fleet Carrier. Built Birkenhead 1935-38, commissioned December 1938, war service Norway, Atlantic and Mediterranean, torpedoed by *U-81* 13 November 1941, sank next day under tow off Gibraltar.

800	Jan 1939-Apr 1941	Skua II
810	Jan 1939-Sep 1941	Swordfish I
814	Jan 1939-Aug 1939	Swordfish I
820	Jan 1939-Sep 1939	Shark I
821	Jan 1939-Apr 1940	Swordfish I
803	Apr 1939-Oct 1940	Skua II/Roc I
818	Aug 1939-Oct 1939	Swordfish I
820	Sep 1939-Jun 1941	Swordfish I
801	Apr 1940-May 1940	Skua II
701	Jun 1940	Walrus I
818	Jun 1940-Jul 1941	Swordfish I
821X	Dec 1940-Jan 1941	Swordfish I
807	Apr 1940-Nov 1941	Fulmar II
800Y	Jun 1941	Fulmar I
825	Jun 1941-Nov 1941	Swordfish I
816	Jul 1941-Nov 1941	Swordfish I
812	Sep 1941-Nov 1941	Swordfish I
808	Oct 1941-Nov 1941	Fulmar II
828	Oct 1941	Albacore I/Swordfish I

HMS ARK ROYAL(3) R09
Ark Royal-class Fleet Carrier. Built Birkenhead 1943-55, ex-HMS *Irresistible*, renamed May 1945, commissioned 22 February 1955, first ship with angled flight deck and steam catapult, major refit 1966-70, parent ship letter O 1955-57, then R 1958-78, paid off 4 December 1978, sold to scrap.

800	Sep 1955-Mar 1956	Sea Hawk FGA.4/6
898	Sep 1955-Apr 1956	Seahawk FGA.6/FGA.4
824	Oct 1955-Apr 1956	Gannet AS.1
849B	Oct 1955-Jun 1958	Skyraider AEW.1
809	Nov 1955-Feb 1956	Sea Venom FAW.21
898	Jul 1956-Jun 1957	Seahawk FGA.6
815	Dec 1956-Jun 1958	Gannet AS.1/4
831	Jan 1957-Nov 1957	Wyvern S.4
802	Feb 1957-Jun 1958	Sea Hawk FB.3/FB.5
804	Feb 1957-May 1958	Seahawk FGA.6
893	Feb 1957-Jun 1958	Sea Venom FAW.21
701B	Jan 1958-Sep 1958	Dragonfly HR.5
800	Jan 1958-Jul 1958	Sea Hawk FGA.6
807	Feb 1960-Feb 1961	Scimitar F.1
800	Mar 1960-Dec 1963	Scimitar F.1
820	Mar 1960-Oct 1960	Whirlwind HAS.7
824	Mar 1960-Feb 1961	Whirlwind HAS.7
849A	May 1960-Feb 1961	Gannet AEW.3
831A	Oct 1960-Nov 1960	Gannet ECM.4
831B	Nov 1960-Dec 1960	Sea Venom ECM.22
893	Nov 1960-Feb 1961	Sea Vixen FAW.1
831A	Mar 1961-Apr 1961	Gannet ECM.4
890	Oct 1961-Dec 1963	Sea Vixen FAW.1
815	Nov 1961-Dec 1963	Wessex HAS.1
849C	Nov 1961-Dec 1963	Gannet AEW.3
831A Dt2	Mar 1962-Dec 1962	Gannet ECM.4
801	Feb 1963-Mar 1963	Buccaneer S.1
803	Dec 1964-Oct 1966	Scimitar F.1
849C	Jan 1965-Oct 1966	Gannet AEW.3
890	Jan 1965-Oct 1966	Sea Vixen FAW.1
815	Jun 1965-Sep 1966	Wessex HAS.1
892	Mar 1969-Dec 1978	Phantom FG.1
809	Jan 1970-Dec 1978	Buccaneer S.2
849B	Jan 1970-Dec 1978	Gannet AEW.3
824	Feb 1970-Dec 1978	Sea King HAS.2

HMS ARROGANT
Hermes-class Fleet Carrier. Building Tyne, cancelled 1945 and scrapped on slip.

HMS ATHELING(1)
Escort Carrier. Was to be HMS *Atheling* but retained by USN as USS *Anguilla Bay*.

HMS ATHELING(2)
Escort Carrier. Was to be HMS *Atheling* but retained by USN as USS *Mission Bay*.

HMS ATHELING(3) D51
Ruler-class Escort Carrier. Built Seattle-Tacoma 1942-43 as USS *Glacier ACV/CVE-33*, transferred to RN on completion and commissioned 31 July 1943. War service East Indies, returned US Navy 13 December 1946, mercantile *Roma* 1950, scrapped Vado 1967.

1838	Feb 1944-Apr 1944	Corsair II
889	May 1944-Jun 1944	Seafire L.IIc/LR.IIc
890	May 1944-Jul 1944	Wildcat V
1838	Aug 1944-Sep 1944	Corsair II

HMS ATHENE
Aircraft Transport. Built Greenock, ex mercantile *Clan Brodie*, launched 12 October 1940 and acquired by RN, no flight deck. Reverted to *Clan Brodie* 1946, scrapped Hong Kong June 1963.

HMS ATTACKER D02
Attacker-class Assault/Escort Carrier. Built San Francisco, laid down as mercantile *US Steel Artisan*, launched 27 September 1941, later USS *Barnes AVG-7*, transferred to RN on completion and commissioned 10 October 1942. War service in Atlantic, Mediterranean and East Indies, returned to USN 5 January 1946, became mercantile *Castel Forte* 1948, *Fairsky* 1958, *Philippine Tourist* 1979, scrapped 1980.

838	Mar 1943-Apr 1943	Swordfish I
840	Mar 1943-Apr 1943	Swordfish I/II
886	Jun 1943-Oct 1943	Seafire L.IIc/ Swordfish II
879	Jul 1943-Nov 1945	Seafire L.IIc/LR.IIc/FXVII
886	Dec 1943-Feb 1944	Seafire L.IIc
809	Nov 1944-Dec 1944	Seafire L.IIc

HMS AUDACIOUS
Ark Royal-class Fleet Carrier. See HMS *Eagle(3)*.
HMS AUDACITY D10
Escort Carrier. Built Bremen, launched 29 March 1939 as German passenger liner MV *Hannover*, captured 8 March 1940 by cruiser HMS *Dunedin* in Mona Passage, West Indies. Renamed *Empire Audacity*, converted to become first Escort Carrier and commissioned July 1941, war service in Atlantic, torpedoed and sunk by *U-751* 21 December 1941 off Portugal.
    802   Sep 1941-Dec 1941   Martlet I/III

HMS AVENGER(1) D14
Archer-class Escort Carrier. Built Chester, Pennsylvania, laid down as mercantile *Rio Hudson*, launched 27 November 1940, converted as *BAVG-2*. Transferred to RN on completion 2 March 1942, war service Arctic and Atlantic, torpedoed and sunk by *U-155* 15 November 1942 west of Gibraltar returning from North Africa.

883	Jun 1942-Nov 1942	Sea Hurricane Ib/IIb
802	Jul 1942-Nov 1942	Sea Hurricane Ib/IIb
825	Jul 1942-Sep 1942	Swordfish I/II
833B Dt3	Oct 1942-Nov 1942	Swordfish II

HMS BATTLER D18
Attacker-class Escort Carrier. Built Pascagoula, Mississippi, laid down as mercantile *Mormactern*, launched April 1942, converted as USS *Altamaha* AVG-6. Transferred to RN on completion 31 October 1942, war service Atlantic, Mediterranean and Indian Ocean, parent ship letter B 1945, returned to USN 12 February 1946 and scrapped at Baltimore.

840	Dec 1942	Swordfish I/II
835	Apr 1943-Jul 1943	Swordfish II
808	Apr 1943-Sep 1943	Seafire L.IIc
807	Aug 1943-Oct 1943	Seafire L.IIc
834	Sep 1943-Oct 1944	Seafire L.IIc/Wildcat V

HMS BEGUM(1)
Escort Carrier. Was to be HMS *Begum* but retained by USN 3 April 1943 as USS *Natoma Bay* AVG-62.

HMS BEGUM(2) D38
Ruler-class Escort Carrier. Built Seattle-Tacoma 1942-43 as USS *Bolinas* ACV/AVG-36, commissioned 22 July 1943 as *CVE-36*. Withdrawn 2 August 1943 and transferred to RN as replacement for AVG-62, HMS *Begum(1)*, war service Indian Ocean, returned to USN 4 January 1946, became mercantile *Raki* 1948 and *I-Yung* 1966, scrapped at Kaohsiung 1974.
    832   May 1944-Feb 1945   Avenger II/Wildcat V

HMS BITER D97
Archer-class Escort Carrier. Built Chester, Pennsylvania, laid down as mercantile *Rio Parana*, launched 18 December 1940, converted to *BAVG-3*, transferred to RN on completion 5 May 1942, war service in Atlantic. Paid off October 1944, transferred to France January 1945 as *Dixmunde*, returned to USN 9 April 1945 and loaned to France the same day, used as transport on Indo-China run, finally returned to USN 10 June 1966. Sunk as test target 1966.

833 Dt3	Sep 1942	Swordfish I
800	Oct 1942-Nov 1942	Sea Hurricane IIc
833A Dt3	Oct 1942-Nov 1942	Swordfish II
811 Dt	Jan 1944-Oct 1944	Wildcat V
811	Feb 1943-Aug 1944	Swordfish II/Wildcat IV

HMCS BONAVENTURE 22
Majestic-class Light Fleet Carrier. Built Belfast 1943-56, ex-HMS *Powerful*, construction suspended 1946-52, sold to Canada 1952, commissioned 17 January 1957, deck identity 22, scrapped in Taiwan 1971.

870	Mar 1957-Sep 1962	F2H-3 Banshee
880	Sep 1957-Dec 1959	Tracker CS2F-1/2
881	Sep 1957-Jul 1959	Tracker CS2F-1
871	Feb 1958-Mar 1959	F2H-3 Banshee

HMS BULWARK R08
Hermes-class Fleet Carrier. Built Belfast 1944-54, commissioned 29 October 1954. Suez 1956, converted to Commando carrier 1959-60, Kuwait 1960, Malaysia and Borneo 1964-65, parent ship letter B, laid up 1975-78. Finally paid off March 1981, broken up at Cairn Ryan from April 1984.

807	Feb 1955-Mar 1955	Sea Hawk F2
898	Apr 1955-Sep 1955	Sea Hawk FB.3/FGA.6
801	May 1955-Jun 1955	Sea Hawk FGA.4
800 Dt	Jun 1955	Sea Hawk FB.3
811	Jun 1955	Sea Hawk FB.3
845	Sep 1955-Oct 1955	Whirlwind HAS.22
895	Apr 1956-Dec 1956	Seahawk FB.3/FGA.4/FGA.6
802	Jun 1956-Jul 1956	Sea Hawk F2/FGA.4
804	Jun 1956-Dec 1956	Sea Hawk FGA.6
810	Aug 1956-Dec 1956	Sea Hawk FGA.4/6
849D	Jun 1957-Nov 1958	Skyraider AEW.1
891	Jun 1957-Oct 1958	Sea Venom FAW.22
898	Jun 1957-Sep 1957	Seahawk FGA.6
820	Jun 1957-Dec 1957	Gannet AS.1
845	Aug 1957-Nov 1958	Whirlwind HAS.7
801	Nov 1957-Nov 1958	Sea Hawk FGA.6
701D	Nov 1957-Dec 1957	Dragonfly HR.5
848	Mar 1960-Dec 1962	Whirlwind HAS.7
847	Mar 1964-Apr 1964	Whirlwind HAS.7
845	Jun 1965-Jan 1966	Whirlwind HAS.7
845	Jan 1966-Oct 1969	Wessex HU.5
848	Sep 1969-Aug 1970	Wessex HU.5
847	Mar 1970-Jun 1970	Wessex HU.5
845	Apr 1971-May 1972	Wessex HU.5
846	Jan 1972-Apr 1972	Wessex HU.5
848	Nov 1972-Mar 1976	Wessex HU.5
814	Jun 1983-Jul 1973	Sea King HAS.1
826	Feb 1979-Sep 1980	Sea King HAS.2
814	Feb 1980-Mar 1981	Sea King HAS.2
845 Dt	Oct 1980-Nov 1980	Wessex HU.5

HMS CAMPANIA D48
Escort Carrier. Built Belfast 1941-43, converted from uncompleted hull of refrigerated cargo ship, commissioned 8 March 1944. War service Atlantic, Norway and Arctic, parent ship letter Z 1945, used as mobile exhibition ship for Festival of Britain 1951, sold to scrap and broken up Blythe from November 1955.

842Q	Oct 1942-Nov 1942	Wildcat V
784B	Mar 1944-Mar 1945	Fulmar IINF/Firefly INF
813	Apr 1944-Mar 1945	Swordfish III/Wildcat V
850 Dt	Oct 1944-Nov 1944	Wildcat V
825	Mar 1945-Apr 1945	Swordfish III/Wildcat VI
821 Dt	Apr 1945-May 1945	Barracuda II
815 Dt	May 1945	Wildcat VI

HMS CENTAUR R06
Hermes-class Fleet Carrier. Built Belfast 1944-53, commissioned 1 September 1953. Kuwait 1960, depot ship from 1966, parent ship letter L 1953-54, then C 1954-67, paid off February 1971, broken up at Cairn Ryan from October 1972.

806	Jul 1954-Nov 1955	Sea Hawk FB.3
810	Jul 1954-Mar 1955	Sea Fury FB.11
820	Jul 1954-Feb 1955	Avenger AS.4
845 Dt	Nov 1954-Mar 1955	Whirlwind HAS.22
814	Feb 1955-Nov 1955	Avenger AS.5
803	Mar 1955-Nov 1955	Sea Hawk FB.3
801	Jan 1956-May 1956	Sea Hawk FGA.4
813	Jan 1956-May 1956	Sea Hawk FB.3
849D	Dec 1958-Jun 1959	Skyraider AEW.1
845	Jan 1959-Mar 1959	Whirlwind HAS.7
801	Jan 1959-Jul 1960	Sea Hawk FGA.6
891	Jan 1959-Jul 1960	Sea Venom FAW.22
810	Jun 1959-Jul 1960	Gannet AS.4
824	Mar 1960-May 1963	Whirlwind HAS.7
807	Apr 1961-May 1962	Scimitar F.1
849A	Apr 1961-Jun 1963	Gannet AEW.3
893	Apr 1961-May 1963	Sea Vixen FAW.1
849B	Nov 1963-Jul 1965	Gannet AEW.3
892	Nov 1963-Jul 1965	Sea Vixen FAW.1
815	Jan 1964-Dec 1964	Wessex HAS.1

HMS CHARGER(1)
Archer-class Escort Carrier. Built Chester Pennsylvania, laid down as mercantile *Rio de la Plata*, launched 1 March 1941, converted to *BAVG-4*. Transferred to RN on completion but returned to USN 4 October 1941 as USS *Charger*, AVG-30 January 1942, commissioned 3 March 1942 as *ACV-30*, later *CVE-30*, used for RN deck landing training. Became liner *Fairsea* 1949, believed scrapped 1968-69.

HMS CHARGER(2)
Ruler-class Escort Carrier. See HMS *Ravager*.

HMS CHASER D32
Attacker-class Escort Carrier. Built Pascagoula, Mississippi, laid down as mercantile *Mormacgulf*, launched 19 June 1942, purchased by USN 9 April 1943 as USS *Breton* ACV-10. Transferred to RN, war service Atlantic, Arctic, Pacific Fleet 1945, returned to USN May 1946, became mercantile *Aagtekerk* 1948 and *E-Yung* 1967, scrapped at Kaohsiung 1972.

835	Nov 1943-Dec 1943	Swordfish II
816	Feb 1944-Mar 1944	Wildcat V
899	Jan 1945-Apr 1945	Seafire L.III

HMS COLOSSUS 15
Colossus-class Light Fleet Carrier. Built Tyne 1942-44, commissioned 16 December 1944, Pacific Fleet 1945-46, parent ship letters C and D 1945-46, then J and S 1946. To France August 1946 as *Arromanches*, five year loan with option to buy, purchased in 1951, deleted 1974, scrapped at Toulon 1978.

827	Jan 1945-Jul 1946	Barracuda II
1846	Jan 1945-Jul 1946	Corsair IV

HMS COURAGEOUS D50
Fleet Carrier. Built Tyne 1915-16 as Cruiser, commissioned 4 November 1916. To reserve 1919, converted 1924-28 and recommissioned 14 February 1928 as Carrier, refit 1936, torpedoed and sunk by *U-29* 17 September 1939 in Atlantic west of Ireland.

404	May 1928-Nov 1932	Flycatcher
407	May 1928-Nov 1931	Flycatcher
445	May 1928-Mar 1933	Fairey IIIF
446	May 1928-Mar 1933	Fairey IIIF
463	May 1928-Mar 1933	Dart
464	May 1928-Mar 1933	Dart
450	Sep 1929-Apr 1933	Blackburn/Fairey IIIF
449	Sep 1930-May 1931	Blackburn
401	Sep 1930-Sep 1932	Flycatcher
442	Oct 1931-Mar 1932	Fairey IIIF
402	Apr 1932-Mar 1932	Flycatcher/Nimrod
404	Nov 1932-Mar 1933	Nimrod/Osprey
800	May 1933-Oct 1938	Nimrod I/II/Osprey
810	May 1933-Nov 1934	Dart/Ripon IIc
820	May 1933-Nov 1934	Fairey IIIF
821	May 1933-Mar 1936	Fairey IIIF/Seal
811	Jul 1934	Ripon IIc
823	Jul 1934-Jul 1935	Fairey IIIF/Seal
820	Nov 1934-Dec 1936	Shark I
810	Nov 1934-Apr 1937	Baffin
822B	Aug 1935-Sep 1935	Fairey IIIF
823A	Jul 1935-Oct 1935	Seal
820	Dec 1936-Oct 1938	Swordfish I
821	Mar 1936-Sep 1937	Shark II
810	Apr 1937-Sep 1937	Shark II
810	Sep 1937-Sep 1938	Swordfish I
821	Sep 1937-Nov 1938	Swordfish I
811	Jan 1939-Apr 1939	Swordfish I
801	Feb 1939-Apr 1939	Sea Gladiator/Skua II
822	Feb May, Sep 1939	Swordfish I
811	Aug 1939-Sep 1939	Swordfish I

HMS DASHER D37
Archer-class Escort Carrier. Built Chester, Pennsylvania 1940-42, laid down as US mercantile *Rio de Janeiro*, converted to *BAVG-5*. Transferred to RN on completion 1 July 1942, war service Atlantic and North Africa, blew up and sank off Arran 27 March 1943.

804	Oct 1942-Nov 1942	Sea Hurricane IIc
837 Dt3	Jan 1943-Feb 1943	Swordfish I/II
891	Jan 1943-Feb 1943	Sea Hurricane IIc
816	Feb 1943-Mar 1943	Swordfish II

HMS EAGLE(1) D94
Fleet Carrier. Built Tyne 1913-24, laid down as Chilean *Dreadnought*-class Battleship *Almirante Cochrane*, construction suspended 1914-17, requisitioned 1918, trials from April 1920. Modified and completed as Carrier 1920-24, commissioned 26 February 1924, deck letter EG 1927, refit 1932, to reserve 5 April 1935, recommissioned 21 January 1937, war service Indian Ocean, Mediterranean and Atlantic, torpedoed and sunk 11 August 1942 by *U-73* north of Algiers during Operation *Pedestal* convoy escort to Malta.

460	Mar 1924-Oct 1930	Dart
440	Mar 1924-Apr 1925	Seagull/Fairey IIID
422	Mar 1924-Mar 1926	Blackburn
402	Mar 1924-May 1931	Flycatcher
440	Aug 1925-Sep 1926	Fairey IIID
441	Jun 1926-Oct 1926	Fairey IIID
423	Feb 1927-Apr 1929	Bison II/Fairey IIIF
421B	Mar 1927-Oct 1927	Bison
448	Jun 1929-May 1931	Fairey IIIF
460	Jan 1931-May 1931	Ripon
803	Apr 1933-Dec 1934	Osprey I
824	Apr 1933-Oct 1934	Fairey IIIF
825	Oct 1934-Mar 1935	Fairey IIIF
824	Jan 1937-Aug 1942	Swordfish I
813	Feb 1937-Mar 1941	Swordfish I
813	Jun 1940-Jan 1942	Sea Gladiator
805 Dt4	Jan 1941-Feb 1941	Fulmar I
804A	Oct 1941	Fulmar II
807	Jun 1942	Fulmar II
801	Jun 1942-Aug 1942	Sea Hurricane Ib
813	Jan 1942-Jun 1942	Sea Hurricane Ib

HMS EAGLE(2)
Ark Royal-class Fleet Carrier. Building on Tyne, cancelled 1945 and scrapped on slip.

HMS EAGLE(3) R05
Ark Royal-class Fleet Carrier. Built Belfast 1942-52, ex-HMS *Audacious*, renamed January 1946, commissioned 1 March 1952, Suez 1956, refit 1964-66, parent ship letter J 1951-57, then E 1957-72, paid off 26 January 1972, scrapped 1978.

800	Mar 1952-May 1954	Attacker FB.1
803	Jun 1952-Dec 1952	Attacker F.1
814	Jun 1952-Nov 1953	Firefly AS.6
827	Mar 1952-Dec 1952	Firebrand TF.5
890	Oct 1952-Dec 1952	Attacker FB.2
849A	Nov 1952-Apr 1959	Skyraider AEW.1
812	Jun 1953-Oct 1953	Firefly AS.6
803	Jan 1953-Apr 1954	Attacker FB.2
809	Jan 1953-Feb 1954	Sea Hornet NF.21
825	Jun 1953-Oct 1953	Firefly AS.5
849C	Jun 1953-Oct 1953	Skyraider AEW.1
815	Jan 1954-May 1954	Avenger AS.4
806	Feb 1954-Jun 1954	Sea Hawk F.1
826	May 1954-Jan 1955	Firefly AS.6
826	Jan 1955-Nov 1955	Gannet AS.1
804	May 1955-Jun 1955	Sea Hawk FGA.4
802	May 1955-Nov 1955	Sea Hawk F.2/FGA.4
827	May 1955-Nov 1955	Wyvern S.4
813	Jun 1955-Nov 1955	Wyvern S.4
845	Aug 1955-Sep 1955	Whirlwind HAS.22
897	Nov 1955-Jan 1957	Sea Hawk FB.3/FGA.6
899	Nov 1955-Jan 1957	Sea Hawk FGA.6
812	Apr 1956-Aug 1956	Gannet AS.6
830	Apr 1956-Dec 1956	Wyvern S.4
892	Aug 1956-Dec 1956	Sea Venom FAW.21
893	Aug 1956-Dec 1956	Sea Venom FAW.21
894	Jan 1957-Apr 1959	Sea Venom FAW.21/22
803	Aug 1957-Mar 1958	Sea Hawk FGA.6
806	Aug 1957-Apr 1959	Sea Hawk FB.5/FGA.6
813	Aug 1957-Apr 1958	Wyvern S.4
814	Aug 1957-Apr 1959	Avenger AS.4
701A	Oct 1957-Sep 1958	Dragonfly HR.5
898	May 1958-Apr 1958	Sea Hawk FGA.6
831B	May 1958-Jul 1958	Sea Venom ECM.22
802	Sep 1958-Mar 1959	Sea Hawk FB.5
824	Feb 1959-Mar 1959	Whirlwind HAS.7
820	May 1960-Jun 1960	Whirlwind HAS.7
800	Dec 1964-Aug 1966	Buccaneer S.1
820	Dec 1964-Oct 1968	Wessex HAS.1
849D	Dec 1964-Jan 1972	Gannet AEW.3
899	Dec 1964-Jan 1972	Sea Vixen FAW.2
826	Apr 1969-Jun 1970	Wessex HAS.3
800	Jun 1967-Jan 1972	Buccaneer S.2
826	Jun 1970-Jan 1972	Sea King HAS.1

HMS EDGAR
Maintenance Carrier. See HMS *Perseus*.

HMS ELEPHANT
Hermes-class Fleet Carrier. See HMS *Hermes(3)*.

HMS EMPEROR(1)
Escort Carrier. Was to be HMS *Emperor* but retained by USN as USS *Nassuk Bay ACV-67*, became USS *Solomons* November 1943.

HMS EMPEROR(2) D98
Ruler-class Assault/Fighter Carrier. Built Seattle-Tacoma 1942-43 as USS *Phybus AVG-34*, commissioned May 1943 as *ACV/CVE-34*. Withdrawn and transferred to RN, war service Norway, Atlantic, Mediterranean and East Indies, returned to USN 12 February 1946 and scrapped.

800	Dec 1943-Sep 1945	Hellcat I/II
804	Dec 1943-Jun 1944	Hellcat I
808 Dt6	Apr 1945	Hellcat II
845	Apr 1945	Avenger I
888	Apr 1945	Hellcat II(PR)
851 Dt	May 1945	Avenger I
896 Dt	Jun 1945	Hellcat IIFB
1700 Dt	Jul 1945-Oct 1945	Walrus I

HMS EMPRESS D42
Ruler-class Assault/Fighter Carrier. Built Seattle-Tacoma 1942-43 as USS *Carnegie CVE/AVG-38*, commissioned 12 August 1943, transferred to RN August 1943, war service Atlantic and East

Indies mainly as Assault CVE, returned to USN 4 February 1946 and scrapped.

850	Jan 1944-Apr 1944		Avenger I
804 Dt4	Feb 1945-Mar 1945		Hellcat II
845	Feb 1945-Mar 1945		Avenger I
888	Feb 1945-Mar 1945		Hellcat II(PR)
804 Dt4	Apr 1945		Hellcat II
845	May 1945-Jun 1945		Avenger I
888	May 1945-Jun 1945		Hellcat II(PR)
896	Jun 1945-Sep 1945		Hellcat IIFB

HMS ENGADINE
Aircraft Transport. Built Dumbarton, ex mercantile *Clan Bucanan*, launched May 1941 and acquired by RN, no flight deck. Reverted to *Clan Bucanan* 1946, scrapped Spain from November 1962.

HMS ETHALION
Maintenance Carrier. See HMS *Pioneer*.

HMS FENCER D64
Attacker-class Escort Carrier. Built San Fransisco, launched April 1942, bought by USN 27 February 1943 as USS *AVG-14*. Transferred to RN 1 March 1943, war service Atlantic, Arctic and Norway, later used as troop transport, returned to USN December 1946. Became mercantile *Roma* 1967, *Galaxy Queen* 1967, *Lady Dina* 1972 and *Caribia 2* 1973, scrapped 1975.

842	Aug 1943-Aug 1944	Swordfish II/Seafire I/II
700W	Sep 1943-Nov 1943	Swordfish
1832A	Nov 1943	Wildcat V
842Q	Nov 1943-Nov 1944	Wildcat V
1832E	Mar 1944	Wildcat V
881	Jun 1944	Wildcat V
850 Dt	Sep 1944-Oct 1944	Wildcat V
852 Dt4	Sep 1944-Oct 1944	Wildcat VI

HMS FORMIDABLE 67
Illustrious-class Fleet Aircraft Carrier. Built Belfast 1937-40, commissioned 31 October 1940, war service Atlantic, Mediterranean and Red Sea, damaged by Luftwaffe 12 May 1941 whilst attempting to cover convoys escaping from Crete. Repaired in USA and returned to service by December 1941, Pacific Fleet 1945, damaged in kamikaze attacks May 1945 and repaired in Australia, laid up December 1945 on return from Far East, parent ship letters R and X 1945. Scrapped at Inverkeithing from November 1953.

827	Jul 1940	Barracuda II
803	Nov 1940-May 1941	Fulmar I
826	Nov 1940-May 1941	Albacore I
829	Nov 1940-Dec 1941	Albacore I/Swordfish I
805 Dt4	Mar 1941-Apr 1941	Fulmar I
806	Mar 1941-May 1941	Fulmar I
810	Dec 1941	Swordfish I
818	Feb 1942-Apr 1942	Albacore I
820	Feb 1942-Nov 1943	Albacore I
888	Feb 1942-Nov 1943	Martlet II/IV
803	Apr 1942	Fulmar II
885	Oct 1942-Nov 1943	Seafire Ib/IIc
893	Oct 1942-Nov 1943	Martlet IV
1841	Jun 1944-Aug 1945	Corsair II
853 Dt4	Jun 1944	Wildcat V
830	Jul 1944	Barracuda II
826	Aug 1944-Sep 1944	Barracuda II
1842	Aug 1944-Aug 1945	Corsair II
848	Sep 1944-Aug 1945	Avenger I

HMS FURIOUS D47
Fleet Carrier. Built Tyne 1915-17, commissioned June 1917 as light battle-cruiser with a forward flying-off deck, decommissioned 1919. Converted to Carrier 1922-25 and recommissioned September 1925, war service Atlantic, Arctic, Norway, North Sea, Mediterranean, to reserve 15 September 1944, used for ship target trials 1945-48. Sold for scrap and stripped at Dalmuir March 1948, broken up at Troon from June 1948.

404	Sep 1925-Oct 1927	Flycatcher
420	Sep 1925-Apr 1929	Blackburn
421	Sep 1925-Apr 1929	Bison
443	Sep 1925-Mar 1930	Fairey IIID/IIIF
461	Nov 1925-Mar 1930	Dart/Ripon
462	Nov 1925-Feb 1929	Dart/Ripon
405	Sep 1926-Mar 1930	Flycatcher
447	May 1929-Mar 1930	Fairey IIIF
449	Oct 1929-Jun 1930	Blackburn
401	Jan 1932-Mar 1933	Flycatcher
407	Jan 1932-Sep 1932	Flycatcher
442	Mar 1932-Mar 1933	Fairey IIIF
465	Mar 1932-Mar 1933	Ripon
466	Mar 1932-Mar 1933	Ripon
801	Apr 1933-Nov 1938	Flycatcher I/Nimrod I/Osprey
811	May 1933-Jan 1935	Ripon IIc
822	Apr 1933-Oct 1938	Fairey IIIF
811	Jan 1935-Nov 1936	Baffin
811	Nov 1936-Oct 1938	Swordfish I
818	Oct 1939-May 1940	Swordfish I
816	Oct 1939-Sep 1940	Swordfish I
801	May 1940-Feb 1941	Skua II
804	May 1940	Sea Gladiator
825	Jul 1940-Apr 1941	Swordfish I
804 Dt5	Sep 1940-Oct 1940	Martlet I
807	Mar 1941-Apr 1941	Fulmar I
800X	May 1941	Fulmar I
800Y	Jun 1941	Fulmar I
800	Jul 1941-Aug 1941	Fulmar II
812	Jul 1941-Aug 1941	Swordfish I
880A Dt4	Jul 1941-Sep 1941	Sea Hurricane Ib
810	Sep 1941	Swordfish I
835	Apr 1942	Swordfish I
822	Jul 1942-Jul 1943	Albacore I
823	Jul 1942-Sep 1942	Albacore I
804	Aug 1942	Hurricane IIb
807	Aug 1942-Feb 1943	Seafire L.IIc
801	Oct 1942-Sep 1944	Seafire
817	Dec 1942-Mar 1943	Albacore I
881 Dt7	Jul 1943	Martlet II
827	Oct 1943-Jun 1944	Barracuda II
830	Oct 1943-Sep 1944	Barracuda II
880	Feb 1944-Oct 1944	Seafire I/F.III
831	Apr 1944-May 1944	Barracuda II
842Q Dt2	Apr 1944	Wildcat V
882 Dt4	May 1944-Jun 1944	Wildcat V
1840	Jul 1944	Hellcat I
842 Dt3	Jul 1944	Swordfish II
827	Aug 1944-Oct 1944	Barracuda II

HMS GIBRALTAR
Gibraltar-class Fleet Attack Carrier. Building on Tyne, cancelled October 1945 and scrapped.

HMS GLORIOUS D77
Fleet Carrier. Built Belfast 1915-17 as light cruiser, commissioned October 1916, to reserve 1919. Converted to carrier 1924-30, recommissioned January 1930, damaged in collision with SS *Florida* 1 April 1931 off Spanish Mediterranean coast, repaired in Malta and returned to service September 1931. Refit 1934-35, war service Indian Ocean and Mediterranean, sunk 8 June 1940 by gunfire from German battlecruisers *Scharnhorst* and *Gneisenau* off Norway.

405	May 1930-Nov 1932	Flycatcher
406	Mar 1930-Feb 1932	Flycatcher
408	Mar 1930-Apr 1931	Flycatcher
441	Apr 1930-Apr 1933	Fairey IIIF
447	Apr 1930-Jan 1932	Fairey IIIF
461	May 1930-Apr 1933	Ripon
462	May 1930-Apr 1933	Ripon
448	May 1931-Apr 1933	Fairey IIIF
460	May 1931-Nov 1932	Ripon
408	Jan 1932-Apr 1933	Nimrod I
409	Jan 1933-Apr 1933	Nimrod I/Osprey
802	Apr 1933-May 1939	Nimrod I/II/Osprey
812	Apr 1933-Jan 1934	Ripon IIc
447	Aug 1933-Apr 1934	Fairey IIIF
812	Jan 1934-Dec 1936	Baffin
822 Dt6	Apr 1934	Fairey IIIF
447 Dt	Oct 1933-Apr 1934	Fairey IIIF
823B	Aug 1935-Oct 1935	Seal
825	Sep 1935-Jul 1936	Fairey IIIF
822B	Sep 1935-Oct 1935	Fairey IIIF
823	Oct 1935-Dec 1936	Seal
823	Dec 1935-Jun 1940	Swordfish I
825	Jul 1936-Apr 1940	Swordfish I
812	Dec 1936-Apr 1940	Swordfish I
802	Aug 1939-Jun 1940	Sea Gladiator
803	Apr 1940	Skua II
804	Apr 1940-May 1940	Sea Gladiator
701	May 1940	Walrus I

HMS GLORY 62 (R62 1947)
Colossus-class Light Fleet Carrier. Built Belfast 1942-45, commissioned 22 April 1945, Pacific Fleet 1945-47, Korea 1951-3,

parent ship letters L and Y 1945-46, then R 1946-54. Sold to scrap at Inverkeithing 23 August 1961.

837	Apr 1945-Oct 1945		Barracuda II
1831	May 1945-Jul 1946		Corsair IV
837	Oct 1945-Oct 1947		Firefly F.1/FR.1
806	Sep 1946-Oct 1947		Seafire F.XV
812	Nov 1949-Sep 1951		Firefly 5
804	Dec 1949-May 1952		Sea Fury FB.11
810	Jul 1951-Apr 1952		Firefly FR.5
812	Sep 1951-May 1952		Firefly AS.6
807	Jul 1952-Aug 1952		Sea Fury FB.11
898	Jul 1952-Oct 1952		Sea Fury FB.11
801	Sep 1952-May 1953		Sea Fury FB.11
821	Sep 1952-May 1953		Firefly FR.5
849C	Nov 1953-Dec 1953		Skyraider AEW.1
801	Oct 1953-Jul 1954		Sea Fury FB.11
826	Nov 1953-Feb 1954		Firefly AS.6

HMS HERCULES
Majestic-class Light Fleet Carrier. Built Tyne 1943-61, construction suspended 1946-57, sold to India January 1957, completed at Belfast and commissioned March 1961 as *Vikrant R11*.

HMS HERMES(1) I95 (D95 1940)
Fleet Carrier. Built Tyne 1918-24 as first British designed Carrier, commissioned 1 May 1923, refit 1933-34, to reserve 19 May 1937, deck letters HR, recommissioned 1 September 1939, war service Atlantic and Indian Oceans, sunk in attack by 50 Japanese aircraft from Carriers *Akagi, Hiryu* and *Soryu* 9 April 1942 off Trincomolee.

403	Mar 1924-Jul 1924		Plover
441	Mar 1924-Mar 1926		Fairey IIID
403	Mar 1925-Jun 1933		Flycatcher
423	Jun 1926-Sep 1926		Bison II
401	Jun 1926-Oct 1927		Flycatcher
440	Sep 1926-Oct 1927		Fairey IIID
442	Feb 1927-Sep 1930		Fairey IIID
406	Feb 1927-Feb 1927		Flycatcher
440	Jan 1928-Jun 1933		Fairey IIIF
824	Oct 1934-May 1937		Seal
803	Jan 1935-Apr 1937		Osprey I
814	Sep 1939-Feb 1942		Swordfish I
710 Dt	May 1940		Walrus I

HMS HERMES(2)
Hermes-class Fleet Carrier. Building on Tyne from June 1944, cancelled October 1945 and scrapped.

HMS HERMES(3) R12
Hermes-class Fleet Carrier. Built Barrow-in-Furness 1944-59, construction suspended 1945-49, ex-HMS *Elephant*, renamed 1945. Commissioned 18 November 1959, converted to Commando carrier 1970-71, Falklands 1982, parent ship letter H. Sold to India March 1986, refitted at Devonport and commissioned May 1987 as *Viraat R22*.

890	Feb 1960-Oct 1961		Sea Vixen FAW.1
804	Jul 1960-Sep 1961		Scimitar F.1
814	Jul 1960-Aug 1961		Whirlwind HAS.7
849C	Jul 1960-Sep 1961		Gannet AEW.3
831A	Jun 1961		Gannet ECM.4
803	May 1962-Feb 1964		Scimitar F.1
814	May 1962-Aug 1963		Wessex HAS.1
849B	May 1962-Oct 1963		Gannet AEW.3
892	May 1962-Nov 1963		Sea Vixen FAW.1
849 Dt	Nov 1963-Dec 1963		Gannet AEW.3
849C	Jan 1964-Dec 1964		Gannet AEW.3
892	Jul 1966-Oct 1968		Sea Vixen FAW.2
849 Dt	Aug 1966-Sep 1966		Gannet AEW.3
809	Sep 1966-Feb 1968		Buccaneer S.2
826	Sep 1966-Feb 1968		Wessex HAS.1
801	May 1968-Jun 1970		Buccaneer S.2
814	May 1968-Jun 1970		Wessex HAS.3
849A	May 1968-Jul 1970		Gannet AEW.3
893	May 1968-Jul 1970		Sea Vixen FAW.2
803 Dt4	Aug 1968-Apr 1969		Buccaneer S.2
814	Aug 1973-Oct 1979		Sea King HAS.1/2
845 Dt8	Aug 1973-Oct 1973		Wessex HU.5
845 Dts	1973-	1977	Wessex HU.5
846	Jun 1977-Jul 1977		Wessex HU.5
820	Jan 1980-Mar 1980		Sea King HAS.2
846 Dts	1981-	1983	Sea King HC.4
845 Dts	1981-	1984	Wessex HU.5
826	May 1981-Jul 1982		Sea King HAS.5
800	Jun 1981-Jul 1983		Sea Harrier FRS.1

HMS HUNTER D80
Attacker-class Escort Carrier. Built Pascagoula Mississippi, laid down as mercantile *Mormacpenn*, purchased 9 January 1943 as USS *Block Island ACV-8*. Transferred to RN and renamed HMS *Trailer*, commissioned 11 January 1943 as HMS *Hunter*, war service Atlantic, Mediterranean and East Indies, returned to USN 29 December 1945, became mercantile *Almdijk* 1948, scrapped at Valencia October 1965.

813 Dt	Mar 1943-Apr 1943	Swordfish II
834	Jul 1943-Aug 1943	Swordfish II
899	Aug 1943-Oct 1943	Seafire IIc
808	Oct 1943-Feb 1944	Seafire L.IIc
807	Jan 1944-Jun 1944	Seafire L.IIc
807 Dt	Oct 1944-Dec 1944	Seafire L.III
1700 Dt	Apr 1945-Jun 1945	Walrus I
1700 Dt	Aug 1945-Sep 1945	Walrus I
807	Mar 1945-Oct 1945	Seafire L.III

HMS ILLUSTRIOUS(1) 87 (R87 1947)
Illustrious-class Fleet Aircraft Carrier. Built Barrow-in-Furness 1937-40, commissioned 16 April 1940. War service Atlantic, Norway, Mediterranean and Indian Ocean, damaged by Luftwaffe dive bombers 10 January 1941 off Malta, East Indies and Pacific Fleet 1945, damaged in kamikaze near miss 6 April 1945. Post war service as trials and training carrier, parent ship letters L and Q 1945, D 1946-54 and Y 1953-55. Broken up Faslane from November 1956.

819	Jun 1940-Dec 1940	Swordfish I
815	Jun 1940-Jan 1941	Swordfish I
806	Jul 1940-Jan 1941	Fulmar I
813 Dt4	Sep 1940	Swordfish I/Sea Gladiator
824 Dt	Nov 1940	Swordfish I
813 Dt4	Nov 1940	Swordfish I/Sea Gladiator
805 Dt4	Jan 1941	Fulmar I
810	Dec 1941	Swordfish I
829	Dec 1941	Swordfish I
829	Mar 1942-Sep 1942	Swordfish II ASV
881	Mar 1942-Feb 1943	Martlet II
810	Mar 1942-Apr 1943	Swordfish I
795 Dt6	Aug 1942-Sep 1942	Fulmar II
806	Oct 1942	Martlet I/II
803	Dec 1942	Fulmar II
810	Apr 1943-Nov 1944	Barracuda II
878	Jun 1943-Oct 1943	Martlet IV
890	Jun 1943-Oct 1943	Martlet IV
894	Jul 1943-Oct 1943	Seafire IIc
847	Nov 1943-Jun 1944	Barracuda II
1830	Dec 1943-Jul 1945	Corsair II
1833	Dec 1943-Jul 1945	Corsair II
832	May 1944	Avenger II
845	May 1944	Avenger I/Wildcat V
1837	Jun 1944-Jul 1944	Corsair II
854	Dec 1944-May 1945	Avenger II
802	Jul 1951-Aug 1951	Sea Fury FB.11
826	Oct 1951	Firefly AS.6
827	Oct 1951	Firebrand TF5
824	Jun 1952-Oct 1952	Firefly AS.6
824	May 1953-Jun 1953	Firefly AS.6
815	Aug 1953-Oct 1953	Avenger TBM-3E
826	Aug 1953-Oct 1953	Firefly AS.6
815	Sep 1954-Oct 1954	Avenger AS.5

HMS IMPLACABLE 86 (R86 1947)
Implacable-class Fleet Aircraft Carrier. Built Clyde 1939-44 commissioned 28 August 1944, war service Atlantic, Norway, Pacific Fleet 1945-46, damaged in kamikaze attack 7 May 1945. Parent ship letters M 1945, N 1945-46, A 1946-47 and C 1948-51. Modernised 1951 but did not return to service, broken up at Inverkeithing from November 1955.

1771	Feb 1944-Oct 1945	Firefly I
828	Aug 1944-Dec 1944	Barracuda II
841	Aug 1944-Oct 1944	Barracuda II
887	Oct 1944	Seafire F.III/L.III
894 Dt	Oct 1944-Nov 1944	Seafire III
880	Oct 1944-Sep 1945	Seafire F.III/L.III
801	Nov 1944-Jun 1946	Seafire
881 Dt10	Dec 1944	Wildcat VI
828	Jan 1946-Jun 1946	Avenger I/II/III
1790	Jan 1946-Jun 1946	Firefly INF
807	Sep 1946-Oct 1946	Seafire F.XVII
801	Nov 1947-Jul 1950	Sea Hornet F.20
813	Oct 1947-Jul 1950	Firebrand TF.5
807	May 1948	Sea Fury F.10

815 Dt6	May 1948		Barracuda TR.3
815	May 1950-Jun	1950	Barracuda TR.3
815	Nov 1950-Dec	1951	Firebrand TF.5

HMS INDEFATIGABLE 10 (R10 1947)
Implacable-class Fleet Aircraft Carrier. Built Clydebank 1939-44, commissioned May 1944. War service Atlantic, Norway, East Indies, Pacific Fleet 1945-46, minor damage in kamikaze attack 1 April 1945. Parent ship letters D 1945, S 1945-46 and B 1946. Reserve from 1946, sold to scrap, hull stripped at Dalmuir from November 1956, broken up at Troon.

894	May 1944-Mar	1946	Seafire II/III
1770	May 1944-Jun	1945	Firefly I
820	Jun 1944-Sep	1944	Barracuda II
826	Jun 1944-Sep	1944	Barracuda II
842 Dt6	Jul 1944		Swordfish II
887	Jul 1944-Mar	1946	Seafire F.III/L.III
1840	Aug 1944		Hellcat I
820	Oct 1944-Mar	1946	Avenger I
888	Dec 1944-Jan	1945	Hellcat II(PR)
1772	Jul 1945-Dec	1946	Firefly I

HMS INDOMITABLE 92 (R92 1947)
Illustrious-class Fleet Aircraft Carrier. Built Barrow-in-Furness 1937-41, commissioned October 1941. War service Atlantic, Mediterranean, Indian Ocean, damaged in attack 12 August 1942, badly damaged in torpedo attack 11 July 1943, repaired in USA, East Indies and Pacific Fleet 1945, minor damage in kamikaze attack 4 May 1945. Parent ship letters N/O/W 1945, C 1946 and A 1947-53. Sold May 1953 and broken up at Faslane from September 1955.

800	Oct 1941-May	1942	Fulmar II
827	Oct 1941-Aug	1942	Albacore I
831	Oct 1941-May	1943	Albacore I/Barracuda I
880	Oct 1941-Aug	1942	Sea Hurricane Ib
806	Apr 1942-Aug	1942	Martlet I/II
796 Dt5	Aug 1941-Sep	1942	Albacore I
800 Dt	Aug 1942		Sea Hurricane Ib
880	Mar 1943-Jul	1943	Seafire IIc
899	Mar 1943-Jul	1943	Seafire IIc
807	Jun 1943-Jul	1943	Seafire L.IIc
815	Jul 1943-Oct	1944	Barracuda II
1839	Jul 1944-Nov	1945	Hellcat I/II
1844	Jul 1944-Nov	1945	Hellcat I/II
857	Nov 1944-Nov	1945	Avenger I/II
800	Nov 1950-Mar	1952	Sea Hornet F.20/ Sea Fury FB.11
815	Apr 1951-Jun	1951	Barracuda TR3
802	May 1951-Jul	1951	Sea Fury FB.11
820	Jan 1952-Jul	1952	Firefly AS.6
826	Jan 1952-Jul	1952	Firefly AS.6
809	Jun 1952-Jul	1952	Sea Hornet F20/NF21/PR22
826	Dec 1952-May	1953	Firefly AS.6
804	Jan 1953-May	1953	Sea Fury FB.11
820	Jan 1953-May	1953	Firefly AS.6

HMS IRRESISTIBLE
Ark Royal-class Fleet Carrier. See HMS *Ark Royal(3)*.

HrMs KAREL DOORMAN(1), Escort Carrier. Ex-HMS *Nairana* .v.), loaned 20 March 1946, returned to UK 9 March 1948, sold as mercantile *Port Victor* 1948, scrapped at Faslane 1971.

860	Jul 1946-Mar 1948	Firefly I

HrMs KAREL DOORMAN(2) R81
Colossus-class Light Fleet Carrier. Ex-HMS *Venerable* (q.v.), bought April 1948 from RN and commissioned 28 May 1948, modernised 1957-58, damaged by boiler fire April 1968, sold to Argentina Oct 1968, refitted at Rotterdam and commissioned March 1969 as *Veinticinco de Mayo*.

860	May 1948-Mar 1950	Firefly I
860	Jul 1950-Jun 1956	Sea Fury FB.50
869	Sep 1957-Oct 1964	Seahawk FB.50

HMS KHEDIVE(1)
Escort Carrier. Was to be HMS *Khedive* but retained by USN as USS *Hehenta Bay*.

HMS KHEDIVE(2) D62
Ruler-class Assault/Fighter Carrier. Built Seattle-Tacoma 1942-43 as USS *Cordova* ACV/AVG-39. Transferred to RN and commissioned 23 August 1943, mainly RCN manned, war service Mediterranean and East Indies. Returned to USN 26 January 1946, became mercantile *Rempang* 1948 and *Daphne* 1969, scrapped around 1975.

899	Apr 1944-Oct 1944	Seafire Vb
808	Jan 1945-Dec 1945	Hellcat II
800 Dt3	May 1945	Hellcat I/II
845	Apr 1945	Avenger I
888	Apr 1945	Hellcat II(PR)
804 Dt8	Feb 1945	Hellcat II
1700 Dt	Jun 1945-Sep 1945	Walrus I

HMS LEVIATHAN
Majestic-class Light Fleet Carrier. Building at Wallsend from October 1942, construction suspended May 1946, scrapped at Faslane from May 1968.

HMS LUCIFER
Ruler-class Escort Carrier. See HMS *Trumpeter*.

HMCS MAGNIFICENT D36
Majestic-class Light Fleet Carrier. Built Belfast 1943-48, loaned to RCN and commissioned 7 April 1948, returned to RN 14 June 1957, parent ship letter X 1948-49, sold to scrap and broken up at Faslane from July 1965.

806	May 1948-Jun 1948	Sea Hornet F.20/ Sea Fury FB.11
803	May 1948-Nov 1950	Sea Fury F.10/FB.11
825	May 1948-Nov 1950	Firefly FR.4/AS.5
826	Mar 1949-Oct 1950	Firefly AS.6
883	Jan 1950-May 1951	Sea Fury FB.11
826	Oct 1950-May 1951	Avenger TBM-3E
871	May 1951-Dec 1955	Sea Fury FB.11
880	May 1951-Nov 1951	Firefly AS.5
881	May 1951-Dec 1952	Avenger TBM-3E
880	Nov 1951-Oct 1956	Avenger TBM-3E
870	Dec 1952-Mar 1954	Sea Fury FB.11
881	Apr 1955-Nov 1956	Avenger AEW

HMS MAJESTIC
Majestic-class Light Fleet Carrier. See HMAS *Melbourne*.

HMS MALTA
Gibraltar-class Fleet Attack Carrier. Building at Clydebank, cancelled 21 December 1945 and scrapped on slip.

HMS MARS
Maintenance Carrier. See HMS *Pioneer*.

HMAS MELBOURNE(1) R21
Majestic-class Light Fleet Carrier. Built Barrow-in-Furness 1943-55, building suspended 1945-49, ex-HMS *Majestic*, transferred and commissioned 28 October 1955, refit 1969 and 1972-73, parent ship letters B 1955-56, Y 1956, then M 1957-82, paid off 30 June 1982, sold and broken up from November 1983.

808	Feb 1956-Dec 1958	Sea Venom FAW.53
816	Feb 1956-Aug 1957	Gannet AS.1
817	Feb 1956-Aug 1958	Gannet AS.1
805	Oct 1958-Jun 1963	Sea Venom FAW.53
825 Dt	Apr 1958-May 1961	Whirlwind HAS.7
814	Apr 1963-May 1963	Wessex HAS.1
817	Aug 1963-Feb 1976	Wessex HAS.31b
738H	Mar 1967-Jul 1967	Sycamore HR.50/51
805	Apr 1969-Jul 1982	Skyhawk A4-G
816	Apr 1969-Jul 1982	Tracker S.2-E/G
817	Feb 1976-Nov 1981	Sea King HAS.50/50a

HMS MONMOUTH(1)
Hermes-class Fleet Carrier. Building at Govan, cancelled October 1945 and scrapped on slip.

HMS NABOB D77
Ruler-class Escort Carrier. Built Seattle-Tacoma from October 1942 as USS *Edisto* ACV/AVG-41, commissioned 7 September 1943 in RCN but remained under RN control, war service Atlantic and Arctic, torpedoed by *U-354* 22 August 1944 off North Cape but limped home, assessed as a constructive total loss, laid up September 1944, returned to USN 16 March 1945, became mercantile *Nabob* 1948 and *Glory* 1967, scrapped 1977.

852	Feb 1944-Aug 1944	Avenger I/Wildcat V
856 Dt3	Aug 1944	Avenger II

HMS NAIRANA D05
Escort Carrier. Built Clydebank 1940-43, uncompleted merchant hull, commissioned 12 December 1943, war service Atlantic and Arctic, parent ship letter Y 1945, loaned Netherlands March 20 1946 as HrMs *Karel Doorman(1)* (q.v.), returned March 1948, sold as mercantile *Port Victor* 1948, scrapped at Faslane 1971.

835	Dec 1943-Sep 1944	Swordfish III/ Sea Hurricane IIc
784B	Feb 1944-Mar 1944	Fulmar IINF
835	Sep 1944-Mar 1945	Swordfish III/Wildcat IV
860	Oct 1945-Nov 1945	Barracuda III

HMS NEW ZEALAND
Gibraltar-class Fleet Attack Carrier. Building at Birkenhead, cancelled February 1946 and scrapped on slip.

HMS OCEAN(1) 68 (R68 1947)
Colossus-class Light Fleet Carrier. Built Clyde 1942-45, commissioned August 1945, Korea 1952-53, Suez 1956, parent ship letter O 1945-53, sold for scrap February 1960, broken up at Faslane from May 1962.

892	Nov 1945-Apr 1946	Hellcat IINF
1792	Dec 1945-Apr 1946	Firefly INF
805	Jun 1946-Aug 1946	Seafire XV
816	Jun 1946-Jul 1948	Firefly FR.1/NF.1
1702 Dt3	Jul 1946-Sep 1946	Sea Otter I
805	Aug 1946-Apr 1947	Firefly FR.1
805	Apr 1947-Jul 1948	Seafire F.17
804	Aug 1948-Dec 1948	Seafire FR.47
804	Apr 1949-Jul 1949	Seafire FR.47
812	Aug 1948-Jun 1949	Firefly NF.1
801	May 1953-Jul 1953	Sea Fury FB.11
807	Jul 1951-Feb 1952	Sea Fury FB.11
810	Jul 1951-Apr 1952	Firefly FR.5
899	Jul 1951-Feb 1952	Sea Fury FB.11
825	Feb 1952-Dec 1952	Firefly FR.5
807	Dec 1952-Dec 1953	Sea Fury FB.11
810	Dec 1952-Dec 1953	Firefly FR.5
899	Dec 1952-Jan 1953	Sea Fury FB.11
845 Dt	Jun 1956-Jul 1956	Whirlwind HAS.22
845	Sep 1956-Oct 1956	Whirlwind HAS.22

HMS PATROLLER D07
Ruler-class Assault Carrier. Built Seattle-Tacoma from November 1942 as USS *Keweenaw ACV/AVG-44*, transferred to RN 2 October 1943 on completion, fitted as Assault Carrier but employed as transport ferry, parent ship letter F, returned to USN 13 December 1946, became mercantile *Almkerk* 1948 and *Pacific Alliance* 1969, scrapped at Kaohsiung 1974.

HMS PEGASUS
Seaplane Carrier. See HMS *Ark Royal(1)*.

HMS PERSEUS R51 (A197)
Maintenance Carrier. Built Tyne 1942-45 as *Colossus*-class Light Fleet Carrier HMS *Edgar*, renamed before commissioning August 1945, to reserve June 1946, Ferry Carrier from June 1953, scrapped at Port Glasgow from May 1958.

845	Apr 1954	Whirlwind HAS.22

HMS PIONEER D76 (R76 1947)
Maintenance Carrier. Built Barrow-in-Furness 1942-45 as *Colossus*-class Light Fleet Carrier HMS *Ethalion*, renamed HMS *Mars*, commissioned 8 February 1945 as Maintenance Carrier, ferry carrier from June 1953, sold to scrap and broken up at Inverkeithing from September 1954.

HMS POLYPHEMUS
Hermes-class Fleet Carrier. Building at Devonport, cancelled October 1945.

HMS POWERFUL
Majestic-class Light Fleet Carrier. See HMCS *Bonaventure*.

HMS PREMIER D23
Ruler-class Escort Carrier. Built Seattle-Tacoma from October 1942 as USS *Estero ACV/AGV-42*, transferred to RN 3 November 1943 on completion, parent ship letter P 1945, war service Atlantic, Norway and Arctic, returned to USN April 1946, became mercantile *Rhodesia Star* 1948 and *Hong Kong Knight* 1967, scrapped at Kaohsiung 1974.

856	Sep 1944-Jun 1945	Wildcat V/VII
881 Dt	Dec 1944-Jan 1945	Wildcat VI

HMS PRETORIA CASTLE F61
Trials Carrier. Built Belfast, launched 1938 as passenger liner SS *Pretoria Castle*, converted to armed merchant cruiser 1939, commissioned for deck trials 1943, used mainly for training, paid off December 1945, became mercantile *Warwick Castle* 1947, scrapped Spain 1962-63.

HMS/HMCS PUNCHER D79
Ruler-class Escort Carrier. Built Seattle-Tacoma from May 1943 as USS *Willapa ACV/AVG-53*, transferred to RN 5 February on completion, Canadian manned, war service Atlantic and Norway, loaned RCN as troopship August 1945, parent ship letter N 1945, returned to USN 16 January 1946, became mercantile *Muncaster Castle* 1949, *Bardic* 1954 and *Ben Nevis* 1959, scrapped at Kaohsiung 1973.

821	Nov 1944-Apr 1945	Barracuda II
881	Feb 1945	Wildcat VI

HMS PURSUER D73
Attacker-class Fighter Carrier. Built Pascagoula, Mississippi, laid down as mercantile *Mormacland*, launched July 1942, purchased by USN 14 June 1943 as USS *St George ACV/CVG-17*, transferred same day to RN, war service Atlantic, Norway, Mediterranean and Normandy, parent ship letter U 1945, returned to USN February 1946 and scrapped.

896	Nov 1943-Jun 1944	Wildcat V
881	Nov 1943-Nov 1944	Wildcat V/VII
881	Mar 1945-Apr 1945	Wildcat VI

HMS QUEEN D19
Ruler-class Escort Carrier. Built Seattle-Tacoma from March as USS *St Andrews ACV/AVG-49*, transferred on completion and commissioned 7 December 1943, war service Atlantic, Norway and Arctic, parent ship letter Q 1945, returned to USN 31 October 1946, became mercantile *Roebiah* 1948, *President Marcos* 1966 and *Lucky One* 1972, scrapped at Kaohsiung 1972.

853	Dec 1944-May 1945	Avenger

HMS RAJAH D10
Ruler-class Assault Carrier. Built Seattle-Tacoma from December 1942 as USS *McLure ACV/AGV-45*, later USS *Prince*, transferred to RN 17 January 1944 on completion, mainly employed on ferry and transport duties, returned to USN 13 December 1946, became mercantile *Drente* 1948, *Lambros* 1966 and *Ulisse* 1969, sold to Spanish shipbreakers 1975.

888	Sep 1944-Oct 1944	Hellcat II(PR)

HMS RANEE D03
Ruler-class Assault Carrier. Built Seattle-Tacoma from January 1943 as USS *Niantic ACV-46*, transferred to RN 8 November 1943 on completion, mainly employed on ferry and transport duties, parent ship letter F 1945, returned to USN November 1946, became mercantile *Friesland* 1948 and *Pacific Breeze* 1967, scrapped 1974.

HMS RAVAGER D70
Ruler-class Escort Carrier. Built Seattle-Tacoma, purchased by USN May 1942 as *AVG-24*, was to be HMS *Charger(2)* but commissioned on completion 26 April 1943 as HMS *Ravager*, war service Atlantic but mainly used for DLT, parent ship letter V 1945, returned to USN 26 February 1946, became mercantile *Robin Trent* 1948 and *Trent* 1971, scrapped at Kaohsiung 1973.

835 Dt	Sep 1943-Oct 1943	Wildcat VI
804	Oct 1943	Hellcat I

HMS REAPER D82
Ruler-class Assault Carrier. Built Seattle-Tacoma from June 1943 as USS *Winjah ACV/AVG-54*, transferred to RN 18 February 1954 on completion, mainly employed on ferry and transport duties, parent ship letter R 1945, returned to USN 20 May 1946, became mercantile *South Africa Star* 1948, scrapped at Milhara 1967.

HMS RULER D72
Ruler-class Assault/Fighter Carrier. Built Seattle-Tacoma from March as USS *St Joseph ACV/AVG-50*, transferred to RN 22 December 1943 on completion, Pacific Fleet 1945, returned to USN 29 January 1946 and scrapped 1947.

885	Dec 1944-Sep 1945	Hellcat I/II
1772	Jan 1945-Mar 1945	Firefly I

HMS SEARCHER D40
Ruler-class Fighter Carrier. Built Seattle-Tacoma 1940-42 as USS *AVG-22*, transferred to RN on completion 20 June 1942, war service Atlantic, Norway and Mediterranean, parent ship letter S 1945, returned to USN 29 November 1945, became mercantile *Captain Theo* 1947 and *Oriental Banker* 1964, scrapped 1976.

882	Dec 1943-Jul 1944	Wildcat V
898	Oct 1943-Jul 1944	Wildcat V
882	Feb 1945-Oct 1945	Wildcat VI
826 Dt	May 1945	Barracuda II

HMS SHAH D21
Ruler-class Escort Carrier. Built Seattle-Tacoma from November 1942 as USS *Jamaica ACV/AVG-43*, transferred to RN 27 September 1943 on completion, war service Indian Ocean and East Indies, returned to USN 6 December 1945, became mercantile *Salta* 1948, scrapped at Buenos Aires 1966.

851	Jun 1944-Sep 1945	Avenger I/Wildcat V
804 Dt4	Apr 1945-May 1945	Hellcat II
888	Apr 1945-May 1945	Hellcat II(PR)
800 Dt8	May 1945	Hellcat I/II
845	Jun 1945-Sep 1945	Avenger I
1700 Dt	Aug 1945	Walrus I

HMS SLINGER D26
Ruler-class Assault Carrier. Built Seattle-Tacoma May 1942-

August 1943 as USS *Chatham AVG-32*, transferred to RN 11 August 1943 on completion, mainly employed on ferry and transport duties, Pacific Fleet 1945, deck letter R 1943, returned to USN 27 February 1946, became mercantile *Robin Mowbray* 1948, scrapped at Kaohsiung 1970.

| 1845 | Dec 1944-Apr 1945 | Corsair IV |

HMS SMITER D55
Ruler-class Escort Carrier. Built Seattle-Tacoma from May 1943 as USS *Vermillion ACV/AVG-52*, transferred to RN 20 January 1944 on completion, operational August 1945 and saw no action, parent ship letter G 1945, returned to USN 6 Apr 1946, became mercantile *Artillero* 1948 and *President Garcia* 1965, wrecked off Guernsey 13 July 1967 and later broken up Hamburg.

| 815 | Jul 1945-Aug 1945 | Barracuda TR3 |
| 888 | Dec 1945 | Hellcat II(PR) |

HMS SPEAKER D90
Ruler-class Assault/Fighter Carrier. Built Seattle-Tacoma from October 1942 as USS *Delgada ACV/AVG-40*, transferred to RN 20 November 1943 on completion, Pacific Fleet 1945, returned to USN 17 July 1946, became mercantile *Lancero* 1948, *President Osmena* 1965 and *Lucky Three* 1971, scrapped at Kaohsiung 1972.

| 1840 | Dec 1944-Apr 1945 | Hellcat II |

HMS STALKER D91
Attacker-class Assault/Fighter Carrier. Built San Francisco 1941-42 as USS *Hamlin AVG-15*, transferred to RN on completion 21 December 1942, war service Atlantic, Mediterranean and East Indies, returned to USN 29 December 1945, became mercantile *Roiuw* 1948 and *Lobito* 1967, scrapped 1975.

833	Jul 1943	Swordfish II/Seafire L.IIc
880	Aug 1943-Oct 1943	Seafire IIc
897	Dec 1943-Feb 1944	Seafire L IIc
809	Dec 1943-Feb 1944	Seafire L.IIc
1700 Dt	Apr 1945-Jun 1945	Walrus I
809	May 1945-Oct 1945	Seafire L.III

HMS STRIKER D12
Attacker-class Escort Carrier. Built San Francisco as USS *Prince William AVG-19*, transferred to RN 28 April 1943, completed 18 May 1943, war service Atlantic, Arctic and Norway, replenishment carrier Pacific Fleet 1945, returned to USN 12 February 1946, scrapped at Baltimore.

| 824 | Oct 1943-Oct 1944 | Sea Hurricane IIc/Wildcat V |

HMAS SYDNEY(1) R17
Majestic-class Light Fleet Carrier. Built Devonport 1943-49, ex-HMS *Terrible*, transferred December 1948, commissioned February 1949, Korea 1951-52, Monte Bello A-bomb tests October 1952, parent ship letter K 1949-58, S 1956-69, training ship from April 1955, recommissioned as Fast Troop Transport 7 March 1962, To Reserve 1958, sold to South Korea for scrap October 1975, left Sydney December 1975.

805	Feb 1949-Mar 1958	Sea Fury F.10/FB.11
816	Feb 1949-Feb 1953	Firefly FR.4/5
808	Aug 1950-Feb 1953	Sea Fury FB.11
817	Aug 1950-Aug 1953	Firefly FR.5/AS.6
816	Sep 1953-Apr 1955	Firefly 5/6
817	Aug 1954-Apr 1955	Firefly AS.6
851	Mar 1956	Firefly AS.6

HMS TERRIBLE
Majestic-class Light Fleet Carrier. See HMAS *Sydney*.

HMS THANE D48, *Ruler*-class Assault Carrier. Built Seattle-Tacoma from February 1943 as USS *Sunset ACV/AVG-48*, transferred to RN 19 November 1943 on completion and commissioned November 1943, used mainly for ferry and transport duties, torpedoed by *U-482* 15 January 1945 and towed to Greenock by frigate HMS *Loring*, to reserve March 1945, returned to USN 5 December 1945 and scrapped at Faslane 1946.

HMS THESEUS 64 (R64 1947)
Colossus-class Light Fleet Carrier. Built Govan 1942-45, commissioned 9 January 1946, Korea 1950-51, Suez 1956, parent ship letter T, sold for scrap February 1960, broken up at Inverkeithing from May 1962.

816	Feb 1946-May 1946	Firefly FR.1
804	Feb 1947-Dec 1947	Seafire F.XV
812	Feb 1947-Dec 1947	Firefly FR.1
810	Aug 1948-Aug 1949	Firefly FR.4
807	Sep 1948-May 1951	Sea Fury FB.11
810	Apr 1950-May 1951	Firefly AS.5
802	Sep 1951-Dec 1952	Sea Fury FB.11
814	Oct 1951-Dec 1951	Firefly AS.6
899	Feb 1952-Jul 1952	Sea Fury FB.11
807	Apr 1952-May 1952	Sea Fury FB.11
804	May 1952-Sep 1952	Sea Fury FB.11
820	Jul 1952-Nov 1952	Firefly AS.6
826	Aug 1952-Nov 1952	Firefly AS.6
807	Oct 1952-Nov 1952	Sea Fury FB.11
810	Oct 1952-Nov 1952	Firefly FR.5
899	Oct 1952-Dec 1952	Sea Fury FB.11
812	Jan 1953-Mar 1953	Firefly AS.6
824	Jan 1953-May 1953	Firefly AS.6
802	Apr 1953-Oct 1953	Sea Fury FB.11
804	Jun 1953-Oct 1953	Sea Fury FB.11
820	Jun 1953-Oct 1953	Firefly AS.6
845 Dt	Jun 1956-Jul 1956	Whirlwind HAS.22
845	Oct 1956-Dec 1956	Whirlwind HAS.22

HMS TRACKER D24
Escort Carrier. Built San Francisco, laid down as mercantile *Mormacmail, BAVG-6,* transferred to RN on completion 31 January 1943, war service Atlantic, Arctic and Normandy, damaged in collision 3 June 1943 on patrol in South West Approaches, returned to service by August 1943, parent ship letters TR 1945, returned to USN 29 November 1945, became mercantile *Corrientes* 1949, scrapped 1964.

816	Aug 1943-Dec 1943	Seafire Ib
846	Jan 1944-Jun 1944	Avenger I
853	Sep 1944-Dec 1944	Avenger I/Wildcat VI

HMS TRAILER
Attacker-class Escort Carrier. See HMS *Hunter*.

HMS TRIUMPH R16 (A108 1965), *Colossus*-class Light Fleet Carrier. Built Tyne 1942-46, commissioned 9 April 1946, active service Korea and Malaya 1950, cadet training ship from 1953, repair ship from 7 January 1964, parent ship letter P 1946-55, laid up 1974, sold to scrap 1982.

| 827 | Jan 1947-Nov 1950 | Firefly FR.1 |
| 800 | Feb 1947-Nov 1950 | Seafire F.XVII/FR.47 |

HMS TROUNCER D85
Ruler-class Assault Carrier. Built Seattle-Tacoma from February 1943 as USS *Perdido ACV/AVG-47*, transferred to RN 31 January 1944 on completion, employed mainly on ferry and transport duties, parent ship letter I 1945, returned to USN March 1946, became mercantile *Greystoke Castle* 1949, *Gallic* 1954 and *Ben Rinnes* 1959, scrapped at Kaohsiung 1973.

HMS TRUMPETER D09
Ruler-class Escort Carrier. Built Seattle-Tacoma 1942-43 as USS *Bastian ACV/AVG-37*, transferred to RN on completion, was to become HMS *Lucifer* but commissioned as HMS *Trumpeter* 4 August 1943, parent ship letter J 1945, returned to USN 6 April 1946 and renamed USS *Bastian*, became mercantile *Alblasserdijk* 1948 and *Irene Valmas* 1966, scrapped at Castellon 1971.

846	Jul 1944-May 1945	Avenger I/Wildcat V
856 Dt3	Aug	Avenger II/Wildcat V
852	Sep 1944-Oct 1944	Wildcat VI
856 Dt3	Dec 1944	Avenger II/Wildcat V
881 Dt2	Dec 1944-Jan 1945	Wildcat VI
828 Dt	Jan 1945	Avenger I
822 Dt	Apr 1945-May 1945	Wildcat VI
822	Jul 1945-Aug 1945	Barracuda TR III

HMS UNICORN I72 (R72 1947, A195)
Maintenance Carrier. Built Belfast 1939-43, commissioned 12 March 1943, operational during 1943 then reverted to supply and repair role, war service in Atlantic, Norway and Mediterranean, repair and ferry carrier Korea 1950-53, parent ship letters X 1945, U 1946 and Y 1946-53, sold to scrap June 1959, stripped at Dalmuir and hull broken up at Troon from March 1960.

800	Mar 1943-Apr 1943	Sea Hurricane IIc
824	Mar 1943-Jul 1943	Swordfish I
818	Mar 1943-Feb 1944	Swordfish II
887	Apr 1943-Oct 1943	Seafire IIc
897	Aug 1943	Spitfire Vb
885 Dt2	Sep 1943-Oct 1943	Seafire IIc
817	Nov 1944-Jan 1945	Barracuda II

HMS VENERABLE 04 (R81 1947)
Colossus-class Light Fleet Carrier. Built Birkenhead from 25 December 1942, commissioned January 1945, Pacific Fleet 1945-46, parent ship letter B 1945-46, variously N/T/Y 1946 and V 1946-48, sold to Netherlands April 1948 as *Karel Doorman(2)* (q.v.), to Argentina 15 October 1968 as *Veinticinco de Mayo*.

802	Sep 1946-Mar 1947	Seafire F.XV
814	Mar 1945-Dec 1945	Barracuda II
814	Jan 1946-Feb 1947	Firefly I
1851	Mar 1945-May 1946	Corsair IV

HMS/HMAS VENGEANCE 71 (R71 1947)

Colossus-class Light Fleet Carrier. Built Wallsend 1942-45, commissioned January 1945, Pacific Fleet 1946, experimental Arctic cruise 1948-49, loaned Australia March 1953-June 1955, parent ship letter A 1945, M and N 1946 and Q 1946-57, sold to Brazil December 1956, reconstructed at Rotterdam 1957-60 and commissioned December 1960 as *Minas Gerais*.

1850	Feb 1945-Aug 1946	Corsair IV
1851	May 1946-Aug 1946	Corsair IV
807	May 1947-Jul 1947	Seafire F.XVII
802	Sep 1947-Nov 1947	Seafire F.XV
814	Sep 1947-Nov 1947	Firefly I
802	Aug 1948-Apr 1951	Sea Fury FB.11
814	Aug 1948-Nov 1950	Firefly FR.4/5
814	May 1951-Jun 1951	Firefly FR.1/AS.6
816	Jun 1953-Aug 1953	Firefly AS.5/6
850	Jul 1953-Aug 1953	Sea Fury FB.11
808	Sep 1953-May 1954	Sea Fury FB.11
817	Sep 1953-May 1954	Firefly AS.6

HMS VICTORIOUS 38 (R38 1947)

Illustrious-class Fleet Aircraft Carrier. Built Tyne from 1937, commissioned 29 March 1941, war service Atlantic, Coral Sea, Arctic, Norway and Mediterranean, Pacific Fleet 1945, minor damage in kamikaze attacks April and May 1945. Trooping ship 1945-46 then service as training ship, modernised and rebuilt 1950-57 with angled deck. Recommissioned January 1958, deck letter variously P/S/V/X 1945, G 1946-50 and V 1957-68. Major fire on board during refit November 1967 and paid off March 1968 as beyond economical repair, crew transferred to HMS *Hermes* (q.v.), broken up at Faslane from July 1969.

809	Jan 1941-Nov 1942	Fulmar II
825	May 1941-Jun 1941	Swordfish I
800Z	May 1941-Jun 1941	Fulmar I
820	Jun 1941	Swordfish I
828	Jul 1941-Aug 1941	Albacore I
827	Jul 1941-Aug 1941	Albacore I
820	Jul 1941-Jan 1942	Albacore I
817	Aug 1941-Nov 1942	Albacore I
832	Aug 1941-Dec 1942	Albacore I
802 Dt8	Sep 1941	Martlet I
885	Jun 1942-Aug 1942	Sea Hurricane Ib
884	Jul 1942-Nov 1942	Spitfire V
801 Dt	Aug 1942	Sea Hurricane Ib
896	Sep 1942-Sep 1943	Martlet IV
898	Oct 1942-Oct 1943	Martlet IV
882	Oct 1942-Sep 1943	Martlet IV
832	Jan 1943-Sep 1943	Avenger TBF1
1834	Feb 1944-Oct 1945	Corsair II/IV
827	Mar 1944-Apr 1944	Barracuda II
829	Mar 1944-Jul 1944	Barracuda II
831	Mar 1944-Aug 1944	Barracuda II
1836	Mar 1944-Oct 1945	Corsair II/IV
1837	Jul 1944-Sep 1944	Corsair II
1838	Jul 1944	Corsair II
822 Dt9	Sep 1944	Barracuda II
849	Dec 1944-Oct 1945	Avenger II
701C	Nov 1957-Jul 1958	Dragonfly HR.3
803	Jun 1958-Mar 1962	Scimitar F.1
824	Aug 1958-Feb 1959	Whirlwind HAS.7
849B	Sep 1958-Jun 1960	Skyraider AEW.1
893	Sep 1958-Feb 1960	Sea Vixen FAW.1
831B	Nov 1958-Dec 1958	Sea Venom FAW.22
894 Dt	Feb 1959	Sea Venom FAW.22
894 Dt	Jun 1959-Aug 1959	Sea Venon FAW.22
892	Jul 1959-Mar 1962	Sea Vixen FAW.1
831B	Sep 1959-Dec 1959	Sea Venom ECM.22
815	Dec 1961	Wessex HAS.1
831A Dt2	Jan 1960-Feb 1960	Gannet ECM.4
849B	Jun 1960-Mar 1962	Gannet AEW.3
825	Aug 1960-Apr 1962	Whirlwind HAS.7
893 Dt	Sep 1960	Sea Vixen FAW.1
819	Jul 1963-Aug 1963	Wessex HAS.1
801	Aug 1963-Jul 1965	Buccanner S.1
814	Aug 1963-Jun 1967	Wessex HAS.1
849A	Aug 1963-Jul 1965	Gannet AEW.3
893	Aug 1963-Jul 1965	Sea Vixen FAW.1
899 Dt	Aug 1963	Sea Vixen FAW.1
893	Nov 1965-Jun 1967	Sea Vixen FAW.2
849A	Jan 1966-Jun 1967	Gannet AEW.3
801	May 1966-May 1968	Buccanner S.2

HMS VINDEX D15

Escort Carrier. Built Tyne 1942-43, uncompleted refrigerated cargo hull *Port Sydney*, bought October 1942, commissioned November 1943, war service Atlantic and Arctic, replenishment carrier in Pacific Fleet 1945, parent ship letters V and X 1945, became MS *Port Vindex* 1947, scrapped at Kaohsiung from August 1971.

825	Dec 1943-Jan 1945	Swordfish I/II
784B	Apr 1944	Fulmar II
811	Sep 1944-Dec 1944	Swordfish II/Wildcat V
813	Apr 1945-May 1945	Swordfish III/Wildcat VI
1790	Jun 1945-Aug 1945	Firefly INF

HMS VINDICTIVE

Seaplane Carrier. Built 1916-18, commissioned 1 October 1918, converted to cruiser 1924 as first RN cruiser with catapult gear. Became training ship 1937, repair ship 1939, laid up Faslane December 1945, broken up from April 1947.

444	Apr 1925-Nov 1929	Fairey IIID

HMS/HMCS WARRIOR 31 (R31 1947)

Colossus-class Light Fleet Carrier. Built Belfast 1942-45, commissioned into RCN 24 January 1946, parent ship letter W 1946-48, J 1953-54. Returned to UK 1956 and modernised, Christmas Island H-bomb tests 1957, to Argentina 4 November 1958 as *Independencia*, paid off 1970 and scrapped 1971.

803	Mar 1946-Aug 1947	Seafire F.XV
825	Mar 1946-Aug 1947	Firefly FR.1
826	Nov 1947	Firefly FR.1
883	Nov 1947	Seafire F.XV
811	Feb 1954-Dec 1954	Sea Fury FB.11
825	Feb 1954-Dec 1954	Firefly AS.5

HMS Begum, possibly at China Bay, with two No.832 Sqdn Avengers on deck. (via R.E.F.Kerrison)

MAC-SHIPS

MV ACAVUS
Tanker. Launched 24 November 1934. Into service October 1943. Withdrawn September 1944. Became mercantile *Iacra* in 1952. Scrapped 1963.

MV ADULA
Tanker. Launched 28 January 1937. Into service February 1944. Withdrawn May 1945. Sold to T.W.Ward, and arrived Briton Ferry 15 May 1953 for scrapping.

MV ALEXIA
Tanker. Launched 20 December 1934. Into service December 1943. Withdrawn June 1945. Became mercantile *Ianthina* in 1951. Scrapped 1954.

MV AMASTRA
Tanker. Launched 18 December 1934. Into service September 1943. Withdrawn September 1944. Became mercantile *Idas* in 1951. Scrapped 1955.

MV ANCYLUS
Tanker. Launched 9 October 1934. Into service October 1943. Withdrawn October 1944. Became mercantile *Imbricaria* in 1952. Scrapped 1954.

MV EMPIRE MACALPINE
Grain Carrier. Launched 23 December 1942. Into service 14 April 1943. Withdrawn May 1945. Became mercantile *Derrynane* in 1947. After many name changes scrapped 1954.

MV EMPIRE MACANDREW
Grain Carrier. Launched 3 May 1943. Into service December 1943. Withdrawn June 1945. Became mercantile *Derryheen* in 1947, *Cape Grafton* in 1950s and *Patricia* in 1964. Scrapped 1970.

MV EMPIRE MACCABE
Tanker. Launched 18 May 1943. Into service December 1943. Withdrawn June 1945. Became mercantile *British Escort* in 1946 and Easthill Escort in 1959. Scrapped 1962.

MV EMPIRE MACCALLUM
Grain Carrier. Launched 12 October 1943. Into service December 1943. Withdrawn June 1945. To mercantile *Doris Clunies* in 1947, *Sunrover* in 1951, *Eudoxin* in 1959 and *Phorkyss* in 1960. Scrapped 1960.

MV EMPIRE MACCOLL
Tanker. Launched 24 July 1943. Into service November 1943. Withdrawn May 1945. Became mercantile *British Pilot* in 1946. Scrapped 1962.

MV EMPIRE MACDERMOTT
Grain Carrier. Launched 24 January 1944. Into service March 1944. Withdrawn May 1945. Became mercantile *La Cumbre* in 1948, *Parnon* in 1960s and *Starlight* in 1969.

MV EMPIRE MACKAY
Tanker. Launched 17 June 1943. Into service October 1943. Withdrawn July 1945. Became mercantile *British Swordfish* in 1946. Scrapped 1960.

MV EMPIRE MACKENDRICK
Grain Carrier. Launched 29 September 1943. Into service December 1943. To mercantile *Granpond* in 1951, *Condor* in 1951, *Saltersgate* in late 1950s and *Vassil Levsky* around 1960.

MV EMPIRE MACMAHON
Tanker. Launched 2 July 1943. Into service December 1943. Withdrawn June 1945. Became mercantile *Navinia* in 1946. Scrapped 1960.

MV EMPIRE MACRAE
Grain Carrier. Launched 21 June 1943. Into service September 1943. Withdrawn June 1945. To mercantile *Alpha Zambesi* in 1947, *Tobon* in mid 1950s and *Despina* in 1967.

MV GADILA
Tanker. Launched 1 December 1934. Into service March 1944. Netherlands Mercantile Marine. Withdrawn May 1945 and reconverted to tanker. Sold to a British shipbreaker and arrived Hong Kong 6 June 1958 for scrapping.

MV MACOMA
Tanker. Launched 31 December 1935. Into service May 1944. Netherlands Mercantile Marine. Withdrawn May 1945 and reconverted to tanker. Sold to a British shipbreaker and arrived Hong Kong 14 December 1959 for scrapping.

MV MIRALDA
Tanker. Launched July 1936. Into service January 1944. Withdrawn May 1945. Became mercantile *Marisa* in 1950. Scrapped 1960.

MV RAPANA
Tanker. Launched April 1935. Into service July 1943. Withdrawn September 1944. Became mercantile *Rotula* in 1950. Scrapped 1958.

MV Empire MacDermott from tail of Swordfish. (G.E.Legg)

MV Macoma. (Royal Netherlands Navy)

MV Empire MacCabe. (Vic Smith)

MV Empire MacAlpine. (Reg Singleton)

WARSHIPS WITH CATAPULTS, CRANES OR FLYING-OFF PLATFORMS 1923 - 1944

HMS Achilles
HMS Ajax
HMS Albatross
HMS Amphion
  (became Perth)
HMS Anson
HMS Apollo
  (became Hobart)
HMS Arethusa
HMS Ark Royal
  (became Pegasus)
HMAS Australia
HMS Barham
HMS Belfast
HMS Bermuda
HMS Berwick
HMS Birmingham
HMS Caledon
HMAS Canberra
HMS Ceylon
HMS Cornwall
HMS Cumberland
HMS Devonshire
HMS Dorsetshire
HMS Duke of York
HMS Edinburgh
HMS Effingham
HMS Emerald
HMS Enterprise
HMS Exeter
HMS Fiji
HMS Frobisher
HMS Galatea
HMS Gambia
HMAS Geranium
HMS Glasgow
HMS Gloucester
HMAS Hobart
HMS Hood
HMS Howe
HMS Jamaica
HMS Kent
HMS Kenya
HMS King George V
HMS Leander
HMS Liverpool
HMS London
HMS Malaya
HMS Manchester
HMS Mauritius
HMS Nelson
HMS Neptune
HMS Newcastle
HMS Newfoundland
HMS Nigeria
HMS Norfolk
HMS Orion
HMS Penelope
HMAS Perth
HMS Prince of Wales
HMS Queen Elizabeth
HMS Ramillies
HMS Renown
HMS Repulse
HMS Resolution
HMS Revenge
HMS Rodney
HMS Royal Oak
HMS Royal Sovereign
HMS Sheffield
HMS Shropshire
HMS Southampton
HMS Suffolk
HMS Sussex
HMAS Sydney
HMS Trinidad
HMS Uganda
HMS Valiant
HMS Vindictive
HMS Warspite
HMS York

ARMED MERCHANT CRUISERS FITTED WITH CATAPULTS

HMS Alcantara
HMS Asturias
HMS Carnarvon Castle
HMS Canton
HMS Cilicia
HMS Corfu
HMS Fidelity
HMAS Manoora
HMS Pretoria Castle
HMS Queen of Bermuda
HMS Ranpura
HMAS Westralia

FIGHTER CATAPULT SHIPS WITH FAA AIRCRAFT

HMS Ariguani
HMS Maplin
HMS Patia
HMS Pegasus
HMS Springbank

CAM-SHIP WITH FAA AIRCRAFT

SS Michael E

HMS Cilicia in 1942. (FAA Museum)

A Swordfish floatplane is visible on HMS Rodney while anchored at Madeira in 1939. (Cdr R.A.B.Phillimore)

MAJOR WW2 WARSHIPS FITTED WITH AIRCRAFT CATAPULTS

HMNZS ACHILLES(1)
Type EIIIH catapult, removed after April 1943. South Atlantic Command September 1939, damaged Guadalcanal 5 January 1943.
Major Action: River Plate 13 December 1939.
Ships Flight: 720 (NZ) Sqdn to 21 January 1940, then flight of 700 Sqdn. Disbanded February 1943.
720	Sep 1939-Jan 1940	1 Walrus		L2236
700	Jan 1940-Feb 1943	1 Walrus		W2724

HMS AJAX(1)
Type EIIIH catapult, removed mid 1941. South Atlantic Command September 1939, Home Fleet July 1940, 4th Cruiser Sqdn Sierra Leone September 1940, Mediterranean September 1940.
Major Actions: River Plate 13 December 1939. Sinking of Italian destroyers *Artigliere* and *Ariel* 12 October 1940.
Ships Flight: 718 Sqdn to 21 January 1940, then flight of 700 Sqdn. Disbanded May 1940. Reformed 1 June 1940. Disbanded February 1941.
718	Sep 1939-Jan 1940	2 Seafox	
700	Jan 1940-May 1940	2 Seafox	
700	Jun 1940-Mar 1941	1 Walrus	P5713

HMS ANSON
Type DIIIH catapult, removed after July 1944.
2nd Battle Sqdn June 1942.
Ships Flight: Formed 1 April 1942. Disbanded August 1943.
700	Apr 1942-Aug 1943	2 Walrus	X9529

HMS ARETHUSA(1)
Believed Type EIIIH catapult, removed by April 1941. 3rd Cruiser Sqdn Mediterranean September 1939, 2nd Cruiser Sqdn Home Fleet January to May 1940, Force H July 1940, 2nd Cruiser Sqdn Home Fleet November 1940.
Ships Flight: 713 Sqdn to 21 January 1940, then flight of 700 Sqdn. Disbanded April 1940.
713	Sep 1939-Jan 1940	2 Seafox	K8587 H9A
700	Jan 1940-Apr 1940	2 Seafox	

HMAS AUSTRALIA
Type EIIIH catapult. Australian Sqdn from Oct 1939, to South American Sqdn Mar 1940, to 1st Cruiser Sqdn Home Fleet July 1940, 4th Cruiser Sqdn March 1941, Australian Sqdn July 1941, attached East Indies Sqdn September 1941, retd Australian Sqdn December 1941.
Major Action: Dakar 24 September 1940.
Ships Flight:
(700)	Jan 1940-Jan 1941	1 Seagull V	A2-4

HMS BARHAM
Type EIT catapult. 2nd Battle Squadron Home Fleet December 1939, 1st Battle Sqdn Mediterranean November 1940. Battle of Matapan 28 March 1941. Ship sunk 25 November 1941.
Major Action: Dakar 24 September 1940.
Ships Flight: 701 Sqdn to 21 January 1940, then flight of 700 Sqdn. Disbanded May 1940. Reformed 1 June 1940 at Lee-on-Solent.
701	Sep 1939-Jan 1940	1 Swordfish	L2751
700	Jun 1940-Nov 1941	1 Walrus	L2293

HMS BELFAST
Type DIH catapult, removed after August 1944. 18th Cruiser Sqdn Home Fleet September 1939, 2nd Cruiser Sqdn Home Fleet November 1939 to July 1940, 1st Cruiser Sqdn Home Fleet November 1942, 10th Cruiser Sqdn Home Fleet January 1943.
Major Action: *Scharnhorst* sinking 26 December 1943.
Ships Flight: 712 Sqdn to 21 January 1940, then flight of 700 Sqdn. Disbanded May 1940, Reformed 1 September 1942 at Donibristle. Disbanded March 1944.
Major Action: *Scharnhorst* sinking 26 December 1943.
712	Sep 1939-Jan 1940	1 Walrus	L2224
700	Jan 1940-May 1940	1 Walrus	P5658
700	Sep 1942-Mar 1944	2 Walrus	X9586

HMS BERMUDA
Type DIVH catapult, removed April 1944. Bermuda Home Fleet August 1942, 10th Cruiser Sqdn Home Fleet November 1942, Plymouth Command July 1943.
Ships Flight: Formed 1 June 1942 at Donibristle. Disbanded August 1943.
700	Jun 1942-Aug 1943	2 Walrus	W3032

HMS BERWICK(1)
Type DIH catapult, removed c.May-August 1942. 8th Cruiser Sqdn American & West Indies September 1939, 1st Cruiser Sqdn Home Fleet December 1939, Mediterranean Fleet November 1940. Damaged by *Hipper* 25 December 1940. 1st Cruiser Sqdn Home Fleet March 1941. Major Action: Spartivento November 1940.
Ships Flight: 718 Sqdn to 21 January 1940, then flight of 700 Sqdn. Disbanded January 1941. Reformed 1 March 1941 at Lee-on-Solent. Disbanded June 1942.
718	Sep 1939-Jan 1940	2 Walrus	L2278
700	Jan 1940-Jan 1941	2 Walrus	L2229
700	Mar 1941-Jun 1942	2 Walrus	W2719

HMS BIRMINGHAM(1)
Type DIH catapult, removed after c.April-August 1943. 5th Cruiser Sqdn China Stn September 1939, 18th Cruiser Sqdn Home Fleet February 1940, detached Immingham May 1940, 18th Cruiser Sqdn Home Fleet July 1940, Mediterranean Fleet September 1941, 4th Cruiser Sqdn East Indies March 1942.
Ships Flight: 715 Sqdn to 21 January 1940, then flight of 700 Sqdn. Disbanded May 1943.
715	Sep 1939-Jan 1940	1 Walrus	L2202
700	Jan 1940-May 1943	1 Walrus	P5709

HMAS CANBERRA(1)
Type EIIIH catapult. Australian Sqdn September 1939, 4th Cruiser Sqdn East India March 1941, Mediterranean Fleet July 1941, East Indies Fleet August 1941, Australian Sqdn September 1941, Sunk Savo Island 9 August 1942.
Major Action: Savo Island 9 August 1942.
Ships Flight:
(700)	Jan 1940-Aug 1942	1 Walrus/		P5715
		Seagull V		A2-22

HMS CEYLON
Type DIVH catapult. Launched 30 July 1942, completed 12 July 1943, Home Fleet from August 1943.
Ships Flight: Formed April 43 at Lee-on-Solent. Never embarked. Disbanded at Donibristle June 1943.
700	Apr 1943-Jun 1943	2 Walrus	Z1819

HMS CORNWALL
Type DIH catapult. 5th Cruiser Sqdn September 1939, Force I Indian Ocean October 1939. 6th Cruiser Sqdn South Atlantic February 1940, 6th Cruiser Sqdn East Indies July 1941, 4th Cruiser Sqdn Far East Fleet March 1942. Sunk off Ceylon 5 April 1942.
Major Action: Sank raider *Pinguin* Seychelles 8 May 1941.
Ships Flight: 715 Sqdn to 21 January 1940, then flight of 700 Sqdn.
715	Sep 1939-Jan 1940	1 Walrus	
700	Jan 1940-Apr 1942	1 Walrus	L2313

HMS CUMBERLAND(1)
Type DIH catapult. South Atlantic Command September 1939, Force G October 1939, South American Division February 1940, 6th Cruiser Sqdn South Atlantic April 1940, South Atlantic Command July 1940, 1st Cruiser Sqdn Home Fleet August 1941.
Ships Flight: 712 Sqdn to 21 January 1940, then flight of 700 Sqdn. Disbanded July 1943.
712	Sep 1939-Jan 1940	1 Walrus	L2235
700	Jan 1940-Jul 1943	1 Walrus	W2702

HMS DEVONSHIRE(1)
Type EIIH catapult, removed after May 1943. 1st Cruiser Sqdn Mediterranean Fleet September 1939, 1st Cruiser Sqdn Home Fleet November 1939, South Atlantic Command November 1940. 4th Cruiser Sqdn Eastern Fleet March 1942. Major Action: Sank raider *Atlantis*, Ascension Island 23 November 1941.
Major Action: Dakar 24 September 1940.
Ships Flight: 711 Sqdn to 21 January 1940, then flight of 700 Sqdn. Disbanded May 1943.
711	Sep 1939-Jan 1940	1 Walrus	L2235
700	Jan 1940-Nov 1941	1 Walrus	L2335

HMS DORSETSHIRE
Type EIVH catapult. 5th Cruiser Sqdn China Station September 1939, Force I October 1939. 6th Cruiser Sqdn South Atlantic March 1940, South Atlantic Command July 1940 to June 1941, East Indies Command September 1941, 4th Cruiser Sqdn Eastern

Fleet March 1942. Ship sunk in Indian Ocean 5 April 1942.
Major Action: *Bismarck* 27 May 1941.
Ships Flight: 715 Sqdn to 21 January 1940, then flight of 700 Sqdn
   715   Sep 1939-Jan 1940 1 Walrus
   700   Jan 1940-Apr 1942 1 Walrus   W2578

HMS DUKE OF YORK
Type DIIIH catapult, removed after September 1944. 2nd Battle Sqdn Home Fleet November 1941, Force H October 1942, 2nd Battle Sqdn November 1942.
Major Actions: Operation Torch November 1942, *Scharnhorst* sinking 26 December 1943.
Ships Flight: Formed 1 September 1941 at Donibristle. Disbanded March 1944.
   700   Sep 1941-Mar 1944 2 Walrus   W2787 "ROMEO II"

HMS EDINBURGH(1)
Type DIH catapult. 18th Cruiser Sqdn Home Sqdn September 1939, 2nd Cruiser Sqdn Home Fleet November 1939, 19th Cruiser Sqdn Home Fleet March 1940. Ship sunk in Arctic 2 May 1942.
Ships Flight: 712 Sqdn to 21 January 1940, then flight of 700 Sqdn.
   712   Sep 1939-Jan 1940 1 Walrus
   700   Jan 1940-May 1942 1 Walrus   P5665

HMS EFFINGHAM
Type EIIH catapult. 12th Cruiser Sqdn Northern Patrol September 1939, detached to Home Fleet October 1939, Halifax Escort Force November 1939. Ship wrecked off Norway 17 May 1940.
Ships Flight: Formed 21 January 1940.
   700   Jan 1940-May 1940 2 Walrus   P5662

HMS EMERALD
Type EIH catapult, removed April 1944. 12th Cruiser Sqdn Northern Patrol September 1939, Halifax Escort Force October 1939, Western Approaches October 1940, 4th Cruiser Sqdn East Indies March 1941, attached East Indies Command July 1941, 4th Cruiser Sqdn East Indies April 1942.
Ships Flight: 700 Sqdn from 21 January 1940, to 703 Sqdn January 1943. Disbanded 1 May 1944.
   700   Jan 1940-Jan 1943 1 Seafox   L4519
   703   Jan 1943-May 1944 1 Kingfisher FN684

HMS ENTERPRISE
Type EIIH catapult, removed February 1944. 12th Cruiser Sqdn Northern Patrol September 1939, Halifax Escort Group October 1939, Home Fleet May 1940, Western Approaches June 1940, North Atlantic Command July 1940, Force H July 1940, South Atlantic Command October 1940, 4th Cruiser Sqdn East Indies Command March 1941, Force T April 1941, East Indies July 1941, 4th Cruiser Sqdn Eastern Fleet March 1942.
Major Action: Sinking of German destroyers Z27, T25 & T26 in Bay of Biscay 28 December 1943.
Ships Flight: 700 Sqdn from January 1940, to 703 Sqdn January 1943. Disbanded 19 April 1944.
   700   Jan 1940-Jan 1943 1 Seafox
   703   Jan 1943-Apr 1944 1 Kingfisher FN662

HMS EXETER(1)
Type SIH catapult. South American Division September 1939, Force G October 1939. River Plate action 13 December 1939. East Indies Command July 1941, 4th Cruiser Sqdn East Indies February 1942. Ship sunk in Java Sea 1 March 1942.
Ships Flight: 718 Sqdn to 21 January 1940, then flight of 700 Sqdn.
   718   Sep 1939-Jan 1940 2 Walrus   K8343
   700   Jan 1940-Mar 1942 2 Walrus   L2236

HMS FIJI
Type DIVH catapult. Portsmouth Command April 1940, 18th Cruiser Sqdn Home Fleet July 1940 to October 1940, attached Mediterranean Fleet April 1941. Lost Crete 22 May 1941.
Ships Flight: Formed 12 February 1940.
   700   Feb 1940-   Walrus   P5710

HMS GALATEA(1)
Believed Type EIIIH catapult. Rear Admiral (Destroyers) Mediterranean September 1939, 2nd Cruiser Sqdn Home Fleet January 1940, Sheerness/Humber May to July 1940, Home Fleet September 1940, 15th Cruiser Sqdn Mediterranean Fleet July 1941. Sunk Alexandria 15 December 1941.
Ships Flight: 713 Sqdn to 21 January 1940, then flight of 700 Sqdn. Disbanded April 1940.
   713   Sep 1939-Jan 1940 Seafox   K8588 H9B
   700   Jan 1940-Apr 1940 Seafox

HMS GAMBIA
Type DIVH catapult, removed c.June-September 1943. Home Fleet March 1942, 18th Sqdn Cruiser Sqdn Home Fleet April 1942, 4th Cruiser Sqdn Eastern Fleet May 1942.
Ships Flight:
   700   Feb 1942-May 1943 Walrus   W3085

HMS GLASGOW(1)
Type DIH catapult, removed after June 1944. 2nd Cruiser Sqdn Humber Force September 1939, 2nd Cruiser Sqdn Home Fleet October 1930, 2nd Cruiser Sqdn Humber Force November 1939, 18th Cruiser Sqdn Home Fleet January 1940, 3rd Cruiser Sqdn Mediterranean Fleet December 1940, 4th Cruiser Sqdn East Indies Fleet March 1941, attached Mediterranean August 1941, attached East Indies Command September 1941, 4th Cruiser Sqdn East Indies Fleet February to August 1942, 10th Cruiser Sqdn Home Fleet November 1942 to April 1943, 10th Cruiser Sqdn Home Fleet July 1943.
Major Action: Sinking of German destroyers Z27, T25 & T26 in Bay of Biscay 28 December 1943.
Ships Flight: 712 Sqdn to 21 January 1940, then flight of 700 Sqdn. Disbanded August 1943.
   712   Sep 1939-Jan 1940 2 Walrus   P5652
   700   Jan 1940-Aug 1943 2 Walrus   P5699

HMS GLOUCESTER(1)
Type DIH catapult. 4th Cruiser Sqdn East Indies Command September1939, attached South Atlantic Command May 1940, 7th Cruiser Sqdn Mediterranean Fleet May 1940 to July 1940, 3rd Cruiser Sqdn Mediterranean September 1940. Ship sunk off Crete 22 May 1941.
Major Action: Sinking of Italian destroyer *Espero* 26 August 1940.
Ships Flight: 714 Sqdn to 21 January 1940, then flight of 700 Sqdn.
   714   Sep 1939-Jan 1940 2 Walrus   L2298
   700   Jan 1940-May 1941 2 Walrus   P5668

HMAS HOBART
Type EIIIH catapult, removed October 1942 (or June 1941). Australian Sqdn September 1939, 4th Cruiser Sqdn East Indies November 1939, Force M/Force I January 1940, Red Sea Force May 1940, Australian Sqdn January 1941, 7th Sqdn Cruiser Sqdn Mediterranean Fleet August 1941, Australian Sqdn December 1941.
Ships Flight: Formed 21 January 1940.
   700   Jan 1940-   2 Walrus   L2321

HMS HOWE
Type DIIIH catapult, removed after December 1943. 2nd Battle Sqdn August 1942. Disbanded March 1943.
Major Action: Operation *Husky* July 1943.
Ships Flight: Formed 15 May 1942 at Donibristle. Disbanded 7 June 1943.
   700   May 1942-Jun 1943 2 Walrus   X9529 H

HMS JAMAICA
Type DIVH catapult. Home Fleet July 1942, 18th Cruiser Sqdn Home Fleet August 1942, 10th Cruiser Sqdn Home Fleet October 1942.
Major Actions: Sinking of Vichy French destroyer *Typhon* 19 November 1942, Sinking of *Scharnhorst* 26 December 1943, Sinking of German destroyer Z7 in Arctic 2 May 1942.
Ships Flight: Formed 15 April 1942 at Donibristle. Disbanded July 1943.
   700   Apr 1942-Jul 1943 1 Walrus

HMS KENT(1)
Type EIVH catapult, removed c.July-November 1942. 5th Cruiser Sqdn China Fleet September 1939, 4th Cruiser Sqdn East Indies Fleet December 1939, 3rd Cruiser Sqdn Mediterranean September to November 1940. Damaged by torpedo Bardia 17 September 1940. 1st Cruiser Sqdn Home Fleet September 1941.
Ships Flight: 715 Sqdn to 21 January 1940, then flight of 700 Sqdn. Disbanded March 1941. Reformed 15 August 1941 at Donibristle. Disbanded September 1942.
   715   Sep 1939-Jan 1940 1 Walrus
   700   Jan 1940-Mar 1941 1 Walrus
   700   Aug 1941-Sep 1942 1 Walrus   P5719

HMS KENYA
Type DIVH catapult. Home Fleet September 1940, 10th Cruiser Sqdn Home Fleet October 1940 to March 1943.
Ships Flight: Formed 1 June 1940 at Lee-on-Solent. Disbanded October 1942.
   700   Jun 1940-Oct 1942 2 Walrus   R6545

HMS KING GEORGE V
Type DIIIH catapult, removed c.February-July 1944. 2nd Battle Sqdn Home Fleet December 1940, Force H May 1943, 2nd Battle Sqdn Home Fleet October 1943.
Major Actions: *Bismarck* 22-27 May 1941. Operation *Husky* July 1943.

Ships Flight: Formed 1 July 1940 at Lee-on-Solent. Disbanded January 1944.
 700   Jul 1940-Jan 1944 2 Walrus   X9564

HMNZS LEANDER(1)
Type EIIIH catapult, removed June 1941. Replaced late 1941, removed 1943. RNZN September 1939, 7th Cruiser Sqdn Mediterranean Fleet June 1940, Red Sea June 1940, 4th Cruiser Sqdn February 1941, 15th Cruiser Sqdn Mediterranean Fleet June 1941.
Major Action: Sank *Ramb I* in Solomon Islands 13 July 1943.
Ships Flight: 720 (NZ) Sqdn to 21 January 1940, then flight of 700 Sqdn. Disbanded March 1943.
 720   Sep 1939-Jan 1940 1 Walrus   L2222 P9A
 700   Jan 1940-May 1942 1 Walrus   L2322

HMS LIVERPOOL(1)
Type DIH catapult, removed after August 1942. Liverpool 4th Cruiser Sqdn East Indies Command September 1939, 5th Cruiser Sqdn China Station December 1939, 4th East Indies Command May 1940, 7th Cruiser Sqdn Mediterranean Fleet July 1940, 3rd Cruiser Sqdn Mediterranean Fleet September to November 1940, 18th Cruiser Sqdn Home Fleet April 1942.
Major Action: Sinking of Italian destroyer *Espero* 26 August 1940.
Ships Flight: 714 Sqdn to 21 January 1940, then flight of 700 Sqdn. Disbanded June 1941. Reformed 1 November 1941 at Donibristle. Disbanded November 1942.
 714   Sep 1939-Jan 1940 2 Walrus   L2257
 700   Jan 1940-Jun 1941 2 Walrus   L2257
 700   Nov 1941-Nov 1942 2 Walrus   W2798

HMS LONDON(1)
Type DIVH catapult, removed early 1943. Rebuilt September 1939 to February 1941, 1st Cruiser Sqdn Home Fleet March 1941 to March 1944, detached West Africa June 1941.
Ships Flight: Formed 15 December 1940 at Lee-on-Solent. Disbanded February 1943.
 700   Dec 1940-Feb 1943 2 Walrus   W2796

HMS MALAYA
Type DIIH catapult, removed c.October-December 1942. 1st Battle Sqdn Mediterranean September 1939, Force J East Indies Command October 1939, North Atlantic Escort Force December 1939, 3rd Battle Sqdn Halifax, 1st Battle Sqdn Mediterranean Fleet May 1940, Force H December 1940 to March 1941, 2nd Battle Sqdn Home Fleet July 1941, Force H October 1941, North Atlantic Command May 1942.
Major Actions: Calabria 9 July 1940, Taranto 11 November 1940.
Ships Flight: 701 Sqdn to 21 January 1940, then flight of 700 Sqdn. Disbanded March 1941. Reformed 15 July 1941. Disbanded 8 October 1942.
 701   Sep 1939-Jan 1940 2 Swordfish
 700   Jan 1940-Mar 1941 2 Swordfish
 700   Mar 1941-Nov 1941 2 Swordfish   K8444
 700   Nov 1941-Oct 1942 2 Walrus   W3042

HMS MANCHESTER(1)
Type DIH catapult. 4th Cruiser Sqdn East Indies Command September 1939, 18th Cruiser Sqdn Home Fleet January 1940, detached Humber Force May 1940, 18th Cruiser Sqdn Home Fleet July to October 1940 and March to July 1941, also from June 1942. Ship sunk during Operation *Pedestal* 13 August 1942.
Ships Flight: 714 Sqdn to 21 January 1940, then flight of 700 Sqdn. Disbanded August 1941. Reformed 15 January 1942.
 714   Sep 1939-Jan 1940 2 Walrus
 700   Jan 1940-Aug 1941 2 Walrus   L2257
 700   Jan 1942-Aug 1942 2 Walrus

HMS MAURITIUS
Type DIVH catapult, removed June 1943. Home Fleet December 1940, 10th Cruiser Sqdn Home Fleet January 1941, attached Mediterranean Fleet at Mombasa July 1941, attached East Indies Fleet August 1941, attached Plymouth Command March 1942, 4th Cruiser Sqdn Eastern Fleet May 1942.
Ships Flight: Formed 1 August 1940 at Lee-on-Solent. Disbanded July 1943.
 700   Aug 1940-Jul 1943 2 Walrus

HMS NEPTUNE
Type EIIIH catapult. 6th Cruiser Sqdn Atlantic Command September 1939 to April 1940, 7th Cruiser Sqdn Mediterranean Fleet June 1940, 4th Cruiser Sqdn East Indies October 1940, attached South Atlantic Command December 1940 to January 1941, attached South Atlantic Command July 1941, 7th Cruiser Sqdn Mediterranean Command September 1941. Ship sunk by mines Tripoli 19 December 1941.
Major Action: Sinking of Italian destroyer *Espero* 26 August 1940.

Ships Flight: 716 Sqdn to 21 January 1940, then flight of 700 Sqdn
 716   Sep 1939-Jan 1940 2 Seafox   K8574
 700   Jan 1940-Dec 1941 2 Seafox

HMS NEWCASTLE(1)
Type DIH catapult, removed October-November 1942. 18th Cruiser Sqdn Home Fleet September 1939, detached Western Approaches July 1940, 18th Cruiser Sqdn Home Fleet September 1940, Force H December 1940, detached South Atlantic January 1941, attached South Atlantic Command March 1941, 4th Cruiser Sqdn Eastern Fleet March 1942.
Ships Flight: 712 Sqdn to 21 January 1940, then flight of 700 Sqdn. Disbanded December 1941. Reformed 15 December 1941 at Donibristle. Disbanded January 1943.
 712   Sep 1939-Jan 1940 2 Walrus   L2331
 700   Jan 1940-Dec 1941 2 Walrus   W2717
 700   Dec 1941-Jan 1943 1 Walrus   W3094

HMS NEWFOUNDLAND
Type DIVH catapult, removed after May 1944. Newfoundland Home Fleet January 1943.
Ships Flight: Formed 15 September 1942 at Donibristle. Disbanded 5 April 1943.
 700   Sep 1942-Apr 1943 2 Walrus   Z1820

HMS NIGERIA
Type DIVH catapult, removed January 1944. 10th Cruiser Sqdn Home Fleet October 1940.
Major Action: Sank *Bremse* 6 September 1941.
Ships Flight: Formed 1 June 1940 at Lee-on-Solent. Disbanded October 1942.
 700   Jun 1940-Oct 1942 2 Walrus   P5706

HMS NORFOLK(1)
Type EIVH catapult, removed March-May 1943. 18th Cruiser Sqdn Home Fleet September 1939, 1st Cruiser Sqdn Home Fleet October 1939. Bombed 16 March 1940. Force K Home Command South Atlantic January 1941, 1st Cruiser Sqdn Home Fleet March 1941, 18th Cruiser Sqdn Home Fleet August 1942, 1st Cruiser Sqdn Home Fleet October 1942.
Major Action: *Scharnhorst* sinking 26 December 1943.
Ships Flight: 712 Sqdn to 21 January 1940, then flight of 700 Sqdn. Disbanded May 1940. Reformed 20 May 1940 at Lee-on-Solent. Disbanded March 1943.
 712   Sep 1939-Jan 1940 1 Walrus   P5648
 700   Jan 1940-May 1940 1 Walrus   L2307
 700   May 1940-Mar 1943 1 Walrus   P5706

HMS ORION
Type EIIIH catapult, removed July-August 1941. 8th Cruiser Sqdn America & West Indies September 1939, Flagship Rear Admiral (Destroyers) Mediterranean May 1940, 7th Cruiser Sqdn (Flagsip) Mediterranean May 1940, Flagship Rear Admiral (Destroyers) Mediterranean July 1940, Flagship Vice Admiral (Destroyers) Mediterranean September 1940.
Major Action: Sinking of Italian destroyer *Espero* 26 August 1940.
Ships Flight: 718 Sqdn to 21 January 1940, then flight of 700 Sqdn. Disbanded March 1941.
 718   Sep 1939-Jan 1940 2 Seafox   K8581
 700   Jan 1940-Mar 1941 2 Seafox   K8571

HMS PENELOPE(1)
Believed Type EIIIH catapult, removed after August 1940. 3rd Cruiser Sqdn Mediterranean Fleet September 1939, 2nd Cruiser Sqdn Home Fleet January to July 1940, damaged in Norway by submarine *X.3*, also twice by grounding & by bombs 9-11.4.40, 2nd Cruiser Sqdn Home Fleet April 1941, 15th Cruiser Sqdn Mediterranean Fleet December 1941 to May 1942, 12th Cruiser Sqdn Mediterranean January to July 1943, Force Q/Force K Mediterranean October 1943, 15th Cruiser Sqdn Mediterranean Fleet December 1943. Sunk Anzio 18 February 1944.
Ships Flight: 713 Sqdn to 21 January 1940, then flight of 700 Sqdn. Disbanded April 1940.
 713   Sep 1939-Jan 1940 1 Seafox   K8588 H9B
 700   Jan 1940-Apr 1940 1 Seafox

HMAS PERTH(1)
Type EIIIH catapult (ex HMS *Ajax*). 8th Cruiser Sqdn America & West Indies September 1939, Australian Sqdn August 1941, Australian Sqdn March 1940, 7th Sqdn Cruiser Sqdn January 1941, Australian Sqdn August 1941; Sunk Sunda Strait 1 March 1942.
Major Action: Bombed Crete 30 May 1941.
Ships Flight: 718 Sqdn to 21 January 1940, then flight of 700 Sqdn
 718   Sep 1939-Jan 1940 1 Walrus
 700   Jan 1940-Mar 1942 1 Walrus/   L2319
                           Seagull V   A2-4

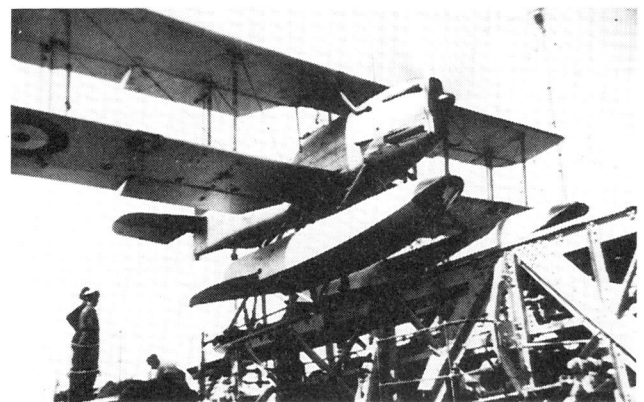

Fairey Seafox K8582 of HMS Ajax. (Capt JC Cockburn)

Walrus W2731 '9S' from HMS Birmingham. (FAA Museum)

Supermarine Walrus W3073 of HMS Glasgow. (G.H.H. Hollands)

Walrus W3099 of HMS Howe being hoisted. (Bill Bailey)

A Walrus being launched from HMS Rodney. (via D. Coombs)

A Walrus 'B' from HMS Sheffield around 1940. (FAA Museum)

A Walrus being launched from HMS Uganda 1943. (I.D. Jones)

Walrus '9B' from HMS Warspite.

HMS PRINCE OF WALES
Type DIIIH catapult, removed July-August 1941. 2nd Battle Sqdn January 1941, Force H September 1941, Force Z November 1941. Ship sunk 10 December 1941.
Major Action: *Bismarck* 23 May 1941.
Ships Flight: Formed 1 October 1940 at Lee-on-Solent
    700   Oct 1940-Dec 1941 2 Walrus

HMS QUEEN ELIZABETH
Type DIIIH catapult, removed after September 1942. 2nd Battle Sqdn Home Fleet May 1941, 1st Battle Sqdn Mediterranean May 1941, 2nd Battle Sqdn Home Fleet July 1943.
Ships Flight: Formed 1 November 1940 at Lee-on-Solent. Disbanded October 1942.
    700   Nov 1940-Oct 1942 2 Walrus   L2289

HMS RENOWN
Type DIIIH catapult, removed February 1943. Battle Cruiser Sqdn August 1939, Force K (Freetown) October 1939, Battle Cruiser Sqdn Home Fleet Match 1940, Force H August 1940 to August 1941, 2nd Battle Sqdn Home Fleet November 1941, Force H October 1942.
Major Actions: 1st Battle of Narvik 9 April 1940, Spartivento 27 November 1940, Operation *Torch* November 1942.
Ships Flight: Formed 1 June 1941 at Lee-on-Solent. Disbanded February 1943.
    700   Jun 1941-Feb 1943 1 Walrus   X9528

HMS REPULSE
Type DIIH catapult. America & West Indies Command October 1939, Battle Cruiser Sqdn December 1939, East Indies Command November 1939, Force Z (Singapore) November 1941. Ship sunk 10 December 1941.
Ships Flight: 705 Sqdn to 21 January 1940, then flight of 700 Sqdn.
    705   Sep 1939-Jan 1940 2 Swordfish   L7687
    700   Jan 1940-Aug 1941 2 Swordfish   P4152
    700   Aug 1941-Dec 1941 1 Walrus   R6586

HMS RESOLUTION
Type EIIIH catapult, removed late 1942. Channel Force August 1939, North Atlantic Escort Force October 1939, 2nd Battle Sqdn Home Fleet April 1940, Force H June 1940, Force M September 1940, 2nd Battle Sqdn Home Fleet October 1941, Eastern Fleet December 1941.
Major Actions: Mers-el-Kebir 3 July 1940, Dakar 23-25 September 1940
Ships Flight: 702 Sqdn to 21 January 1940, then flight of 700 Sqdn. Disbanded January 1941. Reformed 1 August 1941 at Halifax. Disbanded September 1943.
    702   Sep 1939-Jan 1940 1 Swordfish   P4199
    700   Jan 1940-Apr 1941 1 Swordfish   P4222
    700   Aug 1941-Sep 1943 1 Walrus/   W3044
                                        Swordfish   V4312

HMS RODNEY
Type EIIT catapult, removed by August 1943. 2nd Battle Sqdn September 1939, Force H September 1941, 2nd Battle Sqdn Home Fleet November 1941, Force H October 1942. Disbanded March 1944.
Major Actions: Operations against *Scharnhorst* & *Gneisenau* 23-29 November 1939, Norway April to June to 1940, *Bismarck* 27 May 1941, Operation *Torch* November 1942, Operation *Husky* July 1943.
Ships Flight: 702 Sqdn to 21 January 1940, then flight of 700 Sqdn. Disbanded March 1944.
    702   Sep 1939-Dec 1939 1 Swordfish   L7670 E8A
    702   Jan 1940-Jan 1940 1 Walrus
    700   Jan 1940-May 1942 1 Walrus   HD831

HMS SHEFFIELD(1)
Type DIH catapult, removed February 1944. 18th Cruiser Sqdn Home Fleet September 1939, detached Immingham May 1940, 18th Cruiser Sqdn Home Fleet July 1940, Force H September 1940, 10th Cruiser Sqdn Gibraltar October 1941, 18th Cruiser Sqdn Home Fleet November 1941, 10th Cruiser Sqdn Home Fleet October 1942.
Major Actions: Spartivento November 1940, *Bismarck* sinking 27 May 1941, Sinking German destroyers *Z7* 25 May 1942 and *Z16* 31 December 1942.
Ships Flight: 712 Sqdn to 21 January 1940, then flight of 700 Sqdn. Disbanded March 1943.
    712   Sep 1939-Jan 1940 2 Walrus   L2228
    700   Jan 1940-Mar 1943 2 Walrus   R6584

HMS SHROPSHIRE
Type EIIH catapult, removed after November 1942. 1st Cruiser Sqdn Mediterranean Fleet September 1939, Force H October 1939. 6th Cruiser Sqdn South Atlantic February 1940, 4th Cruiser Sqdn East Indies October 1940, detached Red Sea November 1940, 4th Cruiser Sqdn East Indies Fleet December 1940, 1st Cruiser Sqdn Home Fleet August 1941, South Atlantic Command March 1942, became HMAS *Shropshire* September 1942 to replace HMAS *Canberra*.
Ships Flight: 711 Sqdn to 21 January 1940, then flight of 700 Sqdn. Disbanded February 1943.
    711   Sep 1939-Jan 1940 1 Walrus
    700   Jan 1940-May 1942 1 Walrus   P5718

HMS SOUTHAMPTON(1)
Type DIH catapult. 2nd Cruiser Sqdn Humber Force September 1939, 2nd Cruiser Sqdn October 1939, 2nd Cruiser Sqdn Humber Force November 1939, 2nd Cruiser Sqdn Home Fleet December 1939, 18th Cruiser Sqdn Home Fleet February 1940. Ship sunk east of Malta 11 January 1941.
Major Action: Sinking of Italian destroyer *Vega* 10 January 1941.
Ships Flight: 712 Sqdn to 21 January 1940, then flight of 700 Sqdn.
    712   Sep 1939-Jan 1940 2 Walrus   L2294
    700   Jan 1940-Jan 1941 2 Walrus   P5641

HMS SUFFOLK
Type DIH catapult, removed early 1943. 18th Cruiser Sqdn Home Fleet October 1939, 1st Cruiser Sqdn Home Fleet January 1940. Damaged Stavanger 17 April 1940.
Ships Flight: 712 Sqdn to 21 January 1940, then flight of 700 Sqdn. Disbanded May 1940. Reformed 1 November 1940 at Lee-on-Solent. Disbanded January 1943.
    712   Sep 1939-Jan 1940 2 Walrus   L2244
    700   Jan 1940-May 1940 2 Walrus   L2284
    700   Nov 1940-Jan 1943 2 Walrus   L2181

HMS SUSSEX
Type EIIH catapult, removed by December 1943. 1st Cruiser Sqdn Mediterranean Fleet September 1939, Force H October 1939, East Indies Sqdn January 1940, 4th Cruiser Sqdn East Indies February & March 1940, 1st Cruiser Sqdn Home Fleet May 1940. Bombed, burnt out, sank Liverpool 18 September 1940. Salvaged & rebuilt October 1940 to August 1942. 1st Cruiser Sqdn Home Fleet September 1942 to January 1943, 4th Cruiser Sqdn Eastern Fleet March 1943.
Ships Flight: 711 Sqdn to 21 January 1940, then flight of 700 Sqdn. Disbanded Sullum Voe January 1941. Reformed 1 July 1942 at Donibristle. Disbanded November 1943.
    711   Sep 1939-Jan 1940 1 Walrus   L2262
    700   Jan 1940-Jan 1941 1 Walrus   P5669
    700   Jul 1942-Nov 1943 1 Walrus   Z1813

HMAS SYDNEY(1)
Type EIIIH catapult. Australian Sqdn September 1939, 7th Cruiser Sqdn Mediterranean Sqdn May 1940, Australian Sqdn February 1941. Ship sank and sunk by raider *Kormoran* 19 November 1941.
Major Actions: Sank *Bartolemeo Colleoni* 19 July 1940, Sinking of Italian destroyer *Espero* 26 August 1940.
Ships Flight: Existed by 1940.
    (700)   Jan 1940-Nov 1941 1 Seagull V/   A2-4
                                          Walrus   K8542

HMS TRINIDAD
Type DIVH catapult, removed early 1943. 10th Cruiser Sqdn Home Fleet December 1941. Ship sunk in Arctic 15 May 1942.
Ships Flight: Formed 1 September 1941 at Donibristle.
    700   Sep 1941-May 1942 2 Walrus

HMS UGANDA
Type DIVH catapult, removed after October 1944. Home Fleet January 1943, detached West Africa April 1943, attached Plymouth Command April 1943.
Ships Flight: Formed 1 September 1942 at Donibristle. Disbanded 4 June 1943.
    700   Sep 1942-Jun 1943 2 Walrus   X9469

HMS VALIANT
Type DIIIH catapult, removed March-April 1943. 2nd Battle Sqdn Home Fleet January 1940, Force H July 1940, 1st Battle Sqdn Home Fleet August 1940 to May 1942, West Africa Command January 1943.
Major Actions: Mers-el-Kebir 3 July 1940, Matapan 28 March 1941, Operation Husky July 1943.

Ships Flight: 700 Sqdn from 21 January 1940. Disbanded January 1943.
```
700      Jan 1940-Mar 1942  2 Swordfish    K8363
700      Mar 1942-Jan 1943  2 Walrus       W2758
```
HMS WARSPITE
Type DIIH catapult, removed May-June 1943. 2nd Battle Sqdn Home Fleet January 1941. Participated 2nd Battle of Narvik 13 April 1940. Mediterranean Fleet May 1940 to June 1941. Battle of Calabria 9 July 1940. Taranto 11 November 1940. Battle of Matapan 28 March 1941. Eastern Fleet March 1942.
Major Action: Operation *Husky* July 1943.
Ships Flight: 701 Sqdn to 21 January 1940, then flight of 700 Sqdn. Disbanded May 1943.
```
701      Sep 1939-Jan 1940   1 Swordfish    P4192
700      Jan 1940-May 1942   1 Swordfish    P4069
700      May 1942-May 1943   1 Walrus       W2701
```

HMS YORK(1)
Type SIH catapult. 8th Cruiser Sqdn America & West Indies September 1939, 1st Cruiser Sqdn Home Fleet January 1940, 18th Cruiser Sqdn May to July 1940, 3rd Cruiser Sqdn Mediterranean Fleet September 1940. Ship sunk 22 May 1941.
Major Actions: Sinking of Italian destroyers *Artigliere* and *Ariel* 12 October 1940.
Ships Flight: 718 Sqdn to 21 January 1940, then flight of 700 Sqdn.
```
718      Sep 1939-Jan 1940   1 Walrus
700      Jan 1940-Mar 1941   1 Walrus       L2278
```

HELICOPTER-CARRYING SHIPS

Listed below are ships which are, or have been, fitted with platforms to operate helicopters, either for use by the Ships Flight, or for occasional use only. Where appropriate, details of flight and squadron embarkations are given in tabular form, with specimen aircraft in the case of Ships Flights. Flight numbers have been allocated to these units in recent years, and a check list of known allocations is given at the end of the listing. In the case of RFAs, squadron embarkations are so complex that only very brief information is given in this list, the actual dates being available in the main squadron listings. Details of relevant pennant numbers, code numbers and deck codes are given in the section on aircraft code markings. Deck letters are not always worn on fins. In addition to Royal Navy ships, the list includes details of ships of the Australian, Canadian, New Zealand and Netherlands navies, where these have some relevance to the text.

HMS ACHILLES(2) F12
Type 12 (modified) *Leander*-class frigate laid down 1 December 1967, completed 9 July 1970 and commissioned 11 September 1970, fitted for Wasp flight. Refit 1978. Paid off January 1990 and sold to Chile September 1990 as *Ministro Zenteno*.
Ships Flight: Formed 19 June 1970 with Wasp, becoming No.052 Flight. Became *Bacchante* Flight 10 March 1978. Reformed c.3 April 1979, becoming No.043 Flight. Disbanded March 1988.
```
829/052  Jun 1970-Feb 1978  Wasp HAS1    XS538 428/AC
829/043  Sep 1978-Mar 1988  Wasp HAS1    XT778 430/AC
```
HMS ACTIVE F171
Type 21 *Amazon*-class-class frigate, laid down 23 July 1971 and completed 17 June 1977, fitted for Wasp flight. Falklands 1982. To refit 1985. Reformed with Lynx flight 1986. Sold to Pakistan June 1994 as *Shah Jahan*.
Ships Flight: Formed 9 August 1977 ex *Rothesay* Flight with Wasp, becoming No.035 Flight. Disbanded June 1985. Reformed November 1986 with Lynx as No.205 Flight. Disbanded July 1994.
```
829/035  Aug 1977-Jun 1985  Wasp HAS1    XT779 322/AV
815/205  Nov 1986-Jul 1994  Lynx HAS3    XZ692 322/AV
```
HMS AJAX(2) F114
Type 12 (modified) *Leander*-class frigate, laid down 12 October 1959 and commissioned 10 December 1963, fitted for Wasp flight. Paid off for refit and Ikara conversion 25 September 1970. Completed September 1973 and recommissioned 7 December 1973. Was to have paid off in March 1985, but instead it became a harbour training ship for HMS *Raleigh*. Sold and broken up in 1988.
Ships Flight: Formed 6 January 1964 at Culdrose, initially as part of No.700W Flight with Wasp. Disembarked Sembawang February 1965, and paid off 29 February 1968. Reformed March 1968. Disbanded 25 September 1970. Reformed 12 November 1973 as No.023 Flight. Disbanded August 1980. Reformed ex *Galatea* Flight 4 April 1981, as No.020 Flight. Disbanded in March 1985.
```
700W     Jan 1964-Mar 1964  Wasp HAS1    XS543 180/AJ
829      Mar 1964-Feb 1968  Wasp HAS1    XS537 460/AJ
  (at Sembawang Oct 1965 - Jan 1966)
829      Mar 1968-Sep 1970  Wasp HAS1    XT433 460/AJ
829/023  Oct 1973-Aug 1980  Wasp HAS1    XT426 421/AJ
829/020  Apr 1981-Mar 1985  Wasp HAS1    XT791 421/AJ
```
HMS ALACRITY F174
Type 21 *Amazon*-class frigate, laid down 5 March 1973, completed 2 July 1977, fitted for Wasp flight 1977-78, then Lynx flight. Falklands 1982. Refit 1986/87. Sold to Pakistan March 1994 as *Badr*.
Ships Flight: Formed 4 July 1977 ex *Danae* Flight with Wasp. Disbanded July 1978. Reformed 5 September 1978 with Lynx, as No.206 Flight. Became HMS *Brave* Flight April 1986. Reformed as No.233 Flight March 1987. Boyd Trophy Award 1989. Disbanded March 1994.

```
829      Jul 1977-Jul 1978  Wasp HAS1    XS572 327/AL
702/206  Sep 1978-Jan 1981  Lynx HAS2    XZ243 327/AL
815/206  Jan 1981-Apr 1986  Lynx HAS2    XZ254 327/AL
815/233  Mar 1987-Mar 1994  Lynx HAS3    XZ250 327/AL
```
HMS AMAZON F169
Type 21 *Amazon*-class frigate, laid down 6 November 1969 and completed 11 May 1974, fitted for Wasp flight, later Lynx flight. Refit 1983-84. Sold to Pakistan May 1993 as *Babur*.
Ships Flight: Formed 22 June 1975 ex *Dido* Flight with Wasp. Disbanded 26 May 1978. Reformed 9 October 1978 with Lynx as No.208 Flight, becoming Gibraltar Flight in May 1983. Reformed October 1984 ex *Ambuscade* Flight as No.219 Flight. Exchanged flights with *Newcastle* March 1991 to become No.223 Flight and disbanded October 1993.
```
829      Jun 1975-May 1978  Wasp HAS1    XT786 320/AZ
702/208  Oct 1978-Jan 1981  Lynx HAS2    XZ246 320/AZ
815/208  Jan 1981-May 1983  Lynx HAS2    XZ246 320/AZ
815/219  Oct 1984-Mar 1991  Lynx HAS3    ZD257 320/AZ
815/223  Mar 1991-Oct 1993  Lynx HAS3CTS ZF562 320/AZ
```
HMS AMBUSCADE F172
Type 21 *Amazon*-class frigate, laid down 1 September 1971 and completed 5 September 1975, fitted for Wasp flight, later Lynx flight. Falklands 1982. Sold to Pakistan July 1993 as *Tariq*.
Ships Flight: Formed 14 October 1975 ex *Londonderry* Flight with Wasp. Disbanded 14 March 1980. Reformed 15 December 1980 with Lynx, becoming No.219 Flight. Became *Amazon* Flight October 1984. Reformed September 1985 from *Birmingham* Flight, becoming No.200 Flight. Became *Nottingham* Flight August 1991. Reformed August 1991 from *Beaver* Flight as No.242 Flight. Disbanded June 1993.
```
829      Oct 1975-Mar 1980  Wasp HAS1    XT428 323/AB
702/219  Sep 1979-Jan 1981  Lynx HAS2    XZ721 323/AB
  (at Aldergrove Oct - Dec 1980)
815/219  Jan 1981-Oct 1984  Lynx HAS2    XZ696 -/-
815/200  Sep 1985-Aug 1991  Lynx HAS3    ZD259 323/AB
815/242  Aug 1991-Jun 1993  Lynx HAS3CTS ZF557 323/AB
```
HMS ANDROMEDA F57
Type 12 (modified) *Leander*-class frigate, laid down 25 May 1966, completed 2 December 1968 and commissioned 6 January 1969, fitted for Wasp flight. Paid off October 1977 for Sea Wolf conversion, completed December 1980, fitted for Lynx flight. Falklands 1982. Refit 1990/91. To Reserve June 1993 and remains in Reserve September 1994.
Ships Flight: Formed 16 December 1968 with Wasp. Became No.044 Flight August 1973. Boyd Trophy Award 1974. Disbanded Jan 1976. Reformed 23 February 1976. Became *Euryalus* Flight 16 December 1977. Reformed November 1979 with Lynx as No.222 Flight. Became *Scylla* Flight March 1990. Reformed ex *Charybdis* Flight August 1991 as No.227 Flight. Disbanded November 1993.

829	Dec 1968-Jun 1971	Wasp HAS1	XV626	472/AM
829	Jul 1971-Aug 1973	Wasp HAS1	XT438	472/AM
829/044	Aug 1973-Dec 1977	Wasp HAS1	XT421	472/AM
702/222	Nov 1979-Jan 1981	Lynx HAS2	XZ722	472/AM
815/222	Jan 1981-Mar 1990	Lynx HAS3	ZD261	472/AM
815/227	Aug 1991-Jun 1992	Lynx HAS3	XZ695	472/AM
829/227	Jun 1992-Mar 1993	Lynx HAS3	ZD253	472/AM
815/227	Mar 1993-Nov 1993	Lynx HAS3	ZD253	472/AM

(on *Broadsword* Jan - Jul 1993)

HMS ANTELOPE F170
Type 21 *Amazon*-class frigate, laid down 6 November 1969, completed 11 May 1974 and commissioned 19 July 1975, fitted for Wasp flight. Lynx Flight from 1980. Lost off Falklands 24 May 1982 as a result of air attack.
Ships Flight: Formed 31 October 1975 ex *Minerva* Flight with Wasp. Disbanded 1979. Reformed 20 February 1980 with Lynx, becoming No.216 Flight until ship sunk 1982.

829	Oct 1975-Apr 1979	Wasp HAS1	XT788	321/AO
702/216	Oct 1979-Jan 1981	Lynx HAS2	XZ691	321/AO
815/216	Jan 1981-May 1982	Lynx HAS2	XZ723	-/-

HMS ANTRIM D18
County-class destroyer, laid down 1966 and commissioned 14 July 1970. Wessex HAS.3 flight 1970-84. Damaged in air attack off Falklands 21 May 1982. Paid off at Plymouth 18 April 1984. Sold to Chile 25 June 1984 as *Almirante Cochrane*.
Ships Flight: Formed 10 August 1970 with Wessex, becoming No.100 Flight. Boyd Trophy Award 1976. Disbanded 20 January 1984.

737/100	Aug 1970-Aug 1982	Wessex HAS3	XS862	406/AN
829/100	Aug 1982-Jan 1984	Wessex HAS3	XM328	406/AN

HMS APOLLO(2) F70
Type 12 (modified) *Leander*-class frigate, laid down 1 May 1969, completed 28 May 1972 and commissioned 21 July 1972, fitted for Wasp flight. Refit for Wasp flight 1974/76. Sold to Pakistan October 1988 as *Zulfiquar*.
Ships Flight: Formed 15 May 1972 ex *Naiad* Flight with Wasp. Disbanded 15 July 1974. Reformed December 1976, becoming No.021 Flight. Disbanded April 1979. Reformed January 1980 ex *Ariadne* Flight as No.041 Flight. Disbanded March 1988.

829	May 1972-Jul 1974	Wasp HAS1	XS566	470/AP
829/021	Dec 1976-Apr 1979	Wasp HAS1	XS567	470/AP
829/041	Jan 1980-Mar 1988	Wasp HAS1	XT783	470/AP

HMS ARDENT F184
Type 21 *Amazon*-class frigate, laid down 26 February 1974 and completed 13 October 1977, fitted for Wasp flight, Lynx flight from 1987. Lost of Falklands 22 May 1982 as a result of air attack.
Ships Flight: Formed August 1977 with Wasp. Disbanded 1978. Reformed 26 July 1978 with Lynx, becoming No.207 Flight. Disbanded May 1982.

829	Aug 1977-Dec 1978	Wasp HAS1	XV632	340/AD
702/207	Jul 1978-Jan 1981	Lynx HAS2	XZ244	340/AD
815/207	Jan 1981-May 1982	Lynx HAS2	XZ251	-/-

HMS ARETHUSA(2) F38
Type 12 (modified) *Leander*-class frigate, laid down 7 September 1962 and completed 24 November 1965, fitted for Wasp flight. Paid off 10 September 1973 for refit and Ikara conversion, recommissioned 22 April 1977. Refit completed February 1986. Paid off June 1991 to be sunk as target.
Ships Flight: Formed June 1965 at Culdrose with Wasp. Disbanded August 1967. Reformed 16 September 1967, becoming No.044 Flight. Disbanded August 1973. Reformed June 1977, becoming No.022 Flight. Disbanded May 1986.

829	Jun 1965-Aug 1967	Wasp HAS1	XT433	426/AR
829/044	Sep 1967-Aug 1973	Wasp HAS1	XT781	426/AR
829/022	Jun 1977-Dec 1985	Wasp HAS1	XT437	426/-

(on *De Ruyter* Jan - Mar 1981)

HMS ARGONAUT F56
Type 12 (modified) *Leander*-class frigate, laid down 27 November 1964 and completed 17 August 1967, fitted for Wasp flight. Refit September 1972 to April 1973. Paid off for Exocet conversion November 1975 and completed March 1980, fitted for Lynx flight. Damaged in air attack off Falklands 21 May 1982. Recommissioned April 1984. Paid off March 1992 to disposals list. For sale 1993.
Ships Flight: Formed 18 November 1967 with Wasp. Disbanded December 1969. Reformed 6 May 1970. Disbanded October 1975. Reformed 25 June 1979 with Lynx as No.211 Flight. Became *Glamorgan* Flight March 1983. Reformed May 1983 ex *Gibralatar* Flight as No.203 Flight. Exchanged identities with *Sirius* Flight April 1989 to become No.243 Flight. Disbanded March 1992.

829	Nov 1967-Dec 1969	Wasp HAS1	XT418	466/AT
829	May 1970-Oct 1975	Wasp HAS1	XS564	466/AT
702/211	Jun 1979-Jan 1981	Lynx HAS2	XZ256	466/AT
815/211	Jan 1981-Mar 1983	Lynx HAS2	XZ233	466/AT
815/203	May 1983-Mar 1987	Lynx HAS2	XZ695	466/AT
829/203	Mar 1987-Apr 1989	Lynx HAS3	ZD251	466/AT
829/243	Apr 1989-Mar 1992	Lynx HAS3	XZ729	466/AT

RFA ARGUS A135
Aviation training ship, ex MV *Contender Bezant* built as Roll-on/Roll-off general cargo ship, commissioned 1981 & requisitioned May 1982 for South Atlantic with its own flight. Later bought and converted 1984-88 as helicopter support ship to replace RFA *Engadine* (q.v.). Arrived Portsmouth November 1987 and commissioned as RFA *Argus* June 1988. Fitted transport up to 12 Sea Harriers or to operate helicopters. Permanent RN party embarked, helicopter squadrons embark for training, exercises and operations at various times. Gulf 1991.
Sea Kings flown from 1988, and Lynxes from 1989.

829/029	May 1982-Aug 1982	Wasp HAS1	XZ562	371/-
829/031	May 1982-Aug 1982	Wasp HAS1	XT427	372/-
810	1988-date	Sea King HAS5/6		
826/B	1989	Sea King HAS5		
702	1989-date	Lynx HAS3		
700L	1990	Lynx HAS3 CTS		
845	1990	Sea King HC4		
846	1990-91 (Gulf)	Sea King HC4		
848	1991 (Gulf)	Sea King HC4		
826/C	1991 (Gulf)	Sea King HAS6		
845/A	1992	Sea King HC4		
846	1993	Sea King HC4		

HMS ARGYLL F231
Type 23 frigate, laid down April 1987 and commissioned May 1991, fitted for Lynx flight.
Ships Flight: Formed January 1992 with Lynx as No.210 Flight. Became *Battleaxe* Flight July 1994. Eventually intended to receive Merlin.

829/210	Jan 1992-Mar 1993	Lynx HAS3CTS	ZD567	365/AY
815/210	Mar 1993-Jul 1994	Lynx HAS3CTS	ZD567	365/AY
815/OEU	Sep 1993-Oct 1993	Lynx HAS3CTS	ZF558	672/PO

HMS ARIADNE F72
Type 12 (modified) *Leander*-class frigate, laid down 1 November 1969, completed 10 February 1973 and commissioned 2 March 1973, fitted for Wasp flight. Paid off for refit January 1980. Recommissioned 1981. Paid off 1988. Sold to Chile May 1992 as *General Baquedano*.
Ships Flight: Formed 24 November 1972 ex *Aurora* Flight with Wasp, becoming No.041 Flight. Became *Apollo* Flight January 1980. Reformed August 1980 ex *Ajax* Flight as No.023 Flight. Disbanded March 1988.

829/041	Nov 1972-Jan 1980	Wasp HAS1	XS570	455/AE
829/023	Aug 1980-Mar 1988	Wasp HAS1	XT426	455/AE

HMS ARROW F173
Type 21 *Amazon*-class frigate, laid down 28 September 1972 & completed 29 July 1976, fitted for Wasp flight. Lynx flight from 1979. Paid off 1988. Recommissioned June 1989 after 15-month refit. Sold to Pakistan January 1994 as *Khyber*.
Ships Flight: Formed 3 May 1976 with Wasp. Disbanded 13 October 1978. Reformed July 1979 with Lynx as No.204 Flight. Disbanded January 1988. Reformed with Lynx as No.231 Flight ex *Scylla* Flight July 1989. Disbanded December 1993.

829	May 1976-Oct 1978	Wasp HAS1	XT422	326/AW
815/204	Jul 1979-Jan 1988	Lynx HAS2	XZ241	326/AW
815/231	Jul 1989-Dec 1993	Lynx HAS3	XZ237	326/AW

HMS ASHANTI F117
Type 81 *Tribal*-class frigate, laid down 15 January 1958 and commissioned 23 November 1961, fitted for Wasp flight. Refit October 1967 to November 1969. Refit May 1977 to 1978. Became tender to *Sultan* 1981-87. Sunk as missile target September 1988.
Ships Flight: Formed 11 March 1964 at Culdrose with Wasp. Disbanded 24 September 1965. Reformed 15 November 1965. Disbanded 1 September 1967. Reformed 2 September 1969. Disbanded 19 August 1970. Reformed. Became *Charybdis* Flight 23 February 1976. Reformed 17 April 1978 ex *Naiad* Flight. Disbanded April 1980.

829	Mar 1964-Sep 1967	Wasp HAS1	XS540	177/AS
829	Sep 1969-Feb 1976	Wasp HAS1	XT794	427/AS
829	Apr 1978-Apr 1980	Wasp HAS1	XS562	427/AS

MV ASTRONOMER
Requisitioned 29 May 1982 for use in South Atlantic, and converted to helicopter transport and support ship. Chartered 22 April 1983 and renamed RFA *Reliant* (q.v.).

SS ATLANTIC CAUSEWAY
Roll-on/Roll-off general cargo ship. Requisitioned 4 May 1982 for use in South Atlantic as helicopter transport and support ship. Converted to maintain and operate helicopters.

SS ATLANTIC CONVEYOR
Roll-on/Roll-off general cargo ship, requisitioned 14 April 1982 for use in South Atlantic. Converted to aircraft ferry role. Embarked Sea Harriers of No.809 Sqdn and Harriers of No.1(F) Sqdn RAF flow off, but a number of Wessex of No.848D Flt, Chinooks of 18 Sqdn RAF and a Lynx of No.815 Sqdn were lost when ship hit in air attack and sank under tow 28 May 1982.

HMS AURORA F10
Type 12 (modified) *Leander*-class frigate, laid down 1 June 1961 and commissioned 9 April 1964, fitted for Wasp flight. Paid off 1972 for refit and Ikara conversion, completed March 1976. Paid off 29 April 1987 and sold for scrap 1988.
Ships Flight: Formed 11 March 1964 at Culdrose with Wasp. Disbanded 19 November 1969. Reformed 29 November 1969 as No.041 Flight. Became *Ariadne* Flight 24 November 1972. Reformed February 1976 as No.030 Flight. Disbanded May 1987.

829/041	Mar 1964-Nov 1972	Wasp HAS1	XS539 185/AU
829/030	Feb 1976-May 1987	Wasp HAS1	XT443 422/AU

MV AVELONA STAR
Chartered 28 May 1982 for use in South Atlantic. Fitted with helicopter pad.

HMS AVENGER(2) F185
Type 21 *Amazon*-class frigate, laid down 30 November 1974 and completed 15 April 1978, fitted for Lynx flight. Falklands 1982. Sold to Pakistan 23 September 1994 as *Tippu Sultan*.
Ships Flight: Formed 8 May 1978 with Lynx as No.205 Flight, temporarily to *Brilliant* March 1982. No.240 Flt formed April 1982, embarked for South Atlantic, disbanded on return September 1982. No.205 Flight became *Active* Flight November 1986. Reformed January 1988 ex *Arrow* Flight as No.204 Flight. Disbanded April 1994.

702/205	May 1978-Jan 1981	Lynx HAS2	XZ242 341/AG
(at Aldergrove May - Jun 1980)			
815/205	Jan 1981-Nov 1986	Lynx HAS2	XZ692 341/AG
(on *Brilliant* Mar - Jul 1982)			
815/240	Apr 1982-Sep 1982	Lynx HAS2	XZ249 341/AG
815/204	Jan 1988-Apr 1994	Lynx HAS3CTS	XZ697 341/AG

HMS BACCHANTE F69
Type 12 (modified) *Leander*-class frigate, laid down 27 October 1966 and completed 17 October 1969, fitted for Wasp flight. Refit 1977-78. Sold to Royal New Zealand Navy 1 October 1982 as HMNZS *Wellington* (q.v.).
Ships Flight: Formed 31 March 1969 with Wasp. Became *Scylla* Flight 1 March 1977 at Gibraltar. Reformed 10 March 1978 ex *Achilles* Flight, becoming No.052 Flight. Disbanded 31 October 1982.

829	Mar 1969-Mar 1977	Wasp HAS1	XT792 425/BC
829/052	Mar 1978-Oct 1982	Wasp HAS1	XS538 425/-

MV BALTIC FERRY
Roll-on/Roll-off general cargo ship. Requisitioned 2 May 1982 for use in South Atlantic. Modified as a logistic/troop transport and fitted with 2 helicopter pads.

HMS BATTLEAXE F89
Type 22 *Broadsword*-class frigate, laid down 4 February 1976, completed 28 March 1980, fitted for double Lynx flight. Refit 1988-89. Refit 1993-94. Reported to be for sale July 1994, possibly to Chile.
Ships Flight: Formed January 1981 ex *Phoebe* Flight 2 Lynx, as No.201 Flight. Became *Broadsword* Flight September 1988. Reformed from *Brazen* Flight April 1989 as No.235 Flight. Three aircraft in *London* May to July 1993. Became *Brave* Flight August 1993. Reformed July 1994 ex *Argyll* Flight as No.210 Flight.

815/201	Jan 1981-Sep 1986	Lynx HAS2	XZ725 403/BX
829/201	Sep 1986-Sep 1988	Lynx HAS2/3	XZ720 403/BX
829/235	Apr 1989-Mar 1993	Lynx HAS3	XZ235 402/BX
(on *London(3)* May - Jul 1989)			
815/235	Mar 1993-Aug 1993	Lynx HAS3	XZ241 403/BX
815/210	Jul 1994-to date	Lynx HAS3	403/BX

HMS BEAVER F93
Type 22 *Broadsword*-class frigate, laid down 20 June 1980 and commissioned 18 December 1984, fitted for double Lynx flight. Refit 1990-91.
Ships Flight: Formed July 1984 with 2 Lynx as No.244 Flight. Boyd Trophy Award 1985. Became Support Flight A July 1990. Reformed from *Phoebe* Flight February 1991 as No.242 Flight, becoming *Ambuscade* Flight August 1991. Reformed from *Danae* Flight September 1991 as No.218 Flight.

815/244	Jul 1984-Sep 1988	Lynx HAS3	ZD268 375/VB
829/244	Sep 1988-Jul 1990	Lynx HAS3	XZ698 374/VB
829/242	Feb 1991-Aug 1991	Lynx HAS3	XZ697 374/VB
829/218	Sep 1991-Mar 1993	Lynx HAS3	XZ726 374/VB
815/218	Mar 1993-to date	Lynx HAS3	XZ723 374/VB

HMS BERWICK(2) F115
Type 12 *Rothesay*-class frigate, laid down 16 June 1958 and commissioned 1 June 1961. Fitted for Wasp flight 1971. Paid off to Standby Squadron December 1980, Re-commissioned to active service June 1982. Paid off 1985 and sunk as target August 1986.
Ships Flight: Formed 4 January 1971 with Wasp. Became *Lowestoft* Flight October 1973. Reformed from *Plymouth* Flight April 1974 as No.032 Flight, becoming *Yarmouth* Flight 19 December 1980. Reformed June 1982, becoming No.040 Flight. Disbanded October 1985.

829	Jan 1971-Oct 1973	Wasp HAS1	XV639 440/BK
829/032	Apr 1974-Dec 1980	Wasp HAS1	XV632 440/BK
(on *Phoebe* Nov 1977 - Jan 1978)			
829/040	Jun 1982-Oct 1985	Wasp HAS1	XT793 440/BK

HMS BIRMINGHAM(2) D86
Type 42 *Sheffield*-class destroyer, laid down 1972 and commissioned 3 December 1976, fitted for Lynx flight. Refit 1985-86, provision for Lynx.
Ships Flight: Formed July 1977 with Lynx, becoming No.200 Flight. Became *Ambuscade* Flight September 1985. Reformed from *Newcastle* Flight September 1986 as No.241 Flight. Became *Marlborough* Flight June 1994.

700L/200	Jul 1977-Jan 1978	Lynx HAS2	XZ232 333/BM
702/200	Jan 1978-Jan 1981	Lynx HAS2	XZ232 333/BM
815/200	Jan 1981-Sep 1985	Lynx HAS2	XZ693 333/BM
815/241	Sep 1986-Jun 1994	Lynx HAS3	ZD256 333/BM
(on *Tidespring* Oct - Dec 1987)			

RFA BLACK ROVER A273
Small Fleet Tanker, laid down 1972 and commissioned 23 August 1974. Flight deck with stores lift, but no hangar.

HMS BLAKE C99
Helicopter Cruiser. Laid down 1942 as *Tiger*-class cruiser HMS *Tiger*, renamed *Blake* before completion. Construction suspended 1946-54. Commissioned 8 March 1961, converted for helicopters from early 1965, and recommissioned 23 April 1969 with hangar and flight deck to operate a squadron of 4 Wessex or Sea King. 820 Squadron reformed 23 May 1969 for service in ship. Paid off December 1979. Sold and to Cairn Ryan October 1982 for breaking up.

820	May 1969-Dec 1972	Wessex HAS3	XM838 412/BL
820	Dec 1972-Jan 1977	Sea King HAS1	XV708 410/BL
820	Jan 1977-Dec 1979	Sea King HAS2	XV647 412/BL

HMS BLOODHOUND
Type 22 *Broadsword*-class frigate, renamed *London* before completion.

RFA BLUE ROVER A270
Small Fleet Tanker, laid down 1968 and commissioned 15 July 1970. Flight deck with stores lift, no hangar. Sold to Portugal March 1993 as *Berrio*.

HMS BOXER F92
Type 22 *Broadsword*-class frigate, laid down 1 November 1979, completed 22 December 1983 and commissioned January 1984, fitted for Lynx flight.
Ship Flight: Formed ex *Glamorgan* Flight December 1984 as No.211 Flight. Became *Brazen* Flight October 1989. Reformed from *Cornwall* Flight as No.246 Flight April 1991. *Iron Duke* Flight on loan May to November 1993.
Operated No.700L Flight January to April 1991.

815/211	Dec 1984-Sep 1986	Lynx HAS3	ZD250 376/XB
829/211	Sep 1986-Oct 1989	Lynx HAS2/3	ZD251 376/XB
700L	Jan 1991-Apr 1991	Lynx HAS3CTS	ZF557 670/PO
829/246	Apr 1991-Mar 1993	Lynx HAS3	XZ735 377/XB
815/246	Mar 1993-to date	Lynx HAS3	XZ227 376/XB
815/203	May 1993-Nov 1993	Lynx HAS3	XZ690 404/XB

HMS BRAVE F94
Type 22 *Broadsword*-class frigate, laid down 5 April 1982 and commissioned 4 July 1986. Fitted Lynx or Sea King Flt. Gulf 1991.
Ships Flight: Formed April 1986 ex *Alacrity* Flight as No.206 Flight. At Rygge/Vaerlose April-May 1987. Became *Chatham* Flight June 1990. Reformed October 1990 ex *Coventry* Flight as No.245 Flight, becoming *Lancaster* Flight November 1993. Reformed August 1993 from *Battleaxe* Flight as No.235 Flight. Sea Kings of No.826A Flight attached October 1987, August-October 1988 and January-November 1990.

815/206	Apr 1986-Sep 1986	Lynx HAS2	XZ265 328/BA
829/206	Sep 1986-Jun 1990	Lynx HAS3	ZD261 328/BA
826/A	Oct 1987		Sea King HAS5

826/A	Aug 1988-Oct	1988	Sea King HAS5		
826/A	Jan 1990-Nov	1990	Sea King HAS5	XV690	135/-
829/245	Oct 1990-Nov	1992	Lynx HAS3	XZ733	328/BA
815/235	Aug 1993-to	date	Lynx HAS3	XZ241	328/BA

HMS BRAZEN F91
Type 22 *Broadsword*-class frigate, laid down 18 August 1978 and completed 2 July 1982, fitted for double Lynx flight. Gulf 1991. Reported to be for sale July 1994, possibly to Chile.
Ships Flight: Formed 14 June 1982 with 2 Lynx as No.235 Flight. Became *Battleaxe* Flight April 1989. Reformed October 1989 from *Boxer* Flight as No.211 Flight.
No.208 Flight attached in Lebanon November 1983.

815/235	Jun 1982-Sep 1986	Lynx HAS2	XZ690	330/BZ
815/208	Nov 1983 (Lebanon)	Lynx HAS2	XZ720	331/BZ
829/235	Sep 1986-Apr 1989	Lynx HAS3	XZ230	331/BZ
829/211	Oct 1989-Mar 1993	Lynx HAS3	ZD258	330/BZ
815/211	Mar 1993-to date	Lynx HAS3	XZ689	330/BZ

HMS BRIGHTON F106
Type 12 *Rothesay*-class frigate, laid down 23 July 1957 and commissioned 28 September 1961. Paid off for refit and modernisation 5 August 1968 to 1971, fitted for Wasp flight. Paid off March 1981. To Medway for scrap 16 September 1985.
Ships Flight: Formed 14 June 1971 with Wasp. Became *Plymouth* Flight 4 November 1974 at Gibraltar. Reformed 14 April 1975 ex *Rhyl* Flight as No.034 Flight. Became *Leander* Flight May 1981.

829	Dec 1971-Nov 1974	Wasp HAS1	XT779	461/BR
829/034	Apr 1975-May 1981	Wasp HAS1	XT415	461/BR

HMS BRILLIANT F90
Type 22 *Broadsword*-class frigate, laid down 25 March 1977 and completed 15 May 1981, fitted for double Lynx flight. Falklands 1982. To refit June 1987. Gulf 1991. Reported to be for sale July 1994, possibly to Chile.
Ships Flight: Formed August 1981 with 2 Lynx as No.220 Flight. Disbanded August 1987. Reformed December 1987 ex *Broadsword* Flight as No.221 Flight, becoming *Cornwall* Flight December 1992. Reformed December 1991 ex *Chatham* Flight as No.201 Flight.
2 Lynx of No.205 Flight attached in Falklands from *Avenger* March-July 1982.

815/220	Aug 1981-Sep 1986	Lynx HAS2	ZD268	342/BT
815/205	Mar 1982-Jul 1982	Lynx HAS2	XZ692	"341/AG"
829/220	Sep 1986-Aug 1987	Lynx HAS2/3	ZD268	342/BT
829/221	Dec 1987-Dec 1992	Lynx HAS3	ZD250	342/BT
829/201	Dec 1992-Mar 1993	Lynx HAS3	XZ722	343/BT
815/201	Mar 1993-to date	Lynx HAS3	XZ231	342/BT

HMS BRISTOL D93
Type 82 destroyer, laid down 1967 and commissioned 31 March 1973. Flight deck but no hangar. Refit 1979-80 and September 1984 to April 1986. Paid off May 1991. Sea Cadet/CCF accommodation and training ship at Whale Island 1993.

HMS BROADSWORD F88
Lead ship of Type 22 *Broadsword*-class frigate, laid down 7 February 1975 and completed 3 May 1979, fitted for double Lynx flight. Damaged in air attack off Falklands 25 May 1982. Reported to be for sale July 1994, possibly to Chile.
Ships Flight: Formed in March 1979 with 2 Lynx as No.221 Flight. Became *Brilliant* Flight in December 1987. Reformed from *Battleaxe* Flight in September 1988 as No.201 Flight. Became *Chatham* Flight in January 1992. Reformed as No.208 Flight in September 1992.
Andromeda Flight/No.227 Flight on loan January to July 1993.

702/221	Mar 1979-Jan 1981	Lynx HAS2	XZ724	347/BW
815/221	Jan 1981-Sep 1986	Lynx HAS2	XZ695	346/BW
829/221	Sep 1986-Dec 1987	Lynx HAS2/3	XZ229	346/BW
829/201	Sep 1988-Jan 1992	Lynx HAS3	XZ722	346/BW
829/208	Sep 1992-Mar 1993	Lynx HAS3	XZ723	347/BW
815/208	Mar 1993-to date	Lynx HAS3	XZ694	346/BW
815/227	Jan 1993-Jul 1993	Lynx HAS3	XZ694	347/BW

HMS CAMPBELTOWN F96
Type 22 frigate, laid down 1985 and commissioned May 1989. Fitted for Sea King or double Lynx flight.
Ships Flight: Formed October 1989 with Lynx as No.226 Flight

829/226	Oct 1989-Mar 1993	Lynx HAS3	ZD265	338/CT
815/226	Mar 1993-to date	Lynx HAS3	XZ229	338/CT

SS CANBERRA
Liner. Requisitioned 4 April 1982 for use in South Atlantic. Fitted with 2 helicopter pads. Returned to Southampton 11 July 1982.

HMS CARDIFF D108
Type 42 *Sheffield*-class destroyer, laid down 1972 and commissioned 24 September 1979, fitted for Lynx flight. Falklands 1982. Refit completed March 1989. Gulf 1991.
Ships Flight: Formed July 1979 with Lynx as No.214 Flight.

702/214	Jul 1979-Jan 1981	Lynx HAS2	XZ255	335/CF
(At Aalborg Apr - May 1980)				
815/214	Jan 1981-to date	Lynx HAS3	XZ234	335/CF

HMS CHALLENGER K07
Seabed operations vessel, laid down 1979 and commissioned August 1984. Major refit 1985-86. Deck for Sea King, no hangar. Parent ship letters CH. Paid off for disposal list 1991. Sold September 1993 as cable layer to Scottish firm.

HMS CHARYBDIS F75
Type 12 (modified) *Leander*-class frigate, laid down 27 January 1967 and completed 2 June 1969, fitted for Wasp and later Lynx flight. Paid off for Seawolf and Exocet conversion 1979. Conversion completed June 1982. Finally paid off August 1991 to be sunk as target.
Ships Flight: Formed 26 May 1969 with Wasp. Became *Cleopatra* Flight 24 November 1975. Reformed 23 February 1976 ex *Ashanti* Flight. Became *Cleopatra* Flight 20 November 1978. Reformed July 1982 with Lynx as No.228 Flight. Became *Glamorgan* Flight April 1986. Reformed December 1986 ex *Jupiter* Flight as No.227 Flight. Became *Andromeda* Flight August 1991.

829	May 1969-Nov 1975	Wasp HAS1	XT430	431/CY
(on *Fearless* May - Jul 1975)				
829	Feb 1976-May 1978	Wasp HAS1	XT781	431/CY
815/228	Jul 1982-Apr 1986	Lynx HAS2	XZ692	431/CY
815/227	Dec 1986-Aug 1991	Lynx HAS3	ZD253	431/CY

HMS CHATHAM F87
Type 22 frigate, laid down 1986 and commissioned May 1990. Fitted for Sea King or double Lynx flight.
Ships Flight: Formed June 1990 with Lynx as No.206 Flight. Became *Coventry* Flight December 1990. Reformed January 1992 ex *Broadsword* Flight as No.201 Flight. Became *Brilliant* Flight December 1992.
Also carried: Sea King HAS.6 of 826A Flight January 1991, to *Cumberland* January 1992. Lynx HAS.3CTS of 815/OEU January-February 1993. Sea King HAS.6 of 826B Flight ex *Cornwall* January 1993 until July 1993. Sea King HAS.6 of 819B Flight from July 1993 to date.

829/206	Jun 1990-Dec 1990	Lynx HAS3	ZD251	348/CM
826/A	Jan 1991-Jan 1992	Sea King HAS5	ZA161	131/-
829/201	Jan 1992-Dec 1992	Lynx HAS3	ZD260	348/CM
815/OEU	Jan 1993-Feb 1993	Lynx HAS3CTS	ZF558	672/PO
826/B	Jan 1993-Jul 1993	Sea King HAS6	XV696	132/-
819/B	Jul 1993-to date	Sea King HAS6	XV696	699/PW

HMS CLEOPATRA F28
Type 12 (modified) *Leander*-class frigate, laid down 19 June 1963, completed 4 January 1966 and commissioned 1 March 1966, fitted for Wasp flight. Refit May to September 1970. Paid off May 1973 for refit and Exocet conversion, completed November 1975. Recommissioned 28 November 1975. Refit 1978, completed April 1979, fitted for Lynx flight. Refit completed March 1988. Paid off January 1992. Sold to India for scrap 1993.
Ships Flight: Wasp of *Sirius* Flight on loan May to July 1966. Own Ships Flight formed 12 February 1968 with Wasp. Disbanded March 1970. Reformed 14 September 1970. Loaned *Engadine* October 1973 to March 1974. Became *Diomede* Flight April 1974. Reformed 24 November 1975 ex *Charybdis* Flight. Disbanded September 1977. Reformed April 1978. Disbanded September 1978. Reformed 20 November 1978 ex *Charybdis* Flight with Lynx as No.209 Flight. Became *Penelope* Flight January 1982.

829	May 1966-Jul 1966	Wasp HAS1	XT437	450/SS
829	Feb 1968-Mar 1970	Wasp HAS1	XT440	463/CL
829	Sep 1970-Apr 1974	Wasp HAS1	XV631	463/-
(*Engadine* Oct 1973 - Mar 1974)				
829	Nov 1975-Sep 1978	Wasp HAS1	XT784	463/-
702/209	Nov 1978-Jan 1981	Lynx HAS2	XZ247	463/CP
815/209	Jan 1981-Jan 1982	Lynx HAS2	XZ730	463/CP

MV CONTENDER BEZANT
Roll-on/Roll-off general cargo ship. Requisitioned 10 May 1982 for use in South Atlantic with Wasps of Nos.029 and 031 Flights. Converted as RFA helicopter support ship becoming RFA *Argus* (q.v.).

HMS CORNWALL F99
Type 22 frigate, laid down 1983 and commissioned 23 April 1988. Fitted for Sea King or double Lynx flight.
Ships Flight: Formed February 1989 as No.246 Flight. Became *Boxer* Flight April 1991. Reformed ex *Brilliant* Flight January 1992 as No.221 Flight.
Sea King HAS.6 of 826B Flight ex *Fearless* Flight July 1991 until to *Chatham* January 1993.

829/246	Feb 1989-Apr 1991	Lynx HAS3	XZ237 412/CW
826/B	Jul 1991-Jan 1993	Sea King HAS6	XV696 132/-
829/221	Jan 1992-Mar 1993	Lynx HAS3	ZD255 412/CW
815/221	Mar 1993-to date	Lynx HAS3	ZD255 412/CW

HMS COVENTRY (1) D118
Type 42 *Sheffield*-class destroyer, laid down 1973 and commissioned 10 November 1978, fitted for Lynx flight. Sunk off Falklands 25 May 1982 as a result of air attack.
Ships Flight: Formed 8 March 1979 with Lynx as No.212 Flight. Lost with ship.

702/212	Mar 1979-Jan 1982	Lynx HAS2	XZ257 336/CV
815/212	Jan 1981-May 1982	Lynx HAS2	XZ700 336/CV

HMS COVENTRY (2) F98
Type 22 frigate, laid down 1984 and commissioned 14 October 1988. Fitted for Sea King or double Lynx flight.
Ships Flight: Lynx of *Minerva* Flight/No.210 Flight on loan November to December 1988. **Ships Flight** formed November 1988 as No.245 Flight, becoming *Brave* Flight October 1990. Reformed ex *Chatham* Flight December 1990 as No.206 Flight.
Sea King HAS.6 of 826B Flight carried May 1990 until February 1991.

829/210	Nov 1988-Dec 1988	Lynx HAS3	ZD567"424/MV"
829/245	Nov 1988-Oct 1990	Lynx HAS3	XZ696 336/CV
826/B	May 1990-Feb 1991	Sea King HAS5	XZ571 136/-
829/206	Dec 1990-Mar 1993	Lynx HAS3	XZ230 336/CV
815/206	Mar 1993-to date	Lynx HAS3	

HMS CUMBERLAND(2) F85
Type 22 frigate, laid down 1984 and commissioned 10 June 1989. Fitted for double Lynx or Sea King flight.
Ships Flight: Formed May 1989 with Lynx as No.237 Flight. Disbanded January 1992.
Lynx of No.210/*Minerva* Flight attached January to February 1989. Sea King HAS.6 of 826A Flight ex *Chatham* Flight attached January 1992, its parent unit becoming 819A Flight July 1993.

829/210	Jan 1989-Feb 1989	Lynx HAS3	ZD567 424/MV
829/237	May 1989-Jan 1992	Lynx HAS3	XZ256 350/-
826/A	Jan 1992-Jul 1993	Sea King HAS6	XV674 135/-
819/A	Jul 1993-to date	Sea King HAS6	XV674 698/-

MV DAGHESTAN
Helicopter deck fitted November 1943 for Hoverfly I trials.

HMS DANAE F47
Leander-class frigate, laid down 16 December 1964, completed 7 September 1967 and commissioned 10 October 1967, fitted for Wasp flight. Refit, recommissioned 19 June 1970. Paid off for refit and Exocet conversion July 1977, completed September 1980, fitted for Lynx flight. Sold to Ecuador April 1991 as *Moran Valverde*.
Ships Flight: Formed 1 September 1967 with Wasp. Disbanded 18 February 1970. Reformed 16 March 1970. Became *Alacrity* Flight 4 July 1977. Reformed July 1979 with Lynx as No.218 Flight. Became *Beaver* Flight September 1991.

829	Sep 1967-Feb 1969	Wasp HAS1	XT415 464/DN
829	Mar 1970-Jul 1977	Wasp HAS1	XV628 464/DN
702/218	Jul 1979-Jan 1981	Lynx HAS2	XZ699 464/DN
815/218	Jan 1981-Apr 1988	Lynx HAS2/3	XZ726 464/DN
829/218	Apr 1988-Sep 1991	Lynx HAS3	XZ726 464/DN

HMS DEVONSHIRE(2) D02
County-class DLG commissioned 15 November 1962, fitted for Wessex flight. Paid off 30 July 1978. Sunk as missile target July 1984.
Ships Flight: Formed 14 March 1963 with Wessex. Disbanded October 1964. Reformed 14 June 1965. Disbanded 20 September 1968. Reformed 28 February 1971 ex *Fife* Flight. Disbanded 28 July 1978.

	Mar 1963-Oct 1964	Wessex HAS1	XM923 989/D
829	Jun 1965-Sep 1968	Wessex HAS1	XS864 404/DV
737	Feb 1971-Jul 1978	Wessex HAS3	XS146 403/DV

HMS DIDO F104
Type 12 (modified) *Leander*-class frigate, laid down 2 December 1959 as HMS *Hastings*, Renamed during building and and commissioned 18 September 1963, fitted for Wasp flight. Paid off July 1975 for refit and Exocet conversion, and recommissioned 27 October 1978. To New Zealand and recommissioned 18 July 1983 as HMNZS *Southland* (q.v.).
Ships Flight: Formed 12 December 1963 with Wasp. Became *Amazon* Flight 22 June 1975. Reformed October 1978, becoming No.055 Flight. Disbanded July 1983.

700W	Dec 1963-Mar 1964	Wasp HAS1	XS536 473/DI
829	Mar 1964-Jun 1975	Wasp HAS1	XT789 473/DI
829/055	Oct 1978-Jul 1983	Wasp HAS1	XT786 473/-

HMS DILIGENCE A132
Forward repair and maintenance ship, ex MSV *Stena Inspector*, completed January 1981 and chartered May 1982 for use in South Atlantic. Purchased October 1983, converted and commissioned as RFA March 1984. Operates mainly in South Atlantic but has deployed in Gulf (1987-89 and 1990-91). Parent ship letters DL.

HMS DIOMEDE F16
Type 12 (modified) *Leander*-class frigate, laid down 30 January 1968, completed 2 April 1971 and commissioned 21 May 1971, fitted for Wasp flight. Decommissioned 15 July 1988 and sold to Pakistan as *Shamsher*.
Ships Flight: Formed 28 September 1970 with Wasp, becoming No.023 Flight. Became *Ajax* Flight October 1973. Reformed ex *Cleopatra* Flight April 1974, becoming *Achilles* Flight September 1978. Reformed ex *Apollo* Flight April 1979 as No.021 Flight. Disbanded March 1988.

829/023	Sep 1970-Oct 1973	Wasp HAS1	XT432 429/DM
829	Apr 1974-Sep 1978	Wasp HAS1	XS528 423/DM
829/021	Apr 1979-Mar 1988	Wasp HAS1	XV634 423/DM

HMS DUMBARTON CASTLE P235
Castle-class offshore patrol vessel, laid down 1980 and commissioned 26 March 1982. Flight deck for Sea King, no hangar. Parent ship letters DC.

HMS EDINBURGH(2) D97
Type 42 *Sheffield*-class cruiser, laid down 1980 commissioned 17 December 1985, fitted for Lynx flight.
Ships Flight: Formed October 1985 with Lynx as No.207 Flight.

815/207	Sep 1985-to date	Lynx HAS3	XZ689 411/EB

MV ELK
Roll-on/Roll-off general cargo ship. Requisitioned for use in South Atlantic and modified to operate helicopters. Returned to Plymouth 12 July 1982.

MV EMPIRE MERSEY
Fitted with a platform for autogyro trials in USA. Was to be used for Hoverfly tests, but sank in 1943 before use.

HMS ENDURANCE(1) A171
Ice Patrol Ship, ex MV *Anita Dan*, built at Rendsburg 1955-56, purchased from Denmark 1967. Conversion completed 1 October 1968. Painted red to be conspicuous in Antarctic ice fields. Whirlwind Flight 1968-76. Wasp Flight 1976-86. Falklands 1982. Major refit 15 May 1986-1987. Lynx Flight 1987-91. Paid off October 1991 as beyond economical repair and sold to scrap in Singapore.
Ships Flight: Formed 27 May 1968 ex *Protector* Flight with Whirlwind. Disbanded May 1976. Reformed with Wasp June 1976, as No.001 Flight. Disbanded 5 May 1986. Reformed February 1987 with Lynx as No.212 Flight, transferring to *Endurance (2)* October 1991.

	May 1968-May 1976	Whirlwind HAR9	XL880 448/ED
829/001	Jun 1976-May 1986	Wasp HAS1	XS539 435/ED
829/212	Feb 1987-Oct 1991	Lynx HAS3	XZ246 434/ED

HMS ENDURANCE(2) A171
Ice Patrol Ship, ex MV *Polar Circle*, chartered October 1991 to replace *Endurance(1)* as HMS *Polar Circle*. Purchased February 1992 and renamed *Endurance(2)* October 1992.
Ships Flight: Ex *Endurance(1)* Flight October 1991 as No.212 Flight.

829/212	Oct 1991-Mar 1993	Lynx HAS3	XZ233 435/ED
815/212	Mar 1993-to date	Lynx HAS3	XZ246 434/ED

RFA ENGADINE K08
Helicopter Training Ship, laid down 1965 and commissioned 15 December 1967. Permanent RN party embarked. Facilities to operate 4 Wessex, or 2 Wasp and 2 Sea King. Most helicopter squadrons embarked for training, exercises and operations at various times. Falklands 1982. Flight deck extended 1984. Paid off March 1989 and sold for scrap 1990. Replaced by HMS *Argus* (q.v.). Parent deck letters EN.

737	1967-78	Wessex HAS1
737	1967-82	Wessex HAS3
814	1968-69	Wessex HAS3
846	1968-69	Wessex HU5
819	1968-70	Wessex HAS3
700S	1969-70	Sea King HAS1
824	1970-73	Sea King HAS1
737	1970-75	Sea King HAS1
820	1971	Wessex HAS3
846	1971	Wessex HU5
819	1971-75	Sea King HAS1
826	1972	Sea King HAS1

703	1972-80	Wasp HAS1	
829	1973-74	Wasp HAS1	

Trials Support Flt Oct 1973 - Mar 1974:

829	Cleopatra Flt	Wasp HAS1	XS528 451/-	
737	Glamorgan Flt	Wessex HAS3	XM871 410/GL	
824		Sea King HAS1	XV705 056/R	
814	1976	Sea King HAS1		
826	1976	Sea King HAS2		
700L	1977	Lynx HAS2		
820	1977	Sea King HAS2		
824	1977	Sea King HAS2		
829	1977	Wasp HAS1		
702	1978-88	Lynx HAS2		
820	1981	Sea King HAS5		
814	1982	Sea King HAS5		
825	1982 (South Atlantic)	Sea King HAS2		
847	1982 (South Atlantic)	Wessex HU5		
702	1982-89	Lynx HAS3		
819	1983	Sea King HAS2		
826/C	1983	Sea King HAS5		
810	1983-89	Sea King HAS5		

HMS ESKIMO F119
Type 81 *Tribal*-class frigate, laid down 22 October 1958 and commissioned 21 February 1963, fitted for Wasp flight. Paid off 1971, recommissioned 1973. Refit 1976-77. Refit 1979. Paid off to Reserve 1980. To Standby Squadron August 1981. Sunk as missile target January 1986.
Ships Flight: Formed 3 February 1965 with Wasp. Disbanded 4 July 1966. Reformed 28 November 1968. Disbanded c.21 August 1969. Reformed 3 March 1970. Disbanded 1 July 1971. Reformed January 1974 as No.027 Flight. Loaned to *Bulwark* September-October 1980. Became *Plymouth* Flight October 1980.

829	Feb 1965-Jul 1966	Wasp HAS1	XT416 183/-
829	Nov 1968-Aug 1969	Wasp HAS1	XV631 453/ES
829	Mar 1970-Jul 1971	Wasp HAS1	XT427 453/-
829/027	Jan 1974-Oct 1980	Wasp HAS1	XT781 453/-

(On *Bulwark* Sep - Oct 1980)

MV EUROPIC FERRY
Roll-on/Roll-off general cargo ship. Requisitioned 19 April 1982 for use in South Atlantic as a logistic/troop transport. Helicopters operated from upper deck. Sailed for UK 23 June 1982.

HMS EURYALUS F15
Type 12 (modified) *Leander*-class frigate, laid down 2 November 1961, completed 16 August 1964 and commissioned 16 September 1964, fitted for double Lynx flight. Ship paid off for refit and conversion March 1973, completed March 1976. Paid off 31 March 1989. Sold to India for scrap 1993.
Ships Flight: Formed 4 June 1964 with Wasp. Disbanded 16 July 1966. Reformed 5 September 1966. Became *Leander* Flight 31 January 1973. Reformed May 1976. Became *Rhyl* Flight 27 June 1977. Reformed 6 January 1978 ex *Andromeda* Flight. Disbanded. Reformed July 1980, becoming No.044 Flight. Disbanded March 1985.

829	Jun 1964-Jul 1966	Wasp HAS1	XS562 188/EU
829	Sep 1966-Jan 1973	Wasp HAS1	XV630 433/EU
829	May 1976-Jun 1977	Wasp HAS1	XT782 433/EU
829/044	Jan 1978-Mar 1988	Wasp HAS1	XT791 433/EU

HMS EXETER(2) D89
Type 42 *Sheffield*-class destroyer, laid down 1976 and commissioned 19 September 1980, fitted for Lynx flight. Falklands 1982. To refit August 1988. Gulf 1991.
Ships Flight: Formed with Lynx, initially as 29 JSTU (q.v.), becoming No.239 Flight. Became *Glasgow* Flight January 1989. Reformed ex *Southampton* Flight January 1989 as No.202 Flight.

815/239	Jun 1981-Jan 1989	Lynx HAS2	XZ733 420/EX
815/202	Jan 1989-to date	Lynx HAS3	XZ697 420/EX

HMS FALMOUTH F113
Type 12 *Rothesay*-class frigate, laid down 23 November 1957 and commissioned 25 July 1961. Refit August 1968. Recommissioned 6 January 1971, fitted for Wasp flight. Paid off to Standby Squadron 1980. Recommissioned 1992. Immobile tender to *Sultan* 1984-86. Broken up 1989.
Ships Flight: Formed 2 November 1970 with Wasp as No.010 Flight. Became *Phoebe* Flight February 1977. Reformed May 1977. Disbanded 2 May 1980. Reformed May 1982, as No.042 Flight. Disbanded December 1984.

829/010	Nov 1970-Feb 1977	Wasp HAS1	XS542 441/FM
829	May 1977-May 1980	Wasp HAS1	XV639 441/FM
829/042	May 1982-Dec 1984	Wasp HAS1	XT786 441/FM

HMS FEARLESS L10
Assault Ship, laid down 1962 and commissioned 25 November 1965. Refit 1989-91. Flight deck with two operating spots, but no hangar. No permanent flight, but squadrons and flights frequently embark for exercises and operations. Falklands 1982. Parent ship letters FS.

845	1967-68	Wessex HU5	
846	1968	Wessex HU5	
846	1968	Wessex HU5	
847	1969-70	Wessex HU5	
846	1971	Wessex HU5	
846	1971	Wessex HU5	
845	1972	Wessex HU5	
848	1972	Wessex HU5	
845	1974-76	Wessex HU5	
829	May 1975-Jul 1975	Wasp HAS1	XT430"431/CY"
846	1976	Wessex HU5	
845	1978	Wessex HU5	
846	1981-82	Sea King HC4	
845	1981-85	Wessex HU5	
846	1982 (Falklands)	Sea King HC4	
846	1983-84 (Lebanon)	Sea King HC4	
846	1984-85	Sea King HC4	
845	1988	Sea King HC4	
826/B	May 1991-Jul 1991	Sea King HAS6	
845	1991-92	Sea King HC4	
846	1992-94	Sea King HC4	

HMS FIFE D20
County-class destroyer [DLG], laid down 1962 and commissioned 21 June 1966. Refit September 1975, completed August 1976. To Harbour Training Ship at Portsmouth November 1979. Refit commenced July 1980. Recommissioned 31 March 1983. To refit January 1986, then to Dartmouth Training Squadron June 1986. Paid off July 1987 and sold to Chile as *Blanco Encalada*.
Ships Flight: Formed 31 October 1966 with Wessex. Disbanded 13 December 1968. Reformed 12 May 1969. Became *Devonshire* Flight 28 February 1971. Reformed ex *Hampshire* Flight 1 April 1976. Boyd Trophy Award 1979. Disbanded January 1980. Reformed September 1982 with Lynx as No.223 Flight. Disbanded November 1990.

829	Oct 1966-Dec 1968	Wessex HAS1	XS887 403/FI
829	May 1969-Jun 1970	Wessex HAS3	XS149 403/FF
737	Jun 1970-Feb 1971	Wessex HAS3	XS149 403/FF
737	Apr 1976-Jan 1980	Wessex HAS3	XP142 404/FF
815/223	Sep 1982-Nov 1990	Lynx HAS2	XZ248 404/FF

RFA FORT AUSTIN A386
Fort Grange-class Fleet Replenishment Ship, laid down 1975 and commissioned 11 May 1979. Fitted with flight deck and hangar for 4 Sea King. Relief landing platform on hangar roof. Often used for ASW Sea King detachments. Falklands 1982. Parent ship letters FA.

814	1980-82	Sea King HAS2	
819	1980	Sea King HAS2	
824/A	1980	Sea King HAS2	
824/B	1980-81	Sea King HAS2	
824/A	1981	Sea King HAS2	
815/203	Apr-Jul 1982 (Falklands)	Lynx HAS2	XZ242 -/-
815/231	1982 (Falklands)	Lynx HAS2	
826	1982 (Falklands)	Sea King HAS5	
845/B	1982 (Falklands)	Wessex HU5	
848/C	1982 (Falklands)	Wessex HU5	
826/A	1983	Sea King HAS5	
826/C	1983-84	Sea King HAS5	
826/B	1984	Sea King HAS5	
845	1984-86	Wessex HU5	
846	1985-86	Sea King HC4	
819	1985-86	Sea King HAS5	
826/C	1986	Sea King HAS5	
814	1987	Sea King HAS5	
824	1987-88	Sea King HAS5/6	
810	1988-date	Sea King HAS6	
826/A	1988-89	Sea King HAS5	
826/C	1989	Sea King HAS5	
702	1989	Lynx HAS3	
826/D	1991	Sea King HAS6	
845	1992	Sea King HC4	
846	1993	Sea King HC4	

RFA FORT DUQUESNE A229
Air Stores Support Ship, commissioned 1944. Fitted with flight deck. Dragonfly trials. Paid off and sold 1968. Broken up in Holland in 1969.

RFA FORT GEORGE A385
Fort Victoria-class Fleet Replenishment Ship, built down 1988-92. Two helicopter operating spots. Hangar to take 3 aircraft. Facilities to repair Sea King and Merlin. Emergency landing facilities for Sea Harrier. Permanent RN party embarked. Parent ship letters FO. First Sea King trials October 1993. 819 Sqdn Sea Kings embarked June to August 1994.

| 819 | Jun 1994-Aug 1994 | Sea King HAS6 | |

RFA FORT GRANGE A385
Fleet replenishment ship, built 1973-78, commissioned 6 April 1978, fitted with flight deck and hangar for four Sea King helicopters, relief landing platform on hangar roof. Often used for ASW Sea King detachments, Falklands 1982. Gulf 1991. Parent ship letters FG.
Ships Flight: Formed 24 February 1978 in No.706 Squadron at Culdrose with Sea King. Absorbed into No.824A Flight 6 December 1978.

706	Feb 1978-Dec 1978	Sea King HAS1	XV714 343/FG
824	1978	Sea King HAS2	
824	1978	Sea King HAS2	
824/A	1979	Sea King HAS2	
824/A	1979	Sea King HAS2	
702	1980	Lynx HAS2	
824/D	1980	Sea King HAS2	
824/C	1980-81	Sea King HAS2	
814	1981	Sea King HAS2	
824/A	1981	Sea King HAS2	
826	1982	Sea King HAS2	
824/C	1982 (Falklands)	Sea King HAS2	
826/B	1983-84	Sea King HAS5	
826/A	1983-84	Sea King HAS5	
820	1984	Sea King HAS5	
826/C	1984	Sea King HAS5	
819	1984-85	Sea King HAS5	
845	1984-86	Wessex HU5	
846	1985	Sea King HC4	
814	1986	Sea King HAS5	
772/B	Aug-Dec1986	Wessex HU5	XS513 519/-
810	1987	Sea King HAS5	
846	1987	Sea King HC4	
845	1988-89	Sea King HC4	
820	1988	Sea King HAS5	
826/B	1989	Sea King HAS5	
846	1990-91 (Gulf)	Sea King HC4	
826/C	1991	Sea King HAS6	
826/D	1991	Sea King HAS6	
845	1992	Sea King HC4	
846	1992	Sea King HC4	
814/A	1993 (Adriatic)	Sea King HAS6	
820	1993 (Adriatic)	Sea King HAS6	

RFA FORT VICTORIA A387
Fleet replenishment ship, built 1988-92, two helicopter operating spots, hangar to take three aircraft and facilities to repair Sea King and Merlin, emergency landing facility for Sea Harrier, permanent RN party embarked. Parent ship letters FV.

| 810/OEU | 1994 | Sea King HAS.6 | |

HMS GALATEA(2) F18
Type 12 (modified) *Leander*-class frigate, laid down 29 December 1961 and commissioned 25 April 1964, fitted for Wasp flight. Paid off for refit and Ikara conversion 1971, completed September 1974. Paid off to Standby Squadron 30 July 1986. Sunk as target June 1988.
Ships Flight: Formed 28 May 1964 at Culdrose with Wasp. Disbanded 9 September 1966. Reformed 7 November 1966. Became *Brighton* Flight December 1971. Reformed ex *Phoebe* Flight 5 August 1974 as No.020 Flight. Became *Ajax* Flight 4 April 1981. Reformed May 1982 as No.038 Flight. Disbanded October 1982. Reformed ex-*Hecla* Flight October 1982 as No.012 Flight. Disbanded September 1986.

829	May 1964-Sep 1966	Wasp HAS1	XS545 152/GA
829	Nov 1966-Dec 1971	Wasp HAS1	XS566 452/GA
829/020	Aug 1974-Apr 1981	Wasp HAS1	XT443 461/GA
829/038	May 1982-Oct 1982	Wasp HAS1	XS529 360/-
829/012	Oct 1982-Sep 1986	Wasp HAS1	XS529 461/GA

MV GEESTPORT Requisitioned 6 May 1982 for use in South Atlantic. Fitted with helicopter pad.

HMS GLAMORGAN D19
County-class destroyer [DLG], laid down 1962 and commissioned 11 October 1966. Fitted for Wessex and later Lynx flight. Refit 1978-81. Damaged by land-launched Exocet missile off Falklands 12 June 1982. Sold to Chile 1 October 1986 as *Latorre*.
Ships Flight: Formed 1 May 1967 with Wessex. Disbanded 18 December 1969. Reformed 18 May 1970. Attached *Engadine* November 1973 to March 1974. Disbanded 31 May 1978. Reformed ex *Norfolk* Flight 6 March 1981 as No.103 Flight. Disbanded 13 August 1982. Reformed March 1983 ex *Argonaut* Flight with Lynx as No.211 Flight. Became *Boxer* Flight December 1984. Reformed April 1986 ex *Charybdis* Flight as No.228 Flight. Became *London* Flight 1 September 1986.
No.208 Flight attached in Lebanon November 1983.
No.231 Flight attached February 1986.

829	May 1967-Dec 1969	Wessex HAS1	XM874 400/GL
737	May 1970-May 1978	Wessex HAS3	XM871 400/GL
737/103	Mar 1981-Aug 1982	Wessex HAS3	XM837 400/GL
815/211	Mar 1983-Dec 1984	Lynx HAS2	XZ240 400/GL
815/208	Nov 1983 (Lebanon)	Lynx HAS2	XZ720"320/-"
815/231	Feb 1986	Lynx HAS3	ZD256 479/PO
815/228	Apr 1986-Sep 1986	Lynx HAS3	XZ734 400/GL

HMS GLASGOW D88
Type 42 *Sheffield*-class destroyer, laid down 1974 and commissioned 24 May 1979, fitted for Lynx Flight. Damaged in air attack off Falklands 12 May 1982.
Ships Flight: Formed 26 June 1979 with Lynx as No.215 Flight. Became *Hermione* Flight November 1987. Reformed ex *Exeter* Flight January 1989 as No.239 Flight.

702/215	Jun 1979-Jan 1981	Lynx HAS2	XZ254 344/GW
815/215	Jan 1981-Nov 1987	Lynx HAS2	XZ232 344/GW
815/239	Jan 1989-to date	Lynx HAS3	XZ227 344/GW

HMS GLOUCESTER(2) D96
Type 42 *Sheffield*-class destroyer, laid down 1979 and commissioned 11 September 1985, fitted for Lynx Flight. Gulf 1991. Refit 1993.
Ships Flight: Formed September 1985 with Lynx as No.216 Flight. Became *Manchester* Flight February 1993. Reformed ex *York* Flight February 1994 as No.217 Flight.

815/216	Sep 1985-Feb 1993	Lynx HAS3	XZ254 410/GC
815/217	Feb 1994-to date	Lynx HAS3	XZ237 410/GC
(on *Sheffield* Jun - Aug1994)			

RFA GOLD ROVER A271
Small fleet tanker, built 1972-74, commissioned 22 March 1974. Flight deck with stores lift, no hangar. Parent ship letters GV. On disposal list 1993.

HMS GRAFTON F80
Type 23 frigate, building from 1993, due to commission October 1996. To be fitted with Lynx or later Merlin. Parent ship letters GT. Callsign 437.

RFA GREEN ROVER A268
Small fleet tanker, built 1967-69, commissioned 15 August 1969, re-engined 1973-74, flight deck with stores lift, no hangar, parent ship letters GN, paid off to reserve 1990, sold to Indonesia May 1992 as *Arun*.

HMS GRENVILLE F197
Type 15 frigate, built 1941-43, commissioned May 1943 as *Ulster*-class destroyer. Converted 1953-54, fitted with helicopter deck and used for Fairey ultra-light helicopter trials. Paid off April 1974. Broken up Queensborough 1983.

RFA GREY ROVER A269
Small fleet tanker, built 1968-70, commissioned 10 April 1970. Re-engined 1973-74. Flight deck with stores lift, no hangar. Parent ship letters GY.

HMS GURKHA F122
Type 81 *Tribal*-class frigate, laid down 3 November 1958 and commissioned 13 February 1963, fitted for Wasp flight. Refit 1968-70. To Standby Squadron 28 July 1980. Re-commissioned 24 July 1982. Paid off 30 March 1984. Sold to Indonesia April 1984 as *Wilhelmus Zakarias Yohannes*.
Ships Flight: Formed March 1965 with Wasp. Disbanded 3 August 1966. Reformed 21 November 1966. Disbanded 15 May 1968. Reformed 14 September 1970 becoming No.021 Flight. Became *Rhyl* Flight 1 August 1976. Reformed 8 November 1976 ex *Hydra* Flight. Disbanded 25 April 1980. Reformed June 1982 as No.049 Flight. Redesignated *Tribal* Flight 29 September 1983 and disbanded April 1984.

829	Mar 1965-May 1968	Wasp HAS1	XS530 444/GU
829/021	Sep 1970-Sep 1976	Wasp HAS1	XS567 444/GU
829	Nov 1976-Apr 1980	Wasp HAS1	XT428 444/GU
829/049	Jun 1982-Apr 1984	Wasp HAS1	XT430 444/GU

HMS HAMPSHIRE D06
County-class destroyer [DLG], commissioned 15 March 1963, fitted for Wessex flight. Refit 1970-73. Paid off April 1976. Scrapped at Briton Ferry April 1979.
Ships Flight: Formed 25 February 1963 with Wessex. Disbanded 30 June 1969. Reformed from *Kent* Flight 1 July 1969. Disbanded 19 January 1970. Reformed 7 May 1973. Became *Fife* Flight 1 April 1976.
London Flight attached May to July 1967.

	Feb 1963-Dec 1964	Wessex HAS1	XP156 472/HA
829	Dec 1964-Jun 1969	Wessex HAS1	XS875 472/HA
829	May 1947-Jul 1967	Wessex HAS1	XM842"405/LO"
829	Jun 1969-Jan 1970	Wessex HAS1	XS875 402/HA
737	May 1973-Apr 1976	Wessex HAS3	XS153 402/HA

HMS HECATE A137
Hecla-class Survey ship, laid down 1964 and commissioned 20 December 1965, fitted for Wasp flight. Refit Devonport October 1985 to March 1986. Paid off late 1987. Disposal list 1990.
Ships Flight: Formed 28 July 1965 with Wasp. Disbanded April 1967. Reformed 1 January 1968 at Brawdy as No.011 Flight. Became *Hecla* Flight 30 November 1969. Reformed ex *Vidal* Flight 3 August 1971. Became *Hecla* Flight 18 July 1975. Reformed 11 July 1977 ex *Hecla* Flight. Became *Hecla* Flight 1 July 1979. Reformed ex *Hecla* Flight 12 April 1981. Disbanded 20 October 1981. Reformed 19 May 1982 as No.013 Flight. Disbanded 15 December 1983.

829	Jul 1965-Apr 1967	Wasp HAS1	XT432 418/HT
829/011	Jan 1968-Nov 1969	Wasp HAS1	XS532 418/HT
829	Aug 1971-Jul 1975	Wasp HAS1	XS562 418/HT
829	Jul 1977-Jul 1978	Wasp HAS1	XT432 414/HT
829	Mar 1981-Oct 1981	Wasp HAS1	XT432 416/-
829/013	May 1982-Dec 1983	Wasp HAS1	XV626 414/HT

HMS HECLA A133
Survey ship, built 1964-65, commissioned 9 September 1965, fitted for Wasp Flight. Falklands 1982. Refit 1988-89. Gulf 1991.
Ships Flight: Formed 28 February 1965 with Wasp. Became *Vidal* Flight 1 January 1968. Reformed 1 December 1969 ex *Hecate* Flight as No.011 Flight. At Prestwick June to September 1973. Became *Hecla* Flight December 1973. Reformed ex *Hecate* Flight 18 July 1975. Became *Hecate* Flight 11 July 1977. Reformed 1 July 1979 ex *Hecate* Flight. Became *Hecate* Flight 12 April 1981. Reformed April 1982 as No.012 Flight. Became *Galatea* Flight October 1982.

829	Feb 1965-Jan 1968	Wasp HAS1	XT429 408/HE
829/011	Nov 1969-Dec 1973	Wasp HAS1	XS532 409/HL
(at Prestwick Jun - Sep 1973)			
829	Jul 1975-Jul 1977	Wasp HAS1	XT432 416/HL
829	Jul 1978-Mar 1981	Wasp HAS1	XT432 416/HL
829/012	Apr 1982-Oct 1982	Wasp HAS1	XT420 (416)/-

HMS HELMSDALE
Frigate, completed October 1943. Used in late 1946 for 771 Sqdn Hoverfly R.1 trials. Scrapped 1957.

HMS HERALD A138
Improved *Hecla*-class survey ship, built 1972-74, commissioned 31 October 1974, fitted for Wasp Flight. Falklands 1982. Refit 1987-88 with deck strengthening for Lynx. Continued in service without Flight after Wasps retired from service 1987. Gulf 1991. Parent ship letters now HR.
Ships Flight: Formed 2 September 1974 with Wasp ex *Hecla* Flight as No.011 Flight. Became *Hydra* Flight 25 July 1977. Reformed October 1977 ex *Phoebe* Flight as No.010 Flight. Disbanded July 1987.

829/011	Dec 1973-Jul 1977	Wasp HAS1	XV624 417/HE
829/010	Oct 1977-Jul 1987	Wasp HAS1	XT794 325/HE

HMS HERMIONE
Type 12 (modified) *Leander*-class frigate, laid down 6 December 1965 and commissioned 11 July 1969, fitted for Wasp and later Lynx Flight. Paid off for refit and Seawolf/Exocet conversion July 1979. Recommissioned 17 June 1983. Refit completed July 1988. Paid off May 1992. Disposals list 1993.
Ships Flight: Formed 20 May 1968 with Wasp. Became *Minerva* Flight 23 September 1968. Reformed 1 August 1969. Disb October 1979. Reformed June 1983 as No.229 Flight with Lynx. Became *Jupiter* Flight March 1987. Reformed November 1987 ex *Glasgow* Flight as No.215 Flight. Became *Liverpool* Flight May 1992.

829	May 1968-Sep 1968	Wasp HAS1	XS545 475/HM
829	Aug 1969-Oct 1979	Wasp HAS1	XV627 475/HM
815/229	Jun 1983-Mar 1987	Lynx HAS2	XZ720 475/HM
815/215	Nov 1987-May 1992	Lynx HAS3	ZD253 475/HM

HMS HYDRA A144
Hecla-class Survey Ship, laid down 1964 and commissioned 5 May 1966, fitted for Wasp flight. Personnel to UK 7 November 1973 while ship refit at Singapore, new personnel arrived from UK 28 December 1973. Falklands 1982. Sold to Indonesia 17 April 1986 as *Dewa Kembar*.
Ships Flight: Formed 23 June 1969 with Wasp. Disbanded 22 June 1970. Reformed 1970. Ashore at Tengah November 1972 to February 1973 and September 1973 to January 1974. Disbanded 1974. Reformed 1974 with same equipment but mainly new personnel. Ashore at Tengah May to August 1975. Became *Gurkha* Flight 8 November 1976. Reformed ex *Herald* Flight 25 July 1977 as No.011 Flight. Disbanded March 1986.

829	Jul 1969-Nov 1976	Wasp HAS1	XT436 419/HD
829/011	Jul 1977-Mar 1986	Wasp HAS1	XT432 415/HD

HMS INTREPID L11
Assault Ship, built 1962-67, commissioned 11 March 1967. Refit 1984-85. Flight deck with two operating spots, no hangar. No permanent flight but Squadrons and Flights frequently embark for exercises and operations. Falklands 1982. Parent ship letters ID. In reserve 1990 until replacement LPD built, then to be sold.

772/B	Jan-Mar 1987	Wessex HU5	XS513 519/-
845	1975	Wessex HU5	
845	1979-82	Wessex HU5	
845	1982 (Falklands)	Wessex HU5	
845	1987-88	Sea King HC4	
845	1990	Sea King HC4	
846	1981	Wessex HU5	
846	1985-90	Sea King HC4	
846	1981	Sea King HC4	
846	1982 (Falklands)	Sea King HC4	
847	1969-70	Wessex HU5	
848	1968	Wessex HU5	
848	1971-72	Wessex HU5	

CS IRIS
GPO cable ship, requisitioned 24 April 1982 for use in South Atlantic. Fitted out as a dispatch ship with a helicopter pad. Arrived UK 30 November 1982.

HMS IRON DUKE F234
Type 23 frigate, built 1988-92, commissioned 20 May 1993, fitted for Lynx flight.
Ships Flight
Formed March 1993 ex *Sirius* Flight with Lynx as No.203 Flight. On *Boxer* May to November 1993.

815/203 Mar 1993-to date	Lynx HAS3	XZ690 404/IR

HMS JERVIS BAY
Training ship. Converted Roll-on/Roll-off vessel *Australian Trader*. Commissioned 1977 but unable to carry helicopter until 1986/87 refit. Can now carry Sea King.

HMS JUNO F52
Type 12 (modified) *Leander*-class frigate, laid down 16 July 1964 and completed 18 July 1967, fitted for Wasp Flight. Paid off for Exocet refit May 1976. Recommissioned October 1978. Paid off for Exocet conversion by February 1981. To Standby Squadron 1981. Refit and conversion halted 1985, then used as navigation and engineering training ship. Paid off to disposals list 1992.
Ships Flight: Formed 24 July 1967 with Wasp. Became *Arrow* Flight May 1976. Reformed ex *Tartar* Flight 10 October 1977. Disbanded February 1981.

829	Jul 1967-May 1976	Wasp HAS1	XT422 465/-
829	Oct 1977-Oct 1980	Wasp HAS1	XT438 465/-

HMS JUPITER F60
Type 12 (modified) *Leander*-class frigate, laid down 3 October 1966 and completed 9 August 1969, fitted for Wasp Flight. Paid off for refit and Exocet/Seawolf conversion 1980. Recommissioned 21 October 1983, fitted for Lynx Flight. Paid off to disposals list April 1992.
Ships Flight: Formed 13 March 1969 with Wasp. Disbanded 16 March 1972. Reformed April 1972. Became *Naiad* Flight August 1975. Reformed 25 June 1976 ex *Scylla* Flight as No.024 Flight. Disbanded in November 1979. Reformed in September 1983 with Lynx as No.227 Flight. Became *Charybdis* Flight in December 1986. Reformed ex *Hermione* Flight in March 1987 as No.229 Flight.

829	Mar 1969-Sep 1975	Wasp HAS1	XV629 443/JP
829/024	Jun 1976-Mar 1980	Wasp HAS1	XT431 443/JP
815/227	Sep 1983-Dec 1986	Lynx HAS2	XZ227 443/JP
815/229	Mar 1987-May 1992	Lynx HAS3	XZ727 443/JP

Lynx HAS.3 XZ721 '327' of HMS Alacrity Flight in 1990. (MAP)

Lynx HAS.3CTS ZF562 '320/AZ' HMS Amazon Flight 1992. (MAP)

Lynx HAS.1 XZ256 '466/AT' of HMS Argonaut Flight. (I.G.Cave)

Lynx HAS.3 XZ235 '403/BX' HMS Battleaxe Flight c.1986. (MAP)

Lynx HAS.2 XZ232 '333/BM' of HMS Birmingham Flight. (MAP)

Lynx HAS.2 XZ690 '330' of HMS Brazen Flight 1984. (MAP)

Lynx HAS.2 XZ721 of HMS Cardiff Fight in 1983. (MAP)

Lynx HAS.1 XZ247 '463' HMS Cleopatra Flight. (I.G.Cave)

HMS KENT(2) D12
County-class destroyer (DLG), commissioned 15 August 1963, fitted for Wessex flight. Major refit 1969, recommissioned 8 December 1972. Refit November 1976 to April 1977. Paid off 20 June 1980 and became alongside training ship. Sold for scrap 1991.
Ships Flight: Formed 30 July 1963 at Culdrose with Wessex. Became *Hampshire* Flight 30 June 1969. Reformed 15 May 1972. Disbanded 20 June 1980.

	Jul 1963-Dec 1964	Wessex HAS1	XP141 181/KE
829	Dec 1964-Jun 1969	Wessex HAS1	XP140 401/KE
737	May 1972-Apr 1980	Wessex HAS3	XP150 401/KE

MV KEREN
Troopship and later accommodation ship at Port Stanley, ex-MV *St Edmund*. Built as Roll-on/Roll-off passenger ferry, requisitioned 12 May 1982, modified as troopship and fitted with two helicopter pads. Taken into Naval service 15 February 1983 and renamed. Returned to owners 1986.

HMS LANCASTER F229
T23 frigate, built 1987-92, ex-F232, renumbered due to superstition with Form 232 (collisions and groundings). Commissioned May 1992, fitted for Lynx flight, later to be Merlin.
Ships Flight: Formed November 1992 ex *Brave* Flight as No.245 Flight.

829/245	Nov 1992-Mar 1993	Lynx HAS3	XZ731 457/LA
815/245	Mar 1993-to date	Lynx HAS3	XZ731 457/LA

HMS LEANDER(2) F109
Lead ship of Type 12 (modified) *Leander*-class frigates, laid down 10 April 1959 and commissioned 27 March 1963, fitted for Wasp flight. Paid off April 1970 for refit and Ikara conversion, and recommissioned 17 January 1973. Refit 1980. Paid off to Standby Squadron 31 July 1986 and sunk as target September 1989.
Ships Flight: Formed 31 August 1963 at Culdrose with Wasp. Disbanded 20 December 1967. Reformed 3 March 1968. Disbanded 22 April 1970. Reformed ex *Euryalus* Flight 31 January 1973. Became *Sheffield* Flight December 1976. Reformed July 1977. Disbanded October 1980. Reformed May 1981 ex *Brighton* Flight as No.034 Flight. Attached *Tidepool* September to October 1981. Disbanded August 1986.

700W	Aug 1963-Mar 1964	Wasp HAS1	XS533 479/LE
829	Mar 1964-Dec 1967	Wasp HAS1	XS571 479/LE
829	Mar 1968-Apr 1970	Wasp HAS1	XS529 476/LE
829	Jan 1973-Dec 1976	Wasp HAS1	XT441 476/LE
829	Jul 1977-Oct 1980	Wasp HAS1	XT434 476/LE
829/034	May 1981-Aug 1986	Wasp HAS1	XT795 476/-
(on *Tidepool* Sep - Oct 1981)			

HMS LEEDS CASTLE P258
Castle-class offshore patrol vessel, built 1980-81, commissioned October 1981, flight deck for Sea King helicopter, no hangar, parent ship letters LC.

HMS LIVERPOOL(2) D92
Type 42 *Sheffield*-class destroyer, commissioned 1 July 1982, fitted for Lynx flight. Refit 1990-92.
Ships Flight: Formed March 1982 with Lynx as No.224 Flight. Ashore at AUTEC March to May 1988. Disbanded November 1990. Reformed ex *Hermione* Flight May 1992.

815/224	Mar 1982-Nov 1990	Lynx HAS2	XT694 332/LP
815/215	May 1992-to date	Lynx HAS3GMS	XZ720 332/LP

HMS LOFOTEN K07
Helicopter Support Ship, built May 1944-Oct 1945 as tank landing craft LST(3) *L3027*. Named HMS *Lofoten* 1947, later harbour accommodation ship. Converted 1964-66, recommissioned 23 June 1966, to operate up to six Wessex, parent ship letters LT. Laid up at Rosyth 1968 and later scrapped.

HMS LONDON(2) D16
County-class destroyer (DLG), laid down 1960 commissioned 4 November 1963, fitted for Wessex flight. Refit 1972-75. Paid off December 1981. Sold to Pakistan 22 April 1982 as *Babur*.
Ships Flight: Formed 22 October 1963 at Culdrose with Wessex. Disbanded 1 September 1965. Reformed 7 March 1966. Attached *Hampshire* May to July 1967. Disbanded June 1970. Reformed 16 June 1970. Disbanded 26 July 1972. Reformed 30 June 1975. Disbanded 31 March 1980.
772C Flt (Wessex HU.5) attached September 1980 to December 1981.

	Oct 1963-Dec 1964	Wessex HAS1	XP151 175/LN
829	Dec 1964-Sep 1965	Wessex HAS1	XP151 175/LN
829	Mar 1966-Jun 1970	Wessex HAS1	XS874 405/LO
(on *Hampshire* May - Jul 1967)			
737	Jun 1970-Jul 1972	Wessex HAS1	XM842 405/LO
737	Jun 1975-Apr 1980	Wessex HAS3	XM327 405/LN
772/C	Sep 1980-Dec 1981	Wessex HU5	XS507 514/-

HMS LONDON(3) F95
Type 22 frigate, ex-HMS *Bloodhound*, built 1983-87, renamed during building. Commissioned 5 June 1987, fitted for Sea King or double Lynx Flight. Gulf 1991.
Ships Flight: Formed 1 September 1986 ex *Glamorgan* Flight with Lynx as No.228 Flight. Became *Montrose* Flight February 1994.
Sea King HAS.5 826A Flt attached October 1987, and HAS.6 January to April 1989.
Lynx of 700L Flt attached February 1992.

815/228	Sep 1986-Feb 1994	Lynx HAS3	XZ228 405/LO
826/A	Oct 1987	Sea King HAS5	
826/A	Jan 1989-Apr 1989	Sea King HAS6	
829/235	May 1989-Jul 1989	Lynx HAS3	XZ698 406/LO
700L	Feb 1992	Lynx HAS3 CTS	ZF563 671/PO

LONDONDERRY F108
Type 12 *Rothesay*-class frigate, laid down 6 November 1956 and commissioned 22 July 1960. Refit 1967 to 1969, fitted for Wasp. Refitted from November 1975 as trials ship, and recommissioned 11 October 1979. Paid off as Portsmouth station training ship 30 March 1984. Sunk as target 1989.
Ships Flight: Formed 10 November 1969 with Wasp. Became *Ambuscade* Flight 13 October 1975.

829	Nov 1969-Oct 1975	Wasp HAS1	XV637 447/LD

HMS LOWESTOFT F103
Type 12 *Rothesay*-class frigate, laid down 19 June 1958 and commissioned 18 October 1961. Paid off refit and modification 29 August 1967. Recommissioned 29 May 1970, fitted for Wasp. Paid off 31 March 1985 and sunk in torpedo test in Bahamas June 1986.
Ships Flight: Formed 9 February 1970 with Wasp. Disbanded 15 June 1971. Reformed c.19 Oct 1971. Disbanded 15 June 1973. Reformed October 1973 as No.036 Flight. Disbanded March 1985.

829	Feb 1970-Jun 1973	Wasp HAS1	XT428 451/LT
829/036	Oct 1973-Mar 1985	Wasp HAS1	XS538 451/LT

RFA LYNESS A339
Stores Support Ship, commissioned 22 December 1966. Flight deck but no hangar. Parent ship letters LY. Chartered by USA Military Sealift Command January 1981, then sold March 1982 as USNS *Sirius*.

HMS MANCHESTER(2) D95
Type 42 *Sheffield*-class destroyer, laid down 1978 and commissioned 16 December 1982, fitted for Lynx flight. Gulf 1991. Refit 1991-93.
Ships Flight: Formed September 1982 with Lynx as No.232 Flight. Became *Marlborough* Flight August 1991. Reformed February 1993 ex *Gloucester* Flight as No.216 Flight.

815/232	Sep 1982-Aug 1991	Lynx HAS2	XZ734 360/MC
815/216	Feb 1993-to date	Lynx HAS3	XZ254 360/MC

HMS MARLBOROUGH F233
Type 23 frigate, laid down 22 October 1987, and commissioned June 1991, fitted for Lynx flight, later to be Merlin.
Ships Flight: Formed August 1991 ex *Manchester* Flight as No.232 Flight. Disbanded March 1994. Reformed June 1994 ex *Birmingham* Flight as No.241 Flight.

829/232	Aug 1991-Mar 1993	Lynx HAS3	XZ240 363/MA
815/232	Mar 1993-Mar 1994	Lynx HAS3	ZD257 363/MA
815/241	Jun 1994-to date	Lynx HAS3	363/MA

HMS MATAPAN D43
Sonar trials ship, built 1944-47, commissioned 1947 as *Battle*-class destroyer. Reserve from 1965, converted 1971-72, and recommissioned 2 February 1973, fitted with flight deck but no hangar. Parent ship letters MP. Decommissioned 1977. Broken up at Blyth August 1979.

HMS MERMAID F76
Built 1965-68 for Ghana but not delivered after the demise of President Nkrumah. Bought from builders Yarrow April 1972 and commissioned 16 May 1973. Flight deck for Wasp, no hangar. Parent ship letters MM. Transferred to Malaysia May 1977 as *Hang Tuah*.

HMS MINERVA F45
Type 12 (modified) *Leander*-class frigate, laid down 3 June 1963, completed 14 May 1966 and commissioned 22 May 1966, fitted for Wasp and later Lynx flight. Paid off December 1975 for refit and Exocet conversion, completed March 1979. Falklands 1982. Paid off April 1992. Sold to India for scrap 1993
Ships Flight: Formed 23 September 1968 ex *Hermione* Flight with Wasp. Became *Antelope* Flight 31 October 1975. Reformed 18 December 1978 with Lynx, becoming No.210 Flight. Attached *Coventry* November to December 1988, *Cumberland* January to February 1989, Aldergrove March 1989 and Tirstrup April to May 1989. Became *Argyll* Flight January 1992.

829	May 1968-Sep 1968	Wasp HAS1	XT437	"450/SS"
829	Sep 1968-Oct 1975	Wasp HAS1	XT788	424/MV
702/210	Dec 1978-Jan 1981	Lynx HAS2	XZ248	424/MV
815/210	Jan 1981-Apr 1988	Lynx HAS2	XZ698	424/-

(on *Fort Austin* Apr 1982 Lynx HAS2 XZ730 -/-)

829/210	Apr 1988-Jan 1992	Lynx HAS3	XZ730	424/MV

(On *Coventry(2)* Nov -Dec 1988)
(On *Cumberland(2)* Jan - Feb 1989)

HMS MOHAWK F125
Type 81 *Tribal*-class frigate, laid down 23 December 1960 and commissioned 29 November 1963, fitted for Wasp flight. To Standby Squadron after refit 15 October 1979. Paid off 1981. Broken up Cairn Ryan November 1982.
Ships Flight: Formed 14 January 1964 at Culdrose with Wasp. Disbanded 9 April 1970. Reformed 22 March 1972. Disbanded 25 May 1979.

700W	Jan 1964-Mar 1964	Wasp HAS1	XS538 474/MO
829	Mar 1964-Apr 1970	Wasp HAS1	XT422 474/MO
829	Mar 1972-May 1979	Wasp HAS1	XS568 474/MO

HMS MONMOUTH(2) F235
Type 23 frigate, built 1989-92, commissioned September 1993, fitted for Lynx flight, later to be Merlin.
Ships Flight: Formed November 1993 ex *Andromeda* Flight with Lynx as No.227 Flight. Became Support Flight B June 1994.

815/227	Nov 1993-Jun 1994	Lynx HAS3	ZD253 415/MM

HMS MONTROSE F236
Type 23 frigate, built 1989-93, commissioned 1994, fitted for Lynx flight, later to be Merlin.
Ships Flight: Formed February 1994 ex *London* Flight with Lynx as No.228 Flight. Disbanded June 1994.

815/228	Feb 1994-Jun 1994	Lynx HAS3	XZ690 444/MR

HMS NAIAD F39
Type 12 (modified) *Leander*-class frigate, laid down 30 October 1962 and completed 15 March 1965, fitted for Wasp flight. Paid off for refit and Ikara conversion c.July 1972. Completed July 1975. Paid off to disposals list April 1987, to be sunk as target.
Ships Flight: Formed at Culdrose January 1965 as No.015 Flight. Disbanded 21 November 1969. Reformed 4 May 1970. Became *Apollo* Flight 15 May 1972. Reformed ex *Jupiter* Flight September 1975. Became *Ashanti* Flight 17 April 1978. Reformed September 1978 as No.045 Flight. Disbanded May 1987.

829/015	Jan 1965-Nov 1969	Wasp HAS1	XT417 470/NA
829	May 1970-May 1972	Wasp HAS1	XS566 470/NA
829	Sep 1975-Apr 1978	Wasp HAS1	XZ562 324/NA
829/045	Sep 1978-May 1987	Wasp HAS1	XT782 324/-

HMS NEWCASTLE(2) D87
Type 42 *Sheffield*-class destroyer, commissioned 23 March 1978, fitted for Lynx flight. Refit April 1986 - 1987.
Ships Flight: Formed January 1978 with Lynx as No.203 Flight. To *Fort Austin* March 1982. Reformed June 1982 as No.241 Flight. Became *Birmingham* Flight September 1986. Reformed October 1987 ex *Fife* Flight as No.223 Flight. Became *Amazon* Flight March 1991. Reformed March 1991 from old *Amazon* Flight as No.219 Flight.

702/203	Jan 1978-Jan 1981	Lynx HAS2	XZ239 345/NC
815/203	Jan 1981-Mar 1982	Lynx HAS2	XZ239 345/NC
815/241	Jun 1982-Sep 1986	Lynx HAS2	XZ732 345/NC
815/223	Oct 1987-Mar 1991	Lynx HAS3	XZ248 345/NC
815/219	Mar 1991-to date	Lynx HAS3	XZ691 345/NC

MV NORDIC FERRY
Roll-on/Roll-on general cargo. Requisitioned 3 May 1982 for use in South Atlantic. Modified as a logistic/troop transport with 2 helicopter pads. Returned to UK 25 August 1982.

HMS NORFOLK(2) D21
County-Class DLG, built 1966-70, completed 7 March 1970 and commissioned 29 May 1970, fitted for Wessex Flight. Paid off 1981. Sold to Chile March 1982 as *Prat*.
Ships Flight: Formed 14 September 1970 ex *Olwen* Flight with Wessex as No.103 Flight. Attached *Olwen* February to March 1976. Became *Glamorgan* Flight 6 March 1981.

737/103	Sep 1970-Mar 1981 Wessex HAS3	XP140 407/NF

(On *Olwen* Feb - Mar 1976)

HMS NORFOLK(3) F230
Lead ship of Type 23-class frigate, built 1985-90, commissioned June 1990, fitted for Lynx flight, later to be Merlin.
Ships Flight: Formed January 1991 with Lynx as No.209 Flight.

829/209	Jan 1991-Mar 1993	Lynx HAS3	XZ248 361/NF
815/209	Mar 1993-to date	Lynx HAS3	XZ234 361/NF

MV NORLAND
Requisitioned 17 April 1982 for use in South Atlantic and fitted with 2 helicopter pads.

HMS NORTHUMBERLAND F238
Type 23 *Duke*-class frigate, building from 1991, due to commission May 1994, to be fitted with Lynx or later with Merlin. Parent ship letters NL, callsign 372.

HMS NOTTINGHAM D91
Type 42 *Sheffield*-class destroyer, built 1978-83, commissioned 8 April 1983, fitted for Lynx flight. Refit 1986, completed April 1986. Refit 1990-91.
Ships Flight: Formed January 1983 with Lynx as No.236 Flight. Disbanded November 1990. Reformed August 1991 ex *Ambuscade* Flight as No.200 Flight.

815/236	Jan 1983-Nov 1990	Lynx HAS2	XZ230 417/NM
815/200	Aug 1991-to date	Lynx HAS3	ZD250 417/NM

HMS NUBIAN F131
Type 81 *Tribal*-class frigate, laid down 7 September 1959 and commissioned 9 October 1962. Fitted for Wasp flight from 1964. To Standby Squadron 1979. Paid off 1983. Sunk as target 1986.
Ships Flight: Formed 21 October 1964 at Culdrose with Wasp. Disbanded 12 April 1966. Reformed May 1966. Disbanded April 1967. Reformed December 1967. Disbanded 22 June 1968. Reformed 1 October 1968. Disbanded c.27 September 1970. Reformed 9 January 1973. Became *Aurora* Flight February 1976. Reformed 1 September 1976. Disbanded 31 August 1979.

829	Oct 1964-Apr 1966	Wasp HAS1	XS566 187/NU
829	May 1966-Jun 1968	Wasp HAS1	XT442 457/NU
829	Oct 1968-Dec 1970	Wasp HAS1	XV623 457/NU
829/030	Jan 1973-Feb 1976	Wasp HAS1	XT420 457/NU
829	Sep 1976-Aug 1979	Wasp HAS1	XS532 457/NU

RFA OLEANDER A124
OL-class tanker, renamed RFA OLMEDA (q.v.) September 1967.

RFA OLMEDA A124
OL-class tanker, ex-RFA *Oleander*, built 1964-65, commissioned 18 October 1965, renamed September 1967 to avoid confusion with frigate HMS *Leander*. Flight deck, hangar for two Sea Kings to port side of funnel. Falklands 1982. Parent ship letters OD. To disposal list Dec 1993.

819	1966	Wessex HAS1	
826	1968	Wessex HAS1	
820	1968	Wessex HAS1	
814	1968	Wessex HAS3	
819	1969-70	Wessex HAS3	
820	1970-71	Wessex HAS3	
824	1972	Sea King HAS1	
819	1973	Sea King HAS1	
829	Oct 1973	Wasp HAS1	XV636 450/SS
824	1976	Sea King HAS1	
772/A	Oct-Dec 1977	Wessex HU5	XT480 436/RG
824	1977-78	Sea King HAS2	
772/B	Apr-Dec 1978	Wessex HU5	XT486 437/RS
820	1980	Sea King HAS5	
814	1980	Sea King HAS2	
824/C	1980	Sea King HAS2	
846	1981	Sea King HC4	
819	1981	Sea King HAS2	
824/B	1981	Sea King HAS2	
845	1982	Wessex HU5	
824/A	1982 (Falklands)	Sea King HAS2	
824/B	1983-84	Sea King HAS5	
826/A	1984	Sea King HAS5	
845	1984-85	Wessex HU5	
824	1985-86	Sea King HAS5	
819	1986	Sea King HAS5	
826/B	1987	Sea King HAS5	
814	1987-88	Sea King HAS5	
826/A	1987-88	Sea King HAS5	
826/C	1987-88	Sea King HAS5	
824	1988	Sea KIng HAS6	
702	1990-91	Lynx HAS3	
810	1990	Sea King HAS6	
814	1990	Sea King HAS6	
826/C	1990	Sea King HAS5	
702	1993	oLynx HAS3	
810/OEU	1993	Sea King HAS6	XZ581
819/A	1993	Sea King HAS6	

RFA OLNA A123
OL-class tanker, built 1965-66, commissioned 1 April 1966. Flight deck, hangar for two Sea Kings to port side of funnel. Falklands 1982. Gulf 1991. Parent ship letters ON.

820	1966	Wessex HAS1	
819	1966	Wessex HAS1	
814	1968	Wessex HAS3	
826	1968	Wessex HAS3	
819	1969	Wessex HAS3	
824	1970	Sea King HAS1	
814	1970	Wessex HAS3	
826	1970	Sea King HAS1	
826	1972	Sea King HAS1	
820	1972-76	Sea King HAS1	
824	1973-74	Sea King HAS1	
737/O	Jan-Mar 1974	Wessex HAS3	XP105 670/PO
845	1975	Wessex HU5	
707	Dec 1975-Jan 1977	Wessex HU5	XS522 347/ON
820	1977	Sea King HAS2	
824	1977	Sea King HAS1	
814	1978	Sea King HAS2	
826	1979	Sea King HAS2	
845	1979	Wessex HU5	
702	1980	Lynx HAS2	
824/B	1980	Sea King HAS2	
824/C	1980	Sea King HAS2	
772/B	Mar-Aug 1981	Wessex HU5	XT486
772/C	Dec 1981-May 1982	Wessex HU5	XS507 314/-
848/B	1982 (Falklands)	Wessex HU5	
824/B	1982	Sea King HAS2	
826/B	1983-84	Sea King HAS5	
824/B	1984	Sea King HAS5	
826/A	1984-85	Sea King HAS5	
845	1985	Wessex HU5	
826/C	1986	Sea King HAS5	
814	1987	Sea King HAS5	
826/A	1987	Sea King HAS5	
826/B	1987-89	Sea King HAS5	
846	1988	Sea King HC4	
826/D	1990	Sea King HAS6	
849/B	1990	Sea King AEW2	
846	1991 (Gulf)	Sea King HC4	
826/C	1992	Sea King HAS5	
819/C	1994	Sea King HAS6	

RFA OLWEN A122
OL-class tanker, ex-RFA *Olynthus*, built 1963-65, commissioned 21 June 1965. Renamed September 1967 to avoid confusion with submarine HMS *Olympus*. Flight deck, hangar for two Sea Kings to port side of funnel. Falklands 1982. Parent ship letters OW.

814	1966-67	Wessex HAS1	
819	1966-67	Wessex HAS1	
814	1967,1969-70	Wessex HAS3	
819	1973	Sea King HAS1	
737/103	Feb-Mar 1976	Wessex HAS3	XM837 407/NF
824	1978	Sea King HAS2	
819	1979	Sea King HAS2	
819	1987	Sea King HAS5	
824/A	1980	Sea King HAS2	
824/D	1980	Sea King HAS2	
824/C	1981	Sea King HAS2	
820	1981	Sea King HAS5	
824/B	1981-83	Sea King HAS2	
848/C	1982 (Falklands)	Wessex HU5	
826/A	1983	Sea King HAS5	
826/B	1983-84	Sea King HAS5	
845	1984-86	Wessex HU5	
824	1986	Sea King HAS5	
820	1988	Sea King HAS6	
824	1989	Sea King HAS5	
702	1991-92	Lynx HAS3	
820/A	1993 (Adriatic)	Sea King HAS6	

RFA OLYNTHUS A122
OL-class tanker renamed RFA *Olwen* (q.v.) September 1967.

HMS PENELOPE(2) F127
Type 12 (modified) *Leander*-class frigate, laid down 14 March 1961 and commissioned 3 October 1963, fitted for Wasp Flight. Recommissioned as Sea Wolf trials ship 23 June 1967. Paid off December 1977. Refit and Exocet conversion 1979, completed 22 January 1981. Fitted for Lynx Flight. Falklands 1982. Paid off January 1986. Recommissioned September 1986. Sold to Ecuador April 1991 as *Presidente Eloy Alfaro*.
Ships Flight: Formed 16 January 1964 at Culdrose with Wasp. Disb October 1966. Reformed January 1982 ex *Cleopatra* Flight with Lynx as No.209 Flight. Became *Norfolk* Flight January 1991.

700W	Jan 1964-Mar 1964	Wasp HAS1	XS534 184/PE
829	Mar 1964-Oct 1966	Wasp HAS1	XS534 454/PE
815/209	Jan 1982-Apr 1988	Lynx HAS2	XZ691 454/PN
829/209	Apr 1988-Jan 1991	Lynx HAS3	XZ723 454/PN

HMS PHOEBE F42
Type 12 (modified) *Leander*-class frigate, laid down 25 July 1963 and commissioned 15 April 1966, fitted for Wasp Flight. Refit and Exocet August 1974, recommissioned 29 April 1977, fitted for Lynx flight. Paid off Dec 1990. Sold to India for scrap 1992.
Ships Flight: Formed 4 November 1968 with Wasp as No.020 Flight. Disbanded 17 December 1970. Reformed 5 April 1971. Became *Galatea* Flight 5 August 1974. Reformed ex *Falmouth* Flight 28 February 1977 as No.010 Flight. Became *Herald* Flight October 1977. Lynx flight formed 1 November 1977 as No.201 Flight. Became *Battleaxe* Flight in January 1981. Reformed June in 1982 as No.242 Flight. Became *Beaver* Flight in February 1991.

829/020	Nov 1968-Aug 1974	Wasp HAS1	XV625 471/PB
829/010	Feb 1977-Oct 1977	Wasp HAS1	XZ542 471/PB
829	Nov 1977-Jan 1978	Wasp HAS1	XV632 440/BK
700L/201	Nov 1977-Jan 1978	Lynx HAS2	XZ233 471/PB
702/201	Jan 1978-Jan 1981	Lynx HAS2	XZ233 471/PB
815/242	Jun 1982-Mar 1987	Lynx HAS3	XZ724 471/PB
829/242	Mar 1987-Feb 1991	Lynx HAS3	XZ729 471/PB

HMS PLYMOUTH F126
Type 12 *Rothesay*-class frigate, laid down 1 July 1958 and commissioned 11 May 1961. Fitted for Wasp Flight from 1968. Major refit/modification 7 September 1978. Commissioned 24 January 1981. Damaged in air attack off Falklands 8 June 1982. Paid off May 1988. Floating museum at Plymouth 1990.
Ships Flight: Formed 20 December 1968 with Wasp. Disbanded 23 July 1971. Reformed 4 October 1971 as No.032 Flight. Became *Berwick* Flight 27 April 1974. Reformed ex *Brighton* Flight 4 November 1974. Disbanded 22 September 1978. Reformed in October 1980 ex *Eskimo* Flight as No.027 Flight. Disbanded in May 1988.

829	Dec 1968-Jul 1971	Wasp HAS1	XS571 445/-
829/032	Oct 1971-Apr 1974	Wasp HAS1	XV632 445/PL
829	Nov 1974-Sep 1978	Wasp HAS1	XS565 445/-
829/027	Oct 1980-May 1988	Wasp HAS1	XT429 445/-

HMS POLAR CIRCLE A176
Ice Patrol Ship, renamed HMS *Endurance*(2) (q.v.).

HMS PROTECTOR A146
Ice Patrol Ship, built 1935-36 as netlaying and target towing vessel. Converted 1954-55, fitted for double Whirlwind Flt. Sold 1968, replaced by HMS *Endurance*(1) (q.v.),
Ships Flight: Formed 11 July 1955 with Whirlwind. Disbanded 25 May 1956. Reformed 31 July 1956. Disbanded 20 May 1957 at Lee-on-Solent. Reformed 22 July 1957. Disbanded 20 May 1958. Reformed 23 July 1958 at Lee-on-Solent, initially as part of No.701 Squadron. Disbanded 13 May 1959. Reformed 15 July 1959. Disbanded 30 April 1960. Reformed 16 May 1960 at Portsmouth. Disbanded 18 May 1961. Reformed 12 June 1961 at Lee-on-Solent. Disbanded 24 May 1962. Reformed 18 June 1962 at Lee-on-Solent. Disbanded June 1963. Reformed 1 July 1963. Disbanded. Reformed 28 September 1964. Became *Endurance* Flight 27 May 1968 at Lee-on-Solent.

	Jul 1955-May 1956	Whirlwind HAR1	XA866 911/PR
	Jul 1956-May 1957	Whirlwind HAR1	XA866 990/-
	Jul 1957-May 1958	Whirlwind HAR1	XA868 990/-
701	Jul 1958-May 1959	Whirlwind HAR1	XA869 991/PR
701	Jul 1959-Apr 1960	Whirlwind HAR1	XA866 920/-
701	May 1960-May 1961	Whirlwind HAR1	XA869 940/-
701	Jun 1961-May 1962	Whirlwind HAR1	XA866 920/-
701	Jun 1962-Jun 1963	Whirlwind HAR1	XA868 940/-
771	Sep 1964- 1966	Whirlwind HAR1	XA868 449/PC
829	1966-May 1968	Whirlwind HAR9	XN359 448/PC

SS QUEEN ELIZABETH II
Liner. Requisitioned 4 May 1982 for use in South Atlantic. Fitted with 2 helicopter pads and converted to troopship.

SS RANGATIRA
Chartered 15 May 1982 for use in South Atlantic. Modified as a troopship and fitted with a helicopter pad. Left for UK in September 1983.

RFA REGENT A486
Fleet support ship, built 1963-67, commissioned 6 June 1967, fitted with hangar and flight deck to take up to Sea King size helicopter. Falklands 1982. Sold to India for scrap Jan 1993.
Ships Flight: Formed 4 October 1966 at Culdrose with Wessex. To *Olmeda* October 1977.
Various attachments.

707	Oct 1966-	1970	Wessex HU5	XT480 468/RG
814	1970		Wessex HAS3	
846	1970-	1975	Wessex HU5	XT480 468/RG
820	1972		Wessex HAS3	
846	1975		Wessex HU5	
707	1975-Sep	1977	Wessex HU5	XT480 436/RG
772/A	Sep 1977-Oct	1977	Wessex HU5	
772/C	Oct 1978-Jan	1980	Wessex HU5	XS522 635/RG
772/A	May 1980-Oct	1981	Wessex HU5	
848/A	1982(Falklands)		Wessex HU5	
845	1985		Wessex HU5	

RFA RELIANT(1) A84
Air stores support ship, ex-MV *Somersby*, built 1953-54 as grain carrier. Bought 1956, converted 1956-58, commissioned as RFA 1958, flight deck but no hangar. To reserve 1972. Broken up August 1977.

RFA RELIANT(2) A131
Aviation support ship, ex-MV *Astronomer*, commissioned 1977, requisitioned May 1982 for South Atlantic. Chartered 22 April 1983 refitted and commissioned as RFA 16 November 1983, operating up to four Sea Kings. Used to test US 'Arapaho' concept for containerised aircraft support. Sold 1986 to Parramatta Shipping Co.

826/A	1985	Sea King HAS5
826/B	1985-86	Sea King HAS5
826/C	1984-85	Sea King HAS5
846	1984 (Lebanon)	Sea King HC4

RFA RESOURCE A480
Fleet support ship, built 1963-67, commissioned 16 May 1967, fitted with hangar and flight deck to take up to Sea King size helicopter. Falklands 1982. Gulf 1991.
Ships Flight: Formed 14 July 1966 at Culdrose with Wessex. Disbanded May 1980.
Various attachments.

707	Jul 1966-Sep	1977	Wessex HU5	XT484 469/RS
772/B	Sep 1977-Jan	1978	Wessex HU5	XT486 437/RS
772/A	Sep 1979-May	1980	Wessex HU5	
845/A	1982 (Falklands)		Wessex HU5	
845	1983-84		Wessex HU5	
826/A	1988		Sea King HAS5	

HMS RHYL F129
Type 12 *Rothesay*-class frigate, laid down 29 January 1958 and commissioned 31 October 1960. Major refit, recommissioned 12 May 1972, fitted for Wasp flight. Refit April 1975 to 1976. Paid off 27 July 1983 as beyond economical repair, sunk as missile target 300 miles off Lands End August 1985.
Ships Flight: Formed 19 January 1972 with Wasp as No.034 Flight. Became *Brighton* Flight 14 April 1975. Reformed ex *Gurkha* Flight 1 August 1976 as No.021 Flight. Became *Apollo* Flight December 1976. Reformed ex *Euryalus* Flight 27 June 1977. Disbanded September 1978. Reformed ex *Zulu* Flight 31 August 1979 as No.026 Flight. Disbanded 1 October 1983.

829/034	Jan 1972-Apr	1975	Wasp HAS1	XT415 470/-
829/021	Sep 1976-Dec	1976	Wasp HAS1	XS567 470/-
829	Jun 1977-Sep	1978	Wasp HAS1	XT782 446/-
829/026	Aug 1979-Jul	1983	Wasp HAS1	XT784 446/-

HMS RICHMOND F239
Type 23 *Duke*-class frigate building from 1992, due to commission Dec 1994, to be fitted with Lynx or later with Merlin. Parent ship letters RM, callsign 474.

HMS ROTHESAY F107
Lead ship of *Rothesay*-class frigates, laid down 1956, commissioned 23 April 1960. Major refit Jul 1966, recommissioned July 1968, fitted for Wasp Flight. Paid off late 1977 for refit as Trials Ship for ASWE. Refit 1985. Paid off 30 March 1988. Broken up 1988.
Ships Flight: Formed 1 July 1968 with Wasp. Disbanded 7 December 1970. Reformed December 1970 as No.035 Flight. Became *Active* Flight 9 August 1977. Reformed March 1980 ex *Jupiter* Flight as No.024 Flight. Disbanded March 1988.

829	Jul 1968-Dec	1970	Wasp HAS1	XS527 462/-
829/035	Dec 1970-Aug	1977	Wasp HAS1	XT779 462/RO
829/024	Mar 1980-Mar	1988	Wasp HAS1	XT785 462/RO

MV ST EDMUND
Roll-on/Roll-off ferry, renamed MV *Keren* (q.v.).

RMS ST HELENA
Chartered May 1982 for South Atlantic service, converted to support ship, fitted with helicopter pad. Wasp Flight for duration of Falkland campaign. Left for UK 14 August 1982. Returned to owners 1984.
Ships Flight: Formed 12 May 1982 with Wasp as No.033 Flight. Disbanded 8 October 1982.

829/033	May 1982-Oct	1982	Wasp HAS1	XT795 373/-

MV SAXONIA
Requisitioned 28 April 1982 for use in South Atlantic. Used as stores carrier and fitted with a helicopter pad.

HMS SCYLLA F71
Type 12 (modified) *Leander*-class frigate, laid down 17 May 1967 and completed 14 February 1970, fitted for Wasp Flight. Paid off for refit and Seawolf conversion November 1980, recommissioned 7 December 1984, fitted for Lynx Flight. Last *Leander*-class in RN service. Paid off to disposal list Dec 1993.
Ships Flight: Formed 13 March 1970 with Wasp as No.024 Flight. Became *Jupiter* Flight 25 June 1976 at Gibraltar. Reformed ex *Bacchante* Flight 4 March 1977 at Gibraltar. Disbanded 19 December 1980. Reformed October 1984 as No.231 Fight. Became *Arrow* Flight July 1989. Reformed March 1990 ex *Andromeda* Flight as No.222 Flight. Disbanded 3 December 1993.

829/024	Mar 1970-Jun	1976	Wasp HAS1	XS534 432/-
829	Mar 1977-Dec	1980	Wasp HAS1	XS543 432/SC
815/231	Oct 1984-Jul	1989	Lynx HAS3	ZD256 432/SC
815/222	Mar 1990-Jun	1992	Lynx HAS3	XZ227 432/SC
829/222	Jun 1992-Mar	1993	Lynx HAS3	XZ691 432/SC
815/222	Mar 1993-Dec	1993	Lynx HAS3	ZD268 432/SC

HMS SHEFFIELD(2) D80
Lead ship of Type 42 *Sheffield*-class destroyers, laid down 1970 and commissioned 16 February 1975. Wasp Flight 1977-79. Refit 1979-80. Lynx Flight from 1979. Sunk off Falklands 10 May 1982 as result of air attack.
Ships Flight: Formed December 1976 ex *Leander* Flight with Wasp. Disbanded October 1979. Reformed 24 October 1979 with Lynx as No.213 Flight. Lost in ship 10 May 1982.

829	Dec 1976-Oct	1979	Wasp HAS1	XT441 337/SD
702/213	Sep 1979-Jan	1981	Lynx HAS2	XZ725 337/SD
815/213	Jan 1981-May	1982	Lynx HAS2	XZ721 337/SD

HMS SHEFFIELD(3) F96
Type 22 frigate, built 1984-88, commissioned July 1988, fitted for Sea King or double Lynx flight.
Ships Flight: Formed August 1988 with Lynx as No.234 Flight. Boyd Trophy Award 1990.

829/234	Aug 1988-Mar	1993	Lynx HAS3	ZD250 352/SD
815/234	Mar 1993-to date		Lynx HAS3	XZ245 352/SD
815/217	Jun 1994-Aug	1994	Lynx HAS3	XZ237 407/GC

RFA SIR BEDIVERE L3004
Logistic landing ship, ex-*LSL 03*, built 1965-67, commissioned 18 May 1967. Transferred from MoD (Army) to RFA January 1970, flight deck but no hangar. Falklands 1982. Gulf 1991. Parent ship letters BD.

RFA SIR GALAHAD(1) L3005
Logistic landing ship, ex-*LSL 02*, built 1965-66, commissioned 17 December 1966. Transferred from MoD (Army) to RFA March 1970, flight deck but no hangar. Parent ship letters GD. Sunk off Falklands as War Grave after air attack 8 June 1982.

RFA SIR GALAHAD(2) L3005
Logistic landing ship, built 1985-87 as replacement for RFA *Sir Galahad*(1) (qv), commissioned November 1987. Larger than other LSLs, flight deck for Chinook, no hangar. Gulf 1991. Parent ship letters GD.

RFA SIR GERAINT L3027
Logistic landing ship, ex-*LSL 03*, built 1965-67, commissioned 12 July 1967. Transferred from MoD (Army) to RFA March 1970, flight deck but no hangar. Falklands 1982. Major refit 1993-94. Parent ship letters GR.

HMS SIRIUS F40
Type 12 (modified) *Leander*-class frigate, laid down 9 August 1963 and completed 15 June 1966, fitted for Wasp flight. Paid off for refit and Exocet conversion March 1975, completed October 1977. Recommissioned 18 February 1978, fitted for Lynx flight. Paid off to disposals list March 1993.
Ships Flight: Formed 4 April 1966 with Wasp. Attached *Cleopatra* May to July 1966. Disbanded 24 November 1967. Reformed 30 October 1967. Attached *Minerva* May to September 1968. Disbanded 4 August 1969. Reformed 27 October 1969. Attached *Olmeda* October 1973. Disbanded 7 February 1975. Reformed 3 January 1978 at Yeovilton with Lynx as No.202 Flight. Became *Southampton* Flight June 1981. Reformed June 1982 as No.243 Flight. Became *Argonaut* Flight April 1989. Reformed April 1989 ex old *Argonaut* Flight as No.203 Flight. Became *Iron Duke* Flight March 1993.

829	Apr 1966-Nov	1967	Wasp HAS1	XT437 450/SS
829	Oct 1967-Aug	1969	Wasp HAS1	XT437 450/SS
829	Oct 1969-Feb	1975	Wasp HAS1	XV636 450/SS
702/202	Jan 1978-Jun	1981	Lynx HAS2	XZ238 450/SS
815/243	Jun 1982-Mar	1987	Lynx HAS2	XZ255 450/SS

829/243	Mar 1987-Apr 1989	Lynx HAS3	XZ255	450/SS
829/203	Apr 1989-Mar 1993	Lynx HAS3	XZ256	450/SS

RFA SIR LANCELOT L3029
Logistic landing ship, ex-*LSL 01*, built 1962-64, commissioned 16 January 1964. Transferred from MoD (Army) to RFA January 1970, flight deck for Wessex, no hangar. Falklands 1982. Parent ship letters LN. Sold 1989.

RFA SIR PERCIVALE L3036
Logistic landing ship, ex-*LSL 06*, built 1966-68, commissioned 23 March 1968. Transferred from MoD (Army) to RFA March 1970, flight deck but no hangar. Falklands 1982. Gulf 1991. Parent ship letters PE, later PV.

RFA SIR TRISTRAM L3505
Logistic landing ship, ex-*LSL 05*, built 1966-67, commissioned 14 September 1967. Transferred from MoD Army to RFA Jan 1970, flight deck but no hangar. Damaged in air attack off Falklands 8 June 1982. Repaired and modernised including flight deck to take Chinooks 1983-85. Gulf 1991. Parent ship letters TM.

HMS SOMERSET F82
Type 23 frigate, building 1993, due to commission May 1996, to be fitted with Lynx or later with Merlin. Parent ship letters SM, callsign 355.

HMS SOUTHAMPTON(2) D90
Type 42 *Sheffield*-class destroyer, laid down 1976 and commissioned 31 October 1981, fitted for Lynx flight. Badly damaged in collision with VLCC in Persian Gulf 1989. Refitted and returned to service 1992.

Ships Flight: Formed June 1981 ex *Sirius* Flight with Lynx as No.202 Flight. Became *Exeter* Flight January 1989. Reformed May 1992 ex *Jupiter* Flight May 1992 as No.229 Flight.

815/202	Jun 1981-Jan 1989	Lynx HAS2	ZD257	334/SN
815/229	May 1992-to date	Lynx HAS3	XZ232	334/SN

MSV STENA INSPECTOR
Oil industry support ship, see RFA *Diligence*.

MSV STENA SEASPREAD
Oil industry support ship with helicopter platform, requisitioned 10 April 1982 for use in South Atlantic. Converted to heavy repair ship. Returned to UK 18 August 1982.

RFA STROMNESS A344
Stores support ship, commissioned 21 March 1967. Parent ship letters ST. Sold to USA Military Sealift Command October 1983 as USNS *Saturn*.

HMS SUTHERLAND F81
Type 23 frigate, building 1994, due to commission April 1997, to be fitted with Lynx or later with Merlin. Parent ship letters SU, callsign 422.

RFA TARBATNESS A345
Stores support ship, commissioned 27 September 1967. Parent ship letters TB. Sold to USA Military Sealift Command September 1982 as USNS *Spica*.

HMS TARTAR F133
Type 81 *Tribal*-class frigate, laid down 22 October 1959 and commissioned 26 February 1962. Wasp Flight 1964-66, 1967-71, 1973-77. Modernised 1972-74. To Reserve October 1977; To Standby Squadron March 1980. Re-commissioned 17 July 1982. Wasp Flight 1982-83. Paid off 29 March 1984. Sold to Indonesia April 1984 as *Hasanuddin*.

Ships Flight: Formed 25 November 1964. Disbanded 18 November 1966. Reformed 12 January 1967. Disbanded 2 December 1971. Reformed 12 January 1973. Became *Juno* Flight 10 October 1977. Reformed 1 June 1982 as No.050 Flight. Disbanded October 1983.

829	Nov 1964-Nov 1966	Wasp HAS1	XS570	477/TA
829	Jan 1967-Dec 1971	Wasp HAS1	XV634	477/TA
829	Jan 1973-Oct 1977	Wasp HAS1	XT438	477/TA
829/050	Jun 1982-Oct 1983	Wasp HAS1	XV636	477/TA

HMS TERRA NOVA
Icebreaker, planned in 1964 as replacement for *Protector*, but cancelled 1967. Endurance became *Protector*'s replacement in 1968.

RFA TIDEPOOL A76
Large fleet tanker, built 1961-63, commissioned 28 June 1963. Fitted with flight deck, hangar to take one Sea King to port side of funnel. Various Squadrons embarked flights for exercises. Parent ship letters TP. Sold to Chile August 1982 (after delay caused by Falklands conflict) as *Almirante Jorge Montt*

Ships Flight: Formed January 1977 ex *Olna* Flight. Became *Regent* Flight October 1978.

819	1964-67	Wessex HAS1
814	1966-67	Wessex HAS1
820	1968	Wessex HAS1
819	1968-70	Wessex HAS3
820	1971	Wessex HAS3
737/A	1974	Wessex HAS3
820	1976	Sea King HAS1
707	Jan 1977-Sep 1977	Wessex HU5	XS522 347/TP
772/C	Sep 1977-Oct 1978	Wessex HU5	XS522 347/TP
845	1979	Wessex HU5
824/A	1980-81	Sea King HAS2
814	1981	Sea King HAS2
829/034	Sep 1981-Oct 1981	Wasp HAS1	XT795 "476/LE"
845/E	1982 (Falklands)	Wessex HU5

RFA TIDESPRING A75
Large fleet tanker, built 1961-63, commissioned 18 January 1963. Fitted with flightdeck and hangar to take one Sea King to port side of funnel. Various squadrons embarked flights for exercises. Dedicated flight for operations 1975-76. Falklands 1982. Parent ship letters TS. Paid off 1992 and sold to India for scrap.

Ships Flight: Formed 1 April 1975 at Yeovilton. Disbanded 14 May 1976 at Yeovilton.

814	1966	Wessex HAS1	
820	1967	Wessex HAS1	
819	1967	Wessex HAS1	
820	1970	Wessex HAS3	
817RAN	Sep 1974-Dec 1974	Wessex HAS31B	
819	1975	Sea King HAS1	
707/846	Apr 1975-May 1976	Wessex HU5	XT468 332/TS
814	1976	Sea King HAS1	
737/O	Apr 1976-May 1976 (Cod War)	Wessex HAS3	XP105 417/-
772/A	May 1978-Dec 1978	Wessex HU5	XT480/"RG"
772/C	Jan 1980-Jul 1980	Wessex HU5	XS522 635/-
702	1981	Lynx HAS2	
826	1982	Sea King HAS5	
772/A	Jan 1982-Apr 1982	Wessex HU5	
845/C	1982 (Falklands)	Wessex HU5	
826/A	1983	Sea King HAS5	
826/C	1983-85	Sea King HAS5	
820	1984	Sea King HAS5	
814	1985	Sea King HAS5	
819	1986	Sea King HAS5	
826/A	1986	Sea King HAS5	
824	1987	Sea King HAS5	
846	1987-88	Sea King HC4	
772/B	Sep 1987	Wessex HU5	XS513 519/-
815/241	Oct 1987-Dec 1987	Lynx HAS3	XZ254 333/BM
826/A	1988	Sea King HAS5	
826/B	1988-90	Sea King HAS5	
846	1990	Sea King HC4	
826/C	1991	Sea King HAS6	

HMS TIGER C20
Tiger-class cruiser, ex-HMS *Bellerophen*, built 1941-59, renamed February 1945. Construction suspended 1946-54, commissioned March 1959. Converted and fitted with hangar and flight deck to operate a squadron of four Sea King helicopters 1965-April 1969. Paid off April 1978. Left Portsmouth 23 September 1986 for Spanish breaker's yard.

826	1972-Dec 1976	Sea King HAS1	XV647 144/TG
814	Jul 1975-Aug 1975	Sea King HAS1	
826	Dec 1976-Apr 1978	Sea King HAS2	XZ573 141/TG

HMS TRIUMPH
Escort Maintenance Ship, converted from aircraft carrier (q.v.). Conversion completed 1965.

SS UGANDA
Liner. Requisitioned 10 April 1982 for use in South Atlantic. Converted to hospital ship and fitted with a helicopter pad. Arrived in UK 9 August 1982.

HMS UNDAUNTED F53
Type 15 frigate, built 1942-44, originally commissioned 3 March 1944 as *Ulster*-class destroyer. Converted 1953-54, fitted with helicopter deck for P.531 suction pad trials 1961. Parent ship letters UD. Sunk as target November 1978.

HMS VIDAL A200
Survey ship, laid down 1950, commissioned 1954, fitted for, and on occasion with, helicopter flight. Paid off August 1971 and laid up August 1972. Sold and broken up at Bruges June 1976.

Ships Flight: Formed August 1954 with Hiller HT.1. Became part of No.701 Squadron on 31 October 1957 at Lee-on-Solent with Dragonfly. Disbanded. No.701V Flt formed with Dragonfly July 1958. Disbanded July 1961. Reformed 14 August 1961 with Dragonfly. Disbanded July 1965. Reformed ex *Hecla* Flight 1 January 1968 with Wasp. Became *Hecate* Flight 3 August 1971.

Lynx HAS.2 XZ699 '464/DN' of HMS Danae Flight in 1980. (MAP)

Lynx HAS.3 ZD264 '411/EB' HMS Edinburgh Flight in 1986.

Lynx HAS.2 XZ733 '420/EX' of HMS Exeter Flight. (MAP)

Lynx HAS.3GM XZ228 '303/JP' HMS Jupiter Flight in 1991. (MAP)

Lynx HAS.2 XZ239 '305' of HMS Liverpool Flight 1983. (MAP)

Lynx HAS.1 XZ248 '424/MV' of HMS Minerva Flight 1978. (MAP)

Lynx HAS.2 XZ250 '337/SD' of HMS Sheffield Flight. (MAP)

Lynx HAS.2 XZ238 '450/SS' HMS Sirius Flight in 1979. (MAP)

	May 1954-Nov 1957	Hiller HT1	XB474
701V	Jul 1958-Jul 1961	Dragonfly HR5	WP501 705/-
	Aug 1961-Jul 1965	Dragonfly HR5	WG671 969/-
829	Jan 1968-Aug 1971	Wasp HAS1	XT429 408/VI

HMS WESTMINSTER F237
Type 23 *Duke*-class frigate, built 1991-93, commissioned November 1993. To be fitted with Lynx or later with Merlin. Parent ship letters WM, callsign 462.

HMS YARMOUTH F101
Type 12 *Rothesay*-class frigate, laid down 29 November 1957 and commissioned 26 March 1960. Major refit 23 May 1966, recommissioned 30 September 1968, fitted for Wasp flight. Major refit 24 November 1978 to 1981. Falklands 1982. Paid off for disposal April 1986
Ships Flight: Formed 15 April 1968 with Wasp. Became *Rhyl* Flight 31 December 1979. Reformed ex *Berwick* Flight 19 December 1980 as No.032 Flight. Disbanded 30 May 1986.

829	Apr 1968-Dec 1978	Wasp HAS1	XV624 456/YM
829/032	Dec 1980-May 1986	Wasp HAS1	XT793 456/-

HMS YORK(2) D98
Type 42 *Sheffield*-class destroyer, laid down 1980 and commissioned 9 August 1985, fitted for Lynx flight. Refit 1994.
Ships Flight: Formed 1 June 1985 with Lynx, as No.217 Flight. Became *Gloucester* Flight February 1994.

815/217	Jun 1985-Feb 1994	Lynx HAS3	ZD265 407/YK

HMS ZULU F124
Type 81 *Tribal*-class frigate, laid down 13 December 1960 and commissioned 17 April 1964, fitted for Wasp flight. To Standby Squadron August 1979. Re-commissoned 9 August 1982. Paid off 30 March 1984. Sold to Indonesia May 1984 as *Martha Kristina Tiyahahu*.
Ships Flight: Formed December 1963 with Wasp ex No.8 Flight. Disbanded 18 August 1965 at Lee-on-Solent. Reformed 16 September 1967. Disbanded 17 December 1969. Reformed February 1970. Disbanded 2 August 1972. Reformed 10 December 1974 as No.026 Flight. Became *Rhyl* Flight 31 August 1979. Reformed 1 July 1982 as No.039 Flight. Disbanded 1 August 1983.

829	Dec 1963-Aug 1965	Wasp HAS1	XS544 482/ZU
829	Sep 1967-Dec 1969	Wasp HAS1	XT438 442/ZU
829	Feb 1970-Aug 1972	Wasp HAS1	XV639 442/ZU
829/026	Dec 1974-Aug 1979	Wasp HAS1	XT439 442/ZU
829/039	Jul 1982-Aug 1983	Wasp HAS1	XT783 442/ZU

UNNAMED SHIPS
Type 23 frigates Nos.14-16, to be built. To commission 1998-2002, to be fitted with Merlin.
LPDs 01-02, to be built as replacements for HMS *Intrepid* (q.v.) and HMS *Fearless* (q.v.).

ARCTIC FLIGHT
Formed for Icelandic Cod War duties, however Cod War ended before deployment. Embarked RFA *Olna* (q.v.) January to March 1974 to accompany Far East deployment of ships to South Africa, returned in company with returning group. Reformed as OSCAR Flight for later Icelandic Cod War duties, deployed in RFA *Tidespring* (q.v.) April-May 1976.

737	Nov 1973-Sep 1974	Wessex HAS3	XP105 670/-
737	Feb 1976-Sep 1976	Wessex HAS3	XP105 417/-

GIBRALTAR FLIGHT
Lynx flight deployed to Gibraltar 1982-91, initially to provide a presence due to unofficial Spanish posturing as a result of the Falklands conflict, later for surveillance and intelligence gathering duties in the Gibraltar Straits choke point.
Dedicated Flight: Formed July 1982 with Lynx ex *Fort Austin* as No.203 Flight. Became *Argonaut* Flight May 1983. Reformed May 1983 ex *Amazon* Flight as No.208 Flight. Disbanded April 1991.

815/203	Jul 1982-May 1983	Lynx HAS2	345/-
815/208	May 1983-Apr 1991	Lynx HAS3	ZD258 321/GIB

SUPPORT FLIGHTS
Lynx Flights operating from Portland from July 1990 to provide aircraft to ships without flights and new build ships before a dedicated flight available.
Support Flight A

829/244	Jul 1990-Mar 1993	Lynx HAS3	XZ698 479/PO
815/244	Mar 1993-to date	Lynx HAS3	XZ698 479/-

Support Flight B

815/227	Jun 1994-to date	Lynx HAS3	XZ690 462/-

SMALL SHIPS TRIALS FLIGHT (SSTF)
Lynx Flight formed in April 1980 to carry out trials in new ships before dedicated flights had been formed. Later also carried out equipment trials, becoming 700L Squadron Lynx Operational Flying Trials Unit (LOFTU) in 1989.

702/230	Apr 1980-Jan 1981	Lynx HAS2	XZ689 479/VL
815/230	Jan 1981-Jun 1988	Lynx HAS3	ZD268 479/PO
(on *Fort Austin* Apr - May 1982 Lynx HAS2 XZ247 -/-)			
(on *Invincible* May - Sep 1982 Lynx HAS2 XZ725 -/-)			
829/230	Jun 1988-Aug 1989	Lynx HAS3	ZF562 479/-

TRIBAL FLIGHT
Formed 29 September 1983 ex *Gurkha* Flight for HMS *Gurkha* and HMS *Zulu* with Wasp. Disbanded 30 March 1984.

AUSTRALIA

HMAS ADELAIDE 01
FFG-7 frigate (FFG-17), built Seattle 1977-80, commissioned 15 October 1980. Modified 1988-89 to operate S-70B Seahawk. Operates on west coast. Gulf 1991.

HMAS ANZAC 150
MEKO 200 frigate, building 1992, to commission June 1996, to be fitted for Seahawk.

HMAS ARRERNTE 151
ANZAC frigate, building from 1994, to commission March 1998, to be fitted for Seahawk.

HMAS BALLARAT 155
ANZAC frigate, to commission 2003, to be fitted for Seahawk.

HMAS CANBERRA(2) 02
FFG-7 frigate (FFG-18), built Seattle 1978-81, commissioned 24 March 1981. Modified 1990-91 to operate S-70B Seahawk (1993-date, 816 Sqdn).

HMAS DARWIN 04
FFG-7 frigate (FFG-44), built Seattle 1981-84, commissioned 21 July 1984, fitted for Seahawk or Squirrel. Gulf 1991.

HMAS JERVIS BAY GT203
Helicopter and logistic support ship, built as Roll-on/Roll-off ship MV *Australian Trader* 1967-69, commissioned in RAN August 1977. Flight deck for Sea King fitted 1986-87. AS350B Squirrel (723 and 817 Sqdns) and Sea King HAS.50 1987-94. To be replaced by *Kanimbla* 1994.

HMAS KANIMBLA
Newport-class LST, built San Diego 1969-70, commisioned January 1971 as USS *Saginaw LST1188*, fitted with helicopter landing deck. Bought 1994 and transferred to RAN as replacement for HMAS *Jervis Bay* (q.v.).

HMAS MANOORA
Newport-class LST, built San Diego 1970-71, commissioned October 1971 as USS *Fairfax County LST1193*, fitted with helicopter landing deck. Bought 1994 and transferred to RAN as replacement for HMAS *Tobruk* (q.v.).

HMAS MELBOURNE(2) 05,
FFG-7 frigate, built 1985-91, commissioned February 1992, fitted for Seahawk. S-70B Seahawk (816 Sqdn) 1993-date.

HMAS MORESBY A73
Survey ship, built 1962-64, commissioned March 1964. Scout 1964-73 (723 Sqdn). Refit 1973, fitted for Bell 206B-1 Kiowa (1973 to date).

HMAS NEWCASTLE 06
FFG-7 frigate, built 1989-93, commissioned Dec 1993, fitted for Seahawk.

HMAS PARRAMATTA 154
ANZAC frigate, to commission 2002, to be fitted for Seahawk.

HMAS PERTH(2) 157
ANZAC frigate, to commission 2005, to be fitted for Seahawk.

HMAS STALWART O215
Destroyer tender, built 1964-68, commissioned 9 February 1968, helicopter flight deck for Sea King. Carried AS350B Squirrel (1984-86 723 Sqdn), Wessex HAS.31B (1968-86 816 Sqdn), Sea King HAS.50 (1982-86 817 Sqdn). Sold Dec 1986 to become Greek Cruise Ship.

HMAS STUART 153
ANZAC frigate, to commission 2001, to be fitted for Seahawk.

HMAS SUCCESS OR304
Durance-class tanker, built 1980-86, commissioned 23 April 1986, fitted for Sea King. Gulf 1991. Wessex HAS.31B (723 Sqdn 1987-89), AS.350B Squirrel (1989-date), S-70B Seahawk (816 Sqdn 1990-date), Sea King HAS.50 (817 Sqdn 1986-date). During standby operation after military coup in Fiji, carried 2 Wessex, 1 Iroquois and 1 Kiowa.

HMAS SYDNEY(2) 03
FFG-7 frigate (FFG-35), built Seattle 1980-82, commissioned 29 January 1983, modified 1988-89 to operate Seahawk, operates on west coast. AS.350B Squirrel (723 Sqdn 1983-91), S-70B Seahawk (816 Sqdn 1992-date).

HMAS TOBRUK L50
Improved *Sir Bedivere*-class amphibious heavy landing ship built 1978-81, commissioned 23 April 1981, flight deck for helicopters, to be replaced by *Manoora* 1994. AS350B (723 Sqdn 1984-94) & Sea King HAS.50 (817 Sqdn 1981-94).
HMAS TOOWOOMBA 156
ANZAC frigate, to commission 2004, to be fitted for Seahawk.
HMAS WARUMUNGU 152
ANZAC frigate, to commission 2000, to be fitted for Seahawk.

CANADA

HMCS ALGONQUIN 283
Tribal-class destroyer, built 1969-73, commissioned 30 September 1973. Systems update 1987-91, fitted for two CH-124A Sea King. Parent ship letters AL.
HMCS ANNAPOLIS 265
Annapolis-class DDH, built 1960-64, commissioned 19 December 1964. Refit 1978-79. Modernisation 1982-85, fitted for CH-124A Sea King. Parent ship letters AS. Pacific fleet.
HMCS ASSINIBOINE 234
St Laurent-class DDH, built 1953-59, commissioned 16 August 1959. Fitted for CH-124A Sea King 1962-63. Parent ship letters AE. Became harbour training ship 1989.
HMCS ATHABASKAN 282,
Tribal-class destroyer, built 1969-72, commissioned November 1972. Systems update 1990-93, fitted for two CH-124A Sea King. Parent ship letters AN.
HMCS CALGARY 335
Halifax-class FFH, built 1991-94, fitted for CH-124A Sea King.
HMCS CHARLOTTETOWN 339
Halifax-class FFH, building 1993, to commission 1995, fitted for CH-124A Sea King.
HMCS FRASER 233
St Laurent-class DDH, built 1951-57, commissioned 28 June 1957. Fitted for CH-124A Sea King from 1965-66. Modernised 1979-82. Parent ship letters FR. Paid off 1991.
HMCS FREDERICTON 337
Halifax-class FFH, building 1992, to commission 1994, fitted for CH-124A Sea King.
HMCS HALIFAX 330
Halifax-class FFH lead ship, built 1987-92, commissioned June 1992, fitted for CH-124A Sea King.
HMCS HURON 281
Tribal-class destroyer, built 1969-72, commissioned 16 December 1972. Systems update 1989-92, fitted for two CH-142A Sea King. Parent ship letters HN.
HMCS IROQUOIS 280
Tribal-class destroyer, built 1969-72, commissioned 29 July 1972. Systems update 1988-91, fitted for two CH-124A Sea King. Parent ship letters IS.
HMCS LABRADOR
Icebreaker, built 1954 for the Canadian Department of Trade, later to RCN. Carried Bell 47 and Piasecki HUP-3 of HU-21.
HMCS MARGAREE 230
St Laurent-class DDH, built 1951-57, commissioned 5 October 1957, fitted for CH-124A Sea King from 1964-65. Modernised 1979-82. Parent ship letters ME. Paid off 1992.
HMCS MONTREAL 336
Halifax-class FFH, built 1991-93, fitted for CH-124A Sea King.
HMCS NIPIGON 266
Annapolis-class DDH, built 1960-64, commissioned 30 May 1964. Refit 1977-78. Modernised 1982-85, fitted for CH-124A Sea King. Parent ship letters NN.
HMCS OTTAWA(1) 229
St Laurent-class DDH, built 1951-56, commissioned 10 November 1956. Modernised 1979-82, fitted for CH-124A Sea King from 1964-65. Parent ship letters OA. Paid off 1991.
HMCS OTTAWA(2) 341
Halifax-class FFH, building 1994, to commission 1997, to be fitted for CH-124A Sea King. Parent ship letters OA.
HMCS PRESERVER AOR510
Operational support ship, built 1967-70, commissioned 30 July 1970. Can be used as Flag ship and troop carrier, fitted for three CH-124A Sea Kings. Parent ship letters PS.
HMCS PROTECTEUR AOR509
Operational support ship, built 1967-69, commissioned 30 August 1969. Can be used as Flag ship and troop carrier, fitted for three CH-124A Sea Kings. Parent ship letters PT.

HMCS PROVIDER AOR508
Operational support ship, built 1961-63, commissioned 28 September 1963, fitted for three CH-124A Sea Kings. Parent ship letters PR. Pacific fleet.
HMCS REGINA 334
Halifax-class FFH, built 1989-93, fitted for CH-124A Sea King.
HMCS ST JOHN'S 340
Halifax-class FFH, building 1994, to commission 1996, to be fitted for CH-124A Sea King.
HMCS ST LAURENT 205
St Laurent-class DDH, built 1950-55, commissioned Oct 1955. Fitted for CH-124A Sea King from 1962-63. Paid off 1975. Sank under tow to breakers yard 1979.
HMCS SAGEUNAY 206
St Laurent-class DDH, built 1951-56, commissioned 15 December 1956. Fitted for CH-124A Sea King from 1964-65. Parent ship letters SA, later SY. Deleted 1990.
HMCS SKEENA 207
St Laurent-class DDH, built 1951-57, commissioned 30 March 1957. Fitted for CH-124A Sea King from 1964-65. Modernised 1979-82. Parent ship letters SA. Paid off 1990.
HMCS TORONTO 333
Halifax-class FFH, built 1989-92, commissioned 1992, fitted for CH-124A Sea King.
HMCS VANCOUVER 331
Halifax-class FFH, built 1988-92, commissioned 1992, fitted for CH-124A Sea King.
HMCS VILLE DE QUEBEC 332
Halifax-class FFH, built 1989-93, commissioned 1993, fitted for CH-124A Sea King.
HMCS WINNIPEG 338
Halifax-class FFH, building 1992, to be commissioned 1995, fitted for CH-124A Sea King.

NEW ZEALAND

HMNZS CANTERBURY F421, Leander class frigate, built in UK 1969-71, commissioned 22 October 1971. Modernised 1988-90, Wasp flight. Parent ship letters CA.
Ships Flight: Wasp HAS1 1971-date (NZ3903 460/-)
HMNZS ENDEAVOUR A11, fleet supply ship, built South Korea 1987-88, commissioned April 1988, fitted for Wasp. Parent ship letters ER
HMNZS MONOWAI A06, survey vessel, built 1957-60 as islands freighter for NZ Government Maori and Island Affairs Dept *Moana Roa*, transferred RNZN 1974, refit 1974-77, commissioned as survey ship 4 October 1977, fitted for Wasp. Parent ship letters MW.
HMNZS SOUTHLAND F104, Leander class frigate, ex-HMS *Dido* (q.v.), transferred July 1983, refit in UK and commissioned 18 September 1983. Limited refit 1990, Wasp flight. Parent ship letters SL.
Ships Flight: Wasp HAS.1 1984-date
HMNZS WAIKATO F55, *Leander*-class frigate, built in UK 1964-66, commissioned 16 September 1966, limited refit 1991, Wasp flight, enlarged hangar for Lynx. Parent ship letters WA.
Ships Flight: Wasp HAS.1 1967-date (NZ3902 420/-)
HMNZS WELLINGTON F69, Leander class frigate, ex-HMS *Bacchante* (q.v.), transferred 1 October 1982, refit in NZ 1983-86, Wasp flight. Parent ship letters WN.
Ships Flight: Wasp HAS.1 1986-date
unnamed, ANZAC frigate (MEKO 200), building in Australia 1993, due to commission February 1997, to be fitted for helicopter.
unnamed, ANZAC frigate, to be built in Australia 1995-98, due to commission November 1998, to be fitted for helicopter

NETHERLANDS

HrMs ABRAHAM CRIJNSSEN F816
Kortenaer-class frigate, built 1978-83, commissioned January 1983, fitted for two Lynx. Parent ship letters AC.
860 Sqdn: Lynx SH-14B/C Feb 1988-Mar 1990 (272), Sep 1992-to date (271)
HrMs ABRAHAM VAN DER HULST D832
Karel Doorman-class destroyer, built 1989-93, commissioned December 1993, fitted for Lynx flight, later to be NH90.
HrMs AMSTERDAM A837
Zuiderkruis-class combat support ship, building 1992-94, to replace HrMs *Poolster* (q.v.).
HrMs BANKERT F810
Kortenaer-class frigate, built 1976-80, commissioned 29 October 1980, fitted for two Lynx. Parent ship letters BK. Sold to Greece

May 1993 as *Aegon*.
860 Sqdn:
Lynx SH-14B   Apr 1982-Oct 1987 (269), Oct-Nov 1987 (266)
Lynx SH-14C   Jan 1990-Feb 1991 (270), Feb-Apr 1992 (271)
HrMs BLOIS VAN TRESLONG F824
Kortenaer-class frigate, built 1978-82, commissioned 25 November 1982, fitted for two Lynx. Parent ship letters BT.
860 Sqdn:
Lynx SH-14B Jan 1983-Nov 1984 (268), Nov 1988-Sep 1989 (274)
Lynx SH-14C Jan-May 1990 (266), Aug 1991-Dec 1993 (276)
HrMs CALLENBURGH F808
Kortenaer-class frigate, built 1975-79, commissioned 26 July 1979, fitted for two Lynx. Parent ship letters CB. Sold to Greece April 1994.
860 Sqdn:
Wasp AH-12A   Aug 1979-Jan 1980 (247)
Lynx SH-14B   Aug 1981-Sep 1982 (275), Jan-Aug 1986 (282),
               Sep 1987-May 1988 (272), Feb 1989-Jul 1990 (270)
Lynx SH-14C   Mar 1992-Jun 1993 (280)
HrMs DE RUYTER F806
Tromp-class frigate, built 1971-76, commissioned 3 June 1976, fitted as Flagship, Wasp and later Lynx flight. Parent ship letters DR, to be replaced by 2000.
829 Sqdn (022 Flt):
Wasp HAS1   Jan-Mar 1981 (XT437 426/AR) (ex *Arethusa*)
860 Sqdn:
Wasp AH-12A   Oct 1976-Jun 1979 (237)
Lynx SH-14B   Mar-Jul 1981 (271), May-Jun 1983 (267),
               Aug-Oct 1987 (269)
Lynx SH-14C   Jan 1991-Nov 1992 (266), Apr-Jul 1993 (267)
HrMs EVERTSEN F815
Van Speijk-class frigate, built 1965-67, commissioned 21 December 1967, mid-life update 1976, Wasp and later Lynx flight. Parent ship letters EV, sold to Indonesia November 1989 as *Abdul Halim Perdana Kusuma*.
860 Sqdn:
Wasp AH-12A   Mar 1978-Jul 1979 (245)
Lynx SH-14B   Jun 1983-Nov 1984 (278)
HrMs ISAAC SWEERS F814
Van Speijk-class frigate, built 1965-68, commissioned 15 May 1968, mid-life update 1978, Wasp and later Lynx flight. Parent ship letters IS, sold to Indonesia November 1990 as *Karel Satsuitubun*.
860 Sqdn:
Wasp AH-12A   Apr 1977-Mar 1980 (242)
Lynx SH-14B   Jan-Nov 1985 (282)
HrMs JAN VAN BRAKEL F825
Kortenaer-class frigate, built 1979-83, commissioned April 1983, fitted for two Lynx. Parent ship letters JB.
860 Sqdn:
Lynx SH-14B   Sep 1984-Sep 1986 (273), Apr 1989 (269)
Lynx SH-14C   Mar-May 1993 (269)
HrMs KAREL DOORMAN(3) D827
Destroyer, built 1985-91, commissioned May 1991, Lynx flight, later to be NH90. Parent ship letters KD.
860 Sqdn:
Lynx SH-14C   Sep 1993-to date (281)
HrMs KORTENAER F807
Frigate, built 1975-78, commissioned 26 October 1978, fitted for two Lynx. Parent ship letters KN, due for disposal 1995.
860 Sqdn:
Wasp AH-12A   Nov 1978-Dec 1979 (240)
Lynx SH-14B   Aug 1980 (270), Aug 1983-Jul 1984 (271),
               May-Oct 1985 (268)
Lynx SH-14C   Jul 1988-Jan 1990 (266), Jan-Oct 1993 (273)
HrMs PHILIPS VAN ALMONDE F823
Kortenaer-class frigate, built 1977-81, commissioned 2 December 1981, fitted for two Lynx. Parent ship letters PA.
860 Sqdn:
Lynx SH-14B   Jan 1984-Jul 1985 (281), Aug-Nov 1986 (282),
               Jan-Oct 1988 (270)
Lynx SH-14C   Jul 1990-Dec 1993 (280)
HrMs PIETER FLORIS F826
Kortenaer-class frigate, ex-HrMs *Willem Van Der Zaan*, built 1981-83, renamed during building, commissioned October 1983, fitted for two Lynx. Parent ship letters PF.
860 Sqdn:
Lynx SH-14B   Jan-Dec 1985 (274), Dec 1986-Sep 1987 (266)
Lynx SH-14C   Apr 1990-Oct 1991 (283)
HrMs PIET HEIJN F811
Kortenaer-class frigate, built 1977-81, commissioned April 1981, fitted for two Lynx. Parent ship letters PH.

860 Sqdn:
Lynx SH-14B   Jan 1983-Apr 1985 (274), Jan-Dec 1986 (266),
               May-Dec 1988 (267), Feb-Aug 1990 (267)
Lynx SH-14C   Jun-Dec 1992 (278); Jan 1994-to date (262)
HrMs POOLSTER A835
Fast combat support ship, built 1962-64, commissioned 10 September 1964. Provision up to five helicopters, often has RN Sea King embarked. Parent ship letters PR, to be replaced by HrMs *Amsterdam* (q.v.). Sold to Pakistan August 1994.
819 Sqdn:
1984 Sea King HAS.2: 1985 Sea King HAS.5, 1989 King HAS.6
819/C&D Flts: 1993-4 Sea King HAS.6 (XV711 709/PW)
824 Sqdn: 1988 Sea King HAS.5
826/A Flt: 1985 Sea King HAS.5
826/C Flt: 1988 Sea King HAS.5; 1993 Sea King HAS.6
826/D Flt: 1991-93 Sea King HAS.6
860 Sqdn: 1965-80 Wasp AH-12A; 1980-1994 Lynx SH-14B/C
HrMs ROTTERDAM (L800)
LPD amphibious transport, to be built 1994-97.
HrMs TJERK HIDDES(1) F804
Van Speijk-class frigate, built 1964-67, commissioned 16 August 1967, mid life update 1976, Wasp flight. Parent ship letters TH, sold to Indonesia November 1986 as *Ahmed Yani*.
860 Sqdn: Nov 1967-Nov 1968 Wasp AH-12A (243)
HrMs TJERK HIDDES(2) D830
Karel Doorman-class destroyer, built 1986-92, commissioned February 1993, fitted for Lynx flight, later to be NH90.
HrMs TROMP F801
Frigate, built 1971-75, commissioned 3 October 1975, fitted as Flag ship, Wasp and later Lynx flight. Parent ship letters TR, to be replaced by 2000.
860 Sqdn:
Wasp AH-12A   Oct 1975-Sep 1976 (238), Jan 1977-May 1978 (247)
Lynx SH-14B/C Feb 1989-Jun 1992 (268)
HrMs TYDEMAN A906
Hydrographic/oceanographic ship, built 1975-76, commissioned November 1976, fitted for Lynx, due for disposal 2000.
HrMs VAN AMSTEL D831
Karel Doorman-class destroyer, built 1988-93, commissioned May 1993, fitted for Lynx flight, later to be NH90.
HrMs VAN GALEN(1) F803
Van Speijk-class frigate, built 1963-67, commissioned 1 March 1967, mid life update 1978, Wasp flight. Parent ship letters VG, sold to Indonesia November 1987 as *Yos Sudarso*.
860 Sqdn: Apr 1970-Jun 1977 (235), Jan-Dec 1980 (236)
HrMs VAN GALEN(2) D834
Karel Doorman-class destroyer, building 1990-94, to be fitted for Lynx flight, later to be NH90. To commission December 1994.
HrMs VAN KINSBERGEN F809
Kortenaer-class frigate, built 1975-80, commissioned 24 April 1980, fitted for two Lynx. Parent ship letters KB. To be sold to Greece February 1995.
860 Sqdn: Jun 1987-Jul 1987 Lynx SH-14C (270)
               Mar 1990-Jan 1992 Lynx SH-14C (280)
               Sep 1993-May 1994 Lynx SH-14C (270)
HrMs VAN NES(1) F805
Van Speijk-class frigate, built 1963-67, commissioned 9 August 1967, mid life update 1979, Wasp and later Lynx flight. Parent ship letters VN, sold to Indonesia Oct 1988 as *Oswald Siahann*.
860 Sqdn:
Wasp AH-12A   Mar 1977-Mar 1978 (244)
Lynx SH-14B   Jan-Jul 1982 (268)
HrMs VAN NES(2) D833
Karel Doorman-class destroyer, building 1990-94, commissioned June 1994, fitted for Lynx flight, later to be NH90.
HrMs VAN SPEIJK(1) F802
Van Speijk (Leander)-class frigate, 1963-67, commissioned 14 February 1967, mid life update 1978, Wasp and later Lynx flight. Parent ship letters VS, sold to Indonesia November 1986 as *Salmet Riyadi*.
860 Sqdn:
Wasp AH-12A   Jan-Nov 1976 (244); Jan 1979-Jun 1980 12A (238)
Lynx SH-14B   Feb-Dec 1982 (274)
HrMs VAN SPEIJK(2) D828
Karel Doorman-class destroyer, building 1991-95, due to commission June 1995, to be fitted for Lynx flight, later to be NH90.
HrMs WILLEM VAN DER ZAAN D829
Karel Doorman-class destroyer, built 1985-91, commissioned November 1991, to be fitted for Lynx flight, later to be NH90.

HrMs ZUIDERKRUIS A832
Poolster-class fast combat support ship, built 1973-75, commissioned 27 June 1975. Provision for up to five helicopters, often has RN Sea King embarked. Parent ship letters ZK.
819 Sqdn: Sea King HAS.2 1982-83
826/A Flt: Sea King HAS.5 1987
826/B Flt: Sea King HAS.5 1987
826/C Flt: Sea King HAS.6 1989-90, 1993
                Sea King HAS.6 1991 (Gulf)
826/D Flt: Sea King HAS.6 1990-91, 1993

860 Sqdn:
Wasp AH-12A   Aug-Oct 1975 (238); Oct 1977-Apr 1980 (247)
Lynx SH-14B   Apr 1989 (269)
Lynx SH-14C   Sep-Oct 1990 (274)
Unnamed
Air Defence Command Frigate (ADCF), to be built, to be fitted for helicopter, replacement for HrMs *De Ruyter* (q.v.).
Unnamed
Air Defence Command Frigate (ADCF), to be built, to be fitted for helicopter, replacement for HrMs *Tromp* (q.v.).

NUMBERED SHIPS HELICOPTER FLIGHTS

From the mid-1960s, ships helicopter flights were given three-digit numbers. *Endurance* flight was numbered 001, and other Wasp flights 010 onwards. From 1970 Wessex flights were numbered 100 onwards, this series becoming defunct by the mid-1970s. In 1977 the Lynx began to replace the Wasp, and these formed a new 200-series of flights. The following lists include such details as are known of the Wasp and Wessex flights, which are not well recorded, with a more comprehensive coverage of the Lynx flights.

WASP SHIPS FLIGHTS

No.	Ship	Dates
001	HMS ENDURANCE(1)	Jun 1976-May 1986
010	HMS FALMOUTH	Nov 1970-Feb 1977
	HMS PHOEBE	Feb 1977-Oct 1977
	HMS HERALD	Oct 1977-Jul 1987
011	HMS HECATE	Jan 1968-Nov 1969
	HMS HECLA	Nov 1969-Dec 1973
	HMS HERALD	Dec 1973-Jul 1977
	HMS HYDRA	Jul 1977-Mar 1986
012	HMS HECLA	Apr 1982-Oct 1982
	HMS GALATEA(2)	Oct 1982-Sep 1986
013	HMS HECATE	May 1982-Dec 1983
015	HMS NAIAD	Jan 1965-Nov 1969
020	HMS PHOEBE	Nov 1968-Aug 1974
	HMS GALATEA(2)	Aug 1974-Apr 1981
	HMS AJAX(2)	Apr 1981-May 1985
021	HMS GURKHA	Sep 1970-Sep 1976
	HMS RHYL	Sep 1976-Dec 1976
	HMS APOLLO(2)	Dec 1976-Apr 1979
	HMS DIOMEDE	Apr 1979-Mar 1988
022	HMS ARETHUSA(2)	Jun 1977-Dec 1985
023	HMS DIOMEDE	Sep 1970-Oct 1973
	HMS AJAX	Oct 1973-Aug 1980
	HMS ARIADNE	Aug 1980-Mar 1988
024	HMS SCYLLA	Mar 1970-Jun 1976
	HMS JUPITER	Jun 1976-Mar 1980
	HMS ROTHESAY	Mar 1980-Mar 1988
026	HMS ZULU	Dec 1974-Aug 1979
	HMS RHYL	Aug 1979-Oct 1983
027	HMS ESKIMO	Jan 1974-Oct 1980
	HMS PLYMOUTH	Oct 1980-May 1988
029	CONTENDER BEZANT	May 1982-Aug 1982
030	HMS NUBIAN	Jan 1973-Feb 1976
030	HMS AURORA	Feb 1976-May 1987
031	CONTENDER BEZANT	May 1982-Aug 1982
032	HMS PLYMOUTH	Oct 1971-Apr 1974
	HMS BERWICK(2)	Apr 1974-Dec 1980
	HMS YARMOUTH	Dec 1980-May 1986
033	RMS ST HELENA	May 1982-Oct 1982
034	HMS RHYL	Jan 1972-Apr 1975
	HMS BRIGHTON	Apr 1975-May 1981
	HMS LEANDER(2)	May 1981-Aug 1986
035	HMS ROTHESAY	Dec 1970-Aug 1977
	HMS ACTIVE	Aug 1977-Jun 1985
036	HMS LOWESTOFT	Oct 1973-Mar 1985
038	HMS GALATEA(2)	May 1982-Oct 1982
039	HMS ZULU	Jul 1982-Aug 1983
040	HMS BERWICK(2)	Jun 1982-Oct 1985
041	HMS AURORA	Nov 1969-Nov 1972
	HMS ARIADNE	Nov 1972-Jan 1980
	HMS APOLLO(2)	Jan 1980-Mar 1988
042	HMS FALMOUTH	May 1982-Dec 1984
043	HMS ACHILLES	Sep 1978-Mar 1988
044	HMS ARETHUSA(2)	Jun 1965-Aug 1973
	HMS ANDROMEDA	Aug 1973-Jan 1978
	HMS EURYALUS	Jan 1978-Mar 1988
045	HMS NAIAD	Sep 1978-May 1987
049	HMS GURKHA	Jun 1982-Apr 1984
050	HMS TARTAR	Jun 1982-Oct 1983
052	HMS ACHILLES	Jun 1970-Feb 1978
	HMS BACCHANTE	Feb 1978-Oct 1982
055	HMS DIDO	Oct 1978-Jul 1983

WESSEX SHIPS FLIGHTS

No.	Ship	Dates
100	HMS ANTRIM	Aug 1970-Jan 1984
103	HMS NORFOLK(2)	Sep 1970-Mar 1981
	HMS GLAMORGAN	Mar 1981-Aug 1982

LYNX SHIPS FLIGHTS

200 HMS BIRMINGHAM   Jul 1977-Sep 1985
    HMS AMBUSCADE   Sep 1985-Aug 1991
    HMS NOTTINGHAM   Aug 1991-to date
    (700L Sqdn Jul 1977, 702 Sqdn Jan 1978, 815 Sqdn Jan 1981)

201 HMS PHOEBE   Nov 1977-Jan 1981
    HMS BATTLEAXE   Jan 1981-Sep 1988
    HMS BROADSWORD   Sep 1988-Jan 1992
    HMS CHATHAM   Jan 1992-Dec 1992
    HMS BRILLIANT   Dec 1992-to date
    (700L Sqdn Nov 1977, 702 Sqdn Jan 1978, 815 Sqdn Jan 1981, 829 Sqdn Sep 1986, 815 Sqdn Mar 1993)

202 HMS SIRIUS   Jan 1978-Jun 1981
    HMS SOUTHAMPTON(2) Jun 1981-Jan 1989
    HMS EXETER   Jan 1989-to date
    (700L Sqdn Jan 1978, 702 Sqdn Jan 1978, 815 Sqdn Jan 1981)

203 HMS NEWCASTLE   Jan 1978-Mar 1982
    RFA FORT AUSTIN   Apr 1982-Jul 1982
    Gibraltar   Jul 1982-May 1983
    HMS ARGONAUT   May 1983-Apr 1989
    HMS SIRIUS   Apr 1989-Mar 1993
    HMS IRON DUKE   Mar 1993-to date
    (702 Sqdn Jan 1978, 815 Sqdn Jan 1981, 829 Sqdn Mar 1987, 815 Sqdn Mar 1993)

204 HMS ARROW   Jul 1979-Jan 1988
    HMS AVENGER   Jan 1988-Apr 1994
    (702 Sqdn Apr 1978, 815 Sqdn Jan 1981, disbanded at Portland Apr 1994)

205 HMS AVENGER   May 1978-Nov 1986
    HMS ACTIVE   Nov 1986-to date
    (702 Sqdn May 1978, 815 Sqdn Jan 1981, disbanded at Portland Jul 1994)

206 HMS ALACRITY   Sep 1978-Apr 1986
    HMS BRAVE   Apr 1986-Jun 1990
    HMS CHATHAM   Jun 1990-Dec 1990
    HMS COVENTRY(2)   Dec 1990-to date
    (702 Sqdn Sep 1978, 815 Sqdn Jan 1981, 829 Sqdn Sep 1986, 815 Sqdn Mar 1993)

207 HMS ARDENT   Jul 1978-May 1982
    HMS EDINBURGH   Sep 1985-to date
    (702 Sqdn Jul 1978, 815 Sqdn Jan 1981, lost off Falklands May 1982, reformed in 815 Sqdn at Portland Sep 1985)

208 HMS AMAZON   Oct 1978-May 1983
    Gibraltar   May 1983-Apr 1991
    HMS BROADSWORD   Sep 1992-to date
    (702 Sqdn Oct 1978, 815 Sqdn Jan 1981, disbanded Apr 1991, reformed in 829 Sqdn at Portland Sep 1992, 815 Sqdn Mar 1993)

209 HMS CLEOPATRA   Nov 1978-Jan 1982
    HMS PENELOPE   Jan 1982-Jan 1991
    HMS NORFOLK(3)   Jan 1991-to date
    (702 Sqdn Nov 1978, 815 Sqdn Jan 1981, 829 Sqdn Apr 1988, 815 Sqdn Mar 1993)

210 HMS MINERVA   Dec 1978-Jan 1992
    HMS ARGYLL   Jan 1992-to date
    (702 Sqdn Dec 1978, 815 Sqdn Jan 1981, 829 Sqdn Apr 1988, 815 Sqdn Mar 1993)

211 HMS ARGONAUT   Jun 1979-Mar 1983
    HMS GLAMORGAN   Mar 1983-Dec 1984
    HMS BOXER   Dec 1984-Oct 1989
    HMS BRAZEN   Oct 1989-to date
    (702 Sqdn Jun 1979, 815 Sqdn Jan 1981, 829 Sqdn Sep 1986, 815 Sqdn Mar 1993)

212 HMS COVENTRY(1)   Mar 1979-May 1982
    HMS ENDURANCE(1) Feb 1987-Oct 1991
    HMS POLAR CIRCLE Oct 1991-Oct 1992
    (ship renamed Oct 1992)
    HMS ENDURANCE(2) Oct 1992-to date
    (702 Sqdn Mar 1979, 815 Sqdn Jan 1981, lost off Falklands May 1982, reformed in 829 Sqdn at Portland Feb 1987, 815 Sqdn Mar 1993)

213 HMS SHEFFIELD(2) Sep 1979-May 1982
    (702 Sqdn Sep 1979, 815 Sqdn Jan 1981, ship lost off Falklands May 1982, flight disbanded)

214 HMS CARDIFF   Jul 1979-to date
    (702 Sqdn Jul 1979, 815 Sqdn Jan 1981)

215 HMS GLASGOW(2)   Jun 1979-Nov 1987
    HMS HERMIONE   Nov 1987-May 1992
    HMS LIVERPOOL(2) May 1992-to date
    (702 Sqdn Jun 1979, 815 Sqdn Jan 1981)

216 HMS ANTELOPE   Oct 1979-May 1982
    HMS GLOUCESTER   Sep 1985-Feb 1993
    HMS MANCHESTER   Feb 1993-to date
    (702 Sqdn Oct 1979, 815 Sqdn Jan 1981, ship lost off Falklands May 1982, flight reformed in 815 Sqdn at Portland Sep 1985)

217 29 JSTU   Aug 1979-Jun 1982
    HMS YORK   Jun 1985-Feb 1994
    HMS GLOUCESTER   Feb 1994-to date
    (702 Sqdn Aug 1979, formed as *Exeter* Flt but immediately became 29JSTU, 815 Sqdn Jan 1981, Boscombe Down May 1980, Aberporth Sep 1980, disbanded at Yeovilton on completion of Sea Skua trials Jun 1982, reformed in 815 Sqdn at Portland Jun 1985)

218 HMS DANAE   Jul 1979-Sep 1991
    HMS BEAVER   Sep 1991-to date
    (702 Sqdn Jul 1979, 815 Sqdn Jan 1981, 829 Sqdn Apr 1988, 815 Sqdn Mar 1993)

219 HMS AMBUSCADE   Dec 1979-Oct 1984
    HMS AMAZON   Oct 1984-Mar 1991
    HMS NEWCASTLE   Mar 1991-to date
    (702 Sqdn Dec 1979, 815 Sqdn Jan 1981)

220 HMS BRILLIANT   Aug 1981-Aug 1987
    (815 Sqdn Aug 1981, 829 Sqdn Sep 1986, disbanded at Portland Aug 1987)

221 HMS BROADSWORD   Mar 1979-Dec 1987
    HMS BRILLIANT   Dec 1987-Dec 1992
    HMS CORNWALL(2)   Jan 1992-to date
    (702 Sqdn Mar 1979, 815 Sqdn Jan 1981, 829 Sqdn Sep 1986, 815 Sqdn Mar 1993)

222 HMS ANDROMEDA   Nov 1979-Mar 1990
    HMS SCYLLA   Mar 1990-Feb 1994
    (702 Sqdn Nov 1979, 815 Sqdn Jan 1981, 829 Sqdn Jun 1992, 815 Sqdn Mar 1993, disbanded at Portland Feb 1994)

223 HMS FIFE   Sep 1982-Jun 1987
    HMS NEWCASTLE   Oct 1987-Mar 1991
    HMS AMAZON   Mar 1991-Jul 1993
    (815 Sqdn Jun 1982, disbanded at Portland Jul 1993)

224 HMS LIVERPOOL   Apr 1982-Nov 1990
    (815 Sqdn Mar 1982, formed as *Minerva* Flt, became *Liverpool* Flt Apr 1982, disbanded at Portland Nov 1990)

225 flight did not form

226 HMS CAMPBELTOWN   Oct 1989-to date
    (829 Sqdn Oct 1989, 815 Sqdn Mar 1993)

227	HMS JUPITER	Sep 1983-Dec 1986	237 HMS CUMBERLAND	May 1989-Jan 1992
	HMS CHARYBDIS	Dec 1986-Aug 1991	(829 Sqdn May 1989, disbanded at Portland Jan 1992)	

227 HMS JUPITER Sep 1983-Dec 1986
HMS CHARYBDIS Dec 1986-Aug 1991
HMS ANDROMEDA Aug 1991-Nov 1993
HMS MONMOUTH Nov 1993-Jun 1994
Support Flight B Jun 1994-to date
(815 Sqdn Dec 1986, 829 Sqdn Jun 1992, 815 Sqdn Mar 1993)

228 HMS CHARYBDIS Jul 1982-Apr 1986
HMS GLAMORGAN Apr 1986-Sep 1986
HMS LONDON(3) Sep 1986-Feb 1994
HMS MONTROSE Feb 1994-Jun 1994
(815 Sqdn Jul 1982, 829 Sqdn Sep 1986, 815 Sqdn Mar 1993)

229 HMS HERMIONE Jun 1983-Mar 1987
HMS JUPITER Mar 1987-May 1992
HMS SOUTHAMPTON(2)
May 1992-to date
(815 Sqdn Jun 1983)

230 SSTF Apr 1980-Aug 1989
(702 Sqdn Apr 1980, 815 Sqdn Jan 1981, 829 Sqdn Jun 1988, disbanded Portland to become LOFTU (700L Sqdn) Aug 1989)

231 HMS SCYLLA Oct 1984-Jul 1989
HMS ARROW Jul 1989-Dec 1993
(815 Sqdn Oct 1984, disbanded at Portland Dec 1993)

232 HMS MANCHESTER Sep 1982-Aug 1991
HMS MARLBOROUGH Aug 1991-Mar 1994
(815 Sqdn Sep 1982, 829 Sqdn Aug 1991, 815 Sqdn Mar 1993)

233 HMS ALACRITY Mar 1987-Jul 1994
(815 Sqdn Mar 1987)

234 HMS SHEFFIELD(3) Aug 1988-to date
(829 Sqdn Aug 1988, 815 Sqdn Mar 1993)

235 HMS BRAZEN Jun 1982-Apr 1989
HMS BATTLEAXE Apr 1989-Aug 1993
HMS BRAVE Aug 1993-to date
(815 Sqdn Jun 1982, 829 Sqdn Sep 1986, 815 Sqdn Mar 1993)

236 HMS NOTTINGHAM Jan 1983-Nov 1990
(815 Sqdn Jan 1983, disbanded at Portland Nov 1990)

237 HMS CUMBERLAND May 1989-Jan 1992
(829 Sqdn May 1989, disbanded at Portland Jan 1992)

238 Director of Naval Recruiting
Jul 1990-Jun 1992
(829 Sqdn Jul 1990, disbanded at Portland Jun 1992)

239 HMS EXETER Jun 1981-Jan 1989
HMS GLASGOW Jan 1989-to date
(815 Sqdn Jun 1981)

240 HMS AVENGER Apr 1982-Sep 1982
(815 Sqdn Apr 1982, disbanded at Yeovilton on return from Falklands service Sep 1982)

241 HMS NEWCASTLE Jun 1982-Sep 1986
HMS BIRMINGHAM Sep 1986-to date
(815 Sqdn Jun 1982)

242 HMS PHOEBE Jun 1982-Feb 1991
HMS BEAVER Feb 1991-Aug 1991
HMS AMBUSCADE Aug 1991-Jun 1993
(815 Sqdn Jun 1982, 829 Sqdn Mar 1987, 815 Sqdn Aug 1991, disbanded at Portland Jun 1993)

243 HMS SIRIUS Jun 1982-Apr 1989
HMS ARGONAUT Apr 1989-Mar 1992
(815 Sqdn Jun 1982, 829 Sqdn Mar 1987, disbanded at Portland Mar 1992)

244 HMS BEAVER Jul 1984-Jul 1990
Support Flight A Jul 1990-to date
(815 Sqdn Jul 1984, 829 Sqdn Sep 1988, 815 Sqdn Mar 1993)

245 HMS COVENTRY(2) Nov 1988-Oct 1990
HMS BRAVE Oct 1990-Nov 1992
HMS LANCASTER Nov 1992-to date
(829 Sqdn Nov 1988, 815 Sqdn Mar 1993)

246 HMS CORNWALL(2) Feb 1989-Apr 1991
HMS BOXER Apr 1991-to date
(829 Sqdn Feb 1989, 815 Sqdn Mar 1993)

Lynx HAS.3 XZ248 '345/NC' of HMS Newcastle Flight on 15 April 1988

FLEET AIR ARM FLIGHTS 1923 - 1936

Under a reorganisation of RAF coastal units on 1 April 1923, several carrier-borne flights were formed with numbers in the 400 series. The sequence was sub-divided, provision being made for expansion in each sub-series. Numbers from 401 onwards were reserved for Fleet Fighter flights, 420 onwards for Fleet Spotter flights, 440 onwards for Fleet Reconnaissance flights and 460 onwards for Fleet Torpedo flights. Exactly a year later, on 1 April 1924, these units became the Fleet Air Arm of the Royal Air Force.

As more carriers came into service, further flights were formed in each category. Introduction of Fairey IIIFs led to a new combined Fleet Spotter Reconnaissance designation, and consequently the 420 series was abandoned on 26 April 1929, the existing flights in this range being renumbered in the 440 series. By 1930 the term Fleet Torpedo Bomber had been adopted for the 460 series of flights.

On 3 April 1933 most of the flights were reorganised into squadrons, numbered in a new 800-series. A few flights, however, had begun to operate by catapult from capital ships and cruisers, and these retained their 400-series numbers until 15 July 1936, when they were given new 700-series numbers, initially still as flights, but all becoming squadrons by the outbreak of war. Both the 700 and 800 sequences have remained in use to the present day.

Brief details of these units are given below.

No.401 Flight

No.401 (Fleet Fighter) Flight formed with Nightjars at Leuchars on 1 April 1923 for HMS *Argus*. Re-equipping with Flycatchers early in 1924, it joined HMS *Hermes* in 1926, returning to HMS *Argus* in 1927. Transferring to HMS *Courageous* in 1930, and then to HMS *Furious* in 1932, it became No.801 Squadron on 3 April 1933.

Aircraft Equipment	Period of Service	Example
Nightjar	Apr 1923 - Jan 1924	J6931
Flycatcher	Feb 1924 - Apr 1933	N9662 (530)

No.402 Flight

No.402 (Fleet Fighter) Flight formed with Flycatchers at Leuchars on 1 April 1923 for HMS *Eagle*. In the Spring of 1932 it transferred to HMS *Courageous*, and shortly afterwards re-equipped with Nimrods. It became part of No.800 Squadron on 3 April 1933.

Aircraft Equipment	Period of Service	Example
Flycatcher	Apr 1923 - Oct 1932	N9662 (507)
Nimrod	Jul 1932 - Apr 1933	S1625 (502)

No.403 Flight

No.403 (Fleet Fighter) Flight formed with Plovers and Nightjars on 1 June 1923 for HMS *Hermes*. It re-equipped with Flycatchers in July 1924, being reallocated for catapult duty with the 5th Cruiser Squadron in June 1933. It began to re-equip with Ospreys in May 1934, and its first Walrus arrived in June 1936, but on 15 July 1936 it became No.715 Flight.

Aircraft Equipment	Period of Service	Example
Plover	Jun 1923 - Jul 1924	
Nightjar	Jun 1923 - 1924	J6952
Flycatcher	Jul 1924 - Apr 1935	N9931 (3)
Osprey III	May 1934 - Jul 1936	K3644 (590)
Walrus	Jun 1936 - Jul 1936	K5780

No.404 Flight

No.404 (Fleet Fighter) Flight formed with Plovers and Nightjars on 1 July 1923 for HMS *Furious*. Re-equipped with Flycatchers late 1924, it split early 1927 into No.404A Flight in HMS *Furious*, and No.404B Flight which joined HMS *Argus*. The sub-flights reunited in May 1928 and No.404 then joined HMS *Courageous*. Towards the end of 1932 the flight re-equipped with Nimrods and Ospreys, but on 3 April 1933 it became part of No.800 Squadron.

Aircraft Equipment	Period of Service	Example
Plover	Jul 1923 - Mar 1925	N9608
Nightjar	Apr 1924 - Sep 1924	J6933
Flycatcher	1924 - Nov 1932	N9948 (4)
Osprey I	Nov 1932 - Apr 1933	S1684 (210)
Nimrod	Oct 1932 - Apr 1933	S1624

No.405 Flight

No.405 (Fleet Fighter) Flight formed with Flycatchers on 31 May 1924 for HMS *Furious*, a few Plovers being also flown at first. It transferred to HMS *Glorious* in 1930, after trials with a number of experimental fleet fighters. In December 1932 it partially re-equipped with Ospreys, but on 4 April 1933 became No.803 Squadron.

Aircraft Equipment	Period of Service	Example
Plover	Jul 1924 - 1924	N9704
Flycatcher	Jul 1924 - Apr 1933	N9909 (19)
Osprey I	Dec 1932 - Apr 1933	K2781 (285)

No.406 Flight

No.406 (Fleet Fighter) Flight formed with Flycatchers on 31 May 1924 for HMS *Furious*. It transferred to HMS *Hermes* in 1927, but shortly afterwards merged into No.401 Flight. In 1930 it was revived for HMS *Glorious*, until becoming a catapult flight for the 4th Cruiser Squadron in January 1933. It re-equipped with Ospreys in June 1934, and a Fairey IIIF was received the following year. On 15 July 1936 it was renumbered to become No.714 Flight.

Aircraft Equipment	Period of Service	Example
Flycatcher	May 1924 - Jun 1934	S1277 (1)
Osprey III	Jun 1934 - Jul 1936	K3630 (304)
Osprey IV	Feb 1936 - Jul 1936	K5750
IIIF	Apr 1935 - Jul 1936	S1548

No.407 Flight

No.407 (Fleet Fighter) Flight formed with Flycatchers on 1 September 1927 for HMS *Courageous*. It transferred to HMS *Furious* early in 1932, and later that year re-equipped with Ospreys. In January 1933 it became a catapult squadron for the 2nd Cruiser Squadron, and the first Walrus was received shortly before it was renumbered to become No.712 Flight on 15 July 1936.

Aircraft Equipment	Period of Service	Example
Flycatcher	Sep 1927 - Nov 1932	N9676 (10)
Osprey III	Nov 1932 - Jul 1936	K3918 (201)
Osprey IV	Oct 1935 - Jul 1936	K5752
Walrus	Apr 1936 - Jul 1936	K5774

No.408 Flight

No.408 (Fleet Fighter) Flight formed with Flycatchers on 30 March 1929 for HMS *Glorious*. In November 1931 it re-equipped with Nimrods, but on 3 April 1933 it became part of No.802 Squadron.

Aircraft Equipment	Period of Service	Example
Flycatcher	Mar 1929 - Nov 1931	S1283 (12)
Nimrod I	Nov 1931 - Apr 1933	S1585 (576)

No.409 Flight

No.409 (Fleet Fighter) Flight formed with Nimrods and Ospreys on 7 October 1932 for HMS *Glorious*. On 3 April 1933 it merged into No.802 Squadron.

Aircraft Equipment Period of Service Example
Nimrod I   Oct 1932 - Apr 1933 S1632 (562)
Osprey I   Oct 1932 - Apr 1933 S1687 (549)

No.420 Flight

No.420 (Fleet Spotter) Flight formed with Walruses on 1 April 1923 for HMS *Furious*. It re-equipped with Blackburns early in 1925, but on 26 April 1929 was renumbered No.449 Flight.

Aircraft Equipment Period of Service Example
Walrus   Apr 1923 - Apr 1925 N9505
Blackburn I   Jan 1925 - Dec 1925 N9829
Blackburn II Jan 1926 - Apr 1929 S1047 (25)

No.421 Flight

No.421 (Fleet Spotter) Flight formed with Walruses on 1 April 1923 for HMS *Furious*. It re-equipped with Bisons in May 1925, and in early 1927 split into No.421A Flight in HMS *Furious* and No.421B Flight in HMS *Eagle*. Later that year No.421A Flight temporarily amalgamated with No.443A Flight as No.443 (Composite) Flight in HMS *Furious*. No.421 Flight was reunited in June 1928, and re-equipped with Fairey IIIFs in January 1929. On 26 April 1929 it became No.447 Flight.

Aircraft Equipment Period of Service Example
Walrus   Apr 1923 - May 1925 N9526
Bison I   May 1925 - Aug 1925 N9598
Bison II   Aug 1925 - Mar 1929 N9849 (36)
IIIF   Jan 1929 - Apr 1929 S1312

No.422 Flight

No.422 (Fleet Spotter) Flight formed with Walruses on 1 April 1923 for HMS *Eagle*. It soon re-equipped with Blackburns, but temporarily received Fairey IIIDs in January 1927 for service in HMS *Argus*. Reverting to Blackburns in May 1928, it became No.450 Flight on 26 April 1929.

Aircraft Equipment Period of Service Example
Walrus   Apr 1923 -   1923 N9507
Blackburn I   Jun 1923 - May 1926 N9682 (21)
Blackburn II Feb 1926 - Jan 1927 N9982 (29)
IIID   Jan 1927 - May 1928 S1008
Blackburn II May 1928 - May 1929 N9826 (27)

No.423 Flight

No.423 (Fleet Spotter) Flight formed on 21 November 1923 with Bisons and Walruses, the latter soon being discarded. It served in HMS *Argus* until transferring to HMS *Eagle* in February 1926. It had a short spell in HMS *Hermes* in mid-1926 then returned to HMS *Eagle* early in 1927. It started to re-equip with Fairey IIIFs in March 1929, but on 26 April 1929 it became No.448 Flight.

Aircraft Equipment Period of Service Example
Walrus   Nov 1923 - Jul 1924 N9502
Bison I   Nov 1923 - Apr 1925 N9602 (1)
Bison II Apr 1925 - Mar 1929 N9848 (21)

No.440 Flight

No.440 (Fleet Reconnaissance) Flight formed on 1 May 1923 with Seagull amphibians for HMS *Eagle*. It re-equipped with Fairey IIIDs in January 1925, with which it transferred to HMS *Hermes* in September 1926. Fairey IIIFs arrived in November 1927, and on 11 June 1933 the flight merged into No.824 Squadron.

Aircraft Equipment Period of Service Example
Seagull III May 1923 - Jan 1925 N9651 (45)
IIID   Jan 1925 - Oct 1927 S1002 (43)
IIIF   Nov 1927 - Jun 1933 S1478 (873)

No.441 Flight

No.441 (Fleet Reconnaissance) Flight formed on 1 April 1923 with Panthers for HMS *Argus*. In March 1924 it transferred to HMS *Hermes*, and shortly afterwards re-equipped with Fairey IIIDs. In June 1926 it went to HMS *Eagle*, then back to HMS *Argus* in February 1927. In March 1929 it received Fairey IIIFs to become a Fleet Spotter Reconnaissance flight. It transferred to HMS *Glorious* in June 1930, becoming No.823 Squadron on 3 April 1933.

Aircraft Equipment Period of Service Example
Panther Apr 1924 - Jun 1924 N7469
IIID   Jul 1924 - May 1929 N9781 (57)
IIIF   Mar 1929 - Apr 1933 S1404 (801)

No.442 Flight

No.442 (Fleet Reconnaissance) Flight formed on 1 April 1923 with Panthers for HMS *Argus*. It re-equipped with Fairey IIIDs in October 1924, and from 1926 spent much of its time in the Far East with periods afloat in HMS *Hermes*. It returned home to re-equip in October 1930 with Fairey IIIFs. In January 1932 it joined HMS *Furious*, becoming part of No.822 Squadron on 3 April 1933.

Aircraft Equipment Period of Service Example
Panther Apr 1923 - Oct 1924 N7489
IIID   Oct 1924 - Oct 1930 S1004
IIIF   Oct 1930 - Apr 1933 S1303 (706)

No.443 Flight

No.443 (Fleet Reconnaissance) Flight formed on 21 May 1923 HMS *Furious*. It existed only on paper at first, initially as No.443A Flight, but Fairey IIIDs arrived by 1925, and the following year it was made up to strength. In January 1927 a sub-flight joined HMS *Argus* as No.443B Flight for service in the Far East. The other sub-flight, No.443A, re-equipped in May with Fairey IIIFs, and these combined with No.421A Flight in October 1927 to form No.443 (Composite) Flight. In June 1928 No.443 recombined, to become a Fleet Spotter Reconnaissance flight, still in HMS *Furious*. In August 1931 it became a catapult flight, initially for the 2nd Cruiser Squadron, and later for the 6th and 8th Cruiser Squadrons. Ospreys began to arrive in May 1935, but on 15 July 1936 the unit disbanded to form Nos.716 and 718 Flights.

Aircraft Equipment Period of Service Example
IIID   Aug 1925 - May 1928 S1075 (51)
IIIF   May 1927 - Jul 1936 S1544 (769)
Osprey III May 1935 - Jul 1936 K5755

No.444 Flight

No.444 (Fleet Reconnaissance) Flight formed on 15 January 1925 with Fairey IIIDs for service in the seaplane carrier HMS *Vindictive*. In April 1929 it was redesignated to become a Fleet Spotter Reconnaissance flight, and in November 1929 was reallocated for catapult use. In September 1931 it re-equipped with Fairey IIIFs, and with these it was attached to the 2nd Battle Squadron, transferring in September 1933 to the 1st Battle Squadron and the 1st Cruiser Squadron. Small numbers of other types of catapult aircraft were flown, including Seal, Seagull V, Walrus, Osprey, Shark and Swordfish. It disbanded on 15 July 1936 into the new 700-series of flights.

Aircraft Equipment Period of Service Example
IIID   Jan 1925 - Sep 1931 N9469
IIIF   Sep 1931 - Jul 1936 S1509 (719)
Seal   Dec 1932 - Dec 1933 K3479 (719)
Seagull V   Feb 1934 - Aug 1934 N-2
Walrus I   Jan 1935 - Jul 1936 K5778
Osprey   Jan 1936 - Jul 1936 K3634
Shark II   Mar 1936 - Jul 1936 K5624 (091)
Swordfish I   Mar 1936 - Jul 1936 K5931 (092)

No.445 Flight

No.445 (Fleet Reconnaissance) Flight formed on 1 September 1927 with Fairey IIIFs for HMS *Courageous*, becoming a Fleet Spotter Reconnaissance flight early in 1930. It disbanded into Nos.820 and 821 Squadrons on 3 April 1933.

The flight reformed on 30 August 1935 for Fleet Spotter Reconnaissance work. Equipped with Ospreys, these undertook catapult duties with the 3rd Cruiser Squadron, until becoming No.713 Flight on 15 July 1936.

Aircraft Equipment Period of Service Example
IIIF   Sep 1927 - Apr 1933 S1220 (42)
Osprey III Aug 1935 - Jul 1936 K4322 (079)

No.446 Flight

No.446 (Fleet Reconnaissance) Flight formed on 1 September 1927 with Fairey IIIFs for HMS *Courageous*, becoming a Fleet Spotter Reconnaissance flight early in 1930. It disbanded into No.821 Squadron on 3 April 1933.

Aircraft Equipment Period of Service Example
IIIF   Sep 1927 - Apr 1933 S1499 (730)

No.447 Flight

No.447 (Fleet Spotter Reconnaissance) Flight formed on 26 April 1929 by renumbering No.421 Flight for service in HMS *Furious* with Fairey IIIFs. It transferred to HMS *Glorious* in April 1930, but in 1932 was earmarked for catapult use with the 1st Cruiser Squadron, and later also the 1st Battle Squadron. Part of the flight rejoined HMS *Glorious* between October 1933 and March 1934, then in January 1935 some Ospreys were received. The flight disbanded on 15 July 1936 to form the basis of Nos.701 and 711 Flights.

Aircraft Equipment Period of Service Example
IIIF   Apr 1929 - Jul 1936 S1316 (46)
Osprey III Jan 1935 - Jul 1936 K3642 (067)

No.448 Flight

No.448 (Fleet Spotter Reconnaissance) Flight formed on 26 April 1929 by renumbering No.423 Flight for service in HMS *Eagle* with Fairey IIIFs. It transferred to HMS *Glorious* in May 1931, but disbanded on 3 April 1933 to form No.823 Squadron.

Aircraft Equipment Period of Service Example
IIIF   Apr 1929 - Apr 1933 S1539 (827)

No.449 Flight

No.449 (Fleet Spotter Reconnaissance) Flight formed on 26 April 1929 by renumbering No.430 Flight for service in HMS *Furious* with Blackburns. It transferred to HMS *Courageous* in June 1930, and in May 1931 re-equipped with Fairey IIIFs. On 3 April 1933 it became No.822 Squadron.

Aircraft Equipment Period of Service Example
Blackburn II Apr 1929 - Jun 1931 S1157 (45)
IIIF   May 1931 - Apr 1933 S1515 (740)

No.450 Flight

No.450 (Fleet Spotter Reconnaissance) Flight formed on 26 April 1929 by renumbering No.422 Flight for service in HMS *Argus* with Blackburns. It transferred to HMS *Courageous* in September, re-equipping soon afterwards with Fairey IIIFs. On 3 April 1933 it became part of No.820 Squadron.

Aircraft Equipment Period of Service Example
Blackburn II Apr 1929 - Nov 1930 S1154 (52)
IIIF   Nov 1930 - Apr 1933 S1259 (745)

No.460 Flight

No.460 (Fleet Torpedo) Flight formed on 1 April 1923 with Darts for HMS *Eagle*. In November 1930 it re-equipped with Ripons, becoming a Fleet Torpedo Bomber flight. In May 1931 it transferred to HMS *Glorious*, receiving Fairey IIIFs in November 1932. On 3 April 1933 it became part of No.824 Squadron.

Aircraft Equipment Period of Service Example
Dart   Apr 1923 - Nov 1930 N9990 (62)
Ripon II/IIa Nov 1930 - Nov 1932 S1431 (81)
IIIF   Nov 1932 - Apr 1933 S1822 (84)

No.461 Flight

No.461 (Fleet Torpedo) Flight formed on 1 April 1923 with Darts for HMS *Furious*. These were replaced in December 1929 with Ripons, and in May 1930 it transferred to HMS *Glorious*, becoming a Fleet Torpedo Bomber flight shortly afterwards. On 3 April 1933 it became part of No.812 Squadron.

Aircraft Equipment Period of Service Example
Dart   Apr 1923 - Jan 1930 N9823 (60)
Ripon II/IIa Dec 1929 - Apr 1933 S1465 (62)

No.462 Flight

No.462 (Fleet Torpedo) Flight was formed on 31 May 1924 with Darts for HMS *Furious*. It re-equipped with Ripons in February 1929, becoming a Fleet Torpedo Bomber flight shortly after joining HMS *Glorious* in May 1930. On 3 April 1933 it became part of No.812 Squadron.

Aircraft Equipment Period of Service Example
Dart   May 1924 - Mar 1929 N9803 (73)
Ripon II/IIa Feb 1929 - Apr 1933 S1265 (75)

No.463 Flight

No.463 (Fleet Torpedo) Flight formed on 1 September 1927 with Darts for HMS *Courageous*. It became a Fleet Torpedo Bomber flight in 1930, and disbanded into No.810 Squadron on 3 April 1933.

Aircraft Equipment Period of Service Example
Dart   Sep 1927 - Apr 1933 S1117 (65)

No.464 Flight

No.464 (Fleet Torpedo) Flight formed on 1 September 1927 with Darts for HMS *Courageous*. It became a Fleet Torpedo Bomber flight in 1930, and disbanded into No.810 Squadron on 3 April 1933.

Aircraft Equipment Period of Service Example
Dart   Sep 1927 - Apr 1933 N9991 (74)

No.465 Flight

No.465 (Fleet Torpedo Bomber) Flight formed on 20 March 1931 with Ripons for HMS *Furious*. It disbanded into No.811 Squadron on 3 April 1933.

Aircraft Equipment Period of Service Example
Ripon IIc   Mar 1931 - Apr 1933 S1555 (6)

No.466 Flight

No.466 (Fleet Torpedo Bomber) Flight formed on 1 April 1931 with Ripons for HMS *Furious*. It disbanded into No.811 Squadron on 3 April 1933.

Aircraft Equipment Period of Service Example
Ripon IIc   Apr 1931 - Apr 1933 S1560 (14)

MISCELLANEOUS FLEET AIR ARM UNITS

Although the majority of FAA units received squadron numbers, there have been some exceptions, such as Ships Flights, Station Flights, ferry units, and civilian-operated units. Brief details of these are given in this appendix. Not included are ship's aircraft controlled by a particular squadron (generally Nos.700, 701, 702, 815 or 829), details of which can be found elsewhere.

NAVAL WINGS

An order was issued in June 1943 that squadrons embarked in carriers were to be grouped into numbered wings. Each wing would bear a distinguishing number, prefixed by its purpose, being either Fighter or Torpedo Bomber Reconnaissance. In order to avoid confusion with RAF wings bearing the same numbers, each had the word Naval in its title.

Commencing on 25 October 1943, 19 naval wings were formed, and others were planned but never materialised. On 30 June 1945, those wings serving with the British Pacific Fleet lost their identities on merging into the new Carrier Air Groups, the remainder being disbanded over the next few months, usually when their ship returned home.

****

2nd Naval TBR Wing

Formed on 24 January 1944 with Nos.828 and 841 Squadrons, and allocated on 11th March to HMS *Implacable*. Its Barracudas first embarked during August, some being detached to HMS *Formidable* that month. No.828 Squadron absorbed No.841 Squadron on 28 November 1944, and the Wing ceased to exist. Reformed at Katukurunda as No.2 Strike Wing on 10 December 1944, with the Avengers of Nos.820 and 849 Squadrons, but evidently short-lived.

Wing Leaders

Lt Cdr E M Britton RN	24 Jan 1944
Not identified	23 Jul 1944
Wing disbanded	28 Nov 1944

3rd Naval Fighter Wing

Unofficial wartime badge

Formed at Burscough on 25 October 1944 for tactical reconnaissance work with Nos.808, 886 and 897 Squadrons, these embarking on occasion in HMS *Hunter*, HMS *Attacker* and HMS *Stalker* respectively. On 25 February 1944 the Wing moved to Lee-on-Solent, where it took over the newly formed No.885 Squadron to become an Air Spotting Pool attached to the 2nd Tactical Air Force. The Wing was active during the Normandy invasion, following which it was reconstituted, No.808 Squadron absorbing No.886, and No.885 absorbing No.897. The Wing headquarters moved to Ballyhalbert on 4 August, and a virtually new wing was formed during September and October 1944. Nos.808 and 885 Squadrons re-equipped with Hellcats, and were joined by the similarly equipped Nos.800 and 1840 Squadrons. The Wildcats of Nos.881 and 882 Squadrons of the 7th Wing were also attached for three weeks in October 1944. By early 1945 the four Hellcat squadrons were on their way east in the escort carriers HMS *Emperor* (No.800), HMS *Khedive* (No.808), HMS *Ruler* (No.885) and HMS *Speaker* (No.1840). The Wing saw active service with the East Indies Fleet, being eventually disbanded on 9 December 1945.

Wing Leaders

Lt Cdr (A) S J Hall RNVR	25 Oct 1943
Lt Cdr (A) R McD Hill RNVR	13 Mar 1944
Lt Cdr N G Hallett DSC RN	22 May 1944
Wing reforming	15 Jul 1944
Lt Cdr R H P Carver DSC RN	30 Sep 1944
Lt Cdr (A) B H C Nation RN	16 Nov 1944
Mjr P P Nelson-Gracie RM	11 Feb 1945
Lt Cdr R H P Carver DSC RN	8 Apr 1945
Wing disbanded	9 Dec 1945

4th Naval Fighter Wing

It was originally proposed that the 4th Naval Fighter Wing consist of six Seafire squadrons embarked in assault carriers, being Nos.807 and 808 Squadron in HMS *Hunter*, Nos.879 and 886 in HMS *Attacker* and Nos.809 and 897 in HMS *Stalker*. In the event, half were earmarked instead for the 3rd Wing, and when the 4th Wing formed at Burscough on 25 October 1943 it comprised only Nos.807, 809 and 879 Squadrons. After embarking in their respective carriers, these took part in operations in Italy in mid-1944, followed by participation in the landings in the South of France in August. Following Army support operations in the Aegean, the Wing went to Egypt for a spell before re-embarking for Ceylon in early 1945. After seeing service with the East Indies Fleet, the Wing returned home later in the year, to disband at Nutts Corner on 25 January 1946.

Wing Leaders

Lt Cdr (A) A C Wallace RNVR	25 Oct 1943
Lt Cdr (A) G C Baldwin DSC RN	3 Jun 1944
None	16 Nov 1945
Wing disbanded	25 Jan 1946

5th Naval Fighter Wing

Nos.1839 and 1844 Hellcat squadrons formed the 5th Naval Fighter Wing at Eglinton in December 1943, sailing for India in HMS *Begum* in February 1944. They joined HMS *Indomitable* in July 1944, and saw action with the Eastern Fleet, and later the British Pacific Fleet. The ship sailed home after VJ-Day, the Wing disbanding on arrival on 30 November 1945.

Wing Leaders

Cdr H P Sears RN	28 Feb 1944
(In command Nos.5, 6, 12 and 45 Wings)	
Cdr T G C Jameson RN (SO/Air)	7 Apr 1944
Lt Cdr (A) T W Harrington RN	9 Sep 1944
Not identified	Apr 1945
Wing disbanded	30 Nov 1945

6th Naval Fighter Wing

Formed at Burscough in February 1944, consisting of only No.1837 Corsair squadron. Sailed almost immediately in HMS *Atheling* to join the Eastern Fleet and worked up in Ceylon before joining HMS *Illustrious* in June for operations. However, the 6th Wing disbanded on 14 August, and No.1837 became briefly part of the 47th Wing in HMS *Victorious*, before disbanding on 9 September 1944.

The 6th Naval Fighter Wing reformed immediately in the United Kingdom, comprising Nos.1841 and 1842 Corsair squadrons for HMS *Formidable*. After taking part in *Tirpitz* operations, and later seeing extensive action with the British Pacific Fleet, it disbanded on 30 June 1945 on being absorbed into the 2nd Carrier Air Group.

Wing Leaders

Cdr H P Sears RN	28 Feb 1944
(In command Nos.5, 6, 12 and 45 Wings)	
Mjr R C Hay DSO & Bar DSC RM	24 May 1944
Wing disbanded	14 Aug 1944
Lt Cdr (A) R L Bigg-Wither RN	14 Aug 1944
Wing disbanded into 2nd CAG	30 Jun 1945

7th Naval Fighter Wing

Formed at Eglinton on 30 October 1943 with Nos.800 and 804 Hellcat squadrons for service in the assault carrier HMS *Emperor*, Nos.881 and 896 Wildcat squadrons for HMS *Pursuer* and Nos.882 and 898 Wildcat squadrons for HMS *Searcher*. Having two fighter squadrons in each carrier proved unwieldy, and in June 1944 Nos.804, 896 and 898 Squadrons disbanded into their respective companions. The Wing participated in the landings in the South of France in August, later undertaking Aegean operations. Returning to Northern Ireland towards the end of the year, it began to lose its squadrons to other wings, disbanding on 16 December 1944.

Wing Leaders
Lt Cdr (A) M F Fell RN   30 Oct 1943
Wing disbanded   16 Dec 1944

8th Naval TBR Wing

Nos.827 and 830 Squadrons comprised the 8th Naval TBR Wing when it formed on 25 October 1943 for service aboard HMS *Furious*. Its Barracudas took part in numerous operations in Norwegian waters, including attacks on the German battleship Tirpitz. The wing ceased to exist when No.830 Squadron was absorbed into No.827 Squadron on 3 October 1944.

Wing Leaders
Lt Cdr R S Baker-Falkner DSC RN   25 Oct 1943
Not identified   18 Jul 1944
Wing disbanded   3 Oct 1944

9th Naval TBR Wing

Formed on 11 February 1944 with Nos.820 and 826 Barracuda squadrons for service in HMS *Indefatigable*. After carrying out operations in Norwegian waters, including *Tirpitz* strikes, the Wing ceased to exist when No.820 Squadron absorbed No.826 on 23 October 1944.

Wing Leaders
Lt Cdr (A) A J I Temple-West RN   11 Feb 1944
Lt Cdr (A) W R Nowell RN   1 Aug 1944
Wing disbanded   23 Oct 1944

10th Naval Fighter Wing

Formed at Eglinton on 14 October 1944 with Nos.1843 and 1845 Corsair squadrons. No.1845 sailed in the escort carrier HMS *Slinger* in December 1944, as replenishment for the British Pacific Fleet, followed in February 1945 by No.1843 in HMS *Arbiter*. The Wing never saw action as such, No.1845 being disbanded on 5 April 1945 to reinforce squadrons in HMS *Formidable* and HMS *Victorious*, whilst No.1843 merged into the 3rd Carrier Air Group on 30 June 1945.

Wing Leaders
Mjr P P Nelson-Gracie RM   14 Oct 1944
Wing disbanded into 3rd CAG   30 Jun 1945

11th Naval TBR Wing

Formed at Ulunderpet in southern India on 21 April 1944 by renumbering the 45th TBR Wing, which consisted of Nos.822 and 823 Barracuda Squadrons. It was short-lived, however, being disbanded when No.823 was absorbed into No.822 on 6 July 1944.

Wing Leaders
Not identified   21 Apr 1944
Wing disbanded   6 Jul 1944

12th Naval TBR Wing

On 23 December 1943, No.831 Barracuda squadron was allocated to a planned 12th Naval TBR Wing for service in HMS *Indomitable*, but instead it was reallocated to the 52nd Wing on 12 January 1944. When the 12th Wing did actually form on 24 January 1944, it comprised Nos.815 and 817 Squadrons. HMS *Indomitable* was still under repair at that time, and consequently the Wing sailed to the Far East in HMS *Begum* in February 1944, eventually joining HMS *Indomitable* in July 1944 for operations. Disembarking in October, the Wing disbanded on 28 December 1944.

Wing Leaders
Lt Cdr E M Britton RN   24 Jan 1944
Wing disbanded   28 Dec 1944

15th Naval Fighter Wing

Formed at Stretton on 8 November 1943 with Nos.1830, 1831 and 1833 Corsair squadrons for service in HMS *Illustrious*. No.1831 soon disbanded, to be divided between the other two squadrons. Sailing to join the Eastern Fleet and later the British Pacific Fleet, the Wing participated in numerous operations before returning to the United Kingdom in May 1945, the squadrons disbanding on arrival on 28 July 1945.

Wing Leaders
Lt Cdr J W Sleigh DSC RN   8 Nov 1943
Lt Cdr (A) R J Cork DSO DSC RN   2 Dec 1943
Lt Cdr (A) A.M.Tritton
    DSC & 2 Bars RNVR   4 Apr 1944
Wing disbanded   28 Jul 1945

18th Naval Mac-ship Wing

This title was allocated to a proposed Wing intended to control squadrons whose aircraft were embarked in Mac-ships. In the event these squadrons were all combined as No.836, and it is doubtful if the Mac-ship Wing, as it was more generally known, ever used its numbered designation.

21st Naval TBR Wing

The 21st Naval TBR Wing was formed at Machrihanish on 25 October 1943 with Nos.810 and 847 Barracuda squadrons. It embarked in HMS *Illustrious* the following month, then sailed for operations with the Eastern Fleet. No.847 Squadron was absorbed into No.810 Squadron on 30 June 1944, and the Wing then ceased to exist.

Wing Leaders
Lt Cdr N R Corbet-Milward RN   25 Oct 1943
Lt Cdr B E Boulding DSC RN   18 Nov 1943
Lt Cdr (A) A J B Forde RN   27 Feb 1944
Wing disbanded   30 Jun 1944

24th Naval Fighter Wing

The 24th Naval Fighter Wing formed at Henstridge on 25 October 1943 with Nos.887 and 894 Seafire squadrons for service in HMS *Indefatigable*. These first embarked in May 1944, carrying out Norwegian operations during August. In November 1944 the ship sailed to join the Eastern Fleet and later the British Pacific Fleet, for operations against the Japanese. The Wing was absorbed by the 7th Carrier Air Group on 30 June 1945.

Wing Leaders
Lt Cdr N G Hallett DSC RN   31 Dec 1943
None   22 May 1944
Lt Cdr (A) A J Thomson DSC RNVR   1 Nov 1944
Lt Cdr N G Hallett   12 Mar 1945
    DSC & Bar RN
Wing disbanded into 7th CAG   30 Jun 1945

30th Naval Fighter Wing

Formation of the 30th Naval Fighter Wing was first planned in September 1943, for service in HMS *Implacable*. Nos.801, 880, 890 and 899 Seafire squadrons were all considered for this carrier, which was then still under construction. In the event, however, the Wing formed at Machrihanish on 10 October 1944 with Nos.801 and 880 Squadrons, still equipped with Seafires. They first embarked the following month, sailing on 15 March 1945 to join the British Pacific Fleet. Before the Wing could go into action, it disbanded on 30 June 1945 to become part of the new 8th Carrier Air Group.

Wing Leader
Lt Cdr C P Campbell-Horsfall RN   10 Oct 1944
Wing disbanded into 8th CAG   30 Jun 1945

31st Naval TBR Wing

It was originally proposed to form the 31st Naval TBR Wing at Hatston on 25 October 1943 with Nos.832 and 845 Barracuda squadrons. Postings were made to the new formation, which was intended to serve in HMS *Victorious*. However, the ship was not then available, and formation of the Wing was cancelled, her intended squadrons being reallocated to HMS *Engadine* for passage to the Far East.

45th Naval TBR Wing

Formed on 25 October 1943 with Nos.822 and 823 Barracuda squadrons, for service in HMS *Indefatigable*. The ship would not be ready for several months, and the two squadrons did not come together until shortly before taking passage in HMS *Atheling* to the Far East in February 1944 to join the Eastern Fleet. However, soon after arriving in Southern India their parent formation was renumbered to became the 11th Naval TBR Wing, never having embarked in its intended carrier.

Wing Leaders

Lt Cdr B E Boulding DSC RN	25 Oct	1943
Lt Cdr G Douglas DFC RN	1 Dec	1943
Not identified	31 Jan	1944
Wing disbanded	21 Apr	1944

47th Naval Fighter Wing

In October 1943 it was proposed to form the 47th Naval Fighter Wing with Nos.1834, 1835 and 1836 Corsair squadrons, for service in HMS *Victorious*. Soon afterwards No.1835 disbanded to form the basis of No.732 Squadron, but the other two squadrons joined the Wing when it eventually formed at Stretton on 17 January 1944. They embarked in March 1944, and participated in attacks on *Tirpitz*. The ship sailed for Ceylon in June 1944 for operations against the Japanese, and No.1837 Squadron joined the Wing in August 1944 only to be disbanded the following month to enlarge the other two squadrons. The Wing was absorbed into the 1st Carrier Air Group on 30 June 1945.

Wing Leaders

Lt Cdr F R A Turnbull DSC RN	17 Jan	1944
Lt Col R C Hay DSO & Bar DSC RM	14 Aug	1944
Wing disbanded into 1st CAG	30 Jun	1945

52nd Naval TBR Wing

First planned in October 1943, for service in HMS *Implacable* with Nos.815 and 829 Barracuda squadrons. When it actually formed on 26 November 1943 it was reallocated to HMS *Victorious* with Nos.815 and 817 Squadrons. However, the ship was not available, so these joined HMS *Begum* to serve with the 12th Wing in the Far East instead. In their place the 52nd Wing received Nos.829 and 831 Squadrons, these being joined briefly by No.827 Squadron in April for a strike on *Tirpitz*. On 9 July 1944 No.829 Squadron was absorbed by No.831, and the Wing ceased to exist.

Wing Leaders

Lt Cdr J C N Shrubsole RN	26 Nov	1943
Lt Cdr E M Britton RN	5 Jan	1944
Lt Cdr (A) F H Fox RN	24 Mar	1944
Lt Cdr V Rance DSO RN	15 Feb	1944
Wing disbanded	9 Jul	1944

A heavily loaded Barracuda of No.830 Squadron, in the 8th Naval TBR Wing, about to take-off up a special ramp carrying a 1,600-lb bomb for an attack on Tirpitz during Operation Goodwood in August 1944. (FAA Museum)

CARRIER AIR GROUPS

Following the ending of the war in Europe, it became possible to allocate the Royal Navy's full carrier strength to the war in the Far East. A decision had already been made that air squadrons embarked in Fleet and Light Fleet carriers should be reorganised into Air Groups, to align with US Navy policy, and this was now implemented. There would be spare groups in each category, so that a 100% reserve would be available for Fleet Carriers and a 50% reserve for Light Fleet Carriers. The organisation would not cover assault carriers, for which no provision was made for spare groups.

Nos.1 to 6 CAGs were earmarked for the *Illustrious*-class of three ships, each Group comprising two Corsair squadrons and one of Avengers, all with 15 aircraft each. The two ships in the *Implacable*-class were allocated Nos.7 to 10 CAGs, each with two squadrons of 24 Seafires, one of 15 Avengers and one of 15 Fireflies. HMS *Indomitable*, the only ship in its class, was to have Nos.11 and 12 CAGs, each with two squadrons of 24 Hellcats, one of 15 Avengers and one of 12 Fireflies. The first four ships in the *Colossus*-class were intended to have Nos.13 to 18 CAGs, each with a Corsair squadron of 21 aircraft and one with 12 Barracudas. The remaining ships in the *Colossus*-class were allocated Nos.19 to 22 CAGs, of which 19 CAG would be manned by the Royal Canadian Navy, and each group would consist of one squadron of 21 Seafires and one of 12 Barracudas. At the time these were approved in June 1945, the squadrons for Nos.1, 2, 7, 8, 11, 13, 14, 15 and 16 CAGs were already available and these were formed at the end of that month.

With the ending of the Pacific War there was no longer any need for an organisation of the proposed size. Construction of several ships ceased, but the Air Group organisation continued for those that remained or were subsequently completed. Commonwealth navies were included in the numbering system, there being both Australian and Canadian Air Groups. The CAG organisation continued into the postwar period, being reorganised in September 1946 so that each Air Group had one Firefly squadron and one of Seafires. This method of controlling first line squadrons eventually ended for Royal Navy squadrons in February 1952, though Australia and Canada continued until 1954.

1st Carrier Air Group

The 1st CAG formed on 30 June 1945 for HMS *Victorious* with No.849 Avenger squadron and Nos.1834 and 1836 Corsair squadrons, disbanding when the ship returned home in September 1945. It reformed in October 1947 with Nos.801 and 813 Squadron equipped respectively with Sea Hornets and Firebrands for service in HMS *Implacable*. The Group transferred to HMS *Indomitable* on 12 September 1950, being disbanded in May 1951 when No.801 re-equipped with Sea Furies.

Air Group Commanders

Cdr J C N Shrubsole RN	30 Jun 1945
Group disbanded	8 Sep 1945
Capt D B Law DSC RN	3 Nov 1948
Lt Cdr S G Orr DSC RN	21 Nov 1949
Group disbanded	31 May 1951

2nd Carrier Air Group

The 2nd CAG formed on 30 June 1945 with No.848 Avenger squadron and Nos.1841 and 1842 Corsair squadrons for service in HMS *Formidable*. It disbanded when the ship arrived home on 31 October 1945.

Air Group Commander

Lt Col P P Nelson-Gracie RM	30 Jun 1945
Group disbanded	31 Oct 1945

3rd Carrier Air Group

The 3rd CAG formed at Nowra on 2 August 1945 as a spare Group, consisting of No.854 Avenger squadron and Nos.1843 and 1845 Corsair squadrons. It never embarked, and after disbanding on 20 October 1945 the crews returned home in SS *Stratheden*.

Air Group Commanders

Cdr N S Luard RN (temp)	2 Aug 1945
Cdr J C N Shrubsole RN	8 Sep 1945
Group disbanded	20 Oct 1945

4th Carrier Air Group

The 4th CAG was planned to form with No.846 Avenger squadron and Nos.1837 and 1853 Corsair squadrons for service in HMS *Illustrious*. With the ending of the Pacific War the Group never materialised.

5th Carrier Air Group

The 5th CAG was intended as a spare Group for service in an *Illustrious*-class carrier with No.852 Avenger squadron and Nos.1832 and 1838 Corsair squadrons. Before any of these could reform, VJ-Day intervened and the new Group never materialised.

6th Carrier Air Group

The 6th CAG was planned as a spare *Illustrious*-class Group with No.853 Avenger squadron and Nos.882 and 1830 Corsair squadrons. It was to have left the UK in January 1946 after No.882 had re-equipped from Wildcats and the squadrons had worked-up, but instead its formation was cancelled after VJ-Day.

7th Carrier Air Group

The 7th CAG formed on 30 June 1945 at Schofields for service in HMS *Indefatigable*. It consisted of Nos.887 and 894 Seafire squadrons, No.820 Avenger squadron and No.1770 Firefly squadron. No.1770 was replaced by No.1772 squadron, and the Group continued until returning home on 15 March 1946. On 7 December 1950 it reformed as the 7th Night Air Group with Nos.809 and 814 Squadrons equipped respectively with Sea Hornets and Fireflies for HMS *Vengeance*. The concept was not a success, and the Group disbanded after a short period afloat.

Air Group Commanders

Lt Cdr N G Hallett DSC & Bar RN	30 Jun 1945
Group disbanded	23 Mar 1946
Lt Cdr J O Armour RN	22 Nov 1950
None	21 Apr 1951
Group disbanded	Jun 1951

8th Carrier Air Group

The 8th CAG formed on 30 June 1945 for HMS *Implacable* with Nos 801 and 880 Seafires squadrons, No.828 Avenger squadron and No.1771 Firefly squadron. Nos.801 and 1771 ceased to exist in September 1945, the former being absorbed by No.880. The Group disbanded on 4 April 1946, shortly before the ship sailed home.

Air Group Commander

Mjr P P Nelson-Gracie RM	30 Jun 1945
Group disbanded	4 Apr 1946

9th Carrier Air Group

The 9th CAG was to have comprised Nos.802 and 899 Seafire squadrons, No.851 Avenger squadron and No.1773 Firefly squadron. It would have been a spare group for service in an *Implacable*-class carrier, with squadrons coming from both the Far East and the UK, No.1773 being a proposed new squadron, but this plan was cancelled after VJ-Day.

10th Carrier Air Group

The 10th CAG was to have formed as a spare *Implacable*-class carrier with Nos.883 and 1833 Seafire squadrons, No.856 Avenger squadron and a planned No.1775 Firefly squadron. Its formation was cancelled after VJ-Day.

11th Carrier Air Group

The 11th CAG formed on 30 June 1945 for HMS *Indomitable* with Nos.1839 and 1844 Hellcat squadrons and No.857 Avenger squadron. It was also planned to include No.1772 Firefly squadron, but this instead replaced No.1770 in the 7th CAG. The Group disbanded on 30 November 1945.

Air Group Commander

None	30 Jun	1945
Group disbanded	30 Nov	1945

12th Carrier Air Group

The 12th CAG was to have formed as a spare Group for HMS *Indomitable* with Nos.881 and 885 Hellcat squadrons, No.845 Avenger squadron and a planned No.1774 Firefly squadron. It was cancelled after VJ-Day.

13th Carrier Air Group

The 13th CAG was formed on 30 June 1945 with Nos.812 and 1850 Squadron equipped with Barracudas and Corsairs respectively. Embarked in HMS *Vengeance*, it was disbanded when the ship returned home on 12 August 1946. It reformed at Eglinton on 1 October 1946 with Nos.800 and 827 Squadrons respectively equipped with Seafires and Firebrands for HMS *Triumph*, disbanding on 15 November 1950 on return from the Far East. The group reformed in 1951 for service in HMS *Eagle*, with Nos.800 and 803 Attacker squadrons, No.826 Firefly squadron and 827 Firebrand squadron. No.826 Squadron left, and on disembarking to Ford on 3 December 1952 the group disbanded.

Air Group Commanders

Not identified	30 Jun	1945
Lt Cdr G R Callingham RN	5 Apr	1946
Group disbanded	12 Aug	1946
Lt Cdr W C Simpson DSC RN	1 Oct	1946
Lt Cdr S G Orr DSC AFC RN	10 May	1949
Lt Cdr P B Jackson RN	10 Jul	1949
Group disbanded	15 Nov	1950
Not identified		1951
Group disbanded	3 Dec	1952

14th Carrier Air Group

The 14th CAG formed on 30 June 1945 for HMS *Colossus* with Nos.827 and 1846 Squadron equipped respectively with Barracudas and Corsairs, disbanding when the ship arrived home on 23 July 1946. It reformed at Eglinton on 1 October 1946 with No.804 Seafire and 812 Firefly squadrons for HMS *Theseus* for service in the Far East, disbanding on return home on 21 December 1947. Reformed at Ford on 15 January 1948 with the same squadrons, it served in HMS *Ocean* until transferring to HMS *Glory* after No.804 re-equipped with Sea Furies in July 1949, seeing action in Korea in 1951/52. The Group disbanded on returning home in May 1952.

Air Group Commanders

Not identified	30 Jun	1945
Group disbanded	23 Jul	1946
Not identified	1 Oct	1946
Lt Cdr G R Callingham RN	1 Jan	1947
Group disbanded	21 Dec	1947
Lt Cdr J W Sleigh DSO DSC RN	15 Jan	1948
Lt Cdr S J Hall DSC RN	24 Oct	1950
Not identified	24 Dec	1951
Group disbanded	May	1952

15th Carrier Air Group

The 15th CAG formed on 30 June 1945 with Nos.814 Barracuda and 1851 Corsair squadrons for service in HMS *Venerable*, No.814 re-equipping with Fireflies in December 1945. No.1851 transferred to HMS *Vengeance* in June 1946, being relieved by No.802 Seafire squadron. The Group disbanded on 30 March 1947 on returning home, but reformed at Eglinton on 16 May 1947, again with Nos.802 and 814 Squadrons for HMS *Vengeance*, No.802 re-equipping with Sea Furies before embarking. In April 1950, No.802 was temporarily replaced by No.809 Sea Hornet squadron, returning when the latter left in September 1950. No.814 left in November 1950, and the Group then had a period ashore with only No.802 until this was joined by No.825 Firefly squadron in June 1951. The latter departed in September 1951 without embarking, and No.814 then rejoined for a spell in HMS *Theseus* with No.802. The group disbanded at Culdrose on 15 January 1952.

Air Group Commanders

Lt Cdr P D Gick RN	30 Jun	1945
Lt Cdr T G V Percy DSC RN	14 Jan	1946
Group disbanded	30 Mar	1947
Lt Cdr W R J MacWhirter DSC RN	16 May	1947
Lt Cdr J G Baldwin DSC RN	15 Mar	1948
Lt Cdr J N Ball DSC RN	16 May	1949
Lt Cdr J O Armour RN	1 Aug	1950
Not identified	22 Nov	1950
Group disbanded	15 Jan	1952

16th Carrier Air Group

The 16th CAG formed on 30 June 1945 with Nos.837 Barracuda and 1831 Corsair squadron for HMS *Glory*. No.837 re-equipped with Fireflies in October 1945, and No.1831 left in July 1946 to be replaced by No.806 Seafire squadron. The Group disbanded on arrival home on 6 October 1947.

Air Group Commanders

Mjr A J Wright RM	30 Jun	1945
None	Nov	1946
Lt Cdr D W Kirke RN	9 Jan	1947
Group disbanded	6 Oct	1947

17th Carrier Air Group

The 17th CAG was intended to form with Nos.824 Barracuda and 1835 Corsair squadrons for a Colossus-class carrier, but the intervention of VJ-Day made this unnecessary. Instead it formed on 7 October 1947 at Eglinton with Nos.807 Sea Fury and 810 Firefly squadrons for HMS *Theseus*. The Group disbanded at St Merryn on 18 October 1949, but immediately reformed with the same squadrons for the same carrier. After a spell in Korean waters the carrier returned home and the Group disbanded on arrival on 29 May 1951. The 1950 Boyd Trophy was awarded to the Group for its activities in Korea. It reformed again at Arbroath the day after disbanding, with the same squadrons, this time for HMS *Ocean*, but disbanded on transfer to HMS *Theseus* on 12 February 1952.

Air Group Commanders

Not identified	7 Oct	1947
Lt Cdr D C E F Gibson DSC RN	19 Apr	1948
Group disbanded	18 Oct	1949
Lt Cdr F Stovin Bradford DSC RN	19 Oct	1949
Lt Cdr M P G Smith DSC RN	12 Jan	1951
Group disbanded	12 Feb	1952

18th Carrier Air Group

The 18th CAG was to have formed with Nos.822 Barracuda and 1852 Corsair squadrons for service in a *Colossus*-class carrier, but this never materialised due to VJ-Day intervening. The number was reallocated to the Royal Canadian Navy, and it formed at Dartmouth on 15 May 1947 with Nos.826 Firefly and 883 Seafire squadrons for service in HMCS *Warrior*. No.883 re-equipped with Sea Furies in September 1948, but was replaced in November 1948 by No.825 Firefly squadron on the 18th CAG becoming a wholly anti-submarine group for service in HMCS *Magnificent*. It returned to its former composition on 15 January 1951, when No.883 was replaced by No.826, now equipped with Avengers, but on 1 May 1951 the group was renumbered to become the 30th CAG, its squadrons being also renumbered at that time.

Air Group Commanders

Lt Cdr W H Bradley RCN	15 May	1947
Lt Cdr R I W Goddard DSC RCN	1 Dec	1948
Lt Cdr R E Bartlett RCN	20 Apr	1950
Group disbanded	1 May	1951

19th Carrier Air Group

The 19th CAG was allocated to the Royal Canadian Navy, and it formed at Dartmouth on 15 May 1947 with Nos.803 Seafire and 825 Firefly squadrons. After sailing to the UK in HMCS *Warrior* to re-equip, No.803 receiving Sea Furies, then returned in HMCS

Magnificent in May 1948. In November 1948 the Group became a wholly fighter formation, and No.825 was replaced by No.883 Sea Fury squadron. It reverted to its former composition on 15 January 1951 when No.883 was in turn replaced by No.825, which had by then received Avengers, and becoming the 19th Support Air Group. This disbanded on 1 May 1951 on being renumbered as the 31st SAG, its squadrons being renumbered at the same time.

Air Group Commanders
Lt Cdr H J Hunter RCN	15 May 1947
Lt Cdr V J Wilgress RCN	30 Sep 1949
Lt Cdr N Cogdon RCN	15 Jan 1951
Group disbanded	1 May 1951

20th Carrier Air Group

The 20th CAG was originally intended to consist of Nos.805 Seafire and 816 Barracuda squadrons for a *Colossus*-class carrier. By the time it actually formed with these squadrons at Lee-on-Solent in March 1946 for, service in HMS *Ocean*, No.816 had become a Firefly squadron. No.805 also re-equipped temporarily with Fireflies in August 1946, but reverted to Seafires in April 1947. After a spell in the Mediterranean the group disbanded on return to Lee-on-Solent on 1 July 1948. It reformed at Eglinton on 28 August 1948, again with Nos.805 Sea Fury and 816 Firefly squadrons, but this time as a Royal Australian Navy group for service in HMAS *Sydney*. No.808 Sea Fury squadron replaced No.816 in 1951, and the group then undertook operations in Korean waters, later participating in the Monte Bello atomic bomb tests, with Nos.805 and 808 Squadrons. No.850 Sea Fury squadron replaced No.808 in September 1953, but the group disbanded at Nowra in 1954.

Air Group Commanders
Not identified	Mar 1946
Lt Cdr J S L Crabbe RN	6 Jan 1947
Lt Cdr A H Abrams DSC RN	9 Dec 1947
Group disbanded	2 Jul 1948
Lt Cdr P C Whitfield DSC RN	28 Aug 1948
Lt Cdr M F Fell RN	26 May 1950
Not identified	3 May 1952
Group disbanded	1954

21st Carrier Air Group

The 21st CAG was originally intended to form in 1946 with Nos.806 Seafire and 817 Barracuda squadrons for a *Colossus*-class carrier. In the event it did not form until 19 March 1950 at St Merryn, as a Royal Australian Navy Group with Nos.808 Sea Fury and 817 Firefly squadrons. After service in HMAS *Sydney* the group disbanded at Nowra on 30 June 1951.

Air Group Commander
Lt Cdr T W Harrington DSC RN	19 Mar 1950
Group disbanded	30 Jun 1951

22nd Carrier Air Group

The 22nd CAG was planned to comprise Nos.818 Barracuda squadron and a reformed No.884 Seafire squadron for service in a *Colossus*-class carrier. In the event, VJ-Day intervened and it failed to materialise.

30th Carrier Air Group

The 30th CAG formed in the Royal Canadian Navy on 1 May 1951 by renumbering the 18th CAG. It comprised the similarly renumbered Nos.871 and 881 Squadrons, equipped respectively with Sea Furies and Avengers for service in HMCS *Magnificent*. The Air Group system in the RCN was abolished in June 1954 and the 30th CAG then ceased to exist.

Air Group Commanders
Lt Cdr R E Bartlett RCN	1 May 1951
Lt Cdr R A B Creery RCN	3 May 1952
Lt Cdr J W Roberts CD RCN	17 Aug 1953
Lt Cdr M H E Page RCN	16 Apr 1954
Group disbanded	Jun 1954

31st Support Air Group

The 31st SAG formed in the Royal Canadian Navy on 1 May 1951 by renumbering the 19th SAG. Its squadrons were also renumbered to become Nos.870 Sea Fury and 880 Avenger squadrons for service in HMCS *Magnificent*. The group disbanded in June 1954 when the the Royal Canadian Navy abolished its Air Group system.

Air Group Commanders
Lt Cdr N Cogdon RCN	1 May 1951
Lt Cdr J B Fotheringham RCN	4 Mar 1952
Lt Cdr D W Knox CD RCN	24 Apr 1953
Group disbanded	Jun 1954

50th Training Air Group

The 50th Training Air Group formed at Yeovilton on 13 May 1948 to administer locally based second line units. These comprised No.700 already based there, and No.799 which arrived at that time. No.700 Squadron disbanded in August 1949, and in its place No.767 Squadron arrived in September 1949. No.799 left for Machrihanish in December 1951, followed by No.767 to Henstridge in January 1952, and the group ceased to exist.

Air Group Commanders
Lt Cdr J N Ball DSC RN	13 May 1948
Lt Cdr J D Nunn RN	15 May 1949
Lt Cdr J W G Wellham DSC RN	18 Aug 1949
Not identified	12 Jun 1950
Group disbanded	Jan 1952

51st Training Air Group

The 51st Training Air Group formed at Eglinton in May 1946 to administer some of the locally based second line training units. Initially it had only No.719 Squadron until No.718 formed in August 1946. The Group was disbanded on 13 November 1946. The number was taken up again in July 1948, when the 51st Miscellaneous Air Group formed at Lee-on-Solent to administer Nos.771 and 783 Squadrons. No.783 disbanded in November 1949, and the group ceased to exist the following year.

Air Group Commanders
Lt Cdr S P Luke RN	May 1946
Group disbanded	13 Nov 1946
Not identified	Jul 1948
Lt Cdr C R Bateman DSC RN	7 Jan 1949
Lt Cdr J G Baldwin DSC RN	6 Oct 1949
Group disbanded	1950

52nd Training Air Group

The 52nd Training Air Group formed at Eglinton on 1 August 1946 to administer Nos.794 and 795 refresher flying squadrons. It took over No.718 Squadron when the 51st TRAG disbanded in November 1946, but all three squadrons disbanded in March 1947 and the Group ceased to exist. It reformed at Culdrose on 1 February 1950, again as the 52nd TRAG, initially comprising only No.736 Squadron. After the crews had taken Easter leave the latter was split and the new No.738 Squadron also became part of the group. The title 52nd TRAG was dropped on 16 August 1951, when Nos.736 and 738 Squadrons became entirely Sea Fury equipped.

Air Group Commanders
Lt Cdr (A) G Dennison RNVR	1 Aug 1946
Lt Cdr S P Luke RN	13 Nov 1946
Group disbanded	Mar 1947
Lt Cdr P J Leckie RN	1 Feb 1950
Lt Cdr W C Simpson DSC RN	19 Jul 1951
Group disbanded	16 Aug 1951

53rd Training Air Group

The 53rd Training Air Group formed at Eglinton on 14 June 1950 with Nos.719 and 737 Squadrons. It was short-lived, disbanding there on 31 January 1952.

Air Group Commanders
Lt Cdr A Turnbull RN	14 Jun 1950
Lt Cdr S S Laurie RN	14 Mar 1951
Group disbanded	31 Jan 1952

MOBILE NAVAL AIR BASES

The concept of Mobile Naval Air Bases, or MONABs as they were more generally known, was that of a series of mobile self-contained units able to repair, and prepare for service, aircraft, engines and components as required for ships of the Fleet. Each initially formed up at HMS *Flycatcher*, which commissioned at Ludham, Norfolk on 4 September 1944 as the headquarters of the MONAB organisation, moving on 16 February 1945 to Middle Wallop. In all, ten MONABs were formed, though the last of these did not appear until after VJ-Day, and was consequently disbanded without leaving the United Kingdom. In addition to MONABs, the organisation also included a Transportable Aircraft Maintenance Yard (TAMY). All these units had ship's names commencing 'Nab'. After the last MONAB had left Middle Wallop the station reverted to normal squadron use. In the event the mobility of these units was never taken up, circumstances requiring the operational Australian air stations to expand beyond the original intention, and they therefore operated as normal Naval Air Stations. Postwar demobilisation resulted in a rapid rundown, and most of the MONABs had paid off by the end of 1945, though some survived into 1946.

MONAB No.1

Commissioned on 28 October 1944 at Ludham under Cdr GA Nunneley, RN, as HMS *Nabbington*. Embarked Liverpool in SS *Empress of Scotland* on 20 November, it landed at Sydney on 20 December, and temporarily based at Warwick Farm. An advanced party left on 22 December for Nowra, followed by the main party on 1 January 1945. The station was taken over on loan from the RAAF next day and commissioned as a Naval Air Station equipped to deal with Avengers and Corsairs. From 7 March until 27 April the airfield at Jervis Bay was used as the Nowra runways were unserviceable. During March, Capt H G Dickinson, DSC, RN took over command. HMS *Nabbington* paid off on 15 November 1945, Nowra then being taken over by HMS *Nabswick* (MONAB No.5).

MONAB No.2

Commissioned 11 November 1944 as HMS *Nabberley* at Ludham under Cdr EPF Atkinson, RN. Shipped to Australia, it disembarked on 26 January 1945 to RAAF Bankstown, which commissioned three days later as a Naval Air Station, on loan. Equipment assembled and test flown included large numbers of Avengers, Corsairs, Expediters, Fireflies, Hellcats, Martinets, Reliants, Seafires and Sea Otters. *Nabberley* paid off on 31 March 1946.

MONAB No.3

Assembled on 18 October 1944 at Ludham, where it commissioned on 4 December under Cdr(A) EW Kenton, RNVR, as HMS *Nabthorpe*. Travelled to Liverpool on 2 December, and embarked SS *Windsor Castle* on 22 December, arriving at Sydney on 27 January 1945. Temporary accommodation was provided at Warwick Farm, then an advance party left on 5 February for Schofields, where the first naval aircraft landed two days later. The airfield was loaned by the RAAF and commissioned as a Naval Air Station, equipped to deal with Fireflies and Seafires. HMS *Nabthorpe* paid off on 15 November, to be replaced at Schofields by HMS *Nabstock* (MONAB No.6).

MONAB No.4

Assembled at Ludham on 15 November 1944, commissioning there on 1 January 1945 as HMS Nabaron. It left for Liverpool on 16 January to join HMT *Dominion Monarch*, arriving at Sydney on 21 February. From there it went to Manus in the Admiralty Islands, an advanced party arriving on 13 March in the *Clan Macauley*, followed next day by a party of ratings who had left Sydney in HMS *Speaker* eight days earlier. Meanwhile the main party had embarked in HMS *Fencer* at Sydney on 30 March, disembarking to Manus on 10 April. The airfield at Pityilu was officially opened as a Naval Air Station on 2 April, being taken over complete from the US Navy. Flight tests were carried out for the Fleet Train aircraft repair organisation anchored in the nearby lagoon. Returning in September to Australia, it paid off on 10 November 1945.

MONAB No.5

Commissioned at Ludham on 1 February 1945 as HMS *Nabswick*, under Capt HG Dickinson, DSC, RN and embarked in SS *Stirling Castle* on 18 February, arriving Sydney on 29 March. Here Cdr IK Masterman, RN assumed command. On 1 May took over Jervis Bay airstrip, a satellite of RAAF Nowra which had commissioned as a Naval Air Station three days earlier, after temporary use by MONAB No.1. Jervis Bay was paid off on 15 November 1945, and *Nabswick* took over Nowra from MONAB No.1. It was paid off 18 March 1946, and Nowra became a Royal Australian Navy base.

MONAB No.6

Assembled on 1 March 1945 at Middle Wallop, where it commissioned on 1 April as HMS *Nabstock*, under Capt HVP McClintoch, DSO, RN. It sailed for Australia on 22 April, arriving at Sydney on 23 May. It disembarked to Maryborough on 1 June, where it had lodger facilities on the RAAF station. On 15 November it was withdrawn to Schofields, which it took over from HMS *Nabthorpe*, eventually disbanding on 8 June 1946.

MONAB No.7

Commissioned as a Receipt and Despatch Unit at Middle Wallop on 1 June 1945 as HMS *Nabreekie*, under Capt FP Frai, RNVR. Sailing in mid-June, it disembarked on 9 August to Meendale Camp, Brisbane, a former USN Sea Bee camp. It used the airfield at Archerfield, which it shared with TAMY No.1. HMS *Nabreekie* paid off on 5 November 1945.

MONAB No.8

Commissioned at Middle Wallop on 1 July 1945 as HMS *Nabcatcher* as a Receipt and Despatch Unit, under Capt VN Surtees, DSO, RN. Sailing later that month to Australia, it set up temporarily in the RN Barracks at Warwick Farm, until re-embarking for Hong Kong. It arrived at Kai Tak in September. HMS *Nabcatcher* paid off on 27 August 1946, and Kai Tak was then transferred to the books of HMS *Tamar*.

MONAB No.9

Assembled on 18 June 1945 at Middle Wallop, where it commissioned as HMS *Nabrock* on 1 August under Capt JS Salter, DSO, RN. Sailing for Australia in HMT *Dominion Monarch*, it arrived at Sydney on 5 October. The personnel then re-embarked in HMT *Largs Bay* for Singapore, where they disembarked to Sembawang later in the month. However, HMS *Nabrock* paid off on 15 December 1945 and the station then became HMS *Simbang*.

MONAB No.10

Assembled at Middle Wallop on 30 July 1945, commissioning there as HMS *Nabhurst* on 1 September under Cdr TS Jackson, RN. Being no longer required, it was paid off on 12 October 1945.

The unit reformed in March 1951 at Henstridge under Lt Cdr LJS Ede, DSO, DSC, RN. Its task was to maintain wartime equipment, such as five-ton trucks and lightweight jeeps, which were housed in railway containers, ensuring that it was kept in working order should the need arise for a Naval Air Base to be set up. Living quarters and workshops were also containers. The unit disbanded on 2 July 1955.

TAMY No.1

Officially commissioned at Ludham on 1 February 1945 as HMS *Nabsford*, under the command of Capt BJL Rogers-Tillstone, RN. Personnel had in the meantime assembled at HMS *Gosling*, at Risley, near Warrington, taking passage in February in SS *Stirling Castle* for Brisbane, along with MONAB No.5. On arrival the unit took over several installations in the Brisbane area, including the civil airfield at Archerfield, the accommodation being at Focklea Camp. The unit assembled Corsair IVs, Seafire IIIs (later XVs) and Reliants, the first Corsair flying on 16 April 1945. HMS *Nabsford* was paid off on 31 March 1946.

SHIPS FLIGHTS (CARRIERS)

Ship	Aircraft	Period	Example
Albion	Dragonfly HR.3	Sep 54 - Nov 55	VZ965 (901/Z)
	Whirlwind HAR.3	Nov 55 - Oct 57	XG588 (980/Z)
	Whirlwind HAS.7	Jun 58 - Jul 58	XK910
Ark Royal	Dragonfly HR.3	Mar 55 - Apr 56	WG752 (970/O)
	Dragonfly HR.5	Jan 60 - Jan 60	WP497 (903)
	Whirlwind HAR.3	Sep 55 - Oct 57	XG574 (999/O)
	Whirlwind HAS.7	Oct 61 - Sep 66	XM684 (41/R)
	Gannet COD.4	Nov 61 - 67	XA430 (-/R)
	Wessex HAS.1	Feb 70 - Jan 77	XP117 (056/R)
	Sea King HAS.1	Mar 72 - Apr 72	XV671 (040/R)
	Wessex HU.5	Jun 77	XT473 (61)
Begum	Swordfish II	Jul 45 - Oct 45	LS353
Bulwark	Firefly FR.5	Sep 54 - Jan 55	VT481 (904)
	Avenger AS.5	Feb 55 - Feb 57	XB374 (981/B)
	Dragonfly HR.3	Dec 54 - Jan 57	WP502 (983/B)
	Whirlwind HAR.3	Mar 57 - Oct 57	XG575 (982/B)
Campania	Dragonfly HR.3	Apr 52 - Dec 52	WG664
	Sea Otter	Apr 52 - Dec 52	RD898
Centaur	Dragonfly HR.3	Jul 54 - May 56	WH991 (976/C)
	Dragonfly HR.5	Jun 59 - Jun 61	WG709 (977/C)
	Whirlwind HAS.7	Oct 63 - Sep 65	XN261 (978/C)
Eagle	Dragonfly HR.3	Jan 53 - Mar 56	WP498 (901/J)
	Dragonfly HR.5	Jun 57 - Sep 57	WP497 (973/J)
	Whirlwind HAR.3	Sep 57 - Apr 59	XG587 (974/J)
	Whirlwind HAS.7	Apr 64 - Sep 64	XN259 (971)
	Gannet COD.4	May 64 - Aug 65	XG790
	Wessex HAS.1	Jan 69 - Jan 72	XM875 (147/E)
Emperor	Walrus	May 44 - Nov 44	L2238
	Swordfish II	Sep 44 - Nov 44	HS170
Formidable	Barracuda II	Jun 44 - Jul 44	BV952
Glory	Walrus	47 - 47	Z1811
	Sea Otter	May 47 - Jun 47	
	Dragonfly HR.1	Apr 52 - May 52	VX596
	Sea Otter	51 - May 52	
	Firefly FR.1	Aug 53 - Oct 53	DK479
	Dragonfly HR.3	Oct 52 - Sep 54	WN495
Hermes	Dragonfly HR.5	May 60 - May 60	WP497
	Whirlwind HAS.7	Mar 62 - Feb 64	XN360 (986/H)
	Whirlwind HAR.9	Jan 66 - Oct 66	XN310 (335/H)
	Gannet COD.4	66 - Dec 69	XA470 (4/H)
	Wessex HAS.1	Feb 68 - Jun 70	XS871 (265/H)
Illustrious	Sea Otter	Aug 46 - Oct 47	JN199
	Barracuda V	47 - 48	RK571 (800/D)
	Firefly FR.1	Jul 49 - May 53	MB755 (201/D)
	Firefly AS.5	May 54 - Nov 54	WB331 (202/Y)
	Dragonfly HR.3	Mar 53 - Dec 54	WN499 (-/Y)
Implacable	Barracuda V	Feb 48 - Jun 48	RK568 (281/C)
	Barracuda III	Aug 49 - Nov 50	RJ905
	Firebrand TF.5		EK779 (911/C)
Indomitable	Swordfish ITT	Nov 41 - Aug 42	V4599
	Barracuda II	May 44 - Jun 44	BV952
	Dragonfly HR.1	Jan 51 - Apr 53	VZ963
	Barracuda 3	Nov 50 - Jul 52	RJ765
	Dragonfly HR.3	Mar 53 - Apr 53	WG753
Ocean	Sea Otter	Nov 46 - Jun 49	JN249 (O2B)
	Dragonfly HR.1	May 52 - Nov 52	VZ965
	Dragonfly HR.3	Aug 52 - Nov 53	WG707
	Dragonfly HR.3	Aug 56 - Sep 57	WN496
Premier	Barracuda II	Aug 45 - Sep 45	DP862
Sydney	Dragonfly HR.1	Oct 51 - Nov 51	
	Dragonfly HR.3	Jan 53 - May 54	WG753
	Sycamore HR.50	Sep 54	XA220
Theseus	Barracuda II	Nov 46	RK409
	Sea Otter	Nov 48 - Jul 49	RD919 (300/T)
	Dragonfly HR.3	Jan 53 - Oct 53	WH990 (911)
Triumph	Sea Otter	Jan 47 - Apr 51	JN179
	Firefly 1	Apr 51 - May 53	DK553 (202/P)
	Firefly AS.6	Oct 51	WD856 (204/P)
	Sea Balliol T.21	Nov 53 - Dec 55	WL715 (931/P)
Unicorn	Sea Otter	Jun 50	JM877
	Firefly 5	Mar 52	WB395
Venerable	Walrus	Apr 46	Z1804
Vengeance	Sea Otter	Apr 47 - Nov 50	RD899
	Barracuda III	47 - Jan 49	RK479 (302/Q)
	Firefly FR.1	Nov 50 - May 51	MB749 (201/Q)
Victorious	Walrus	Jan 45 - Apr 45	
	Dragonfly HR.5	Apr 59 - Oct 60	WP495 (967/V)
	Gannet COD.4	Sep 64 - May 67	XA466 (3/V)
Warrior	Dragonfly HR.3	Oct 53 - Dec 54	WG665
	Dragonfly HR.3	Oct 56 - Jul 57	VZ962
	Whirlwind HAR.3	Nov 56 - Oct 57	XG588 (995/J)
	Avenger AS.5	Nov 56 - Jul 57	XB386 (997/J)

STATION FLIGHTS

Station	Aircraft	Period	Example
Abbotsinch (inc MTPS)	Reliant	Nov 43 - Jan 44	FK902
	Sea Otter	Jan 46	
	Dominie	Sep 55 - Sep 57	HG709 (901/AC)
	Sea Hawk FB.3	Apr 58 - Jul 58	WM976
	Gannet T.2	Sep 58 - 62	XA529
	Gannet T.5	Sep 58 - May 59	XG882
	Sea Vampire T.22	Nov 59 - Jul 62	XA130 (970/AC)
	Sea Balliol T.21	Oct 59 - Sep 63	WP325 (971/AC)
Anthorn	Oxford	Oct 44 - Nov 47	MP293
	Traveller	Nov 44 - Nov 45	FT498
	Swordfish II	Nov 44 - Feb 45	NF141
	Seafire III	Feb 45 - Aug 46	LR839
	Tiger Moth II	Jun 45 - Jul 46	BB731
	Anson I	Jul 45 - Sep 46	EG696
	Harvard IIa	Apr 46 - Jul 52	EZ345 (-/AH)
	Seafire F.17	Jan 47	SW988
	Dominie	Nov 49 - Feb 53	HG708 (901/AH)
	Dragonfly HR.3	Dec 53 - Nov 56	WP494 (900/AH)
	Firefly FR.5	Jul 54 - Aug 54	WB259
	Gannet T.2	May 56 - Sep 57	XA529
	Firefly T.2	Jun 56 - Feb 58	DK550
	Sea Hawk F.1	Jun 56 - May 57	WF210
	S Venom FAW.20	Feb 57 - Sep 57	WM562
Arbroath	Tiger Moth II	Sep 43 - Jun 60	T8191 (Z)
	Proctor II	Aug 43	Z7246
	Reliant	Jul 44 - Aug 45	FK909
	Dominie	Aug 45 - Mar 62	NF848 (901/AR)
	Expeditor C.2	Mar 47 - Oct 53	FT995 (900/AO)
	Sea Otter	Apr 47 -	RD917 (902/AO)
Arbroath contd	Anson I	Jul 47	NK952
	Swordfish II	48	NF399 (912/AO)
	Martinet TT.1	Dec 48 - Feb 49	
	Firefly T.1	Apr 52 - Feb 54	MB437 (902/AO)
	Firefly T.2	Jun 51 - Dec 52	DK531 (902/AO)
	Firefly FR.5	Jul 54 - Aug 54	WB259
	Harvard T.2b	Oct 50 - May 51	KF512 (901/AO)
	Harvard T.3	Aug 51 - Jul 55	EZ253 (903/AO)
	Sea Fury T.20	Feb 53 - Feb 54	VZ354
	Sea Prince T.1	Mar 62 - Jul 68	WP309 (880/A)
	Sea Prince C.1	May 57	WF137 (901/AO)
	Sea Prince C.2	Jun 55 - Oct 59	WM756 (c/s900)
	Sea Devon C.1	Mar 56 - Nov 56	XJ321 (901)
Ayr	Reliant	Mar 45 - Nov 45	FB559 (BR0Q)
	Sea Otter	Mar 45 - Jan 46	JM974 (BR9A)
	Tiger Moth		
Ballyhalbert	Oxford	Oct 45	V3634
	Reliant	Jan 44 - Jan 45	FL160
Bankstown	Tiger Moth	May 45	A17-70
Belfast	Reliant	Dec 43 - Jan 46	FK925 (Q9D)
	Walrus	May 44 - Dec 44	W2682
	Tiger Moth	Jun 44 -	
	Oxford	Dec 44 - Dec 45	HM613 (Q9F)
	Sea Otter	Apr 45 - Aug 45	JM754
	Swordfish II	May 45 - Aug 45	NF115
	Traveller	Oct 45 - Nov 45	FT485
	Firefly 1	Jan 46	DK445
	Anson 1	Jun 54 - Dec 55	NK201 (999/SZ)
Bramcote	Dominie	Aug 55 - Jan 58	X7332 (890/BR)

Avro Anson NL121 '900/BR' of Stn Flt Bramcote in 1954

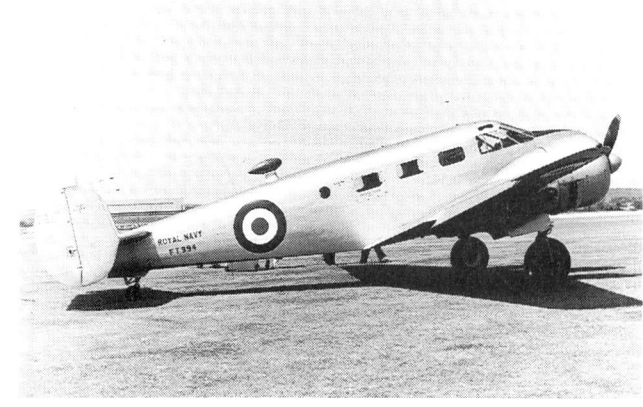
Expediter C.2 FT994 of Stn Flight Arbroath in 1973. (FAA Museum)

Tiger Moth XL717 of Station Flight Lossiemouth in 1968. (MAP)

Dominie HG709 '901/AC' of Stn Flt Abbotsinch in 1955. (John Huggon)

Sea Vampire T.22 XA107 '681' of Stn Flight Lossiemouth 1966. (MAP)

Stinson Reliant FB568 of Station Flight Eglinton in 1944.

Supermarine Sea Otter RD921 '902/O' of Ships Flight HMS Ocean in 1947. (Handley via Ray Williams)

Westland Dragonfly HR.3 WG671 '901'/C' of Ships Flight HMS Centaur in 1954/5. (FAA Museum)

Station	Aircraft	Period	Example		Station	Aircraft	Period	Example	
Brawdy	Dominie	Sep 52 - Jul 58	X7341	(910/BY)	Drem contd	Traveller	Sep 45	FT508	
	Sea Fury T.20	Nov 52 - Sep 53	VX290	(906/BY)	Dunino	Reliant	Dec 45	FK966	
	Dragonfly HR.3	Mar 53 - Jan 58	WG749	(905/BY)		Harvard III	Dec 45	EZ250	
	Dragonfly HR.5	Jul 57 - Jun 63	VZ962	(904/BY)	East Haven	Seafire Ib	Dec 43	MB359	
	Anson 1	Dec 54 - Feb 56	LT304	(601/BY)		Tiger Moth II	Jun 44 - Apr 45	T7696	
	Vampire FB.5	Feb 55 - Sep 56	VV631	(903/BY)		Reliant	Nov 44 - Nov 45	FK903	
	Sea Vampire T.22	Aug 55 - Jun 70	XG743	(798/BY)		Barracuda II	Jan 45	?	(E8D)
	Tiger Moth T.2	Jul 56 - Dec 69	BB694	(F)	Eastleigh	ST.25	Sep 43 - Apr 44	X9543	(I9B)
	Meteor T.7	Sep 57 - Aug 60	WS116	(906/BY)		Albacore	Dec 43 - Aug 44	N4263	
	Meteor TT.20	Dec 59 - Dec 59	WD585			Hornet Moth	Dec 43	P6785	
	Sea Hawk F.1	Feb 57 - 59	WF218	(906)		Reliant	Jan 44 - Oct 45	FK883	(ELOO)
	Sea Hawk FGA.4	Dec 56 - Aug 57	WV837	(965)		Sea Otter	Jul 44 - Feb 47	JM870	(I9B)
	Sea Hawk FGA.6	Nov 59 - May 60	XE342			Oxford		DF482	(I9A)
	Sea Prince T.1	Jun 61 - Sep 70	WP317	(908/BY)		Tiger Moth II	Dec 44 - Aug 45	BB858	(ELOG)
	Sea Prince C.1	Mar 62 - Dec 63	WF138	(907/BY)		Dauntless	Aug 45 - Jun 46	JS998	(ELOC)
	Sea Prince C.2	Jul 67 - Sep 68	WJ349	(-/BY)		Wellington Ic		HF845	(ELOS)
	Whirlwind HAS.7	May 63 - Sep 68	XL835	(905/BY)	Eglinton	Tiger Moth II	Aug 43	X5106	
	Whirlwind HAR.9	Dec 68 - Jan 71	XN311	(14/BY)		Proctor Ia	Oct 43	P6106	
	Hunter GA.11	Sep 64 - Jan 65	XF301			Proctor IIa	Oct 43	P6006	
	Scimitar F.1	May 68 - Nov 68	XD219			Reliant	Jan 44 - Oct 45	FK935	(J9C)
Brunswick	Expeditor C.II	Aug 44 - Dec 44	HD754			Traveller	Jul 45 - Oct 45	FT495	
Burscough	Reliant	Feb 44 - Dec 45	FB660	(O9G)		Anson I	Sep 45 - Nov 49	LT304	
	Firefly F.1	May 45 - Feb 46	Z2015			Harvard T.2b	Apr 47 - Nov 48	KF511	
	Swordfish II	Jun 45 - Sep 45	LS158			Harvard T.3	Jun 48 - Jul 49	EZ388	(903/JR)
	Anson I	Aug 45 - Sep 45	DJ545	(O9Y)		Sea Otter	Jan 48 - Oct 52	JM866	(903/GN)
	Oxford	Nov 45 - Apr 46	PH296			Dominie	Sep 49 - Mar 53	NF861	(900/GN)
China Bay/	Hellcat I	Jul 45 - Sep 45	FN400			Hoverfly II	Jan 51 - Jun 52	KN843	
Trincomalee	Hellcat II	Jul 45 - Sep 45	JZ805			Firefly T.1	Feb 55 - Jun 55	Z1943	(905/GN)
	Expeditor C.II	Jul 45	FT986			Firefly T.2	Jan 51 - Jul 56	MB578	(906/GN)
	Wildcat II	Jul 45	JV440			Firefly FR.5	Sep 54 - Jan 55	VT393	
	Harvard III	Jul 45	EZ432			Dragonfly HR.3	Dec 52 - Mar 59	WG720	(902/GN)
	Seafire III	Jul 45	LR808			Whirlwind HAS.22	Oct 53 - Oct 53	WV201	(901/GN)
	Corsair III	Jul 45	JS640			Sea Fury T.20	Mar 54 - Sep 56	WE820	(916/GN)
Colombo	Reliant	Jul 44 - Aug 44	FL133			Sea Prince T.1	May 54 - Apr 56	WP307	(909/GN)
	Swordfish I	Nov 44	V4651			Avenger AS.5	Feb 55 - Sep 55	XB300	
	Harvard III	Jul 45 - Aug 45	KF544			Gannet T.2	Jul 57 - Nov 58	XA509	(920/GN)
Church Fenton	Sea Prince T.1	Feb 69 - Mar 71	WP312	(-/CF)		Whirlwind HAS.7	Jun 58 - Sep 58	XK935	
Crail	Tiger Moth II	Mar 43 - Jun 45	T5535		Evanton	Reliant	Oct 43 - Jul 45	FK928	
	Gladiator	May 43 - Jun 43	K7979			Dominie	Sep 47 - Oct 47	X7341	
	Proctor Ia	May 43 - Jul 43	P6050			Oxford	47	PH261	(901/EV)
	Anson I	Jul 45 - Jan 47	MH210	(C9B)	Fearn	Reliant	Mar 44 - 45	FK913	
	Oxford	Mar 46 - Sep 46	NM606			Swordfish II	Mar 44 - Jun 44	HS214	
Culdrose	Harvard T.3	Dec 47 - Sep 48	EZ400	(900/CW)		Tiger Moth II	44 - Nov 44	BB696	
	Sea Otter	Feb 49 - Jul 52	RD895	(901/CW)		Traveller	Nov 44 - Apr 45	FT471	
	Firefly F.1	Jun 54 - Sep 54	DK554	(918)	Fleetlands	Gazelle HT.2	Dec 79 - Feb 82	ZA942	(-/FL)
	Firefly T.1	Sep 54 - Feb 55	Z2021	(917/CU)	Ford	Anson I	Oct 44 - Aug 45	MG730	(804/FD)
	Firefly T.2	Jan 51 - Feb 55	MB745	(918/CU)		Reliant	Aug 45 - Dec 45	FK953	
	Sea Fury T.20	Oct 51 - Oct 52	WG652	(997/CW)		Sea Fury FB.11	Mar 52 - Apr 52	VX655	
	Meteor F.8	Feb 52	WA960	(904/CW)		Sea Fury T.20	Jul 50 - Feb 55	WE824	(902/FD)
	Dragonfly HR.3	May 53 - Mar 58	WG667	(901/CU)		Firebrand TF.5	Jul 51	EK737	
	Dragonfly HR.5	Jan 59 - Sep 64	WG664	(915/CU)		Firefly T.1	Aug 51 - Aug 54	Z2027	(901/FD)
	Sea Balliol T.2	Jun 58 - Jan 61	WL721	(994/CU)		Meteor T.7	May 52 - Oct 53	WL332	(905/FD)
	Gannet T.5	Apr 59 - Sep 66	XG889	(995/CU)		Attacker FB.2	Jul 52 - May 53	WA528	
	Dominie	Dec 58 - Jun 63	NF881	(999/CU)		Dragonfly HR.3	Apr 53 - Jul 58	WP495	(982/FD)
	Whirlwind HAR.3	Aug 58 - Jul 61	XG586	(914)		Dragonfly HR.5	Sep 57 - Sep 58	WG664	(923/FD)
	Whirlwind HAS.7	Dec 59 - Oct 67	XK940	(588/CU)		Sea Vampire T.22	May 54 - May 58	XA153	(923/FD)
	Whirlwind HAR.9	Jul 66 - Jun 75	XN258	(589/CU)		Dominie	Jun 56 - Feb 57	NF880	
	Avenger AS.6	Nov 60 - 62	XB446	(992)		Gannet T.2	Nov 56 - Feb 58	XG880	(923/FD)
	Tiger Moth T.2		T8191			Sea Hawk FGA.6	Aug 57 - Sep 57	XE338	
	Sea Vampire T.22	Jun 62 - Sep 62	XA162	(990/CU)	Gosport	Hoverfly I	Mar 46 - May 47		
	Wasp HAS.1	Jul 63	XS530	(992/CU)		Oxford	May 46 - Nov 49	PH325	(901/GJ)
	Sea Prince C.1	May 64 - 65	WF137	(999/CU)		Barracuda II	Nov 47	RK461	
	Sea Devon C.20	65 - Feb 78	XJ348	(c/s599)		Harvard T.2a	Jun 51 - Nov 54	EZ316	(-/GJ)
	Chipmunk T.10	Mar 72 - Oct 74	WP906	(c/s516)		Tiger Moth T.2	Dec 50 - Jan 55	T6296	(-/GJ)
	Devon C.2/2	Jan 78 - Apr 81	VP967	(c/s599)		Anson T.1	May 52 - Jan 56	NK201	
	Sea Devon C.20	Apr 81 - Jan 83	XK895	(c/s519)	Hal Far	Harvard T.3	Mar 47 - Mar 52	EZ275	
	Sea Heron C.1	Apr 81 - Mar 82	XR443	(c/s517)		Sea Otter	Sep 48 - Apr 50	JN183	
Culham	Reliant	Mar 45	FB555			Expeditor C.2	Dec 49 - Jun 55	KP115	(811/HF)
	Dominie		HG694	(900/CH)		Sea Fury FB.11	Oct 52 - Mar 53	WG597	
	Anson 1	Jan 49 - Jul 50	NK287	(601/CH)		Sea Fury T.20	May 51 - Apr 54	VZ364	(200/HF)
Dale	Reliant	Nov 45 - Nov 45	FB567	(P9D)		Firefly FR.1	Nov 50 - Oct 51	DK536	
	Oxford	Oct 46	V4146	(P9C)		Firefly T.2	Jul 51 - Jan 55	DK486	
	Tiger Moth II	Aug 47 - Oct 47	N6847			Firefly 5	Aug 51 - Oct 51	WB404	
	Mosquito B.25		KB602	(POE)		Dragonfly HR.3	Dec 52 - Sep 59	WG723	(902/HF)
Dekheila	Beaufighter II	45 - Jun 45	R2301			Dragonfly HR.5	Jun 59 - Dec 62	WG708	(960/HF)
Donibristle	Swordfish I	May 43	K8876			Meteor T.7	Apr 54 - Oct 55	WS116	(410/HF)
	Tiger Moth II	Dec 44 - Jan 45	BD142			Sea Devon C.20	Aug 54 - Aug 59	XK896	(956/HF)
	Dominie	Sep 45	X7341			Sea Hawk FB.5	Aug 58 - Jul 60	WM994	
	Oxford	Nov 45 - Feb 46	NM600			Sea Vampire T.22	Mar 59 - Apr 60	XA115	(961/HF)
Drem	Reliant	Sep 45	FB657			Whirlwind HAS.22	Sep 59 - Oct 64	WV224	(958/HF)

Station	Aircraft	Period	Example	
Hal Far contd	Whirlwind HAS.7	Jun 52 - Apr 63	XN382	
	Hunter T.8	Apr 57	XE457	
	Sea Heron C.2	Sep 64 - 65	XR444	(794/HF)
Hatston	Hornet Moth	40 - May 40	P6787	
	Proctor Ia	Feb 41 - Aug 43	P6037	
	Reliant	Nov 44 - Dec 44	FB531	
	Dominie	Aug 45 - Sep 45	X7341	
Henstridge	Reliant	Jan 44 - Jul 45	FB561	(G9B)
	Sea Gladiator	Aug 43 - Oct 43	N2273	
	Tiger Moth II	Sep 45	T7695	(G9E)
Heston	Traveller	Sep 45	FT507	
Inskip	Gladiator I	Jul 43	K8052	
	Reliant	Oct 43 - Oct 45	FK903	
	Tiger Moth II	Sep 45 - Oct 45	X6984	
Jervis Bay	Reliant	Aug 45	FB767	
Kai Tak	Sea Otter	Apr 47 - May 47	JM874	
Katukurunda	Reliant	Mar 45 - Sep 45	FL130	(K8A)
Lee-on-	Walrus	Oct 44 - Dec 44	K8564	
Solent	Sea Fury FB.11	Mar 50 - Jun 50	VX282	
	Firefly 5	Apr 51 - Sep 51	VT411	
	Whirlwind HAR.3	Sep 55 - Sep 55	XG573	(c/s900)
	Sea Balliol T.21	Nov 56 - Dec 58	WL721	(928)
	Sea Vampire T.22	57 - Nov 62	XA156	(927)
	Sea Prince T.1	Jul 57 - Sep 59	WF127	(929)
	Sea Hawk FGA.6	Mar 60 - Jul 63	WV856	(c/s928)
	Tiger Moth T.2	Jun 68	T6296	(-/LS)
	Whirlwind HAR.9	Oct 72 - Mar 77	XN384	(811/LS)
	Wessex HU.5	Feb 77 - Sep 82	XS510	(814/LS)
		May 85 - Mar 88	XT517	(814)
Linton-on-Ouse	Sea Prince T.1	Jul 58 - Jan 69	WP311	(903/LO)
Lossiemouth	Hellcat II	Jun 46 - Jan 62	KE209	
	Sea Otter	Oct 46 - Jul 52	JN205	
	Martinet TT.1	47	NR472	
	Dominie	Mar 48 - Dec 58	NF847	(901/LM)
	Harvard T.2b	Nov 53	KF549	
	Harvard T.3	Sep 48	EZ409	
	Anson I	May 49 - Aug 53	NK610	(900/LM)
	Firefly FR.1	Jan 49 - Oct 53	Z2020	
	Oxford	Mar 50 - Jan 55	PH453	(901)
	Sea Fury T.20	May 52 - Aug 52	WG653	
	Expeditor C.2	Jul 53	KP116	
	Tiger Moth T.2	Sep 53 - Jan 62	BB694	(-/LM)
	Meteor T.7	Dec 53 - Jan 62	WS103	(937/LM)
	Dragonfly HR.3	Mar 53 - Jan 58	WN492	(934/LM)
	Vampire FB.5	May 55 - Jun 57	VV631	(906/LM)
	Sea Devon C.20	May 56 - Jul 67	XJ322	
	Dragonfly HR.5	May 58 - May 63	WN492	(934/LM)
	Sea Hawk F.2	Aug 58 - Jun 59	WF259	(-/LM)
	Sea Hawk F.B.3	Apr 57 - Oct 58	WM982	
	Sea Hawk FGA.4	Dec 56 - Jun 59	WV799	(938/LM)
	Sea Hawk FGA.6	Mar 59 - May 64	XE374	(982/LM)
	Sea Vampire T.22	Sep 59 - Jan 69	XG769	(682/LM)
	Sea Prince T.1	Sep 60 - Dec 71	WM739	(608/LM)
	Sea Prince C.2	Sep 60 - Sep 65	WP309	(931/LM)
	Scimitar F.1	Jul 61 - Jun 62	XD316	
	Whirlwind HAS.7	Oct 62 - Sep 72	XM660	(933/LM)
	Whirlwind HAR.9	Nov 69 - Feb 73	XN387	(86/LM)
	Chipmunk T.10	Oct 71 - Jan 72	WK574	(680)
Machrihanish	Swordfish I	Nov 43	V4634	
	Anson I	May 45 - Sep 46	MH229	
	Reliant	Sep 45 - Oct 45	FB709	
	Traveller	Sep 45 - Oct 45	FT499	(M9F)
	Sea Otter	Sep 45 - Apr 46	JN257	
	Dominie	Oct 51 - Jul 52	X7508	(901/MA)
	Sea Otter	Nov 51 - Sep 52	JM951	(915/MA)
	Firefly T.2	Dec 51 - Oct 52	MB731	(905/MA)
Maryborough	Tiger Moth II	Jul 45 - Oct 45	A17-72	
Maydown	Tiger Moth II	Aug 43 - 43	X5106	
Merryfield	Sea Venom FAW20	Dec 56 - Dec 57	WM555	
	Sea Venom FAW21	May 57 - Aug 57	WW273	
Piarco	Tiger Moth II	Aug 43 - Mar 44	N9378	
Ponam	Reliant	May 45 - Sep 45	FB760	
Portland	Dragonfly HR.5	May 59 - Nov 59	WG718	
Prestwick	Sea Devon C.20	Jan 74 - Jun 75	XJ322	(c/s317)
Puttalam	Reliant	May 45	FB598	(P-75)
Rattray	Reliant	Mar 45	FB644	
Ronaldsway	Reliant		FK917	(RON)
	Oxford	Sep 44 - Nov 45	ED295	(AR83)
	Tiger Moth II	Dec 44 - Jun 45	BB805	
	Anson I	Apr 45 - Dec 45	LT417	

Station	Aircraft	Period	Example	
Ronaldsway ctd	Expeditor C.II	Apr 46	FE882	(ROQ)
St Merryn	Proctor Ia	Nov 40	P6069	
	Reliant	Mar 44 - Oct 45	FK895	(S9O)
	Tiger Moth II	45	BB865	
	Seafire Ib	Apr 45	MB349	
	Seafire F.17	Jan 46 - Sep 46	SX220	
	Oxford	Jul 45 - Jan 50	JN185	(980/MF)
	Anson I	May 46 - Jul 53	NK829	(901/MF)
	Harvard IIb	47 - 50	KF553	
	Firefly FR.1	Oct 45 - Mar 52	PP479	(914/MF)
	Firefly T.1	Jan 52 - Nov 53	Z1873	(917/MF)
	Firefly T.2	May 50 - Jan 55	MB578	(915/MF)
	Martinet TT.1	Feb 50 - Feb 51	RG974	
	Sea Fury T.20	Aug 51 - Oct 51	WG652	(901/MF)
	Dragonfly HR.3	Jun 53 - Apr 54	WP494	(903/SR)
Schofields	Reliant	Mar 45 - Oct 45	FB751	
	Seafire L.III	Mar 45	NF430	
Sembawang	Seafire XV	Jun 47 - Jul 47		
	Firefly 5	May 54 - Jan 57	WB377	(-/BW)
Speke	Traveller	Mar 45	FT503	
Stretton	Hornet Moth	Aug 42	DZ213	
	Proctor Ia	Aug 42		
	Reliant	Jan 44 - 45	FK940	(R9A)
	Traveller	Dec 44 - Nov 45	FT484	
	Wellington GR	Apr 45		
	Seafire F.17	Sep 45 - Nov 45		
	Dominie	Oct 45 - Jan 57	NF848	(902/JA)
	Oxford		PH362	(ST9H)
	Anson I/ASH	Apr 50 - Jul 51	MH118	(750/JA)
	Meteor T.7	Oct 52 - Mar 54	WA652	(901/ST)
	Sea Vampire T.22	Oct 54 - Oct 56	XA168	(901/ST)
Tambaram	Reliant	Jun 44 - Nov 45	FB601	
	Swordfish I	Feb 45	L2745	
	Harvard IIb	Nov 45	KF550	
Tanga	Swordfish I	Mar 45		
	Reliant	Mar 45		
Twatt	Reliant	Apr 45 - Aug 45	FL163	
Woodvale	Reliant	May 45 - Sep 45	FK954	
	Dominie	Jun 45 - Aug 45	X7507	
	Anson I	Aug 45	LV137	
Worthy Down	Tiger Moth II	Nov 42 - 47	W6420	
	Anson I	Nov 46 - Jan 47	MH210	
Yeovilton	Proctor IIa	Aug 43	BV544	
	Reliant	Nov 43 - Nov 45	FK910	(Y9J)
	Master II	Feb 45	AZ666	
	Wellington XI	Apr 45 - Dec 45	MP504	(Y9R)
	Seafire L.IIc	Jul 45	LR728	
	Anson I	Dec 45 - Apr 46	LT346	
	Beaufort T.I	Dec 44 - Mar 45	LR901	(Y9P)
	Dominie	Jun 50 - Sep 62	HG709	(801/VL)
	Sea Fury T.20	Sep 50 - Jul 56	VX299	(904/VL)
	Vampire FB.5	Jun 51 - Dec 54	VZ143	(902)
	Sea Vampire F.20	Sep 53 - May 54	VV144	(902/VL)
	Sea Vampire T.22	Aug 56 - Sep 67	XG742	(944/VL)
	Expeditor C.2	Jul 53 - Jul 54	HD775	(900/VL)
	Firefly T.2	Oct 53 - Mar 54	MB673	(904/VL)
	Oxford	May 54 - Aug 54	PG979	
	Dragonfly HR.3	Dec 55 - Apr 58	WG751	(948/VL)
	Dragonfly HR.5	Apr 58 - Dec 63	WG670	(941/VL)
	Hiller HT.1	56 - May 57	XB474	(952/VL)
	Sea Balliol T.21	Jul 56 - Jun 60	WL734	(944/VL)
	Sea Venom FAW21	Jul 56 - Feb 58	XG630	
	Gannet T.2	May 59 - Jun 59	XG873	
	Gannet AS.4	Feb 61 - May 62	XG832	(943/VL)
	Sea Hawk FGA.6	Jun 62 - Jul 62	WV836	
	Sea Prince T.1	Feb 63 - Jul 66	WM739	(950/VL)
	Sea Prince C.2	May 54 - Jan 71	WJ350	(c/s749)
	Sea Devon C.20	Jun 65 - Dec 89	XK896	(c/s710)
	Tiger Moth 2	Jul 65 - Sep 73	T6296	(G)
	Whirlwind HAS.7	Nov 63 - Nov 70	XL853	(941/VL)
	Meteor T.7	Aug 66 - Jan 67	WS103	(709/VL)
	Hunter T.7	Dec 69 - Sep 70	XF310	(738)
	Hunter T.8	Oct 59 - Jul 70	XL580	(946/VL)
	Hunter GA.11	Mar 69 - Nov 70	XE685	(708/VL)
	Wessex HAS.1	Dec 70 - Jan 74	XP151	(719/VL)
	Chipmunk T.10	Jun 71 - Mar 93	XK574	(738/VL)
	Sea Heron C.2	Nov 72 - Dec 89	XM296	(c/s709)
	Sea Devon C.2	Nov 72 - Dec 89	XW296	(709)
	Gazelle HT.2	Sep 88 - to date	ZB649	(-/VL)
	Jetstream T.3	Nov 89 - to date	ZE438	(576)

FERRY UNITS

Detailed information on the various FAA ferry units appears not to have survived. The following information has been pieced together and is believed to be substanially accurate, though there are some apparent anomolies and gaps.

FERRY POOL, ANTHORN
Formed at 1 RDU Anthorn in November 1945. Became No.4 Ferry Pool on 1 February 1945 (later No.3 Ferry Flight). Reverted to Ferry Pool Anthorn in 1949 until the RDU closed down in early 1958.

Aircraft	Period	Example
Dominie	Aug 1949	NF867
Harvard T.2b	Aug 1949	KF504
Firefly T.1	Aug 1955 - Jul 1956	MB698
Sea Balliol T.21	May 1956 - Jul 1957	WP332

FERRY POOL, ARBROATH
Existed at AHU Arbroath in 1955.

Aircraft	Period	Example
Sea Fury FB.11	Jun 1955 - Jul 1955	VW581

FERRY POOL, BELFAST
Formed at RNAY Belfast in September 1945 under Lt M.A.Button. Disbanded 17 March 1946.

Aircraft	Period	Example
Traveller	Oct 1945	FT533
Hellcat I	Dec 1945	JV101

FERRY POOL, CULHAM
Formed at Culham in September 1945. Commanded by Lt G.R.Blackburn. Probably disbanded January 1946.

Aircraft	Period	Example
Anson I	Sep 1945 - Jan 1946	MH117
Reliant	Sep 1945 - Jan 1946	FK987

FERRY POOL, DONIBRISTLE
Existed by April 1942 at Donibristle. Became No.5 Ferry Squadron in November 1945.

Aircraft	Period	Example
Fulmar II	Apr 1942 - Jul 1942	X8573
Dominie	Apr 1942	X7494
Proctor I	Jan 1943 - May 1943	Z7241
Proctor Ia	Apr 1943 - Oct 1943	P6074
Proctor IIa	Apr 1943	BV538
Tiger Moth II	Mar 1943 - Oct 1943	T7054
Swordfish I	Jul 1943 - Oct 1943	K8876
Swordfish II	May 1943 - Mar 1944	DK782
Walrus	May 1943 - Jun 1943	Z1819
Reliant	Feb 1944 - Mar 1944	FK960
Seafire L.IIc	Mar 1944	MB216
Traveller	Nov 1944 - Apr 1945	FT525

FERRY POOL, STRETTON
Formed at AHU Stretton by September 1945, becoming Ferry Pool No.5 late in that year.

Aircraft	Period	Example
Traveller	Sep 1945 - Jan 1946	FT484
Anson I	Oct 1945	EF867
Dominie	Oct 1945 - Dec 1945	NF849

FERRY POOL, WORTHY DOWN
Existed by June 1945 attached to the local Storage Section. Became Ferry Pool No.6 in November 1945.

Aircraft	Period	Example
Tiger Moth II	Jun 1945 - Aug 1945	T7054
Leopard Moth	Jun 1945 - Aug 1945	ES945
Reliant	Jun 1945 - Aug 1945	FL163
Traveller	Jun 1945 - Aug 1945	FT483
Master II	Jun 1945 - Aug 1945	DL944
Hoverfly I	Jun 1944 - Aug 1944	KK990
Swordfish III	Jun 1945 - Aug 1945	NR913
Anson I	Jun 1945 - Aug 1945	EG695
Avenger I	Jun 1945 - Aug 1945	FN806
Avenger II	Jun 1945 - Aug 1945	JZ338
Barracuda II	Jun 1945 - Aug 1945	ME178

FERRY POOL NO.1
Formed on 2 February 1946 under Lt E.A.Moore at Henstridge, moving to Yeovilton on 2 April 1946. Became No.1 Ferry Flight on moving to 2 RDU Culham on 26 September 1946.

Aircraft	Period	Example
Oxford	Jul 1946 - Sep 1946	PH264

FERRY POOL NO.2
Formed in February 1946 at AHU Stretton; Existed until January 1948.

Aircraft	Period	Example
Seafire F.45	May 1946	LA480
Firefly FR.I	Jul 1946	MB666
Oxford	Feb 1946 - Jun 1947	V4269
Anson I	Feb 1946 - Apr 1946	LT490
Dominie	Feb 1946 - Apr 1947	X7497

FERRY POOL NO.4
Formed by numbering Ferry Pool Anthorn on 1 February 1946. Became No.3 Ferry Flight on 20 Jun 1947.

Aircraft	Period	Example
Tiger Moth	Jan 1946 - Feb 1946	T6975
Avenger III	May 1946	

FERRY POOL NO.5
Existed at Stretton by January 1946.

Aircraft	Period	Example
Sea Otter	Jan 1946	RD870
Martinet TT.1	Jan 1946	RG890
Hellcat II	Jan 1946	KE151
Wildcat VI	Jan 1946	JV804
Corsair III	Jan 1946	JS536
Corsair IV	Jan 1946	KD978
Anson I	Jan 1946	N9608
Barracuda III	Jan 1946	RJ965

FERRY POOL NO.6
Formed November 1945 from Worthy Down. Disbanded February 1946.

Aircraft	Period	Example
Leopard Moth	Dec 1945 - Jan 1946	ES945
Anson I	Dec 1945 - Jan 1946	EG695

NO.2 FERRY SQUADRON
Existed by January 1946 at AHU Stretton, becoming No.2 Ferry Flight in 1947.

Aircraft	Period	Example
Dominie	Jan 1946 - Jun 1947	HG727
Oxford	Apr 1946 - Jun 1946	DF361
Anson I	Oct 1946	NK834
Hellcat NF.II	Apr 1946 - Jun 1946	JZ995
Seafire XVII	Jul 1946	SX280

NO.5 FERRY SQUADRON
Formed from Ferry Pool Donibristle in November 1945, with a satellite at Evanton. Moved to Crail on 7 February 1946 due to congestion, poor approaches and runway conditions at Donibristle, with Lt F.H.Borlance in command. Became No.4 Ferry Flight in September 1946.

Aircraft	Period	Example
Anson I	Mar 1946	1946 NK164
Tiger Moth II	Feb 1946 - Apr 1946	N6545
Dominie	Jun 1946 - Sep 1946	HG717
Oxford	Jul 1946 - Sep 1946	NM600

NO.1 FERRY FLIGHT
Formed at 2 RDU Culham on 26 Sep 1946 by redesignating No.1 Ferry Pool on its move from Yeovilton. The unit disbanded on 31 Aug 1950.

Aircraft	Period	Example
Anson I	Sep 1946 - Oct 1947	NK287 (601/CH)
Oxford	Sep 1946 - Nov 1947	PH264
Seafire F.17	Oct 1947 - Jan 1947	SX155
Dominie	Dec 1947 - Nov 1950	NF849 (602/CH)
Firefly II	Dec 1946 - Jan 1947	DK442
Firefly FR.4	Apr 1947 - Sep 1948	TW729
Firefly AS.5	Oct 1949 - Jan 1950	WB333

NO.2 FERRY FLIGHT
Existed at AHU Stretton by February 1947 until at least 1950.

Aircraft	Period	Example
Seafire F.17	Feb 1947 - Mar 1949	SX305
Dominie	Oct 1947 - Nov 1949	X7507 (902/JA)
Harvard IIb	Jul 1948	KF507
Harvard III	Feb 1948 - Jul 1948	EZ425

NO.3 FERRY FLIGHT
Formed by restyling No.4 Ferry Pool at 1 RDU Anthorn on 20 June 1947; Became Ferry Pool Anthorn around 1949.

Aircraft	Period	Example
Dominie	Jan 1948 - Mar 1950	NF867
Tiger Moth 2	Jan 1949 - Feb 1949	T8191
Anson 1	Dec 1949	MH186

NO.4 FERRY FLIGHT
Formed from No.5 Ferry Squadron at Crail in September 1946. Moved to AHU Arbroath on 22 March 1947, and disbanded there in 1950.

Aircraft	Period	Example
Anson I	Sep 1946 - May 1947	NK952
Oxford	Mar 1947 - Dec 1947	NM600
Harvard IIb	Jul 1947 - Aug 1947	KF500
Firefly I	Jul 1947 - Oct 1947	Z1904
Firefly IV	Jul 1947 - Oct 1947	TW716
Seafire F.15	Jun 1948	PR477

NAVAL FERRY FLIGHT, BELFAST
Civilian-operated by Short & Harland from November 1950.

Aircraft	Period	Example
Dominie	Nov 1950 - Feb 1954	NF873

SHORTS FERRY FLIGHT, ROCHESTER
Civilian-operated by Shorts from November 1950.

Aircraft	Period	Example
Dominie	Nov 1950 - Jul 1958	NF871
Sea Devon C.20	May 1955 - Sep 1956	XJ323
Sea Prince C.1	Sep 1956 - Apr 1957	WJ349
Sea Prince T.1	Sep 1956 - Jun 1960	WP311

COMMUNICATIONS FLIGHTS

Station	Aircraft	Period	Example
Ceylon	Albacore I	Mar 43 - May 43	X9014
Christchurch	Reliant	Mar 44	FK917
Coimbatore	Walrus	Jul 43	HD808
	Albacore I	Sep 43 - Dec 43	X9012
Dekheila	Fulmar II	Sep 42 - Oct 42	DR665
Donibristle	Proctor Ia	Apr 40 - Dec 40	P6074
	DH.86	Jul 40 - Dec 40	AX844
	Rapide	Aug 40 - Dec 40	R9563
Fayid	Fulmar I	Jan 43	N1936
	Fulmar II	Nov 44	N4118
Malta (Ta Kali)	Anson I	Aug 45	LT115
	Beaufighter II	Aug 45	T3051
	Martinet TT.I	Aug 45	NR310
	Baltimore IV	Jun 46 - Jul 46	FA435
	Baltimore V	Apr 46 - Aug 46	FW376

OTHER UNITS

FLEET REQUIREMENTS UNIT
Formed on 11 August 1938 in HMS *Argus* (shore base Lee-on-Solent). Redesignated No.770 Squadron 24 May 1939.

Aircraft	Period	Example
Swordfish I	Aug 1938 - May 1939	L7677

RN FIGHTER FLIGHT
Formed at Aboukir on 21 August 1941, being attached to No.700 Sqdn and initially known as the RN Night Fighter Unit. Moved to Dekheila on/by 17 October 1941, being there attached to No.775 Sqdn and referred to as the RN Fighter Flight. Went on 21 November 1941 to Fuka, where it was redesignated No.889 Sqdn on 16 March 1942.

Aircraft	Period	Example
Fulmar II	Nov 1941 - Mar 1942	X8526

RN FIGHTER SQUADRON
A temporary amalgamation in July 1941 of Nos.803, 805 and 806 Squadrons for operations in the Western Desert, with a total equipment of 16 Hurricanes and 8 Martlets. Moves are listed under the individual squadrons, which regained their own identities in February 1942.

TEST FLIGHT, TRINCOMALEE

Aircraft	Period	Example
Wildcat V	Aug 1945 - Oct 1945	JV466
Hellcat II	Aug 1945 - Oct 1945	JX706

RN AIR SIGNAL SQUADRON
Formed at Hamble on 16 November 1949 to take over the aircraft and radar training task of No.783 Squadron. Operated by Air Service Training Ltd under Admiralty contract to meet the requirements of the Naval Air Signals School, Seafield Park. Contract terminated 30 November 1953.

Aircraft	Period	Example
Anson T.1	Nov 1949 - Nov 1953	NK324 (604/D)

RN SECTION, JOINT WARFARE ESTABLISHMENT
Formed by 1946 at Old Sarum, attached to the School of Air Support. This later became the School of Land/Air Warfare, and on 1 April 1963 the name was again changed, to the Joint Warfare Establishment, its aircraft being then operated as the Joint Helicopter Trials and Development Unit. The RN element came under the parentage of RNAS Yeovilton until disbandment on 22 July 1976.

Aircraft	Period	Example
Dominie	May 1946 - Apr 1956	HG709 (801/VL)
Sea Fury F.10	Apr 1948 - Feb 1950	TF945
Sea Fury FB.11	Feb 1950 - Feb 1952	VW229
Firefly FR.1	Jun 1949 - Jan 1954	MB738
Hiller HT.1	Jan 1954 - 1956	XB523
Sea Balliol T.21	Nov 1955 - Sep 1961	WP324
Dragonfly HR.5	Sep 1961 - Oct 1962	WP500
Whirlwind HAR.3	Sep 1966	XG587 (758)
Whirlwind HAS.7	Oct 1970 - Jul 1976	XN299 (758)

English Electric Canberra T.22 WT535 '852' of FRADU, Yeovilton in August 1981.

Chipmunk T.10 WK634 '902' of Britannia Flight in 1968. (MAP)

Hunter T.8 WT722 '742/VL' of FRADTU in 1973. (MAP)

Avro Anson I DJ331 '606:G' of the RN Air Signal Squadron, Hamble in 1952 (R.M.Rayner)

Airspeed Oxford PH319 '609' of the Admiralty Flight, Rochester in 1950

ADMIRALTY FLIGHT
Formed 16 November 1949 at Rochester and took over from No.780 Sqdn the task of familiarisation flying for out of practice naval officers. Operated as the Naval Instrument and Refresher Flying School. Contract terminated May 1955.

Aircraft	Period	Example
Oxford	Nov 1949 - May 1955	PH140 (611)
Harvard T.2b	Nov 1949 - Jan 1952	KF558
Harvard T.3	Jun 1951 - May 1955	EZ428 (205)
Firefly FR.1	Jul 1950 - May 1955	DK548 (102)
Firefly T.1	Oct 1952 - May 1955	Z2015
Firefly T.2	Aug 1950 - May 1955	MB756 (261)

WYVERN CONVERSION UNIT
Formed in February 1957 from the Wyvern Flight of No.764 Squadron Ford. Disbanded in December 1957.

Aircraft	Period	Example
Wyvern S.4	Feb 1957 - Dec 1957	VZ793 (360/FD)

AIRWORK
A civilian-operated unit run by Airwork Ltd. Commenced operating on 5 January 1950 at Brawdy to provide aircraft to exercise the Aircraft Direction School at Kete. Also undertook a Heavy Twin Conversion Course for FAA pilots, using Sea Hornets and Sea Mosquitoes. Moved to St.Davids in September 1951, and operated a jet conversion course with Meteor T.7s. Returned to Brawdy in October 1958 but continued to use St.Davids as a satellite. To Yeovilton in January 1961 and operated as the Air Direction Training Unit. Merged into the Fleet Requirements and Air Direction Training Unit on 1 December 1972.

Aircraft	Period	Example
Auster 5	Jan 1950 - Sep 1954	TJ651
Mosquito T.3	Jan 1950 - Sep 1956	VT622 (412/BY)
Sea Mosquito TR.33	Jan 1950 - Aug 1952	TW249
Sea Hornet F.20	Jul 1952 - Jun 1953	TT213 (421/BY)
Sea Hornet NF.21	Jul 1952 - Oct 1955	VZ694 (427/BY)
Meteor T.7	Oct 1953 - Sep 1957	WL334 (007/BY)
Attacker F.1	Dec 1955 - Jan 1957	WA521 (021/BY)
Attacker FB.2	Sep 1956 - Jan 1957	WZ297 (022/BY)
Sea Venom FAW.20	Oct 1955 - Jun 1959	WM557 (017/BY)
Sea Venom FAW.21	Feb 1957 - Apr 1961	XG666 (019/BY)
Sea Venom FAW.22	Jan 1961 - Oct 1970	XG733 (013/VL)
Sea Vampire T.22	Mar 1958 - Jul 1970	XA129 (747/VL)
Hunter T.8/T.8c	Jun 1970 - Nov 1972	XE665 (741/VL)
Hunter GA.11	Sep 1972 - Nov 1972	WV381 (732/VL)
Sea Vixen FAW.2	Jan 1971 - Nov 1972	XP954 (753)

AIRWORK FLEET REQUIREMENTS UNIT
A civilian-operated unit run by Airwork Ltd. Opened at Hurn on 1 September 1952 to provide some, and eventually all, of the Royal Navy's FRUs needs. To Yeovilton on 16 October 1972, becoming part of the FRADU on 1 December 1972.

Aircraft	Period	Example
Mosquito PR.16	Sep 1952 - Sep 1953	RF985
Sea Mosquito TR.33	Sep 1952 - May 1953	TW249 (416/BQ)
Sea Hornet F.20	Mar 1953 - Oct 1955	TT213 (421/BQ)
Sea Hornet NF.21	Mar 1953 - Oct 1955	VZ672
Attacker FB.2	Oct 1955 - Feb 1957	WP285 (038)
Sea Fury FB.11	Oct 1955 - Apr 1961	WJ224 (030)
Sea Hawk F.1	Nov 1956 - Aug 1958	WF229 (039)
Sea Hawk FB.5	Apr 1958 - May 1964	WM993 (034)
Sea Hawk FGA.6	Jun 1961 - Feb 1969	XE334 (036)
Meteor TT.20	May 1958 - Mar 1971	WM159 (040)
Dragonfly HR.3	Sep 1958 - Jul 1961	WG719
Scimitar F.1	Dec 1965 - Dec 1970	XD333 (837)
Meteor T.7	Jul 1967 - Mar 1971	WL350 (844)
Hunter T.8/T.8c	1969 - Aug 1971	XL603 (738)
Hunter GA.11	Mar 1969 - Oct 1972	WV267 (833)
Canberra B.2	Sep 1969 - Jun 1972	WK142 (847)
Canberra T.4	Nov 1969 - Nov 1972	WJ866 (849)
Canberra TT.18	Sep 1969 - Oct 1972	WJ636 (842)

FLEET REQUIREMENTS AND AIR DIRECTION UNIT
A civilian-operated unit, formed on 1 December 1972 at Yeovilton to combine the functions of the locally based Air Direction Training Unit with those of the Airwork FRU which had recently moved from Hurn. Known initially as the Fleet Requirements and Air Direction Training Unit, the title was later shortened by omitting the word Training. Part of the unit moved out to Boscombe Down in August 1983 whilst runway repairs were undertaken, returning to Yeovilton on 3 October. The Contract transferred to Flight Refuelling Ltd in 1983.

Aircraft	Period	Example
Hunter T.8c	Dec 1972 - to date	XL580 (743/VL)
Hunter GA.11/PR.11	Dec 1972 - to date	XE668 (832/VL)
Sea Vixen FAW.2	Dec 1972 - Feb 1974	XN696 (751)
Canberra T.4	Dec 1972 - Mar 1986	WJ869 (848)
Canberra TT.18	Dec 1972 - Nov 1992	WK123 (840)
Canberra T.22	Nov 1973 - Sep 1985	WT525 (855)
Hunter T.7	Aug 1981 - Mar 1993	XF310 (876/VL)
Hunter T.8M	Mar 1994 - to date	XL602
Hawk T.1	Apr 1994 - to date	XX248

NO.29 JOINT SERVICES TRIALS UNIT
Formed on 1 August 1979 at Yeovilton for evaluation of the Sea Skua missile system. To Boscombe Down on 1 May 1980, and to Aberporth on 15 September 1980. Disbanded on 30 Jun 1982.

Aircraft	Period	Example
Lynx HAS.2	Aug 1979 - Jun 1982	XZ227 (478)

ROYAL NAVAL HISTORIC FLIGHT
Formed out of Heron Flight at Yeovilton in 1973. Operates two or three vintage aircraft during the flying display season each year.

Aircraft	Period	Example
Swordfish II	Sep 1960 - to date	LS326
Sea Fury FB.11	Jan 1972 - Jun 1989	TF956 crashed
Tiger Moth T.2	1972 - to date	T8191 in reserve
Firefly 5	Oct 1972 - to date	WB271
Sea Fury T.20	Jun 1976 - Jul 1990	WG655 crashed
Sea Hawk FGA.6	1976 - to date	WV908
Sea Fury T.20	Oct 1992 - to date	VZ345
Swordfish II	May 1992 - to date	W5856
Chipmunk T.10	Mar 1993 - to date	WK608
Chipmunk T.10	Mar 1994 - to date	WB657

RNEC MANADON FLIGHT
Based at Roborough it gave air experience to pupils of the nearby RN Engineering College, Manadon, Plymouth.

Aircraft	Period	Example
Tiger Moth T.2	Apr 1950 - Aug 1958	T7693 (B)
Harvard T.3	Oct 1951 - Dec 1954	FT958
Oxford	Oct 1951 - Mar 1955	PH190
Sea Balliol T.21	Aug 1955 - Oct 1957	WL717

BRITANNIA FLIGHT
Formed on 14 June 1960 to provide air experience for the pupils of the Britannia Royal Naval College, Dartmouth, fixed wing aircraft being based at Roborough, and helicopters at Norton, Dartmouth. Airwork Ltd was responsible for maintenance and flying activities at Roborough. In the early eighties the flight was officially restyled the Naval Flying Grading Flight, though still unofficially known as Britannia Flight. After the Falklands campaign the dedicated Wasp Flight was withdrawn and disembarked Ships Flights detached occasionally to Norton until the Wasp was withdrawn from service in March 1988. Airwork was acquired by Shorts in January 1994, and the Chipmunk Flight was disbanded in March 1994 when the flying grading task was taken over by them as civilian contractors, using five Grob G115 D2s with civil registrations G-BVHC to G-BVHG and named the Heron.

Aircraft	Period	Example
Dragonfly HR.5	Jun 1960 - Jun 1967	WG667 (901)
Tiger Moth T.2	Nov 1960 - Oct 1966	NL879
Chipmunk T.10	Jun 1966 - Mar 1994	WP795 (901)
Wasp HAS.1	Nov 1967 - Apr 1982	XS535 (95/DM)

Westland Sea King HAR.3 XZ592 'S' of the RAF Sea King Training Unit, Culdrose in 1991.

NORTHERN COMMUNICATIONS SQUADRON
Formed on 9 October 1953 at Donibristle to take over the task of No.782 Squadron. Operated by by Airwork Services Ltd. Contract terminated late 1958 and duties taken over by No.781 Squadron.

Aircraft	Period	Example
Dominie	Oct 1953 - Mar 1957	NF864 (049/DO)
Sea Prince C.1	Nov 1955 - Sep 1956	WF136 (045/DO)
Sea Prince C.2	Nov 1955 - Sep 1956	WJ349 (046/DO)
Sea Fury T.20	Mar 1955 - Mar 1956	WE826 (049/DO)
Sea Devon C.20	Sep 1956 - 1958	XJ324

RAF SEA KING TRAINING UNIT
Formed on 1 November 1977 at Culdrose with 6 Sea King HAR.3 to train RAF Sea King crews. From 26 October 1979 the unit temporarily lost its independence and operated as the Sea King Training Flight of No.706 Squadron. The unit finally departed from Naval overview on 5 April 1993 on transfer to St.Mawgan.

Aircraft	Period	Example
Sea King HAR.3	Nov 1977 - Oct 1979	XZ589 (c/s 533)
Sea King HAR.3	Jan 1982 - Apr 1993	ZE369

ROYAL NAVAL ELEMENTARY FLYING TRAINING SQUADRON (RNEFTS)
Formed April 1973 within No.2 Flying Training School, RAF at Church Fenton. Moved to Leeming 29 November 1974, then to Linton-on-Ouse 26 April 1984. The squadron closed in March 1994 when the task was taken over by civilian contractors.

Aircraft	Period	Example
Bulldog T.1	Apr 1973 - Mar 1994	XX531 (14)

LYNX OPERATIONAL FLYING TRAINING UNIT
Formed June 1990 at Portland. Redesignated No.700L Squadron on 16 July 1990.

Aircraft	Period	Example
Lynx HAS.3	Jun 1990 - Jul 1990	ZF563 (671)

SEA KING HAS.6 INTENSIVE FLYING TRIALS UNIT
Formed early 1988 within No.824 Squadron at Prestwick.

Aircraft	Period	Example
Sea King HAS.6	Apr 1988 - 1988	ZA136 (251)

TRIALS UNIT, LOSSIEMOUTH
In the later summer of 1948 a Trials Unit equipped with Barracudas was based at Lossiemouth to carry out dive-bombing using armour piercing bombs dropped from 12,000ft against the battleship HMS *Nelson*, which was moored in the Firth of Forth, west of the island of Inchkeith. Working up was done at a bombing range near Kinloss. The bombs, which were unarmed, scored several hits and caused considerable damage. The ship was then towed to Rosyth to be broken up.

OPERATIONAL EVALUATION UNITS
From 1991 a series of Operational Evaluation Units (OEUs) was created to evaluate tactics of, and modifications to, in-service aircraft. Parented by the aircraft type lead squadrons, details are given in the squadron section.

Aircraft	Period	Example	Sqdn
Sea King HAS.6	Jun 1991 - Jul 1993	XZ581 (133)	826
	Jul 1993 - to date	XZ922 (514)	810
Lynx HAS.3(CTS)	Jul 1992 - Jun 1994	ZF558 (672/PO)	815
Lynx HAS.8	Jul 1994 - to date	XZ732 (670/PO)	815
Sea Harrier FRS.2	Jun 1993 - to date	ZD615 (712/OEU)	899

Bulldog T.1 XX515 '7' of the RNEFTS. (MAP)

Sea Prince T.2 WJ349 '046' of the Northern Communications Squadron, Donibristle in 1956. (MAP)

NAVAL AIRCRAFT CODE MARKINGS

It has been the practice throughout the history of the Fleet Air Arm for the majority of its aircraft to carry code markings as a means of identification. These have been known variously as side numbers, Fleet numbers or call signs. The latter is a reference to their use for radio identification purposes. For the historian they have the great advantage that they very often enable the parent squadron or unit of an aircraft depicted in a photograph or referred to in a document to be readily identified.

When the first few 400-series flights were formed in April 1923 as part of the RAF, the latter had no standard system of identification markings. Consequently, although a few of the new units adopted codes, such as single letters or single numbers, the majority did not. However, this state of affairs was not to last long, and at a meeting towards the end of 1923 aboard the battleship HMS *Queen Elizabeth*, it was decided that aircraft of these flights would adopt standardised markings.

The new markings would consist of single or double digit numbers painted in a coloured band along the fuselage sides. The colour of each band would indicate the parent carrier of the flight concerned. Thus, of the carriers then in service or shortly to commission, HMS *Argus* aircraft would carry green fuselage bands, those in HMS *Furious* red, HMS *Hermes* white and HMS *Eagle* black. When HMS *Courageous* came into service it adopted blue, and this was followed by yellow for HMS *Glorious*. Finally, just before the outbreak of war, HMS *Ark Royal* adopted a three-coloured band consisting of two blue strips separated by a red one, all of equal size. The only exceptions to the colour band system were the later catapult flights, which carried their code numbers painted directly on to the fuselage sides.

The system of numbering which was adopted was based on the numbers of the flights to which they were allocated. Thus the fleet fighter flights, being numbered in the 401-419 range (though not all taken up), used codes 1-19. Similarly 20-39 were allocated to fleet spotters (420-439 range), 40-59 to fleet reconnaissance aircraft (440-459 range) and finally 60-89 to fleet torpedo aircraft (460 onwards). To avoid the possibility of signalling error, no digit was duplicated within a code, so that numbers 11, 22, 33 and so on were never taken up. These numbers were painted on to the appropriately coloured fuselage band, which was generally a diagonal one, though many variations were employed, especially in the early days.

The first change in the numbering system occurred in April 1929 when the 420-series of flights was abolished. The fleet reconnaissance flights were being phased out, except in the case of some catapult flights, and consequently an extended 450-series of flights absorbed the four existing flights in the 420-series. The direct connection with flight number allocations was now relaxed, and the fleet fighter range of codes was extended to become 1-29. The newly-titled fleet spotter reconnaissance flights then adopted 30-59, the fleet torpedo bomber flights (as they were to become) used 60-89, and fleet reconnaissance flights 90-98.

By this time, however, the system was getting cumbersome, the number of new flights steadily increasing as newer and bigger carriers came into service. In January 1932, therefore, a completely new system came in to use. Codes could now comprise up to three digits, and no two codes would be identical at any one time, irrespective of the fuselage band colour. They continued to avoid duplication of digits, but this was extended so that no digit was ever used twice within a particular combination. Thus such numbers as 221, 212 and 122 were not to be taken up within a sequence. As a further refinement, separate sub-series of codes in each of these sequences were reserved for the different areas of the world in which the Fleet then operated. Thus torpedo bomber flights now adopted codes in the range 1-99, and also 01-09. Reconnaissance aircraft used 201 onwards, fighters 501 onwards and spotter reconnaissance aircraft 701 onwards (Home) and 801 onwards (Mediterranean).

The next change occurred in April 1933, when most of the flights were regrouped into squadrons. For the most part these simply adopted the code sequences inherited from their predecessors, extended where necessary to cope with increases in complement. A further reorganisation of the system took place, however, during 1935-1936, probably for security reasons, this being the time of the Abyssinian Crisis and the emergence of Nazi Germany. Catapult aircraft now generally carried codes in the 001-099 series, the 102-series was reserved for fighters, the 501-series for fleet reconnaissance, and 601 onwards for fleet spotter reconnaissance. There were a few minor exceptions to these sequences. When the catapult flights were re-grouped in July 1936 to become 700-series flights, they retained the code allocations for the most part, extended as required.

A short-lived identification scheme which came into use in some squadrons early in 1937 was the use of two-letter combinations in place of the number codes. In this, each squadron was allocated a block of such codes, such as AA to AL and AM to AX, but only a few actually adopted them before the system was abandoned.

Tension in Europe continued to mount, and both the RAF and the FAA gave further consideration to new systems of aircraft code markings. By the Spring of 1938 these had both been formulated, the RAF settling for two-letter squadron combination plus an individual letter, whilst the FAA was to have a basically similar system in which the unit code was to be a letter/number combination. However, whereas in the RAF system the unit code was placed one side of the fuselage roundel and the individual letter to the other, the FAA code was to be painted left to right (letter/number/letter) irrespective of its relation to the position of the roundel. In most instances it was painted entirely on one side of the roundel, though in some early cases it appeared on the vertical tail surfaces in various layouts.

The new FAA code markings were first painted on the aircraft in May 1939, when the Admiralty finally regained control of its Air Arm from the RAF. Unlike the RAF, though, the new codes were adopted not only by the first line squadrons, but by the catapult squadrons (as they had now become) and also the training units and second line units which adopted squadron numbers from 750 onwards. In the case of first line squadrons the new codes were initially painted as before on the coloured fuselage carrier bands, but these were quickly painted out on the outbreak of war.

Although this wartime FAA code system appears baffling, the basic principles were quite simple. The problem is that its pattern changed as the war progressed, and also that it was quite possible for two units to use identical codes, though not generally in the same theatre of war.

The central number was a class number indicating its function. In the case of operational carrier aircraft there were by 1939 only two main categories, being spotter reconnaissance for which numbers 1 to 5 were allocated, and fighter for which numbers 6 and 7 were used. The prefix letter to these indicated the parent carrier, the initial letter of whose name was usually adopted for this purpose. Thus TSR squadrons in HMS *Ark Royal* were initially coded A2 (810 Sqdn), A3 (814 Sqdn), A4 (820 Sqdn) and A5 (821 Sqdn), whilst her fighters used A6 (800 Sqdn) and A7 (803 Sqdn).

In the original allocation, numbers 8 and 9 were used by catapult aircraft. Number 8 was reserved for wheeled aircraft fitted with floats for this purpose (i.e. Swordfish seaplanes), whilst 9 was for catapult amphibians and fixed float seaplanes (i.e. Walruses and Seafoxes). Number 0 was to be for autogyros, experimental aircraft and the like.

The original prefix allocations, not all of which were taken up, were A - HMS *Ark Royal*, C - HMS *Courageous*, E - HMS *Eagle*, F - HMS *Formidable*, G - HMS *Glorious*, H - HMS *Hermes*, L - HMS *Illustrious*, M - a new carrier under construction, N - HMS *Indomitable*, O - Observer training aircraft, P & Q - converted liner carrier, R - HMS *Argus* (TSRs), T - Flying training aircraft. U - HMS *Furious*, V - HMS *Victorious*, W - Shore station aircraft, X - Experimental, Y & Z Shore station aircraft.

Catapult squadrons had their own series of prefix letters. Some of these duplicated the main sequence, but since they were restricted to suffix numbers 8 and 9 there was no danger of duplicating codes. The allocations made were A - HMS *Albatross* (floatplane), B - Battle Cruiser Squadron, C - 1st Battle Squadron, D - Battleships in reserve, E - 2nd Battle Squadron, F - 1st Cruiser Squadron, G - 2nd Cruiser Squadron, H - 3rd Cruiser Squadron, J - 4th Cruiser Squadron, K - 5th Cruiser Squadron, L - 6th Cruiser Squadron, M - Cruisers in reserve, N - 8th Cruiser Squadron, P & Q - Armed Merchant Cruisers, U & V - spare. Some minor alterations were made to these allocations in practice, but essentially they were used as originally intended, until being largely superseded in January 1940, when all the catapult squadrons were amalgamated as No.700 Squadron which was then allocated code G9, though it probably never took this up.

The code system was basically geared to the first line squadrons, and had to be adapted to meet the needs of the training and other second line squadrons. Initially this was not too difficult a problem, though a little licence had to to be taken with the basic rules. To allow for the fact that many would have mixed equipment, it was laid down that they would use the class figure relating to their main equipment. Thus at Ford and Lee-on-Solent most of the observer training squadrons used codes in ther W1 to W5 range, being equipped mainly with TSR aircraft, but No.751 Squadron used W9 being a Walrus-equipped unit. In effect W-prefixes were reserved for observer training squadrons.

Similarly, X-prefixes were used in practice by TAG training squadrons, except that X8 was reserved for use by No.778 Squadron, the Service Trials Unit. Deck landing training squadrons used T-prefixes, and Fleet requirements units used R-prefixes. O-prefixes were earmarked for operational pools, though it is not certain that these were taken up. Y-prefixes were used by fighter schools (Y6 and Y7), torpedo schools (Y2, Y3, Y4 and Y5), and seaplane schools (Y8 and Y9), and in all of these the suffix numbers were correctly employed for their main equipment. It was recognised that some training squadrons might become unusually large, and these were authorised to use the class number 0 for the overflow. Thus at Ford both Nos.750 and 752 Squadrons had to use codes in the W0 series, and No.750 continued to do so after moving to Trinidad.

The first important change occurred in April 1940, when some changes were announced to the original prefix allocations, though some of these simply recognised what had actually been happening in practice. In the carrier series, B became HMS *Indefatigable*, while C became vacant with the loss of HMS *Courageous*. In the shore-based series, O became Armament training, P - pools, Q - Communications and Miscellaneous, R - FRUs, S - Shore-based operational squadrons and Y - Torpedo and fighter schools. At the same time it was announced that in future only shore-based aircraft would carry the full code, and those which were carrier based would abandon the prefix letter. In actual fact, some carrier squadrons, such as No.810, continued to carry prefix letters until well into 1941. Another anomaly was that during the North African landings (Operation Torch) squadrons embarked in HMS *Formidable* adopted the identification marking Ø as a prefix to their codes.

In May 1941 permission was given for stations with more than one non-operational squadron to modify the class numbering system to meet local needs. It was suggested that numbers 1 and 2 would be appropriate where these used multi-seater aircraft.

By May 1942 there were so many second line squadrons, and some were becoming so large, that a revised coding system was introduced in which the prefix letter indicated the parent station. The initial allocation of these was A - Arbroath (and Dundee satellite), B - Easthaven, C- Crail, D-Donibristle, E - Eastleigh, F - Lawrenny Ferry, H - Hatston, K - Machrihanish, L - Lee-on-Solent, M - St.Merryn, N - Henstridge, P - Campbeltown, R - Stretton, S - Sandbanks, T - Twatt, V - Evanton, W - Worthy Down and Y - Yeovilton. A further modification at that time was that instead of using 0-codes for additional aircraft, they would retain these original code with a horizontal bar over the individual letter.

Further changes took place in January 1943 in the allocation of shore base letters, and eventually it became necessary to use two-letter combinations, when there became more UK stations than available single letters. These later allocations included B - Donibristle, D - Dunino (later Drem), E - Easthaven, F - Fearn, G - Henstridge, I - Eastleigh (later Crimond), J - Eglinton, K - Inskip, M - Machrihanish, N - Maydown, O - Burscough, P - Dale, Q - Belfast (Sydenham), R - Ronaldsway, S - St.Merryn, U - Hinstock, V - Woodvale, X - Abbotsinch, Z - Grimsetter (later Zeals), AA - Dundee, AH - Burscough, AN - Campbeltown, AN - Anthorn, AR - Ronaldsway (later Ayr), AT - Crimond (renamed Rattray), AY - Haldon, BH - Ballyhalbert, BY - Charlton Horethorne, CM - Culham, DO - Dunino, EL - Eastleigh (previously I), EV - Evanton, FD - Ford, GM Grimsetter, HA - Halesworth, GP - Gosport, IT - Milltown and ST - Stretton.

Another change in January 1943 was the abolition of barred letters in the repeated alphabets used by large units. Instead these gave way to black individual letters where these were used a second time. Seemingly a rather confusing means of identification, and one which not all units adopted. Hinstock, for instance, used duplicated individual letters (e.g. U2AA) on the Oxfords of No.758 Squadron. Another variant was No.765 Squadron at Sandbanks, which used a B-prefix for its L3 code on some aircraft (e.g.BL3S). No.736 Squadron, the School of Air Combat at St.Merryn, chose to ignore the standard system entirely and coded its aircraft AC-A, AC-B, AC-C etc.

By 1944 quite a number of shore bases had been established overseas, and prefix letter allocations were also made for these, as follows. A - Addu Attoll (Gan) (later Brisbane), B - Bankstown, C - China Bay (Trincomalee), D - Dekheila, G - Gibraltar, H - Hastings (later Cochin), J - Jervis Bay, K - Katukurunda, L- Colombo, M - Ta Kali, N - Kantali (later Nowra), P - Puttalam (later Ponam), Q - Coimbatore, R - Port Reitz (later Sulur), T - Tambaram and W - Wingfield.

Under this new system, squadron identification numbers for second line squadrons were allocated on a station basis, rather than centrally as hitherto. Numbers 1 to 7 were earmarked for training squadrons, and 8, 9 and 0 for FRUs, communications units, trials units and other miscellaneous formations. It was again suggested that in the training squadrons numbers 1 and 2 be used for multi-seaters.

The advent of central servicing meant that on the larger training stations aircraft would be taken from a pool as required, irrespective of which squadron they were nominally allocated to. Thus serial numbers and codes noted in flying log books would not necessarily relate to the actual squadron to which the person concerned belonged, except where it was the only squadron on the station with that equipment.

Many British naval squadron working up in the United States used carrier-type number/letter combinations for identification purposes. These were in fact an abbreviated form of the full call-sign, which also included the central letter B (for British). Some squadrons, however, carried the full combination until embarking for the United Kingdom, in the form, for example, 2BA, 2BB, 2BC etc. Another variation amongst American-trained squadrons, particularly on Corsairs, was the allocation of V-codes to each squadron, to be used in combination with individual numbers. An example of this was No.1852 Squadron, which numbered its aircraft 1V10, 2V10, 3V10 etc until embarking, when it adopted individual letters as the only identification.

Developments were, in the meantime taking place amongst the the markings borne by aircraft of carrier-based first line squadrons. From October 1943 these had largely been grouped as Wings. Some of these continued to use number/letter codes as identification, but many of those in escort carriers used a combination of a letter denoting the carrier concerned plus an individual letter. In August 1944 the fighter wings standardised on a letter/number/ letter combination, the first letter in each case denoting the wing concerned, the number the particular squadron within the wing, and the last letter the individual aircraft.

Not every wing to which a code was allocated actually formed, and of those that did form, not all troubled to use the new system. Allocations under this system were A - 15 Wing, B - 26, C - 29, D - 4, E - 16, F - 35, G - 28, H - 24, I - 11, J - 44, K - 3, L - 6, M - 18 (aircraft of Macships), N - 40, O - 10, P - 30, Q - 43, R - 5, S - 49, T - 47, U - 22, V - 42, W - 7, X - 33, Y - 37 and Z - 13. These could be changed periodically by local Commanders-in-Chief if extra security was required. In fact, although intended basically for fighter wings, their use was not entirely confined to these, the Swordfish of No.836 Squadron, for instance, using their own variation for a time, being a combination consisting of the Wing letter M, an individual number and the flight letter. Thus, the Swordfish of 'B' Flight of No.836 Squadron carried codes M1B, M2B, and M3B at that time, later reverting to their more normal B1, B2 and B3.

Aircraft in anti-submarine escort carriers began to carry two letter markings, of which the first denoted the carrier and the second the individual aircraft. The class numbers for other first line squadrons were now changed, so the TBR squadrons were to use 1 to 3, two-seater fighter and dive bomber squadrons 4 and fighter squadrons 5 to 9 and also 0.

A further development, in April 1945, was the allocation of deck identification letters for all forms of carrier, which in many cases were to be identical with the carrier letter prefixes borne by its aircraft. Where the carriers were operational, these letters could be changed periodically for security reasons. The letters initially allocated to home-based fleet and escort carriers were B - HMS *Battler*, F - HMS *Ranee*, G - HMS *Smiter*, I - HMS *Trouncer*, J - HMS *Trumpeter*, L - HMS *Glory*, N - HMS *Puncher*, O - HMS *Pretoria Castle*, P - HMS *Premier*, Q - HMS *Queen*, R - HMS *Reaper*, S - HMS *Searcher*, T - HMS *Patroller*, U - HMS *Pursuer*, V - HMS *Ravager*, X - HMS *Vindex*, Y - HMS *Nairana* and Z - HMS *Campania*.

Macships were similarly marked, though such markings were never carried on the aircraft. The allocations were MA - *Acavus*, MB - *Empire MacColl*, MD - *Amastra*, MF - *Ancylus*, MH -

Empire MacAlpine, MJ - Empire MacMahon, MK - Empire MacAndrew, ML - Empire MacCabe, MM - Empire MacKay, MN - Empire MacCallum, MO - Empire MacKendrick, MP - Alexia, MQ - Adula, MR - Gadila, MS - Empire MacDermott, MU - Empire MacRae, MV - Rapana, MW - Miralda and MX - Macoma.

The East Indies Fleet fell into line in July 1945, carrier letters then allocated being A - HMS Attacker, B -HMS Begum, D - HMS Searcher, E - HMS Emperor, H - HMS Hunter, J - HMS Smiter, K - HMS Khedive, M - HMS Empress, O - HMS Trumpeter, R - HMS Ameer, S - HMS Shah and T - HMS Stalker.

In June 1945 the carrier aircraft identification systemn was again changed. General purpose escort carriers would continue to use the letter/letter code system, but those in assault carriers, and all those in fleet and light fleet carriers would revert to a letter/figure/letter system. In this system the initial letter would denote the tactical unit to which the squadron belonged, the other two symbols continuing as before to denote the particular squadron and the individiual aircraft. In order to avoid overlapping in neighbouring theatres of war, initial letters A to J were to be used only by the Home Fleet and East Indies Fleet, whilst N to Z could only be used by the Mediterranean Fleet and the British Pacific Fleet.

The British Pacific Fleet had, however, by this time adopted yet another system of identification on its aircraft, somewhat akin to that of the US Navy alongside which it was operating. From April 1945 the parent carrier letters were used as fin marking, and the fuselages carried a three-digit number for individual identification. Each carrier used the same basic combination of codes, those in the 111 to 169 range being reserved for single seat aircraft, 270 to 298 for two-seaters and 370 to 398 for three seaters.

In 1946 this system was used as a basis for a universal coding system which in essence has survived to the present day, though in modified form. All FAA aircraft, whether at home or abroad, would carry a three digit fuselage number of which the first digit would denote its layout or function. Thus single-seater aircraft would use codes 100 - 199, two-seaters 200 - 299, three-seaters 300 - 399 and multi-engined aircraft 400-499. The remaining numbers were to be used by units with a specialised function, and thus FRU aircraft used 500-599, multi-engined light trainers 600-699, a spare series was 700-799, communications were 800-899, station flights used 900-999 and experimental, tactical trials and development aircraft used 000-099. These numbers were to be used as call signs, but the call sign 99 was specifically reserved for Air Group Commanders, therefore British Pacific Fleet squadrons were told to avoid using 299 or 399. At least one Corsair carried code 99, and examples are known of Training Air Group Commanders using codes 199 or 299 on their aircraft.

As in the British Pacific Fleet system, each ship or station used the same sequence of numbers, allocations to individual aircraft being made locally. Also as in that system, fin letters were used to denote the parent ship, but in the case of shore bases a two-letter combination was used, this being the call sign of the station concerned. Commonwealth carriers were encompassed by this system, to aid identification when operating together. The Royal Australian Navy also used the three-digit sytem, and used the two-letter fin code NW for its shore base at Nowra, but the Royal Canadian Navy preferred to adopt its own aircraft identification system, which it used in conjunction with that of the Royal Canadian Air Force. The Australians have continued to use a fairly similar system to that of the FAA, changing to 900-series codes for second line units in 1955, and then to 800-series codes for both first and second line units in 1958, fin codes being dropped in recent years.

The FAA changed the system of code allocations in January 1956, though not their appearance. Codes were no longer to be allocated by stations, but would be issued centrally to each squadron, though again on a function basis. Thus FRUs and Communications squadrons would be given codes in the range 000-099, first line squadrons 100-499, training and auxiliary squadrons 500-799, reserve squadrons 800-899 and station and ships flights 900-999. The use of the 800 series by reserve squadrons was short-lived as they disbanded in March 1957.

In the initial allocations under the new system, blocks of numbers were allocated to squadrons in their numerical sequence. Thus No.800 Squadron had 100-114, No.801 had 115-129, No.802 had 130-144 and so on. Second line squadron were similarly allocated codes in numerical sequence, whilst those of station and ships flights were in alphabetical sequence. With the constant formation of new units and the disbandment of those which had served their purpose, it was inevitable that this neat series of allocations could not last very long. Attempts were made at first to reallocate blocks of codes to new squadrons in something like their correct sequence, but this gradually became more difficult, and in some instances codes blocks had to be allocated outside those for which they were intended.

By July 1965 the situation had become very confused, and as a consequence a fresh start was made. Codes were once again to be allocated to squadrons on a station basis, but this time within broad blocks without any regard for their function. This would give greater flexibility provided no big organisational changes took place.

Under the initial allocations the broad range 0 - 199 was reserved for first line carrier squadrons, 400-499 to helicopters attached to small ships and 500-999 to aircraft of shore-based units. Each of these ranges was sub-divided, so that in the 001-399 range HMS Ark Royal took 001-057, HMS Eagle 060-147, HMS Victorious 230-277 and HMS Hermes 301-347. Carrier aircraft did not have codes containing 8 or 9, to avoid signalling confusion. Ashore, Portland used 500-539, Culdrose 540-599, Lossiemouth 600-699, Yeovilton 700-759 and Brawdy 760-817, with other miscellaneous units taking 818-999. It is not uncommon under this system for second line aircraft to omit the first digit of their code.

Essentially this system remains in use to the present day, though with some modifications. It no longer includes Commando squadrons, which in 1971 adopted their own system comprising a unit letter and an individual letter. Some reorganisation within the blocks had taken place by 1975. HMS Ark Royal retained its 001-057 range, but HMS Eagle had gone out of service and its codes largely reallocated. 060-063 were now for use by a Sea King pool, 064-065 by RSRE Malvern, 100-127 by a Sea Harrier pool, 140-145 by HMS Tiger and 200-227 by HMS Bulwark. The former HMS Victorious air group had transferred to HMS Hermes in 1968, taking with it the code range 250-277. This had left vacant the 301-347 range, which was partially used to provide codes 300-317 to the new FAA base at Prestwick, and partly to make further codes available for small ships flights, these by now using 320-347 in addition to the 400-477 range. HMS Invincible, then under construction, was allocated 350-357, but in the event never took it up.

Ashore, Portland was now using four ranges, 500-517, 610-617, 630-637 and 650-677. Culdrose had increased its single range to 540-599, whilst Yeovilton still used 700-759. By now Lossiemouth was at a much reduced strength and consequently had given up its 600-699 range in favour of 760-777. Apart from the Portland allocations already mentioned, this was reallotted as 600-607 to Honington, 620-627 to Leuchars and 640-647 to Yeovilton. As to the miscellaneous units, 810-829 was given to Lee-on-Solent, 830-880 to FRADU Yeovilton, 895-897 to BRNC Dartmouth and 901-912 to the BRNC AEF at Roborough.

Not all of these allocations were taken up, but they remain substantially the same at the time of writing. Honington and Leuchars no longer have a FAA presence, and their code allocations have been taken over by Culdrose and Portland respectively. HMS Invincible used 360-362 for a time on its helicopters, before taking over part of the old HMS Ark Royal range. Recent usage has been in the ranges 000-021 HMS Invincible, 123-127 HMS Illustrious, 264-275 814 Squadron, 300-319 Portland (station to close in 1999), 320-377 small ships flights, 400-479 small ships flights, 490-499 reserved for Royal New Zealand Navy, 500-599 Culdrose, 600-677 Portland, 700-708 Prestwick, 710-790 Yeovilton, 830-879 FRADU Yeovilton and 895-912 Dartmouth/Roborough.

Blackburn Baffin K4071 '536' of No.810 Squadron, HMS Courageous in 1936. (A.Curtis)

FLEET AIR ARM CODES 1933 - 1939

Codes	Sqdn	Ship	Years	Aircraft	Example
034-035	407	2nd Cruiser Sqdn	1936/37	Osprey	K3918 (034)
061	705	HMS Frobisher	1937	Seatutor	K2893 (061)
067-071	447/711	1st Cruiser Sqdn	1935/39	Osprey	K3642 (067)
				Walrus	L2194 (069)
072-073	444/701	1st Battle Sqdn	1935/37	IIIF	S1809 (072)
				Osprey	K3640 (073)
075-076	444	1st Battle Sqdn	1935/36	Walrus	
075-076	-	HMAS Sydney/HMAS Australia	1936	Seagull V	A2-2 (076)
073-076	701	1st Battle Sqdn	1937/39	Swordfish	K5930 (073)
078-079	445/713	3rd Cruiser Sqdn	1935/38	Osprey	K4322 (079)
081-082	447/711	1st Cruiser Sqdn	1936	Osprey	K3647 (082)
089-093	444/705	Capital ships	1936/39	Shark	K5624 (091)
				Swordfish	K5931 (092)
01-09) 1-3)	810	HMS Courageous	1933/36	Dart	N9823 (2)
				Ripon	S1562 (03)
				Baffin	K4078 (08)
4-16	811	HMS Furious	1933/35	Ripon	S1652 (14)
				Baffin	S1266 (13)
34-42	712	2nd Cruiser Sqdn	1937/39	Walrus	L2269 (38)
40-46	820A	HMS Courageous	1935/36	Baffin	S1553 (46)
43-45	715	5th Cruiser Sqdn	1938/39	Walrus	L2190 (43)
60-65) 70-75) 81-83)	812	HMS Glorious/HMS Furious/HMS Eagle	1933/36	Ripon	S1358 (83)
				Baffin	K3554 (60)
				Swordfish	K8868 (71)
71-76) 81-86)	824	HMS Eagle	1933/34	IIIF	S1821 (83)
71-76) 81-86)	825	HMS Eagle	1934/35	IIIF	S1474 (74)
102-125	800	HMS Courageous/HMS Ark Royal	1936/39	Nimrod	K2826 (106)
				Osprey	K5742 (108)
134-143	801	HMS Furious/HMS Courageous	1936/39	Nimrod	K2818 (135)
				Osprey	K3916 (138)
			1939	S Gladiator	N5502 (135)
147	712	2nd Cruiser Sqdn	1938/39	Walrus	L2280 (147)
178-206	FRU	Lee/Portland	1939	Swordfish	L2772 (182)
201-209	800	HMS Courageous	1933/34	Nimrod	S1619 (206)
206-207	407	2nd Cruiser Sqdn	1933/36	Osprey	K2774 (206)
208-210	800	HMS Courageous	1933/36	Osprey	K2779 (208)
214	407	2nd Cruiser Sqdn	1936	Osprey	K4329 (214)
234-236	801	HMS Furious	1934/36	Osprey	K3622 (234)
285-295	803	HMS Eagle/HMS Hermes	1933/37	Osprey	K2782 (286)
304-307	406/714	4th Cruiser Sqdn	1934/39	Osprey	K3630 (304)
				Walrus	L2255 (305)
501-510	800	HMS Courageous	1933/36	Nimrod	K2913 (503)
512-514	801	HMS Furious	1933/34	Flycatcher	
516-521	801	HMS Furious	1933/36	Nimrod	K2831 (519)
523-537	810	HMS Courageous/HMS Ark Royal	1936/39	Baffin	S1650 (530)
				Shark	K8486 (531)
				Swordfish	K8441 (534)
548-560	802	HMS Glorious	1933/34	Osprey	K3628 (548)
561-563) 571-578)	802	HMS Glorious	1933/39	Nimrod	K3656 (561)
580-590	813	HMS Eagle	1937/39	Swordfish	K8396 (587)
590-594	403	5th Cruiser Sqdn	1935/36	Osprey	K3644 (590)
601-614	811	HMS Furious/HMS Courageous	1935/39	Baffin	K4074 (610)
				Swordfish	K6006 (602)
645-659	820	HMS Courageous	1935/39	Shark	K4356 (653)
				Swordfish	L2718 (652)
678-691	821	HMS Courageous/HMS Ark Royal	1936/39	Shark	K5610 (685)
				Swordfish	K6000 (678)
701-714	822	HMS Furious	1933/35	IIIF	S1489 (709)
701-710	814	HMS Ark Royal	1938/39	Swordfish	K9779 (702)
716-720	444	Capital ships	1933/36	IIIF	S1807 (716)
				Seal	K3479 (719)
				Osprey	
721-735	821	HMS Courageous	1933/36	IIIF	S1189 (726)
738-750	820	HMS Courageous	1933/35	IIIF	S1546 (741)
				Seal	K3521 (750)
				Shark	K4354 (742)
769-781	718	8th Cruiser Sqdn	1936/39	IIIF	S1859 (780)
				Walrus	K8340 (769)
790-791	718	8th Cruiser Sqdn	1936/38	Osprey	K5746 (791)
801-807	823	HMS Glorious	1933/34	IIIF	S1356 (820)
801-814	823	HMS Courageous	1935/39	Seal	K3542 (801)
				Swordfish	K5973 (806)
810-816	447	Capital ships	1933/36	IIIF	S1395 (815)
				Osprey	K3634 (816)
820-834	823	HMS Glorious	1933/34	IIIF	S1312 (829)
830-843	825	HMS Eagle/HMS Glorious	1935/36	IIIF	S1785 (840)
870-891	824	HMS Hermes/HMS Eagle	1934/37	Seal	K4222 (871)
901-921	822	HMS Furious/HMS Courageous	1936/39	IIIF	S1395 (918)
				Seal	K4780 (907)
				Shark	K5657 (902)
				Swordfish	K6009 (912)
945-954	824	HMS Eagle	1937/39	Swordfish	K8389 (951)
967-981	825	HMS Glorious	1937/39	Swordfish	K5976 (978)

Fairey Seal K3519 '804' of No.823 Squadron, HMS Courageous bearing the pennant of Rear Admiral Sir Alexander Ramsey.

FLEET AIR ARM CODES 1939 - 1947

Code	Sqdn	Ship or Base	Years	Aircraft	Example		Code	Sqdn	Ship or Base	Years	Aircraft	Example	
A1	754	Arbroath	1943	Lysander	?	(A1M)	C3	815	HMS Courageous	1939	not used	-	-
				Albacore	?	(A1F)	C3	711/785/786	Crail	1943/45	Anson I	?	(C3B)
A1	767/769	Arbroath	1943	Swordfish							Barracuda II	LS778	(C3R)
A1	737	Arbroath	1945	Barracuda II	DP851	(A1Z)	C3	800	29th Naval F Wg	1945	Hellcat IINF	JZ999	(C3H)
				Barracuda III			C4	816	HMS Courageous	1939	not used		
A1	827	HMS Colossus	1945	Barracuda II	MX637	(A1X)	C4	711/785/786	Crail	1943/45	Barracuda II	LS588	(C4S)
A2	810	HMS Ark Royal	1939/40	Swordfish I	L2739	(A2G)					Avenger	?	(C4Y)
A2	812	HMS Argus	1942	Swordfish I	?	(A2F)					Swordfish I	L9739	(C4X)
A2	741	Arbroath	1943	Swordfish	?	(A2H)	C5	817	HMS Courageous	1939	not used	-	-
A2	737	Arbroath	1944/45	Swordfish I	LS446	(A2C)	C5	711/785/786	Crail	1943/45	Albacore I	X9157	(C5M)
				Anson I	NK834	(A2T)					Barracuda II	MD708	(C5F)
A3	814	HMS Ark Royal	1939	Swordfish I	?	(A3H)					Avenger	?	(C5X)
A3	818	HMS Ark Royal	1939	Swordfish I	?	(A3A)	C6	804	HMS Courageous	1939	not used		
A3	753	Arbroath	1943	Swordfish I	?	(A3S)	C6	711	Crail	1944/45	Barracuda II	BV695	(C6L)
A3	741	Arbroath	1943/44	Swordfish I	W5917	(A3Z)					Reliant	?	(C6B)
				Swordfish II	HS223	(A3C)					Avenger	?	(C6A)
A4	820	HMS Ark Royal	1939/40	Swordfish I	L2731	(A4G)	C6	804	29th Naval F Wg	1945	Hellcat II		
A4	740	Arbroath	1943	Albacore	?	(A4X)	C7	805	HMS Courageous	1939	not used		
A4	751	Arbroath	1943	Walrus	?	(A4D)	C7	786	Crail	1944/45	Anson I	NK764	(C7C)
A4	753	Arbroath	1943/45	Swordfish	?	(A4F)					Swordfish	?	(C7G)
				Albacore	BF737	(A4X)					Reliant	?	(C7G)
				Barracuda II			C7	808	29th Naval F Wg	1945	Hellcat II	JZ788	(C7J)
A4	719/794/795	HMS Implacable	1946/47	Firefly FR.I	MB745	(A4P)	C8	705	Battle Cr Sq	1939	used B8 instead	-	-
							C8	701	1st Battle Sqdn	1939/40	Swordfish I	K8362	(C8A)
A5	821	HMS Ark Royal	1939/40	Swordfish I	L7682	(A5Z)	C8	770	Crail	1942/44	Skua II	L2952	(C8S)
A5	818	HMS Ark Royal	1940	Swordfish I	?	(A5C)	C8	786	Crail	1945	Anson I	?	(C8B)
A5	754	Arbroath	1943	Lysander	?	(A5F)					Reliant	?	(C8B)
				Albacore	?	(A5C)							
A5	740	Arbroath	1943	Walrus	?	(A5A)	C8	804	29th Naval F Wg	1945	Hellcat II	JX808	(C8Q)
A5	753	Arbroath	1943/45	Albacore	X9022	(A5N)	C8	733	China Bay	1945/46	Barracuda II	LS672	(C8K)
				Barracuda II	MX655	(A5B)					Avenger I	JZ144	(C8B)
				Reliant	?	(A5H)					Avenger II	JZ357	(C8G)
A5	794	HMS Implacable	1946/47	Seafire III	RX248	(A5G)	C9	718	8th Cruiser Sq	1939/40	Seafox	K8591	(C9M)
A6	800	HMS Ark Royal	1939/40	Skua II	L2938	(A6M)	C9	St F	Crail	1945	Anson I	NK840	(C9A)
				Roc I			C9	733	China Bay	1944/45	Wildcat V	JV430	(C9O)
A6	783	Arbroath	1943	Anson I	?	(A6N)	C0	778	Crail	1943/44	Swordfish I	P4213	(C0)
				Swordfish	?	(A6E)					Barracuda II	BV810	(C0)
A6	753	Arbroath	1944/45	Barracuda II	LS868	A6Q					Martlet IV	FN153	(C0)
A6	1833	15th Naval F Wg	1944/45	Corsair II	JT672	(A6K)					Firefly I	?	(C0)
A7	803	HMS Ark Royal	1939	Skua II	L2874	(A7C)					Corsair	?	(C0)
A7	801	HMS Ark Royal	1940	Skua II	L2907	(A7A)	D1	737	Dunino	1943	Walrus I	X9571	(D1X)
A7	753	Arbroath	1944/45	Barracuda II	?	(A7B)	D1	784	Drem	1945/46	Firefly INF	MB558	(D1E)
A7	1830	15th Naval F Wg	1944/45	Corsair II	JT443	(A7R)	D1	790B	Drem	1946	Firefly INF	MB440	(D1U)
A8	803	HMS Ark Royal	1940	Skua II	L3010	(A8B)	D2	732/784	Drem	1945/46	Anson I	?	(D2E)
A8	791	Arbroath	1942/44	Swordfish I	L9737	(A8J)					Hellcat IINF	JZ907	(D2W)
				Swordfish II	HS367	(A8T)	D3	784	Drem	1945/46	Anson I	MG473	(D3A)
				Skua II	L3034	(A8Q)	D4	?	Donibristle?	1943	Albacore I	L7173	(D4S)
				Roc I	L3092	(A8A)	D4	879	4th Naval F Wg	1944/45	Seafire IIc		
				Defiant TT.I	N1617	(A8N)					Seafire III	PR292	(D4Y)
				Sea Hurricane Ib	?	(A8X)	D5	779	not used	1939	not used		
				Blenheim IV	?	(A8J)	D5	807	4th Naval F Wg	1944/45	Seafire III	NF630	(D5H)
A9	710	HMS Albatross	1939/40	Walrus I	L2334	(A9K)	D5	784	Drem	1945/46	Hellcat IINF	KE122	(D5K)
A9	791?	Arbroath	1944	Albacore	?	(A9Y)	D6	885	3rd Naval F Wg	1942/43	Seafire IIc	MB145	(D6K)
A9	St F	Arbroath	1945	Reliant	?	(A9D)					Seafire III	NN189	(D6D)
				Swordfish	L9780	(A9N)	D6	809	3rd Naval F Wg	1945	Seafire III	NF497	(D6Y)
A0	783	Arbroath	1943/47	Anson I	NK211	(A0Z)	D8	722	battleships	1939	not used		
				Wellington I	L4244?	(A0F)	D8	770	Drem	1944/45	Seafire IIc	LR639	(D8J)
				Firefly FR.I	?	(A0P)					Blenheim IV	R3871	(D8W)
				Avenger I	FN897	(A0F)	D9	723	catapult ship	1939	not used	-	-
				Barracuda II	MD652	(A0M)	E1	?	East Haven	?	Anson I	NK954	(E1V)
				Walrus	?	(A0D)	E1	767/769	East Haven	1944/46	Firefly I	Z1889	(E1J)
				DH.86	AX840?	(A0P)					Barracuda II	BV737	(E1P1)
				Swordfish II	LS442	(AOR)	E2	767/769	East Haven	1943/45	Swordfish	?	(E2R)
B1	814	HMS Venerable	1945	Barracuda II	PM687	(B1L)					Albacore I	X9109	(E2A)
B2	768	East Haven/Donibristle	1944/45	Spit Vb/hooked	?	(B2M)	E2	768	East Haven	1945/46	Seafire III	NF855	(E2A)
				Swordfish	?	(B2B)					Corsair IV	KD431	(E2M)
				Barracuda	?	(B2J)					Barracuda II	DP887	(E2N)
				Traveller	FT516	(B2G)	E3	731	East Haven	1943/5	Swordfish	HS158	(E3E)
				Firefly I	?	(B2H)					Seafire Ib	MB335	(E3Y)
B7	896	HMS Empress	1945	Hellcat II							Barracuda II	P9805	(E3G)
B8	701	1st Battle Sqdn	1939	used C8 instead	-	-					Firefly I	Z2116	(E3J)
B8	705	Battle Cr Sqdn	1939/40	Swordfish I	L7680	(B8F)					Fulmar II	?	(E3F5)
B8	770	Donibristle	1944/45	Blenheim IV	Z6271	(B8X)					Corsair III	JS853	(E3S)
B8	896	HMS Empress	1945	Hellcat II	JX688	(B8H)	E4	813	HMS Eagle	1939/42	Swordfish I	P4159	(E4G)
B8	782	Donibristle	1946	Dominie I	NF881	(B8H)	E4	769	East Haven	1943/45	Barracuda II	LS535	(E4K)
B9	?	carrier	1945	Wildcat			E4	731?	East Haven	1945	Firefly I	?	(E4H)
B9	898	HMS Pursuer	1945	Hellcat II	JX995	(B9R)	E5	824	HMS Eagle	1939/42	Swordfish I	K8414	(E5G)
B0	784	Drem	1944/45	Fulmar I	N4146	(B0J)	E6	731?	East Haven	1944/45	Firefly I	Z1870	(E6E)
				Fulmar I	DR725	(B0A)	E8	702	2nd Battle Sq	1939/40	Swordfish	P4199	(E8F)
				Anson I	N9608	(B0AC)	E8	St F	East Haven	1944/45	Barracuda II	?	(E8D)
				Reliant I	FK913	(B0S)					Reliant	?	(E8B)
B0	898	HMS Pursuer	1945	Hellcat II	JX731	(B0Q)					Tiger Moth II	?	(E8C)
C1	711/785/786	Crail	1943/45	Swordfish I	V4505	(C1L)	F1	714/717/747	Fearn	1944	Barracuda II	DP894	(F1E)
				Swordfish II	HS427	(C1X)	F2	714/717/747	Fearn	1944	Barracuda II	LS683	(F2G)
				Albacore I	N4221	(C1N)							
				Barracuda II	LS873	(C1V)	F3	826	HMS Formidable	1939	not used	-	-
				Avenger I	JZ150	(C1J)	F4	829	HMS Formidable	1940	not used	-	-
C2	711/785/786	Crail	1943/45	Swordfish I	W5904	(C2G)	F4	826	HMS Formidable	1940	Albacore I?		
				Albacore I	?	(C2G)	F4	747?	Fearn	1945	Barracuda II		
				Anson I	?	(C2W)	F5	830	HMS Formidable	1939	not used	-	-
				Barracuda II	LS649	(C2A)	F5	829	HMS Formidable	1940	Albacore I?		
				Avenger I	FN795	(C2Y)	F6	808	HMS Formidable	1939/40	not used	-	-

Code	Sqdn	Ship or Base	Years	Aircraft	Example		Code	Sqdn	Ship or Base	Years	Aircraft	Example	
F8	721	not formed	1939	not used	-	-	L1	780	Lee-on-Solent contd		Swordfish I Proctor Ia	?	(L1R)
F9	711	1st Cruiser Sq	1939/40	Walrus	L2261	(F9C)	L1	798	Lee-on-Solent	1943/44	Barracuda II		
F9	St F	Fearn	1945	Reliant	FK9..	(F9C)					Blenheim I	L6764	(L1N)
G1	?	Henstridge		Swordfish III	NS200	(G1I)					Beaufort I	LR927	(L1L)
G1	718/761	Henstridge	1943/45	Spitfire Vb	AB201	(G1U)					Beaufighter II	T3223	(L1P)
				Seafire Ib	NX957	(G1A)					Seafire IIc	?	(L1P)
				Seafire III	NN568	(G1E)	L1	799?	Lee-on-Solent	1946	Oxford	?	(L1A)
G2	761	Henstridge	1944/45	Seafire III	NN257	(G2R)	L2	760	Lee-on-Solent	1945	Seafire III	NN174	(L2T)
G3	812	HMS Glorious	1939/40	Swordfish I	K8867	(G3P)	L2	798	Lee-on-Solent	1943/45	Master II	?	(L2C)
G3	718	Henstridge	1944/45	Spitfire PR.XIII	P8784	(G3L)					Barracuda II	?	(L2X)
G3	718/761	Henstridge	1945	Seafire III	NF482	(G3I)					Firefly I	?	(L2J)
G4	823	HMS Glorious	1939/40	Swordfish I	L9763	(G4H)					Harvard III	FT962	(L2W)
G4	761	Henstridge	1944/45	Seafire III	NF536	(G4L)	L3	815	HMS Illustrious	1940	Swordfish I	?	(L3R)
G5	825	HMS Glorious	1939/40	Swordfish I	P3992	(G5K)	L3	765	Lee-on-Solent/Sandbanks	1942/43	Walrus I	R6552	(L3T)
G5	761	Henstridge	1944	Seafire III	NF510	(G5P)							
				Defiant TTIII	N1726	(G5H)	L3	798	Lee-on-Solent	1944/45	Spitfire Vb		
G6	802	HMS Glorious	1939/40	Sea Gladiator	N5519	(G6A)					Seafire IIc	?	(L3L)
G6	761	Henstridge	1944/45	Seafire III	PP973	(G6R)					Tiger Moth II	T7034	(L3D)
G8	700	Hatston HQ Flight	1940	Walrus?							Harvard IIb	KF555	(L3D)
G9	712	2nd Cruiser Sq	1939/40	Walrus I	L2280	(G9K)					Harvard III	FT957	(L3M)
G9	St F	Henstridge	1943/46	Reliant I	FB526	(G9A)					Avenger II	JZ467	(L3A)
				Tiger Moth	T7695	(G9E)	L4	819	HMS Illustrious	1939	used L5 instead	-	-
H1	845	HMS Empress	1945	Avenger II	JZ100	(H1P)	L4	815	HMS Illustrious	1940	Swordfish I	?	(L4Q)
H2	New	HMS Hermes	1939	not formed	-	-	L4	826	HMS Illustrious (not embarked)	1940	Albacore I	?	(L4G)
H3	814	HMS Hermes	1939/41	Swordfish I	?	(H3G)							
H5	818	HMS Hermes	1939	not used	-	-	L4	798	Lee-on-Solent	1945	Seafire IIc	?	(L4B)
H5	887	24th Naval F Wg	1944/45	Seafire III	LR628?	(H5S)	L5	826	HMS Illustrious	1939	not used	-	-
H6	894	24th Naval F Wg	1944/45	Seafire III	NN460	(H6Z)	L5	819	HMS Illustrious	1940/41	Swordfish I	P4075	(L5Q)
H8	713	3rd Cruiser Sq	1939	used H9 instead	-	-	L6	806	HMS Illustrious	1940	Skua II	L3012	(L6K)
H9	713	3rd Cruiser Sq	1939/40	Seafox I	K8587	(H9A)					Roc I	L3075	(L6R)
H9	712	Hatston	1944/45	Reliant	?	(H9B)	L8	781	Lee-on-Solent	1843	Oxford II	L6180	(L8O)
				Sea Otter	?	(H9S)	L8	765	Lee-on-Solent	1944/45	Wellington X	NC826	(L8F)
I1	714	Rattray	1945	Barracuda II							Wellington XI	HZ361	(L8B)
I1	766	Rattray	1946	Firefly FR.I	MB722	(I1B)	L8	799	Lee-on-Solent	1945/46	Firefly I	Z2051	(L8A)
I2	714	Rattray	1945	Barracuda II	P9744	(I2C)					Anson I	DJ561	(L8J)
I2	766	Rattray	1946	Firefly FR.I	MB641	(I2A)	L9	716	6th Cruiser Sq	1939/40	Seafox?		
I3	714/717	Rattray	1945	Barracuda II	?	(I3L)	L9	781	Lee-on-Solent	1942/45	Oxford I	V3390	(L9B)
											Dominie	X7350	(L9C)
I3	766	Rattray	1946	Firefly FR.I	DK526	(I3X)					Vega Gull	P5987	(L9H)
I4	717	Rattray	1945	Barracuda II	?	(I4V)					Walrus	?	(L9U)
I5	769	Rattray	1945	Barracuda II	?	(I5F)					Proctor Ia	P6068	(L9F)
I6	769	Rattray	1945	Barracuda II	?	(I6A)					Swordfish I	V4378	(L9S)
I6	766	Rattray	1946	Firefly FR.I	MB731	(I6C)					Fulmar II	DR635	(L9E)
I6		Rattray?		Seafire III	NN497	(I6J)	L9	762	Lee-on-Solent	1944	Beaufort I	LR901	(L9J)
I7	815	Rattray	1945/46	Barracuda III	ME248	(I7K)	L9	797	Colombo Rcse	1945	Beaufighter II	T3431	(L9Y)
I7	766	Rattray	1946	Firefly FR.I	MB641	(I7L)	L0	746	Wittering	1944	Fulmar II	DR714	(L0F)
I8	821	Rattray	1945/46	Barracuda III	?	(I8H)	L0	781	Lee-on-Solent	1944	Swordfish I	L8085?	(L0Z)
I9	St F	Eastleigh	1944/45	Oxford I	DF482	(I9A)	L0	781	Heath Row	1945	Hudson IV	AE635	(L0B)
				Monospar ST25	X9543	(I9B)	L0	701	Heston	1945/46	Oxford I	NM641	(L0A)
				Sea Otter I	JM870	(I9B)					Traveller	FT467	(L0F)
I0	716	Eastleigh	1945/46	Sea Otter I	JM801	(I0A)					Harvard III	EZ424	(L0E)
J1	794	Eglinton	1945/46	Corsair III	JS793	(J1R)					Dominie I	HG714	(L0R)
J2	794	Eglinton	1945/46	Seafire III							Seafire XV	SR485	(L0Z)
J3	794	Eglinton	1945	Wildcat VI	JV851	(J3V)					Expeditor I	FT976	(L0G)
J4	758X	Eglinton	1944	Oxford	?	(J4R)					Anson C.X	NK836	(L0Z)
J4	854	HMS Illustrious	1944	Avenger I			M1	836	Mac Wing	1944/45	Swordfish II	NF193	(M1B)
J4	794	Eglinton	1945	Martinet TT.I	NR654	(J4M)	M2	768	Machrihanish	1943	Wildcat II	AL241	(M2K)
J9	714	4th Cruiser Sq	1939/40	Walrus I	L2253	(J9G)					Sea Hurricane Ib	P2886	(M2B)
J9	St F	Eglinton	1944/45	Traveller	FT485	(J9A)					Spit Vb/hooked	?	(M2Y)
				Reliant	FK935	(J9C)					Seafire IIc	MA904	(M2T)
K1	756	Katukurunda	1945	Avenger I	JZ179	(K1N)	M2	836	Mac Wing	1944/45	Swordfish II	NE941	(M2B)
				Avenger II	JZ512	(K1B)	M3	836	Mac Wing	1944/45	Swordfish III	NS151	(M3V)
K1	760	Inskip	1944	Sea Hurricane IIc	NF739	(K1K)	M4	836	Mac Wing	1944/45	Swordfish III	NS173	(M4K)
K1	766	Inskip	1944/46	Swordfish II	HS435	(K1P)	M8	728	Ta Kali	1944/46	Martinet TT.I	?	(M8H)
				Swordfish III							Seafire L.IIc	MB281	(M8A)
				Firefly I	Z1902	(K1R)					Seafire L.III	NF521	(M8L)
				Sea Hurricane IIc	NF728	(K1F)					Mosquito B.25	KB647	(M8B)
K2	747	Inskip	1943/44	Barracuda II	P9828	(K2L)					Beaufort I ?		
K2	766	Inskip	1944/46	Swordfish II	LS423	(K2G)	M8	772	Machrihanish	1943/44	Chesapeake I	AL951	(M8E)
				Swordfish III							Fulmar II	BP786	(M8G)
K2	766	Inskip	1944/46	Firefly I	Z1890	(K2H)					Skua II	L2907	(M8L)
K3	766	Inskip	1944/46	Swordfish II	LS114	(K3L)					Walrus	?	(M8F)
				Swordfish III							Blenheim IV		(M8J)
				Master GT.II	DL487	(K3B)	M9	-	Reserve Cruiser	1939	not used		
K3	800	3rd Naval F Wg	1945	Hellcat II	JV304	(K3G)	M9	740	Machrihanish	1943/45	Walrus I	W2778	(M9N)
K4	737	Inskip	1944	Anson	?	(K4Y)					Reliant I	FL157	(M9L)
				Swordfish II	?	(K4B)					Oxford	?	(M9B)
K5	763	Inskip	1944/45	Avenger I	FN766	(K5M)	M9	SF	Machrihanish	1945	Traveller	FT499	(M9F)
				Avenger II	JZ353	(K5A)	N1	812	HMS Vengeance	1945	Barracuda II	PM758	(N1W)
K5	766	Inskip	1945/46	Firefly I	MB641	(K5L)	N3	831	HMS Indomitable	1939	not used	-	-
K6	808	3rd Naval F Wg	1944/45	Hellcat I	JV118	(K6Y)	N4	832	HMS Indomitable	1939	not used	-	-
				Hellcat II	JV321	(K6J)	N4	744	Maydown	1945	Barracuda II	?	(N4B)
K6	804	3rd Naval F Wg	1945	Hellcat II	JX807	(K6U)	N5	833	HMS Indomitable	1939	not used	-	-
K7	1840	3rd Naval F Wg	1944/45	Hellcat II	JX750	(K7P)	N5	1850	HMS Vengeance	1945	Corsair IV	KD269	(N5N)
K7	744	Machrihanish	1944	Swordfish II	?	(K7P)	N6	809	HMS Indomitable	1939	not used	-	-
K7	729	Katukurunda	1945/46	Oxford	PH137	(K7B)	N6	744	Maydown	1945	Barracuda II	?	(N6H)
K8	SF	Katukurunda	1944/45	Barracuda II							Barracuda III	RJ916	(N6C)
				Reliant	FL130	(K8A)					Avenger II	JZ...	(N6R)
K8	885	3rd Naval F Wg	1945	Hellcat II	JW740	(K8B)	N6	810	HMS Queen	1945	Barracuda III	ME226	(N6A)
K9	715	5th Cruiser Sq	1939/40	Walrus I	L2212	(K9C)	N7	880	HMS Indomitable	1940	not used	-	-
K9	772	Machrihanish	1942	Fulmar I	N4147	(K9B)	N7	744	Maydown	1944	Swordfish II	HS330	(N7F)
K9	SF	Inskip	1945	Firefly FR.I	?	(K9A)					Swordfish III	NS120	(N7X)
L1	780	Lee-on-Solent	1943	Barracuda II	?	(L1Y)	N8	723	Nowra	1945/46	Corsair	?	(N8AL)
				Blenheim I	L6764	(L1N)					Martinet TT.I	?	(N8O)
				Tiger Moth II	T7045	(L1B)	N9	718	8th Cruiser Sq	1939/40	not used?	-	-

455

Code	Sqdn	Ship or Base	Years	Aircraft	Example	
O1	735	Burscough	1945	Barracuda II		
				Barracuda III	MD849	(O1X)
O2	1702	HMS Ocean	1946	Sea Otter I	JN252	(O2C)
O4	774	Aldergrove	1939/40	Shark IITT ?		
				Swordfish I ?		
O4	735	Burscough	1945	Barracuda II	?	(O4F)
O4	1792	HMS Ocean	1945/46	Firefly INF	MB747	(O4F)
O5	775	Lee-on-Solent	1939/40	not used	-	-
O5	892	HMS Ocean	1945	Hellcat IINF	?	(O5B)
O5	805	HMS Ocean	1946/47	Seafire XV	PR477	(O5C)
				Firefly FR.I	PP561	(O5X)
O6	776	Allocation only	1939/40	not used	-	-
O6	816	HMS Ocean	1946/47	Firefly FR.I	PP553	(O6F)
Ø6	885	HMS Formidable	1942/43	Seafire IIc	MB119	(Ø6G)
Ø7	888	HMS Formidable	1942/43	Wildcat II	AJ148	(Ø7A)
O7	707	Burscough	1945	Swordfish II	LS445	(O7B)
				Swordfish III	NF309	(O7A)
O8	707	Burscough	1945	Barracuda III	ME166	(O8U)
O8	772	Burscough	1946	Martinet TT.I	?	(O8C)
O9	777	Allocation only	1939/40	not used	-	-
O9	St F	Burscough	1945	Reliant I	FB660	(O9G)
				Anson I	DJ545	(O9Y)
O9	772	Burscough	1946	Seafire III	NF559	(O9B)
Ø9	893	HMS Formidable	1942/43	Wildcat IV	FN148	(Ø9C)
O0	772?	Burscough?	1946?	Martinet TT.I	MS662	(O0E)
P1	794	Dale	1943	Sea Hurricane Ib	AF966	(P1V)
P1	762	Dale	1944/45	Beaufort TII	ML716	(P1U)
				Wellington XI	MP547	(P1Y)
P1	849	HMS Victorious	1945	Avenger I	JZ214	(P1L)
				Avenger II	JZ487	(P1J)
P2	794	Dale	1943	Master II	W9026	(P2P)
P2	762	Dale	1944/45	Oxford	MP292	(P2J)
P2	790?	Dale	1946	Firefly I	?	(P2N)
P3	784	Dale	1946	Anson I	?	(P3A)
P3	790?	Dale	1945/46	Oxford	HN705	(P3Y)
				Seafire III	NN609	(P3N)
P3	1701?	Ponam	1946	Sea Otter	?	(P3A)
P5	763	Lee-on-Solent	1940	Swordfish I	?	(P5H)
P5	887	24th Naval F Wg	1944	Seafire III	LR887	(P5H)
P6	894	24th Naval F Wg	1944	Seafire III	?	(P6N)
P6	801	30th Naval F Wg	1945	Seafire III		
P7	760	Eastleigh/Yeovilton	1940	Skua II ?		
				Roc I ?		
P7	801/880	30th Naval F Wg	1945	Seafire III	PR189	(P7N)
P7	748	Dale	1944/45	Corsair III	JS511	(P7AE)
				Hellcat I	FN332	(P7AP)
P8	794	Dale	1943	Defiant TT.I	DR974	(P8M)
				Martinet TT.I	JN588	(P8E)
P8	801	30th Naval F Wg	1945	Seafire III	PP994	(P8Q)
P8	784	Dale	1946	Firefly I	MB577	(P8P)
P8	790B	Dale	1946/47	Firefly I	MB577	(P8P)
P9	720	New Zealand Sq	1939/40	Walrus I	L2222	(P9A)
P9	766	Lee-on-Solent	1940	not used	-	-
P9	St F	Dale	1945/46	Reliant I	FB567	(P9D)
				Oxford I	V4146	(P9C)
				Anson I	..995	(P9K)
P0	SF	Dale	1945/46	Mosquito B25	KB602	(P0E)
Q1	781	Lee-on-Solent	1940			
Q2	?	?		Firefly FR.I	MB465	(Q2K)
Q4	854	HMS Illustrious	1944/45	Avenger I	JZ110	(Q4Q)
Q6	780	Lee-on-Solent	1939/40	no evidence of use		
Q9	St F	Belfast	1944/45	Oxford I	HM613	(Q9F)
				Reliant I	FK925	(Q9D)
R1	FP?	Stretton	1943	Proctor	?	(R1B)
R1	814	HMS Venerable	1945	Barracuda	MX710	(R1L)
R2	812	HMS Argus	1942	Swordfish I		
R2	710/713/747	Ronaldsway	1945	Barracuda II	LS835	(R2R)
				Barracuda III	MD901	(R2B)
R3	772	Portland/Lee	1939	Swordfish I	?	(R3C)
R3	710/713/747	Ronaldsway	1945	Barracuda II	MD617	(R3P)
				Barracuda III	MD892	(R3M)
R4	773	Bermuda	1940/41	Swordfish I	P4203	(R4A)
				Walrus I	L2266	(R4C)
R4	710/713/747	Ronaldsway	1945	Barracuda II	?	(R4W)
R5	771	Hatston/Twatt	1939/43	Swordfish I	L7679	(R5G)
				Henley III	L3368	(R5M)
				Skua II	L3046	(R5G)
				Roc I	L3177	(R5D)
				Defiant TTI	DR885	(R5Q)
				Chesapeake	AL927	(R5S)
R5	1839	5th Naval F Wg	1944/45	Hellcat I	FN434	(R5K)
				Hellcat II	JW859	(R5B)
R5	710/713/747	Ronaldsway	1945	Barracuda II	?	(R5Z)
R6	1844	5th Naval F Wg	1944/45	Hellcat I	FN383	(R6F)
				Hellcat II	JX723	(R6R)
R6	1851	HMS Venerable	1945	Corsair IV	KD215	(R6L)
R6	710/713/747	Ronaldsway	1945	Barracuda II	MD530?	(R6N)
R7	710/713/747	Ronaldsway	1945	Barracuda III	MX776	(R3M)
R7	776	Woodvale	1945	Hurricane FB.IIc	LF656	(R7B)
R8	797	Colombo	1944/45	Defiant TT	?	(R8S)
R8	776	Woodvale	1944/45	Martinet TT.I	MS585	(R8Q)
				Swordfish II	LS234	(R8M)
				Traveller I	FT535	(R8F)
				Hurricane FB.IIc	LF798?	(R8L)
R9	St F	Stretton	1944/45	Reliant I	FK940	(R9A)
				Wellington	?	(R9P)
R0	St F	Ronaldsway	1945/46	Reliant I	FK917	(R0N)
				Expeditor	FR882	(R0Q)
S1	719	St Merryn	1944/45	Spitfire Vb	AB929	(S1K)
				Wildcat IV	?	(S1S)
S1	794	St Merryn	1945	Seafire IIc	MA977	(S1G)
S2	741	St Merryn	1946/47	Firefly FRI	PP479	(S2Q)
S3	709	St Merryn	1944/46	Harvard IIb	KF559	(S3V)
				Harvard III	EZ274	(S3N)
S3	736/741	St Merryn	1946/47	Firefly FRI	MB723	(S3E)
				Barracuda II	?	(S3F)
S4	826	Dekheila	1941/43	Albacore I	X8980	(S4K)
S4	715	St Merryn	1945	Seafire III	NF551	(S4B)
				Seafire XVII	SX115	(S4L)
				Corsair III		
S5	828	Hal Far	1941/43	Albacore I	X8942	(S5B)
S5	821	Dekheila	1942	Albacore I	T9207	(S5L)
S5	709	St Merryn	1944/45	Hellcat I	JV152	(S5A)
				Hellcat II	JV247	(S5H)
				Seafire III	NF493	(S5N)
				Seafire F.45	LA449	(S5A)
S5	741	St Merryn	1946/47	Firefly FR.I	MB755	(S5M)
				Seafire XVII	SX198	(S5N)
S6	803	Wick/Hatston	1940	Skua II		
S6	774	St Merryn	1942/44	Swordfish I	P4086	(S6D)
				Albacore I	X9041	(S6K)
				Barracuda II	?	(S6H)
S6	815	Mersa Matruh	1943	Swordfish II	HS180	(S6B)
S6	709	St Merryn	1944/45	Hellcat I	JV129	(S6A)
S7	804	Hatston/Belfast	1940/42	Wildcat I	BJ561	(S7L)
				Sea Hurricane Ia		
				Sea Hurricane Ib	Z7148	(S7D)
S7	815	Mersa Matruh	1943	Albacore I	N4242	(S7A)
S7	748	St Merryn	1943/46	Wildcat I	AX829	(S7O)
				Wildcat V		
				Wildcat VI	?	(S7D)
				Corsair III	JS498	(S7.)
				Corsair IV		
				Spitfire Va	R6722	(S7H)
				Seafire Ib	PA110	(S7B)
				Seafire III	NN336	(S7P)
S8	792	St Merryn	1944	Martinet TT.I	MS660	(S8C)
				Defiant TT.III	?	(S8S)
S9	St F	St Merryn	1944/45	Reliant I	FK895	(S9O)
T3	758?		1943/44	Anson I	LT346	(T3R)
T4	767	Donibristle/Hyeres/Arbroath	1939/42	Swordfish I	L2719	(T4G)
				Albacore I	?	(T4C)
T5	768	Donibristle	1940	not taken up	-	-
T6	769	Donibristle	1939	Sea Gladiator	N5500	(T6L)
T7	770	Lee-on-Solent/Hyeres	1939/40	no information on use		
T7	1834	47th Naval F Wg	1945	Corsair II	JT696	(T7M)
T8	771	Twatt	1942/45	Blenheim IV	T2322	(T8A)
				Martinet TT.I	NR632	(T8Q)
				Boston III	W8282	(T8B)
				Corsair II	JT487	(T8N)
				Roc I	L3104	(T8G)
				Skua II	L3025	(T8M)
				Swordfish I	W5918	(T8W)
				Gladiator	N2299	(T8K)
				Hurricane IIc	PG47.	(T8N)
				Boston II, III	AH507	(T8A)
				Havoc I	AW396	(T8C)
T8	722	Tambaram	1944/45	Reliant	?	(T8A)
T8	1836	47th Naval F Wg	1945	Corsair II	JT422	(T8B)
T9	722	Tambaram	1944/45	Martinet TT.I	PX134	(T9Z)
T9	St F	Twatt	1945	Reliant	FK889	(T9.)
TΘ	767	Donibristle/Hyeres	1939/40	Swordfish	P4020	(TΘC)
T0	767	Arbroath	1941	Albacore I	?	(T0G)
U1	758		1942/46	Oxford	DF393	(U1G)
U1	827	HMS Colossus	1945	Barracuda II	PM769	(U1B)
U1	780	Hinstock	1946	Seafire XV	SR593	(U1H)
				Oxford	?	(U1G)
				Firefly I	MB475	(U1L)
U2	758	Hinstock	1942/46	Oxford	PH248	(U2JJ)
				Harvard III	EZ381	(U2S)
				Tiger Moth II	?	(U2FF)
U2	798	Hinstock/Peplow	1945/46	Harvard III	EZ396	(U2K)
U2	780	Hinstock/Peplow	1946	Harvard IIb	KF522	(U2R)
				Harvard III	EZ381	(U2S)
U3	815	HMS Furious	1939/40	Swordfish I	L2810	(U3F)
U3	818	HMS Furious	1940	Swordfish I	?	(U3F)
U3	758	Hinstock	1942/46	Oxford	NM458	(U3S)
				Anson I	K6288	(U3F)
				Tiger Moth	BB723	(U3K)
				Harvard IIb	KF528	(U3XX)
				Harvard III	EZ421	(U3O)
U3	780	Hinstock	1945/46	Oxford	PG982	(U3EE)
U4	811	HMS Furious/HMS Courageous	1939	Swordfish I	?	(U4G)

Code	Sqdn	Ship or Base	Years	Aircraft	Example		Code	Sqdn	Ship or Base	Years	Aircraft	Example	
U4	816	HMS Furious	1939/40	Swordfish I	P4167	(U4B)	Y6	759	Eastleigh	1939/40	not taken up?		
U5	822	HMS Furious/ HMS Courageous	1939	Swordfish I	?	(U5G)	Y6	759	Yeovilton	1943/46	Seafire III Harvard III Wildcat V	PP999 EZ425	(Y6F) (Y6Q)
U5	1846	HMS Colossus	1945	Corsair IV	KD477	(U5A)					Corsair III	JS751	(Y6K)
U6	801	HMS Furious	1940	Skua II			Y7	760	Eastleigh	1940	Skua II		
U6	1846	HMS Colossus	1945	Corsair IV	KD344	(U6K)					Roc I		
U7	1846	HMS Colossus	1945	Corsair IV	KD681	(U7F)	Y7	759	Yeovilton	1944/45	Seafire		
V4	827	HMS Victorious	1939	not used	-	-					Corsair III	JS759	(Y7X)
V4	812	HMS Vengeance	1946	Firefly I	MB471	(V4C)	Y8	765	Lee-on-Solent	1939	Swordfish I	P4084	(Y8L)
V5	828	HMS Victorious	1939	not used	-	-					Seafox I	K8613	(Y8Q)
V6	807	HMS Victorious	1939	not used	-	-	Y8	794	Charlton Horethorne	1943/44	Defiant TT.I	DR974	(Y8L)
V8	1850	HMS Vengeance	1946	Corsair IV	KD849	(V8B)	Y8	1831	HMS Glory	1945	Corsair IV	KD413	(Y8.)
V9	776?	Woodvale?	1945	Martinet TT.I	RG888	(V9S)	Y9	766	Lee-on-Solent	1939	not taken up	-	-
W1	750	Ford/Piarco	1939/42	Shark II	L2361	(W1W)	Y9	764	Lee-on-Solent	1940	Swordfish I	?	(Y9F)
W1	857	HMSIndomitable	1945	Avenger II	JZ592	(W1S)	Y9	St F	Yeovilton	1944/45	Reliant I	FK954	(Y9K)
W2	749	Piarco	1941/45	Walrus	P5666	(W2QB)					Beaufort T.II	LR901	(Y9P)
				Goose	FO475	(W2A)					Anson I	LT346	(Y9G)
W3	752	Ford/Piarco	1939/45	Proctor I	P6030	(W3.)					Wellington XI	MP504	(Y9R)
				Proctor II/IIa	Z7239	(W3AS)	Y0	790	Charlton Horethorne	1942/45	Oxford	T1098	(Y0T)
W4	753	Lee-on-Solent/ Arbroath	1939/43	Shark II Swordfish I Albacore I	K8518 V5969 N4326	(W4F) (W4Z) (W4C)	Y0	St F	Yeovilton	1945	Oxford	T1098	(Y0T)
W4	760?	Yeovilton	1942	Sea Hurricane			YΘ	787	Wittering/ Tangmere	1943/45	Fulmar I Sea HurricaneIIc Swordfish	N4023 NF721 DK747	(YΘE) (YΘF) (YΘG)
W5	754	Lee-on-Solent/ Arbroath	1939/40	Seafox I Walrus	K8579 ?	(W5N) (W5B)							
W5	752	Piarco	1942/45	Reliant I	FK978	(W5V)	YΘ	736B	Speke/ Woodvale/Fearn	1945	Seafire L.III	NF586	(YΘH)
W6	793	Piarco	1942/45	Roc I Albacore	?	(W6C)	Z1	790	Zeals	1945	Mosquito B.25	KB576?	(Z1X)
W6	755	Worthy Down	1941/44	Lysander III Lysander IIIa Proctor IIa Seamew I	T1445 V9295 BV644 FN628	(W6K) (W6I) (W6F) (W6D)	Z8 Z8 Z0	771 790 790	Zeals Zeals Zeals	1945 1945 1945	Wildcat IV Firefly I Firefly I	FN270 Z2030 ?	(Z8M) (Z8M) (Z0H)
W7	760	Yeovilton	1941/42	Sea Hurricane Ib	V6700	(W7E)	AA4	751	Dundee	1944	Walrus	W2688	(AA4Y)
W7	793	Piarco	1942/45	Fulmar I, II	?	(W7C)	AA5	740	Arbroath	1943	Walrus	?	(AA5F)
W7	857	HMS Indomitable	1944	Avenger II	JZ565	(W7N)	AA5	751	Dundee	1944	Walrus	W3040	(AA5R)
W8	760	Yeovilton	1941/42	Sea Hurricane 1b	P3090	(W8E)	AC	736	St Merryn	1943/45	Barracuda II	DN633	(ACF)
W8	793	Piarco	1944/45	Martinet TT.I	?	(W8B)					Seafire Ib	NX908	(ACA)
W8	789	Wingfield	1944/45 1945	Martinet TT.I Beaufighter II	NR646 T3137	(W8A) (W8R)					Avenger II Wellington XI	?	(ACF) (ACX)
W9	789	Wingfield	1944/45	Beaufighter II	T7099	(W9Q)					Corsair III		
W9	751	Ford/Arbroath	1939/43	Walrus	L2172	(W9C)	AH4	735	Burscough	1944/45	Barracuda II Hellcat I	? JV198	(AH4D) (AH4P)
W9	760	Yeovilton	1941/44	Sea Hurricane Ib	Z4922	(W9D)	AH7	735	Burscough	1944/45	Anson I	NK762	(AH7S)
W0	750	Ford/Piarco	1940/42	Shark II	?	(W0Q)	AH8	St F	Burscough	1944/45	Reliant I	FK987	(AH8C)
W0	752	Ford	1940	Proctor 1a	?	(W0S)	AH8	707	Burscough	1945	Avenger III	JZ670	(AH8X)
W0	734	Worthy Down	1944/45	Whitley VII	Z9379	(W0X)	AR	772?	Ayr	1945	Defiant TT.III	N4001	(AR)
X2	755	Worthy Down	1939				AR1	705	Ronaldsway	1945	Swordfish II	?	(AR1A)
X3	756	Worthy Down	1939	not used?	-	-	AR2	710/ 713/747	Ronaldsway	1944/45	Barracuda II	?	(AR2L)
X3	755	Worthy Down	1939	Shark II	K5656	(X3L)					Anson I	NK738	(AR2Y)
X5	758	Worthy Down	1939/41	Skua II Osprey III Shark	M1296? K3618	(X5W) (X5B)	AR3	710/ 713/747	Ronaldsway	1944/45	Barracuda II	LS958	(AR3K)
X6	757	Worthy Down	1939	Osprey III	K3619	(X6P)	AR4	710/ 713/747	Ronaldsway	1944/45	Barracuda II	?	(AR3A)
X0	-	Exp autogyro	1939	not taken up?	-	-							
X0	778	Lee-on-Solent/ Arbroath	1939/40				AR5	710/ 713/747	Ronaldsway	1944/45	Barracuda II	?	(AR4L)
Y1	759	Yeovilton	1943/46	Sea Hurricane Ib Wildcat IV Wildcat V Spitfire I Spitfire Vb Seafire Ib Corsair III Wellington?	V7438 FN245 JV326 R7193 NX895 JS526 ?	(Y1C) (Y1R) (Y1A) (Y1M) (Y1O) (Y1M) (Y1N)	AR6 AR7 AR8	710 710 St F	Ronaldsway Ronaldsway Ronaldsway	1945 1945 1944/45	Barracuda II Barracuda II Oxford Anson I	? ? ED295 ?	(AR6F) (AR7X) (AR83) (AR8Z)
							AR8	772	Ayr	1945/46	Martinet TT.I Mosquito B.XVI Mosquito B.25	? MM364 KA948	(AR8H) (AR8O) (AR8Q)
Y1	837	HMS Glory	1945	Barracuda II	PM812	(Y1L)	AR9	772	Ayr	1945/46	Boston III Corsair III	W8274 JS549	(AR9L) (AR9R)
Y2	761	Gosport	1939	not taken up	-	-	AR0	730	Ayr	1945	Firefly I	Z2104	(AR0K)
Y2	759	Yeovilton	1943/46	Oxford Master I Spitfire Va/b Seafire III Sea HurricaneIb Corsair III Harvard III Wildcat IV Wildcat V	HN490 N7444 L1096 ? V6604 JS599 EZ406 FN125	(Y2H) (Y2H) (Y2W) (Y2B) (Y2O) (Y2G) (Y2Z) (Y2E)	AT1 AT2 AT3 AT4 BH1 BH2	714 714 717 717 718 718	Rattray Rattray Rattray Rattray Ballyhalbert Ballyhalbert	1944/45 1944/45 1944/45 1944/45 1945 1945	Barracuda II Barracuda II Barracuda II Barracuda II Seafire III Corsair III Corsair IV	? ? P9921 BV831 JS479	(AT1K) (AT2J) (AT3Q) (AT4B) (BH2Q)
							BH6	718	Ballyhalbert	1945	Seafire III		
							BL3	765	Sandbanks	1942/43	Kingfisher I Walrus	FN678 L2266	(BL3P) (BL3Y)
Y2	700	Yeovilton	1946	Firefly Seafire XV Oxford Harvard III	Z1986 SW907 DF453 EZ447	(Y2J) (Y2C) (Y2C) (Y2M)	BR8	772	Ayr	1944/45	Blenheim IV Firefly NF.II Beaufighter X	V5655 Z1874 RD323	(BR8J) (BR8W) (BR8N)
Y3	762	Gosport	1939	not taken up	-	-	BR8	772?	Ayr		Corsair III		
Y3	759	Yeovilton	1943/46	Wildcat IV Wildcat V Tiger Moth II Spitfire I Spitfire Vb Seafire IIc Seafire III Harvard III Corsair III	FN143 JV579 BB731 X4643 NM981 RX341 EZ433 JS771	(Y3O) (Y3V) (Y3T) (Y3.) (Y3I) (Y3C) (Y3U) (Y3L)	BR9 BR9 BR0 BY1 BY8 BY0	772? St F St F 780 794 790	Ayr Ayr Ayr Charlton Horethorne Charlton Horethorne Charlton Horethorne	1943/44 1943/44 1943/45	Corsair III Sea Otter Reliant Swordfish I Swordfish II Defiant TT.III Oxford	? JM974 FB559 L2265 HS549 ? MP293	(BR9C̄) (BR9P) (BR0Q) (BY1S) (BY1R) (BY8A) (BY0X)
Y4	763	Worthy Down	1939	Swordfish ?			EL0	St F	Eastleigh	1945/46	Reliant I	FK883	(EL0O)
Y4	759	Yeovilton	1943/46	Seafire III Wildcat V Corsair III	RX345 JV442 JS507	(Y4B) (Y4F) (Y4O)					Dauntless I Sea Otter I Tiger Moth II Wellington Ic	JT923 JM866 BB858 HF845	(EL0B) (EL0A) (EL0G) (EL0S)
Y5	764	Gosport	1939	not taken up	-	-							
Y5	759	Yeovilton	1943/46	Seafire III Corsair III Harvard III	NN577 JS517 EZ378	(Y5G) (Y5V) (Y5F)	FD1 FD3 FD3	813 704 704	Ford Ford Thorney Is	1945/46 1945 1945	Firebrand TF.IV Mosquito FB.VI MosquitoT.III	EK665 RF825 TV964	(FD1L) (FD3B) (FD3E)

457

CodeSqdn	Ship or Base	Years	Aircraft	Example		CodeSqdn	Ship or Base	Years	Aircraft	Example	
FD4 811	Ford	1945/46	Mosquito FB.VI	TE701	(FD4A)	GP9 771	Gosport	1945/47	Seafire L.III	RX345	(GP9R)
			Mosquito TR.33	TW238	(FD4Q)				Seafire XV	PR402	(GP9K)
FD5 762	Ford	1946/47	Oxford I	RR362	(FD5M)	GP0 771	Gosport	1945/47	Oxford I	RR361	(GP0A)
FD6 762	Ford	1946/47	Beaufort T.II	ML718	(FD6R)	HA3 762	Halesworth	1945/46	Beaufort T.II	ML716	(HA3U)
		1946/47	Mosquito T.III	TV954	(FD6H)			1945/46	Mosquito B.25	KA962	(HA3L)
			Mosquito FB.VI	TE813	(FD6R)	IT1 767	Milltown	1946/47	Firefly FR.I	Z1973	(IT1E)
FD8 720	Ford	1945/47	Anson I	NL122	(FD8Y)	IT2 767	Milltown	1946/47	Firefly FR.I	DK447	(IT2S)
			Oxford	V4201	(FD8F)	IT3 767	Milltown	1946/47	Firefly FR.I	?	(IT3M)
FD9 778	Ford	1946/47	Seafire III	RX173	(FD9R)				Seafire III	LR858	(IT3U)
			Seafire XV	SW862	(FD9M)	IT4 767	Milltown	1946/47	Firefly FR.I	?	(IT4W)
			Barracuda II	RK427	(FD9F)	IT5 767	Milltown	1946/47	Firefly FR.I	?	(IT5Z)
GP2 727	Gosport	1946/47	Tiger Moth II	DE373	(GP2F)	IT6 767	Milltown	1946/47	Firefly FR.I	Z2054	(IT6E)
			Harvard III	EZ442	(GP2Z)	IT7 767	Milltown	1946/47	Firefly FR.I	?	(IT7P)
			Seafire XV	SW807	(GP2X)	KM2 ?	?	c 1943/44	Wildcat	?	(KM2R)
GP8 771	Gosport	1945/47	Mosquito B.25	KA950	(GP8O)	ST9 St F	Stretton	1945	Dominie I	Z7253	(ST9A)
			Martinet TT.I	RG882	(GP8K)				Oxford I	PH362	(ST9H)

****

SINGLE LETTER UNIT CODES 1944-1945

CodeSqdn	Ship or Base	Years	Aircraft	Example		CodeSqdn	Ship or Base	Years	Aircraft	Example	
A 879	HMS Attacker	1943/44	Seafire IIc	MB317	(A:E)	O 806B	HMS Illustrious	1942	Fulmar II	BP782	(O:R)
			Seafire III	NF595	(A:V)	O 708	Gosport	1944	Firebrand TF.II	DK383	(O:C)
B 881	HMS Illustrious	1942	Wildcat V	AM974	(B:J)	P 856	HMS Premier	1945	Avenger II	JZ603	(P:D)
B 750	Piarco	1944/45	Barracuda II	LS787	(B:9)				Wildcat VI	JV761	(P:S)
C 899	HMS Chaser	1945	Seafire III	NF575	(C:V)	P 757	Puttalam	1945	Reliant I	FB598	(P75)
E 800	HMS Emperor	1944/45	Hellcat I	JV102	(E:B)				Harvard IIb	KF552	(P93)
			Hellcat II	JV227	(E:F)				Seafire III	NN178	(P35)
F 842	HMS Fencer	1944	Wildcat V	JV596	(F:3)	Q 853	HMS Queen	1945	Avenger II	JZ456	(Q:K)
			Swordfish II	LS354	(F:H)				Wildcat VI	JV706	(Q:T)
G 813	HMS Campania	1944/45	Swordfish II	NR988	(G:A)	S 809	HMS Stalker	1944/45	Seafire IIc	MB269	(S:A)
H 807	HMS Hunter	1944	Seafire IIc	LR747	(H:J)				Seafire III	NN390	(S:L)
			Seafire III	NM995	(H:F)	S 882	HMS Searcher	1945	Wildcat VI	JV768	(S:X)
J 846	HMS Trumpeter	1945	Avenger I	FN903	(J:Q)	S 851	HMS Shah	1945	Avenger I	FN939	(S:V)
			Avenger II	JZ590	(J:F)	T 853	HMS Tracker	1944/45	Avenger II	JZ397	(T:F)
			Wildcat VI	JV665	(J:F)				Wildcat VI	JV729	(T:Z)
K 756	Katukurunda	1943/44	Swordfish II	LS348	(K:L)	T 757	Tambaram	1945	Corsair IV	KD361	(T79)
K 899	HMS Khedive	1943/44	Seafire III	NN344	(K:O)	U 881	HMS Pursuer	1944/45	Wildcat VI	JV705	(U:Y)
N 821	HMS Puncher	1945	Barracuda II	?	(N:Y)	Y 835	HMS Nairana	1944/45	Swordfish III	NR939	(Y:C)
			Barracuda III	MD841	(N:L)	Z 835	HMS Nairana	1945	Swordfish III	NS196	(Z:B)

****

V-CODES USED IN USA 1944-1945

CodeSqdn	Ship or Base	Years	Aircraft	Example		CodeSqdn	Ship or Base	Years	Aircraft	Example	
V4 1846	Brunswick	7-10.44	Corsair III	JS882	(4V4)	V9 1848	Brunswick	7-10.44	Corsair I	JT102	(16V9)
V7 738	Brunswick	1945	Avenger I	FN843	(20V7)				Corsair II	JT601	(12V9)
			Avenger II	JZ387	(7V7)	V10 1852	Brunswick	2-5.45	Corsair IV	KD817	(12V10)
			Avenger III	JZ695	(18V7)	V11 1849	Brunswick	8-11.44	Corsair III	JS661	(8V11)
V7 1845	Brunswick	6-8.44	Corsair III	JS834	(4V7)				2-seater	?	(9V11)
V7 1851	Brunswick	9-12.44	Corsair IV	KD213	(5V7)	V11 1835	Brunswick	12.44-3.45	Corsair IV	KD774	(7V11)
V8 738?	Bar Harbour	1945	Corsair II	JT683	(16V8)	V11 1853	Brunswick	4-7.45	Corsair IV	KD796	(2V11)
						V16 1850	Brunswick	8-11.44	Corsair	?	(4V16)

An oddity. This Barracuda at Ronaldsway in 1945 appears to be coded 'R3Y', but with the '3' painted in reverse. (RAF Museum 6061-2)

FIN CODES SINCE 1945 - SHORE BASES

Code	Shore Base	Years
AC	Abbotsinch	1946 - 1963
AH	Anthorn	1946 - 1957
AO	Arbroath	1946 - 1970
BL	Belfast	1972
BQ	St.Davids	1953 - 1956
BR	Bramcote	1946 - 1958
BW	Sembawang	1954 - 1955
BY	Brawdy	1952 - 1971
CF	Church Fenton	1969 - 1970
CH	Culham	1947 - 1953
CM	Culham	1945 - 1946
CU	Culdrose	1953 - date
CW	Culdrose	1947 - 1953
DL	Dale	1946 - 1947
DM	Dartmouth	1974 - 1982
DO	Donibristle	1946 - 1959
EV	Evanton	1946 - 1948
FD	Ford	1946 - 1958
FL	Fleetlands	1983 - date
FN	Fearn	1946
GJ	Gosport	1946 - 1956
GN	Eglinton	1950 - 1963
HF	Hal Far	1946 - 1965
HR	Henstridge	1951 - 1952
JA	Stretton	1946 - 1953
JB	St.Merryn	1946 - 1951
JR	Eglinton	1946 - 1949
LM	Lossiemouth	1946 - 1972
LO	Linton-on-Ouse	1967
LO	Lossiemouth	1969
LP	Lee-on-Solent	1946 - 1955
LS	Lee-on-Solent	1955 - 1988
LU	Leuchars	1972
MA	Machrihanish	1951 - 1952
MF	St.Merryn	1951 - 1953
MV	Milltown	1946 - 1953
NW	RAN Nowra	1946 - date
PO	Portland	1959 - date
PQ	Belfast	1953 - 1955
PW	Prestwick	1971 - date
SJ	Syerston	1954
SR	St.Merryn	1953 - 1956
ST	Stretton	1953 - 1958
SZ	Belfast	1955
VL	Yeovilton	1946 - date
VM	Worthy Down	1946 - 1947
WU	Wroughton	1972 - 1992

DECK LETTERS SINCE 1945 - FLEET CARRIERS

Code	Carrier	Years
A	HMS Vengeance	1945
A	HMS Implacable	1946 - 1947
A	HMS Indomitable	1947 - 1953
A	HMS Albion	1958 - 1972
B	HMS Venerable	1945 - 1946
B	HMS Indefatigable	1946
B	HMAS Melbourne	1955 - 1956
B	HMS Bulwark	1954 - 1981
C	HMS Colossus	1945
C	HMS Indomitable	1946
C	HMS Implacable	1948 - 1951
C	HMS Centaur	1954 - 1967
D	HMS Indefatigable	1945
D	HMS Colossus	1945
D	HMS Illustrious	1946 - 1954
E	HMS Formidable	1948
E	HMS Eagle	1957 - 1972
F	HMS Formidable	1952 - 1953
G	HMS Victorious	1946 - 1950
H	HMS Hermes	1958 - 1984
J	HMS Colossus	1946
J	HMS Eagle	1951 - 1957
J	HMS Warrior	1953 - 1954
K	HMS Terrible (became HMAS Sydney)	Not used
K	HMAS Sydney	1949 - 1958
L	HMS Illustrious	1945
L	HMS Glory	1946
L	HMS Centaur	1953 - 1954
L	HMS Illustrious	1982 - date
M	HMS Implacable	1945
M	HMAS Melbourne	1957 - 1982
N	HMS Indomitable	1945
N	HMS Implacable	1945 - 1946
N	HMS Vengeance	1946
N	HMS Venerable	1946
N	HMS Invincible	1980 - date
O	HMS Indomitable	1945
O	HMS Ocean	1945 - 1953
O	HMS Ark Royal	1955 - 1957
O	HMS Ocean from	1997
P	HMS Victorious	1945
P	HMS Triumph	1946 - 1955
Q	HMS Illustrious	1945
Q	HMS Vengeance	1946 - 1957
R	HMS Ruler	1944
R	HMS Formidable	1945
R	HMS Glory	1946 - 1954
R	HMS Ark Royal	1958 - 1978
R	HMS Ark Royal	1985 - date
S	HMS Victorious	1945
S	HMS Indefatigable	1945 - 1946
S	HMS Colossus	1946
S	HMAS Sydney	1956 - 1969
T	HMS Venerable	1946
T	HMS Theseus	1946 - 1960
U	HMS Unicorn	1946
V	HMS Vengeance	1945
V	HMS Victorious	1945
V	HMS Venerable	1946 - 1948
W	HMS Indomitable	1945
W	HMS Arbiter	1945
W	HMS Warrior	1946 - 1948
X	HMS Unicorn	1945
X	HMS Victorious	1945
X	HMS Formidable	1945 - 1947
X	HMCS Magnificent	1948 - 1949
Y	HMS Glory	1945 - 1946
Y	HMS Venerable	1946
Y	HMS Unicorn	1946 - 1953
Y	HMS Illustrious	1953 - 1955
Y	HMAS Melbourne	1956
Z	HMS Colossus	1945 - 1946
Z	HMS Albion	1954 - 1957
TR	HMS Tracker	1945

Percival Sea Prince T.1 WM739 of the RN detachment at RAF Church Fenton bore the fin code 'CF' in 1969/70. (MAP)

DECK LETTERS - SHIPS OTHER THAN CARRIERS

Code	Ship	Years	Pennant
B	HMS Blake	1979-1982	C99
D	HMS Devonshire	1962	D02
E	HMS Endurance	1976	A171
F	HMS Fearless	1974-1975	L10
M	HMS Mohawk	1964	F125
T	HMS Tidespring	1963-1965	A75
Y	HMS Yarmouth	1970	F101
AB	HMS Ambuscade	1975-1993	F172
AC	HMS Achilles	1970-1990	F12
AC	HrMS Abraham Crijnsen	1983-date	F816
AD	HMS Ardent	1977-1982	F184
AE	HMS Ariadne	1973-1992	F72
AE	HMCS Assiniboine	1957-1989	DD234
AG	HMS Avenger	1975-1994	F185
AJ	HMS Ajax	1964-1985	F114
AL	HMCS Algonquin	1973-date	DD283
AL	HMS Alacrity	1977-1994	F174
AM	HMS Andromeda	1968-1993	F57
AN	HMS Antrim	1969-1984	D18
AN	HMCS Athabaskan	1972-date	DD282
AO	HMS Antelope	1975-1982	F170
AP	HMS Apollo	1972-1988	F70
AR	HMS Arethusa	1965-1985	F38
AS	HMS Ashanti	1964-1987	F117
AS	HMCS Annapolis	1964-date	DD265
AS	RFA Argus	1988-date	A135
AT	HMS Argonaut	1967-1992	F56
AU	HMS Aurora	1964-1987	F10
AV	HMS Active	1977-1994	F171
AW	HMS Arrow	1976-1993	F173
AY	HMS Argyll	1991-date	F231
AZ	HMS Amazon	1974-1993	F169
BA	HMS Brave	1986-date	F94
BC	HMS Bacchante	1969-1982	F69
BD	RFA Sir Bedivere	1967-date	L3004
BE	RFA Blue Rover	1970-1992	A270
BK	HMS Berwick	1970-1985	F115
BK	HrMs Bankert	1980-1993	F810
BL	HMS Blake	1969-1979	C99
BM	HMS Birmingham	1976-date	D86
BR	HMS Brighton	1971-1981	F106
BS	HMS Bristol	1973-1993	D23
BT	HMS Brilliant	1981-date	F90
BT	HrMs Blois van Treslong	1982-date	F824
BV	RFA Black Rover	1974-1991	A273
BW	HMS Broadsword	1979-date	F88
BX	HMS Battleaxe	1980-date	F89
BZ	HMS Brazen	1982-date	F91
CA	HMNZS Canterbury	1973-date	F421
CB	HrMs Callenburgh	1979-1994	F808
CF	HMS Cardiff	1979-date	D108
CH	HMS Challenger	1984-date	
CL	HMS Cleopatra	1966-1973	F28
CL	HMS Cumberland	1989-date	F85
CM	HMS Chatham	1990-date	F87
CO	HMS Coventry	1978-1979	D118
CP	HMS Cleopatra	1975-1992	F28
CS	HMS Charybdis	1969-1970	F75
CT	HMS Campbeltown	1989-date	F86
CV	HMS Coventry	1980-1982	D118
CV	HMS Coventry	1988-date	F96
CW	HMS Cornwall	1988-date	F99
CY	HMS Charybdis	1970-1991	F75
DA	HMS Danae	1967-1976	F47
DC	HMS Dumbarton Castle	1982-date	P265
DI	HMS Dido	1963-1975	F104
DL	RFA Diligence	1983-date	A132
DM	HMS Diomede	1970-1988	F16
DN	HMS Danae	1976-1991	F47
DO	HMS Dido	1978-date	F104
DR	HrMs De Ruyter	1976-1995	F806
DV	HMS Devonshire	1965-1978	D02
EB	HMS Edinburgh	1984-date	D97
ED	HMS Endurance	1967-1976	A171
ED	HMS Endurance	1976-1991	A171
ED	HMS Endurance	1994-date	A171
EE	HMS Endurance	1992-1994	A171
EN	RFA Engadine	1967-1989	K08
ER	HMNZS Endeavour	1988-date	A11
ES	HMS Eskimo	1963-1980	F119
EU	HMS Euryalus	1964-1989	F15
EV	HrMs Evertsen	1968-1989	F815
EX	HMS Exeter	1980-date	D89
FA	RFA Fort Austin	1979-date	A386
FF	HMS Fife	1969-1987	D20
FG	RFA Fort Grange	1978-date	A385
FI	HMS Fife	1966-1969	D20
FM	HMS Falmouth	1970-1984	F113
FO	RFA Fort George	1992-date	A388
FR	HMCS Fraser	1965-1991	DD233
FS	HMS Fearless	1965-date	L10
FV	RFA Fort Victoria	1992-date	A387
GA	HMS Galatea	1964-1986	F18
GC	HMS Gloucester	1984-date	D96
GD	RFA Sir Galahad	197.-1982	L3005
GL	HMS Glamorgan	1966-1986	D19
GN	RFA Green Rover	1969-1990	A268
GR	RFA Sir Geraint	1967-date	L3027
GT	HMS Grafton	from 1997	F80
GU	HMS Gurkha	1964-1984	F122
GV	RFA Gold Rover	1974-date	A271
GW	HMS Glasgow	1979-date	D88
GY	RFA Grey Rover	1970-date	A269
HA	HMS Hampshire	1963-1976	D06
HD	HMS Hydra	1974-1986	A144
HE	HMS Hecla	1965-1969	A133
HE	HMS Herald	1978-1987	A138
HL	HMS Hecla	1969-1993	A133
HM	HMS Hermione	1969-1992	F58
HN	HMCS Huron	1972-date	DD281
HR	HMS Herald	1972-1977	A138
HR	HMS Herald	1987-date	A136
HT	HMS Hecate	1965-1987	A137
HY	HMS Hydra	1969-1972	A144
ID	HMS Intrepid	1967-date	L11
IR	HMS Iron Duke	1990-date	F234
IS	HMCS Iroquois	1972-date	DD280
IS	HrMs Isaac Sweers	1968-1990	F814
JB	HrMs Jan van Brakel	1983-date	F825
JH	HrMs Jacob van Heemskerk	1986-date	F812
JO	HMS Juno	1967-1992	F52
JP	HMS Jupiter	1969-1992	F60
KE	HMS Kent	1963-1980	D12
KN	HrMs Kortenaer	1978-date	F807
KP	HrMs van Kinsbergen	1980-1994	F809
LA	HMS Lancaster	1992-date	F229
LC	HMS Leeds Castle	1982-date	P258
LD	HMS Londonderry	1969-1984	F108
LE	HMS Leander	1973-date	F109
LN	HMS London	1966-1981	D16
LN	RFA Sir Lancelot	1964-1989	L3029
LO	HMS London	1963-1965	D16
LO	HMS London	1987-date	F95
LP	HMS Liverpool	1982-date	D92
LR	HMS Leander	1963-1970	F109
LT	HMS Lowestoft	1970-1985	F103
LT	TLC Lofoten	1965	K07
LY	RFA Lyness	1966-1981	A339
MA	HMS Marlborough	1991-date	F233
MC	HMS Manchester	1982-date	D95
ME	HMCS Margaree	1965-1991	DD230
MI	HMS Minerva	1966-1968	F45
MM	HMS Mermaid	1973-1977	F76
MM	HMS Monmouth	1992-date	F235
MO	HMS Mohawk	1964-1981	F125
MP	HMS Matapan	1975-1977	D43
MR	HMS Montrose	1993-date	F236
MV	HMS Minerva	1968-1992	F45
MW	HMNZS Monowai	1977-date	A06
NA	HMS Naiad	1965-1987	F39
NC	HMS Newcastle	1978-date	D87
NF	HMS Norfolk	1970-1982	D21
NF	HMS Norfolk	1990-date	F230
NL	HMS Northumberland	1994-date	F238
NM	HMS Nottingham	1983-date	D91
NN	HMCS Nipigon	1964-date	DD266
NU	HMS Nubian	1962-1986	F131
OA	RFA Olna	1966-197.	A123
OA	HMCS Ottawa	1965-1991	DD229
OD	RFA Olmeda	1965-date	A124
ON	RFA Olna	1975-date	A123
OW	RFA Olwen	1965-date	A122
PA	HrMs Philips van Almonde	1981-date	F823
PB	HMS Phoebe	1966-1991	F42
PC	HMS Protector	1959-1966	A146
PC	HMS Polar Circle	1991-1992	A176
PE	HMS Penelope	1963-1982	F127
PF	HrMs Pieter Florisz	1983-date	F826
PH	HrMs Piet Heijn	1981-date	F811
PL	HMS Plymouth	1961-1988	F126
PN	HMS Penelope	1982-1991	F127
PR	HrMs Poolster	1964-1994	A835
PR	HMS Protector	1966-1967	A146
PR	HMCS Provider	1963-date	AOR508
PS	HMCS Preserver	1970-date	AOR510
PT	RFA Protecteur	1969-date	AOR509
PV	RFA Sir Percivale	1968-date	L3036
RE	RFA Regent	1969-1970	A486
RG	RFA Regent	1970-1992	A486
RL	HMS Rhyl	1960-1984	F129
RM	HMS Richmond	1995-date	F239
RO	HMS Rothesay	1960-1988	F107
RS	HMS Resource	1967-date	A480
SA	HMCS Skeena	1957-1990	DD207
SC	HMS Scylla	1970-date	F71
SD	HMS Sheffield	1975-1982	D80
SL	HMNZS Southland	1983-date	F104
SM	HMS Somerset	from 1996	F82
SN	HMS Southampton	1981-date	D90
SS	HMS Sirius	1966-1993	F40
ST	RFA Stromness	1967-1983	A344
SU	HMS Sutherland	from 1997	F81
SY	HMCS Saguenay	1965-1990	DD206
TA	HMS Tartar	1962-1984	F133
TB	RFA Tarbatness	1967-1981	A345
TG	HMS Tiger	1959-1978	C20
TH	HrMs Tjerk Hiddes	1957-1986	F804
TH	HrMS Tjerk Hiddes	1992-date	D830
TM	RFA Sir Tristram	1967-date	
TP	RFA Tidepool	1963-1982	A76
TR	HMS Triumph	1965-1974	A108
TR	HMS Tromp	1975-date	F801
TS	RFA Tidespring	1974-1993	A75
UD	HMS Undaunted	1961-1978	F53
VB	HMS Beaver	1984-date	F93
VI	HMS Vidal	1954-1976	A200
VN	HrMS Van Nes	1967-1988	F805
VN	HrMS Van Nes	1994-date	D833
WA	HMNZS Waikato	1966-date	F55
WM	HMS Westminster	1996-date	F237
WN	HMNZS Wellington	1982-date	F69
WW	HrMs Witte de With	1986-date	F813
XB	HMS Boxer	1984-date	F92
YK	HMS York	1985-date	D96
YM	HMS Yarmouth	1968-1986	F101
ZK	HrMs Zuiderkruis	1975-date	A832
ZU	HMS Zulu	1964-1984	F124

Australian Ships:

Code	Ship
01	HMAS Adelaide
02	HMAS Canberra
03	HMAS Sydney
04	HMAS Darwin
50	HMAS Tobruk
73	HMAS Moresby
203	HMAS Jervis Bay
215	HMAS Stalwart
304	HMAS Success

BRITISH PACIFIC FLEET CODES 1945 - 1947

	Ship	Codes	Sqn	Years	Aircraft	Example		Ship	Codes	Sqn	Years	Aircraft	Example
A	Vengeance	111 - 131	1850	1945/46	Corsair IV	KD427 (126/A)	S	Indefatigable	111 - 134	887	1945/46	Seafire III	PP930 (122/S)
		270 - 281	812	1946	Firefly I	MB501 (280/N)			135 - 159	894	1945/46	Seafire III	NN507 (148/S)
		370 - 381	812	1945/46	Barracuda II	PM939 (374/A)			270 - 281	1770	1945	Firefly I	DT987 (275/S)
B	Venerable	111 - 127	1851	1946	Corsair IV	KD838 (111/B)			270 - 281	1772	1945/46	Firefly I	DK551 (276/S)
		270 - 281	814	1945/46	Firefly I	DK490 (281/B)						Martinet I	RG909 (274/S)
		370 - 381	814	1945	Barracuda II	PM939 (379/B)						Harvard IIb	KF534 (273/S)
C	Colossus	111 - 123	1846	1945/46	Corsair IV	KD412 (122/C)			370 - 389	820	1945	Avenger II	JZ434 (387/S)
		370 - 379	827	1946	Barracuda II	?)378/D)	T	Venerable	111 - 123	1851	1946	Corsair IV	KD619 (113/T)
D	Colossus	111 - 131	1846	1945	Corsair IV	KD856 (131/D)			270 - 281	814	1946	Firefly I	MB640 (272/T)
		370 - 382	827	1945/46	Barracuda II	PM760 (373/D)			370 - 381	814	1945	Barracuda II	
L	Glory	111 - 123	1831	1945	Corsair IV	? (123/L)	V	Vindex	282 - 298	1790	1945	Firefly INF	MB587 (289/V)
		370 - 381	837	1945	Barracuda II	MX767 (372/L)	V	Venerable	131 - 145	802	1946	Seafire XV	? (132/V)
M	?	131 - 138	?	1945	Corsair IV	KD789 (138/M)			285 - 296	814	1946	Firefly I	PP564 (291/V)
M	Vengeance	270 - 281	812	1946	Firefly I	MB435 (----/N)	W	Indomitable	111 - 128	1839	1945	Hellcat I	JV141 (116/W)
N	Implacable	111 - 122	880	1945	Seafire III	NN621 (115/N)						Hellcat II	JW859 (112/W)
		111 - 151	801	1945/46	Seafire XV	SR596 (125/N)			131 - 146,	1844	1945	Hellcat I	FN439 (1 ../W)
		270 - 281	1771	1945	Firefly I	DK432 (274/N)			162 - 163			Hellcat II	JX762 (135/W)
					Martinet I	RG958 (277/N)			370 - 377,	857	1945	Avenger I	FN915 (382/W)
		282 - 298	1790	1945/46	Firefly I	MB620 (282)			380 - 386			Avenger II	JZ386 (386/W)
		370 - 381	828	1945	Avenger		X	Formidable	111 - 128	1841	1945	Corsair IV	KD349 (121/X)
N	Vengeance	270 - 281	812	1946	Firefly I	MB501 (280/N)			129 - 145	1842	1945	Corsair II	JT687 (141/X)
N	Venerable	270 - 281	814	1946	Firefly I	MB617 (274/N)						Corsair IV	KD625 (142/X)
P	Victorious	111 - 128	1834	1945	Corsair II	JT633 (120/P)			370 - 391	848	1945	Avenger I	JZ114 (376/X)
		131 - 150	1836	1945	Corsair II	JT365 (137/P)						Avenger II	JZ466 (380/X)
		370 - 385	849	1945	Avenger II	JZ678 (377/P)	X	Victorious	111 - 125	1834	1945	Corsair II	JT632 (116/X)
Q	Illustrious	111 - 128	1830	1945	Corsair II	JT359 (118/Q)	Y	Glory	111 - 123	1831	1945/46	Corsair IV	KD905 (123/Y)
		129 - 147	1833	1945	Corsair II	JT528 (143/Q)			111 - 122	806	1946	Seafire XV	SW786 (114/Y)
		370 - 381	854?	1945	Avenger I	? (374/Q)			270 - 283	837	1945/46	Firefly I	MB522 (273/Y)
R	Glory	111 - 123	806	1946/47	Seafire XV	? (116/R)	Y	Venerable	111 - 133	1851	1946	Corsair IV	KD505 (112/Y)
		270 - 283	837	1946/47	Firefly I	PP648 (276/R)							

Chance Vought Corsair IVs of No.1846 Squadron from HMS Colossus in 1945. (via Peter Arnold)

FLEET AIR ARM CARRIER CODES 1946 - 1956

Ship	Codes	Sqdn	Year	Aircraft Type	Example
A Implacable	100-116	794	1947	Seafire F.3	NF510 (114/A)
	200-215	795	1946/47	Firefly FR.1	MB745 (215/A)
A Indomitable	100-103, 110-113, 120-123	813	1950/52	Firebrand TF.5	EK628 (112/A)
	150-162	801	1951/52	Sea Fury FB.11	WE711 (162/A)
	271-280	826	1952/53	Firefly AS.6	WD913 (275/A)
	281-288	824	1952/53	Firefly AS.6	WD907 (286)
	450-461	801	1950/51	Sea Hornet FR.21	VR861 (461/A)
	481-489	809	1952	Sea Hornet NF.21	VW953 (484/A)
B Bulwark	901-905	Sh F	1954	Dragonfly HR.3	VX600 (905/B)
				Avenger AS.5	XB389 (902/B)
C Implacable	100-103, 110-113, 120-123	813	1947/50	Firebrand TF.5	EK786 (112/C)
	281	Sh F		Barracuda TR.5	RK568 (281/C)
	450-467	801	1948/51	Sea Hornet F.20	TT196 (450/C)
				Sea Hornet PR.22	VX658 (465/C)
	800	Sh F	1948	Barracuda TR.5	RK579 (800/C)
	911-913	Sh F		Firebrand TF.5	EK779 (911/C)
C Centaur	100-111	810	1954/55	Sea Fury FB.11	VX634 (105/C)
	141-152	803	1954/55	Sea Hawk FB.3	WM912 (142/C)
	146-158	801	1955	Sea Hawk FGA.4	WV871 (150/C)
	158-169	811	1955/56	Sea Hawk FB.3	WM961 (165/C)
	161-173	806	1954/55	Sea Hawk FB.3	WM906 (167/C)
				Sea Hawk FGA.4	WV855 (171/C)
	371-378	820	1954/55	Avenger AS.4	XB446 (372/C)
	381-388	814	1954/55	Avenger AS.5	XB392 (383/C)
	401-409	820	1955	Gannet AS.1	WN445 (403/C)
	901-902	Sh F	1954/55	Dragonfly HR.3	WG671 (901/C)
D Illustrious	201-206	Sh F	1949/51	Firefly FR.1	MB755 (201/D)
	800-801	Sh F	1947/48	Barracuda TR.5	RK542 (801/D)
J Eagle	101-112	800	1951/54	Attacker F.1	WA473 (102/J)
				Attacker FB.1	WA531 (102/J)
				Attacker FB.2	WP275 (102/J)
	100-118	811	1953/54	Sea Fury FB.11	VX621 (107/J)
	104-107	890	1952	Attacker F.1	WA494 (105/J)
				Attacker FB.2	WK327 (104/J)
	111-119	803	1951/53	Attacker F.1	WA512 (115/J)
	111-119	890	1952	Attacker F.1	WA513 (118/J)
				Attacker FB.2	WK321 (111/J)
	120-131	827	1952	Firebrand TF.5	EK691 (123/J)
	121-129	813	1955	Wyvern S.4	VZ780 (121/J)
	131-136	827	1954/55	Wyvern S.4	WL882 (137/J)
	131-136	830	1855	Wyvern S.4	WL888 (134/J)
	141-149	890	1952	Attacker F.1	WA478 (142/J)
				Attacker FB.2	WK327 (147/J)
	140-154	803	1952/54	Attacker FB.2	WK320 (151/J)
	143-149	831	1955	Wyvern S.4	WN330 (144/J)
	161-174	806	1953/54	Sea Hawk F.1	WM902 (165)
	171-182	802	1954/55	Sea Hawk FGA.4	WV837 (175/J)
	186-199	804	1955	Sea Hawk F.1	WF208 (188)
				Sea Hawk FGA.4	WV833 (197/J)
	211-220	812	1952/53	Firefly AS.6	WB426 (212)
	221-228	820	1951/52	Firefly AS.6	WD909 (221/J)
	255-263	814	1952/53	Firefly AS.6	WD889 (256/J)
	271-279	826	1952	Firefly AS.6	WJ105 (276/J)
	283-288	703A	1954	Firefly AS.5	WB359 (286/J)
				Firefly AS.6	WD847 (283/J)
	280-291	825	1953/54	Firefly AS.5	VT470 (283/J)
	292	813	1953	Firefly FR.1	PP392 (282/J)
	301-306	849 HQ Flight	1953	Skyraider AEW.1	WT944 (301/J)
	307-312	849A	1952/55	Skyraider AEW.1	WT954 (310/J)
	311-314	849B	1954	Skyraider AEW.1	WT956 (314/J)
	343-350	826	1955	Gannet AS.1	WN373 (344/J)
	361-369	815	1954	Avenger AS.4	XB326 (365)
	440-447	812	1955	Gannet AS.1	WN357 (445/J)
	481-489	809	1953/54	Sea Hornet NF.21	VV437 (484/J)
	901-903	Sh F	1953/55	Dragonfly HR.3	WG750 (901/J)
J Warrior	100-116	811	1953/54	Sea Fury FB.11	WG590 (105/J)
	280-287	825	1953/54	Firefly AS.6	VX436 (281/J)
O Ocean	101-118	805	1947/48	Seafire F.17	SX234 (104/O)
	101-121	802	1952	Sea Fury FB.11	WE683 (112/O)
	130-151	807	1951/53	Sea Fury FB.11	WF590 (146/O)
	131-140	804	1948/49	Seafire FR.47	VP444 (133/O)
	143-149	898	1951/42	Sea Fury FB.11	WF615 (146/O)
	200-215	816	1947/48	Firefly FR.1	PP560 (205/O)
	200-211	812	1948/49	Firefly FR.5	VT369 (211/O)
	212-215	812 Black Flight	1948/49	Firefly NF.1	PP555 (213/O)
O Ocean contd	217	816 Black Flight	1947/48	Firefly NF.1	PP557 (217/O)
	226-228	816?		Firefly FR.1	
	230-239	810	1951/53	Firefly FR.5	WB349 (232/O)
	281-292	825	1952	Firefly AS/FR.5	WB427 (284/O)
	291-299	810	1952/53	Firefly FR.5	VT405 (292/O)
	902	Sh F	1948	Sea Otter ABR.2	RD921 (902/O)
O Ark Royal	100-113	800	1955/56	Sea Hawk FB.3	WN108 (108/O)
				Sea Hawk FGA.4	WV906 (110/O)
				Sea Hawk FGA.6	XE339 (109/O)
	130-139	898	1955	Sea Hawk FGA.6	XE367 (133/O)
	226-235	809	1955/56	Sea Venom FAW.20	WM521 (235)
				Sea Venom FAW.21	WW151 (231)
	281-283	891	1955	Sea Venom FAW.21	WW139 (281/O)
	315-318	849B	1955	Skyraider AEW.1	WT957 (317/O)
	411-419	824	1955	Gannet AS.1	WN396 (411/O)
	900,990, 999	Sh F	1955	Dragonfly HR.3	WG718 (990/O)
				Whirlwind HAR.3	XG574 (999/O)
P Triumph	171-182	800	1948/49	Seafire F.17	SX345 (179/P)
				Seafire FR.47	VP461 (178/P)
	199	13CAG Ldr	1948/49	Seafire F.17	SX387 (199/P)
				Seafire F.47	VP431 (199/P)
	201-211	Sh F	1951/53	Firefly FR.1	DK553 (202/P)
				Firefly AS.6	WD869 (211/P)
	251-254	827?	1947	Firefly FR.1	
	271-282	827	1947/50	Firefly FR.1	PP596 (273/P)
	299	13CAG Ldr	1949/50	Firefly FR.1	PP648 (299/P)
	931-934	Sh F	1953/55	S Balliol T.21	WL715 (931/P)
Q Vengeance (see also RAN)	100-121	802	1947/51	Seafire F.15	PR407 (103/Q)
				Sea Fury F.10	TF912 (110/Q)
				Sea Fury FB.11	VW657 (101/Q)
	201-211	814	1947/48	Firefly FR.1	MB510 (208/Q)
	201-202	St F	1950/51	Firefly FR.1	MB745 (202/Q)
	211-224	814	1948/51	Firefly FR.4	VG995 (222/Q)
				Firefly FR.5	VT465 (216/Q)
				Firefly AS.6	WD890 (220/Q)
	301-302	Sh F	1947/49	Barracuda TR.3	RK479 (302/Q)
	481-489	809	1950/52	Sea Hornet NF.21	VW954 (484/Q)
R Glory	100-120	804	1949/52	Sea Fury FB.11	VW670 (111/R)
	151-170	801	1952.54	Sea Fury FB.11	VW570 (158/R)
	201-211	812	1950/52	Firefly FR.5	WB259 (205/R)
	205-209	821	1952/53	Firefly FR.5	VT439 (206/R)
	212-215	812 Black Flight		Firefly NF.1	PP491 (213/R)
	230-237	810	1952	Firefly FR.5	VX438 (232/R)
	271-279	826	1953/54	Firefly AS.6	VT406 (278/R)
T Theseus	101-115	802	1951/52	Sea Fury FB.11	WE717 (108/T)
	110-131	807	1947/51	Sea Fury FB.11	VW577 (113/T)
	130-144	804	1947	Seafire F.15	SW845 (139/T)
	143-149	898	1952/53	Sea Fury FB.11	WG597 (145/T)
	150-159	804	1952/53	Sea Fury FB.11	VR924 (157/T)
	171-182	802	1953/54	Sea Fury FB.11	VW547 (173/T)
	219-220	814	1951/52	Firefly AS.6	WH627 (219/T)
	221-229	820	1953	Firefly AS.6	WD908 (226/T)
	230-241	810	1947/51	Firefly FR.4	VG991 (236/T)
				Firefly AS.5	WB338 (239/T)
	287-298	812	1946/48	Firefly FR.1	MB758 (294/T)
	300	Sh F	1948/49	Sea Otter ABR.2	RD919 (300/T)
	911	Sh F	1951	Dragonfly HR.3	WM990 (911)
Y Illustrious	201-203	Sh F	1951/53	Firefly FR.1	PP645 (203/Y)
				Firefly AS.5	WB331 (202/Y)
Z Albion	100-112	898	1954/55	Sea Hawk FB.3	WM920 (107/Z)
	120-131	807	1955	Sea Hawk FB.3	WN105 (126/Z)
				Sea Hawk FGA.4	WV918 (127/Z)
	170-179	810	1955	Sea Hawk FGA.4	XE335 (174/Z)
	181-192	813	1954/55	Wyvern S.4	VZ778 (183/Z)
	200-208	890	1955	Sea Venom FAW.20	WM554 (208/Z)
	251-258	892	1955	Sea Venom FAW.21	WW190 (258/Z)
	319-322	849C	1954/55	Skyraider AEW.1	WV105 (320/Z)
	381-389	814	1955	Avenger AS.5	XB309 (387/Z)
	901-902	Sh F	1954/55	Dragonfly HR.3	VZ965 (901/Z)
PR Protector	910-911	Sh F	1955	Whirlwind HAR.1	XA866 (911/PR)

FLEET AIR ARM SHORE CODES 1946 - 1956

	Base	Codes	Sqdn	Years	Aircraft Type	Example		Base	Codes	Sqdn	Years	Aircraft Type	Example
AC	Abbotsinch	200-261	SAD	1947/55	Anson T.1		CH	Culham	100-112	SAD	1947/55	Seafire F.15	SR575 (122/CH)
					Seafire F.17							Seafire F.17	SP343 (126/CH)
					Firefly FR.1	DK501 (206/AC)						Seafire FR.46	LA551 (109/CH)
					Firefly T.2	DK489 (200/AC)						Sea Fury FB.11	WE732 (108/CH)
					Firefly FR.4	TW752 (261/AC)						Attacker FB.2	WK323 (106)
					Firefly FR.5	VX392 (222/AC)			151-160	SAD	1951/55	Sea Fury FB.11	VR949 (153/CH)
					Firefly AS.6	WD881 (224/AC)			200-206	SAD	1947/55	Harvard T.2b	KF524 (206/CH)
					Harvard T.2a	EX272 (202/AC)						Harvard T.3	EZ418 (201/CH)
					Harvard T.2b	KF517 (239/AC)						Sea Fury T.20	VZ355 (201/CH)
					Harvard T.3	EZ383 (207/AC)			271-279	SAD	1954/55	Harvard T.3	KF578 (277/CH)
					Avenger AS.5	XB437 (226/AC)						Sea Fury T.20	VZ345 (272)
					Sea Balliol T.21	WP324 (206/AC)						Sea Balliol T.21	WL734 (275)
					Sea Fury T.20	VZ363 (235/AC)						Sea Vampire	
		320-322	SAD	1955	Avenger AS.5	XB397 (322/AC)						T.20	XG722 (278)
		600-601	SAD	1954/55	Oxford T.1	PH408 (601/AC)			601-602	No.1	1947/50	Dominie C.1	NF849 (602/CH)
					Sea Prince					Ferry Flight		Anson C.1	NK287 (601/CH)
					T.1	WP312 (600/AC)			701	739	1949	Sea Mosquito	
		611-612	SAD	1953/54	Oxford T.1	PH297 (612/AC)						TR.33	
					Sea Prince T.1	WP312 (611/AC)			900	St F		Dominie C.1	HG694 (900/CH)
		901	St F	1955	Dominie C.1	HG709 (901/AC)	CU	Culdrose	100-119	736	1953	Attacker F.1	WA486 (105/CU)
AH	Anthorn	900-903	St F	1949/55	Dragonfly HR.3	WP494 (903/AH)						Attacker FB.1	WT851 (111/CU)
					Harvard T.3	EZ345 (---/AH)						Attacker FB.2	WP283 (117/CU)
					Dominie C.1	HG708 (901/AH)			121-141	738	1953	Sea Fury FB.11	VR952 (141/CU)
AO	Arbroath	450-467	801	1948	Sea Hornet F.20	TT211 (458/AO)			161-169	759	1953	Seafire FR.47	PS951 (168/CU)
		501-509	772	1947/48	Mosquito PR.34	RG297 (503/AO)			180-182	759	1953	Sea Vampire	
		900-912	St F	1947/55	Sea Otter	RD917 (902/AO)						F.20	VV136 (180)
					Expeditor C.2	FT995 (900/AO)			200-206	738	1953	Sea Fury T.20	WE826 (200/CU)
					Swordfish 2	NF399 (912/AO)			200-255	766	1953/54	Firefly FR.1	DT985 (230/CU)
					Firefly T.1	MB437 (902/AO)			210-215	759	1953/54	Sea Fury T.20	WE822 (213/CU)
					Firefly T.2	DK531 (902/AO)			236-239	744	1954/55	Firefly AS.6	WB261 (236/CU)
					Dominie C.1	NF847 (903/AO)			272-280	765	1955	Firefly T.2	DK513 (280/CU)
					Harvard T.2b	KF512 (901/AO)			282-294	ScAD	1954	Firefly FR.4	VH129 (293)
					Harvard T.3	EZ432 (900/AO)				(Temp)		Firefly AS.6	WD909 (283/CU)
					Sea Prince C.2	WM756(c/s 900)			301-304	849	1953/55	Skyraider	
BQ	Brawdy	415-425	A/W	1952/55	Sea Hornet F.20	TT213 (421/BQ)				HQ Flt		AEW.1	WT968 (303/CU)
			FRU		Sea Hornet				315-318	849C	1953/54	Skyraider	
					NF.21	VW950 (418/BQ)						AEW.1	WV179 (317/CU)
					Mosquito T.3	VT624 (417/BQ)			315-318	849B	1954/55	Skyraider	
					Sea Mosquito							AEW.1	WT959 (315/CU)
					TR.33	TW249 (416/BQ)			319-322	849D	1953/54	Skyraider	
BR	Bramcote	151-166	1833	1947/55	Seafire F.15	SR542 (162/BR)						AEW.1	WV105 (320/CU)
					Seafire F.17	SX220 (158/BR)			323-326	849E	1954	Skyraider	
					Seafire FR.47	VP474 (156/BR)						AEW.1	WV179 (324/CU)
					Sea Fury FB.11	WJ288 (153/BR)			323-326	849D	1954/55	Skyraider	
					Sea Fury T.20	VX292 (166/BR)						AEW.1	WT121 (326)
					Attacker FB.2	WZ295 (160/BR)			329-336	765	1955	Firefly T.7	WJ159 (329/CU)
		201-206	MAD	1954/55	Firefly AS.6	WD201 (201/BR)			340-350	750	1954/55	Firefly T.7	WJ172 (347/CU)
		252-264	MAD	1947/55	Harvard T.2b	KF549 (253/BR)			360-380	796	1954/55	Firefly T.7	WM768 (368/CU)
					Harvard T.3	EZ438 (253/BR)			381-389	815	1954/55	Avenger AS.5	XB396 (382/CU)
					Sea Fury T.20	VX291 (254/BR)			394-399	744	1955	Avenger AS.5	XB383 (397/CU)
					Firefly FR.1	PP534 (253/BR)			401-403	744	1954/55	Gannet AS.1	WN462 (403/CU)
					Firefly T.2	MB752 (251/BR)			402-404)	759	1953	Meteor T.7	WS116 (410/CU)
					Firefly T.3	PP478 (256/BR)			410-417)				
					Firefly FR.5	VH140 (262/BR)			405-408	736	1953	Meteor T.7	WS112 (406/CU)
					Sea Balliol T.21	WL728 (258/BR)			410-417	825	1955	Gannet AS.1	WN422 (414/CU)
		271-273	MAD	1954/55	Sea Fury T.20	VX290 (272/BR)			419	825	1955	Gannet T.2	ZA516 (419/CU)
		401	MAD	1954/55	Sea Prince T.1	WM740(401/BR)			601-614	764	1954	Sea Prince T.1	WP308 (612/CU)
		900-903	St F	1949/55	Anson T.1	NL121 (900/BR)			623-624	765	1955	Oxford T.1	NM355 (624/CU)
			FRU		Dominie C.1	X7332 (903)			901-902	St F	1953/55	Dragonfly HR.3	WN498 (902/CU)
BW	Sembawang		St F	1954/55	Firefly 5	WB377 (---/BW)			917-918	St F	1954/55	Firefly FR.1	DK554 (918/CU)
BY	Brawdy	100-111	898	1953/54	Sea Hawk F.1	WF182 (101/BY)						Firefly T.1	Z2021 (917/CU)
		120-131	807	1954/55	Sea Hawk F.1	WF184 (122)						Firefly T.2	MB745 (918/CU)
					Sea Hawk F.2	WF242 (129)	CW	Culdrose	100-110	790	1947/48	Seafire F.15	? (103/CW)
		161-174	806	1953/54	Sea Hawk F.4	WF175 (167)						Seafire F.17	SX288 (108/CW)
		290-291	A/W	1955	Sea Venom				100-149	736/	1950/53	Sea Fury F.10	TF911 (118/CW)
			FRU		FAW.20	WM567(290)				738		Sea Fury FB.11	VR938 (122/CW)
		411-450	A/W	1949/55	Sea Hornet F.20	TT213 (421/BY)			100-119	736	1952/53	Attacker F.1	WA476 (100/CW)
			FRU		Sea Hornet							Attacker FB.1	WT851 (111/CW)
					NF.21	VV439 (420/BY)						Attacker FB.2	WP299 (109/CW)
					Mosquito T.3	VT626 (422/BY)			150-156	790	1947/49	Seafire F.15	PR424 (152/CW)
					Meteor T.7	WL352 (442/BY)			151	?	1950	Firebrand TF.5	EK731 (151/CW)
		901-906	St F	1952/55	Dominie C.1	NF881 (901/BY)			161-179	736/	1950/52	Seafire F.17	SX113 (165/CW)
					Dragonfly HR.3	WG664 (905/BY)				738/			
					Sea Fury T.20	VX290 (906/BY)				759			
					Meteor T.7	WL337 (903/BY)			161-169	759	1952/53	Seafire FR.47	VP493 (162/CW)
					Vampire FB.5	VV631 (903/BY)			180-189	736	1950	Seafire F.17	SX276 (189/CW)
					Sea Vampire				180-183	738	1950/51	Firebrand TF.5	EK745 (183/CW)
					T.22	XA115 (906/BY)							

463

Base		Codes	Sqdn	Years	Aircraft Type	Example
CW	Culdrose contd	180-183	759	1951/53	Firebrand TF.5	EK844 (182/CW)
					Sea Vampire F.20	VV141 (181/CW)
		190-199	702	1951/52	Sea Vampire F.20	VV142 (199/CW)
					Vampire FB.5	VZ142 (192/CW)
					Attacker F.1	WA523 (194/CW)
		200-207	738	1950/53	Sea Fury T.20	VZ350 (205/CW)
		201-206	780	1947/49	Harvard T.2b	KF558 (206/CW)
					Harvard T.3	EZ240 (204)
		210-215	759	1951/53	Sea Fury T.20	VZ825 (210/CW)
		220-227	792	1948/50	Firefly FR.1	PP435 (221/CW)
		220-221	759	1952/53	Vampire T.11	WL461 (220)
		270-271	736	1949	Firefly FR.1	DK449 (271/CW)
		282-294	SAD (Temp)	1954	Firefly FR.4	VH129 (293)
					Firefly AS.6	WD881 (284)
		291-296	736	1950/52	Sea Fury T.20	VX285 (292/CW)
		299	52TRAG Ldr	1950/51	Firefly T.1	MB412 (299/CW)
		301-304	778	1951/52	Skyraider AEW.1	WT947 (304/CW)
		301-304	849 HQ Flt	1953	Skyraider AEW.1	WT944 (301/CW)
		400-404	702	1949/52	Meteor T.7	WA652 (404/CW)
		402-404	759	1953	Meteor T.7	WL353 (402/CW)
		403-414	790	1947/49	Sea Mosquito TR.33	TW257 (405/CW)
		405-408	736	1952/53	Meteor T.7	WL336 (403/CW)
		410-417	759	1952/53	Meteor T.7	VW447 (412/CW)
		450-466	762	1948/49	Sea Mosquito TR.33	TW283 (466/CW)
					Mosquito T.3	VA878 (457/CW)
					Mosquito FB.6	TE829 (465/CW)
		450-457	738	1950/51	Sea Hornet F.20	VR837 (454/CW)
					Sea Hornet PR.22	VW931 (450/CW)
		451-456	759	1951/53	Sea Hornet F.20	VR837 (454/CW)
					Sea Hornet PR.22	VZ664 (451/CW)
		481-489	809	1949/52	Sea Hornet NF.21	VW947 (482/CW)
		491-494	792	1950	Sea Hornet NF.21	VX248 (491/CW)
		601-614	780	1947/49	Oxford T.1	NM758 (603/CW)
		640-642	792	1949/50	Oxford T.1	PH140 (640/CW)
					Anson T.1	DJ545 (642/CW)
		650-662	762	1948/49	Oxford T.1	ED295 (656/CW)
		900-905	St F	1949/53	Sea Otter ABR.2	RD893 (902/CW)
					Harvard T.3	EZ400 (900/CW)
					Meteor F.8	WA960 (904/CW)
		997-999	St F	1951/52	Sea Fury T.20	WG652 (997/CW)
DL	Dale	104	790	1947/48	Seafire F.15	
		402-411	790	1946/48	Mosquito FB.6	TE720 (402/DL)
					Sea Mosquito TR.33	? (408/DL)
		481-495	790	1947	Sea Mosquito TR.33	? (485/DL)
DO	Donibristle	201-205	782	1951/52	Firefly FR.1	PP584 (201/DO)
					Firefly T.2	DK540 (203/DO)
					Firefly FR.4	TW687 (201/DO)
					Sea Fury T.20	VZ352 (205/DO)
		206-251	SAD	1950/51	Firefly FR.1	DK548 (226/DO)
					Firefly T.1	MB727 (236/DO)
					Firefly T.2	DK495 (212)
					Firefly AS.6	WD859 (243/DO)
					Harvard T.2b	KF517 (239/DO)
		801-815	782/ NCS	1946/55	Expeditor C.2	KP116 (c/s 807)
					Oxford 1	NM241 (801/DO)
					Dominie C.1	NF864 (804/DO)
					Firefly FR.1	PP655 (814/DO)
					Firefly T.2	DK540 (811/DO)
EV	Evanton	211-213	RNARY	1946/48	Firefly F.1	Z1901 (213/EV)
		901	St F		Oxford	PH261 (901/EV)
FD	Ford	000-042	778	1946/48	Oxford	PH185 (002/FD)
					Sea Hornet F.20	WE239 (009/FD)
					Sea Hornet PR.22	VZ655 (005/FD)
					Seafire F.17	SX305 (017/FD)
					Seafire F.45	LA450 (012/FD)
					Dominie 1	NF871 (002/FD)
					Firefly F.1	Z1955 (026/FD)
					Mosquito PR.16	RG171 (042/FD)
FD	Ford contd	000-042 contd			Sea Mosquito TR.33	RF904 (042/FD)
					Barracuda TR.3	MD989 (031)
		001-045	703	1948/55	Sturgeon TT.2	TS477 (004)
					Sea Mosquito TR.33	TS241 (043/FD)
					Firefly FR.4	VG957 (022/FD)
					Firefly 5	WB373 (023/FD)
					Firefly AS.6	WD853 (025/FD)
					Sea Hornet F.20	WE239 (009/FD)
					Sea Hornet NF.21	VW958 (001/FD)
					Sea Hornet PR.22	WE247 (007/FD)
					Sea Hawk F.1	WF152 (032/FD)
					Seafire F.17	SX347 (019/FD)
					Meteor F.3/hooked	EE337 (031/FD)
					Sea Balliol T.21	VR596 (031/FD)
					Blackburn YA.8	WB788 (015)
					Firefly FR.4	TW733 (025/FD)
					Firefly AS.5	WB259 (025/FD)
					Firefly AS.6	WD845 (021/FD)
		052-056	703	1952	Attacker F.1	WA470 (052)
					Attacker FB.1	WA527 (054/FD)
		061-099	703	1950/55	Avenger 3	KE442 (064/FD)
					Avenger AS.4	XB365 (065/FD)
					Avenger TBM-3E	XB364 (066/FD)
					Sea Vampire F.20	VV141 (074/FD)
					Sea Vampire F.21	VG701 (076/FD)
					Meteor T.7	WS103 (075/FD)
					Sea Hawk F.1	WF152 (073/FD)
					Sea Hawk FB.3	WM906 (073/FD)
					Sea Fury F.10	TF955 (094/FD)
					Sea Fury FB.11	VX608 (098/FD)
					Sea Fury T.20	VZ369 (097/FD)
					Attacker FB.2	WZ277 (076/FD)
					Wyvern S.4	VZ782 (082/FD)
					Gannet AS.1	WN465 (083/FD)
					Firebrand TF.5	EK636 (082/FD)
					Sturgeon TT.2	TS491 (093/FD)
					Skyraider AEW.1	WT945 (088)
					Anson 1	MG731 (097/FD)
		071-084	700	1955	Gannet AS.1	WN376 (084/FD)
					Wyvern S.4	VZ796 (081/FD)
					Sea Vampire F.20	VV152 (071/FD)
					Sea Hawk F.1	WF233 (074/FD)
					Sea Hawk FB.3	WF294 (074/FD)
					Sea Hawk FGA4	WV801 (072/FD)
		100-103) 110-113) 120-123)	813	1946	Firebrand TF.4	EK790 (113/FD)
		100-103) 110-113) 120-123)	813	1947	Firebrand TF.5	EJ766 (121/FD)
		120-131	827	1950/52	Firebrand TF.4	EK780 (121/FD)
		150-161	801	1947/48	Sea Hornet FR.20	TT204 (154/FD)
		161-179	764	1955	Sea Hawk F.1	WF201 (162/FD)
					Sea Hawk F.2	WF249 (168/FD)
					Wyvern S.4	VZ799 (173/FD)
					Sea Vampire F.20	VT803 (178)
		201-225	CAD	1951/55	Firefly T.2	MB725 (216/FD)
					Firefly AS.6	WH631 (206/FD)
					Harvard T.2b	KF514 (219/FD)
					Harvard T.3	EZ372 (221)
					Sea Balliol T.21	WL720 (224/FD)
		251-259	764	1955	Sea Vampire T.22	XG742 (254/FD)
		271-278	826	1951	Firefly AS.6	WD902 (273/FD)
		293-294	813	1953	Meteor T.7	WL335 (293)
		361-369	815	1954	Avenger AS.5	XB445 (364/FD)
		400-411	762	1947/48	Oxford T.1	PH260 (406/FD)
					Anson T.1	MG725 (401/FD)
		450-459	762	1947/49	Mosquito T.3	TW103 (450/FD)
		470-476	762	1947/49	Mosquito FB.6	RF782 (476/FD)
					Sea Mosquito TR.33	TW293 (472/FD)

Base		Codes	Sqdn	Years	Aircraft Type	Example	Base		Codes	Sqdn	Years	Aircraft Type	Example
FD	Ford contd	501-516	771	1947/55	Firefly FR.1	MB719 (508/FD)	GN	Eglinton contd	401-409	820	1955	Gannet AS.1	WN426 (404/GN)
					Firefly TT.4	TW723 (515/FD)			411-419	824	1955	Gannet AS.1	WN396 (411/GN)
					Sea Vampire F.20	VV140 (503/FD)			421-434	737	1955	Gannet AS.1	WN412 (431/GN)
					Sea Vampire F.21	VG701 (505/FD)						Gannet T.2	XA508 (421/GN)
					Sea Hawk FB.2	WF294 (514/FD)			455	812	1955	Gannet T.2	XA520 (455/GN)
					Meteor T.7	WA649 (516/FD)			456-459	719	1955	Gannet AS.1	XA357 (459/GN)
		501-515	700	1955	Sea Vampire F.20	VV149 (505/FD)						Gannet T.2	XA522 (456/GN)
					Firefly TT.4	VG974 (501/FD)			900-910	St F	1948/55	Sea Otter ABR.2	RD881 (901/GN)
		542-545	771	1950/52	Sea Mosquito TR.33	TW250 (543/FD)						Sea Fury T.20	WE824 (910/GN)
					Mosquito FB.6	TE705 (545/FD)						Firefly T.1	Z1943 (905/GN)
		585-599	771	1948/52	Sturgeon TT.2	TS484 (590/FD)						Firefly T.2	MB578 (906/GN)
					Anson 1	MH160 (591/FD)						Dragonfly HR.3	WG720 (902/GN)
					Mosquito PR.16	MM361 (595/FD)						Whirlwind HAS.22	WV201 (901/GN)
					Sea Mosquito TR.33	TW286 (598/FD)						Dominie C.1	NF861 (900/GN)
					Mosquito TT.39	ML980 (599/FD)						Sea Prince T.1	WP307 (909/GN)
					Sea Vampire F.20	VV150 (593/FD)	HF	Hal Far	200-201	IF F	1953/55	Sea Fury T.20	VZ364 (200/HF)
					Sea Vampire F.21	VG701 (594/FD)			410-412	IF F	1954/55	Meteor T.7	VW446 (412/HF)
		591-592	700	1955	Anson 1	NK834 (591/FD)			500-535	728	1948/55	Mosquito PR.16	NS742 (526/HF)
		600-603	720	1946/48	Anson 1	MG673 (601/FD)						Mosquito B.25	KA959 (521/HF)
		601-602	CAD	1954/55	Sea Prince T.1	WP311 (601/FD)						Mosquito TT.39	RV295 (511/HF)
		804	St F		Anson 1	MG730 (804/FD)						Martinet TT.1	RH114 (513/HF)
		900-905	St F	1951/55	Sea Vampire T.22	XA130 (900/FD)						Seafire F.17	SX294 (502/HF)
					Firefly T.1	Z2027 (901/FD)						Sea Hornet F.20	WE238 (530/HF)
					Sea Fury T.20	VZ369 (902/FD)			570-599	728	1951/55	Meteor T.7	WL350 (574/HF)
					Meteor T.7	WL332 (905/FD)						Sturgeon TT.2	TS480 (599/HF)
		981-983	St F	1953/55	Dragonfly HR.3	WP495 (982/FD)						Sturgeon TT.3	TS488 (581/HF)
GJ	Gosport	201-202	727	1946/50	Harvard T.2b	KF521 (201/GJ)						Sea Vampire F.20	VV153 (582/HF)
					Harvard T.3	EZ404 (202/GJ)			801	728	1946/47	Baltimore IV	FA435 (801/HF)
		210-239	727	1946/50	Tiger Moth T.2	T7045 (211/GJ)			811-812	728	1949/55	Expeditor C.2	FT994 (811/HF)
		501-515	705	1947/50	Hoverfly 1	KL112 (506/GJ)			901-903	728/	1952/55	Dragonfly HR.3	WG723 (902/HF)
					Hoverfly 2	KN879 (501/GJ)				St F			
		501	St F	1950	Tiger Moth T.2	BB865 (501/GJ)			913	St F	1948	Harvard T.3	EZ436 (913/HF)
		591	St F	1955	Anson 1	NK895 (591/GJ)	HR	Henstridge	-	767	1952	Sea Fury F.10	TF903 (---/HR)
		600-603	720	1948/50	Anson 1	MG721 (603/GJ)						Firefly FR.1	PP399 (---/HR)
		700-711	705	1950/55	Dragonfly HR.1	VX596 (710/GJ)	JA	Stretton	101-120	1831	1947/53	Seafire F.15	SR578 (111/JA)
					Dragonfly HR.3	WG705 (705/GJ)						Seafire F.17	SX159 (102/JA)
					Whirlwind HAR.1	XA862 (704)						Sea Fury FB.11	VR929 (102/JA)
					Whirlwind HAS.3	XG576 (703)			160-169	767	1952/53	Sea Fury F.10	TF903 (160/JA)
					Whirlwind HAS.22	WV221 (701/GJ)			171-173	767	1953	Attacker F.1	WA487 (173/JA)
		780-787	706	1953/54	Whirlwind HAS.22	WV219 (c/s 781)						Attacker FB.1	WA535 ?
									201-210	1831	1947/52	Harvard T.2b	KF505 (202/JA)
		901-902	St F	1947	Oxford 1	DF518 (901/GJ)						Harvard T.3	EZ408 (202/JA)
GN	Eglinton	022-023	744	1951/53	Firefly AS.6	VT499 (022/GN)						Sea Fury T.20	VX287 (201/JA)
		103	813	1950	Firebrand TF.5	EK723 (103/GN)			260-263	767	1953	Firefly FR.4	VG976 (263/JA)
		100-119	737	1949/50	Seafire F.17	SP324 (119/GN)			750	St F	1950/51	Anson 1/ASH	MH118 (750/JA)
		200-231	737	1950/55	Firefly T.1	MB496 (220/GN)			900-905	St F/ 2 FF	1947/53	Dominie C.1	X7507 (905/JA)
					Firefly FR.1	DV121 (225/GN)	JB	St Merryn	105	736	1949	Seafire F.17	SX253 (105/JB)
					Firefly TT.4	TW739 (217/GN)			100-136	736	1949/50	S Fury FB.11	VW234 (124/JB)
					Firefly AS.5	VT466 (206/GN)			151-153	741	1947	Harvard T.3	
					Firefly AS.6	WD900 (223/GN)			161-199	736	1947/49	Seafire F.15	PR399 (163/JB)
		211-220	812	1952/53	Firefly AS.6	VT474 (211)						Seafire F.17	SX311 (179/JB)
		211	815	1953	Avenger TBM-3E	XB318 (c/s 211)			201-205	736	1947/50	Harvard T.3	EZ327 (202/JB)
		226-231	719	1949	Firefly AS.5	VT467 (226/GN)			202-287	736/ 796	1947/50	Firefly FR.1	DK504 (254/JB)
		240	815	1952/53	Firefly Tr							Firefly T.1	DK499 (271/JB)
		242-247	744	1952/55	Sea Fury FB.11	WG655 (246/GN)			204-253	741	1947	Firefly FR.1	MB616 (253/JB)
					Firefly T.1	Z1943 (245/GN)			218-238	816	1948/49	Firefly FR.4	TW732 (227/JR)
					Firefly T.2	DK478 (247/GN)			300	SNAW	1947	Avenger III	JZ671 (300)
		255-279	719	1950/53	Firefly AS.5	VX436 (277/GN)			551-553	736	1947/50	Martinet TT.1	RG967 (551)
					Firefly AS.6	WD842 (267/GN)			600	St F	1947/50	Oxford 1	LB413 (600/JB)
		256-259	814	1954	Firefly AS.6	VT426 (256/GN)	JR	Eglinton	100-112	805	1948/49	Sea Fury F.10	TF925 (110/JR)
		280-287	825	1951	Firefly AS.5	WB362 (283/GN)						Sea Fury FB11	VR930 (105/JR)
		300-312	815	1950/53	Barracuda TR.3	RJ797 (300/GN)			100-117	737	1948	Seafire F.15	
												Seafire F.17	SX138 (100/JR)
		320-341	719	1953/55	Firefly T.7	WJ157 (321/GN)			213-214	768	1948/49	Firefly 1	Z2100 (213/JR)
		350-361	815	1953/54	Avenger TBM-3E	XB318 (361/GN)			218-233	816	1948/49	Firefly FR.4	TW731 (227/JR)
												Firefly AS.5	VX378 (218/JR)
		381-388	814	1954	Avenger AS.5	XB367 (381/GN)			220-225	737	1949	Firefly FR.1	DT933 (225/JR)
		391-398	824	1954/55	Avenger AS.4	XB324 (395)						Firefly T.1	MB496 (220/JR)
		400-410	744	1951/55	Sea Prince T.1	WP320 (405/GN)			300-311	744	1946/47	Barracuda TR.3	RJ937 (304/JR)
					Anson I	LT346 (401/GN)			300-318	815	1947/49	Barracuda TR.3	ME284 (300/JR)
									400-405	719	1947/49	Anson 1	NK867 (405/JR)
									900-903	St F	1948/49	Sea Otter	RD881 (902/JR)
												Harvard T.3	EZ388 (903/JR)
												Dominie 1	X7332 (900/JR)

465

Base		Codes	Sqdn	Years	Aircraft Type	Example		Base		Codes	Sqdn	Years	Aircraft Type	Example
LM	Lossie-mouth	100-141	766	1946/53	Seafire F.15	PR374 (130/LM)	LP	Lee-on-Solent contd		267-269	781	1949/54	Harvard T.2b	KF514 (268/LP)
					Seafire F.17	SX113 (106/LM)				290-293	781/JOAC	1954/55	Sea Balliol T.21	WL723 (291)
		100-119	736	1953/55	Attacker F.1	WA481 (100/LM)				301-310	824	1953/54	Avenger TBM-3E	XB373 (305)
					Attacker FB.2	WP299 (109/LM)				311-315	781	1947/52	S Otter ABR.2	RD873 (312/LP)
					Sea Hawk F.1	WF162 (102/LM)				323-335	783	1947/48	Barracuda TR.5	RK558 (325/LP)
					Sea Hawk F.2	WF271 (113/LM)				391-398	824	1954	Avenger AS.4	XB362 (363)
					Sea Hawk FB.3	WF296 (119/LM)				441-442	781	1951/54	Meteor T.7	WL352 (442)
		100-149	738	1953/54	Sea Fury FB.11	VX660 (120/LM)				451-453	781/JOAC	1954/55	Sea Vampire T.22	XA112 (451)
					Sea Hawk F.1	WF165 (123/LM)				504	771	1950	Firefly FR.1	? (504/LP)
					Sea Hawk F.2	WF261 (125/LM)				510-515	773	1950	Seafire F.15	PR368 (510/LP)
					Sea Hawk FB.3	WF299 (124/LM)				550-599	771	1947/53	Anson 1	MG726 (550/LP)
					Sea Hawk FGA.4	WV843 (122/LM)							Sea Hornet NF.21	VW958 (552/LP)
		120-131	802	1954	Sea Hawk F.1	WF216 (123)							Firefly FR.1	MB436 (556/LP)
		120-135	738	1954/55	Sea Hawk F.1	WF165 (122/LM)							Seafire F.45	LA482 (564/LP)
		157	801	1953	Sea Fury FB.11	VR928 (157/LM)							Martinet TT.1	PX119 (575/LP)
		150-158) 176)	736	1953/54	Attacker F.1	WA484 (151/LM)							Mosquito PR.16	NS775 (597/LP)
					Attacker FB.1	WA530 (150/LM)							Mosquito B.25	KB584 (589/LP)
					Attacker FB.2	WZ275 (153/LM)							Sea Mosquito TR.33	TW257 (590/LP)
		150-156	736	1954/55	Sea Hawk F.2	WF257 (150/LM)							Mosquito PR.34	PF628 (590/LP)
					Sea Hawk FB.3	WF282 (153/LM)							Sea Mosquito T.39	? (598/LP)
		200-268	766	1947/53	Firefly FR.1	MB698 (207/LM)							S Fury FB.11	VX291 (590/LP)
					Firefly T.1	Z2111 (252/LM)							Meteor T.7	WA649 (591/LP)
					Firefly T.2	MB585 (520/LM)				601-608	783	1947/49	Anson 1	MH117 (601/LP)
					Harvard T.3	FT967 (239/LM)				601-608	781	1949/54	Oxford 1	DF518 (608/LP)
		201-206	738	1953/54	Sea Fury T.20	VX301 (201/LM)				751-787	799	1946/48	Harvard T.2b	KF532 (751/LP)
		204-212	738	1954/55	Sea Vampire T.22	XA107 (210/LM)							Seafire 3	PP928 (769/LP)
		211-215	736	1953/54	Sea Vampire T.22	XA106 (211/LM)							Seafire F.15	PR377 (772/LP)
		221-242	759	1954	Sea Vampire T.22	XA152 (239/LM)							Barracuda TR.3	RK469 (782/LP)
		221-242	736	1954/55	Sea Vampire T.22	XA159 (236/LM)							Firefly FR.1	? (781/LP)
		243-250	766	1953	Firefly T.2	MB585 (250/LM)				850-869	781/St F	1946/53	Expeditor C.2	KP110 (852/LP)
		250-251	764	1953	Firefly T.2	MB662 (250/LM)							Dominie C.1	X7448 (854/LP)
		270-275	766	1951/52	Sea Fury T.20	VX309 (272/LM)							Oxford	
		400-402	766	1947/49	Anson T.1	NK669 (402/LM)							Anson 1	NK837 (869/LP)
		402-404	759	1953/54	Meteor T.7	WL353 (402/LM)							S Prince C.1	WF137 (850/LP)
		405-408	736	1953/54	Meteor T.7	WS107 (405/LM)							S Prince C.2	WJ348 (851/LP)
		410-417	759	1953/54	Meteor T.7	WS106 (415/LM)							S Devon C.20	XJ320 (c/s 852)
		900-907	St F	1953/55	Sea Otter	? (904/LM)	LS	Lee-on-Solent		201-237	781	1955	Firefly T.1	MB693 (221/LS)
					Anson 1	NK610 (900/LM)							Sea Fury T.20	VZ351 (228/LS)
					Oxford 1	PH453 (901)				271-279	826	1954/55	Firefly AS.6	WB246 (275/LS)
					Dragonfly HR.3	WP493 (903/LM)	MA	Machri-hanish		201-208	799	1951/52	Harvard T.2b	KF509 (205/MA)
					Meteor T.7	WS103 (907/LM)				222-235	799	1951/52	Firefly FR.1	PP393 (233/MA)
					Dominie C.1	NF847 (901/LM)							Firefly T.1	MB412 (222/MA)
					Vampire FB.5	VV631 (906/LM)				241-248	820	1951/52	Firefly FR.5	VT370 (242/MF)
LP	Lee-on-Solent	000-029	778	1947/48	Sea Hornet FR.20	VR844 (000/LP)							Firefly AS.6	WB439 (244/MA)
					Seafire F.17	SX283 (016/LP)				901-915	St F	1951/52	Dominie C.1	X7508 (901/MA)
					Firefly FR.4	VG968 (028/LP)							Sea Otter	JN243 (902/MA)
		001-029	778	1948/50	Firefly FR.4	VG993 (029/LP)							Firefly T.2	MB731 (905/LM)
					Firefly 5	VT362 (025/LP)	MF	St Merryn	210-290	796	1950/53	Firefly FR.1	DK504 (254/MF)
					Sea Hornet FR.20	VR844 (006/LP)							Firefly T.3	PP435 (262/MF)
					Sea Hornet NF.21	VW958 (001/LP)							Firefly AS.5	VT479 (231/MF)
					Dominie 1	NF861 (002/LP)				300-313	796	1950/51	Firefly AS.6	WD892 (217/MF)
					Seafire F.17	SX161 (012/LP)							Barracuda TR.3	ME179 (310/MF)
		031-099	703	1947/50	Mosquito FB.6	TE720 (041/LP)				300-316	750	1952/53	Barracuda TR.3	ME264 (310/MF)
					Sea Mosquito TR.37	VT728 (048/LP)							Firefly T.7	WJ192 (302/MF)
					Firebrand TF.5	EK741 (031/LP)				360-378	796	1953	Firefly T.7	WJ195 (367/MF)
					Avenger 3	KE443 (068/LP)				600-612	750	1952/53	Anson 1	MH229 (603/MF)
					Anson 1	MG735 (081/LP)							Sea Prince T.1	WF127 (608/MF)
					S Fury FB.11	VR941 (098/LP)				901-902	St F	1951/53	Anson 1	NK829 (901/MF)
					Sea Vampire F.20	VF315 (072/LP)							Dragonfly HR.3	WH992 (902/MF)
		101-125	781	1949/54	Seafire F.17	SX194 (103/LP)							Sea Fury T.20	WG652 (901/MF)
		103-106	773	1949	Sea Fury FB.11	VR928 (120/LP)				914-918	St F	1951/53	Firefly FR.1	PP479 (914/MF)
		154-167	781	1949/52	Seafire F.17	SX161 (166/LP)							Firefly T.1	Z1873 (917/MF)
					Sea Fury FB.11	VR951 (165/LP)							Firefly T.2	MB578 (915/MF)
		201-239	781	1949/54	Firefly T.1	MB496 (220/LP)				980-985	St F	1951/52	Sea Otter 2	RD889 (980/MF)
					Firefly FR.1	MB726 (205/LP)	MV	Milltown	100-120	767	1947/49	vSeafire L.3	PP972 (120/MV)
					Firefly T.2	DK550 (226/LP)							Seafire F.15	PR497 (109/MV)
					Firefly FR.4	TW250 (238/LP)				201-244	767	1947/49	Firefly FR.1	MB732 (202/MV)
					Firefly FR.5	? (239/LP)	RO	Lee-on-Solent (attd Roborough?)	900-901	St F	1955	Whirlwind HAR.3	XG572 (c/s RO901)
					Sea Fury T.20	VX310 (207/LP)								
		214-217	824	1953	Avenger TBM-3E	XB387 (c/s 214)								

	Base	Codes	Sqdn	Years	Aircraft Type	Example		Base	Codes	Sqdn	Years	Aircraft Type	Example
SJ	Syerston	-	22FTS	1954	Sea Fury T.20	VZ353 (---/SJ)	VL	Yeovilton	100-154	contd		Sea Fury FB.11	TF973 (119/VL)
SR	St Merryn	300-310	750	1953/54	Firefly T.7	WJ193 (309/SR)		contd	100-116	764	1953/54	Seafire F.17	SX280 (107/VL)
		360-378	796	1953/54	Firefly T.7	WM807(365/SR)			120-127	764	1954	Sea Hawk F.1	WM905(122)
		603-611	750	1953/54	Sea Prince				150-156	1834	1954/55	Sea Fury FB.11	VW663 (154/VL)
					T.1	WF127 (608/SR)			162	799	1949	Seafire F.15	SR583 (162/VL)
		902-903	St F	1953/54	Dragonfly				200-206	700/	1946/49	Firefly FR.1	MB401 (200/VL)
					HR.3	WP494 (903/SR)				767/		Harvard T.3	EZ284 (203/VL)
ST	Stretton	100-112	1831	1953/55	Sea Fury F.10	TF941 (110/ST)				799			
					Sea Fury FB.11	WM489(109/ST)			200-208	890	1954/55	Sea Venom	
		120-128	767	1954/55	Sea Hawk F.1	WF159 (125)						FAW.20	WM516(205/VL)
		160-166)	718	1955	Attacker FB.2	WZ302 (163/ST)			200-207	766	1955	Sea Venom	
		170-176)										FAW.20	WM562(200/VL)
		161-163	767	1953	Sea Fury F.10	TF916 (163/ST)			226-235	809	1954/55	Sea Venom	
		171-176	767	1953/54	Attacker F.1	WA513 (176/ST)						FAW.20	WM545(228)
					Attacker FB.2	WZ373 (170/ST)			240	50	1948	Tiger Moth T.2	T5900 (240/VL)
		180-181	767	1954	Sea Hawk F.1	WF210 (181/ST)				TRAG			
		201-213	SAD	1953/55	Harvard T.2b	KF525 (205/ST)			243-251	764	1953/54	Firefly T.1	Z2119 (243/VL)
					Harvard T.3	EX405 (203/ST)						Firefly T.2	MB673 (244/VL)
					Sea Balliol				260-270	1834	1954/55	Sea Balliol T.21	WL734 (265/VL)
					T.21	WP326 (202/ST)						Sea Fury T.20	WE823 (260/VL)
					Firefly T.2	MB747 (205/ST)						Harvard T.2b	KF552 (265/VL)
					Sea Fury T.20	VX307 (210/ST)			261-268	808	1955	Sea Venom	
		260-264	767	1953	Firefly FR.4	TW749 (261/ST)						FAW.20	WM550(266)
		260-264	718	1955	Sea Vampire				277	?	?	Firefly FR.1	PP620 (277/VL)
					T.22	XG774 (261)			300-322	700	1946/49	Barracuda	
		280-289	NAD	1952/55	Firefly FR.1	DK542 (282/ST)						TR.3	RJ766 (302/VL)
					Firefly T.2	DK530 (285/ST)			701	700	1947/48	Sea Otter 2	JN201 (701/VL)
					Firefly T.3	PP491 (282/ST)			801	St F	1950/51	Dominie C.1	HG709 (801/VL)
					Firefly FR.5	VT493 (286/ST)			901-908	St F	1950/55	Vampire FB.5	VZ148 (901/VL)
					Firefly AS.6	VT499 (285/ST)						Oxford	? (902)
		309-311	NAD	1955	Avenger AS.5	XB442 (309/ST)						Sea Vampire	
		361-365	767	1954/55	Avenger AS.4	XB310 (362/ST)						F.20	VV144 (902/VL)
		409	NAD	1953/55	Sea Prince T.1	WF132 (409/ST)						Sea Vampire	
		901-902	St F	1952/55	Sea Vampire							T.22	XA156 (908/VL)
					T.22	XA164 (901/ST)						Meteor T.7	WS107 (c/s906)
					Dominie C.1	NF848 (902/ST)						Sea Fury T.20	VX291 (905/VL)
					Meteor T.7	WA652 (901/ST)						Firefly T.2	MB673 (904/VL)
SZ	Belfast	999	St F	1954/55	Anson 1	NK201 (999/SZ)						Expeditor C.2	HD775 (900/VL)
VL	Yeovilton	100-154	767/	1948/51	Seafire F.15	SR485 (154/VL)	-	Rochester	203-205	Ad F	1951/55	Harvard T.3	EZ364 (203)
			799		Seafire F.17	SX232 (105/VL)			601-615	Ad F	1950/55	Oxford	PH140 (611)
					Seafire F.46	LA545 (110)	-	Hamble	601-608	AST	1949/53	Anson 1	NK941 (603'C')
					Sea Fury F.10	TF912 (120/VL)							

Hawker Hunter GA.11 WT721 '694/LM' of No.764 Squadron, Lossiemouth in 1970. (MAP)

FLEET AIR ARM CODES 1956 - 1965

Codes	Fin	Sqdn	Base	Years	Aircraft Type	Example
000-023	BY	A/W FRU	Brawdy, St Davids	1956/60	Mosquito T.3	VA878 (001/BY)
					Meteor T.7	WA652 (004/BY)
					Sea Venom FAW.20	WM513(010/BY)
					Sea Venom FAW.21	WW283(017/BY)
					Attacker F.1	WA519 (019/BY)
011-022	VL	A/W FRU	Yeovilton	1961/65	Sea Venom FAW.21	WW188(019/VL)
					Sea Venom FAW.22	XG695 (016/VL)
025-045	-	A/W FRU	Hurn	1956/65	Sea Fury FB.11	VR936 (031)
					Sea Hawk F.1	WF191 (035)
					Sea Hawk FB.5	WF296 (038)
					Sea Hawk FGA.6	WV825 (034)
					Scimitar F.1	XD232 (031)
					Firefly TT.4	VG957 (041)
					Meteor T.7	WL350 (044)
					Meteor TT.20	WM255(046)
					Attacker FB.2	WK342 (034)
045-049	DO	NCS	Donibristle	1956/58	Sea Prince C.1	WF136 (045/DO)
					Sea Prince C.2	WJ349 (045/DO)
					Dominie	NF864 (049/DO)
					Sea Fury T.20	WE826 (049/DO)
056-057	-	A/W FRU	Hurn	1957/58	Firefly TT.4	TW739 (057)
070-083	W	300 RIN	Brawdy	1960/61	Sea Vampire T.22	XA102 (070/W)
					Sea Hawk FGA.6	IN-152 (072/W)
086-088	HF	847	Hal Far, Nicosia	1956/59	Gannet AS.1	XA355 (088/HF)
					Gannet AS.4	XA455 (088)
090-099	J O	893	Eagle, Ark Royal	1956/57	Sea Venom FAW.21	WW265(092/O)
100-111	J Z O/R	800	Eagle, Albion, Ark Royal	1956/59	Sea Hawk FGA.4	WV832 (106/Z)
					Sea Hawk FGA.6	XE454 (101/Z)
100-113	R	800	ArkRoyal	1959/64	Scimitar F.1	XD264 (108/R)
100-111	E	800	Bulwark	1964/65	Buccaneer S.1	XN953 (109/E)
111-117	E	800B	Eagle	1964/65	Scimitar F.1	XD271 (114/E)
116-127	C	801	Centaur	1956	Sea Hawk FGA.4	WV846 (124/C)
115-128	B C	801	Bulwark, Centaur	1957/60	Sea Hawk FGA.6	XE398 (121/B)
115-124	R V	801	ArkRoyal, Victorious	1962/65	Buccaneer S.1	XN955 (124/V)
130-142	E Z R/O	802	Eagle, Albion, Ark Royal	1956/59	Sea Hawk FB.3	WM971(133/O)
					Sea Hawk FB.5	WF281 (136/R)
141-159	H R V	803	Hermes, Ark Royal, Victorious	1958/65	Scimitar F.1	XD248 (151/V)
145-156	J/E	803	Eagle	1957/58	Sea Hawk FGA.6	XE337 (155/J)
160-173	B A O	804	Bulwark, Albion, Ark Royal	1956/59	Sea Hawk FGA.6	WV919 (168/A)
161-166	H	804	Hermes	1960/61	Scimitar F.1	XD236 (163/H)
173?	-	829	Dido	1963/64	Wasp HAS.1	XS536 (173)
174?	-	829	Mohawk	1964/65	Wasp HAS.1	XS532 (174)
175-190	A J/E	806	Albion, Eagle	1957/60	Sea Hawk FB.5	WN119 (180/J)
					Sea Hawk FGA.6	XE439 (178/E)
175	LO	829	London	1964/65	Wessex HAS.1	XP151(175/LO)
177	AS	829	Ashanti	1964/65	Wasp HAS.1	XS540 (177/AS)
180	AJ	700W /829	Ajax	1964/65	Wasp HAS.1	XS537(180/AJ)
181	KE	829	Kent	1964/65	Wessex HAS.1	XP140 (181/KE)
182	-	829	Zulu	1964/65	Wasp HAS.1	XS544 (182)
183	ES	829	Eskimo	1964/65	Wasp HAS.1	XT416 (183/ES)
184	PE	700W /829	Penelope	1964/65	Wasp HAS.1	XS534 (184/PE)
185	AU	829	Aurora	1964/65	Wasp HAS.1	XS539 (185/AU)
187	NU	829	Nubian	1964/65	Wasp HAS.1	XS566 (187/NU)
188	EU	829	Euryalus	1964/65	Wasp HAS.1	XS562 (188/EU)
190-201	B	895	Bulwark	1956	Sea Hawk FGA.6	XE439 (200/B)
190-201	J	897	Eagle	1956/57	Sea Hawk FGA.6	WV907 (190/J)
190-198	C R	807	Centaur, Ark Royal	1958/62	Scimitar F.1	XD245 (192/R)
207-219	H C R V	892	Hermes, Centaur, Ark Royal, Victorious	1959/65	Sea Vixen FAW.1	XJ486 (212/R)
220-229	Z A	809	Albion	1956/59	Sea Venom FAW.21	XG667 (224/A)
220-233	R LM	809	ArkRoyal Lossiemouth	1962/65	Buccaneer S.1	XK531 (227/LM)
230-239	B Z	810	Bulwark Albion	1956	Sea Hawk FGA.4	WV860 (239/Z)
230-236	C	810	Centaur	1959/60	Gannet AS.4	XA432 (233/C)
240-251	C	811	Centaur	1956	Sea Hawk FB.3	WN116 (250/C)
240-254	H R	890	Hermes, Ark Royal	1960/65	Sea Vixen FAW.1	XJ574 (240/R)
250-267	J GN	812	Eagle, Eglinton	1956	Gannet AS.1	WN357 (265/J)
					Gannet T.2	XA520 (255/GN)
255-259	V	893	Victorious	1959/60	Sea Venom FAW.22	WW215(255/V)
265-280	-	831	Culdrose	1958/62	Gannet AS.1	XA340 (279)
					Gannet ECM.6	XA472 (278)
					Sea Vampire T.22	XA155 (279)
					Sea Venom 21ECM	XG608 (273)
					Avenger AS.6	XB328 (266)
270-278	J/E CU	813	Eagle Culdrose	1956/58	Wyvern S.4	VZ761 (274/J)
280-288	J/E CU	814	Eagle, Culdrose	1957/59	Gannet AS.4	XA425 (286/J)
281-288	H	814	Hermes	1959/60	Whirlwind HAS.7	XN308 (287/H)
290-299	O/R	815	Ark Royal	1956/58	Gannet AS.1	XA342 (292/O)
					Gannet AS.4	XA425 (296/R)
290-295	R	820	Ark Royal	1959/60	Whirlwind HAS.7	XK944 (290/R)
292	-	815	Eglinton	1958	Whirlwind HAS.7	XL869 (292)
290-297	E	820	Eagle	1964/65	Wessex HAS.1	XS126 (294/E)
300-301	J	813	Eagle	1956	Wyvern S.4	VZ787 (300/J)
300-311	-	815	Eglinton, Portland	1958/59	Whirlwind HAR.3	XG577 (301)
					Whirlwind HAS.7	XL882 (307)
301-308	A	815	Albion	1959/60	Whirlwind HAS.7	XL867 (301/A)
300-307	C R	815	Centaur, Ark Royal	1961/65	Wessex HAS.1	XP106 (300/R)
310-318	V	825	Victorious	1960/62	Whirlwind HAS.7	XL882 (312/V)
321-329	C	820	Centaur	1956	Gannet AS.1	WN448 (326/C)
320-328	B	820	Bulwark	1956/57	Gannet AS.1	WN404 (324/B)
					Gannet T.2	XA524 (320/B)
320-327	A GN	820	Albion, Eglinton	1958/59	Whirlwind HAS.7	XL841 (323/A; 'V')
320-325	H CU R	819	Hermes, Culdrose, Ark Royal	1961/65	Wessex HAS.1	XM872 (320/H)
331-338	O	824	Ark Royal	1956	Gannet AS.1	WN396 (330/O)
330-339	Z/ A	824	Albion	1956/57	Gannet AS.1	WN363 (333/O)
					Gannet AS.4	XA420 (333/Z)
330-337	V	824	Victorious	1958/59	Whirlwind HAS.7	XL846 (331/V; 'V')
330-338	R C	824	Centaur, Ark Royal	1959/63	Whirlwind HAS.7	XN303 (333/C)
340-348	Z	825	Albion	1956	Gannet AS.1	WN377 (340/Z)
340-349	CU	825	Culdrose	1957/58	Gannet AS.4	XA462 (346/CU)
					Gannet T.2	XG869 (349/CU)
340-347	H V	814	Hermes, Victorious	1961/66	Wessex HAS.1	XM870 (344/V)
350-356	O	890	Ark Royal	1956	Sea Venom FAW.21	WW201(352/O)
351-355	-	848	Hal Far	1958/59	Whirlwind HAS.22	not carried
360-367	FD	Wyvern CU	Ford	1957	Wyvern S.4	VZ762 (264/FD)
370-379	J	830	Eagle	1956/57	Wyvern S.4	WN326 (375/J)
380-388	J FD O	831	Eagle, Ford, Ark Royal*	1956/57	Wyvern S.4	WN325 (380/O)
385-388	-	751	Culdrose	1958	Sea Venom FAW.21	XG608 (388)

Codes	Fin	Sqdn	Base	Years	Aircraft Type	Example
380-398	CU - R	831	Culdrose, Watton, Ark Royal	1958/65	Avenger AS.6 Sea Vampire T.22 Sea Prince T.1 Sea Venom 21ECM Sea Venom 22ECM	XB364 (380) XA109 (385) WF122 (390) XG608 (386/CU) XG629 (380)
390-397	-	845	Bulwark, Centaur	1957/59	Whirlwind HAS.7	XK942 (395 'F')
410-413	CU HQ	849	Culdrose	1956/58	Skyraider AEW.1	WT963 (411/CU)
410-418	CU HQ	849	Culdrose	1958/60	Skyraider AEW.1	WT950 (416/CU)
410-416	CU BY	849 HQ	Culdrose, Brawdy	1960/65	Gannet AEW.3	XL465 (413/BY)
414-417	J E	849A	Eagle	1956/58	Skyraider AEW.1	WT954 (417/J)
418-421	O	849B	Ark	1956/58	Skyraider AEW.1	WT952 (418/O)
418-421	E	849A	Eagle	1958/60	Skyraider AEW.1	WT953 (421/E)
420-423	C R V	849A	Centaur, Ark Royal, Victorious	1960/65	Gannet AEW.3	XL456 (420/R)
422-425	Z/ A	849C	Albion	1956/60	Skyraider AEW.1	WT947 (422/Z)
425-428	H C V	849B	Hermes, Centaur, Victorious	1960/65	Gannet AEW.3	XL481 (428/V)
426-429	C B Z/A	849D	Centaur, Bulwark Albion	1956/60	Skyraider AEW.1	WT097 (429/C)
430-433	V	849B	Victorious	1958/60	Skyraider AEW.1	WV181 (430/V)
430-433	H R	849C	Hermes, Ark Royal	1960/65	Gannet AEW.1	XL493 (437/R)
435-444	B C O	891	Bulwark, Centaur, Ark Royal	1956/61	Sea Venom FAW.21 Sea Venom FAW.22	WW290(443/B) XG674 (436/C)
435-438	E	849D	Eagle	1964/65	Gannet AEW.3	XL480 (436/E)
442-443	A	849C	Albion	1959/60	Skyraider AEW.1	WT966 (452/A)
445-452	J	892	Eagle	1956	Sea Venom FAW.21	WW209(446/J)
445-454	CU HQ	849	Culdrose	1960/65	Gannet COD.4 Gannet T.2	XA463 (445/CU) XG886 (454/CU)
450-453	A	849D	Albion	1960	Skyraider AEW.1	WT966 (452/A)
451-453	V	849B	Victorious	1960	Skyraider AEW.1	WT945 (453/V)
455-469	J B	897	Eagle, Bulwark	1956	Sea Hawk FB.3	WM916(460/J)
455-469	C O V	893	Centaur, Ark Royal, Victorious	1957/60	Sea Venom FAW.21	WW188(466/O)
455-468	C R V	893	Centaur, Ark Royal, Victorious	1960/65	Sea Vixen FAW.1	XN651 (461/C)
470-481	B E O	898	Bulwark, Eagle, Ark Royal	1956/59	Sea Hawk FGA.4	WV919 (482/O)
470	NA	829	Naiad	1965	Wasp HAS.1	XT417 (470/NA)
472	HA	Sh F /829	Hampshire	1963/65	Wessex HAS.1	XP156 (472/HA)
473	DI	700W /829	Dido	1963/65	Wasp HAS.1	XS536 (473/DI)
474	MO	700W /829	Mohawk	1964/65	Wasp HAS.1	XS538 (474/MO)
479	LE	700W /829	Leander	1963/65	Wasp HAS.1	XS533 (479/LE)
481	KE	Sh F	Kent	1963	Wessex HAS.1	XP141 (481/KE)
481	-	829	Hecla	1965	Wasp HAS.1	XT423 (481)
482	ZU	829	Zulu	1964/65	Wasp HAS.1	XS544 (482/ZU)
484	GU	829	Gurkha	1965	Wasp HAS.1	XS530 (484/GU)
485-496	J	899	Eagle	1956/57	Sea Hawk FGA.6	XE340 (485/J)
485-499	A J/E	894	Albion, Eagle	1957/60	Sea Venom FAW.22	WW205(490/O)
485-498	E VL	899	Eagle, Yeovilton	1961/65	Sea Vixen FAW.1 Sea Vixen FAW.2	XJ567 (487/VL) XP923 (493/E)

Codes	Fin	Sqdn	Base	Years	Aircraft Type	Example
500-524	FD VL	700	Ford, Yeovilton	1956/61	Avenger AS.5 Gannet AS.1 Gannet AS.4 Wyvern S.4 Firefly TT.4 Sea Vampire F.20 Sea Vampire T.22 Sea Venom FAW.20 Sea Venom FAW.21 Sea Hawk F.2 Sea Hawk FB.3 Sea Hawk FGA.4 Sea Hawk FGA.6 Whirlwind HAR.3 Whirlwind HAS.7 Seamew AS.1 Scimitar F.1 Anson 1 Sea Fury FB.11 Meteor TT.20	XB300 (508/FD) WN453 (522/FD) XG797 (505/VL) VZ796 (518/FD) VG697 (505/FD) VV152 (510/FD) XA165 (520/FD) WM523(521/FD) WW208(519/VL) WF259 (511/FD) WF294 (514/FD) WV904 (516/VL) WV834 (515/VL) XJ402 (501/VL) XK939 (502) XE179 (507) XD221 (512/FD) NK834 (520/FD) VW633 (523/FD) WM242(511)
501-511	CU	706	Culdrose	1962/65	Wessex HAS.1 Wasp HAS.1	XM871 (507/CU) XS529 (510)
505-508	-	700H	Lee-on-Solent	1957	Whirlwind HAS.7	XG597 (507'G')
506-512	-	700H	Culdrose	1960/62	Wessex HAS.1	XM833 (507)
520-541	LP CU	705	Lee-on-Solent Culdrose	1956/65	Dragonfly HR.3 Hiller HT.1 Hiller HT.2 Whirlwind HAR.1 Whirlwind HAR.3 Whirlwind HAS.7 Whirlwind HAS.22	VZ965 (532) XB477 (538) XS164 (536/CU) XA862 (527 'N') XG576 (526 'D') XG592 (531) WV218 (528)
541-559	GN	719	Eglinton	1956/59	Firefly T.7 Gannet AS.1 Gannet T.2 Gannet T.5	WJ165 (550/GN) WN461 (543/GN) XA510 (544/GN) XG887 (545/GN)
543-549	CU	705	Culdrose	1960/65	Hiller HT.2 Dragonfly HR.3	XS171 (543) WG722 (548)
555-568	BY	727	Brawdy	1956/60	Sea Vampire T.22 Sea Balliol T.21 Sea Prince T.1 Dragonfly HR.5	XA170 (562/BY) WL724 (564/BY) WF118 (567/BY) WG664 (562/BY)
570-599	HF	728	Hal Far	1956/65	Meteor T.7 Meteor TT.20 Sturgeon TT.2	WS115 (575/HF) WM147(580/HF) TS495 (583/HF)
590-599	HF	750	Hal Far	1963/65	Sea Vampire T.22 Sea Venom FAW.22	XA110 (599/HF) XG721 (592/HF)
595-599	LM	736	Lossiemouth	1956/58	Sea Vampire T.22	XA169 (596/LM)
590-599	-	728B	Hal Far	1958/61	Firefly U.9 Canberra D.14	VT364 (593) WD941 (591)
600-616	LM	736	Lossiemouth	1956/65	Sea Hawk F.2 Sea Hawk FB.3 Sea Hawk FGA.4 Sea Hawk FGA.6 Sea Vampire T.22 Scimitar F.1 Hunter T.8	WF257 (613/LM) WN105 (616/LM) WV864 (609/LM) XE370 (603/LM) XA163 (600/LM) XD273 (612/LM) XL581 (619/LM)
611-618	LM	764	Lossiemouth	1965	Scimitar F.1	XD215 (611/LM)
617-627	GN	737	Eglinton	1956/57	Gannet AS.1 Gannet T.2	WN415 (618/GN) XA509 (626/GN)
617-625	LM	736	Lossiemouth	1957/63	Sea Hawk FGA.4 Sea Hawk FB.5 Sea Hawk FGA.6 Scimitar F.1	WV833 (618/LM) WF302 (615/LM) XE338 (621/LM) XD217 (617/LM)

469

Codes	Fin	Sqdn	Base	Years	Aircraft Type	Example
621-624	-	728C	Hal Far	1958	Whirlwind HAS.22	WV222 (622)
625-627	-	719	Eglinton	1960/61	Whirlwind HAS.7	XN359 (627)
629-656	LM BY	738	Lossiemouth Brawdy	1956/65	Sea Hawk F.1	WF232 (647/LM)
					Sea Hawk F.2	WF265 (638/LM)
					Sea Hawk FB.3	WF299 (650/LM)
					Sea Hawk FGA.4	WV891 (637/LM)
					Sea Hawk FGA.6	WV795 (646/LM)
					Sea Venom FAW.21	WW195 (644/LM)
					Sea Vampire T.22	XA107 (633/LM)
					Hunter T.8	XL582 (631/LM)
					Hunter GA.11	XF297 (644/BY)
655-659	-	728B	Hal Far	1959/61	Meteor U.15	VT104 (656)
					Meteor U.16	WE932 (656)
655-664	BY	759	Brawdy	1963/65	Hunter T.8	XL603 (659/BY)
					Hunter T.8c	XL604 (663/BY)
657-661	CU	744	St Mawgan	1956	Gannet AS.1	WN421 (657/CU)
664	HF	750	Hal Far	1963	Sea Vampire T.22	XA110 (664/HF)
665-679	HF CU	750	Hal Far, Culdrose	1956/65	Sea Prince T.1	WF120 (665/CU)
					Sea Venom FAW.21	XG627 (676/HF)
					Sea Venom FAW.22	WW199 (675/HF)
					Sea Devon C.20	XJ349 (665/CU)
680-688	-	751	Watton, Culdrose	1956/58	Firefly AS.6	WD923 (680)
					Avenger AS.5	XB357 (687)
					Avenger AS.6	XB360 (680)
					Sea Venom FAW.21	XG608 (688)
680-689	LM	700Z	Lossiemouth	1961/63	Buccaneer S.1	XK532 (681/LM)
					Hunter T.8	WV319 (689/LM)
					Hunter T.8b	WW664 (686/LM)
689-714	FD LM	764	Ford, Lossiemouth	1956/65	Sea Hawk F.1	WF163 (690/FD)
					Sea Hawk F.2	WF260 (708/FD)
					Sea Hawk FB.3	WF298 (713/FD)
					Sea Hawk FGA.4	WV804 (694/LM)
					Sea Hawk FGA.6	XE407 (696/LM)
					Wyvern S.4	VZ799 (690/FD)
					Hunter T.8	WV322 (697/LM)
					Hunter T.8b	XF995 (698/LM)
					Hunter T.8c	XF991 (688/LM)
					Hunter PR.11	WT723 (692/LM)
					Hunter GA.11	XE716 (699/LM)
					Sea Vampire F.20	VV151 (712/LM)
					Sea Vampire F.21	VG701 (714/FD)
					Sea Vampire T.22	XA171 (691/FD)
704-715	FD	767	Ford	1956/57	Sea Hawk F.2	WF248 (706/FD)
					Sea Hawk FB.3	WM981 (710/FD)
705	-	701	Vidal	1958	Dragonfly HR.5	WP501 (705)
706-707	-	701 HQ	reservation	1957/58	Dragonfly HR.3	?
708-709	V	701C	Victorious	1957/58	Whirlwind HAR.3	XG574 (709/V)
710-711	-	701D	Bulwark	1957	allocation only	
710-722	VL	766	Yeovilton	1959/65	Sea Vixen FAW.1	XJ565 (718/VL)
712-713	E	701A	Eagle	1957/58	Whirlwind HAR.3	XG585 (713/E)
714-715	O/R	701B	Ark Royal	1957/58	Whirlwind HAR.3	XG583 (714/O)
716-717	-	701 Trials	Lee-on-Solent	1957/58	Whirlwind HAR.3	XG582 (717)
717-724	VL	766	Yeovilton	1956	Sea Venom FAW.20	WM563 (719/VL)
717-730	CU	765	Culdrose	1956/57	Firefly T.2	MB726 (722/CU)
					Firefly T.7	WJ168 (725/CU)
					Oxford T.1	PH326 (729/CU)
718	-	701 VIP	Lee-on-Solent	1957/58	Whirlwind HAS.22	WV219 (718)
719-720	-	701 HQ	Lee-on-Solent	1957/58	Dragonfly HR.5	WG671 (720)
721	-	701	Vidal?	1957/58	Dragonfly HR.5	?
722-723	-	701 Trials	Lee-on-Solent	1957/58	Whirlwind HAR.3	XJ402 (723)
725-734	LM	700B	Lossie Solent	1965	Buccaneer S.2	XN978 (726/LM)
726-739	VL	766	Yeovilton	1957/60	Sea Venom FAW.21	XG621 (729/VL)
731-740	VL	766	Yeovilton	1956/60	Sea Venom FAW.20	WW207 (737/VL)
					Sea Venom FAW.21	XG655 (736/VL)
					Sea Vampire T.22	XA130 (740/VL)
740-752	LP	781	Lee-on-Solent	1956/62	Dominie C.1	HG713 (c/s 745)
					Sea Devon C.20	XJ321 (c/s 749)
					Sea Heron C.2	XR441 (c/s 740)
					Whirlwind HAS.1	XA862 (c/s 747)
					Whirlwind HAS.22	WV219 (c/s 747)
					Sea Balliol T.21	WL722 (750)
					Sea Prince C.1	WP318 (c/s 756)
750-756	-	702	Ford	1957/58	Sea Balliol T.21	WL715 (752)
					Sea Vampire T.22	XA108 (754)
					Sea Prince T.1	WP318 (756)
750-759	PO	771	Portland	1961/64	Dragonfly HR.5	VZ965 (755/PO)
					Whirlwind HAR.3	XJ402 (751/PO)
					Whirlwind HAS.7	XN385 (755/PO)
					Whirlwind HAS.22	WV205 (753)
					P.531 O/N	XN332 (759)
					Wasp HAS.1	XS563 (759)
750-756	PO	771	Portland	1965	Whirlwind HAS.7	XN358 (750/PO)
761-784	CU	796	Culdrose	1956/58	Firefly T.7	WJ193 (761/CU)
					Gannet AS.1	XA396 (761/CU)
					Gannet T.2	XA523 (769/CU)
760-766	-	737	Portland	1959/60	Whirlwind HAS.3	XG587 (765)
767-779	PO	737	Portland	1959/62	Whirlwind HAS.7	XG596 (775)
770-776	PO	737	Portland	1962/65	Wessex HAS.1	XP147 (772/PO)
780-782	-	737	Portland	1960/61	Whirlwind HAR.3	XJ401 (780)
					Whirlwind HAS.22	WV203 (782)
					Wessex HAR.1	XM326 (780)
784-789	PO	737	Portland	1960/62	Whirlwind HAS.7	XL868 (786)
791-794	CU	765	Culdrose	1957	Sea Balliol T.21	WP325 (791/CU)
791-794	CU	796	Culdrose	1957/58	Sea Balliol T.21	WP321 (791/CU)
790-795	HF	728/750	Hal Far	1961/65	Sea Prince T.1	WF934 (790/HF)
					Sea Devon C.20	XJ348 (795/HF)
					Sea Heron C.2	XR444 (794/HF)
795-798	GN	745	Eglinton	1956/57	Avenger AS.5	XB398 (798/GN)
800-807	AC	SAD	Abbotsinch	1956/57	Avenger AS.5	XB308 (807/AC)
800-809	FD	700X	Ford	1957/58	Scimitar F.1	XD221 (801/FD)
					Sea Vampire T.22	XG769 (809)
810-818	ST	NAD	Stretton	1956/57	Attacker FB.2	WK321 (813/ST)
					Sea Vampire T.22	XA106 (818/ST)
810-815	-	751	Culdrose	1957/58	Sea Venom FAW.21	WW294 (812)
820-834	-	SAD	Benson	1956/57	Attacker FB.2	WK325 (830)
					Sea Hawk F.1	WF233 (822)
833-844	-	MAD	Bramcote	1956/57	Attacker FB.2	WZ292 (838)
					Sea Vampire T.22	XG775 (844)
845-854	-	SAD	Benson	1956/57	Sea Fury FB.11	VW556 (849)
					Sea Fury T.20	VX286 (852)
					Sea Hawk F.1	WF187 (851)
					Sea Vampire T.22	XA159 (854)
855-864	FD	CAD	Ford	1956/57	Firefly T.2	MB755 (862)
					Firefly AS.6	WB436 (855/FD)
					Firefly T.7	WK364 (858)
					Gannet AS.1	WN396 (855/FD)
					Gannet T.2	XA525 (864/FD)
					Sea Vampire T.22	XG772 (853)
867-868	ST	NAD	Stretton	1956/57	Sea Balliol T.21	WP327 (867/FD)
869-874	ST	NAD	Stretton	1956/57	Avenger AS.5	XB442 (869/ST)

Codes	Fin	Sqdn	Base	Years	Aircraft Type	Example
875-884	FD	CAD	Ford	1956/57	Firefly T.1	DK495 (882/FD)
					Firefly T.2	MB725 (884/FD)
					Firefly AS.6	WD854 (875/FD)
					Sea Prince T.1	WF133 (881/FD)
					Gannet AS.1	XA399 (878/FD)
885-888	AC	SAD	Abbotsinch	1956/57	Avenger AS.5	XB386 (888/AC)
					Sea Balliol T.21	WP324 (887/AC)
					Sea Prince T.1	WP312 (888/AC)
890-898	BR	MAD	Bramcote	1956/57	Firefly AS.6	WJ118 (896/BR)
					Avenger AS.5	XB391 (892/BR)
					Dominie 1	X7332 (890/BR)
					Sea Prince T.1	WM740 (897/BR)
					Sea Balliol T.21	WL728 (898/BR)
900	AH	St F	Anthorn	1956	Dragonfly HR.3	WP494 (900/AH)
900-902	-	BRNC	Dartmouth	1960/65	Dragonfly HR.5	WG667 (901)
901-903	AO	St F	Arbroath	1956/59	Dominie 1	NF847 (903/AO)
					Sea Prince C.1	WT137 (901/AO)
					Sea Prince C.2	WM756 (901/AO)
					Sea Devon C.20	XJ321 (901/AO)
902	-	JOAC	Lee-on-Solent	1956/57	Sea Vampire T.22	XA110 (902)
902	HA	Sh F	Hampshire	1963	Wessex HAS.1	XP156 (902/HA)
903	LO	St F	Linton-on-Ouse	1958/60	Sea Prince T.1	WP311 (903/LO)
903	-	Sh F	Ark Royal	1960	Dragonfly HR.5	WP497 (903)
904-910	BY	St F	Brawdy	1956/65	Dragonfly HR.3	WP500 (905)
					Dragonfly HR.5	VZ962 (904/BY)
					Sea Prince C.1	WF138 (907/BY)
					Sea Prince T.1	WP317 (908/BY)
					Dominie C.1	X7341 (910/BY)
					Meteor T.7	WA652 (910/BY)
					Whirlwind HAS.7	XL835 (905/BY)
					Sea Vampire T.22	XA115 (906/BY)
					Sea Hawk F.1	WF218 (906)
911-915	CU	St F	Culdrose	1956/65	Dragonfly HR.3	WP495 (912/CU)
					Dragonfly HR.5	WG607 (914/CU)
					Whirlwind HAR.3	XG586 (914)
					Whirlwind HAS.7	XK940 (911/CU)
					Gannet T.2	XA516 (915)
916-920	GN	St F	Eglinton	1956/59	Sea Fury T.20	WE824 (916/GN)
					Sea Prince T.1	WP307 (920/GN)
					Dragonfly HR.3	WG722 (918/GN)
					Firefly T.2	DK531 (919/GN)
					Gannet AS.1	WN366 (916/GN)
					Gannet T.2	XA509 (920/GN)
918-919	R	Sh F	Ark	1960/65	Whirlwind HAS.7	XK911 (918/R)
920	-	Sh F	Protector	1959/65	Whirlwind HAR.1	XA866 (920)
921-924	FD	St F	Ford	1956/59	Dragonfly HR.3	WG709 (922/FD)
					Dragonfly HR.5	WG664 (923/FD)
					Gannet T.2	XG880 (923/FD)
					Sea Vampire T.22	XA153 (923/FD)
					Gannet T.2	XG880 (923/FD)
927-929	LM	St F	Lee-on-Solent	1956/61	Sea Vampire T.22	XA156 (927)
					Sea Prince T.1	WP320 (929)
					Sea Balliol T.21	WL721 (928)
					Swordfish 2	NF389 (c/s 929)
					Sea Hawk FGA.6	XE390 (c/s 928)
931-939	LM	St F	Lossiemouth	1956/65	Dragonfly HR.3	WG676 (932/LM)
					Dragonfly HR.5	WN492 (934/LM)
					Dominie C.1	NF847 (931/LM)
					Whirlwind HAS.7	XM660 (933/LM)
					Sea Prince T.1	WF125 (935/LM)
					Sea Prince C.2	WJ349 (931/LM)
					Meteor T.7	VW447 (935/LM)
					Sea Hawk FGA.4	WV799 (939/LM)
					Sea Vampire T.22	XA164 (931/LM)
940	ST	St F	Stretton	1956	Sea Vampire T.22	XA168 (940/ST)
940	-	Sh F	Protector	1959/65	Whirlwind HAR.1	XA868 (940)
941-954	VL	St F/ FOFT/ IRF/ CIFE Flt	Yeovilton	1956/65	Hiller HT.1	XB474 (952/VL)
					Hunter T.8	XL580 (946/VL)
					Sea Prince T.1	WM739 (950/VL)
					Gannet AS.4	XG832 (943/VL)
					Sea Vampire T.22	XA118 (945/VL)
					Sea Fury T.20	WE822 (946/VL)
					Dragonfly HR.3	WG751 (948/VL)
					Dragonfly HR.5	WG670 (948/VL)
					Whirlwind HAS7	XL853 (941/VL)
					Sea Balliol T.21	WL719 (944/VL)
956-961	HF	728/ 728B/ St F	Hal Far	1956/65	Dragonfly HR.3	WN494 (960/HF)
					Dragonfly HR.5	WG708 (960/HF)
					Whirlwind HAR.3	XG573 (958/HF)
					Whirlwind HAS.22	WV224 (958/HF)
					Sea Devon C.20	XK896 (956/HF)
					Expeditor C.2	? (956/HF)
					Hunter T.8	XF322 (962/HF)
					Sea Vampire T.22	XA115 (961/HF)
961-962	GN	St F	Eglinton	1956	Dragonfly HR.3	WP504 (961/GN)
963	ST	St F	Stretton	1956/57	Dominie C.1	HG714 (963/ST)
963-966	LP	St F	Lee-on-Solent	1964/65	Sea Devon C.20	XJ319 (963)
964	FD	St F	Ford	1956	Sea Vampire T.22	XG744 (964/FD)
965	BY	St F	Brawdy	1956/57	Sea Hawk FGA.4	WV837 (965)
967-969	V	Sh F	Victorious	1959/60	Dragonfly HR.5	VX598 (968/V)
969	-	Sh F	Vidal	1961/62	Dragonfly HR.5	WG671 (969)
970-971	O	Sh F	Ark Royal	1956/57	Dragonfly HR.3	WG718 (971/O)
					Whirlwind HAR.3	XG572 (971/O)
970-971	AC	St F	Abbotsinch	1959/63	Sea Vampire T.22	XA130 (970/AC)
					Sea Balliol T.21	WP325 (971/AC)
					Sea Hawk FGA.6	WV793 (c/s970)
971	E	Sh F	Eagle	1964	Whirlwind HAS.7	XN259 (971)
972	B	Sh F	Bulwark	1957	Whirlwind HAR.3	XG581 (972/B)
973-974	J	Sh F	Eagle	1956/59	Dragonfly HR.3	WH989 (974/J)
					Dragonfly HR.5	WP497 (973/J)
					Whirlwind HAR.3	XJ399 (974/J)
973-975	LP	St F	Lee-on-Slnt	1964/65	Sea Heron C.2	XR442 (c/s974)
976-978	C	Sh F	Centaur	1956/65	Dragonfly HR.3	WP493 (977/C)
					Dragonfly HR.5	WG709 (977/C)
					Whirlwind HAS.7	XN261 (978/C)
979-980	Z	Sh F	Albion	1956/57	Whirlwind HAR.3	XG578 (980/Z)
980-984	LM	St F	Lossiemouth	1959/65	Sea Vampire T.22	XG769 (980/LM)
					Sea Prince T.1	WF122 (984/LM)
					Sea Hawk FGA6	WV909 (983/LM)
981-985	B	Sh F	Bulwark	1956/57	Dragonfly HR.3	WG750 (985/B)
					Avenger AS.5	XB389 (982/B)
981-982	B	701	Bulwark	1957	Whirlwind HAR.3	XG581 (982/B)
984	LP	St F	Lee-on-Slnt	1964/65	Sea Heron C.2	XR442 (c/s 984)
985-986	H	Sh F	Hermes	1962/64	Whirlwind HAS.7	XN360 (986/H)
989	D	Sh F	Devonshire	1962/64	Wessex HAS.1	XM923 (989/D)
990-991	PR	Sh F	Protector	1956/59	Whirlwind HAR.1	XA866 (990/PR)
990-991	-	701	Protector	1958	Whirlwind HAR.1	XA869 (991)
990-999	CU	St F /829	Culdrose	1958/65	Sea Prince C.1	WF137 (999/CU)
					Sea Balliol T.21	WL716 (992/CU)
					Dominie C.1	NF881 (999/CU)
					Avenger AS.6	XB446 (992)
					Sea Vampire T.22	XA162 (990/CU)
					Gannet T.5	XG889 (995/CU)
					Wasp HAS.1	XS530 (992/CU)
991-994	-	700W	Culdrose	1963/64	Wasp HAS.1	XS531 (993)
992	-	Sh F	Eagle	1956	Whirlwind HAR.3	XG573 (992)
992-998	J	Sh F	Warrior	1956/57	Whirlwind HAR.3	XG584 (994/J)
					Avenger AS.5	XB320 (998/J)

471

FLEET AIR ARM CODES 1965 - TO DATE

Codes	Fin	Sqdn	Ship/Base	Years	Aircraft Type	Example
001-007) 010-014)	R	890	Ark Royal	1965/66	Sea Vixen FAW.1	XN704 (006/R)
000-008) 010-018)	R	892	Ark Royal	1969/78	Phantom FG.1	XT862 (015/R)
000-008	N, R	801	Invincible, Ark Royal	1981/94	Sea Harrier FRS.1 Sea Harrier FRS.2	ZA175 (004/N)
008-021	N, R, L	820	Invincible, Ark Royal, Illustrious	1981/94	Sea King HAS.5 Sea King HAS.6	XZ921 (017/N) ZA169 (101)
015-017) 020-027) 030-034)	R	803	Ark Royal	1965/66	Scimitar F.1	XD271 (030/R)
020-027) 030-036)	R	809	Ark Royal	1969/78	Buccaneer S.2 Buccaneer S.2c Buccaneer S.2d	XV357 (034/R) XV359 (035/R) XV868 (025/R)
034-037) 040)	R	849C	Ark Royal	1965/66	Gannet AEW.1	XL498 (040/R)
040-041	R	SAR	Ark Royal	1969	Wessex HAS.1	?
040-044	R	849B	Ark Royal	1970/78	Gannet AEW.3 Gannet COD.4	XP229 (043/R) XG790 (040/R)
040	R	SAR	Ark Royal	1972	Sea King HAS.1	XV671 (040/R)
041-042	R	SAR	Ark Royal	1965/66	Whirlwind HAS.7	XM684 (41/R)
046-047	R	SAR	Ark Royal	1972/77	Wessex HAS.1	XS881 (046/R)
046-047	CU	771	Culdrose (attd)	1979	Wessex HAS.1	XS881 (046/CU)
050-057	R	815	Ark Royal	1965/66	Wessex HAS.1	XM832 (056/R)
050-056	R, EN	824	Ark Royal Engadine	1970/79	Sea King HAS.1 Sea King HAS.2	XV705 (051/R) XZ577 (052/R)
056-057	R	SAR	Ark Royal	1970/72	Wessex HAS.1	XS880 (057/R)
060-067	E	820	Eagle	1965/68	Wessex HAS.1	XS125 (063/R)
060-063	-	Pool	Culdrose	1972/76	Sea King HAS.1	XV670 (062/R)
064	-	RRE/ RSRE	(Malvern)	1972	Sea King HAS.1	XV651 (064)
067	-	Pool	Culdrose	1974	Sea King HAS.1	XV670 (067)
070-074	E	849B	Eagle	1965/72	Gannet AEW.3	XL503 (072/E)
100-107) 109-115)	E	800	Eagle	1965/72	Buccaneer S.1 Buccaneer S.2	XN953 (107/E) XT271 (105/E)
100-127	-	-	Harrier Pool	1976	allocation only	
100-105	VL	700A	Yeovilton	1979/80	Sea Harrier FRS.1	XZ455 (102/VL)
100-106	VL	899	Yeovilton	1980/81	Sea Harrier FRS.1	XZ452 (101/VL)
120-127) 130-137)	E	899	Eagle	1965/72	Sea Vixen FAW.2	XN656 (134/E)
120-128 130	H, VL, L, N	800	Hermes, Yeovilton, Illustrious, Invincible	1981/94	Sea Harrier FRS.1	XZ459 (125/H)
127, 129-139	-, H	826	Culdrose Hermes	1985/93	Sea King HAS.5 Sea King HAS.6	XZ916 (130) XV657 (132)
133-134	- -	826OEU 810OEU	Culdrose Boscombe Down	1991/94	Sea King HAS.6	XZ922 (134)
140-147	E, TG, EN, B, H	826	Eagle, Tiger, Engadine, Bulwark, Hermes	1968/84	Wessex HAS.3 Sea King HAS.1 Sea King HAS.2/2A	XP153 (143/E) XV663 (141/EN) XZ571 (140/TG)
146-148	E	SAR	Eagle	1969/72	Wessex HAS.1	XM326 (147/E)
150-160	VL, LU	767	Leuchars Yeovilton	1969/72	Phantom FG.1	XT867 (152/VL)
158	LU	767	Leuchars	1972	Phantom FG.1	XT866 (158/LU)
180-189	CU R, N, L	849	Culdrose Ark Royal, Invincible, Illustrious	1984/94	Sea King AEW.2/2A	XV672 (182/R)
200-227	-	-	Bulwark	1976	allocation only	
230-233) 236,240)	LM	700B	Lossiemouth	1965	Buccaneer S.2	XN978 (231/LM)
230-237) 240-241)	H, V	801	Hermes, Victorious	1965/70	Buccaneer S.2	XV333 (234/H)
238-239	LM	801	Lossiemouth	1968	Buccaneer S.2	XV336 (238)
240-247) 250-257)	H, V	893	Hermes, Victorious	1965/70	Sea Vixen FAW.2	XJ578 (243/V)
250-253	H	814	Hermes	1973	Sea King HAS.1	XV643 (250/H)
250-254	H, N	800	Hermes, Invincible	1980/81	Sea Harrier FRS.1	XZ492 (254/N)
250-259	-	809	Hermes, Invincible, Illustrious	1982	Sea Harrier FRS.1	XZ459 (256)
250-258	-	824	Culdrose, Prestwick	1985/94	Sea King HAS.5 Sea King HAS.6	ZA130 (257) XV676 (252)
260-264	H, V	849A	Hermes, Victorious	1965/70	Gannet AEW.3 Gannet COD.4 Gannet AS.4	XL471 (263/V) XA454 (264/H) XA430 (264)
264-267	H	814	Hermes	1976/77	Sea King HAS1	XV646 (264/H)
264-275	H, B, L, N	814	Hermes, Bulwark, Illustrious, Invincible	1977/94	Sea King HAS.2/2A Sea King HAS.5 Sea King HAS.6	XZ581 (273/H) XZ919 (271)B ZA169 (266/N)
265-266	V	SAR	Victorious	1967/78	Wessex HAS.1	XP160 (265/V)
265-266	H	SAR	Hermes	1968/70	Wessex HAS.1	XS871 (265/H)
268	-	825	Atlantic Causeway	1982	Sea King HAS.2/2A	XV696 (268)
270-277	H, V	814	Hermes, Victorious	1965/70	Wessex HAS.1 Wessex HAS.3	XM843 (271/V) XM916 (270/H)
270-274	H	814	Hermes	1973/77	Sea King HAS.1	XV677 (270/H)
300-319	PW		Portland		(allocation)	
300-308) 310)	CU PW	819	Culdrose, Prestwick	1971/94	Sea King HAS.1 Sea King HAS.2/2A	XV706 (307/PW) XV658 (304/PW)
300-307	PO	815	Portland	1982/94	Lynx HAS.2/3	XZ230 (301/PO)
301-307) 311-315)	H, VL	892	Hermes, Yeovilton	1965/68	Sea Vixen FAW.2	XN705 (302/VL)
314-315	L, OL	772	Illustrious, Olna	1982/84	Wessex HU.5	XT458 (315/L)
317	-	St F	Prestwick	1974/76	Sea Devon C.20	XJ322 (c/s317)
317	-	Director of Naval Recruiting		1991/92	Lynx	
320-327	H, LM	809	Hermes, Lossiemouth	1966/70	Buccaneer S.2	XV344 (325/H)
320	AZ	829	Amazon	1975/78	Wasp HAS.1	XT786 (320)
320	AM AZ	815	Amazon	1978/93	Lynx HAS.2/3	XZ246 (320/AZ)
321	-	829	Antelope	1976/79	Wasp HAS.1	XT788 (321)
321	AO	702/ 815	Antelope	1979/82	Lynx HAS.2	XZ691 (321/AO)
321	GIB	815	Gibraltar Flight	1983/94	Lynx HAS.3	ZP258 (321/GIB)
322	AV	829	Active	1977/94	Wasp HAS.1 Lynx HAS.2/3	XT739 (322/AV) XZ238 (322/LP)
323	-	829	Ambuscade	1975/80	Wasp HAS.1	XT428 (323)
323	AB	702 815	Ambuscade	1982/94	Lynx HAS.2/3	XZ721 (323/AB)
324	NA	829	Naiad	1975/87	Wasp HAS.1	XZ562 (324)
325	HE	829	Herald	1976/87	Wasp HAS.1	XS568 (325)
326	-	829	Arrow	1976/78	Wasp HAS.1	XT422 (326)
326	AW	702/ 815	Arrow	1978/94	Lynx HAS.2/3	XZ241 (326/AW)
327	-	829	Alacrity	1977/78	Wasp HAS.1	XS572 (327)
327	AL	702/ 815	Alacrity	1978/94	Lynx HAS.2/3	XZ243 (327/AL)
328	BA	815/ 829	Brave	1986/94	Lynx HAS.2/3	ZD265 (328/BA)
329		815	Brave allocation only			
330-333	H, BY	849B	Hermes, Brawdy	1965/68	Gannet AEW.3	XL498 (333/H)
330-331	ED	829	Endurance	1975/77	Whirlwind HAR.9	XL898 (330/ED)
330-331	BZ	815	Brazen	1982/94	Lynx HAS.2/3	XZ690 (330/BZ)
332	TS	846	Tidespring	1974/75	Wessex HU.5	XT468 (332/TS)
332	LP	815	Liverpool	1982/94	Lynx HAS.2/3	XZ239 (332/LP)
333	BM	702/ 815	Birmingham	1977/94	Lynx HAS.2/3 Lynx HAS.3	XZ695 (333/BM) ZD259 (333/BM)
334	SN	815	Southampton	1981/94	Lynx HAS.2/3	XZ238 (334/SN)
335-336	H	SAR	Hermes	1966	Whirlwind HAR.9	XN310 (335/H)
335	CF	702/ 815	Cardiff	1979/94	Lynx HAS.2/3	XZ255 (335/CF)
336	CO, CV	702/ 829/ 815	Coventry	1979/82	Lynx HAS.2/3	XZ257 (336/CV)
336	CV	815	Coventry	1989/94	Lynx HAS.3?	XZ239 (338/CT)
337	-	829	Sheffield	1975/79	Wasp HAS.1	XV632 (337)

Codes	Fin	Sqdn	Ship/Base	Years	Aircraft Type	Example
337	SD	815	Sheffield	1980/82	Lynx HAS.2	XZ725 (337/SD)
337	CV	815	Coventry	1991/94	Lynx HAS.3	ZD255 (371/CV)
338	CT	815	Campbeltown	1989/94	Lynx HAS.3	ZD265 (338/CT)
339	CT	815	Campbeltown	allocation only		
340-347	H, CU	826	Hermes, Culdrose	1966/68	Wessex HAS.1	XS878 (341/H)
340	AD	829	Ardent	1977/78	Wasp HAS.1	XV632 (340)
340	AD	702/815	Ardent	1978/82	Lynx HAS.2	XZ244 (340/AD)
341	AG	702/815	Avenger	1978/94	Lynx HAS.2/3	XZ252 (341/AG)
342	-	-	Fort Austin	1977	allocation only	
342-343	BT	815/829	Brilliant	1981/94	Lynx HAS.2/3	XZ729 (342/BT)
343	FG	706	Fort Grange	1978	Sea King HAS1	XV714 (343/FG)
344	GW	702/815	Glasgow	1979/94	Lynx HAS.2/3	XZ732 (344/GN)
345	NC	702/815	Newcastle	1978/94	Lynx HAS.2/3	XZ242 (345/NC)
346	BW	702/815/829	Broadsword	1979/94	Lynx HAS.2/3	XZ695 (346/BW)
347	ON	829	Olna	1975/77	Wessex HU.5	XS522 (347/ON)
347	TP	829	Tidepool	1978	Wessex HU.5	XT480 (436/TP)
347	RG	772	Regent	1981	Wessex HU.5	XS522 (347)
347	BW	829/815	Broadsword	1982/94	Lynx HAS.2	XZ724 (347)
348	CM	815	Chatham	1990/94	Lynx HAS.3	ZD251 (348/CM)
349	CM	815	Chatham	1990/94	allocation only	
350-357	-	-	Invincible	1976	allocation only	
350-356	CU PW	824	Culdrose Prestwick	1981/89	Sea King HAS.2/2A	XZ579 (356)
					Sea King HAS.5	XV711 (353/CU)
350	CL	815	Cumberland	1989/94	Lynx HAS.3	XZ256 (350/-)
351	CL	815	Cumberland	1989/94	allocation only	
352-353	SD	829/815	Sheffield	1988/94	Lynx HAS.3	ZD260 (352/SD)
355	SM	815	Somerset	1996	due	
360-362	N	820	Invincible	1980/81	Sea King HAS.2/2A	XV647 (360/N)
					Sea King HAS.5	XV711 (361/N)
360	MC	815	Manchester	1982/94	Wasp HAS.1	XS562 (360)
					Lynx HAS.2/3	XZ736 (360)
361-362	-	824D	Illustrious	1982/83	Sea King HAS.2/2a(AEW)	XV704 (361)
361-362	NF	829/815	Norfolk	1991/94	Lynx HAS.3	XZ234A(361/NF)
			(362 not used)			
363-370	-	849	Culdrose	1984/85	Sea King AEW.2	XV706 (363)
363	MA	829/815	Marlborough	1991/94	Lynx HAS.3	XZ723 (363/MA)
			(364 not used)			
365	AY	815	Argyle	1992/94	Lynx HAS.3	ZD567 (365/AY)
			(365 not used)			
371-372	-	829	Contender Bezant	1982	Wasp HAS.1	XS562 (371)
372	NL	815	Northumberland	1994	Lynx HAS.3	
373	-	829	St Helena	1982	Wasp HAS.1	XT795 (373)
374-375	VB	815/829	Beaver	1984/94	Lynx HAS.2/3	ZD268 (375/VB)
376	XB	815/829	Boxer	1984/94	Lynx HAS.2/3	ZD262 (376/XB)
377	-	815	FIR	1985/88	Lynx HAS.2	XZ719 (377)
400	GL	829/737	Glamorgan	1967/83	Wessex HAS.1	XM874 (400/GL)
					Wessex HAS.3	XM919 (400/GL)
400	GL	815	Glamorgan	1983/86	Lynx HAS.2	XZ240 (400/GL)
401	KE	829/737	Kent	1965/80	Wessex HAS.1	XP140 (401/KE)
					Wessex HAS.3	XP150 (401/KE)
402	HA	829/737	Hampshire	1965/76	Wessex HAS.1	XS875 (402/HA)
					Wessex HAS.3	XS153 (402/HA)
402-403	BX	829/815	Battleaxe	1981/94	Lynx HAS.2/3	XZ235 (402/BX)
403	FI/FF	829/737	Fife	1967/71	Wessex HAS.1	XS867 (403/FF)
					Wessex HAS.3	XS149 (403/FI)
403	DV	737	Devonshire	1971/78	Wessex HAS.3	XP105 (403/DV)
404	DV/DE	829/737	Devonshire	1965/70	Wessex HAS.1	XP159 (404/DV)
404	FF	737	Fife	1971/80	Wessex HAS.3	XM836 (404/FF)
404	FF	815	Fife	1983/87	Lynx HAS.3	XZ248 (404/FF)
404	IR	815	Iron Duke	1993/94	Lynx HAS.3	XZ690 (404/IR)
405	LO/LN	829/737	London	1965/82	Wessex HAS.1	XM842 (405/LO)
					Wessex HAS.3	XM327 (405/LN)
405-406	LN	829/815	London	1986/94	Lynx HAS.2/3	XZ734 (405/LN
406	AN	829/737	Antrim	1970/84	Wessex HAS.3	XP137 (406/AN)
407	NF	737	Norfolk	1970/81	Wessex HAS.3	XP140 (407/NF)
407	YK	829/815	York	1985/94	Lynx HAS.2/3	XZ254 (407/YK)
408	-	829	Vidal	1968/71	Wasp HAS.1	XT429 (408)
408	GL	737	Glamorgan	1974	Wessex HAS.3	XM919 (408/VL)
409	HE	829	Hecla	1967/72	Wasp HAS.1	XT423 (409/HE)
410-414	BL/B	820	Blake	1969/80	Wessex HAS.1	XM327 (411/BL)
					Sea King HAS.1	XV696 (411/BL)
					Sea King HAS.2/2A	XV647 (412/BL)
410	GC	815	Gloucester	1985/94	Lynx HAS.2	XZ722 (410/GC)
411	EB	815	Edinburgh	1985/94	Lynx HAS.3	ZD264 (411/EB)
412-413	CW	815	Cornwall	1989/94	Lynx HAS.3	ZD255 (412/CW)
414-417	-	829	Portland	1971/73	Wasp HAS.1	XT781 (414)
414	HT	829	Hecate	1973/84	Wasp HAS.1	XT632 (414/HT)
415	HD	829	Hydra	1974/83	Wasp HAS.1	XS568 (415/HD)
415	MM	815	Monmouth	1994	Lynx HAS.3	ZD253 (415/MM)
416	-	829	Hecla	1975/84	Wasp HAS.1	XT432 (416)
417	-	829	Herald	1973/76	Wasp HAS.1	XV624 (417)
417	-	737	Oscar	1976	Wessex HAS.1	XP105 (417)
417	NM	815	Nottingham	1983/94	Lynx HAS.2	XZ241 (417/NM)
418	HT	829	Hecate	1965/73	Wasp HAS.1	XS562 (418)
418-419	PO	772	Portland	1986/87	Wessex HU.5	ZS513 (419/PO)
419	-	829	Hydra	1969/74	Wasp HAS.1	XS531 (419)
420	S	829	Sembawang	1969/72	Wasp HAS.1	XS543 (420/S)
420-421	PO	771	Portland	1972	Wessex HAS.1	XS888 (420/PO
420	-	-	Waikato	1976	Wasp HAS.1	NZ3902 (420/-)
420	EX	815	Exeter	1981/94	Lynx HAS.2/3	XZ733 (420/EX)
421	AJ	829	Ajax	1965/85	Wasp HAS.1	XV634 (421)
422	AU	829	Aurora	1976/87	Wasp HAS.1	XT420 (422)
422	SU	815	Sutherland	1997		
423	DM	829	Diomede	1970/88	Wasp HAS.1	XS572 (423/DM)
424	MI/MV	829	Minerva	1969/75	Wasp HAS.1	XT424 (424/MV)
424	MV	702/815/829	Minerva	1978/92	Lynx HAS.2/3	XZ748 (424/MV)
425	BC	829	Bacchante	1969/82	Wasp HAS.1	XT792 (425/BC)
426	AR	829	Arethusa	1965/85	Wasp HAS.1	XT421 (426/AR)
427	AS	829	Ashanti	1965/81	Wasp HAS.1	XT438 (427/AS)
428	-	829	Achilles	1970/71	Wasp HAS.1	XS538 (428)
429	-	829	Diomede	1970	Wasp HAS.1	XT423 (429)
429	-	-	Waikato	1970/71	Wasp HAS.1	NZ3902 (430)
430	-	829	Achilles	1978/88	Wasp HAS.1	XS538 (430)
430	EE	815	Endurance	1993/94	(not used)	
431	CY	815	Charybdis	1969/78	Wasp HAS.1	XT430 (431)
431	CY	815	Charybdis	1982/91	Wasp HAS.2	XZ734 (431/CY)
432	-	829	Scylla	1970/81	Wasp HAS.1	XS534 (432)
432	SL	829/815	Scylla	1984/93	Lynx HAS.3	ZD256 (432/SL)
433	EU	829	Euryalus	1964/88	Wasp HAS.1	XT780 (433/EU)
434-437	PO	737	Portland	1968/73	Wessex HAS.1	XS868 (435/PO)
					Wessex HAS.3	XS119 (434/PO)
434-435	ED	829	Endurance	1973/76	Whirlwind HAS.9	XN386 (434/ED)
434-435	E	829	Endurance	1976/86	Wasp HAS.1	XS527 (435/E)
434-435	ED	829	Endurance	1987/91	Lynx HAS.3	XZ233 (435/ED)
434-435	PC	829	Polar Circle	1991/92	Lynx HAS.3	XZ233 (435/PC)
434-435	ED	829/815	Endurance	1991/94	Lynx HAS.3	XZ233 (435/EE)
435	ED	829	Endurance	1987	Lynx HAS.3	XZ233 (435/ED)
436	RG	829	Regent	1973/74	Wessex HU.5	XT480 (436/RG)
436	-	772	Regent	1981	Wessex HU.5	XT480 (436)
437	RS	829	Resource	1973/84	Wessex HU.5	XT484 (437/RS)
437	N	772	Invincible	1981	Wessex HU.5	XT486 (437/N)
437	GT	815	Grafton	1997	due	
440	BK	829	Berwick	1971/85	Wasp HAS.1	XV624 (440/BK)
441	-	829	Falmouth	1971/85	Wasp HAS.1	XS542 (441)
442	ZU	829	Zulu	1967/84	Wasp HAS.1	XT438 (442/ZU)
443	JP	829	Jupiter	1969/79	Wasp HAS.1	XV629 (443)
443	JP	815	Jupiter	1983/92	Lynx HAS.2/3	XZ227 (443/JP)
444	GU	829	Gurkha	1966/83	Wasp HAS.1	XT434 (444/GU)
444	-	829	Tribal	1983/84	Wasp HAS.1	XT430 (444)
444	MR	814	Montrose	1994	Lynx HAS.3	XZ690 (444/MR)
445	PL	829	Plymouth	1968/88	Wasp HAS.1	XS571 (445)
446	RO	829	Rhyl	1971/83	Wasp HAS.1	XS527 (446)
447	LD	829	Londonderry	1969/75	Wasp HAS.1	XV637 (447/LD)
448-449	PR	829	Protector	1965/68	Whirlwind HAR.1	XA866 (448)
448-449	ED	829	Endurance	1970/74	Whirlwind HAS.7	XM666 (448/ED)

Codes	Fin	Sqdn	Ship/Base	Years	Aircraft Type	Example
450	SS	829	Sirius	1966/75	Wasp HAS.1	XV636 (450/SS)
450	SS	702/ 815/ 829	Sirius	1977/94	Lynx HAS.2/3	XZ238 (450/SS)
451	LO	829	Lowestoft	1970/85	Wasp HAS.1	XT420 (451/LO)
452	GA	829	Galatea	1968/76	Wasp HAS.1	XS566 (452/GA)
452	BR	829	Brighton	1976/81	Wasp HAS.1	XT415 (452/BR)
453	ES	829	Eskimo	1965/81	Wasp HAS.1	XV631 (453/ES)
454	PE	829	Penelope	1965/66	Wasp HAS.1	XS534 (454/PE)
454	PN	815/ 829	Penelope	1982/91	Lynx HAS.2/3	XZ730 (454/PN)
455	AU	829	Aurora	1965/72	Wasp HAS.1	XS540 (455/AU)
455	AE	829	Ariadne	1973/88	Wasp HAS.1	XS570 (455)
456	Y/ YM	829	Yarmouth	1968/86	Wasp HAS.1	XV624 (456/Y)
457	NU	829	Nubian	1967/79	Wasp HAS.1	XT420 (457/NU)
457	LA	829/ 815	Lancaster	1992/94	Lynx HAS.3	XZ731 (457/LA)
460	AJ	829	Ajax	1965/76	Wasp HAS.1	XT433 (460/AJ)
460	-	-	Canterbury	1971/72	Wasp HAS.1	NZ3903 (460)
461	BR	829	Brighton	1971/76	Wasp HAS.1	XT415 (461/BR)
461	GA	829	Galatea	1976/86	Wasp HAS.1	XT443 (461)
462	RO	829	Rothesay	1968/88	Wasp HAS.1	XS565 (462/RO)
462	WM	815	Westminster	1994	Lynx HAS.3	
463	CL	829	Cleopatra	1968/78	Wasp HAS.1	XS534 (463/CL)
463	CP	702 815	Cleopatra	1978/92	Lynx HAS.2	XZ247 (463/CP)
464	DA	829	Danae	1967/77	Wasp HAS.1	XT415 (464/DA)
464	DN	702/ 815 829	Danae	1979/91	Lynx HAS.2/3	XZ699 (464/DN)
465	-	829	Juno	1967/80	Wasp HAS.1	XS542 (465)
466	AT	829	Argonaut	1967/75	Wasp HAS.1	XS564 (466/AT)
466	AT	702/ 815/ 829	Argonaut	1979/94	Lynx HAS.2/3	XS233 (466/AT)
468	RG	829	Regent	1966/73	Wessex HU.5	XT480 (468/RG)
469	RS	829	Resource	1966/73	Wessex HU.5	XT484 (469/RS)
470	NA	829	Naiad	1965/74	Wasp HAS.1	XT416 (470/NA)
470	AP	829	Apollo	1974/88	Wasp HAS.1	XS569 (470)
471	PH	829	Phoebe	1967/77	Wasp HAS.1	XV625 (471/PH)
471	PB	702 815/ 829	Phoebe	1977/90	Lynx HAS.2/3	XZ233 (471/PB)
472	AM	829	Andromeda	1968/78	Wasp HAS.1	XV626 (472/AM)
472	AM	815	Andromeda	1980/94	Lynx HAS.2/3	XZ722 (472/AM)
473	DI	829	Dido	1965/83	Wasp HAS.1	XS565 (473/DI)
474	MO	829	Mohawk	1965/76	Wasp HAS.1	XV638 (474/MO)
474	RM	815	Richmond	1994		
475	HM	829	Hermione	1969/81	Wasp HAS.1	XT428 (475)
475	HM	815	Hermione	1983/92	Lynx HAS.2/3	XZ720 (475/HM)
476	LE	829	Leander	1965/86	Wasp HAS.1	XS529 (476/LE)
477	TA	829	Tartar	1965/83	Wasp HAS.1	XV634 (477/TA)
478	-	815	29JSTU	1980/82	Lynx HAS.2	XZ227 (478)
479	BX	702	Battleaxe	1982	Lynx HAS.2	XZ689 (479/BX)
479	VL, PO	702/ 815/ 829	Trials Flt	1983/88	Lynx HAS.2 Lynx HAS.3	XZ289 (479/VL) ZD268 (479/PO)
479	PO	815	Support Flt	1990/94	Lynx HAS.3	XZ698 (479/PO)
480	-	702	29JSTU	1979/80	Lynx HAS.2	XZ691 (480)
490-499			RNZN allocation			
500-599			Culdrose allocation			
500-507	PO	829/ 703	Portland	1966/80	Wasp HAS.1	XS537 (503/PO)
501-512	CU	810	Culdrose	1983/94	Sea King HAS.5 Sea King HAS.6	XV706 (502) XV663 (501/CU)
508-527	PO	771	Portland	1967/74	Whirlwind HAS.7 Wessex HAS.1	XK940 (515/PO) XS873 (517/PO)
510-517	PO	772	Portland	1974/81	Wessex HAS.1 Wessex HU.5	XS885 (512/PO XS521 (511/PO)
510-512	-	829	Portland	1981/84	Wasp HAS.1	XT423 (512)
512-514	-	810OEU Boscombe	1994	Sea King HAS.6	XZ581 (512)
513-519	PO	829	Portland	1965/67	Whirlwind HAS.7	XL852 (513/PO)
516-518	CU	St F	Culdrose	1981/84	Chipmunk T.10 Sea Heron C.1 Sea Devon C.20	WP906 (c/s516) XR443 (c/s517) XJ324 (c/s518)
516-519	CU	771	Culdrose	1983/84	Chipmunk T.10 Sea Devon C.20	WP906 (516) XJ319 (c/s518)
520-529	PO	737	Portland	1965/75	Wessex HAS.1 Wessex HAS.3 Sea King HAS.1	XS862 (525/PO) XP147 (521/PO) XV644 (528/PO)
520-530	CU	771	Culdrose	1974/84	Wessex HAS.1 Wessex HU.5	XS150 (524/CU) XT482 (527/CU)
520-539	-	826	Culdrose	1983/84	Sea King HAS.2/2A Sea King HAS.5	XZ579 (536) XV712 (578)
520-521	-	MTPS	Culdrose	1988	NASU delivery call sign	
530-533	-	819	Ballykelly	1965/71	Wessex HAS.1 Wessex HAS.3	XP113 (531) XP118 (531)
530-536	CU	RAF SKTU	Culdrose	1978/79	Sea King HAS.3	XZ587 (c/s531)
531-536	CU	SKTU	Culdrose	1978/79	Sea King HAS.3	XZ587 (c/s531)
531-538	CU	824	Culdrose	1980/81	Sea King HAS.2/2A	XV660 (536/CU)
538	CU	705	Culdrose	1984	Gazelle HT.2	XX441 (38/CU)
539	CU	St F	Culdrose	1979/80	Chipmunk T.10	WP776 (c/s539)
540-552	CU	705	Culdrose	1965/75	Hiller HT.2	XS169 (44)
540-559	CU	705	Culdrose	1975/94	Gazelle HT.2	XW854 (47/CU)
553-567	CU	705	Culdrose	1965/74	Whirlwind HAR.3 Whirlwind HAS.7	XG583 (563) XL836 (55/CU)
					Gazelle HT.2	XW886 (58/CU)
560-576	CU	750	Culdrose	1978/94	Sea Prince T.1 Jetstream T.2 Jetstream T.3	WF133 (567/CU) XX487 (568/CU) ZE438 (576/CU)
564-565	-	706	Culdrose	1965/67	Wasp HAS.1	XS531 (65)
566-571	CU	706	Culdrose	1967/70	Wessex HAS.3	XM872 (569/CU)
568-578	CU	750	Culdrose	1972/78	Sea Prince T.1	WP321 (575/CU)
575-584	CU	824	Culdrose	1979/81	Sea King HAS.2/2A	XZ577 (582/CU)
575-576	CU	706/ SKTF	Culdrose	1979/84	Sea King HAR.3	XZ585 (576)
576-579	CU	750	Culdrose	1986/93	Jetstream T.3	ZE438 576/CU)
577-584	CU	824	Culdrose	1979/81	Sea King HAS.2/2A	XZ577 (582/CU)
579-584	CU	706	Culdrose	1967/75	Wasp HAS.1.	XS545 (579/CU)
579	CU	St F	Culdrose	1978/79	Chipmunk T.10	WP776 (c/s579)
580-586	CU	700H	Culdrose	1967	Wessex HAS.3	XS121 (582/CU)
580-582	CU	706	Culdrose	1981/88	Sea King HAS.5	XZ922 (580/CU)
580-599	CU	706	Culdrose	1979/84	Sea King HAS.2/2A Sea King HAR.3 Sea King HAS.5 Sea King AEW.5 Sea King HAS.6	XZ581 (593/CU) XZ578 (589/CU) XZ573 (593/CU) XV650 (588/CU) ZE418 (583)
589-599	CU	706	Culdrose	1970/78	Sea King HAS.1	XV649 (594/CU)
585-598	CU	706	Culdrose	1979/94	Sea King HAS.2/2A	XZ581 (593/CU)
586	CU	St F	Culdrose	1972	Chipmunk T.10	WP776 (586)
587-590	CU	SAR	Culdrose	1965/75	Whirlwind HAS.7 Whirlwind HAR.9	XK940 (588/CU) XL875 588/CU)
591	-	706	Culdrose	1969/72	Wasp HAS.1	XV633 (91)
599	-	St F	Culdrose	1969/79	Sea Devon C.20 Devon C.2/2	XJ348 (c/s599) VP599 (c/s599)
599	-	781		1981	Devon C.2/2	VP967 (c/s599)
600-607	-	-	Honington	1976	allocation only	
600-677			Portland allocation			
600-607)	PO	829	Culdrose	1980/93	Wasp HAS.1	XT799 (603)
610-614)					Lynx HAS.2/3	XZ732 (601/PO)
608-609	LM	St F	Lossiemouth	1965/72	Sea Prince T.1 Sea Prince C.2	WM739(608/LM) WM756(609/LM)
610-617	LM	803	Lossiemouth	1967/79	Buccaneer S.1 Buccaneer S.2	XN959 (610/LM) XV357 (612/LM)
610-617	PO	772	Portland	1981	Wessex HU.5	XT766 (512/PO)
614-617)	LM	764B	Lossiemouth	1965	Scimitar F.1	XD215 (611/LM)
620-621)						
624)						
614-617	-	829 HQ	Portland	1973/77	Wasp HAS.1	XT781 (614)
615-617	-	829 HQ	Portland	1981	Wasp HAS.1	XV626 (617)
618-619)	LM	750	Lossiemouth	1965/72	Sea Prince T.1	WF120 (618/LM)
628-629)						
638-639)						
648-649)						
658-659)						
620-627	-	-	Leuchars	1976	allocation only	
620-629	PO	772	Portland	1981/94	Wessex HU.5 Sea King HC.4	XT680 (621/PO) ZF121 (21)
630-637)	LM/736		Lossiemouth	1965/72	Buccaneer S.2	XK534 (633/LM)
640-644)	LO					
650-657						
630-637	PO	702	Portland	1982/94	Lynx HAS.2/3	ZD251 (631/PO)
634-636	-	703	Portland	1975/80	Wasp HAS.1	XS571 (634)
635-637	-	772	Portland	1981	Wessex HU.5	XR480 (636)

Codes	Fin	Sqdn	Ship/Base	Years	Aircraft Type	Example
640-647	-	-	Yeovilton	1976	allocation only	
640-648	PO	702	Portland	1982/87	Lynx HAS.2/3	XZ231 (645/PO)
650-657	PO	737	Portland	1973/77	Wessex HAS.3	XM872 (662/PO)
660-666)						
668-669)	LM	750	Lossiemouth	1965/70	Sea Venom FAW.21	WW151(679/LM)
678-680)					Sea Venom FAW.22	XG692 (668/LM)
670	-	737	Arctic Flight	1973	Wessex HAS.3	XP105 (670)
670-672	-	700L		1990/92	Lynx HAS3CTS	ZF557 (670)
670-672	-	815OEU	Portland	1992/94	Lynx HAS3CTS	ZF557 (670)
					Lynx HAS.8	XZ732 (670/PO)
677-680)	LM	764	Lossiemouth	1965/72	Hunter T.8	WV322 (687/LM)
687-699)					Hunter T.8c	XL604 (689/LM)
					Hunter GA.11	WV256 (698/LM)
					Hunter PR.11	WT723 (692/LM)
680	-	St F	Lossiemouth	1971/72	Chipmunk T.10	WK574 (680)
681-683	LM	St F	Lossiemouth	1965/72	Sea Vampire T.22	XA107 (681/LM)
					Chipmunk T.10	WK574 (681)
683-686	LM	SAR	Lossiemouth	1965/73	Whirlwind HAS.7	XM660 (86/LM)
					Whirlwind HAR.9	XN387 (86/LM)
695-709	PW	819	Prestwick	1993/94	Sea King HAS.6	XV708 (708/PW)
698	CL	819	Cumberland	1994	Sea King HAS.6	XV674 (698/-)
700-707)	VL	766	Yeovilton	1965/70	Sea Vixen FAW.1	XK556 (705/VL)
710-717)						
720-727)					Sea Vixen FAW.2	XN647 (707/VL)
700-709	PW, N	819	Prestwick	1981/93	Sea King HAS.2a	XV707 (707/PW)
					HAS.5	XV663 (703)
					HAS.6	XV676 (707/PW)
701-706	VL	890	Yeovilton	1971	Sea Vixen FAW.2	XN687 (704/VL)
708-709)	VL	StF/ Base	Yeovilton	1965/88	Hunter T.7	XF321 (728/VL)
718-719)		Flt/			Hunter T.8	WV396 (748/VL)
728-729)		SAR			Hunter T.8c	XF994 (718/VL)
738-739)		Flt			Hunter GA.11	XE685 (708/VL)
748-749)					Sea Prince C.2	WJ350 (749)
					Chipmunk T.10	WK574 (738/VL)
					Meteor T.7	WS103 (709/VL)
					Heron C.4	XM296 (c/s 729)
					Gazelle HT.2	ZB649 (c/s 728/VL)
709-710	-	FONFT	Yeovilton	1975/81	Sea Devon C.20	XJ319 (c/s710)
710-790			Yeovilton allocation			
710-718)	VL, N	899	Yeovilton Invincible	1981/94	Sea Harrier FRS.1	XZ457 (714/VL)
721-725)					Sea Harrier FRS.2	ZD615 (712/OEU)
					Hunter T.8M	XL580 (719/VL)
					Harrier T.4N/T.4A	XB604 (717)
712-714	-	899OEU	Boscombe /Yeovilton	1992/94	Sea Harrier FRS.2	ZE694 (714/OEU)
722-727) 757)	VL	700P	Yeovilton	1968/69	Phantom FG.1	XT859 (725/VL)
730-737)	VL	ADS/ ADTU/ FRADU	Yeovilton	1965/74	Sea Venom FAW.22	XG691 (737/VL)
740-747)					Hunter T.8	XL584 (744/VL)
740-747)					Hunter T.8c	WV363 (747/VL)
					Hunter GA.11	WV381 (732/VL)
					Hunter PR.11	WT723 (736/VL)
					Sea Vampire T.22	XA129 (747/VL)
723-724	-	899OEU	Yeovilton	1994	Sea Harrier FRS.2	ZD615 (723/OEU)
730	-	702	Yeovilton	1982	Lynx HAS.3	ZD250 (730)
734-737		StF	Yeovilton	1983/88	Sea Heron C.1	XR443 (c/s736)
740-745	VL	700L	Yeovilton	1976/77	Lynx HAS.2	XZ229 (740/VL)
740-747	VL	702	Yeovilton	1978/82	Lynx HAS.2	XZ230 (741/VL)
747	-	?	Culdrose	1973	Gazelle HT.2	XW864 (747)
750-755	VL	890	Yeovilton	1967/71	Sea Vixen FAW.1	XJ577 (752/VL)

Codes	Fin	Sqdn	Ship/Base	Years	Aircraft Type	Example
750-755	-	FRU/ ADTU/ FRADU	Yeovilton	1971/74	Sea Vixen FAW.2	XN658 (750)
750-751	-	StF	Yeovilton	1993/94	Jetstream T.3	ZE440 (c/s 751)
751-753	VL	815	Yeovilton	1981	Lynx HAS.2	XZ230 (751/VL)
754	CF	St F	Church Fenton	1970	Sea Prince T.1	WP312 (---/CF, c/s 754)
755	-	781	Lee-on-Solent	1968	Sea Devon C.20	XJ350 (c/s755)
758	-	JHTDU	JWE Old Sarum	1966/76	Whirlwind HAR.3	XG587 (758)
					Whirlwind HAS.7	XN299 (758)
760-767)	BY	849	Brawdy, Lossiemouth	1965/78	Gannet AEW.3	XL449 (763/BY)
770-774)	LM	HQ			Gannet COD.4	XG797 (766/BY)
777)		Trg F			Gannet T.5	XG882 (771/LM)
776	P	RRE	Pershore	1969/70	Gannet AEW.3	XL502 (76/P)
777-780	BY	738	Brawdy	1965/70	Hunter T.8	XF357 (779/BY)
781-795	BY	738	Brawdy	1965/70	Hunter GA.11	XF300 (783/BY)
796-799	BY	St F	Brawdy	1965/70	Sea Vampire T.22	XG772 (799/BY)
798	BY	849 HQ	Brawdy	1968/69	Gannet T.5	XG882 (708/BY)
800-811	BY	759	Brawdy	1965/69	Hunter T.8	XF988 (810/BY)
					Hunter T.8c	XL604 (803/BY)
800-829			Culdrose allocation			
810-812	LS	SAR Flt	Lee-on-Solent	1972/81	Whirlwind HAR.9	XN310 (810/LS)
					Wessex HU.5	XS496 (813/LS)
813 815	BY	SAR Flt	Brawdy	1965/71	Whirlwind HAS.7	XL846 (14/BY)
					Whirlwind HAR.9	XN311 (14/BY)
814-817	LS	781	Lee-on-Solent	1971/81	Chipmunk T10	WP906 (c/s815)
					Wessex HU.5	XT487 (c/s815)
					Sea Devon C.20	XJ322 (c/s815)
816-826	CU	771	Culdrose	1984/94	Wessex HU.5	XT474 (c/s820)
					Chipmunk T.10	WP906 (c/s816)
					Sea Devon C.20	XK895 (c/s818)
					Sea King HAR.5	XV647 (820)
817	BY	St F	Brawdy	1970	Sea Prince C.2	WM739(---/BY, c/s817)
818-829	LS	781	Lee-on-Solent	1965/81	Whirlwind HAS.22	WV223 (c/s827)
					Sea Devon C.20	XJ322 (c/s826)
					Sea Heron C.2	XR442 (c/s822)
					Heron C.4	XM296 (c/s824)
					Chipmunk T.10	WK574 (c/s818)
					Sea Hawk FGA.6	WV856 (c/s828)
					Wessex HU.5	XT770 (c/s827)
830-859	VL	A-W FRU/ FRADU	Hurn, Yeovilton	1965/94	Scimitar F.1	XD267 (834)
					Hunter T.8c	WT799 (839/VL)
					Hunter GA.11	WT804 (831/VL)
					Meteor T.7	WL350 (844)
					Meteor TT.20	WM242(842)
					Canberra B.2	WK142 (847)
					Canberra T.4	WJ869 (849)
					Canberra TT.18	WK142 (848)
					Canberra T.22	WH803 (856)
					Hawk T.1	XX242 (8..)
860-866	HF	728	Hal Far	1965/67	Meteor T.7	WL332 (860/HF)
					Meteor TT.20	WD612 (865/HF)
860-880	VL	FRADU	Yeovilton	1974/94	Hunter T7	XF310(876/VL)
					Hunter T.8c	XF357 (870)
					Hunter GA.11	XE685 (861)
					Hunter PR.11	XF977 (865)
					Hawk T.1	XX181
880	A	St F	Arbroath	1966/68	Sea Prince T.1	WP309 (880/A)
881-887			Prestwick allocation			
890	-	NASU	Changi	1966	Hunter T.8b	XF967 (890)
895-897	DM	BRNC	Dartmouth	1965/84	Dragonfly HR5	WG719 (97)
					Wasp HAS.1	XS541 (95)
901-912	-	BRNC/	Dartmouth Roborough	1966/94	Chipmunk T.10	WP809 (912)
989	-	Sh F	Hecla	1965/67	Wasp HAS.1	XT423 (989)
990	-	Sh F	Hecate	1965/66	Wasp HAS.1	XT427 (990)

FLEET AIR ARM HELICOPTER CODES SINCE 1971

Code	Fin	Sqdn	Base	Years	Aircraft Type	Example	Code	Fin	Sqdn	Base	Years	Aircraft Type	Example
V	A	848	Albion,	1971/76	Wessex HU.5	XS511 (VP/B)	X	CU	846	Culdrose,	1971/75	Wessex HU.5	XT461 (XD/VL)
	B		Bulwark,					VL		Yeovilton			
	VL		Yeovilton				X	-	847	South	1982	Wessex HU.5	XT471 (XW)
V	H	846	Hermes,	1976/77	Wessex HU.5	XT465 (VR/VL)				Atlantic Task Force			
	VL		Yeovilton				X	-	845	Yeovilton	1982	Wessex HU.5	XT478 (XL)
V	B	846	Bulwark,	1979/94	Wessex HU.5	XT451 (VL/VL)			(ex 847 Sqdn codes)			
	H		Hermes,		Sea King HC.4	ZA294 (VT/B)	Y	-	845	Yeovilton	1979/94	Wessex HU.5	XT468 (YD)
	VL		Yeovilton						(Y not displayed)		Sea King HC.4	ZE438 (YD)
W	CU	707	Culdrose,	1971/82	Wessex HU.5	XT479 (WX/VL)	Z	-	848	South	1982	Wessex HU.5	XT479 (ZA)
	VL		Yeovilton							Atlantic Task Force			
W	-	848	Yeovilton	1982	Wessex HU.5	XT482 (WL)	Z	VL	707	Yeovilton	1982/95	Wessex HU.5	XS507 (ZG/VL)
W	-	848	Yeovilton,	1990/91	Sea King HC.4	ZA298 (WA)						Sea King HC.4	ZD625 (ZX)
			Kuwait				Z	VL	848	Yeovilton	1995	Sea King HC.4	

ROYAL AUSTRALIAN NAVY FLEET AIR ARM CODES SINCE 1948

RAN CODE ALLOCATIONS 1948-1955

Codes	Fin	Sqdn	Base	Years	Aircraft Type	Example
100-129	K	805	Sydney,	1948/55	Sea Fury F.10	TF950 (107/JR)
	Q		Vengeance,		Sea Fury FB.11	WZ645 (103/K)
	JR/		Eglinton			
	GN					
130-139	K	808	Sydney,	1950/54	Sea Fury FB.11	WE676 (138/K)
	Q		Vengeance			
160-171	K	850	Sydney,	1953/54	Sea Fury FB.11	WJ246 (168/K)
	Q		Vengeance			
201-213	K	817	Sydney,	1950/55	Firefly T.2	MB696 (212/K)
	Q		Vengeance		Firefly FR.5	WB351 (202/K)
					Firefly AS.6	WD891 (202/K)
218-241	K	816	Sydney,	1948/55	Firefly FR.4	TW726 (228/JR)
	Q		Vengeance,		Firefly FR.5	WB243 (236/K)
	JR/		Eglinton		Firefly AS.6	WJ109 (238)
	GN					
901-916	-	723	Nowra	1952/55	Wirraway	
					C-47B	? (901)
					Sycamore HR.50	XA220 (907)
					Sycamore HR.51	XD654 (909)
					Firefly T.5	VX373 (916/NW)
					Firefly 6	VX386 (912/NW)
					Sea Fury FB.11	
					Sea Otter 2	

RAN CODE ALLOCATIONS 1955-1958

Codes	Fin	Sqdn	Base	Years	Aircraft Type	Example
100-129	K	805	Sydney,	1955/58	Sea Fury FB.11	VW645 (109/K)
	NW		Nowra			
200-211	Y	808	Melbourne	1955/58	Sea Venom FAW.53	WZ937 (211/Y)
260-272	-	851	Sydney,	1955/56	Firefly FR.5	VX373 (263)
			Nowra		Firefly AS.6	WD866 (271)
					Firefly TT.6	WB518 (268)
300-307	Y	816	Melbourne	1955/58	Gannet AS.1	XA330 (302/Y)
310-316	Y	817	Melbourne	1955/58	Gannet AS.1	XA326 (311/Y)
421-426	B	816	Melbourne	1955	Gannet AS.1	XA332 (421/B)
431-435	B	817	Melbourne	1955	Gannet AS.1	XA326 (432/B)
903-907	NW	723	Nowra	1958	Firefly TT.6	WB518 (903/NW)
911	NW	724	Nowra	1956	Firefly 6	WB508 (911/NW)
920-922	NW	723	Nowra	1955/56	Sea Fury FB.11	WG628 (920/NW)
930-931	-	725	Nowra	1958	Autocar	A11-301 (931)
950-953	NW	724	Nowra	1955/56	Sea Fury FB.11	
958-960	NW	724	Nowra	1955/58	Vampire T.34a	A79-840 (958/NW)
961-963	NW	724	Nowra	1955/56	Firefly T.5	VX373 (962/NW)
964-968	NW	724	Nowra	1955/56	Firefly AS.6	WB504 (965/NW)
971-972	NW	724	Nowra	1955/56	Wirraway	A20-168 (972/NW)
					Sea Fury FB.11	VW660 (972/NW)
973-975	NW	725	Nowra	1958	Gannet AS.1	XA329 (973/NW)
980-982	-	724	Nowra	1955/58	Vampire T.34	A79-8.. (980)
986-989	NW	724	Nowra	1955/58	Sea Venom FAW.53	WZ909 (987/NW)
991-996	NW	724	Nowra	1955/58	Sycamore HR.50	XA219 (996)
					Sycamore HR.51	XK902 (992)

RAN CODE ALLOCATIONS 1958 - 1963

Codes	Fin	Sqdn	Base	Years	Aircraft Type	Example
113-115	NW	724	Nowra	1961/62	Sea Fury FB.11	WH588 (114/NW)
800-810	M	805	Melbourne	1958/63	Sea Venom FAW.53	WZ943 (805/M)
810-819	M	816	Melbourne	1962/63	Gannet AS.1	XA389 (814/M)
824-833	M	816	Melbourne	1961/62	Gannet AS.1	XG787 (828/M)
841-842	-	723	Nowra	1963	Scout	WS101 (841)
842-847	NW	723	Nowra	1958/63	Firefly TT.6	WD826 (845/NW)
848-853	NW	723	Nowra,	1958/63	Sycamore HR.50	XA220 (849/M)
	M		Melbourne		Sycamore HR.51	XN448 (852)
854	NW	725	Nowra	1958/59	Gannet T.2	XA514 (854/NW)
856-857	NW	723	Nowra	1961/63	Autocar	A11-300 (856/NW)
863-867	NW	724	Nowra	1958/63	Sea Venom FAW.53	WZ928 (866/NW)
					Sea Venom TT.53	WZ930 (865)
871-875	NW	724	Nowra	1958/63	Sea Vampire T.22	XA167 (872/NW)
					Vampire T.34a	A79-838 (871/NW)
876-884	NW	724	Nowra	1961/63	Gannet AS.1	XA350 (881/NW)
					Gannet T.2	XA514 (878/NW)
878	NW	724	Nowra	1963	Firefly TT.6	WD901 (878/NW)
880-887	-	725	Nowra	1962/63	Wessex HAS.31	WA206 (886)
889	-	725	Nowra	1958/61	Firefly TT.5	WB271 (889)
894	NW	725	Nowra	1958/61	Sea Fury FB.11	WH590 (894/NW)

RAN CODE ALLOCATIONS 1963 - 1968

Codes	Fin	Sqdn	Base	Years	Aircraft Type	Example
800-803	NW	724	Nowra	1963/68	C-47B	N2-23 (801/NW)
802-806	NW	724	Nowra	1963/68	Vampire T.34a	A79-840 (804/NW)
806-809	NW	724	Nowra	1963/68	Sea Vampire T.22	XA167 (807/NW)
810-836	-	725/	Nowra,	1963/68	Wessex HAS.31a	WA213 (823)
		817	Sydney,			
			Stalwart,			
			Melbourne			
817-818	M	816	Melbourne	1964/67	Sea Venom FAW.53	WZ903 (817/M)
841-860	NW	724/	Nowra,	1963/67	Gannet AS.1	XA434 (846)
	M	816	Melbourne		Gannet T.2	XA517 (855)
853-858	-	723	Nowra	1964/68	Iroquois	N9-881 (856)
860-861	NW	724	Nowra	1968/78	C-47B	N2-43 (860/NW)
862-889	NW	724	Nowra,	1963/68	Sea Venom FAW.53	WZ937 (862/M)
	M		Melbourne Moresby			
891-892	-	723	Nowra, Moresby	1963/68	Scout	WS101 (892)
893-897	-	723	Nowra	1965/66	Iroquois	N9-3103 (895)

RAN CODE ALLOCATIONS SINCE 1968

Codes	Fin	Sqdn	Base	Years	Aircraft Type	Example
800-803	-	724/851	Nowra	1966/74	C-47B	N2-23 (801)
800-801	-	851/723	Nowra	1983/84	HS-748	N15-709 (800)
801-810	-	817	Nowra, Melbourne	1975/84	Sea King HAS.50	N16-125 (10)
804-807	-	724	Nowra	1968/71	Sea Venom FAW.53/TT.53	N4-946 (807)
808-809	-	724	Nowra	1968/70	Sea Vampire T.22	N6-966 (808)
810-836	-	725/817/723	Nowra, Melbourne, Sydney, Stalwart, Tobruk	1968/84	Wessex HAS.31A/31B	N7-210 (820)
810-836	-	816	Nowra	1984/88	Wessex HAS.31B	N7-209 (819)
820	-	817	Nowra	1983/84	Sea King HAS.50a	N16-238 (20)
824-828	-	723	Nowra	1984	Squirrel	N22-017 (27)
840-853	-	816/851	Nowra, Melbourne	1968/77	Tracker S-2E	N12-153595 (840)
840-843	-	816/851	Nowra, Melbourne	1977/84	Tracker S-2E	N12-153598 (841)
844-859	-	816/851	Nowra, Melbourne	1977/84	Tracker S-2G	N12-153580 (858)
860-869	-	724	Nowra	1973/83	Macchi MB.326H	N14-074 (865)
860-865	-	723	Nowra	1984/88	Squirrel	N22-014 (861)
864-877	-	724	Nowra	1968/71	Sea Venom FAW.53/TT.53	N4-904 (868)
870-889	-	724/805	Nowra	1968/84	Skyhawk A-4G	N13-154906 (885)
					Skyhawk TA-4G	N13-154912 (881)
890-899	-	723	Nowra, Moresby	1974/88	Kiowa	N17-013(892)
891-892	-	723	Nowra, Moresby	1968/74	Scout	N8-101 (891)
891-892	-	723	Nowra, Moresby	1974/84	Kiowa	N17-013 (892)
893-899	-	723	Nowra	1968/84	Iroquois	N9-882 (897)
75	-	817	Nowra (75th Anniversary code)	1986	Sea King HAS.50	N16-125 (75)

ROYAL CANADIAN NAVY AIRCRAFT CODES 1948 - 1952

Codes			Sqdn	Years	Aircraft Type	Example
VG-AAA	to	VG-AAZ	883	1948/51	Seafire F.15	SW860 (AA-H)
					Sea Fury FB.11	TG129 (AA-D)
VG-AAA	to	VG-AAZ	871	1951/52	Sea Fury FB.11	VW227 (AA-H)
VG-ABA	to	VG-ABZ	826	1948/51	Firefly FR.1	PP460 (AB-.)
					Avenger TBM-3E	53545 (AB-Z)
VG-ABA	to	VG-ABZ	881	1951/52	Avenger TBM-3E	53420 (AB-G)
VG-BCA	to	VG-BCZ	803	1948/51	Sea Fury FB.11	TG114 (BC-L)
VG-BDA	to	VG-BDZ	825	1948/51	Firefly FR.4	VH134 (BD-C)
					Firefly AS.5	VH138 (BD-A)
VG-BDA	to	VG-BDZ	880	1951/52	Firefly AS.5	
					Avenger TBM-3E	53437 (BD-B)
VG-BGC			Air Group Cdr	1948/51	Sea Fury FB.11	TG120 (BG-C)
VG-TFA	to	VG-TFZ	743	1948/52	Swordfish II	
					Harvard II	3233 (TF-Y)
					Avenger AS.3	86-28 (TF-Z)

A 'VG-BCx' coded Hawker Sea Fury FB.11 of No.803 Squadron, Royal Canadian Navy at RCAF Centralia in December 1951. (D.W.Warne)

Grumman Hellcat II KE209, seen here as a gate guardian at Lossiemouth in 1969, is now in the Fleet Air Arm Museum collection. (MAP)

Vought Corsair IV KD431 of the Fleet Air Arm Museum collection

NAVAL AIRCRAFT MUSEUMS

NAVAL AIRCRAFT HELD BY THE FLEET AIR ARM MUSEUM AT YEOVILTON

Aircraft	Serial	Status
Blackburn Buccaneer S.1	XK488	Static Display [outside]
Blackburn Buccaneer S.1	XN957 (630/LM)	Static Display
Blackburn Skua	L2940 Wreck	Static Display
Douglas Skyraider AEW.1	WV106 (427/C)	Flambards, Helston
Douglas Skyraider AEW.1	WV121 (415/CU)	Stored Yeovilton
D.H. Sea Vampire T.22	XA127 Nose	Stored Yeovilton
D.H. Sea Vampire T.22	XA129	Stored Wroughton
D.H. Sea Venom FAW.21	WW138 (227/Z)	Stored Yeovilton
D.H. Sea Vixen FAW.1	XJ481 (-/VL)	Pres Fleetlands
D.H. Sea Vixen FAW.2	XS590 (131/E)	Stored Yeovilton
D.H. Sea Vampire F.1	LZ551/G	Static Display [Science Museum loan]
D.H. Sea Vixen FAW.1/2	? Nose	Stored Yeovilton
D.H. Tiger Moth T.2	XL717/"G-ABUL"	Static Display
Fairey IIIF	? Fuselage frame	Static Display
Fairey Albacore I	(N4172) marked "N4389/4M"	Static Display
Fairey Barracuda II	DP872 Nose	Static Display
Fairey Barracuda II	DP872 Main section	Stored Wroughton
Fairey Firefly TT.4	VH127 (200/R)	Static Display
Fairey Fulmar I	N1854/(G-AIBE)	Static Display
Fairey Gannet AEW.3	XL503 (070/E)	Static Display
Fairey Gannet COD.4	XA466 (770/LM)	Stored Wroughton
Fairey Gannet T.5	XG883 (773/BY)	WAM Rhoose
Fairey Gannet T.2	XA508 (627/GN)	MAM Baginton
Fairey Swordfish II	(HS618/A2001) marked "P4139"	Static Display
Gloster Gladiator II	(N5903) marked "N2276/H"	Static Display [Shuttleworth loan]
Gloster Meteor TT.20	WM292 (841)	WAM Rhoose
Gloster Meteor T.7	WS103 (709/VL)	Restoration, Crowley Technical College
Grumman Avenger ECM.6B	XB446	Stored Yeovilton
Grumman Hellcat II	KE209	Static Display
Grumman Martlet I	AL246	Static Display
Hawker P.1052	VX272 [7174M]	Stored Lee
Hawker P.1127	XP980 [A2700]	Static Display
Hawker Sea Fury FB.11	WJ231 (115/O)	Static Display
Hawker Sea Hawk FGA.6	XE340 (131/Z)	East Fortune
Hawker Sea Hawk FGA.6	WV856 (163/-)	Stared Yeovilton
Hiller HT.1	XB480 (537/-)	Static Display
McDonnell-Douglas Phantom FG.1	XT596	Static Display
North American Harvard 3	(1657) [ex FAA EX976]	Static Display [ex-Portuguese AF]
Northrop Chukar D.2	XW994	Stored Wroughton
Percival Sea Prince T.1	WP313 (568/CU)	Stored Wroughton
Short 184	8359	Forward fuselage Static Display
Sopwith Baby	"N2078" [composite with 8214/8215]	Static Display
Supermarine 510	VV106 [7175M]	Stored Lee
Supermarine Attacker F.1	WA473 (102/J)	Stored Yeovilton
Supermarine Scimitar F.1	XD220	USS Intrepid, New York
Supermarine Scimitar F.1	XD317 (112/R)	Stored Yeovilton
Supermarine Seafire F.17	SX137	Static Display
Supermarine Walrus I	L2301/(G-AIZG)	Static Display
Vought Corsair F.4	KD431 (E2M)	Static Display
Westland Dragonfly HR.5	VZ962	Weston-super-Mare [at International Helicopter Museum]
Westland Dragonfly HR.5	WN493	Static Display
Westland Wasp HAS.1	XS527	Static Display
Westland Wasp HAS.1	XT427 (606/-)	Flambards, Helston
Westland Wessex HU.5	XT769 (823/-)	Stored Yeovilton
Westland Wessex HAS.3	XP142 "Humphrey"	Static Display
Westland Wessex HU.5	XS508	Static Display
Westland Whirlwind HAS.7	XG594 (517/-)	East Fortune
Westland Whirlwind HAR.1	XA864	Stored Wroughton
Westland Whirlwind HAR.3	XG574 [A2575]	Static Display
Westland Wyvern TF.1	VR137	Static Display

NAVAL AIRCRAFT HELD BY THE NAVAL AVIATION MUSEUM AT NOWRA

Aircraft	Serial	Status
Auster Autocar J/5G	A11-300 (856)	Static Display
Bell Iroquois UH-1B	N9-3092 (894)	Static Display
Bristol Sycamore HR.50	XA220 (850)	Static Display
Bristol Sycamore HR.51	XD653 (849)	Static Display
D.H. Sea Venom FAW.53	WZ895 (870/M)	To Flight
D.H. Sea Venom FAW.53	WZ931 (877/M)	Static Display
D.H. Sea Venom FAW.53	WZ935 (878/M)	Static Display
D.H. Sea Venom FAW.53	WZ937 (211/Y)	Static Display
D.H. Sea Vampire T.22	XA770 (875/NW)	Static Display.
D.H. Vampire	A79-375	Restoration
Douglas Dakota C-47	N2-43 (800/NW)	Static Display
Douglas Dakota C-47	N2-90 (802/NW)	Flying
Fairey Firefly Mk.5	WD826 (245/K)	Flying
Fairey Firefly Mk.6	WJ109 (207/K)	Static Display
Fairey Gannet AS.1	XA434 (895/M)	Static Display
GAF Radioplane KD-2R	N10-	Static Display
Grumman Tracker S-2G	N12-152333 (844)	Flying
Grumman Tracker S-2G	N12-153589 (859)	Static Display
Grumman Tracker S-2E	N12-153600 (845)	Restoration
Hawker Sea Fury FB.11	VW623 (102/K)	Restoration
McDonnell-Douglas A-4B	BuNo142871 (888) As A4G -N13-154906	Static Display
Supermarine Sea Otter	JN200	Nose only
Westland Scout	N8-101 (891)	Static Display
Westland Scout	XR603 (892)	To be restored
Westland Wessex HAS.31A	N7-217 (827)	Static Display
Westland Wessex HAS.31B	N7-204 (814)	Static Display
Westland Wessex HAS.31B	N7-205 (815)	Static Display
Westland Wessex HAS.31B	N7-221 (831)	Static Display
Westland Wessex HAS.31B	N7-224 (834)	Static Display

AIR-BRITAIN - THE INTERNATIONAL ASSOCIATION OF AVIATION HISTORIANS - FOUNDED 1948

Since 1948, Air-Britain has recorded aviation events as they have happened, because today's events are tomorrow's history. In addition, considerable research into the past has been undertaken to provide historians with the background to aviation history. Over 15,000 members have contributed to our aims and efforts in that time and many have become accepted authorities in their own fields.

Every month, *AIR-BRITAIN NEWS* covers the current civil and military scene. Quarterly, each member receives *AIR-BRITAIN DIGEST* which is a fully-illustrated journal containing articles on various subjects, both past and present.

For those interested in military aviation history, there is the quarterly *AEROMILITARIA* which is designed to delve more deeply into the background of, mainly, British and Commonwealth military aviation than is possible in commercial publications and whose format permits it to be used as components of a filing system which suits the readers' requirements. This publication is responsible for the production of the present volume and other monographs on military subjects. Also published quarterly is *ARCHIVE*, in a similar format but covering civil aviation history in depth on a world-wide basis. Both magazines are well-illustrated by photographs and drawings.

In addition to these regular publications, there are monographs covering type histories, both military and civil, airline fleets, Royal Air Force registers, squadron histories and the civil registers of a large number of countries. Although our publications are available to non-members, prices are considerably lower for members who have priority over non-members when availability is limited. Normally, the accumulated price discounts for which members qualify when buying monographs far exceed the annual subscription rates.

A large team of aviation experts is available to answer members' queries on most aspects of aviation. If you have made a study of any particular subject, you may be able to expand your knowledge by joining those with similar interests. Also available to members are libraries of colour slides and photographs which supply slides and prints at prices considerably lower than those charged by commercial firms.

There are local branches of the Association in Bournemouth, Central Scotland, Exeter, Gwent, Heston, London, Luton, Manchester, Merseyside, Rugby, Sheffield, Southampton, South-West Essex, Stansted and West Midlands.

If you wish to receive samples of Air-Britain magazines, please write to the following address enclosing 50p and stating your particular interests. If you would like only a brochure, please send a stamped self-addressed envelope to the same address (preferably 230mm by 160mm or over) -
Air-Britain Membership Enquiries (Mil), 1 Rose Cottages, 179 Penn Road, Hazlemere, High Wycombe, Bucks., HP15 7NE.

MILITARY AVIATION PUBLICATIONS
[* Currently out of print]

Royal Air Force Aircraft series: (prices are for members/non-members and are post-free)

J1-J9999	(£8.00/£12.00)	K1000-K9999	(£2/50/£3.75)*	L1000-N9999	(£12.00/£18.00)
P1000-P9999	(£2.00/£3.00)*	R1000-R9999	(£2.50/£3.75)*	T1000-T9999	(£3.00/£4.50)*
V1000-W9999	(£4.00/£6.00)*	X1000-Z9999	(£4.00/£6.00)*	AA100-AZ999	(£6.00/£9.00)*
BA100-BZ999	(£6.00/£9.00)	DA100-DZ999	(£5.00/£7.50)	EA100-EZ999	(£5.00/£7.50)
FA100-FZ999	(£5.00/£7.50)	HA100-HZ999	(£6.00/£9.00)	JA100-JZ999	(£6.00/£9.00)
KA100-KZ999	(£6.00/£9.00)	LA100-LZ999	(£7.00/£10.50)	MA199-MZ999	(£8.00/£12.00)
NA100-NZ999	(£8.00/£12.00)	PA100-RZ999	(£10.00/£15.00)	SA100-VZ999	(£6.00/£9.00)
		WA100-WZ999	(£5.00/£7.50)*		

Type Histories

The Halifax File	(£6.00/£9.00)*	The Lancaster File	(£8.00/£12.00)*	The Washington File	(£2.00/£3.00)*
The Whitley File	(£4.50/£6.75)*	The Typhoon File	(£4.00/£6.00)*	The Stirling File	(£6.00/£9.00)*
The Anson File	(£15.00/£22.50)	The Harvard File	(£7.00/£10.50)	The Hampden File	(£11.00/£16.50)
The Hornet File	(£9.00/£13.50)	The Beaufort File	(£10.00/£15.00)	The Camel File	(£13.00/£19.50)

Hardbacks

The Squadrons of the Royal Air Force and Commonwealth (£15.00/£15.00)

The Squadrons of the Fleet Air Arm (£24.00/£36.00)

Both the above cover the histories of all squadrons with precise tables of movements and equipment. Squadron badges are included and both are profusely illustrated.

Royal Navy Shipboard Aircraft Developments 1912 - 1931 (£15.00/£15.00))

Royal Navy Aircraft Serials and Units 1911 - 1919 (£15.00/£15.00))

Central American and Caribbean Air Forces (£12.50/£18.75)

Individual Squadron Histories

Strike True - The History of No.80 Squadron, Royal Air Force (£4.00/£6.00)

With Courage and Faith - The History of No.18 Squadron, Royal Air Force (£5.00/£7.50)*

Scorpions Sting - The Story of No.84 Squadron, Royal Air Force (£11.00/£16.50)

The above are available from Air-Britain Sales Department, 5 Bradley Road, Upper Norwood, London SE19 3NT